THE BRITISH YEAR BOOK OF
INTERNATIONAL LAW

THE
BRITISH YEAR BOOK OF
INTERNATIONAL LAW

2008

SEVENTY-NINTH YEAR OF ISSUE

OXFORD
AT THE CLARENDON PRESS
2009

OXFORD

UNIVERSITY PRESS

Great Clarendon Street, Oxford OX2 6DP

Oxford University Press is a department of the University of Oxford.
It furthers the University's objective of excellence in research, scholarship,
and education by publishing worldwide in

Oxford New York

Auckland Cape Town Dar es Salaam Hong Kong Karachi
Kuala Lumpur Madrid Melbourne Mexico City Nairobi
New Delhi Shanghai Taipei Toronto

With offices in

Argentina Austria Brazil Chile Czech Republic France Greece
Guatemala Hungary Italy Japan Poland Portugal Singapore
South Korea Switzerland Thailand Turkey Ukraine Vietnam

Oxford is a registered trade mark of Oxford University Press
in the UK and in certain other countries

Published in the United States
by Oxford University Press Inc., New York

© Oxford University Press, 2009

British Library Cataloguing in Publication Data

Data available

Library of Congress Cataloging in Publication Data

Data available

Typeset by Macmillan Publishing Solutions
Printed in Great Britain
on acid-free paper by
CPI Antony Rowe, Chippenham, Wiltshire

ISBN 978–0–19–958039–2

1 3 5 7 9 10 8 6 4 2

Editorial Communications should be addressed as follows:

Articles and Notes:
  PROFESSOR JAMES CRAWFORD
  Lauterpacht Centre for International Law,
  5 Cranmer Road, Cambridge, CB3 9BL.
  JRC1000@hermes.cam.ac.uk

Books for Review:
  PROFESSOR J. CRAIG BARKER
  Sussex Law School, University of Sussex,
  Brighton, East Sussex BN1 9QQ.
  J.C.Barker@sussex.ac.uk

The Editors and members of the Editorial Committee do not make themselves in any way responsible for the views expressed by contributors.

The British Year Book of International Law is indexed in *Current Law Index*, published by Information Access Company, and in *Legal Journals Index*, published by Legal Information Resources Limited.

SIR DEREK BOWETT (1927–2009), Whewell Professor of International Law, University of Cambridge (1981–1991)

As this volume was going to press, news came of the death of Professor SIR DEREK BOWETT CBE, QC, FBA, Whewell Professor of International Law at Cambridge and co-editor of this Year Book from 1982 (vol. 52) to 1993 (vol. 64). A notice of his contribution to international law will appear in the next volume.

CONTENTS

LIST OF ABBREVIATIONS

ABM	Anti-Ballistic Missile (Treaty)
AC	Appellate Court
ACHR	American Convention on Human Rights
ACP	African, Caribbean and Pacific
AIDS	Acquired Immune Deficiency Syndrome
AIT	Asylum and Immigration Tribunal
AMA	Agreement on Movement and Access
AML	Anti-money laundering
ANC	African National Congress
ASAT	Anti-Satellite
ASIL	American Society of International Law
ATCA	Alien Tort Claims Act
ATT	Arms Trade Treaty
AU	African Union
AVR	Assisted Voluntary Return
AWE	Atomic Weapons Establishment
BERR	Business, Enterprise and Regulatory Reform
BIOT	British Indian Ocean Territory
BIT	Bilateral Investment Treaty
BNSC	British National Space Centre
BP	British Petroleum
CAT	United Nations Convention Against Torture
CBD	Convention on Biological Diversity
CCAA	China Center of Adoption Affairs
CCW	Convention on Conventional Weapons
CEDAW	Convention on the Elimination of All Forms of Discrimination against Women
CEDAW OP	Optional Protocol to the Convention on the Elimination of All Forms of Discrimination against Women
CEFAS	Centre for Environment, Fisheries and Aquaculture Science
CESCR	Committee on Economic, Social and Cultural Rights
CFSP	Common Foreign and Security Policy
CFT	Combating the financing of terrorism
CHR	Commission on Human Rights
CIA	Central Intelligence Agency
CITES	Convention on International Trade in Endangered Species of Wild Fauna and Flora
CJ	Chief Justice
CLCS	Commission on the Limits of the Continental Shelf
COI	Central Office of Information (service)
CORC	Convention on the Rights of the Child

COTWs	Coalitions of the willing
CPPNM	Convention on the Physical Protection on Nuclear Material
CPS	Crown Prosecution Service
CPT	European Committee for the Prevention of Torture
CRC	Committee on the Rights of the Child
CSCE	Conference on Security and Co-operation in Europe (predecessor to the OSCE)
CTBT	Comprehensive Nuclear Test Ban Treaty
DEFRA	Department for Environmental, Food and Rural Affairs
DFID	Department for International Development
DPO	Disabled People's Organisation
DPRK	Democratic People's Republic of Korea
DRC	Democratic Republic of the Congo
DRF	Disability Rights Fund
DSB	Dispute Settlement Body
DSU	Dispute Settlement Understanding
EAW	European Arrest Warrant
EBA	Everything But Arms Scheme
EC	European Community
ECAs	Export Credit Agencies
ECGD	Export Credits Guarantee Department
ECHR	European Convention on Human Rights
ECJ	European Court of Justice
ECmHR	European Commission of Human Rights
ECOSOC	United Nations Economic and Social Council
ECT	Energy Charter Treaty
ECtHR	European Court of Human Rights
EEA	European Economic Area
EEC	European Economic Community
EEZ	Exclusive Economic Zone
EFTA	European Free Trade Association
EPA	Economic Partnership Agreement
EPO	European Patent Office
ESPD	European Security and Defence Policy
EU	European Union
EUCT	European Union Constitutional Treaty
EUECJ	Court of Justice of the European Communities (law reports of the British and Irish Legal Information Institute)
EULEX Kosovo	European Union Rule of Law Mission in Kosovo
EURATOM	European Atomic Energy Community
EWCA	England and Wales Court of Appeal
EWHC	High Court of England and Wales
FAC	Foreign Affairs Committee

FATF	Financial Action Task Force
FCO	Foreign and Commonwealth Office
FET	Fair and Equitable Treatment
FRY	Federal Republic of Yugoslavia
G7	Group of seven industrialized nations
GA	General Assembly of the United Nations
GAERC	General Affairs and External Relations Council
GATS	General Agreement on Trade in Services
GATT	General Agreement on Tariffs and Trade
GBE	Knight Grand Cross of the Order of the British Empire
GSP	Generalised System of Preferences
HC	High Court
HCNM	High Commissioner for National Minorities of the OSCE
HIPCs	Heavily indebted poor countries
HIV	Human Immunodeficiency Virus
HM	Her Majesty
HMG	Her Majesty's Government
HMRC	Her Majesty's Revenue and Customs
HMS	Her Majesty's Ship
HRA	Human Rights Act
HRC	United Nations Human Rights Council
HRCttee	Human Rights Committee
IACmHR	Inter-American Commission on Human Rights
IACtHR	Inter-American Court of Human Rights
IAEA	International Atomic Energy Agency
ICAO	International Civil Aviation Organisation
ICC	International Criminal Court
ICCPR	International Covenant on Civil and Political Rights
ICED	International Convention for the Protection of All Persons from Enforced Disappearance
ICERD	International Convention on the Elimination of All Forms of Racial Discrimination
ICES	International Council for the Exploration of the Sea
ICESCR	International Covenant on Economic, Social and Cultural Rights
ICJ	International Court of Justice
ICRC	International Committee of the Red Cross
ICRMW	International Convention on the Protection of the Rights of All Migrant Workers and Members of Their Families
ICRPD	The Convention on the Rights of Persons with Disabilities
ICRW	International Convention for the Regulation of Whaling

ICSID	International Centre for the Settlement of Investment Disputes
ICTY	International Criminal Tribunal for Former Yugoslavia
IDA	International Development Association
IEHC	The High Court of Ireland
ILC	International Law Commission
ILO	International Labour Organisation
IMO	International Maritime Organisation
INF	Irradiated Nuclear Fuel
IOM	International Organisation for Migration
IP	Intellectual Property
IRA	Irish Republican Army
IRGC	Iranian Revolutionary Guards Corps
ISAF	International Security Assistance Force
ISC	Intelligence and Security Committee
ISI	Inter-Services Intelligence
ITA	International Territorial Administration
ITO	International Trade Organization
ITUC	International Trade Union Confederation
IWC	International Whaling Commission
JARPA	Japanese research programme in the Antarctic
JHA	Justice and Home Affairs
KB	King's Bench
KCMG	Knight Commander of the Order of St Michael and St George
KFOR	Kosovo Force (NATO-led)
KPS	Kosovo Police Service
LCIA	London Court of International Arbitration
LDC	Least Developed Countries
LITTE	Liberation of Tigers Tamil Eelam
LJ	Lord Justice
LJJ	Lords Justices
LLB	Bachelor of Laws
LLM	Master of Laws
LNG	Liquefied Natural Gas
LRA	Lord's Resistance Army
LSE	London School of Economics
MAI	Multilateral Agreement on Investments
MANPADs	Man portable air defence systems
MARPOL	International Convention for the Prevention of Pollution from Ships
MCC	Military Co-ordination Commission
MDC	Movement for Democratic Change
MDG	Millennium Development Goals
MFN	Most-favoured-nation

MoD	Ministry of Defence
MONUC	United Nations Organization Mission in the Democratic Republic of the Congo
MoU	Memorandum of Understanding
MP	Member of Parliament
MR	Master of the Rolls
NAFTA	North American Free Trade Agreement
NAM	Non-Aligned Movement
NATO	North Atlantic Treaty Organization
NGO	Non-Governmental Organisation
NHRIs	National Human Rights Institutions
NISR	Nuclear Industries Security Regulations
NNDR	National Non-Domestic Rates
NPM	Non-Precluded Measure
NPT	Treaty on the Non-Proliferation of Nuclear Weapons
NSG	Nuclear Suppliers Group
NWCU	National Wildlife Crime Unit
OAS	Organisation of American States
OCHA	Office for the Co-ordination of Humanitarian Affairs
OCNS	Office for Civil Nuclear Security
OECD	Organisation for Economic Co-operation and Development
OHCHR	Office of High Commissioner for Human Rights
ONUC	United Nations Operation in the Congo
OPCAT	Optional Protocol to the United Nations Convention Against Torture
OPRC	International Convention on Oil Pollution Preparedness, Response and Co-operation
ORF	Operational Reserve Force
OSCE	Organization for Security and Co-operation in Europe
OSPAR	Protection of the Marine Environment of the North-East Atlantic
OUP	Oxford University Press
PCA	Partnership and Co-operation Agreement
PCIJ	Permanent Court of International Justice
PF	Popular Front
PKK	Kurdistan Workers Party
PMOI	People's Mujaheddin Organisation of Iran
PPA	Programme Partnership Agreement
PSI	Proliferation Security Initiative
QB	Queen's Bench
QBD	Queen's Bench Division
QC	Queen's Counsel
QF	Qods Force of the IRGC

QSR	Quality Status Report
RAF	Royal Air Force
RMP	Revenue Management Programme
SCC	Standards Council of Canada
SCR	Security Council Resolution
SFO	Serious Fraud Office
SFRY	Socialist Federal Republic of Yugoslavia
SIA	State Immunity Act
SOFA	Status of Forces Agreement
SOLAS	International Convention for Safety of Life at Sea
SOSREP	Secretary of State's Representative for Maritime Salvage and Intervention
SSR	Soviet Socialist Republic
SUA	Suppression of Unlawful Acts Against the Safety of Maritime Navigation Protocol
TBVC	Transkei, Bophuthatswana, Venda and Ciskei
TEC	Treaty establishing the European Community
TFG	Transitional Federal Government
TFSC	Turkish Federated State of Cyprus
TRIPS	Trade Related Intellectual Property Rights
TRNC	Turkish Republic of Northern Cyprus
TVPA	Torture Victims Protection Act
UAE	United Arab Emirates
UCR	United Cyprus Republic
UDI	Unilateral Declaration of Independence
UK	United Kingdom
UKAIT	United Kingdom Asylum and Immigration Tribunal
UKHL	United Kingdom House of Lords
UKMIL	United Kingdom Materials on International Law
UN	United Nations
UNAMID	African Union - United Nations Mission in Dafur (Hybrid operation)
UNCITRAL	United Nations Commission on International Trade Law
UNCLOS	United Nations Convention on the Law of the Sea
UNCRC	United Nations Convention on the Rights of the Child
UNCTAD	United Nations Conference on Trade and Development
UNESCO	United Nations Educational, Scientific and Cultural Organization
UNHCR	United Nations High Commissioner for Refugees
UNIFIL	United Nations Interim Force in Lebanon
UNITAF	Unified Task Force (Somalia)
UNMEE	UN Mission in Ethiopia and Eritrea
UNMIK	United Nations Mission in Kosovo

UNOSOM	United Nations Operation in Somalia
UNPROFOR	United Nations Protection Force
UNSCR	United Nations Security Council Resolution
UNTAET	United Nations Transitional Administration in East Timor
US	United States
USA	United States of America
USSR	Union of Soviet Socialist Republics
USVF	United States Visiting Forces
VCCR	Vienna Convention on Consular Relations Concerning the Compulsory Settlement of Disputes Protocol
VCLT	Vienna Convention on the Law of Treaties
VERTIC	Verification Research, Training and Information Centre
WH	Westminster Hall
WMD	Weapons of Mass Destruction
WS	Written Statements
WTO	World Trade Organisation

ALBERICO GENTILI (1552–1608)

The four-hundredth anniversary of the death of Alberico Gentili, one of the greatest of the early modern scholars and practitioners of international law, fell on 19 June 2008, and was marked by celebratory conferences in San Ginesio, the town of his birth in the Italian Marche, in Oxford, where he held the Regius Chair in Civil Law, and in London, where he was admitted to Gray's Inn and practised as a barrister and where his body was interred in St Helen's church, Bishopsgate. A protestant refugee from religious turmoil in Italy, Gentili arrived in England via Slovenia with his father Matteo, a doctor, and his brother, Scipione. Under the patronage of Robert Dudley, Earl of Leicester, Alberico Gentili began a career at Oxford in 1581 and was appointed to the Regius Chair six years later. He became increasingly busy with legal practice in London, where he served as the lawyer to the Spanish Embassy. He drew on this part of his life for the fascinating notes of cases assembled in *Hispanicae advocationis libri duo*, which was published posthumously in 1613.

Though described by T E Holland, who almost single-handedly rehabilitated Gentili's reputation at the end of the nineteenth century, as "a civilian of the old school",[1] Gentili's writings on international law are in some ways strikingly modern. His analysis of the law on the use of force, for example, in his text *De Jure Belli Libri Tres*[2] is both subtle and less dependent upon classical allusions than are the writings of many of his contemporaries. The combination of his civilian training and his practical experience give his analyses of legal principles a refreshing clarity and directness, anticipating modern doctrinal arguments. Coleman Phillipson[3] wrote, for example, of Gentili's "precise and vigorous statement of the doctrine of territorial sovereignty (including exclusive jurisdiction in adjacent seas) as the fundamental principle underlying the mutual rights and obligations of belligerents and neutrals", and said that "[i]n reference to this great question Gentili makes a decided advance, and we find that

---

[1] Thomas Erskine Holland, *Studies in International Law*, (Clarendon Press, Oxford, 1898), p. 16. As Chichele Professor of International Law and Diplomacy, Holland devoted his Inaugural Lecture in 1874 to the subject of Alberico Gentili. Holland recorded the revived interest in Gentili that followed the lecture: *ibid.*, pp. 37–39. Holland's role in the rehabilitation of Gentili was marked by the naming of a *piazza* in San Ginesio in honour of Holland, establishing a link between San Ginesio and Oxford which endures to the present day.

[2] Published posthumously in 1612. For a discussion of this contribution see Vaughan Lowe, "The Use of Force in the British Tradition of International Law", in *Alberico Gentili, L'uso Della Forza Nel Diritto Internazionale*, (Centro Internazionale di Studi Gentiliani, San Ginesio, Dott. A. Giuffrè Editore, 2006), pp. 71–95 (in Italian, pp. 99–125).

[3] Another sadly neglected scholar of international law, who wrote much on the early history of the subject and edited later editions of the textbook on International Law written by F. E. Smith (the Earl of Birkenhead).

his conclusions forestall, for the most part, those of modern international law."[4]

In recent years the scale and the particularity of Gentili's contribution to the development of the doctrine of international law has been increasingly recognized and studied. Much of the credit for the intensification of interest in his work must go to Dr Pepe Ragoni and Professor Diego Panizza, of the Centro Internazionale di Studi Gentiliani in San Ginesio, which has organized annual conferences and published a distinguished series of books and essays, in English and Italian, focusing on aspects of Gentili's life and works.[5]

[4] Coleman Phillipson, "Introduction", in *De Iure Libri Tres* (Classics of International Law. Clarendon Press, Oxford, 1933), p. 17a.
[5] <http://www.cisg.it/index_html_originale>

Sir Francis Vallat
(1912–2008)

Sir Francis Vallat gbe, kcmg, qc
(1912–2008)

Francis Aimé Vallat, who died on April 6 2008, was born in 1912 to a British father and a French mother. Returning from the First World War as a colonel, his father took the family to Canada but he died not long afterwards, leaving them in rather straitened circumstances. After a shaky start academically, Francis recovered himself to such an extent that he won a prize and bursary that enabled him to attend the newly established University of Toronto Law School, where he obtained a good degree. It was there that he developed his love, not only of academic life, but also of sport, for which his large and athletic frame equipped him well, and which he continued to enjoy for many years.

On the strength of his first degree at Toronto, Vallat was able to go to Cambridge, where he studied under Arnold McNair and became a devotee of international law and the League of Nations. Having obtained first class honours in the LLB, he taught for a year at Bristol University and in 1935 was called to the Bar by Gray's Inn. He began a common-law practice, but it was interrupted by World War II, in which he served in the RAF Volunteer Reserve.

After the war, he became an Assistant Legal Adviser at the Foreign Office, rising through the ranks to become the Legal Adviser in 1960. By all accounts he was a skilled negotiator with his overseas counterparts. His commanding physical presence and dignified demeanour were considerable assets, but he was also a shrewd judge of character and of the diplomatic possibilities. As the representative of his country he made major contributions at the United Nations General Assembly and at important international conferences, including those that established the World Health Organization and the Inter-Governmental Maritime Consultative Organization (as it then was); the 1954 Geneva Conference on Korea and Indo-China; and the Nicosia discussions that led to the independence of Cyprus in 1960. He led the United Kingdom delegation at the Vienna Conferences on Diplomatic Relations in 1961 and on the Law of Treaties in 1968–9. During his time at the FCO he was also involved (initially behind the scenes, but in later cases as Agent or Counsel) in a number of important cases in international courts and tribunals: at the International Court of Justice in *Minquiers and Ecrehos*,[1] *Monetary Gold Removed from Italy*,[2] *Effect of Awards of Compensation by the UN Administrative Tribunal*,[3] *South-West Africa (Petitioners)*,[4] *Constitution of the Maritime Safety Committee of the Inter-Governmental Maritime Consultative Organization*,[5]

---

[1] *ICJ Reports* 1953, p. 47.   [2] *ICJ Reports* 1954, p. 19.   [3] *ICJ Reports* 1954, p. 47.
[4] *ICJ Reports* 1956, p. 23.   [5] *ICJ Reports* 1960, p. 150.

Certain Expenses of the UN,[6] and *Northern Cameroons (Preliminary Objections)*;[7] in the European Commission of Human Rights in the *Cyprus (Greece v UK) case*;[8] in the *Ambatielos* arbitration;[9] and in the *Red Crusader* enquiry.[10] In 1961 he was appointed Queen's Counsel, and in 1962 Knight Commander of the Order of St. Michael and St. George.

He was not, it is said, a very 'hands-on' Legal Adviser: he tended to delegate more than his immediate predecessors, and was not a frequent attender at the traditional departmental tea at which current problems were discussed. This, and his reserved and dignified demeanour, led some to think him rather remote. But he could be very encouraging and helpful to younger colleagues and had a forward-looking attitude. It was due to him that Miss Joyce Gutteridge (later an eminent figure) became the first woman Assistant Legal Adviser; and when, in the 1960s, another young female member of his department (Eileen Denza) got married, Vallat refused to allow the Office to enforce the contractual provision that required her to resign. When she had a baby the following year, he insisted that she be kept on and given an established post, and in due course promotion. In that place and at that time, this was a decidedly unconventional and progressive attitude.

It was also an indication of Vallat's non-conformity that he took a year's sabbatical from the Foreign Office (as it had by then become) to go as Acting Director and Visiting Professor to McGill University Institute of Air and Space Law in 1965; and also that he took early retirement from Whitehall in 1968. He left to become Director of International Law Studies, and subsequently Professor of International Law, at King's College, in the University of London, where he remained for 8 years.

Vallat enjoyed academic life. His writings were few, however, and it would be fair to say that his taste was neither for theory nor for the minutiae of footnote-bedecked scholarship: he had a more practical and practice-oriented approach. This is reflected in his most useful work, the Melland Schill lectures on *International Law and the Practitioner* (1966), which offered helpful advice to private practitioners faced with questions of international law—not least by offering guidance on how to deal with the Foreign Office and on what it could or could not do to assist. His articles on the powers and functions of the UN General Assembly and Security Council were similarly sound and businesslike rather than innovative or prophetic.[11] He was a conscientious teacher who had a good rapport with

---

[6] *ICJ Reports* 1962, p. 151.   [7] *ICJ Reports* 1963, p. 15.

[8] Applications no. 175/56 and 299/57, *Yearbook of the European Convention on Human Rights* 1958–59, 175ff.; 25 *ILR* 27 & 168.

[9] (1956) 23 ILR 306.

[10] (1962) 35 *ILR* 485.

[11] 'The General Assembly and the Security Council of the United Nations' (1952) 29 this *Year Book* 63; 'Voting in the General Assembly of the United Nations' (1954) 31 this *Year Book* 273; 'The Competence of the United Nations General Assembly' (1959-II) 97 *RCADI* 203. Other works (apart from that mentioned in the following footnote) were: 'Law Reform in England' (1937–38)

the young, as many can testify. He encouraged and promoted the careers of junior colleagues; and was an energetic and imaginative academic administrator. He built international law studies at King's into a force to be reckoned with, and helped develop the London University LLM into one of the most important international law programmes in the world. It is another sign of his forward-looking approach that, together with the present writer, he established the first postgraduate course in human rights law in the country, at a time when there was not much interest in the subject.[12]

These were by no means his only contributions to the study and progressive development of international law. In 1982 was appointed a member of the Curatorium of the Hague Academy of International Law, eventually becoming its Vice-President. He was first an associate, then a member, of the Institute of International Law. He also served as Director of Studies of the International Law Association; as a member of the UK National Group of the Permanent Court of Arbitration; as a member of the Board of Editors of this Year Book (from 1947); and so on. From 1973–1981 he was a member of the International Law Commission, and its Chairman in 1977–1978. He was the Commission's Special Rapporteur (following Sir Humphrey Waldock) on the succession of States in respect of treaties, and the UN's Expert Consultant to the international conference that finalized a Convention on that subject. That the 1978 Vienna Convention on Succession of States in Respect of Treaties proved not to be very popular with States[13] is not an adverse reflection on Vallat's work. The subject matter was exceptionally complex: if one considers the variety of different causes of change of sovereignty and the variety of the different types of treaty involved, the permutations are very numerous indeed. Furthermore, the State practice was in many respects inconsistent and often dictated merely by temporary expediency. Above all, aspects of the topic were the subject of irreconcilable political differences between governments. That the Convention has nevertheless made *some* contribution to the development of customary law on the subject is, in the circumstances and with the benefit of hindsight, probably the most that could have been expected.

Other marks of recognition kept coming. In 1971 Vallat was made a Bencher of Gray's Inn; and in 1982, and most unusually, he received a second knighthood, the GBE—Knight Grand Cross of the Order of the British Empire.

---

2 *University of Toronto Law Journal* 233; 'The Function of the International Court of Justice in the World Community' (1972) 2 *Georgia Journal of International & Comparative Law* 55; and (with Gerald Fitzmaurice) 'Sir (William) Eric Beckett KCMG, QC (1896–1966): An Appreciation' (1968) 17 *ICLQ* 267.

[12] A book he edited in the early 1970s was connected with this initiative: *An Introduction to the Study of Human Rights: Based on Lectures Delivered at King's College, London, in the Autumn of* 1970 (undated). This volume comprises lectures not only by distinguished international lawyers such as René Cassin, but also by a theologian, a political scientist, and so on.

[13] It was only in 1996 that it entered into force, and at the time of writing has attracted only 21 ratifications.

All the while, since he left the Foreign Office, Francis had continued his important practice at the international law Bar, representing and advising governments and other major clients. In the ICJ, during this period, he represented Libya in its disputes with Tunisia and with Malta;[14] and Qatar in its dispute with Bahrain over *Maritime Delimitation and other Questions*.[15] He treated the representatives of his clients with the consideration that their position merited, but—even if they were heads of State or government—without obsequiousness. In return, clients treated him with the greatest respect, not just because of his eminence, but for the quality of the advice that he gave them. What was particularly impressive was his judgment— he knew what would work forensically and diplomatically, whatever might be an idea's purely theoretical merits or demerits. He was in such demand that he carried on his practice until he was very advanced in years.

In recounting all of his achievements, one should not forget that there was of course another side to the man, for he had many interests outside the law. He was an enthusiastic sailor and skier, carrying on the latter beyond an age where most people would consider it prudent. He loved gardening, the theatre and, later in life, music. He was an expert uphol- sterer, branching out, in due course, into antique restoration. Above all, he had a great gift for friendship, and a jolly sense of humour. He loved to tease, and if occasionally his remarks verged too much on the personal (which caused some to take offence) it was not through malice. And he was certainly willing to take from his friends as good as he got.

He was married three times. First, to Mary Cockell, in 1939, with whom he had a son and a daughter. The marriage was dissolved in 1973. In 1988 he married Patricia Morton Anderson, who had been his personal assist- ant at the Foreign Office; she died in 1995. The following year he married a family friend, Lady Joan Parham, and they were a devoted couple for over a decade. She survives him.

MAURICE MENDELSON

---

[14] *Continental Shelf (Tunisia v Libyan Arab Jamahiriya)*, *ICJ Reports* 1981, p. 3 (*Application by Malta to Intervene*) and *ICJ Reports* 1982, p. 18 (*Merits*) and *Application for Revision and Interpretation … ICJ Reports* 1985, p. 192; *Continental Shelf (Libyan Arab Jamahiriya v Malta)*, *ICJ Reports* 1984, p. 3 (*Application by Italy to Intervene*) and *ICJ Reports* 1985, p. 13 (*Merits*).

[15] *ICJ Reports* 1994, p. 112 (*Jurisdiction and Admissibility*); *ICJ Reports* 1995, p. 6 (*Jurisdiction and Admissibility*); *ICJ Reports* 2001, p. 40 (*Merits*).

THE DOCTRINE OF
INCORPORATION REVISITED

By ROGER O'KEEFE*

I. INTRODUCTION

The case of *R v Jones (Margaret)*[1] in 2006 was the first occasion on which the House of Lords has been called upon to examine in any depth the shibboleth that customary international law is part of the law of England and Wales—what Lord Denning MR in *Trendtex Trading Corporation v Central Bank of Nigeria* referred to as the doctrine of incorporation.[2] In *Jones (Margaret)*, where the issue was whether the crime of aggression known to customary international law was a crime under English law in the absence of a statute to this effect, Lord Bingham[3] was willing to accept, as had the Crown, the 'general truth' of the appellants' core contention, for which there was 'old and high authority',[4] that customary international law is part of the law of England and Wales, even if he hesitated to embrace the proposition 'in quite the unqualified terms in which it has often been

* University Senior Lecturer in Law and Deputy Director, Lauterpacht Centre for International Law, University of Cambridge; Fellow and College Lecturer in Law, Magdalene College, Cambridge. The following article is based on a paper presented by the author at *International Law and the English Legal System*, SLS Public International Law Group-British Institute of International and Comparative Law Seventeenth Conference on Theory and International Law, BIICL, London, 14 April 2008.

[1] [2006] UKHL 16; [2007] 1 AC 136.

[2] [1977] QB 529, 554. Reference to the 'doctrine of incorporation' as such does not appear prior to this in English case-law, although Lord Atkin in *Chung Chi Cheung v The King* [1939] AC 160, 167–8 speaks of the English courts' treating rules of customary international law 'as incorporated into the domestic law'. The label does, however, appear in pre-*Trendtex* academic writings: see eg E D Dickinson, 'Changing Concepts and the Doctrine of Incorporation' (1932) 26 *American Journal of International Law* 239; H Lauterpacht, 'Is International Law a Part of the Law of England?' (1939) 25 *Transactions of the Grotius Society* 51; J G Starke, *An Introduction to International Law* (8th edn, Butterworths, London, 1977), 89–94. Lauterpacht, ibid, refers synonymously to the doctrine of 'adoption', taking his cue from the verb used by Blackstone when, as discussed below, he states at W Blackstone, *Commentaries on the Laws of England*, book IV, chap 5, 67, that 'the law of nations (wherever any question arises which is properly the object of it's [*sic*] jurisdiction) is here adopted in it's full extent by the common law, and is held to be part of the law of the land'. (The edition referred to here is the four-volume University of Chicago Press facsimile of the First Edition of 1765–1769 (University of Chicago Press, Chicago, 1979).) See also D P O'Connell, *International Law* (2nd edn, Stevens & Sons, London, 1970), vol I, 49–50, albeit with a difference of emphasis.

[3] Lords Rodger, Carswell, and Mance agreed, the last adding a few paragraphs of his own. The same three Lords also agreed with Lord Hoffmann.

[4] [2007] 1 AC 136, 155, para 11, citing *Triquet v Bath* (1764) 3 Burr 1478, 1481; Blackstone, above n 2, book IV, chap 5, 67; *Duke of Brunswick v King of Hanover* (1844) 6 Beav 1, 51–2; *The Emperor of Austria v Day* (1861) 2 Giff 628, 678; *Chung Chi Cheung v The King* [1939] AC 160, 167–8; *Trendtex Trading Corporation v Central Bank of Nigeria* [1977] QB 529, 554; and *J H Rayner (Mincing Lane) Ltd v Department of Trade and Industry* [1989] Ch 72, 207.

stated', sympathizing as he did with Brierly's view that customary international law 'is not a part, but is one of the sources, of English law'.[5] (Lord Hoffman preferred to 'say nothing about the reception into English law of rules of international law which may affect rights and duties in civil law',[6] an issue Lord Mance also thought unnecessary to address.[7]) Pointing to Blackstone's examples of violation of safe-conducts, infringement of the rights of ambassadors and piracy *jure gentium*, as well as, he thought it 'at least arguable', war crimes,[8] Lord Bingham accepted 'that a crime recognised in customary international law may be assimilated into the domestic criminal law of this country'.[9] But this did not follow automatically:[10] 'a crime recognised as such in customary international law (such as the crime of aggression) may', his Lordship stated, 'but need not, become part of the domestic law of England and Wales without the need for any domestic statute'.[11] Lord Bingham's reading of the authorities led him to conclude 'that "customary international law is applicable in the English courts only where the constitution permits"'.[12] On this last basis, he held that the crime of aggression was not a crime under English law: first, it was up to Parliament, not the courts, to create new crimes;[13] secondly, the courts' slowness to review the exercise of prerogative powers over the conduct of foreign affairs and the deployment of the armed forces and their slowness to adjudicate upon transactions between sovereign States on the international plane was to be taken into account '[i]n considering whether the customary international law crime of aggression has been, or should be, tacitly assimilated into [English] domestic law'.[14] Lords Hoffmann and Mance came to the same conclusion for essentially the same reasons.

Jones (Margaret) is not the only recent case in which the doctrine of incorporation has been invoked by counsel and/or the court. There have been at least seventeen others since 1999 alone.[15] This apparent enthusiasm

---

[5] Ibid, citing J L Brierly, 'International Law in England' (1935) 51 *Law Quarterly Review* 24, 31.

[6] Ibid, 170, para 59.

[7] Ibid, 179, para 100.

[8] Ibid, 158, paras 20–2, quote at 22. See also 179, para 101 (Lord Mance).

[9] Ibid, 159, para 23.

[10] Ibid. See, similarly, 179, para 101 (Lord Mance).

[11] Ibid, 161, para 27. See, similarly, 179, para 101 (Lord Mance).

[12] Ibid, 160, para 23, quoting the present author, 'Customary International Crimes in English Courts' (2001) 72 *British Yearbook of International Law* 293, 335.

[13] Ibid, 160–2, paras 23–9. See, similarly, 170–1, paras 60–2 (Lord Hoffmann) and 179, para 101 (Lord Mance).

[14] Ibid, 163, para 30. See also 171–2, paras 63–7 (Lord Hoffmann).

[15] See *R v Metropolitan Stipendiary Magistrate, Ex parte Pinochet Ugarte (No 1)* [2000] 1 AC 61 and *R v Metropolitan Stipendiary Magistrate, Ex parte Pinochet Ugarte (No 3)* [2000] 1 AC 147; *Holland v Lampen-Wolfe* [2000] 1 WLR 1573 (insofar as the customary international law of State immunity was applied as common law); *Hutchinson v Newbury Magistrates' Court* (2000) 122 ILR 499; *R (Marchiori) v Environment Agency* [2002] EWCA Civ 3; (2002) 127 ILR 574; *R (Abbasi) v Secretary of State for Foreign and Commonwealth Affairs* [2002] EWCA Civ 1598; (2002) 126 ILR 685; *R (Campaign for Nuclear Disarmament) v Prime Minister* [2002] EWHC 2777; (2002) 126 ILR 727; *R v Lyons* [2002] UKHL 44; [2003] 1 AC 976; *Chagos Islanders v Attorney General and Her Majesty's British Indian Ocean Territory Commissioner* [2003] EWHC 2222, unreported, 9 October 2003, QBD, Ouseley J; *R (Manson) v Bow Street Magistrates' Court* [2003] EWHC 2720 (Admin),

stands in marked contrast to their Lordships' colder eye in *Jones (Margaret)*, which was perhaps foreshadowed in the briefest of statements in *R (European Roma Rights Centre) v Immigration Officer at Prague Airport*, where the failure to prove the existence of the customary international rule of refugee law at issue made it, in Lord Bingham's view, unnecessary to address the question of 'the extent to which and the manner in which international law is or may become part of the common law'.[16] Not dissimilarly, in *R (Marchiori) v Environment Agency*, Laws LJ, recalling counsel's submission 'that it is trite law that the law of nations is part of the law of England', remarked that 'there are nice conceptual questions as to what is precisely meant by this'.[17]

In his judgment in *In re McKerr* in 2004, Lord Steyn concluded a digression on the possible role of the doctrine of incorporation in the case before their Lordships with the observation that '[t]he impact of evolving customary international law on our domestic legal system is a subject of increasing importance'.[18] And so it is. In this light, now seems an opportune time to revisit the place of customary international law in English law and English judicial decision-making.[19]

II. The Doctrine as Stated

A. Prefatory clarification

What has come to be known as the doctrine of incorporation is taken to state that customary international law is automatically part of the law of England and Wales, without the need for legislative intervention. In other words, rules of customary international law are taken *ipso facto* to be rules of common law. In reliance on this doctrine, one or other party to a case

---

unreported and judgment not made public, 15 October 2003, QBD (DC), judgment as approved by the court obtained from Smith Bernal Wordwave Limited (official shorthand writers to the court); *Tatchell v Mugabe* (2004) 36 *ILR* 572; *Re Mofaz* (2004) 128 ILR 709; *In re McKerr* [2004] UKHL 12; [2004] 1 WLR 807; *R (European Roma Rights Centre) v Immigration Officer at Prague Airport* [2004] UKHL 55; [2005] 2 AC 1; *Re Bo Xilai* (2005) 128 ILR 713; *A and others v Secretary of State for the Home Department (No 2)* [2005] UKHL 71; [2006] 2 AC 221 (see counsel's submission at 237); *R (Mohamed) v Secretary of State for Foreign and Commonwealth Affairs* [2008] EWHC 2048 (Admin), unreported, 21 August 2008, QBD (DC); *R (Al-Saadoon) and another v Secretary of State for Defence* [2009] EWCA Civ 7, unreported, 21 January 2009, CA (Civ Div).

[16] [2004] UKHL 55; [2005] 2 AC 1, 39, para 28. Lord Hope, Baroness Hale and Lord Carswell were in full agreement with Lord Bingham on the refugee-law questions in the case, and Lord Steyn (ibid, 45, para 43) thought there was 'no answer' to Lord Bingham's reasoning in this respect.

[17] [2002] EWCA Civ 3; (2002) 127 ILR 620, 644, para 43, referring also to 'the principle, whatever its precise reach, that the law of nations is part of the law of England'.

[18] [2004] UKHL 12; [2004] 1 WLR 807, 824, para 52.

[19] Each generation seems to feel the need to engage in this exercise afresh. See eg J Westlake, 'Is International Law a Part of the Law of England?' (1906) 22 *Law Quarterly Review* 14; Lauterpacht, above n 2; J G Collier, 'Is International Law Really Part of the Law of England?' (1989) 38 *International & Comparative Law Quarterly* 924.

has frequently sought to rely on a rule of customary international law as a rule of common law capable of direct application by an English court, in the manner of any other rule of common law.[20] The doctrine of incorporation stands in opposition to what Lord Denning MR in *Trendtex* labelled the doctrine of transformation,[21] the theoretically competing view that rules of customary international law, like rules in treaties to which the UK is party, do not become part of English law unless and until Parliament enacts them.[22] The English courts have adhered since the eighteenth century to the doctrine of incorporation.

In more general terms, English law has never subscribed to a Manichaean antinomy between itself and international law. In the English courts, international law is not *res inter alios acta* but rather a body of law known to English law of which the court may properly take judicial notice, so that it has long been the case that international law is pleaded in the

---

[20] By way of more-or-less random introductory example, in the application to the Bow Street Magistrates' Court which lay at the heart of *R (Manson) v Bow Street Magistrates' Court* [2003] EWHC 2720 (Admin), the applicant sought the issue of summonses against the Prime Minister, the Secretary of State for Foreign and Commonwealth Affairs and the Secretary of State for Defence in respect of their alleged commission of crimes against peace, as recognized by customary international law and therefore, it was submitted, by the common law of England. Not dissimilarly, the defendants in *R v Jones (Margaret)* [2006] UKHL 16; [2007] 1 AC 136—charged under, variously, section 1(1) of the Criminal Law Act 1977 and section 3(b) of the Criminal Damage Act 1971 (conspiracy to cause criminal damage) and section 68(1) of the Criminal Justice and Public Order Act 1994 (aggravated trespass)—argued that crimes against peace (*sub nom.* the crime of aggression), as recognized by customary international law, constituted common-law crimes, and thus provided them with defences under, variously, section 3(1) of the Criminal Law Act 1967 (use of reasonable force to prevent a crime) and section 68(2) of the Criminal Justice and Public Order Act 1994 (aggravated trespass relating only to disruption, etc of activity not involving the commission of an offence). See, similarly, *Hutchinson v Newbury Magistrates' Court* (2000) 122 ILR 499. In *R (European Roma Rights Centre) v Immigration Officer at Prague Airport* [2004] UKHL 55; [2005] 2 AC 1, the applicant argued that customary international law provided that 'if a national of country A, wishing to travel to country B to claim asylum, applies in country A to officials of country B, he may not be denied leave to enter country B without appropriate enquiry into the merits of his asylum claim' ([2005] 2 AC 1, 38, para 26); and that since customary international law was part of the common law, this rule served to render unlawful the actions of the UK's immigration officer at Prague airport. Many other examples are considered below at Parts III and IV.

[21] Prior reference to 'transformation' in this context can be found in Lauterpacht, above n 2, 60, 64, 65, 75, 76, 84 and 86. O'Connell, above n 2, vol I, 49, speaks explicitly of a 'transformation doctrine'.

[22] The doctrine of transformation, which at its simplest states that statute is required to turn a rule of customary international law into a rule of English law, is often stated additionally to provide that rules of customary international law do not become part of English law 'except in so far as they have been already adopted and made part of our law by the decisions of the judges', in the words of Lord Denning MR in *Trendtex Trading Corporation v Central Bank of Nigeria* [1977] QB 529, 553. To the extent that this further statement could be taken to mean that the courts must await a prior judicial decision which adopts and makes the customary international rule part of the law of England, it can be dismissed as self-defeatingly circular: a first judicial adoption into English law has to come sometime. On the other hand, a different understanding of the doctrine of 'judicial transformation' (or 'judicial adoption'), which—at least insofar as the gist of the inquiry is whether legislation is required before a rule derived from customary international law can be relied on in the English courts—can equally and more usefully be characterized as a variant of the doctrine of incorporation, is considered below at Part IV.A. On a different and purely terminological point, note that when Parliament enacts *treaty*-based international rules into domestic law, it is said, somewhat confusingly, to have 'incorporated' the treaty. In Lord Denning MR's terminology, we would say that Parliament 'transforms' a treaty.

English courts as law and that the court is presumed to know its content. (This is in contrast with the position in relation to foreign national law, which is pleaded as fact and on which, therefore, evidence may be led.[23]) But parties and judges have traditionally felt no compulsion to cite the doctrine of incorporation to justify having regard in the English courts to customary international law *quâ* international law—and, it might be added, to craft common-law conflicts rules,[24] to construe statutes[25] and so on[26] by unabashed reference to it. The reason for this is simple: that international law is treated as law in the English courts is a proposition distinct from the doctrine of incorporation.[27] It is a proposition applicable as much to treaties, which most certainly do not form part of English law in the absence of statutory enactment,[28] as it is to customary international law; and it is a proposition relevant to the consideration of rules of international law as rules of international law—that is, as rules applicable on the international plane. In contrast, the doctrine of incorporation, which is limited in its

[23] See eg *Trendtex Trading Corporation v Central Bank of Nigeria* [1977] QB 529, 569 (Stephenson LJ), citing for support *The Cristina* [1938] AC 485, 497 (Lord Macmillan): '[R]ules of international law … must be in some sense "proved", and they are not proved in English courts by expert evidence like foreign law: they are "proved" by taking judicial notice of "international treaties and conventions, authoritative textbooks, practice and judicial decisions" of other courts in other countries which show that they have "attained the position of general acceptance by civilised nations"' (reference omitted). See also *Halsbury's Laws of England* (4th edn, reissue, 2002), vol 17(1), para 565 and vol 18(2), para 601; Lauterpacht, above n 2, 59; J L Brierly, *The Law of Nations. An Introduction to the International Law of Peace* (4th edn, Clarendon Press, Oxford, 1949), 77; O'Connell, above n 2, vol I, 53; I A Hunter, 'Proving Foreign and International Law in the Courts of England and Wales' (1978) 18 *Virginia Journal of International Law* 665, 674 and 685–6; F A Mann, *Foreign Affairs in English Courts* (Clarendon Press, Oxford, 1986), 126; Collier, above n 19, 935; R Jennings & A Watts (eds), *Oppenheim's International Law. Volume I: Peace* (9th edn, Longman, London, 1992), 57; I Brownlie, *Principles of Public International Law* (7th edn, Oxford University Press, Oxford, 2008), 41.

[24] See eg *Wolff v Oxholm* (1817) 6 M & S 92, 99–106; *Oppenheimer v Cattermole* [1976] 1 AC 249, 278 (Lord Cross); *Kuwait Airways Corporation v Iraqi Airways Company (Nos 4 and 5)* [2002] UKHL 19; [2002] 2 AC 883; *Société Eram Shipping Company Limited v Compagnie Internationale de Navigation* [2003] UKHL 30; [2004] 1 AC 260, 283–4, paras 54–5 (Lord Hoffmann) and 290 and 298, paras 80 and 109 (Lord Millett). In the words of Mann, 'when they develop their conflicts rules, English judges frequently adhere to … public international law': F A Mann, 'International Delinquencies before Municipal Courts' (1954) 70 *Law Quarterly Review* 181, 185 n 14.

[25] See the canon of construction recognized in *R v Keyn* (1876) 2 Ex D 63, 85 (Sir Robert Phillimore) and 210 (Lord Cockburn CJ); and, more recently, in *Salomon v Commissioners of Customs and Excise* [1967] 2 QB 116, 143 (Diplock LJ) and *Alcom Ltd v Republic of Colombia* [1984] AC 580, 588 (Sir John Donaldson MR, the expression 'the general principles of international law' referring in this context to rules of customary international law). See also, in a related but distinct vein, the use made of (customary) international law by Lord Rodger in *R (Al-Skeini) v Secretary of State for Defence* [2007] UKHL 26; [2008] 1 AC 153, 193, 194 and 195, paras 46, 49 and 54. Consider too Lord Hoffmann's statement in *R v Lyons* [2002] UKHL 44; [2003] 1 AC 976, 992 which extended what his Lordship called the 'strong presumption in favour of interpreting English law … in a way which does not place the United Kingdom in breach of an international obligation' to encompass the common law.

[26] Consider eg *Buck v Attorney-General*, 770–2 (Diplock LJ). See also [1965] Ch 745, 768 (Harman LJ) and 773–4 (Russell LJ).

[27] That said, the two are not, in the final analysis, unrelated, as explained below at Parts IV.A and VI.

[28] This rule is so well established that in *In re McKerr* [2004] UKL 12; [2004] 1 WLR 807, 826, para 63, Lord Hoffmann stated that 'it should no longer be necessary to cite authority for the proposition that the Convention [in question], as an international treaty, is not part of English domestic law'.

application to rules of customary international law, goes to reliance on these rules as rules of English law.

B. *The origin of the doctrine*

The statement that customary international law is part of English law is traceable to Lord Mansfield CJ's account in *Triquet v Bath*[29] in 1764 of Lord Talbot CJ's judgment of 1736 in *Barbuit*'s case.[30] Lord Mansfield CJ, quoting passages from *Barbuit* not actually found in the judgment as reported,[31] recalls:

Lord Talbot declared a clear opinion—'That the law of nations, in its full extent was part of the law of England.' ...

I was counsel in this case; and have a full note of it.

I remember, too, Lord Hardwicke's declaring his opinion to the same effect; and denying that Lord Chief Justice Holt ever had any doubt as to the law of nations being part of the law of England, upon the occasion of the arrest of the Russian Ambassador.

Mr Blackstone's principles are right ...[32]

(Blackstone appeared in *Triquet* as plaintiff's counsel.) Lord Mansfield CJ's recollection in *Triquet* was strictly obiter, since the case, like *Barbuit*'s case before it,[33] turned on the construction of an Act of Parliament, 7 Anne c 12, also known as the Diplomatic Privileges Act 1708.[34] Lord

---

[29] (1764) 3 Burr 1478.   [30] (1736) Cases t Talbot 281.
[31] The absence is noted by Stephenson LJ in *Trendtex Trading Corporation v Central Bank of Nigeria* [1978] QB 529, 567. A footnote to the final line of the judgment does contain the phrase 'the law of nations (which in its fullest extent was and formed part of the law of *England*)', but this is artefactual, added by Forrester, the reporter of the 'Cases in Equity, temp Ld Talbot': see Cases t Talbot 281, 283. Adair has suggested that what Forrester reported was Lord Mansfield CJ's recollection of *Barbuit*'s case, rather than Lord Talbot CJ's actual words: E R Adair, *The Exterritoriality of Ambassadors in the Sixteenth and Seventeenth Centuries* (Longmans, Green & Co, London, 1929), 239; E R Adair, 'The Law of Nations and the Common Law of England: A Study of 7 Anne cap. 12' (1928) 2 *Cambridge Historical Journal* 290, 296. Lauterpacht sees 'no reason to assume [this]': Lauterpacht, above n 2, 79 n (q). But Dickinson sees Adair's suggestion as 'confirmed by the fact that [the footnote in question] is found neither in the first edition of the Talbot decisions, published in 1741, nor in the second edition of 1753, but appears for the first time, insofar as we have been able to determine, in the London edition of 1792': E D Dickinson, 'L'Interprétation et l'application du droit international dans les pays anglo-américains', 40 *Recueil des Cours* (1932-II) 305, 339 n 1, present author's translation.
[32] 3 Burr 1478, 1481.
[33] Lord Talbot CJ was not called on in *Barbuit* to determine the relationship between the law of nations and the law of England *in abstracto*. The case turned on 'whether the defendant [was] such a person as 7 *Anne, cap* 10 [*sic*, read '12'] describes', as was expressly 'declaratory of the antient universal *jus gentium*': see Cases t Talbot 281, 282.
[34] The long title is 'An Act for preserving the Privileges of Ambassadors and other publick Ministers of Foreign Princes and States'. The Act was passed in urgent response to the arrest, manhandling and brief detention, by properly accredited officers of justice, of the Russian ambassador to Great Britain in execution of a writ relating to debts owed by him to certain merchants. The preamble records: 'Whereas several turbulent and disorderly persons having in a most outrageous Manner

Mansfield CJ was quick to add, however, that 'the Act was not occasioned by any doubt "whether the law of nations, particularly the part relative to public ministers, were not part of the law of England; and the infraction, criminal"'.[35] A year after *Triquet v Bath*, in *Lockwood v Coysgarne*, his Lordship reiterated 'that the Statute of 7 Ann. was only declaratory of the law of nations, and that the law of nations was in full force in these kingdoms'.[36] He reprised the motif two years later in *Heathfield v Chilton*, where he stated that '[t]he privileges of public ministers and their retinues depend on the law of nations; which is part of the common law of England'.[37] His Lordship added that '[t]he law of nations will be carried as far in England, as any where'.[38] He later took the point for granted in *Clarke v Cretico*.[39]

An equally influential early statement of the place occupied in English law by the law of nations is found in the 1760s in Chapter 5 ('Offences against the Law of Nations') of Book IV of Blackstone's *Commentaries on the Laws of England*. Blackstone writes:

In arbitrary states [the law of nations], whenever it contradicts or is not provided for by the municipal law of the country, is enforced by the royal power: but since in England no royal power can introduce a new law, or suspend the execution of the old, therefore the law of nations (wherever any question arises which is properly the object of it's [*sic*] jurisdiction) is here adopted in it's full extent by the common law, and is held to be part of the law of the land. And those acts of parliament, which have from time to time been made to enforce this universal law, or to facilitate the execution of its decisions, are not to be considered as introductive of any new rule, but merely as declaratory of the old fundamental constitutions of the kingdom; without which it must cease to be part of the civilized world.[40]

insulted the Person of His Excellency Andrew Artemonowitz Matueof Ambassador Extraordinary of his Czarish Majesty Emperor of Great Russia Her Majesties [*sic*] good Friend and Ally by arresting him and taking him by Violence out of his Coach in the publick Street and detaining him in Custody for several Hours in Contempt of the Protection granted by Her Majesty contrary to the Law of Nations and in Prejudice of the Rights and Privileges which Ambassadors and other publick Ministers authorized and received as such have at all Times been thereby possessed of and ought to be kept sacred and inviolable ...' Section 3 of the Act provides: '[A]ll Writs and Processes that shall at any Time hereafter be sued forth or prosecuted whereby the Person of any Ambassador or publick Minister of any foreign Prince or State authorized and received as such by Her Majesty Her Heirs or Successors or the Domestick or Domestick Servant of any such Ambassador or other publick Minister may be arrested or imprisoned or his or their Goods or Chattels may be distrained seized or attached shall be deemed and adjudged to be utterly null and void to all Intents Constructions and Purposes whatsoever.' Section 4 made it a criminal offence to initiate the proceedings referred to in section 3, perpetrators being deemed 'Violators of the Law of Nations and Disturbers of the publick Repose'.

[35] 3 Burr 1478, 1480. M'Kean CJ expressed a similar view in the early US case of *Respublica v De Longchamps*, 1 US (1 Dall) 111, 117 (Court of Oyer and Terminer, Philadelphia, 1784).

[36] (1765) 3 Burr 1676, 1678.

[37] (1767) 4 Burr 2015, 2016. The case was another under 7 Anne c 12.

[38] 4 Burr 2015, 2016.

[39] (1808) 1 Taunt 106. This also fell to be determined under 7 Anne c 12.

[40] Blackstone, above n 2, book IV, chap 5, 67. Blackstone summarizes his chapter on offences against the law of nations as an account of 'the principal cases, in which the statute law of England interposes, to aid and enforce the law of nations, as a part of the common law; by inflicting an adequate punishment upon offences against that universal law, committed by private persons': ibid, 73.

Turning to specifics, Blackstone states that '[t]he principal offences against the law of nations, animadverted on as such by the municipal laws of England, are of three kinds: 1. Violation of safe-conducts; 2. Infringement of the rights of embassadors [*sic*]; and 3. Piracy'.[41] 'As to the rights of embassadors, which are ... established by the law of nations', Blackstone avers that 'the common law of England recognizes them in their full extent, by immediately stopping all legal process, sued out through the ignorance or rashness of individuals, which may intrench upon the immunities of a foreign minister or any of his train'.[42]

The assertions by Lord Mansfield CJ, Blackstone and, if he ever actually uttered the words ascribed to him, Lord Talbot CJ that the law of nations was adopted in its full extent[43] by the common law and held to be part of the law of England were in fact baseless.[44] Prior to the Civil War and the later Glorious Revolution, the relationship between international law and English law 'had not begun to be considered by the common lawyers'.[45] Leaving aside the ancient maritime law applied by the civil-law Admiralty courts, '[t]he rules of international law were regarded as matters which concerned the Crown, and fell within its wide prerogative in relation to foreign affairs'.[46] In other words, prior to the post-1689 constitutional dispensation, any rules of international law not within the jurisdiction of the Admiralty[47] were enforced in England 'by prerogative

---

[41] Ibid, 68. Blackstone's label 'offence against the law of nations' treated as identical what were actually two distinct legal phenomena: see the discussion below at nn 143 and 145.

[42] Ibid, 70, emphasis omitted.

[43] It is important to distinguish in this regard between those rules of the sixteenth- to eighteenth-century law of nations pertinent to relations between States (what today we would call public international law) and those rules of the law of nations, within the broad meaning then accorded the term, which pertained to relations between individuals, most notably the law merchant: as regards the latter, which did not *per se* fall within the Crown's prerogative in respect of foreign affairs, see the discussion in the following paragraph below, including in n 55.

[44] Referring to that part of the law of nations pertaining to relations between States, Crawford speaks of 'the historically untenable claim that "international law was part of the law of England"': J Crawford, 'Public International Law in Twentieth-century England', in J Beatson & R Zimmermann (eds), *Jurists Uprooted. German-speaking Émigré Lawyers in Twentieth-century Britain* (Oxford University Press, Oxford, 2004), 681, 686. Holdsworth similarly describes Lord Mansfield CJ and Blackstone's assertions as 'historically incorrect': W S Holdsworth, *A History of English Law* (Methuen, London, 1923–66), vol X, 373. Adair is more damning still, characterizing Lord Mansfield CJ's dictum in *Heathfield v Chilton* that the law of nations is part of the common law of England, affirming and rendering more directly what he had said in *Triquet v Bath*, as 'all nonsense so far as the seventeenth and eighteenth centuries are concerned': Adair, *Exterritoriality*, above n 31, 88. See also ibid, 238 and Adair, 'The Law of Nations', above n 31, 295–6 and 297, the latter calling Lord Mansfield CJ's statement 'radically unsound'.

[45] W S Holdsworth, 'The Relation of English Law to International Law' (1941–42) 26 *Minnesota Law Review* 141, 141. See also Holdsworth, above n 44, vol XIV, 23.

[46] Holdsworth, above n 45, 141. See also Holdsworth, above n 44, vol XIV, 23.

[47] '[T]hat part of the law of England which is directed to the enforcement of international obligations, and the regulation of the rights of foreigners [was] ... [u]p to the [nineteenth] century ... a very meagre branch of English law; and this is due to the fact that it was a branch of law which fell outside the purview of the ordinary courts. ... [I]n the Middles Ages it was regarded as falling within the jurisdiction of the admiral, the chancellor, or special officials. More especially it fell, as a branch of maritime law, under the jurisdiction of the admiral. ... [T]he peculiar history of the Admiralty jurisdiction in

action, not by the ordinary courts or the common law'.[48] Nor is there any evidence to suggest that the relationship between international law and the common law had been raised in the common-law courts between 1688 and *Barbuit*'s case in 1736. As to specifics, there is no indication whatsoever that the common-law courts recognized the immunities of ambassadors prior to the passage of 7 Anne c 12[49]—a point freely admitted by Blackstone himself.[50] Even less (if less than nought is possible) did they treat the violation of these immunities as criminal before the same Act made them so.[51] As for the other two 'offences against the law of nations'

England for a long time prevented the development of such branches of law.': Holdsworth, above n 44, vol II, 474.

[48] Adair, 'The Law of Nations', above n 31, 294. See also Adair, *Exterritoriality*, above n 31, 239, 241, 242, and 243. Lauterpacht, above n 2, 68 and 70 concedes the point, yet claims ibid, 68 that '[t]he substance of most of the available evidence points to the fact that principles of international law, especially with regard to diplomatic immunities, were recognized and given effect by English law', arguing ibid, 70 that '[t]he law relating to the royal prerogative was and is part of the law of England'. He concludes ibid that '[a]ny criticism of Blackstone's view by reference to the fact that the relevant portions of the Law of Nations were enforced by the royal prerogative and not by the common law courts must be regarded as being based on a controversial technicality'. But he later admits ibid, 79–80: 'It is possible that at the beginning of the eighteenth century international law was not part of the common law; it is possible that Blackstone and Lord Mansfield in 1765 [*sic*] and Lord Talbot in 1737 [*sic*] were mistaken in assuming that this was the position in the seventeenth and in the preceding centuries.'

[49] Holdsworth takes the view that '[t]he statute of 1708, which dealt with the immunities of ambassadors, though said by Lord Mansfield and others to be only declaratory of the common law, really introduced this principle of international law into the common law ...': Holdsworth, above n 45, 149. See also Holdsworth, above n 44, vol XIV, 31. He speaks of 'the historically incorrect view that the statute was merely in affirmance of a common law rule which had received and admitted the binding force of the rules of international law': ibid, 52. See also ibid, 62. Adair, 'The Law of Nations', above n 31, 295 makes the same point even more strikingly: 'The statute was specifically passed because international law was not part of the common law of England, because its breach, therefore, could not be legally prevented [after the Glorious Revolution put paid to prerogative interference with the courts] unless it was incorporated in the law of England by act of Parliament or by long-continued action of the ordinary courts. It was avowedly declaratory, but it was declaratory not of the common law, but of international law and of the custom of the English government in certain international questions, and in these questions the statute gave the government just that legal support which the common law could not provide.' See also Adair, *Exterritoriality*, above n 31, 238. *Cf contra* Lauterpacht, above n 2, 68–70.

[50] See Blackstone, above n 2, book I, chap 7, 247: 'And the truth is, we find no traces in our lawbooks of allowing any privilege to embassadors or their domestics, even in civil suits, previous to the reign of queen Anne ...' Blackstone recounts ibid, 247–8 how Queen Anne informed the Czar of Russia, on the occasion of his ambassador's arrest and mistreatment in 1708, '"that the law of England had not yet protected embassadors from the payment of their lawful debts; that therefore the arrest was no offence by the laws; and that she could inflict no punishment upon any, the meanest, of her subjects, unless warranted by the law of the land"' (reference omitted). He concludes ibid, 248, reference omitted: 'And, in consequence of this statute [viz 7 Anne c 12], thus enforcing the law of nations, these privileges are now usually allowed in the courts of common law.'

[51] The denial by Lord Mansfield CJ in *Triquet v Bath* of any doubt on the part of the Court of Queen's Bench, in the celebrated case of the Russian ambassador, as to whether violations of the rights of ambassadors were criminal under the law of England is simply wishful thinking, and is contradicted by Blackstone, ibid, book I, chap 7, 247–8. Those responsible for the insult to the ambassador were convicted by the jury of the fact of having arrested and detained him, but whether this constituted a criminal offence was never determined. See *Case of Andrew Artemonowitz Mattueof, Ambassador of Muscovy* (1709) 10 Mod 5, 5 n (a). Indeed, the inability of the English courts to convict the perpetrators of a criminal offence fuelled the dispute between Russia and Great Britain: see C de Martens (ed), *Causes célèbres du droit des gens* (2nd edn, Brockhaus, Leipzig, 1858), vol I, 86–96.

identified by Blackstone, namely violations of safe-conducts and piracy, neither was triable in the ordinary common-law courts or, indeed, under the common law; rather, in accordance with respective special procedures laid down in Acts cited by Blackstone himself, the first, abolished by Blackstone's time, had been triable under statute, while the second was tried under the species of civil law applied by the Admiralty courts.[52]

In reality, Blackstone and Lord Mansfield CJ's statements are more in the way of jusnaturalist professions of faith: both the law of nations and the common law of England proceeded from universal tenets of right reason, they asserted, so that the two bodies of law naturally coincided on coincident subject-matters.[53] Peremptory statements such as those in *Triquet v Bath* and subsequent cases are also typical of Lord Mansfield CJ's energetic, expansive and distinctly pre-popular democratic[54] vision of the 'law-declaring' role of the English judge. It pays too to appreciate that the term 'the law of nations' as used in Lord Mansfield CJ and Blackstone's day meant something significantly different from its use after the mid-nineteenth century at the latest and from the use of the term 'public international law' today. The seventeenth- and eighteenth-century law of nations represented a mélange of rules governing relations

---

Holdsworth, above n 45, 149 draws the unequivocal conclusion that 7 Anne c 12 'for the first time provided for penalties' for breach of diplomatic immunity. See also Holdsworth, above n 44, vol XIV, 31; Adair, 'The Law of Nations', above n 31, 294–7 and *Exterritoriality*, above n 31, 87–8, 238, 240 and 241. Even Lauterpacht agrees: see Lauterpacht, above n 2, 69.

[52] See the discussion below at Part III.A.3.

[53] See also eg C M Picciotto, *The Relation of International Law to the Law of England and of the United States of America* (McBride, Nast & Co, London, 1915), 75–6, para 41 and 107, para 66; H Triepel, 'Les rapports entre le droit interne et le droit international', 1 *Recueil des Cours* (1923) 77, 88–9; Dickinson, above n 2, 253 and above n 31, 336 and 344; Lauterpacht, above n 2, 67–8; Brierly, above n 23, 77–8; I A Shearer, 'The Relationship between International Law and Domestic Law', in B R Opeskin & D R Rothwell (eds), *International Law and Australian Federalism* (Melbourne University Press, Melbourne, 1997), 34, 36; M Lobban, 'Custom, common law reasoning and the law of nations in the nineteenth century', in A Perreau-Saussine & J B Murphy (eds), *The Nature of Customary Law. Legal, Historical and Philosophical Perspectives* (Cambridge University Press, Cambridge, 2007), 256, 264–5. As William Murray, Solicitor-General, Mansfield—in a report of 18 January 1753 by the Committee appointed by His Britannic Majesty to reply to the complaints of Frederick II of Prussia as to certain captures of Prussian vessels made by British ships during the war with France and Spain—described the law of nations as 'founded upon justice, equity, convenience, and the reason of the thing, and confirmed by long usage': see *The Zamora* [1916] 2 AC 77, 94. For his part, Blackstone, above n 2, book I, intro, sec 2, 42–3 writes: 'Upon these two foundations, the law of nature and the law of revelation, depend all human laws; ... human laws are only declaratory of, and act in subordination to [these].' To these foundations Blackstone adds 'a third kind of law ... called "the law of nations"; which ... depends entirely upon the rules of natural law, or upon mutual compacts, treaties, leagues, and agreements between several communities'. See also ibid, book IV, chap 5, 66: 'The law of nations is a system of rules, deducible by natural reason, and established by universal consent among the civilized inhabitants of the world ...'

[54] Although by Mansfield's day the constitutional dispensation ushered in by the Glorious Revolution had limited the power of the monarchy vis-à-vis Parliament, the latter was not yet a body genuinely representative of the population. See similarly, in relation to Blackstone, P Sales & J Clement, 'International Law in Domestic Courts: The Developing Framework' (2008) 124 *Law Quarterly Review* 388, 415: '[H]e was writing at a time before the full development of democratic legal theory in the 19th and 20th centuries, and before the full development of credible democratic credentials of Parliament with the expansion of the franchise over that period.'

between States, rules governing transactions spanning more than one State's jurisdiction between individuals of different nationalities, such as maritime law and the law merchant, and (to the extent that these differed from the immediately foregoing) rules of what we would now call private international law regulating conflicts between different national systems of law.[55] By the mid-nineteenth century, however, the law of nations had become almost exclusively a body of rules between States; and while exceptions have proliferated over time, modern public international law remains for the most part an inter-State law.

Any debate, however, is academic, given that it is the reception of Lord Mansfield CJ and Blackstone's views that counts, and this reception was unquestioning, at least to the extent that the question was whether statute was *per se* required before a rule of customary international law could become a rule of English law.

C. The reception of the doctrine

In the early nineteenth-century case of *Viveash v Becker*,[56] Lord Ellenborough CJ took it as axiomatic that the law of nations as to diplomatic immunity, although reflected in 7 Anne c 12, was otherwise applicable in the English courts without the need for parliamentary intervention. In the event, his Lordship held that the law of nations did not assist the defendant, a mere consul; but he added that, '[i]f we saw clearly that the law of nations was in favour of the privilege, it would be afforded to the defendant'.[57] In 1823, in *Novello v Toogood*, Abbot CJ referred to 'the common law, of which the law of nations must be deemed a part'.[58] The following year, in *De Wütz v Hendricks*, Best CJ went as far as to say that 'the law of nations [was] in all cases of international law ... adopted into the municipal code

---

[55] See *Sosa v Alvarez-Machain*, 542 US 692, 743 (2004). See also eg H Triepel, *Droit international et droit interne* (R Brunet trans, Pédone, Paris, 1920), 138–9, especially 139 n 1; Lauterpacht, above n 2, 52; E D Dickinson, 'The Law of Nations as Part of the National Law of the United States' (1952) 101 *University of Pennsylvania Law Review* 26, 26–9; M Rheinstein, 'The Constitutional Bases of Jurisdiction' (1955) 22 *University of Chicago Law Review* 775, 804–8; M Akehurst, 'Jurisdiction in International Law' (1972–73) 46 *British Yearbook of International Law* 145, 212–4; Hunter, above n 23, 675; S Jay, 'The Status of the Law of Nations in Early American Law' (1989) 42 *Vanderbilt Law Review* 819, 821–2. Blackstone characterizes the law merchant as 'a branch of the law of nations' recognized by the common law, observing that 'in civil transactions and questions of property between the subjects of different States, the law of nations has much scope and extent, as adopted by the law of England': Blackstone, above n 2, book IV, chap 5, 67. See also eg *Mogadara v Holt* (1691) 1 Show KB 317, 318 (Eyres J); *Scrimshire v Scrimshire* (1752) 2 Hag Con 395, 420 (Sir Edward Simpson). For maritime law as part of the law of nations, see eg *Luke v Lyde* (1759) 2 Burr 882, 887 (Lord Mansfield CJ). As regards rules of private international law, see eg *Roach v Garvan* (1748) 1 Ves Sen 157, 159 (Lord Hardwicke LC); *Scrimshire v Scrimshire* (1752) 2 Hag Con 395, 416–7, 419, 421 and 422 (Sir Edward Simpson); *Robinson v Bland* (1760) 1 Black W 256, 258 (Lord Mansfield CJ). For a good example of the admixture of public and private international law in this earlier law of nations, see dicta in *Madrazo v Willes* (1820) 3 B & Ald 353.

[56] (1814) 3 M & S 284.

[57] Ibid, 298.

[58] (1823) 1 B & C 554, 562. This was another diplomatic immunity case under 7 Anne c 12.

of every civilized country'.[59] A degree of modesty was restored in *Duke of Brunswick v King of Hanover*, when Lord Langdale MR limited himself to the statement that 'the law of nations, ... when ascertained, is to be deemed part of the common law of England'.[60] In 1861, in *The Emperor of Austria v Day and Kossuth*,[61] Sir John Stuart V-C stated that '[a] public right, recognised by the law of nations, is a legal right; because the law of nations is part of the common law of England'.[62] His Lordship cited with approval Blackstone's view—'and', he added, 'it has so always been held in our Courts'—that 'the law of nations, whenever any question arises, which is properly the object of its jurisdiction, is adopted in its full extent by the common law of England, and held to be part of the law of the land'.[63]

The celebrated late nineteenth-century case of *The Queen v Keyn*[64] is often taken as authority for the proposition that customary international law is not part of English law without statutory enactment. But of the thirteen judges and seven-strong majority of the Court for Crown Cases Reserved, only the judgments of Lord Cockburn CJ[65] and Lush J cast doubt on whether the law of nations formed part of the law of England in the absence of legislation, and even then ambiguously. For example, Lord Cockburn CJ states:

At all events, I am prepared to abide by the distinction taken in the statutes of Richard II between the realm and the sea. For centuries our judicial system in the administration of the criminal law has been divided into two distinct and independent branches, the one having jurisdiction over the land and any sea considered to be within the land; the other over the sea external to the land. No concurrent assent of nations, that a portion of what before was treated as the high sea, and as such common to all the world, shall now be treated as the territory of the local state, can of itself, without the authority of Parliament, convert that which before was in the eye of the law high sea into British territory, and so change the law, or give to the Courts of this country, independently of legislation, a jurisdiction over the foreigner where had it not before.[66]

Lush J states similarly:

In the reign of Richard II the realm consisted of the land within the body of the counties. All beyond low-water mark was part of the high seas. At that period the three-mile radius [of the territorial sea] had not been thought of. International

---

[59] (1824) 2 Bing 314, 315–6.
[60] (1844) 6 Beav 1, 45. On appeal, the House of Lords took it as read that the applicable rule was to be derived from the law of nations: see (1848) 2 HLC 1.
[61] (1861) 2 Giff 628.
[62] Ibid, 678.
[63] Ibid.
[64] (1876) 2 Ex D 63.
[65] Pollock B and Field J concurred in a single sentence. Kelly CB 'agree[d] substantially' with both Sir Robert Phillimore and Cockburn CJ: ibid, 151.
[66] Ibid, 197–8.

law, which, upon this subject at least, has grown up since that period, cannot enlarge the area of our municipal law, nor could treaties with all the nations of the world have that effect. That can only be done by Act of Parliament. As no such Act has been passed, it follows that what was out of the realm then is out of the realm now, and what was part of the high seas then is part of the high seas now; and upon the high seas the Admiralty jurisdiction was confined to British ships.[67]

These passages could be read to support the need for statutory enactment of the law of nations. But they equally (and, in the event, actually[68]) support the view that the reception of the law of nations into English law, while possible in principle, is trumped by the constitutional supremacy of Parliament—whose will was embodied in the instant case in 'the statutes of Richard II',[69] which divided the criminal jurisdiction of the English courts between the courts of common law (the realm, viz land) and the courts of the admiral (the sea)—and by the constitutional separation of powers, in accordance with which the jurisdiction of the courts can be enlarged by Parliament alone. The second of these propositions is what the other famous, and frequently misconstrued, dicta of Lord Cockburn CJ in *Keyn* are directed towards.[70] (For what it is worth, in *The Charkieh* three years earlier, Lord Cockburn CJ referred to 'international law, which is part of the municipal law of this country'.[71]) For his part, Lord Coleridge CJ, referring in dissent to the law of nations as 'that collection of usages which civilized states have agreed to observe in their dealings with one another', affirmed that 'when [appropriate circumstances] arise, the English Courts give effect, as part of English law, to such agreement'.[72]

At the turn of the last century, in *West Rand Central Gold Mining Company v The King*[73] in the Divisional Court of King's Bench, Lord Alverstone CJ, while wary of authors as a source of the law of nations, was in no doubt as to that law's domestic applicability:

It is quite true that whatever has received the common consent of civilized nations must have received the assent of our country, and that to which we have assented along with other nations in general may properly be called international law, and as such will be acknowledged and applied by our municipal tribunals when legitimate occasion arises for those tribunals to decide questions to which doctrines of international law may be relevant.[74]

---

[67] Ibid, 239.   [68] See the discussion below at Part III.B.2.

[69] The statutes referred to are 13 Rich II st I c 5 and 15 Rich II c 3, considered by his Lordship at 2 Ex D 63, 167–8.

[70] See ibid, 203 and 207–8.

[71] (1872–73) LR 8 QB 197, 199.

[72] 2 Ex D 63, 154.

[73] [1905] 2 KB 391.

[74] Ibid, 406–7.

His Lordship cited *Barbuit, Triquet v Bath* and *Heathfield v Chilton* with approval.[75] He did, however, enter a proviso, namely that the law of nations formed part of the law of England only to the extent that it was not 'contrary to the principles of her laws as declared by her Courts'.[76] Lord Alverstone CJ's words in *West Rand* were quoted and accepted as a correct statement of the law by Bankes LJ in *Commercial and Estates Company of Egypt v Board of Trade*.[77] Three years later, Lord Phillimore in *Engelke v Musmann* referred simply to 'international law, which is part of the common law of this country'.[78]

Like *Keyn* in the century before it, the Privy Council case of *Chung Chi Cheung v The King*[79]—strictly speaking not an English authority, but subsequently treated by the courts as effectively such—is sometimes taken to stand for the proposition that customary international law is not part of the law of England until made so by statute. But, like *Keyn, Chung Chi Cheung* in fact states something significantly different. A much-quoted dictum of Lord Atkin, delivering the judgment of the Board, reads:

It must always be remembered that, so far, at any rate, as the Courts of this country are concerned, international law has no validity save in so far as its principles are accepted and adopted by our own domestic law. There is no external power that imposes its rules upon our own code of substantive law and procedure.[80]

But his Lordship goes on immediately to say:

The Courts acknowledge the existence of a body of rules which nations accept among themselves. On any judicial issue they seek to ascertain what the relevant rule is, and, having found it, they will treat it as incorporated into the domestic law, so far as it is not inconsistent with rules enacted by statutes or finally declared by their tribunals.[81]

Far from denying the incorporation of customary international law, the passage as a whole in fact endorses it, subject to the proviso that statute and finally declared rules of common law are trumps. The statement that 'international law has no validity save in so far as its principles are accepted and adopted by our own domestic law' is clearly not intended to mean that customary international law is not applicable as English law. On the contrary, Lord Atkin is seeking to explain why in fact it is, his reasoning being that customary international law does not force itself upon English law; rather, in his Lordship's view, English law admits customary

---

[75] Ibid, 407–8, warning, however, that 'the expressions used by Lord Mansfield ... that the law of nations forms part of the law of England, ought not to be construed so as to include as part of the law of England opinions of text-writers ...'.

[76] Ibid, 408.

[77] [1925] 1 KB 271, 283.

[78] [1928] AC 433, 449.

[79] [1939] AC 160.

[80] Ibid, 167–8.

[81] Ibid, 168.

international law on English law's terms.[82] Not dissimilarly, in *Commercial and Estates Company of Egypt v Board of Trade*, his Lordship (or Atkin LJ, as he then was), in giving effect at English law to the customary international right of angary, states:

> The right of angary of the Sovereign is a right recognized by our municipal law, giving rise to rights and obligations in the full sense. ... International law as such can confer no rights cognizable in the municipal courts. It is only in so far as the rules of international law are recognized as included in the rules of the municipal law that they are allowed in the municipal Courts to give rise to rights or obligations. The right of angary therefore is a right recognized by English law ...[83]

The year before *Chung Chi Cheung* in *The Cristina*, Lord Atkin had spoken of 'propositions of international law engrafted into our domestic law'.[84]

Any lingering uncertainty over the status of customary international law in English law as there may have been was formally dispelled by the Court of Appeal's decision in *Trendtex Trading Corporation v Central Bank of Nigeria*,[85] where Lord Denning MR subscribed to the view that 'the rules of international law are incorporated into English law automatically and considered to be part of English law unless they are in conflict with an Act of Parliament'.[86] Shaw LJ agreed, declaring that 'the law of nations ... [is] applied in the courts of England'.[87] Like Lord Denning MR, the only limitation his Lordship acknowledged on the applicability of customary international law in English courts was the primacy of statute.[88]

'[T]hat the rules of international law from time to time in force are automatically incorporated into the common law and, subject always to statute, are supreme' was subsequently affirmed by Nourse LJ, dissenting on a separate point, in *J H Rayner (Mincing Lane) v Department of Trade and Industry*.[89] In turn, citing Nourse LJ in *J H Rayner*, Mantell J in *Al-Adsani v Government of Kuwait*[90] 'accepted the proposition that international forms part of the law of this country', subject to the proviso that 'where the clear language of [a] statute is to the contrary ... the statute must prevail'.[91]

Turning to this century, Lord Lloyd referred in *R v Metropolitan Stipendiary Magistrate, Ex parte Pinochet Ugarte (No 1)* to 'the requirements

---

[82] See also the discussion below at Part IV.A.   [83] [1925] 1 KB 271, 295.
[84] [1938] AC 485, 490.
[85] [1977] QB 529.
[86] Ibid, 553. See also 554: '[T]he rules of international law, as existing from time to time, do form part of our English law.'
[87] Ibid, 579.
[88] Ibid, 577 and 578.
[89] [1989] Ch 72, 207.
[90] (1995) 103 ILR 420.
[91] Ibid, 428.

of customary international law, which are observed and enforced by our courts as part of the common law',[92] saying later that 'the common law incorporates the rules of customary international law'.[93] In the subsequent *R v Bow Street Metropolitan Stipendiary Magistrate, Ex parte Pinochet Ugarte (No 3)*, Lord Millet stated plainly that '[c]ustomary international law is part of the common law'.[94] Even more forthrightly, when *Jones (Margaret)* was before the Court of Appeal, Latham LJ (giving the judgment of the court)—having recalled Blackstone,[95] Lord Alverstone CJ in *West Rand*,[96] Lord Denning MR in *Trendtex*[97] and Nourse LJ in *J H Rayner*[98]—declared there to be '[n]o doubt ... that a rule of international law is capable of being incorporated into English law if it is an established rule derived from one or more of the recognised sources, [including] a clear consensus'.[99] Away from the superior courts of record, Judge Workman, Senior District Judge sitting in the Bow Street Magistrates' Court, stated in *Tatchell v Mugabe* that 'international customary law ... is embodied in our Common Law'.[100] In the subsequent cases of *Re Mofaz* and *Re Bo Xilai*, he gave effect at common law to the immunities supposedly accorded a serving Minister for Defence and a serving Minister for Commerce and International Trade by customary international law.[101]

It will be recalled, however, that in *R (Marchiori) v Environment Agency*, Laws LJ, recounting the applicant's submission that the law of nations is part of the law of England, observed that 'there are nice conceptual questions as to what is precisely meant by this'.[102] It will also be recalled that in *Jones (Margaret)*, while accepting the 'general truth' of the contention that customary international law is part of the law of England, Lord Bingham was wary of formulating the doctrine of incorporation 'in quite the unqualified terms in which it has often been stated'.[103] Although not needing to determine, and so not determining, the point, his Lordship leant towards Brierly's view that customary international law 'is not a part, but is one of the sources, of English law'[104]—a distinction flagged

---

[92] [2000] 1 AC 61, 89.
[93] Ibid, 90, going on to quote from Jennings & Watts, above n 23, 57.
[94] [2000] 1 AC 147, 276.
[95] [2004] EWCA Crim 1981; [2005] QB 259, 270–71, para 19, quoting Blackstone, above n 2, book IV, chap 5, 66–7.
[96] [2005] QB 2 271, para 20, quoting [1905] 2 KB 391, 406–7.
[97] Ibid, 271, paras 21–2, quoting [1977] QB 529, 554.
[98] Ibid, 271–72, para 23, quoting [1989] Ch 72, 207.
[99] Ibid, 272, para 24.
[100] [2004] 136 ILR 572, 573. The case actually fell under section 20 of the State Immunity Act 1978 (c 33).
[101] See (2004) 128 ILR 709 and (2005) 128 ILR 713 respectively.
[102] [2002] EWCA Civ 3; (2000) 127 ILR 620, 644, para 43, referring also to 'the principle, whatever its precise reach, that the law of nations is part of the law of England'.
[103] [2006] UKHL 16; [2007] 1 AC 136, 155, para 11.
[104] [2007] 1 AC 136, 155, para 11, citing Brierly, above n 5, 31.

earlier by Stephenson LJ in *Trendtex*.[105] For their parts, Lords Hoffmann and Mance eschewed any general statement 'about the reception into English law of rules of international law which may affect rights and duties in civil law'.[106]

III. The Doctrine in Practice

A. Seldom applied

Since its judicial inception in the eighteenth century, the doctrine of incorporation, as variously formulated, has been accepted many times and without dissent by the English courts as representing an accurate statement of the relationship between customary international law and the common law of England. In the great majority of these cases, however, acceptance of the doctrine has been purely obiter. Despite the plethora of occasions on which the courts have affirmed or not denied that customary international law is part of the common law of England, only in relation to a single area of customary international law has this proposition, whether explicitly advanced or simply assumed, led unambiguously to the international rule's actual application, by the ordinary common-law courts, as a rule of English law. Perhaps just as strikingly, in only two other cases, both of them arising out of the same facts, has the doctrine of incorporation been determinative of the outcome. The examples given by Blackstone and cited by the House of Lords in *Jones (Margaret)* are fallacies, except for the common-law crime of piracy, which instead is historically anomalous and has nothing to do with the doctrine of incorporation. Several other cases sometimes cited as examples of the doctrine in action are also deceptive. As for prize law, this is a wholly sui generis corpus of rules, the applicable law before an English prize court being avowedly international law as such, and not the common law.

Each of these clusters of cases will be looked at in turn.

1. The sole line of established case-law

The single field of consistent practical application of the doctrine of incorporation has been in certain cases involving the procedural immunity of foreign sovereigns and foreign States and their property from the jurisdiction of the English courts,[107] namely cases on the immunity of a foreign sovereign himself or herself prior to the coming into force of section 20 of the State Immunity Act 1978;[108] cases on the immunity of a

---

[105] See *Trendtex Trading Corporation v Central Bank of Nigeria* [1977] QB 529, 569, referring to 'rules of [customary] international law, whether they be part of our law or a source of our law'.

[106] [2007] 1 AC 136, 170, para 59 (Lord Hoffmann). See, similarly, 179, para 100 (Lord Mance).

[107] As regards diplomatic immunity, this has been embodied in statute since 7 Anne c 12, passed in 1708.

[108] See *Duke of Brunswick v King of Hanover* (1844) 6 Beav 1, upheld (1848) 2 HLC 1; *De Haber v Queen of Portugal* (1851–1852) 17 QB 196; *Mighell v Sultan of Johore* [1894] 1 QB 149. Consider

foreign State, its emanations and officials and the property of a foreign State, especially State vessels, prior to the coming into force of Part I of the State Immunity Act;[109] and cases on the immunity of a foreign State in respect of its armed forces both before and after the advent of the State Immunity Act,[110] section 16(2) of which provides that Part I of the Act does not apply to proceedings relating to anything done by or in relation to the armed forces of a State while present in the United Kingdom. There have also been two criminal cases, which are excluded from the application of Part I of the State Immunity Act by section 16(4), in the Bow Street Magistrates' Court (and thus not of precedential value), one involving the immunity of a foreign Minister for Defence and the other a foreign Minister for Commerce and International Trade.[111] In all these cases, the immunity to which the relevant natural or legal person or property was entitled as a matter of customary international law was given effect by the English courts by way of a common-law rule barring the impleading or prosecution of the former and/or barring execution against them.

2. The two isolated cases

The two stand-alone cases in which the doctrine of incorporation has determined the result are *Commercial and Estates Company of Egypt v Ball*[112] and *Commercial and Estates Company of Egypt v Board of Trade*.[113] These factually complicated cases require some explanation.

Both actions arose after the UK government had, during the First World War, requisitioned a British vessel in a neutral port carrying a cargo of timber belonging to the claimants, nationals of another neutral State. Without the consent and over the protest of the owners, the ship was brought back to the UK, where the timber was requisitioned by the Controller of Timber Supplies on behalf of the Board of Trade in purported application of the Defence of the Realm Regulations, promulgated pursuant to the Defence of the Realm Act 1914.

In 1918, the plaintiffs first brought an action against the Controller of Timber in the High Court, seeking a declaration that the requisition was *ultra vires* and void, along with associated injunctive relief, and a

---

also the implicit finding in *R v Bow Street Metropolitan Stipendiary Magistrate, Ex parte Pinochet Ugarte (No 3)* [2000] 1 AC 147 that Senator Pinochet enjoyed immunity at common law in respect of acts performed by him as head of State prior to the coming into force of the UK's State Immunity Act 1978.

[109] See eg *The Parliament Belge* (1880) 5 PD 197; *The Cristina* [1938] AC 485; *United States of America and Republic of France v Dollfus Mieg et Cie SA and Bank of England* [1952] 1 AC 582; *Trendtex Trading Corporation v Central Bank of Nigeria* [1977] QB 529; *I° Congreso del Partido* [1983] 1 AC 244.

[110] See eg *Littrell v Government of the United States of America (No 2)* [1995] 1 WLR 82; *Holland v Lampen-Wolfe* [2000] 1 WLR 1573.

[111] See *Re Mofaz* (2004) 128 ILR 709 and *Re Bo Xilai* (2005) 128 ILR 713 respectively.

[112] (1920) 36 Times LR 526.

[113] [1925] 1 KB 271.

declaration that if the defendant kept the cargo he was obliged to compensate the plaintiffs for its full value. The defendant sought to justify the
requisition by reference to the Defence of the Realm Regulations and,
alternatively, as an exercise on behalf of the Crown of the royal prerogative in relation to the defence of the realm and of the right of angary, the
latter being the right of a belligerent, recognized by customary international law, to requisition the goods of neutrals found within its territory
or territory of which it is in military occupation, subject to an obligation
to pay full compensation. In *Commercial and Estates Company of Egypt v
Ball*, in which no written judgment was handed down, Bailhache J rejected
the first of the defendant's arguments but accepted the second. He further held that the right of angary carried with it the right on the part of
the owner of the goods to full compensation. Judgment, however, was
given for the defendant, since compensation could be payable only by the
Crown, rather than by the defendant personally, and the former was not a
formal party to the action (this being possible only via a petition of
right).[114]

Subsequently the Indemnity Act 1920 was passed, which prohibited
proceedings in respect of any act done in good faith and done or purporting to be done in defence of the realm but which provided for the award
of compensation via a War Compensation Court. Section 2(1)(b) of the
Act provided that persons who had, during the War, incurred direct loss
by reason of interference with property of theirs in the UK through the
exercise or purported exercise of any prerogative right of the Crown or of
any regulation made or purporting to be made under any enactment relating to the defence of the realm were entitled to compensation in respect
of their loss. Section 2(2) dealt with how this compensation was to be
calculated. Pursuant to subsection (i), where, under any regulation made
or purporting to be made under any enactment relating to the defence of
the realm, any special principle for assessment of compensation was contained in the regulation, compensation was to be assessed in accordance
with that principle. Pursuant to subsection (iii)(a), if the claimant would,
apart from the Act, have had a legal right to compensation, the tribunal
was to give effect to that right; but in assessing compensation, it was to
have regard to the amount of the compensation to which, apart from the
Act, the claimant would have been legally entitled, and to the existence of
a state of war and to all other circumstances relevant to a just assessment
of compensation. The claimants sought compensation under the Indemnity
Act in the War Compensation Court, whose judgment denying them full
compensation they appealed to the Court of Appeal.

In *Commercial and Estates Company of Egypt v Board of Trade*, in the
Court of Appeal, Bankes and Atkin LJJ held that the Defence of the Realm
Regulations did not apply to the seizure of a neutral's goods brought into

---

[114] See 36 Times LR 526.

the UK against that person's will, so that the special principle for assessment of compensation laid down in the Regulations was inapplicable.[115] But the requisition of the claimants' timber was justified as an exercise of the prerogative right of angary, a prerogative right of the Crown within the meaning of section 2(1)(b) of the Indemnity Act. This right on the part of the Crown gave the claimants a corresponding legal right to compensation 'apart from the Act' for the purposes of section 2(2)(iii)(a), meaning that the court was obliged to give effect to that right and, in doing so, to have regard to the amount of compensation to which the claimants would have been entitled by reference to the right of angary, viz full compensation.

Leaving aside the construction of the Defence of the Realm Regulations, the principal issue for the Court of Appeal was 'whether if the Act had never been passed the claimants would have had a right to compensation enforceable in the Courts of this country in accordance with the municipal law of this country'.[116] In addressing this, Bankes LJ cited the judgment of Lord Parker in *The Zamora*, on appeal before the Privy Council from the Prize Court, where his Lordship discusses the origins of and State practice on the right of angary,[117] a right recognized by customary international law but also recognized as involving an obligation to make full compensation. Bankes LJ then asked whether 'the right thus described by Lord Parker [was] a branch of international law which constitute[d] part of the law of the land'.[118] By way of reply, his Lordship quoted at length from *West Rand*, where Lord Alverstone CJ explained what was meant by the proposition that customary international law forms part of the law of England, before concluding:

Accepting this as a correct statement of the law it would seem that the Courts of this country, apart from the Indemnity Act, would not have hesitated at the instance of a neutral to have administered the law of angary in its entirety had the neutral taken the proper steps to claim the exercise of their jurisdiction.[119]

The 'right [was] so well established in international law that it form[ed] part of the municipal law of this country'.[120] Bankes LJ earlier referred in

[115] Scrutton LJ's dissent centred on this aspect of the case.
[116] [1925] 1 KB 271, 282 (Bankes LJ).
[117] Ibid, 282, citing [1916] 2 AC 77, 101–2.
[118] Ibid, 283. In *The Zamora* [1916] 2 AC 77, 106, the Privy Council concluded that '[a] belligerent Power has by international law the right to requisition vessels or goods in the custody of its Prize Court pending a decision of the question whether they should be condemned or released, but such right is subject to certain limitations'. Since the case came on appeal from the Prize Court, where customary international law as such, and not the common law of England, was the applicable law (see below), the Board was not required to inquire into whether the customary right of angary had been received into English law. See *Attorney-General v De Keyser's Royal Hotel Ltd* [1920] AC 508, 564 (Lord Sumner): 'As to the judgment in *The Zamora*, ... [w]hat has to be borne in mind is that no issue as to the Royal Prerogative arose for consideration in that case.'
[119] [1925] 1 KB 271, 283.
[120] Ibid, 284.

passing to the claimants' 'common law right'.[121] For his part, Atkin LJ first stated:

[T]here is a well ascertained right of a belligerent Sovereign to take possession of the property of neutrals so found within his territory or territory occupied by his forces for the purposes of warfare. This is the right of angary. It appears to me to be well recognized by the conventions of civilized nations, which constitute the body of international law, and it is equally clear that it is only so recognized on the footing that the Sovereign so exercising this right makes full compensation for the property he so seizes.[122]

His Lordship next considered whether the right of angary was a prerogative right of the Crown for the purposes of section 2(1) of the Indemnity Act, which seemed to him 'to admit of little doubt'.[123] The final inquiry was whether the obligation to pay compensation associated with the right of angary could be enforced only at the international level through the intervention of the affected neutral's State, as argued by the defendant, or whether it gave rise under English law to a right to compensation enforceable at the instance of the former owner in the English courts, as argued by the claimant. In Atkin LJ's view, it was the latter:

The right of angary of the Sovereign is a right recognized by our municipal law, giving rise to rights and obligations in the full sense. The simplest illustration that can be given is the successful plea of the Timber Controller in the action brought against him by the present claimants [before Bailhache J]. He established his immunity by showing authority from the Crown under the right of angary. If no such power in the Crown was recognized by the municipal law of this country, the defendant would have remained with an undefended liability for conversion of the timber. Once the goods are seized under the right of angary, the property or the right to possession passes from the neutral owner to the Crown by our municipal law. The Crown could enforce in the Courts of this country the ordinary rights coming from that property or possession against any trespasser; and similarly the original owner or his assignee would fail in the municipal Courts to establish his rights against any person dealing with the goods who derived title, or the right of possession, through the Crown.[124]

His Lordship immediately continued:

International law as such can confer no rights cognizable in the municipal Courts. It is only in so far as the rules of international law are recognized as included in the rules of the municipal law that they are allowed in the municipal Courts to give rise to rights or obligations. The right of angary therefore is a right recognized by English law, and falls within the definition [of the prerogative] of Professor Dicey as a right legally left in the hands of the Crown. Does it give rise to 'a legal right to compensation' in the owner of the goods seized? It is plain that one of the conditions of the right of angary as recognized by international law is that full compensation shall be made to the neutral owner. I see no reason for holding that our municipal law recognizes the right to seize, but rejects the obligation

---

[121] Ibid, 281.   [122] Ibid, 293.
[123] Ibid, 294.   [124] Ibid, 295.

to compensate. ... It was contended that the sole right to compensation was the right of the Sovereign of the injured neutral to claim compensation on behalf of his subject. I can see no reason for any such restriction. ... No doubt international usage would justify the Sovereign of the neutral owner in claiming on behalf of his subject if fair compensation was withheld. This is usual practice between States and does not depend upon the absence of legal right in the neutral to sue in the municipal Courts of the country where he has been wronged in person or property. It may well be that in some States the municipal law does not recognize the right to compensation, either by denying its existence or by reason of its procedure not admitting process against the Sovereign. In our law legal rights can be put in action against the Sovereign by petition of right, and it was, as I think, rightly conceded by the Attorney-General that apart from the Indemnity Act, if a petition of right could have been brought for compensation in this case, the claimants must be held to have a legal right to compensation.[125]

In this light, the case was remitted to the War Compensation Court to be heard on the footing that the claimants had a legal right to compensation for their timber under the right of angary.

Bankes and Atkin LJJ's respective judgments are straight applications of the doctrine of incorporation.[126] They are significant in that they suggest that the doctrine can give rise at common law not only to disabilities on the part of the relevant organ of government, as in the immunity cases in relation to the courts, but also to rights or, more accurately, powers—specifically, prerogative powers on the part of the Crown.[127] In this light, the statement that customary international law is part of the common law of England would seem to extend beyond rules of law established by the courts themselves to encompass that 'residue of discretionary or arbitrary

---

[125]   Ibid, 295–6.
[126]   See, subsequently, Viscount Radcliffe in *Burmah Oil Co Ltd v Lord Advocate* [1965] AC 75, 123, referring to *The Zamora* (wrongly) and *Commercial Estates Company of Egypt v Board of Trade*: 'Angary, ... as those cases made plain, was only a Crown right recognised by our municipal law because it was a belligerent right recognised by international law and there acknowledged to be subject to the condition of providing compensation to the deprived neutral.'
[127]   The *Commercial Estates* litigation is not the only case-law in which the prerogative has been considered in the light of customary international law. *In re Ferdinand, Ex-Tsar of Bulgaria* [1921] 1 Ch 107 turned on whether the Crown enjoyed a prerogative power in time of war to seize the property of enemy nationals. All three members of the Court of Appeal made detailed reference to the position under customary international law. But it was in reliance on Hale's *Pleas of the Crown*, the Year Books and dicta in more recent English authorities that the court held 'that by the common law of England the Crown has the right, if it chooses to exercise it, to seize as forfeited to itself the property of enemies found within the realm at the outbreak of war': ibid, 136 (Warrington LJ). See also ibid, 124 (Lord Sterndale MR) and 143 (Younger LJ). That is, 'the right in question [was] a part of the ancient common law of England': ibid, 138 (Warrington LJ). Warrington LJ seemingly contemplated, by reference to *West Rand*, that the Crown's established prerogative in this regard could be extinguished by a subsequent change in the customary international rule, at least where the UK government had accepted this rule as binding: see ibid, 136 and 138–9. This also seems to have been the purpose for which Younger LJ looked to customary international law, and is the most likely explanation for Lord Sterndale's recourse to the latter: see ibid, 114–5 and 125 respectively. All of their Lordships were, however, firmly of the view that customary international law served instead to support the common-law position.

authority, which at any given time is legally left in the hands of the Crown',[128] 'out of the ordinary course of the common law',[129] not created but merely declared by the courts.[130]

3. *Three fallacies and an anomaly*

In *Jones (Margaret)*, Lord Mance held that the crimes of piracy, violation of safe-conducts, infringement of the rights of ambassadors and, 'very arguably', war crimes 'have in the past been received and recognised at common law as domestic crimes'.[131] Lord Bingham effectively stated the same.[132] Both of their Lordships took their first three examples from Blackstone, while the example of war crimes was based on the appellants' citation of the case of *Re Sandrock*[133] as representative of the war crimes trials conducted by British forces in the immediate wake of the Second World War. But the reality is that of the offences listed by Lords Mance and Bingham only piracy has ever been tried as a common-law crime, and this for particular historical reasons which have nothing to do with the doctrine of incorporation.

At the international level, the crime of piracy predates international law in its identifiably modern, inter-State form, having its origins in the various medieval bodies of transnational maritime law applied in the different European ports—the Rhodian laws, the *Consolato del Mare*, the Wisby (Visby) code, the Lübeck code, the laws of Amalfi, the laws of Trani, the code of Oléron and so on[134]—which eventually coalesced into a maritime law that constituted, by the time of Lord Mansfield CJ's statement in *Luke v Lyde*, 'the general law of nations'.[135] In England, piracy became triable not under the common law but directly under this maritime law,

---

[128] *Burmah Oil Co Ltd v Lord Advocate* [1965] AC 75, 99 (Lord Reid), 117 (Viscount Radcliffe), 137 (Lord Hodson) and 165 (Lord Upjohn), quoting A V Dicey, *Introduction to the Study of the Law of the Constitution* (10th edn, Macmillan, London, 1959), 424. The same statement, albeit from an earlier edition of Dicey, is quoted with approval in *Attorney-General v De Keyser's Royal Hotel Ltd* [1920] AC 508, 526 (Lord Dunedin); *In re Ferdinand, Ex-Tsar of Bulgaria* [1921] 1 Ch 107, 139 (Warrington LJ); *Council of Civil Service Unions v Minister for the Civil Service* [1985] AC 374, 398 (Lord Fraser); and *R (Bancoult) v Secretary of State for Foreign and Commonwealth Affairs* [2008] UKHL 61; [2008] 3 WLR 955, 977, para 69 (Lord Bingham). See, similarly, *Burmah Oil Co Ltd v Lord Advocate* [1965] AC 75, 148 (Lord Pearce)('the residue of the power of sovereignty that has not been superseded or abridged or supplanted temporarily by the power of the King in Parliament').

[129] Blackstone, above n 2, book 1, chap 7, 232.

[130] 'The prerogative is not, strictly speaking, the product of the common law, but it is defined by common law judges.': S Payne, 'The Royal Prerogative', in M Sunkin & S Payne (eds), *The Nature of the Crown. A Legal and Political Analysis* (Oxford University Press, Oxford, 1999), 77, 106. 'Though these powers were "known to the common law", they should more accurately be understood as having been accommodated within our law.': M Loughlin, 'The State, the Crown and the Law', in Sunkin & Payne, ibid, 33, 64, quoting G H L Le May, *The Victorian Constitution* (Duckworth, London, 1979), 6.

[131] [2006] UKHL 16; [2007] 1 AC 136, 179, para 101. Confusingly, his Lordship almost immediately states that 'crimes under public international law can no longer be, *if they ever were*, the subject of any automatic reception or recognition in domestic law by the courts': ibid, emphasis added.

[132] [2007] 1 AC 136, 158, paras 20–2.

[133] Ibid, 158, para 22, citing (1945) 13 ILR 297.

[134] See Holdsworth, above n 44, vol I, 526–8.

[135] (1759) 2 Burr 882, 887.

a species of civil law[136] applied by the Admiralty courts.[137] Even when piracy became triable by the idiosyncratic Admiralty Sessions according to a modified common-law procedure, the relevant statute, 28 Hen VIII c 15 of 1536,[138] provided only for its trial and punishment: 'piracy itself remained an offence unknown to the common law and was felony only by the marine law',[139] although by then piracies were described by Sir John Hawles, Solicitor General, as 'crimes against the law of nations'.[140] It was not until the abolition of the Admiralty Sessions in the nineteenth century and the transfer of their exclusive jurisdiction over crimes at sea to the Central Criminal Court[141] that piracy was tried as a common-law crime, and it was tried as such not thanks to the doctrine of incorporation but simply by virtue of the fact that the common law inherited those crimes previously recognized and applied by the Admiralty.[142] It was termed piracy *'jure gentium'* not on account of the view that customary international law was part of the common law of England[143] but because

[136] See, among others, M Hale, 'A Disquisition touching the Jurisdiction of The Common Law and Courts of Admiralty in relation to Things done upon or beyond the Sea, and touching Maritime and Merchant Contracts', in M Prichard & D Yale (eds), *Hale and Fleetwood on Admiralty Jurisdiction* (Selden Society, London, 1993), 1, 58; M Hale, *The History of the Common Law of England* (C M Gray ed, University of Chicago Press, London, 1971), 20 and 23–5; J F Stephen, *A History of the Criminal Law of England* (Macmillan, London, 1883), vol II, 17; Holdsworth, above n 44, vol IV, 272. For the material sources of this law as applied in England, see *The Black Book of the Admiralty* (T Twiss ed, Longman/Trübner, London, 1871–6), vol II, 209–41 and 431–81, vol III and vol IV; Hale, 'Disquisition', ibid, 58–64; Hale, *History*, ibid, 24; Pritchard & Yale, ibid, xxxiii–vi.

[137] Before the mid-fourteenth century, cases of piracy had sometimes been prosecuted at common law. But in 1361 a commission of oyer and terminer issued to, *inter alia*, several justices to try a case of piracy by the common law 'was recalled upon the express ground that by the law of England such offences were triable, not by the common law before justices, but by the maritime law before the admiral': R G Marsden, 'Early Prize Jurisdiction and Prize Law in England' (1909) 24 *English Historical Review* 675, 681. See also the reproduction of the royal revocation of the commission in R G Marsden (ed), *Documents relating to Law and Custom of the Sea* (Navy Records Society, London, 1915–6), vol I, 88. '[N]o record has been found of pirates having been tried at common law' after this: Marsden, 'Early Prize Jurisdiction', ibid, 683. See also R G Marsden (ed), *Select Pleas in the Court of Admiralty. Volume I* (Selden Society, London, 1894), liv, recalling an incident which shows that by 1429 'the criminal jurisdiction of the common law courts in cases of piracy seems to have fallen into desuetude'. Although reference is often made in the literature, in relation to subsequent years, to 'piracy at common law', the label is used in order to distinguish piracy under the maritime law, and ultimately under the law of nations, from piracy within the extended meaning given to it over the years by various statutes. See eg Stephen, above n 136, vol II, 27: 'It must ... be observed that there are two kinds of piracy, namely, first, piracy at common law, or (as it is often called) piracy by the law of nations; and secondly, piracy by statute ...'

[138] See also, the previous year, 27 Hen VIII c 4.

[139] Prichard & Yale, above n 136, cxlviii. In the words (and spelling) of Hale, 'Disquisition', above n 136, 1, 87, 'pyracy, though it be Capital by the Marine Law, yet the Common Law takes no Notice of [it]'.

[140] *Trial of Joseph Dawson and others* (1696) 13 Howell's St Tr 451, col 477.

[141] See section 22 of 4 & 5 Will IV c 36, affirmed by section 4 of 7 Vict c 2, which conferred Admiralty's criminal jurisdiction on the courts of assize.

[142] 'The criminal jurisdiction of the Admiralty, having been administered by the common law judges, has become part and parcel of the common law ...': Holdsworth, above n 44, vol I, 552.

[143] For example, the doctrine of incorporation is never so much as mentioned in the Privy Council's judgment in *In re Piracy jure gentium* [1934] AC 586, in which the common law of crime of Hong Kong was implicitly treated as consonant with that of England. As it is, it is worth pointing out that— whatever the position under the old pan-European maritime law and perhaps even under the law of

the definition of piracy before the defunct Admiralty Sessions was determined by reference to the law of nations.[144]

Violations of safe-conducts were triable not at common law but pursuant to statute.[145] By 2 Hen V st I c 6, they were deemed to be high treason,

nations of Blackstone's time—the crime of piracy, described by Blackstone as an 'offence against the law of nations', is probably not in its modern form what we would today call a crime against (or, more commonly, under) international law. That is, in all likelihood modern international law does not itself prohibit, on pain of punishment, the commission by an individual of piracy. Rather, the better view is that contemporary customary international law posits a special jurisdictional rule permitting each State to apply its municipal criminal law on the basis of universality to conduct amounting to piracy, as defined by customary international law itself—in other words, to criminalize piracy wherever and by whomever it is committed: see eg Harvard Law School Research in International Law, 'Jurisdiction with Respect to Crime' (1935) 29 *American Journal of International Law Supplement* 435, 755–6 and 760; Brownlie, above n 23, 306, including n 47; J Crawford & S Olleson, 'The Nature and Forms of International Responsibility' in M Evans (ed), *International Law* (2nd edn, Oxford University Press, Oxford, 2006), 451, 453. See also *The SS 'Lotus'*, PCIJ Rep Series A No 10, 70 (sep op Moore). In short, today there is no substantive crime of piracy under customary international law which could possibly be incorporated into the common law. The crime, although defined by customary international law, is substantively one under municipal law alone.

[144] The position remains the same today, so that, for example, when the UK wished to make sure that the definition of piracy given in the Convention on the Law of the Sea 1982 was reflected in domestic criminal law, the relevant statutory provision, section 26(1) of the Merchant Shipping and Maritime Security Act 1997 (c 28), stipulated that '[f]or the avoidance of doubt it is hereby declared that for the purposes of any proceedings before a court in the United Kingdom in respect of piracy, the provisions of the United Nations Convention on the Law of the Sea 1982 that are set out in Schedule 5 shall be treated as constituting part of the law of nations'.

[145] 'It is to these statutes that we must look for the germs of that part of the law of England which is directed to the enforcement of international obligations, and the regulation of the rights of foreigners.': Holdsworth, above n 44, vol II, 474. As it is, even in the eighteenth century, the violation of safe-conducts granted to foreigners and attacks on foreign ambassadors, both characterized by Blackstone as 'offences against the law of nations', were not what we would today call crimes against or under international law—that is, international law did not itself prohibit, on pain of punishment, their commission by an individual. Any criminalization was under national law alone. Moreover, even in Blackstone's day, violations of safe-conducts and attacks on ambassadors were not 'offences against the law of nations' in the same way that piracy was. What the label referred to in the former context was the criminalization and ultimately punishment under national law of acts constituting a breach of the law of nations by the receiving State, either because they were performed by a servant of the State or because they resulted from what we would now call its failure of due diligence. The receiving State's prosecution of the persons responsible for the breach amounted to a form of reparation to the victim's State. See eg the reference to 'reparation' and the repeated reference to 'satisfaction' in the extended diplomatic correspondence over the attack on the Russian ambassador in 1708, the abortive attempt to prosecute those responsible and the consequent passage of 7 Anne c 12, section 4 of which made the suit or prosecution of an ambassador a criminal offence, in Martens, above n 51, 86–7 and 75, 76, 78, 86, 87, 89, 90, 91, 93, 94, and 95. See also *Triquet v Bath* (1765) 3 Burr 1676, 1480 (Lord Mansfield CJ)('No punishment would have been thought, by [the Czar], an adequate reparation'; 'this Act of Parliament passed, as an apology ... from the whole nation'); *Respublica v De Longchamps*, 1 US (1 Dall) 111, 117 (1784)(M'Kean CJ)('no punishment less than death would have been thought by the Czar an adequate reparation for the arrest of his Ambassador'; 'However, the Princes of the world, at this day, are more enlightened, and do not require impracticable nor unreasonable reparations for injuries of this kind.'); *Viveash v Becker* (1814) 3 M & S 284, 291 (Lord Ellenborough CJ)('the Act of Parliament was passed by way of apology, and in order to conciliate the powers offended'). Blackstone, above n 2, book IV, chap 7, 68 writes: '[W]here the individuals of any state violate this general law [viz the law of nations], it is then the interest as well as the duty of the government under which they live, to animadvert upon them with a becoming severity, that the peace of the world may be maintained. … It is … incumbent upon the nation injured, first to demand satisfaction and justice to be done on the offender, by the state to which he belongs …' In modern terms, we would say that such prosecution acquitted the responsible State's obligation to afford satisfaction to the injured State, within the

triable, if committed at sea, by specially-appointed conservators of truces and safe-conducts in the ports according to the procedure of the maritime law or, if committed within the body of a county, by the local port's con-servator and two men learned in the law of the land according to the pro-cedure of the common law. This Act was revived[146] by 29 Hen VI c 2, which extended the power to adjudicate such cases to the Lord Chancellor, sitting with either Chief Justice. But if these Acts survived 14 Edw IV c 4, they were finally repealed by statutes passed under Edward VI and Mary which abolished novel treasons.[147] In short, violations of safe con-ducts were not as such crimes by Blackstone's day, although 31 Hen VI c 4 still provided for a special civil remedy.

As for violations of the rights of ambassadors, these were punished in Blackstone's day pursuant to statute, namely 7 Anne c 12. They were never punishable at common law.[148]

Pace Lords Bingham and Mance, war crimes have never been tried with-out statute in the common-law courts. As a matter of English law, crimi-nal jurisdiction over the army in time of war, traceable all the way back to the court of the Constable and the Marshal[149] and subsequently exercised by courts-martial, has always constituted a separate criminal jurisdiction,[150] one in which the applicable law was originally civil law[151] in character (comprising ordinances issued by the King at the start of each war[152]), later

meaning of articles 34 and 37 of the International Law Commission's Articles on Responsibility of States for Internationally Wrongful Acts, annexed to UNGA res 56/83, UN Doc A/RES/56/83, 12 December 2001. In short, as with piracy, in neither case does there exist a substantive offence under customary international law even potentially capable of incorporation into the common law.

[146]   It had previously been suspended by 14 Hen VI c 8 and repealed by 20 Hen VI c 11.
[147]   See Blackstone, above n 2, book IV, chap 5, 70.
[148]   See the discussion above at Part II.B.
[149]   For the jurisdiction of this court, see 13 Rich II st I c 2, translated at 2 Statutes of the Realm 61: 'To the Constable it pertaineth to have Cognisance ... of War out of the Realm, and also of Things that touch War within the Realm that cannot be determined nor discussed by the Common Law, with other Usages and Customs to the same matters pertaining ...'.
[150]   See, generally, W S Holdsworth, 'Martial Law Historically Considered' (1902) 18 *Law Quarterly Review* 117, 119–22; R O'Sullivan (ed), *Military Law and the Supremacy of the Civil Courts* (Stevens & Sons, London, 1921), 1–12; D P O'Connell, 'The Nature of British Military Law' (1963) 19 *Military Law Review* 141; J Stuart-Smith, 'Military Law: Its History, Administration and Practice' (1969) 85 *Law Quarterly Review* 478.
[151]   See, among many others, E Coke, *Institutes of the Laws of England* (19th edn, F Hargrave & C Butler eds, Clark *et al*, London, 1832), 391b; Hale, *History*, above n 136, 20 and 27–8; Holdsworth, above n 44, vol IV, 272.
[152]   See Hale, *History*, above n 136, 26; M Hale, *The Prerogatives of the King* (D Yale ed, Selden Society, London, 1976), 119–20; Stuart-Smith, above n 150, 479–81. Hale, *Prerogatives*, ibid, 119 notes in the Constable and Marshal's jurisdiction over the army something of an 'intermixture' between this military law, properly so called, and the *jus belli* or law of war. For examples of ordinances issued by the King, see the Ordinances of War made by Richard II at Durham in 1385 and the Ordinances of War made by Henry V at Mantes in 1419, reproduced in *Black Book*, above n 136, vol I, 453–8 and 459–72 respectively. As for procedure, proceedings in the court of the Constable and Marshal 'held anciently the form of common law proceedings, though in later times [the court] hath held the course of summary proceedings according to the civil law', according to Hale, *Prerogatives*, ibid, 120.

partly prerogative and partly statutory,[153] and finally wholly statutory.[154] Jurisdiction over enemy prisoners of war was also originally exercised by the civil-law Constable and Marshal's court,[155] applying the *jus belli* or law of war directly,[156] and later, in rare cases where recourse was had to adjudication, by ad hoc courts composed of officers applying the same. The British military courts sitting in occupied Germany after the Second World War—which, pursuant to a Royal Warrant of 1945,[157] tried enemy war criminals under the customary international law of war crimes—represented a more formalized and regularized species of the last. They were not implanted within the criminal justice system of England and Wales (nor of Scotland or Northern Ireland, for that matter) but were simply designated as 'Military Courts', standing wholly outside the civilian court system, in the same way that the regular courts-martial (from which they were completely distinct) stand outside it;[158] and the law they applied was not English law but 'the laws and usages of war',[159] viz the customary international laws of war, as a sui generis applicable law. Today, leaving aside certain Second World War offences,[160] war crimes are triable under the International Criminal Court Act 2001[161] or the earlier Geneva Conventions Act 1957,[162] as amended by the Geneva Conventions (Amendment) Act 1995.[163]

[153] See Holdsworth, above n 150, 121–2, on the articles of war promulgated by the king at the commencement of war and the annual Mutiny Act, first passed in 1689, as well as the later Army Act 1881, which did not wholly dispense with the theoretical possibility of prerogative promulgation of articles of war. See also O'Connell, above n 150, 141–7.

[154] See Army Act 1955 (c 18). See also Air Force Act 1955 (c 19) and Naval Discipline Act 1957 (c 53). These Acts will be superseded by the Armed Forces Act 2006 (c 52) when its relevant provisions enter into force. All of this legislation not only provides for specific military offences but also deems the ordinary ('civil') criminal law to be applicable to service personnel wherever they may be, although the charge in the event of a violation of the latter is not an offence against the latter as such but rather (except, under the 1950s Acts, as regards the commission of certain offences in the UK) an offence against the deeming provision of the relevant legislation, viz Army Act 1955, section 70; Air Force Act 1955, section 70; Naval Discipline Act 1957, section 42; Armed Forces Act 2006, section 42. Until very recently, the practice was that service personnel suspected of conduct amounting to a war crime would be charged not with a war crime as such but with murder, manslaughter, assault, etc within the meaning of the ordinary criminal law or with a relevant offence under military law, such as looting, an offence against the civilian population, disgraceful conduct, disobedience to standing orders, disobedience to a lawful command, etc.

[155] See Hale, *History*, above n 136, 26; Holdsworth, above n 44, vol IV, 574 and 577; H E Richards, 'Martial Law' (1902) 18 *Law Quarterly Review* 133, 133.

[156] See Hale, above n 152, 119 and 121, although noting at 120 a degree of intermixture with military law.

[157] Royal Warrant, Regulations for the Trial of War Criminals, 14 June 1945, AO 81/1945, reproduced in War Office, *The Law of War on Land being Part III of the Manual of Military Law* (HMSO, London, 1958), appendix XXV, 347.

[158] In constitutional terms, these military courts were prerogative courts, and thus prohibited from sitting within the realm.

[159] Royal Warrant 1945, section 1, cross-referable to sections 2 and 4.

[160] War crimes involving homicide committed in Germany or German-occupied Europe during World War II by persons who were on 8 March 1990 or who became subsequently UK citizens or residents may be tried under the War Crimes Act 1991 (c 13). They are tried not as war crimes *eo nomine* but as murder, manslaughter, or culpable homicide within the meaning of English law.

[161] c 17.   [162] c 52.   [163] c 27.

4. *Four deceptive cases*

a. *De Wütz v Hendricks*

Some commentators treat the judgment of Best CJ in the early nineteenth-century case of *De Wütz v Hendricks*[164] as an application of the doctrine of incorporation.[165] But closer examination reveals this not to be so.

The plaintiff, with a view to raising a loan to fund the Greek War of Independence against the Ottomans, lodged with the defendant, a London stockbroker, a power of attorney (which turned out to be a fabrication) purportedly signed by the Exarch of Ravenna. For his part, the defendant, at the former's request, arranged the printing of stamped scrip receipts. The deal for the loan fell through after suspicions were raised as to the truth of the plaintiff's claims, and the defendant refused to return the supposed power of attorney and withheld the scrip receipts. The plaintiff sued in trover for the return of both. At the trial before Best CJ, the jury found for the defendant on the ground that the transaction was a fraud on the part of the plaintiff. The plaintiff moved for a new trial, again before Best CJ, arguing that the fraudulent transaction did not deprive him of his property in the papers.

Best CJ stated:

It occurred to me at the trial that it was contrary to the law of nations (which in all cases of international law is adopted into the municipal code of every civilized country), for persons in England to enter into engagements to raise money to support the subjects of a government in amity with our own, in hostilities against their government, and that no right of action could arise out of such a transaction. I stated my opinion to the counsel for the Defendant, but he did not ask for a nonsuit, so I permitted the cause to proceed. In consequence of what I said, a note has since been sent me of a case that occurred lately in Chancery, in which the Lord Chancellor is reported to have said that English courts of justice will afford no assistance to persons who set about to raise loans for subjects of the king of Spain to enable them to prosecute a war against that sovereign. Had I been aware that my opinion was supported by such high authority (although the counsel for the Defendant would not take the objection), I should have nonsuited the Plaintiff. On further consideration, I think that my opinion at the trial was right, and on that ground we ought not to grant a new trial.[166]

His Lordship's reference to the case in Chancery before the Lord Chancellor is to *Jones v Garcia del Rio*,[167] decided the year before. In this earlier case, holders of scrip or shares in a loan raised for the benefit of the Peruvian government, to be secured in part by Peruvian government bonds payable to the bearer, sought an injunction, on behalf of themselves and all other subscribers to the loan, compelling the defendant

---

[164] (1824) 2 Bing 314.
[165] See eg Lauterpacht, above n 2, 54–5; Jennings & Watts, above n 23, 57 n 12.
[166] 2 Bing 314, 315–6.
[167] (1823) 1 Turn & R 297. That this is the case referred to by Best CJ in *De Wütz v Hendricks* is made clear at 2 St Tr NS 125, 127 n (a), in an alternative report of the latter case.

bankers to return their subscriptions. They alleged fraud and misrepresentation and an inability to perfect the security, their argument being that no State of Peru had ever been recognized by His Majesty's government and that no such State existed, Peru remaining a province and dependency of the kingdom of Spain.[168] The injunction was granted *ex parte*, upon which the defendant made motion to dissolve it, submitting *inter alia* that, while it was true that His Majesty's government had not recognized an independent State of Peru, such a State did in fact exist, after the people of Peru had risen in revolution, ousted the Spanish viceroy and established a State of their own. In responding to this argument, Lord Eldon LC had cause to state the following:

> We all know that Peru was part of the dominions of Spain, and that Spain and this country are at peace, and that this country has not acknowledged the government of Peru; I want to know, whether, ... if individuals in this country choose to advance their money for the purpose of assisting a colony opposed to its parent state, that parent state being at peace with this country, the Courts of Justice here will assist them to recover their money, and will not leave them to get it as they can? Practically speaking great inconvenience may result from these transactions, for if at any future time the government of this country shall be disposed to say, Peru shall still continue annexed to Spain, these creditors will immediately come to the government and say, do not accede to the arrangement unless Spain will pay us what we have advanced to the colony.[169]

In the event, however, Lord Eldon LC decided the case on a completely different basis, namely that the plaintiffs, having distinct demands, could not file a single bill. '[A]nd upon that ground alone, his Lordship, without again adverting to the question of public policy, dissolved the injunction'.[170] The maxim that the law of nations forms part of the common law of England appears nowhere either in counsel's argument or in the judgment.

On its own, Best CJ's judgment in *De Wütz v Hendricks* is equivocal. What is clear—both from his use of the word 'ought' and his reference to Lord Eldon's dicta in *Jones v Garcia del Rio*, where the issue is expressly characterized as such—is that his Lordship's denial of a right of action was a function of public policy. But his precise reasoning is inscrutable. Best CJ could be saying that because it is contrary to the law of nations[171]

---

[168] 1 Turn & R 297, 298. Counsel's submissions and the judgment refer consistently to recognition of the government of Peru, when what is clearly meant is the State of Peru. The same goes in relation to Spain.

[169] Ibid, 299–300. It should be noted that of equal, if not greater concern to His Lordship was 'whether, supposing Peru to be so far absolved from the government of Spain that it never can be attached to it again, the King's Courts will interfere at all while the Peruvian government is not acknowledged by the government of this country': ibid, 299. 'What right have I, as the King's Judge', he asked ibid, 'to interfere upon the subject of a contract with a country which he does not recognize?'

[170] Ibid, 301.

[171] This was probably not, in fact, true at the time. It is certainly not true today. Modern customary international law imposes on individuals no obligation of loyalty to their sovereign. Nor does it prohibit individuals from providing material support to rebels against a foreign sovereign. What it

quâ the law of nations for an individual to fund a revolt against a foreign sovereign in amity with the United Kingdom, an English court should not recognize any cause of action purporting to arise out of such conduct. On this reading, his reference to international law being adopted into municipal law is either merely by way of justification *ex abundante cautela* for his taking notice of international law at all in the municipal context or is simply gratuitous and literally parenthetical commentary expressive of a mind shaped by eighteenth-century nostrums. Alternatively, his Lordship could be saying that because it is contrary to the law of nations for individuals to support a rebellion against a foreign sovereign at peace with their own, it is contrary to English law to do so, and an English court should not recognize any cause of action purporting to arise out of a breach of English law. On this second reading, Best CJ's invocation of the doctrine of incorporation is part of the ratio of the judgment. Even on the judgment's own terms, however, the second construction is less likely than the first. As a rhetorical matter, his Lordship's nod to the doctrine of incorporation simply does not read like a crucial part of his reasoning. Moreover, it would perhaps be surprising (although by no means out of the question) were the common law of England, a law traditionally governing relationships between individuals within the realm and the relationship between the English sovereign and her subjects, to concern itself with the relationship between a foreign sovereign and his.

The second construction of *De Wütz v Hendricks* is rendered less likely still by cross-reference to *Jones v Garcia del Rio*, prayed in aid by Best CJ. The statement that the law of nations forms part of the law of the land does not feature at all in the former. Lord Eldon CJ's musings in that case would appear to be directed towards customary international law as customary international law.

All in all, *De Wütz v Hendricks* is better seen as yet one more of the many nineteenth-century cases, most of them proceeding under 7 Anne c 12, in which the maxim that the law of nations is part of the law of England is repeated to no genuinely useful end.

b. *The Emperor of Austria v Day and Kossuth*

The judgment of Sir John Stuart V-C in the mid-nineteenth-century case of *The Emperor of Austria v Day and Kossuth*[172] is also sometimes taken as a clear example of the doctrine of incorporation in action.[173] But the reality is far more equivocal—even leaving aside the fact that, when

does do is impose on States an obligation of due diligence in relation to acts by individuals directed against the safety of a foreign State or its government—that is, an obligation to take all measures within their power to prevent their territory being used by individuals for acts inimical to this safety.

[172] (1861) 2 Giff 628.
[173] See eg Lauterpacht, above n 2, 56; O'Connell, above n 2, vol I, 57–8; Jennings & Watts, above n 23, 57 n 12 ('a striking application of the doctrine').

the Lord Chancellor and Lords Justice upheld the decision on appeal, they did so on a different ground,[174] and the fact that the alleged right under the law of nations cited by the Vice-Chancellor, the so-called *jus cudendae monetae*, really 'has nothing to do with international law', in the words of defendant's counsel on appeal.[175] In the final analysis, the case does not appear to be one where a rule of customary international law was applied as a rule of common law.

The plaintiff, in his capacity as the king of Hungary and thus representative of the Hungarian State, moved to restrain the defendants, a firm of London printers and the Hungarian nobleman and revolutionary Lajos Kossuth, from counterfeiting Hungarian paper money, and sought the delivery up to be destroyed of counterfeit notes already produced and the plates from which they were printed. He argued that he enjoyed the exclusive right under Hungarian law to issue Hungarian paper money.[176] The account given in the law reports of the submissions of plaintiff's counsel to the Court of Chancery evidences no argument based on the law of nations, let alone on the doctrine of incorporation, although, going on the fact that the doctrine makes its way into the judgment, such an argument seems to have been made. In response, the defendants submitted that the English courts had no jurisdiction to grant relief, since the right sought to be protected was 'a mere public and political right'[177]—that is, either a prerogative right of a foreign sovereign or a political right of his subjects, neither of which could be enforced in an English court.

The Vice-Chancellor granted the relief sought. He first addressed the defendants' argument that the right in question was merely 'public and political':

> If the question merely related to an affair of State it would be a question, not of law, but for mere political discussion. But the regulation of the coin and currency of every State is ... a great public right recognised and protected by the law of nations. A public right, recognised by the law of nations, is a legal right; because the law of nations is part of the common law of England.[178]

---

[174] *The Emperor of Austria v Day and Kossuth* (1861) 3 De G F & J 217. In argument before the Lord Chancellor and Lords Justice, 'counsel for the Plaintiff ... entirely repudiated any claim to the injunction on the ground of a mere invasion of any prerogative of the Plaintiff as a reigning sovereign': ibid, 232.

[175] Ibid, 227. But *cf* ibid, 251 (Turner LJ). The better view is that the right to stamp coin and print money is a right not under customary international law but under domestic law alone. It is a domestic-law right for the protection of which, however, customary international law lends its support in certain ways. For example, going beyond the usually territorial and nationality-based grounds of prescriptive jurisdiction, customary international law has long permitted a State to criminalize the counterfeiting of its currency by non-nationals based in another State's territory; and the counterfeiting by one State of another's currency with a view to destabilizing the latter's economy would constitute an impermissible interference in the domestic affairs of that State, as prohibited by customary international law.

[176] See 2 Giff 628, 628 and 639–41.

[177] Ibid, 678.   [178] Ibid.

The last statement was 'supported by unquestionable authority', by which his Lordship meant Blackstone, whose views he faithfully reproduced.[179] He continued:

To apply these acknowledged principles of the law of nations and law of England to the present case, it appears that the British Parliament, by the Act 11 Geo 4 and 1 Wm 4, c. 66, has enacted that the forgery or counterfeiting the paper money of any foreign sovereign or State is a felony punishable by the law of England. This statute is a legislative recognition of the general right of the sovereign authority in foreign States to the assistance of the laws of this country to protect their rights as to the regulation of their paper money as well as their coin, and to punish, by the law of England, offences against that power.

The friendly relations between civilized countries require, for their safety, the protection by municipal law of an existing sovereign right of the kind recognised by the law of nations. ...[180]

His Lordship then turned to the relief sought in the case, which was not itself a criminal prosecution under 11 Geo 4 and 1 Wm 4, c 66 but instead a suit at equity:

[I]f the avowed and single purpose, for which this property is now in the hands of the Defendant, be a purpose hostile to the Plaintiff's rights, if this Court were to refuse its interference, the refusal would amount to a decision that it has no jurisdiction to protect the legal right of the Plaintiff—a legal right recognised by the law of nations, and, therefore, by the law of England. ...

Foreign States at peace with this country have always been held entitled to the assistance of the law of England to vindicate and protect their rights ...[181]

Sir John Stuart V-C concluded:

[W]here, as in the present case, the existing rights of the Plaintiff, as sovereign of Hungary, are recognised by the Crown of England, the relief which he seeks for this cause is for the protection of a legal right of universal public importance against the acts of the Defendants. That protection can only be effectively afforded by the relief prayed for in this suit; and there must be a decree against the Defendants, according to the prayer of the bill.[182]

The decree was thus given.

It is not easy to discern the ratio of Sir John Stuart V-C's judgment; but close reading suggests that his Lordship did not, in fact, apply the putative rule of customary international law at issue, the *jus cudendae monetae*, as a rule of common law. His use of the law of nations is more by way of evidentiary affirmation of the legal nature of the exclusive domestic right of the king of Hungary to issue paper money and by way of legitimation of his Lordship's decision to protect that domestic legal

---

[179] Ibid, 678–9.   [180] Ibid, 679.
[181] Ibid, 680–1.   [182] Ibid.

right by means of an equitable remedy at English law.[183] His Lordship's reasoning appears to be as follows: that the king of Hungary's exclusive right under Hungarian law to issue Hungarian currency is indeed a legal and not merely political right is evidenced by the fact that the law of nations recognizes it as such—and since the law of nations recognizes the right as a legal one, so too should the law of England, the law of nations being part of the common law of England; foreign States at peace with England have always been held entitled to the assistance of the law of England to vindicate and protect their legal rights; *ergo* the king of Hungary should be granted the relief he seeks to vindicate and protect his exclusive right under Hungarian law to issue Hungarian currency. What Sir John Stuart V-C is not saying is that the king of Hungary enjoys the exclusive right under the common law of England to issue Hungarian currency—which, as it is, would be a curious and extremely doubtful proposition.[184] The invocation of the doctrine of incorporation is superfluous at best.

c. The Rose Mary

The 1953 case of *Anglo-Iranian Oil Co Ltd v Jaffrate (The Rose Mary)*[185] was heard not in the English courts but in the Supreme Court of the then Colony of Aden. But to the extent that it proceeded under principles taken directly from English law, and insofar as it was subsequently considered in the English courts,[186] it merits mention. The case involved an action in detinue for delivery up of oil contained in a tanker. Pursuant to a concession agreement of 1933 between the plaintiffs (until 1935, the Anglo-Persian Oil Company) and the government of Persia (after 1935, Iran), the former enjoyed the exclusive right to extract oil in a given area of Iran. In 1951, the government of Iran legislated to expropriate without compensation and to nationalize all property vesting in the plaintiffs by virtue of the 1933 agreement. The plaintiffs' suit was part of a worldwide strategy to resist the nationalization. The legal obstacle in the present case was that, under English common-law conflicts rules, transfer of title to tangible movable property is generally governed by the law of the State where the property was situate at the time of the purported transfer, and, in an application of the foreign act of State doctrine, an English court is generally bound to give effect to a foreign law pertaining to property situate, at the time of the law's passage, within the territory of the foreign

---

[183] See, arguably similarly, 3 De G F & J 217, 251 (Turner LJ).

[184] Also extremely doubtful is his Lordship's enforcement of a foreign sovereign prerogative—so doubtful, in fact, that when the case went on appeal, counsel for the plaintiff disavowed his Lordship's reasoning: see ibid, 232. The Lord Chancellor stated obiter that he would have upheld the appeal had it turned on this ground: ibid, 238. See, similarly, 251–2 (Turner LJ).

[185] [1953] 1 WLR 246.

[186] See *In re Claim by Helbert Wagg & Co Ltd* [1956] 1 Ch 323.

State in question. The plaintiffs' challenge to the application in the instant case of the foreign act of State doctrine was summarized by Campbell J:

The plaintiffs' contention can be based on two grounds: first, that no state can be expected to give effect within its territorial jurisdiction to a foreign law that is contrary to its own public policy or essential principles of morality; and secondly, that a foreign law that is contrary to international law ... need not be regarded.[187]

His Lordship accepted that customary international law required an expropriating State to pay compensation to parties whose property was expropriated, and concluded:

... I am satisfied that, following international law as incorporated in the domestic law of Aden, this court must refuse validity to the Persian Oil Nationalization Law in so far as it relates to nationalized property of the plaintiffs which may come within its territorial jurisdiction.[188]

He held the disputed oil to be the property of the plaintiffs.

Campbell J's reasoning is unclear to the extent that, when recounted as part of the plaintiffs' submission, the principle on which he relies is a negative, essentially discretionary one ('a foreign law that is contrary to international law ... need not be regarded'), but when referred to in his own conclusion on the point it is positive and mandatory ('this court must refuse validity'). It is significant, however, that the two relevant passages from English case-law to which his Lordship looks for support—neither of which, it should be noted, invoke the doctrine of incorporation—are couched in the negative.[189] Secondly, his Lordship never makes clear which of the two possible grounds underpinning the plaintiffs' contention he prefers. But although his conclusion would seem to favour the latter alone, the fact that he relies on authorities in which the court is avowedly declining to apply, rather than being compelled not to apply, the foreign law in question and the fact that a third English case he cites has nothing to do with international law but turns purely on English public policy[190] strongly suggest that he sees the two grounds as one and the

---

[187] [1953] 1 WLR 246 at 253.

[188] Ibid, 259. According to Campbell J, this refusal did not run counter to *Luther v Sagor* [1921] 3 KB 532 and *Princess Paley Olga v Weisz* [1929] 1 KB 718, which laid down that an English court was bound to apply a law of a foreign State which purported to confiscate property situate within that State's territory, since those cases related only to the property of the confiscating State's own nationals and therefore did not implicate international law: ibid, 253 and 258. See also the plaintiffs' argument: ibid, 248. Campbell J's reading of *Luther v Sagor* and *Princess Paley Olga v Weisz* was disapproved by Upjohn J in *In re Claim by Helbert Wagg & Co Ltd* [1956] 1 Ch 323, 346–8. As for the doctrine of incorporation, Campbell J had earlier cited Lord Atkin's famous dictum in *Chung Chi Cheung v The King* [1939] AC 160, 168.

[189] See [1953] 1 WLR 246, 254, quoting *Wolff v Oxholm* (1817) 6 M & S 92, 106 (Lord Ellenborough) ('nor are [the plaintiffs] or we bound to regard' the ordinance in question); and [1953] 1 WLR 246, 255, quoting *In re Fried Krupp AG* [1917] 2 Ch 188, 193 (Younger J)(an ordinance which 'neither [the plaintiffs] nor we are bound to regard').

[190] See ibid, quoting *Kaufman v Gerson* [1904] 1 KB 591, 599–600 (Romer LJ)('to enforce a contract so procured would be to contravene what by the law of this country is deemed an essential moral interest').

same—that is, that a foreign law that is contrary to international law, and thereby contrary to domestic public policy, need not be regarded.[191] This is certainly how the principle enunciated in the case has been conceived of since.[192]

Ultimately, it can be seen that *The Rose Mary* has nothing to do with the doctrine of incorporation. Campbell J does not apply the obligation to pay compensation imposed on an expropriating State by customary international law as a rule of common law.[193] Rather, he looks to the former in its quality as a rule of customary international law and, by reference to it, crafts a common-law, public policy-based exception to a common-law conflicts rule. It is telling that in subsequent cases in the English courts in which international law has been invoked as English public policy to justify—either obiter, as in *In re Claim by Helbert Wagg & Co Ltd* and *Oppenheimer v Cattermole*, or by way of ratio, as in *Kuwait Airways Corporation v Iraqi Airways Company (Nos 4 and 5)*—the court's refusal to give effect to foreign law, the doctrine of incorporation has never been so much as mentioned. In this light, reference to the doctrine of incorporation in the *Rose Mary* is otiose.

d. R v Mills

The fourth deceptive case is not from a superior court of record and calls for only the briefest of mentions. In *R v Mills*, an unreported ruling on jurisdiction and abuse of process in the Croydon Crown Court in 1995,[194]

---

[191]   See also D P O'Connell, 'A Critique of the Iranian Oil Litigation' (1955) 4 *International & Comparative Law Quarterly* 267, 278, reference omitted: 'In effect these two separate propositions were not separate grounds, but the second was rather a corollary or restatement of the first. The court made reference to *Kaufman v Gerson*, apparently in support of the view that English courts will not give effect to foreign legislation contrary to public policy as it is conceived by them. ... From this citation it would seem that the proposition on which Campbell J really based his decision might have been more aptly framed as follows: foreign legislation "not conformable" in its operations "to the usage of nations" is contrary to public policy as understood in English courts, and therefore such legislation need not be recognised.'

[192]   See *In re Claim by Helbert Wagg & Co Ltd* [1956] 1 Ch 323, 349 (Upjohn J): 'In my judgment the true limits of the principle that the courts of this country will afford recognition to legislation of foreign States in so far as it affects title to movables in that State at the time of the legislation or contracts governed by the law of that State rests in considerations of international law, or in the scarcely less difficult considerations of public policy as understood in these courts. Ultimately I believe the latter is the governing consideration.' See also *Oppenheimer v Cattermole* [1976] 1 AC 249, 278 (Lord Cross), with whom the other Lords agreed: 'I think—as Upjohn J thought (see *In re Claim by Helbert Wagg & Co Ltd* [1956] Ch 323, 334)—that it is part of the public policy of this country that our courts should give effect to clearly established rules of international law.' As to the Nazi denaturalization law at issue in that case, Lord Cross stated obiter that 'a law of this sort constitutes so grave an infringement of human rights that the courts of this country ought to refuse to recognise it as a law at all' (ibid). The public policy basis for the exception to the foreign act of State doctrine first suggested in *The Rose Mary* was put beyond doubt by the House of Lords in *Kuwait Airways Corporation v Iraqi Airways Company (Nos 4 and 5)* [2002] UKHL 19; [2002] 2 AC 883.

[193]   See also O'Connell, above n 191, 279, concluding that Campbell J 'did not, ... in fact, apply international law as a rule of decision ...'.

[194]   Noted in W Gilmore, 'Hot Pursuit: The Case of *R v Mills and others*' (1995) 44 *International & Comparative Law Quarterly* 949. Transcript of judgment on file with author, per kind favour of Professor Bill Gilmore and, in turn, the Solicitors' Office, HM Customs and Excise, London.

the defendants, who had been arrested on the high seas by HM Customs and Excise, sought a stay of the indictment in reliance on the abuse of process doctrine developed in *R v Horseferry Road Magistrates' Court, Ex parte Bennett*,[195] arguing that their arrest had been in breach of international law. Judge Devonshire held that the actions of the customs officers were in accordance with a State's customary international right of 'hot pursuit', which 'had been incorporated in the Common Law of England'.[196]

Again it can be seen that what the court is really doing here is looking to the relevant rule of customary international law *quâ* customary international law.[197] There was simply no need, in order to refute the defendants' contention that their arrest was in breach of international law, to establish that the UK's right of hot pursuit under customary international law was part of the common law. Judge Devonshire's invocation of the doctrine of incorporation was gratuitous. As it is, it must seriously be doubted whether the common law of England, which, as distinct from the law of Admiralty and from statute, was historically a terrestrial and territorially-limited law, can give rise to rights on the high seas.

5. *A sui generis area*

Finally, it is worth mentioning, if only to emphasize its sui generis character, one body of law traditionally applied by courts in England in which customary international law has long played a direct part. This is the law of prize, viz the body of rules regulating the capture of foreign vessels by a State, in this case the UK, in the course of declared war. Like the law of piracy, this too originated, prior to the rise of the modern, inter-State law of nations, in the old transnational maritime law applied in the ports of medieval and renaissance Europe, a form of civil, not common law given effect in England by the Admiralty courts.[198] This corpus of rules eventually passed into the law of nations, and English jurisdiction in matters of prize—which came to be exercised by the High Court of Admiralty by virtue of a commission issued by the Crown under the Great Seal at the

---

[195] [1994] 1 AC 942.
[196] Transcript, 9, citing in support *Regina v Sunila and Solayman* (1986) 28 DLR (4th) 450, 459 (Hart JA). See also Gilmore, above n 194, 954.
[197] See, in this light, Transcript, 10: 'I cannot accept the argument that no domestic court has any power to consider and adjudicate on the power to arrest pursuant to a right conferred by international law. The right of "hot pursuit" under which the *Poseidon* was arrested is a power conferred by the general principles of international law [viz customary international law] of which the Geneva Convention [on the High Seas 1958] was merely declaratory. The Court is being asked to adjudicate on the proper application of those powers …'. See also ibid, 22: 'I hold that the *Poseidon* was properly arrested in international waters under the terms of the Geneva Convention and in accordance with the provisions of the international law of the sea.'
[198] Prior to the fourteenth century, prize cases, which were originally treated as a species of proceedings against piracy, 'had been heard sometimes by the Council, and sometimes by the common law courts; but … their inability to cope with the difficulties caused by the piratical propensities of Englishmen had led to the establishment of a court of Admiralty': Holdsworth, above n 44, vol I, 562. See also Marsden, 'Early Prize Jurisdiction', above n 137.

commencement of each war[199]—was exercised by direct reference to this law of nations: that is, the law of nations, rather than the common law, was the law to be applied by the court.[200] When, via the Naval Prize Act 1864,[201] the High Court of Admiralty was vested with the powers of a permanent Court of Prize independently of any commission issued under the Great Seal, section 55 of the Act kept on foot the court's pre-existing competence to decide cases in accordance with customary international law, a competence unaffected by the substitution by the Judicature Act 1873, as explained by the Judicature Act 1891, of the High Court of Justice for the High Court of Admiralty as the permanent Court of Prize in the UK.[202] Although by this point it was perhaps not inaccurate to talk of an English common law of prize, this was avowedly expressive of the customary international rules on the subject; and although this law was applied by the High Court, it was applied by the Probate, Divorce and Admiralty Division sitting as the Prize Court,[203] with appeals going not to the Court of Appeal and the House of Lords but to the Privy Council.[204] In sum, the case-law of English prize courts cannot, for historical and jurisdictional reasons, be considered indicative of the general relationship between customary international law and the common law.[205] All this said, the application of prize law by English prize courts after 1873 is not irrelevant to certain questions discussed below, and will be referred to when occasion arises.

---

[199] This system of special commissions meant that the prize court 'became a court almost entirely distinct from the instance court [of Admiralty]': Holdsworth, above n 44, vol I, 564. In *Lindo v Rodney*, reported in a note appended to *Le Caux v Eden* (1781) 2 Dougl 594, 613–20, Lord Mansfield CJ states at 614 that '[t]he whole system of litigation and jurisprudence in the Prize Court, is peculiar to itself: it is no more like the Court of Admiralty than it is to any Court in Westminster-Hall'.

[200] See eg the commission conferring jurisdiction in prize on the Court of Admiralty cited by Lord Mansfield CJ in *Lindo v Rodney*, as indirectly reported at 2 Dougl 613, 614. This authorized and required the Court of Admiralty 'to proceed upon all and all manner of captures, seizures, prizes, and reprisals, of all ships and goods, that are, or shall be, taken; and to hear and determine, according to the course of the Admiralty, and the law of nations'.

[201] 27 & 28 Vict c 25. The High Court continues to enjoy jurisdiction as a prize court pursuant to section 27 of the Supreme Court Act 1981 (c 54).

[202] The jurisdiction of the High Court of Admiralty was transferred to the newly-created High Court of Justice by the Supreme Court of Judicature Act 1873 (c 66), section 16. But a degree of confusion arose as to whether the transfer included Admiralty's prize jurisdiction. For the avoidance of doubt, section 4 of the Supreme Court of Judicature Act 1891 (c 53) was passed, paragraph (1) of which made it clear that the High Court of Justice was to be considered a prize court within the meaning of the Naval Prize Act 1864.

[203] Supreme Court of Judicature Act 1891, section 4(2).

[204] Ibid, section 4(3).

[205] See, in this light, *Trendtex Trading Corporation v Central Bank of Nigeria* [1977] QB 529, 568, where Stephenson LJ, referring to the view expressed by Sir Samuel Evans P in the First World War prize case of *The Odessa* [1915] P 52, 62 that, when dealing with customary international law, '[p]recedents handed down from earlier days should be treated as guides to lead, and not as shackles to bind', observed insightfully that Sir Samuel 'may have felt a greater freedom in the Prize Court than a judge of a court of common law to let precedents lead him on to the future and not bind him to the past'.

B. Reasons for not applying

So why is it that there have been so few occasions on which the English courts have actually applied the doctrine of incorporation to give rise to a common-law rule? There is a range of reasons, some of them prosaic. In many instances where the English courts have invoked the maxim that customary international law is part of the law of England, they have not in the event had cause to rely on it on account of the fact that the customary international rule at issue was implemented in statute.[206] In other cases, the rule of customary international law alleged was not established to the satisfaction of the court[207] or the facts of the case fell outside the alleged rule.[208] Three other reasons, however, merit closer consideration.

1. Rule of customary international law one between States alone

In *R v Secretary of State for the Home Department, Ex parte Thakrar*, the applicant argued that customary international law obliged a State to accept its nationals expelled from another State and that, as customary international law was part of the law of England, the Secretary of State was obliged to admit him to the UK. The Court of Appeal rejected the submission. Lord Denning MR, after explaining that the customary international rule at issue did not apply to the UK and its former colonies anyway but only to what his Lordship called 'self-contained countries', continued:

Even in regard to self-contained countries, however, the rule of international law [in question] is only a rule as between two states. It is not a rule as between an individual and a state. The expelling state—if it had a good case—might call upon the home state to receive the person whom it expelled. But the individual could not pray the rule in aid for his own benefit.[209]

Orr LJ came to the same conclusion on the point.[210] Analogous reasoning also underpins a passage from the judgment of Kerr LJ in *J H Rayner*

---

[206] Consider the plethora of diplomatic immunity cases brought under 7 Anne c 12.

[207] See eg *J H Rayner (Mincing Lane) Ltd v Department of Trade and Industry* [1989] Ch 72, 242–9 (Ralph Gibson LJ) and [1990] 2 AC 418, 512–3 (Lord Oliver); *Hutchinson v Newbury Magistrates' Court* (2000) 122 ILR 499, 504–6 (Buxton LJ, delivering the judgment of the court); *R (Marchiori) v Environment Agency* [2002] EWCA Civ 3; (2002) 127 ILR 620, 645–6, paras 46–8 (Laws LJ); *R (Abbasi) v Secretary of State for Foreign and Commonwealth Affairs* [2002] EWCA Civ 1598; (2002) 126 ILR 685, 714, para 69 (Lord Phillips MR, delivering the judgment of the court); *R v Jones (Margaret)* [2004] EWCA Crim 1981; [2005] QB 259, 277, para 43 (Latham LJ)(judgment upheld on different grounds by House of Lords); *R (European Roma Rights Centre) v Immigration Officer at Prague Airport* [2004] UKHL 55; [2005] 2 AC 1, 38, para 27 (Lord Bingham); *R (Mohamed) v Secretary of State for Foreign and Commonwealth Affairs* [2008] EWHC 2048 (Admin), paras 166–9 and 183; *R (Al-Saadoon) and another v Secretary of State for Defence* [2009] EWCA Civ 7, paras 62–3.

[208] See eg *Viveash v Becker* (1814) 3 M & S 284, 291–8 (Lord Ellenborough CJ); *R v Secretary of State for the Home Department, Ex parte Thakrar* [1974] QB 684, 701–2 (Lord Denning MR) and 709–10 (Lawton LJ); *Chagos Islanders v Attorney General and Her Majesty's British Indian Ocean Territory Commissioner* [2003] EWHC 2222, para 382 (Ouseley J). See also *R (Al-Saadoon) and another v Secretary of State for Defence* [2009] EWCA Civ 7, para 70 (insufficient evidence to make out claim, whatever customary position).

[209] [1974] QB 684, 702.

[210] Ibid, 708–9.

(Mincing Lane),[211] and traces of it can be found, elided with considerations of justiciability, in Lord Alverstone CJ's judgment in *West Rand*.[212]

2. *Constitutional principles*

It was stated by Lord Bingham in *Jones (Margaret)* 'that "customary international law is applicable in the English courts only where the constitution permits"'.[213] Constitutional principles have frequently been cited, although often not in so many words, as a reason for not giving effect through a rule of common law to a rule of customary international law. The two constitutional principles implicated in this regard have been the supremacy of Parliament and the separation of powers.

There are consistent and uncontroversial statements throughout the case-law to the effect that a putative rule of common law derived from a rule of customary international law is, like any rule of common law, inapplicable where the content of an unambiguous statutory provision is to the contrary.[214] This is a straightforward function of the doctrine of parliamentary supremacy. By related operation of this doctrine, Parliament can oust the jurisdiction of the courts in relation to rules of common law, including rules giving expression to customary international law. For example, by choosing to put on a legislative footing some rules of customary international law but not others *ejusdem generis*, Parliament can, by implication, displace any residual jurisdiction over the unenacted rules, *quâ* common-law rules, that would otherwise vest in the courts. This was the case in *Viveash v Becker*,[215] where the question before Lord Ellenborough CJ was whether the diplomatic immunity provided for in 7 Anne c 12 was to be read as encompassing consuls. His Lordship '[could] not help thinking that the Act of Parliament which mentions only "embassadors and public ministers" and which was passed at a time when it was an object studiously to comprehend all kinds of public ministers entitled to these privileges, must be considered as declaratory not only of what the law of nations is, but of the extent to which that law is to be carried [in the English courts]'.[216] Nor is this the only way that statute can prevent the courts from giving effect to customary international law by way of common law. In *R v Secretary of State for the Home Department,*

---

[211] [1989] Ch 72, 184–5. But *cf contra*, on the particular rule in question, ibid, 219–20 (Nourse LJ).

[212] [1905] 2 KB 391, 409–12.

[213] [2006] UKHL 16; [2007] 1 AC 136, 160, para 23, quoting the present author, above n 12, 335.

[214] See *Chung Chi Cheung v The King* [1939] AC 160, 167–8 (Lord Atkin); *Trendtex Trading Corporation v Central Bank of Nigeria* [1977] QB 529, 553 (Lord Denning MR) and 577 and 578 (Shaw LJ); *J H Rayner (Mincing Lane) v Department of Trade and Industry* [1989] Ch 72, 207 (Nourse LJ); *Al-Adsani v Government of Kuwait* (1995) 103 ILR 420, 428 (Mantell J); *Bolkiah v The State of Brunei Darussalam* [2007] UKPC 62, para 29. Despite the implication in some dicta to the converse, the existence of contrary statute goes to the applicability of the common-law rule in the given instance, rather than to its existence in principle—as is the case in relation to any common-law rule. For what it is worth, note that an English prize court is also bound by the will of Parliament as expressed in statute: *The Zamora* [1916] 2 AC 77, 93.

[215] (1814) 3 M & S 284.

[216] Ibid, 298.

Ex parte Thakrar,[217] the applicant, who had been expelled from Uganda and was not a British 'patrial', argued that customary international law obliged the respondent to admit him into the UK in these circumstances. Section 3(1) of the Immigration Act 1971, however, provided that '[e]xcept as otherwise provided by or under this Act, where a person is not a patrial—(a) he shall not enter the United Kingdom unless given leave to do so ...'. Orr LJ stated:

[I]t is common ground (see *per* Lord Atkin in *Chung Chi Cheung v The King* [1939] AC 160, 167–168) that a rule of international law cannot be treated as incorporated into English municipal law where to do so would be inconsistent with the provisions of a statute. In the present case it is, in my judgment, clear beyond any doubt that the right which the applicant claims under international law is in conflict with the opening words of section 3(1) of the Immigration Act 1971 ... The Act is there saying that any exception to the rule that a non-patrial requires leave to enter the United Kingdom is to be found in the Act itself or in the regulations made under the Act, and it would plainly, in my judgment, be inconsistent with this provision to recognise any further exception based on international law.[218]

Lawton LJ was of the same view:

Whatever may be the nature and extent of the rule, I am satisfied that Parliament can decide whether it should be accepted and adopted within the realm; and by implication it has made its decision in the Immigration Act 1971 which regulates all entry into and stay in the United Kingdom. No person has any right of entry which is not given by that Act. Such rights as may be given by public international law to individuals are not rights given by the Act. It follows that they are of no value in municipal law.[219]

The Divisional Court had held the same.[220] Not too dissimilarly, while Mantell J in *Al-Adsani v Government of Kuwait*[221] was prepared for the sake of argument to accept that customary international law could give rise to a common-law tort of 'torture', this was no use to the claimant in the instant case, since the State Immunity Act 1978 made it clear that the Government of Kuwait was immune from the jurisdiction of the English courts in respect of the impugned conduct. The Court of Appeal upheld this decision,[222] and, while the customary international law basis of the tort of torture subsequently alleged in *Jones v Saudi Arabia*[223] was not made explicit, the House of Lords similarly ruled there that the State Immunity Act prevailed.

A combination of parliamentary supremacy and the separation of powers explains the decision in the great nineteenth-century case of *The*

---

217 [1974] 1 QB 684.   218 Ibid, 708.
219 Ibid, 710.
220 Ibid, 690–2 (Lord Widgery CJ), with whom May and Bridge JJ agreed.
221 (1995) 103 ILR 420.
222 (1996) 107 ILR 536.   223 [2006] UKHL 26; [2007] 1 AC 270.

Queen v Keyn,[224] which centred on a putative rule of customary international law which would have permitted a coastal State to exercise criminal jurisdiction over a three-mile territorial sea, including over foreigners on board foreign ships within that sea. Taken by some to support the view that customary international law is not applicable in the English courts unless and until Parliament legislates for this, *Keyn* is in fact a straightforward instance of the trial court's procedural incompetence, which in turn reflects constitutional principle. The necessary background to the case is somewhat involved. Original jurisdiction in England and Wales over indictable offences committed on land derives from the commissions of oyer and terminer and gaol delivery, common-law jurisdictions exercised in the past by the courts of assize and quarter sessions. Original jurisdiction over crimes at sea derives from the Admiralty courts. Both common law and Admiralty jurisdiction over crimes were extensions of royal power. With parliamentary victory in the Civil War and the evolution of the constitution to reflect the sovereignty of the Crown in Parliament, the criminal justice dispensed by the royal courts came to be viewed with some suspicion.[225] The Glorious Revolution and the Bill of Rights entrenched this stance. Common law and Admiralty jurisdiction over crimes, where not truncated, was not permitted to exceed its existing limits. Reflecting the nascent separation of powers between legislature and judiciary, Parliament alone was entitled to extend the jurisdiction of the English criminal courts. Only Parliament, too, could rightfully create new criminal courts *stricto sensu*. Now, when the Central Criminal Court was created by an Act of 1834, it was vested by Parliament with Admiralty's exclusive jurisdiction over crimes at sea.[226] The prisoner in *Keyn*, a foreigner, had been convicted at trial in the Central Criminal Court of murder committed on board a foreign ship. The question put to the Court for Crown Cases Reserved was whether the Central Criminal Court had jurisdiction to try the prisoner as charged.[227] The answer arrived at by seven of the thirteen judges was that it did not. The only common ratio was that the criminal jurisdiction of Admiralty, conferred by statute unaltered on the Central Criminal Court, had never extended to crimes committed by foreigners on foreign ships,[228] 'and no assent on the part of

---

[224] (1876) 2 Ex D 63.

[225] It is no coincidence that one of the first legislative acts of the Long Parliament had been to abolish the infamous Court of Star Chamber, a prerogative court detested for its criminal jurisdiction.

[226] See section 22 of 4 & 5 Will IV c 36, affirmed by section 4 of 7 Vict c 2, the Act which conferred Admiralty's criminal jurisdiction on the courts of assize.

[227] 2 Ex D 63, 64.

[228] See, in this regard, the detailed analysis of the ratio of the case conducted in G Marston, *The Marginal Seabed: United Kingdom Legal Practice* (Clarendon Press, Oxford, 1981), 136–7, which concludes: 'On this analysis, the *ratio decidendi* of *R v Keyn* is confined to the extent, *ratione materiae*, of the Admiral's power of adjudication ...'. Of the dissentients in *Keyn*, Lindley J, conceding at 2 Ex D 63, 98 that 'the jurisdiction contended for by the Crown has never been exercised', explained simply that 'no case appears ever to have arisen for its exercise'. Amphlett JA, noting similarly at 124 'that no precedent can be found for the exercise by the Court of Admiralty of criminal jurisdiction over a foreigner on board a foreign vessel', reminded the Court that '[s]uch a case must be rare, and

foreign nations to the exercise of dominion and jurisdiction over these waters [could], without an Act of Parliament, confer on the Admiral or any other judge of this country a larger jurisdiction than he possessed before'.[229] 'How', Lord Cockburn CJ asked, 'when exercising the functions of a British judge, can [the Admiral], or those acting in substitution for him, assume a jurisdiction which heretofore he did not possess, unless authorized by statute?'[230] 'Every such usurped exercise of judicial power [was]', according to his Lordship, 'in the highest degree unconstitutional.'[231]

Similarly, the scope of the power conferred on an administrative decision-maker by a statute is limited by the terms of that statute, and this was significant in *R (Marchiori) v Environment Agency*,[232] where the applicant sought to rely on the doctrine of incorporation. She sought judicial review of the legality of authorizations granted by the respondent, under section 13(1) of the Radioactive Substances Act 1993, to contractors to the Ministry of Defence to permit them to discharge radioactive waste from military installations in England at which Trident nuclear warheads were manufactured. She submitted that the respondent had applied in a legally impermissible manner the 'justification principle' laid down in article 6(a) of Council Directive 80/836/Euratom, made pursuant to the EURATOM Treaty, Chapter III, Title 2—viz that 'every activity resulting in exposure to ionizing radiation [be] justified by the advantages which it produces'—by characterizing the UK's nuclear defence programme as an advantage for the purposes of the principle. The applicant argued that customary international law, as elucidated by the International Court of Justice in its advisory opinion in *Legality of the Threat or Use of Nuclear Weapons*,[233] required the respondent to treat the Trident nuclear deterrent as a detriment, not an advantage, since the law of nations was part of the law of England and a condition of the respondent's *vires* was compliance

very probably was never under the consideration of the Court before'. Nor, it should be added, could the criminal jurisdiction of the courts of common law, which was historically limited to the realm (ie land), extend to offences by foreigners on foreign ships.

[229]   2 Ex D 63, 229 (Lord Cockburn CJ).

[230]   Ibid, 230–1.

[231]   Ibid, 231. Consider also, in this light, the passages from the judgments of Lord Cockburn CJ and Lush J quoted above at Part II.C. See too ibid, 203 (Lord Cockburn CJ): 'Nor, in my opinion, would the clearest proof of unanimous assent on the part of other nations be sufficient to authorize the tribunals of this country to apply, without an Act of Parliament, what would practically amount to a new law. In doing so we should be unjustifiably usurping the province of the legislature. The assent of nations is doubtless sufficient to give the power of parliamentary legislation in a matter otherwise within the sphere of international law; but it would be powerless to confer without such legislation a jurisdiction beyond and unknown to the law, such as that now insisted on, a jurisdiction over foreigners in foreign ships on a portion of the high seas.' See also ibid, 68 (Sir Robert Phillimore), not deciding the issue: 'It is, indeed, a most grave question whether, if this statement of international law is correct, nevertheless an Act of Parliament would not be required to empower the Court to exercise jurisdiction ...' In the wake of *Keyn*, the jurisdiction of the Central Criminal Court was extended by legislation over a three-mile territorial sea, although the preamble to the Territorial Waters Jurisdiction Act 1878 (c 73) asserted the immemoriality of the new dispensation.

[232]   [2002] EWCA Civ 3; (2002) 127 ILR 620.

[233]   [1996] ICJ Rep 226, especially at 257, paras 78–9.

with the relevant prevailing general law. In the Court of Appeal, Laws LJ (with whom Thorpe LJ and Morland J agreed) held that, even if the Trident nuclear programme were unlawful under international law (which the ICJ's advisory opinion showed, in fact, not to be the case), the appeal would still have failed, since the respondent's relevant functions were conferred on it and limited by the Radioactive Substances Act: the respondent was 'neither the author nor the judge of any policy of national defence', and 'it would be far beyond the scope of the provision made by [the Act] for the respondent to embark upon the least consideration of it'.[234]

The doctrine of the separation of powers primarily explains the decision in *West Rand*.[235] In that case, a gold mining company brought a petition of right against the Crown seeking the return of gold taken from its mine prior to the outbreak of the Anglo-Boer War by officials acting on behalf of the government of the subsequently-conquered South African Republic. The claimant argued that customary international law provided that the sovereign of a conquering State was liable for the obligations of the conquered State; that customary international law formed part of the law of England; and that therefore rights and obligations binding upon the former South African Republic could be enforced against the Crown in the English courts. Lord Alverstone CJ, delivering the judgment of the Divisional Court of King's Bench, expressed doubt as to whether the international rule argued for existed; but, even if it did, it was 'inconsistent with the law as recognised for many years in the English courts':

[I]t is sufficient for us to cite the language of Lord Mansfield in *Campbell v Hall* in a passage the authority of which has, so far as we know, never been called in question: 'It is left by the Constitution to the King's authority to grant or refuse a capitulation. ... If he receives the inhabitants under his protection and grants them their property he has a power to fix such terms and conditions as he thinks proper. He is entrusted with making the treaty of peace; he may yield up the conquest or retain it upon what terms he pleases. These powers no man ever disputed, neither has it hitherto been controverted that the King might change part or the whole of the law or political form of government of a conquered dominion.'[236]

The matter was thus non-justiciable, since 'matters which fall properly to be determined by the Crown by treaty or as an act of State are not subject to the jurisdiction of the municipal Courts, and ... rights supposed to be acquired thereunder cannot be enforced by such Courts'.[237]

---

[234] 127 ILR 620, 646, para 48.   [235] [1905] 2 KB 391.

[236] Ibid, 406.

[237] Ibid, 408–9. See also, not dissimilarly, the Privy Council case of *Cook v Sprigg* [1899] 1 AC 572. An action was brought under the Crown Liabilities Act 1888 (Cape Colony) by which the plaintiffs sought to enforce against the Crown concessions granted to them by the paramount chief of Pondoland prior to the chief's cession of Pondoland to the United Kingdom, after which the territory was annexed to the Cape Colony. It was argued, *inter alia*, that customary international law

Under the Westminster constitutional dispensation, the power to enter into treaties is a prerogative of the Crown, while the power to legislate for the rights and obligations of individuals under English law is the province of Parliament. One upshot of this delineation of powers is that a treaty to which the UK is party cannot have effect in English law unless Parliament enacts legislation to implement its provisions.[238] In certain cases, this can in turn pose an obstacle to the incorporation into the common law of rules of customary international law. In *R v Lyons*,[239] the applicants, whose respective convictions had been held by the European Court of Human Rights (ECtHR) to have involved a violation of their right to fair trial under the then-unincorporated European Convention on Human Rights (ECHR), argued that the UK (and thus, they submitted, the court as an organ of State) was bound under customary international law by the secondary obligation to make restitution (*restitutio in integrum*) for its internationally wrongful act,[240] which in the present case meant quashing their convictions. The House of Lords rejected the argument as one whose 'foundations rest[ed] upon sand', being as it was 'nothing more than an

imposed an obligation on a State which accepts territory by way of cession to respect private property within that territory. While the maxim that customary international law is part of the law of land does not feature as such in the report's account of counsel's submission or in the judgment, counsel for the plaintiffs did cite *Triquet v Bath* in support of his argument '[a]s to obligations resulting from international law ... being enforceable in municipal courts': see [1899] 1 AC 572, 576. In response, the Board stated at [1899] 1 AC 572, 578: 'It is a well-established principle of law that the transactions of independent States between each other are governed by other laws than those which municipal courts administer. It is no answer to say that by the ordinary principles of international law private property is respected by the sovereign which accepts the cession and assumes the duties and legal obligations of the former sovereign with respect to such private property within the ceded territory. All that can be properly meant by such a proposition is that according to the well-understood rules of international law a change of sovereignty by cession ought not to affect private property, but no municipal tribunal has authority to enforce such an obligation. And if there is an express or well-understood bargain between the ceding potentate and the Government to which the cession is made that private property shall be respected, that is only a bargain which can be enforced by sovereign against sovereign in the ordinary course of diplomatic pressure.' (It might be observed, by way of aside, that the Privy Council here conflates two distinct forms of non-justiciability, namely the non-justiciability of the prerogative acts of the Crown, which is surely what was at issue in the instant case, and the non-justiciability of pure questions of international law between sovereign States. *Cf*, in this light, Holdsworth, above n 44, vol XIV, 34, in line with the approach taken by the Board, and, *contra*, Stephen, above n 136, vol II, 65, prefiguring the modern approach.) Note that, in the distinct context of prize law, the Crown by tradition expressly submitted to the jurisdiction of the Prize Court in the prize rules promulgated at the commencement of war. See *The Zamora* [1916] 2 AC 77, 91: 'In the first place, all those matters upon which the Court is authorized to proceed are, or arise out of, acts done by the sovereign power in right of war. It follows that the King must, directly or indirectly, be a party to all proceedings in a Court of Prize. In such a Court his position is in fact the same as in the ordinary Courts of the realm upon a petition of right which has been duly fiated. Rights based on sovereignty are waived and the Crown for most purposes accepts the position of an ordinary litigant.' See also [1916] 2 AC 77, 92: 'The acts of a belligerent Power in right of war are not justiciable in its own Courts unless such Power, as a matter of grace, submit to their jurisdiction.'

[238] In *In re McKerr* [2004] UKHL 12; [2004] 1 WLR 807, 826, para 63, Lord Hoffmann stated that 'it should no longer be necessary to cite authority for [this] proposition'.

[239] [2003] 1 AC 976.

[240] See Articles on Responsibility of States for Internationally Wrongful Acts, above n 145, arts 34 and 35.

attempt to give direct domestic effect to an international treaty'[241] in violation of the separation of powers. Lord Hoffman, with whom most of the other Lords agreed, explained:

The obligation to make restitution ... is in the present case ancillary to a treaty obligation. It is infringement of the treaty obligation ... that is said to give rise to the obligation to make restitution. [Counsel for the applicants] himself described it as a secondary obligation in the sense used by Lord Diplock in *Photo Production Ltd v Securicor Transport Ltd* [1980] AC 827, 848–849. But if there is no enforceable primary obligation, how can its breach give rise to an enforceable secondary obligation?[242]

Analogous reasoning is found in the judgment of Lord Oliver in *J H Rayner (Mincing Lane)*, where the claimants sought to rely on an alleged rule of customary international law that where States, by means of treaty (in this case, the Sixth International Tin Agreement) brought into being an international organization (here, the International Tin Council) which was intended to engage in commercial transactions, the member States were secondarily liable for the organization's debts to third parties. To this Lord Oliver replied:

Now assuming that such a rule could be established, I can see that it might be said that it forms part of English law ... [But i]f such a rule exists, it is at highest a rule of construction, and however the matter is looked at, the question of liability or no liability stems from an unincorporated treaty which, without legislation, can neither create nor destroy rights under domestic law.[243]

Most of the other Lords agreed with his Lordship.[244]

The constitutional separation of powers between the executive and Parliament, between the courts and Parliament and between the courts and the executive lay at the heart of the Lords' decision *Jones (Margaret)* that the customary international crime of aggression was not a crime at common law.[245] Lord Bingham agreed with Sir Franklin Berman that

---

[241] [2002] UKHL 44; [2003] 1 AC 976, 995, para 39 (Lord Hoffman).
[242] [2003] 1 AC 976, 995, para 39 (Lord Hoffman).
[243] *J H Rayner (Mincing Lane) Ltd v Department of Trade and Industry* [1990] 2 AC 418, 512.
[244] See also, directly on point, ibid, 480 (Lord Templeman).
[245] The ruling in *Jones (Margaret)* that statute is required before a crime under customary international law can become a crime under English law was prefigured in *Hutchinson v Newbury Magistrates' Court* (2002) 122 ILR 499, 506 (Buxton LJ, delivering the judgment of the court) ('impossible to reconcile [the claimant's] contention with the debate in *Pinochet (No 3)* which concluded, illuminatingly subject to the specific dissent on this point by Lord Millett, that although State torture had long been an international crime ..., it was only with the passing of Section 134 of the Criminal Justice Act 1998 that the English criminal courts acquired jurisdiction over "international", that is to say extra-territorial torture'); and in paragraph 4 (no explanation being given) of the Divisional Court's judgment in *R (Manson) v Bow Street Magistrates' Court* [2003] EWHC 2720 Admin, unreported and judgment not made public, judgment as approved by the court obtained from Smith Bernal Wordwave Limited, official shorthand writers to the court. The incorporation argument was not in fact put to the Lords in *R v Bow Street Metropolitan Stipendiary Magistrate, Ex parte Pinochet Ugarte (No 3)* [2000] 1 AC 147. Lord Millet nonetheless expressed the view that a crime under customary international law was automatically a crime under the common law, although his Lordship did not press the point, since the other Lords apparently considered that statutory

'[i]nasmuch as the reception of customary international law into English law takes place under common law, and inasmuch as the development of new customary international law remains very much the consequence of international behaviour by the Executive, in which neither the Legislature nor the Courts, nor any other branch of the constitution, need have played any part, it would be odd if the Executive could, by means of that kind, acting in concert with other States, amend or modify specifically the *criminal* law, with all the consequences that flow for the liberty of the individual and rights of personal property'.[246] As it was, since *Knuller (Publishing, Printing and Promotions) Ltd v Director of Public Prosecutions*,[247] in which the House of Lords surrendered its common-law power to create crimes, statute was now the sole source of new criminal offences;[248] and a raft of Acts showed that, when domestic effect was sought to be given to crimes under customary international law, the practice was to legislate.[249] (In the latter regard, Lord Bingham noted that Parliament had consciously opted not to legislate for the crime of aggression during the passage of the International Criminal Court Act 2001.[250]) All this reflected 'what has become an important democratic principle in this country: that it is for those representing the people of the country in Parliament, not the executive and not the judges, to decide what conduct should be treated as lying so far outside the bounds of what is acceptable in our society as to attract criminal penalties'.[251] Lord Hoffman also invoked 'the democratic principle', deferred to by the courts since *Knuller*[252] and equally applicable to the incorporation into domestic law of crimes under international law,[253] 'that it is nowadays for Parliament and Parliament alone to decide whether conduct not previously regarded as criminal should be made an offence'.[254] New domestic offences should, his Lordship said, 'be debated in Parliament, defined in a statute and come into force on a prescribed date', 'not creep into existence as a result

authority was required 'before our courts can exercise extraterritorial criminal jurisdiction even in respect of crimes of universal jurisdiction': ibid, 276. In this light, the reason for the other Lords' insistence on statute seems to have been the extraterritorial jurisdictional element, rather than anything to do with the relationship between customary international crimes and the common law. This is how *Pinochet (No 3)* was read in *R v Jones (Margaret)* [2004] EWCA Crim 1981; [2005] QB 259, 275, para 38 by the Court of Appeal, which, in a ruling overturned by the House of Lords (upholding the Court of Appeal's decision on other grounds), held that a crime under customary international law was 'capable of being incorporated into English law so as to create a crime punishable in domestic law': [2005] QB 259, 273, para 30.

[246] [2006] UKHL 16; [2007] 1 AC 136, 160, para 23, original emphasis, quoting F Berman, 'Jurisdiction: The State', in P Capps, M Evans & S Konstantinidis (eds), *Asserting Jurisdiction: International and European Legal Perspectives* (Hart, Oxford, 2003), 3, 11. 'There [were], besides, powerful reasons of political accountability, regularity and legal certainty for saying that the power to create crimes should now be regarded as reserved exclusively to Parliament, by Statute.': ibid.

[247] [1973] AC 435.
[248] [2007] 1 AC 136, 161–2, para 28.
[249] Ibid, 162, para 28.
[250] Ibid.
[251] Ibid, para 29.
[252] Ibid, 171, para 61.   [253] Ibid, para 62.   [254] Ibid, 170, para 60.

of an international consensus to which only the executive of this country is a party'.[255] Lord Mance agreed that the courts' power to recognize new crimes did not survive *Knuller*: the creation and regulation of crimes was, in a modern parliamentary democracy, 'a matter *par excellence* for Parliament to debate and legislate'.[256] 'Even crimes under public international law [could] no longer be, if they ever were, the subject of any automatic reception or recognition in domestic law by the courts.'[257] In the opinion of Lord Bingham, and in a qualification peculiar to his Lordship's judgment alone, one needed very compelling reasons to depart from this principle.[258] In the case of aggression, the compelling reasons were to the contrary, among them the courts' slowness to review the exercise of prerogative powers over the conduct of foreign affairs and the deployment of the armed forces.[259] These were not issues of justiciability; rather, they were factors to be taken into account '[i]n considering whether the customary international law crime of aggression has been, or should be, tacitly assimilated into [English] domestic law'.[260] Lord Hoffmann similarly took the view that, since aggression was 'a crime in which the principal is always the state itself',[261] the liability of individuals being 'in a sense secondary', the prosecution of aggression in the domestic courts would, in the absence of statutory authority, be 'inconsistent with a fundamental principle of [the] constitution',[262] in that 'the making of war and peace and the disposition of the armed forces has always been regarded as a discretionary power of the Crown into the exercise of which the courts will not inquire'.[263] His Lordship thought that to say that these matters are not justiciable 'may be simply another way of putting the same point'.[264] But he did not accept the implication that one could start by determining whether aggression is a crime under English law and then proceed to consider whether the issues it raises are justiciable: the 'discretionary nature or non-justiciability of the power to make war' was 'simply one of the reasons why aggression is not a crime in domestic law'.[265]

---

[255] Ibid, 171, para 62.　　[256] Ibid, 179, para 101.　　[257] Ibid.

[258] Ibid, 162, para 29. It is, with respect, hard to see how any such departure could be reconciled with the constitutional principles emphasized by his Lordship and by Lords Hoffmann and Mance. In the later case of *R (Gentle) v Prime Minister* [2008] UKHL 20; [2008] 2 WLR 879, 896, para 49, Baroness Hale summarized *Jones (Margaret)* without reference to Lord Bingham's qualification: the case stood for the proposition that '[c]rimes under customary international law are not automatically incorporated into domestic law and it is no longer open to the courts to recognise new common law crimes'.

[259] [2007] 1 AC 136, 162–3, para 30. His Lordship also referred in support of his argument to the courts' slowness to adjudicate upon transactions between sovereign States on the international plane.

[260] Ibid, 163, para 30. In *R (Gentle) v Prime Minister* [2008] UKHL 20; [2008] 2 WLR 879, 885, para 8, in the different context of the ECHR, Lord Bingham subsequently stated: '[I]n deciding whether a right exists it is relevant to consider what exercise of the right would entail. Thus the restraint traditionally shown by the courts in ruling on what has been called high policy—peace and war, the making of treaties, the conduct of foreign relations—does tend to militate against the existence of the right: *R v Jones (Margaret)* [2006] UKHL 16, [2007] 1 AC 136, paras 30, 65–67.'

[261] See also [2007] 1 AC 136, 180, para 103 (Lord Mance).

[262] Ibid, 171, para 63.　　[263] Ibid, 172, para 65.　　[264] Ibid, para 67.　　[265] Ibid.

3. *Other common-law principles and rules*

In *West Rand*, Lord Alverstone CJ, accepting that customary international law formed part of the law of England, added the proviso that this was only to the extent that it was not 'contrary to the principles of her laws as declared by her Courts'.[266] Lord Atkin in *Chung Chi Cheung* similarly recognized that the English courts will treat customary international law as incorporated into English law only 'so far as it is not inconsistent with rules ... finally declared by their tribunals'.[267] Some of these judicially-enunciated principles and rules are of a constitutional import, as seen already. But others are not.

An example of how the latter, more prosaic common-law principles and rules have prevented the reception into the common law, at least in the form argued for, of a rule of customary international law is Ouseley J's judgment in the Queen's Bench Division in *Chagos Islanders v Attorney General and Her Majesty's British Indian Ocean Territory Commissioner*,[268] where his Lordship rejected a claim for damages based, in reliance on the doctrine of incorporation, on the UK's alleged breach of the customary international human right not to be exiled from one's home State. His Lordship reasoned that, even if one were to accept the hypothetical possibility that a customary international human right could be recognized as a common-law human right, there was no reason why the breach of a common-law human right would give rise to an action in damages. This would, Ouseley J said, be 'no more and no less than a particular example of a tort for unlawful administrative acts', and the House of Lords had made it 'clear for many years that an *ultra vires* act does not of itself give rise to tortious liability'.[269] In short, even if an English court accepted, on the basis of the doctrine of incorporation, that an individual had a right as a matter of common law not to be exiled, this 'provide[d] no reason for a tort to be created'.[270] Any such remedy as may exist would be strictly by way of judicial review.[271]

An earlier example comes from the appeal to the Lord Chancellor and Lords Justice in *The Emperor of Austria v Day and Kossuth* in 1861, an appeal dismissed on grounds different from those on which the Court of Chancery had based its decision at first instance. Purely obiter, Turner LJ considered the argument put at first instance by the plaintiff, in his capacity as king of Hungary, in an action to restrain the defendants from counterfeiting Hungarian paper money and for the delivery up of the

---

[266] [1905] 2 KB 391, 408.   [267] [1939] AC 160, 167–8.
[268] [2003] EWHC 2222.
[269] Ibid, para 378, citing in support of this well-established proposition *Three Rivers DC v Bank of England (No 3)* [2003] 2 AC 1, 190 (Lord Steyn), citing in turn *X (Minors) v Bedfordshire CC* [1995] 2 AC 633.
[270] Ibid, para 379. His Lordship seemingly left the door slightly ajar by pointing out that the claimants had put forward no reason why the aforementioned principle should not apply in the instant case. But it is difficult to see what reasons could compellingly be adduced.
[271] Ibid.

notes already produced and the plates from which they were printed. His Lordship accepted the plaintiff's contention 'that the right of coining money, the *jus cudendae monetae*, was universally acknowledged to be a prerogative of sovereigns vested in them for the benefit of their subjects—that this right extended no less to the creation of paper money than to the stamping of coin—that it was acknowledged by all nations and recognized by international law, and that, international law being part of the law of England, [the] Court would interfere in favour of the rights recognized by and founded upon it'.[272] His Lordship, however, continued:

[B]ut the argument failed to satisfy my mind that this Court can or ought to interfere in aid of the prerogatives of a foreign sovereign. The prerogative rights of sovereigns seem to me, as at present advised, to stand very much upon the same footing as acts of State and matters of that description, with which the municipal Courts of this country do not and cannot interfere. Such acts and matters are recognized by international law no less than the prerogative rights of sovereigns; but the municipal Courts of this country have disclaimed all right to interfere with respect to them. … The same reasoning which applies to the prerogative rights of sovereigns seems to me to apply also to the political rights of nations; and so far, therefore, as this bill is founded upon the prerogative rights of the Plaintiff, or upon the political rights of his subjects, my present opinion, speaking with all respect of [*sic*] what fell from the Vice-Chancellor in the course of his judgment, is against the decree which he has made.[273]

In short, even if the alleged rule of customary international law was in principle capable of incorporation into the common law,[274] established case-law prevented its enforcement by an English court.[275]

IV. The Doctrine As More Accurately Conceived

A. *An act of discerning judicial lawmaking*

As has been seen above, it is only in certain immunity cases and in two cases on the right of angary and its concomitant obligation to pay compensation that a rule of customary international law has actually been applied or conclusively recognized by the English courts as part of English law. The point to be made now is that, if one stops to think about it, were customary international law truly *automatically part* of the common law,

---

[272] (1861) 3 De G F & J 217, 251.
[273] Ibid, 251–2.
[274] On closer analysis, it is not clear that this is, in fact, what his Lordship was suggesting by his reference to the doctrine of incorporation. As with Sir John Stuart V-C at first instance, it is arguable that Turner LJ's invocation of customary international law and the doctrine of incorporation was more by way of legitimation of the English court's hypothetical intervention to support a right vesting in the king under Hungarian law.
[275] Like the question of contrary statute, this is an example going to the application of the putative common-law rule, rather than to its existence as such.

it could not have been applied at common law even in these cases. Something subtly different must explain what the courts are doing.

Take first the immunity cases, considering by way of preface the nature of the entity bound by the relevant international obligation.

By and large,[276] international obligations direct the conduct of States, and international law conceives of the State as a legal person wholly distinct from the several branches of government and from the individual officers and agents which together constitute its domestic legal and political reality and which, as a function of its constitution, carry out its business.[277] If we were to draw the analogy with company law, there exists a form of corporate veil.[278] Putting it simply and adapting it to the present context, in those situations where customary international law imposes an obligation, only the United Kingdom as such, and not the Crown[279] or

[276]   The exceptions are those obligations aimed at international organizations and those directed towards the conduct of individuals, the latter being the province of international criminal law. There are also certain obligations under international humanitarian law, namely those applicable during non-international armed conflict, that are binding on non-State insurgent groups, although this remains disputed by some writers.

[277]   See eg paragraph (6) of the International Law Commission's commentary to article 2 of its Articles on Responsibility of States for Internationally Wrongful Acts: *International Law Commission, Report on the work of its fifty-third session (23 April-1 June and 2 July-10 August 2001)*, UN Doc A/56/10, 71: 'Under many legal systems, the State organs consist of different legal persons (ministries or other legal entities), which are regarded as having distinct rights and obligations for which they alone can be sued and are responsible. For the purposes of the international law of State responsibility the position is different. The State is treated as a unity, consistent with its recognition as a single legal person in international law.' See also J Combacau & S Sur, *Droit international public* (4ème édn, Montchrestien, Paris, 1999), 221, present author's translation: 'The State is a legal person. It is in this capacity that international law thinks of it and treats it. ... Personality implies first of all that the legal order which recognizes it conceives of the State as a corporate entity, separate from the elements that comprise it. ... [T]he State ... is held to be a body distinct from its constitutive elements ...' In Oppenheim's straightforward words, 'States only, and neither their Courts nor officials ..., are subjects of International Law': L Oppenheim, *International Law. A Treatise* (2nd edn, Longmans, Green & Co, London, 1912), vol II, 554, para 434. See also D Anzilotti, *Cours de droit international* (G Gidel trans, first published 1929, Editions Panthéon-Assas, Paris, 1999), 122–3; W E Beckett, 'Les questions d'intérêt générale au point de vue juridique dans la jurisprudence de la Cour Permanente de Justice Internationale', 39 *Recueil des Cours* (1932-I) 131, 155; G G Fitzmaurice, 'The General Principles of International Law Considered from the Standpoint of the Rule of Law', 92 *Recueil des Cours* (1957-II) 1, 74–8 and 87–8; Sales & Clement, above n 54, 415 n 126.

[278]   'The state ... is a so-called juristic person, or, what amounts to the same, a corporation': H Kelsen, *Principles of International Law* (Rinehart & Co, New York, 1952), 100. See also Combacau & Sur, above n 277, 221; Crawford & Olleson, above n 143, 460.

[279]   Note that the Crown, which, when referred to in this context, 'personifies the executive government of the country' (*British Broadcasting Corporation v Johns (Inspector of Taxes)* [1965] Ch 32, 79 (Diplock LJ)), is not coextensive with the State as an international legal person, since the organs of the State comprise not just the executive but also the legislature and the judiciary: see eg Articles on Responsibility of States for Internationally Wrongful Acts, above n 145, article 4(1). Even more to the point, the aggregation of these organs still does not equate to the State as such, the latter being a purely formal legal abstraction which is greater than the sum of its parts. In the words of Kelsen, above n 278, 100, '[a]s a juristic person the state is the personification of a social order, constituting the community we call "state"'. The attribution to the State of the conduct of its various organs and officials is simply a pragmatic recognition of 'the elementary fact that the State cannot act of itself', and 'is necessarily a normative operation': *International Law Commission, Report on the work of its fifty-third session*, above n 277, 35, paras (5) and (6) respectively. See also, generally, Beckett, above n 277, 155; Kelsen, ibid, 107; Fitzmaurice, above n 277, 87–8; Combacau & Sur, above n 277, 221; Crawford & Olleson, above n 143, 460; M Shaw, *International Law* (6th edn, Cambridge University

Parliament or the courts,[280] is bound by it.[281] As a consequence, a rule to the effect that customary international law is automatically part of the common law is of no help to a claimant seeking to argue that the Crown or the courts are compelled to adopt a particular course of action, since the only entity bound by the putative common-law rule (and this only for the sake of 'argument, since the statement speaks to its own impossibility[282]) is the United Kingdom.

Acknowledgment of the hurdle posed by the indivisibility of the State as a subject of international law is glimpsed in *Lyons*, where the House of Lords dismissed as a 'fallacy'[283] the argument that the court, as an organ of State, was bound to give effect to the UK's customary international obligation to make restitution (*restitutio in integrum*) for an internationally wrongful act. Lord Hoffmann, with whom most of the other Lords agreed, stated:

International law does not normally take account of the internal distribution of powers within a state. It is the duty of the state to comply with international law, whatever may be the organs which have the power to do so. And likewise, a [rule of international law] may be infringed by the actions of the Crown, Parliament or the courts. From the point of view of international law, it ordinarily does not matter.[284]

Lord Millet touched on the same point.[285]

In the immunity cases, the rule of customary international law in question—that each State is obliged to ensure that the organs, individual officials and property of a foreign State are immune from the jurisdiction of its courts—is a rule binding on the United Kingdom, not on the English courts. As such, if we were to give effect to a rule which says that customary international law is automatically part of the common law, the result

---

Press, Cambridge, 2008), 786. Conversely, in English law, when the word 'State' is found in legislation, '[i]t does not mean [only] the Government or the Executive': *Chandler v Director of Public Prosecutions* [1964] AC 763, 790 (Lord Reid). 'Perhaps the country or the realm are as good synonyms as one can find', and Lord Reid for one was 'prepared to accept the organised community as coming as near to a definition as one can get': ibid.

[280] See also Oppenheim, above n 277, vol I, 26–7, para 21; F A Mann, 'The Consequences of an International Wrong in International and National Law' (1976–77) 48 *British Yearbook of International Law* 1, 48, citation omitted: 'The decisive question is not (as it has been wholly unjustifiably put in Germany) whether ... public international law imposes upon the municipal judge the duty to [give effect to its rules]. That question was rightly answered in the negative, but misses the point altogether, for *ex hypothesi* public international law which, as a rule, addresses the State provides no answer.'

[281] See, generally, Triepel, above n 55, 120; Anzilotti, above n 277, 469 and 471–2.

[282] It goes almost without saying that the United Kingdom is not bound by the common law of England.

[283] [2002] UKHL 44; [2003] 1 AC 976, 995, para 40 (Lord Hoffman).

[284] [2003] 1 AC 976, 995, para 40. Conversely, in *In re McKerr* [2004] UKHL 12; [2004] 1 WLR 807, 826, para 63, Lord Hoffmann, emphasizing the differences between the domestic rights enforceable under the Human Rights Act and the international rights enforceable under the ECHR, stated that the former 'are available against specific public authorities, not the United Kingdom as a state'.

[285] [2003] 1 AC 976, 1011, para 105. The full text of the passages from the respective judgments of Lords Hoffmann and Millet excerpted here are somewhat confusing in their elision of two distinct arguments: the first, that international law binds the State as such, and not any of its domestic constitutional organs; the second, that the British constitution's separation of powers and parliamentary supremacy place restrictions on the doctrine of incorporation.

would simply be (and this is impossible) that the United Kingdom was bound by an English common-law rule to the same effect as the customary international rule. To posit that the English courts themselves are bound by this common-law rule would amount to holding X to account for the breach by Y of an obligation owed by Y. So in the immunity cases, where the latter was indeed posited, more must be going on than meets the eye.

In reality, what is happening in the immunity cases is that the courts are taking a rule of customary international law binding on the United Kingdom, but at the same time a rule which, in terms of its structural logic, lends itself readily to application by the English courts, and turning it into a rule of common law directed towards and binding on those courts.[286] This was effectively acknowledged by Lord Wright in *The Cristina*, where his Lordship explained that the rule of State immunity at issue '[was] binding on the municipal Courts of this country in the sense and to the extent that it has been received and enforced by these Courts'.[287] In other words, there is an additional link in the chain of logic, and that link is an active, albeit unstated and perhaps even unselfconscious judicial mediation between the international and domestic legal spheres, an act of judicial lawmaking in which the court translates—in the sense of renders into another language—the customary international rule binding on the United Kingdom into a common-law rule binding on the relevant branch of government, in this case the courts. In short, the model is one not of automatic incorporation but of what Capps, coming at the question from a different angle, has termed 'judicial transformation'[288] or what O'Connell calls 'judicial adoption'.[289] Putting it another way, Lord Bingham's instinct in *Jones (Margaret)* was unerring: as others have said before[290] (including Brierly, whom his Lordship quoted[291]), customary international law is a source, rather than a part, of the common law of England, and a legitimate source, all other things being equal—indeed, a source that, all other things again being equal, an English court must,[292] as a matter of common

---

[286]   See Triepel, above n 55, 110–1 and 144–5; Anzilotti, above n 277, 61–3.

[287]   [1938] AC 485, 502.

[288]   P Capps, 'The court as gatekeeper: customary international law in English courts' (2007) 70 *Modern Law Review* 458, 464. See also, using the language of 'transformation', Anzilotti, above n 277, 62–3.

[289]   O'Connell, above n 2, vol I, 49–50. See also, using the language of 'adoption', Triepel, above n 55, 144–52; Oppenheim, above n 277, vol I, 26–7, para 21; Picciotto, above n 53, 106, para 65; Sales & Clement, above n 54, 388.

[290]   Picciotto, above n 53, 105–6, para 65; Collier, above n 19, 935; Sales & Clement, above n 54, 413. See also, from a historical point of view, Dickinson, above n 2, 260; Holdsworth, above n 45, 147 and 150–1 and above n 44, vol XIV, 32; Lobban, above n 53, 256–7 and 277–8. See too, to the same effect but not using the word 'source', Triepel, above n 55, 110–1 and 144–5; Oppenheim, above n 277, vol I, 26–7, para 21; Anzilotti, above n 277, 61–3; Mann, above n 23, 121–3 and 124.

[291]   Brierly, above n 5, 31, quoted in part at [2007] 1 AC 136, 155, para 11.

[292]   See Westlake, above n 19, 26 (the statement being limited to rights under customary international law pertaining to individuals); Lauterpacht, above n 2, 79 and 81; O'Connell, above n 2, vol I, 50–1; Starke, above n 2, 92; G Sawer, 'Australian Constitutional Law in Relation to International Relations and International Law', in K W Ryan (ed), *International Law in Australia* (2nd edn, Law

law,[293] endeavour to draw upon when occasion arises. What Lord Denning MR in *Trendtex* referred to as the doctrine of incorporation[294] is in reality a statement to the effect that the English courts, where appropriate, may and must create rules of common law by reference to rules of customary international law. It is a licence and a direction to the judge to look, where relevant, to a rule of customary international law operative on the international plane and, in appropriate circumstances, to coin in near enough its image a rule of common law applicable in an English court.

The same goes, *mutatis mutandis*, for the right of angary and its associated obligation to pay compensation as given effect at common law in the *Commercial Estates Company of Egypt* litigation. Just as with obligations, so too with rights it is the case that international law regulates the conduct of the United Kingdom and not of the Crown, Parliament, or the courts. The customary international right of angary thus vests in the United Kingdom as such, not in the Crown, and if customary international law were automatically part of the common law of England, the English common-law right of angary would equally vest in the United Kingdom—an incoherent proposition. What happened in the *Commercial Estates Company of Egypt* cases, rather, is that the court looked to the customary international right of angary and fashioned—or, in the context of a prerogative power, it is perhaps better to say 'creatively recognized' via the

Book Co, Sydney, 1984), 35, 51. See also, more cautiously, Mann, above n 23, 121 ('may and probably must'); P J Duffy, 'English Law and the European Convention on Human Rights' (1980) 29 *International & Comparative Law Quarterly* 585, 599 ('may and should').

[293] See the discussion three paragraphs hence below.

[294] There is no compelling need to discard the label, which, apart from being arbitrary anyway, serves usefully to distinguish English law's relationship with customary international law from its relationship with treaty, where parliamentary intervention is generally required before a rule of international law becomes one of English law. Lord Atkin uses the term 'incorporated' in *Chung Chi Cheung*, even though the model he endorses is actually one of judicial transformation or judicial adoption: see [1939] AC 160, 167–8. Among scholars, Brierly, above n 23, 78–9 characterizes the approach taken by Lord Atkin in *Chung Chi Cheung* as a manifestation of what he expressly terms the doctrine of incorporation. The same goes for Starke, above n 2, 91–2. Lauterpacht, above n 2, 77–84 treats not only Lord Atkin's statement in *Chung Chi Cheung* but also the statements of Lords Atkin and Wright in *The Cristina* [1938] AC 485, 490 (Lord Atkin) and 502 (Lord Wright) and the words of Atkin LJ, as he then was, in *Commercial Estates Company of Egypt* [1925] 1 KB 271, 295 as applications of what he too explicitly refers to as the doctrine of incorporation or, synonymously, adoption. Mann, above n 23, 120–3, while acknowledging 'a purely theoretical difference of opinion or, perhaps one should say, of formulation' (ibid, 122), also treats Lord Atkin's various dicta and those of Lord Wright as statements of the doctrine of incorporation. Indeed, he states ibid, 121 that '[i]t is in [the Atkin and Wright] sense (and cannot have been in any other sense)' that Lord Mansfield CJ and Blackstone spoke of the law of nations being part of the common law of England. (In this last he is seemingly joined by Oppenheim, who cites Blackstone, above n 2, book IV, chap 5, along with Westlake, above n 19, and *West Rand*, as illustrations of his model of adoption: see Oppenheim, above n 277, vol I, 26, para 21.) For his part, Brownlie, above n 23, 44 describes Lord Atkin's dictum in *Chung Chi Cheung* as 'by no means incompatible with the principle of incorporation'. Cunningham goes so far as to call this dictum the 'classic formulation' of the doctrine of incorporation: A J Cunningham, 'The European Convention on Human Rights, Customary International Law and the Constitution' (1994) 43 *International & Comparative Law Quarterly* 537, 547. And in a case-note on *Trendtex*, Crawford (1976–77) 48 *British Yearbook of International Law* 353, 358 suggests that '[p]robably the *dicta* which have been regarded as embodying the "doctrine of [judicial] transformation" have been … qualifying rather than displacing the basic principle that international law is part of the law of England'.

common law—a domestic power modelled on it, vesting in what the court perceived to be the relevant branch of government. It is in this light that we can read the passage of Atkin LJ's judgment in *Commercial Estates Company of Egypt v Board of Trade* where his Lordship states:

International law as such can confer no rights cognizable in the municipal Courts. It is only in so far as the rules of international law are recognized as included in the rules of the municipal law that they are allowed in the municipal Courts to give rise to rights or obligations.[295]

In short, the model is that of judicial transformation or judicial adoption. This is also the case with the customary international obligation to pay compensation that is the concomitant of the right of angary: licensed and charged, as it were, by the doctrine of incorporation, the court took an international obligation binding on the United Kingdom and transposed it—in the sense of rewriting it in a different musical key—into a common-law obligation binding on the Crown.

It pays to emphasize at this point that the terms 'incorporation' (as conceptualized here), 'transformation', 'adoption', 'translation', 'transposition' and the like are no more than metaphors for what is actually going on, and, like many metaphors, they tend to obscure as much as they promise to enlighten. All that really happens when an English court applies the doctrine of incorporation is that, mindful of the operation on the international plane of a relevant rule of customary international law, the judge enunciates an as-near-as-possible-analogous common-law rule. Incorporation has nothing to do with the metaphysical unity of customary international law and the common law. The former is not immanent in the latter. Nor is the act of incorporation some sort of quasi-alchemical transmutation of the customary international rule into a common-law one. The customary international rule serves merely as the 'historical or persuasive source'[296] of the common-law rule: inspired, as it were, by customary international law, the court lays down the common-law rule in the usual way.

It is also important to stress that the source of the court's duty, *ceteris paribus*, to incorporate a rule of customary international law is not the relevant customary international rule itself, whether *quâ* customary international law or *quâ* common law, since, as has already been said, this rule is binding on the UK alone, not on the English courts. Rather, the obligation is a freestanding common-law one, imposed on the courts by the courts themselves through their enunciation and consistent affirmation of the doctrine of incorporation.[297] To the extent that the word 'must' is never used in the various judicial formulations of the doctrine of incorporation,

---

[295] [1925] 1 KB 271, 295.   [296] Sawer, above n 292, 50, emphasis omitted.
[297] See Lauterpacht, above n 2, 79 (excepting cases of overriding statute and of at least certain contrary rules of common law): 'Courts treat the relevant rules of international law as incorporated into the domestic law because they are bound to do so ... by virtue of an established rule which bids them to act in that way. It is a rule of law ... that the courts acknowledge the existence and the appli-

the mandatory nature of this common-law rule is not as explicit as it could be. But there is no indication in any of the various judicial iterations of the doctrine that, absent persuasive arguments against incorporation, an English court would be at liberty not to give effect at common law to a relevant rule of customary international law.[298] The obligatory nature of the common-law rule is also inherent in the repeated characterization of customary international law as a part—or, as preferred by Lord Bingham in *Jones (Margaret)* and as suggested here, a source—of the common law: if the former is a part or equally a source of the latter, it follows that, in the absence of satisfactory reasons to the contrary, the court must give effect to it, since a court is not free for no or no satisfactory reason to decline to have recourse to a part or source of its applicable law when the latter is relevant to the determination of the case before it. The mandatory common-law rule is reinforced, independently of the doctrine of incorporation, by the entrenched proposition that in the English courts international law is treated as law, the argument being that it is in the nature of legal reasoning and the judicial function to give effect to law.[299] One important upshot of the basis of the mandatory rule in the common law, rather than in international law, is that the obligation to give effect at common law to a rule of customary international law is independent of whether the latter is itself mandatory: the obligation on the English court applies equally to customary international rules which merely permit the UK to adopt a course of conduct.[300]

Most crucially, it is essential to underline that the judicial interposition that is the reality of incorporation is not mechanical. It involves discernment of what is appropriate and what is not.[301] Its outcome in a given case

cability of the relevant rules of international law. The courts themselves have engrafted that mandatory rule upon the common law.'

[298] See O'Connell, above n 2, vol I, 50; Starke, above n 2, 92; Sawer, above n 292, 51; Mason, 'International Law as a Source of Domestic Law', in Opeskin & Rothwell, above n 53, 210, 214.

[299] See, in this light, Mann, above n 280, 48: 'Where ... transformation of customary international law occurs, the judge will implement it in pursuance of the principle of effectiveness, ie so that within the national system of law the international rule can most effectively be worked out and the court can reach results most closely conforming to the international rule.'

[300] *R v Keyn* is sometimes explained by reference to the distinction between mandatory and permissive rules of customary international law: see eg Jennings & Watts, above n 23, 57. But the explanation is based on a misreading.

[301] See O'Connell, above n 2, vol I, 50–1: 'The outcome is ... no[t] the automatic application of rules of international law on every occasion. Rather it is that international law is channelled with municipal law as guiding the judicial process. Whenever appropriate, the norms of international law will govern the decision. When not appropriate they will not.' See also *Nulyarimma v Thompson* (1999) 165 ALR 621, 629–30, paras 25–6 (Full Federal Court of Australia, Wilcox J): '[I]t is difficult to make a general statement covering all the diverse rules of international customary law. It is one thing, it seems to me, for courts of a particular country to be prepared to treat a civil law rule like the doctrine of foreign sovereign immunity as part of its domestic law, whether because it is accepted by those courts as being "incorporated" in that law or because it has been "transformed" by judicial act. It is another thing to say that a norm of international law criminalising conduct that is not made punishable by the domestic law entitles a domestic court to try and punish an offender against that law. ... Perhaps this is only another way of saying that domestic courts face a policy issue in deciding whether to recognise and enforce a rule of international law.'

depends on the court's discriminating assessment of a range of factors born out by the case-law. The courts have declined to give effect at common law to a customary international rule of a purely State-to-State character, as distinct from a rule providing for the rights of individuals as against a State. They have decided against crafting a common-law rule from customary international law where to do so would have run counter to a competing, indeed overriding constitutional principle. They have likewise refused to apply at common law a customary international rule on the ground that it would have contradicted some basic principle or rule of the common law itself.

In sum, the reception into English law of a rule of customary international law does not follow automatically. Even less is customary international law immanent in the common law. Rather, to adapt the words of Lord Bingham in *Jones (Margaret)*, 'a [rule] recognised as such in customary international law ... may but need not, become part of the domestic law of England and Wales without the need for any domestic statute';[302] or, in the modified words of Lord Mance in the same case, not all rules of customary international law 'must or should be received and recognised as domestic law [rules]'.[303] This is precisely what was meant by Lord Atkin in *Chung Chi Cheung* when he said:

It must always be remembered that, so far, at any rate, as the Courts of this country are concerned, international law has no validity save in so far as its principles are accepted and adopted by our own domestic law. There is no external power that imposes its rules upon our own code of substantive law and procedure.[304]

Taken out of context, the first sentence could be misleading: it would be an exaggeration to say that international law 'has no validity' in the English courts until those courts have chosen to receive it. As outlined already, this brand of stark dualism has never been the way of English law. To the extent that the determination of a point of domestic law calls for it, the courts may rightly have regard to international law as international

---

[302] [2006] UKHL 16; [2007] 1 AC 136, 161, para 27. In practice, as stated above, there would seem, according to their Lordships' analysis, no circumstances in which a customary international crime could today become part of English law without statute.

[303] [2007] 1 AC 136, 179, para 101.

[304] [1939] AC 160, 167–8. See, similarly, *Chow Hung Ching v The King* (1948) 77 CLR 449, 462 (High Court of Australia, Latham CJ), references omitted: 'International law is not as such part of the law of Australia (*Chung Chi Cheung v The King* ...), but a universally recognized principle of international law would be applied by our courts: *West Rand Central Gold Mining Co v The King*.' See also ibid, 477 (Dixon J): '[T]he theory of *Blackstone (Commentaries*, (1809), vol 4, p 67) that "the law of nations (whenever any question arises which is properly the object of its jurisdiction) is here adopted in its full extent by the common law, and is held to be a part of the law of the land" is now regarded as without foundation. The true view, it is held, is "that international law is not a part, but is one of the sources, of English law" (Article by Prof *J L Brierly* on International Law in England, (1935), 51 *Law Quarterly Review*, p 31.).'

law, be it custom or treaty.[305] Rather, Lord Atkin's statement is directed towards how and when a rule of customary international law can be relied on as a rule of English law, and in this context it is spot on. Indeed, in *Thakrar*, only a few years before *Trendtex*, Lord Denning MR himself not only paraphrased but agreed with Lord Atkin to the effect that 'rules of international law only become part of our law in so far as they are accepted and adopted by us'.[306] The incorporation of customary international law is an act of judicial lawmaking in which, as the immunity and angary cases show, a common-law court is, in the absence of persuasive contraindications, empowered and even directed to engage.

B. Considerations relevant to the appropriateness of incorporation

As already seen, the case-law suggests that whether incorporation is contraindicated in a given case depends on at least three considerations.[307] These will now be considered in more detail.

1. Is the rule of customary international law structurally amenable to domestic application?

The first consideration is the extent to which the relevant customary international rule lends itself as a structural matter to application by a domestic court—in other words, the logical ease or naturalness with which the court would be able to transform the rule from one operative on the international plane to one applicable in the English courts.[308] The foremost question in this regard is whether the rule of customary international law is one of a strictly State-to-State character or whether it implicates

---

[305] As regards treaty, see *R (Campaign for Nuclear Disarmament) v Prime Minister* [2002] EWHC 2777 (Admin); (2002) 126 ILR 727, 744, para 36 and 749, para 47 (Simon Brown LJ), endorsed in *Republic of Ecuador v Occidental Exploration and Production Co* [2005] EWCA Civ 1116; [2006] QB 432, 456–7, para 31 (Mance LJ).

[306] [1974] QB 694, 701.

[307] Crawford, above n 294, 358 argues that '[t]he vice in the proposition that a clearly established rule of [customary] international law is not part of the law of England unless adopted as such *by the courts* is that no criteria are provided by which the courts are to decide whether or not to adopt a particular rule' (emphasis added). Similarly, Sales and Clement suggest, above n 54, 417 that '[t]he task now facing the courts in the United Kingdom is to articulate a set of criteria by reference to which relevant rules of CIL can be identified as properly applicable by those courts'. It is submitted that the courts have already, albeit unsystematically, gone quite some way towards enunciating such criteria.

[308] While it is not clear, this seems to be what Brownlie is referring to when he states that 'the courts still have to ascertain the ... effect [of rules of customary international law] *within the municipal sphere*': Brownlie, above n 23, 41–2, original emphasis. Crawford and Edeson speak of 'the need for clear and satisfactory evidence that the customary rule ... is capable, according to its terms, of having direct legal effects as part of municipal law': J Crawford & W R Edeson, 'International Law and Australian Law', in Ryan, above n 292, 71, 73, including n 12. Shearer, above n 53, 43 states that 'the automatic incorporation doctrine is limited to those rules of international law that are ... susceptible of direct application in domestic law without the need for adaptation or choice of means', and although it is never actually the case that a rule of international law is susceptible of direct application without the need for adaptation, the thrust of the statement is accurate. Consider also Westlake, above n 19, 14–5 and 16–7.

the rights of individuals.[309] This is the point made at its clearest by Lord Denning MR in *R v Secretary of State for the Home Department, Ex parte Thakrar*.[310]

Take first individual rights, and specifically human rights. While the transposition is not seamless given the indivisibility of the State as an international legal person,[311] it does no violence to the structural logic of the rule to transform a customary international human right, an individual right opposable as against the State on the international plane, into a common-law human right opposable as against whichever organ of State is in a position to cause that State to breach it. In the event of the breach of a customary international human right, international law itself envisages that an individual can have a remedy against the State at the international level; in this light, even though as a formal matter it involves piercing the veil of the State as a subject of international law, no conceptual contortions are required for the common law to envisage that the individual can have a remedy against the organ of State in whose conduct the international breach in practice consists, at least where that organ forms part of the executive and is thus in principle amenable to judicial review.

The vast majority of international rules, however, provide not for individual rights but for the rights and obligations of States vis-à-vis each other. In the event of the breach of these rules, international law does not envisage anything other than a State-to-State remedy, and from here it is more of a conceptual leap to a common-law rule capable of enforcement by a court. The implication seemingly to be drawn from Lord Denning MR and Orr LJ in *Thakrar* and from Kerr LJ in *J H Rayner* is that this is a leap too far.

That said, there is at least one body of international rules of a strictly State-to-State character which lend themselves readily to domestic application. These are the rules on the various immunities from the jurisdiction of foreign courts to which States are entitled. Although a State-to-State right, the right of a State to see that its organs and officials and its property are accorded immunity (within the bounds of the relevant international rules) from the jurisdiction of another State's courts envisages both specified beneficiaries[312] and the specific foreign State organ implicated by the right. From here it is only a short distance to a common-law rule, enforceable in the courts, entitling a specified beneficiary to the procedural

---

[309] In principle, the *obligations* of individuals can also be implicated by a rule of customary international law. But at present the only sphere of international law that imposes obligations on individuals (by and large negative obligations, ie prohibitions) is international criminal law, and it will be recalled that the House of Lords held in *Jones (Margaret)* that today, for constitutional reasons, crimes under customary international law do not give rise to novel common-law crimes.

[310] See also the other judicial statements to similar effect cited above at Part III.B.1.

[311] Note that the indivisibility issue does not arise in the context of crimes recognized by customary international law, where it is not a State's but an individual's obligations that are in issue. But recall again the Lords' ruling in *Jones (Margaret)* in relation to novel common-law crimes based on customary international law.

[312] The word is not used here in the sense in which it is used in the English law of equity.

immunity in question (subject, of course, to its waiver by the benefici-ary's State). Putting it another way, if a foreign State is entitled under customary international law to see that its various organs and officials and its property enjoy immunity from the jurisdiction of the courts of the UK, it is a natural progression to say that a foreign State is entitled under the common law to see that its various organs and officials and its prop-erty enjoy immunity from the jurisdiction of the English courts.

In this regard, the Court of Appeal's decision in *Commercial Estates Company of Egypt v Board of Trade* is less straightforward. While the cus-tomary international right of angary involves a concomitant obligation to compensate, international law neither provides the owner of the requisi-tioned goods with an individual right to compensation as against the req-uisitioning State—in other words, the requisitioning State's obligation is owed strictly towards the owner's State of nationality—nor specifically envisages that the owner shall enjoy such a right in that State's courts. The latter is in contrast to the customary law of prize, which, although by the mid-nineteenth century a body of rules as between States, itself fore-saw and indeed mandated that, in certain situations, a private shipowner would be entitled to a remedy in a State's prize courts for that State's violation of the customary international rules on taking in prize. From here it was an unproblematic proposition for an English prize court to give effect to a private right of action against the Crown, whose warship it would have been that took the prize[313] (and which expressly submitted, via prize rules promulgated at the outbreak of war, to the court's exercise of jurisdiction over its relevant acts of State). The leap from the UK's cus-tomary international obligation, when exercising the right of angary, to compensate the owner of the goods to the owner's common-law right to compensation from the Crown is somewhat greater. That said, the inter-national obligation to compensate, owed to the owner's State of nationality, does foresee a specified beneficiary, viz the owner, even if it does not pre-scribe that the latter is entitled to a remedy in the courts of the requisi-tioning State. In short, the logical leap is not too daunting.

2. *Is the proposed common-law rule contraindicated by constitutional principle?*

The second consideration is whether the conversion of the relevant cus-tomary international rule into a judicially enforceable rule of common law is contraindicated by the constitutional principles of the supremacy of Parliament or the separation of powers, as has transpired in numerous cases.[314]

---

[313] The Declaration respecting Maritime Law, Paris, 16 April 1856 (entered into force same day), 46 BFSP (1855–1856) 26–7, which was in fact a treaty, provided in article 1 that '[p]rivateering is, and remains, abolished'.

[314] See the discussion above at Part III.B.2. See also, albeit arguing explicitly normatively, Sales & Clement, above n 54, 414: '[D]omestic constitutional law operates as a filter governing the extent to

3. Is the proposed common-law rule contraindicated by the common law itself?

To constitutional considerations can be added, finally, whether the recognition of the rule of common law derived from customary international law would run counter to some rule or principle of the common law itself as finally declared by the courts.[315] A prime example of this restriction, recognized by Lord Alverstone CJ in *West Rand* and by Lord Atkin in *Chung Chi Cheung*, is Ouseley J's judgment in *Chagos Islanders*.

C. The settled cases in light of the doctrine as more accurately conceived

How, then, does the doctrine of incorporation as understood here measure up against those few cases, namely the immunity and angary cases, in which a rule of customary international law has successfully been relied on in the English courts as a rule of common law or, in the context of the prerogative right of angary, as a power recognized by the common law? One would hope well, given that the doctrine as conceptualized and systematized in this article represents little other than a distillation and reconciliation of the authorities and first principles. But the fit cannot be taken for granted. In this light, it may be useful to hold the cases up to the doctrine as conceived here. The starting point of the analysis is that the passage from a customary international obligation binding on the United Kingdom to a common-law duty binding on the courts, or from a customary international right vesting in the United Kingdom to a common-law power vesting in the Crown, is an act of judicial lawmaking, the appropriateness of which depends on a weighing of the three considerations sketched out above.

Starting with the immunity cases, the first factor to be taken into account is that the customary international rules on immunities lend themselves readily to application by a domestic court: they expressly envisage the availability to specified beneficiaries of a procedural defence in the various courts of the United Kingdom, in this case England and Wales. Next, as regards the constitutional implications of common-law immunities, it is arguable that a decision as fundamental to the rule of law as the exempting of certain natural and legal persons from judicial process is a decision more appropriately taken by Parliament, which, unlike the courts, enjoys a democratic mandate and, to a greater extent than the courts, has the logistical and procedural wherewithal to engage in the requisite consultation and debate on relevant policy questions. In this light, it is debateable whether reliance on the doctrine of incorporation is defensible in the context of immunities. If the issue were to arise for the first time today, the courts might hesitate. But the historical reality is that the reception

---

which the domestic courts should recognise norms taken from CIL and treat them as forming part of the common law and hence as directly enforceable in domestic law.'

[315] See the discussion above at Part III.B.3.

into the common law of the customary international law on immunities happened long ago, when the English courts had a more robust approach to their lawmaking powers. Indeed, it is not by chance that the first avowed invocation of the doctrine of incorporation in the context of immunities, in *Triquet v Bath*, was by the activist Lord Mansfield CJ.[316] As it is, regardless of the origins of this line of authority, the fact is that Parliament in the past saw nothing wrong with leaving the question of foreign immunities to the courts, which, after all, were traditionally the custodians of their own process. The reason the legislature eventually intervened by means of the State Immunity Act 1978 was the constitutional necessity to do so in order to give domestic effect to the European Convention on State Immunity 1972, a treaty designed to establish a common Council of Europe regime on the matter. Moreover, sections 16(2) and 16(4) of the State Immunity Act, respectively excluding from the Act's purview proceedings relating to anything done by or in relation to the armed forces of a foreign State while present in the United Kingdom and criminal proceedings, manifest Parliament's equanimity with the prospect that questions of State immunity in proceedings excluded from the scope of the Act should continue to be left to the courts. In this light, the application of the doctrine of incorporation to give effect via the common law to the customary international law of immunities is defensible as a constitutional matter, although perhaps not ideal. Finally, no rule or principle of the common law itself militates against the incorporation of the immunities recognized by customary international law. Overall, then, the doctrine of incorporation as explained here is consistent with the immunity cases.

Turning to the angary cases, it is necessary to tease apart the customary international right of angary as such from the associated obligation to pay reparation to the owner of the requisitioned goods. Starting with the first, in terms of the amenability of the right of angary to application by an English court, the international right vesting in the UK to requisition the property of the nationals of neutral States translates easily into a domestic power vesting in the Crown to requisition the property of the nationals of neutral States. As for the constitutional considerations, on the other hand, it is highly questionable whether the courts can, via the doctrine of incorporation, add to 'the remaining portion of the Crown's original authority'.[317] That said, the recognition of a common-law power of angary can plausibly be characterized as no more than the elucidation of a particular aspect of the Crown's traditional prerogative in respect of the

---

[316] See above at Part II.B.

[317] Dicey, above n 128, 425. In the famous words of Diplock LJ, 'it is 350 years and a civil war too late for the Queen's courts to broaden the prerogative': *British Broadcasting Corporation v Johns (Inspector of Taxes)* [1965] Ch 32, 79. See also *R (Bancoult) v Secretary of State for Foreign and Commonwealth Affairs* [2008] UKHL 61; [2008] 3 WLR 955, 977, para 69 (Lord Bingham).

defence of the realm in wartime,[318] which has long been held to include the power to requisition property.[319] Indeed, this is how the parties argued the point in the *Commercial Estates Company of Egypt* cases;[320] and when inquiring in *Commercial Estates Company of Egypt v Board of Trade* into whether the right of angary was 'a prerogative right of His Majesty' within the meaning of the Indemnity Act 1920, Atkin LJ, holding that this could 'admit of little doubt', emphasized that the phrase 'ha[d] to be construed as occurring in an Act passed in 1920 in respect of acts done ... for the defence of the realm'.[321] Alternatively, the view expressed by Viscount Radcliffe in the post-Second World War case of *Burmah Oil Co Ltd v Lord Advocate* was that the assertion of the right of angary, as given effect at common law in *Commercial Estates Company of Egypt v Board of Trade*, 'was in fact an aspect of the Crown's [prerogative in respect of] foreign relations'.[322] Either way, in the words of Lord Reid in *Burmah Oil*, 'there is nothing novel in the idea that a prerogative right to take property carries with it an obligation to pay compensation'.[323] So incorporation would seem tolerable from a constitutional angle. Finally, no rule or principle of the common law itself is implicated. Taking all three considerations together, then, the judicial recognition in the *Commercial Estates Company of Egypt* cases of a prerogative right of angary derived from customary international law is acceptable. It was certainly not

---

[318] 'Although the source of the royal prerogative is not the common law, it is the common law that declares what the royal prerogative is ...': Payne, above n 130, 79. Moreover, 'it [is] generally accepted that ... it [is] the judiciary's duty to determine the boundaries of prerogative powers ...': Loughlin, above n 130, 64. In short, the courts 'ha[ve] jurisdiction to decide what [are] the nature and the limits of the prerogative powers of the Crown ...': W Wade, 'The Crown, Ministers and Officials: Legal Status and Liability', in Sunkin & Payne, above n 130, 23, 29. They 'can determine whether the prerogative power exists [and] what is its extent ...': S A de Smith, *Judicial Review of Executive Action* (3rd edn, Stevens & Sons, London, 1973), 253. See also *Council of Civil Service Unions v Minister for the Civil Service* [1985] AC 374, 398 (Lord Fraser); *R (Bancoult) v Secretary of State for Foreign and Commonwealth Affairs* [2008] UKHL 61; [2008] 3 WLR 955, 977, para 69 (Lord Bingham).

[319] See *Rex v Hampden* (1637) 3 St Tr 826 (the '*Ship Money*' case); *In re a Petition of Right* [1915] 3 KB 649; *Attorney-General v De Keyser's Royal Hotel Ltd* [1920] AC 508; *Crown of Leon (Owners) v Lords Commissioner of the Admiralty* [1921] 1 KB 595.

[320] See defendant's counsel in *Commercial Estates Company of Egypt v Ball* (1920) 36 Times LR 526, 527 ('in the exercise of the Royal Prerogative for the Defence of the Realm, and of the right of angary') and claimants' counsel in *Commercial Estates Company of Egypt v Board of Trade* [1925] 1 KB 271, 274 ('The prerogative rights of the Crown include the right of angary, which enables the Crown to seize the property of neutrals within its jurisdiction in time of war for the defence of the realm ...').

[321] [1925] 1 KB 271, 294. Similarly, when addressing whether the common law 'recognize[d] the right to seize, but rejected the obligation to compensate', his Lordship observed: 'So to hold would be to impute to our law a remarkable distinction between its treatment of those subject to British law and neutrals not so subject. In the former case municipal law by a series of statutes, if not by the common law, provides for compensation either in full or with some restrictions when the subject's property is taken for the defence of the realm. ... It would indeed be remarkable if our law granted compensation to subjects who had a direct interest in the defence of the realm and denied it to neutrals whose goods were here against their will.'

[322] [1965] AC 75, 123.

[323] Ibid, 102. Lord Reid continued that this 'has apparently always been recognised with regard to the prerogative rights of purveyance and angary': ibid. Given that the prerogative right of angary was recognized for the first time in the *Commercial Estates Company of Egypt* litigation, his Lordship's use of the word 'always' is, in this respect, an overstatement.

challenged when referred to in the House of Lords in *Burmah Oil*.[324] But what of the court's parallel recognition in the *Commercial Estates* cases of a common-law right to compensation on the part of the owner of the requisitioned goods? While a non-negligible leap of logic is required to go from this customary international rule to the common-law one, the leap is arguably not prohibitive. No constitutional principles are implicated by the judicial recognition of a common-law right to compensation on the part of the owner of the goods. Nor does any rule or principle of the common law stand in the way: prior to 1947, the procedure for claiming such compensation in the event that it was withheld would have been an action in unjust enrichment by way of petition of right; and with the abolition of the petition of right in 1947,[325] an unjust enrichment claim could now be brought against the Crown in the ordinary way.

D. The doctrine as more accurately conceived applied to three further questions

So what can the doctrine of incorporation as conceived here tell us about those cases in which reliance on it to ground an action or defence remains something of an open question? The first such case is an action for judicial review to overturn a decision to go to war in circumstances in which the UK would stand in breach of the customary international prohibition on the unlawful use of armed force by one State against another. The second is reliance on a customary international human right as the common-law basis for an application for judicial review of executive conduct. The last is an action in tort for the violation of a customary rule of either international human rights law or international criminal law.

1. The prohibition on the use of force

In *R (Campaign for Nuclear Disarmament) v Prime Minister*,[326] the applicant—seeking to establish, against the backdrop of the UK's military build-up along Iraq's southern border in late 2002, that the English courts had jurisdiction to interpret United Nations Security Council resolution 1441 (2002)[327]—argued as follows: the prohibition on the unlawful[328] use of force by one State against another was a rule of customary international law, and customary international law formed part of the law of England; the use of force not in self-defence was unlawful unless authorized by the Security Council, and resolution 1441 did not provide such authorization; *ergo*, an application for an advisory declaration from the

---

[324] See ibid, 102 (Lord Reid) and 123 (Viscount Radcliffe).
[325] See Crown Proceedings Act 1947 (c 44), section 1.
[326] [2002] EWHC 2777 (Admin); (2002) 126 ILR 727.
[327] UN Doc S/RES/1441, 8 November 2002.
[328] That is, not in the lawful exercise of the inherent right to individual or collective self-defence and not, in the alternative, authorized by the United Nations Security Council under article 42 of the United Nations Charter.

Administrative Court aimed at preventing a breach of customary international law fell within the court's common-law supervisory jurisdiction.
But in the Divisional Court, Simon Brown LJ, with whom Maurice Kay
and Richards JJ agreed, ruled that the English courts did not have jurisdiction to interpret resolution 1441, stating:

> All of the cases relied upon by the applicants in which the court has pronounced
> upon some issue of international law are cases where it has been necessary to do
> so in order to determine rights and obligations under domestic law. ... [But] there
> is in the present case no point of reference in domestic law to which the interna-
> tional law issue can be said to go; there is nothing here susceptible of challenge
> in the way of the determination of rights, interests or duties under domestic law
> to draw the court into the field of international law.[329]

By holding, without more, that the applicant's case did not sound in
domestic law, the Divisional Court appeared to give the shortest of shrifts
to the argument that the prohibition on the unlawful use of inter-State
force, being a rule of customary international law, formed part of the law
of England. But the case is complicated by the fact that the relief sought
was merely an advisory declaration, there being at that point no decision
by the executive to invade Iraq capable of being challenged.

What, however, if a decision had been take to invade Iraq? Would the
doctrine of incorporation have grounded an action for judicial review of
the decision? The familiar point of departure is that customary international law obliges the UK, not the Crown, to refrain from the unlawful
use of force against another state. In this light, the recognition of a common-law cause of action against the Crown founded on customary international law would be an act of judicial creativity whose appropriateness
is to be measured against the three yardsticks previously suggested.

The prohibition on the use of inter-State force is not readily amenable
to application by a domestic court. In the words of Baroness Hale in *R
(Gentle) v Prime Minister*, '[t]he lawfulness of war is an issue between
states, not between individuals or between individuals and the state'.[330]
There is no individual right under customary international law to see that
a State does not launch an unlawful war. Additionally, the prohibition
envisages no specific beneficiaries. Nor does it implicate any specific organ
of State: whereas obviously only the courts are capable of causing a State
to violate the immunity to which a foreign State is entitled in its courts,
the prohibition on the use of force can be violated as much through the
conduct of the legislature which votes for the war as through the acts of
the executive which conceives and implements it. This militates almost
irremediably against the judicial recognition of the prohibition as one of

---

[329] 126 ILR 727, 744–5, para 36.
[330] [2008] UKHL 20; [2008] 2 WLR 879, 899, para 57. See also, similarly, [2008] 2 WLR 879, 890,
para 24 (Lord Hope): 'The issue of legality in this area of international law belongs to the area of
relations between states. ... It is not part of domestic law reviewable here or, under the Convention,
in the European Court at Strasbourg.'

common law. That said, it is, for the sake of argument, not wholly unthinkable that the prohibition could give rise to a common-law rule restraining the Crown from launching an internationally unlawful war. But the argument is killed stone dead by constitutional impediments.[331] First, as held by the Lords in *Jones (Margaret)*, the fact that the adjudication of the common-law rule argued for by reference to customary international law would involve the courts in areas traditionally deemed non-justiciable—in this case, the exercise of the prerogative power to go to war—is a strong argument against its incorporation in the first place. Secondly, any such move by the courts would amount in substance to the creation of a novel administrative-law action for procuring the UK's breach of public international law, and it is difficult to see on what constitutional basis this might be justified. It could not, strictly speaking, be illegality, since only the UK, not the Crown, would act unlawfully by starting an internationally unlawful war.[332] Nor could it be irrationality, since the House of Lords has held, albeit in the treaty context, that it is not irrational for a decision-maker to act in a manner contrary to the UK's international legal obligations.[333]

2. Human rights obligations and judicial review

In dicta in *R v Secretary of State for Foreign and Commonwealth Affairs, ex parte Pirbhai*,[334] Woolf J—rejecting an argument based on the doctrine of incorporation, as stated in *Trendtex*, to the effect that it was the court's duty to ascertain for itself the content of the relevant customary international law, viz the requirement to exhaust local remedies, where the Secretary of State had purported to rely on this in declining to espouse a claim by the applicants against Uganda—stated:

... I cannot accept [this] argument. In my view, it overlooks the fact that the rule of international law which was being considered in the *Trendtex* case was a rule which had undoubtedly been adopted and incorporated into English law. The principle of sovereign immunity is applied as part of the domestic law. All rules of international law are not so applied. There are rules or principles of international law, for example relating to human rights, which are no part of our domestic law and the domestic courts cannot apply or interpret them in the same way as they apply and interpret domestic law.[335]

---

[331] In this light, an examination of the third consideration would be otiose.

[332] That said, it would by no means be absurd to argue that the Crown had in substance acted *ultra vires*, given the practical reality of its authorship of the UK's unlawful conduct.

[333] See *R v Secretary of State for the Home Department, Ex parte Brind* [1991] 1 AC 696.

[334] 7 September 1984, QBD (Crown Office List), Woolf J, 129 SJ 756, official transcript from LexisNexis® Butterworths.

[335] Consider also the scepticism expressed by Onseley J in *Chagos Islanders v Attorney General and Her Majesty's British Indian Ocean Territory Commissioner* [2003] EWHC 2222, para 375, in the context of the customary international human right not to be exiled from one's homeland: 'It may be that [counsel for the claimants] has put somewhat too broad an interpretation on *Trendtex* if he regards it as authority for the proposition that international law is enforceable without more by subject against Crown so long as no Act of Parliament is contravened.'

On the other hand, in *In re McKerr*, Lord Steyn wondered aloud and wholly obiter whether customary international human rights law might avail an applicant for judicial review of executive conduct:

[T]here may be an argument that the right to life has long been recognised in customary international law, which in the absence of a contrary statute has been part of English law since before the 1998 Act came into force. … The point has not been in issue in the present case. It has not been researched, and it was not the subject of adversarial argument. It may have to be considered in a future case.[336]

As it was, his Lordship acknowledged that it was perhaps unrealistic to suggest that the particular human right at issue in the case 'was already part of customary international law at a time material to [the] proceedings'.[337]

So could a customary international human right be invoked as a common-law right such as to ground an application in the English courts for judicial review of executive conduct? An inquiry into whether it could must again be premised on the understanding that it is the UK, not the Crown, that is bound by international law, so that the provision by the English courts of an administrative-law remedy against the Crown in respect of the UK's violation of a customary international human right would represent a creative act of judicial interposition which may or may not be appropriate, all things considered.

Arguing in favour of the recognition of common-law human rights by reference to customary international human rights law is the fact that we are dealing here with rights vested in individuals by international law itself and opposable as a matter of international law as against States. That is, customary international human rights lend themselves to domestic application without the need for fundamental reconfiguration: all that is needed is to pierce the veil of the State to permit the transfer of the obligation from the UK to the Crown. It is the constitutional implications, however, that give pause.[338] As with the prohibition on the use of force, the courts' restraint of Crown conduct by reference to common-law human rights drawn from customary international law would be the judicial coining of an administrative-law action for procuring a breach of public international law by the UK, an action for which the constitutional underpinnings would be highly uncertain. Moreover, there is an argument that the Human Rights Act (HRA) manifests a parliamentary intention to 'cover the field' in relation to human rights—that is, that by providing in domestic law for the enforcement of some international human rights standards binding on the UK as a matter of international law, Parliament has, by implication, excluded the domestic enforcement of others.[339] This is essentially the same reasoning that dissuaded the court in *Viveash v Becker*

---

[336] [2004] UKHL 12; [2004] 1 WLR 807, 824, para 52.   [337] Ibid.
[338] Note that the third consideration is neither here nor there in such a case.
[339] See *Anisminic Ltd v Foreign Compensation Commission* [1969] 1 All ER 208.

from giving effect to a customary international rule on consular immunity, although there the original source of the relevant statutory rule was also customary, not conventional; and an analogous argument persuaded Orr and Lawton LJJ in the Court of Appeal and Lord Widgery CJ and May and Bridge JJ in the Divisional Court in *Thakrar*.[340] That said, the 'covering the field' argument is not watertight, given that a more than *de minimis* logical distinction can be drawn between those international human rights secured to individuals as a function of treaty-law by the ECHR and those enuring by virtue of customary international law, so that the enactment of the one is not necessarily to be taken as the exclusion of the other. Also on the other side of the equation is, more generally, the courts' traditional role as the safeguard of individual liberty against overweening executive power and today's heightened judicial concern for human rights, the latter manifest in a stricter standard of review when human rights are in play.

In the final analysis, when it comes to judicial review of executive conduct by reference to common-law human rights derived from customary international law, the constitutional cons possibly outweigh the pros, although it is by no means certain, and it would be rash to rule out such judicial creativity.

3. *Human rights/international criminal obligations and actions in tort*

In *Chagos Islanders*, Ouseley J in the Queen's Bench Division rejected a claim for damages brought against the Attorney General and Her Majesty's British Indian Ocean Territory Commissioner and based, in reliance on the doctrine of incorporation, on the UK's alleged breach of the customary international human right not to be exiled from one's home State. In *Jones v Saudi Arabia*,[341] the claimants, seeking damages from the Kingdom of Saudi Arabia and certain Saudi officials, asserted the novel tort of 'torture', as distinct from the established torts of assault and battery, seemingly basing their case on the argument run in *Al-Adsani v Government of Kuwait*[342] that torture is prohibited by customary international law and that customary international law is part of the common law. The court in *Al-Adsani* was willing to entertain the submission for the sake of argument; but *Al-Adsani*, like *Jones v Saudi Arabia* itself, turned on and was dismissed on the basis of State immunity, and neither Mantell J in the High Court nor the Court of Appeal went so far as to recognize the tort of torture at common law.[343] The claim in *Al-Adsani* was unspecific as to the precise customary international prohibition in question, but the fact that it was brought against the government of Kuwait suggests that the putative

---

[340] See [1974] QB 684, 708 (Orr LJ) and 710 (Lawton LJ); ibid, 690–2 (Lord Widgery CJ, with whom May and Bridge JJ agreed).
[341] [2000] 1 AC 147.
[342] See *Al-Adsani v Government of Kuwait* (1995) 103 ILR 420 (Mantell J) and (1996) 107 ILR 536 (CA).
[343] See 103 ILR 420, 427; 107 ILR 536, 540 (Stuart-Smith LJ).

tort was envisaged as a remedy for the breach by the State of Kuwait of the prohibition on torture embodied in customary international human rights law, although it was far from helpful that Mantell J—after referring to the relevant provisions of the Universal Declaration of Human Rights, the International Covenant on Civil and Political Rights, the ECHR, the Declaration on Torture and the Torture Convention, reproducing, *inter alia*, the right not to be subjected to torture in ECHR, Article 3—referred to torture as 'an offence against public international law'.[344] Similarly, in *Jones v Saudi Arabia*, the claim against the Kingdom would also seem to have been based on the State of Saudi Arabia's breach of its customary international human rights obligation in respect of torture. The claim against the individual defendants, on the other hand, could either have been derivative of the State's breach of its human rights obligation or premised instead on the violation by the individuals of the customary international criminal prohibition on torture binding on them directly as individuals. It is by no means clear on which argument the claimants were relying. Either way, if the case had not been dismissed on the ground of State immunity, should the claimants' argument for a common-law tort of torture based on customary international law have been accepted? Equally, was Ouseley J right to reject the claim in *Chagos Islanders*?

Take first a claim for damages against the Crown in respect of the UK's breach of a customary international human right. The structural amenability of customary international human rights to domestic application favours a common-law remedy for their breach. As regards the constitutional implications, we must again wonder whether Parliament, through the passage of the HRA, has displaced the common-law jurisdiction of the courts in relation to human rights. But even if one were not to rule out on constitutional grounds the possibility that a customary international human right could be recognized as a common-law human right, there is no reason why the breach of a common-law human right would give rise to an action in damages, as correctly pointed out by Ouseley J in *Chagos Islanders*.[345] This would be 'no more and no less than a particular example of a tort for unlawful administrative acts', and the House of Lords has made it 'clear for many years that an *ultra vires* act does not of itself give rise to tortious liability'.[346] Moreover, as reiterated by Lord Steyn in *Three Rivers DC v Bank of England (No 3)*, 'there is no overarching principle

---

[344] 103 ILR 420, 426–7.

[345] [2003] EWHC 2222, para 379. The appropriate remedy, as made clear by Ouseley J, would be by way of judicial review; and, needless to say, in a case such as the present not involving the British executive, the idea of an English court reviewing the lawfulness, by reference to common-law rules of English administrative law, of the conduct of the executive of a foreign sovereign State—let alone seeking to restrain such conduct—is preposterous.

[346] Ibid, para 378, citing in support of this well-established proposition of the law of tort *Three Rivers DC v Bank of England (No 3)* [2003] 2 AC 1, 190 (Lord Steyn), citing in turn *X (Minors) v Bedfordshire CC* [1995] 2 AC 633. In *X (Minors)*, Lord Browne-Wilkinson stated at [1995] 2 AC 633, 730: 'The breach of a public law right by itself gives rise to no claim for damages. A claim for damages must be based on a private law cause of action.'

in English law of liability in tort for "unlawful, intentional and positive acts"'.[347] In short, even if an English court accepted, on the basis of the doctrine of incorporation, that an individual had a human right as a matter of common law, this 'provides no reason for a tort to be created'.[348] In other words, the third of our three considerations bars recovery. Nor can one circumvent this conclusion by relying on the incorporation not of the primary customary international obligation to refrain from torture but of the secondary customary international obligation to make reparation, in this case to pay compensation. As Lord Hoffmann made clear in *Lyons*, there cannot be a secondary obligation of reparation (in that case restitution[349]) at common law for the breach of a primary obligation binding purely as a matter of international law: in his Lordship's words, 'if there is no enforceable primary obligation, how can its breach give rise to an enforceable secondary obligation?'[350]

As for a claim in tort against a foreign State, the fact that the customary international rule in question is an individual right opposable as against the foreign State plays to its transposition into the common law, since such transposition is possible at little cost to the structural logic of the rule. Indeed, in purely conceptual terms,[351] it would be easier to grant a tortious remedy in English law when it is a foreign State that stands in breach of a customary international human right than it would be in relation to the UK. Whereas the Crown is not the same as the United Kingdom and the United Kingdom cannot be sued in the English courts, English law has no trouble conceiving of a foreign State as a notionally unitary legal person. In simple terms, unlike the UK, a foreign State can be sued in the English courts as a State *per se*. But the basic principles of tort law highlighted above again pose very serious obstacles.

Turning to a claim against an individual State official based on the State's customary international human rights obligations, this ought to fail for the same reasons as those already outlined. Reliance instead for the primary obligation on any relevant customary international crime—a prohibition binding as a matter of international law on the individual official, not the State, and (with the exception of aggression) binding as much on a private individual as on a State functionary—would do nothing to assist the

---

[347] [2003] 2 AC 1, 190, citing *Lonrho Ltd v Shell Petroleum Co Ltd (No 2)* [1982] AC 173, 187.

[348] [2003] EWHC 2222, para 379. The words of Bork J, of the US Court of Appeals for the District of Columbia Circuit, in *Tel-Oren v Libyan Arab Republic*, 726 F 2d 744, 811 (DC Cir 1984) are apposite: 'To say that international law is part of … common law is to say only that it is nonstatutory … law to be applied, in appropriate cases, in municipal courts. It is not to say that, like the common law of contract and tort, for example, by itself it affords individuals the right to ask for judicial relief. Thus, the step appellants would have us take—from the phrase "common law" to the implication of a cause of action—is not a simple and automatic one.'

[349] Restitution is only one mode of reparation under customary international law, the others being compensation and satisfaction: see Articles on Responsibility of States for Internationally Wrongful Acts, above n 145, arts 34, 36 and 37. The decision in *Lyons* is equally applicable to the latter two.

[350] [2002] UKHL 44; [2003] 1 AC 976, 995, para 39.

[351] That is, leaving aside the procedural hurdle of State immunity and the further tort-law arguments above.

claimant.[352] As held for constitutional reasons in *Jones (Margaret)*, crimes under customary international law are not crimes under English law, and, even if they were, it is trite English law that a crime does not *ipso facto* constitute a tort. Nor could one attempt to rely, via the doctrine of incorporation, on a secondary obligation under customary international law to make reparation, since, *pace* Stuart-Smith LJ in *Al-Adsani*,[353] individual delictual responsibility is unknown to present international law.

In addition, in all these cases, the recognition by the courts of a cause of action in tort for the violation of a rule of customary international law would be no less than the judicial creation of a new tort, something which has not truly happened since the coining of the unified tort of negligence in *Donoghue v Stephenson*[354] in 1932. The reason for this is essentially constitutional: given its wide-reaching implications, economic and sometimes political, the creation of a novel head of tort is now generally recognized as better left to Parliament, on account of the latter's democratic legitimacy and superior capacity to engage beforehand in the necessary research and consultation.

In sum, a claim in tort, in reliance on the doctrine of incorporation, for the violation of a rule of customary international human rights law or customary international criminal law should be rejected on principle.

It is worth adding that there is nothing to stop a victim suing under the ordinary law of tort in respect of conduct which, on the international plane, would amount to a violation of customary international law. Torture contrary to customary international law, for example, is clearly compensable as the traditional tort of battery. Arbitrary detention contrary to customary international law would constitute the tort of false imprisonment. Certain acts by State officials contrary to customary international law could be actionable as the tort of misfeasance in public office. In such cases, customary international law would be irrelevant to the claim.

Finally, it should be noted by way of postscript that tort actions for violations of customary international law are commonplace in the federal courts of the United States. But the only reason that this step has been taken there is on account of the interposition of legislation, first the Alien Tort Claims Act (ATCA)[355] and then, as specifically regards torture and extrajudicial killing contrary to customary international law, section 2(a) of the Torture Victims Protection Act (TVPA).[356] The former has, since

---

[352]   The same goes in respect of any customary international crime.

[353]   See his Lordship's erroneous statement, obiter, that '[i]n international law torture is ... a tort for which the victim should be compensated': (1996) 107 ILR 536, 540.

[354]   [1932] AC 562. Even then, it is unclear to what extent Lord Atkin saw himself as creating a new tort.

[355]   28 USC §1350.

[356]   Pub L 102–256, 12 March 1992, 106 Stat 73. Section 2(a) of the TVPA explicitly provides for a cause of action in tort. The relevant part of section 2 reads: '(a) Liability.—An individual who, under actual or apparent authority, or color of law, of any foreign nation—(1) subjects an individual to torture shall, in a civil action, be liable for damages to that individual; or (2) subjects an individual

1789,[357] provided that '[t]he district courts shall have original jurisdiction of any civil action by an alien for a tort only, committed in violation of the law of nations ...'. It lay virtually dormant until 1980, when Judge Kaufman of the US Court of Appeals for the Second Circuit held in the landmark case of *Filártiga v Peña-Irala*[358] that it vested the federal courts with original jurisdiction over claims for damages in respect of violations 'of the rights already recognized by international law',[359] in that case over a tort of torture contrary to customary international law. This interpretation, which has given rise to an abundant jurisprudence, only just survived challenge in the Supreme Court in *Sosa v Alvarez-Machain*,[360] which whittled down the availability of ATCA actions to those in respect of a limited range of violations of customary international law; but the Supreme Court nonetheless upheld the idea that claims for damages could be brought in the federal courts under the common law for torts such as 'torture', 'genocide' and the like. The Supreme Court's reasoning is premised on the belief that Blackstone's eighteenth-century offences against the law of nations, namely violations of safe-conducts, infringements of the rights of ambassadors and piracy, were compensable as such in tort. But, with respect, this is simply not true. Insofar as these offences were compensable in tort, they were compensable without reference to the law of nations as ordinary torts such as trespass to the person and trespass to goods, not as the torts of 'violation of a safe-conduct', 'infringement of the rights of an ambassador' and 'piracy'. In this light, the better view is that ATCA was intended to grant the federal courts jurisdiction over garden-variety torts such as trespass to the person and trespass to goods where the impugned conduct amounted to a violation by the United States of its positive duty of protection in respect of the victim.[361] But be that as it

---

to extrajudicial killing shall, in a civil action, be liable for damages to the individual's legal representative, or to any person who may be a claimant in an action for wrongful death.'

[357] The Act was originally part of the first Judiciary Act, ch 20, §9, 1 Stat 73, 77 (1789).

[358] 630 F 2d 876 (2d Cir 1980).

[359] Ibid, 887.

[360] 542 US 692 (2004).

[361] See the discussion above at n 145. Similarly, an attentive reading of *Respublica v De Longchamps*, 1 US (1 Dall) 111 (Court of Oyer and Terminer, Philadelphia, 1784) reveals something quite different from what the case is often taken to stand for. The case involved two attacks upon the French Consul-General to the United States. The charges were framed in ordinary terms as 'unlawfully and violently threatening and menacing bodily harm and violence' and 'Assault and Battery' (see 1 US 111, 115), rather than as any violation of the law of nations as such; and the court's reference at the beginning of its judgment to the law of nations was directed towards the three questions put to it by the President and the Supreme Executive Council and reproduced at 1 US 111, 115, in particular the first and second, namely: '1st. Whether [the defendant] could be legally delivered up by Council, according to the claim made by the late Minister of France? 2ndly. If [he] could not be thus legally delivered up, whether [his] offences in violation of the law of nations, being now ascertained and verified according to the laws of th[e] Commonwealth, [he] ought not to be imprisoned, until his most Christian Majesty [the King of France] shall declare, that the reparation is satisfactory?' In short, the crimes in question were ordinary common-law crimes, and their occurrence amounted to a violation of the law of nations in the sense that it amounted to a wrongful failure by the United States to ensure the Consul-General's inviolability. See, in this light, the court's summing up at 1 US 111, 117: 'You then have been guilty of an atrocious violation of the law of nations; you have grossly

may. The point here is simply that the explicit reference in ATCA to 'a tort ... committed in violation of the law of nations' has, rightly or wrongly, been taken to vest the US federal courts with power to award damages at common law in respect of violations of customary international law. In short, the express words of the statute have been crucial in influencing how the common law has developed in this regard. The situation is different under English law. That said, the statement by the Supreme Court in *Sosa* that 'a judge deciding in reliance on an international norm will find a substantial element of discretionary judgment in the decision'[362] is as applicable to the English courts as to the American.

V. THE PROBLEM OF PRECEDENT

A central question at issue in *Trendtex* was whether an English court is bound by an earlier, otherwise precedential decision based on a rule of customary international law when the relevant rule of customary international law has itself changed in the interim. There the Court of Appeal was asked to give effect in English law to the doctrine of restrictive State immunity allegedly embodied in contemporary customary international law. The problem was that previous authority of the Court of Appeal, founded on what was said to be the defunct customary international doctrine of absolute State immunity, had laid down that the immunity from the jurisdiction of the English courts enjoyed by a foreign State was absolute.[363] By a 2:1 majority, the Court of Appeal held that it was permitted to apply the new rule of customary international law without waiting for the House of Lords to overrule the previous decisions. Lord Denning MR elaborated:

[T]he rules of international law, as existing from time to time, do form part of our English law. It follows ... that a decision of this court—as to what was the ruling of international law 50 or 60 years ago—is not binding today. International law knows no rule of stare decisis. If this court is satisfied that the rule of international law on a subject has changed from what it was 50 or 60 years ago, it can give effect to that change—and apply the change in our English law—without waiting for the House of Lords to do it.[364]

---

insulted gentlemen, the peculiar objects of this law ... in a most wanton and unprovoked manner: And it is now the interest as well as duty of the government, to animadvert upon your conduct with a becoming severity, such a severity as may tend to reform yourself, to deter others from the commission of the like crime, preserve the honor of the State, and maintain peace with our great and good Ally, and the whole world.'

[362]   542 US 692, 749.

[363]   See *Compania Mercantil Argentina v United States Shipping Board* (1924) 131 LT 388. See also, in the context of Admiralty actions in rem, *The Parlement Belge* (1880) 5 PD 197 and *The Porto Alexandre* [1920] P 30. Dicta to the same effect were also to be found in judgments of the House of Lords, namely *The Cristina* [1938] AC 485, 490 (Lord Atkin)(an action in rem) and *Rahimtoola v Nizam of Hyderabad* [1958] AC 379, 394 (Viscount Simonds).

[364]   [1977] QB 529, 554.

'After all', his Lordship added, 'we are not considering here the rules of English law on which the House has the final say. We are considering the rules of international law.'[365] Shaw LJ agreed:

May it not be that the true principle as to the application of international law is that the English courts must at any given time discover what the prevailing international rule is and apply that rule? ... [T]he law of nations ... [is] applied in the courts of England. The rule of stare decisis operates to preclude a court from overriding a decision which binds it in regard to a particular rule of (international) law, it does not prevent a court from applying a rule which did not exist when the earlier decision was made if the new rule has had the effect in international law of extinguishing the old rule.[366]

Trendtex settled before the Lords were able to hear and rule on the appeal. In the subsequent case of *I° Congreso del Partido*, Robert Goff J considered himself bound by *Trendtex* on this point, concluding, 'I must in the present case likewise give effect to the rules of international law, irrespective of any previous English decision to the contrary'.[367] In *R v Metropolitan Stipendiary Magistrate, ex parte Pinochet Ugarte (No 1)*, Lord Slynn stated that '[r]ules of customary international law change ... and as Lord Denning MR said in Trendtex Trading Corporation v Central Bank of Nigeria [1977] QB 529, "we should give effect to those changes and not be bound by any idea of stare decisis in international law"'.[368] In *R v Jones (Margaret)*, the Court of Appeal applied 'the principle which Lord Denning MR affirmed in *Trendtex Trading Corporation v Central Bank of Nigeria* [1977] QB 529, namely that English law reflects the state of international law from time to time, and does not apply the principle of binding precedent to a determination of its content'.[369] The court there held obiter that, although crimes against peace (now known as the crime of aggression) had been tried at Nuremberg, customary international law had changed since then with the result that the crime of aggression was no longer defined with sufficient clarity to enable it to constitute a crime at common law.[370]

  Trendtex stands in direct opposition to the Court of Appeal's earlier decision in *Thai-Europe Tapioca Service Limited v Government of Pakistan, Ministry of Food and Agriculture, Directorate of Agricultural Supplies (Imports and Shipping Wing) (The Harmattan)*.[371] There Lawton LJ, after referring to the same prior decisions of the Court of Appeal as were later at issue in *Trendtex*, stated:

[T]he ordinary rule of stare decisis must follow. ... It was submitted on behalf of the plaintiffs that since 1924 the views of jurists all over the world about the

---

[365] Ibid, 555.   [366] Ibid, 579.   [367] [1978] 1 QB 500, 518.
[368] [2000] 1 AC 61, 77.
[369] [2004] EWCA Crim 1981; [2005] QB 259, 273, para 31.
[370] See [2005] QB 259, 277, para 43.
[371] [1975] 1 WLR 1485. See also the earlier case in the Queen's Bench Division of *Swiss Israel Trade Bank v Government of Salta and Banco Provincial de Salta* [1972] 1 Lloyd's Rep 497, 507 (McKenna J).

immunity of sovereign states which engage in trade have changed; and that in many parts of the world courts have decided that states engaging in trade should lose their sovereign immunity when so doing. We have to concern ourselves with the law of this country. It may be that at some future date the House of Lords will consider the three cases to which I have referred; but they have not done so yet.[372]

Scarman LJ was of the same view:

I think it is important to realise that a rule of international law, once incorporated into our law by decisions of a competent court, is not an inference of fact but a rule of law. It therefore becomes part of our municipal law and the doctrine of stare decisis applies as much to that as to a rule of law with a strictly municipal provenance. This has been stated again and again in the cases to which Mr Kemp drew our attention and it is to be found I think by necessary implication in the speech of Lord Macmillan in *The Cristina* [1938] AC 485, 497 in a passage to which I need not refer. I think therefore that it is not open to this court to apply a new rule or view developing in the international field if it be inconsistent with a rule already incorporated into our law by a decision of the Court of Appeal or the House of Lords.[373]

Lord Denning MR did not address the point. In *Trendtex*, Stephenson LJ, dissenting on this point, followed the approach taken by Lawton and Scarman LJJ in *Thai-Europe Tapioca Service*. In the subsequent case of *The Uganda Co (Holdings) Ltd v The Government of Uganda*, Donaldson J, faced with inconsistent authority from the Court of Appeal in the form of *Thai-Europe Tapioca Service* and *Trendtex*, preferred (as he considered himself free to do) the earlier *Thai-Europe Tapioca Service* on the curious ground that 'a decision which asserts the doctrine of precedent must logically have more weight as a precedent than one which denies or modifies that doctrine'.[374]

It is interesting that in none of these cases did the court mention either the words of Lord Alverstone CJ in *West Rand* that the law of nations forms part of the law of England only to the extent that it is not 'contrary to the principles of her laws as declared by her courts'[375] or those of Lord Atkin in *Chung Chi Cheung* that the English courts 'will treat [customary international law] as incorporated into the domestic law, so far as it is not inconsistent with rules ... finally declared by their tribunals'.[376] Perhaps these dicta can be distinguished as referable only to other rules of the common law, rather than to the rule based on customary international law—that is, on allegedly outdated customary international law—actually at issue before the court, although it is by no means clear that they can be. Another explanation may be that at least the Court of Appeal was bound by neither, *West Rand* being a decision of the Divisional Court and *Chung Chi Cheung* of the Privy Council. Be all this, however, as it may.

---

[372] [1975] 1 WLR 1485, 1493.   [373] Ibid, 1495.   [374] [1979] 1 Lloyd's Rep 481, 487.
[375] [1905] 2 KB 391, 408.   [376] [1939] AC 160, 167–8.

It has to be said that the reasoning of Lord Denning MR and Shaw LJ in *Trendtex* is far from compelling. The former's argument that international law knows no doctrine of stare decisis is beside the point: the issue is the common law's doctrine of the same. For its part, Shaw LJ's attempt to show that the common-law doctrine of stare decisis is not even implicated in a case such as *Trendtex* is unconvincing in its failure to grapple with the logical consequences of the fact that the upshot of the incorporation of a rule of customary international law is a rule of common law, and a rule of common law that says 'X', rather than one that says 'customary international law says X'—in other words, in the case of *Trendtex*, a common-law rule to the effect that 'a foreign State is immune from the jurisdiction of the English courts only in respect of *acta jure imperii*', rather than one to the effect that 'customary international law provides that a foreign State is immune from the jurisdiction of the English courts only in respect of *acta jure imperii*'. In the final analysis, it is impossible to fault the words of Scarman LJ in *Thai-Europe Tapioca Service* that an incorporated rule of customary international law 'becomes part of [English] municipal law and the doctrine of stare decisis applies as much to that as to a rule of law with a strictly municipal provenance'.[377] The problem of contrary common-law authority cannot be wished away.

What, then, is the solution to this problem?

There is no reason why the question whether to give effect at common law to a rule of customary international law should in principle be approached any differently in situations where the as-yet-unincorporated customary international rule is a new one which has had the effect of replacing an incorporated predecessor. The point of departure remains that the doctrine of incorporation serves as a standing direction to an English court to craft rules of common law by reference to customary international law but that the court's decision to do so is one the appropriateness of which in any given case depends on a weighing of three factors. The first of these, namely whether the rule lends itself structurally to domestic application, will depend on the content of the rule in question, and so cannot be assessed in the abstract. But the third will have particular resonance in the cases at issue here. The doctrine of precedent is a fundamental principle of the common law. It is no exaggeration to call it quasi-constitutional. It weighs heavily in the balance. Given this, it must be doubted whether it is appropriate to transpose a (new) rule of customary international law into English law where the common-law rule created would fly in the face of binding authority.

An analogy could be drawn with the courts' traditional approach to the law merchant, a customary law established by reference to the practice of merchants which, like the law of nations (of which, indeed, it was described

377 [1975] 1 WLR 1485, 1495. See also Picciotto, above n 53, 85, para 48 and 103–4, para 63; Mann, above n 23, 123–4.

as being part[378]), was considered part of the common law of England. Once a rule of the law merchant had been recognized by a common-law court as part of English law, its existence was subsequently to be established by reference to this prior case-law, rather than by direct reference to the practice of merchants.[379] This was something on which none other than Lord Mansfield CJ was emphatic. In *Edie and Laird v The East India Company*, noting that the content of the rule at issue had already been determined by two judgments of the English courts, he declared, 'But the point of law is here settled: and, when once solemnly settled, no particular usage shall be permitted to weigh against it: this would send everything to sea again.'[380]

There is also an analogy between cases like *Trendtex* and the sort of case at issue in *Kay v Lambeth London Borough Council*.[381] On 25 October 2004, Judge Bush, sitting as a judge of the High Court at Leeds District Registry, held that, despite in the interim the decision of the ECtHR to the contrary in *Connors v United Kingdom*,[382] he was bound by the House of Lords' decision in *Harrow London Borough Council v Qazi*[383] and by the Court of Appeal's decision in *Kay v Lambeth London Borough Council*[384] to rule that the second set of defendants in the case before him could not raise as a defence to an order for possession sought by Leeds City Council a plea that their rights under article 8 of the ECHR, as secured to them by the HRA, would be infringed. The Court of Appeal, also holding itself bound by the Lords' decision in *Qazi*, dismissed the defendants' appeal,[385] but, considering *Qazi* incompatible with the subsequent Strasbourg decision in *Connors*, granted leave to appeal to the House of Lords. It was argued before the Lords that, where an English court was acting pursuant to the mandatory duty imposed on it by section 2 of the HRA to take into account judgments of the ECtHR, the doctrine of precedent should be relaxed in cases of clear inconsistency between an otherwise-binding domestic authority and a subsequent decision of the court in Strasbourg. The two appeals were disposed of on other grounds, but Lord Bingham— with whose reasons on point Lord Nicholls, Lord Hope, Lord Walker, Baroness Hale and Lord Brown agreed—addressed the precedent issue.

---

[378]   See above at Part II.B, especially n 55.

[379]   See *Edie and another v East-India Company* (1761) 2 Burr 1216, 1222 and 1224 (Lord Mansfield CJ), 1224 and 1225 (Denison J), 1225–6 (Foster J) and 1226–8 (Wilmot J). See also *Brandao v Barnett* (1846) 12 Cl & F 787, 805 (Lord Campbell) and 810 (Lord Lyndhurst). See too Lobban, above n 53, 262–3.

[380]   *Edie and Laird v The East India Company* (1761) 1 Black W 295, 298. The passage is not found in the alternative report of the same case found at 2 Burr 1216, as cited immediately above n 379.

[381]   [2006] UKHL 10; [2006] 2 AC 465.

[382]   (2004) 40 EHRR 189.

[383]   [2003] UKHL 43; [2004] 1 AC 983.

[384]   [2004] EWCA Civ 926; [2005] QB 352. The Court of Appeal in this case saw no inconsistency between *Qazi* and *Connors*.

[385]   See *Leeds City Council v Price* [2005] EWCA Civ 289; [2005] 1 WLR 1825.

After describing the doctrine of precedent as 'a cornerstone of [the English] legal system',[386] his Lordship stated:

As Lord Hailsham observed ... , 'in legal matters, some degree of certainty is at least as valuable a part of justice as perfection'. That degree of certainty is best achieved by adhering, even in the Convention context, to our rules of precedent. It will of course be the duty of judges to review Convention arguments addressed to them, and if they consider a binding precedent to be, or possibly to be, inconsistent with Strasbourg authority, they may express their views and give leave to appeal, as the Court of Appeal did here. Leap-frog appeals may be appropriate. In this way, in my opinion, they discharge their duty under the 1998 Act. But they should follow the binding precedent, as again the Court of Appeal did here.[387]

There is no satisfying reason why the principles applicable to the reception into English law of decisions of the ECtHR should not extend to the incorporation of rules of customary international law. It should be noted, however, that the House of Lords has since refined what it said in *Kay*. In *R (RJM) v Secretary of State for Work and Pensions*,[388] Lord Neuberger— with whom Lords Hope, Rodger, Walker and Mance agreed—emphasized that *Kay* was a situation where the Court of Appeal was forced to choose between a decision of the House of Lords and a subsequent decision of the ECtHR. His Lordship held that it was different where the English decision confronting the Court of Appeal was one of its own,[389] since the Court of Appeal was freer to depart from its own prior rulings than from those of the Lords.[390] Moreover, his Lordship added,

[t]he principle promulgated in *Young v Bristol Aeroplane Co Ltd* [1944] KB 718 [that the Court of Appeal is bound to follow one of its own decisions unless there is conflicting Court of Appeal authority, unless it is inconsistent with a subsequent decision of the House of Lords or unless it was rendered *per incuriam*]

---

[386] [2006] 2 AC 465, 496, para 42.
[387] Ibid, 497, para 43. Lord Bingham was, however, willing to make 'one partial exception': ibid, para 45. In *D v East Berkshire Community NHS Trust* [2003] EWCA Civ 1151; [2004] QB 558, the Court of Appeal had departed from the decision of the House of Lords in *X (Minors) v Bedfordshire County Council* [1995] 2 AC 663, holding that the latter could not survive the introduction of the HRA, which had undermined the policy considerations on which the House of Lords had largely based its decision. On appeal, the Lords had not criticized the Court of Appeal's 'bold course', had agreed that the policy considerations underpinning *X v Bedfordshire* had been 'very largely eroded', and had accepted that the latter was no longer good law. But there were other considerations, too, which made *X v Bedfordshire* 'a very exceptional case': judgment had been given in 1995, 'well before the 1998 Act', and had made no reference to the ECHR; and, 'importantly', the children whose claim in negligence the Lords had rejected as unarguable had succeeded before the ECtHR in establishing a breach of article 3 of the Convention, 'recovering what was, by Strasbourg standards, very substantial reparation'. 'On these extreme facts', the Court of Appeal had been entitled to hold, as it did, that the Lords' decision in *X v Bedfordshire*, in relation to children, could not survive the HRA. 'But such a course [was] not permissible save where the facts [were] of that extreme character.' See [2006] 2 AC 465, 498, para 45, referring to *Z v United Kingdom* (2001) 34 EHRR 97.
[388] [2008] UKHL 63; [2008] 3 WLR 1023.
[389] [2008] 3 WLR 1023, 1042, paras 63 and 65.
[390] Ibid, para 65.

was, of course, laid down at a time when there were no international courts whose decisions had the domestic force which decisions of the ECtHR now have, following the passing of the 1998 Act, and in particular section 2(1)(a). In my judgment, the law in areas such as that of precedent should be free to develop, albeit in a principled and cautious fashion, to take into account such changes. Accordingly, I would hold that, where it concludes that one of its previous decisions is inconsistent with a subsequent decision of the ECtHR, the Court of Appeal should be free (but not obliged) to depart from that decision.[391]

In this light, while the general statements of principle enunciated in *Trendtex* in relation to the doctrine of precedent and customary international law fare poorly in the light of *Kay*, the actual decision in *Trendtex*, involving as it did the Court of Appeal's departure from one of its own previous decisions, may nonetheless, in the light of *RJM*, be reconcilable with it. That said, Lord Neuberger's emphasis in *RJM* on the role played by an international court (there, the ECtHR) with formal powers of authoritative interpretation and application could be taken to suggest that where, as in *Trendtex*, the putative emergent rule of customary international law is one needing to be ascertained by the Court of Appeal itself without the benefit of a decision of the International Court of Justice, the Court of Appeal may be far less justified, and perhaps not justified at all, in departing from its own authority.

In the final analysis, then, the better view is that the doctrine of precedent ought to apply as much to rules of common law derived from customary international law as to other common-law rules.[392] This does not, it should be emphasized, mean that a rule of common law derived from a rule of customary international law need remain static in the face of a change in the customary international rule. It simply means that it is up to a hierarchically superior court to make any common-law adjustment.

VI. The Doctrine in Wider Context

When understood as really a doctrine of judicial transformation or judicial adoption, whereby the courts, in appropriate cases, are empowered and even directed to fashion rules of common law by reference to rules of customary international law, the doctrine of incorporation reveals itself as really just a particular manifestation of a more general principle of English law that customary international law is, all other things being equal, a legitimate source of common-law decision-making and one to

---

[391] Ibid, para 66.

[392] See also Mann, above n 23, 124–5. But *cf* Brierly, above n 5, 33–4 (criticizing '[a] rigid adherence to the English doctrine of precedents' in matters of international law); Crawford, above n 294, 361; Hunter, above n 23, 695–6; C Schreuer, 'The Applicability of Stare Decisis to International Law in English Courts' (1978) 25 *Netherlands International Law Review* 234, 238 (based, however, on the mistaken belief that an Act of Parliament, rather than simply a decision of a higher court or the House of Lords' deployment of the 1966 Practice Statement, would be necessary to overrule a precedent).

which the courts must endeavour to give effect. Although directed towards the specific end of applying a rule of customary international law as a common-law rule in more or less its own right, the doctrine of incorporation, properly understood, is not fundamentally different from the courts' crafting common-law conflicts rules by reference to the customary international rules on jurisdiction;[393] from the court's use of customary international law to arrive at common-law rules of decision in *De Wütz v Hendricks, The Emperor of Austria v Day and Kossuth, The Rose Mary* (and, ultimately, *Kuwait Airways*) and *R v Mills*; and so on.[394] In each instance, the courts are authorized and indeed directed to look to customary international law in its quality as customary international law and, insofar as this is otherwise appropriate, to give effect to it by means of the common law. In each instance, customary international law is a source of the common law. The only difference is that in cases where the doctrine of incorporation is invoked, what is asked of the court is to give effect to the customary international rule via a common-law rule in the former's more or less mirror image. In the other cases, the customary international rule is acknowledged and given effect at one further remove.

VII. CONCLUSION

In 1617, George Abbot, Archbishop of Canterbury, declared that, 'as thinges now stand throughout the whole worlde, there is no place so remote, but that the consideration thereof is mediately or immediately of consequence to our affairs here'.[395] Today, when our affairs here are adjudicated in the English courts and when things global are manifest in customary international law, the consequence of consideration thereof is, *pace* His Grace, more accurately characterized as strictly 'mediate'. The doctrine of incorporation, when more accurately understood as a doctrine of judicial transformation or judicial adoption, provides that customary international law is a source, and not as such a part, of the common law. To the extent that it is made a part, it is through the subtly modifying interposition of an English court. The model is one not of immanence or inexorable necessity but of discerning judicial agency. It is an agency that the judges would do well to exercise in as conscious and transparent a way as possible, by reference to considerations treated as determinative by their predecessors.

---

[393] See above at Part II.A. See also Dickinson, above n 2, 260: 'The law of nations [is] a source, rather than an integral part, of the national system. Indeed, in its modern version, the doctrine is essentially like the modern Anglo-American doctrine underlying the so-called conflict of laws of private international law. It means simply that the national law governing matters of international concern is to be derived, in the absence of a controlling statute, executive decision, or judicial precedent, from ... relevant principles of the law of nations ...'; and Dickinson, above n 31, 344–5.

[394] See the discussions above at Parts II.A and III.A.4.

[395] J Scott, 'What the Dutch taught us. The late emergence of the modern British State', *Times Literary Supplement*, 16 March 2001, 4.

THE DENUNCIATION OF
HUMAN RIGHTS TREATIES

By YOGESH TYAGI*

* © Yogesh Tyagi, 2009. Professor of International Law and Director, Centre for Promotion of Human Rights Teaching and Research, School of International Studies, Jawaharlal Nehru University, New Delhi; and Professor of Law, City University of Hong Kong. For comments on earlier drafts of this article, I am grateful to two anonymous reviewers and Professors James Crawford, Vaughan Lowe, Michael Reisman, Laurence Helfer, Rahmatullah Khan, V S Mani, and Detlev Vagts. I am also indebted to Dr Pemmaraju Sreenivasa Rao, Dr Markus Schmidt, Dr Romesh Weeramantry, Dr Jan Wetzel, Dr Rebecca Everly, Mr Brian Gorlick, and Ms Liv Herriot for their suggestions. I want to thank Dean Guiguo Wang, Dr Chandra Jeet, Dr Ravindra Pratap, Dr Udayakumara Ramakrishna B N, Dr Margaret Young, and Librarians Anne Burnett, Lai Chu Lau, and Petra Weiler.

I. INTRODUCTION

The promotion and protection of human rights is a principal and perpetual obligation of States. The moment a State violates human rights, it begs questions about its moral authority, political legitimacy, and legal sanctity. Human rights treaties occupy a pride of place in the global rule of law because of their codification of solemn obligations of States. The denunciation of a human rights treaty by the government of a State party is a matter of serious concern. Denunciation is a formal statement with substantial effects on the beneficiaries and trustees of the target treaty,[1] although a treaty can be denounced in effect without a formality.[2] Denunciation creates an atmosphere that is not favourable to human rights. It undermines the significance of the target treaty. Moreover, it tests the authority of the treaty monitoring body, where such a body exists. Even the possibility, threat, or rumour of denunciation may affect the confidence, image, and efficiency of the treaty body.

When a State decides to denounce a human rights treaty, it generally compels the international community to react. Although national interests invariably guide State responses to instances of denunciation, considerations of political convenience do not necessarily constrain the reaction of the international community. Even if the community of States fails to respond to an act of denunciation, civil society may not endorse it and the persons affected by it may find a new cause for action. The disapproval of denunciation may not result in a coercive measure like humanitarian intervention on the part of others concerned. Lack of such a response cannot however be a basis for the denouncing State to assume endorsement of its action. Denial of treaty obligations is always a matter of concern for all involved. There are numerous cases of the denunciation of international labour conventions, but far fewer denunciations of human rights treaties. An isolated instance of denunciation may not lead to the breakdown of the treaty regime. Nevertheless, it could restrict the growth of a human rights culture.

---

[1] This article does not use the terms 'beneficiary' and 'trustee' in the same sense as that developed by the law of trust at the domestic level and the trusteeship system under the auspices of the United Nations. Rather, it employs these terms in a generic sense. Accordingly, the term 'beneficiary' mainly applies to individuals, groups of individuals, and communities, who have inherent and inalienable rights and freedoms. Likewise, the term 'trustee' primarily covers States, human rights institutions, and their functional partners, which have a responsibility to promote and protect human rights. When individuals, groups of individuals, or communities bear or share a responsibility to promote and protect human rights, they also become 'trustees'. Civil society qualifies itself to be both a beneficiary and a trustee of human rights. In any case, the term 'trustee' does not imply an entity to which human rights are transferred in any manner.

[2] For instance, without denouncing the 1989 Second Optional Protocol to the International Covenant on Civil and Political Rights, which is aimed at the abolition of the death penalty (the ICCPR Second Protocol), on 22 July 2008 Liberia enacted a law to permit the imposition of the death penalty. This was claimed to be 'a robust response to the increasing level of crime against innocent citizens'. Visit <www.tlcafrica.com/tlcnews10.htm> (last accessed 10 December 2008).

The promotion and protection of human rights is a common objective of humankind. Human rights jurisprudence is built on the basis of respect for the principles of good faith, universality, interdependence and inseparability. The denunciation of a human rights treaty is the antithesis of some of these principles. It may give rise to the question of compliance with obligations *erga omnes*, especially when treaty obligations become part of customary law. Since some human rights are peremptory norms of international law, the denunciation of a treaty enunciating those rights may undermine those norms.

The focus of this study is to understand and appreciate the ways and means by which the international human rights system deals with incidents of denunciation. It begins with a sketch of the concept of denunciation. It reviews both traditional and modern sources of international law to identify relevant prescriptions applicable to denunciation of treaties in general and human rights treaties in particular. As part of its examination of State practice of denunciation of human rights treaties, this study pays particular attention to the responses of the monitoring bodies of those treaties. There have been attempts to redefine positive morality in a few cases of denunciation. The formulation of a general comment on the nature of a treaty, the special status of the target treaty and the assertiveness of the treaty monitoring body are some of the features of the process that redefines treaty obligations. This study underlines the limits of positive morality and advocates a pragmatic approach to meet the challenge of denunciation. It presents a perspective on fashioning an appropriate response to incidents of denunciation. The development of confidence-building measures through a proactive but judicious use of the monitoring mechanisms of human rights treaties is at the heart of the proposed perspective. This may be useful in addressing the challenge posed by denunciation of human rights treaties.

II. The Concept of Denunciation

The concept of denunciation involves at least five aspects: the use of terminology, forms of denunciation, causes for denunciation, consequences of denunciation, and basic issues. In addition, denunciations can be legal or illegal. The present section enquires into these aspects and refers to issues of legality wherever necessary, while the next section on the law of denunciation considers the subject of legality in depth.

A. Terminology

In essence, the terms 'abrogation', 'denunciation', 'revocation', 'termination', and 'withdrawal' imply the same thing. Still, different treaties employ them differently. Certain provisions of the 1969 Vienna Convention on the Law of Treaties (VCLT)[3] apply the same rules to both denunciation and suspension of a treaty.[4] However, the term 'suspension' does not apply in respect of human rights treaties. The terms 'denunciation' and 'withdrawal' are prominent in connection with international human rights law: withdrawal having a more narrow meaning in relation to exit from procedural obligations, and denunciation generally referring more broadly to exit from some or all of a treaty's substantive provisions. Although the terms 'denunciation' and 'withdrawal' are treated as interchangeable,[5] they have different meanings in international law. There is a view that '[a]lthough denunciation is also used in relation to a multilateral treaty, the better term is withdrawal'.[6] Not many follow this prescription. In spite of the fact that the term 'denunciation' has an ancient origin and appears less elegant than the term 'withdrawal', it finds expression in many multilateral treaties. For Lord McNair:

Termination means simply the ending of a treaty, by whatever method that may occur and whether by the act of one party or of all, or by the operation of the treaty itself or of the law in certain events, such as a State succession or the outbreak of war.

Denunciation ... means the act of a party, whether lawful or not, in giving notice that it considers itself no longer bound by the treaty.[7]

Following this approach, the UN Handbook on Final Clauses of Multilateral Treaties also distinguishes the term 'denunciation' from the term 'termination'.[8] However, the VCLT treats the terms 'denunciation' and 'termination' as synonyms. The International Labour Organization (ILO) employs the term 'denounce' as a substitute for the 'termination' of ILO conventions.[9] In the scholarly world, however, the term 'denouncement' is not a substitute for 'denunciation'. The term 'exit' as a substitute for the term 'denunciation' is rare in the literature. One may use the term 'denouncer' for a State that makes a 'denunciation' or

---

[3] (1969) 8 ILM 679. The VCLT was adopted on 22 May 1969 and opened for signature on 23 May 1969 by the United Nations Conference on the Law of Treaties, which was held at the Neue Hofburg in Vienna, Austria, from 26 March to 24 May 1968 and 9 April to 22 May 1969. As of 31 January 2009, there are 108 States parties to the VCLT: search <http://treaties.un.org> (last accessed 31 January 2009).

[4] Articles 30(5), 42(2), 43, 59, 60 and 65.

[5] For example, the Department of International Law of the Organization of American States (OAS) uses two expressions in the context of Peru: 'withdrawal of declaration' and 'withdrawal of denunciation'. While the former refers to Peru's decision to withdraw its acceptance of the optional jurisdiction of the Inter-American Court of Human Rights (IACtHR), the latter denotes Peru's decision to withdraw its earlier decision. Visit <www.oas.org/juridico/english/Sigs/b-32.html> (last accessed 10 December 2008).

[6] A Aust, *Modern Treaty Law and Practice* (Cambridge University Press, Cambridge, 2000) 224.

[7] Lord McNair, *The Law of Treaties* (Clarendon Press, Oxford, 1961) 491.

[8] *Final Clauses of Multilateral Treaties: Handbook* (United Nations, New York, 2003), UN Sales No. E.04.V.3, 117 (hereinafter '*UN Handbook on Final Clauses*'). Available at <http://untreaty.un. org/English/FinalClauses/english.pdf> (last accessed 10 December 2008).

[9] See below n 29.

'withdrawal', but the term 'denouncing State' is more appropriate for two reasons: an act of denunciation is always an act of State, and the old instruments of the law of treaties employ it.

A survey of treaties indicates that there is 'no consistency in employment of the terms denunciation, termination and withdrawal'.[10] In addition, a review of the literature on the law of treaties reveals that a number of new terms appear as substitutes for the term 'denunciation'. In spite of this increasing inconsistency, the use of terminology rarely gives rise to controversy in denunciation matters. The main reason is that the denunciation of a treaty puts an end to a well-defined legal relationship, preceded by a formal notification that consists of a precise formulation altering the inter se obligations among the parties to the target treaty. In the event of any controversy, the language of the notification, the intention of the denouncing State and the effect of its action on the rights and obligations of the parties to, and the beneficiaries and trustees of, the target treaty may help in the characterization of the act involved as 'denunciation'.

B. Forms

The denunciation of a treaty may appear in different forms, such as unilateral or collective, complete or partial, executive or legislative, and express or implied. An explanation of each one of these forms is useful. The implied right of denunciation will be discussed at the end of this section because of its complexity and the controversy surrounding it.

1. Unilateral or Collective

Armed with innumerable examples, Lord McNair identified three situations of denunciation of a treaty: termination by agreement of both or all parties; termination by act of one party; and termination by operation of the treaty itself or by operation of law.[11] A unilateral denunciation is the most common form of ending a treaty relationship. Indeed, every unilateral denunciation has multilateral effects. This means that a State may make a unilateral denunciation only in accordance with the law applicable to the target treaty. In case of a conflict between the law of treaties and the law of the target treaty, the latter prevails as long as it is compatible with peremptory norms of international law. Since a unilateral denunciation is likely to lead to more serious challenges than those arising out of a collective denunciation, the VCLT pays relatively more attention to the former.

When States parties to a treaty decide to terminate their treaty-based relationship with mutual consent, common intention and joint action, this amounts to a collective denunciation. Sometimes, States parties may

---

[10]   K Widdows, 'The Unilateral Denunciation of Treaties Containing No Denunciation Clause' (1982) 53 *British Year Book of International Law* 83, 95, n 26.

[11]   Above n 7, 506–19.

effect a fundamental change in a treaty by a revision, an amendment, a supplement, or another device. They can achieve the same objective by adopting another treaty to supersede the earlier one. However, not every revision, amendment, or supplement constitutes a collective denunciation. The intention of the parties, the expression of their common will, the form of the change introduced by them, and the effect of the change may help in determining whether the target treaty has been denounced. Like a unilateral denunciation, every collective denunciation ought to comply with the provisions of the target treaty or the relevant understanding among the parties concerned. A collective denunciation is the least controversial form of ending a treaty relationship, but it is the most difficult one to achieve.

One of the interesting examples of distinguishing a collective denunciation from a fundamental change of a multilateral treaty is the development of the 1966 International Covenant on Economic, Social and Cultural Rights (ICESCR).[12] In 1985 the Economic and Social Council (ECOSOC) introduced a new mechanism for the implementation of the ICESCR by establishing the Committee on Economic, Social and Cultural Rights (CESCR).[13] There was no provision in the ICESCR for the establishment of such a body. It was a fundamental change in the ICESCR without any amendment thereto. Yet, it has not been construed as a partial or collective denunciation of the ICESCR, for justifiable reasons. First, the fundamental change was made without any intention to denounce the target treaty. Secondly, it was introduced to help achieve the object and purpose of the target treaty. Finally, it did not affect the substantive rights and obligations enshrined in the target treaty. Thus, the intention of the parties, the nature of the treaty and the effect of change on the substantive obligations enshrined in the target treaty are critical factors in the characterization of 'denunciation'.

2. *Complete or Partial*

Some treaties are subject to denunciation in their totality, some permit partial withdrawal, and some others allow both possibilities. However, the VCLT envisages the partial denunciation of a treaty in exceptional

---

[12] 999 UNTS 3. On 19 December 1966 the UN General Assembly adopted the ICESCR and opened it for signature. The ICESCR entered into force on 3 January 1976. As of 31 January 2009, there are 160 States parties to it: search <http://treaties.un.org> (last accessed 31 January 2009).

[13] Following the failure of two previous monitoring bodies, namely, the Sessional Working Group and the Sessional Working Group of Government Experts, the 18-member CESCR was established under ECOSOC Resolution 1985/17 (28 May 1985) (for details, see M C R Craven, *The International Covenant on Economic, Social, and Cultural Rights: A Perspective on its Development* (Clarendon Press, Oxford, 1995)). It deploys a reporting procedure, which includes the consideration of State reports, the adoption of concluding observations on those reports, and the formulation of general comments on the provisions of the ICESCR. After the entry into force of the 2008 Optional Protocol to the ICESCR (the ICESCR Protocol), the CESCR shall have competence to consider individual and inter-State communications and also to conduct inquiry into grave or systematic violations by a State party of any of the rights set forth in the Covenant. See UN Doc A/RES/63/117 (10 December 2008).

situations.[14] A multilateral treaty covering a large subject matter with elaborate arrangements generally needs flexibility with regard to the application of its provisions. Accordingly, it may have one provision governing its complete denunciation and another regulating its partial denunciation.[15] Conversely, a treaty may have a provision for either complete or partial denunciation. When a treaty provides for only partial denunciation, the prohibition of its complete denunciation is not an automatic assumption.

There are several examples of one treaty terminating another.[16] Sometimes the integration of a treaty into another treaty may amount to an act of denunciation. For instance, the adoption of the 1994 Marrakesh Agreement Establishing the World Trade Organization (the WTO Agreement) involved the incorporation of the 1947 General Agreement on Tariffs and Trade (GATT) into the new agreement. As a result, GATT 1947 as an agreement, as well as GATT as an international institution, ceased to exist, even though its law is incorporated into the new regime. Accordingly, GATT 1994 is 'legally distinct' from GATT 1947.[17]

The VCLT recognizes partial suspension of a multilateral treaty temporarily and as between two or more parties, if the treaty provides for the possibility of such a suspension.[18] Further, the suspension in question is permissible if: (*a*) it is not prohibited by the treaty; (*b*) it does not affect the enjoyment by the other parties of their rights under the treaty or the performance of their obligations; and (*c*) it is not incompatible with the object and purpose of the treaty.[19] The parties concerned have to notify the other parties of their intention to conclude the agreement and of those provisions of the treaty the operation of which they intend to suspend. The exercise of the sovereign right to suspend certain human rights during a state of emergency does not amount to the suspension of the treaty relationship. On the contrary, it attracts the application of a set of additional obligations on the part of the derogating State.[20] This necessarily

---

[14] Article 44(2) of the VCLT states: 'A ground for invalidating, terminating, withdrawing from or suspending the operation of a treaty recognized in the present Convention may be invoked only with respect to the whole treaty except as provided in the following paragraphs or in article 60.'

[15] For example, the 1996 European Social Charter (Revised) provides for its general denunciation under paragraph 1 of Article M and partial denunciation under paragraphs 2 and 3 of the same article. See *Human Rights: A Compilation of International Instruments: Volume II: Regional Instruments* (United Nations, New York, 1997), UN Doc ST/HR/1/Rev.5 (Vol. II), 181, 203–204 (hereinafter '*Compilation of Regional Human Rights Instruments*').

[16] For example, Article 44 of the 1961 Single Convention on Narcotic Drugs provides for the termination of a number of earlier treaties in the narcotics field as between parties to the Single Convention. Interestingly, the Single Convention itself is subject to denunciation under Article 46. See 520 UNTS 151 (entered into force 13 December 1964).

[17] Article 2(4) of the WTO Agreement, <www.wto.org/english/docs_e/legal_e/04-wto.doc> (last accessed 10 December 2008).

[18] VCLT, article 58.

[19] Ibid.

[20] For instance, Article 4, in conjunction with Article 5 of the 1966 International Covenant on Civil and Political Rights (ICCPR), subjects the right of derogation to a set of conditions and restrictions, including the necessity of official proclamation of public emergency and the duty of the derogating

requires a closer relationship between the derogating State and other States parties to the target treaty.

The entry into force of a treaty is not necessary for denouncing the treaty in whole or part. The abrogation of Part XI of the 1982 United Nations Convention on the Law of the Sea (UNCLOS)[21] by the adoption of the 1994 Agreement relating to the Implementation of Part XI illustrates the partial denunciation of a treaty even before its entry into force. Indeed, both the Agreement and the Convention came into force together in 1996. In the event of an inconsistency between the Agreement and Part XI, the former shall prevail.[22] The partial denunciation of the UNCLOS escaped closer legal scrutiny because of the circumstances prevailing at that time and also because of the influence of its protagonists. This kind of exercise signifies a power-centric dynamism in State practice. Sometimes, it facilitates the realization of the broad objectives of the target treaty; otherwise, it signals the premature frustration of functionalism.

The *Peruvian* cases illuminate the debate on complete and/or partial denunciation.[23] There, Peru withdrew its consent to the optional jurisdiction of the IACtHR under Article 62 of the 1969 American Convention on Human Rights (ACHR), also known as 'Pact of San José, Costa Rica'.[24] The Inter-American Commission on Human Rights (IACmHR) opposed it. Article 62 is silent on the withdrawal of a declaration, and Article 78 of the ACHR embodies the applicable law without any indication of the possibility of a partial denunciation.[25] The IACtHR considered the withdrawal inadmissible on the grounds that the ACHR was of a unitary nature and that the Convention had no scope for its partial denunciation.[26] Michael Reisman and Mahnoush Arsanjani are sceptical of the legal basis of these judgments,[27] implying that there is scope for controversy in the absence of a clear provision on the partial denunciation of, or withdrawal from, a treaty.

3. *Executive or Legislative*

The VCLT describes the person(s) who have the authority to sign a treaty,[28] but it does not mention the person(s) who can denounce a treaty. On the other hand, the ILO provides that the instrument of denunciation

---

State to notify the other States parties to the Covenant. See 999 UNTS 171 (entered into force 23 March 1976).

[21] 1833 UNTS 3 (entered into force 16 November 1994).

[22] Visit <www.un.org/Depts/los/convention_agreements/convention_overview_part_xi.htm> (last accessed 10 December 2008).

[23] For details, see below nn 290–293.

[24] Below n 292.

[25] Below n 338.

[26] Below nn 297–298.

[27] W M Reisman and M H Arsanjani, 'No Exit? A Preliminary Examination of the Legal Consequences of United States' Notification of Withdrawal from the Optional Protocol to the Vienna Convention on Consular Relations' in M G Kohen (ed) *Promoting Justice, Human Rights and Conflict Resolution through International Law/La promotion de la justice, des droits de l'homme et du règlement des conflits par le droit international:* Liber Amicorum *Lucius Caflisch* (Brill NV, Leiden, 2007) 920.

[28] VCLT, article 7.

must be signed by a person with authority to engage the State (such as the Head of State, Prime Minister, and Minister responsible for Foreign Affairs or Labour).[29] The VCLT takes for granted that the denunciation of a treaty is the prerogative of the executive branch of the denouncing State. The denunciation of a treaty is a formal, political, and international act. The executive branch performs this act by communicating with the outside world, especially the depository of the instruments of accession, ratification, succession and denunciation of the target treaty.

It is important to note that the denunciation of a treaty is the product of a process. Logically, the process of denunciation of a treaty should match the procedure of acceptance of the treaty. However, this logic does not shape State practice. There is no uniformity in State practice on the acceptance of a treaty. Different States follow different procedures for assuming obligations under different kinds of treaties. A State may have a divergent practice regarding different categories of treaties, and it may sometimes adopt a divergent practice for the same kind of treaties.[30] In principle, if a State cannot become a party to a treaty without its ratification by its legislature, the denunciation of the treaty may come into effect only after its approval by the legislature. In other words, a legislative action is expected to precede an executive denunciation in a democratic State. However, this approach is not applicable to those States that do not subscribe to the doctrine of separation of powers *stricto sensu*. Since the separation of powers need not necessarily make the legislature indispensable in the treaty ratification process, the denunciation of a treaty may remain essentially an executive act.

In India, for instance, the executive not only concludes treaties but also ratifies them. Under the practice followed since the adoption of the Constitution of India in 1950, as a default procedure, treaties and international agreements are submitted to the Cabinet (the Council of Ministers of the Government of India) for ratification or accession. Legislative control of treaty ratification is exercised in an indirect way when the Government seeks to enact necessary implementing legislation to give full effect to the provisions of the treaty in question. With coalition governments as the order of the day, Cabinet approval is delayed until either a 'sense' of the House of the People (Lok Sabha) is established in its favour or a suitable implementation is in place. The 2008 Indo-US nuclear deal is the latest

---

[29] 'Section X: Denunciation of Conventions (ILS Handbook of Procedures)', <http://training.itcilo.it/ILS/FOA/library/handbook_en/2911.htm> (last accessed 10 December 2008).

[30] For instance, on 26 May 1972 the Soviet Union and the United States signed the Treaty on the Limitation of Anti-Ballistic Missile Systems (the ABM Treaty) and the Interim Agreement on Certain Measures with respect to the Limitation of Strategic Offensive Arms (the Interim Agreement). While the ABM Treaty limited the deployment of anti-ballistic missile systems to two designated areas, the Interim Agreement limited the overall level of strategic offensive missile forces. President Nixon submitted the ABM Treaty to the Senate for its 'advice and consent' to ratification, while he sought an expression of support from both houses of Congress for the Interim Agreement. Visit <www.fas.org/nuke/control/abmt/text/abm-art.htm> (last accessed 10 December 2008).

example.[31] Treaties involving boundary agreements sometimes require amendment to the Constitution.[32] Such constitutional amendments cannot come into force in the absence of their approval by the concerned State legislatures as well. Failure to adopt/approve such a constitutional amendment may compel the executive to denounce the treaty containing a boundary agreement. If a treaty containing a boundary agreement were to be implemented without a constitutional amendment, it would be *ultra vires* under domestic law[33] and a *fait accompli* in international law. The first impression one can gather from this practice is that the executive branch of the government and/or the political party with a parliamentary majority may indirectly control (or affect) the process of ratification of a treaty in India. Secondly, given the Cabinet system of ratification in India, the question of a legislative denunciation does not normally arise there. Finally, the executive's treaty-making power has become an issue since the early 1990s, particularly after India signed and ratified the WTO Agreement, which did not have broad support in Parliament.[34] This has led to litigation[35] and a quest for reform.[36]

In a country like the United States, where treaties, together with domestic sources, are 'the supreme Law of the Land',[37] a legislative action

---

[31] The Indo-US nuclear deal consists of a series of communiqués and agreements. It culminated in the 2008 Agreement for Cooperation between the Government of the United States of America and the Government of India Concerning Peaceful Uses of Nuclear Energy (the 123 Agreement) only after the enactment of the 2008 United States–India Nuclear Cooperation Approval and Nonproliferation Enhancement Act. It created a controversy that prompted a meeting of Lok Sabha to decide on the vote of confidence in the government led by Prime Minister Manmohan Singh. See S Sengupta, 'Indian Government Survives Confidence Vote', *New York Times*, 23 July 2008, <www.nytimes.com/2008/07/23/world/asia/23india.html?_r=2&ref=world&oref=slogin&oref=slogin> (last accessed 10 December 2008).

[32] For instance, the 1958 Agreement between India and Pakistan on Border Disputes (East Pakistan) (subsequently Bangladesh) necessitated the adoption of the Constitution (Ninth Amendment) Act, 1960. The amendment never came into force because of the conclusion of the boundary agreements between Bangladesh and India in 1974 and 1982, which terminated or modified the 1958 Agreement. For details, see P C Rao, *The Indian Constitution and International Law* (Taxman Publications, Delhi, 1993) 134–39.

[33] For instance, the controversy regarding the ceding of Kachatheevu Island by India to Sri Lanka. See *J Jayalalitha v Union of India and Others*, Writ Petition (Civil) No. 561 of 2008. See also 'Island handover to Lanka: Centre gets SC notice on Jaya PIL', *Times of India*, 6 January 2009.

[34] See, for instance, S K Jha, *Final Act of WTO: Abuse of Treaty-Making Power* (Centre for Study of Global Trade System and Development, New Delhi, 2006).

[35] In *Shiva Kant Jha v Union of India et al.*, the petitioner requested the Delhi High Court to declare, inter alia, that the executive has no power to enter into any agreement that is binding on India without the agreement's ratification by Parliament and that the Government's treaty-making powers are subject to constitutional limitations, which operate both against the executive and Parliament. The petitioner also requested the Court to determine constitutional principles in conformity with which the treaty-making procedure can be prescribed. See CWP (PIL) No. 1357 of 2007, <www.shivakantjha. org/openfile.php?filename=pil/writ_petition_226.htm> (last accessed 10 December 2008).

[36] In 2002 the National Commission to Review the Working of the Constitution of India under the chairmanship of Justice Venkatachaliah made recommendations either for having an amendment to the Constitution or for enacting legislation to regulate the treaty power of the Union Government whenever necessary after consulting the State Governments and Legislatures 'for giving effect to international agreements'. Visit <http://lawmin.nic.in/ncrwc/finalreport/v1ch11.htm>, para 77 (last accessed 10 December 2008).

[37] Constitution of the United States of America, article 6 § 2.

prior to the denunciation of a law-making, self-executing, or private rights–bearing treaty is a reasonable expectation. This need not be the case with regard to other treaties. In fact, different species of treaties are subject to different legal processes in the United States. The US Constitution specifies the process for making treaties, but it is silent on the question of denunciation. Louis Henkin points out that, although the federal government has the constitutional power to terminate treaties, '[a]t various times, the power to terminate treaties has been claimed for the President, for the President-and-Senate, for President-and-Congress, for Congress'.[38] Michael Reisman and Myres McDougal state that 'it is simply preposterous to conclude in the absence of express provision that a comprehensive, exclusive power goes to the president'.[39] They suggest congressional approval for the termination of a treaty. This view would strengthen the spirit of constitutional democracy. It has some support in both academic and legislative circles.[40] Even if the President terminates a treaty without congressional approval[41] and escapes judicial disapproval,[42] the Senate Foreign Relations Committee contends that the termination of treaties requires the participation of the Senate or Congress.[43] In the final analysis, however, the President holds the political power to terminate a treaty. Although many experts support the presidential prerogative in treaty matters, there is a suggestion that the United States should discontinue its traditional treaty-making practice and that almost every treaty should be approved by both houses of Congress as a congressional-executive agreement.[44] If this suggestion were accepted, it would become more difficult to denounce a treaty-turned agreement without congressional approval.

While expressing the view that Congress is unlikely to succeed 'in establishing a right to terminate a treaty (or to share in the decision to

---

[38] L Henkin, *Foreign Affairs and the United States Constitution* (2nd edn, Clarendon Press, Oxford, 1996) 211.

[39] M Reisman and M McDougal, 'Who Can Terminate Mutual Defense Treaties?' 36 *National Law Journal*, 21 May 1979, 19. However, Reisman does not maintain this view as discussed with the author.

[40] See, among others, J H Riggs Jr, 'Termination of Treaties by the Executive without Congressional Approval: The Case of the Warsaw Convention' (1966) 32 *Journal of Air Law & Commerce* 526, 533–34.

[41] For instance, President Bush unilaterally terminated the 1994 Convention for the Avoidance of Double Taxation and the Prevention of Fiscal Evasion with Respect to Taxes on Income, a bilateral treaty between Sweden and the United States, with effect from 1 January 2008, and the Senate did not express any public objection. See O A Hathaway, 'Treaties' End: The Past, Present, and Future International Lawmaking in the United States' (2008) 117 *Yale Law Journal* 1236, 1326, n 266.

[42] In *Goldwater v Carter*, for instance, the Court of Appeals refused to invalidate President Carter's unilateral termination of the 1954 Sino-American Mutual Defense Treaty; the Supreme Court declined to consider the legality of that termination because it involved a nonjusticiable political question: 444 US 996 (1979). Similarly, in *Kucinich v Bush*, the District Court dismissed the petition of a group of legislators, who had challenged the constitutionality of President Bush's unilateral termination of the ABM Treaty: 236 F. Supp. 2d 1, 2–3 (DDC 2002). There is still no judicial verdict on the question of whether the President has the power to terminate a treaty without the approval of Congress. See Hathaway, above n 41, 1324.

[43] Hathaway, ibid, 1325.

[44] Ibid, 1357.

terminate)',[45] Henkin draws attention to some of the means available to Congress that can be used to seal the fate of a treaty. Apart from legislative means, 'Congress can also declare war and terminate or suspend treaty relations with the other belligerent'.[46] The case law of the United States recognizes that 'Congress can denounce treaties if it sees fit to do so'.[47] It suggests that an Act of Congress is on full parity with a treaty, and that when a statute which is subsequent in time is inconsistent with a treaty, the statute, to the extent of conflict, renders the treaty null.[48] Several experts support the doctrines of the 'well-settled' relationship between US statutes and treaties that give subsequently enacted statutes precedence.[49] They admit that 'the later-in-time' rule generates violations of international law even though it has been effective domestically since the mid-nineteenth century.[50] It is obvious, therefore, that 'the later-in-time' rule presents the possibility of a legislative denunciation internally of a treaty even without following the treaty-based process.[51] Such denunciations might not survive the test of international law,[52] including the VCLT in general[53] and the law of the target treaty in particular, but the burden of undoing the damage to the treaty lies on its beneficiaries, trustees, and parties. In short, while the executive remains the key functionary in the processes of both making and unmaking treaties, the legislature finds various opportunities to influence those processes.

If a treaty allows a State to participate in its application prior to its ratification, the ratification process in due course may offer an opportunity to the legislature of the State concerned to terminate the treaty as well as its provisional application. For instance, Article 45 of the 1994 Energy Charter Treaty (ECT) envisages its provisional application by those States that have not yet ratified it.[54] The Russian Federation is one such State, which applies the ECT's provisions to the extent that they are consistent with Russia's

---

[45] Henkin, above n 38, 214.

[46] Ibid, 212.

[47] [1972] *Diggs v Shultz*, 470 F.2d 461, 466.

[48] [1998] *Breard v Greene*, 523 US 371.

[49] See, for example, C Bradley and L F Damrosch, '*Medellin v Dretke*: Federalism and International Law' (2005) 43 *Columbia Journal of Transnational Law* 667, 680.

[50] D F Vagts, 'The United States and Its Treaties: Observance and Breach' (2001) 95 *American Journal of International Law* 313–34.

[51] J G Ku, 'Treaties as Laws: A Defense of the Last-in-Time Rule for Treaties and Federal Statutes' (2005) 80 *Indiana Law Journal* 319–90.

[52] Hathaway states that the enactment of subsequent contrary legislation may very well leave the United States in violation of international law, but that international law would be unenforceable in domestic courts. She believes that, in order for a treaty to no longer be binding according to international law, the United States must formally withdraw from it: see Oona Hathaway, 'International Delegation and State Sovereignty' (2008) 71 *Law & Contemporary Problems* 115, 132–33, n 58.

[53] Article 27 of the VCLT, titled 'Internal law and observance of treaties', lays down: 'A party may not invoke the provisions of its internal law as justification for its failure to perform a treaty'. Internal law includes both legislation and case law.

[54] Energy Charter Secretariat (2004) at <www.encharter.org/fileadmin/user_upload/document/EN.pdf> (last accessed 10 December 2008).

constitution, laws and regulations.[55] In view of Article 45(3)(a) of the ECT, the State legislature has the right to terminate the Treaty and its provisional application.[56] It is true that the option of a provisional application was given only to initial signatories and only for a short period so no other ECT member, future or present, can choose to apply the Treaty provisionally. It is also true that there are only two States applying the ECT provisionally (Belarus and Russia) and that neither of them has yet terminated the Treaty or its provisional application. Moreover, the saving clauses envisage that the provisions of the ECT shall continue to apply to the existing investments for a period of twenty years from the date when the withdrawal from the Treaty takes effect.[57] In spite of all these constraints, the option of either an executive or a legislative action against the ECT is available to both the States even before ratifying the Treaty.

Since the judiciary of a democratic State generally has power to review the validity of its domestic laws, which include a wide range of instrumentalities,[58] it may consider an instrument of accession to, or ratification of, a treaty invalid on the ground of its incompatibility with the constitution of the State concerned. Unless the legislature overrules a judgment of the highest court of appeal, which is not a common practice, the judgment remains binding on the executive as well as the legislature.[59] Consequently, a judicial pronouncement against an instrument of accession to, or ratification of, a treaty may lead to a formal denunciation on the part of the executive or simply amount to the de facto denunciation of the treaty. Alternatively, the executive or any other person with a *locus standi* in the matter may seek judicial review of the judgment and its prospective overruling may exempt the executive from taking the step of denunciation.

The chain of events following the judgment of the Supreme Court of Sri Lanka in the case of *Nallaratnam Singarasa v Attorney General* illustrates the role of the judiciary in treaty matters in at least some jurisdictions.[60] There, the Court held that Sri Lanka's accession to the Optional

---

[55] As of 18 December 2008, there are 48 Contracting Parties to the ECT. In addition, 2 States apply the whole ECT provisionally, and 3 States apply Part VII provisionally. Observers include 21 States, the Palestinian National Authority and 10 international organizations: visit <www.encharter.org/index.php?id=61&L=0> (last accessed 18 December 2008).

[56] Article 106(d) of the Constitution of the Russian Federation states: 'Liable to obligatory consideration by the Council of the Federation shall be the federal laws adopted by the State Duma on the ... ratification and denunciation of international treaties and agreements of the Russian Federation'. Visit <www.constitution.ru/en/10003000-06.htm> (last accessed 10 December 2008).

[57] ECT, article 45(3)(b).

[58] According to Article 13(3)(a) of the Constitution of India, for instance, the term 'law' includes 'any Ordinance, order, bye-law, rule, regulation, notification, custom or usage having in the territory of India the force of law'. Visit <http://lawmin.nic.in/coi/coiason29july08.pdf> (last accessed 10 December 2008).

[59] For instance, Article 141 of the Constitution of India states: 'The law declared by the Supreme Court shall be binding on all courts within the territory of India.' Ibid.

[60] SC Spl (LA) No. 182/99. Available at <www.ahrchk.net/statements/mainfile.php/2006statements/735> (last accessed 10 December 2008).

Protocol to the International Covenant on Civil and Political Rights (the first ICCPR Protocol) was unconstitutional and that the views of the Human Rights Committee (HRCttee) were not binding on the State.[61] In October 2006 the HRCttee discussed this judgment and met informally with the Permanent Mission of Sri Lanka to the United Nations to express concern over the judgment. It has not taken any official position on the judgment for fear that a negative position would prompt the Sri Lankan Government to denounce the Protocol. In order to dilute the negative effect of the judgment, on 4 March 2008 the President of Sri Lanka sought the Court's opinion on two questions. First, whether individuals within the territory of Sri Lanka would derive the benefit and the guarantee of rights as contained in the ICCPR through the medium of the legal and constitutional processes prevailing in Sri Lanka? Secondly, whether the rights recognized in the ICCPR are justiciable through the medium of legal and constitutional process prevailing in Sri Lanka?[62] On 17 March 2008 the Court answered both questions in the affirmative.[63] One may wonder whether the Court has corrected its earlier view that 'the rights under the Covenant are not rights under the law of Sri Lanka'.[64] Since the Court has not yet overruled its earlier judgment, the fear of a formal denunciation of the Protocol has merely receded after the above advisory opinion. In any case, it is important to mention that this kind of judicial review is not common. In fact, State practice generally demonstrates the opposite: '[C]ourts do not terminate treaties, but they may interpret political acts or even political silences to determine whether they implied or intended termination. Courts do not sit in judgment on the political branches to prevent them from terminating or breaching a treaty'.[65] In other words, judicial review is a rare vehicle of denunciation.

The withdrawal of its declaration by Peru, consenting to the optional jurisdiction of the IACtHR under Article 62 of the ACHR, is an instance of the different limbs of the State synchronizing their moves towards an act of denunciation. In 1999 the Peruvian declaration of withdrawal originated from the judiciary (the Supreme Council of Military Justice of Peru), approved by the legislature (the Congress of the Republic of Peru) and effected by the executive (the Minister of Foreign Affairs of Peru).[66] It could be easily identified as a collective act.

The VCLT has oversimplified the relationship between domestic law and a treaty to which the denouncing State was a party. Though

---

[61] The HRCttee is an 18-member body of independent experts representing different civilizations and the principal legal systems. It monitors the implementation of the ICCPR by administering three procedures: the reporting procedure under Article 40 of the ICCPR; the inter-State communication procedure in terms of Articles 41 and 42 of the Covenant; and the individual communication procedure under the first ICCPR Protocol. For details, see M Nowak, *U.N. Covenant on Civil and Political Rights: CCPR Commentary* (2nd edn, N P Engel Publisher, Kehl, 2005).

[62] SC Reference No. 01/2008. A copy is available with the author.

[63] Ibid.

[64] The *Singarasa* case, above n 60.

[65] Henkin, above n 38, 214.   [66] For details, see below nn 290–293 and surrounding text.

understandable in terms of the broad policy goals of the global rule of law, where the State essentially means the executive branch of the government, the Vienna prescription of the said relationship does not truly reflect State practice and certainly not the complexities of the domestic law procedures governing treaties. Moreover, it has no rule to deal with the denunciation of a treaty by an international body. There are some instances of an international body terminating a treaty,[67] indicating that the government of a State is not the sole denouncer of treaties.

Since human rights treaties require each State party to take the necessary steps, in accordance with its constitutional processes, to adopt such laws or other measures as may be necessary to give effect to the rights recognized therein, the involvement of the legislature is essential. The whole exercise may also include judicial review of enabling legislation, if not the treaty as such. In the absence of enabling legislation, the judiciary may or may not recognize a treaty-based obligation. These processes may lead to a situation where the executive may feel obligated to reconsider the State party's commitment to the treaty in question. Accordingly, executive control over human rights treaties has its limitations. In any case, denunciation is not merely an executive act. It is a formal product, which depends on a legal process. The objectives and purposes of human rights treaties can best be served only when executive denunciation (product) is seen in the light of the process from which it resulted.

4. *Express or Implied*

The US Restatement of the Foreign Relations Law points out that '[a] right to terminate an agreement is often expressed but may also be implied'.[68] Theoretically, an express provision on the denunciation of a treaty minimizes the possibility of a controversy relating to its application. It derives strength from the identification of an authority to receive the notification of denunciation, the conditions applicable to denunciation, and a general rule relating to the entry into force of the notification. It obtains further strength from the inclusion of safety clauses, a statement of the effects on pending matters concerning the target treaty, and the monitoring of these aspects by the treaty body, if such a body exists. Generally, an express provision on denunciation symbolizes the good governance of treaty affairs.

However, an express provision on denunciation may not be helpful in respect of some human rights treaties. It may represent the lowest common denominator at the time of drafting a treaty. It need not necessarily reflect the nature, object, purpose and importance of the treaty. Since this is the case with several human rights treaties, such as the 1948 Convention

---

[67] For example, Article 63(4) of the 2001 International Cocoa Agreement provides that the International Cocoa Council may terminate this agreement. See UNCTAD Doc TD/COCOA.9/7 and Corr 1 (13 March 2001) 33. Available at <www.icco.org/pdf/agree01english.pdf> (last accessed 31 January 2009).

[68] *Restatement (Third) of the Foreign Relations Law of the United States*, Vol 1 (American Law Institute, St. Paul, 1987) 210 (hereinafter '*US Restatement of the Foreign Relations Law*').

on the Prevention and Punishment of the Crime of Genocide (the Genocide Convention)[69] and the 1965 International Convention on the Elimination of All Forms of Racial Discrimination (ICERD),[70] the denunciation clauses of these treaties are misleading. Because of the lack of opportunity to subject them to an authoritative interpretative process or judicial review,[71] the denunciation clauses remain a dormant source of conflict or confusion.

An implied denunciation may come into reckoning when a treaty does not have any express provision relating to the permissibility or prohibition of its denunciation. The silence of the target treaty may invite competing interpretations about its denunciation. It may give rise to confusion, controversy, or uncertainty. As a matter of policy, therefore, the drafters of a treaty should always consider the question of denunciation. Even if their deliberations failed to incorporate a denunciation clause in the treaty, the drafting history would help in determining the intention of the parties to the treaty and the scope of competence of its monitoring body, if such a body exists. Also, it may help in assessing the continuity of the obligations incorporated in the treaty.

Having played a leading role in the codification of the modern law of treaties, Taslim Olawale Elias highlighted the conceptual differences with regard to the implied right of denunciation. He stated:

There are two schools of thought on this question. On the one hand, some jurists consider that where the treaty itself is silent on the point, it is to be presumed that no such right exists, since the parties themselves would have made express provision for it. On the other hand, there are other jurists who take the view that the mere absence of a specific provision of a right of termination or withdrawal in the treaty should not be interpreted to mean that the right is thereby taken away, since, in their view, the right exists under customary international law in any case. The latter view is to be preferred, as it is consistent with principle and makes for a certain degree of flexibility, provided that reasonable notice is given, by the party wanting to denounce or withdraw, to the other parties to the treaty.[72]

This statement underlines the importance of flexibility in treaty relations. It is in line with general State practice. It seeks to favour a regime without bias against denunciation. It may not find equal support in the province of human rights law, which accords greater importance to the integrity of a treaty and the continuity of treaty obligations.

Whether States have a right to denounce a treaty in the absence of an express provision to that effect has been a matter of widespread interest. James Brierly rightly observed that '[o]ne of the most difficult and

---

[69] 78 UNTS 277 (entered into force 12 January 1951), article 14.
[70] 660 UNTS 195 (entered into force 4 January 1969), article 21.
[71] The application of the Genocide Convention and the ICERD was the main issue in the *Armed Activities on the Territory of the Congo* case (*Democratic Republic of the Congo v Rwanda*) [2006] ICJ Rep 6, but their denunciation clauses were not in contention there.
[72] T O Elias, *The Modern Law of Treaties* (A W Sijthoff, Leiden, 1974) 105.

practically important questions of the law of treaties relates to the termination of treaties which contain, at any rate in their expressed terms, no provision for that purpose'.[73] He held the view that '[t]here is certainly no general right of denunciation of a treaty of indefinite duration'.[74] At the same time, he recognized that 'there are some [treaties] which, from the nature of the subject-matter or the circumstances in which they were concluded, we may fairly presume were intended to be susceptible of denunciation even though they contain no express term to that effect'.[75] While observing that 'there is a general presumption against the existence of any right of unilateral termination of a treaty',[76] Lord McNair acknowledged the implied right of denunciation in a complex formulation:

Just as there is nothing juridically impossible in the existence of a treaty which is incapable of termination except by the consent of all parties, so also there is nothing juridically impossible in the existence of an implied term giving a party the right to terminate it unilaterally by denunciation. It is a question of the intention of the parties which can be inferred from the terms of the treaty, the circumstances in which it was concluded, and the nature of the subject-matter.[77]

In a liberal tone, Sir Gerald Fitzmaurice observed that 'there are certain sorts of treaties which, unless entered into for a fixed and stated period or expressed to be in perpetuity, are *in their nature* such that any of the parties to them have an implied right to bring them to an end or to withdraw from them'.[78] As an architect of contemporary treaty law, Sir Humphrey Waldock identified four types of treaties with scope for denunciation in the absence of an express provision. These are commercial or trading treaties (other than those intended to establish an international regime of an economic kind for a particular area, river system or waterway and intended to be of permanent duration); treaties of alliance or military cooperation; treaties of technical cooperation; and treaties of arbitration, conciliation, or judicial settlement.[79] Similarly, drawing a distinction between 'permanent' and other treaties, the Rapporteur of the US Restatement of the Foreign Relations Law illustrates: 'Treaties of alliance and commercial treaties are ordinarily not meant to be indefinite, and in the absence of provisions stating or implying the contrary, a right to withdraw may be implied.'[80] There is a mass of bilateral treaties of a

---

[73]   J L Brierly, *The Law of Nations: An Introduction to the International Law of Peace*, 6th edn by Sir Humphrey Waldock (Oxford University Press, Oxford, 1963) 330.

[74]   Ibid, 331.

[75]   Ibid.

[76]   McNair, above n 7, 493.

[77]   Ibid, 511.

[78]   *Second Report on the Law of Treaties by Mr. G.G. Fitzmaurice, Special Rapporteur*, UN Doc A/CN.4/107 (15 March 1957) 38–39, para 16. Available at <http://untreaty.un.org/ilc/documentation/english/a_cn4_107.pdf> (last accessed 10 December 2008).

[79]   *Second Report on the Law of Treaties, by Sir Humphrey Waldock, Special Rapporteur*, UN Doc A/CN.4/156 and Add. 1–3 (20 March, 10 April, 30 April and 5 June 1963) 68, paras 15–18. Available at <http://untreaty.un.org/ilc/documentation/english/a_cn4_156.pdf> (last accessed 10 December 2008).

[80]   Above n 68, 210.

commercial nature, and they are subject to either express or implied denunciation.

Neither Sir Humphrey nor the US Restatement considered it necessary to place human rights treaties in the category of 'permanent' treaties, although none of those treaties is of limited duration. The VCLT does not regard human rights treaties as a special case with respect to the question of denunciation. Only Article 60(5) of the VCLT provides that the legal consequences of a material breach of a treaty 'do not apply to provisions relating to the protection of the human person contained in treaties of a humanitarian character'.[81] This provision is vague concerning the scope of the term 'humanitarian character'.[82] While Egon Schwelb became one of the first proponents of the inadmissibility of any act of denunciation of the International Covenants on Human Rights,[83] Kelvin Widdows referred to these instruments in a footnote without any indication of the permissibility or prohibition of their denunciation.[84] Many scholars who are more sensitive to new developments relating to human rights treaties do not put these treaties in the category of instruments immune from denunciation.[85] In other words, with only a few exceptions, scholarly opinion on the law of treaties is not generally opposed to the implied right of denunciation of human rights treaties. This position is consistent with the final clauses of several human rights treaties. However, it does not match the soft law on denunciation.[86] It also appears to be inconsistent with world public opinion, which considers human rights treaties sacrosanct. Therefore, new developments in international law have glossed over a number of writings on denunciation.

The above discussion suggests that the form of denunciation of a treaty invariably indicates the broad parameters of the law applicable to the treaty. The form may help determine the validity of an instrument of denunciation. In denunciation matters, therefore, the form matters no less than the substance.

C. Causes

Generally, the denunciation clause of a treaty is concerned with the procedure by which the act of denunciation can be performed. The denouncing State is not required to specify the reasons that underlie its act of

---

[81] This provision did not exist in the draft prepared by the International Law Commission. It was incorporated into the final text at the initiative of Switzerland at the Vienna Conference on the Law of Treaties. For details, see E Schwelb, 'The Law of Treaties and Human Rights' in H Schlochauer (ed) *Archiv des Völkerrechts* (J C B Mohr (Paul Siebeck), Tübingen, 1974/1975) 2–6 and 21–26.

[82] While the drafting history reveals that Article 60(5) was incorporated in view of the 1949 Geneva Conventions on the Protection of War Victims and similar conventions and agreements, Schwelb advocated a liberal interpretation by including conventions for the 'protection of human rights in general' within the scope of this provision. Ibid, 23.

[83] Ibid, 26–27.

[84] Widdows, above n 10, 103, n 49.

[85] See, among others, Aust, above n 6, 234.

[86] See below nn 235–255 and surrounding text.

denunciation of a human rights treaty. Failure to specify reasons need not necessarily affect the validity of denunciation.[87] Like ILO conventions, most of the treaties on arms control or disarmament constitute an exception in this regard. For instance, the 2008 Convention on Cluster Munitions requires that the 'instrument of withdrawal shall include a full explanation of the reasons motivating withdrawal'.[88]

Generally, the denouncing State does specify some reasons to justify its act. Even if the notice of denunciation does not mention the reasons, one can glean them from other sources.[89] A reasoned instrument of denunciation demonstrates its sensitivity towards the rule of law, which seeks to promote transparency in the legal processes of public interest. On the other hand, when a notification of denunciation is not accompanied by reasons, this is likely to give rise to protests and objections from a far wider group of participants than those directly affected. In the event of a dispute over an act of denunciation, it is incumbent on the denouncing State to establish its case by adducing reasons for its action.

The denouncing State may adduce a variety of reasons for the denunciation of a treaty. Such reasons may include a fundamental change of circumstances, emergence of new norms of international law, or vital interests. Couched in legal language, an ideological change or strategic shift may also be a reason for denunciation. Invariably, the politically motivated redefinition of national interests serves as a catalyst for denunciation. The denunciation of the ABM Treaty by the United States in 2002 is one example.[90] The denunciation of the 1965 Washington Convention on the Settlement of Investment Disputes between States and Nationals of Other States by Bolivia in 2007 is another.[91] The infectious effect of the Bolivian denunciation is evident from Ecuador's withdrawal of its consent to the jurisdiction of the International Centre for the Settlement of Investment Disputes (ICSID) in 2007.[92] There is concern that Venezuela

---

[87] See, for example, Article 317(1) of the UNCLOS.

[88] Article 20(2). On 30 May 2008 the Dublin Diplomatic Conference on Cluster Munitions adopted the Convention, which was opened for signature on 3 December 2008. Visit <www.clusterconvention. org/pages/pages_ii/iia_textenglish.html#art20> (last accessed 23 August 2009).

[89] For instance, on 7 March 2005 the US Secretary of State gave a 60-day notice to the UN Secretary-General regarding the US withdrawal from the 1963 Optional Protocol to the Vienna Convention on Consular Relations Concerning the Compulsory Settlement of Disputes without stating reasons. Three days later, however, the Deputy Spokesman of the US Department of State explained the reasons. See Reisman and Arsanjani, above n 27, 899, n 3.

[90] To establish its missile defence system, the United States sought the revision of the ABM Treaty. On 13 December 2001, when it realized that it could not convince the Russian Federation (successor to the Soviet Union) to agree to the revision, the United States denounced the Treaty in accordance with its Article 15(2). Visit <www.acronym.org.uk/docs/0112/doc01.htm> (last accessed 31 January 2009).

[91] Since 2006, Bolivia has nationalized several industries to exercise greater government control over its natural resources. On 2 May 2007, in order to avoid international arbitrations in the nationalization cases, Bolivia denounced the Washington Convention in accordance with its Article 71. Visit <www.skadden.com/Index.cfm?contentID=51&itemID=1267> (last accessed 31 January 2009).

[92] To pursue '21st century socialism', Ecuador has adopted the policy of nationalizing its key industries since 2007 but has become embroiled in a number of arbitrations at the ICSID. On 4

may also follow suit.[93] These incidents demonstrate the extent to which ideology can contribute to the contraction of a treaty relationship.

Traditionally, a material breach of a treaty by one party could be used by an innocent party to question the reason for the existence of the treaty.[94] However, modern treaty law does not favour this. As noted earlier, Article 60(5) of the VCLT provides that a material breach of a treaty does not affect the application of provisions relating to the protection of the human person contained in treaties of a humanitarian character. While a State may invoke the right of denunciation in the event of a material breach of a bilateral treaty (not a boundary agreement), the same is not true with a multilateral treaty. On the same lines, Judge Fitzmaurice,[95] Sir Ian Sinclair,[96] the US Restatement of the Foreign Relations Law[97] and several other authorities maintain that a material breach is not a valid ground for the unilateral denunciation of a treaty in general. Since denunciation is not an appropriate remedy for a material breach of a human rights treaty, in particular, it is impermissible to denounce such a treaty on the ground of its serious violation even if the treaty as such recognizes the right of denunciation. If 'material breach' were to be allowed to operate as a basis for denunciation, no human rights treaty would survive for long.

The irrelevance of change in the form of the government of a State party or in the persons composing that government is one of the major contributions of juristic opinion, and this has proved to be very useful for dealing with the question of both denunciation of and succession to human rights treaties. It inspired the HRCttee to emphasize the obligation of the former republics of the Soviet Union and Yugoslavia to succeed to the ICCPR after the disintegration of these two socialist States in the early 1990s. However, it is difficult to apply the analogies of human rights treaties to other treaties in general. In practice, the change of government, leadership, or ideology in a country invariably affects its relationship with other countries. Obviously, it is likely to have its effects on some treaties. For instance, in 2008 the change of regime in Nepal led to the renewed demand for the abrogation/revision of the 1950 Treaty of Peace and Friendship between the Government of India and the Government of Nepal,[98] which

December 2007 it notified the Secretary-General of the ICSID under Article 25(4) of the Washington Convention of its intention to withdraw from the jurisdiction of the Centre. Article 25(4) allows a Contracting State to notify the ICSID of the class or classes of disputes which the State would or would not consider submitting to the jurisdiction of the Centre. Search publications at <http://icsid.worldbank.org> (last accessed 10 December 2008).

[93] Above n 91.

[94] See, among others, B P Sinha, *Unilateral Denunciation of Treaty because of Prior Violations of Obligations by other Party* (Martinus Nijhoff Publishers, The Hague, 1966) 207 and 214–5.

[95] Cf Sir Ian Sinclair, *The Vienna Convention on the Law of Treaties* (2nd edn, Manchester University Press, Manchester, 1984) 190 and 201, n 134.

[96] Ibid, 190.

[97] Above n 68, § 335, 217.

[98] Having secured victory in the 2008 parliamentary elections, Maoist leader Pushpa Kamal Dahal 'Prachanda', later the Prime Minister of Nepal, said that 'we want to scrap that treaty [with India]

recognizes the right of denunciation.[99] Thus, a political change may influence diplomatic postures and treaty affairs. This influence may extend to the possibility of a review, revision, or denunciation of a treaty, particularly that of a political nature.

A few studies provide an insight into the causes of denunciation of certain human rights treaties.[100] One common factor is the poor state of human rights in the denouncing States. Besides this sociological dimension, the denunciation clauses of human rights treaties merit scrutiny in the light of their autonomous meaning as well as their relationship with both substantive and procedural obligations of States parties. According to Laurence Helfer, who deals with the denunciation clauses of various kinds of treaties, 'deciding whether and when to invoke these clauses is a concern of government officials when changed circumstances, shifting domestic preferences, or dissatisfaction with treaty-based institutions create tensions between national interests and international commitments'.[101] This observation requires examination in the light of State practice of human rights treaties.

Because incidents of denunciation are not many when compared with instruments of accession or ratification, one may wonder why most treaties escape denunciation. A number of treaties hardly come into operation, and this factor does not justify their denunciation. From diplomatic constraints to practical inconvenience, various factors prevent denunciation. Sometimes, cumbersome denunciation procedure, the lack of a better alternative, or the prospects of success in adapting the treaty regime to the more contemporary expectations of the parties concerned may dissuade them from denouncing the target treaty. For instance, in spite of their dissatisfaction with the 1960 Indus Waters Treaty, neither India nor Pakistan is ready to denounce it. Both States parties consider the dissatisfactory application of the Treaty more acceptable than its denunciation.[102] The involvement of a third party as the guarantor of the Treaty further restrains both States parties from terminating their water relations.[103]

---

and replace it with a new one in the changed context'. See 'Maoists to scrap 1950 Indo-Nepal Treaty', 24 April 2008, <www.rediff.com/news/2008/apr/24nepal.htm> (last accessed 10 December 2008).

[99]   Article 10 of the Indo-Nepal Treaty reads: 'The Treaty shall remain in force until it is terminated by either party by giving one year's notice.' See 94 UNTS 4 (entered into force 31 July 1950).

[100]   For instance, Laurence Helfer has discussed the rationales asserted in connection with the denunciation of the ACHR by Trinidad and Tobago and that of the first ICCPR Protocol by Guyana, Jamaica, and Trinidad and Tobago. See L R Helfer, 'Overlegalizing Human Rights: International Relations Theory and the Commonwealth Caribbean Backlash Against Human Rights Regimes' (2002) 102 *Columbia Law Review* 1832–1911.

[101]   L R Helfer, 'Exiting Treaties' (2005) 91 *Virginia Law Review* 1579, 1647.

[102]   Article 12(4) of the Indus Waters Treaty contains a denunciation clause: 'The provisions of this Treaty ... shall continue in force until terminated by a duly ratified treaty concluded for that purpose between the two Governments.' See (1960) 1 *Indian Journal of International Law* 341, 365.

[103]   The World Bank was instrumental in the adoption of the Indus Waters Treaty and acts as its guarantor in the sense that, in case of a dispute relating to the interpretation and implementation of the Treaty, either party may request the Bank to appoint an arbiter/expert to help settle the dispute.

If the denunciation clause of a treaty cannot help a State party in achieving the objective of ending its treaty obligations effectively, there is no point in denouncing it. For instance, the ECT allows its denunciation along with a provision that in respect of the existing investments the denunciation shall come into effect only after twenty years.[104] The provision for the 20-year waiting period gives the impression that the drafters of the ECT wanted to discourage its unilateral denunciation by a Contracting Party. The absence of any instance of denunciation of the ECT supports this viewpoint. Conceptually, it seems that the waiting period levels the playing field for all States, reducing fear that the remaining States will be taken advantage of, and eliminating any advantage in withdrawing.[105] Considering the stability of expectations of foreign investors, Reisman and Arsanjani express the view that '[t]he withdrawal regime of the ECT is quite logical'.[106] However, this regime is very radical. It is different from other regimes of denunciation. It lacks wider acceptance in the law of treaties.

A study of human rights treaties reveals that the need for the denunciation of such treaties rarely arises. Human rights treaties recognize the right of derogation to meet emergency needs. They grant States parties a margin of appreciation to exercise functional flexibility in normal circumstances. They allow States parties to determine the direction, speed and priority of their implementation measures. Moreover, if a State can bear the accusations of violating its obligations under a treaty, it need not denounce the treaty. As a result, generally, only extraordinary developments trigger the denunciation of a human rights treaty.[107] Since most States consider the continuity of treaty obligations as a demonstration of good faith, they do not want to give up an inherent advantage by taking an extreme action that may attract hostile public attention. That is why a number of States manage their treaty obligations without exercising the right of denunciation. Instead of rushing to formal denunciations of treaties, States with developed systems of law resort to amending domestic legislation, restructuring administrative arrangements, or changing policy prescriptions.[108] Others simply ignore troubling treaties or respect them in breach.

---

[104] ECT, articles 45(3)(*b*) and 47(3).
[105] B Koremenos and A Nau, 'Explaining the Variation in Formal Withdrawal Clauses', presentation at the Annual Convention of the International Studies Association, 28 February–3 March 2007, Chicago, IL, USA, <www.allacademic.com//meta/p_mla_apa_research_citation/1/8/0/9/9/pages180990/p180990-1.php> (last accessed 10 December 2008).
[106] Above n 27, 906.
[107] For a discussion on such cases, see below nn 322–456 and surrounding text.
[108] For instance, following the HRCttee's views in the *Dutch Social Security* cases (for example, *S.W.M. Broeks v Netherlands* (Communication No. 172/1984) and *F.H. Zwaan-de Vries v Netherlands* (Communication No. 182/1984), *Report of the Human Rights Committee*, GAOR, forty-second session (1987), supplement no. 40, UN Doc A/42/40, Annex VIII.B and D, 139–50 and 160–69 respectively), the Netherlands felt obligated to change its law. When Article 26 of the ICCPR became a catchall provision for a number of complaints against the Netherlands, the State party considered the

In sum, the most important reasons for avoiding denunciation of a treaty are the principle of good faith, imperatives of stability, international comity, and diplomatic constraints. Functional necessities, reciprocal benefits, international reputation, and apprehension of retaliatory action also operate as barriers to the denunciation of a treaty. Comparatively, there are always more reasons for continuing with treaty relations than for their termination. Hence, the corpus of formal denunciations remains small.

D. Consequences

The consequences of the denunciation of a treaty depend on a number of factors, such as whether the target treaty is bilateral or multilateral, whether the denunciation is consensual or unilateral, whether it is legal or illegal, and whether the denouncing State and other parties are ready to develop an alternative relationship to their satisfaction. The provisions of the target treaty, the importance of its subject matter, the influence of the denouncing State, and the impact on the interests of the remaining parties also determine the consequences of denunciation.

Generally, lawful countermeasures follow a unilateral denunciation of a bilateral treaty. The affected party may make a claim for compensation, submit the matter to dispute resolution, demand new treaty relations, or embark on another course of action compatible with the Charter of the United Nations. Drawing from municipal law analogies, the law and practice governing the consequences of the denunciation of a bilateral treaty is very rich and sometimes controversial too. In the case of an unlawful denunciation, which is difficult to establish through due process of law, the affected party may have the provocation to resort to peaceful and/or coercive measures if its vital interests are at stake.[109] However, a unilateral coercive action against an unlawful unilateral denunciation is impermissible under international law.

The entire range of consequences of the denunciation of a multilateral treaty is not generally clear from its text. Even the Charter of the United Nations, which establishes the supremacy of its law under Article 103, neither precludes its denunciation nor describes the consequences of its denunciation. The main reasons for the inadequate articulation of the consequences are that few multilateral treaties prohibit denunciation, and that the minimal codification of the applicable rules has been considered

---

possibility of denunciation of the first ICCPR Protocol. A memorandum was submitted to the Dutch Parliament, but the Dutch Government received a legal opinion against denunciation.

[109]   For instance, in 1951 the United Kingdom considered that the Iranian termination of the 1931 oil concession agreement between the Government of Iran and the Anglo-Iranian Oil Company was illegal. It imposed an economic and oil embargo against Iran. This was followed by a *coup d'état* against the Mosaddeq Government of Iran by some Iranian military officers along with the sympathizers of the Anglo-Iranian Oil Company and the establishment of the pro-Western regime of Shah Mohammad Reza Pahlavi. Finally, the *Anglo-Iranian Oil Company* case (*United Kingdom v Iran*) came before the International Court of Justice (ICJ). See [1952] ICJ Rep 93.

a sound approach for dealing with denunciation. Further, the difficulty of obtaining a formal decision from the multilateral forum in charge of the target treaty may dissuade the affected party from taking a strong position against the act of denunciation.

The inapplicability of the provisions of the target treaty to the denouncing State is one of the main consequences of denunciation. There are two exceptions: first, if the provisions of the target treaty have become part of customary rules or peremptory norms of international law, the denouncing State cannot escape their application; and secondly, the denunciation of a treaty need not necessarily affect its dispute settlement clause, if such a clause exists. While the first exception demands an extensive exercise with considerable scope for disagreement,[110] the second involves the principle of fairness. In the context of commercial contracts, Reisman explains:

[T]he "sanctity of contracts" is too simplistic a policy notion. The importance of honoring agreements and the extent to which they should be honored in each case is relative to numerous contextual demands. An unfair or demonstrably unequal agreement should not be honored. If the inequality extends to the compromissary aspects of the agreement, the jurisdictional component as well should be susceptible to denunciation. Hence the entire compromissary process must be examined in order to determine whether it is so unfair to one of the parties as to merit denunciation. The effects of denunciation must also be considered.[111]

This formula rejects the application of a general rule either in favour or against the continuing validity of a dispute settlement clause after the denunciation of an international contract. Indeed, it is a judicious approach towards bilateral commercial contracts. In spite of its sensitivity towards the principle of fairness, however, the Reisman formula seems to be inapplicable to a multilateral treaty. It may not serve community interests by denying the possibility of a denunciation-related dispute resolution by a designated body under the auspices of a multilateral treaty. As a result, for a limited purpose, the dispute settlement clause of a multilateral treaty may survive its unilateral denunciation. There is some jurisprudence to support this impression,[112] although one can cite some cases to prove the contrary as well. Therefore, it is incumbent upon the denouncing State to make a special case for obtaining the complete frustration of its specific multilateral treaty relationship.

There are several studies on the consequences of denunciation of treaties, but most of these mix up 'breach' and 'denunciation', as well as 'effect' and 'remedy'. For instance, Lord McNair identified the consequences

---

[110] See, among others, T Meron, *Human Rights and Humanitarian Norms as Customary Law* (Clarendon Press, Oxford, 1989).

[111] W M Reisman, *Nullity and Revision: The Review and Enforcement of International Judgments and Awards* (Yale University Press, New Haven, 1971) 357–58.

[112] See, for example, the *Appeal Relating to the Jurisdiction of the ICAO Council* case (*India v Pakistan*), below n 268.

of, and remedies for, the breach of a treaty. According to him, these consequences-cum-remedies are the right of unilateral abrogation; retaliatory suspension of performance; the right to receive reparation and to institute arbitral or judicial proceedings; the right to take certain non-forcible measures to secure reparation; the right to invoke sanctions, if any, stipulated in the treaty; and the right in certain circumstances to prosecute individuals.[113] There is a need to draw attention to each aspect of denunciation and its consequences.

Making a distinction between 'breach' and 'denunciation', Helfer points out the reputational consequences of denunciation of a treaty and highlights the unseen benefits associated with denunciation.[114] He observes that '[a]n exiting state faces different burdens and benefits, different prospects of being sanctioned, different reputational consequences, and different responses by other parties than a state that breaches an international agreement'.[115] Influenced by game theory, he claims that the denunciation of a treaty 'helps to resolve certain theoretical and doctrinal puzzles that have long troubled scholars of international affairs'.[116] Obviously, he treats the denunciation of a treaty as a fresh opportunity to rearrange international relations in a given field. This viewpoint is unlikely to impress human rights advocates, who consider the integrity of human rights treaties inviolable.

Some commentators deal with the consequences of denunciation of the ACHR,[117] the ICCPR,[118] and the first ICCPR Protocol.[119] While a few calculate the damage to the cause of human rights after the denunciations of these treaties,[120] fewer look at the brighter side that an accession with a reservation is better than an act of denunciation.[121] Reisman and Arsanjani enquire into the direct and indirect, immediate and distant, and legal and other consequences of the United States' withdrawal from the optional jurisdiction of the ICJ under the 1963 Optional Protocol to the Vienna Convention on Consular Relations Concerning the Compulsory Settlement of Disputes (the VCCR Protocol).[122] They point out that the withdrawal from the Protocol has not affected the substantive obligations of the United States under the

---

[113]   McNair, above n 7, 539–80.   [114]   Helfer, above n 101, 1621–28.
[115]   Ibid, 1582.
[116]   Ibid, 1579.
[117]   See, for instance, N Parassram Concepcion, 'The Legal Implications of Trinidad & Tobago's Withdrawal from the American Convention on Human Rights' (2001) 16 *American University International Law Review* 847, 879–84.
[118]   See, for instance, I Boerefijn, 'Denunciations of Human Rights Instruments Jeopardise Universal Ratification' (1998) 16 *Netherlands Quarterly of Human Rights* 3–4.
[119]   See, for instance, N Schiffrin, 'Current Development: Jamaica Withdraws the Right of Individual Petition under the International Covenant on Civil and Political Rights' (1998) 92 *American Journal of International Law* 563–67.
[120]   See, for instance, Parassram Concepcion, above n 117.
[121]   See, for instance, G McGrory, 'Reservations of Virtue? Lessons from Trinidad and Tobago's Reservation to the First Optional Protocol' (2001) 23 *Human Rights Quarterly* 769–826.
[122]   Above n 27.

VCCR, which enshrines certain human rights. As for the procedural obligations, Reisman and Arsanjani observe an uncertain legal outcome, which
depends on whether the VCCR is regarded as a human rights treaty and
whether the withdrawal is questioned before the ICJ. In general, they consider that the consequences of an act of denunciation considerably depend
on the exercise of 'power' by the denouncing State. As a result, '[i]t is possible that a state caught in an optional dispute resolution mechanism whose
gate-keepers decree has "no exit" will simply tear its own way out by ignoring the decisions of the court or tribunal that purports to operate under
it'.[123] By implication, the impact of a unilateral denunciation on the target
treaty remains a matter of curiosity not confined to a legal analysis. In any
case, it is difficult to justify a unilateral coercive action as a response to the
denunciation of a treaty.

The denunciation of a treaty may lead to its termination altogether in
certain situations. Article 15 of the Genocide Convention illustrates this:

If, as a result of denunciations, the number of Parties to the present Convention
should become less than sixteen, the Convention shall cease to be in force as from
the date on which the last of these denunciations shall become effective.

Considering this situation a special case, however, the UN Handbook on
Final Clauses states that '[u]nless the treaty otherwise provides, a multilateral treaty does not terminate by the reason only that the number of
parties falls below the number necessary for its entry into force'.[124] This
observation seeks to reduce the negative impact of an act of denunciation.

Concisely, the consequences of denunciation of a treaty need not necessarily follow a cause-and-effect approach. The law of denunciation does
not have complete control over the consequences of denunciation. A general impression is that, unlike a collective denunciation, a unilateral
denunciation does not lead to healthy developments. While the legal consequences of a valid denunciation are relatively simple and predictable,
other consequences depend on innumerable variables. In case of a controversy over the validity of an act of denunciation, an uncertain legal
outcome is inevitable. Generally, lack of certainty about consequences
operates as a constraint on the decision of a State to denounce a treaty.

E. Issues

The denunciation of a treaty involves a host of issues. Some issues are
general and others peculiar to the target treaty. Whether the act of denunciation follows the provisions of the target treaty is always the first and
foremost issue. The most contentious issue is whether a State has an
implied right of denunciation in the absence of an express provision.
Further, whether a material breach of a treaty, a fundamental change of

---

[123] Ibid, 926.   [124] Above n 8, 117.

circumstances, or a threat to the vital interests of a State party can allow it to invoke the right of denunciation remains a matter of debate. There is an issue as to whether a fundamental change of circumstances relates to facts only or extends to law as well. The period of the notice of denunciation and the role of the depository of the instruments of signature/ratification/accession/succession are issues when the target treaty contains no denunciation clause.

Identifying the consequences of denunciation is a practical problem, especially when the target treaty contains customary law obligations, general principles of law, peremptory norms, or basic rules of a minimum world public order. The question of consequences is critical when the beneficiaries or trustees of the target treaty oppose its denunciation. The response of the beneficiaries and trustees of the target treaty to an act of denunciation and its impact on domestic and international law, particularly when treaty obligations need no further incorporation in domestic law, raise their own important issues.

Given the implied powers of international institutions,[125] the role of the treaty monitoring body in denunciation matters acquires special significance. This role becomes crucial in cases of a nexus between denunciations and reservations. Besides the limits of implied powers, the objectivity of the monitoring body remains a perennial issue. Where there is no monitoring body, the choice of forum to raise questions concerning the consequences of denunciation is an issue by itself.

The possibility of a conflict between the nature and certain provisions of the target treaty, between the nature of the target treaty and the intention of the parties to that treaty, between the soft law of the treaty monitoring body and the intention of the parties, or between the *lex specialis* and the Vienna regime presents an image of some prospective issues. Moreover, an act of denunciation may give rise to some unpredictable issues even beyond the scope of the target treaty. In any case, how to minimize the damage to the target treaty is likely to be an issue for those States parties that want to continue with their treaty relationship. In brief, the issues involved in the denunciation of a treaty may engage both domestic and international law and also extraneous and unpredictable considerations.

F. Synthesis

Technically, the term 'denunciation' signifies a specific act (a formal statement), by a specific limb of a State (the executive government), and for a specific purpose (the end of a treaty relationship). In this conception, both the source and the effect of the statement are equally important. In substance, however, who makes a statement is not as important

---

[125] See, among others, R Khan, *Implied Powers of the United Nations* (Vikas Publications, Delhi, 1970).

as its effect. The law of treaties is good at generalities, obsessed with formalities, and weak at confronting realities in the field of human rights. It considers that denunciation is merely an executive act. This understanding emerges from traditional thinking, prevalent practice and practical convenience. However, a deeper understanding of State practice shows that the role of the executive in respect of human rights treaties is crucial but that the legislature and the judiciary play an equally important role in many cases. This reality does not find recognition in the law of denunciation. That is why the concept of denunciation has considerable scope for development. The concept needs a host of clarifications regarding the meaning, manifestations, and several other aspects of denunciation.

The term 'denunciation' has several synonyms in the law of treaties, but not all of them are in use in human rights law. Human rights treaties use only two terms: denunciation and withdrawal. While denunciation reduces or eliminates the substantive obligations of the denouncing State or its subjection to monitoring or adjudication procedures, withdrawal affects the procedural obligations of the State. Sometimes, the denouncing State may use the term 'withdrawal' for its act of denunciation.[126] When the procedural obligations as such constitute the exclusive subject matter of a treaty, the withdrawal of a State from those obligations may amount to an act of denunciation. That is why a State party's withdrawal from the individual communication procedure of the first ICCPR Protocol is an act of denunciation, whereas the same action against the same procedure of the ICERD is merely a withdrawal. If a treaty is silent on this matter, the choice of term is the prerogative of the denouncing State.[127] Indeed, other States parties are free to make objections.

A State party to a treaty may accomplish its objectives in connection with the treaty by any branch of its government. Any branch of a government may violate a treaty. Likewise, any limb of a State may target a treaty in a manner that is as prejudicial to the treaty as its denunciation. As a result, there is a possibility of legislative or judicial action against a treaty without the tag of denunciation. It is true that the law of treaties does not recognize a legislative or judicial denunciation, but the situation is different at the domestic level. In any case, the possibility of a legislative denunciation cannot be dismissed as a legal fiction. Since international law recognizes only an executive denunciation, there is a tendency

---

[126]   See, for example, below n 376 and surrounding text.
[127]   For instance, Senegal used the term 'denunciation' for its withdrawal from the 1958 Convention on the Territorial Sea and the Contiguous Zone, the 1958 Convention on the Living Resources of the High Seas (see <http://treaties.un.org/Pages/ViewDetails.aspx?src=TREATY&id=454&chapter=21& lang=en> (last accessed 31 January 2009)), and the 1958 Convention on the Continental Shelf (see <http://treaties.un.org/Pages/ViewDetails.aspx?src=TREATY&id=457&chapter=21&lang=en> (last accessed 31 January 2009)). In contrast, the United States employed the term 'withdrawal' while denouncing the VCCR Protocol (see <http://treaties.un.org/Pages/ViewDetails.aspx?src=TREATY& id=238&chapter=3&lang=en> (last accessed 31 January 2009)).

to treat a legislative or judicial denunciation as a case of inappropriate State practice not amounting to denunciation *stricto sensu*. This is a reasonable interpretation, but it seems to focus on the form rather than the substance of the act in question. A legislative denunciation may not be an act of denunciation for international law purposes, but this makes little difference for the purpose of domestic law. Just as a domestic court may declare an executive act or legislation invalid, it may also declare an instrument of accession or ratification invalid. Although there are not many examples of this kind, the isolated ones indicate the need to revisit the concept of denunciation.[128]

Several reasons require the present study to employ the term 'denunciation' in a restrictive sense, implying an action taken by the executive. First, the law of treaties is designed to deal with an executive denunciation, not a legislative or judicial denunciation. Secondly, States are unwilling to introduce any radical change in the law of treaties. Thirdly, considering the expansion of the term 'treaty', the complexities of the law of treaties are already too many, and a flexible use of the term 'denunciation' may compound them. Fourthly, while promoting a better understanding of State practice with regard to human rights treaties, a flexible use of the term 'denunciation' is unlikely to lead to the reconfiguration of the rights and obligations enshrined in those treaties. Fifthly, domestic legislative, judicial or political acts rejecting the application of a treaty or some or all of its substantive obligations are analytically distinct from formal acts of denunciation for the purposes of the law of treaties. Concisely, the present study subscribes to the conventional meaning of the term 'denunciation' without neglecting the need to better capture its sense with a focus on the process surrounding the act of denunciation.

The identification of the causes of denunciation of a treaty may help in addressing them, thus paving the way for bringing the denouncing State back into the fold of the treaty. It is a challenging task to trace the causes of denunciation if the denouncing State fails to explain them. Even an official statement may not help much, as the denouncing State may not be forthcoming in sharing information on its internal deliberations regarding denunciation. Transparency in governance, freedom of the press, and a healthy civil society may help in this regard. An extensive analysis of the State practice of denunciations and surrounding circumstances may also help identify both causes and consequences of denunciations. While the consequences of denunciation of a human rights treaty are mostly negative, the merits or demerits of denunciation of other treaties are arguable. The denunciation of a treaty involves a number of issues, which may vary from case to case. A study of the law applicable to those issues is the subject matter of the next part.

---

[128]   See, for example, the *Singarasa* case, above n 60 and surrounding text.

III. THE LAW OF DENUNCIATION

Generally, essaying the law on a particular subject matter can never be too precise. The law of treaties is no exception. Sir Hersch Lauterpacht noted this point well before the conclusion of the VCLT:

> [O]nce we approach at close quarters practically any branch of international law, we are driven, amidst some feeling of incredulity, to the conclusion that although there is as a rule a consensus of opinion on broad principle—even this may be an overestimate in some cases—there is no semblance of agreement in relation to specific rules and problems. Thus, for instance, with regard to the law of treaties, perhaps the only principle of wider import as to which there is no dissent is that treaties ought to be fulfilled in good faith. Even that statement is accurate only if we reduce the emanations of the so-called *rebus sic stantibus* doctrine to the manageable confines of a general principle of law applied by an international tribunal at the instance of the state which claims to be released from the treaty on account of a change in vital circumstances. Apart from that general and unavoidable acceptance of the basic principle, *Pacta sunt servanda,* there is little agreement and there is much discord at almost every point.[129]

The underlying message of this observation remains true even today, to wit, it is difficult to expect too much precision in any normative analysis. Keeping this constraint in perspective, there is a need to explore the law of denunciation beyond its generalities in order to serve the cause of human rights.

Broadly, the main sources of the law of denunciation consist of customary law, general treaty law, human rights treaty law, international labour law, soft law, and case law. Since a rich body of literature on the law of treaties is already available, a brief discussion of customary law and general treaty law may be adequate to facilitate an elaborate study of the human rights treaty law on denunciation. Further, international labour law offers useful analogies for human rights law. The applicable soft law considerably supplements the law of human rights treaties, especially where denunciation clauses are absent, ambiguous, inadequate, or outdated. Relevant case law helps us to appreciate the issues involved in the law of denunciation in the context of a specific set of facts. The case law on denunciation involving human rights is too modest but still worthy of consideration. The limited literature on the denunciation of human rights treaties provides perspectives on some aspects of State practice. There is scope for a conflict of opinion on the relative significance of the applicable sources of law. An examination of all these sources may enable us to understand the essence of applicable law and to evaluate the practice of denunciation of human rights treaties.

---

[129] H Lauterpacht, 'Codification and Development of International Law' (1955) 49 *American Journal of International Law* 16, 17.

A. Customary Law

Customary law is evidence of State practice, a part of the domestic law of several States, and a recipient of scholarly attention. Yet, it is not easy to reach consensus on what rules have become part of customary law. A perceptive commentator rightly observes: 'An impediment to effective participation in the process of identifying the customary rule is that many developing states do not publish or record their practices in international affairs.'[130] As a result, State practice emanating from developed States remains the principal evidence of the customary rule. This is hardly a scientific method of identifying customary rules in the age of globalization. The process of codification brings some transparency in the course of identifying customary rules. Happily, the law of treaties has been a beneficiary of this process.

Most of the customary rules relating to the law of treaties find expression in a series of instruments, ranging from the 1871 London Declaration[131] to the 1986 Vienna Convention on the Law of Treaties between States and International Organizations or between International Organizations (the Second VCLT).[132] Whether the VCLT's provisions on the denunciation of treaties have the status of customary rules has been a matter of debate,[133] although there is a momentum in favour of treating most of the Convention as an embodiment of customary law.[134] The identification of the customary law of denunciation is an indispensable exercise in the event of a denunciation of a treaty without a denunciation clause. To avoid repetition, it seems appropriate to study the customary law on denunciation along with an analysis of the written law on the subject in the following section.

B. General Treaty Law

There are innumerable treaties of a wide variety. Some of these are not even registered. In the absence of any comprehensive data on treaties, it is not easy to get a clear picture of treaty practice on the various types of

---

[130] G D Triggs, *International Law: Contemporary Principles and Practices* (LexisNexis Butterworths, Sydney, 2006) 61.

[131] For details, see D J Bederman, 'The 1871 London Declaration, Rebus Sic Stantibus and a Primitivist View of the Law of Nations' (1988) 82 *American Journal of International Law* 1–40.

[132] On 21 March 1986 the Second VCLT was adopted at Vienna. As of 31 January 2009, there are 39 signatories and 40 parties to the Convention. The Convention shall come into force following the date of deposit of the thirty-fifth instrument of ratification or accession by States. International organizations, which are party to the Convention, are not counted for entry into force purposes. Because only 28 States are parties to the Second VCLT as of 31 January 2009, the Convention has not yet entered into force. Search <http://treaties.un.org> (last accessed 31 January 2009).

[133] See, among others, M E Villiger, *Customary International Law and Treaties: A Manual on the Theory and Practice of the Interrelation of Sources* (2nd edn, Kluwer Law International, The Hague, 1997); and N Kontou, *The Termination and Revision of Treaties in the Light of New Customary International Law* (Clarendon Press, Oxford, 1994).

[134] See, among others, Aust, above n 6, 11.

provisions on denunciation. Broadly, there are seven types of denunciation clauses in the treaties concluded under the auspices of the Council of
Europe, the ILO, and the United Nations:

(*a*)   Treaties that permit denunciation at any time;
(*b*)   Treaties that preclude denunciation for a fixed number of years,
        calculated either from the date the agreement enters into force or
        from the date of ratification by the State;
(*c*)   Treaties that permit denunciation only at fixed time intervals;
(*d*)   Treaties that may be a subject of denunciation only on a single
        occasion, identified either by time period or upon the occurrence of
        a particular event;
(*e*)   Treaties whose denunciation occurs automatically upon the State's
        ratification of a subsequently negotiated agreement;
(*f*)   Treaties that are silent on denunciation; and
(*g*)   Treaties that are silent on denunciation of their substantive parts
        but contain a provision for withdrawal from their procedural
        arrangements.[135]

One can draw some general conclusions from treaty practice concerning
denunciation. First, treaties with a provision for denunciation are common. Secondly, treaties that expressly preclude unilateral denunciation are
uncommon. Thirdly, boundary agreements and other territorial settlements are generally presumed to be permanent. Fourthly, there is no uniform pattern of denunciation clauses even within a uniform category of
treaties. Fifthly, treaty provisions on withdrawal from procedural arrangements are clearer than those governing the denunciation of substantive
matters. Sixthly, procedural obligations in the exercise of the right of
denunciation are weaker than those applicable to implementation measures and reservation matters. Seventhly, denunciation clauses incorporate
certain safety valves to prevent an abrupt disruption of relations between
the denouncing States and other parties. Finally, the scope of safety valves
has some influence on a decision pertaining to denunciation.

    Treaty making is an ancient practice, but the codification of the law of
treaties is a relatively recent phenomenon. The 1871 London Declaration
by seven European States (Austria, Germany, Hungary, Italy, Great Britain,
Russia, and Turkey) was an initial attempt to enunciate the customary
principle of international law on denunciation.[136] By subjecting the unilateral denunciation of a treaty to the consent of all the parties to the treaty,
the 1871 Declaration represented a rather rigid position on this matter.[137]
Interestingly, most States maintained this position for a long time[138] and

---

[135]   Adapted from Helfer, above n 101, 1597.
[136]   Reisman and Arsanjani, above n 27, 907.
[137]   For details, see Bederman, above n 131.
[138]   Widdows, above n 10, 94.

a few hold it even now.[139] In fact, in 1997 the UN Secretary-General took a similar position in respect of the denunciation of the ICCPR by the Democratic People's Republic of Korea (DPRK).[140] Thus, the consent of the parties as a criterion for determining the validity of denunciation of the target treaty is a lasting contribution of the 1871 Declaration.

The 1928 Havana Convention on Treaties was the maiden exercise to codify the law of treaties.[141] Though applicable only to a small number of Latin American States (Brazil, Dominican Republic, Ecuador, Haiti, Honduras, Nicaragua, Panama, and Peru), it did include rules governing treaty denunciation. In spite of their outdated formulation, these rules help understand the development of ideas on the subject. Articles 10 and 14(D) of the Havana Convention provided the possibility of denunciation of a treaty by the agreement of the contracting parties.[142] Article 14(F) envisaged total or partial denunciation of a treaty if agreed upon by the contracting parties.[143] Most important, Article 17 stipulated:

Treaties whose denunciation may have been agreed upon and those establishing rules of international law, can be denounced only in the manner provided thereby.

In the absence of such a stipulation, a treaty may be denounced by any contracting State, which State shall notify the others of this decision, provided it has complied with all obligations covenanted therein.

In this event the treaty shall become ineffective, as far as the denouncing State is concerned, one year after the last notification, and will continue in force for any other signatory States, if any.[144]

Article 17 contained the seeds of some of the provisions of the modern law on denunciation. The percentage of the provisions dealing with denunciation was very high in the Havana Convention. This implied that the denunciation of treaties in the Americas was not considered incompatible with the application of the principle of *pacta sunt servanda* during the period preceding the Havana Convention. Certainly, human rights treaties were not the focus of attention during that period.

The VCLT embodies the most authoritative statement of law on treaties. While most of the provisions of the VCLT amount to the codification of

---

[139]   See, for instance, § 332 of the *US Restatement of the Foreign Relations Law*, above n 68 and below n 160 and surrounding text.

[140]   For the notification of withdrawal and the aide-mémoire of the Secretary-General, see UN Doc C.N.467.1997.TREATIES-10 (12 November 1997), noted at <http://treaties.un.org/Pages/ViewDetails.aspx?src=TREATY&id=322&chapter=4&lang=en> (last accessed 31 January 2009).

[141]   The Sixth International Conference of the International Commission of American Jurists adopted the Havana Convention in 1927. For details, see O J Lissitzyn, 'Efforts to Codify or Restate the Law of Treaties' (1962) 62 *Columbia Law Review* 1166, n 4.

[142]   (1935) 29 *American Journal of International Law, Supplement*, 1206.

[143]   Ibid.

[144]   Ibid, 1207.

the customary rules of international law, some provisions represent a 'progressive' development with considerable scope for conflict of opinion. The provisions relating to the denunciation of treaties fall in the mixed category; some of them are simple formulations (as, for example, the requirement of notice) while others are difficult propositions (as, for example, the implied right of denunciation). Even some simple formulations have scope for controversy; for example, there are three options in respect of the requirement of notice, namely, three months (Article 65), twelve months (Article 56(2)), and 'cases of special urgency' (Article 65). That is why it is not considered appropriate to regard the notice-related provisions as declaratory of existing law.[145] In the absence of an express stipulation, the reasonable period of notice depends on the facts and circumstances of the denunciation of the treaty relationship in question.

The VCLT envisages the possibility of denunciation or termination of or withdrawal from a treaty under the following conditions:

(a)   In accordance with the provisions of the treaty (Articles 42(2) and 54(a));
(b)   In accordance with the provisions of the VCLT (Article 42(2));
(c)   By consent of the parties to the treaty (Article 54(b));
(d)   Based on the intention of the parties to the treaty (Article 56(1)(a));
(e)   Based on the nature of the treaty (Article 56(1)(b));
(f)   By conclusion of a later treaty relating to the same subject-matter (Article 59);
(g)   As a consequence of a material breach of the treaty (Article 60);
(h)   Owing to the impossibility of performing the treaty (Article 61(1));
(i)   Owing to a fundamental change of circumstances (Article 62(1)); or
(j)   Owing to incompatibility with a new peremptory norm of international law (Article 64).

Broadly, the VCLT divides the applicable law into two categories: the law of denunciation of a treaty with a denunciation clause, and the law of denunciation of a treaty without a denunciation clause. As for validity and continuance in force of treaties belonging to the first category, Article 42 of the VCLT states:

1.   The validity of a treaty or of the consent of a State to be bound by a treaty may be impeached only through the application of the present Convention.
2.   The termination of a treaty, its denunciation or the withdrawal of a party, may take place only as a result of the application of the provisions of the treaty or of the present Convention. The same rule applies to suspension of the operation of a treaty.

---

[145] H Thirlway, 'The Law and Procedure of the International Court of Justice 1960–1989. Supplement, 2007: Parts Four, Five and Six' (2007) 78 *British Year Book of International Law* 17, 86.

This article is a partial codification of customary law relating to denunciation.[146] On the other hand, the uncustomary formulation of Article 56 of the VCLT deals with the validity and continuance in force of treaties without a denunciation clause:

1.   A treaty which contains no provision regarding its termination and which does not provide for denunciation or withdrawal is not subject to denunciation or withdrawal unless:
    (a)   it is established that the parties intended to admit the possibility of denunciation or withdrawal; or
    (b)   a right of denunciation or withdrawal may be implied by the nature of the treaty.
2.   A party shall give not less than twelve months' notice of its intention to denounce or withdraw from a treaty under paragraph 1.

In particular, subparagraph 1(b) did not appear in the text of the article prepared by the International Law Commission (ILC). It was proposed by the United Kingdom delegation and inserted by the Drafting Committee at the Vienna Conference on the Law of Treaties by the smallest possible majority.[147] Initially, there was weak support for the inclusion of the right of implied denunciation. When the Committee of the Whole discussed the draft, the representative of Finland said that the subparagraph 'introduced an element of uncertainty into article 53 [Article 56 of the VCLT] and thus weakened the principle of the stability of treaties'.[148] Therefore, he asked for a separate vote on the subparagraph, in the hope that it would be deleted. However, the Committee of the Whole approved the subparagraph by an overwhelming majority.[149] This change in the voting behaviour of States was not an indication of any transformation in the normative status of the right of implied denunciation; it merely reflected the dynamics of conference diplomacy.

Finally, the conflict of views on subparagraph 1(b) resurfaced in the plenary of the Vienna Conference. The United Kingdom delegation argued that a broadening of the availability of implied denunciation would lessen the likelihood of resort to the more drastic grounds of termination set forth in the VCLT.[150] On the other hand, the Australian delegation doubted whether it was a good reason for inserting a ground of

---

[146]   The reference to 'the present Convention' in Article 42 indicates the absence of the customary law character of this provision because there was no VCLT earlier.

[147]   The proposal was adopted by 26 votes in favour, 25 against, and 37 abstentions. See United Nations Conference on the Law of Treaties (Second session, Vienna, 9 April–22 May 1969), *Summary Records of the Plenary Meetings and of the Meetings of the Committee of the Whole*, Vol 2 (United Nations, New York, 1970), UN Doc A/CONF.39/11/Add.1, 109 (hereinafter *'Vienna Conference Records II'*).

[148]   United Nations Conference on the Law of Treaties (First session, Vienna, 26 March–24 May 1968), *Summary Records of the Plenary Meetings and of the Meetings of the Committee of the Whole*, Vol 1 (United Nations, New York, 1969), UN Doc A/CONF.39/11, 477.

[149]   The subparagraph was adopted by 73 votes to 2, with 4 abstentions. Ibid.

[150]   *Vienna Conference Records II*, above n 147, 109.

termination in the VCLT.[151] It therefore called for a separate vote on the subparagraph, whereas the Cuban delegation opposed the motion. This was an interesting situation where the question of denunciation brought Cuba closer to the United Kingdom than its Commonwealth family member Australia. To facilitate the Conference's work, the Australian delegation decided not to press for a separate vote. As a result, the plenary adopted Article 53 (Article 56 of the VCLT) without any opposition. The Cuban delegation justified it as follows:

The article struck a proper balance between the subjective and objective elements involved in setting a term to treaties which contained no provision regarding termination, denunciation or withdrawal. Article 53, considered as a whole, made a positive contribution to the progressive development of international law by curbing the abusive practice of perpetual treaties, the purpose of which was to impose a policy enabling the strong to dominate the weak. A treaty of indefinite duration could now be brought to an end by application of the *rebus sic stantibus* clause implicit in all such treaties. History showed how circumstances could change fundamentally in a comparatively short period of time. Again, the right to withdraw from a treaty was a factual matter which was necessarily governed by the circumstances of each particular case, especially by reference to the character of the treaty.[152]

From the opposite side, the representative of Italy stated that 'the provision in subparagraph 1(*b*) enabling a party to invoke the nature of a treaty in order to denounce it or to withdraw from it held a danger for the stability of treaties'.[153] He submitted that '[t]he provision was incompatible with the principle of *pacta sunt servanda*'.[154] Since then, it remains arguable whether the provision envisaging the right of implied denunciation is really a 'progressive' development of international law. According to Michael Akehurst, the provision reflects the views of most British writers, but many Continental writers think that there could never be an implied right of denunciation under customary international law.[155] He observes:

The rules of law concerning the termination of treaties try to steer a middle course between the two extremes of rigidity and insecurity. They work fairly well, because every State is a party to hundreds of treaties on a wide range of topics, and therefore has an interest in ensuring that the right balance between security and flexibility is maintained in practice.[156]

Not many commentators share the view that the VCLT's rules on denunciation work 'fairly well'.[157] Yet, Article 56 of the VCLT mirrors Article 56 of the Second VCLT.[158] Also, the UN Handbook on Final Clauses

---

[151] Ibid.   [152] Ibid.   [153] Ibid, 110.   [154] Ibid.
[155] M Akehurst, 'Treaties, Termination' in R Bernhardt (ed) *Encyclopaedia of Public International Law*, Vol 7 (North-Holland, Amsterdam, 1984) 507.
[156] Ibid.
[157] Among the critics are Arsanjani, Reisman and Widdows. Above nn 10 and 27.
[158] Visit <http://untreaty.un.org/ilc/texts/instruments/english/conventions/1_2_1986.pdf> (last accessed 10 December 2008).

reaffirms Article 56.[159] In the same spirit, § 332 of the US Restatement of the Foreign Relations Law consolidates VCLT Articles 42 and 56:

(1) The termination or denunciation of an international agreement, or the withdrawal of a party from an agreement, may take place only
  (a) in conformity with the agreement or
  (b) by consent of all the parties.
(2) An agreement that does not provide for termination or denunciation or for the withdrawal of a party is not subject to such action unless the right to take such action is implied by the nature of the agreement or from other circumstances.[160]

In comparison to the VCLT, the US Restatement accords greater importance to the consent of the parties to a treaty by presenting the consent test as an alternative criterion for denunciation in conformity with that treaty. Also, it provides wider scope to the implied right of denunciation by referring to 'other circumstances', which is an open expression. Accordingly, the intention of the parties to a treaty, the nature of the treaty and other circumstances become the alternative criteria for its denunciation in the absence of an express provision and common consent. How to ascertain the intention of the parties, how to determine the nature of a treaty, how to know the details of behind-the-scenes negotiations, and who will perform all these tasks remain difficult questions. Myres McDougal presented a complex prescription to deal with some of them:

Where it is impossible to determine the genuine shared expectations of the parties [to a treaty], the decision-maker has the task of augmenting such expectations in the light of community policies; we might call this a task of supplementation. Where the shared expectations of the parties run counter to community policies, the decision-maker must exercise an integrating or policing function. These are not, however, mutually exclusive.[161]

Emphasizing that '[e]verything is changing, including the demands and expectations of the parties and outside circumstances', McDougal 'counselled a search for the facts: the kind of agreement which is in question (is it a treaty on human rights? ...)'.[162] Widdows holds that these considerations are more in the nature of 'political guides' to a decision maker; that they are not indications of intent or of 'nature'; and that they are indications of alteration in expectation.[163] According to him:

Such an interpretation would allow a large number of external considerations to be imported into a dispute about a right of unilateral denunciation, thus confusing the rule with those of termination under the doctrine of *rebus sic stantibus* or impossibility of performance. It would indeed turn Article 56 into a minor *clausula*

---

[159] Above n 8, 112.   [160] Above n 68, 209.
[161] *Proceedings of the American Society of International Law at its Sixty-first Annual Meeting, held at Washington, D.C., April 27–29, 1967* (American Society of International Law, Washington, 1967) 204.
[162] Ibid, 204–205.   [163] Above n 10, 113.

rebus sic stantibus and would more than negative the whole justification of the rule as a certain residual rule to be applied in cases where the particular treaty in question is silent on the point.[164]

This is a cautious reflection on the potential policy-oriented interpretations of the 'nature' test and 'other circumstances'. Obviously, it points out the possibility of conflicts arising out of the inadequacies of the Vienna regime on denunciation. In spite of those inadequacies, Anthony Aust reaffirms Sir Arthur Watts's statement that the contemporary law of treaties is authoritatively set out in the VCLT.[165] Widdows does not share this opinion: '[T]he Vienna Conference, the *fons et origo* of contemporary treaty law and practice, failed to provide an absolute rule on the question of unilateral denunciation of treaties not containing a governing clause. More than that, it provided a rule of uncertain content and ambit and may have clouded the issue for ever.'[166] This is a brief evaluation of a limited aspect of the Vienna regime on denunciation. It gives little confidence about the Vienna regime, which is the mainstay of the modern law of treaties.

On the one hand, the VCLT reflects considerable sophistication through its various formulations such as the special treatment of treaties of a humanitarian character (Article 60(5)), the separability of treaty provisions (Article 44), and distinguishing the law on denunciation of a bilateral treaty from that of a multilateral treaty (Article 60(1) and (2)). On the other, it creates a cloud of confusion over the classification of treaties based on the nature of each one of them. It leaves the question of the nature of the target treaty wide open, thus allowing a number of uncertain processes and products to occupy the huge normative space. It contains an ambiguous provision on the intention of the 'parties' as a relevant factor in the matter of denunciation. While recognizing the intention of the parties and the nature of the treaty as alternatives for determining the admissibility of denunciation, the VCLT does not indicate which of them shall prevail in case of a conflict. It has no safeguard against capricious denunciations. Obviously, the VCLT does not enshrine the entire body of law on denunciation. Nor is it of universal application. Most important, it is not in many respects in conformity with international human rights law.[167] Besides the VCLT, therefore, there is a need to search for an appropriate body of law in the province of human rights regimes.

C. Human Rights Treaty Law

There are many human rights treaties at both international and regional levels, but few at the bilateral level. Like a number of other treaties, human rights treaties are not uniform with regard to the question of

---

[164] Ibid, 113–14.   [165] Above n 6, 11.   [166] Above n 10, 83.
[167] The continuity of obligations, reservations to treaties, rules of interpretation, and succession to treaties are some of the areas where the VCLT does not meet the special requirements of a human rights regime.

denunciation. While most of the African human rights treaties have no provision on denunciation, most of the European and Inter-American human rights conventions incorporate denunciation clauses. Even the 'core' UN human rights treaties do not present a uniform position on denunciation.[168] Some permit denunciation at any time. Some others allow denunciation only after the expiry of a certain period. Quite a few have scope for withdrawal from their procedural arrangements. Just a few are silent on denunciation or withdrawal altogether. Ranging from the first to the latest 'core' treaties, a majority of them recognize the right of denunciation. These are:

(a) The ICERD (Article 21);[169]
(b) The Convention against Torture and Other Cruel, Inhuman or Degrading Treatment or Punishment, 1984 (CAT) (Article 31);[170]
(c) The Convention on the Rights of the Child, 1989 (CORC) (Article 52);[171]
(d) The International Convention on the Protection of the Rights of All Migrant Workers and Members of Their Families, 1990 (ICRMW) (Article 89);[172]
(e) The Convention on the Rights of Persons with Disabilities, 2006 (ICRPD) (Article 48);[173]
(f) First ICCPR Protocol (Article 12);[174]
(g) The ICESCR Protocol (Article 20);[175]
(h) Optional Protocol to the Convention on the Elimination of All Forms of Discrimination against Women, 1999 (Article 19);[176]
(i) Optional Protocol to the Convention on the Rights of the Child on the involvement of children in armed conflict, 2000 (Article 11);[177]
(j) Optional Protocol to the Convention on the Rights of the Child on the sale of children, child prostitution and child pornography, 2000 (Article 15);[178]
(k) Optional Protocol to the Convention against Torture and Other Cruel, Inhuman or Degrading Treatment or Punishment, 2002 (Article 33);[179]
(l) Optional Protocol to the Convention on the Rights of Persons with Disabilities, 2006 (Article 16).[180]

---

[168] Legally, there is no distinction between the 'core' and other treaties. However, the United Nations maintains this distinction. Common features of the 'core' treaties are that they have monitoring bodies and their implementation measures are stronger than those of other human rights treaties.
[169] See above n 70.
[170] 1465 UNTS 85 (entered into force 26 June 1987).
[171] 1577 UNTS 3 (entered into force 2 September 1990).
[172] UN Doc A/RES/45/158 (18 December 1990).
[173] UN Doc A/RES/61/106 (24 January 2007).
[174] 999 UNTS 171 (entered into force 23 March 1976).
[175] UN Doc A/RES/63/117 (5 March 2009).
[176] 2131 UNTS 83 (entered into force 22 December 2000).
[177] UN Doc A/RES/54/263 (16 March 2001).
[178] Ibid.
[179] UN Doc A/RES/57/199 (9 January 2003).   [180] See above n 173.

Most of these treaties contain a common formulation on denunciation, as illustrated by Article 21 of the ICERD: 'A State Party may denounce this Convention by written notification to the Secretary-General of the United Nations. Denunciation shall take effect one year after the date of receipt of the notification by the Secretary-General.' The main reason behind this common formulation is that the drafters generally copy the 'final clauses' of the previously concluded treaty. This is not merely a matter of convenience; it is also a result of a policy to incorporate as many similar provisions in similar kinds of treaties as possible.[181] A familiar formulation on denunciation or any other aspect of a treaty may encourage States to join the treaty regime with fewer inhibitions, whereas a unique provision may make States overcautious about joining the regime.[182]

Article 89(1) of the ICRMW incorporates an uncommon formulation on denunciation: 'Any State Party may denounce the present Convention, not earlier than five years after the Convention has entered into force for the State concerned, by means of a notification in writing addressed to the Secretary-General of the United Nations.'[183] It is uncommon in the sense that no other 'core' human rights treaty of the United Nations system contains a similar provision. However, it resembles Article 58 of the European Convention on Human Rights (ECHR) and Article 78 of the ACHR. It imposes a restriction of five years on the right to denounce the ICRMW. The logic of this restriction seems to be that, if a State party can embrace the ICRMW regime for the initial period of five yeas, it is unlikely to separate thereafter. It would be unreasonable to single out this provision as an impediment to the wider acceptance of the ICRMW, which remains to be ratified by a host of States.[184]

Wherever a 'core' treaty provides for an optional individual communication procedure or inter-State communication procedure, it allows for withdrawal from this procedure after due notice by the State party concerned. Likewise, a 'core' treaty with a dispute settlement clause either permits reservations to the clause or allows the declaring State to withdraw its declaration after due notice. As a result, quite a few human rights treaties incorporate not only a general denunciation clause but also additional clauses of a comparable nature. For instance, in addition to a provision on reservations (Article 91), the ICRMW has clauses relating to

---

[181] In 1952 the UN General Assembly requested the drafters of the two covenants on human rights to incorporate 'as many similar provisions as possible'. See General Assembly Resolution 543 (VI) (5 February 1952), in *Yearbook of the United Nations, 1951* (United Nations, New York, 1952) 484.

[182] For example, one of the main reasons for India's objection to the adoption of the 1996 Comprehensive Nuclear Test Ban Treaty (CTBT) was its final clauses. India holds that CTBT Article 14(1) (entry into force), along with Annex II (list of States whose participation is mandatory to bring the Treaty into force), seeks to deny a sovereign right to join or not to join the Treaty. For the text of the CTBT, see UN Doc A/50/1027 (10 September 1996).

[183] Above n 172.

[184] As of 31 January 2009, there are forty States parties to the ICRMW. Most of the developed countries are conspicuous by their absence in the list of the parties: search <http://treaties.un.org> (last accessed 31 January 2009).

denunciation (Article 89), withdrawal from the inter-State communication procedure (Article 76(2)), withdrawal from the individual communication procedure (Article 77(8)), withdrawal from the dispute settlement clause (Article 92(3)), and revision (Article 90). Obviously, this appears to be a comprehensive body of the *lex specialis* on the subject. It ignores an old ILC understanding that a revision clause makes unnecessary any clause on denunciation.[185]

On the other side, the 1979 Convention on the Elimination of All Forms of Discrimination against Women (CEDAW) does not have any denunciation or withdrawal clause, but provides for both revision[186] and reservations to the dispute settlement clause.[187] The ICCPR[188] and the 2006 International Convention for the Protection of All Persons from Enforced Disappearance (ICED)[189] are without any general denunciation clause, but both have a specific withdrawal provision relating to their procedural arrangements. The only 'core' treaties free from any denunciation or withdrawal clause are the ICESCR[190] and the ICCPR Second Protocol.[191] No human rights treaty prohibits its denunciation *expressis verbis*.

The absence of a denunciation clause in some treaties and the presence of such clauses in the larger number of treaties of a similar nature give the impression that their drafters paid no heed to the work of Harold Tobin, who devised a test for the inclusion or exclusion of a denunciation clause long ago:

In general those treaties setting up differing rights and obligations for the different parties are not apt to provide for unilateral denunciation. The same is true if the drafting of the convention has involved a considerable amount of diplomatic bargaining in order to secure the participation of one or of several states. In the cases of both these types of treaties, if such a provision is made it is frequently accompanied by a statement that denunciation by one of the parties releases all the others, or by a provision that in such a case all the parties should meet to confer on their subsequent action.[192]

One may wonder whether the Tobin test is suitable for human rights treaties, because they reflect a broad collective understanding, not a narrow

---

[185] *Yearbook of the International Law Commission, 1966, Vol II* (United Nations, New York, 1967), UN Doc A/CN.4/SER.A/1966/Add.1, 251.

[186] 1249 UNTS 13 (entered into force 18 December 1979), article 26.

[187] Ibid, article 29(2) and (3).

[188] Article 41. See above n 20 and below n 195 and surrounding text.

[189] Article 42(3). Visit <www2.ohchr.org/english/law/disappearance-convention.htm> (last accessed 10 December 2008).

[190] See above n 12; see also *Human Rights: A Compilation of International Instruments: Volume I (First Part): Universal Instruments* (United Nations, New York, 2002), UN Doc ST/HR/1/Rev.6 (Vol I/Part 1) 7–16 (hereinafter '*Compilation of International Human Rights Instruments I*').

[191] On 15 December 1989 the UN General Assembly adopted the ICCPR Second Protocol and opened it for signature. The Protocol entered into force on 11 July 1991. As of 31 January 2009, there are 70 States parties to the Protocol. Search <http://treaties.un.org> (last accessed 31 January 2009).

[192] H J Tobin, *The Termination of Multipartite Treaties* (Columbia University Press, New York, 1967) 204.

diplomatic bargaining. Yet, there is a need to enquire why drafters follow no criterion for the recognition of the right of denunciation in some human rights treaties and the codification of silence on the subject in others. Negotiators generally do not keep any particular criterion or formula for adopting provisions of a treaty under negotiation. Their national briefs guide them. Those briefs are developed in view of the importance of the subject matter and the need to achieve a consensus, which maintains some balance of interests involved. Negotiations are by definition free from legal restraints, except for certain procedures and formalities related to putting together a legally binding instrument.

This indicates that, in spite of their long-standing involvement in the treaty-making process, States generally lack perspective when it comes to the question of denunciation. Alternatively, some States are perhaps very clear about their objectives and do not treat the denunciation clauses as an appropriate tool for attaining those objectives. In any case, inconsistent treaty formulations on the question of denunciation illustrate the difficulties of developing customary rules on the subject. They underline the limitations of the rules of general international law on denunciation.

Like the UN human rights treaty system, the International Bill of Human Rights is incoherent on the question of denunciation.[193] The first ICCPR Protocol and the ICESCR Protocol are the only constituents of the International Bill with an almost identical denunciation clause. The first ICCPR Protocol is the result of a compromise on the adoption of the Protocol based on the Netherlands proposal. In 1966 the representative of Ivory Coast (Marie-Antoinette Berrah) remarked that the 'withdrawal of declaration' clause in the Netherlands proposal would make the HRCttee virtually ineffective, since any State could withdraw at any time. She wanted a compulsory individual petition system.[194] However, she had little support in the Third Committee of the UN General Assembly, which adopted the Protocol with a denunciation clause.

Unlike the first ICCPR Protocol and the ICESCR Protocol, the remaining constituents of the International Bill of Human Rights do not mention the word 'denounce'. The closest terminology in the ICCPR refers to 'withdrawal' with regard to a limited aspect of the procedural arrangements envisaged in the Covenant. Indeed, the ICCPR, the ICESCR, the first ICCPR Protocol and the ICESCR Protocol contain a provision for amendment, implying the possibility of a collective denunciation.

---

[193] The ICCPR system represents a number of subsystems and units. Individuals, groups of individuals, States, the HRCttee, the specialized agencies of the United Nations, and the Secretary-General of the Organization fall in the category of 'units'. Along the same lines, three implementation procedures—reporting under Article 40 of the ICCPR, inter-State communications pursuant to Articles 41 and 42 of the Covenant, and individual complaints under the Optional Protocol—represent 'subsystems'.

[194] *Summary Records of Meetings of the Third Committee*, GAOR, twenty-first session (1966), UN Doc A/C.3/SR.1375–1464, agenda item 62, mtg 1438, para 48 (hereinafter '*Third Committee Records* (1966)').

Unlike the traditional style of treaty formulation, the provision for a limited withdrawal is not among the final clauses of the ICCPR. It is present only in Article 41(2) of the ICCPR, which lays down the terms and conditions for the acceptance and application of the inter-State communication procedure. This makes a difference, implying the inapplicability of withdrawal in a general sense. Article 41(2) reads in part as follows:

A declaration [for the acceptance of the inter-State communication procedure by a State party] may be withdrawn at any time by notification to the Secretary-General. Such a withdrawal shall not prejudice the consideration of any matter which is the subject of a communication already transmitted under this article; no further communication by any State Party shall be received after the notification of withdrawal of the declaration has been received by the Secretary-General, unless the State Party concerned has made a new declaration.[195]

Obviously, this provision is applicable only to those States that have made a declaration under Article 41 of the ICCPR.[196] Some of them have revised their declarations in terms of their temporal application,[197] implying that they have withdrawn their earlier declarations. Except for the question on the propriety of Resolution (70) 17 of the Committee of Ministers of the Council of Europe,[198] which seeks to establish the supremacy of the European procedure over the ICCPR procedure,[199] there is no dispute over the right of withdrawal as such.[200]

The absence of any instance of invoking the inter-State communication procedure under the auspices of any 'core' UN human rights treaty has been a blessing in disguise because it has not allowed any controversy that could lead to denunciation.[201] This is not the case with the first ICCPR Protocol, which attracts considerable action[202] and some amount of controversy too. Although the denunciation law of the Protocol is similar to

---

[195]   999 UNTS 171.

[196]   As of 31 January 2009, forty-eight States have made declarations under Article 41. Visit <http://treaties.un.org/Pages/ViewDetails.aspx?src=TREATY&mtdsg_no=IV-4&chapter=4&lang=en> (last accessed 22 August 2009).

[197]   See, for example, Germany and Switzerland. Ibid.

[198]   See, among others, A A Cançado Trindade, 'Co-existence and Co-ordination of Mechanisms of International Protection of Human Rights (At Global and Regional Levels)' (1987-II) 202 *Recueil des cours* 9, 405.

[199]   See *Yearbook of the European Convention on Human Rights, 1970* (Martinus Nijhoff Publishers, The Hague, 1972) 74.

[200]   In contrast, the Peruvian withdrawal from the optional jurisdiction of the IACtHR under Article 62 of the ACHR became controversial. See below nn 290–293 and surrounding text.

[201]   The use of the inter-State complaint procedure in the *Greek* case triggered the denunciation of the ECHR (see below nn 324–335 and surrounding text). For a study of the procedure, see S Leckie, 'The Inter-State Complaint Procedure in International Human Rights Law: Hopeful Prospects or Wishful Thinking?' (1988) 10 *Human Rights Quarterly* 249–303.

[202]   As of 28 November 2008, the HRCttee registered 1819 complaints concerning 82 States parties to the first ICCPR Protocol. Out of these, 645 have been concluded by adopting 'Views' under Article 5(4) of the Protocol; 518 have been declared inadmissible; 255 have been either discontinued or withdrawn; 16 have been declared admissible but not yet concluded; and 385 are pending at the pre-admissibility stage. The HRCttee has found violations of human rights in 512 cases and no violation in 133. Search <www2.ohchr.org/english/bodies/hrc/docs/SURVEYCCPR94.xls> (last accessed 25 February 2009).

that of Article 41, their practice is divergent. Certain States have denounced the Protocol,[203] a few have harboured the idea of denunciation,[204] and several others have acted in a worse manner.[205]

Unlike the Article 41 arrangement, there is scope for controversy relating to the denunciation of the ICCPR as a whole. Neither the ICCPR nor its drafting history helps in resolving this controversy. One can seek guidance from the VCLT, juristic opinion, general international law, State practice, the soft law of the HRCttee, and the practices of human rights bodies and their functional partners. The expectations of civil society count in this calculation because of its involvement in the promotion and protection of human rights.

Considering that the VCLT is not applicable with retrospective effect,[206] one may argue that its provisions relating to denunciation are not applicable to the ICCPR, the ICESCR and the first ICCPR Protocol. The three human rights instruments were adopted (16 December 1966) *before* the adoption (22 May 1969) of the VCLT. Likewise, they came into force (23 March 1976) *before* the VCLT's entry into force (27 January 1980). About one-third of the States parties to the ICCPR are not parties to the VCLT.[207] Obviously, the Vienna regime on denunciation is not applicable to these States, even if one ignored the non-retroactivity rule. However, exceptions exist for those provisions of the VCLT that have become part of customary international law. Almost the same is true with the ICESCR. The ICCPR Second Protocol and the ICESCR Protocol are the only constituents of the International Bill of Human Rights to which the VCLT is applicable by virtue of its earlier entry into force, except for those States parties to the Protocols that are not parties to the Convention.[208]

---

[203] See Jamaica, Guyana, and Trinidad and Tobago, discussed below nn 389–423 and surrounding text.

[204] For the example of the Netherlands, see above n 108.

[205] For instance, on 7 February 2000 Darmon Sultanova, an Uzbek national and the mother of death-row inmates Uigun and Oibek Ruzmetov, complained to the HRCttee against the violation of their right to freedom from torture, the right to fair trial, and other rights. The Special Rapporteur for New Communications requested the State party not to carry out the death sentence against the Ruzmetov brothers, pending the determination of their case by the HRCttee. The State party did not reply, but the complainant informed the HRCttee that her sons had been executed and the State party had forged its death records. See *Ruzmetov v Uzbekistan*, Communication No. 915/2000, *Report of the Human Rights Committee*, GAOR, sixty-first session (2006), supplement no. 40, UN Doc A/61/40, vol II, Annex V.F, 33 (para 1.2), 37 (para 5.1) and 40 (para 8).

[206] VCLT, article 4.

[207] As of 31 January 2009, the following parties to the ICCPR are not parties to the VCLT: Afghanistan, Angola, Azerbaijan, the Bahamas, Bahrain, Bangladesh, Belize, Benin, Bolivia, Botswana, Brazil, Burundi, Cambodia, Cape Verde, Chad, Côte d'Ivoire, DPRK, Djibouti, Dominica, Dominican Republic, El Salvador, Equatorial Guinea, Eritrea, Ethiopia, France, the Gambia, Ghana, Grenada, Iceland, India, Indonesia, Iran, Iraq, Israel, Jordan, Kenya, Lebanon, Libya, Madagascar, Malta, Mauritania, Moldova, Monaco, Namibia, Nepal, Nicaragua, Norway, Papua New Guinea, Romania, Samoa, San Marino, the Seychelles, Sierra Leone, Samoa, Somalia, South Africa, Sri Lanka, Swaziland, Thailand, Timor-Leste, Trinidad and Tobago, Turkey, Uganda, the United States, Vanuatu, Venezuela, Yemen, and Zimbabwe.

[208] These are: Azerbaijan, Cape Verde, Djibouti, France, Iceland, Malta, Monaco, Namibia, Nepal, Norway, Romania, San Marino, the Seychelles, South Africa, Timor-Leste, Turkey, and Venezuela.

The inapplicability of the uncustomary rules of the VCLT to the ICCPR and the ICESCR is not a cause for concern, because the Convention does not provide 'an absolute rule on the question of unilateral denunciation of treaties not containing a governing clause'.[209] In addition, the VCLT does not help serve the purpose of maintaining the special status of human rights treaties.[210] To highlight the special status of human rights treaties, the ILC Special Rapporteur on reservations takes into account the indivisibility, interdependence, interrelatedness, and importance of the rights set out in those treaties.[211] Instead of the Vienna regime, therefore, a human rights treaty–specific regime for governing the denunciation of the ICCPR, the ICESCR, the first ICCPR Protocol and the ICESCR Protocol makes more sense. Consequently, the second and not the first paragraph of Article 42 of the VCLT is relevant in the context of these human rights instruments.[212] Since neither the ICCPR nor the ICESCR has a general clause governing its denunciation, Article 56 of the VCLT becomes relevant for them in spite of its arguable applicability. As noted earlier, it allows the denunciation of a treaty without a denunciation clause in two situations: if the nature of the treaty permits denunciation and if the parties to the treaty intended to permit denunciation.[213] The relevance of Articles 42(2) and 56 of the VCLT originates from their status as evidence of the most widely acceptable formulations on the subject rather than their binding nature *stricto sensu*.

Article 56 of the VCLT gives rise to a few questions. How does one ascertain the intention of States parties to a human rights treaty that may become the target of denunciation? Does the nature of a treaty such as the ICCPR allow any right of denunciation? What is the role of the treaty monitoring body in the whole process? Answers to these questions may help clarify the position of those treaties that do not have a denunciation clause.

First, before ascertaining whether the 'parties intended to admit the possibility of denunciation or withdrawal' from the ICCPR, for instance, it is necessary to understand who 'the parties' are—parties to the ICCPR drafting process, parties at the time of entry into force of the Covenant, or parties at the time of denunciation. Clearly, the intentions of these three categories of States are not identical. In treaty interpretation matters, the intention of the drafters is relevant if it is part of the *travaux préparatoires* of the treaty and the circumstances of its conclusion.[214]

---

[209] Widdows, above n 10, 83.
[210] See below nn 211, 220 and 222 and surrounding texts.
[211] *Report of the International Law Commission, Sixtieth session* (5 May–6 June and 7 July–8 August, *GAOR, sixty-third session, 2008*), supplement no. 10, UN Doc A/63/10, (2008) 173.
[212] See above at 119.
[213] See above at 120.
[214] VCLT, article 32.

In other matters, the intention of the parties to a treaty is relevant.[215] Both primary[216] and secondary[217] sources of the *travaux préparatoires* of the ICCPR reveal nothing regarding denunciation. None of the participants in the drafting process provides any account of even informal discussion on the subject.

However, the silence of the *travaux préparatoires* does not imply the permission or prohibition of denunciation, unless some special circumstances exist or one applies an innovative interpretation.[218] This gives rise to the question of whether the States 'parties intended to admit the possibility of denunciation or withdrawal' from the ICCPR. It is difficult to ascertain how many States considered the possibility or permissibility of denunciation before acceding to or ratifying the ICCPR. Keeping in view the records of Senate hearings for the ratification of the ICCPR by the United States, for instance, one may observe that even the most vocal States have not expressed any intention about denunciation at the time of assuming obligations under the Covenant.[219] None of the instruments of ratification/accession/succession indicates any State party's intention to claim or renounce the right of denunciation concerning the ICCPR. Perhaps States generally assumed that the absence of a denunciation clause in the ICCPR did not constrain their inherent rights as well as their freedoms under customary international law. Since the ICCPR does not contain any provision against denunciation, it is possible to argue that States parties felt free to do what was not prohibited as long as they did not violate customary rules, general principles of law, and peremptory norms of international law. This seems logical to argue especially for those States that became parties to the ICCPR prior to the 'prohibition' of denunciation pursuant to an authoritative interpretation of the subject matter.

---

[215] See the following articles of the VCLT: 7 (Full powers); 12(1)(c) (Consent to be bound by a treaty expressed by signature); 14(1)(d) (Consent to be bound by a treaty expressed by ratification, acceptance or approval); 18(a) (Obligation not to defeat the object and purpose of a treaty prior to its entry into force); 20(4)(b) (Acceptance of and objection to reservations); 25(2) (Provisional application); 28 (Non-retroactivity of treaties); 29 (Territorial scope of treaties); 40(5) (Amendment of multilateral treaties); 41(2) (Agreements to modify multilateral treaties between certain of the parties only); 56(2) (Denunciation of or withdrawal from a treaty containing no provision regarding termination, denunciation or withdrawal); 58(2) (Suspension of the operation of a multilateral treaty by agreement between certain of the parties only); and 59(2) (Termination or suspension of the operation of a treaty implied by conclusion of a later treaty).

[216] UN Docs A/2929 (1955), A/5411 (1963), A/6546 (1966), A/C.3/SR.1375–1464 (1966), E/1371 (1949), E/1681 (1950), E/2256 (1952), E/2447 (1953) and E/2573 (1954).

[217] M J Bossuyt, *Guide to the* 'Travaux Préparatoires' *of the International Covenant on Civil and Political Rights* (Martinus Nijhoff Publishers, Dordrecht, 1987).

[218] See, for example, E Evatt, 'Democratic People's Republic of Korea and the ICCPR: Denunciation as an Exercise of the Right of Self-Defence' (1998) 5 *Australian Journal of Human Rights* 215–24.

[219] See *International Human Rights Treaties: Hearings before the Committee on Foreign Relations, United States Senate, Ninety-sixth Congress, First Session on November 14, 15, 16 and 19, 1979* (The US Government Printing Office, Washington, 1980); and 'Senate Committee on Foreign Relations Report on the International Covenant on Civil and Political Rights (24 March 1992)' (1992) 31 ILM 648–60.

A comparative study of the 'core' UN human rights treaties may help in this context. If the ICERD could recognize the right of denunciation in 1965, there was no reason to relinquish that right one year later when adopting the ICCPR and the ICESCR. The absence of any drafting history on the right of denunciation concerning the ICCPR simply means that the drafters, who after all represented sovereign States, never thought of it as an issue worthy of consideration. Perhaps they had taken for granted the implied right of denunciation as a manifestation of their national sovereignty, if not a direct rule of customary international law. If the drafters of the ICCPR could not do inadvertently what their counterparts did deliberately with the ICERD the year before, it is not a valid justification for an extraordinary interpretation of treaty relations at the cost of sovereign discretion.

It is important to mention that the original intention of the drafters was different from the present view of the States parties to the ICCPR. While the drafters wanted to create a human rights regime with a monitoring body of limited competence, most of the States parties are not too worried about the liberal use of powers by the HRCttee. For its part, the HRCttee has been bold enough to redefine both written and unwritten provisions of the ICCPR. In brief, the practice of the HRCttee proves that the intention of the drafters is of little consequence in the interpretation of implementation provisions of the ICCPR. One may not be sure whether the same approach is sound in denunciation matters.

In the event of a denunciation, States parties to a treaty can express their intention in different forms: approval, acquiescence, or objections. However, there is no obligation on the part of States parties to express their intention. That is why a State party's silence may imply either intentional ambiguity or unintentional acquiescence. In either case, it is not easy to determine the validity of an act of denunciation. Since there is no obligation on the part of States parties to respond to an act of denunciation within a definite time period, the uncertainty over the prospective expression of intention constrains the process of determining whether the act is valid. For instance, States parties to the ICCPR meet at least every alternate year to elect half of the members of the HRCttee, and issues relating to denunciation have not been discussed at those meetings. The meaning of the silence of States parties is difficult to interpret. It also raises a few questions of law and policy. Is it permissible for the HRCttee to act as an arbiter in the absence of a compromissary clause in the ICCPR? What happens if neither the HRCttee nor States parties respond to an act of denunciation in a resolute manner? Is it wise not to harmonize the position of the HRCttee with that of the other treaty bodies in denunciation matters?

Secondly, there is a growing belief that human rights treaties have a special status by virtue of their altruistic approach, lofty objectives, substantive provisions, overriding effects, transnational monitoring, and implications for the sovereignty of States. These treaties embody a number of inherent, inalienable and natural rights that outshine other negotiated rules. Except for their procedural arrangements[220] and reservation-laden provisions,[221] human rights treaties are not normally restrained by the rule of reciprocity. Nor are they governed by the theory of positivism alone, which regards the consent of States as the principal basis of obligation.[222] They place emphasis on each State party's capacity and willingness to make constant progress towards the enjoyment of human rights. They represent the perpetual necessities of every human being, and this belief places them at a higher level of normative order. In sum, human rights treaties constitute the moral foundation of the international community.

The presence of a denunciation clause in a majority of the 'core' treaties does not go well with their special status. At best, the nature test comes into conflict with the express clauses. It is difficult to argue that the nature of the ICERD is different from that of the ICCPR merely because the former includes a denunciation clause and the latter does not. Similarly, it is not easy to discern the difference between the nature of the CEDAW (without any denunciation clause) and that of the CORC (with a denunciation clause). Since human rights treaties are not of a monolithic nature, the claim of their collective special status is questionable. Indeed, some of them are of a special nature.

Thirdly, neither the ICCPR (without a denunciation clause) nor the first ICCPR Protocol (with a denunciation clause) envisages a role for the HRCttee in denunciation matters. However, the HRCttee of today is different from that of the early days. By exercising its implied powers in order to enhance its institutional effectiveness in view of the rising expectations of individuals and activists, the HRCttee has expanded its ambit of activity over the years. It has become an assertive body with considerable influence and rich jurisprudence. If the HRCttee can give an effective interpretation to its self-defined mandate in reservation matters,[223] for instance, it sees no obstacle to doing so in denunciation matters as well. It is difficult to predict all the problems that might arise if the HRCttee were to act as an arbiter in denunciation matters. Yet, it is

---

[220] For instance, the principle of reciprocity rules the inter-State communication procedure under a human rights treaty. Accordingly, no inter-State complaint shall be received by the treaty monitoring body (a) if it concerns a State party that has not made a declaration accepting the competence of the body, and (b) if it is made by a State that has not made such a declaration.

[221] For a study of reservations to human rights treaties, see among others, Y Tyagi, 'The Conflict of Law and Policy on Reservations to Human Rights Treaties' (2000) 71 *British Year Book of International Law* 181–258.

[222] For the insignificance of consent in respect of human rights treaties, see L R Helfer, 'Nonconsensual International Lawmaking' (2008) *University of Illinois Law Review* 71, 78 and 86.

[223] On 2 November 1994 at its fifty-second session, the HRCttee adopted General Comment 24. See UN Secretariat, *Compilation of General Comments and General Recommendations adopted by Human Rights Treaty Bodies*, UN Doc HRI/GEN/1/Rev.9 (Vol I) (27 May 2008) 210–17 (hereinafter 'Compilation of General Comments').

unclear who would deal with ICCPR-related denunciation matters if the HRCttee failed to do so.

States parties appear to be the most effective referee on denunciation matters relating to the ICCPR, especially given the important factor of State intent, yet they avoid acting in that capacity. Because of its role as the monitor of the ICCPR system, the HRCttee is an appropriate body with the most authoritative view on Covenant matters. Unlike States parties, most of which maintain silence, the HRCttee responds to incidents of denunciation. Perhaps other actors lack the confidence to believe that they can also influence situations related to denunciation. States parties generally consider such questions in the light of diplomatic convenience. Rarely, some of the States parties regard the denunciation of a human rights treaty as a matter of serious concern requiring a commensurate response.

Incidents of denunciation have largely affected the ICCPR system, and the other treaty systems have shown only modest concern regarding this matter. Even the political organs of the United Nations system, some of which are generally vocal in human rights matters, have not taken any action in the wake of denunciation of human rights treaties. As a result, unlike implementation measures, denunciation matters are not always a subject of common concern. Except for the HRCttee's initiative and the ensuing response in 1997,[224] the question of denunciation has not contributed to the development of any arrangements for joint and separate action by the treaty bodies and their functional partners. This is not surprising because international procedural law in the field of human rights is still in the process of evolution. Indeed, there is scope for drawing lessons from other branches of international law.

D. International Labour Law

International labour law is a forerunner of international human rights law in institutional terms, and their convergence is mutually reinforcing.[225] As the main constituents of international labour law, ILO conventions recognize the possibility of denunciation.[226] In the absence of a provision in the Constitution of the ILO on the possibility of denouncing a ratified convention, any provision allowing for denunciation must be included in the relevant convention, along with a time limit within which denunciation can take place. Almost all ILO conventions contain a denunciation clause of one kind or another; every convention determines the conditions under which States that have ratified it may denounce it and

---

[224] Below nn 381–383 and surrounding text.

[225] See generally, C W Jenks, *Human Rights and International Labour Standards* (Stevens and Sons, London, 1961).

[226] For details, see K Widdows, 'The Denunciation of International Labour Conventions' (1984) 33 *International and Comparative Law Quarterly* 1052–63.

thereby terminate their obligations. Even the 'core'[227] and 'priority'[228] conventions are within the ambit of denunciation.

The only exceptions to the general rule of denunciation under ILO conventions are the Final Articles Revision Conventions (Nos. 80 and 116). These two conventions do not have a denunciation clause, with the exception of a provision on automatic denunciation that is based on their revision by a future revising convention either wholly or in part. Unlike other conventions, the Final Articles Revision Conventions do not provide for domestic implementation by member States, except for administrative purposes. In fact, these two conventions obligate the ILO itself to effect certain procedural changes in the administration of ILO conventions. As such, all the substantive conventions of the ILO are subject to denunciation by their States parties. Thus, they are a class apart from a number of human rights treaties such as the ICCPR, the ICESCR, and the ICCPR Second Protocol.

Broadly, ILO conventions envisage two types of denunciation: those denunciations that follow automatically from the ratification of a convention revising an earlier convention,[229] and 'pure' denunciations effected by an act of denunciation communicated to the Director-General of the International Labour Office.[230] Article 24 of the Safety and Health in Agriculture Convention, 2001 (No.184), is an example of 'pure' denunciation:

1.   A Member which has ratified this Convention may denounce it after the expiration of ten years from the date on which the Convention first comes

---

[227] The eight 'core' conventions are: the Freedom of Association and Protection of the Right to Organise Convention, 1948 (No.87); the Right to Organise and Collective Bargaining Convention, 1949 (No.98); the Forced Labour Convention, 1930 (No.29); the Abolition of Forced Labour Convention, 1957 (No.105); the Equal Remuneration Convention, 1951 (No.100); the Discrimination (Employment and Occupation) Convention, 1958 (No.111); the Minimum Age Convention, 1973 (No.138); and the Worst Forms of Child Labour Convention, 1999 (No.182). Visit <www.ilo.org/ilolex/english/docs/declworld.htm> (last accessed 10 December 2008).

[228] The four 'priority' conventions are: the Labour Inspection Convention, 1947 (No.81); the Employment Policy Convention, 1964 (No.122); the Labour Inspection (Agriculture) Convention, 1969 (No.129); and the Tripartite Consultation (International Labour Standards) Convention, 1976 (No.144). Visit <www.ilo.org/global/What_we_do/InternationalLabourStandards/Introduction/Conventionsand Recommendations/lang--en/index.htm> (last accessed 10 December 2008).

[229] In this case, ratification by a member State of the new revising convention shall *ipso jure*—i.e., automatically and without the need for a special declaration to that effect—involve the immediate denunciation of the revised convention. Moreover, unless otherwise provided, the earlier convention shall cease to be open to ratification. For instance, a standard *ipso jure* denunciation clause can be found in Article 28 of the Safety and Health in Agriculture Convention, 2001 (No.184):
1.   Should the Conference adopt a new Convention revising this Convention in whole or in part, then, unless the new Convention otherwise provides—
   (a) the ratification by a Member of the new revising Convention shall *ipso jure* involve the immediate denunciation of this Convention, notwithstanding the provisions of Article 24 above, if and when the new revising Convention shall have come into force;
   (b) as from the date when the new revising Convention comes into force, this Convention shall cease to be open to ratification by the Members.
2.   This Convention shall in any case remain in force in its actual form and content for those Members which have ratified it but have not ratified the revising Convention. Visit <www.ilo.org/ilolex/english/convdisp.htm> (last accessed 10 December 2008).

[230] ILO, *Manual for Drafting ILO Instruments* (International Labour Office, Geneva, 2006) 19.

into force, by an act communicated to the Director-General of the International Labour Office for registration. Such denunciation shall not take effect until one year after the date on which it is registered.

2.   Each Member which has ratified this Convention and which does not, within the year following the expiration of the period of ten years mentioned in the preceding paragraph, exercise the right of denunciation provided for in this Article, will be bound for another period of ten years and, thereafter, may denounce this Convention at the expiration of each period of ten years under the terms provided for in this Article.[231]

This article provides for a number of time periods: (*a*) an initial period of validity of the convention, deemed from the date on which it first enters into force; (*b*) the period during which it may be denounced; (*c*) a period during which the convention remains in force if it has not been denounced, at the end of which the denunciation-validity cycle is repeated; and (*d*) a period of 'notice' between the date on which denunciation is registered and the date on which it takes effect.[232] The different periods make up the system of 'windows' of denunciation and their main objective is to ensure a certain degree of stability of standards. These 'windows' are 'open' parameters. In the case of the initial period of validity, for instance, the ten-year period was considered necessary to enable an initial evaluation to be made of the functioning of a convention, given that ILO conventions apply to the social and labour sphere, where the impact of new regulation often is only visible after a long period of application.[233]

The law of denunciation of ILO conventions has evolved over the years in an organized manner.[234] During the first phase, covering 1919–1927, the earliest conventions contained a provision enabling a State to denounce a convention after it had been in force for a certain period. The second phase encompassing 1928–1970 employed a formula under which, after an initial period of ten (or occasionally five) years, a convention was open to denunciation for a period of one year at ten-yearly (or occasionally five-yearly) intervals. In the third phase, since 1971, the applicable law aimed at ensuring that the ILO Governing Body was properly informed of the reasons for each denunciation so that it might make recommendations to the State concerned and bear in mind the problems encountered in the drafting of future conventions.

The ILO law of denunciation has three key features: proper notification, democratic consultation, and written explanation. The most impressive aspect of the ILO law is that it has been adopted unanimously, practiced continuously, and violated rarely. Unlike both general treaty law and

---

[231]   Visit <www.ilo.org/ilolex/english/convdisp1.htm> (last accessed 10 December 2008).

[232]   ILO, *Possible Improvements in the Standard-Setting Activities of the ILO: Final Provisions of the International Labour Conventions*, ILO Governing Body Doc GB.286/LILS/1/2 (March 2003) 7–8.

[233]   Ibid, 9.

[234]   For the legislative history of the applicable law, see Widdows, above n 226, 1052–56.

human rights treaty law, the ILO law does not allow free play of narrow interests and escape from international accountability. Obviously, it has much to offer international law in general and human rights law in particular.

E. Soft Law

Soft law is an important feature of modern human rights law. Yet, although those who contribute to the development of soft law have been active in several human rights matters, there has been less concern about the question of denunciation of human rights treaties. The main reason is the isolated incidents of denunciation, which rarely hurt those who control the decision-making processes in the international system. The lack of compulsion to lift the veil of denunciation is also responsible for the inadequate development of soft law on the subject.

As a reaction to the denunciation of the ICCPR by the DPRK in 1997, the HRCttee adopted General Comment 26 on the 'Continuity of Obligations under the International Covenant on Civil and Political Rights'.[235] It appears as the only body of soft law on denunciation. It is useful to understand the essential aspects of the General Comment and evaluate its significance.

General Comment 26 indicates that its drafters used the VCLT as their guidebook. Five statements reinforce each other: the content of the ICCPR does not allow its denunciation;[236] the nature of the ICCPR does not permit its denunciation;[237] the drafters of the ICCPR deliberately excluded the possibility of its denunciation;[238] the ICCPR does not have a temporary character typical of treaties where a right of denunciation is considered permissible;[239] and, since the rights enshrined in the ICCPR belong to the people living in the territory of the State party, no act of a State may take away those rights, and denunciation cannot be an exception in this regard.[240] Never before in the history of human rights has any treaty body dealt with the normative aspects of denunciation in such a creative manner.

However, General Comment 26 also includes the inaccurate statement that 'the drafters of the Covenant deliberately intended to exclude the possibility of denunciation'.[241] As noted earlier, the drafting history of the ICCPR is silent on the question of denunciation.[242] According to Egon Schwelb, who had first-hand knowledge of the drafting process, the preparatory work of the ICCPR did not contain any proposal, amendment,

---

[235] See *Compilation of General Comments*, above n 223, 222–23.
[236] Ibid, 222, para 1.
[237] Ibid, para 3.   [238] Ibid, para 2.
[239] Ibid, 223, para 3.
[240] Ibid, para 4.   [241] Ibid, 222, para 2.
[242] Above nn 216–217.

or statement from which it could be inferred, much less established, that it was intended to make denunciation permissible.[243] This is not an erroneous conclusion, but its basis may also lead to the equally authentic opposite view. Since the meaning of the silence of the preparatory work is difficult to interpret, it is an imaginary claim that 'the drafters of the Covenant deliberately intended to exclude the possibility of denunciation'.[244] How could the drafters do something 'deliberately' without having deliberations on it?

It seems that, in their enthusiasm to uphold the integrity of the ICCPR, the drafters of General Comment 26 sought to enhance the normative value of the Covenant. In the process, they ignored Lord Wilberforce's admonition that 'the use of *travaux préparatoires* in the interpretation of treaties should be cautious'.[245] Recognizing that there may be cases where *travaux préparatoires* can be useful, he laid down a criterion: 'These cases should be rare, and only where two conditions are fulfilled, first, that the material involved is public and accessible, and secondly, that the *travaux préparatoires* clearly and indisputably point to a definite legislative intention.'[246] The historical logic of the General Comment does not satisfy the Wilberforce criterion.

In spite of its unintentional limited inaccuracy, General Comment 26 is a clear, concise, and compelling statement of soft law against the denunciation of the ICCPR. At the same time, it is neither conclusive evidence of the intention of the drafters of the ICCPR nor the final statement on the soft law of denunciation. The HRCttee has revised a number of its General Comments,[247] and it is free to revise the General Comment on denunciation as well. None of the other human rights treaty bodies of the United Nations system has adopted a similar statement against denunciation. They are generally silent on the subject, and a majority of them have constituent instruments with denunciation clauses. This shows the idiosyncrasy of the HRCttee's soft law on denunciation.

General Comment 26 articulates the essence of the applicable law, even if it is in soft form. The line of argument in the General Comment seems to be conveying four messages. First, the VCLT is relevant to the question of denunciation of human rights treaties in spite of their special nature. Secondly, the ICCPR Second Protocol has as much immunity against denunciation as the ICCPR does. Thirdly, the ICESCR is expected to enjoy a similar immunity in the absence of a denunciation clause therein

---

[243]   E Schwelb, 'The International Measures of Implementation of the International Covenant on Civil and Political Rights and of the Optional Protocol' (1977) 12 *Texas International Law Journal* 141, 166.

[244]   See *Compilation of General Comments*, above n 223, 222, para 2.

[245]   *Forthergill v Monarch Airlines* [1981] AC 251.

[246]   Ibid, 278.

[247]   For instance, the initial general comments on Articles 2, 3, 7, 10, 14 and 40 of the ICCPR have been revised (*Compilation of General Comments*, above n 223, 172–268). Interestingly, the Consolidated Guidelines for State Reports superseded General Comment 2.

and also in view of its inseparability from and interdependence with, the ICCPR. Finally, in spite of embodying a peremptory norm of international law on the right to freedom from all forms of racial discrimination, the ICERD does not enjoy immunity against denunciation because of the presence of a denunciation clause therein. In brief, there is no common law on the denunciation of human rights treaties. In addition, there is no uniform soft law on denunciation because the General Comment of the HRCttee is not binding on other treaty bodies and none of them has yet adopted a similar general comment or an interpretative statement on the subject.

The legal significance of General Comments is a matter of debate. The HRCttee considers its General Comments binding on States parties. It expects States parties to take cognizance of General Comments, adopt them in State practice, and reflect them in their periodic reports.[248] General Comments are a new species of soft law, which invariably refine hard law. An institutional mechanism to monitor the implementation of not only hard law contained in the ICCPR but also soft law developed by the HRCttee has been in place for quite some time. There is a belief that 'General comments constitute a jurisprudential commitment, making it difficult for the [Human Rights] Committee to take a different view later'.[249] The HRCttee cannot take a position to allow the denunciation of its constituent instrument. This is not only against the nature of the ICCPR but it is also incompatible with the principle of institutional effectiveness and the soft law of the monitoring body.

Whether States parties to the ICCPR can ignore the HRCttee's General Comments is also a matter of debate. According to one commentator, 'general comments are fundamentally transcendental, in that they encompass a variety of factual circumstances and are directed at all State parties; they are therefore clarifying, norm-creating and quasi-adjudicatory in nature as well'.[250] There is a view that General Comments constitute 'subsequent practice in the application of the treaty [ICCPR] which establishes the agreement of the parties regarding its interpretation' within the sense of Article 31(3)(b) of the VCLT (general rule of interpretation), or, alternatively, the acquiescence of States parties in those determinations constitutes such practice.[251] This means that States parties are not free to take any stand on General Comments. Although States parties may question

---

[248] In its general guidance for the contents of reports of States parties to the ICCPR, the HRCttee states: 'The terms of the articles in Parts I, II and III of the Covenant must, together with general comments issued by the Committee on any such article, be taken into account in preparing the report.' See UN Doc CCPR/C/66/GUI/Rev.2 (26 February 2001), para C.1.

[249] UN Doc CCPR/C/133 (22 December 1997), para 57.

[250] E Marsh, 'General Comments', <www.icva.ch/doc00000486.html>, para 26 (last accessed 10 December 2008).

[251] Committee on International Human Rights Law and Practice, Final Report on the Impact of Findings of the United Nations Human Rights Treaty Bodies (Report of the 71st Conference of the International Law Association, Berlin, 2004) 5–6. Available at <http://web.abo.fi/instut/imr/research/seminars/ILA/Report.pdf> (last accessed 31 January 2009).

the contents of General Comments, and a few of them have actually done so on isolated occasions,[252] none has challenged General Comment 26 since its adoption in 1997. As a result, one may assume that States parties acquiesce to the HRCttee's position on the prohibition of denunciation of the ICCPR. It is difficult to establish this assumption as a determination of law. In 2000 Aust observed that 'the views of the Committee are not determinative of the matter, and must be treated with due caution'.[253] Now, he holds the view that 'such of its General Comments as have received wide support may be regarded as a secondary source of international law'.[254] However, he does not mention whether General Comment 26 is a 'primary' or 'secondary' source of law. In sum, scholarly opinion is neither decisive nor dismissive of the legal significance of General Comment 26.

The above discussion leads to several interpretations of the legal status of General Comment 26. First, the substance of General Comment 26 is an authoritative interpretation of the ICCPR insofar as the question of denunciation. Secondly, in the absence of any ICCPR provision on denunciation *expressis verbis*, General Comment 26 is the primary source of law. Thirdly, because its origin was not in a legal vacuum on its subject matter, General Comment 26 is a secondary source of law. Fourthly, considering its non-binding nature *stricto sensu*, General Comment 26 is soft law applicable to the ICCPR and the Optional Protocols thereto. Fifthly, since it relates to the continuity of obligations under the ICCPR, General Comment 26 is a *lex ferenda* for other human rights treaties of a similar nature. Finally, following the rationale of General Comment 26, denunciations are prohibited in respect of those human rights treaties that do not expressly permit States to denounce them.[255] In short, General Comment 26 seeks to supplement the International Bill of Human Rights with regard to the law of denunciation.

Even if it is considered merely an internal regulation, General Comment 26 provides guidance on denunciation until its repudiation by the HRCttee or by States parties to the ICCPR and the Second Optional Protocol thereto. Since a good amount of time has passed without any amendment or challenge to it from any source, the General Comment has developed into well-established law on the question of denunciation of the ICCPR. At the same time, it is not a final version of soft law. Nor is it a statement of soft law on the question of denunciation of human rights treaties in

---

[252] See the observations of the following States parties on General Comment 24: France (*Report of the Human Rights Committee*, GAOR, fifty-first session (1996), supplement no. 40, UN Doc A/51/40, vol I, Annex VI, 104–106); the United Kingdom (*Report of the Human Rights Committee*, GAOR, fiftieth session (1995), supplement no. 40, UN Doc A/50/40, vol I, Annex VI, 130–34); and the United States (at 126–29).

[253] Above n 6, 234.

[254] A Aust, *Modern Treaty Law and Practice* (2nd edn, Cambridge University Press, Cambridge, 2007) 411.

[255] S Joseph, J Schultz, and M Castan, *The International Covenant on Civil and Political Rights: Cases, Materials, and Commentary* (2nd edn, Oxford University Press, Oxford, 2005) 821.

general. It is *lex specialis* in the normative setting of *lex ferenda*. By virtue of the credentials of its drafters, in particular, the General Comment has considerable value.

F. Case Law

Although the doctrine of precedent is not applicable in the international legal system, judicial decisions occupy a pride of place. While the breach of a treaty has been the subject of international adjudication in innumerable cases, there are not many instances of litigating a denunciation matter. Lord McNair referred to a few relevant cases, such as the German Supreme Court decision of 1925 on the recognition of the tacit termination of a bilateral treaty between Germany and Russia[256] and the Lebanese Court of Appeal decision of 1927 on the illegality of the denunciation by Turkey of the Capitulations at the outbreak of the First World War.[257] Yet, none of them appears as a leading case on denunciation. The present section briefly refers to selected cases decided by a domestic court, an international court, a regional court, and a quasi-judicial body. These cases do not all directly concern denunciation, although they seem to raise issues that have relevance for an examination of denunciation of human rights treaties.

1. Luzern v Aargau

One of the earliest instances of adjudicating a denunciation matter is the Swiss inter-cantonal case of *Luzern v Aargau*.[258] The Reitnau *Gemeinde* (municipality), inhabited by the Aargau community and situated in the canton Luzern, had the right to levy taxes for local needs until 1817. Luzern considered that this right violated its territorial sovereignty. In 1830 both cantons settled their dispute by a treaty, which determined the boundaries of the Aargau community in Luzern's territory and that of the Luzern community in Aargau's territory.[259]

In 1869 Luzern sought to apply its new taxation law in Reitnau but found that the 1830 treaty was obstructing the application of the new law. It argued that the treaty was not legally binding because of its incompatibility with territorial sovereignty. Aargau objected to this. In 1870 the Swiss Federal Council decided that the treaty was binding and that Luzern had no right to levy taxes in Reitnau. In 1881 Luzern terminated the treaty.[260] When Aargau refused to accept the termination, Luzern took the matter to the Federal Court to secure the acceptance of its unilateral termination.

---

[256]   McNair, above n 7, 508.
[257]   Ibid, 514, n 2.
[258]   Entscheidungen des Schweizerischen Bundesgerichtes aus dem Jahr 1882, Amtliche Sammlung, VIII. Band, 43–58. Available at <www.servat.unibe.ch/dfr/dfr_bge00.html> (last accessed 10 December 2008). Translation by Christiane Eifler.
[259]   Ibid, 44–45.   [260]   Ibid, 45.

A couple of issues in this case involved the law of treaties: first, the scope of the 1830 treaty, particularly whether the treaty determined territorial boundaries; and second, whether Luzern had a right to unilateral termination of the treaty. Regarding the first issue, while Luzern relied on the wording of the treaty, Aargau referred to its object and purpose, which provided a clear statement that a permanent solution of the dispute was intended. As for the second issue, Luzern claimed to have a right to unilateral termination owing to its territorial authority, which had been guaranteed by the constitution of Luzern since 1875. It argued that, in general, treaties concerning matters under public law could be terminated unilaterally. On the other hand, Aargau claimed that treaties, even those affecting sovereignty, could not be unilaterally terminated. It submitted that, although a legislative act may terminate contracts affecting sovereignty, this right to legislate should be limited by the contractual obligation. Otherwise, there may be a breach of contract that should not be accepted by a federal State.

On 17 February 1882 the Federal Court decided that the wording, content, and history of the 1830 treaty provided no indication that Luzern wanted to be bound just for a certain time. In contrast, the treaty determined boundaries and the nature of boundaries required them to remain unaltered.[261] Hence, the unilateral right of termination could not be interpreted from the treaty. Regarding the unilateral termination, the Court considered public and international law and held:

It may be admitted that in State treaties which do not concern the regulation of concrete juridical relations, but contain merely agreements on rules of objective law ... it is to be assumed, even in default of special treaty stipulations to this effect, that the parties have the right of unilateral denunciation, since in such treaties it is not to be assumed in the nature of the matter that the parties had desired to bind themselves forever and irrevocably. But this follows simply from the presumptive will of the parties, or from the special nature of these State treaties. On the other hand, it is utterly incorrect to postulate as a general rule such a unilateral right of withdrawal on the part of the party bound, by such State treaties, concerning public law relations whereby concrete juridical relations are regulated and subjective rights and duties of the contracting States are determined.[262]

Furthermore, the general acceptance of the principle of liability under international law was found incompatible with a unilateral right to termination, although the 1830 treaty limited the sovereignty rights of the parties. The Federal Court recognized that the parties might have a particular reason for termination. However, it pointed out that to cause such an extraordinary right of termination, the limitation of sovereignty through a treaty must arise from its incompatibility with the continuance

---

[261]   Ibid, 57.
[262]   Cf D Schindler, 'The Administration of Justice in the Swiss Federal Court in International Disputes' (1921) 15 *American Journal of International Law* 149, 164.

of the living conditions in the State under commitment as an independent community or be the result of a substantial change since the signing of the contract.[263] Such a particular reason for termination did not exist in this case. Whether Aargau could be committed to accept the termination by simultaneous payment of compensation was not required to be decided, because such a claim had not been submitted for adjudication. For these reasons, the claim made by Luzern was defeated. This case law recognized the limited right of implied denunciation.

2. *The Namibia case*

The termination of the South African mandate in South West Africa (Namibia) by the UN General Assembly in 1966 was the cause of controversy in the *Legal Consequences for States of the Continued Presence of South Africa in Namibia (South West Africa) notwithstanding Security Council Resolution 276 (1970)* case. On 29 July 1970 the UN Security Council requested the ICJ to give an advisory opinion on the legal consequences of the continuing presence of South Africa in Namibia even after the termination of the mandate there. South Africa objected to the jurisdiction of the ICJ, challenged the validity of the termination of its mandate over South West Africa, and justified its continuing presence in the territory. Regarding the status of the VCLT, the ICJ said that '[t]he rules laid down by the Vienna Convention on the Law of Treaties concerning termination of a treaty relationship on account of breach (adopted without a dissenting vote) may in many respects be considered as a codification of existing customary law on the subject'.[264] Which aspects of the VCLT are not a codification of customary law was not a matter of concern to the ICJ. On the right of denunciation, the ICJ observed:

The silence of a treaty as to the existence of such a right cannot be interpreted as implying the exclusion of a right which has its source outside of the treaty, in general international law, and is dependent on the occurrence of circumstances which are not normally envisaged when a treaty is concluded.[265]

This observation goes well with the *ratio* of the *Lotus* case, where the Permanent Court of International Justice (PCIJ) held that the rules of law binding upon States emanate from their own free will and that restrictions upon the independence of States cannot be presumed.[266] Although the *Namibia* opinion was appreciated, its confusion over 'the right to terminate' and the 'right to invoke a breach as a ground for termination' came under attack. For example, Herbert Briggs criticized it as an

---

[263] Above n 258, 57.
[264] [1971] ICJ Rep 47, para 94.
[265] Ibid, 47, para 96.
[266] See the *Case of the S.S. 'Lotus' (France v Turkey)* [1927] PCIJ, Series A, No. 10, 18.

'unfortunate dictum'.[267] This viewpoint may get support from those who want to restrict the right to implied denunciation. In any case, the dictum appears irrelevant to human rights treaties and outdated in view of General Comment 26.

3. The ICAO Council Jurisdiction case

The *Appeal Relating to the Jurisdiction of the ICAO Council* case originated from the breach of treaty obligations regarding civil aviation between India and Pakistan.[268] On 30 January 1971 a couple of Kashmiri militants hijacked an Indian Airlines aircraft from Srinagar (India). They took the aircraft to Lahore (Pakistan) and burnt it there in the presence of Pakistani security forces. India considered this a material breach of the 1944 Convention on International Civil Aviation (the Chicago Convention), the 1944 International Air Services Transit Agreement (the Transit Agreement), and a bilateral understanding of 1966. It suspended flights of Pakistani aircraft over Indian territory. Pakistan complained about this suspension to the Council of the International Civil Aviation Organization (the ICAO Council), which monitors the implementation of the Chicago Convention, the Transit Agreement, and civil aviation matters. India challenged the jurisdiction of the ICAO Council on the ground that the Chicago Convention and the Transit Agreement were not applicable to it because of their suspension in its relations with Pakistan. When the ICAO Council declined to accept its position, India asked the ICJ to declare the Council's jurisdiction in this matter illegal. On the other hand, Pakistan claimed that the ICAO Council had jurisdiction in this matter because India's unilateral suspension of the Chicago Convention and the Transit Agreement was unlawful. At the same time, it argued that the ICJ had no jurisdiction in this case because both the multilateral treaties, on the basis of which the Court was seized of the matter, had already been suspended by India. In this way, both the parties relied on competing interpretations of the unilateral suspension or termination of the target treaties.

The issue was whether a State party had the unilateral right to suspend or terminate multilateral treaties for a breach of their provisions by another State party. If yes, what was the impact of suspension or termination on the jurisdictional clauses of the target treaties? Even without going into the merits of the case, the ICJ made certain observations that rejected the positions of both the parties on the unilateral suspension or termination of the treaties in question.[269] The spirit of those observations was to prevent the parties to a treaty from exercising sweeping powers in denunciation matters.

---

[267] H W Briggs, 'Unilateral Denunciation of Treaties: The Vienna Convention and the International Court of Justice' (1974) 68 *American Journal of International Law* 51, 53.
[268] [1972] ICJ Rep 46.
[269] Ibid, paras 67 and 70.

4. *The Iceland Fisheries Jurisdiction cases*

Following the Cod War, the unilateral extension of its exclusive fisheries jurisdiction by Iceland in conflict with the 1961 Exchange of Notes with the United Kingdom was the cause of action in the *Iceland Fisheries Jurisdiction* case (*United Kingdom v Iceland*).[270] Treated as treaties, the Exchange of Notes contained a jurisdictional clause, but Iceland refused to appear before the ICJ. By letters and telegrammes, Iceland submitted that the Exchange of Notes was made under difficult conditions; that the relevant international law had developed since then; and that it considered the Exchange of Notes terminated. Since its vital interests were at stake, Iceland refused to confer jurisdiction on the ICJ in any case involving the extent of its fishery limits. It submitted that treaties containing jurisdictional clauses were by their nature subject to a unilateral right of denunciation.

The ICJ found that it had jurisdiction in this case, and considered it on merits along with the case of *Federal Republic of Germany v Iceland*, because both raised similar issues. It held that Iceland was not entitled unilaterally to exclude the fishing vessels of the United Kingdom from the disputed area, and that the parties were under mutual obligations to undertake negotiations in good faith for the equitable solution of their differences. Implicitly recognizing the right of denunciation, however, the Court held:

> It appears to the Court that, although the compromissory clause in the 1961 Exchange of Notes contains no express provision regarding duration, the obligation it embraces involves an inherent time-factor conditioning its potential application. It cannot, therefore, be described accurately as being of a permanent nature or as one binding the parties in perpetuity. This becomes evident from a consideration of the object of the clause when read in the context of the Exchange of Notes.[271]

In other words, the ICJ did not assume the exclusion of the unilateral right of denunciation in the absence of an express provision to that effect. In the context of human rights, however, this position is incompatible with General Comment 26.

5. *The Gabčíkovo-Nagymaros Project case*

In the case concerning *Gabčíkovo-Nagymaros Project (Hungary/Slovakia)*,[272] the ICJ dealt with the question of the termination of the 1977 Treaty on the Construction and Operation of the Gabčíkovo-Nagymaros Barrage System and related instruments between Hungary and Czechoslovakia (and subsequently Slovakia as successor State).[273] In 1989 Hungary unilaterally suspended and then abandoned work on the project for the construction and operation of dams on the river Danube. Three years later,

---

[270] [1973] ICJ Rep 3.   [271] Ibid, 15, para 26.
[272] [1997] ICJ Rep 7.
[273] For an analysis, see Thirlway, above n 145, 86–100.

Czechoslovakia put an alternative provisional solution into operation as a unilateral measure. Considering the alternative solution as a material breach, Hungary notified its termination of the 1977 Treaty in 1992. By their Special Agreement in 1993, Hungary and Slovakia requested the ICJ to decide whether Hungary was entitled to suspend and subsequently abandon the works on the project for which the 1977 Treaty attributed responsibility to Hungary; whether the Czech and Slovak Federal Republic was entitled to proceed to the 'provisional solution' and to put into operation this system; what were the legal effects of the notification of the termination of the 1977 Treaty by Hungary; and what were the legal consequences, including the rights and obligations for the parties, arising from its judgment on these questions.

There was no provision in the 1977 Treaty regarding its termination. Also, there was no indication that the parties intended to admit the possibility of termination. In fact, the 1977 Treaty established a long-standing and durable regime of joint investment and joint operation. The VCLT was not applicable to the 1977 Treaty because of the non-retroactivity rule. The ICJ considered that, in many respects, Articles 60 to 62 of the VCLT relating to termination or suspension of the operation of a treaty were declaratory of customary rules of international law.[274] It found both Hungary and Slovakia in breach of their obligations, but it could not determine which one of them was more decisive. Therefore, the ICJ refused to consider the 1977 Treaty terminated. It asked both the parties to negotiate in good faith in the light of the prevailing situation, and to take all necessary measures to ensure the achievement of the objectives of the 1977 Treaty.[275]

This case has enriched the law relating to the conditions, grounds and consequences of denunciation. Accordingly, a material breach of a treaty may arise out of facts and/or law. However, it does not necessarily lead to the denunciation of even a bilateral treaty. A premature material breach cannot be a valid ground for the denunciation of a treaty. A material breach of a treaty cannot justify the denunciation of another treaty. Denunciation of a treaty on the ground of a material breach is different from denunciation owing to a fundamental change of circumstances. The denouncing State cannot invoke a fundamental change of circumstances if that State itself is responsible for introducing that change. A fundamental change of circumstances must have been unforeseen. The stability of treaty relations requires that the plea of a fundamental change of circumstances be applied only in exceptional cases. The impossibility of performance of a treaty as a ground for its denunciation is a narrow concept. Finally, while the requirement of notice for the denunciation of a treaty is a general principle of law, there is no uniform rule on what should

---

[274] [1997] ICJ Rep 7, 38, para 46.
[275] Ibid, 77, para 139.

be a minimum period of notice and Article 65 of the VCLT does not enshrine an established law on the subject.

6. *The Armed Activities on the Territory of the Congo case (DRC v Uganda)*

In 1999 the Democratic Republic of the Congo (DRC) filed a case against Uganda concerning acts of armed aggression allegedly perpetrated by Ugandan troops on the territory of the DRC.[276] Uganda argued that its troops were present in the Congo since May 1997 with the consent of the Congolese Government,[277] whereas the Congo claimed that it had withdrawn its consent on 28 July 1998 by issuing an official statement for the withdrawal of foreign troops from its territory.[278] A key question was whether, and if so with effect from what date, the DRC had withdrawn its consent.[279] There was no written agreement for the entry and exit of Ugandan troops. In other words, there was an issue regarding the termination of an informally created treaty relationship.[280]

Uganda argued that any withdrawal of consent for the presence of Ugandan troops would have required a formal denunciation, by the DRC, of the April 1998 Protocol on Security along the Common Border of the two countries.[281] Unimpressed by this argument, the ICJ distinguished the Protocol-based relationship from the informally created relationship between the Congo and Uganda. It observed that the consent for the entry of Ugandan troops into the Congo was not an open-ended consent. It also observed that the Congolese Government could withdraw its consent for the presence of Ugandan troops at any time, without further formalities being necessary.[282] It concluded that 'any earlier consent by the DRC to the presence of Ugandan troops on its territory had at the latest been withdrawn by 8 August 1998'.[283] It therefore held that by engaging in military activities against the Congo on the latter's territory, Uganda had violated the principle of non-use of force in international relations and the principle of non-intervention.[284]

This case has contributed to the development of the law on denunciation by clarifying a few points. First, an unwritten agreement is also subject to the rules of denunciation. Secondly, a written agreement does not necessarily override an earlier unwritten agreement between the same parties if the subject matter of one is not identical with that of the other. Thirdly, the standard of formalities such as notice for the denunciation of an unwritten agreement is lower than that for a written agreement.

---

[276] See *Case Concerning Armed Activities on the Territory of the Congo (Democratic Republic of the Congo v Uganda)* (19 December 2005): see <www.icj-cij.org/docket/files/116/10455.pdf> (last accessed 10 December 2008).
[277] Ibid, para 36.
[278] Ibid, paras 30 and 49–51.
[279] Thirlway, above n 145, 88.   [280] Ibid.
[281] *DRC v Uganda*, above n 276, para 50.
[282] Ibid, para 47.   [283] Ibid, para 53.   [284] Ibid, para 345.

7. *The Armed Activities on the Territory of the Congo case (DRC v Rwanda)*

In 2002 the DRC filed a case in respect of 'massive, serious and flagrant violations of human rights and of international humanitarian law' resulting from acts of armed aggression allegedly perpetrated by Rwanda on the territory of the DRC.[285] To establish the jurisdiction of the ICJ, the DRC referred to a host of international instruments, including the Genocide Convention and the ICERD. It also contended that Article 66 of the VCLT established the jurisdiction of the ICJ to settle disputes arising from the violation of peremptory norms in the area of human rights, as those norms were reflected in a number of international instruments. The ICJ rejected the DRC's request for the indication of provisional measures along with Rwanda's request to remove the case from its list of cases. It considered the question of the applicability of the VCLT to the Genocide Convention as well as the ICERD. It held that 'in the present case the rules contained in the Vienna Convention are not applicable, save in so far as they are declaratory of customary international law', and that 'the rules contained in Article 66 of the Vienna Convention are not of this character'.[286]

The ICJ found that it had no jurisdiction in this case. Still, the ICJ's observations on the applicability of the VCLT are useful. Clearly, the VCLT as such is not applicable to those human rights treaties that were adopted before the conclusion of the Convention.[287] Although the above-quoted observations of the ICJ do not have a direct effect on the question of denunciation, they provide clear indications that not all provisions of the VCLT are customary rules of international law and that not all VCLT rules are binding on every State.

8. *The Peruvian cases*

In 1994 Jaime Francisco Sebastián Castillo Petruzzi and three other Chilean citizens complained to the IACmHR that they had been illegally detained, falsely implicated, unfairly tried, and wrongly convicted for the alleged crime of treason against the Republic of Peru. The IACmHR found some of these allegations true and proposed a friendly settlement, which was rejected by Peru. On 30 May 1999 the IACtHR held that Peru had violated several rights of the four Chileans.[288] It ordered, inter alia,

---

[285] [2006] ICJ Rep 6; see also <www.icj-cij.org/docket/files/126/10435.pdf> (last accessed 10 December 2008).

[286] Ibid, para 125.

[287] See, for example, the ICCPR, the ICERD, the ICESCR, the first ICCPR Protocol, the 1951 Convention relating to the Status of Refugees, the 1954 Convention relating to the Status of Stateless Persons, the 1961 Convention on the Reduction of Statelessness, and the 1968 Convention on the Non-Applicability of Statutory Limitations to War Crimes and Crimes Against Humanity. For the texts of these instruments, visit <www2.ohchr.org/english/law> (last accessed 31 January 2009).

[288] Judgment of 30 May (Merits, Reparations and Costs), para 226, <www.corteidh.or.cr/docs/casos/articulos/seriec_52_ing.doc> (last accessed 10 December 2008).

that the four Chileans be judged anew in a regular court with due process guarantees.[289] On 11 June 1999 the Supreme Council of Military Justice of Peru decided that the judgment given by the IACtHR was 'non-performable'.[290] Although the IACmHR insisted on the binding nature of the judgment,[291] Peru refused to comply with the judgment.

Following its failure to implement the *Castillo Petruzzi* judgment and fearing similar judgments in the pending cases against it, Peru decided to withdraw from the optional jurisdiction of the IACtHR under Article 62 of the ACHR.[292] On 9 July 1999 it informed the OAS General Secretariat that its declaration of withdrawal 'shall go into effect immediately and shall apply to all cases in which Peru has not responded to a petition filed before the Court'.[293] On the basis of this decision, on 16 July 1999 Peru returned to the IACtHR the *Baruch Ivcher-Bronstein* case[294] and the *Constitutional Court* case,[295] both of which had been submitted for the

---

[289] Ibid.

[290] OAS, *Annual Report of the Inter-American Court of Human Rights, 1999* (OAS, San José, 2000), OAS Doc OEA/Ser.L/V/III.47/Doc 6 (24 January 2000) 41. Available at <www.corteidh.or.cr/docs/informes/info_99_ing.pdf> (last accessed 10 December 2008).

[291] OAS, *Inter-American Commission on Human Rights: Second Report on the Situation of Human Rights in Peru*, OEA/Ser.L/V/II.106 Doc 59 rev (2 June 2000), chapter 3, paras 15–23 (hereinafter 'IACmHR Second Report on Peru (2000)'). Available at <www.cidh.oas.org/countryrep/Peru2000en/chapter3.htm> (last accessed 10 December 2008).

[292] Article 62 reads:
1. A State Party may, upon depositing its instrument of ratification or adherence to this Convention, or at any subsequent time, declare that it recognizes as binding, *ipso facto*, and not requiring special agreement, the jurisdiction of the Court on all matters relating to the interpretation or application of this Convention.
2. Such declaration may be made unconditionally, on the condition of reciprocity, for a specified period, or for specific cases. It shall be presented to the Secretary General of the Organization, who shall transmit copies thereof to the other member states of the Organization and to the Secretary of the Court.
3. The jurisdiction of the Court shall comprise all cases concerning the interpretation and application of the provisions of this Convention that are submitted to it, provided that the States Parties to the case recognize or have recognized such jurisdiction, whether by special declaration pursuant to the preceding paragraphs, or by a special agreement.
See *Compilation of Regional Human Rights Instruments*, above n 15, 32.

[293] Above n 290, 18 n 3.

[294] In 1997 the IACmHR received a petition concerning Baruch Ivcher-Bronstein, an Israeli-born naturalized citizen of Peru, who was chairperson of the board of directors and majority shareholder of Television Channel 2. Channel 2 had disseminated news on corruption in, and human rights violations by, the Fujimori regime. Peru considered the news detrimental to national security. It derecognized Ivcher-Bronstein's nationality, suspended his shareholder rights, revoked his appointment as president of the company, and brought judicial actions against him, his family, and other persons close to him. Both the IACmHR and the IACtHR found those acts in violation of the ACHR. The IACtHR asked Peru to investigate the violations in order to identify and punish the guilty parties, to take the necessary steps to restore Ivcher-Bronstein's rights, and to pay him compensation. See IACtHR Judgment of 6 February 2001 (Merits, Reparations and Costs), <www.corteidh.or.cr/docs/casos/articulos/seriec_74_ing.pdf> (last accessed 10 December 2008).

[295] In 1997 the IACmHR received a petition concerning the illegal dismissal of the justices of the Constitutional Court by the Peruvian Government led by President Fujimori. The IACmHR found that Peru had violated the Court's independence and autonomy (Article 25 of the ACHR), the right to a fair trial (Article 8(1) of the Convention) and the guarantee of security in a position in public service (Article 23(c) of the Convention). The IACtHR upheld the findings of violation of Articles 8 and 25 along with Article 1 of the ACHR. It asked Peru to punish the persons responsible for the

consideration of the Court before the declaration of withdrawal. The IACmHR deplored the withdrawal and challenged the validity of the declaration of withdrawal. On the other hand, Peru argued: 'The accession of the Peruvian State to the Inter-American Court's contentious jurisdiction was a unilateral and sovereign act. The withdrawal of such recognition, accordingly, is also a unilateral and sovereign act'.[296] Claiming that the withdrawal did not mean denouncing the ACHR in part or in whole, Peru questioned the IACtHR's competence to consider the pending cases against it. Thus, the effect of the declaration of withdrawal on the pending cases became the key issue.

On 24 September 1999 the IACtHR delivered judgments on its jurisdiction in the *Constitutional Court* case[297] and the *Ivcher-Bronstein* case.[298] It declared that the attempt of Peru to withdraw from the optional jurisdiction of the Court with immediate effect was inadmissible. It therefore resolved to continue hearing and processing the pending cases. Within a week, Peru informed the OAS Secretary General that the Peruvian State was not a party to the proceedings in question. Apart from a few domestic institutions such as the Office of Human Rights Ombudsman,[299] some civil society organizations, governments, legislatures, and international organizations expressed their rejection of the position taken by the Peruvian Government vis-à-vis its obligations under the ACHR.[300] As a result, Peru explored a friendly settlement in a few pending cases. On 31 January 2001 Peru terminated its declaration of withdrawal.

Three sets of factors influenced the *Peruvian* judgments: legal, social and political. Legally, the IACtHR took into account the special status of the ACHR, the unitary nature of the Convention embodying both substantive and procedural obligations, the unconditional acceptance of the jurisdictional clause by Peru, the unlimited duration of the acceptance of the jurisdictional clause by that State, and the absence of a provision for withdrawal in the jurisdictional clause. Widespread opposition to the Peruvian withdrawal provided the IACtHR with the necessary social support to construct a higher standard of morality in the matter of denunciation/withdrawal. Finally, the downfall of the Fujimori regime created a political atmosphere that was conducive to a reconstruction of the concept of consent as a basis of obligation in international law.

As noted earlier, Reisman and Arsanjani question the legal basis of the *Peruvian* judgments:

violations, to pay the arrears of salary and other benefits to the justices, and to reimburse the victims for costs and expenses. See IACtHR Judgment of 31 January 2001 (Merits, Reparations and Costs), <www.corteidh.or.cr/docs/casos/articulos/seriec_71_ing.doc> (last accessed 10 December 2008).

    [296] *IACmHR Second Report on Peru* (2000), above n 291, para 26.
    [297] *Case of the Constitutional Court v Peru*, Judgment of 24 September 1999 (Competence); see <www.corteidh.or.cr/docs/casos/articulos/seriec_55_ing.doc> (last accessed 10 December 2008).
    [298] *Case of Ivcher-Bronstein v Peru*, Judgment of 24 September 1999 (Competence); see <www.corteidh.or.cr/docs/casos/articulos/seriec_54_ing.doc> (last accessed 10 December 2008).
    [299] *IACmHR Second Report on Peru* (2000), above n 291, para 27.   [300] Ibid, para 45.

The Court's reasoning is not without difficulty, for the treaty in question does not require states parties to accept jurisdiction at all, let alone accept it without conditions and limitations. It is not clear why a state party that accepts jurisdiction unconditionally should thereafter be denied the benefits that accrue to a state party which never accepted jurisdiction or accepted it conditionally. If the objectives of the treaty can be accomplished by parties that never accept jurisdiction why would they be disserved by a state that accepted but then withdrew a jurisdictional commitment?[301]

Reflecting on the assessments that the *Peruvian* judgments are a progressive development of international law, Reisman and Arsanjani observe that 'most of these assessments appear to be based less on the soundness of the policy innovation and more on the facts of the respective cases'.[302] They fear that the judgments set a trend that might make States overcautious about the presence of both substantial obligations and the jurisdictional clause in the same instrument.[303]

9. *Christopher Bethel v Trinidad and Tobago*

The denunciation of the first ICCPR Protocol by Trinidad and Tobago in 1998 provoked the submission of this case to the HRCttee. There, the complainant on death row claimed that the actions taken by the State party through the denunciation of the Protocol, thereby frustrating his legitimate expectations, constituted a breach of Article 1 of the Protocol (the right to submit a communication to the HRCttee) and of Article 26 of the ICCPR (the principle of non-discrimination).[304] The HRCttee refused to examine the complainant's allegation concerning the legal effect of the denunciation and the State party's reaccession with a serious reservation about the Committee's competence to deal with death penalty cases. Even the joint individual opinion of Fausto Pocar and Martin Scheinin concurred with the majority and merely reiterated the HRCttee's desire to deal with the issue of incompatibility and legal effect of the reservation 'in due course'.[305] This conclusion implied that the HRCttee had no inclination to examine the legality of the Trinidadian denunciation and that it had maintained its reluctance to determine the compatibility of reservations with the provisions of the ICCPR and the Protocol.

10. *Damian Thomas v Jamaica*

In the case of Damian Thomas, a Jamaican minor who was sentenced for a double murder, a complaint was addressed to the HRCttee on 16 August 1997, alleging that he was being held in a prison with adult inmates in

---

[301] Above n 27, 920–21.
[302] Ibid, 924.
[303] Ibid.
[304] Communication No. 830/1998, *Report of the Human Rights Committee*, GAOR, fifty-fourth session (1999), supplement no. 40, UN Doc A/54/40, vol II, Annex XII.S, 376, para 3.
[305] Ibid.

violation of the ICCPR.[306] On 11 May 1998 the complainant further sub-mitted that the prison wardens had systematically beaten the minor pris-oner several times in 1996 and 1997.[307] The HRCttee transmitted these allegations to the Government of Jamaica for its comments. The Government promised to investigate the allegations, but failed to forward its findings to the HRCttee. Since Jamaica had denounced the first ICCPR Protocol with effect from 23 January 1998, the HRCttee faced the dilemma of whether to examine the case because it was submitted before the denunciation but contained certain allegations made after the denuncia-tion. It considered the case partly admissible and held that the post-de-nunciation allegations were inadmissible under Article 1 of the Protocol.[308] Relying on the relevance of the date of the alleged ill-treatment, however, Hipólito Solari Yrigoyen issued a dissenting opinion:

> Although the State party denounced the Optional Protocol, a measure which took effect on 23 January 1998, the events described in the author's complaint occurred before that date and are handled in the same manner as the original complaint. The terms of the Optional Protocol therefore continue to apply to the communication, as provided in article 12, paragraph 2 thereof.[309]

A leading commentator also disagreed with the majority decision of the HRCttee, stating that Article 12(2) of the first ICCPR Protocol only refers to the submission of the communication as the relevant date and not to the transmission of a communication (or specific allegations) to the respondent State.[310] Therefore, like the dissenting opinion, this comment advocates a narrow interpretation of the instrument of denunciation. Later, unlike the HRCttee, the IACtHR adopted a narrow interpretation of the Trinidadian instrument of denunciation of the ACHR.[311] Concisely, the *Thomas* case conveys the message that it is possible for the treaty monitoring body to minimize the adverse effects of an act of denunciation in situations of continuing violations that come before it for consideration.

This limited body of case law highlights certain aspects of the law of treaties with a significant bearing on the question of denunciation. For example, there is no general right of unilateral denunciation; there is scope for the implied right of denunciation; the breach of a treaty does not necessarily lead to its denunciation; a narrow interpretation of an instrument of denunciation is permissible; and the principle of good faith remains applicable to the consequences of denunciation. Further, not all

---

[306]   Communication No. 800/1998, ibid, Annex XI.II, 276–77.
[307]   Ibid, 278, para 6.3.
[308]   Ibid.
[309]   Ibid, 280.
[310]   Nowak, above n 61, 907.
[311]   In the *Case of Caesar v Trinidad and Tobago*, relying on Article 78 of the ACHR, the IACtHR held: '[A] denunciation will not release the denouncing State from its obligations under the Convention with respect to acts of that State occurring prior to the effective date of the denunciation that may constitute a violation of the Convention'. Visit <www.corteidh.or.cr/docs/casos/articulos/seriec_123_ing.doc> (last accessed 10 December 2008).

provisions of the VCLT are customary norms of international law; for example, while Articles 60 to 62 of the Convention have become part of customary international law, Article 65 and 66 of the same instrument cannot claim the same status. Also, the VCLT has no retrospective effect even in respect of human rights treaties. As a matter of policy, a negotiated settlement of a dispute involving the question of denunciation is a welcome alternative to the determination of competing claims in strict legal terms.

Case law makes a modest contribution to the body of law on denunciation. The modesty of case law recalls Lord McNair's observation: 'It is perhaps not surprising that the relevant authority on the subject is diplomatic rather than judicial or arbitral, because Governments are hesitant about submitting such issues to adjudication.'[312] Case law helps in understanding the attitude of the adjudicatory bodies towards the target treaties. It may also help in formulating policy guidelines for those actors that deal with denunciation matters.

G. Synthesis

The elaborate set of sources of law gives the impression that a large body of law on the denunciation of treaties exists, but the reality is that only a small body of law emerges out of these sources. The law of denunciation is heavily dependent on the law of treaties, and other sources are merely modest contributors. Historically, the law of treaties has developed through three phases: the law before the adoption of the VCLT, the VCLT regime, and the VCLT plus. The evolution of the principle of *pacta sunt servanda* is the most important feature of the law developed well before the adoption of the VCLT. This principle remains a core content of the law governing the denunciation of a treaty. The London Declaration and the Havana Convention were the most significant developments of the pre-VCLT phase. The 1935 Harvard Draft Convention on the Law of Treaties gave expression to the Anglo-Saxon practice of the law of treaties during that phase. It recognized the right of denunciation.[313] Like the London Declaration, the Harvard Draft had no scope for an implied right of denunciation. Unlike these two, however, the Havana Convention enshrined the right of implied denunciation.

When the ILC assumed responsibility for drafting a convention on the law of treaties, there was no consensus on the implied right of denunciation. Partly owing to the contribution of the United Kingdom, the VCLT's provisions on the right of denunciation reflect British practice to a significant extent. These provisions recognize the implied right of denunciation. In this regard, the US Restatement of the Foreign Relations Law makes a useful point: 'Modern agreements generally specify either a term for the agreement, or procedures whereby a party may withdraw; therefore, there will rarely be occasion to decide whether a right of with-drawal is implied.'[314] In most cases, therefore, *lex generalis* need not con-front *lex specialis* insofar as the question of denunciation is concerned.

The VCLT's provisions on the implied right of denunciation leave the matter open to the intention of the parties and the nature of the treaty. Both aspects may give rise to a conflict of opinion. This kind of conflict becomes unmanageable if the drafting history is silent, the intention of the parties is not discernible, the nature of the target treaty is debatable, or the target treaty does not have a monitoring body. Even if the target treaty has a monitoring body, it may not have the competence to act as a dispute settler in denunciation matters. As a result, a treaty without a denunciation clause has vast scope for disputes in the event of its denun-ciation. Such a denunciation invariably leads to an uncertain legal outcome.

Considering the difficulties in the application of the implied right of denunciation, the UN Office of Legal Affairs holds the view that specific provisions on denunciation/withdrawal contribute to assisting in the effective implementation of a multilateral treaty.[315] While the experience of the ILO upholds this view, human rights treaty practice is inconsis-tent. One may argue in favour of the idea that all treaties must contain explicit denunciation clauses in order to avoid confusion, curtail capri-cious denunciations, and impose reasonable conditions. Since human rights treaties do not follow a uniform practice of incorporating denunciation clauses, they are not able to promote normative consistency in respect of denunciation. This exhibits a fragmentation of law relating to denuncia-tion. Most of the human rights treaty law on denunciation is outdated in view of the growing status of human rights norms. Indeed, the soft law on denunciation has rendered the denunciation clauses of the leading human rights treaties vulnerable.

The permissibility of denunciation of a treaty depends on the provi-sions of the treaty, the nature of the treaty, the circumstances of its con-clusion, the intention of the parties, an agreement among the parties, and the interpretation of these aspects by the treaty monitoring body, where such a body exists. The drafters of the VCLT did not realize that the nature of a treaty might not allow its denunciation though the treaty as such may have a denunciation clause. For instance, the ICERD permits its denunciation but its nature does not, since it provides the multilateral framework for the implementation of the peremptory norm of interna-tional law on the elimination of all forms of racial discrimination and States cannot break such framework with impunity. In a similar vein, the test of the intention of the States parties to determine the permissibility of denunciation may come into conflict with the nature of the target

---

[314] Above n 68, 210.
[315] See *UN Handbook on Final Clauses*, above n 8, 118.

treaty. European history proves that the Contracting Parties to the ECHR cannot tolerate its denunciation even though it contains a denunciation clause.[316] As a result, the treaty law of denunciation has problems with its own logic and content. Because of its incoherence, human rights treaty law does not help resolve those problems. Obviously, there is a need to further develop human rights treaty law.

In the form of General Comment 26, the soft law on denunciation has produced the VCLT plus. It is authentic, idealistic and attractive to the community of human rights advocates. However, it is the contribution of only one treaty body, namely, the HRCttee. Moreover, it is not a common law of denunciation. It has potential for conflict with the law applicable to various human rights treaties. For instance, the logic of General Comment 26 places the ICESCR in the category of treaties beyond the scope of denunciation without recognizing that such interpretation finds no support from the provisions of the Covenant and that its monitoring body need not necessarily corroborate that interpretation. Likewise, the General Comment considers the ICERD subject to denunciation without realizing that its denunciation clause has become obsolete in view of the importance of the Convention in the global rule of law. Most important, unlike some other fields,[317] the soft law on denunciation has little influence on the treaty-making process. A majority of the human rights treaties formulated after the adoption of the General Comment contain a denunciation clause, although their nature does not allow denunciation. Both case law and scholarly works on denunciation are limited, indicating their inadequacies for addressing the issues involved in the denunciation of human rights treaties. In these circumstances, State practice is an attractive subject of study to understand the challenge of denunciation, the mindset of denouncers, the response of others, and related matters.

IV. THE PRACTICE OF DENUNCIATION

Although cases of denunciation of human rights treaties are not numerous, some of the vital interests of the beneficiaries and trustees of those treaties are involved therein. Not all affected parties react in every case of denunciation and their reactions are not always coherent. They are invariably selective and rarely effective. The main reason for this asymmetrical equation is that every case of denunciation is special and presents a challenge to the effectiveness of the treaty system. It is useful to study the reasons for denunciation, the consequences of denunciation, and the reactions of the affected parties and others following the denunciation of

---

[316] See below nn 323–335 and surrounding text.
[317] P S Rao, 'Role of Soft Law in the Development of International Law: Some Random Notes' in Asian-African Legal Consultative Organization, *Fifty Years of AALCO: Commemorative Essays in International Law* (AALCO, New Delhi, 2007) 62–91.

specific human rights treaties. The following treaties are identified for this purpose: the Convention relating to the Status of Stateless Persons; the ACHR; the ECHR; the ICCPR; the first ICCPR Protocol; and the International Labour Conventions. These treaties have been the targets of denunciation in the fields of human rights and workers rights. This section concludes with a comparative analysis of these cases of denunciation.

A. The Convention relating to the Status of Stateless Persons

The 1954 Convention relating to the Status of Stateless Persons[318] belongs to the category of human rights treaties, even though the official documents differ in this regard.[319] In accordance with Article 40 of the Convention,[320] Madagascar gave notice to the UN Secretary-General on 2 April 1965 denouncing the Convention.[321] The denunciation took effect one year later and Madagascar became the first denouncer of a human rights treaty. There was no controversy over this incident. Neither the depository of the instruments of signature/ratification/accession/denunciation nor any State party to the Convention sought to learn the reasons for denunciation. No one tried to bring Madagascar back into the fold of the Convention. Even the academic world ignored the incident. It is difficult to find any discussion or analysis relating to this incident. In the absence of any authentic account of the events preceding and following the denunciation, one can speculate as to why the international community remained silent on this unprecedented development in the history of international human rights law.

In the first place, the denunciation of the Convention relating to the Status of Stateless Persons came at a time when human rights were not a matter of serious concern in international relations. Apart from setting a negative precedent in State practice, the consequences of denunciation were perhaps not serious enough to provoke reactions. Since the Convention had not established any monitoring body, there was no entity

---

[318]   360 UNTS 117 (entered into force 6 June 1960).

[319]   While one UN publication entitled *Multilateral Treaties Deposited with the Secretary-General: Status as at 31 December 2004* (United Nations, New York, 2004) does not include the Convention relating to the Status of Stateless Persons in the category of 'Human Rights', another UN publication entitled *Human Rights: A Compilation of International Instruments: Volume I (Second Part): Universal Instruments* (United Nations, New York, 2002), UN Doc ST/HR/1/Rev.6 (Vol I/Part 2) 617–28 does (hereinafter '*Compilation of International Human Rights Instruments II*').

[320]   Article 40 reads:

1.   Any Contracting State may denounce this Convention at any time by a notification addressed to the Secretary-General of the United Nations.

2.   Such denunciation shall take effect for the Contracting State concerned one year from the date upon which it is received by the Secretary-General of the United Nations.

3.   Any State which has made a declaration or notification under article 36 may, at any time thereafter, by a notification to the Secretary-General of the United Nations, declare that the Convention shall cease to extend to such territory one year after the date of receipt of the notification by the Secretary-General.

[321]   See <http://treaties.un.org/Pages/ViewDetailsII.aspx?&src=TREATY&id=143&chapter=5& Temp=mtdsg2&lang=en> (last accessed 31 January 2009).

to discharge the responsibility of responding to the denunciation in question. Civil society in Madagascar was not sensitive towards human rights at the time of denunciation. Also, human rights NGOs were not a force to reckon with at that time. Most important, the act of denunciation was consistent with the applicable law. One can also point out that the Convention is not among the 'core' UN human rights treaties. However, these factors cannot be considered sufficient justification for ignoring the first instance of denunciation of a human rights treaty.

Although the Convention relating to the Status of Stateless Persons is not much in discussion, the problem of statelessness remains alive, albeit to a decreasing extent. The fact that a few States have acceded to the Convention as late as 2008 indicates the continuing relevance of the law incorporated therein to deal with the problem of statelessness. Ignoring the absence of Madagascar from the Convention regime shows the poor response of the international community to the problem under discussion. This does not sit well with the spirit of international human rights law.

B. The European Convention on Human Rights

The ECHR laid down the foundation of the first regional human rights regime. It also has the unenviable distinction of being the first regional convention on human rights to face denunciation. Greece signed the ECHR within a month of its adoption by the Council of Europe in the autumn of 1950, and ratified it on 28 March 1953, well before its entry into force in the autumn of 1953. On 21 April 1967 a coterie of colonels overthrew the democratically-elected government of Prime Minister Panagiotis Kanellopoulos, manipulated the support of King Constantine, and established themselves as a junta under the de facto leadership of Colonel George Papadopoulos. The right-wing junta shut down parliament, revoked the Constitution, and instituted military law. Exercising the right of derogation under Article 15 of the ECHR, which allowed the suspension of some human rights during a state of emergency, the military junta took a series of draconian measures, arrested hundreds of citizens, and used torture as the standard method for control over Greek society.[322]

Within a week of the coup, the Parliamentary Assembly of the Council of Europe deplored the suspension of constitutional law in Greece, protested against all measures contrary to the ECHR, and called upon the Greek authorities to restore parliamentary democracy.[323] On 9 June 1967 the Political Committee of the Parliamentary Assembly adopted a resolution, which became the basis of joint and separate action by Council members.

---

[322] For details, see J Becket, *Barbarism in Greece: A Young American Lawyer's Inquiry into the Use of Torture in Contemporary Greece* (Walker and Company, New York, 1970).

[323] Order 256 directed to the Bureau of the Assembly (26 April 1967), <http://assembly.coe.int/Mainf.asp?link=/Documents/AdoptedText/ta67/EDIR256.htm> (last accessed 10 December 2008).

Invoking the inter-State complaint procedure of the ECHR under Article 24,[324] Denmark, Norway, and Sweden filed a case against Greece, and the Netherlands followed suit immediately. This was the first time a Contracting Party to the ECHR had complained against another in the former European Commission of Human Rights (ECmHR), not to promote its own interests, but in the interest of general principles, namely, the maintenance of European public order (*ordre public*).[325] The complaining States alleged that the Greek Government had violated ECHR Articles 3 (the right to freedom from torture), 5 (the right to liberty and security of person), 6 (the right to a fair and public hearing), 8 (the right to respect for private and family life), 9 (the right to freedom of thought, conscience and religion), 10 (the right to freedom of expression), 11 (the right to freedom of peaceful assembly and to join trade unions), 13 (the right to marry and to found a family) and 14 (the right to non-discrimination). On 14 December 1967 the former ECmHR began its hearings in the *Greek* cases. It heard the testimonies of torture victims and others, sent representatives to investigate the allegations, intervened to save some detainees, and asked the military junta to present its case.

While the inter-State complaints were still pending before the former ECmHR, the Parliamentary Assembly declared that Greece was in violation of conditions that would allow it to remain a member of the Council of Europe. It therefore recommended to the Committee of Ministers to consider expulsion as a necessary measure. On 6 May 1969 the Council decided to wait for the report of the former ECmHR. In November 1969 the former ECmHR decided by a majority vote that Greece could not rely on Article 15 of the ECHR to justify a military coup because there was no serious threat to the State's public order. It concluded that Greece had violated Articles 3, 5, 6, 8, 9, 10, 11, 13, and 14 of the ECHR and Article 3 of the First Protocol to the Convention.[326]

The former ECmHR sent its confidential report to the Ministers of Foreign Affairs. On 12 December 1969 the Committee of Ministers had to decide whether to expel or suspend Greece for its violation of the ECHR. While Sweden asked for expulsion, Germany suggested suspension. On the other hand, Cyprus, France, and Turkey were against taking any action at all. Even without membership of the Council of Europe, the United States had considerable interest in its NATO ally Greece and

---

[324] Article 24 laid down: 'Any High Contracting Party may refer to the Commission, through the Secretary-General of the Council of Europe, any alleged breach of the provisions of the Convention by another High Contracting Party.': see *Compilation of Regional Human Rights Instruments*, above n 15, 81.

[325] Andreas Papandreou Foundation, 'The Council of Europe Fights for Democracy in Greece, 1967–1969' (Athens, 1998), <www.agp.gr/agp/content/Document.aspx?d=7&rd=5499005&f=1426&r f=1866356962&m=4735&rm=9703031&l=1> (last accessed 10 December 2008).

[326] *Denmark, Norway, Sweden and the Netherlands v Greece*, Application Nos. 3321/67, 3322/67, 3323/67 and 3344/67, in European Commission and European Court of Human Rights, *Yearbook of the European Convention on Human Rights, 1969, Vol 12* (Martinus Nijhoff Publishers, The Hague, 1972) 512 (hereinafter '*ECHR Yearbook* (1969)').

developed a soft spot for the Greek military junta.[327] Before the Committee of Ministers could take any formal decision, the military junta decided to denounce the ECHR. Indeed, it had a right to do so under Article 65 of the original ECHR (Article 58 of the present text).[328] On 12 December 1969 it served a notice of denunciation.[329] Consequently, Greece ceased to be a party to the ECHR with effect from 13 June 1970.[330] In this way, Greece denounced three treaties: the ECHR, the First Protocol to the Convention, and the Statute of the Council of Europe.

Instead of voting to suspend Greece, the Committee of Ministers considered it a foregone conclusion that the denouncing State would, from then on, absent itself from all activities of the Council of Europe, and made it clear that Greece's exit was a result of the Council's activities and pressure.[331] It urged the Government of Greece to restore, without delay, human rights and fundamental freedoms in Greece, in accordance with the ECHR and the First Protocol thereto, taking into account the proposals made by the ECmHR; to abolish immediately torture and other ill-treatment of prisoners; and to release immediately persons detained under administrative order.[332] In other words, Greece remained obligated to respect substantive human rights obligations under the ECHR regime.

The Greek denunciation of the ECHR was a challenge to the moral foundation of a progressively united Europe. The collective response was prompt, effective, and admirable: 'The Council of Europe wrote a dramatic chapter in the fight against the Greek dictators. The country's "suspension" from the Council in 1969 undermined the legitimacy of the military regime and landed one of the first important international blows against the junta.'[333] The Cyprus policy of the military junta led to its

---

[327] For an account of US involvement in Greece, see W Blum, *Killing Hope: U.S. Military and CIA Interventions since World War II* (Common Courage Press, Monroe, 1995). Excerpts available at <http://thirdworldtraveler.com/Blum/Greece_KH.html> (last accessed 31 January 2009).

[328] Article 65 laid down:

1. A High Contracting Party may denounce the present Convention only after the expiry of five years from the date of which it became a Party to it and after six months' notice contained in a notification addressed to the Secretary-General of the Council of Europe, who shall inform the other High Contracting Parties.

2. Such a denunciation shall not have the effect of releasing the High Contracting Party concerned from its obligations under this Convention in respect of any act which, being capable of constituting a violation of such obligations, may have been performed by it before the date at which the denunciation became effective.

3. Any High Contracting Party which shall cease to be a Member of the Council of Europe shall cease to be a Party to this Convention under the same conditions.

4. The Convention may be denounced in accordance with the provisions of the preceding paragraphs in respect of any territory to which it has been declared to extend under the terms of Article 63.

See *Compilation of Regional Human Rights Instruments*, above n 15, 90.

[329] S Greer, *The European Convention on Human Rights: Achievements, Problems and Prospects* (Cambridge University Press, Cambridge, 2006) 26.

[330] For details, see *ECHR Yearbook* (1969), above n 326, Vol 12a, 78–84.

[331] See Andreas Papandreou Foundation, above n 325.

[332] Committee of Ministers Resolution DH (70) 1 (15 April 1970), in *ECHR Yearbook* (1969), above n 326, 511.

[333] See Andreas Papandreou Foundation, above n 325.

downfall and the restoration of democracy in Greece in 1974.[334] This enabled Greece to rejoin the ECHR regime on 28 November 1974, when it acceded again to the Statute of the Council of Europe. On 1 May 1998 George Papandreou, the then Minister of Foreign Affairs of Greece, offered a tribute to the Council of Europe and commemorated 'all those, both within the Council and without, who supported the struggle for the return of democracy to the country of its origin'.[335]

After 1969, no Contracting Party to the ECHR has exercised the right of denunciation. However, the political constituents of a few European States such as the United Kingdom have unsuccessfully explored the possibility of denunciation of the ECHR.[336] Happily, the ECHR remains the model of a moral code with comprehensive institutional support.

C. The American Convention on Human Rights

Both the ACHR and the ECHR have several things in common, including the recognition of the right of denunciation *expressis verbis*. Like the ECHR, the ACHR has been a target of a solitary denunciation. Unlike the former, however, the latter does not have adequate institutional support against denunciation. Since the Peruvian withdrawal from the optional jurisdiction of the IACtHR has not been considered an act of denunciation,[337] the present section is confined to an analysis of the Trinidadian denunciation of the ACHR.

On 26 May 1998 the Minister of Foreign Affairs of Trinidad and Tobago notified the OAS Secretary General that it was withdrawing its ratification of the ACHR in accordance with Article 78 of the Convention.[338] The notice mentioned the cause of denunciation, the Trinidadian Government's efforts to avoid denunciation, and the process of denunciation followed by the Government.[339] The Government indicated that it could not reconcile the law enunciated by the Judicial Committee of the Privy Council in the case of *Pratt and Morgan v The Attorney General for*

---

[334]   See, among others, C M Woodhouse, *The Rise and Fall of the Greek Colonels* (Granada, London, 1985).

[335]   See Andreas Papandreou Foundation, above n 325.

[336]   Helfer observes: 'Reputational concerns also led Tony Blair to withdraw his proposal to denounce and re-ratify the European Convention on Human Rights.' See L R Helfer, 'Not Fully Committed? Reservations, Risk, and Treaty Design' (2006) 31 *Yale Journal of International Law* 367, 374.

[337]   Above nn 297–298.

[338]   Article 78 reads:

1.   The States Parties may denounce this Convention at the expiration of a five-year period from the date of its entry into force and by means of notice given one year in advance. Notice of the denunciation shall be addressed to the Secretary General of the Organization, who shall inform the other States Parties.

2.   Such a denunciation shall not have the effect of releasing the State Party concerned from the obligations contained in this Convention with respect to any act that may constitute a violation of those obligations and that has been taken by that State prior to the effective date of denunciation.

[339]   See denunciation notified May 26, 1998, reproduced in OAS, *Basic Documents Pertaining to Human Rights in the Inter-American System* (OAS, San José, 2003) 74. Available at <www.corteidh. or.cr/docs/libros/Basinglo1.pdf> (last accessed 10 December 2008).

Jamaica[340] with the Constitution of Trinidad and Tobago as well as the applicable international measures of implementation.

In the *Pratt and Morgan* case, the Privy Council had asked for the observance of strict guidelines by States in the hearing and determination of appeals from death row prisoners. It observed that, in any case in which execution was to take place more than five years after the sentence of death, there would be strong grounds for believing that the delay was such as to constitute 'inhuman or degrading punishment or other treatment'. It therefore required that a State that wished to retain capital punishment must accept the responsibility of ensuring that execution followed as swiftly as practicable after sentence, allowing a reasonable time for appeal and consideration of reprieve. Accordingly, it recommended that domestic courts should complete capital appeals within twelve months of conviction; that the entire domestic appeal process (including an appeal to the Privy Council) should be completed within approximately two years; and that the international human rights bodies, such as the HRCttee and the IACmHR, should dispose of complaints to them in death penalty cases at most within eighteen months.

The Government of Trinidad and Tobago realized that inordinate delay in carrying out the death penalty within its jurisdiction constituted cruel and inhuman punishment and was accordingly a contravention of Article 5(2)(*b*) of the ACHR.[341] Recognizing the Privy Council's ruling as the constitutional standard for the State, the Government decided to ensure that the appellate process was expedited by the elimination of delays within the system so that capital sentences imposed in accordance with its domestic law could be enforced before their characterization as an inhuman treatment or punishment. In the same direction, the Government sought the cooperation of the IACmHR in implementing the relevant timeframes for completion of the consideration of petitions to the Commission in capital cases so that the mandatory sentence of death for convicted persons could be carried out without delay. Following its rules of procedure for the handling of petitions, the IACmHR refused to give any assurances that capital cases would be completed within the timeframe sought. This became the basis of the Government's decision to denounce the ACHR:

The government of Trinidad and Tobago is unable to allow the inability of the [Inter-American] Commission to deal with applications in respect of capital cases expeditiously to frustrate the implementation of the lawful penalty for the crime of murder in Trinidad and Tobago. Persons convicted and sentenced to death after due process of law can have the constitutionality of their death sentence determined before the Courts of Trinidad and Tobago. Sufficient safeguards therefore exist for the protection of the human and fundamental rights of condemned prisoners.[342]

---

[340] [1994] 2 AC 1 (PC).   [341] Above n 339.
[342] Ibid.

The denunciation became effective on 26 May 1998, barely seven years after the ratification of the ACHR by Trinidad and Tobago. Consequently, the Government of Trinidad and Tobago resumed executions, defied the IACmHR's orders in a few cases, and weakened the regional human rights regime. Moreover, it created a fear of denunciation by other States.[343] Fortunately, Article 78(2) of the ACHR ensured that the Government maintained its responsibility with regard to those cases that were under consideration by the IACmHR and those that had continuing effects. Moreover, the denunciation did not release Trinidad and Tobago from its customary law obligation to respect the right to life and due process of law. The denunciation had an infectious effect in the sense that subsequently Trinidad and Tobago denounced the first ICCPR Protocol on the same ground[344] and that Peru withdrew from the jurisdiction of the IACtHR because of its inability to implement the Court's decisions.[345]

It is disappointing that no State party to the ACHR sought to dissuade Trinidad and Tobago from denouncing the Convention and that no efforts were made to bring the denouncing State back into the fold. While Trinidad and Tobago had shown its domestic law compulsions to withdraw from the ACHR, the treaty regime demonstrated no creativity in meeting the challenge to its own integrity. At least, the IACmHR could have sought an advisory opinion of the IACtHR on the limits of denunciation. In turn, the IACtHR could then have used this opportunity to elaborate the customary law obligations of the denouncing State. The European experience suggests that, had the Trinidadian denunciation been dealt with more effectively, the Government of Guyana might not have jumped to denounce the first ICCPR Protocol and the Peruvian Government would have been restrained in its withdrawal from the optional jurisdiction of the IACtHR.

D. The International Covenant on Civil and Political Rights

The ICCPR is a principal pillar of the International Bill of Human Rights. It stands at 'the apex of human rights law'.[346] It is considered one of 'the most important legal instrument[s] in the hierarchy of international

---

[343]   Parassram Concepcion, above n 117, 847–90.

[344]   See United Nations Treaty Collection, Status of Treaties, Chapter IV.5, at <http://treaties.un.org/Pages/ViewDetails.aspx?src=TREATY&mtdsg_no=IV-5&chapter=4&lang=en> (last accessed 23 August 2009) ('On 26 May 1998 the Government of Trinidad and Tobago informed the Secretary-General of its decision to denounce the Optional Protocol with effect from 26 August 1998. On 26 August 1998, the Government of Trinidad and Tobago re-acceded to the Optional Protocol with a reservation. On 27 March 2000, the Government of Trinidad and Tobago notified the Secretary-General that it had decided to denounce the Optional Protocol for the second time with effect from 27 June 2000.').

[345]   Above n 293 and surrounding text.

[346]   R Higgins, 'The United Nations: Still a Force for Peace' (1989) 52 Modern Law Review 1.

agreements'.[347] However, all these distinctions proved to be inadequate to safeguard the integrity of the ICCPR from acts of denunciation by the DPRK and Yugoslavia (Serbia and Montenegro). Because of these incidents, the HRCttee reviewed the law of denunciation and introduced some innovative ideas. An examination of both incidents is in order.

1. *Former Yugoslavia*

The denunciation of the ICCPR by Yugoslavia (Serbia and Montenegro) was an offshoot of the Balkan crisis in the 1990s. After the break up of the Socialist Federal Republic of Yugoslavia (SFRY), there was controversy as to whether the Serbian-dominated Federal Republic of Yugoslavia (FRY) should be regarded as a continuation of the SFRY or whether it should be treated as a new State. The FRY claimed that it was continuing the State, international legal and political personality of the SFRY, and notified the UN Secretary-General accordingly.[348] The other former Yugoslav republics and their supporters opposed the claim. The HRCttee considered all the independent republics successors to the SFRY in respect of the ICCPR. On the other hand, the Arbitration Commission of the Conference for Peace in Yugoslavia (commonly known as the Badinter Commission)[349] expressed the opinion that the FRY was a new State that could not be considered the sole successor to the SFRY.[350] The General Assembly,[351] the Security Council,[352] the United States,[353] the West European States, the Islamic countries, and several others more or less adopted the Badinter approach.

Armed with the Badinter Commission's opinion and distancing themselves from the HRCttee's approach, Bosnia-Herzegovina and Croatia requested the UN Legal Counsel to clarify the legal situation created by the General Assembly resolution on the FRY's ineligibility to continue

---

[347] Evgeny Nasinovsky (the Union of Soviet Socialist Republics), in *Third Committee Records* (1966), above n 194, mtg 1433, para 35.

[348] UN Doc A/46/915 (7 May 1992), Annex, Declaration (27 April 1992) 4, para 1. Available at <www.bayefsky.com/pdf/serbia_t2_cedaw.pdf> (last accessed 23 December 2008).

[349] Set up by the Council of Ministers of the European Economic Community on 27 August 1991, the 5-member Badinter Commission consisted of Robert Badinter (President of the Constitutional Council of France), Roman Herzog (President of the Federal Constitutional Court of Germany), Aldo Corasaniti (President of the Constitutional Court of Italy), Francisco Tomás y Valiente (President of the Constitutional Court of Spain), and Irene Petry (President of the Constitutional Court of Belgium). It delivered fifteen opinions on major legal questions arising from the disintegration of the SFRY. For details, see P Radan, 'Post-Secession International Borders: A Critical Analysis of the Opinions of the Badinter Arbitration Commission' (2000) 24 *Melbourne University Law Review* 50–76.

[350] Opinion No. 10 (4 July 1992), reproduced in (1992) 31 ILM 1526.

[351] General Assembly Resolution 47/1 (22 September 1992), UN Doc A/47/485, Annex (30 September 1992).

[352] Resolution 777 (1992) adopted by the Security Council at its 3116th meeting on 19 September 1992 (S/RES/777), (search <www.un.org/documents/scres.htm>) (last accessed 25 February 2009).

[353] E D Williamson and J E Osbom, 'A U.S. Perspective on Treaty Succession and Related Issues in the Wake of the Breakup of the USSR and Yugoslavia' (1993) 33 *Virginia Journal of International Law* 261–73.

the membership of the SFRY.[354] On 29 September 1992 the Legal Counsel stated that the only practical consequence of the resolution was that the FRY could not participate in the work of the General Assembly and its subsidiary organs, conferences and meetings.[355] At the same time, he clarified that the resolution did not take away the right of the FRY to participate in the work of other UN organs.[356]

Bosnia-Herzegovina, Croatia, and Slovenia ignored the distinction between the 'subsidiary organs' and 'other organs' of the United Nations system on the one hand and such organs and the 'treaty bodies' on the other. They argued that the FRY could not be treated as a party to treaties such as the ICCPR. They objected to the participation of the FRY in the meetings of States parties to the UN human rights treaties. In particular, they sought a ban on the participation of the FRY in the eighteenth meeting of the States parties to the ICCPR at New York on 16 March 1994; the meeting was held to conduct the periodic elections of HRCttee members. By an overwhelming majority, States parties decided to bar the FRY from the meeting.[357] This was an unprecedented case of suspension without any reference to any provision of the ICCPR. It had no basis in the rules of procedure of the meeting of States parties to the ICCPR.[358] There was no precedent or procedure to test the legality of the FRY suspension.

Following the controversial decision of the States parties to the ICCPR, the FRY declared its withdrawal from the Covenant without submitting a formal notification to the UN Secretary-General.[359] In fact, the notification came in the form of a letter dated 26 January 1995 addressed to the HRCttee Chairperson. The letter stated that in view of the fact that the rights of the FRY under the ICCPR, particularly the right to participation in the meetings of States parties, had been denied, the FRY Government would only submit its next periodic report to the HRCttee when the FRY was treated as an equal party to the Covenant.[360] The letter nowhere used the word 'denounce'. It indicated the FRY's intention to suspend its reporting obligation, not substantive obligations, under the ICCPR. Still, it was interpreted as an act of denunciation because the reporting obligation was the key to the implementation system of the ICCPR. This was a

[354] Letter dated 25 September 1992 from the Permanent Representatives of Bosnia and Herzegovina and Croatia to the United Nations addressed to the Secretary-General, UN Doc A/47/474 (27 September 1992).
[355] Letter dated 29 September 1992 from the Under-Secretary-General, the Legal Counsel, addressed to the Permanent Representatives of Bosnia and Herzegovina and Croatia to the United Nations, available at <www.bayefsky.com/pdf/serbia_t2_cedaw.pdf> (last accessed 27 February 2009).
[356] Ibid.
[357] While the FRY was the only voter in its favour, fifty-two States parties voted against it and seventeen abstained from the voting. Among the abstainers were India and the Russian Federation. See UN Doc CCPR/SP/SR.18 (8 December 1994).
[358] UN Doc CCPR/SP/2 (Rev 1) (10 August 1984).
[359] *Report of the Human Rights Committee*, GAOR, fiftieth session (1995), supplement no. 40, UN Doc A/50/40, vol I, Annex VI, 13, para 53.
[360] Ibid.

curious case of denunciation by a State party in retaliation against suspension by the other States parties to the ICCPR.[361]

The Chairperson of the HRCttee observed that it was not for the Committee to take a position on the action of the meeting of States parties with regard to the FRY. He stated that the submission of reports under the ICCPR constituted a legal obligation assumed by each State party and was indispensable for carrying out the HRCttee's basic function of establishing 'a constructive dialogue' with States parties in the field of human rights. Therefore, he urged the FRY to continue to comply with its ICCPR obligations in general and the reporting obligation in particular.[362] However, the FRY refused to comply with its reporting obligation. This quarrel was 'most unfortunate' from the point of view of the international protection of human rights.[363] It created fissures in the ICCPR system at a time when the system was extremely relevant for the fragile States of the Balkans. It undermined the authority of the HRCttee, weakened the protection of human dignity, and subjected human rights to new power politics.

There was no apparent reaction to the FRY denunciation from any other actor in the ICCPR system—the UN Secretary-General, States parties, specialized agencies, or civil society; if there was one, it remained unheard. None of them had the courage to take a position different from the West's decision to ostracize the principal perpetrator of the 'ethnic cleansing' in the Balkans. The members of the Non-Aligned Movement (NAM), which had come into existence with a major contribution of Yugoslavia and played an important role in the drafting of the ICCPR, were unable to act in a meaningful manner owing to their lack of mutual understanding. The Russian Federation, the greatest supporter of the FRY, was incapable of engaging in a diplomatic confrontation with the West at that time. The Western States were keen to see the FRY exposed with regard to its ICCPR obligations. As a result, the balance of power went against the FRY. In the process, the first case of denunciation of the ICCPR met with an asymmetrical legal response. It conveyed an uncomfortable message that a balanced approach to a problem of international law depends on the balance of power in international relations.

A scholarly reaction came from Rosalyn Higgins, who was a member of the HRCttee at the time of the FRY denunciation. When she was no longer a member of the HRCttee, Judge Higgins presented 'a personal perspective' that questioned the legality of the suspension of the FRY from the meeting of States parties to the ICCPR.[364] Another commentator

---

[361] For a relevant discussion, see L Sicilianos, 'The Relationship between Reprisals and Denunciation or Suspension of a Treaty' (1993) 4 *European Journal of International Law* 341–59.

[362] *Report of the Human Rights Committee*, above n 359, para 54.

[363] M T Kamminga, 'State Succession in Respect of Human Rights Treaties' (1996) 7 *European Journal of International Law* 469, 478.

[364] R Higgins, 'Opinion: Ten Years on the UN Human Rights Committee: Some Thoughts upon Parting' (1996) 6 *European Human Rights Law Review* 580.

criticized the course taken by a country like Bosnia-Herzegovina, which opposed the continuation of the FRY as a successor to the SFRY in respect of the ICCPR on the one hand, and then filed a case against the same enemy as a successor to the parent State in respect of the Genocide Convention on the other.[365] The commentator observed: 'The Bosnian attitude smacks of bad faith or at least of serious inconsistency.'[366] According to the commentator, '[b]y refusing to accept the attitude adopted by the Human Rights Committee, the other parties have provided the FRY with excellent grounds on which to dodge international scrutiny of its human rights record'.[367] The dubious nature of the FRY's suspension is evident from Yehuda Blum's observations that the 1992 resolutions of the Security Council and the General Assembly 'had been adopted without any *legal* justification and in violation of the relevant provisions of the UN Charter';[368] that those resolutions represented 'a political compromise';[369] and that they created 'the grave legal difficulties'.[370] Obviously, the questionable approach of some of the States parties, as well as that of the General Assembly and the Security Council, created a climate of confusion over the legal status of the FRY. It was unhelpful to the progressive development of the law of succession to human rights treaties. Later, it became a source of disputes over State responsibility for the serious violations of human rights in the Balkans. Some of those disputes remain unresolved.[371]

In 1999 Operation Allied Force, a NATO-led intervention, created a new situation in the Balkans. It led to the destruction of the FRY infrastructure, the downfall of the Milošević regime, and the establishment of a pro-Western government in Belgrade under the leadership of Vojislav Koštunica. On 1 November 2000, when Yugoslavia (Serbia and Montenegro) joined the United Nations as a new member and renounced its claim to have continued the international legal personality of the former Yugoslavia,[372] the FRY denunciation of the ICCPR became obsolete. Since the former denouncing State had lost its international legal personality, the successor State became a party to the ICCPR with

---

[365] See *Case Concerning the Application of the Convention on the Prevention and Punishment of the Crime of Genocide (Bosnia and Herzegovina v Yugoslavia (Serbia and Montenegro))* (see Provisional Measures, Order of 8 April 1993, summarized at <www.icj-cij.org/docket/files/91/7369.pdf> (last accessed 10 December 2008)).

[366] Kamminga, above n 363.

[367] Ibid.

[368] Y Z Blum, 'Was Yugoslavia a Member of the United Nations in the Years 1992–2000?' (2007) 101 *American Journal of International Law* 800, 814.

[369] Ibid, 801.

[370] Ibid.

[371] See, for instance, the ICJ judgment of 18 November 2008 on the Preliminary Objections in the *Case Concerning Application of the Convention on the Prevention and Punishment of the Crime of Genocide (Croatia v Serbia)*, <www.icj-cij.org/docket/files/118/14891.pdf> (last accessed 10 December 2008).

[372] On 1 November 2000 the General Assembly admitted the FRY (now Serbia) to membership of the United Nations. See UN Doc A/RES/55/12 (10 November 2000), available at <www.un.org/documents> (last accessed 24 February 2009).

effect from 12 March 2001 under a new name. In short, political forces, not legal norms, helped resolve the crisis of the maiden denunciation of the ICCPR. Certainly, this was not a pleasant experience for those who sought to safeguard international law from the vagaries of world politics.

2. DPRK

Unlike its closest ally (the People's Republic of China), the DPRK became a party to the ICCPR in 1981. Also, unlike its southern neighbour (the Republic of Korea), the DPRK had attached no reservation to the ICCPR. Because of its poor human rights record and serious reporting defaults, the DPRK was a target of criticisms at the UN General Assembly and the former Sub-Commission on Prevention of Discrimination and Protection of Minorities (the predecessor of the Sub-Commission on the Promotion and Protection of Human Rights) in the 1990s. Additionally, it had been at loggerheads with the United States, which had considerable influence in the former Sub-Commission. On 23 August 1997 the former Sub-Commission adopted a resolution on the 'Situation of Human Rights in the Democratic People's Republic of Korea'.[373] It expressed concern over 'persistent and concordant allegations that grave violations of human rights' were being committed in the DPRK.[374] It asked the DPRK to respect its human rights obligations, submit its overdue report under Article 40 of the ICCPR, and cooperate with other UN human rights procedures. It invited the international community to devote greater attention to the situation of human rights in the DPRK.

Because of the former Sub-Commission's resolution, the DPRK notified its withdrawal from the ICCPR on 25 August 1997. It accused the former Sub-Commission of encroaching on the country's sovereignty and dignity. It alleged that 'dishonest elements' had abused the ICCPR. The DPRK claimed that the step of withdrawal was taken in self-defence against 'the dangerous and hostile acts'.[375] It asserted thus: 'Although the Government of the DPRK has been compelled to withdraw from the ICCPR, it will, as ever, fully guarantee its citizens all the rights enshrined in the Covenant'.[376] In other words, the DPRK did not use the denunciation of the ICCPR as a pretext to ignore its substantive obligations under the Covenant.

Since the UN Secretary-General was the first entity to receive the DPRK notification of withdrawal from the ICCPR, the UN Secretariat's response was prompt, precise, and precarious. It forwarded on 23 September 1997 an aide-mémoire to the Government of the DPRK explaining the legal position arising from the notification. Acting at the

---

[373] Sub-Commission Resolution 1997/3 (21 August 1997) was adopted by a secret ballot and the majority of 13 to 9 with 3 abstentions. Available at Office of the High Commissioner for Human Rights (<www.unhchr.ch>) (last accessed 24 February 2009).

[374] Ibid.

[375] Cf Evatt, above n 218, 216.

[376] Ibid, 217.

advice of the UN Legal Counsel, the Secretary-General expressed the opinion that 'a withdrawal from the Covenant would not appear possible unless all States Parties to the Covenant agree with such a withdrawal'.[377] Later, the Secretariat circulated the notification and the aide-mémoire to all States parties. The United Nations has not disclosed any State party's reaction to the aide-mémoire, but the Danish Ministry of Foreign Affairs claims that Denmark and some other States denied their consent to the purported denunciation.[378] Finally, the Secretariat published the summary of this course of action in the relevant official documents[379] and placed it on the UN web site.[380] Thus, unlike the FRY denunciation, the DPRK denunciation followed the traditional procedure, albeit incorrectly ignoring the practice of notice.

From 15 to 19 September 1997, the eighth meeting of the persons chairing the UN human rights treaty bodies was held at Geneva and the HRCttee Chairperson used this opportunity to engineer a collective response to the DPRK denunciation.[381] The chairpersons expressed 'serious concern' over the denunciation, 'strongly questioned' the conformity of the proposed course of action with existing international law, and opposed the admissibility of the 'unilateral denunciation'.[382] Moreover, they called on the international community 'to do everything possible to uphold the integrity of the human rights treaty system in general, and that of the International Covenant on Civil and Political Rights in particular'.[383] In spite of the chairpersons' appeal, not many States parties to the ICCPR reacted. If this course of events had gone unchallenged, it would have led to a recognition of the implied right of denunciation of the ICCPR.

Since the HRCttee was not in session at the time of notification of the DPRK denunciation, Chairperson Chanet acted on behalf of the Committee and sought to dissuade the DPRK from implementing the denunciation.[384] On 29 August 1997 she issued a press statement, expressing deep concern about the DPRK's action. She recalled that the State party had ceased all cooperation with the HRCttee since 1984, and that it had failed to respond to all efforts to resume a dialogue. Further, she observed:

The very regrettable attempt of the DPRK to breach its obligations under the Covenant constitutes a further step in a process aimed at denying its population

---

[377]   UN Secretary-General, above n 140.
[378]   H Klingenberg, 'Elements of Nordic Practice 1998: Denmark' (1999) 68 *Nordic Journal of International Law* 163–64.
[379]   *Multilateral Treaties Deposited with the Secretary-General: Status as at 31 December 1997* (New York, United Nations, 1998), UN Doc ST/LEG/SER.E/16, 159, n 5.
[380]   Above n 140.
[381]   Boerefijn, above n 118, 3.
[382]   See *Report of the Eighth Meeting of Persons Chairing the Human Rights Treaty Bodies*, UN Doc A/52/507 (21 October 1997), para 29.
[383]   Ibid.
[384]   Evatt, above n 218, 217.

the international protection of the rights guaranteed by the Covenant ... This is unprecedented in international human rights law; in effect, this is the first time since the entry into force of the Covenant on 23 March 1976 that a State has tried to renounce commitments undertaken of its own full accord.[385]

While disapproving the DPRK denunciation, Chairperson Chanet expressed the hope that the State authorities would reconsider their action. On the other hand, the DPRK refused to retreat. In their reaction of 8 September 1997, the State authorities alleged that the Chairperson's statement of 29 August 1997 was a distortion of the facts and an infringement of national sovereignty and dignity. The DPRK rejected as irresponsible the claim that it had ceased cooperation with the HRCttee since 1984. It accused the Chairperson of a renunciation of the impartiality of the chair. On 23 October 1997 the DPRK made it clear that it would not reconsider its position without the withdrawal of the former Sub-Commission's resolution against it. Influenced by the opponents of the DPRK, the former Sub-Commission was not willing to withdraw its resolution. There was no precedent or procedure to test the legality of the Sub-Commission's resolution, which had uncertain legal value and political implications. Since it had no authority to annul another body's resolution, the HRCttee decided to deal with the matter at its autumn session in 1997.

During its sixty-first session at Geneva, in October 1997, the HRCttee adopted General Comment 26, claiming that international law does not permit any State party to denounce the ICCPR or to withdraw from it.[386] The HRCttee sought the implementation of its anti-denunciation law when it sent the General Comment to the DPRK with a covering letter to that effect. Unsurprisingly, however, there was no positive response from the DPRK.

While the UN Secretary-General had expressed the opinion that a withdrawal from the ICCPR would be possible with the agreement of all States parties to the Covenant, the HRCttee maintained its opposition to denunciation in all circumstances. The former Commission on Human Rights (CHR) supported the HRCttee's view,[387] implying that the leading human rights bodies had differences with the Secretary-General on the question of denunciation. In July 1999 the HRCttee renewed its request to the DPRK to submit its overdue report under Article 40 of the ICCPR. Realizing the limits of its defiance, the DPRK submitted its second periodic report in May 2000. One year later, the HRCttee considered the report in the presence of the DPRK delegation and welcomed 'the opportunity to resume the dialogue with the State party after an interval of

---

[385] Ibid.
[386] Above n 235 and surrounding text.
[387] See, for example, CHR Resolution 1993/23 (5 March 1993) in *Commission on Human Rights: Report of the Forty-Ninth Session (1 February to 12 March 1993)*, ESCOR, UN Doc E/1993/23, 108–9.

more than 17 years'.[388] The DPRK had not formally withdrawn its instrument of denunciation, but the HRCttee interpreted the receipt of the State's second periodic report to the same effect. Thus, the DPRK denunciation lasted less than three years.

The DPRK incident shows the importance of the HRCttee's perseverance based on the progressive role of international law in contrast with the customary reticence of States parties and some other actors in denunciation matters. It demonstrates the HRCttee's militancy against denunciation. Although its statements seem to suggest that the HRCttee sees itself as interpreting the ICCPR rather than 'creating' new norms, the process of adopting General Comment 26 proves the capacity of the Committee to create instant norms without commensurate competence to seek their acceptance and compliance by States parties. This is an interesting example of the structural asymmetry of the ICCPR system, where the sustainable development of hard law depends on the growth of soft law in the sense that the latter expands and strengthens the framework for the promotion and protection of the former. It illustrates the process of redefining positive morality, emerging out of the twilight zone of hard law and soft law relating to the same subject matter. While the denunciation of the ICCPR would not have been unlawful *stricto sensu*, the soft law became a new benchmark of legality. It represents an additional standard of positive morality because States have acquiesced to it in spite of their freedom not to do so. In sum, the DPRK incident led to an instant normative revolution. It offered an important lesson about the limits of involvement of other bodies in the functioning of the ICCPR system. Most important, it proved that the denunciation of a human rights treaty is not a final event in the process of promotion and protection of human rights.

E. Optional Protocol to the International Covenant on Civil and Political Rights

The first ICCPR Protocol is an integral part of the International Bill of Human Rights. It is one of the 'core' UN human rights treaties. It recognizes the right of an individual to seek a remedy at the international level for the violation of his or her rights under the ICCPR. However, it has been a target of denunciation by three Caribbean States: Guyana, Jamaica, and Trinidad and Tobago. Since these States have much in common, a joint assessment of their denunciations follows their individual examinations.

1. Jamaica

On 23 October 1997 Jamaica became the first State to denounce the first ICCPR Protocol. Several factors were responsible for this. First, the

---

[388] See the HRCttee's concluding observations on the second periodic report of the DPRK, UN Doc CCPR/CO/72/PRK (27 August 2001).

complaints of hundreds of prisoners on death row, who claimed to be victims of unfair trial, degrading treatment, and inhuman punishment, exposed the state of human rights in Jamaica. Certain London-based law firms[389] and NGOs[390] represented most of those prisoners in their pursuit of international remedies. Secondly, numerous complainants successfully requested the HRCttee to grant them interim measures of protection against their impending execution, pending the consideration of their cases. Thirdly, most of the death penalty cases against Jamaica disclosed violations of the ICCPR, and the HRCttee invariably asked the State party to release the victims and pay them compensation.[391] Fourthly, the HRCttee addressed 'a barrage of follow-up requests' to the Jamaican authorities during 1995–1996 and the Jamaican Government could not cope with them.[392] Fifthly, the Privy Council in the *Pratt and Morgan* case observed that detention on death row for over five years constituted inhuman or degrading treatment.[393] Consequently, the Jamaican Government was not allowed to execute those prisoners who had spent more than five years on death row. Sixthly, the Privy Council imposed an eighteen-month timetable for review of a capital case by the HRCttee.[394] Finally, the HRCttee refused to give an assurance that it would complete its consideration of every death penalty case within the period prescribed by the Privy Council.[395] Instead of resolving its human rights problems, Jamaica decided to dissolve its relationship with the first ICCPR Protocol. Indeed, it had the right to do so under Article 12(1) of the Protocol.[396]

Jamaica expressed no desire to rejoin the first ICCPR Protocol after its denunciation. There was no State reaction to the Jamaican denunciation, but several civil society members reacted sharply. One commentator observed that Jamaica's actions 'may roll back the international legal protection of human rights'.[397] Similarly, Amnesty International expressed

---

[389] The leading law firms involved in the HRCttee-related work were Allen & Overy, Bennison Garrett & Brown, Clifford Chance, D J Freeman & Ingledew, Duthie Hart & Duthie, Frere Cholmeley, Herbert Smith, Linklaters & Paines, Lovell White & Durrant, Norton Rose, Simons Muirhead and Burton, Simmons & Simmons, S J Berwin & Co, and Theodore Goddard.

[390] Amnesty International, *Jamaica: A Summary of Concerns: A Briefing for the Human Rights Committee* (Amnesty International, London, 1997). Available at <web.amnesty.org/library/Index/ ENGAMR380071997? open&of=ENG-JAM> (last accessed 10 December 2008).

[391] More than 83 per cent of cases decided on the merits disclosed violations: see above n 202.

[392] M Schmidt, 'Follow-Up Activities by UN Human Rights Treaty Bodies and Special Procedures Mechanisms of the Human Rights Council: Recent Developments' in G Alfredsson et al. (eds) *International Human Rights Monitoring Mechanisms: Essays in Honour of Jacob Th. Muller* (N P Engel Publisher, Kehl) (in press).

[393] [1994] 2 AC 1 (PC).

[394] According to the Privy Council, in death penalty cases, 'it should be possible for the Committee [HRCttee] to dispose of them with reasonable dispatch and at most within eighteen months'. Ibid, 20.

[395] Joseph, Schultz, and Castan, above n 255, 813.

[396] First ICCPR Protocol, article 12(1) ('Any State Party may denounce the present Protocol at any time by written notification addressed to the Secretary-General of the United Nations. Denunciation shall take effect three months after the date of receipt of the notification by the Secretary-General.')

[397] Schiffrin, above n 119, 563.

concern that the Jamaican denunciation cut off an avenue of international scrutiny for redress of human rights violations in Jamaica and that this unprecedented step could undermine the system of international human rights promotion and protection. It therefore urged the Jamaican Government to reverse its decision and reaccede to the Protocol.[398] There was no response from the Government.

Occasionally, the HRCttee tried to influence developments relating to the Jamaican denunciation. In November 1997, when the Jamaican notification of denunciation had not yet become effective, it considered the second periodic report of Jamaica. Apparently, this was the most opportune moment to deflect the impending denunciation. Kenneth Rattray, the then Solicitor-General of Jamaica and the leader of the country's delegation to the HRCttee, announced the denunciation *during* the examination of the second periodic report. One HRCttee member 'deplored Jamaica's decision, which had made the day a bleak one for human rights'.[399] The Chairperson of the HRCttee stated her position thus:

The head of the Jamaican delegation himself had acknowledged that it was a sad day, and she could only agree: sad for human rights, for Jamaica, for the community of nations that adhered to the Covenant and for the Committee, which deeply regretted that the decision had been taken and considered it a step in the wrong direction.[400]

The HRCttee noted with 'the utmost regret Jamaica's notification of denunciation of the Optional Protocol' and cautioned, '[u]nless withdrawn, this denunciation will become effective on 23 January 1998'.[401] The Chairperson pleaded that 'it should be possible to chart a new course, to find a way of restoring the bonds that were being loosened and perhaps even reversing the decision'.[402] Jamaica ignored the plea and withdrew from the Protocol. Since then, it has not submitted any report under Article 40 of the ICCPR,[403] thus denying the HRCttee its role to review the situation arising out of the denunciation. In other words, the denunciation of the Protocol has had a spin-off effect on the ICCPR as well.

In 2003 the Committee on the Rights of the Child (CRC)[404] considered the second periodic report of Jamaica under Article 44 of the CORC and

---

[398]   See, for instance, Amnesty International, *Amnesty International Report 1998: Jamaica*, 1 January 1998, available at <www.unhcr.org/refworld/docid/3ae6a9f63c.html> (last accessed 25 February 2009).

[399]   Evatt, UN Doc CCPR/C/SR.1623/Add.1 (27 October 1997), para 29.

[400]   Ibid, para 2.

[401]   UN Doc CCPR/C/79/Add.83 (19 November 1997), para 10.

[402]   Ibid.

[403]   UN Doc CCPR/C/42/Add.15 (7 March 1997), available at <www.bayefsky.com/reports/jamaica_ccpr_c_42_add.15_1997.php> (last accessed 10 December 2008).

[404]   Established in 1991, the CRC is an 18-member body of independent experts who consider State reports on the implementation of the CORC and the Optional Protocols thereto. Like other UN human rights treaty bodies, it adopts concluding observations on State reports and general comments on the provisions of the CORC. However, it does not have the power to consider complaints concerning the violation of the rights of the child. For details, see M Verheyde and G Goedertier,

expressed concern over the State party's withdrawal from the first ICCPR Protocol.[405] Because the withdrawal directly affects persons under 18 years, the CRC recommended that the State party consider reacceding to the Protocol.[406] The recommendation remains unfulfilled, but it proves that the denunciation of the Protocol is too serious a matter to be left solely with the denouncing State or the monitoring body. It underlines the interdependence of the UN human rights treaty bodies.

2. *Guyana*

On 5 January 1999 Guyana notified the UN Secretary-General that it had decided to withdraw from the first ICCPR Protocol with effect from 5 April 1999. Within four months, however, it reacceded to the Protocol with a death penalty–related reservation.[407] Unlike the Jamaican denunciation, the reaccession-cum-reservation by Guyana became the target of a series of objections from Finland, France, Germany, the Netherlands, Poland, Spain, and Sweden.[408] The main reason for this differential treatment was that, while no State party had the right to challenge the denunciation of the Protocol by another party, every State party had freedom to object to the reservations of any State party. The objectors acknowledged the right of denunciation but questioned the propriety of the applied procedure on the following grounds:[409]

(*a*) The procedure of denunciation followed by the immediate reaccession with a reservation is highly undesirable as circumventing the rule of law of treaties that prohibits the formulation of reservations after accession;

Articles 43–45: The UN Committee on the Rights of the Child (Martinus Nijhoff Publishers, Leiden, 2006).

[405] *Committee on the Rights of the Child: Report on the Thirty-Third Session (Geneva, 19 May–6 June 2003)*, UN Doc CRC/C/132 (23 October 2003) 88, para 405.

[406] Ibid, para 406.

[407] Guyana's instrument of reaccession reads as follows:
Guyana re-accedes to the Optional Protocol to the International Covenant on Civil and Political Rights with a Reservation to article 6 thereof with the result that the Human Rights Committee shall not be competent to receive and consider communications from any person who is under sentence of death for the offences of murder and treason in respect of any matter relating to his prosecution, detention, trial, conviction, sentence or execution of the death sentence and any matter connected therewith.
Accepting the principle that States cannot generally use the Optional Protocol as a vehicle to enter reservations to the International Covenant on Civil and Political Rights itself, the Government of Guyana stresses that its Reservation to the Optional Protocol in no way detracts from its obligations and engagements under the Covenant, including its undertaking to respect and ensure to all individuals within the territory of Guyana and subject to its jurisdiction the rights recognised in the Covenant (in so far as not already reserved against) as set out in article 2 thereof, as well as its undertaking to report to the Human Rights Committee under the monitoring mechanism established by article 40 thereof.
See United Nations Treaty Collection, Status of Treaties, Chapter IV. 5, at <http://treaties.un.org/Pages/ViewDetails.aspx?src=TREATY&id=&chapter=&lang=en#> (last accessed 22 August 2009).

[408] Ibid.

[409] Ibid.

(b) The practice constitutes a misuse of the procedure;
(c) The practice contravenes the principle of *pacta sunt servanda*;
(d) The practice undermines the basis of international treaty law;
(e) The practice prejudices the protection of human rights;
(f) The practice violates the first ICCPR Protocol;
(g) The practice of the reaccession with reservation may set a bad precedent.

As the target of these objections, Guyana offered no response. Since Guyana had not made a declaration under Article 41 of the ICCPR, there was no scope for filing a case against it under the inter-State communication procedure of the HRCttee. The objectors did not consider it necessary to address the question of procedural propriety at the meetings of States parties to the ICCPR. They felt no need to raise the question at any other forum. No one explored the possibility of requesting the ECOSOC or the General Assembly to seek an advisory opinion of the ICJ on the question of whether the denunciation-driven reservations were compatible with the object and purpose of the first ICCPR Protocol.

About one year after Guyana's denunciation of, and reaccession to, the first ICCPR Protocol, the HRCttee considered the second periodic report of that State under Article 40 of the ICCPR. Although its concluding observations on the report do not mention anything about the denunciation, implying its involuntary acquiescence to the unfortunate action, the HRCttee urged the State party 'to formally withdraw its reservation made on its reaccession to the Optional Protocol'.[410] Guyana has not yet done so. This failure of the State party invites the involvement of the Special Rapporteur for follow-up on concluding observations,[411] the Office of High Commissioner for Human Rights (OHCHR) and their functional partners, which have a role in the implementation of the recommendations and suggestions of the treaty bodies.[412] The Special Rapporteur and others have yet to convince Guyana to comply with the HRCttee's recommendation by withdrawing its reservation to the Protocol.

3. *Trinidad and Tobago*

On 26 May 1998 Trinidad and Tobago informed the UN Secretary-General of its decision to denounce the first ICCPR Protocol. Three

---

[410] UN Doc CCPR/C/79/Add.121 (25 April 2000), para 9.

[411] At the conclusion of its consideration of a State report under Article 40 of the ICCPR, the HRCttee adopts comments/observations reflecting the views of the body as a whole. In July 2002 the HRCttee appointed a Special Rapporteur for follow-up on concluding observations. For the mandate of the Special Rapporteur, see *Report of the Human Rights Committee*, GAOR, fifty-seventh session (2002), supplement no. 40, UN Doc A/57/40, vol I, Annex III.A.

[412] This was reaffirmed by the Chief of the Treaties and Council Branch of the OHCHR on 15 October 2007: see 'Human Rights Committee Opens Ninety-First Session' (Doc CT07014E), available at <www.unog.ch> (last accessed 7 March 2009).

months later, the denunciation came into effect and Trinidad and Tobago reacceded to the Protocol with a death penalty–related reservation.[413] Like the Guyanese instrument, the Trinidadian reaccession-cum-reservation became the target of a series of objections on similar grounds by Denmark, France, Germany, Ireland, Italy, the Netherlands, Norway, Spain, and Sweden.[414] Those objections and public opinion motivated the HRCttee's decision in the case of *Kennedy v Trinidad and Tobago*, where the denunciation-driven reservation was found invalid.[415] Following this decision, Trinidad and Tobago again denounced the Protocol on 27 March 2000 without any indication of its return.

In October 2000, when it considered the combined third and fourth periodic reports of Trinidad and Tobago, the HRCttee placed on record 'its profound regret at the denunciation of the Optional Protocol'.[416] It however abstained from making a formal recommendation to Trinidad and Tobago to reaccede to the Protocol. Indeed, Trinidad and Tobago knows the HRCttee's expectations but is not yet ready to meet them. There is no initiative to bring Trinidad and Tobago back into the Protocol framework.

Since the aggrieved persons and the monitoring body of the target treaty endure most of the pain of an act of denunciation, it is mainly for them to respond to the challenges stemming from the act. When an aggrieved person brings a case of violation of his or her rights under the target treaty, it is incumbent on the monitoring body to administer remedies according to the applicable law. A major policy consideration is to prevent the unlawful effects of the denunciation in question. Generally, the treaty itself has some provisions for this purpose. In the case of the first ICCPR Protocol, for instance, Article 12 has two safety provisions: the requirement of a three-month notice, and the continuing application of the procedure to the pending cases. Relying on these provisions, the HRCttee continued to deal with several cases against Guyana,[417] Jamaica,[418] and Trinidad and Tobago.[419] In some of these cases, it issued interim

---

[413] The Trinidadian instrument of reaccession of 26 August 1998 is identical to the one made by Guyana: see above n 407.

[414] Ibid.

[415] Communication No. 845/1999, *Report of the Human Rights Committee*, GAOR, fifty-fifth session (2000), supplement no. 40, UN Doc A/55/40, vol II, Annex X, 265–66, para 6.7. The following HRCttee members appended their joint separate opinion: Nisuke Ando, Prafullachandra Natwarlal Bhagwati, Eckart Klein, and David Kretzmer (at 268–71).

[416] UN Doc CCPR/CO/70/TTO (10 November 2000), para 7.

[417] See, for example, *Hussain et al. v Guyana*, Communication No. 862/1999, *Report of the Human Rights Committee*, GAOR, sixty-first session (2006), supplement no. 40, UN Doc A/61/40, vol II, Annex V.B, 7–11; *Persaud v Guyana*, Communication No. 812/1998 (at Annex V.A, 1–6); *Chan v Guyana*, Communication No. 913/2000 (at Annex V.E, 23–31).

[418] See, for example, *Pryce v Jamaica*, Communication No. 793/1998, *Report of the Human Rights Committee*, GAOR, fifty-ninth session (2004), supplement no. 40, UN Doc A/59/40, vol II, Annex IX.B, 10–14; *Lobban v Jamaica*, Communication No. 797/1998 (at Annex IX.C, 15–20); *Howell v Jamaica*, Communication No. 798/1998 (at Annex IX.D, 21–28).

[419] See, for example, *Girjadat Siewpersaud et al. v Trinidad and Tobago*, Communication No. 938/2000, ibid, Annex IX.R, 132–37.

measures of protection and consequently the States parties concerned granted stays of execution.[420] In a few cases, however, the States parties concerned failed to participate in the procedure and the HRCttee expressed its displeasure over such failures.[421]

The HRCttee has now completed consideration of the remaining cases that were pending against Jamaica and Trinidad and Tobago. The number of cases against Guyana was negligible, partly because of its reservation-laden reaccession to the first ICCPR Protocol. There is an unenviable record: Jamaica is out of the Protocol after completing one hundred cases where violations of the ICCPR were found. There is another unenviable record: Trinidad and Tobago is the only country to have denounced the same treaty twice. Finally, another record is that, among all human rights treaties, the first ICCPR Protocol has become the target of the largest number of denunciations. This conveys a message that, in spite of accepting most of the ICCPR's substantive obligations, States remain apprehensive of international procedural obligations in the field of human rights.

Occasional opportunities to examine the Caribbean denunciations and their effects arise at the time of consideration of the periodic reports of the States parties concerned under Article 40 of the ICCPR. While the inter-State communication procedure is inapplicable because none of the denouncing States has accepted that procedure, the reporting procedure is ineffective as a means to establish the accountability of the Caribbean States in respect of their denunciations. Only the first ICCPR Protocol procedure could be of some help in the given circumstances. While expressing its concerns about the denunciation and subsequent reaccession with serious reservations,[422] Amnesty International proposed a set of measures to discourage such practice.[423] These measures are not focussed

---

[420]   See, for example, *Persaud v Guyana*, above n 417.

[421]   See, for example, ibid, para 5.

[422]   *Report of the Persons Chairing the Human Rights Treaty Bodies on Their Eleventh Meeting*, UN Doc A/54/805 (21 March 2000), para 32.

[423]   At the eleventh meeting of the chairpersons of the monitoring bodies of the UN human rights treaty system, in mid-2000, Amnesty International made the following recommendations in response to the denunciation of human rights treaties:

We call on you to consider some or all of the following measures in response to this threat to the system;

Calling on all States Parties to the human rights treaties to condemn the practice of entering reservations which are clearly contrary to the object and purpose of treaties or their Optional Protocols;

Calling on all States Parties to reiterate that in ratifying or acceding to the human rights treaties states accept the competence of the Committee established by that treaty and cannot simply refuse to implement their recommendations in certain cases;

Including in the follow-up procedures currently being discussed in the context of the Plan of Action a procedure for dealing with situations where States openly refuse to implement recommendations by a treaty body, particularly in cases where human life is in danger;

Calling on the High Commissioner [for Human Rights] to do everything in her power to promote and defend the human rights treaty system including, where necessary, condemnation of actions by governments which undermine it.

The International Secretariat of Amnesty International provided this information.

on the question of denunciation and their impact on the denouncing State is invisible. The scholarly world has been rather economical in paying attention to the challenge of denunciations of the Protocol. The victims of the Caribbean denunciations are not able to intensify their campaign against their plight, and their cause is no longer a priority of civil society. In other words, the age of globalization is not free from the tendency to forget some serious human rights challenges.

F. International Labour Conventions

Both the ICCPR[424] and the ICESCR[425] incorporate certain international labour standards. The ILO itself characterizes its 'core' conventions as 'fundamental human rights conventions';[426] the UN basic documents on human rights include certain ILO conventions;[427] and some publicists do likewise.[428] The writings of Sir Wilfred Jenks[429] and some others strengthen the bonds between 'human rights' and 'social justice'.[430]

Since its inception in 1919, the ILO has sought to monitor the implementation of both ratified and unratified conventions. Unlike the isolated instances of denunciation of other species of human rights treaties, the denunciation of ILO conventions is a common phenomenon. The ILO database of the International Labour Standards provides up-to-date information on their denunciations, which appear in yellow boxes. It proves that 'Member States of the International Labour Organisation have taken advantage of the standard denunciation provisions of International Labour Conventions to free themselves from the obligations of the Conventions'.[431] Obviously, denunciation is not a foul in international labour law. Considering the widespread practice of their

---

[424] For instance, Article 22 of the ICCPR enshrines the right to freedom of association with others, including the right to form and join trade unions for the protection of one's interests.

[425] For instance, Article 8 of the ICESCR recognizes the right of everyone to form trade unions and join the trade union of his or her choice, the right of trade unions to establish national federations or confederations, and the right to strike.

[426] ILOLEX, the database of the International Labour Standards, is titled 'Ratifications of the Fundamental Human Rights Conventions by Country'. Above n 227.

[427] *Compilation of International Human Rights Instruments I*, above n 190, 91–103, 109–17 and 214–26; and *Compilation of International Human Rights Instruments II*, above n 319,501–16 and 530–42.

[428] See, among others, I Brownlie and G Goodwin-Gill (eds) *Basic Documents on Human Rights* (5ᵗʰ edn, Oxford University Press, Oxford, 2006) 497–591 (hereinafter '*Basic Documents on Human Rights*').

[429] C W Jenks, 'Human Rights, Social Justice and Peace: The Broader Significance of the ILO Experience' in A Eide and A Schou (eds) *International Protection of Human Rights: Proceedings of the Seventh Nobel Symposium, Oslo, September 25–27, 1967* (Almqvist and Wiksell, Stockholm, 1968) 227–60.

[430] See, among others, V A Leary, 'Lessons from the Experience of the International Labour Organisation' in P Alston (ed) *The United Nations and Human Rights: A Critical Appraisal* (Clarendon Press, Oxford, 1992) 580–619; and P Alston (ed) *Labour Rights as Human Rights* (Oxford University Press, Oxford, 2005).

[431] Widdows, above n 226, 1052.

denunciations, Widdows rightly suggests that ILO conventions are worthy subjects for analysis.[432]

On 16 April 1938 India under British rule became the first denouncer of an ILO convention. It denounced the Unemployment Convention, 1919 (No.2), because the Government of India Act, 1935, had substantially altered the relations between the Central Government and the provinces and, under its terms, the subject matter of the Convention had passed exclusively to the provinces.[433] Essentially, this was the British Government's decision. It was driven by the introduction of the 1935 Act, which was a product of the gradual process of granting autonomy to the colonial territory in the face of the freedom struggle.

There are only two cases of the denunciation of the 'core' conventions: on 19 April 1979 Singapore denounced the Abolition of Forced Labour Convention, 1957 (No.105), and Malaysia did likewise on 10 January 1990.[434] Singapore denounced the Convention because of its failure to reach an understanding with the ILO Committee of Experts on the Application of Conventions and Recommendations on the practical difficulties the country faced with regard to the implementation of the Convention. In particular, it disagreed with the interpretation of the term 'forced labour' as applicable to prisoners under certain domestic legislation.[435] The ILO Office, several member States and trade unions were quite upset with the denunciation. In July 2008 the International Trade Union Confederation (ITUC) recommended that the Government of Singapore should ratify once again the Convention.[436] Singapore has yet to respond positively.

Malaysia decided to denounce the Abolition of Forced Labour Convention in response to continuing criticism of the existence of compulsory prison labour.[437] It defended its decision for 'perfectly valid and cogent reasons', whereas the worker members of the ILO Conference Committee on the Application of Conventions and Recommendations regarded that decision as 'a giant leap backwards'.[438] The worker members observed that '[d]enunciation of an ILO Convention was always regrettable, but even more so when its subject was forced labour'.[439]

---

[432]   Ibid.

[433]   *ILO Official Bulletin*, 1938, 66.

[434]   Above n 227.

[435]   Cornell University ILR School, *The Elimination of All Forms of Forced or Compulsory Labour* (2002) (Cornell University, Ithaca, New York, 2002) 218–19. Available at <http://digitalcommons.ilr.cornell.edu/cgi/viewcontent.cgi?article=1010&context=forcedlabor> (last accessed 31 January 2009).

[436]   ITUC, 'Internationally Recognised Core Labour Standards in Singapore: Report for the WTO General Council Review of the Trade Policies of Singapore (Geneva, 14 and 16 July 2008)' 10, <www.ituc-csi.org/IMG/pdf/Singapore_11-July-2008.final.pdf> (last accessed 31 January 2009).

[437]   See 'ILCCR: Examination of individual case concerning Convention No. 105, Abolition of Forced Labour, 1957 Malaysia (ratification: 1958) Published: 1990', ILOLEX Doc 131990MYS105 (1990). Available as Conference Committee observations at <www.ilo.org/ilolex/english/iloquery.htm> (last accessed 1 March 2009).

[438]   Ibid.

[439]   Ibid.

A worker member of Malaysia registered the Malaysian workers' disagreement with the denunciation. A worker member of Japan warned that there could be grave consequences if Malaysia was allowed to denounce the Convention. The member proposed that the ILO Conference Committee ask the Government to reconsider its position, and to bring its law and practice into conformity with the Convention. Consequently, the ILO Director-General had undertaken a mission to Kuala Lumpur in April 1990 to examine possible solutions that would enable Malaysia to revoke its decision.[440] The Government welcomed the mission, but maintained its decision. In 2001 the International Confederation of Free Trade Unions mentioned that the Government should provide legal guarantees for protection against forced labour and again ratify the Convention.[441] Since 2005, the ILO Declaration Expert-Advisers were concerned that the Government had not yet opened a dialogue with the ILO Office and its employers' and workers' organizations with a view to reconsidering its decision. They urged Malaysia to take action in this regard.[442]

There is only one case of denunciation and re-ratification of the same 'priority' convention. On 5 April 1971 Brazil denounced the Labour Inspection Convention, 1947 (No.81),[443] but subsequently changed its decision and again ratified the Convention on 11 October 1989.[444] It had encountered certain difficulties in applying the Convention, specifically concerning the status of inspection staff (Articles 6) and the reimbursement of their travelling and incidental expenses (Article 11(2)). Later, when it managed to overcome those difficulties, the Brazilian Secretariat for Labour Protection recommended the ratification of the Convention.[445] As a result, none of the 'priority' conventions stands denounced.

The Night Work (Women) Convention (Revised), 1948 (No.89), has been the subject of the largest number of denunciations.[446] Although about one-tenth of the instruments of ratification of ILO conventions have been the targets of denunciation,[447] only 0.15 per cent of the instruments of

[440] Ibid.
[441] See 'Country Baseline under the ILO Declaration Annual Review (2000–2008): Malaysia': search <www.ilo.org> (last accessed 27 March 2009).
[442] Ibid.
[443] 'General Survey on Labour Inspection by the Committee of Experts on Application of Conventions and Recommendations', Report III, Part 4B, International Labour Conference, 71st Session, 1985, endnote 7 (ILOLEX General Survey Doc 251985G02). Available at <www.ilo.org/ilolex/english/iloquery.htm> (last accessed 10 December 2008).
[444] Visit <www.ilo.org/ilolex/cgi-lex/ratifgroupe.pl?class=g03_06&country=Brazil> (last accessed 10 December 2008).
[445] Above n 443.
[446] The 21 denouncing States are: Austria, Belgium, Cuba, Cyprus, the Czech Republic, the Dominican Republic, France, Greece, Ireland, Italy, Luxembourg, Malta, the Netherlands, New Zealand, Portugal, Slovakia, Spain, Sri Lanka, Switzerland, Uruguay, and Zambia. Visit <www.ilo.org/ilolex/english/newratframeE.htm> (last accessed 10 December 2008).
[447] As of 31 October 2008, there are 188 conventions. The total number subject to 'pure' denunciations is 127. The total number of ratifications of conventions is 6887, and the total number of denunciations is 700. Visit <www.ilo.org/ilolex/english/convdisp2.htm> (last accessed 10 December 2008).

ratification of the 'core' conventions have been denounced. Uruguay has denounced the largest number of conventions.[448] Among developed States, France has made the largest number of denunciations,[449] closely followed by the United Kingdom.[450] On the other hand, except for its withdrawal from the ILO during 1977–1980,[451] the United States has not denounced any ILO convention. This is understandable because, unlike its European allies, the United States maintains a very low ratification rate of ILO conventions.

Rarely does a State fail to explain the reasons for its denunciation of an ILO convention.[452] According to the official records, major reasons for denunciation are:

(a) The conceptual inflexibility of the convention;
(b) The inappropriateness of the convention in modern circumstances;
(c) The continuity of contravention between domestic law and the convention;
(d) The denouncing State's belief that it is difficult to implement the convention in local conditions;
(e) The denouncing State's conclusion that it is impracticable to carry out the precise terms of the convention;
(f) The denouncing State's assessment that the convention is no longer relevant under the domestic conditions;
(g) Substantial change of domestic law relating to the convention;
(h) Profound changes in socio-economic life in the jurisdiction of the denouncing State;
(i) Substantial developments in economic conditions and relationships between employers and workers within the jurisdiction of the denouncing State;
(j) Intended revisions of legislation that might affect the denouncing State's ability to satisfy the terms of the convention.

One can gather some impressions from State practice with respect to the denunciation of ILO conventions. First, States have been slow to move towards denunciation and there is no discernible movement to denounce precipitately.[453] Secondly, there is no evidence that certain States have shown

---

[448] The 27 denounced conventions bear the following numbers: 2; 3; 4; 5; 6; 7; 10; 12; 15; 17; 18; 20; 24; 25; 33; 42; 45; 52; 58; 59; 60; 62; 67; 89; 96; 101; and 112. Visit <www.ilo.org/ilolex/english/newratframeE.htm> (last accessed 10 December 2008).

[449] The 19 denounced conventions have the following numbers: 4; 5; 9; 10; 15; 32; 33; 41; 45; 54; 58; 72; 75; 89; 91; 108; 109; 112; and 123. Ibid.

[450] The 17 denounced conventions bear the following numbers: 4; 5; 6; 7; 10; 15; 18; 26; 41; 43; 45; 63; 88; 94; 95; 99; and 101. Ibid.

[451] For details, see W Galenson, *The International Labor Organization: An American View* (The University of Wisconsin Press, Madison, 1981).

[452] For example, on 7 June 1974 Czechoslovakia denounced the Unemployment Provision Convention, 1934 (No.44), without stating any reasons. Likewise, on 19 April 1979 Singapore denounced the Abolition of Forced Labour Convention, 1957 (No.105), without mentioning any reasons.

[453] Widdows, above n 226, 1060.

a propensity towards denunciation.[454] Thirdly, the denouncing States had trouble in applying the convention in the period immediately before the denunciation.[455] Fourthly, those ILO conventions that are least denounced have the most liberal denunciation clauses. Fifthly, a preponderant majority of the denounced conventions are the old ones and their denunciation becomes inevitable owing to the substantial change of circumstances. Finally, in spite of the recognition of the right of denunciation, the practice of this right against a 'core' convention is considered an unhealthy development.

Although all ILO conventions are subject to denunciation, the 'core' conventions have been the targets of minimal denunciations and the 'priority' conventions have so far escaped denunciation almost altogether. In spite of their recognition as 'fundamental human rights conventions', the issue of customary law or *jus cogens* has not been raised to question the right of denunciation in the case of 'core' conventions. The process of globalization has not made any discernable difference in the State practice of the denunciation of ILO conventions because a number of them have been denounced in the new millennium.

The ILO Office itself has not only urged States to denounce outmoded conventions but it has also proposed an amendment to the ILO Constitution authorizing the ILO Conference to abrogate outmoded conventions still in force.[456] The denunciation of ILO conventions is a transparent phenomenon by virtue of the officially recognized procedure. It is also a very democratic process in the sense that the principal parties (States, employers, and workers) have an opportunity to engage in consultations prior to an act of denunciation. While States and employers rarely disagree with each other in denunciation matters, workers generally find themselves on the other side. The ILO monitoring mechanism obtains an advance warning of denunciation and this offers an opportunity to engage in preventive diplomacy if necessary. In sum, the ILO law and practice on denunciation is a model of maturity in both normative and functional terms.

G. Synthesis

The State practice of the denunciation of human rights treaties in formal terms is very limited, and the denunciations of ILO conventions constitute a unique phenomenon. The solitary denunciation of the Convention relating to the Status of Stateless Persons was an aberration, and the same is true with the ACHR and the ECHR. The five cases of denunciation by the DPRK, Guyana, Jamaica, Trinidad and Tobago, and Yugoslavia (Serbia and Montenegro) are less than two per cent of the total number of accessions to and ratifications of the target instruments, namely, the

---

[454] Ibid, 1062.　[455] Ibid.
[456] L R Helfer, 'Understanding Change in International Organizations: Globalization and Innovation in the ILO' (2006) 59 *Vanderbilt Law Review* 649, 714.

ICCPR and the first Optional Protocol thereto. This percentage is much lower than the denunciations of ILO conventions as a whole, but much higher than the percentage of the denunciations of the 'core' ILO conventions. While 10.16 per cent of the instruments of ratification of ILO conventions have been denounced, only 0.15 per cent of the instruments of ratification of the 'core' conventions of the same organization have been subjected to denunciation. In other words, in spite of having a denunciation clause, the 'core' ILO human rights conventions are less prone to denunciations than the 'core' UN human rights treaties.

Most of the denunciations have had a short span. Greece rejoined the ECHR within five years of denunciation. Guyana reacceded to the first ICCPR Protocol immediately. Trinidad and Tobago also reacceded to the Protocol immediately and denounced it again only after its reservation was found invalid. The DPRK returned to the fold of the ICCPR within three years of denunciation, and Yugoslavia (Serbia) did likewise within six years. In addition, Peru terminated its partial withdrawal from the ACHR within two years. Apart from these instances, Jamaica has so far not been able to overcome the difficulties that forced it to denounce the first ICCPR Protocol in 1997. Therefore, most of the States parties remain committed to most of the human rights treaties most of the time. This is in contrast to the practice of denunciation of or withdrawal from treaties in general; since 1975, a State denounces or withdraws from a treaty every ten days.[457] Evidently, human rights treaties are relatively less prone to denunciation.

One can generalize that the denunciation of a human rights treaty is a consequence or a direct response of a State party that is held in violation of the treaty rights in question by a judicial, quasi-judicial, or administrative body at the international level. Such a finding generally provokes the government concerned. Occasionally, the politicization of international human rights processes has incited denunciations. Although every denunciation has its own cause and effect, the Caribbean denunciations originated under the same circumstances and led to the same consequences. Those denunciations appeared because of intolerance towards capital crimes, reaction to a precedent set by the highest court of appeal, disillusion with the assertiveness of international monitoring bodies, and embarrassment caused by civil society. They produced frustration among the beneficiaries of the target treaties and their monitoring bodies. Each one of the denouncing States can still offer a justification for its action against the target treaty. Concisely, States have considered acts of denunciation for a variety of reasons, such as diplomatic provocation, international condemnation, legal compulsion, economic burden, political machination, moral degradation, and normative evolution.

In fact, the cause of denunciation is not as important as its cost. A potential denouncer calculates the cause and cost before taking a decision

---

[457] Helfer, above n 101, 1608.

in this regard. The cost-benefit analysis with regard to the denunciation of ILO conventions is different from other treaties. While the denunciation of a 'core' ILO convention may harm the image of the denouncing State as much as the denunciation of any human rights treaty, the same is not true with regard to other ILO conventions. Therefore, the causes and consequences of denunciation of the ICCPR and the first Optional Protocol thereto are not similar to the causes and consequences of denunciation of those ILO conventions that are not 'core' or 'priority' conventions. Thus, in terms of their respective law and practice of denunciation, the ICCPR system and the ILO system must be treated separately.

In spite of relying on denunciation clauses, none of the denouncing States can escape the accusation of lowering the standard of protection in respect of human rights. States avoid formal denunciations of human rights treaties because of the high reputational costs involved therein. They do not want to suffer economic loss following hostile reactions from those States that impose human rights conditionality on international trade. The diplomatic disadvantage resulting from the alienation from a forum of multilateral discourse arrests the option of denunciation. States also consider an act of denunciation unnecessary when they can exercise less risky options to attain the same objective. Because of their publicity, most of the incidents of formal denunciation have been the subject of concern at the international level, though not all have generated substantial scrutiny. Local remedies hardly exist in denunciation matters. Generally, the target treaties without monitoring bodies are defenceless against denunciation.

The incidents of denunciation indicate that, though they are not many, they present serious challenges to the confidence of the human rights regimes in question. Meeting these challenges resourcefully is a question of law and policy. There is a need to develop a better perspective in order to meet these challenges.

V. PERSPECTIVE ON DENUNCIATION

Unlike States, human rights advocates believe in the special status of human rights treaties. This is also the belief of most of the human rights bodies, such as the HRCttee,[458] the IACmHR,[459] and the IACtHR.[460]

---

[458]   General Comment 26, above n 235 and surrounding text.

[459]   In the *Constitutional Court* case, the IACmHR submitted: 'International human rights law has the supreme objective of protecting individual rights and freedoms. In light of that objective, this legal regime possesses specialized attributes which in some moments differ from those of other branches of international law.' See *IACmHR Second Report on Peru* (2000), above n 291, chapter 3, para 39.

[460]   In its advisory opinion on *The Effect of Reservations on the Entry Into Force of the American Convention on Human Rights* (*Arts. 74 and 75*), the IACtHR observed that 'modern human rights treaties ... are not multilateral treaties of the traditional type concluded to accomplish the reciprocal

Human rights treaties have enormous implications for individuals and denunciation/reservations, even if legally permissible, raise questions related to morality and legitimacy. However, the hard law of denunciation of human rights treaties does not reflect their special status. The nature test and General Comment 26 seek to establish the special status of human rights treaties in denunciation matters. Both are valuable guides but not without problems. First, the nature test serves little purpose in the presence of denunciation clauses; a majority of human rights treaties have such clauses. Secondly, even if the General Comment is the *lex specialis* of the ICCPR and the *lex ferenda* for other treaties of similar nature, there is no general hard or soft law to make human rights treaties immune from denunciation. In the backdrop of this reality, human rights treaties have to reconcile their special status with their vital need to remain an integral part of international law.

Normally, the denunciation of a treaty is a lawful act if it is permissible under the treaty. This may not be the case, however, if we apply the nature test, the special status of human rights treaties, or General Comment 26; the presence of a denunciation clause as such would hardly make any difference by itself without the help of some additional factors. This is perhaps the most progressive interpretation of the law of denunciation of human rights treaties. It is favourable to the cause of human rights but uncomfortable to the community of States. It seems to have little recognition under the present state of international law, where the adoption of a treaty with a denunciation clause is a common phenomenon.

Irrespective of its legality, the denunciation of a human rights treaty affects its beneficiaries, trustees and parties. It creates an immediate need to make a determination as to whether the provisions of the treaty have a continuing application. The proponents of continuity have to prove that the provisions of the treaty have become customary rules, general principles of law, or peremptory norms of international law. This is not an easy task. Since human rights treaties enshrine some peremptory norms of international law,[461] the denunciation of any one of those treaties presents a challenge to the implementation of those norms. The monitoring body of the target treaty encounters an issue of credibility, because it has to prove its effectiveness in all circumstances; unlike States, it cannot dilute its responsibility even during a state of emergency. An act of denunciation

---

exchange of rights for the mutual benefit of the contracting States.' See Advisory Opinion OC-2/82 (24 September 1982), IACtHR, Series A, No. 2, para 29.

[461] In its Commentary to the Draft Articles on State Responsibility in 2001, the ILC included the following in the category of peremptory norms of international law: the prohibition of slavery and slave trade, genocide, racial discrimination and apartheid, torture (as defined in the CAT), basic rules of international humanitarian law applicable in armed conflict, and the right to self-determination. See Draft Articles on State Responsibility, Commentary on Article 40, in *Yearbook of the International Law Commission, 2001: Report of the Commission to the General Assembly on the work of its fifty-third session, Vol II, Part II* (United Nations, New York, 2007), UN Doc A/CN.4/SER.A/2001/Add.1 (Part 2) 112–13, paras 4–6.

ends the denouncing State's treaty relationship with the remaining States parties. It leaves civil society with a sense of insecurity, especially when the target treaty covers non-derogable rights. Those persons who are under the jurisdiction of the denouncing State lose a forum for the expression of their grievances, if any. The denouncing State appears as 'an odd man out' and must address the issues of isolation and damaged reputation. The remaining States parties are deprived of an opportunity to engage the denouncing State in a constructive dialogue within the framework of the target treaty.

An act of denunciation undermines the efforts to universalize the target treaty.[462] Because all human rights are interrelated[463] and their monitoring bodies recognize their interdependence,[464] any harm to any of them is likely to have adverse effects on the rest. In brief, denunciation disrupts relations between different participants in the treaty system, strains limited resources, sets wrong priorities, and derails the process of sustainable development of a human rights culture. Obviously, there is a powerful case against the denunciation of any human rights treaty even if it contains a denunciation clause *expressis verbis*. This is also true with the 'core' and 'priority' conventions of the ILO, although denunciation is admissible there.

At the same time, no human rights regime can be effective without its wider acceptance. That is why the United Nations pursues the goal of universal acceptance of the 'core' human rights treaties in particular.[465] In fact, universalization is only possible if conditions conducive to it are in place. One of the conditions of universalization is that States should have the confidence of exercising their sovereign discretion, particularly in extreme situations. Like the right of derogation,[466] the recognition of the right of denunciation derives its logic from this perspective. In this sense, the presence of a denunciation clause in a treaty should not be viewed as antithetical to international cooperation including in the area of human rights. In fact, it operates as a centripetal force in a treaty relationship.

The UN human rights treaty system would be too ambitious to seek to achieve what is not possible even in the most developed regional system, namely, the European human rights system. Even after facing the Greek

---

[462] Boerefijn, above n 118, 3.

[463] Almost every international human rights instrument affirms the interdependence and inseparability of human rights. Adopted by the representatives of 171 States by consensus, the 1993 Vienna Declaration on Human Rights sums up the issue thus: 'All human rights are universal, indivisible and interdependent and interrelated.' See UN Doc A/CONF.157/24 (1993), part I, para 5.

[464] See, for instance, above n 405 and accompanying text.

[465] See, for instance, '2008 Treaty Event: Towards Universal Participation and Implementation—Dignity and Justice for All of Us', <http://untreaty.un.org/English/CNs/2008/101_200/158E.pdf> (last accessed 10 December 2008).

[466] ICCPR, article 4(1) ('In time of public emergency which threatens the life of the nation and the existence of which is officially proclaimed, the States Parties to the present Covenant may take measures derogating from their obligations under the present Covenant to the extent strictly required by the exigencies of the situation, provided that such measures are not inconsistent with their other obligations under international law and do not involve discrimination solely on the ground of race, colour, sex, language, religion or social origin.').

denunciation, the ECHR expressly retains the right of denunciation in its latest version[467] and implicitly reaffirms the logic of having the same right in several other conventions.[468] Similarly, in spite of the denunciation of the ACHR by Trinidad and Tobago, some of the subsequently adopted American conventions contain a provision on denunciation.[469] Although most of the African human rights treaties do not contain any denunciation clause,[470] their freedom from denunciation remains uncertain. It seems that, besides the applicable law of treaties, African legal traditions would help determine the admissibility of denunciation of the African conventions.

Some of the latest 'core' UN human rights treaties incorporate the right of denunciation.[471] Almost 200 ILO conventions contain denunciation clauses and a majority of them have actually been denounced with little controversy on the subject. Even a historic treaty like the Rome Statute of the International Criminal Court is subject to denunciation.[472] Similar is the situation with several big treaties, such as the CTBT,[473] the UNCLOS[474] and the WTO Agreement,[475] as well as a few new millennium treaties, such as the Convention on Cluster Munitions[476] and the International Convention for the Suppression of Acts of Nuclear Terrorism.[477]

This widespread practice allowing for the possibility of denunciation of a treaty shows that international law recognizes the realities of the contemporary world. Human rights treaties do likewise. The denial of the right to denunciation as such might not necessarily prevent States from denouncing a treaty to which they are a party. In a case of need, or perceived need, States might adopt soft and silent ways and means, such as indifference towards

---

[467] Article 58 (former Article 65) of the ECHR, as amended by Protocol 11, which came into force on 1 November 1998. See *Basic Documents on Human Rights*, above n 428, 623.

[468] See, for example, Article 37 of the 1977 European Convention on the Legal Status of Migrant Workers (ibid, 715); Article 22 of the 1987 European Convention for the Prevention of Torture and Inhuman or Degrading Treatment or Punishment (ibid, 722); Article 22 of the 1992 European Charter for Regional or Minority Languages (ibid, 743–44); Article 31 of the 1995 European Framework Convention for the Protection of National Minorities (ibid, 752); Article 46 of the 2005 European Convention on Action against Trafficking in Human Beings (ibid, 805).

[469] See, for example, Article 13 of the 1999 Inter-American Convention on the Elimination of All Forms of Discrimination Against Persons with Disabilities (ibid, 988).

[470] An old exception is Article 13 of the 1969 Convention Governing the Specific Aspects of Refugee Problems in Africa. See *Compilation of Regional Human Rights Instruments*, above n 15, 329.

[471] See, for example, Article 20(1) of the ICESCR Protocol: 'Any State Party may denounce the present Protocol at any time by written notification addressed to the Secretary-General of the United Nations. Denunciation shall take effect six months after the date of receipt of the notification by the Secretary-General.' Above n 175.

[472] 2187 UNTS 3 (entered into force 1 July 2002), article 127(1).

[473] CTBT, article 9(2) reads: 'Each State Party shall, in exercising its national sovereignty, have the right to withdraw from this Treaty if it decides that extraordinary events related to the subject matter of this Treaty have jeopardized its supreme interests.' Above n 182.

[474] UNCLOS, above n 21, article 317(1).

[475] WTO Agreement, above n 17, article 15.

[476] Convention on Cluster Munitions, above n 88, article 20.

[477] Article 27. Adopted by the General Assembly on 15 April 2005: see UN Doc A/RES/59/290; see article 25 on the information on entry into force. Text available at <http://treaties.un.org/doc/publication/ctc/ch_xviii_15.pdf>. (last accessed 26 February 2009).

treaty provisions or procedural obligations. Many States parties to the ICCPR and the Optional Protocols thereto do so even without risking the opprobrium of being designated as a denouncer.[478] Similarly, when some pressure groups wish their State would denounce a treaty but are unable to convince the State to denounce that treaty, they may rely on a restrictive interpretation of the provisions of the treaty to serve more or less the same purpose. Contraction of human rights of persons detained, indicted and accused in the prosecution of the war on terror proves this point.

The presence or absence of a provision on denunciation in a treaty is not an indication of the importance of that treaty. For instance, the fact that the ICERD contains an express provision on denunciation does not make it inferior to the CEDAW that does not have a comparable provision. Likewise, the presence of a denunciation provision in the 1949 Geneva Conventions for the Protection of War Victims[479] and the Additional Protocols thereto[480] does not mean that one can denounce them, escape the application of international humanitarian law, and feel free to commit grave breaches such as war crimes. The inclusion or exclusion of a provision on denunciation may be the result of a number of factors, known or unknown, such as diplomatic convenience, drafting difficulties, urgency of adopting a convention with consensus, or simply a lack of time to resolve the issue at the drafting stage.

The incorporation of an express provision on denunciation in a treaty is no guarantee of its dispute-free interpretation, application, or implementation. For instance, the DPRK denunciation of the 1968 Treaty on the Non-Proliferation of Nuclear Weapons (NPT) has been a cause of disagreement in spite of the recognition of the right of denunciation in the treaty itself.[481] This means that the inclusion or exclusion of a provision on denunciation cannot meet the expectations of all the generations to

---

[478] See examples at above n 205 and accompanying text.

[479] The common denunciation provision states: 'Each of the High Contracting Parties shall be at liberty to denounce the present Convention.' See Article 63 of the Convention (I) for the Amelioration of the Condition of the Wounded and Sick in Armed Forces in the Field; Article 62 of the Convention (II) for the Amelioration of the Condition of Wounded, Sick and Shipwrecked Members of Armed Forces at Sea; Article 142 of the Convention (III) relative to the Treatment of Prisoners of War; and Article 158 of the Convention (IV) relative to the Protection of Civilian Persons in Time of War. Visit <www.icrc.org/Web/Eng/siteeng0.nsf/htmlall/genevaconventions> (last accessed 10 December 2008).

[480] Article 99 of the 1977 Protocol relating to the Protection of Victims of International Armed Conflicts (Protocol I); Article 25 of the 1977 Protocol relating to the Protection of Victims of Non-International Armed Conflicts (Protocol II); and Article 14 of the 2005 Protocol relating to the Adoption of an Additional Distinctive Emblem (Protocol III) (ibid).

[481] Article 10(1) of the NPT states: 'Each Party shall in exercising its national sovereignty have the right to withdraw from the Treaty if it decides that extraordinary events, related to the subject matter of this Treaty, have jeopardized the supreme interests of its country. It shall give notice of such withdrawal to all other Parties to the Treaty and to the United Nations Security Council three months in advance. Such notice shall include a statement of the extraordinary events it regards as having jeopardized its supreme interests.' See 729 UNTS 169 (entered into force 5 March 1970).

come. It requires the development of a more dynamic treaty law than the one at present.

The progressive development of the law of treaties should take into account the imperatives of the global rule of law, which may not tolerate the denunciation of a certain treaty even if it contains a denunciation clause. For instance, it is difficult to perceive the United Nations to be 'a centre for harmonizing the actions of nations' in the attainment of the common ends of the Organization, if the UN Charter becomes a target of denunciation because of the absence of a prohibitory clause therein. In the same spirit, States parties to human rights treaties should review the applicable law and its ambiguities relating to denunciation. For instance, it does not serve any purpose to have a codified myth that the CAT is subject to denunciation. If the budgetary arrangements of the CAT can be amended in view of new financial realities, the denunciation clause of the Convention can also be amended pursuant to new moral imperatives. Considering that States parties would not like to open a Pandora's Box on the law and policy of denunciation, the soft law-making process may help bring about this kind of reform.

The HRCttee should revise General Comment 26 to enrich its content. The urgency of the matter in the face of the DPRK denunciation was a sound justification for the quick adoption of General Comment 26 in 1997,[482] but its revision should reflect the HRCttee's capacity to take into account the views of others, particularly States parties to the ICCPR. Besides addressing issues relating to denunciation, the revised general comment should reflect on denunciation-like situations that affect the ICCPR and the Optional Protocols thereto. It should highlight the potential consequences of denunciation to dissuade States parties from departing too radically from their treaty commitments. It should also enumerate the benefits of the continuity of obligations enshrined in a human rights treaty. Some guidance regarding the role of civil society in denunciation matters and denunciation-like situations should find expression in the revised general comment.

The HRCttee and other treaty bodies could jointly draft and adopt a general comment on the issues relating to the denunciation of the UN human rights treaties because most of these treaties are of similar nature. The process of formulation of a joint general comment should be used to strengthen the bonds between the treaty bodies on the one hand and States parties on the other. Besides its own experience, as well as the practices of other treaty bodies, the HRCttee should study some new and sophisticated clauses relating to denunciation.[483] A joint general comment

---

[482]   The HRCttee began its sixty-first session on 19 October 1999. Ten days later, it adopted the General Comment. Even General Assembly resolutions generally take longer for their negotiation, drafting and adoption.

[483]   For example, Article 20(2) of the Convention on Cluster Munitions (above n 88 and accompanying text) and Article M of the European Social Charter (Revised) (above n 15).

would promote the harmonization of human rights norms. It could potentially lead to the avoidance of normative conflicts and promote a common
law of denunciation. To some extent, it could also respond to those who
worry about the fragmentation of international law.

Besides strengthening the moral force of international human rights
law, it is necessary to make its practice more sensitive to political realities.
Those who intend to react to denunciations should think carefully about
their objectives before going public. If the main objective is to encourage
the denouncing State to reconsider its position, the response needs to be
less legalistic and more pragmatic. Instead of making formal statements,
the objectors may engage in bilateral discussions to understand and appreciate the problems of the denouncing State and try to explore the possibility of resolving those problems. This approach can encourage the objectors
to do justice to the principle of international cooperation, which requires
all States to extend cooperation to each other and to take 'joint and separate' action to help resolve human rights problems.[484] It may inspire the
denouncing State to reclaim its treaty rights and obligations. The history
of human rights treaties suggests that no denouncing State wants to remain
outside the denounced regime forever. Therefore, condemnation of the
denouncing State need not be the main objective. Rather, the main objective should be bringing the denouncing State back into the fold.

The need to expedite the process of correcting the wrongs of denunciation should be the principal policy consideration of the treaty regime
in question. As soon as it detects the danger of denunciation of a treaty,
the treaty body should try to deflect the danger by engaging in a constructive dialogue with the denouncing State and by drawing attention to the
consequences of denunciation in terms of their adverse effects on human
rights in particular and the rule of law in general. It may resort to preventive diplomacy with the help of well-meaning interlocutors such as
NHRIs and regional or sub-regional organizations. It may try to impress
on the denouncing State its sovereign obligation to explore a constructive
alternative to denunciation. In case of its inability to do so, the treaty body
should encourage its functional partners to devise a collaborative response,
to minimize the adverse effects of denunciation and to create conditions
conducive to the denouncing State's return to the treaty system. In this
regard, the treaty bodies can learn from the NPT model.[485] To help the

---

[484]   Articles 1(3) and 56 of the UN Charter provide the foundation of the principle of international
cooperation. The 1970 Declaration on Principles of International Law concerning Friendly Relations
and Cooperation among States in Accordance with the Charter of the United Nations elaborates this
principle (General Assembly Resolution 2625 (XXV) (24 October 1970)). Every international human
rights instrument gives expression to the principle of international cooperation.

[485]   In 1993, when the DPRK gave notice to withdraw from the NPT, the most concerned States
entered into negotiations to avert the crisis. Within three months, they reached an agreement and the
DPRK suspended its withdrawal notice. In 2003 also, when the DPRK announced that it was ending
the suspension of its previous withdrawal notification, the most concerned States intensified their
diplomatic efforts to convince the DPRK to return to the NPT. If it had adopted this kind of
approach after the DPRK notification of withdrawal from the ICCPR in 1997, the HRCttee could

treaty bodies in the implementation of their denunciation-dissuading policy, the OHCHR may offer its advisory services to those States parties that are in the danger zone of denunciation; civil society may take the discussion on the subject to the grassroots-level; and human rights experts may develop action-oriented and situation-specific solutions. The whole exercise may help reconstruct a fruitful structure of functional relationships that may eventually relegate the possibility of denunciation to an academic interest.

The international community as a whole, not a treaty body alone, has the responsibility for dealing with the cracks in the treaty system whenever they occur. The task of a treaty body is to monitor the implementation of its constituent instrument, not to change its content, spirit and procedure. Human rights instruments are 'drafted in such a way as to limit the possibilities of dramatic change from within, by processes of interpretation and application as distinct from amendment'.[486] Therefore, the adoption of remedial measures relating to denunciation need not be the sole responsibility of the treaty body that is directly affected. States parties to a treaty in danger of denunciation have a special responsibility to demonstrate creativity and to maintain unity as a collegiate entity. They may seek the help of the OHCHR, which can arrange advisory services to address the root causes of the act or threat of denunciation if there is any. The collective role of States parties and the OHCHR is crucial in respect of those human rights treaties that have no monitoring bodies. Indeed, this course of action is possible when the principle of international cooperation finds expression in State practice in both spirit and substance.

VI. CONCLUSION

A treaty brings States together and its denunciation clause gives them a sense of security. On the other hand, an act of denunciation operates as a centrifugal force and disrupts a treaty relationship. Although treaty making is an old phenomenon, the law of treaties cannot claim the status of universality in its entirety. As a result, some sources of the law are more pertinent to address the question of denunciation than other questions. The principle of *pacta sunt servanda* provides stability for international relations, and the rule *rebus sic stantibus* introduces flexibility. Accordingly, the principle of good faith coexists with the possibility of denunciation of a treaty. Conceptually, the doctrine of national sovereignty empowers a State not only to enter into a treaty but also to exit from it. The absence

---

have avoided acrimonious exchanges with the State party and their constructive dialogue would have been restored much earlier.

[486] P Alston, 'Beyond "them" and "us": Putting Treaty Body Reform into Perspective' in P Alston and J Crawford (eds) *The Future of UN Human Rights Treaty Monitoring* (Cambridge University Press, Cambridge, 2000) 522.

of righteous howls over denunciations reflects a sense of tolerance and pragmatism among the parties.

However, States parties to a treaty or its monitoring body, where such a body exists, may employ, as appropriate, the following devices to deny the right of denunciation: an express provision, a supplementary instrument, an authoritative interpretation, an interpretative declaration, the nature of the treaty in question, the intention of the parties concerned, or a combination of some of these devices. The same objective can be achieved with the help of an agreement making another remedy exclusive. The pressure of public opinion or the special status of the treaty in the global rule of law can do likewise. Although these special circumstances may exist in respect of several treaties, only the ICCPR and the Second Optional Protocol thereto have so far been considered worthy of claiming immunity against denunciation. It seems that not many human rights treaties would be able to establish a similar claim. Since the present state of law is not sensitive to all the special circumstances under discussion, the progressive development of the law on denunciation is overdue. Indeed, the questions of interpretation arising in this context are likely to be tricky.

There is no human rights treaty with a provision on the prohibition of denunciation. In fact, a majority of the 'core' UN human rights treaties contain denunciation clauses. Denunciation is permissible even in respect of some of the treaties with one or more of their provisions having the character of peremptory norms of international law. A majority of the human rights treaties adopted in the new millennium contain denunciation clauses. The process of globalization has not made any significant difference in a normative sense concerning denunciation, because it cannot amend the final clauses of a treaty, but it has enhanced the benefits of continuing with international human rights arrangements.

The denunciation of a human rights treaty invariably attracts international attention. That is why States parties do not lightly consider denunciation of human rights treaties and the same accordingly remains rare. The prospect of economic integration creates stakes that operate as a constraint in the freedom of the unilateral denunciation of a treaty. For instance, a Member State of the Council of Europe and the European Union cannot afford to denounce the ECHR without taking the risk of expulsion from these organizations. The process of globalization has increased the economic and social costs of denunciation. It has certainly ensured that no act of denunciation can go unnoticed, as happened with the first case of denunciation of a human rights treaty. In other words, globalization may not have reduced the prospects of denunciation of human rights treaties, but it has increased both the cost of denunciation and the means of accountability of the denouncing State.

No State considers it prudent to pay a high price for the exercise of its right to denounce a treaty. The right of denunciation continues to carry unwritten inhibitions. Considering the economic price, reputational cost, and comparative disadvantage of an act of denunciation, some States invent alternatives to achieve almost the same objectives. The persistent defiance of critical treaty obligations is a striking instance of de facto denunciations. If a State party can exercise the right of derogation with an imaginative justification and without making a notification, for instance, why should it proceed with the denunciation of the target treaty? Similarly, if a State party to a human rights treaty can afford to ignore its indispensable obligation to submit its report to the treaty monitoring body for over a decade or so, what is the need to make a formal denunciation? Quite a few States parties have fallen into this kind of situation[487] and the number of 'serious defaulters' has been increasing.[488] As a result, unhappily, the breach of obligations becomes a substitute for the act of denunciation.

Denunciation is an executive act, although an initiative to this effect may originate from any arm of a State party—the executive, the legislature, or the judiciary—or its political parties. The possibilities for such initiatives may differ in different domestic jurisdictions. Denunciation may also come from a collective stand of a group of States. As a State is responsible for the acts of its organs or federal units, the State party should ensure internal accountability in order to prevent the possibility of an illegal denunciation. The denunciation of a human rights treaty as such may not affect the normative value of its provisions but it may disturb their translation in State practice, international implementation and progressive development.

Although denunciations of human rights treaties are not common, the possibility of denunciation continues to hang like the Sword of Damocles over the treaty monitoring bodies. Because of the necessity of safeguarding the integrity of its constituent instrument, the HRCttee has responded to the incidents of denunciation of the ICCPR and the first Optional Protocol thereto in a resolute manner, although it failed to make an instant impact on the denouncing States. It has made a significant contribution to the progressive development of international law by adopting General Comment 26 against the denunciation of the ICCPR and the Second Optional Protocol thereto. Following the General Comment, some scholars observe that denunciations are impermissible in respect of those human rights treaties that do not expressly permit denunciation.[489] Like the General Comment, which is the main body of soft law on denunciation,

---

[487] For instance, Syria did not submit any report under Article 40 of the ICCPR for more than twenty years (July 1978 to January 2000) (see reporting history of the Syrian Arab Republic available at <www.bayefsky.com/./html/syria_t3_ccpr.php> (last accessed 10 December 2008)). Likewise, Sierra Leone has not submitted any report under Article 9 of the ICERD for more than thirty years (since April 1974) (see reporting history of Sierra Leone available at <www.bayefsky.com/./html/sierraleone_t3_cerd.php> (last accessed 31 January 2009)).

[488] As of 31 July 2008, as many as 48 States parties were in 'serious default' of their reporting obligations under the ICCPR. See *Report of the Human Rights Committee*, GAOR, sixty-third session (2008), supplement no. 40, UN Doc A/63/40, vol I, 15–16.

[489] Joseph, Schultz, and Castan, above n 255.

this view seeks to redefine the applicable law. The soft law constitutes a challenge to the traditional basis of obligation in international law. Because of the morally powerful content of the General Comment, States have not come out openly against the new positive morality on denunciation. One may wonder whether the silence of sovereigns on the effect of General Comment 26 constitutes an *opinio juris* to give rise to a new customary norm of international law against the denunciation of the ICCPR-type of treaties.

History shows that only a small number of States have come to the stage of denunciation of human rights treaties; ILO conventions present an exception in this regard; and State practice makes the 'core' ILO conventions an exception within that exception. While treaty bodies such as the CRC and the HRCttee are sensitive to the need to rebuild the relationship between the denouncing States and the denounced regimes, most of their functional partners have not contributed to this field to the best of their abilities. All the trustees of human rights treaties and their functional partners have a duty to take joint and separate action not only to promote and protect human rights but also to meet the actual and potential challenges of denunciation of human rights treaties.

Apart from the adoption of a joint general comment on the issues relating to denunciation, the UN human rights treaty bodies should regularly engage in a constructive dialogue with States parties with a view to forestalling any situation that may lead to the denunciation of a human rights treaty. This type of confidence building measure would bridge the gap between the monitors and their targets. It can produce better results by involving civil society at various stages of monitoring procedures. Because of the availability of greater opportunities to participate in the functioning of the treaty monitoring process, innumerable actors are in a position to contribute to the evolution of new normative standards and functional solutions to the challenge of denunciation, even if it arises only occasionally. This unprecedented opportunity must be used to enrich the content and practice of human rights in general and the law of denunciation in particular.

As a matter of policy, the drafters of human rights treaties should discuss the question of denunciation not only to take a well-informed decision on the inclusion or exclusion of the relevant clause but also to educate others about their understanding of the subject matter. In case its inclusion is agreed upon, the denunciation clause in a human rights treaty ought to have a provision on pending matters, a specified period of notice, a long period before the denunciation comes into effect, and a role for civil society, the States parties and the monitoring body, where such a body exists. Most important, it should require the denouncing State to make a statement about the steps taken to avoid denunciation and to explain the reasons for denunciation. This may introduce greater transparency in the law and practice of denunciation of human rights treaties.

Status of Settlers Implanted by Illegal Territorial Regimes

By Yaël Ronen[*]

  * Yaël Ronen, Post-doctoral fellow, Minerva Center for Human Rights at the Hebrew University of Jerusalem. E-mail: yael.ronen@cantab.net. Research for this study was generously funded by the Minerva Center for Human Rights, Hebrew University in Jerusalem. I am grateful to Prof. Yuval Shany, to participants in the Hebrew University Law Faculty seminar, and to the anonymous reviewer for their comments. Usual disclaimers apply.

I. INTRODUCTION

This article concerns settlers introduced into a territory by a territorial regime that is illegal under international law. Such regimes usually fall within one of two categories. The first category includes entities which effectively operate as States and claim statehood on the basis of acts that are unlawful under international law; the second category includes established States which act as sovereigns over areas outside their recognized national territories, in violation of international law. The article focuses on one specific phenomenon associated with both categories of illegal territorial regimes, namely the introduction or implantation of large settler populations into the territories under dispute. It examines this phenomenon at a specific moment, namely when the illegal territorial regime is replaced by a lawful, or 'post-transition', one.

Illegal regimes characteristically take measures to change the demographic composition of the territory under dispute. Two main strategies are employed. One is the forced removal of the local population from the territory and change of nationality and residence status of those persons.[1] The other is the transfer of their own populations or populations loyal to them into the territory, and the subsequent granting to these populations of residence or nationality[2] in the territory. This article is concerned with the response of the post-transition regime to this second strategy.

At the time of transition from the illegal regime to the new, lawful regime, it is not surprising that there are calls at various levels, either for the physical removal of settlers from the country or at least for their exclusion from the body politik. These calls represent a variety of interests and sentiments. Common to most situations is resentment towards the settlers as representatives of the exploiting regime, and a common thirst for retribution. This sentiment is not limited to situations where an illegal territorial regime ends; it is common to many post-colonial regimes. Another motive for expulsion is the concern of the post-transition regime that despite formal withdrawal, the previous, illegal regime will continue to exert political, economic or military pressure on the territory under the new regime, through its diaspora population of settlers. A further source of indigenous objection to settlers remaining in the territory is scarcity of local resources.

The post-transition regime must therefore determine what it may and should do with persons who had settled in the territory during the existence of the illegal territorial regime and under its instruction or with its acquiescence. The legal power of the post-transition regime to reverse the acts of the illegal regime by removal of settlers may be limited in various ways. There may be an obligation to give effect to whatever status the illegal regime conferred upon the settlers; expulsion may also be limited by the operation of human rights law and standards applicable to long-term

---

[1] A post-transition regime wishing to reverse the situation is doubtlessly entitled to offer nationality and residence status to persons who had previously been denied it. It may be queried whether the post-transition regime is also entitled to impose such status. It is generally accepted that a State may not impose its nationality to persons not resident in its territory. The question is whether the post-transition regime may *restore* status to a non-resident without that person's consent.

[2] The terms 'nationality' and 'citizenship' are used here interchangeably, depending on the context in which they appear. Ordinarily 'nationality' reflects the international dimension of the relationship between a State and the individual, while 'citizenship' reflects the domestic, constitutional dimension of the same relationship. In some cases, the phenomenon of secondary citizenship or nationality (for example in federated States) complicates this delineation. In the cases examined in this article this matter does not arise.

residents, regardless of the original impermissibility of their arrival in the territory and subsequent invalidity of their status.[3]

This article examines these questions through a study of five cases of transition from illegal territorial regimes. In four of them the process of transition to a legal regime has been completed: the transition from Ian Smith's regime in Rhodesia to independent Zimbabwe (1980), the restoration of the independence of the Baltic States following the annexation by the Soviet Union (1990–1991), South Africa's transition from apartheid to democracy and the elimination of the TBVC States (Transkei, Bophuthatswana, Venda and Ciskei) (1994), and East Timor's independence following annexation by Indonesian rule (2002). The fifth case is the prospective reunification of the Republic of Cyprus with the Turkish Republic of Northern Cyprus (TRNC), which at the time of writing is being negotiated.[4]

This is not an exhaustive catalogue of settler implantation by regimes that have been regarded internationally as illegal. Conspicuously (but not exclusively) absent from its coverage are South Africa's administration of Namibia (1966–1990) and Israel's purported annexation of East Jerusalem in 1967 and of the Golan Heights in 1981.[5] The case of Namibia, while fundamental to the law applicable to illegal regimes, does not raise questions of settlers' implantation as no such phenomenon occurred. The case of Israel differs from others in that should the Golan Heights revert to Syrian control or should Israeli control in East Jerusalem be relinquished, Israeli settlers are unlikely to wish to remain in the territory.

Part II sets out the historical and legal circumstances of each of the cases examined. Part III focuses on potential constraints on expulsion of settlers based on their purportedly acquired status, Part IV focuses on constraints on expulsion of settlers arising from substantive human rights law. Part V concludes with a comparison of the practice in the various cases by reference to the parameters established earlier.

---

[3] There are other limitations. The Special ILC Rapporteur on the expulsion of aliens (hereafter 'Special Rapporteur') also catalogues limits inherent in the international legal order and limits relating to the procedure of expulsion, UN Doc A/CN.4/581 para 27. The latter category is generally unaffected by the identity of potential expellees or the circumstances of expulsion (except with respect to national security grounds for expulsion, eg ICCPR art 13, ECHR Protocol 7, 22 November 1984, CETS 155 (entered into force 1 November 1998) art 1(2)). Therefore it is of limited interest in the present context. Moreover, procedural guarantees, around which a large part of jurisprudence revolves, usually affect actual acts of expulsion, rather than the adoption of a policy on expulsion.

[4] For a discussion of the illegality of these regimes see John Dugard, *Recognition and the United Nations* (Grotius, Cambridge, 1987). The process of their transition to legal regimes is discussed in Yaël Ronen, *Legal Aspects of Transition from Unlawful regimes in International Law (PhD Thesis)* (Cambridge, 2005) and 'The Dispossessed and the Distressed: Land Rights in Transition from Unlawful Territorial Regimes' in Eva Brems (ed) *Conflicts between Fundamental Rights* (Intersentia, Antwerp, 2008) 521.

[5] Examples of other cases of an illegal regime are Iraq's annexation of Kuwait in 1990–1991, Western Sahara under Moroccoan rule, and possibly the purported statehood of Transdnistria, South Ossetia, and Abkhazia.

II. The Phenomenon

A. Rhodesia

1. Background[6]

Until 1965 Southern Rhodesia[7] was a British colony enjoying extensive self-government powers. In the early 1960s, the British Government and the Southern Rhodesian Government negotiated independence for the colony, without success. The point of contention was the transition to majority rule. On 11 November 1965 the Southern Rhodesian Government, headed by Ian Smith, issued a unilateral declaration of independence (UDI) of Rhodesia.[8]

Both the UN General Assembly and the Security Council repeatedly called upon all States not to recognize the illegal racist minority regime in Southern Rhodesia.[9] Other international organizations also took action.[10]

---

[6] On Rhodesia's declaration of independence, the international reaction and the reversion to colony status, see: Douglas G Anglin 'Zimbabwe: Retrospect and Prospect' (1979–1980) 35 *International Journal* 663; Simon Beynam (ed) *Zimbabwe in Transition* (Almqvist and Wiksell, Stockholm, 1992), James Crawford *The Creation of States* (2nd ed, Oxford University Press, Oxford, 2006) 128–131; Jeffery Davidow, *A Peace in Southern Africa: The Lancaster House Conference on Rhodesia,* 1979 (Westview Press, Boulder, 1984); John Dugard, 'Rhodesia: Does South Africa Recognize it as an Independent State?' (1977) 94 *The South African Law Journal* 127, Dugard, above n 4, 90; Vera Gowlland-Debbas, *Collective Responses to Illegal Acts in International Law: United Nations Action in the Question of Southern Rhodesia* (Martinus Nijhoff, Dordrecht, 1990); Desmond William Lardner-Burke, *Rhodesia: The Story of the Crisis* (Oldbourne, London, 1966); Adolphe Lawson, *Les Accords de Lancaster House en 1979: l'Aboutissement de Deux Décennies de Débats sur les Conditions de l'Indépendance du Zimbabwe* (Almqvist & Wiksell International, Uppsala, 1988); Robert O Matthews, 'Talking Without Negotiating: The case of Rhodesia' (1979–1980) 39 *International Journal* 91; Myres S McDougal and W Michael Reisman, 'Rhodesia and the United Nations: The Unlawfulness of International Concern' (1968) 62 *American Journal of International Law* 1; Wyndraeth H Morris-Jones, *From Rhodesia to Zimbabwe: Behind and Beyond Lancaster House* (Frank Cass, London, 1980); Jericho Nkala, *The United Nations, International Law and the Rhodesian Independence Crisis* (Clarendon, Oxford, 1985); Claire Palley, *The Constitutional History and Law of Southern Rhodesia, 1888–1965 with Special Reference to Imperial Control* (Clarendon Press, Oxford, 1966); John Parker, *Rhodesia: Little White Island* (Pitman, London 1972), Alison Quentin-Baxter, *Rhodesia and the Law A Commentary on the Constitutional and International Law Aspects of the Rhodesian Situation* (New Zealand Institute of International Affairs, Wellington, 1970); Brad R Roth, *Governmental Illegitimacy in International Law* (Clarendon, Oxford, 1999); Peter Slinn, 'Zimbabwe Achieves Independence' (1980) 6 *Commonwealth Law Bulletin* 1038; Lord Christopher Soames, 'From Rhodesia to Zimbabwe' (1980) 56 *International Affairs* 405.

[7] Until the Declaration of Independence the territory was called Southern Rhodesia. After the Declaration it renamed itself Rhodesia. Following the internal settlement of 1978 the name changed to Rhodesia-Zimbabwe, and upon independence it became Zimbabwe. For convenience, this work will use the name 'Rhodesia' for the period until 1980, and 'Zimbabwe' for the following period. 'Zimbabwe' is the African name for the territory, and its use reflects the realization of Black African self-determination.

[8] 'Proclamation by Prime Minister' (1966) 5 *International Legal Materials* 230. This was clearly in excess of the Rhodesian government's powers under the 1961 constitution. Initially Rhodesia purported to remain a monarchy, with the Queen as head of State, but in 1970 it proclaimed itself a Republic.

[9] Eg GA Res 2024(XX) (11 Nov 1965), GA Resolution 2012 (XX) (12 October 1965), GA Res 2022(XX) (5 Nov 1965), SC Res 216 (11 November 1965), SC Res 217 (12 November 1965), SC Res 277 (18 March 1970), SC Res 288 (17 November 1970).

[10] Eg Second Ordinary Session of the Assembly of Heads of States of the Organization of African Unity held in Accra, Ghana from 21 to 26 Oct 1965, AHG/Res 25 (II) (22 Oct 1965) para 5, Sixth

The UDI was considered illegal because it had been carried out without consultation with the Black majority and in order to perpetuate the existing White minority rule.[11] Both were violations of the right of the Black population to self-determination.[12] The adherence to the policy of non-recognition was universal. No State recognized the statehood of Rhodesia, although South Africa's practice came close to such recognition.

During a decade of abortive attempts to resolve the Rhodesia problem through negotiated settlements and pressure placed on the Smith regime through the UN-imposed sanctions,[13] fighting within Rhodesia escalated, resulting by 1978 in some 12,000 victims of guerrilla action.[14] The conflict was finally resolved in December 1979, when the British Government brokered the Lancaster House Agreement.[15] Under the Agreement, Rhodesia temporarily reverted to colony status under direct control of a Governor appointed by the British government.[16] Elections were held in February 1980,[17] leading to the transition of Rhodesia in April of the same year into independent, majority-ruled Zimbabwe.[18] Zimbabwe adopted the Independence Constitution,[19] also agreed upon at Lancaster House.

2. *Settlers under the Rhodesian regime*

In 1965, the population of Rhodesia comprised about five million people, 4% (210,000) of whom were White.[20] The UDI was followed by a brief period of emigration of non-Blacks, arising from insecurity about the political future of the country. Thereafter, the emigration of Whites, Asians,

Ordinary Session of the Council of Ministers of the Organization of African Unity held in Addis Ababa, Ethiopia from 28 Feb to 6 Mar 1966, CM/Res 75 (VI) para 1.

[11] Under Rhodesian law, a distinction was made between Whites, Blacks, Coloureds, and Asians.

[12] Eg GA Resolution 2022 (XX) (5 Nov 1965), preambular paras 4, 5; Gowlland-Debbas, above n 6, 221–237; Nineteenth Ordinary Session of the Council of Ministers Held in Rabat, Morocco from 5 to 12 June 1972, CM/Res 267 (XIX) preambular paras 5, 7; Twenty-Ninth Ordinary Session of the Council of Ministers Held in Libreville, Gabon from 23 June to 3 July 1977 CM/Res 547 (XXIX) preambular para 5.

[13] Nkala, above n 6; Gowlland-Debbas, above n 6, 17–23; Matthews, above n 6; Stephen J Stedman *Peacemaking in Civil War, International Mediation in Zimbabwe, 1974–1980* (Lynne Rienner, Boulder, 1991).

[14] Margaret Doxey, 'The Making of Zimbabwe: From Illegal to Legal Independence' (1982) 36 *The Year Book of World Affairs* 150, 161.

[15] For an analysis of the negotiations and their outcome see Lawson, above n 6; Davidow, above n 6.

[16] Pre-Independence Arrangements, annexed to the Report of the Constitutional Conference, Lancaster House (1979) (1980) 19 *International Legal Materials* 387, para 2.

[17] Elections for the White seats were held on 14 Feb 1980, and for the Black seats on 27, 28, and 29 Feb 1980.

[18] Because of the short period of time between the reversion to Colony status and Zimbabwe's independence, this article considers the process of transition to independence and not only reversion to colony status.

[19] United Kingdom Southern Rhodesia—Report of the Constitutional Conference, Lancaster House, London, September–December 1979 (Lancaster House, 21 December 1979) (Cmnd 7802 1979).

[20] Barry M. Schutz, 'European Population Patterns, Cultural Persistence, and Political Change in Rhodesia' (1973) 7 *Canadian Journal of African Studies/Revue Canadienne des Études Africaines* 3, 21.

and Coloureds from the country slowed. In contrast, immigration increased during the late 1960s and early 1970s.[21] This was partly the result of a governmental immigration campaign which began in 1964 to attract a million White settlers to the country.[22] The Government's campaign involved considerable financial and social integration incentives. In addition, as African States gradually achieved independence, Rhodesia became the destination of many Whites who sought to preserve a colonial lifestyle. Even in the late 1970s, by which time Rhodesia's deteriorating political and economic situation[23] discouraged immigration and emigration was again on the rise, large numbers of immigrants were still arriving from newly-independent Mozambique and Angola.[24]

Overall, from 1966 to 1980, the net population of non-Blacks grew only marginally, by less than 5%. Moreover, because the growth rate of the Black population increased, the relative size of the non-Black population consistently grew smaller.[25] Yet the composition of the non-Black population changed dramatically: by 1980, about half of it was post-UDI immigrants.[26]

3. Transitional arrangements

During the Lancaster House negotiations on withdrawal of the Smith regime and establishment of Zimbabwe, the Popular Front (PF), representing the Black population of Rhodesia, objected to the validation of citizenships granted since 1965. It was particularly concerned that validating such citizenships would create a large population of dual nationals of both Zimbabwe and South Africa, which by 1980 had become an island of White minority dominance over a Black majority. The PF assumed that post-UDI settlers were for the most part supporters of the illegal regime, who were therefore perceived as a security risk for Zimbabwe. This assumption was not without basis, given the motives for immigration noted above.[27] Moreover, the PF was concerned that dual nationality would result in excessive South African involvement in Zimbabwe under the guise of protection of its nationals.[28] The PF therefore suggested that potential dual nationals would be required to opt for either Zimbabwean or their other nationality within one year of independence.

---

[21] Lovemore M. Zinyama, 'International Migrations to and from Zimbabwe and the Influence of Political Changes on Population Movements, 1965–1987' (1990) 24 *International Migration Review* 748, 751.
[22] Glenn V Stephenson, 'The Impact of International Economic Sanctions on the Internal Viability of Rhodesia' (1975) 65 *Geographical Review* 377, 385.
[23] Zinyama, above n 21, 751–752.
[24] Schutz, above n 20, 21–22.
[25] Ibid, 20.
[26] In the 1969 census their total number was only 252,414. The net immigration of about 11,000 non-Blacks consisted of some 145,000 immigrants and 134,000 emigrants. Based on data provided in Zinyama, above n 21, 751–752.
[27] Schutz, above n 20, 21–22.
[28] Lawson, above n 6, 145.

These proposals were not adopted in the Lancaster House Agreement. In line with a general validation of pre-1980 law,[29] the Independence Constitution confirmed the validity of pre-transition Rhodesian citizenship, and provided that persons holding it immediately prior to the date on which Zimbabwe became independent would automatically become Zimbabwean citizens. The Constitution did not distinguish the date on which that citizenship had been acquired. Moreover, persons not holding Rhodesian citizenship but entitled to it under pre-transition law would have an unqualified right to claim Zimbabwean citizenship for a period of five years following independence.[30] On the basis of *ius sanguinis*, descendants of Zimbabwean citizens were also entitled to Zimbabwean citizenship, regardless of the basis on which their parents had acquired that citizenship.[31]

The status of Whites as Zimbabwean citizens and residents was thereby guaranteed. In practice the Zimbabwean Government took measures to encourage the White population to emigrate from the country, mostly through economic incentives such as the right to remove funds from the country under favourable terms. The precise composition of the White population, namely whether it was recently-arrived settlers or long-term inhabitants, was of little significance. Zimbabwe acted in this respect, as in others, as a State emerging from colonial rule, similar to other newly independent States in Central and Southern Africa, and the incentives were not related in any way to the illegality of the previous regime.

B. The TBVC States

1. Background[32]

Between 1976 and 1981 South Africa granted independence to four States within its territory: Transkei, Bophuthatswana, Venda, and Ciskei (hereinafter 'the TBVC States'[33]). This was perhaps the ultimate extension of the South African government's apartheid policy. It was an attempt to

---

[29] Constitution (Interim Provisions) Ordinance 1979, s. 4.

[30] Independence Constitution, above n 1, B1.

[31] Ibid, B3. At the same time, the Agreement empowered Parliament to make provisions for taking away the Zimbabwean citizenship of a person who had acquired it other than by birth or descent. Theoretically this left the door open to deny citizenship of post-UDI settlers, ibid, B6(B).

[32] On the establishment of the TBVC States, the international reaction and the reincorporation of the TBVC States into South Africa, see George N Barrie, 'The "Absorption" of Bophuthatswana March 1994: Extinction of State Personality from a South African perspective, Irrelevancy from an International Perspective' (1994) *Tydskrif Vir Die Suid-Afrikaanse Reg* (Journal of South African Law) 348; AJ Christopher, *The Atlas of Changing South Africa* (2nd ed, Routledge, London, 2001); Andries Cilliers, 'Reincorporation of Bophuthatswana and Certain Other States in to the Republic of South Africa' (1993/1994) 19 *South African Yearbook of International Law* 93; Paul Daphne, 'Undoing Apartheid is Going to Cost Us' (1994) 96 *Work in Progress* 14; Donald E deKieffer and David A Hartquist, 'Transkei: A legitimate Birth' (1978) 13 *New England Law Rev* 428; Dermott J Devine, 'International Law Tensions Arising from the South African Situation 1976–1986' (1987) *Acta Juridica* 165; Dugard, above n 4, 98; John Dugard, 'The Future of the TBVC 'States'' (1992) 8 *South African Journal on Human Rights* iii.

[33] Also referred to as 'Bantustans', together with six non-independent units within South Africa.

produce a new version of racial segregation, seemingly in line with contemporary international standards. The South African Government presented the granting of so-called independence to the TBVC States as 'internal decolonization'.[34] It claimed that it was responding to requests by the representatives of these entities. The independence of Transkei in 1976, Bophuthatswana in 1977, Venda in 1979, and Ciskei in 1981 was effected by domestic legislation entitled Status Acts,[35] which created each of the TBVC States and severed them from South Africa. The TBVC States were governed by civil and military dictatorships, often subjected to states of emergency and always prone to coups. Their governments depended on the South African Government to maintain power, which was held through repression of opposition and frequent resort to violence. Ordinarily, these governments followed policies demanded by the South African Government.[36]

The grant of independence to the TBVC States was condemned by the UN General Assembly as a tool for the perpetuation of apartheid and for dispossessing the black population of its right to self-determination.[37] The TBVC States were never recognized as independent by any State except South Africa and the other TBVC States.[38] Their existence was also vehemently opposed by the leading opposition movement, the African National Congress (ANC), as well as by residents of the TBVC States themselves, who resented the material deprivation which characterized the TBVC States in comparison with the rest of South Africa.[39]

The 1989 elections in South Africa marked the beginning of a new era and the gradual renunciation of apartheid. In February 1990 the South African Government began to dismantle the apartheid regime.[40] It soon became clear that the TBVC States would be reincorporated within the new democratic South Africa.[41] On 27 April 1994, elections were held

---

[34] John Dugard, 'Collective Non-recognition: the Failure of South Africa's Bantustan States' in *Boutros Boutros-Ghali Amicorum Discipulorumque: Liber, Peace Development, Democracy, Vol 1* (Bruylant, Bruxelles, 1998) 383–387.

[35] Status of Transkei Act 1976, Status of Bophuthatswana Act 1977, Status of Venda Act 1979, Status of Ciskei Act 1981.

[36] Interview with Mr. Zam Titus, Special Advisor to the minister of Provincial and Local Government and formerly Director-General of the Ministry of Constitutional Development, Administrator-General of Ciskei, participant in the multiparty negotiating forum (Pretoria, 7 April 2004).

[37] GA Res 31/6A (26 October 1976) on Transkei, GA Res 32/105 N (14 Dec 1977) on Bophuthatswana, S/13549 Note by the President of the Security Council (21 Sept 1979) on Venda, GA Res 37/69 A (9 Dec 1982) on Ciskei.

[38] Although not being recognized themselves, they were incapable of recognizing the statehood of other entities. Dermott J Devine, 'Recognition, Newly Independent States and General International Law' (1984) 10 *South African Yearbook of International Law* 18.

[39] South African Institute of Race Relations, *Race Relations Survey* 1989–90 (SAIRR, Johannesburg, 1990) 435.

[40] South African Institute of Race Relations, *Race Relations Survey* 1991/92 (SAIRR, Johannesburg, 1992) 79.

[41] Tanya Woker & Sue Clarke, 'Homelands' (1991) 2 *South African Human Rights Yearbook* (1991) 104, 105; South African Institute of Race Relations, *Race Relations Survey* 1992–93 (SAIRR, Johannesburg, 1993) 506, Firoz Cachalia, 'A Report on the Convention for a Democratic South Africa' (1992) 8 *South African Journal on Human Rights* 249, 261; Titus, above n 36, Interview with

throughout South Africa, including the TBVC States. After the elections the Interim Constitution came into force, repealing the provisions granting independence to the TBVC States.[42]

2. Settlers in the TBVC States

A large number of persons became citizens of the TBVC States, who had not been South African citizens previously. These naturalized TBVC citizens fell within two main categories. One group consisted of criminals and mafia members from around the world, who profited from the lack of international relations and cooperation with the TBVC States to evade the law. They often acquired TBVC citizenship through illegal payment to the TBVC States' despot leaders. The other, much larger, group comprised people from various African States, such as Ugandan doctors, who wanted to immigrate to South Africa. They preferred to naturalize in the TBVC States since this was more easily done than in South Africa, and because the rural TBVC States were more similar to their States of origin than urban South Africa.[43]

3. Post-Apartheid arrangements

At the early stages of the negotiations over the transition from apartheid, there was a debate on the status of naturalized TBVC citizens. Eventually it was decided to give legal effect to previous grants of status.[44] The resultant 1993 Restoration and Extension of South African Citizenship Act, which generally reversed the apartheid-era legislation on nationality, adopted the principle that persons who were citizens of the TBVC States but not of South Africa, namely post-'independence' naturalized citizens, would have to apply for South African citizenship by naturalization. This provision was criticized as discriminatory because it applied to former TBVC States' citizens only.[45] Accordingly, the 1995 South African Citizenship Act made the acquisition of South African citizenship by these persons automatic.[46] At the same time, the Act permitted the Minister of Home Affairs to deprive a person of South African citizenship if his or

---

Prof. Francois Venter, University of Potchefstroom, participant in the MPNF (Potschefstroom, 6 April 2004); Interview with Mr. Rolf Meyer, South Africa's Minister of Defence, of Communication and of Constitutional Affairs 1991–1996 (Pretoria, 8 April 2004).

[42] Interim Constitution art 230. The Interim Constitution was later replaced by the Constitution of the Republic of South Africa, 1996, which entered into force on 7 February 1997.

[43] Interview of the author with Dr. Jonathan Klaaren, Witwatersrand University (Johannesburg, 5 April 2004).

[44] Klaaren, ibid.

[45] Restoration and Extension of South African Citizenship Act 196 of 1993 art 4. Jonathan Klaaren, 'Post-Apartheid Citizenship in South Africa' in T. Alexander Aleinikoff and Douglas Klusmeyer (eds) *From Migrants to Citizens: Membership in a Changing World* (Carnegie Endowment for International Peace, Washington DC, 2000) 221, 228, 234–235.

[46] South African Citizenship Act no. 88 of 1995 art 4(1)(iii). The Act was amended by the South African Citizenship Act Amendment Act no. 69 of 1997, deleting this subparagraph, to rectify the fact that the 1995 wording did not grant South African citizenship as of right to persons who were citizens of the former TBVC states by registration, see South African Citizenship Act Amendment Bill, 1997, 8.

her certificate of naturalization had been obtained by fraudulent means.[47] This paved the way for a distinction between good-faith settlers and criminals fleeing the law.

C. East Timor

1. Background[48]

East Timor was until the mid-1970s a colony of Portugal.[49] In 1974 Portugal began a process of decolonization, which included the territory of East Timor. Neighbouring Indonesia opposed independence for East Timor.[50] In 1975, disagreement among factions within East Timor on its future spurred a civil war. Indonesian forces intervened and on 7 December 1975 occupied East Timor. In July 1976 Indonesia annexed East Timor as its 27th province.[51]

Portugal claimed that Indonesia's annexation of East Timor was illegal[52] because it rested on a violation of the prohibition on the use of force and on

---

[47]   South African Citizenship Act no. 88 of 1995 art 8(1)(a).

[48]   For general reference on the annexation of East Timor, the international reaction and the transition to independence, see: Mari Alkatiri, The Democratic Republic of East Timor (Statement in the Fourth Committee of the United Nations General Assembly) (1977) 7 *Journal of Contemporary Asia* 280; Antonio Cassese, *Self-Determination of Peoples, A Legal Reappraisal* (Cambridge University Press, Cambridge, 1995) 223–230; Roger S Clark, 'Obligations of Third States in the Face of Illegality—Ruminations Inspired by the Weeramantry Dissent in the Case Concerning East Timor' in Antony Anghie and Garry Stugess (eds) *Legal Visions of the 21ˢᵗ Century: Essays in Honour of Judge Christopher Weeramantry* (Martinus Nijhoff, The Hague, 1998); Roger S Clark, 'The "Decolonization" of East Timor and the United Nations Norms on Self Determination and Aggression' (1995) updated and corrected version (on file with the author) of Roger S Clark, 'The "Decolonization" of East Timor and the United Nations Norms on Self Determination and Aggression' (1980) 7 *Yale Journal of World Public Order* 2; Catriona Drew, 'The East Timor Story: International Law on Trial' (2001) 12 *European Journal of International Law* 651; James Dunn, *East Timor: A People Betrayed* (Jacaranda, Milton, 1983); Geoffrey C Gunn, *East Timor and the United Nations, the Case for Intervention* (Red See Press, Lawrenceville,1997); Lauri Hannikainen, 'The Case of East Timor from the Perspective of *Jus Cogens*', in *International Law and the Question of East Timor* 103 (Catholic Institute for International Relations and International Platform of Jurists for East Timor, London, 1995); Sharon D Korman, *The Right of Conquest: The Acquisition of Territory by Force in International Law and Practice* 281–292 (Oxford University Press, Oxford, 1996); Heike Krieger (ed) *East Timor and the International Community: Basic Documents* (Cambridge University Press, 1997); James J Fox and Dionisio Babo Soares (eds) *Out of the Ashes: Destruction and Reconstruction of East Timor* (Australian National University Press, Canberra 2003); Ian GM Scobbie and Catriona J Drew, 'Self-Determination Undetermined: The Case of East Timor' (1996) 9 *Leiden Journal of International Law* 185; Hansjoerg Strohmeyer, 'Policing the Peace: Post-Conflict Judicial System Reconstruction in East Timor' (2001) 24 *University of New South Wales Law Journal* 171; Conflict, Security and Development Group, *A Review of Peace Operations: A Case of Change* (King's College, London, 2003) 215–323; Commission for Reception, Truth and Reconciliation in East Timor (CAVR) *Chega! (CAVR Final Report)* 31 October 2005, available at <http://www.ictj. org/en/news/features/846.html> (last accessed 29 June 2009).

[49]   GA Res 1542 (15 December 1961).

[50]   Clark (1980), above n 48, 19–43.

[51]   Indonesia, Law 7/76 on the Legalization of the Integration of East Timor into the Unitary State of the Republic of Indonesia and the Formation of the Province of East Timor (1976).

[52]   Eg UN Doc A/52/152, Note Verbale dated 19 May 1997 from the Permanent Mission of Portugal to the UN addressed to the Secretary-General (20 May 1997), para 1.

the denial of the East Timorese population's right to self-determination.[53] Individual States accepted the Portuguese contention,[54] although few concrete measures were taken to sanction the delinquency.[55] The collective international position was expressed in General Assembly Resolution 3485 (XXX) of 12 December 1975, which called upon Indonesia:

to desist from further violation of the territorial integrity of Portuguese Timor and to withdraw without delay its armed forces from the territory in order to enable the people of the Territory freely to exercise their right to self-determination and independence.

Subsequent resolutions were less explicit with regard to the unlawfulness of the Indonesian intervention.[56]

In 1999 Indonesia agreed to hold a referendum in East Timor to determine its political future,[57] presenting the population with a choice between independence and integration within Indonesia as an autonomous region. In August 1999, over 78% of the half million voters put ballots in favour of independence.[58] Once the results of the vote were released, pro-integration militia groups went on a violent rampage, assisted by the Indonesian military.[59] In October 1999 the UN Security Council established the United Nations Transitional Administration in East Timor (UNTAET),

---

[53] Statement of the representative of Portugal, S/PV.1864 (15 December 1975) para 59; GA Res 31/53 (1 December 1976); Cassese, above n 48, 226.

[54] For the UK, see statement of the Minister of State, Foreign and Commonwealth Office (Mr. John Battle) that 'East Timor was invaded by Indonesia in 1975,' Hansard HC Vol 334 (6th Series) Col 764 (15 February 2000); An exception is Australia, which on 14 February 1979 announced it recognized the incorporation of East Timor into Indonesia *de jure*. It also claimed that other States have recognized the annexation, *Case Concerning East Timor (Portugal/Australia)*, Counter-memorial of the Government of Australia, 1 June 1992, paras 175–176, *East Timor (Portugal/Australia)*, Rejoinder of the Government of Australia, 1 July 1993, paras 44–54 Judge Skubiszewski opined that certain of the following States might have recognized the annexation *de facto*: Bangladesh, India, Iran, Iraq, Jordan, Malaysia, Morocco, Papua New Guinea, the Philippines, and the US, *Case Concerning East Timor (Portugal/Australia)*, [1995] ICJ Rep 90, Dissenting Opinion of Judge Skubiszewski, para 26.

[55] Thomas D Grant, 'East Timor, the UN System, and Enforcing Non-Recognition in International Law' (2000) 33 *Vanderbilt Journal of Transnational Law* 273, 298–99.

[56] SC Res 384 (22 December 1975), SC Res 389 (22 April 1976); GA Res 31/53 (1 December 1976), GA Res 32/34 (28 November 1977), GA Res 33/39 (13 December 1978), GA Res 34/40 (21 November 1979), GA Res 35/27 (11 November 1980), GA Res 36/50 (24 November 1981), GA Res 37/30 (22 November 1982). In 1983 the Commission on Human Rights adopted a resolution on the right of the East Timorese to self-determination which reaffirmed the inalienable right of the people of East Timor to self-determination and independence Commission of Human Rights Res 1983/8, UN Yearbook (1983) 833–834. For the position of the ICJ see *Case Concerning East Timor*, above n 54.

[57] Agreement between the Republic of Indonesia and the Portuguese Republic on the Question of East Timor, 5 May 1999, 2062 UNTS 8 (entered into force 5 May 1999); Agreement Regarding the Modalities for the Popular Consultation of the East Timorese through a Direct Ballot (Portugal-Indonesia), 5 May 1999, 2062 UNTS 40 (entered into force 5 May 1999).

[58] UN Secretary-General Press Release SG/SM/7119 SC/6722 of 3 September 1999.

[59] By late September, hundreds of people were killed and an estimated 400,000—over half the population—was forced to flee their homes. Geoffrey Robinson, *East Timor 1999: Crimes Against Humanity* Report commissioned by the UNOHCR (Geneva, 2005) 42–44.

to administer East Timor before handing it over to an elected Timorese government. On 20 May 2002 East Timor became independent.

Independent East Timor took the position that it had been occupied by Indonesia in violation of the prohibition on the use of force and of the right of the people of East Timor to self-determination.[60] The overall implications of this position on the applicable law in East Timor are yet to be settled,[61] although East Timorese law generally provides for continuity from Indonesian law applicable prior to 1999.[62]

2. Settlers under the Indonesian administration

It is estimated that in 1974 East Timor's population numbered around 650,000.[63] During Indonesia's rule, East Timor was a migration destination for Indonesian migrants under the Indonesian 'transmigration' policy (aimed at dispersing populations from dense and poor areas to outlying islands of the archipelago),[64] as well as for voluntary Indonesian migrants, for the most part attracted by economic incentives which Indonesia offered to settlers in East Timor. Non-governmental sources estimate a fall of over 20% in the indigenous population by 1980, primarily because of mass killings by Indonesia, and as a result of famine and of the departure of refugees.[65]

Although Indonesia conducted a number of censuses, exact data on the demographic composition of East Timor are hard to obtain. This is due to suspected excess counts and undercounts, as well as to lack of information on internal migration. Low counts provided by the Indonesian government suggest that East Timor was a migration destination for little

---

[60]   The preamble to the East Timorese Constitution; Indonesia has attempted to justify its use of force against East Timor on four grounds: self defence, invitation by the East Timorese, the future stability of Indonesia and Southeast Asia, and humanitarian purposes. However, none of these claims are sustainable as a matter of fact or of law: Clark (1980), above n 48, 37–43.

[61]   East Timor, Court of Appeal Judgment, Criminal Offence No. 3/2002 in the name of the appellant *Armando dos Santos v the Prosecutor General*, Dili, 15 July 2003, available in English at <http://www.jsmp.minihub.org/judgmentspdf/courtofappeal/Ct_of_App-dos_Santos_English22703.pdf> (last accessed 1 July 2009). Although the majority's ruling as to the validity of Indonesian legislation was rejected by lower courts and later superseded by legislation, its statement on the fact of unlawful occupation was not contested; Preamble of Law on the Juridical regime Real Estate Part 1—Ownership over Real Estate, No. 1/2003, adopted on 10 March, 2003. The original version in Portuguese ('A ocupação de Timor-Leste, entre 1975 e 1999, foi um acto ilegal, conforme reconhecido a nível internacional') is available at <http://www.gov.east-timor.org/L1bens.htm> (last accessed 29 June 2009).

[62]   Lei No. 2/2002 de 7 de Agosto Interpretação do Direito Vigente em 19 de Maio de 2002, and Lei No. 10/2003 de 10 de Dezembro Interpretação Do Artigo 1 da Lei No. 2/2002, de 7 de Agosto e Fontes do Direito.

[63]   Ben Kiernan 'The Demography of Genocide in Southeast Asia, The Death Tolls in Cambodia, 1975–79, and East Timor, 1975–80' (2003) 35 *Critical Asia Studies* 585, 590.

[64]   Mark J Miller, 'Demography and Security (MIT Center for International Studies, December 11–12, 1998)' (1999) 33 *International Migration Review* 193, 195.

[65]   Kiernan, above n 63, 594, Graeme Hugo, 'Forced Migration in Indonesia: Historical Perspectives' (2006) 15 *Asian and Pacific Migration Journal* 53.

over 10,000 persons,[66] and that overall, only about 6% of East Timor's population was previously resident in another province. This data only accounts for first-generation migrants, as government censuses would count subsequent generations of Indonesian internal migrants as native East Timorese despite their non-East Timorese ethnicity. High estimates of non-governmental sources suggest that by 1997 there were 160,000–180,000 non-Timorese inhabitants in East Timor in the 15–60 age group,[67] constituting 20% of the population.

Indonesian settlers in East Timor constituted a favoured military and commercial elite,[68] often given the best land while the local population was forced onto poorer land. Only a small percentage of native East Timorese occupied public service positions.[69]

3. East Timor's policy on nationality and residence

In view of the demographic composition of the territory, namely the Indonesian dominance of the political and economic elite, the presence of Indonesians in independent East Timor might have given cause for concern. However, following the referendum and in the midst of the ensuing violence, Indonesia conducted a massive pre-planned evacuation. About 250,000 persons were evacuated, comprising 70,000 military personnel and other non-Timorese, and 180,000 East Timorese.[70] By 2002, when East Timor's Nationality Law[71] was formulated and came into effect, the residence and nationality of Indonesian-era settlers was of little practical significance, although there have been isolated incidents of disputes concerning the expulsion of non-indigenous East Timorese.[72] The matter may re-emerge as the regulation of land rights progresses, since East Timorese law reserves the ownership of land to East Timorese nationals.[73]

East Timor's 2002 Nationality law determines its original citizens without any reference to previous citizenship, neither under Portuguese nor under Indonesian law. Article 8(1) of the Nationality Law provides

---

[66] Graeme Hugo, 'Pengungsi—Indonesia's Internally Displaced Persons' (2002)11 *Asian and Pacific Migration Journal* 297–332. This is less than one percent of all official transmigrants in the period 1968–2000, Riwanto Tirtosudarmo, 'Mobility and Human Development in Indonesia' Human Development Reports Research Paper 2009/19 8 table 2.2 (UNDP, June 2009).

[67] Kiernana, above n 63, 597. A different estimate is that of 5000 transmigrant families; Miller, above n 64, 195.

[68] Stephen Sherlock 'Political Economy of the East Timor Conflict' (1996) 36 *Asian Survey* 835, 837–838.

[69] UNDP, 'East Timor: Building Blocks for a Nation' (2000) 22–23.

[70] Robinson, above n 59, 78–81.

[71] Lei 9/2002 of 5 Nov 2002 (hereinafter 'East Timor Nationality Law').

[72] US Department of State, 2005 Country Reports on Human Rights Practices, East Timor, Section 2(c).

[73] It is not clear whether this reservation operates prospectively or applies also to existing ownership. Once the criteria for ownership are clarified, and if transactions carried out under the Indonesian administration receive any measure of validity, a problem may arise with respect to Indonesian owners of property who under the current legislation are not entitled to East Timorese citizenship.

that an original national of East Timor is one who was born in the national territory to a parent born in East Timor; or to a foreign parent and who, being over seventeen years old, declares to become an East Timorese national of his or her own accord.[74]

Section 8(1)(a) thus provides original nationality to second-generation natives of the territory. While this applies to most ethnic East Timorese, few Indonesian-era settlers are likely to benefit from this provision.[75] Article 1(c) allows adult second-generation settlers to acquire East Timorese nationality by declaration.

In addition, the Nationality Law provides for discretionary naturalization on the basis of long-term residence for persons who have been 'usual and regular resident of Timor-Leste [East Timor] for at least ten years prior to 7 December 1975 or after 20 May 2002' and able to speak one of the official languages of East Timor.[76] Settlers under Indonesian rule may thus acquire nationality on the same footing as other foreigners, but in the calculation of their lawful residence period, the period of Indonesian rule would not be counted. The law emphasizes that '[a] foreign citizen who has settled in Timor-Leste as a result of transmigration policy or foreign military occupation shall not be considered as a usual or regular resident'.[77]

Furthermore, Article 131(1) of the Immigration and Asylum Act (2003) clarifies that Indonesian-era settlers can not rely on residential status granted by Indonesia, but must obtain permission to reside in East Timor from the new East Timorese government:

Foreigners who entered the country after December 7, 1975, and who are conducting activities in the national territory for which under the present provisions it is mandatory to be a resident or holder of a proper visa, must, within 90 days from the entry into force of this Act, request a visa that will allow them to stay or to practice a professional activity.

Unlike the status of post-independence immigrants, residence of settlers under Indonesian rule is regulated by the instruction of the Minister of Interior, rather than by the standard immigration authorities.[78] Indonesian-era settlers are therefore subject to stricter control in acquiring permanent status in East Timor.

---

[74] East Timor Nationality Law, above n 71, art 8(1)(a), (c). Subarticle (b) grants original nationality to a person born in East Timor to incognito parents, stateless parents or parents of unknown citizenship. These provisions more or less duplicate art 3 of the East Timor Constitution (2002).

[75] Only third-generation settlers could benefit from this provision, if their parents were born from 1976 onwards in East Timor; they themselves would be not much older than 10 years old in 2002. Minors are unlikely to acquire East Timorese nationality if their parents do not.

[76] East Timor Nationality Law, above n 71, art 12(1)(b), (c). Since during the Indonesian administration the use of both languages was suppressed by the dominant Indonesian, the majority of settlers from that period were unlikely to be fluent in either of the two official languages, Portuguese and Tetum.

[77] Ibid, art 12(2).

[78] East Timor Immigration and Asylum Act (2003) art 131(2).

D. The Baltic States

1. Background[79]

The signing of the Molotov-Ribbentrop Pact in August 1939[80] marked the beginning of the active Soviet campaign for taking over Estonia, Latvia and Lithuania (the Baltic States).[81] On 16 June 1940 the Soviet Union issued ultimatums to all three States, requiring full occupation and the reconstruction of their governments under Soviet supervision. All three States caved in.[82] The puppet governments established in each of them under Soviet military guard arranged for elections, following which the elected assemblies in each State petitioned the Supreme Soviet of the USSR for admission to the Union. In August 1940 the Supreme Soviet passed legislation admitting Estonia, Latvia and Lithuania into the USSR as Soviet Republics.[83]

International reaction to the annexation was neither uniform nor clear.[84] Some States refused to recognize the annexation altogether because it was based on a threat to resort to force.[85] Other States recognized the absorption

---

[79] For general references on the annexation of the Baltic States, the international reaction and the restoration of independence, see: Cassese, above n 48, 258–264 (1995), Inesis Feldmanis, The Occupation of Latvia: Aspects of History and International Law (2004) <http://www.mfa.gov.lv/en/latvia/history/occupation-aspects/> (last accessed 29 June 2009), William JH Hough III, 'The Annexation of the Baltic States and its Effect on the Development of Law Prohibiting Forcible Seizure of Territory' (1985) 6 New York Law School Journal of International & Comparative Law 303, Anton Lieven, The Baltic Revolution, Estonia, Latvia, Lithuania and the Path to Independence (Yale University Press, New Haven, 1993), Lauri Mälksoo, Illegal Annexation and State Continuity: The Case of the Incorporation of the Baltic States by the USSR (Brill, Leiden, 2003), Rein Müllerson, International Law, Human Rights and Politics: Developments in Eastern Europe and the CIS (Routledge, London, 1994), Vello Pettai, 'The Construction of State Identity and its Legacies: Legal Restorationism in Estonia' (2007) 3 Ab Imperio 1, Peter van Elsuwege, 'State Continuity and its Consequences: The Case of the Baltic States' (2003) 16 Leiden Journal of International Law 17, Robert A Vitas, 'The Recognition of Lithuania—The Completion of the Legal Circle' (1993) 24 Journal of Baltic Studies 247, Romain Yakemtchouk, 'Les Républiques Baltes en Droit International Echec d'Une Annexion Opérée en Violation du Droit des Gens', (1991) 37 Annuaire français de droit international 259, Dainius Žalimas, 'Legal Issues on the Continuity of the Republic of Lithuania' (2001) 1 Baltic Yearbook of International Law 1, Ineta Ziemele, State Continuity and Nationality: The Baltic States and Russia (Martinus Nijhoff, Leiden, 2005). This article refers to the three States jointly because much of their relevant history is similar. However, specific differences between them are noted. Needless to say, each of the three States has independent policy and character.

[80] Treaty of Nonaggression Between Germany and the Union of Soviet Socialist Republics (signed 23 August 1939) and Secret Supplementary Protocol (USSR-Germany) (signed 23 August 1939, amended 28 September 1939) reproduced in I Shishcanu, V Varatec (eds) The Pact Molotov-Ribbentrop and its Consequences for Bessarabia: Documents (Universitas, Chişinău, 1991) 6.

[81] Susan E Himmer, 'The Achievement of Independence in the Baltic States and its Justifications' (1993) 6 Emory International Law Review 253, 266.

[82] Lieven, above n 79, 79–80.

[83] On 3, 5 & 6 August 1940; Boris Meissner, 'The Occupation of the Baltic States from a Present-Day Perspective' in: Talvas Jundzis (ed) The Baltic States at Historical Crossroads (Latvia Academy of Sciences, Rīga, 1998) 480.

[84] Hough, above n 79, Pierre M Eisemann and Martti Koskenniemi (eds) State Succession: Codification Tested against the Facts 52 (Martinus Nijhoff, The Hague, 2000); Mälksoo, above n 79, 122; Rytis Satkauskas, 'The Practice of France with Respect to the Baltic States' (2001) 1 Baltic Yearbook of International Law 111, 113.

[85] It has also been suggested that the annexation violated the right of the Baltic peoples to self-determination, Jean Salmon, 'Pays Baltes' (2001) 24 Revue Belge de Droit International 262, 266.

of the Baltic States into the USSR only *de facto*.[86] Some States recognized it *de jure*,[87] and others remained silent.[88]

The reversion of the Baltic States to independence formed part of, and indeed precipitated, the breakdown of the Soviet Union. In 1990 all three States began legislative processes towards renewing their independence.[89] By September 1991 all three Baltic States were admitted to the United Nations.

An important element in the policies of the Baltic States and common to all three was their self-perception as having emerged from an illegal regime of occupation to restore their pre-1940 independence.[90] This position was generally accepted by other States and organizations[91] although some controversy remained.[92] This self-perception was expressed,

See also Meissner, above n 83, 381–385; Mälksoo, above n 79, 91 on self-determination in the peace treaties with the USSR; Resolution 189 (1960) of the Council of Europe; but Cassese notes that the right to self-determination did not ripen until the 1960s. Cassese, above n 48, 262.

[86] Hough, above n 79, 430–442. For the United Kingdom see Court of Appeal, *A/S Tallinna Laevauhisus v Tallinna Shipping Co* (1946); *Hansard* HC Deb vol 433 (5th Series) col 5 (10 February 1947) cited in the High Court, *In re Pikelny* (1955); *Hansard* HC Deb vol 776 (5th series) col 583 (22 January 1969); Hansard HC Deb vol 172 (6th series) col 172 (8 May 1990). For Canada see Exchequer Court, *Estonian States Cargo and Passenger Line v S S Elise and Messrs Laane and Balster* (1949).

[87] Mälksoo, above n 79, 121.

[88] Hough, above n 79, 437, 440–443.

[89] Eg Latvian SSR, Supreme Council, Declaration on the Restoration of Independence of the Republic of Latvia (4 May 1990); Act on the Re-establishment of the State of Lithuania (11 March 1990); Resolution on the National Independence of Estonia (20 August 1991) noted in Mälksoo (2003), above n 79, 47; Law on the Statehood of Latvia (21 August 1991).

[90] For Estonia see statement on crimes committed by the occupation regimes in Estonia during the Second World War, June 17–23, 2002 Estonian Review, available at: <http://www.vm.ee/eng/kat_137/2484.html> (last accessed 29 June 2009). The Persons Repressed by Occupying Powers Act defines such persons as those 'unlawfully repressed by the powers that occupied Estonia between 16 June 1940 and 20 August 1991'. This includes both the USSR and Germany. June 16 is the day of the Baltic States' annexation into the USSR. Persons Repressed by Occupying Powers Act, passed 17 December 2003, RT [Riigi Teataja (State Gazette)] I 2003, 88, 589, available at <http://www.legaltext.ee/text/en/X80010.htm> (last accessed 29 June 2009); for Latvia see preamble to the Declaration on the Renewal of Independence (4 May 1990), ECtHR 9 October 2003, *Slivenko v Latvia*, application no. 48321/99, judgment of 9 October 2003, para 76; for Lithuania see the Act on the Re-establishment of the State.

[91] On the question whether by 1940 the prohibition on the threat or use of force had become part of customary international law see Ian Brownlie, *International Law and the Use of Force by States* (Clarendon, Oxford, 1963) 364; Hersch Lauterpacht (ed) *Oppenheim's International Law* (6th ed, Longmans, Green and Co, London, 1940) 153 n 6; Boris Meissner, 'The Right to Self-Determination after Helsinki and its Significance for the Baltic Nations', (1981) 13 *Case Western Reserve Journal of International Law* 375, 380–381; Žalimas, above n 79; Herbert Wright, 'The Legality of the Annexation of Austria by Germany', (1944) 38 *American Journal of International Law* 621; James W Garner, 'Non-Recognition of Illegal Territorial Annexations and Claims to Sovereignty', (1936) 30 *American Journal of International Law* 679; Robert Y Jennings, *The Acquisition of Territory in International Law* 52–67, 81 (Manchester University Press, Manchester 1963); International Law Commission (ILC), *Law of Treaties: Report by Mr Hersch Lauterpacht, Special Rapporteur*, UN Doc A/CN.4/63 (1953), Commentary (3) to Draft art 12; International Military Tribunal September 1946—1st October (1946), *The Trial of German Major War Criminals*, 19.

[92] The Russian Federation (as successor of the USSR) maintains that the Baltic States had been annexed lawfully and their independence is the result of secession. V Socor, Kremlin Assails Baltic States, 2(93) *Eurasia Daily Monitor* (12 May 2005) <http://www.jamestown.org/single/?no_cache=1&tx_ttnews[tt_news]=30393> (last accessed 29 June 2009); van Elsuwege, above n 79.

inter alia, in the reversion to pre-1940 in certain areas of law, including citizenship.

2. *Settlers under the Soviet regime*

From the 1940s, the Soviet Government carried out a policy of Russification[93] of the Baltic States in order to give permanence to Soviet rule.[94] This policy was particularly prominent in Estonia and Latvia. Large waves of immigration took place in 1945–1950 and in 1961–1970.[95] Many Russophones were encouraged to migrate by the higher than average socio-economic conditions in Estonia and Latvia and the cultural incentives derived from the perceived 'Europeanness' of the Baltic region. Significant numbers of Russophone residents of the three States had been posted there while on military duty and then remained in place upon retirement, particularly in Latvia, where the Soviet Army's Baltic region's headquarters was located.[96] By the late 1980s, when the USSR was disintegrating, the Russophone minority in Estonia and Latvia was much larger than any comparable migrant group in any European country. In Estonia, the share of Estonians decreased from over 88% in 1934 to 61.5% in 1989,[97] while that of Eastern Slavs grew from 8% to 35%. In Latvia, Latvians declined from 77% to 52% during the same period, while the Eastern Slavs population grew from 12% to 42%.[98] Only in Lithuania did the share of the indigenous population remain almost constant, at 88%. Inhabitants of the three States were considered nationals of the Soviet Union and residents of the respective Soviet Republic.

At the time of reversion to independence, the status of Soviet-era Russophone settlers was by far the most pressing and contentious issue, particularly in Estonia and Latvia. The Baltic independence movements argued that the mass immigration of Soviet settlers violated international law on the transfer of civilian population to occupied territory.[99] The elected transitional Congresses of Estonia and Latvia[100] considered Soviet-era

[93] The term 'Russification' indicates the introduction of a Russophone population. Ethnically this population comprises not only Russians but is characterized by being non-Baltic. For the purpose of this article its designation as Russophone is sufficient, to indicate its non-Baltic character and the fact that its dominant language is Russian.

[94] For a detailed review of this policy see Mälksoo, above n 79, 216–221.

[95] Estonia, UN Doc CERD/C/329/Add.2. (5 July 1999) para 41.

[96] Ziemele, above n 79, 364.

[97] Estonia, UN Doc CERD/C/329/Add.2 (5 July 1999) para 38.

[98] European Parliamentary Assembly of the Council of Europe Doc 7169 (6 October 1994) Report on the application by Latvia for membership of the Council of Europe (Rapporteur: Mr Espersen, Denmark, Socialist Group) annex VII; James Hughes, 'Exit in Deeply Divided Societies: Regimes of Discrimination in Estonia and Latvia and the Potential for Russophone Migration' (2005) 43 *Journal of Common Market Studies* 739, 743–744.

[99] Convention Relative to the Treatment of Civilian Persons in Time of War, 12 August 1949, 75 UNTS 287 (entered into force 21 October 1950, hereinafter 'Geneva Convention IV'), art 49.

[100] Established by elections organized in 1990 by the Citizens Committees (restorationist grass-roots organizations led by former anti-Soviet dissidents). Vello Pettai and Klara Hallik, 'Understanding Processes of Ethnic Control: Segmentation, Dependency and co-optation in Post-communist Estonia' (2002) 8 *Nations and Nationalism* 505, 509.

settlers 'as at worst colonial occupiers, and at best immigrants',[101] and in both States policies developed that contained an element of seeking revenge on the settler communities. Calls were made for 'a counter-attack against the colonists' by a strong policy of discouraging them from remaining in the restored States.[102] However, radical nationalism in the guise of legalistic restorationism was not the only voice in the Baltic States.[103] Eventually the moderate forces in Estonia and Latvia, who advocated a more liberal policy, toned down the debate, which gradually coalesced around a consensus that the expulsion of the immigrant population was politically impossible.[104] Instead, the debate focused on whether settlers would be entitled to citizenship and under what conditions.

3. Transitional arrangements common to all three Baltic States

The formal citizenship policy in all three States reflected their formal legal position: all three States reinstated their pre-1940 legislation. Consequently, original citizenship was made available only to pre-1940 citizens and their descendants.[105] Post-1940 settlers could naturalize in the same manner as other foreigners. In addition, in all three States, military personnel both active and retired were generally excluded from naturalization. The details and specific implementation of these policies and subsequent practice differed among the three States.

4. Transitional arrangements in Lithuania

In Lithuania the small Russophone population, of less than 12%, was not perceived as a serious threat. Accordingly, the Lithuanian citizenship legislation is much more inclusive than those of Estonia and Latvia. Under the 1989 Citizenship Law of Lithuania (at the time still called the Lithuanian SSR), persons residing permanently in Lithuania on the date of enactment of the law but not regarded as original citizens on the basis of pre-1940 nationality, i.e. post-1940 settlers and their descendants, were given two years to opt for Lithuanian citizenship.[106] The only condition

---

[101] Helsinki Watch, 'New Citizenship Laws in the Republics of the Former USSR' (1992) 1–2, quoted by Jean-Marie Henckaerts, *Mass Expulsion in Modern International Law and Practice*, (Martinus Nijhoff, The Hague, 1995) 93.

[102] Peet Kask, 'National radicalization in Estonia: Legislation on Citizenship and Related Issues' (1994) 22 *Nationalities Papers* 379, 386–7; Hughes, above n 98, 748.

[103] Helen M Morris, 'EU Enlargement and Latvian Citizenship Policy' (2003) *Journal on Ethnopolitics and Minority Issues in Europe* 3, 3–4.

[104] Hughes, above n 98, 747; Mälksoo, above n 79, 223–224.

[105] Estonia: Resolution of the Supreme Council of the Republic of Estonia 'On Implementation of Citizenship Act' (RT 1992, 7, 109); Latvia: On 15 October 1991 the Supreme Council of the Latvian SSR adopted the Resolution on the Renewal of Republic of Latvia's Nationals' Rights and fundamental Principles of Naturalization. The Resolution declared the invalidity of the 'USSR Decree on the Order in which the Lithuania, Latvia and Estonia SSR Nationals are Granted USSR Citizenship' of 7 September 1940, and restored the rights of Latvian nationals. Under the resolution, Latvian nationality was reserved to nationals on 17 June 1940 and their descendants, as well as to persons who had been permanent residents in Latvia on that date. Ziemele, above n 79, 155.

[106] Lithuania, Citizenship Law, 1989, art 1(3). The deadline was 4 November 1991.

for eligibility was to have a permanent place of employment or constant legal source of support.[107] One category that was ineligible for Lithuanian nationality was retired servicemen, which in early 1995 numbered in Lithuania almost 10,000, and 30,000 with their families.[108] Their presence in Lithuania was deemed illegal, and their employment in the military not a lawful source of income.[109] On the same ground, Lithuania refused to commit itself to granting permanent residence to military personnel.[110] By implication, family members of military personnel who arrived in connection with their service could also be prevented from remaining in Lithuania.

After the expiry of the opting-in period, Soviet-era settlers could naturalize under the same terms as other foreigners.[111] They were neither discriminated against nor entitled to any concessions. By 2000, 99% of the residents of Lithuania held Lithuanian citizenship.[112]

5. *Transitional arrangements in Estonia*

Upon regaining independence, Estonia reintroduced its pre-Soviet, 1938 Law on Citizenship (later replaced by the 1995 Law on Citizenship). Persons seeking Estonian nationality other than its pre-1940 nationals and their descendants had to fulfill the requirements for naturalization, which included long-term residence and knowledge of Estonian. The earliest date of residence qualifying for naturalization was 30 March 1990, the date on which the Supreme Council of the Estonian Soviet Republic proclaimed the illegality of Soviet rule and the restoration of the Republic of Estonia.[113] In other words, as in East Timor, Soviet-era settlers could not benefit from their residence in the territory during the period of purported annexation in order to satisfy the requirements for naturalization. The greatest obstacle for Soviet-era settlers in naturalization was not, however, the requirement of residence, but their poor command of Estonian. Language requirements underwent various changes, eventually

---

[107] W Rogers Brubaker, 'Citizenship Struggles in Soviet Successor States' (1002) 26 *International Migration Review* 269, 280. Constitutional Court of the Republic of Lithuania ruling on the compliance of the Seimas of the Republic of Lithuania Resolution 'On amending item 5 of the resolution of the Supreme Council of the Republic of Lithuania "On the procedure for implementing the Republic of Lithuania Law on Citizenship", adopted 22 December 1993', with the Constitution of the Republic of Lithuania, Case 7/94, 13 April 1994.

[108] Ceslovas Stankevicius, 'Enhancing Security of Lithuania and Other Baltic States in 1992–94 and Future Guidelines' (1996) Final Report of Individual Democratic Institutions Research Fellowships 1994–1996 <http://www.nato.int/acad/fellow/94–96/stankevi/home.htm> (last accessed 29 June 2009) Chapter 6, para 21.

[109] Constitutional Court of the Republic of Lithuania, above n 107.

[110] Stankevicius, above n 108, Chapter 6.

[111] Lithuania, 1991 Law on Citizenship, above n 1.

[112] Statistical Office of Estonia, Central Statistical Bureau of Latvia and Statistics Lithuania, '2000 Round of Population and Housing Censuses in Estonia, Latvia and Lithuania' (Vilnius, 2003) 33.

[113] Resolution of the Supreme Soviet of the Estonian SSR 'On the State Status of Estonia'.

relaxed under pressure by the EU, OSCE and Council of Europe.[114] This allowed greater access for settlers to Estonian nationality.

The status of persons who did not acquire Estonian nationality is regulated under the 1992 Aliens Law, which required all aliens, including pre-1990 long-term residents, to apply for a residence permit within two years.[115] The requirements were not such that Russophone settlers could not, on the whole, satisfy, although the financial cost was high.[116] By 1996 practically all settlers could register for residence permits.[117]

Special arrangements apply to retired servicemen, who in 1995 numbered 10,500 and 40,000 with their families.[118] Active and retired foreign military personnel are entirely prevented from acquiring Estonian nationality, with the exception of retirees who have been married for five years to an Estonian national by birth.[119] Under the Agreement between the Republic of Estonia and the Russian Federation on Social Guarantees for Pensioners of the Armed Forces of the Russian Federation in the Territory of the Republic of Estonia,[120] Estonia undertook to secure residential status for retired servicemen and their families who do not constitute a threat to national security; only in 2004 was Estonian domestic law amended to reflect this commitment,[121] allowing retired servicemen to obtain temporary residence permits.[122] Active members of a foreign army are deemed a threat to national security[123] and are thus not entitled even to temporary residence.[124]

By 2006, 82% of the population resident in Estonia held Estonian nationality. Estonia's naturalization legislation is still criticized for being overly exclusive,[125] as 8% of the resident population have remained with no nationality at all.[126]

---

[114] For an account of these organizations' involvement until 1999 see Lowell W Barrington, 'The Making of Citizenship Policy in the Baltic States' (1999) 13 *Georgetown Immigration Law Journal* 159, 191–197.

[115] The deadline was later extended.

[116] Ziemele, above n 79, 316–317.

[117] 'Honouring of obligations and commitments by Estonia', Report by the Committee on Legal Affairs and Human Rights PACE Doc 7715 (20 Dec 1996) explanatory n para 16: 'It can be expected of the aliens currently living in Estonia that they register themselves with the state, instead of simply not acting at all. These people have only themselves to blame, if they are open to deportation now.'

[118] Stankevicius, above n 108, Chapter 6.

[119] Estonian 1995 Law on Citizenship art 21(1)(6), (2). The discrimination of citizens by naturalization by this particular legal clause was unsuccessfully challenged in Estonian courts. The general scheme of art 21 (without reference to the differentiation by status of spouse) was confirmed as justified on grounds of national security by the Human Rights Committee in *Vjatšeslav Borzov v Estonia*, Communication No. 1136/2002, UN Doc CCPR/C/81/D/1136/2002 (2004).

[120] RT II 1995, 46, 203, cited in Vadim Poleshchuk, 'Non-citizens in Estonia' (Legal Information Centre for Human Rights, 2004) 11.

[121] Estonia, Combined Sixth and Seventh Periodic Reports, UN Doc CERD/C/46/Add.1 (1 April 2005) para 91.

[122] Estonia Aliens Law, art 12(2¹)(5) As amended on 17 December 2003 and entered into force on 16 January 2004—RT I 2004, 2, 2.

[123] Ibid, art 12(2¹)(6).

[124] Ibid, art 12(6). The same applies to reserve forces, ibid.

[125] Concluding observations of the Committee on the Elimination of Racial Discrimination, Estonia, UN Doc CERD/C/EST/CO/7 (19 October 2006) para 15.

[126] Estonia Citizenship and Migration Board 2006 Yearbook, 13 (on file with the author).

6. *Transitional arrangements in Latvia*

Latvia's transitional nationality policy was the most exclusive of the three Baltic States, reflecting what it perceived as a threat posed by a large non-titular minority.[127] As a result, over half a million individuals (most of whom were Soviet-era settlers), constituting over 22% of the population, found themselves stateless.[128] Latvia's immediate post-transition policy excluded such settlers not only from nationality but potentially even from residence. In 1993 the CSCE High Commissioner for National Minorities (HCNM) expressed his concern that denial of citizenship and expulsions on a massive scale would be contrary to generally accepted international humanitarian principles, might endanger the stability of the country, and would probably have very serious international repercussions.[129]

Subsequent legislation regulated the acquisition of Latvian nationality by naturalization. However, this became a real option only in 1994, when the Law on Citizenship was promulgated.[130] Naturalization was contingent upon a minimum residence of five years. Similarly to Estonia and East Timor, the earliest date qualifying for residence was the day on which the previous regime formally ended, namely 4 May 1990, the date of Latvia's Declaration of Restoration of Independence. Additional requirements were fluency in the Latvian language, Constitution and history, a loyalty oath to the State, a legitimate source of income,[131] and an application fee.[132] As in Estonia, the residence requirement, despite its late qualifying date, was not the main obstacle to naturalization. Rather, the standards required with regard to fluency in Latvian and knowledge of the Constitution and history were excessively high[133] and together with the exorbitant fee (a month's wages) discouraged applications and resulted

---

[127] CSCE High Commissioner for National Minorities (hereinafter 'HCNM') letter to the Minister of Foreign Affairs of Latvia, attached to Recommendations by the CSCE High Commissioner on National Minorities upon his visits to Estonia, Latvia and Lithuania, CSCE Communication No. 124 (Prague, 23 April 1993) <www.osce.org/item/2959.html> (hereinafter 'CSCE 1993 Recommendations') 7 (last accessed 1 July 2009).

[128] European Commission 2002 regular report on Latvia's progress towards accession, cited by Caroline Taube, 'Latvia: Political Participation of Linguistic Minorities' (2003) 1 *International Journal of Constitutional Law* 511, 512.

[129] HCNM letter to the Minister of Foreign Affairs of Latvia, ref No 1463/93/L dated 10 December 1993, CSCE Secretariat, contained in CSCE Communication No. 8, 31 January 1994 (hereafter 'CSCE 1994 Communication') 3, <http://www.minelres.lv/count/latvia/931210r.htm> (last accessed 1 July 2009).

[130] Ziemele, above n 79, 150.

[131] Latvia 1994 Law on Citizenship art 12.

[132] Application for naturalization was possible from 1998 through 'naturalization windows', reserving certain periods of time for persons of different ages. Following international criticism, these 'windows' were abolished in 1999. Eg the letter of the Minister of Foreign Affairs of the Republic of Latvia to OSCE High Commissioner on National Minorities, dated 10 December 1996, OSCE Doc REF HC/2/97 (7 Jan 1997) <www.osce.org/documents/hcnm/1997/01/2731_en.pdf> (last accessed 1 July 2009).

[133] For examples of ludicrous questions see HCNM letter dated 23 May 1997 to the Minister for Foreign Affairs of the Republic of Latvia and the letter of reply, dated 11 September 1997, HCNM. GAL/1/97 (11 September 1997), <http://www.osce.org/documents/html/pdftohtml/2733_en.pdf.html> (last accessed 12 Oct 2007, no longer available).

in a large population of non-nationals, primarily Soviet-era settlers and their families.

In 1998 there were demonstrations in Riga in protest over this policy and violence erupted. Russia threatened to place sanctions on Latvia.[134] Throughout this period the OSCE and the European Commission were heavily involved and exerted pressure on Latvia, whose aspirations to join the EU and NATO led it to gradually relax the requirements for naturalization.[135] There have since been waves of requests for naturalization, with surges in 1999 and in 2004, shortly before the entry of Latvia into the EU. By April 2007, the number of non-nationals resident in Latvia was reduced to about 418,000,[136] making up about 18% of the entire population.

In view of the obstacles facing Soviet-era settlers in obtaining Latvian nationality, their status as residents gained importance. Latvian legislation on the matter was for a long time inconsistent and unclear, leading to arbitrary executive decisions, including expulsion.[137] Ziemele argues that executive action resulted from lack of detailed analysis of the situation of different groups of residence and lack of clear political and legal guidance, rather than from a unified government view that all Soviet-era settlers should be expelled or that their residence should be challenged *en masse*.[138] But the inability to formulate clear policy[139] was itself the result of the heated political debate on the future identity of Latvia.

In 1995 the Law on the Status of Former USSR Citizens who are not Citizens of Latvia or any Other State finally determined the right to permanent residence of former USSR nationals resident and registered in Latvia before 1992, although inconsistencies remain because the Soviet system provided for various types of registration.[140] Latvia is still criticized for not sufficiently integrating Russophone residents into Latvian society.[141] For example, non-nationals still cannot hold offices in public administration and the court system, they may not acquire ownership of land in borderland zones and in protective zones for public water bodies, and they may not work as lawyers,[142] private detectives, or armed guards.[143]

---

[134] Aivars Stranga, 'The End Product, a Crisis in Latvian-Russian Relations (March–August 1998)', NATO Research Fellowships Programme 1996–1998 <www.nato.int/acad/fellow/96–98/stranga.pdf> (last accessed 1 July 2009).

[135] Above n 133.

[136] Data of the Board for Citizenship and Migration Affairs—1 January 2008, <http://www.np.gov.lv/index.php?en=fakti_en&saite=residents.htm> (last accessed 30 September 2008).

[137] Ziemele, above n 79, 160–162.

[138] Ibid, 164.

[139] Pettai, above n 79.

[140] Art 1: see Ziemele, above n 79, 162.

[141] PACE Doc 11094 from 2006, Concluding observations of the Committee on the Elimination of Racial Discriminatio, Latvia, UN Doc CERD/C/63/CO/7 (10 December 2003) paras 12, 13.

[142] Latvian Centre for Human Rights and Ethnic Studies 'Human Rights in Latvia in 2004' (Rīga, 2005) 23.

[143] Latvia Second Periodic Report, UN Doc CCPR/C/LVA/2002/2 (29 November 2002) para 15.

Article 11 of the 1994 Law on Citizenship bars both active and retired military servicemen of foreign States from acquiring Latvian nationality,[144] with the exception of those who had been permanent residents prior to conscription. This is similar to the arrangements in Lithuania and Estonia. Following the withdrawal of Russian troops from Latvia on 31 August 1994, there were in Latvia some 22,000 retired military personnel, numbering 87,000 with their families.[145] Their right to remain in Latvia and related rights were regulated in a 1994 Latvian-Russian treaty on social protection of retired military personnel of the Russian Federation and their family members.[146] Active military personnel (persons who retired from active military service after 28 June 1992) and their immediate families are barred from permanent residence in Latvia under the 1992 Aliens and Stateless Persons (Entry and Residence) Act[147] (unless they had been permanent residents when taking up service or are family members of Latvian nationals) if, irrespective of the date of their arrival, they arrived in Latvia in connection with that service.[148]

E. Cyprus

1. Background[149]

The population of the island of Cyprus, all together over a million persons today,[150] comprises approximately 80% Greek Cypriots of Christian faith and 20% Turkish Cypriots of Muslim faith. In 1960 Cyprus gained independence from British rule. Ethnic conflict erupted in civil disturbances

---

[144] Latvia 1994 Law on Citizenship art 11(3), (4), (5), (6).

[145] Stankevicius, above n 108, Chapter 6 para 21.

[146] Agreement between the Government of the Republic of Latvia and the Government of the Russian Federation on Social Protection of Retired Military Personnel of the Russian Federation and Their Family Members Residing on the Territory of Latvia, signed at Moscow, 30 April 1994, 1887 UNTS 42 (entered into force 30 April 1994).

[147] Act of 9 June 1992.

[148] As amended in 1996, art 23(2), (3). A similar outcome was achieved earlier by the Immigration Law of 1992 and also under the 1995 Law on the Status of Those Former USSR Citizens who do not have the Citizenship of Latvia or that of any Other State, art 1(3).

[149] For general references on the establishment of the TRNC, on the international reaction and on proposals for solutions, see: Samuel KN Blay, Self-Determination in Cyprus: The New Dimensions of an Old Conflict, (1981–1983) 10 *Australian Yearbook of International Law* 67, Rauf R Denktaş, 'The Crux of the Cyprus Problem' (1999) IV *Perceptions* 5, Clement H Dodd, *The Cyprus Imbroglio* (Eothen, Huntingdon, 1998) 78–82, Dugard, above n 4, 108–111, Zaim M Necatigil [published as Nedjatigil], *The Cyprus Conflict—A Lawyer's View (2ⁿᵈ edn)* (A–Z Publications, Lefkoşa, 1982); Zaim M Necatigil [published as Nejatigil], *Our Republic in Perspective* (Tezel Offset, Lefkoşa), Zaim M Necatigil, *The Cyprus Question and the Turkish Position in International Law (2ⁿᵈ edn)* (Oxford University Press, Oxford, 1993), Zaim M Necatigil, The Legal System of the Turkish Republic of Northern Cyprus (1998) 4 *Journal of Cyprus Studies* 213; Claire Palley, *An International Relations Debacle The UN Secretary-General's Mission of Good Offices in Cyprus 1999–2004* (Hart, Oxford, 2005); Oliver P Richmond, *Mediating in Cyprus, the Cypriot Communities and the United Nations* (Frank Cass, London, 1998).

[150] The Government of Cyprus estimates the population of Government-controlled areas at 867,600. Government of Cyprus Statistical Service Demographic Report 2006, 11. Estimates on the population of the TRNC vary as discussed below, but exceed 150,000.

in 1963,[151] resulting in a retreat of the Turkish Cypriot population into enclaves. Violence peaked again in July 1974, when Greek Cypriots favouring a union of Cyprus with Greece staged a coup d'état. In response, Turkey invaded Cyprus, claiming that it was exercising its rights under the 1960 Treaty of Guarantee to protect the Turkish-Cypriot population. During the military conflict, which continued until early 1975, practically all Greek Cypriots fled their homes in the northern part of the island and moved to the south, while most Turkish Cypriots fled from their homes in the southern part of the island to the north. The Turkish-held territory set up its own administration under the name Turkish Federated State of Cyprus (TFSC). In November 1983 the Turkish-Cypriot community declared the independence of the Turkish Republic of Northern Cyprus (TRNC).[152]

The TRNC was immediately recognized as an independent State by Turkey. The UN Security Council condemned the declaration of independence as legally invalid and called upon all States not to recognize any Cypriot State other than the Republic of Cyprus.[153] This call has been adhered to by all States[154] except Turkey. The refusal to recognize the statehood of the TRNC is based on the violation by Turkey in 1974 of the prohibition on the use of force and of the right of Cyprus to self-determination.[155]

Attempts to resolve the conflict[156] climaxed in April 2004, when the UN Secretary-General presented the populations of both parts of the island with a draft Comprehensive Settlement of the Cyprus Problem (the

---

[151] SC Res 186 (4 March 1964).
[152] Declaration of Independence by Turkish Cypriot Parliament on 15 November 1983; UN Doc A/38/586-S/16148 (16 November 1983).
[153] SC Res 541 (18 November 1983), SC Res 550 (11 May 1984).
[154] European Community (EC) Bulletin 11–1983 point 2.4.1, 16 November 1983; Press communiqué of the Commonwealth Heads of Government, 29 November 1983, cited in ECtHR Grand Chamber 18 December 1996, *Loizidou v Turkey (Merits)*, Judgment of 18 December 1996 Reports of Judgments & Decisions 1996–VI 2216, para 23.
[155] See eg Council of Europe Parliamentary Assembly Recommendation 974 (1983) on the Situation in Cyprus (23 November 1983) para 12(c). Dugard, above n 4, 110. This aspect of the affair is entirely absent from the opinion of Sir (then Mr) Eli Lauterpacht CBE QC, 'Turkish Republic of Northern Cyprus, the Status of the Two Communities in Cyprus' UN Doc A/44/968 S/21463 Letter from the Permanent Representative of Turkey to the United Nations Addressed to the Secretary-General (9 August 1990). The TNRC argues that Turkey's recourse to force was within its rights—and obligation—under the 1960 Treaty of Guarantee, to protect the Turkish-Cypriot population, Necatigil (1993), above n 149. Yet even if the Treaty of Guarantee permits the use of force, it could not override the customary prohibition on the use of force embodied in the UN Charter. For a discussion of this debate, see Dodd, above n 149, 80, Necatigil (1982), above n 149, Ch 4. Security Council Resolutions give the impression that the unlawfulness with which the Security Council was concerned was the violation of the 1960 Treaties (a point disputed by the TRNC: see eg Necatigil (1993), above n 149, 324), and possibly the secession. It is submitted that the violation of the 1960 Treaties is not opposable to States not parties to the Treaties, while secession is not an unlawful act: James Crawford, 'State Practice and International Law in Relation to Succession' (1998) 69 *British Year Book of International Law* 85, 86–87.
[156] Richmond above n 149; Necatigil (1982), above n 149, 147–164; Palley, above n 149, 15–16; eg UN Doc S/24472 Report of the Secretary-General on his Mission of Good Offices in Cyprus, containing Proximity Talks Leading to Set of Ideas on an Overall Framework Agreement on Cyprus (21 August 1992).

'Annan Plan'), proposing a federated United Cyprus Republic (UCR).[157] In simultaneously-held referenda on 24 April 2004, a majority of TRNC voters approved the Annan Plan, while in the south, the majority of voters rejected it. Without acceptance on both sides, the Plan did not materialize. Nonetheless, at the time of writing the Plan serves as the unprofessed basis for negotiations between the two sides which have resumed in 2008.[158] It is also an indication of what the international community, acting through the UN Secretary-General, considers an acceptable compromise.[159]

2. Settlers in the TRNC

In 1974 Turkish Cypriots numbered about 118,000.[160] Since then the composition of this population, residing mostly in the territory now under TRNC rule, has changed dramatically.

In addition to the flight of Greek Cypriots from the north,[161] the arrival of displaced Turkish Cypriots from the south, and massive emigration of Turkish Cypriots in later years,[162] the most significant demographic change in the TRNC, and on which this article focuses, is the settlement in it of mainland Turks, with the encouragement of both Turkey and the TRNC. Large waves of settlers arrived in 1975 and 1977. These were estimated to make up more than 10% of the population in the territory at the time.[163] Another wave of mainland Turks arrived in the early 2000s as construction workers, following a building boom in the TRNC.

Until 2004 TRNC legislation was very permissive with regard to acquisition of TRNC citizenship. TFSC legislation had made it discretionary upon request and, in particular, available to members of the Turkish armed forces who had served in Cyprus and their families.[164] In 1981

---

[157] The discussion in this work is based on the Comprehensive Settlement of the Cyprus Problem as finalized on 31 March 2004, <http://www.hri.org/docs/annan/> (last accessed 29 June 2009). It is not suggested that the Plan in any way binds either party to the dispute or the UN Secretary-General.

[158] Interview with Dr. Kudret Özersay, advisor to the TRNC negotiating team, Lefkoşa, 27 November 2008; see also UK House of Commons Foreign Affairs Committee 'Visit to Turkey and Cyprus' Fifth Report of Session 2006–07 Doc No. HC 473 (9 May 2007) (hereinafter 'UK House of Commons 2006–07 Report') paras 55, 81.

[159] European Parliament Resolution 21 April 2004, 'Prospects for the Unification of Cyprus'; Matthew Bryza, Deputy Assistant Secretary for European and Eurasian Affairs, Roundtable with Turkish Journalists, Washington, DC (1 February, 2007) <http://turkey.usembassy.gov/statement_020107.html> (last accessed 29 June 2009).

[160] Department of Statistics and Research of the Republic of Cyprus, quoted in 'The Demographic Structure of Cyprus', PACE Doc 6589 (27 April 1992), Report of the Committee on Migration, Refugees and Demography, Rapporteur: Mr Alfons Cuco ('Cuco Report') para 35.

[161] UN and ICRC estimates of 43,000, quoted in 'Colonisation by Turkish settlers of the Occupied part of Cyprus' PACE Doc 9799 (2 May 2003) Report of the Committee on Migration, Refugees and Demography, Rapporteur: Mr Jaakko Laakso ('Laakso Report') para 18. The TRNC reports 65,000 displaced Turkish Cypriots.

[162] UK House of Commons Foreign Affairs Committee 'Cyprus' Second Report of Session 2004–5 Doc No. 113-I (22 February 2005) (hereinafter 'UK House of Commons 2004–5 Report') para 201, based on the Laakso Report, above n 161, appendix 5.

[163] Cuco Report, above n 160, para 89.

[164] Law no. 3/1975. On the practical consequences of this law see Mete Hatay, 'Beyond Numbers: An Inquiry into the Political Integration of the Turkish 'Settlers' in Northern Cyprus' PRIO Report 4 (Nicosia, 2005) 11.

complementary provisions extended nationality to persons permanently resident in the territory for at least one year, those who made or could make an important contribution to the economy, or social and cultural life of the TFSC, and those who have rendered services to the security forces.[165] The 1983 Constitution of the TRNC provides that original citizens of the TRNC include original citizens of the Republic of Cyprus ordinarily resident in the TRNC when it declared independence, and citizens of the TFSC.[166] TRNC legislation of 1993 confers original TRNC citizenship on persons born to a TRNC parent. TRNC citizenship is also available to spouses of TRNC citizens. In addition, the law provides for discretionary naturalization for various categories of foreigners. Ordinarily, naturalization is contingent upon a five-year residence in the TRNC. However, certain categories of individuals are exempt from this requirement. These include veterans of the 1974 Peace Operation and their families; and persons 'who have rendered services after 1 August 1958 in the cadres of the Turkish Resistance Organization in the TRNC and their families'.[167] Finally, according to the Government of Cyprus, on 12 October 2004 a protocol was signed between Turkey and the TRNC to regularize the presence of the construction workers arriving in the 2000s, adding some 40,000 new residents—and potential citizens—to the TRNC.[168] Since 2004, the granting of TRNC citizenship has become more selective,[169] and mass grants, which had apparently been a common occurrence, subsided.[170]

Turkish nationals may retain their nationality even when acquiring a new one.[171] Their children are Turkish nationals from birth.[172] At the same time, under Cypriot law, descendants of pre-1974 Cypriot nationals are eligible for citizenship.[173] Accordingly, children of mixed marriages

---

[165] Laakso Report, above n 161, 37–38.

[166] TRNC Constitution art 67.

[167] Law 52/1993 of 27 May 1993, Articles 4(1), 7, 8(1)(B), 9(1)D, 9(1)(E). The Turkish Resistance Organization (TMT) was a locally-established paramilitary force.

[168] The Protocol authorized the residence of Turkish nationals present in the TRNC and employed there at the time of the protocol's entry into force, namely 1 January 2005. This means that Turkish nationals who on 12 October 2004 were residing in Turkey, had a 3-month window wherein to transfer to the TRNC so as to take advantage of the protocol. Observations made by the Ministry of Foreign Affairs of Cyprus, annexed to European Commission against Racism and Intolerance (ECRI) Third Report on Cyprus (adopted 16 December 2005) 42. The mass arrival of construction workers was partly linked to the release of bonds related to Greek-Cypriot abandoned property that until then prevented building improvements.

[169] UK House of Commons 2006–07 Report, above n 158, para 106.

[170] There are indications that the toughening of requirements is causing tension in TRNC-Turkish relations. See eg 'Fifty thousand persons will reportedly be gradually made "citizens" of the "TRNC"' Turkish Mass Media Bulletin 18/12/2007, Republic of Cyprus Press and Information Office, <http://www.pio.gov.cy/moi/pio/pio.nsf/All/93E64B0FF93CE004C22573B5003F5F17?Open Document> (last accessed 29 June 2009).

[171] The Turkish Nationality law as amended in 1981 permits the acquisition of another nationality (TRNC nationality being recognized by Turkey) without renunciation of Turkish Nationality. The only condition for dual nationality is to obtain permission of the Ministry of Interior. Dual nationality has been encouraged since the 1980s. Bilgin Tıryakıoğlu, 'Multiple Citizenship and its Consequences in Turkish Law' (2006) 3 Ankara Law Review 1, 5–6, 9.

[172] Turkey, Nationality law, art 1 as amended in 2004.

[173] The Republic of Cyprus, Citizenship Law, No 43 of 1967, art 4.

between settlers and local Turkish Cypriots are nationals of the Republic of Cyprus, although the Republic does not routinely acknowledge their status.[174]

The demographic composition of the TRNC is difficult to establish. Censuses carried out by the TRNC are rejected by the Government of Cyprus as unreliable and intentionally misleading as to the number of Turkish settlers. The population categories used by the opposing sides are defined differently, frustrating any attempt at comparing data.[175] The Council of Europe has initiated its own studies on the population of the TRNC.[176] Data on the number of settlers therefore vary enormously: from a Turkish Government estimate of 31,000 settlers in 2003–4,[177] to a 2006 Government of the Republic of Cyprus estimate of 150,000–160,000 settlers.[178] A 2006 TRNC census, on which the Cypriot estimate is based, quotes the total number of immigrants since the 1970s at little over 100,000.[179] In 2003 the Council of Europe endorsed an estimate of 115,000 settlers, concluding that by 2000, at the latest, mainland Turkish settlers have outnumbered indigenous Turkish Cypriots.[180]

Turkish settlers fall into two main categories. The vast majority are peasants and shepherds who arrived between 1975 and 1977 from poor regions in Turkey. These farmers were invited by radio and by announcements by muhtars made in Turkish village coffee-shops. A small minority holding significant political clout comprises professionals, businessmen, retired military officers, and former students.[181] They live mainly in mixed neighbourhoods in urban areas and are often married to Turkish Cypriots.[182] Rural Turks have low professional skills and their

---

[174] US Department of State 2006 Country Reports on Human Rights Practices, Cyprus. UK House of Commons 2006–07 Report, above n 158, para 113.

[175] 'How Many Turkish Cypriots Remain in Cyprus' Written evidence before the select committee of the House of Commons <http://www.publications.parliament.uk/pa/cm200405/cmselect/cmfaff/113/113we33.htm> (last accessed 7 July 2009).

[176] Eg Cuco Report, above n 160. For detailed analysis of data see Laakso Report, above n 161; UK House of Commons 2004–5 Report, above n 162, 62–63. Palley argues that the TRNC Government objected to these initiatives because it was reluctant to expose the large number of Turkish settlers, Palley, above n 149.

[177] Laakso Report, above n 161, para 24.

[178] Analysis of the '2006 Population Census' in the Occupied Area of Cyprus and Aide Memoire, produced by the Government of Cyprus PIO (undated), on file with the author.

[179] The Final Results of TRNC General Population and Housing Unit Census, Additional Tables, <http://nufussayimi.devplan.org/Kesin-sonuc-index_en.html> (last accessed 10 Feb 2009).

[180] Laakso Report, above n 161, paras 24–27 and the appendices provide detailed (and conflicting) data, concluding that settlers have outnumbered the local population since 2000. Additional data is available in the UK House of Commons 2004–5 Report, above n 162. In 2007 The UK House of Commons quoted the number of 200,000 permanent residents, of which only about 50,000 are permanent Turkish settlers and another 100,000 are short-term residents, mostly Turkish. UK House of Commons 2006–07 Report, above n 158, para 104.

[181] Cuco Report, above n 160, para 90, Hatay, above n 164, 11–13.

[182] UK House of Commons 2004–5 Report, above n 162, para 54. In 1992, the Cuco Report quoted the figure of 1500 intermarriages notified between 1974 and 1990 to the Turkish Consulate in the TRNC, Cuco Report, above n 160, para 82. Hatay, above n 164, 12 quotes the number of Peace Force veterans married to Turkish Cypriots at around 800.

customs and traditions differ in a significant way from those in Cyprus.[183] The Government of the Republic of Cyprus claims (with the endorsement of the Council of Europe) that these differences are the main reason for the tensions and dissatisfaction of the indigenous Turkish-Cypriot population, who tends to view the settlers as a foreign element.[184] Although their immigration to the TRNC was politically motivated and facilitated by the Turkish and TRNC Governments, the settlers themselves were not politically motivated in coming, and a substantial number of them may even have had little or no clear idea of where Cyprus was located before their arrival. They do not form a monolithic group and they do not all support a nationalist agenda.[185] The UK House of Commons mission to Cyprus reported that the settlers, unlike Turkish Cypriots, feel they have nothing in common with Greek Cypriots.[186] Because of their number, Turkish settlers have a growing impact on the political climate in the TRNC.

3. *Transitional arrangements under the Annan Plan*

The Annan Plan does not spell out the legal status of the TRNC. This is an obvious consequence of the attempt to satisfy both Greek and Turkish Cypriots. Main Article 12 of the Foundation Agreement, entitled 'Past Acts', provides for legal continuity between the TRNC and UCR:

1. Any act, whether of a legislative, executive or judicial nature, by any authority in Cyprus whatsoever, prior to entry into force of this Agreement, is recognised as valid and, provided it is not inconsistent with or repugnant to any other provision of this Agreement or international law, its effect shall continue following entry into force of this Agreement. No-one shall be able to contest the validity of such acts by reason of what occurred prior to entry into force of this Agreement.
2. Any claims for liability or compensation arising from acts prior to this Agreement shall, insofar as they are not otherwise regulated by the provisions of this Agreement, be dealt with by the constituent state from which the claimant hails.

An observation appended to Main Article 12 indicates:

This reference, like the whole draft Article, is without prejudice to the question of the legitimacy or status of the relevant authorities under international law.

---

[183] Hatay, ibid, 49–50.

[184] Laakso Report, above n 161, paras 40–43; PACE Recommendation 1197 (1992) on the demographic structure of the Cypriot communities adopted on 7 Oct 1992 para 7; Leonard W Doob, 'Cypriot Patriotism and Nationalism' (1986) 30 *Journal of Conflict Resolution* 383, 394.

[185] For an analysis of Turkish settlers' politics see Hatay, above n 164, 7; Othon Anastasakis, Gilles Bertrand & Kalypso Nicolaïdis, 'Getting to Yes: Suggestions for Embellishment of the Annan Plan for Cyprus' (South East European Studies Programme (SEESP) European Studies Centre, St Anthony's College, University of Oxford, February 2004) 4.

[186] UK House of Commons 2006–07 Report, above n 158, para 77.

Another observation to Main Article 12 excludes citizenship and immigration from this arrangement, and provides:

Matters of citizenship, immigration, and properties affected by events since 1963 are dealt with in a comprehensive way by this Agreement; any validity of acts prior to entry into force of this Agreement regarding these matters shall thus end unless they are in conformity with the relevant provisions of this Agreement.

The point of departure in the Annan Plan is that original citizenship in the UCR would not cover persons who received such citizenship from the TRNC (or its precursor the TFSC), that is mainly settlers from mainland Turkey. Instead they are subject to specific provisions.

The Draft Federal Law on Citizenship of the United Cyprus Republic[187] defines original citizens of the UCR as persons who had Cypriot citizenship in 1963 and their descendants. However, although the Government of the Republic of Cyprus argues that under the law of occupation[188] Turkey is obligated to remove its citizens from the TRNC, it conceded that the consequences for individual settlers of long-standing should nonetheless be examined in a humane fashion.[189] Accordingly, from the outset of the negotiations on the Annan Plan it has been accepted that in addition to pre-1963 nationals and their descendants, concessions would be made towards long-term residents with respect to nationality and residence. On 31 August 2002, Rauf Denktaş, then leader of the TRNC, declared that there were only about 30,000 Turkish settlers and that persons who had gained citizenship of the TRNC should be accommodated. The Republic of Cyprus' then President Clerides agreed that subject to these being the correct numbers he would accept the principle that whoever was a 'citizen' of either side would become a citizen of the new federation.[190] From that time until the final drafting of the Annan Plan, the numbers and categories of persons entitled to original citizenship have undergone various changes. The final version of the Annan Plan contains the following provision on original citizenship:[191]

Article 3—Cypriot citizenship upon entry into force of the Foundation Agreement
    Upon entry into force of the Foundation Agreement, the following persons shall be considered citizens of the United Cyprus Republic:

a.   Any person who held Cypriot citizenship in 1963 and his or her descendants and the spouses of such citizens...

---

[187] Foundation Agreement, Annex III Attachment IV.
[188] Geneva Convention IV, above n 99, art 49(6), Statute of the International Criminal Court, 17 July 1998, 2187 UNTS 90 (entry into force 1 July 2002), art 8.
[189] Observations attached to ECRI Report, above n 168, 44.
[190] Palley, above n 149, chapter XVII.
[191] Draft Federal Law on Citizenship of the United Cyprus Republic, Annex III Attachment IV art 3. Part F of the Annan Plan (entitled 'Measures to be taken during April 2004') includes the following item: 'Hand over by 10 April 2004 to the Secretary-General the list numbering no more than 45,000 persons as specified in the proposed Federal Law on Citizenship of the United Cyprus Republic (failing which the Citizenship Board shall, after entry into force of the Foundation Agreement, prepare the list in accordance with that law).'

b. Any person whose name figures on a list handed over to the Secretary-General of the United Nations by each side no later than 25 March 2003. Each side's list may number no more than 45,000 persons, inclusive of spouses and children, unless there are specific reasons preventing such spouses and children from being considered Cypriot citizens. The list shall contain the name of each person and the basis for their inclusion on the list, as well as, where relevant, the date of their entry into Cyprus. Applicants shall be included on the list based on the following criteria and in the following order of priority:

i) persons 18 years of age or older who enjoyed permanent residence in Cyprus for at least seven years before reaching the age of 18 and for at least one year during the last five years and their minor children who enjoy permanent residence in Cyprus;

ii) other persons who have enjoyed permanent residence in Cyprus for more than seven consecutive years, based on the length of their stay.

The list would be made public, and individuals may appeal against their own omission or the inclusion of others. Under the Annan Plan, there are no bars to naturalization for Turkish military personnel. When the negotiations resumed in 2008, Cyprus's President Christofias announced unilaterally that the 45,000 quota would be increased to 50,000.[192]

Persons outside the quota may acquire UCR nationality by naturalization in accordance with the Draft Federal Law on Citizenship. The requisites for naturalization include nine years' consecutive residence in the UCR. Up to five years' residence under the TRNC may be counted towards naturalization.[193] In this the Annan Plan differs from the arrangements in the Baltic States and East Timor, where residence under the illegal regime was not counted at all towards naturalization. In order to benefit from this provision, Turkish settlers need permission to remain in Cyprus until the 9-year period completes. Main Article 3 of the Foundation Agreement[194] provides:

In addition, for a transitional period of 19 years or until Turkey's accession to the European Union, whichever is earlier, Cyprus may limit the right of Greek nationals to reside in Cyprus if their number has reached 5% of the number of resident Cypriot citizens holding Greek Cypriot internal constituent state citizenship status, or the right of Turkish nationals to reside in Cyprus if their number has reached 5% of the number of resident Cypriot citizens holding Turkish Cypriot internal constituent state citizenship status.

In other words, when the Foundation Agreement comes into force, settlers numbering up to 5% of the population of the Turkish-Cypriot constituent

---

[192] 'Christofias firm on settlers' <http://www.cyprusemb.se/dbase/cypemb/svenska/ref1162.asp> (last accessed 10 Feb 2009).

[193] Draft Federal Law on Citizenship, art 5.

[194] Echoed in art 3 of the Draft act of Adaptation of the Terms of Accession of the United Cyprus Republic to the European Union.

State, estimated at about 10,000, may remain in the UCR as residents in expectation of eventual naturalization.

Conclusions on the implications of the plan remain vastly disparate. The Government of the Republic of Cyprus warns that under the 2004 version of the Plan, 111,000 Turkish settlers are entitled to either UCR citizenship or residence;[195] the UK House of Commons concludes that thousands of the Turkish settlers would have to leave the territory.[196] The uncertainty is the result not only of the lack of knowledge as to the actual number of settlers in the various categories, but also of different readings of the agreement. Palley reports that the UN team made a different representation to each of the parties, for example with respect to whether spouses of Turkish Cypriots would be entitled to citizenship outside the quota.[197] Different expectations also exist with regard to thousands of students and academic staff. The ambiguity of the situation is apparent in the difference between the July 2003 statement of the Secretary-General's Special Adviser's own legal adviser, that 'the Plan does not foresee that anybody will be forced to leave';[198] and the Secretary-General's 2004 statement that 'about half' of the settlers would have to leave the island.[199] These ambiguities suggest that the removal of Turkish settlers might not be as dramatic as the Annan Plan appears to suggest. Indeed, it is reported that the Turkish Cypriot side prepared a list of candidates for immediate naturalization, which contained no more than 41,000 names. However, this limited number may be based on the assumption that various categories, such as spouses, are entitled to original citizenship outside the quota.

The provisions of the Annan Plan and of any prospective alternative would require a derogation from EU principles on the *acquis communautaire*, such as the freedom of movement and establishment. Accordingly, the Republic of Cyprus' instrument of Accession to the EU provides that since the EU is ready to accommodate the terms of a settlement of the Cyprus conflict in line with the principles on which the EU is founded, in the event of such settlement the Council will decide on the adaptations to the terms of accession to the EU with regard to the Turkish-Cypriot

---

[195] UK House of Commons 2004–5 Report, above n 162, para 59.

[196] Ibid. The UK Foreign Affairs Committee pointed out that about 42,000 Turkish settlers who are not married to Turkish Cypriots would have to leave, UK House of Commons 2006–07 Report, above n 158, para 105.

[197] Draft Federal Law on Citizenship of the United Cyprus Republic, Annex III Attachment IV art 6. See also Statement by the Secretary-General's Special Adviser on Cyprus, Alvaro de Soto, at the Joint meeting of the Foreign Affairs Committee and the Delegation of the European Parliamentary Committee with the Republic of Cyprus, Brussels, 14 April 2004.

[198] Didier Pfirter, Statement at a conference on 'The Annan Plan: Myths and Realities,' at Bögaziçi University in Istanbul on 17 July 2003 quoted in Comments by the Government of Cyprus on the Report of the Secretary General on his Mission of Good Offices in Cyprus (UN Doc S/2004/437 (28 May 2004) para 41, UK House of Commons Foreign Affairs Committee, Cyprus—Second Report Volume II, Oral and written evidence HC113-II Incorporating HC 1172 i-iv, Session 2003–04 (22 February 2005) 85.

[199] Report of the Secretary-General on his mission of good offices in Cyprus, UN Doc S/2004/437, para 60.

Community. Until then, the application of the *acquis* is suspended in those areas of the Republic of Cyprus where the Government of the Republic does not exercise effective control.[200]

F. Summary

The practice of post-transition regimes with regard to the rights of settlers under the illegal regime to remain in the territory is not uniform. In Zimbabwe and South Africa, complete continuity of status was offered. In these cases, the core question was the status of the White community, which was not synonymous with the settler community. The main problems were therefore only marginally related to the illegal regime, and mostly reflected the challenges characteristic of decolonization. In East Timor and the Baltic States, and in Cyprus as envisaged under the Annan Plan, there is formal discontinuity. In East Timor this did not generate any practical problems, because Indonesian-era settlers had already left of their own accord. In contrast, in the Baltic States and in the TRNC, strict adherence to the reversal would have had major repercussions. Additional arrangements were made which in practice allowed at least some of the settlers to remain in the territory as residents and eventually to naturalize. Parts III and IV examine whether this was the result of benevolence, political pressure or legal constraints, or a combination of these.

III. STATUS-BASED LIMITATIONS ON EXPULSION

A. National and long-term residents

International law protects certain categories of individuals from expulsion, first and foremost nationals. Their expulsion is practically prohibited in both universal and regional instruments. Relevant provisions for present purposes include ECHR Protocol 4 Article 3(1) and ICCPR Article 12(4) of the International Covenant on Civil and Political Rights (ICCPR).[201]

---

[200] Protocol No. 10 attached to the Treaty of Accession of Cyprus, signed on 16 April 2003 by the Republic of Cyprus, art 4. See also the Draft Act of Adaptation to the Terms of Accession of the United Cyprus Republic to the European Union, which addressed, *inter alia*, issues of residence, arts 2, 3, 5.

[201] See below n 245. See also American Convention on Human Rights, 22 November 1969, 1144 UNTS 123 (entered into force 18 June 1978, hereinafter 'ACHR') art 22(5), Arab Charter on Human Rights, reprinted in (1997)18 *Human Rights Law Journal* 151, art 22. The prohibition in art 12(4) is not absolute but is limited to 'arbitrary' denial of the right to enter one's country, that is unreasonable in the circumstances; the HRC nonetheless 'considers that there are few, if any, circumstances in which deprivation of the right to enter one's own country could be reasonable'. Furthermore, art 12(4) has been interpreted as not only permitting entry into one's own country, but also as prohibiting expulsion from one's own country, Committee Member Bhagwati in *Stewart v Canada*, Communication No 538/1993 UN Doc CCPR/C/58/D/538/1993 (1996), For a discussion of the prohibition on expulsion of nationals see UN Doc A/CN.4/581. There are limitations on expulsion of

Long-term residents, in contrast, are not protected as such by any of the major human rights instruments. This matter was considered in *Stewart v Canada* in 1996 with respect to ICCPR Article 12(4), which stipulates: 'No one shall be arbitrarily deprived of the right to enter his own country'. The applicant was a British citizen who had resided in Canada since the age of seven. He was facing deportation from Canada on grounds of his criminal activity. The Human Rights Committee (HRC) majority was of the view that the term 'his own country' in Article 12(4) 'applies to individuals who are nationals and to certain categories of individuals who, while not nationals in a formal sense, are also not 'aliens' within the meaning of article 13, although they may be considered as aliens for other purposes'.[202] The Committee added[203] that the concept 'his own country'

embraces, at the very least, an individual who, because of his special ties to or claims in relation to a given country cannot there be considered to be a mere alien. This would be the case, for example, of nationals of a country who have there been stripped of their nationality in violation of international law and of individuals whose country of nationality has been incorporated into or transferred to another national entity whose nationality is being denied them... The language of article 12, paragraph 4, permits a broader interpretation, moreover, that might embrace other categories of long-term residents, particularly stateless persons arbitrarily deprived of the right to acquire the nationality of the country of such residence.

Since Mr. Stewart's failure to acquire Canadian nationality was attributed to his own inaction, the HRC found that he was not protected by Article 12(4).

In *Madafferi v Australia* the Committee summarized its jurisprudence thus:[204]

... a person who enters a State under the State's immigration laws, and subject to the conditions of those laws, cannot normally regard that State as his 'own country', when he has not acquired its nationality and continues to retain the

---

additional categories of persons, such as stateless persons and refugees. These categories are discussed only briefly, where the circumstances of settlement under illegal regimes are particularly significant.

[202] *Stewart v Canada*, ibid, para 12.3.

[203] Ibid, para 12.4. see also *Francesco and Anna Madafferi and their children v Australia*, Communication no 1011/2001, views of 26 July 2004, UN Doc CCPR/C/81/D/1011/2001. This jurisprudence was incorporated in the HRC's General Comment 27: Freedom of movement (Art 12), UN Doc CCPR/C/21/Rev.1/Add.9 (1999), para 20. See also *Simalae Toala et al. v New Zealand*, Communication no 675/1995, views of 2 November 2000 UN Doc CCPR/C/70/D/675/1995.

[204] *Madafferi v Australia*, above n 203, para 9.6. It can be argued that the Committee limited the scope of art 12(4) further than member States had expected it to. In 1981, Canada claimed that the right under art 12(4) was available to nationals or permanent residents. Communication 68/1980 *AS v Canada*, decision on admissibility, 31 July 1980, para 5.1. But in *Canepa v Canada*, Communication No. 558/1993, UN Doc CCPR/C/59/D/558/1993 (1997), Canada claimed that a person cannot acquire a right under art 12(4) by virtue only of long-term residence, para 9.2. *Madafferi v Australia*, above n 203, followed *Stewart v Canada*, above n 201.

nationality of his country of origin. An exception might only arise in limited circumstances, such as where unreasonable impediments are placed on the acqui-sition of nationality.

Accordingly, under the HRC's jurisprudence, attachment to the territory through long-term presence does not suffice to protect a person from expulsion. What is required is a formal link to the State of residence such as nationality, or special circumstances that justify substitution of that formal link, generally linked to victimization of the person in formalizing the relationship with the State of residence or in maintaining the nation-ality of another State.[205] Persons holding an effective nationality of another State who have not been unfairly denied the possibility of naturalization in the State of residence, are not protected by Article 12(4).[206] Thus, Turkish settlers in the TRNC and their descendants, all of whom generally retain effective Turkish nationality,[207] Indonesian nationals who have remained in East Timor, and Soviet-era settlers in the Baltic States who hold another nationality, are all excluded from the ambit of protection under Article 12(4).

An interesting question concerns settlers who become stateless follow-ing State succession.[208] This was an acute problem with respect to settlers in the Baltic States who had become stateless as a result of the Soviet Union's break up, and the lack of coordination of the domestic legislation between Russia, the various newly-independent States, and the Baltic States. If protection under Article 12(4) is contingent upon nationality being 'denied' in bad faith on the part of the post-break up States, then inadvertently-stateless persons are not protected, just as foreign nationals are not. If statelessness is sufficient for triggering the application of Article 12(4) even when it results from acts in good faith, then stateless Soviet-era settlers are protected from expulsion.

Turkish settlers in the TRNC may also be stateless (since the Annan Plan rejects the validity of TRNC nationality). However, their situation is different. If Turkey withdrew its nationality from persons who acquired purported TRNC nationality, then from an international legal perspec-tive it unlawfully created a situation of statelessness. Accordingly it is obligated to re-confer its nationality on the individual in question. Until it does so, Article 12(4) may well benefit the settlers and prevent their expulsion from the UCR.

Extensive protection for long-term residents exists under EU law, appli-cable to the Baltic States and to the future UCR. Directive 2003/109, which forms part of a process of assimilating permanent residents (nationals of

---

[205] *Stewart v Canada*, ibid.
[206] In other words, a person can only have one 'own country'. It is not a matter of comparative strength of links but of one attachment excluding another.
[207] See above n 171.
[208] HRC General Comment 27, above n 203, para 20.

third countries) to nationals of member States,[209] stipulates the rights of long-term lawful residents in Member States. Those include protection from expulsion, with one exception, namely when the presence of the foreign resident constitutes an actual and sufficiently serious threat to public policy or public security. Until the implementation of the Directive, the Council of Europe's Committee of Ministers' Recommendation (2000)15 calls for assimilation of long-term residents to nationals by severely limiting the possibility of their expulsion.[210]

To conclude, ICCPR Article 12(4), ECHR Protocol 4 Article 3(1) and Directive 2003/109 protect individuals from expulsion on the basis of their status as nationals (or quasi-nationals) or long-term residents. In order to establish whether settlers under an illegal regime can benefit from this protection, the validity of the status granted to them by the illegal regime must be established. Such validity can be examined against two bodies of law: the law of occupation, where applicable; and the law of non-recognition applicable to illegal territorial regimes. Even if status granted by the regime is valid under either of these bodies of law, a second question is whether this validity survives the transition to the post-transition regime.

B. Status granted to settlers by an occupying power

The Baltic States, East Timor, and the TRNC can all be regarded as cases of occupation.[211] The Soviet takeover of the Baltic States was peaceful in the sense that there were no armed clashes, but it was the threat of the use of force by the military and its presence that achieved the takeover, which resulted in the territory of the Baltic States being under the authority of a hostile (Soviet) military force. During the Soviet era, there were only isolated references by States and international organizations to the Baltic States as occupied territories.[212] Yet most pertinently for present purposes, the Baltic States now consider themselves to have been

---

[209] EU Directive 2003/109 of 25 November 2003, in effect from 23 January 2006, not applicable to the UK, Ireland and Denmark. At the time of writing, judgments for failure to interpose have already been given in *Commission v Portugal* [2007] ECR I-120, Case C-59/07, *Commission v Spain* [2007] ECR I-161, Case C-5/07, Case C-34/07, *Commission v Luxemburg* [2007] ECR I-175.

[210] The Council of Europe's Parliamentary Assembly in Rec 1504(2001) called on the Committee of Ministers to recommend further steps for assimilation of long-term residents. The Committee of Ministers replied on 6 December 2002 that Rec (2000)15 addressed many of the concerns of the Assembly and that the Committee was thus not minded to devise new standards. *Üner v The Netherlands* [GC] Application no. 46410/99, judgment of 18 October 2006, para 37.

[211] Adam Roberts, 'What is Military Occupation?' (1985) 55 *British Year Book of International Law* 249.

[212] Report of the Select Committee of the US House of Representatives to Investigate the Incorporation of Lithuania, Latvia, and Estonia into the Soviet Union (the Kersten Committee) in 1954; US Department of Defence Authorization Act, 1983; See eg Proclamation 5068—Baltic Freedom Day, June 13, 1983, available at <http://www.reagan.utexas.edu/archives/speeches/1983/61383d.htm> (last accessed 1 July 2009); Resolution 189 (1960) of the Parliamentary Assembly of the Council of Europe, on the situation in the Baltic States; Document I-777/80.

liberated from occupation.[213] East Timor and the TRNC[214] are clear cases of occupation, where a hostile army gained effective control over the territory as a consequence of armed conflict.[215] East Timor's legislation and jurisprudence reflect the State's perception of having emerged from occupation.[216]

Article 49 of the Fourth Geneva Convention prohibits the occupying power from deporting or transferring parts of its own civilian population into the territory it occupies. According to the ICRC study on customary international law, the prohibition on transferring parts of the occupying power's own civilian population into the occupied territory constitutes customary law.[217] Articles 85(4)(a) and 85 of Additional Protocol I and Article 8(2)(b)(viii) of the ICC statute designate the transfer by the Occupying Power of parts of its own civilian population into the territory it occupies as a war crime.[218] Yet the precise scope of prohibition is debated. In particular, controversy revolves on whether the prohibition covers only forcible transfers, or also permissive transfers and facilitation of relocation of settlers in occupied territories. The common interpretation of Article 49 is that it prohibits any transfer of settlers to occupied territories, whether forcibly or by actively organizing or encouraging it.[219]

---

[213] See eg 2002 statement of the Estonian parliament on crimes committed by the occupation regimes in Estonia during the Second World War: Estonian Review, June 17–23, 2002, <http://www.vm.ee/eng/kat_137/2484.html> (last accessed 1 July 2009); Estonia's 2003 Persons Repressed by Occupying Powers Act; Latvia's Declaration on the Renewal of Independence, May 4, 1990; Lithuania's Law on Rehabilitation of Persons Repressed for Resistance to the Occupying Regime 2 May 1990; Lithuania's Resolution of the Supreme Council of the Republic of Lithuania regarding the Process of Enforcement and Application of the Law of the Republic of Lithuania on the Procedures and Conditions of the Restoration of the Ownership Rights of Existing Real Property 16 July 1991.

[214] See eg GA Res 33/15 of 9 November 1978 preambular para 6, GA Res 34/30 of 20 November 1979 preambular para 9, GA Res 37/253 of 13 May 1983 preambular para 8, European Parliament resolution on the 1999 regular report from the Commission on Turkey's progress towards accession, adopted on 15 November, 1999, Bulletin EU 11–2000, *Loizidou v Turkey* (Preliminary Objections) (1995) A310, paras 62, 63, *Loizidou v Turkey* (Merits) (1996) 23 *EHRR* 513 para 52; *Cyprus v Turkey (The Forth Interstate Case)*, (2002) 35 *EHRR* 30 para 76, and partly dissenting opinion of Judge Palm, joined by Judges Jungwiert, Levits, Pantîru, Kovler and Marcus-Helmons, and partly dissenting opinion of Judge Marcus-Helmons.

[215] The Turkish army is still heavily present in the TRNC, without authorization of the Government of the Republic of Cyprus, which is the recognized sovereign over the territory.

[216] See preamble to the East Timorese Constitution, Preamble of Law on the Juridical regime Real Estate Part 1—Ownership over Real Estate, No. 1/2003, *Armando dos Santos* case, above n 61.

[217] Jean Marie Henckaerts and Louise Doswald-Beck (eds) *Customary International Humanitarian Law Vol I: Rules* (ICRC, Geneva, 2005) Rule 130, 462–463, and sources cited there.

[218] None of the occupying powers discussed here are or have been parties to the Protocol Additional to the Geneva Conventions of 12 August 1949, and relating to the Protection of Victims of International Armed Conflicts, 8 June 1977, 1125 UNTS 609 (entered into force 7 December 1978). The provisions of the ICC Statute, above n 188, are not directly applicable to any of the cases examined here, because implantation occurred before 2002, possibly with the exception of the TRNC.

[219] David Kretzmer, 'The Advisory Opinion: The Light Treatment of International Humanitarian Law' (2005) 99 *American Journal of International Law* 88, 91. There are other opinions, to the effect that *any* measure of transfer is prohibited. Commission on Human Rights, Sub-Commission on Prevention of Discrimination and Protection of Minorities, Human Rights and Population Transfer: Final Report of the Special Rapporteur, Mr. Al-Khasawneh, UN Doc E/CN.4/Sub.2/1997/23 14–15 para 46. This report seems to suggest that implantation of settlers is a violation of *ius cogens*, para 46.

A different view, advanced primarily by Israel, is that the prohibition covers only forcible transfer.[220]

The mobilization of Soviet military personnel to the Baltic States and of Indonesian transmigrants to East Timor was undoubtedly forcible. The voluntary relocation of other Russophones to the Baltic States, Indonesians to East Timor, and mainland Turks to the TRNC, was organized and encouraged by Turkey and Indonesia, respectively.[221] The responsibility of all three occupying powers is thus engaged.

The remedy, in the case of breach of the prohibition, is reversion to the *status quo ante*:[222] the occupying power should repatriate its nationals. If the settler population has in the meantime been deprived of the nationality of the occupying power through measures in violation of international law, the occupying power must restore its nationality and allow that population entry, although until it does so, technically that population might not be repatriated.

At any rate, since the occupying power cannot grant what it does not have, the settler population cannot acquire status in the territory during the period of occupation. Consequently, the question of survival of status through transition to the post-transition regime does not arise. The consequences of this rather arcane perception of individuals as pawns which States can move around may be mitigated by other bodies of law, such as human rights law, discussed in Part IV.

C. Status granted to settlers under an illegal regime

1. The Namibia exception

During the period of the illegal territorial regime's existence, the regime's authority is usually unchallenged within the territory under dispute.[223] Accordingly, the question whether to give legal effect to its acts arises primarily before foreign authorities. The International Law Commission's Articles on Responsibility of States for Internationally Wrongful Acts codify the customary rule of international law that States are under an obligation not to recognize as lawful a situation created by a serious breach of an obligation arising under a peremptory norm of general international

---

Legal Consequences of the Construction of a Wall in the Occupied Palestinian Territory (Advisory Opinion) [2004] ICJ Rep 136 (hereinafter '*Wall* Advisory Opinion') para 120.

[220] Israeli Ministry of Foreign Affairs, 'Israel, the Conflict and Peace: Answers to frequently asked questions (November 2007), <http://www.mfa.gov.il/MFA/Terrorism-+Obstacle+to+Peace/ Palestinian+terror+since+2000/Israel-+the+Conflict+and+Peace-+Answers+to+Frequen. htm#settlements> (last accessed 7 July 2009).

[221] See eg Adi Schwartz, 'The Settlers of Cyprus failed to Settle in the Hearts' Ha'aretz (Israeli Daily Newspaper) 25 May 2005 B6 (in Hebrew, on file with author).

[222] ILC Draft Articles on Responsibility of States for Internationally Wrongful Acts (2001), UN Doc A/56/10, art 30(1); Al-Khasawneh, above n 219, paras 60–63.

[223] For a unique exception see the *S v Banda and Others Bophuthatswana General Division* 1989(4) SA 519, where the legality of the South African administration of Namibia was challenged and considered in a South African court.

law, nor render aid or assistance in maintaining that situation.[224] This is a specific expression of the principle *ex injuria ius non oritur*. The violations at the root of the illegal territorial regimes described here, namely the unlawful use of force and the denial of the right to self-determination, are both regarded as serious breaches of peremptory norms. The applicability of the obligation of non-recognition to illegal territorial regimes was confirmed in the *Namibia* Advisory Opinion in 1971 on the legal consequences of South Africa's continuing illegal presence in Namibia.[225] In 2004 the Court reiterated its position on the obligation of non-recognition of an unlawful act under international law.[226]

The principle *ex injuria ius non oritur* entails invalidity of the acts of the illegal regime. Opposite it operates the principle *ex factis ius oritur*, which mandates that acts of the illegal regime may have legal consequences despite the illegality of the regime that performed them.[227]

The ICJ provided some guidance on the balance between the two principles in the *Namibia* Advisory Opinion:[228]

In general, the non-recognition of South Africa's administration of the Territory should not result in depriving the people of Namibia of any advantages derived from international co-operation. In particular, while official acts performed by the Government of South Africa on behalf of or concerning Namibia after the termination of the Mandate are illegal and invalid, this invalidity cannot be extended to those acts, such as, for instance, the registration of births, deaths and marriages, the effects of which can be ignored only to the detriment of the inhabitants of the Territory.

In other words, the general invalidity of domestic acts carried out under an illegal regime is qualified where it would act to the detriment of the inhabitants of the territory. This is the '*Namibia* exception'. The reference in the Advisory Opinion to the 'inhabitants of the Territory' was clearly

---

[224] ILC Draft Articles on Responsibility of States for Internationally Wrongful Acts, above n 222, arts 40, 41 and their commentaries. See also Alexander Orakhelashvili, *Peremptory Norms in International Law* (Oxford University Press, Oxford, 2006) 189–203. Milano argues that the obligation covers all unlawful territorial situations, including ones generated not through a violation of a peremptory norm. Enrico Milano, *Unlawful Territorial Situations in International Law* 141 (Brill, Leiden, 2006). For law and practice preceding the ILC Articles see Dugard, above n 4.

[225] *Legal Consequences for States of the Continued Presence of South Africa in Namibia (South West Africa) notwithstanding Security Council Resolution 276 (1970)* ICJ Rep [1971] 16 (hereinafter '*Namibia* Advisory Opinion') paras 123–124. The violation of international law that prompted the Advisory Opinion was not of a peremptory norm, but of the obligation in art 25 of the UN Charter: see 54. However, the revocation of the South African Mandate over Namibia was brought about following the violation of norms regarded as peremptory, primarily the right to self-determination.

[226] *Wall* Advisory Opinion, above n 219. The regime to which the Court referred as 'illegal' was the restrictions on movement across the Wall in the Occupied Palestinian Territories. One of the arguments against the construction of a wall was that it was creating an illegal territorial situation, ie the forcible annexation of territories. However, there was no discussion of the lawfulness of Israel's control of the West Bank as such.

[227] Crawford, above n 6, 166–67; Robert Y Jennings, 'Nullity and Effectiveness in International Law' in *Cambridge Essays in International Law (Essays in Honour of Lord McNair)* (Oceana Publications, London, 1965) 75.

[228] *Namibia* Advisory Opinion, above n 225, para 125.

to the indigenous population as in Namibia there was no significant settler population to speak of. A general question therefore arises whether the
'inhabitants' protected by the *Namibia* exception can also include settlers,
in which case their status may acquire validity despite the illegality of the
regime as a whole; and whether such exceptional recognition survives the
transition from the illegal regime to the post-transition regime.

The *Namibia* exception has received various interpretations, which in
many instances overlap.[229] In the *Namibia* advisory opinion itself, Judge
de Castro suggested[230] that a distinction must be made between the private
and the public sector. The acts and rights of private persons (such as entries
in the civil registers and in the Land Registry, marriages and judgments
of civil courts) should be regarded as valid even if carried out under the law
of the illegal regime. On the other hand, other States should not regard as
valid any acts and transactions of the authorities in Namibia relating to
public property, concessions, etc. States will thus not be able to exercise
protection of their nationals with regard to any acquisitions of this kind.[231]
Granting of civic status, whether it is nationality or residence, is a public
sphere activity and therefore under this interpretation merits no validity.
It does not appear to matter whether the individuals involved belong to
the indigenous population or are settlers.

A different interpretation of the *Namibia* exception was put forward by
Judge Onyeama, who suggested in the *Namibia* advisory opinion that the
prohibition on giving legal effect to acts of the illegal regime concerns only
acts that aim at entrenching the illegal regime or are capable of doing so.[232]
Ordinary day-to-day acts would fall within the validating scope of the
exception. Under this interpretation, nationality purportedly granted under
the illegal regime, the epitome of entrenchment of the regime, would not
be given validity. With respect to residence the situation is less clear-cut.
On the one hand, its purpose is to change the demographic character of
the territory so as to entrench the illegal regime in it. On the other hand,
the grant of residence is more easily reversible than the grant of nationality, so its capacity to achieve this goal is limited. Yet as the immunity to
expulsion of long-term residents grows,[233] long-term residence begins to
resemble nationality, and the justification for validating it diminishes.

According to a third interpretation, paragraph 125 of the *Namibia*
Advisory Opinion should be read literally. Since non-recognition is not
qualified, then *a priori* no act of any kind should be recognized, whether or
not it entrenches the illegal regime.[234] The exception calls for a case-by-case
examination whether under the specific circumstance, non-recognition of
nationality or residence would be detrimental to the inhabitants of the

---

[229] For a discussion of the three interpretations see Ronen (2005), above n 4, 78–82.
[230] *Namibia* Advisory Opinion, above n 225, 218–219.
[231] *Cf* in the UK *Emin v Yeldag* [2002] 1 FLR 956.
[232] *Namibia* Advisory Opinion, above n 225; see further Ronen (2005), above n 4, 79.
[233] Part IV below.
[234] *Namibia* Advisory Opinion, above n 225, 99–100.

territory. This allows greater flexibility, which may also include protection of settlers. At the same time, since this interpretation gives weight to considerations of justice and fairness, it is presumably available only to persons acting in good faith.[235] This might limit protection to settlers who have come into the territory under compulsion or in ignorance of the legal situation. There may also be circumstances where exceptional validity of a settler's status would be necessary to avoid detriment to a local inhabitant of the territory. Recognition of settlers' status in the territory is also important to ensure stability and reliability of commercial interaction.

The claim that nationality granted by the illegal regime should be recognized on the basis of the *Namibia* exception was made in *Veysi Dag*, an asylum request made in the UK by a Turkish-Cypriot claiming to be a national of the TRNC. The Immigration Appeal Tribunal first rejected the relevance of the *Namibia* exception to the TRNC, noting that unlike South Africa, which was recognized as a sovereign State, albeit over different territory to the one it claimed, the TRNC is not recognized at all. The Tribunal assumed that the *Namibia* exception would have been formulated differently had the ICJ had in mind a situation equivalent to that of the TRNC. Furthermore, the Immigration Appeal Tribunal considered that 'nobody has identified any disadvantage which would accrue to the appellant by reason of the international non-recognition of the "Turkish Republic of Northern Cyprus"'.[236] Accordingly it found that the *Namibia* exception did not apply on the facts. This statement seems to be a mistaken framing of the question. The non-recognition of the TRNC is not under debate. What the *Namibia* exception may require is that the Immigration Appeal Tribunal consider the potential detriment to TRNC inhabitants as a result of the non-recognition of the legal validity of the TRNC's conferment of nationality. In asylum requests, for example, not to acknowledge the purported nationality of the applicant in a manner which would result in denial of otherwise-justified asylum would be detrimental to the inhabitant.[237] It seems that the decision whether to give validity to nationality or residence, under this interpretation, can only be made on a case-by-case basis.

2. *Survival of status recognized under the* Namibia *exception through transition to a lawful regime*

The *Namibia* exception was formulated with respect to the situation during the existence of the illegal regime. It ensured that individuals would not be held hostage to enforcement measures aimed at releasing them from the grasp of that regime. It did not address the post-transition stage. The effect of

---

[235] *Cf Lamar v Micou*, 112 US 452 (1884) at 473.

[236] UK Immigration Appeal Tribunal (determination notified 14 March 2001) *Veysi Dag v The Secretary of State for the Home Department*, CG [2001] 00002 Appeal No: HX/70783/98 *(01 TH 0075)* para 23.

[237] In *Veysi Dag* the Immigration Appeal Tribunal pointed out that in the circumstances, even if TRNC nationality were recognized, the appellant would not have succeeded in his asylum request, ibid, para 33.

change of responsibility of international relations of a territory on nationality is ordinarily regulated by the law on state succession,[238] codified in the ILC Draft Articles on Nationality of Natural Persons in relation to the Succession of States.[239] However, the Draft Articles are limited to State succession occurring in conformity with international law. The commentary provides that the Draft Articles do not apply to situations of illegal annexation of territory.[240] Equally, then, they cannot apply to situations of emergence from illegal annexation (or other territorial situations in violation of international law). In the absence of legal norms governing the survival of exceptionally-recognized status under the *Namibia* exception, the matter is one of policy.

The significance of continuity of status in providing stability and security did not escape policy makers. But policy makers did not necessarily aim to provide stability and security. In Estonia, when in 1993 the debate turned to the right of non-nationals to remain in the country, the draft Aliens Law rejected the possibility that Soviet-era residence 'registration' could be automatically exchanged for a new Estonian residence permit, instead requiring settlers to apply for new permits. One of the drafters expressed it most frankly: 'By means of the present law we have to create a situation where the colonists feel the earth shaking under their feet'.[241] Indeed, the goal of the draft law was to create extreme uncertainty among non-national residents about their future status in Estonia. This policy choice was greatly criticized, and following pressure by European institutions, the draft was subsequently amended so that residence granted by the Soviet authorities was automatically given validity.[242] Shaking the ground underneath Soviet-era settlers was regarded as illegitimate if not outright illegal.

Another example of the refusal of the post-transition regimes to give validity even to residential status under the illegal regime concerns the qualifying date of residence for the purpose of naturalization. In both Estonia and Latvia, the period of lawful residence is calculated (at the earliest) from the day on which each of the States declared its reversion to independence. The period of residence under Soviet rule is not taken into account. In contrast, the Annan Plan allows residence of up to five years in the TRNC prior to transition into the UCR to be counted towards fulfilling the requisites for naturalization in the UCR.[243]

Although neither the law of occupation nor the law of non-recognition require the post-transition regime to recognize the validity of status granted to individuals by the illegal regime, in most of the cases examined here, the

---

[238] There are other constraints, mostly based on international human rights law. However, they are not status-based and are considered in Part IV.
[239] Yearbook of the International Law Commission, vol II, Part Two (1999).
[240] ILC Draft art 3 and commentary (2) to ILC Draft art 3; ibid.
[241] Kask, above n 102, 386.
[242] Ibid, 385–388.
[243] A separate question is whether the same period would be counted towards the fulfilment of a lawful residence period for the purpose of Directive 2003/109.

settler population was eventually given the opportunity to remain in the territory, either unreservedly (as in Zimbabwe and South Africa), or with qualifications (in the Baltic States only to the civilian population, in the TRNC on a numerical basis). These policy and practices may be explained by another relevant body of norms, namely international human rights law.

IV. International Human Rights-Based Limitations on Expulsion

A. Introduction

New factual situations come to exist which may have legal consequences because of their effectiveness. This part examines how the presence of settlers may generate legal consequences, embodied in international human rights law, that limit the post-transition regime's discretion in expelling them, despite the original illegality of the transfer of settlers to the territory.

Various international human rights may be implicated in measures of expulsion. These include the right to a hearing, the prohibition on racial and other discrimination, the right to property,[244] the right to family and private life, the prohibition on inhuman treatment and more. The discussion here focuses on certain norms which are particularly pertinent to expulsion of long-term settlers implanted under an illegal regime. It also focuses on two international instruments: the 1966 International Covenant on Civil and Political Rights (ICCPR), which is binding on all post-transition regimes examined here,[245] and the European Convention on Human Rights and Fundamental Freedoms (ECHR), which is binding upon the Baltic States and is expected to be binding upon the UCR.[246] This Part begins with a discussion of the relevant rights, and then examines potential grounds for interfering with those rights.

B. The prohibition on discrimination

International law prohibits discrimination, which means unreasonable inequality in treatment of individuals or groups, which has the purpose

---

[244] Eg when the freedom of ownership is conditional upon status, as in East Timor, or when expulsion is carried out in a manner that prevents individuals from benefiting from their property.

[245] International Covenant on Civil and Political Rights, 16 December 1966, 999 UNTS 171 (entered into force 23 March 1976, hereinafter 'ICCPR'), in force for Estonia since 21 January 1992, for Latvia since 14 August 1992, for Lithuania since 20 February 1992, for East Timor since 18 December 2003, Annan Plan, Foundation Agreement, Annex V, Item 112 in the multilateral treaty list binding upon the UCR.

[246] European Convention on Human Rights and Fundamental Freedoms, 4 November 1950, 213 UNTS 222 (entered into force 3 September 1953, hereinafter 'ECHR'), in force for Estonia since 16 April 1996, for Latvia since 27 June 1997, for Lithuania since 20 June 1995; Annan Plan, above n 157, Foundation Agreement, Annex V, Item 204 in the multilateral treaty list binding upon the UCR. This right is also guaranteed by the Constitution of Estonia, art 33; Constitution of Latvia, art 96; Constitution of Lithuania, art 24, Constitution of East Timor, art 37, Annan Plan, Foundation Agreement, Annex V, Item 204 in the multilateral treaty list binding upon the UCR and Draft Constitution art 11(1), enshrining the ECHR in the Constitution, and UCR Constitution Attachment 5, arts 19, 20.

or effect of nullifying or impairing their exercise on an equal footing of human rights and fundamental freedoms.[247] A distinction among persons is not discriminatory if the criteria used are reasonable and objective and their effect is proportionate to the aim pursued;[248] at the same time, some distinctions are regarded as absolutely prohibited, namely those based on race, colour, descent, national or ethnic origin.[249]

As a matter of fact, in the UCR and the Baltic States potential expellees are overwhelmingly Turkish and Russophones (respectively). This has been justified as non-discriminatory policy, because the expulsion is not ethnically-based but tied to the distinction between a national or as a foreigner, which is not regarded *prima facie* as discriminatory.[250] The expulsion of a foreigner can not be regarded as discriminatory merely because a national cannot be expelled under similar circumstances. Thus, where the right to remain hinges on eligibility for nationality, the question whether the post-transition regime acted in a discriminatory manner shifts from the issue of expulsion to the determination of eligibility for nationality.

It is generally accepted that States may lay out conditions for the acquisition of nationality, provided that these do not discriminate against any particular national origin.[251] The policies of the post-transition regime in the Baltic States, East Timor and under the Annan Plan did not single out the Russophones, Indonesians, or Turks. They were drafted neutrally in terms of nationality or ethnicity.

In the Baltic States, the fact that excluded settlers were predominantly Russophones was therefore claimed to be merely a consequence of the immigration patterns under the illegal regime. Moreover, because the legislation was not ethnically-defined, there was not an absolute correlation between ethnicity and eligibility for nationality. Defenders of the Baltic States' restorationalist policies point out that the reversion to pre-1940 legislation did not reserve nationality only to ethnic Balts. All pre-1940 nationals of the Baltic States were entitled to reacquire their nationality, regardless of their ethnicity.[252] Conversely, where reversion to the pre-1940 situation was qualified, this also affected persons of Baltic descent, too. For example, at the early stages some former nationals of Lithuanian descent were prevented from

---

[247] ICCPR, above n 245, art 2, 26, ECHR, ibid, art 14, ECHR Protocol 12, 4 November 2000, CETS 177 (entered into force 1 April 2005), Convention on the Elimination of All Forms of Racial Discrimination, 7 March 1966, 660 UNTS 195 (entered into force 4 January 1969, hereinafter 'CERD')) art 1(1), ACHR, above n 201, art 1(1), Universal Declaration of Human Rights, GA Res 217A (III) (10 December 1948), art 7. HRC General Comment 18: Non-discrimination (9 November 1989) para 1. The prohibition on racial discrimination is almost unanimously recognized as *ius cogens*.

[248] Ibid, para 13.

[249] CERD, above n 247, art 2(1).

[250] Ibid, art 1(2), UN Doc A/CN.4/565 para 280.

[251] CERD, ibid, art 1(3). The term 'nationality' used in the Convention should be read as 'national origin', which is similar but not clearly identical to 'ethnic origin'. Natan Lerner, *The UN Convention on the Elimination of all Forms of Racial Discrimination* (Sijthoff & Noordhoff, Alphen aan den Rijn, 1980) 29–30.

[252] Estonia: Resolution of the Supreme Council of the Republic of Estonia 'On Implementation of Citizenship Act'; Latvia: 1994 Citizenship Law, art 2(1); Lithuania: 1991 Law on Citizenship art 1(3).

reacquiring Lithuanian nationality.[253] The exclusion of Russophones from nationality was therefore claimed to be only an incidental consequence of legitimate legislation rather than an ethnically-related measure.[254]

The same can be said with respect to the UCR and its treatment of Turkish settlers. Under the Annan Plan, all post-1963 settlers, not only mainland Turks, would not be regarded as nationals. Yet although this includes many other foreign nationals, of which there are over 8,000 currently in the TRNC,[255] the political debate focuses on the future of Turkish settlers.

Unlike the Baltic States and UCR, East Timor did not revert to earlier legislation, but adopted original nationality legislation. The 2002 Nationality Law largely limits nationality to ethnic East Timorese, but there is nothing in the legislation singling out Indonesian settlers. Moreover, East Timorese-born individuals may acquire nationality by declaration, thereby allowing Indonesians and other second-generation immigrants to become nationals.

If the neutrally-drafted distinction is merely a cover-up for ethnic discrimination, it is prohibited. But it may be that the distinction between settlers under the illegal regime and other foreigners reflects a legitimate concern, in which case it would be lawful as long as it is necessary and proportionate to the aim pursued, and applied without bias against any ethnicity. The justifications for the legislation adopted and its effect on the right of settlers to acquire nationality or residence is examined below in the context of the grounds for expulsion.

Similarly to the provisions on original nationality, formally the legislation on naturalization in all three cases is also ethnically and nationally-neutral.[256] In practice, there are provisions that affect only settlers under the illegal regime, such as the inability to rely on residence under the illegal regime in calculating the length of residence for the purpose of naturalization (in East Timor, Estonia, Latvia, and partly under the Annan Plan). *Prima facie*, these provisions are not discriminatory because they do not impair the settlers' enjoyment on equal footing of any human right. Their effect is that the settlers under the illegal regime are not better placed than other foreigners. At the same time it may be queried whether disregard of the period of residence in the territory is proportionate to the aim pursued by the legislation. Again, the examination of the aim pursued follows in the context of the grounds for expulsion.

---

[253] If they were not resident in Lithuania or had acquired other nationality: 1991 Law on Citizenship art 1(3).

[254] Although legally there was no singling out of the settler population, there is no doubt that the political motivation for the legislation was ethnically-oriented. Pettai, above n 79; Kask, above n 102, 379.

[255] The Final Results of TRNC General Population and Housing Unit Census, Additional Tables, <http://nufussayimi.devplan.org/Kesin-sonuc-index_en.html> (last accessed 10 Feb 2009).

[256] In the Baltic States there are limitations on holding dual nationality. This does not prevent the acquisition of nationality by foreign nationals, but only requires them to renounce their previous nationality.

A different type of provision gives preferential treatment to certain set-tlers, such as the residence (and eventual naturalization) arrangement of 50,000 persons entitled to remain in the Turkish-Cypriot constituent State of the UCR. Preferential treatment is permitted under international law within certain limitations.[257] Moreover, inclusion on the list was never lim-ited by any ethnic or national criteria. Nonetheless, if in practice the entire list will contain only persons of Turkish origin, it may be queried whether the exclusion of other foreigners is discriminatory.

C. Protection from severance from one's social environment— the right to private life

Although formally residential status granted under the illegal regime may be disregarded by the post-transition regime,[258] long-term residence is a fact which may carry legal consequences. When the illegal regime lasts over two decades, as has happened in the cases examined here, there are likely to be many members of the settler community who consider the territory their home both geographically and socially, having lived there a large part of their life or even all of it. They may have never been to their State of origin (possibly their State of nationality but not necessarily). This attachment is protected under international human rights instruments.

1. ECHR Article 8

ECHR Article 8 stipulates:

1. Everyone has the right to respect for his private and family life, his home and his correspondence.
2. There shall be no interference by a public authority with the exercise of this right except such as is in accordance with the law and is necessary in a dem-ocratic society in the interests of national security, public safety or the eco-nomic well-being of the country, for the prevention of disorder or crime, for the protection of health or morals, or for the protection of the rights and freedoms of others.

Under ECHR jurisprudence, the concept of 'private life' within the meaning of Article 8 encompasses the totality of social ties between individuals and the community in which they live.[259] The right to private life protects 'the right to establish and develop relationships with other human beings and the outside world' and 'can sometimes embrace aspects of an individual's social identity'.[260] The expulsion of an integrated immigrant therefore

---

[257] CERD, above n 247, art 1(4).   [258] Above Part III.
[259] *Üner v Netherlands*, above n 210, para 59.
[260] *Pretty v United Kingdom*, Application No. 2346/02 ECHR 2002-III para 61 *cf* ACHR, above n 201, art 11(2). According to the jurisprudence of the Inter-American Commission on Human Rights, 'The requirements of art 11 encompass a range of factors pertaining to the dignity of the

constitutes an interference with his or her right to respect for private life.[261] The criteria for assessing a person's integration within the State were developed mostly with respect to expulsion of criminal convicts, but are applicable *mutatis mutandis* to expulsion on other grounds, including settlement under an illegal territorial regime. The extent of integration is measured through the solidity of social, cultural and family ties with the State of residence and with the State of destination (usually the State of nationality).[262] Those depend on the length of the person's stay in the country from which he or she is to be expelled; the nationalities of other persons affected; the person's family situation; and the seriousness of the difficulties which family members are likely to encounter in the country of origin of the expellee. The European Court of Human Rights (ECtHR) has emphasized that the longer a person has been residing in a particular State, the stronger his or her ties with that country will be, and the weaker the ties with the State of nationality. Therefore the Court has regard to the special situation of foreigners who have spent most, if not all, their childhood in the State of residence, were brought up there and received their education there.[263]

There is a striking difference between the protection from expulsion available under ICCPR Article 12(4)[264] and that offered under ECHR Article 8. Protection under the former depends on formal status, while under the latter it depends on the factual situation. Interestingly, in both the HRC and the ECtHR there have been attempts to move from one type of protection to the other. In both cases, these attempts appear to have failed.

ECtHR judges have in a number of cases advocated an approach which assimilates long-term residents to nationals, rendering them practically immune to expulsion.[265] In *Üner v the Netherlands*, however, the majority

---

individual, including, for example, the ability to pursue the development of one's personality and aspirations, determine one's identity, and define one's personal relationships. Report No. 4/01 Case 11.625 María Eugenia Morales de Sierra, Guatemala, (19 January 2001) para 46.

[261] *Üner v Netherlands*, above n 210, para 59, uses the term 'settled' in the sense of 'integrated', which is more common in Council of Europe documents and ECHR judgments.

[262] Ibid, para 58.

[263] In *Cyprus v Turkey*, *Application* 8007/77, 13 Decision and Reports 85, decided by the European Commission on Human Rights, Judge Schermers in a separate opinion on rights in residential property in the TRNC wrote: 'As Article 8 guarantees the right to respect for his home to everyone, the rights of the new occupant should be taken into account, even if the occupation was originally established on an invalid title. After a long period of time restoration of the *status quo ante* will become a violation of Article 8 with respect to the new occupant. It is difficult to establish how long this period is to be, because in fact it is a gradual process. ...children will be born in the house who have no other place which they could consider as their home... I cannot accept as the only possible remedy that Turkey should be obliged to break up the homes of all present occupants in order to allow the original occupants to return.' This reasoning is all the more applicable to issues of personal status, where validation of the settler's status given his association with the territory does not come at the expense of an identifiable dispossessed other.

[264] Above Part III.

[265] Judge Martens in *Beldjoudi v France* 14 EHRR (1992) 801; also his dissenting opinion in *Boughanemi v France*, 22 EHRR (1996) 228; Judge Morenilla partly dissenting and Judge Wildhaber concurring in *Nasri v France* (1996) 21 EHRR 458 Judge Baka dissenting in *Boughanemi v France* and

opinion squarely rejected the proposition that this assimilation be read into Article 8, insisting that States should be permitted to maintain the functionability of Article 8(2). Thus, an 'integrated alien' is not a separate category of persons enjoying immunity from expulsion by virtue of quasi-status alone.[266]

An opposite trend was discernable in the HRC, namely the attempt to introduce factual criteria for protection under Article 12(4) rather than formal classification. As noted above, under Article 12(4) protection from expulsion is dependent on either nationality or a quasi-formal link to the State of residence.[267] This jurisprudence was criticized by a minority of Committee members, in *Stewart* and subsequently.[268] The dissenting view (on this point held by at least six of the Committee members)[269] was that the ICCPR is concerned with the 'strong personal and emotional links an individual may have with the territory where he lives and with the social circumstances obtaining in it'. Therefore a State is 'one's own country' not by virtue of formal ties, but by virtue of 'the web of relationships that form his or her social environment'.[270] Accordingly, the dissenting Committee members considered that Article 12(4) invites consideration of such matters as long-standing residence, close personal and family ties and intentions to remain, as well as to the absence of such ties elsewhere.[271] These are factual, not formal, criteria.

The minority view in *Stewart* attached to Article 12(4) a meaning similar to that of ECHR Article 8, rather than of a status-based right. It may

in *Boujlifa v France* 30 EHRR (1997) 419; Judge Morenilla dissenting in *Boujlifa*; joint dissenting opinion of Judges Baka and Van Dijk in *Boujlifa*; Joint Dissenting Opinion of Judges Costa, Zupančič and Türmen in *Üner v Netherlands*, above n 210, para 5.

[266] *Slivenko v Latvia*, above n 90, para 95. *Üner v Netherlands*, above n 210, para 56–58, which examines this issue in light of the Committee of Ministers Recommendation Rec (2000) 15 and Parliamentary Assembly Recommendation 1504 (2001).

[267] *Madafferi v Australia* (2004) above n 203. In *Simalae Toala et al v New Zealand* (2000), above n 203, the Committee went even further in restricting recourse to art 12(4), this time on factual grounds, by suggesting that nationals who have no effective links with the state of nationality cannot claim the right under art 12(4) with respect to that State: para 11.4.

[268] *Canepa v Canada* (1997) above n 204, individual opinions by Committee Members Evatt and Medina Quiroga (dissenting), and Chanet (dissenting).

[269] *Stewart v Canada* (1996), above n 201, individual opinions by Committee Members Evatt, Medina Quiroga, Aguilar Urbina (dissenting) paras 5–7, and Bhagwati, Chanet and Prado Vallejo. Committee Member Klein's opinion does not address the matter squarely but his agreement with the other dissenting judges may be inferred from his dissatisfaction with the delineation of the relationship between arts 12(4) and 13.

[270] Both quotes from the dissenting opinion by Committee Members Evatt, Medina Quiroga, Aguilar Urbina, para 5.

[271] Dissenting opinion by Committee Members Evatt, Medina Quiroga, Aguilar Urbina, paras 5, 6. See also Manfred Nowak *UN Covenant on Civil and Political Rights: CCPR Commentary* (2nd ed, NP Engel, Kehl, 2005) 287–288, Stig Jagerskiold 'The Freedom of Movement' in Louis Henkin (ed) *The International Bill of Rights; The Covenant on Civil and Political Rights* (Columbia University Press, New York, 1981) 166, 180–181, Henckaerts, above n 101, 83, Hurst Hannum, *The Right to Leave and Return in International Law and Practice* (Martinus Nijhoff, Dordrechet, 1987) 59–60. See also 'The Right to Leave and the Right to Return: A Declaration Adopted by the Uppsala Colloquium, Sweden, June 21, 1972', reprinted in (1973) 7 International Migration Review 62–66. Art 12 restricts the possibility of limiting the right to return of long-term residents.

be preferable to the majority opinion, which implies that a State of residence becomes a person's own country only through the cumulative failures by two States—the State of nationality and the State of residence itself. In addition, it is difficult to imagine that the drafters of Article 12(4) intended to attach the specific meaning attributed to it in the General Comment, to a very general terminology. On the other hand, it is also difficult to read a requirement of a factual link to the state of residence into 'his own country' or 'arbitrarily'.[272]

In *Canepa v Canada*, Mr. Scheinin, in critique of the majority opinion in *Stewart* as overly limited, added other potential categories of persons entitled to protection under Article 12(4), namely 'if the person is stateless or if it would be impossible or clearly unreasonable for him or her to integrate into the society corresponding to his or her de jure nationality'.[273] Like the majority view in *Stewart*, Mr. Scheinin placed the emphasis on the inability to relocate to the State of nationality; but he expanded this 'inability' from formal to practical obstacles, resulting from strong integration of the person in the State of residence.[274] This modification incorporates the minority view within that of the majority's. In this respect it shifts slightly, from reliance on formal status alone to incorporation of factual considerations.

Although the majority's limited interpretation was adopted in the General Comment on Article 12(4) adopted in 1999, the Committee attached significance to the positive link with the State of residence, noting that 'other factors may in certain circumstances result in the establishment of close and enduring connections between a person and a country', and requested States to report on the rights of permanent residents to return to their country of residence.[275]

In conclusion, despite attempts to duplicate elements of ECHR Article 8 into ICCPR Article 12(4) and vice versa, the two instruments remain distinct. The ICCPR concerns the formal status of a person with reference to how this status came to exist, while the ECHR examines the circumstances of the individual by reference to their future implications.

2. *ICCPR Article 17*

Article 17 of the ICCPR protects everyone from 'arbitrary or unlawful interference with his privacy, family, home...'. The term 'privacy' has been interpreted narrowly, in the sense of isolation from society and the public, rather than the forging of social ties. It thus differs from 'private life' under the ECHR. The term 'family' has originally been interpreted

---

[272] See also Amnesty International: 'The Right to Return: The Case of the Palestinians, Policy Statement, Amnesty International's position on forcible exile and the right to return', AI Index: MDE 15/013/2001 (30 March 2001) para 7.

[273] *Canepa v Canada* (1997) above n 204, Individual opinion by Committee Member Scheinin (concurring).

[274] cf *Üner v Netherlands*, above n 210, para 58.

[275] HRC General Comment 27, above n 203, para 20.

narrowly so as to cover immediate formal relationships rather than social ties. This changed in *Winata v Australia*, which concerned an alien couple about to be deported from Australia after residing there illegally for many years. They had a 13-year old child, a citizen of Australia who was thereby entitled to remain in the country. The majority view was that expulsion of the parents would have compelled the family to choose whether the child remains alone in the country or accompanies his parents. The Committee found this to be an 'interference' with the 'family', because 'substantial changes to long-settled family life would follow' whatever choice the parents made.[276] Similar circumstances were presented in *Madafferi v Australia*. The Committee noted that the State's reasons for the removal of a person concerned must be weighed against the degree of hardship the family and its members would encounter as a consequence of such removal.[277] In *Winata* the Committee took into consideration the fact that the complainants' son 'has grown in Australia from his birth 13 years ago, attending Australian schools as an ordinary child would and developing the social relationships inherent in that'.[278] In *Madafferi* it noted the alien environment that the spouse and children would have faced (moving from Australia to Italy), the language barrier for the children, and the difficulty in caring under such circumstances for the expellee, whose mental health had been seriously troubled, in part by acts that could be ascribed to the State wishing to expel the individual.[279] The *Winata* and *Madafferi* jurisprudence expands 'interference' with the family where the family has a free-standing right to remain in that State of residence, by combining the candidate expellee's right to family life with the attachment of his or her family to the State of residence (or 'private life' in terms of ECHR Article 8). Several members of the Committee objected to this interpretation of Article 17 on the ground that it assimilated Article 17 to ECHR Article 8.[280] The two provisions still differ with respect to adult second-generation immigrants who are attached to the State of residence, but have no formal family relationships there.[281]

The ECtHR has in a number of cases faced situations similar to that of *Winata*, namely where the main obstacle to expulsion was that it would entail difficulties for the families to stay together because of obstacles to the integration of the spouse or children in the candidate expellee's country of origin.[282] However, once Article 8 was expanded to cover a person's social environment, the need to rely on the right to respect for family life

---

[276] *Winata v Australia* Communication no 930/2000, views of 26 July 2001, UN Doc CCPR/C/72/D/930/2000, para 7.2.

[277] *Madafferi v Australia* (2004) above n 203, paras 9.7, 9.8.

[278] *Winata v Australia*, above n 276, para 7.3.

[279] *Madafferi v Australia* (2004) above n 203, para 9.8.

[280] *Winata v Australia*, above n 276, Individual opinion by Committee Members Bhagwati, Khalil, Kretzmer and Yalden (dissenting), individual opinion of Committee Member Wedgewood in *Madafferi v Australia*, above n 203.

[281] Eg *Canepa v Canada*, above n 204.

[282] Eg *Boultif v Switzerland*, application no. 54273/00, ECHR 2001-IX.

was reduced to rare situations where the only link that an individual has to the State of residence is marriage to one of its nationals or long-term residents.[283]

Article 17 also protects the individual from interference with the 'home', which may reasonably include the social environment of a person, and in this respect can also assimilate Article 17 to ECHR Article 8. An argument to this effect was put forward in *Canepa v Canada*. After establishing that there would not be a disruption of immediate family relations, the Committee concluded: 'There appear to be no circumstances particular to the author [of the complaint] or to his family which would lead the Committee to conclude that his removal from Canada was an arbitrary interference with his family, nor with his privacy or home.'[284] It thus attached no weight to social ties as 'home' for the purpose of Article 17. The HRC's General Comment on Article 17 also suggests that the acceptable interpretation is limited to 'home' as institutional or even tangible structures.[285]

D. *The prohibition on collective expulsion*

If the post-transition regime is contemplating the removal of a large number of individuals on the basis of their group affiliation, namely their being settlers brought in by an illegal regime, the collective character of removal becomes pertinent. Collective expulsion has been understood by the ECtHR,[286] and subsequently by the ILC Rapporteur on the Expulsion of Aliens, as 'any measure by the competent authorities compelling aliens, as a group, to leave a country, except where such a measure is taken after and on the basis of a reasonable and objective examination of the particular case of each individual alien of the group'.[287] In other words, collective expulsion is defined—and prohibited—as lacking individual review. It is prohibited by ECHR Protocol 4 Article 4 and other regional instruments.[288] The ICCPR contains no specific provisions on collective

---

[283] As was the case of Mr. Boultif, ibid.

[284] *Canepa v Canada*, above n 204, 11.5. There were no individual opinions on this issue.

[285] HRC General Comment 16: Article 17 (Right to Privacy) (23 March 1988).

[286] *Sultani v France*, application No. 45223/05, judgment of 20 Sept 2007; see also *Becker v Denmark*, Decision of the European Commission of Human Rights as to the Admissibility of Application 7011/75 19 *Yrbk of European Convention on Human Rights* 416 (1976) quoted in Henckaerts, above n 101, 12 footnote 35: the decision to expel must be based on 'a reasonable and objective examination of the particular cases of each individual alien of the group'. See also *Conka v Belgium*, application no 51564/99, judgment of 5 February 2002, para 56.

[287] A/CN.4/581 para 107.

[288] ACHR, above n 201, art 22(9) provides: 'The collective expulsion of aliens is prohibited.' The African Charter on Human and Peoples' Rights art 12(5) provides: 'The mass expulsion of non-nationals shall be prohibited.' African [Banjul] Charter on Human and Peoples' Rights, adopted June 27, 1981, OAU Doc CAB/LEG/67/3 rev. 5, 21 *International Legal Materials* 58 (1982), entered into force Oct. 21, 1986. The preparatory memorandum of the UN Secretariat for the ILC distinguished collective expulsion from mass expulsion, which it defined by the quantitative element. According to the memorandum, mass expulsion is prohibited (even if it is not collective) where it imposes an excessive burden on the receiving State or when it constitutes an abuse of rights, UN Doc A/CN.4/565 paras 993–994. For present purposes, it is collective expulsion as defined by the Rapporteur which is pertinent. At any rate, it is doubtful whether the distinction proposed by the memorandum is reflected

expulsion, but Article 13 (which generally prohibits arbitrary expulsion of aliens lawfully within the territory of a State) has been interpreted as requiring an individual inspection of the circumstances of each individual. By implication this prohibits any collective measure. Henckaerts argues that collective expulsion is qualitatively similar to individual expulsion, because the requirement of a review process exists also with respect to individual expulsions. Nonetheless, collective expulsion merits a separate prohibiting provision because the massive scale of expulsions creates a presumption that certain norms, particularly the prohibition on discrimination and the right to review, have been violated.[289] The ILC Special Rapporteur concludes that 'it seems reasonable to suggest that there is a general principle of international law on this matter that is "recognized by civilized nations" and prohibits collective expulsion'.[290]

Expulsion of settlers under an illegal regime from the territory of the post-transition regime because of their status as such would appear to be a collective expulsion based on group affiliation. The collective appearance of the expulsion (in the form of numerous identical orders relying on a legislative authorization without reference to the specific circumstances of the potential expellee) would transfer the burden of proof to the post-transition regime to show that the expulsion is lawful. The post-transition regime may discharge this burden if it provides for a genuine process of review for each individual which revolves on the specific ground for expulsion.

E. The prohibition on inhuman treatment

Another basis for protection of long-term residents against expulsion was offered by Judges de Meyer and Morenilla of the ECtHR. Both have argued that the expulsion of second-generation immigrants, born or raised from an early age in the host State, may constitute inhuman treatment prohibited under ECHR Article 3.[291]

In *Beldjoudi*, Judge de Meyer merely pointed out that the applicant 'would be ejected, after over forty years, from a country which has always in fact been "his" since birth, even though he does not possess its "nationality"'. This statement suggests that long-term residence—from birth in

---

in the international instruments. The ILC Special Rapporteur, for example, considered the prohibition in art 12(5) of the Banjul Charter as that of collective expulsion, even though is it termed 'mass expulsion'. Indeed, art 12(5) appears to reflect the Secretariat's criteria for 'collective expulsion', because the prohibition is based on the discriminatory nature of the expulsion in targeting a group, rather than the number of expellees. In the context of settlers under an illegal regime, it is appropriate to speak of 'collective expulsion', because *prima facie* the issue is that of targeting a group without considering the particulars of each individual.

[289] Henckaerts, above n 101, 14–15.
[290] UN Doc A/CN.4/581 para 115.
[291] Judge de Meyer in separate opinion in *Beldjoudi*, above n 265 and in a partly dissenting opinion in *Nasri v France*, above n 265; Judge Morenilla in a partly dissenting opinion in *Nasri v France* above n 265.

this case—is sufficient to render expulsion a violation of Article 3. In *Nasri,* Judge de Meyer reiterated his position, but added that he did so 'in particular in view of Mr Nasri's disability' (deaf-mutism). This addition suggests that residence from birth in the host State might not always be sufficient to grant a person immunity from expulsion.

Judge Morenilla in *Nasri* provided a different rationale for his reliance on Article 3. First he noted that he would have followed the approach of the majority of the Commission in that application, which concluded that there had been a violation of Article 3 because of the sensory and social isolation to which the applicant would have been exposed to if expelled to Algeria.[292] However, he suggested that Article 3 might be applicable regardless of the future awaiting the expellee. He considered the general question which underlies the application of Article 3 to be 'the limits to be imposed on administrative measures—or sanctions—of deportation to the country "of origin", on account of criminal or antisocial behavior on the part of "second generation" aliens, including those who, like the applicant, came as children accompanying their migrant worker parents'.[293] He noted:

A State which, for reasons of convenience, accepts immigrant workers and authorizes their residence becomes responsible for the education and social integration of the children of such immigrants as it is of the children of its 'citizens'. Where such social integration fails, and the result is antisocial or criminal behavior, the State is also under a duty to make provision for their social rehabilitation instead of sending them back to their country of origin, which has no responsibility for the behavior in question and where the possibilities of rehabilitation given the foreign social environment, are virtually non-existent. The treatment of offenders whether on the administrative or criminal level should not therefore differ according to the national origin of the parents in a way which—through deportation—makes the sanction more severe in a clearly discriminatory manner.

According to Judge Morenilla, the 'inhuman treatment' consists of the host State's invitation of immigrants and failure to discharge the responsibilities that accompany such invitation, resulting in second-generation immigrants finding themselves facing expulsion to a State of origin where their chances of rehabilitation are virtually non-existent. Unlike Judge de Meyer, Judge Morenilla attached significance to the conduct of the State of long-term residence. It remains unclear whether Judge Morenilla interpreted Article 3 as protecting all second-generation immigrants; only those born to lawful immigrants; only those whom the State has failed to integrate; or those who in addition face hardship in their State of origin for the same reasons for which they did not integrate in the host State.

In *Nasri,* Judge Wilderhaber interpreted the statements of both partly-dissenting judges as extending protection under Article 3 to all second-generation immigrants. For this reason he objected to the reliance on

---

[292] *Nasri v France,* ibid.
[293] Ibid, Judge Morenilla in a partly dissenting opinion, para 2.

Article 3, and commented that such reliance 'might have implied that no balancing of public interests can take place but rather that immigrants of the "second generation" cannot be expelled at all'.[294]

Judge Wilderhaber alluded to the difference between ECHR Article 8, which allows the balancing of the hardship of expulsion with other considerations such as the interests of the State of residence and the circumstances of the individual's arrival in it, and ECHR Article 3, which does not. But in determining the pertinence of Article 3, both Judge de Meyer and Judge Morenilla took account of the history of the candidate expellees. They also took account of what those persons were expected to face in the State of destination. Thus, while protection under Article 3 is absolute once its applicability in a particular case is established, entering within its scope is not guaranteed to all second-generation immigrants.

Article 3 therefore does not necessarily protect all second-generation settlers under an illegal regime. They may be denied such protection altogether because they arrived in the territory through violation of international law, although, as discussed below, not of their own will. Individual circumstances may be relevant, such as whether they acted in good faith. If protection under Article 3 depends on fault on the part of the State of residence, settlers are clearly unprotected. Finally, if protection under Article 3 depends on the prospects of integration in the State of origin, the circumstances of each settler have to be examined separately. To conclude, the prohibition on inhuman treatment does not seem to create a blanket prohibition on expulsion of settlers brought in under an illegal regime.

F. Grounds for expulsion

1. Introduction

As noted above, the fact that an act of expulsion interferes with a person's family or private life does not mean that it is impermissible. Similarly, not every distinction between persons is prohibited as discriminatory. ECHR Article 8 provides an exhaustive list of grounds that would justify interference with one's private life: 'national security, public safety or economic well-being of the country, for the prevention of disorder or crime, for the protection of health or morals, or for the protection of rights and freedoms of others.'[295] If an aim is regarded as legitimate and proportionate for the purposes of Article 8, it will also be non-discriminatory under the ECHR. Furthermore, it will probably also be regarded as non-arbitrary for the purposes of ICCPR Articles 12(4), 13, and 17. The justification for expulsion is assessed under ECHR Article 8 in relation to the aim and effects of

---

[294] Concurring Opinion of Judge Wilderhaber in *Nasri v France* (1996) above n 265.

[295] The ACHR allows a wider scope of restriction, requiring that restrictions be placed only in accordance with law, for reasons of general interest and in accordance with the purpose for which such restrictions have been established. ACHR, above n 201, art 30.

the measure under consideration. The requirement that the interference be 'necessary in a democratic society' has been interpreted to mean that the interference must be justified by a pressing social need and in particular, there must be a 'reasonable relationship of proportionality between the means employed and the aim sought to be realized'.[296] In short, since only the ECHR sets out an exhaustive list of grounds for expulsion, as well as other specific limitations, it presents the highest threshold for permissible interference with rights.[297] The following discussion will therefore focus on whether expulsion of settlers is permitted under ECHR Article 8. It considers whether expulsion serves a legitimate aim, and whether it is a proportionate means to achieving that aim. Since this determination should be made by reference to each individual potential expellee's circumstances and not *in abstractu*, the discussion here will only highlight some general considerations.

2. *'Prevention of disorder'—illegality of the settlers' presence*

Since the transfer of settlers is prohibited both under international law and under the domestic law of the ousted regime, the expulsion of settlers may formally fall within the category of 'prevention of disorder and crime' for the purpose of the ECHR, which includes enforcement of immigration law.[298] Legislation which requires persons who have arrived in violation of domestic immigration law to leave is not discriminatory if it is applied equally towards all foreigners. However, legislation that singles out persons who entered the country under the illegal regime may be discriminatory, unless the specific circumstances of arrival are shown to be relevant for the maintenance of order, and the consequences of the distinction are not disproportionate to its aim. This raises the question as to the 'order' that the post-transition regime wishes to maintain.

The ECtHR clearly had domestic law in mind when it confirmed that the prevention of disorder entitles the State to take dissuasive measures such as expulsion against persons who have violated immigration law. If so, there is no reason to single out settlers under the illegal regime from other entrants. Indeed, it is questionable whether the domestic law of the ousted regime, which was purportedly violated, was even applicable at the time that the settlers arrived. In addition, dissuasive measures such as expulsion are valuable against people who act in bad faith with knowledge of the domestic law that they are violating. This is not clearly the case of settlers. Not only does their knowledge of the actual situation differ from one individual to another, but the legal status of the territory may have been sufficiently indeterminate that it might be excessive to hold them in

---

[296] Case Relating to Certain Aspects of the Laws on the Use of Languages in Education in Belgium (Merits) 6 ECtHR (Ser. A) at 34, para 10 (1968), cited by Henckaerts (1995), above n 101, 24; see also *Üner v Netherlands*, above n 210, para 55.

[297] *Cf* the Universal Declaration of Human Rights, above n 247, art 29.

[298] *Shevanova v Latvia* (application no. 58822/00) judgment of 15 June 2006, para 74; *Kaftailova v Lithuania* (application no. 59643/00) judgment of 22 June 2006, para 66.

full knowledge of the implications of their conduct. Finally, the expulsion of persons who had not exercised any choice in relocating to the territory (whether they knew of the illegality or not) or were born in it carries little weight in the way of ensuring domestic order and preventing crime.[299]

The weighty violation of law generated by the transfer of settlers is not of domestic law but of international law. The 'order' which their expulsion may maintain is the international one. But the link between the individual and the disruption of international order is so distant that it seems inappropriate to rely on it under the 'prevention of disorder and crime' ground. Furthermore, the responsibility for disruption of order does not attach directly to the settlers themselves but to the illegal regime. In addition to the issues of faith and knowledge of the law, it can be queried whether individuals should be held accountable for the illegal regime's action, even in the limited context of imposing administrative measures such as expulsion.

To conclude, formally it may be possible to justify the expulsion of settlers by the illegality of their presence. However, because of its weakness this ground is likely to be outbalanced by the hardship it causes when the proportionality test is applied to individual cases. By way of comparison, in both *Winata* and *Shevanova*, where the individuals knowingly and consciously violated immigration law, State interest gave way to individual circumstances. Such an outcome is all the more expected when individual conduct is in good faith.

3. 'Protection of the rights and freedoms of others'—the right to self-determination

A common concern of a post-transition regime is that the settler community would constitute an obstacle to asserting the new regime's national identity. This fear was explicitly noted in an Estonian Congress resolution:[300]

Subsequent to its annexation of the Republic of Estonia, the Soviet Union organized extensive immigration by its citizens into Estonia. As a result of this, non-citizens form over one-third of the population of Estonia, which is now threatening the preservation of the native population of Estonia and the security and unity of the entire Estonian nation.

Radical nationalists in Estonia emphasized the need to 'guarantee the existence of the Estonian nation and culture in the future' by excluding Russophones from citizenry.[301] Russophones and even ethnic Estonians who held moderate positions were labelled 'internal enemies' who were

---

[299] In 2005, 11% of the residents of Estonia were stateless. Over half of them had been born in Estonia. European Commission against Racism and Intolerance Third Report on Estonia (adopted on 24 June 2005, published 21 February 2006) 32, para 124.

[300] Quoted in Barrington, above n 114, 188, quoting Congress of Estonia Position on the Immigrants from the Former USSR Residing in the Republic of Estonia (1992).

[301] Andrus Ristkok (politician, in 2006 awarded presidential State decoration in recognition of his activities in the restoration and strengthening of the Estonian State), quoted in Kask, above n 102, 382.

attempting to 'help the external enemy, strengthening their conquest and their achievements here'. Further concern was expressed that if Russophone settlers were to obtain citizenship rights, new waves of immigration would follow, which would eventually make Russophones a majority of the population.[302]

Similar sentiments were voiced in Latvia. Gvido Zemrido, the Chief Justice of the Latvian Supreme Court, said in 1993:[303]

It is clear that Latvians want to regain their national identity and that they are trying to preserve that identity against what they consider foreign intruders.

The National Independence Movement, one of the influential nationalist parties, believed that independent Latvia would be threatened with extinction given the Russophones' higher birth rate.[304]

The same concern, that the settler population would perpetuate the illegal regime's identity despite the transition, has been voiced with respect to the UCR.[305] Turkish settlers are regarded as culturally different from Turkish Cypriots; it is feared that they will change the character of Cyprus, and turn the northern part in effect into another province of Turkey.[306] This concern is heightened by the fact that Turkish settlers are already a majority on the electoral rolls of the TRNC, which under the Annan Plan is the future Turkish-Cypriot constituent State of the UCR. They would therefore control its government and consequently share in the federal system, as representatives of the Turkish-Cypriot constituent State.[307]

Such concerns cannot be dismissed as abstract when they are a reaction to actual detriment already caused to the lawful regime's national identity through a violation of international law. The HCNM[308] acknowledged Latvia's concern for its national character:

I fully understand and respect the determination of your Government to maintain and strengthen the Latvian identity after 50 years of Soviet occupation which greatly endangered the maintenance of that identity.[309]

---

[302] Ibid, 387–388; Andris Spruds, 'Minority Issues in the Baltic States in the Context of the NATO Enlargement' NATO Individual Research Fellowship Final Report 9 (2001).

[303] Quoted in Barrington, above n 114, 190.

[304] Visvaldis Lacis quoted in Spruds, above n 302, 7.

[305] Loukis G Loucaides 'Expulsion of Settlers from Occupied Territories: The Case of Turkish Settlers in Cyprus' in his *Essays on the Developing Law of Human Rights* (Martinus Nijhoff, Dordrecht, 1995) 108, 129.

[306] Palley (2005), above n 149, 227, Doob, above n 184.

[307] Observations made by the Ministry of Foreign Affairs of Cyprus, annexed to European Commission against Racism and Intolerance (ECRI) Third Report on Cyprus, above n 168, 42 footnote 43.

[308] According to Zurjari-Ossipova, the establishment of the HCNM post was a Russian initiative. Olga Zurjari-Ossipova, 'Human Rights as the Political-Juridical Issues of the Estonian-Russian Inter-State Relations' 18 NATO Research Fellowships programme 1995–1997 (June 1997), <www.nato.int/acad/fellow/95–97/zurjari.pdf> (last accessed 7 July 2009).

[309] HCNM letter to the Minister of Foreign Affairs of Latvia, CSCE 1994 Communication, above n 129, 2.

At the same time, the HCNM was unwilling to accept that the group as a whole was expellable. In commenting on the Latvian policy with regard to the Russophone community (at the time when the right of the latter to remain in the territory of Latvia and its status there had not yet been formulated), the HCNM wrote to the Latvian authorities:

As I pointed out in my recommendation of 7 April 1993, your Government has of course the right to remove from Latvia territory non-citizens whose continuous presence could be damaging to its vital interest, such as persons who have been found in proper judicial procedures to have committed grave crimes. But on the other hand, massive expulsion of non-Latvian residents would be contrary to generally accepted international humanitarian principles even more so because the overwhelming majority of the non-Latvians living in your country have not been actively engaged in oppressive practices during the years of the Soviet occupation of Latvia. I am glad that your Government is not considering this option.[310]

Although Latvia's aim to preserve its national identity and political independence was legitimate, it was not entitled to pursue it by expelling settlers unless they had been personally jeopardizing the achievement of that aim.

The protection of national identity can be phrased as 'protection of the rights and freedoms of others' to realize the right to self-determination. But maintaining the identity of the local population does not necessarily require that the settler population be expelled. Theoretically, protection of the national identity against 'dilution' may be achieved through less severe measures. In Estonia and Latvia, the strategy first attempted, of denial of nationality combined with permission to remain, was vehemently rejected by the European institutions as disproportionate. The latter exerted heavy pressure on both States to enable the settler minority to naturalize, as well as to minimize the differences with regard to political and other rights between nationals and permanent residents. In Cyprus this midway arrangement was not attempted. The Annan Plan provides either for acquisition of original nationality or removal from the territory, with an exception for persons entitled to remain with the prospect of eventual naturalization. Permanent residence without an option of naturalization and with restrictions on civil rights was perceived as unacceptable.

The HCNM advocated a strategy to defuse the danger. He encouraged Estonia and Latvia to provide the Russophone population with a genuine opportunity to integrate within the State, formally by acquiring citizenship and substantively through cultural and educational means. He pointed out:[311]

The alternative policy is to aim at the integration of the non-Estonian population by a deliberate policy of facilitating the chances of acquiring Estonian citizenship

---

[310] Recommendations by the CSCE High Commissioner on National Minorities about the Latvian Draft Citizenship Law, CSCE 1994 Communication, above n 129, 3.

[311] HCNM to the Minister of Foreign Affairs of Estonia, in CSCE 1993 Recommendations, above n 127, 3, HCNM letter to the Minister of Foreign Affairs of Latvia, CSCE 1994 Communication, above n 129, 3.

for those who express such a wish, and of assuring them full equality with Estonian citizens... Furthermore, such a policy would certainly not be incompatible with the wish of the Estonians to ensure and strengthen their political, cultural and linguistic identity.

And:[312]

I am fully aware that the policy I advocate does not only require an effort on the part of the Latvian Government, but equally a contribution on the part of the non-Latvian population. Adaptation to the reality of the re-emergence of Latvia as an independent state requires that at any rate those who have not yet retired from work and who do not yet speak the Latvian language make a determined effort to master that language to such a degree that they are able to conduct a simple conversation in Latvian. In this way they would, without having to sacrifice their cultural or linguistic identity, provide a convincing proof of their willingness to integrate.

The HCNM considered that integration would increase the chances that the Russophone minority would embrace Estonian or Latvian identity rather than act to modify it or prevent its consolidation.[313] Programs have subsequently been undertaken to adapt non-titular citizens into the titular-dominant State and society.[314]

The strategy proposed by the HCNM, if successful, will reduce the threat emanating from the presence of a specific minority community to the national identity by disintegrating the minority's threatening collective character. It confronts the threat by a less intrusive measure than expulsion, indeed by one that does not necessarily interfere with any right. As such, it is clearly an alternative which makes expulsion or exclusion from citizenship an excessive and therefore prohibited measure. However, while theoretically useful, the viability of this strategy is not guaranteed.

First, alongside the right of the post-transition regime to protect its identity there is the right of the minority to preserve its character. In other words, while the post-transition regime may encourage the integration of the settler community in the State's national society, it may not demand that the settler community abandon its own identity. Yet it is precisely that identity, with its particular history and weight, which threatens the identity of the State.[315]

Second, integration goes only a limited way towards breaking the attachment of the minority to its State of origin. This is particularly pertinent when the State of origin maintains a formal role with respect to the post-transition regime. For example, the ethnic link between Turkey and Turkish Cypriots was recognized and was given concrete expression when Cyprus

---

[312] HCNM letter to the Minister of Foreign Affairs of Latvia, CSCE 1993 Recommendations, above n 127, 8–9.
[313] HCNM letter to the Minister of Foreign Affairs of Latvia and HCNM letter to the Minister of Foreign Affairs of Estonia, in CSCE 1993 Recommendations, above n 127.
[314] For a description of Estonia's policy see Pettai and Hallik, above n 300, 520.
[315] Spruds, above n 302, 9.

became independent, in the 1960 Treaties of Guarantee and Alliance.[316] The Annan Plan retains the Treaties through Additional Protocols that apply the Treaties *mutatis mutandis* to the UCR.[317] It may be overly ambitious to expect a settler population to integrate in the post-transition regime's society while sanctioning a formal role for the State of origin with regard to the post-transition regime.

4. 'National security'—continued influence of the former illegal regime

The link between the settlers and their State of origin raises another concern, particularly when that link is formalized, that the withdrawn, illegal regime would use the presence of its diaspora to exert political and economic pressure over the post-transition regime. This concern has already proven justified in the Baltic States, when Russia's support for ethnic Russians played significantly into its negotiations with the three States on withdrawal of troops, on economic measures and more. Russia went so far as to indicate in its 1993 Military Doctrine that it reserved the right to use military force if the rights of Russian citizens in other countries were violated.[318]

Intervention may go so far as to involve military force, as the Turkish military intervention in Cyprus in 1974 demonstrates. Yet non-military pressure can be even more pervasive than military pressure, because it is less overt and there are fewer constraints on resorting to it. For example, the presence of the Turkish settlers in Cyprus is regarded as a means by which Turkey will have direct influence over the whole of the UCR, since most Turkish settlers are highly susceptible to Turkish influence.[319] This concern was reinforced by Turkey's characterization of the settlers as 'security' for Turkey, giving rise to the fear that in the case of inter-communal clashes, Turkey would jump at the opportunity to intervene in the Greek-Cypriot Constituent State of the UCR.[320]

Theoretically, integration may be the answer to this problem, too. By distancing the settlers from their State of origin, both formally (through acquisition of the post-transition regime's nationality) and substantively (through personal identification with the post-transition regime), integration would weaken the capacity of the State of origin—the withdrawn illegal regime—to intervene. However, as pointed out, granting the State of origin a formal international status with respect to the post-transition regime, as Turkey has with respect to the UCR under the Annan Plan, hinders integration.

---

[316] Treaty of Guarantee of the Independence of Cyprus, 1960, 382 UNTS 3, Treaty of Alliance, 1960, 397 UNTS 287.

[317] Annexes II, III, IV, to the Annan Plan Part c: Treaty on Matters related to the New State of Affairs in Cyprus. The 'special relations and strong ties' between Turkey and Turkish Cypriots are also recognized in the Draft act of Adaptation of the Terms of Accession of the United Cyprus Republic to the European Union, para 14.

[318] Stankevicius, above n 108, chapter 6 paras 57–60; Spruds, above n 302, 22, 26–27.

[319] Cuco Report, above n 160, para 93.

[320] Palley, above n 149, 223, 227.

Moreover, as real as the danger may be that Turkey would use the presence of its diaspora as a pretext to intervene in the island, it is paradoxically weak as a justification for the expulsion of the Turkish settlers. Even if all mainland Turks leave the island, there is still a substantial population—Turkish Cypriots—that Turkey regards as its kin and claims to protect. The Treaty of Guarantee acknowledges and accepts this relationship as legitimate. Expulsion of the settlers would therefore not eliminate Turkey's interests. Precisely because of this, Greek Cypriots objected to the Annan Plan's perpetuation of Turkish involvement and influence. In their view, Turkish influence should have been limited rather than expanded as it was by the inclusion of the security and constitutional order of the constituent States under the amended Treaty of Guarantee.[321]

5. 'National security'—fear of a fifth column

A State may legitimately regard the presence of foreign military forces on its territory as a national security threat.[322] On this ground, all three Baltic States excluded active military personnel from eligibility for nationality and even permanent residence. The question is, however, how far beyond active military personnel this ground for expulsion can expand without constituting excessive interference with private life. Ordinarily, previous military training does not justify a presumption of danger emanating from a person. Yet Estonia, for example, has argued that it may remove former military personnel and reservists from its territory because in time of conflict (or precipitating such time) they might act as a fifth column, facilitating military intervention by the withdrawn illegal regime.[323] The same was argued in Cyprus. Many Turkish settlers are military reservists, who have immigrated after completing compulsory military service.[324] Greek Cypriots are concerned that even if the UCR is demilitarized, Turkey would have a ready army waiting, merely requiring air drops of equipment and some target practice.[325]

Here too, the HCNM's strategy was intended to minimize the risk and the concern. In his words, the integration policy[326]

---

[321] Preamble to Protocol amending the Treaty. Palley, above n 149, 223.
[322] *Slivenko v Latvia*, above n 90, HCNM letter to the Minister of Foreign Affairs of Estonia and HCNM letter to the Minister of Foreign Affairs of Latvia, in CSCE 1993 Recommendations, above n 127.
[323] Eg Estonia's position in *Vjatšeslav Borzov v Estonia*, Communication No. 1136/2002, UN Doc CCPR/C/81/D/1136/2002 (2004) para 4.10.
[324] The majority, according to Greek Cypriots: Palley, above n 149. Professional Turkish military personnel have for the most part left the TRNC in the 1980s.
[325] Observations made by the Ministry of Foreign Affairs of Cyprus, annexed to European Commission against Racism and Intolerance (ECRI) Third Report on Cyprus (adopted 16 December 2005) 43 footnote 44.
[326] HCNM letter to the Minister of Foreign Affairs of Estonia CSCE 1993 Recommendations, above n 127, 3; see also Recommendations by the CSCE High Commissioner on National Minorities about the Latvian Draft Citizenship Law, CSCE Communication No. 8, above n 129, 3.

would greatly reduce the danger of destabilization, because it would consider-ably enhance the chances of the non-Estonian population developing a sense of loyalty toward Estonia.

And:[327]

It is my opinion that such a policy would be the most effective way to ensure the loyalty of non-Latvian's towards Latvia...

The status of non-active military personnel came before the ECtHR in 2003 in *Slivenko v Latvia*. The question was whether retired military personnel and their families should be treated similarly to military per-sonnel on active duty, or whether this would constitute a disproportionate interference with their private life. The first applicant, Tatjana Slivenko, was a permanent Latvian resident of Russian origin. She had moved to Latvia when she was one month old. Her father was then an actively serv-ing officer in the Soviet army. She later married Nikolay Slivenko, who was also a serving Soviet military officer in Latvia. Their daughter Karina, the second applicant, was born in Riga in 1981. In 1994, Nikolay Slivenko was required to leave Latvia, being a military person on active duty.[328] Tatjana Slivenko's parents were allowed to remain in Latvia. Tatjana and Karina Slivenko were also required to leave, under domestic Latvian law, which applied to family members who had arrived in Latvia as a result of accompanying a military person.

The applicants claimed that their removal from Latvia would violate their right under ECHR Article 8. They claimed that their presence in Latvia did not result from a family connection with a serving military person who was required to leave, Tatjana having arrived in Latvia long before she met her husband.

The Latvian government maintained that its policy pursued the legiti-mate aims of protecting national security and preventing disorder and crime.[329] It claimed that under the Latvian-Russian treaty, family mem-bers of active military personnel could be required to leave regardless of the circumstances of their arrival in Latvia. Under Latvian law, family members that have arrived in connection with the military service could be required to leave regardless of whether the military person was active or retired. Accordingly, Tatjana and her daughter were not protected by either, because they were family members of Nikolay, an active military person (for the purpose of the Treaty), and had arrived in Latvia in connection with the military service of Tatjana's father (for the purpose of Latvian law). Thus, while the father himself was not subject to expul-sion, his daughter and granddaughter were. Effectively, the Latvian policy was that expulsion may satisfy either the Treaty or Latvian law, expand-ing the population of expellees so as to include family members that have

---

[327] HCNM letter to the Minister of Foreign Affairs of Latvia, CSCE 1993 Recommendations, above n 127, 8–9.
[328] See text at n 147–148.   [329] *Slivenko v Latvia*, above n 90, para 77.

arrived with any military personnel, and any family members of active personnel, regardless of how they arrived in Latvia.[330]

The ECtHR accepted that the Latvian-Russian treaty sought to protect legitimate interests with respect to military personnel. First, it noted that 'the withdrawal of the armed forces of one independent State from the territory of another, following the dissolution of the State to which they both formerly belonged, constitutes, from the point of view of the Convention, a legitimate means of dealing with the various political, social and economic problems arising from that dissolution'.[331] It was also evident to the Court that the continued presence of active servicemen of a foreign army, with their families, may be seen as incompatible with the sovereignty of an independent State and as a threat to national security.[332] The Court found that the obligation upon family members to leave the country was not in itself objectionable from the point of view of the ECHR. The Latvian-Russian treaty even respected the family life of the persons concerned by obligating Russia to accept the whole family unit within its territory, irrespective of the origin or nationality of individual family members. The Court then examined the claims that the family could be expelled either on the ground that they were relatives of a retired military officer or on the ground that they were relatives of an active military officer against the right to private life. It ruled that expulsion of family members of active servicemen under the treaty, regardless of the circumstances of their arrival in Latvia, would normally not be a disproportionate interference, having regard to the conditions of service of military officers who occasionally transfer from one place to another, but was nonetheless the subject to an Article 8 test.[333] The Court also noted that the justification for removal of troops, namely national security and routine military transfer, does not apply to the same extent to retired military officers and their families. Instead, greater importance must be attached to their legitimate private interests.[334] Accordingly, the ECtHR found that the expulsion under Latvian law of family members of a retired officer, who was himself entitled to remain in Latvia, on the basis of an unsubstantiated presumption of danger to national security because they were also family members of an active serviceman, was a disproportionate infringement on the right to private life.

The dissenting minority saw no reason to distinguish between military personnel and their families, or between active and retired personnel. They argued that the purpose of the treaty was to repatriate the 'totality of a foreign army'. Since a condition of actual danger to territorial security

---

[330] This policy was subject to the prohibition on expulsion of Latvian nationals and permanent residents.

[331] *Slivenko v Latvia*, above n 90, para 117.

[332] Ibid.

[333] It is not clear to what extent the Court took into consideration the fact that the family had not arrived in Latvia as a result of the active serviceman's service.

[334] *Slivenko v Latvia*, above n 90, para 118.

would rarely be satisfied in relation to family members, setting such a condition for expelling family members would undermine the effectiveness of the Treaty.[335] It is questionable why the 'totality' of an army necessarily includes retirees and their families. Moreover, the minority was willing to accept expulsion based on a familial relationship with retired military persons, even though they were entitled to remain in Latvia, and despite the fact the domestic Latvian law did not allow expulsion based merely on a familial relationship with active military persons.

The treatment of family members of foreign troops as inextricably linked to the military may be related to the dissenting judges' perspective on the political context in which the removal of troops was taking place. Unlike the majority,[336] the dissenting judges took account of 'the specific historical context and purpose for which the treaty was signed, namely the elimination of the consequences of the Soviet rule of Latvia'.[337] If expulsion is considered in this wider context, namely the reversal of the occupation and purported annexation of Latvia by the Soviet Union, then there is less of a difference between retired and active military personnel, given that both groups had taken part in the consolidation of the Soviet annexation. Even then it is not clear that civilian family members share the same responsibility for the consolidation of the annexation. An argument along these lines concerns the reversal of historic injustice, a matter addressed expressly by Judge Maruste in a dissenting opinion, and which merits separate discussion.

6. Redressing historical injustice

In *Slivenko*, Judge Maruste opined that 'the restoration of the independence of the Baltic States on the basis of legal continuity and the withdrawal of the Soviet/Russian troops has to be regarded as redress for a historical injustice', and that 'the withdrawal of the armed forces of one independent State from the territory of another constitutes an appropriate way of dealing with the various political, social and economic problems arising from that historical injustice'.[338]

'Redress of historical injustice' is not listed in ECHR Article 8 as a ground for expulsion. It might be regarded as a matter of 'prevention of disorder'. However, since 'disorder' does not appear to have been drafted with international law and order in mind, this category is appropriate if one takes account of the injustices caused under domestic law. In many cases the domestic law, particularly that applicable under the illegal regime, actually permitted the injustices.[339] Alternatively, 'protection of

---

[335] Ibid, Joint dissenting opinion of Judges Wildhaber, Ress, Sir Nicolas Bratza, Cabral Barreto, Greve, and Maruste para 7.

[336] Ibid, Majority opinion, para 111.

[337] Ibid, Joint dissenting opinion of Judges Wildhaber, Ress, Sir Nicolas Bratza, Cabral Barreto, Greve, and Maruste, para 4. Judge Maruste also appended a separate dissenting opinion, in which he detailed further the circumstances leading to the presence of Soviet forces and civilians in Latvia.

[338] Ibid, separate Dissenting Opinion of Judge Maruste.

[339] Again, the applicability of the ousted regime's law is at least debatable.

the rights and freedoms of others' might cover redress for the violation of international norms.

However, reliance on both 'prevention of disorder' and 'protection of rights and freedoms of others' blurs the distinction between individual and State responsibility. Where individuals are responsible for specific injustices, their exclusion from the State is acceptable, falling easily within 'order and prevention of crime' or 'national security'. Indeed, all three Baltic States deny residence (let alone nationality) to persons involved in crimes against the State, crimes against humanity, or war crimes.[340] However, removal of an entire group on the ground of historical injustice caused by the consequences of political manoeuvring is more problematic. It is true that the presence of the settler community facilitated large-scale deprivation of the titular communities, through political alienation, economic marginalization, etc. Such deprivation may even constitute a violation of the obligation to respect the right of peoples to internal self-determination. But this obligation does not govern the conduct of individuals.[341] Accordingly, it is doubtful that individuals may be held responsible for violating it. Moreover, it is doubtful that they may be expelled because of their membership in the group whose presence led to the violation, without any specific responsibility attached to them individually. Notably, Judge Maruste only relied on this ground to justify expulsion of military personnel. As active guardians of the illegal regime they each can be said to bear a particular responsibility for the historical injustice. But Judge Maruste's opinion made no reference to the requirement of proportionality between the aim and the means to achieve it, particularly with respect to family members of military personnel. Their expulsion may lead to excessive injury to their private life and as such discriminate against them in comparison with other civilian settlers. To conclude, redress for historical injustice is a weak ground for expulsion of individuals. Just as the injustice was not individually-addressed, neither should be its redress.

7. 'Protection of the rights and freedoms of others'—property

The presence of settlers may have immediate, tangible repercussions for the local population. One particular problem is that of immovable property.

---

[340] Estonia, Citizenship Act 1995, art 21(1)3) excludes from nationality a person who has acted against the Estonian state and its security. Estonia, Aliens Act, arts 12(4)3), 12), 13) exclude from residence a person if there is good reason to believe that such activities have been or are directed against Estonia and its security; there is good reason to believe that he or she has participated in punitive operations against civil population; or there is good reason to believe that he or she has committed a crime against humanity or a war crime. Latvia, 1994 Citizenship Law art 11(1) excludes from nationality persons who have, by unconstitutional methods, acted against the independence of Latvia, the democratic parliamentary structure of the State or the existing State power in Latvia, if such has been established by a judgment of a court. Lithuania, Citizenship Law, Arts. 13(1), (2), excludes from nationality persons who have committed crimes against humanity or acts of genocide, and persons who took part in criminal activities against Lithuania.

[341] International instruments do not attach to individual persons the responsibility for violations of the right to self-determination of peoples.

Turkish settlers were given, under a variety of legislative and other arrangements, rights in property previously owned by Greek Cypriots. The Annan Plan regulates these property issues. Formally this regulation is unrelated to the residence issue; in practice the residence of settlers in the territory will exacerbate potential conflicts between original owners and current occupants. Thus, the presence of Turkish settlers was perceived as rendering remote the prospect of reinstatement of Greek Cypriots in their home and properties, and was one of the main grounds for the rejection of the Annan Plan by Greek Cypriots.[342]

The phenomenon of settlers acquiring local property is not unique to Cyprus. It was prevalent in East Timor, and in part in the Baltic States.[343] However, in those cases the matter took on different forms. In East Timor the settlers have for the most part departed. In the Baltic States settlers have possibly depleted local resources, but for the most part they were not housed in properties owned by the local population.[344] Accordingly, in both places the conflict of rights is not so much between the local population and the settlers as between the local population and the State or among local individuals. Moreover, the process of privatization has made many such competing claims moot.

V. CONCLUSIONS

A. Diversity in transitional arrangements

It appears that the post-transition regime is not obligated to recognize the validity of formal status granted by the illegal regime. This status is possibly invalid *ab initio* under international law, and even if it merits partial or *ad hoc* recognition under the *Namibia* exception, it does not appear to transcend the change of regime. However, international human rights law places limitations on the powers of the post transition regime to expel settlers, requiring it to take account of factual developments, regardless of their original illegality. The objectives pursued by the post-transition regimes and the political environment within which they operate affect the scope and extent of the emerging individual human rights and inform the permissibility of the post-transition regimes' policies. There is consequently not a single response to the question whether settlers may be expelled or

---

[342] Palley, above n 149, 222. On the link between property disputes and residence see Ronen (2008), above n 4, 547–553.

[343] It is also a characteristic post-armed conflict issue. See on the work of the Property Commission in Bosnia and Herzegovina, Marcus Cox, 'The Right to Return Home: Ethnic Cleansing in Bosnia and Herzegovina', (1998) 47 *International and Comparative Law Quarterly* 599. For materials on the link between refugee and displaced persons' return and property restitution see Scott Leckie (ed) *Housing Land, and Property Restitution Rights of Refugees and Displaced Persons* (Cambridge University Press, Cambridge, 2007).

[344] Pettai, above n 79, 13–14.

not. This is evident when comparing the arrangements adopted by the various post-transition regimes.

Most notable is the difference between the arrangements in the Southern African cases and those in the Baltic States, East Timor, and Cyprus. In the former, illegality of the settlement had no perceptible effect on post-transition regime policy. In the latter, there was formal discontinuity. This difference can be explained party by the daunting challenges of decolonization which made this illegality insignificant. But there is another, significant difference between the two groups of cases. In the Southern African cases, once transition took place there was no formerly illegal regime which continued to threaten the post-transition regime. There was no danger of the settlers being used as pawns in a grand design by a usurper regime. This allowed for the regulation of individuals' status to be carried out on an almost individual basis.

The situation was very different in the Baltic States, East Timor, and the TRNC. In all three cases, the termination of the illegal regime did not eliminate the perceived threat from its government—Russia, Indonesia, and Turkey—which continues to exist. The fear of those former occupants affected the arrangements sought with respect to their diasporas. East Timorese legislation totally excludes Indonesian settlers from acquiring any status in East Timor on the basis of their residence there, although the viability of this approach was never put to the test. In the Baltic States and in Cyprus, strict adherence to the reversion to *status quo ante* would have had major repercussions. Additional arrangements were therefore made which in practice allowed at least some of the settlers to remain in the territory as residents and eventually to naturalize. Even then, the arrangements adopted in each case are dissimilar. In the Baltic States, expulsion of the settlers was taken off the table at an early stage. The pressure exerted on the post-transition regimes concerned the regulation of nationality, not of residence. With respect to Cyprus, the internationally-sponsored agreement provided for large-scale removal of settlers, even if not large enough for the liking of Greek Cypriots.

The legal principles underlying the two cases are similar, yet the practical outcomes differ greatly. It could be argued that the difference is not a legal but a political one. The international community, represented primarily by Western European States, was loath to upset Russia, which still retained significant political and military power. In addition, in the euphoria of the demise of Soviet rule, it may have seemed unjustifiable to castigate individuals for the misdeeds of a dead empire. Therefore it was deemed acceptable that Russophone settlers would remain in place. In contrast, with respect to the Cyprus conflict, the international community more readily aligns with the prospective post-transition regime. This follows from the declaration by the UN Security Council that the establishment of the TRNC was illegal, and from Cyprus' membership in the EU.

Another, less cynical, explanation for the difference is that although the claim of the Baltic States was accepted that they were reverting to independence rather than newly-independent, there was little expectation to truly turn the clock half a century backwards. To start with, until the late 1980s reversion to independence was not seriously envisaged. The international community had been more or less resigned to the annexation. In contrast, the unlawfulness of the TRNC has been consistently dealt with by legal means from the first moment. It was also upheld by the ECtHR, an international judicial institution, the decisions of which are binding on all parties to the conflict. Under these circumstances, pursuing the logical conclusions does not appear in conflict with reasonable expectations.

However, beyond the general political and legal policies, the two situations also differ in the outcome of balancing the post-transition regime's interests against the settlers' human rights. First, the perceived threat presented by mainland Turks to the character of Cyprus may appear greater than that presented by Russophones in the Baltic States, since mainland Turks already comprise, according to estimates, the majority of the population in the TRNC. The short-term provisions of the Annan Plan are regarded as the tip of an iceberg of Turkish migration to the EU, which the latter may regard as undesirable. The perceived military threat for the UCR might also be greater than that which was perceived with respect to Russia. Turkey's military involvement in Cyprus was much more recent than the Soviet Union's in Estonia. Importantly, the statuses of the two illegal regimes are not on par. The Russian Federation has renounced any claims over the Baltic States, not only in practice but even formally, by declaring the Molotov-Ribbentrop Pact null and void.[345] In contrast, Turkey's status as guarantor of Cyprus' security under the Treaty of Guarantee preserves the concern regarding intervention.

Differences exist also with regard to the hardship which expulsion is likely to cause to mainland Turks compared with Russophone settlers. First, the mainland Turkish community was only three decades old (or two, counting from 1983) when the Annan Plan was formulated, while the Russophone population in the Baltic States went back fifty years. There is an entire generation's difference between the two; there are therefore likely to be many third-generation settlers in the Baltic States, but fewer in the TRNC. Third-generation immigrants are generally less familiar with the culture of the State of origin than second-generation ones, and their integration there is likely to be more difficult. Needless to say, in neither case is language an obstacle to integration in the State of origin. Another pertinent difference is the fact that following the breakdown of the Soviet Union, many Russophone settlers found themselves stateless. They may be protected from expulsion either under the Convention relating to the Status of Stateless Persons[346] or under ICCPR Article 12(4). Moreover, had it been decided to expel them, it would have been technically difficult.

---

[345] Congress of People's Deputies Resolution on a Political and Legal Appraisal of the Soviet-German Non-Aggression Treaty of 1939 (1989).
[346] Adopted on 28 September 1954, entered into force 6 June 1960, art 30(1).

Statelessness is less of a problem in the case of Turkish settlers. Finally, the proportionality of expulsion is measured, *inter alia*, in light of the behaviour of the individual. A person acting in good faith is entitled to greater consideration than one who has deliberately acted in bad faith.[347] Mainland Turks were not formally forced to move to the TRNC. In contrast, many Russophones had little choice when they relocated to the Baltic States. On this ground too, they (and their descendants) might have won more sympathy. The time that has passed since the wrongful act (settlement) may play a role, analogous to the length of time from the commitment of an offense in the case of expulsion because of criminal activity.[348] In short, the circumstances of the Russophone community and the mainland Turkish community differ in such a way that expulsion was deemed a disproportionate—and therefore unlawful—measure with respect to Russophones in the Baltic States, but not with respect to mainland Turks in the TRNC.

A comparison of the regulation under the Annan Plan of nationality and residence issues with that of property is instructive. The Plan included a letter from the leaders of Cyprus to the Secretary-General of the Council of Europe, requesting that the ECtHR strike out any proceedings currently before it concerning affected property in Cyprus, in order to allow the domestic mechanism established to solve these cases to proceed.[349] This indicates the understanding of the drafters of the Plan that the provisions on property were not compatible with ECtHR jurisprudence. There is no similar letter with respect to nationality and residence. This suggests that the Plan's drafters regarded the provisions as compatible with the obligations of the prospective UCR under the ECHR.[350]

B. Human rights and conflict resolution

Many of the concerns of the post-transition regime arise from the presence in the territory of a large settler population, although no risk emanates from any specific individual. There is therefore something troubling about the notion that the scope of a person's right depends on whether his or her plight is shared by other individuals for whom that person is not legally responsible and on the political circumstances in which that plight arises.

---

[347] Compare *Shevanova v Latvia*, above n 298, para 75 and *Shevanova v Latvia* (application no. 58822/00), judgment of 7 December 2007 para 49, as well as *Sisojeva and Others v Latvia* (application no. 60654/00, judgment of 16 June 2005, para 95, with *Kaftailova v Latvia*, above n 298, para 68.

[348] Cf *Boultif v Switzerland*, above n 282.

[349] Foundation Agreement, Annex IX, Attachment 3: Letter to the Secretary-General of the Council of Europe.

[350] The scope of judicial review of the Plan requires further study, and is outside the scope of the present enquiry. The Plan would have been endorsed by the Security Council: Part E: Matters to be Submitted to the United Nations Security Council for Decision. In view of *Behrami and Behrami v France* (Application No. 71412/01), this endorsement might have precluded any further review by the ECtHR. See also *Saramati v France, Germany and Norway* (Application No. 78166/01), Grand Chamber decision (Admissibility) 2 May 2007.

Arguably, few human rights are absolute, and in most cases the right of the individual may be balanced against the interests of the community, which include considerations on the allocation of resources. In this vein, it has been questioned whether international human rights law should be fully applicable in situations of mass movement of persons. For example, when the prohibition on *refoulment* was incorporated in the Refugee Convention of 1951, it was suggested by some delegations that it should not apply in situations of mass influx. Some scholars argue that ICCPR Article 12(4) is intended to apply only to individuals asserting an individual right, and that there was no intention to address claims resulting from mass displacement following political transfers of population.[351] A more general argument is that human rights discourse is not the appropriate tool for immigration issues. In order to discharge their special duties of security, welfare, self determination and community to their own citizens and residents, States must have greater control over who comes within these categories. Accordingly, the regulation of entry into the country of foreigners should be made not through human rights discourse but through policy considerations.[352] All these arguments posit not that the right in question may be interfered with, but that in certain circumstances, it does not exist at all.

There are various reasons to reject the relevance of these arguments with respect to the permissibility of expelling settlers under an illegal regime, since there is a legal distinction between not allowing persons into the country—refugees, returnees or ordinary migrants—and forcing them out. First, as pointed out earlier, as a matter of *lex lata* there is an express prohibition under international law on collective expulsion. Second, there is no claim that the post-transition regimes do not have the resources to accommodate the settlers.

For the most part, the problem is not quantitative but qualitative: the argument is that the settler community *as a community* presents a risk to the post-transition regime (in terms of its identity, national security, etc). Relevant human rights instruments clearly do not address this problem. That does not mean, however, that they can be dismissed as irrelevant. Thus, while international human rights law does not dictate any single solution, any political arrangement sought should be compatible with the post-transition regime's human rights obligations.

---

[351] Jagerskiold, above n 271, 180, Hannum, above n 271, 59–60, but see Guy Goodwin-Gill and Jane McAdam, *The Refugee in International Law* 206–208 (Oxford University Press, Oxford, 2007).

[352] Ruth Gavison, 'Immigration and the Human Rights Discourse: The Universality of Human Rights and the Relevance of States and of Numbers' (July 2008, draft cited by permission and available with the author).

Investment Arbitration and the Law of Countermeasures

By Martins Paparinskis*

* D Phil candidate, University of Oxford, the Queen's College, AHRC and Commercial Bar Scholar. I am very grateful to Professor Vaughan Lowe for pointing out the legal issues discussed in this contribution. Valuable comments and criticisms of Dr Andrés Rigo Sureda, Dr Johannes Koepp, Gleider Hernández, Markos Karavias, Antonios Tzanakopoulos, and James Upcher, and of the two anonymous referees are acknowledged. An early version of this paper was presented at the Society of International Economic Law 2008 inaugural conference in Geneva. I am grateful for the questions and comments received there, and to the Law Faculty of the University of Oxford for its financial support for my attendance at the conference. The views expressed and the errors or omissions made are the responsibility of the author alone.

I. Introduction

The international law of foreign investment protection has, throughout the last century of its development, been concerned with the search for the most appropriate rules and the best means for the settlement of disputes concerning the application of those rules. In general, the shift has been away from vague and crude substantive rules (set out in customary law, general principles and evocations of equity) discretionarily enforced by the home State, and in the direction of 'treatyfied' law of investment protection, implemented by means of investor-State arbitration. Idelson very astutely observed the direction of this change already in 1931:[1]

protection of its nationals (including companies) would be much easier for the State concerned if the rights of such nationals were defined by elaborate treaties and not allowed to rest on general principles of International Law. Those principles were formulated in times when the economic life of nations was much simpler than it is today.[2]

The contemporary law of foreign investment protection could therefore be said to consist of several strata of legal arguments. The results of the more recent efforts of law-making sometimes accept and incorporate the classic rules; sometimes clarify the classic ambiguities or replace the unsatisfactory solutions; sometimes permit different approaches in parallel; and quite often maintain constructive ambiguity regarding the precise relationship between different rules. The present contribution seeks to examine the contemporary relationship between the two concepts that

---

[1] Idelson's insight may have partly come from his own recent experience of arbitrating the treatment of foreign investors with host States. He was the lead counsel for the claimant in the *Lena Goldfields* arbitration, where his argument for the internationalization of applicable law through the application of general principles was 'a gigantic first step for the international commercial arbitration, almost equivalent to the caveman's discovery of fire', VV Veeder, 'The *Lena Goldfields* Arbitration: The Historical Roots of Three Ideas' (1995) 47 *International and Comparative Law Quarterly* 747, 772. When Idelson made his intervention in the Grotius Society on 10 December 1931, the very considerable award against the USSR had been rendered more than a year ago (on 3 September 1930), but the USSR had not yet complied with the award and did not seem likely to do so in the nearest future (and indeed the agreement on the compensation between USSR and UK for noteholders of the already-defunct *Lena* was agreed upon only in 1968, with the funds coming from the Baltic gold in the British banks in apparent breach of the UK obligation of non-recognition of the annexation of Baltic States) (at 789); RB Lillich, 'The Anglo-Soviet Claims Agreement of 1968' (1972) 21 *International and Comparative Law Quarterly* 1.
[2] WE Beckett, 'Diplomatic Claims in Respect of Injuries to Companies' (1931) 17 *Transactions of the Grotius Society* 175, 194.

typify the contrast between classic and modern approaches to investment protection law in perhaps the starkest terms: the law of countermeasures and investment arbitration.

The application of countermeasures in disputes regarding foreign investment was a natural and effective approach of acting in the classic international legal order.[3] The 1905 first edition of Oppenheim's *International Law* reflects precisely this kind of thinking, relying on the 1837– 1842 *Sicilian Sulphur* dispute to explain the working of countermeasures. Great Britain took the view that the Two Sicilies had breached the 1816 treaty of commerce (*inter alia* providing for the protection of property rights of British nationals) by the grant of sulphur monopoly rights to a company of French merchants, and therefore in 1840 embargoed Sicilian ships until the grant of the monopoly was withdrawn after a French mediation.[4] In the *Sicilian Sulphur* dispute the British countermeasures were employed 'for the purpose of compelling [Two Sicilies] to consent to a satisfactory settlement of a difference created by its own international delinquency'.[5] However, countermeasures and foreign investment could also interact in the opposite manner, with the countermeasures being applied against foreign property. To quote Oppenheim once again, '[a]n act of reprisal can be performed against anything and everything that belongs or is due to the delinquent State and its citizens.'[6]

The more recent developments have taken a profoundly negative view about these practices, and indeed some of the modern rules have been created precisely to preclude them. As the Tribunal explained in the *Banro American Resources, Inc. and Société Aurifère du Kivu et du Maniema S.A.R.L. v DRC* award, '[o]ne of the main objectives of the mechanisms instituted by the Washington [ICSID] Convention was to put an end to international tension and crises, leading sometimes to the use of force, generated in the past by the diplomatic protection accorded to an investor by the State of which it was a national.'[7] An investment treaty dispute regarding indirect expropriation—because that is what the *Sicilian Sulphur* dispute was, albeit in a very rudimentary form—would now most likely be resolved through investment arbitration pursuant to a claim brought by the investor against the host State. The home State of the investor would not come into the picture at all, let alone apply countermeasures in defence of the investor. Conversely, the mistreatment of foreign investment in response to the investor's home State would now *prima facie* constitute

---

[3] Writing in 1885, Phillimore observed that '[i]t most commonly happens that *Reprisals* are resorted to for the purpose of redressing injuries inflicted upon the Right of Individuals', R Phillimore, *Commentaries upon International Law* (Volume 3, 3rd edn, Butterworths, London, 1885) 19 (emphasis in the original).

[4] L Oppenheim, *International Law* (Volume 2, Longmans, Green, and Co., London, 1905) 35; see below n 32.

[5] Ibid, 34.

[6] Ibid, 38; see discussion at n 302, n 304 and surrounding text.

[7] *Banro American Resources, Inc. and Société Aurifère du Kivu et du Maniema S.A.R.L. v Democratic Republic of the Congo*, ICSID Case No. ARB/98/7, Award, September 1, 2000 (2002) 17 *ICSID Review—Foreign Investment Law Journal* 382, 386 (para 15).

only an additional ground of wrongfulness because of the lack of legitimate public purpose for the particular conduct.[8]

With these radical changes in mind, the examination of the relationship between investment arbitration and the law of countermeasures will be taken in four steps. First of all, the general relationship of countermeasures and investment protection law will be sketched, and the historical and contemporary perspectives of the relationship will be explained (Part II). The second and third parts will address the role of countermeasures 'as a sword', employed by the home State to ensure the implementation of the investor's rights. The Convention on the Settlement of Investment Disputes between States and Nationals of Other States (ICSID Convention) that created the International Centre for the Settlement of Investment Disputes (ICSID) expressly excluded the use of diplomatic protection (and, as will be further suggested, also countermeasures). The legal argument is conceptually different from other, non-ICSID investment treaty arbitrations. The application of countermeasures in the context of non-ICSID and ICSID arbitrations will therefore be considered separately, respectively in Parts III and IV. Fourthly, the role of countermeasures 'as a shield' will be addressed, applied by host States to preclude the wrongfulness of breach of investment protection treaties (Part V).[9]

With the exception of the ICSID Convention, States have not dealt with the relationship between countermeasures and investment arbitration in clear and express terms. Therefore, the analysis will consider the relevance of general developments in State practice and the evolution of the international legal order, as well as of the nature of the rights of investors and the obligations of States. It will be argued that, even though diplomatic protection and the accompanying countermeasures have 'somewhat faded' from contemporary State practice, being factually replaced by investment arbitration, in legal terms the entitlement of the State still very much maintains its parallel existence.[10] Diplomatic protection and countermeasures, considered as a measure to induce compliance with investment protection law, are not generally precluded, despite express suspension during ICSID arbitrations. There does not seem to be any customary law rule coordinating dispute settlement, and the investor's invocation of responsibility neither imposes over that of the State nor replaces it as *lex specialis*. It is therefore up to the interpretation of the dispute settlement rules of each particular treaty and the customary law of countermeasures to establish the procedural conditions for the application of countermeasures.

---

[8] *BP v Libyan Arab Republic*, Award, October 10, 1973 (1979) 53 International Law Reports 297, 329.

[9] To borrow the framework from Pauwelyn's offensive / positive and defensive / negative models of relationship between human rights and WTO law, J Pauwelyn, 'Human Rights in WTO Dispute Settlement' in T Cottier, J Pauwelyn and E Bürgi (eds) *Human Rights and International Trade* (Oxford University Press, Oxford, 2005) 205, 206.

[10] *Case Concerning Ahmadou Sadio Diallo (Republic of Guinea v Democratic Republic of Congo)* [2007] ICJ Rep <http://www.icj-cij.org/docket/files/103/13856.pdf> (last accessed 28 February 2009), para 88.

In its defensive capacity, the relationship between countermeasures as a circumstance precluding wrongfulness and investment protection obligations is not entirely clear. It will be argued that the most persuasive conceptualization would treat countermeasures as not excluded in principle but as not applicable to the investor's rights under the treaty, provided that these rights are considered to be direct. Since the nature of investors' rights is far from settled, the debate about the limits of countermeasures is effectively dependant on the debate about the nature of investors' rights. This correlation between the nature of the rights and the applicability of countermeasures may provide a pragmatic reason for States in general and home States in particular to express their views regarding these theoretical questions in clearer terms. In particular, States could be likely to adopt the direct rights approach in the future efforts of law-making and law-application, whatever the possible short-term benefits of the derivative rights arguments for host States in particular arbitrations may be.

II. COUNTERMEASURES AND INVESTMENT PROTECTION LAW

A. Countermeasures

The first edition of Oppenheim's *International Law* in 1905 defined countermeasures in the following terms:

injurious and otherwise internationally illegal acts of a State against another as are exceptionally permitted for the purpose of compelling the latter to consent to a satisfactory settlement of a difference created by its own international delinquency.[11]

Classical international law seems to have generally accepted the permissibility of otherwise wrongful acts taken for the purpose of implementing international responsibility,[12] and the general proposition remains valid in the contemporary legal order.[13] Countermeasures (or reprisals, as they

---

[11] Oppenheim, above n 4, 34.

[12] Eg Phillimore, n 3, 18–43; Ф Мартенс, *Современное международное право цивилизованных народов* (Том II, Типогрфия А. Бенке, Санктпетербург, 1905) 506–509; GS Baker (ed) *Halleck's International Law* (Volume 1, 4th ed, Kegan Paul, Trench, Trubner & Co. Ltd., 1908) 505–507; AP Higgins (ed) *Hall's Treatise on International Law* (8th ed, Clarendon Press, Oxford, 1924) 433–436; F von Liszt, *Le droit international: Exposé systématique* (9e édn, A. Pedone, Paris, 1927) 296–298; A Verdross, 'Règles générales du droit international de la paix' (1929) 30 *Recueil des Cours* 271, 491–493; K Strupp, *Éléments du droit international public* (2e edn, Les Éditions internationales, Paris, 1930) 344–347; R Ago, 'Le délit international' (1939) 68 *Recueil des Cours* 419, 536–537.

[13] ILC, '2001 Draft Articles on Responsibility of States for Internationally Wrongful Acts with Commentaries' in *Official Records of the General Assembly, Fifty-Sixth Session, Supplement No.10* (A/56/10) 20, arts 22, 49–54; also R Ago, 'Eighth Report on State Responsibility' in *Yearbook of the ILC 1979, Vol. II(1)* A/CN.4/318 39–47; E Zoller, *Peacetime Unilateral Remedies: An Analysis of Countermeasures* (Transnational Publishers, Inc., New York, 1984); OY Elagab, *The Legality of Non-Forcible Counter-Measures in International Law* (Clarendon Press, Oxford, 1988); L-A Sicilianos, *Les réactions décentralisées a l'illicité: des contre-mesures a la légitime défense* (LGDJ, Paris, 1990); N White and A Abass, 'Countermeasures and Sanctions' in M Evans (ed) *International Law* (2nd edn, Oxford University Press, Oxford, 2006) 509–521.

were called before the change in the international law treatment of the use of force transformed the terminology)[14] were one of the classic rules of the decentralized international legal order, and provided the right of self-help to the injured State.[15]

Countermeasures are adopted unilaterally by States,[16] and not in accordance with or through any collective institutionalized settings.[17] Countermeasures are not automatic but are voluntarily adopted as a reaction to certain acts.[18] Countermeasures are adopted as a reaction to internationally wrongful acts. While the State will in most cases formulate its own view on the issue, the wrongfulness is an objective concept and a mere belief in the wrongfulness is insufficient.[19] Countermeasures themselves are in principle wrongful, and are thus different from retorsions, acts that are unfriendly (and may indeed be adopted unilaterally as a response to a wrongful act) but that are not themselves wrongful.[20]

It is also broadly agreed that countermeasures have to comply with certain procedural and substantive criteria. Logically, countermeasures can be adopted only in response to an earlier internationally wrongful act; therefore, in the absence of such an act, there can *ab initio* be no preclusion of wrongfulness.[21] The injured State must first call upon the wrongdoing State to comply with its obligations of cessation and reparation,[22] and the countermeasure must also be proportionate.[23] There is somewhat less agreement about the relationship of countermeasures to judicial methods of dispute settlement and the scope of obligations that are not subject to

---

[14] 2001 ILC Articles on State responsibility, ibid, 128.

[15] Third States' rights to take countermeasures are more controversial, see 2001 ILC Articles on State responsibility, above n 13, art 54; S Talmon, 'The Constitutive versus the Declaratory Theory of Recognition: *Tertium non Datur?*' (2004) 75 *British Yearbook of International Law* 101, 162–181; M Dawidowicz, 'Public Law Enforcement without Public Law Safeguards? An Analysis of State Practice on Third-Party Countermeasures and Their Relationship to the UN Security Council' (2006) 77 *British Yearbook of International Law* 333; see discussion at n 417–n 420 and surrounding text.

[16] JL Brierly, 'Sanctions' (1932) 17 *Transactions of the Grotius Society* 67, 68.

[17] Sicilianos, above n 13, 2–5.

[18] Ibid, 6.

[19] J Crawford, 'Counter-measures as Interim Measures' (1994) 5 *European Journal of International Law* 65, 66.

[20] 2001 ILC Articles on State responsibility, above n 13, 128.

[21] *Responsabilité de l'Allemagne à raison des dommages causés dans les colonies portugaises du sud de l'Afrique (sentence sur le principe de la responsabilité) (Portugal contre Allemagne)* (1928) II Reports of International Arbitral Awards 1011, 1025–1028; 'Régime des représailles en temps de paix' in *Résolutions de l'Institut de Droit International:* 1873–1956 (Editions juridiques et sociologiques S.A., Bâle, 1957) 167, 168, art 1; *Air Service Agreement of 27 March 1946 between the United States of America and France* (1978) XVIII Reports of International Arbitral Awards 417, 443 (para 81); *Gabčíkovo-Nagymaros Project (Hungary/Slovakia)* [1997] ICJ Rep 7, 56 (para 83); 2001 ILC Articles on State responsibility, above n 13, art 49.

[22] *Naulilaa,* ibid, 1027–1028; 'Régime des représailles en temps de paix', ibid, art 6(1); *Air Service Agrement,* ibid, 444 (paras 85–87); *Gabčíkovo-Nagymaros Project,* ibid, 56 (para 84); 2001 ILC Articles on State responsibility, above n 13, art 52(1).

[23] *Naulilaa,* ibid, 1027–1028; 'Régime des représailles en temps de paix', ibid, art 6(2); *Air Service Agrement,* ibid, 443 (para 83); *Gabčíkovo-Nagymaros Project,* ibid, 56 (paras 85–87); 2001 ILC Articles on State responsibility, above n 13, art 51; T Franck, 'On Proportionality of Countermeasures in International Law' (2008) 102 *American Journal of International Law* 715.

countermeasures. These are issues of particular importance in the context of investment arbitration regarding the use of countermeasures respectively 'as a sword' and 'as a shield', and will be further discussed in greater detail.[24]

The 2001 International Law Commission's (ILC) Articles on State Responsibility ('2001 ILC Articles on State responsibility') reflect the most recent thinking on the topic of countermeasures. The 2001 ILC Articles on State responsibility address countermeasures in two places, in Article 22 under the rubric of circumstances precluding wrongfulness, and in Articles 49–54 under the rubric of implementation of the international responsibility of the State. This approach accurately captures the dual context *vis-à-vis* a specific primary rule that countermeasures may occupy: both to preclude the wrongfulness of the breach of that primary rule, and as a measure undertaken to ensure implementation of the responsibility for its breach.

In investment law countermeasures could appear in two guises: as a shield used by the host State to preclude the wrongfulness of a breach of the primary obligations under investment protection law and as a sword used by the home State to ensure the implementation of those primary obligations (and perhaps applying countermeasures regarding investment protection rules as well). It is from this perspective that the present contribution will address the relationship of investment arbitration and countermeasures: on the one hand, countermeasures as a sword used by the home State to ensure the implementation of investment protection obligations, and on the other hand, as a shield used by the host State to preclude the wrongfulness of the breach of these obligations.

B. Historical perspective

Countermeasures have traditionally been connected with the treatment and protection of economic interests of aliens. Even before the emergence of international law, the XIV century practices recognized the right of a prince to grant rights of private reprisals to an individual in case of denial of justice by foreign princes,[25] and the concept of denial of justice and procedures for invoking reprisals was described in surprisingly modern terms.[26] The link of denial of justice and reprisals turned out to have

---

[24] 'Régime des représailles en temps de paix', ibid, arts 5 and 6(4); 2001 ILC Articles on State responsibility, above n 13, arts 50 and 52(3), (4). See discussion at III.G and V.A.

[25] *De Bello, de Represaliis et De Duello* (Oxford University Press, Oxford, 1917) 307–329, esp. 324; J Paulsson, *Denial of Justice* (Cambridge University Press, Cambridge, 2005) 101.

[26] *De Bello*, ibid, 310–311 (reprisals may be granted to mere residents that contribute to the State; an argument relying on effective economic link as an alternative to nationality), 311 (citizens not subject to jurisdiction by their own free will are not protected; an argument relying on lack of effective nationality), 312 (reprisals against the State of citizenship may not be ordered in principle, but can in cases of double citizenship), 313 (citizens of other States may be protected pursuant to special documents), AV Freeman, *The International Responsibility of States for Denial of Justice* (Longmans, Green and Co., London, 1938) 54–56; Paulsson, ibid, 13. The similarities are even more striking if

a lasting impact on legal thinking,[27] leading to extensive analyses of the definition of denial of justice in the classic texts.[28] The main reason appears to be that reprisals, even after the monopolization by the State of the use of military force changed them from public to private,[29] were still considered available only against actions that fell within the concept of denial of justice.[30] Even after denial of justice and reprisals were finally conceptually divorced, the focus on denial of justice still informed the pre-Second World War debate about the international standard on the treatment of aliens, in particular regarding the possibility of creating such rules outside the concept of denial of justice.[31] In that sense, it may be said that the link between the archaic rules on the treatment of aliens and countermeasures mutually reinforced each other and strengthened the law-making arguments that elucidated the broader international standard of treatment regarding the protection of property.[32]

one does not rely on what appears to be a somewhat unpersuasive translation by Brierly. De Legnano analysed the possible situations of denial of justice, drawing distinction between the situation where the judgment is pronounced 'ob gratiam partis' (and the remedy is restitution), 'ob gratiam illorum qui regnunt' (and the remedy is compensation) and 'ex solo iuidicis motu' (and there is no remedy), *De Bello,* above n 25, 168. Brierly translates these sentences as meaning 'from favour to the other parties', 'favour to the rulers' and 'from the judge's own motion', and this translation is certainly grammatically plausible, ibid, 323. However, the contrast between the bias in favour of parties or the State on the one hand and the judge's action *proprio motu* on the other hand seems illogical, because the examples are not incompatible, describing the judge's motivations and the nature of his acts. A more persuasive translation would distinguish between judgments unjust because of 'favour / gratitude *from* / influence *of* parties / the State' (CT Lewis, *A Latin Dictionary* (Oxford University Press, Oxford, 1991) 825–826, 1233) and simply erroneous uninfluenced judgments, mirroring the contemporary differentiation of wrongfulness of corrupt or dependent judicial administration and lack of wrongfulness for substantive judicial errors, eg Freeeman, at 287–303, 308–361; Paulsson, ibid, 73–81, 157–163, 164–167, 195–196.

[27] HW Spiegel, 'Origin and Development of Denial of Justice' (1938) 32 *American Journal of International Law* 63, 63–64; Freeman, above n 26, 53–67.

[28] Eg H Grotius, *De jure belli ac pacis libri tres* (Clarendon Press, Oxford, 1925) 626–627; E de Vattel, *The Law of Nations or the Principles of Natural Law* (Carnegie Institute, Washington, 1916) 228–230; RH Dana (ed) *Wheaton's Elements of International Law* (8th edn, Sampson Lowe, Son, and Company, London, 1866) 269–370; Phillimore, above n 3, 19–20; Halleck, above n 12, 505–506; E Nys, *Le droit international* (M. Weissenbruch, Bruxelles, 1912) 266; Hall, above n 12, 59–60.

[29] Мартенс, above n 12, 506–508; G Clark, 'English Practice with Regard to Reprisals by Private Persons' (1933) 27 *American Journal of International Law* 695, 721–722; F Kalshoven, *Belligerent Reprisals* (Leyden, A.W. Sijthoff, 1971) 1–10.

[30] C de Visscher, 'Le déni de justice en droit international' (1935) 52 *Recueil des Cours* 369, 369–374; EJ de Aréchaga, 'International Responsibility' in M Sorensen (ed) *Manual of Public International Law* (Macmillan, London, 1968) 553, 555.

[31] Proceeding from different levels of appreciation of the concreteness of the law on treatment of aliens, the spectrum of views ranged from addressing all rules under the rubric of denial of justice to addressing denial of justice as the only rule, with the intermediate (and ultimately successful) approach considering denial of justice as one and non-exhaustive rule in the law of treatment of aliens, G Fitzmaurice, 'The Meaning of the Term "Denial of Justice"' (1932) 13 *British Yearbook of International Law* 93, 93–105; OJ Lissitzyn, 'The Meaning of the Term Denial of Justice in International Law' (1935) 19 *American Journal of International Law* 632; Freeman, above n 26, 84–186.

[32] One of the early cases of indirect expropriation was the *Sicilian Sulphur* dispute where the UK applied reprisals to ensure implementation of responsibility for what it considered to be a treaty breach, Great Britain, *State Papers* 1839–1840 *Volume* 28 (Harrison and Sons, London, 1857) 1163–1242; *State Papers* 1840–1841 *Volume* 29 (James Ridgway and Sons, London, 1857) 175–204; *State Papers* 1841–1842 *Volume* 30 (James Ridgway and Sons, London, 1858) 111–120; AP Fachiri, 'Expropriation and

However, in another sense, reprisals very much undermined the argument for developing a sophisticated international standard for the treatment of aliens and their property interests. From the Latin American perspective the procedural aspect was perceived, as Álvarez wrote in 1909, to constitute simply the 'use of force, such as the seizure of customs houses, pacific blockades, etc., in order to compel the recognition of claims'. This procedural context influenced the perception of the underlying substantive rules as an attempt by the US and European States to 'assur[e] unduly for their citizens who came to those countries a specially privileged situation'.[33] As Jennings later noted, the substance of the law was not necessarily bad law, but the perception of it as a rationalization of European policies at a period of their dominance could not be dismissed.[34] It is perhaps not surprising that one of the first exercises in multilateral universal treaty-making to restrict the use of force was directed precisely at reprisals for economic reasons: the 1899 Hague Convention Respecting the Employment of Force for the Recovery of Contract Debts.[35]

Even after the prohibition of forcible reprisals, the consistently unsuccessful attempts at multilateral treaty-making regarding treatment of aliens both between the World Wars and after the Second World War[36] suggested a continuing distrust of the perceived earlier misuse of law and procedure by former colonial and imperial powers.[37] Consequently, in order to move beyond the normatively and emotionally contentious customary law[38] and particularly its methods of dispute settlement reminiscent of reprisals, the focus of investment law-making gradually moved to treaty law both in substantive and procedural terms.

International Law' (1925) 6 *British Yearbook of International Law* 159, 163–164. Great Britain relied on the authority of this case regarding the law on the treatment of aliens both in the context of codification and adjudication, see respectively S Rosenne (ed) *League of Nations Conference for the Codification of International Law [1930]* (Volume II, Oceana Publications, Inc., New York, 1975) 551; *Oscar Chinn Case (Great Britain v Belgium)* PCIJ Rep Series C 75 51–57.

[33] A Álvarez, 'Latin America and International Law' (1909) 3 *American Journal of International Law* 269, 300; see the historical perspective in W Shan, 'Calvo Doctrine, State Sovereignty and the Changing Landscape of International Investment Law' in W Shan, P Simons and D Singh (eds) *Redefining Sovereignty in International Economic Law* (Hart Publishing, Oxford, 2008) 247.

[34] RY Jennings, 'State Contracts in International Law' (1961) 37 *British Yearbook of International Law* 156, 159.

[35] I Brownlie, *International Law and the Use of Force by States* (Clarendon Press, Oxford, 1963) 24; also AS Hershey, 'The Calvo and Drago Doctrines' (1907) 1 *American Journal of International Law* 26; LM Drago, 'State Loans in Their Relation to International Policy' (1907) 1 *American Journal of International Law* 692; JB Scott, 'The Work of the Second Hague Peace Conference' (1908) 2 *American Journal of International Law* 1, 15; H Accioly, *Traité de droit international public* (Recueil Sirey, Paris, 1940) 290–293.

[36] G van Harten, *Investment Treaty Arbitration and Public Law* (Oxford University Press, Oxford, 2007) 18–21.

[37] S Rosenne, 'State Responsibility: *Festina Lente*' (2004) 75 *British Yearbook of International Law* 363, 364.

[38] See Nervo's and Fitzmaurice's 1957 debate at the ILC, *Yearbook of the ILC* 1957, *Vol. I* A/CN.4/SER.A/1957 156, 163–164 respectively; cf RB Lillich, 'Duties of States Regarding Civil Rights of Aliens' (1978) 161 *Recueil des Cours* 329, 360–365.

Against this background and faced with an argument for closer integration of customary and treaty investment law-making processes in the *Barcelona Traction, Light and Power Company, Limited* case, the International Court of Justice chose to treat the processes as largely autonomous with little potential for normative influence either way, a solution generally perceived at that time as having a profoundly negative and limiting effect on the protection of investors' rights.[39] Counter-intuitively, the long-term consequences of the Court's approach have been beneficial for investors: showing the States the inadequacy of customary law-making efforts in the area; pushing the law-making resources into treaty-making; and clearly recognizing and confirming the rights of States to provide more beneficial treatment to investors through treaty law unhindered by archaic and inappropriate customary law concepts.[40] As a result, the apparently ineffective customary law of diplomatic protection and the treaty law of investment arbitration seemed to be developing independently from one another.

In light of these developments and in particular after the strong emergence of an investor-State centred system of dispute settlement, diplomatic protection and countermeasures seemed to have parted the ways with investment protection law. Given law-making efforts to create both a substantively[41] and procedurally depoliticized model of investment dispute settlement to replace that of diplomatic protection,[42] the contemporary relevance of countermeasures—the aspect of secondary rules probably most prone to politicizing the underlying dispute—may not be immediately clear.[43]

---

[39] Eg R Higgins, 'Aspects of the Case Concerning Barcelona Traction, Light and Power Company, Ltd.' (1970–1971) 11 *Virginia Journal of International Law* 327, 341; RB Lillich, 'The Rigidity of Barcelona' (1971) 65 *American Journal of International Law* 522, 552–557; C de Visscher, 'La notion de reference (renvoi) au droit interne dans la protection diplomatique des actionnaires de societés anonymes' (1971) 7 *Revue Belge de Droit International* 1, 6.

[40] S Schwebel, 'Some Aspects of International Law in Arbitration between States and Aliens' in S Schwebel, *Justice in International Law* (Cambridge University Press, Cambridge, 1994) 196, 210–211; F Berman, 'The Relevance of the Law on Diplomatic Protection in Investment Arbitration' in F Ortino et al (eds) *Investment Treaty Law: Current Issues II* (BIICL, London, 2007) 67, 69; *RomPetrol Group N.V. v Romania*, ICSID Case No. ARB/06/03, Decision on Respondent's Preliminary Objections to Jurisdiction and Admissibility, April 18, 2008, <http://ita.law.uvic.ca/documents/RomPetrol.pdf> (last accessed 28 February 2009), para 91; M Paparinskis, '*Barcelona Traction*: A Friend of Investment Protection Law' (2008) 8 *Baltic Yearbook of International Law* 105, 105–133.

[41] Eg KJ Vandevelde, 'The BIT Program: A Fifteen-Year Appraisal' (1992) 86 *ASIL Proceedings* 532, 534–535; A Newcombe and L Paradell, *Law and Practice of Investment Treaties: Standards of Treatment* (Walter Kluwer Law and Business, the Hague, 2009), in particular Chapter 1.

[42] Eg A Broches, 'The Convention on the Settlement of Investment Disputes between States and Nationals of Other States' (1972) 136 *Recueil des Cours* 331, 344; IFI Shihata, 'Towards a Greater Depoliticization of Investment Disputes: The Roles of ICSID and MIGA' (1986) 1 *ICSID Review— Foreign Investment Law Journal* 1 et seq. As Lowenfeld stated in his separate opinion in the *Corn Products* decision on responsibility, '[t]he essence of each of these arrangements [ICSID Conventions, BITs and NAFTA] is that controversies between foreign investors and host states are insulated from political and diplomatic relations between states', *Corn Products*, Separate Opinion of Arbitrator Lowenfeld, below n 49, para 1.

[43] While the vocabulary of depoliticization remained generally uncontested, it was quite ironic how the argument sought to characterize the discretion within the law of diplomatic protection as political. The argument drew the distinction between 'legal' legal and 'political' legal disputes in

C. Contemporary perspective

There are a number of reasons, both theoretical and practical, why the examination of the role that the seemingly archaic gunboat diplomacy-reminiscent countermeasures play within the refined treaty structures of modern investment protection law is both valuable and necessary.

First of all, there is considerable conceptual ambiguity regarding the role of the law of State responsibility in investment protection law,[44] *inter alia* regarding the 'sword' perspective of invocation and the 'shield' perspective of preclusion of wrongfulness. The former aspect is exemplified in Douglas' argument for investment law as a sub-system of the law of responsibility[45] and Leben's rebuttal situating investment law within and not outside general international law.[46] The latter aspect may be seen in the application of the law of necessity as a circumstance precluding wrongfulness in the investment arbitrations arising out of the Argentinian financial crisis, and the very divergent solutions adopted in this regard by Tribunals[47] and legal writers.[48] More recent arbitral awards have also directly addressed

---

ratione personae terms of the parties, thus transforming the earlier debates that had unsuccessfully attempted to distinguish legal and political in *ratione materiae* terms, H Lauterpacht, *Function of Law in the International Community* (Clarendon Press, Oxford, 1933) 144–145.

[44] J Crawford, 'Similarity of Issues in Disputes Arising under the Same or Similarly Drafted Investment Treaties' in Y Banifetami (ed) *Precedent in International Arbitration* (Juris Publishing, Inc., New York, 2008) 97, 100.

[45] Z Douglas, 'The Hybrid Foundations of Investment Treaty Arbitration' (2003) 74 *British Yearbook of International Law* 151, 184–193.

[46] C Leben, 'La responsabilité internationale de l'État sur le fondement des traités de promotion et de protection des investissements' (2004) 50 *Annuaire français de droit international* 683, 691–697.

[47] *CMS Gas Transmission Company v Republic of Argentina*, ICSID Case No. ARB 01/08, Final Award, May 12, 2005, 44 *International Legal Materials* 1205, 1238 (paras 304–394); *Enron Corporation and Ponderosa Assets, L.P. v Republic of Argentina*, ICSID Case No. ARB/01/3, Award, May 22, 2007, <http://ita.law.uvic.ca/documents/Enron-Award.pdf> (last accessed 28 February 2009), paras 294–345; *LG&E v Republic of Argentina*, ICSID Case No. ARB/02/1, Decision on Liability, October 3, 2006, <http://ita.law.uvic.ca/documents/ARB021_LGE-Decision-on-Liability-en.pdf> (last accessed 28 February 2009), paras 245–261; *CMS Gas Transmission Company v Republic of Argentina*, ICSID Case No. ARB 01/08, Decision of the *ad hoc* Committee on the Application for Annulment, September 25, 2007, <http://ita.law.uvic.ca/documents/CMSAnnulmentDecision.pdf> (last accessed 28 February 2009), paras 101–136; *Sempra Energy International v Republic of Argentina*, ICSID Case No. ARB/02/16, Award, September 28, 2007, <http://ita.law.uvic.ca/documents/SempraAward.pdf> (last accessed 28 February 2009), paras 325–397; *BG Plc. v Republic of Argentina*, UNCITRAL arbitration, Final Award, December 24, 2007, <http://ita.law.uvic.ca/documents/BG-award_000.pdf> (last accessed 28 February 2009), paras 367–412; *Metalpar S.A. and Buen Aire S.A. v Argentina*, ICSID Case No. ARB/03/5, Award on the Merits, June 6, 2008, <http://ita.law.uvic.ca/documents/MetalparAwardEng.pdf> (last accessed 28 February 2009), paras 208–213; *Continental Casualty Company v Republic of Argentina*, ICSID Case No. ARB/03/9, Award, September 5, 2008, <http://ita.law.uvic.ca/documents/ContinentalCasualtyAward.pdf> (last accessed 28 February 2009), paras 162–168, 175, 192, 222; *National Grid P.L.C. v Republic of Argentina*, UNCITRAL Case, Award, November 3, 2008, <http://ita.law.uvic.ca/documents/NGvArgentina.pdf> (last accessed 28 February 2009), paras 250–262.

[48] Eg M Raux, 'La reconnaissance de l'état de nécessité dans la dernière sentence relative au contentieux Argentin: LG&E c/Argentine' (2006) 125 *Gazette du Palais* 3799, 3799–3803; S Ripinsky, 'State of Necessity: Effect on Compensation' (2007) 4 (6) *Transnational Dispute Management* (online subscription e-journal); A Reinisch, 'Necessity in International Investment Arbitration—An Unnecessary Split of Opinions in Recent ICSID Cases? Comments on *CMS v Argentina* and *LG&E v Argentina*' (2007) 8 *Journal of World Investment and Trade* 191, 191–214; S Schill, 'International

the law of countermeasures. The *Archer Daniels Midland Company and Tate & Lyle Ingredients Americas, Inc. v Mexico ('ADM')* and the *Corn Products International, Inc. v Mexico ('Corn Products')* Tribunals proposed divergent solutions to the possible application of countermeasures to investors, with one arbitrator of each Tribunal writing further separate opinions on the issue.[49] Indeed, the complexity of the broader legal argument between the general and particular in international law[50] suggests that the debate in investment protection law is not likely to lead to straightforward and clear answers.[51]

Secondly, recent investment arbitrations have both dealt with countermeasures directly and have addressed issues raising similar concerns. Since depoliticized settlement of investor-State disputes was an express and important consideration in the creation of parts of the present regime,[52] one could expect the use of countermeasures 'as a sword' to be limited (at least outside rules expressly providing for these rights).[53] On the other hand, the use of circumstances precluding wrongfulness to shield the State from the investor's claims was not a direct consideration in creating

Investment Law and the Host State's Power to Handle Economic Crises—Comment on the ICSID Decision in *LG&E v Argentina*' (2007) 24 *Journal of International Arbitration* 265, 277–286; G Bottini, 'Protection of Essential Interests in the BIT Era' in T Weiler (ed) *Investment Treaty Arbitration and Treaty Law* (JurisNet, LLC, New York, 2008) 145; RA Luizi, 'BITs & Economic crises: Do States have *carte blanche*?', at 165; AK Björklund, 'Emergency Exceptions' in P Muchlinski, F Ortino and C Schreuer (eds) *The Oxford Handbook of International Investment Law* (Oxford University Press, Oxford, 2008) 459; J Kurtz, 'Adjudging the Exceptional at International Law: Security, Public Order and Financial Crisis' (2008) *Jean Monnet Working Paper* 06/08, <http://www.jeanmonnetprogram. org/papers/08/080601.pdf> (last accessed 28 February 2009); WW Burke-White and A von Staden, 'Investment Protection in Extraordinary Times: The Interpretation and Application of Non-Precluded Measures Provisions in Bilateral Investment Treaties' (2008) 48 *Virginia Journal of International Law* 307.

[49] *Archer Daniels Midland Company and Tate & Lyle Ingredients Americas, Inc. v Mexico,* ICSID AF Case No. ARB/(AF)/04/5, Award, November 21, 2007, <http://ita.law.uvic.ca/documents/ ADMTateRedactedAward.pdf> (last accessed 28 February 2009), paras 110–184; Concurring Opinion of Arbitrator Rovine, <http://ita.law.uvic.ca/documents/ADM-Concurring.pdf> (last accessed 28 February 2009); *Corn Products International, Inc. v Mexico,* ICSID AF Case No. ARB/(AF)/04/1, Decision on Responsibility, January 15, 2008, <http://ita.law.uvic.ca/documents/CPI-DecisiononResponsibility-eng. pdf> (last accessed 7 April 2009); Separate Opinion of Arbitrator Lowenfeld, <http://ita.law.uvic.ca/ documents/CPI-DecisiononResponsibility-LowenfeldOpinion.pdf> (last accessed 7 April 2009).

[50] B Simma and D Pulkowski, 'Of Planets and Universe: Self-Contained Regimes in International Law' (2006) 17 *European Journal of International Law* 483, 506.

[51] Report of the Study Group of the ILC, 'Fragmentation of International Law: Difficulties Arising from Diversification and Expansion of International Law' A/CN.4/L.682, paras 46–194; J Pauwelyn, *Conflict of Norms in Public International Law* (Cambridge University Press, Cambridge 2003); see discussion at V.B.

[52] Broches, above n 42, 344; Shihata, above n 42, 1. As Broches pointed out, '[t]he [ICSID] would therefore offer a means of settling directly, on the legal plane, investment disputes and insulate such disputes from the realm of politics and diplomacy', *Convention on the Settlement of Investment Disputes between States and Nationals of Other States: Documents Concerning the Origin and the Formulation of the Convention* (Volume II, ICSID, Washington, 1968) 242.

[53] The *lex specialis* regimes dealing with countermeasures could have some relevance, especially in situations when the same disputes or different aspects of the same disputes are brought before different dispute settlement bodies, see J Pauwelyn, 'Adding Sweeteners to Softwood Lumber: the WTO-NAFTA "Spaghetti Bowl" is Cooking' (2006) 9 *Journal of International Economic Law* 197, 197–206.

the contemporary system, thus one could expect that legal rules would not deal with countermeasures in a clear and express manner.

These propositions are supported by practice. Retorsions have been used to compel States to consent to investment arbitration[54] and might be considered in cases when host States do not comply with the awards.[55] There is so far no publicly available information about States going further and using countermeasures to ensure the implementation of investment treaty obligations. At the same time, the lack of practice may simply reflect the so-far generally satisfactory compliance by host States with the awards, giving no practical incentive for home States to interfere in the dispute. The global economic downturn, taken together with the very considerable amounts at stake in some pending arbitrations, may lead to the States failing to satisfy investment awards, whether through inability[56] or unwillingness,[57] and thus raising the question about the possible role of home States in starker terms.

From the defensive perspective, Mexico has in two cases expressly invoked countermeasures to preclude wrongfulness of its breaches of investment protection rules.[58] Argentina has relied on necessity in a number of cases arising out of its economic crisis,[59] raising similar conceptual issues regarding conduct voluntarily undertaken in breach of international obligations.[60] In addition, the so-called non-precluded measure clauses (NPM clauses) have an unclear relationship with rules on necessity,[61] and could *mutatis mutandis* refer to countermeasures.[62] To the extent (if any) that the law of State responsibility plays a direct role in the interpretation of NPM clauses, the law of countermeasures should similarly be fully implied in

[54] *Compañía del Desarrollo de Santa Elena S.A. v Republic of Costa Rica*, ICSID Case No. ARB(AF)/00/01, Final Award, February 17, 2000, (2000) 15 *ICSID Review—Foreign Investment Law Journal* 169, 179 (paras 24–26); C Brower and J Wong, 'General Valuation Principles: The Case of *Santa Elena*' in T Weiler (ed) *International Investment Law and Arbitration: Leading Cases from the ICSID, NAFTA, Bilateral Treaties and Customary International Law* (Cameron May, London, 2005) 747, 751–754.

[55] L Caplan, 'Post-Annulment Options: Possible Resources by Investor's Home State' (2009) 6 (1) *Transnational Dispute Management* 7–8.

[56] The arbitrations regarding the Argentinean financial crisis could provide one example, V Lowe, 'Some Comments on Procedural Weaknesses in International Law' (2004) 98 *ASIL Proceedings* 37, 39; V Lowe, 'Fair and Equitable Treatment in International Law: Remarks' (2006) 100 *ASIL Proceedings* 73, 74.

[57] AS Alexandroff and IA Laird, 'Compliance and Enforcement' in P Muchlinski, F Ortino and C Schreuer (eds) *The Oxford Handbook of International Investment Law* (Oxford University Press, Oxford, 2008) 1171, 1175–1185.

[58] See above n 49.

[59] See above n 47, n 48.

[60] As Hungary (Dupuy) explained the similarity, 'l'état de nécessité se distingue également des contre-mesures, avec lesquelles il partage pourtant ce caractère volontaire. Contrairement à elle en effet, cette cause exonératoire peut être invoquée *même sans constituer une réaction à un fait illicite initial commis par l'autre Etat*', *Gabčíkovo-Nagymaros Project (Hungary/Slovakia)* ICJ Pleadings CR 97/3, <http://www.icj-cij.org/docket/files/92/11035.pdf> (last accessed 28 February 2009), 70 (emphasis in the original).

[61] See above n 47, n 48.

[62] *Military and Paramilitary Activities in and against Nicaragua (Nicaragua v US)* (Merits) [1986] ICJ Rep 14, Dissenting opinion of Judge Sir Robert Jennings 528, 541, see discussion at V.B.

the treaties (when the preclusion of wrongfulness is sought not in a protection of essential interests but in a response to an anterior wrongful act). Consequently, the idea of conduct voluntarily undertaken in apparent breach of some substantive obligations has been (and most likely will be) extensively debated before and by Tribunals.

Investment awards and particular arguments explained in them play a considerable role in presenting and deciding subsequent cases.[63] It is possible that the idea of applying countermeasures to investment protection rules, now openly discussed, will also be internalized both in the arguments of host States in particular cases and possible longer-time strategies for (mis)treating foreign investments. For these reasons, it is necessary to clearly identify the framework of law within which home, host States and investors could operate.

Thirdly, countermeasures against foreign property or investments do take place in practice. The Fourth Special Rapporteur on State Responsibility Arangio-Ruiz pointed to the 1958 Indonesian expropriation of Dutch property, the 1959–1960 Cuban expropriation of property belonging to the Americans and the 1971 Libyan expropriation of the investment belonging to British Petroleum as examples of such countermeasures.[64]

---

[63] JP Commission, 'Precedent in Investment Treaty Arbitration: A Citation Analysis of a Developing Jurisprudence' (2007) 24 *Journal of International Arbitration* 129; OK Fauchald, 'The Legal Reasoning of ICSID Tribunals: An Empirical Analysis' (2008) 19 *European Journal of International Law* 301, 333–343; 'Cross References in Investment Arbitration Case Law: Salient Topics' in Y Banifetami (ed) *Precedent in International Arbitration* (Juris Publishing, Inc., New York, 2008) 473. The argument for following earlier cases or at least established approaches has been presented from different perspectives both in case law and legal writings, see respectively *SGS Société Générale de Surveillance S.A. v Republic of the Philippines*, ICSID Cases No. ARB/02/6 and ARB/04/08, Decision of the Tribunal on Objections to Jurisdiction, January 29, 2004, <http://ita. law.uvic.ca/documents/SGSvPhil-final_001.pdf> (last accessed 28 February 2009), para 97; *Saipem S.p.A. v Bangladesh*, ICSID Case No. ARB/05/07, Decision on Jurisdiction and Recommendation on Provisional Measures, March 21, 2007, (2007) 22 *ICSID Review—Foreign Investment Law Journal* 100, 117 (para 67); *Victor Pey Casado and President Allende Foundation v Republic of Chile*, ICSID Case No. ARB/98/2, Award, May 8, 2008, <http://ita.law.uvic.ca/documents/Peyaward.pdf> (last accessed 28 February 2009), para 119; and J Paulsson, 'International Arbitration and the Generation of Legal Norms: Treaty Arbitration and International Law' (2006) 3 (5) *Transnational Dispute Management*; G Kaufmann-Kohler, 'Arbitral Precedent: Dream, Necessity or Excuse?' (2007) 23 *Arbitration International* 357; D Di Pietro, 'The use of precedents in ICSID arbitration. Regularity or certainty?' (2007) 10 *International Arbitration Law Review* 92; T-H Cheng, 'Precedent and Control in Investment Treaty Arbitration' (2007) 30 *Fordham International Law Journal* 1014; J Paulsson, 'Awards—and Awards' in AK Björklund, IA Laird and S Ripinsky (eds) *Investment Treaty Law: Current Issues III* (BIICL, London, 2008) 95; AK Björklund, 'Investment Treaty Arbitral Decisions as Jurisprudence Constante' in CB Picker, ID Bunn and DW Arner (eds) *International Economic Law: State and Future of the Discipline* (Hart Publishing, Oxford, 2008) 265; CH Schreuer and M Weiniger, 'Conversations Across Cases—Is There a Doctrine of Precedent in Investment Arbitration?' in P Muchlinski, F Ortino and CH Schreuer (eds) *The Oxford Handbook of International Investment Law* (Oxford University Press, Oxford, 2008) 1188; contributions by Prosper Weil, James Crawford, Gilbert Guillaume, Thomas Wälde, and Gabrielle Kaufmann-Kohler to Y Banifetami (ed) *Precedent in International Arbitration* (Juris Publishing, Inc., New York, 2008).

[64] G Arangio-Ruiz, 'Fourth Report on State Responsibility' in *Yearbook of the ILC* 1992, *Vol. II (1)* A/CN.4 SER.A/1992/Add.1 7 fn 7; I Seidl-Hohenveldern, 'Reprisals and the Taking of Private Property' in *De Conflictu Legum: Essays Presented to Kollewijn and Offerhaus* (A.W. Sijthoff, Leiden, 1962) 470–474. Bowett gives an example of a 1970 Libyan nationalization of the property of Italian nationals as an alleged reprisal for obtaining the property during the period of colonization and

Bank accounts of foreign nationals have also been frozen as apparent countermeasures against their home States.[65]

The factual background to the three Libyan arbitrations illustrates the reasons that may lead States to the application of countermeasures against foreign investments. In 1971, Libya nationalized the BP interests and property of the BP/Hunt deed of concession in retaliation for the failure of the UK to protect certain islands in the Persian Gulf from the Iranian occupation. In 1973, Libya nationalized the remaining Hunt interests and property from the deed of concession as a reprisal for US support for Israel. In 1973 and 1974, Libya nationalized property and interests of TOPCO, CALASIATIC and LIAMCO, apparently at least partly in retaliation for US support for Israel in the Arab-Israeli conflict and its efforts to consolidate the position of oil-importing nations through the 1974 Washington conference.[66]

The point made here is not that such obligations were indeed owed to Libya by the home States of the investors, that they were breached or that the response complied with procedural requirements and was proportionate:[67] what is important is that Libya used or at least attempted to use the conceptual framework of countermeasures. Tomuschat has noted that countermeasures against property seem the most used device in major conflicts, and would even put developing countries in a position of superiority since most foreign investment is situated precisely in these countries.[68] The policies that Libya expressed and the ways it went about to implement them do not look out of place in the twenty-first century, therefore strengthening the necessity for a conceptual framework for addressing the law of countermeasures and investment protection law. The general legal framework, the particular legal arguments, the factual potential for controversy and already existing cases and disputes all suggest the relevance of analysis of the role of countermeasures in investment protection law.

---

causing irreparable damage to Libyan people, D Bowett, 'International Law and Economic Sanctions' (1975–1976) 16 *Virginia Journal of International Law* 245, 252 fn 82.

[65] The 1956 UK freezing of Egyptian sterling accounts during the Suez crisis, the 1980 US freezing of Iranian accounts during the Tehran hostage crisis and the 1982 UK freezing of Argentinian accounts during the Falkland crisis, Sicilianos, above n 13, 359–360.

[66] RB von Mehren and PN Kourides, 'International Arbitrations between States and Foreign Parties: the Libyan Nationalisation Cases' (1981) 75 *American Journal of International Law* 476, 483–487; C Greenwood, 'State Contracts in International Law—The Libyan Oil Arbitrations' (1982) 53 *British Yearbook of International Law* 27, 28–31.

[67] It is not clear whether in the Libyan and Indonesian cases one can actually identify the anterior breach of the obligation owed to the State that would justify countermeasures, Bowett, above n 64, 252. It has been reported that Italy and Libya were close to concluding a deal to compensate Libya for the colonial rule ('Undoing the Damage', *Economist*, 31 July 2008), with the Italian apology suggesting an acknowledgment of the breach ('Who's Sorry Now?', *Economist*, 2 October 2008). In the Libyan arbitrations, only the *BP* Tribunal concluded that the purpose of the action was related to extraneous political issues (*BP*, above n 8, 329), while the *Texaco* and *LIAMCO* Tribunals found an economic purpose to the nationalizations, Greenwood, above n 66, 30–31.

[68] C Tomuschat, 'Are Countermeasures Subject to Prior Dispute-Settlement Procedures?' (1994) 5 *European Journal of International Law* 77, 78. In the 2000 ILC debate, Galicki pointed to 'the right to protection of property, which was violated so often in practice as a result of the application of countermeasures', *Yearbook of the ILC 2000, Vol. I* A/CN.4/SER.A/2000 298, para 62.

III. COUNTERMEASURES AS A SWORD: NON-ICSID ARBITRATION

A. Diplomatic protection and countermeasures

Most modern investment protection treaties contain arbitration offers by both States to the investors of the other State, giving the investor a choice between different arbitral venues that could include ICSID, ICSID Additional Facility, UNCITRAL, SCC or LCIA. It is generally accepted that the investor's claim under the treaty is treated as its consent to investment arbitration, providing jurisdiction to the arbitral Tribunal.[69] The role of countermeasures is not expressly addressed in any of these documents. However, their legal effect may be identified indirectly from the position they take regarding the right of diplomatic protection.

Diplomatic protection is described in the following terms by Article 1 of the 2006 ILC Draft Articles on Diplomatic Protection (2006 ILC Articles) (reflecting customary law):[70]

diplomatic protection consists of the invocation by a State, through diplomatic action or other means of peaceful settlement, of the responsibility of another State for an injury caused by an internationally wrongful act of that State to a natural or legal person that is a national of the former State with a view to the implementation of such responsibility.[71]

The law of countermeasures and the law of diplomatic protection both belong to the secondary rules of international law that come into operation when a primary rule is breached, but they address somewhat different issues. The law of diplomatic protection deals with secondary rules addressing the invocation of State responsibility if the primary rule breached covers the treatment of nationals of the home State.[72] The law of countermeasures deals with secondary rules addressing the measures taken to induce the compliance of the State with its obligations under the law of responsibility pursuant to breaches of primary rules of any content whatsoever.[73]

The 2001 ILC Articles on State responsibility address the diplomatic protection rules of nationality and local remedies in Article 44 under the rubric of admissibility, stating that the responsibility of the State may not be invoked if any applicable rules of nationality and local remedies have not been complied with. The rules of diplomatic protection and State responsibility thus connect at the point of admissibility of claims: to the

---

[69] Eg C McLachlan, L Shore and M Weiniger, *International Investment Arbitration: Substantive Principles* (Oxford University Press, Oxford, 2007) 45–56; CF Dugan et al, *Investor-State Arbitration* (Oxford University Press, Oxford, 2008) 77–80; R Dolzer and C Schreuer, *Principles of International Investment Law* (Oxford University Press, Oxford, 2008) 222–229; C Schreuer, 'Consent to Arbitration' in P Muchlinski, F Ortino and C Schreuer (eds) *The Oxford Handbook of International Investment Law* (Oxford University Press, Oxford, 2008) 830.

[70] *Diallo*, above n 10, para 39.

[71] ILC, 2006 'Draft Articles on Diplomatic Protection with Commentaries' in *Official Records of the General Assembly, Sixty-First Session, Supplement No.10* (A/61/10) 22, 24, art 1.

[72] Ibid, 24.

[73] ILC 2001 Articles, above n 13, art 49; CF Amerasinghe, *Diplomatic Protection* (Oxford University Press, Oxford, 2008) 327.

extent that the primary rules in question deal with injury to aliens, compliance with diplomatic protection determines the admissibility; to the extent that the primary rules address any other issues whatsoever, diplomatic protection has no application.

The right to take countermeasures to induce compliance with obligations under the law of responsibility is therefore logically predicated on the right to invoke responsibility in the first place. Article 52 of the 2001 ILC Articles on State responsibility reflects this logic by requiring the injured State to call upon the responsible State according to Article 43 that deals with notice of the claim, thus inescapably excluding the application of countermeasures to cases when responsibility has not (or may not) be invoked.[74] The suspension of the right to invoke responsibility would therefore result in an inadmissibility of the international claim, effectively similar to a case of inadmissibility where the domestic remedies have not been exhausted.[75] In the latter case, the inadmissibility results from the factual failure to satisfy the requirement of admissibility, while in the former case the reason is the legal impermissibility of the conduct satisfying the requirement, but the conceptual situation is similar. Since the claim is inadmissible during the suspension of diplomatic protection, it is also not possible to take countermeasures to induce compliance with such a claim.

The ICSID Convention is the only set of investment protection rules that expressly addresses diplomatic protection. It states in Article 27(1):

No Contracting State shall give diplomatic protection, or bring an international claim, in respect of a dispute which one of its nationals and another Contracting State shall have consented to submit or shall have submitted to arbitration under this Convention, unless such other Contracting State shall have failed to abide by and comply with the award rendered in such dispute.[76]

Since Article 27(1) sets ICSID arbitrations apart from disputes arbitrated under other rules, the place of countermeasures in ICSID and non-ICSID arbitrations will be addressed separately. For the sake of convenience, the latter case will be taken first, since due to Article 27(1) possible arguments for excluding or limiting countermeasures in non-ICSID arbitrations will most likely also apply to ICSID arbitrations but not *vice versa*.

There are three somewhat overlapping but conceptually distinct reasons why diplomatic protection would not apply in non-ICSID arbitrations: either there is a general rule paralleling Article 27(1) in content that suspends

---

[74] Even though Article 52(2) permits taking urgent countermeasures without giving notice, the commentary (countermeasures may be taken 'even before any notification of the intention to do so') confirms that this rule addresses only the situations where notification could be given in principle but it would frustrate the purpose of countermeasures. It does not extend the right to take countermeasures to situations where no right to invoke responsibility and notify about it exists in the first place at all, 2001 ILC Articles on State responsibility, above n 13, 136.

[75] To follow the procedural approach to exhaustion of local remedies, CF Amerasinghe, *Local Remedies in International Law* (2nd edn, Cambridge University Press, Cambridge, 2004) 385–421.

[76] Convention on the settlement of investment disputes between States and nationals of other States, 18 March 1965, 575 UNTS 160 (entered into force 14 October 1966), art 27(1); see discussion at IV.

diplomatic protection when any kind of investment arbitration takes place (*B.*), or investment arbitration addresses very different issues from diplomatic protection and thus States opt out of diplomatic protection in favour of the special regime of invocation of State responsibility (*C.*), or investment arbitration addresses the same issues as diplomatic protection and thus excludes it as *lex specialis* (*D.*). These arguments will be considered in turn, and it will be argued that none of them is fully persuasive. Since diplomatic protection and countermeasures would accordingly be still available at least in principle, it will be further explored how the rendering of an arbitral award (*E.*), exhaustion of local remedies (*F.*) and the procedural conditions for the application of countermeasures would operate in their regard (*G.*).

B. Diplomatic protection excluded by invocation of investment arbitration

Non-ICSID arbitration rules do not provide for express exclusion of diplomatic protection. While the particular treaty can expressly suspend the right of the State to engage in diplomatic protection, such rules are not widespread.[77] The existence of an ICSID arbitration clause in the particular treaty does not *per se* exclude diplomatic protection, because Article 27(1) would apply only from the moment that the consent becomes mutual through the investor's claim.[78] The issue is rarely clearly settled in terms of treaty interpretation.

It is also not clear whether there is a customary law rule that would suspend or waive the exercise of diplomatic protection during investor-State arbitration. Amerasinghe has suggested that:

> once the procedures directly involving the investor are invoked, the treaty does not permit resort to diplomatic protection directly with the involvement in arbitration of the investor's national State; otherwise, the settlement procedures provided for would duplicate rather than simplify the procedures for the settlement of disputes which would not be a logically consistent result.[79]

Amerasinghe seems to be saying that there exists a customary law fork-in-the-road rule similar in effect to Article 27(1) of the ICSID Convention, permitting the use of investor-State and State-State dispute settlement only alternatively. While the policy wisdom of the proposition is evident, it is less obvious that there exists sufficient State practice to justify its existence as a rule of law.

The issue of coordination of State-State and investor-State dispute settlement proceedings could arise only when treaties, traditionally having only the former kind of dispute settlement clauses, started to provide also for investor-State arbitration. The 1959 Abs-Shawcross Draft

---

[77] See discussion on treaty practice at n 97–n 104 and surrounding text.
[78] See discussion at Part IV.C.
[79] Cf Amerasinghe *Diplomatic Protection*, above n 73, 341.

Convention on Investment Abroad provided for both compulsory State-State adjudication and optional investor-State arbitration, without any express attempt made to coordinate these proceedings.[80] The doctrine likewise did not identify the Convention as setting down alternatives, most probably because the very idea of individual-State arbitration was still controversial.[81]

The 1960 and 1967 OECD Draft Conventions on the Protection of Foreign Property similarly provided for compulsory State-State and optional investor-State arbitration. It also coordinated the two by permitting the latter only after the failure of the home State to institute proceedings for six months. More importantly in the present context, the Draft Conventions suspended the investor-State arbitration if the State at some point began its proceedings.[82] However, this rule alternated only investor-State and State-State arbitrations and not investor-State arbitration and diplomatic protection in general,[83] thus leaving the non-adjudicative methods of espousal of the claim unaffected,[84] as the Commentary expressly confirmed regarding the possibility of overlapping claims.[85] In any event, the suspension applied to investor-State proceedings, thus reflecting logic different from that of Article 27(1) of the ICSID Convention. To the extent that the Draft Conventions can be taken into account at least to assess the general perception of certain States and authorities, they do not support the existence of any underlying customary rule.

Since Article 27(1) of the ICSID Convention expressly excludes diplomatic protection, one would expect to find guidance in the Convention itself or its preparatory materials if the rule codified pre-existing customary

---

[80] Note, 'The Proposed Convention to Protect Private Foreign Investment: An Introduction' (1960) 9 *Journal of Public Law* 115, 117. The commentary notes that 'when proceedings are instituted by a national, jurisdiction is conferred exclusively upon the arbitral tribunal', (at 123) without making it clear whether the exclusivity operates *vis-à-vis* State-State adjudication or the domestic remedies in the host State.

[81] Eg G Schwarzenberger, 'The Abs-Shawcross Draft Convention on Investments Abroad: A Critical Commentary' (1960) 9 *Journal of Public Law* 147, 162–163; G Schwarzenberger, *Foreign Investment and International Law* (Stevens & Sons, London, 1969) 124 (criticizing the very idea of granting individual access to arbitration that would undermine the exclusiveness of State's control of the claims); I Seidl-Hohenveldern, 'The Abs-Shawcross Draft Convention to Protect Private Foreign Investment: Comments on the Round Table' (1961) 10 *Journal of Public Law* 100, 109 (noting the broad purpose of depoliticization *inter alia* by individual access); AA Fatouros, 'An International Code to Protect Private Investment-Proposals and Perspectives' (1961) 14 *University of Toronto Law Journal* 77, 97–98 ('private individuals as well as States would be entitled to rights under [the Draft Convention]').

[82] 'OECD Draft Convention on the Protection of Foreign Property' (1963) 2 *International Legal Materials* 241, art 7, 257–258; 'OECD Draft Convention on the Protection of Foreign Property' (1968) 7 *International Legal Materials* 117, art 7, 132–133.

[83] 2006 ILC Articles, above n 71, art 1 ('diplomatic protection consists of the invocation by a State, through diplomatic action or other means of dispute settlement').

[84] Commentary 8(a) to both Draft Conventions explains the right of espousal to consist both of diplomatic and adjudicatory presentation of the claim, and Article 8(c) excludes the suspension when the claim is espoused only through diplomatic channels, 1960 OECD, above n 82, 260–261, Commentary 8(a) and (c); 1967 OECD, above n 82, Commentary 8(a) and (c).

[85] Ibid, 261, Commentary 8 (a) and (c); ibid, 136, Commentary 8 (a) and (c).

law. Interpreting Article 27 according to its ordinary meaning and in its context (in particular the preamble), nothing supports the view that the suspension of diplomatic protection would be a codification. Looking at the negotiations of the ICSID Convention, it appears that Article 27 was not considered to be a codification. The early drafts were not unequivocal, speaking about exclusion of the home State's action as a natural[86] and reasonable concomitant of individual access to arbitration[87] that could be read either in terms of reasonableness of treaty-making or of the rule of general international law behind it. However, Broches expressly and consistently described the rule that was to become Article 27 as an important innovation.[88]

The most relevant discussion took place in the Santiago consultative meeting. The Venezuelan delegate argued that the rule was superfluous since diplomatic protection could only apply if the State had failed to comply with the arbitration agreement with the national,[89] and was supported by the Canadian delegate.[90] The Venezuelan delegate's critique seemed to be part of the broader Latin American scepticism about diplomatic protection.[91] More importantly, Broches responded that the rule would be superfluous provided that the Venezuelan delegate's view was generally shared, but it appeared not to be.[92] In this light, criticism of Article 27 would support its customary nature, while support of Article 27 would support its innovative treaty character. Since no other States supported the view of the Venezuelan and Canadian delegates, State practice of the 1960s is in favour of the view that Article 27 did not codify pre-existing customary law. The *Banro* award's extensive discussion of the balance of investment arbitration and lack of diplomatic protection in the ICSID Convention also supports this conclusion, by emphasizing the uniqueness and innovation of the depoliticizing element of the particular treaty deal.[93]

---

[86] *Convention: Documents,* above n 52, 23–24 (Working Paper in the Form of a Draft Convention, art II (5)), 163–164 (First Preliminary Draft of the Convention).

[87] Ibid, 221–222 (Preliminary Draft of the Convention).

[88] Ibid, 242, 303, 372, 464.

[89] Ibid, 348–349 (Espinosa).

[90] Ibid (Summers).

[91] Ibid (Espinosa, Meneses), see generally DR Shea, *The Calvo Clause* (University of Minnesota Press, Minneapolis, 1955) 19–32; AH Roth, *The Minimum Standard of International Law Applied to Aliens* (A.W. Sijthoff's Uitgeversmaatschappij N.V., Leiden, 1949); OM Garibaldi, 'Carlos Calvo Redivivus: The Rediscovery of Calvo Doctrines in the Era of Investment Treaties' (2006) 3 (5) *Transnational Dispute Management.*

[92] *Convention: Documents,* above n 52, 348–349.

[93] *Banro,* above n 7, 386 (paras 15–23); also *Autopista Concesionada de Venezuela, C.A. v Bolivarian Republic of Venezuela,* ICSID Case No. ARB/00/5, Decision on Jurisdiction, September 27, 2001 (2001) 16 *ICSID Review—Foreign Investment Law Journal* 469, 492 (para 74). Schreuer's discussion of diplomatic protection and investment arbitration implicitly confirms this view, addressing 'remnants of diplomatic protection' only in the ICSID context and not more generally, C Schreuer, 'Investment Protection and International Relations' in A Reinisch and U Kriebaum (eds) *The Law of International Relations: Liber Amicorum Hanspeter Neuhold* (Eleven International Publishing, Utrecht, 2009) 345, 347–348; similarly Dolzer and Schreuer, above n 69, 213.

Article 27 does not appear to have contributed to a subsequent emergence of such a rule. States have not invoked it as reflecting customary law. The fact that States have not engaged in diplomatic protection of investments covered by investment treaties containing an investor-State arbitration clause does not contradict this conclusion. Diplomatic protection is a right and not an obligation;[94] thus one would have to show that the abstention has followed from a feeling of legal obligation.[95]

There are at least two ways in which the argument could be made on the basis of treaty practice, relying either on the exclusion of diplomatic protection or the coordination of dispute settlement proceedings. There is considerable controversy whether and in what way investment protection treaties can contribute to customary law;[96] however, there is no reason of principle why a sufficiently general and consistent treaty practice of suspension of diplomatic protection could not give rise to a customary rule of such a nature. A review of BITs conducted at the beginning of the 1990s concluded that 32 out of about 400 BITs included rules modelled on Article 27 addressing ICSID arbitration.[97] A number of recent Model BITs may be considered as reflective of the broader trends in investment treaty-making[98] and a demonstration of the views of the States regarding the preferable content of investment protection rules. From 34 Model BITs formulated from 1991 to 2007, five BITs prohibit diplomatic protection during investment arbitration in general (Italy, Kenya, Bolivia, Mongolia, Chile),[99] four BITs prohibit diplomatic protection during ICSID investment arbitration (Malaysia, Switzerland, UK, Germany),[100] and 25 BITs do not address the issue at all (Norway, US, Canada, India, Ghana, Romania, Uganda, Guatemala, Burkina Faso, Benin, Burundi, Mauritius, Sweden, Thailand, Greece, Finland, Denmark, Peru, Turkey, France,

---

[94] *Barcelona Traction, Light and Power Company, Limited, (New Application: 1962) (Second Phase)* [1970] ICJ Rep 3, 44 (paras 78–79). Even under contemporary international law, the ILC could not agree to do anything more than recommend States to consider the exercise of diplomatic protection, 2006 ILC Articles, above n 71, art 19.

[95] *The Case of the S.S. "Lotus"* [1927] Series A No 10 1, 28.

[96] Eg R Baxter, 'Treaties and Custom' (1970) 129 *Recueil des Cours* 25, 80–91; RY Jennings, 'What is International Law and How Do We Tell It When We See It?', in *Collected Writings of Sir Robert Jennings* (Volume 2, Kluwer Law International, the Hague, 1998) 730, 736; M Mendelson, 'The Formation of Customary International Law' (1998) 272 *Recueil des Cours* 155, 329–330; S Schwebel, 'The Influence of Bilateral Investment Treaties on Customary International Law' (2004) 98 *ASIL Proceedings* 27, 27–30.

[97] P Peters, 'Dispute Settlement Arrangements in Investment Treaties' (1991) 22 *Netherlands Yearbook of International Law* 91, 145–146.

[98] Douglas, above n 45, 159.

[99] Respectively 2003 Italian Model BIT art X(5); 2003 Kenya Model BIT 10(d); Bolivia Model BIT, *International Investment Instruments: A Compendium* (Volume X, United Nations, New York, 2002) 275, 284, art 10(3); 1998 Mongolia Model BIT art 8(6); 1994 Chile Model BIT art 8(6). A similar rule was also included in the 1986 Asian-African Legal Consultative Committee Revised Draft of Model Agreements for Promotion and Protection of Investments Model A art 10(vi), Model B art 10(vi). Unless otherwise indicated, the BITs are available at <http://www.unctadxi.org/templates/DocSearch_780.aspx> (last accessed 28 February 2009).

[100] Respectively 1998 Malaysia Model BIT art 10(4); 1995 Switzerland Model BIT art 8(4); 1991 UK Model BIT art 8(4); 1991 Germany Model BIT art 10(6).

Croatia, South Africa, Germany, Netherlands, China).[101] To the extent that the Model BITs accurately reflect broader practice, they do not support a creation of a new customary law rule. The multilateral treaties providing for formalized dispute settlement between States also reflect the same kind of thinking, not providing for express exclusion of State dispute settlement during investor-State arbitration.[102]

While exclusion of diplomatic protection from all cases of investment arbitration is the policy that some States follow,[103] it is a practice of only a small minority of States and therefore is not sufficiently widespread to create a customary rule. The divergences do not follow North-South divisions, as each approach is reflected in the practice of both developed and developing States. The exclusion of diplomatic protection in ICSID cases does not contribute to customary law, because it only superfluously restates the anyway binding Article 27, *a contrario* implying that diplomatic protection is not excluded in non-ICSID arbitrations. The coordination of investor-State dispute settlement proceedings in investment protection treaties is also not sufficiently quantitatively widespread and qualitatively uniform, and in any event would be directed only at the adjudicative methods of dispute settlement and would not affect other methods of espousal.[104] To conclude, there is no practice that would support the existence of customary law analogous to Article 27 and applicable to all investment arbitrations.

The First Rapporteur on Diplomatic Protection Bennouna suggested, in light of his broader criticism of the fiction of diplomatic protection as a protection of the State's rights,[105] that the existence of an internationally available remedy meant that the fiction could be dispensed with and

---

[101] Respectively 2007 Norway Model BIT; 2004 US Model BIT; 2004 Canada Model BIT; 2003 India Model BIT; 2003 Ghana Model BIT; Romania Model BIT in UNCTAD, *International Investment Instruments: A Compendium* (Volume XIII, United Nations, New York, 2005) 287; Uganda Model BIT in UNCTAD, *International Investment Instruments: A Compendium* (Volume XII, United Nations, New York, 2003) 313; Guatemala Model BIT, ibid, 292–293; Burkina Faso Model BIT in UNCTAD, *International Investment Instruments: A Compendium* (Volume X, United Nations, New York, 2002) 287; Benin Model BIT; Mauritius Model BIT; 2002 Sweden Model BIT; 2002 Thailand Model BIT; 2001 Greece Model BIT; 2001 Finland Model BIT; 2000 Denmark Model BIT; 2000 Peru Model BIT; 2000 Turkey Model BIT; 1999 France Model BIT; 1998 Croatia Model BIT; 1998 South Africa Model BIT; 1998 Germany Model BIT art 10; 1998 US Model BIT (1994 revised); 1998 Netherlands Model BIT; 1994 China Model BIT; 1994 US Model BIT.

[102] Energy Charter Treaty, 17 December 1994, 2080 UNTS 95 (entered into force 16 April 1998), art 27(2); North American Free Trade Agreement (1993) 32 *International Legal Materials* 612, 694, art 2004.

[103] UNCTAD, *Bilateral Investment Treaties 1995–2006; Trends in Investment Law-Making*, (United Nations, New York, 2007) 118–119.

[104] Peters, above n 97, 116–117; W Ben Hamida, 'L'arbitrage État-investisseur face à un désordre procédural: la concurrence des procédures et les conflits juridictions' (2005) 51 *Annuaire français de droit international* 564, 575–577; CH Schreuer, *The ICSID Convention: A Commentary* (Cambridge University Press, Cambridge, 2001) 402–405.

[105] M Bennouna, 'La protection diplomatique, un droit de l'État?' in *Boutros Boutros-Ghali Amicorum discipulorumque liber* (Bruylant, Bruxelles, 1998) 245–250.

the home State's exercise of diplomatic protection put aside.[106] The argument did not receive much support in the ILC at that point.[107] Juliane Kokott in her 2002 Report to the International Law Association[108] and the Second Rapporteur on Diplomatic Protection Dugard in his Fourth Report argued that the invocation of BIT or ICSID procedures clearly excluded diplomatic protection,[109] and the 2004 ILC Draft Articles on Diplomatic Protection adopted in the first reading stated that the invocation of BIT and ICSID dispute resolution clauses excluded diplomatic protection at least in most cases.[110] The 2006 ILC Articles excluded the sentence and adopted a more nuanced position, maintaining diplomatic protection to the extent that it was not incompatible with investment protection rules.[111]

At the end of the day, whether the right protected is that of the individual or that of the State, the right to exercise diplomatic protection is a

---

[106] M Bennouna, *First Report on Diplomatic Protection* A/CN.4/484, para 40. It is not clear whether (now Judge) Bennouna's argument only explained the policy behind the ICSID system or made a broader legal argument regarding all investment arbitrations. The express reference to ICSID arbitration (ibid, para 39) and the description of local remedies and diplomatic protection as being put aside (a rule characteristic to ICSID arbitration) supports the former view. If Judge Bennouna instead intended to make the latter and broader point, the *LaGrand* judgment supports the contrary view that the existence of an individual right does not preclude a State's rights to espouse them before an international court, *LaGrand Case (Germany v US)* [2001] ICJ Rep 466, 482 (para 42). While the *Avena* judgment is less clear, finding the particular claim to be interdependent (mixed) and not one of diplomatic protection, *Case Concerning Avena and Other Mexican Nationals (Mexico v US)* [2004] ICJ Rep 12, 35 (para 40), it does not suggest that individual rights cannot be protected by diplomatic protection (cf Separate Opinion of Judge Veresschetin, 79 (paras 1–13), Separate Opinion of Judge Parra-Arranguren, 84, 88 (paras 16–28), Separate Opinion of Judge Tomka, 94 (paras 2–13), Separate Opinion of Judge *ad hoc* Sépulveda, 99, 104 (paras 16–24)); the contrary suggestion by Vice-President Ranjeva appears to be motivated by an overly rigorous view of what exhaustion of local remedies would require, Declaration, 75, 77 (paras 8–13).
[107] *Yearbook of the ILC* 1998 *Vol. I* A/CN.4/SER.A/1998 8, para 37 (Lukashuk), 27, paras 13–14 (Al-Khasawneh), 28, paras 18, 21 (Pellet).
[108] J Kokott, 'Interim Report on "The Role of Diplomatic Protection in the Field of the Protection of Foreign Investment"' in *Report of the Seventieth ILA Conference* (ILA, London, 2002) 265.
[109] J Dugard, *Fourth Report on Diplomatic Protection*, A/CN.4/530/Add.1, para 108.
[110] ILC, 2004 'Draft Articles on Diplomatic Protection with Commentaries' in *Official Records of the General Assembly, Sixty-First Session, Supplement No.10* (A/59/10) 89. The only authority on which the commentary relies is Article 27(1) of the ICSID Convention, so the Commission's position is not without ambiguity: Article 27(1) would exclude diplomatic protection in *all* (and not just most) cases when ICSID arbitration is invoked, while in other cases it would be up to the interpretation of particular treaties and arbitration rules to identify the exclusion (unless the Commission *sub silentio* considered Article 27(1) to reflect customary law). Lowenfeld makes a similar argument in his separate opinion in the *Corn Products* decision on responsibility, stating that '[i]n return for agreeing to independent international arbitration, the host state is assured that the state of the investor's nationality (as defined) will not espouse the investor's claim or otherwise intervene in the controversy between an investor and a host state, for instance by denying foreign assistance or attempting to pressure the host state into some kind of settlement,' *Corn Products*, Separate Opinion of Arbitrator Lowenfeld, above n 49, para 1. It is not clear what the source of the assurance of the host State would be: apart from Article 27(1) of the ICSID Convention, investment protection treaties rarely exclude the home State's rights of protection. In NAFTA cases, the express exclusion will not come into play in any arbitration as long as Canada and Mexico are not parties to the ICSID Convention.
[111] 2006 ILC Articles, above n 71, art 17.

right of the State.[112] States are entitled to waive or suspend the exercise of diplomatic protection by treaties (as they have done in the ICSID Convention), by customary law rules or by unilateral acts, but in the absence of a normatively determinable expression of the State's will the laudable goal of coordination of investment dispute settlement mechanisms is not a sufficient reason to presume a tacit waiver. To paraphrase the passage regarding exhaustion of local remedies from the *Elettronica Sicula S.p.A.* case of the International Court of Justice:

> the parties to a treaty can therein either agree that the [right to exercise diplomatic protection] shall not apply to claims based on alleged breaches of that treaty; or confirm that it shall apply. Yet the Chamber finds itself unable to accept that an important principle of customary international law should be held to have been tacitly dispensed with, in the absence of any words making clear an intention to do so.[113]

The point made regarding exhaustion of local remedies in the exercise of diplomatic protection *a fortiori* applies to the right to exercise diplomatic protection itself. Indeed, both within the context of investment dispute settlement and more generally, the proliferation of courts and tribunals has created situations when the same dispute or different facets of the same dispute can be brought before different tribunals.[114] The existence of the parallel right to diplomatic protection and investment arbitration is in that sense not an aberration but a natural element of an increasingly multifaceted international legal order.

C. Diplomatic protection excluded by investor's invocation of State responsibility

Even if one accepts the lack of treaty or customary law that would suspend the exercise of diplomatic protection, it could be said that these arguments are not determinative. Since the first investment protection treaties with investor-State arbitration clauses appeared only after the drafting of the ICSID Convention, the premise of the negotiators was that the

---

[112] Eg A Pellet, 'The Second Death of Euripide Mavrommatis? Notes on the International Law Commission's Draft Articles on Diplomatic Protection' (2008) 7 *Law and Practice of International Courts and Tribunals* 33, 33–58; C Dominicé, 'Regard actuel sur la protection diplomatique' in *Liber amicorum Claude Reymond, Autour de l'arbitrage* (Litec, Paris, 2004) 73, 77–79; G Gaja, 'Droits des États et droits des individus dans le cadre de la protection diplomatique' in J-F Flauss (ed) *La protection diplomatique* (Nemesis et Bruylant, Bruxelles, 2003) 63; F Orego Vicuña, *International Dispute Settlement in an Evolving Global Society* (Cambridge University Press, Cambridge, 2004) 31–33; 2006 ILC Articles, above n 71, 26.

[113] *Elettronica Sicula S.p.A. (ELSI) (US v Italy)* [1989] ICJ Rep 15, 42 (para 50); also *Maffezini v Spain*, ICSID Case No. ARB/97/7, Decisions on Objections to Jurisdiction, January 25, 2000, (2001) 16 *ICSID Review—Foreign Investment Law Journal* 207, 220 (para 22).

[114] Eg Y Shany, *The Competing Jurisdictions of International Courts and Tribunals* (Oxford University Press, Oxford, 2003); Y Shany, 'Contract Claims v Treaty Claims: Mapping Conflicts between ICSID Decisions on Multi-Sourced Investment Claims' (2005) 99 *American Journal of International Law* 835.

State's consent would be contained in a different instrument from that containing the substantive rules of international law. This approach would accurately reflect the consent given in a contract or an investment law but not one in an investment protection treaty. Consequently, it is necessary to consider the legal implications of the emergent investor's treaty rights on the State's rights.

Douglas has argued that investment arbitration cannot be conceptualized merely as a reinforced right of diplomatic protection, because of its qualitatively different nature (*inter alia* because of the functional control that the investor enjoys over the claim, the absence of exhaustion of domestic remedies requirement even in non-ICSID cases and the calculation of damages by reference to the investor's damages).[115] Of direct relevance to the present analysis is his conclusion that because the investor's rights are direct rights, the substantive investment protection rules should be excluded from applying to State-State legal relations:

The contracting states to investment treaties have legislated for a new legal regime or sub-system to define the legal consequences that follow a violation of the minimum standards of treatment towards a qualified investment. In relation to the investor/state sphere, a breach of a treaty standard by the host state certainly creates new obligations upon that state. But these new obligations do not correspond to new rights of the national state of the investor because the injury is caused exclusively to the investor. This is so because the contracting states have opted out of the *inter*-state secondary rules of state responsibility in relation to a limited group of wrongs causing damage to a particular sphere of private interests. The national state of the investor thus has no immediate secondary rights within the investment treaty regime to challenge the commission of this breach of treaty; instead the new rights arising upon the breach of treaty vest directly in the investor.[116]

If Douglas' argument is correct, then the home State would not be entitled to engage in diplomatic protection over breaches of primary rules addressing the standards of treatment of investors and investment, because the implementation of those rules would have been carved out from the *lex generalis* and could be implemented solely through the *lex specialis* regime of investor arbitration. At the same time, the argument is problematic on a number of levels. A more persuasive conceptualization would be to consider the investor's rights and remedies as complimenting and not excluding the State's rights and remedies. As Pellet stated in the 1998 ILC debate, 'diplomatic protection ... operated in ... areas ... such as the protection of private economic interests, where it existed side by side with other mechanisms like ICSID, which gave private individuals direct access to international law.'[117]

First of all, in general terms, to the extent that the 2001 ILC Articles on State responsibility accurately reflect customary international law,

---

[115] Douglas, above n 45, 167–184.
[116] Ibid, 190–191.
[117] *Yearbook of the ILC 1998*, above n 107, 28, para 18.

there is no inevitability in excluding the responsibility owed to other States if it accrues to non-State entities. Article 33(2) provides a without prejudice clause to rights arising out of international responsibility of the State which may accrue to non-State entities.[118] The 'without prejudice' language avoids the negative inference that such rights may not accrue,[119] but it does not require a superimposition of these rights on top of the rights existing for States under the law of State responsibility.[120] The commentary expressly refers to investment agreements as one example of primary rules owed to a non-State entity that can be directly invoked by it.[121] The Fifth Special Rapporteur Crawford has pointed out that 'the secondary obligations arising from a breach may be owed directly to the beneficiary of the obligation, in this case the investor, who effectively opts in to the situation as a secondary right holder by commencing arbitral proceedings under the treaty.'[122] It is difficult to discern any opt-out by the States from their right to claim responsibility; the language used by Crawford suggests precisely the opposite process.

Secondly, with all due caution, both the 2001 ILC Articles on State responsibility and the ILC Draft Articles on Responsibility of International Organizations have addressed the plurality of injured States[123] and international organizations in terms of each State or international organization being entitled to claim responsibility.[124] This shows at the very least that the idea of parallel invocation of responsibility for the breach of the same primary rule is not alien to the international law of responsibility. As the International Court pragmatically observed in *Reparation for Injuries Suffered in the Service of United Nations* advisory opinion regarding the concurrency of claims by the UN and States, there was 'no rule of law which assigns priority to the one or to the other, or which compels either the State or the Organization to refrain from bringing an international

---

[118] 2001 ILC Articles on State responsibility, above n 13, 94.

[119] J Crawford, 'The ILC's Articles on Responsibility of States for Internationally Wrongful Acts: A Retrospect' (2002) 96 *American Journal of International Law* 874, 887.

[120] Discussion in the ILC showed concern about not prejudicing individual rights, *Yearbook of the ILC* 2000, above n 68, 15, para 33 (Gaja), 28, para 17 (Crawford), 73, para 14 (Simma), 74, para 19 (Crawford), 78, para 52 (Kamto), 84, para 46 (Badan), 85, para 51 (Tomka), 91, para 26 (Kabatsi).

[121] 2001 ILC Articles on State responsibility, above n 13, 95.

[122] Crawford 'Retrospect', above n 119, 888; similarly J Crawford, 'Treaty and Contract in Investment Arbitration' (2009) 6 (1) *Transnational Dispute Management* 5–6.

[123] 2001 ILC Articles on State responsibility, above n 13, art 46; J Crawford, *The International Law Commission's Articles on State Responsibility: Introduction, Text and Commentaries* (Cambridge University Press, Cambridge, 2002) 45–56. The preference for plurality is confirmed in the opposite scenario of the law of responsibility regarding multiplicity of responsible States, 2001 ILC Articles on State responsibility, above n 13, art 47; cf C Chinkin, 'The Continuing Occupation? Issues of Joint and Several Liability and Effective Control' in P Shiner and A Williams (eds) *The Iraq War and International Law* (Hart Publishing, Oxford, 2008) 161, 168–179 and S Talmon, 'A Plurality of Responsible Actors: International Responsibility for Acts of the Coalition Provisional Authority in Iraq', at 185, 209–216.

[124] ILC, 'Draft Articles on Responsibility of International Organizations' in *Official Records of the General Assembly, Sixtieth Session, Supplement No.10 (A/63/10)* 291, art 50 and Commentary; G Gaja, *Sixth Report on the Responsibility of International Organisations* A/CN.4/597, para 24.

claim. The Court sees no reason why the parties concerned should not find solutions inspired by goodwill and common sense.'[125] Since the grain of thinking in the law of responsibility appears to be in favour of parallelism of responsibility, the argument for exclusiveness should bear the burden of explaining why investment protection diverges from this path.[126]

Thirdly, in historical terms, diplomatic protection on the basis of Friendship, Commerce and Navigation Treaties and subsequently BITs has long been the central element of investment treaty dispute settlement mechanisms and was confirmed by the International Court in the *ELSI* case.[127] It would be a rather odd result if by supplementing the classic treaty models with the untested investor-State arbitration option, States had lost all rights to diplomatic protection by tacitly opting out of the State-State responsibility regime. It would also raise the question about the rationale for continued inclusion in BITs of broadly worded State-State dispute settlement clauses, which would now have very limited if any legal effect (a questionable conclusion in terms of treaty interpretation and the principle of effectiveness). Finally, it would also mean that for the last third of the last century, from the first investor-State arbitration clauses in BITs to the relatively recent appreciation by investors of

---

[125] [1949] ICJ Rep 174, 184–186.

[126] The *Barcelona Traction* judgment relied on multiplicity of claims as one of the reasons to reject the general right of diplomatic protection of shareholders, *Barcelona Traction*, above n 94, 49 (paras 97–98). However, the Court distinguished the *Reparation for Injuries* parallel protection by States and international organizations, both in legal terms as involving two separate basis of protection, at 38 (para 53) and in pragmatic terms as normally involving clearly identifiable few protectors, at 50 (para 98). The parallelism of investor-State and State-State claims seems closer to the *Reparation for Injuries* paradigm. It involves the invocation of responsibility by different types of entities, and not *inter se* within a particular regime, L Caflisch, 'The Protection of Corporate Investments Abroad in the Light of the Barcelona Traction Case' (1971) 31 *Zeitschrift für ausländisches öffentliches Recht und Völkerrecht* 161, 191. The number of potential claimant States and investors due to corporate structuring and broad *ratione personae* coverage of investment protection treaties may indeed be large and not immediately identifiable. Still, the legally uncontroversial existence of a multiplicity of claimants in investor-States proceedings suggests that a similar multiplicity of claimant States would not go against the grain of the particular area of law. In any event, to apply *mutatis mutandis* Judge Fitzmaurice's argument, 'once the principle of claims ... had been admitted for such circumstances, it would not be difficult to work out ways of avoiding a multiplicity of *proceedings,* which is what would really matter', *Barcelona Traction,* above n 94, Separate Opinion of Judge Fitzmaurice, 64, 77 (fn 21) (emphasis in the original); also Separate Opinion of Judge Jessup, 161, 199 (paras 66–72); Dissenting Opinion of Judge Riphagen, 334, 350 (para 22); Higgins, above n 39, 339. Article 27(1) of the ICSID Convention and the existing treaty practice shows the ease with which 'ways of avoiding multiplicity of proceedings' by investors and States may be worked out, see preceding discussion at n 76 and n 99 and surrounding text.

[127] Eg RR Wilson, 'Postwar Commercial Treaties of the United States' (1949) 43 *American Journal of International Law* 262; RR Wilson, 'Property-Protection Provisions in United States Commercial Treaties' (1951) 45 *American Journal of International Law* 83; RR Wilson, 'Access-to-Courts Provisions in United States Commercial Treaties' (1953) 47 *American Journal of International Law* 20; H Walker, 'Provisions on Companies in United States Commercial Treaties' (1956) 50 *American Journal of International Law* 373; KJ Vandevelde, 'A Brief History of International Investment Agreements' (2005–2006) 12 *U C Davis Journal of International Law and Policy* 157, 157–184; ELSI, above n 113, 42 (paras 50, 52), see generally B Stern, 'La protection diplomatique des investissements internationaux: de Barcelona Traction à Elettronica Sicula ou les glissements progressifs de l'analyse' (1990) 117 *Journal du droit international* 897.

their practical impact, host State responsibility for breaches of the treaties could never have been invoked in any legally permissible way.

Fourthly, the total exclusion of States' rights would produce curious results in practice. The State would be prevented from protecting investors who do not consent to arbitration (eg because of threats by the host State or insufficient monetary resources) in a dispute where the home State sees an important principle that needs to be arbitrated. It is also not entirely clear how the opt-out from State responsibility would operate in situations where some but not all substantive rules are excluded from investor-State arbitration despite being binding for the State. If the implication of the position is that the State is entitled to invoke responsibility to the extent that the investor is not, different *ratione materiae* limitations to the arbitral jurisdiction could lead to odd results.[128]

Fifthly, in comparative terms, it may be instructive to consider the position of human rights bodies, the other example apart from investment treaties given in the ILC commentary to Article 33. The systems under the International Covenant on Civil and Political Rights and the European Convention of Human Rights (ECHR) include procedures for both State-State and individual-State complaints. Even though the former procedure has not been utilized,[129] the practice of inter-State complaints under the ECHR, regarding both cases where the interest is abstract and particularly where States have special interests,[130] could be read to support the general tendency in international law to permit parallel invocation of responsibility.[131]

---

[128] The Soviet-era BITs sometimes limit the investor's rights to claim to the remedial consequences of expropriation, eg *RosInvestCo UK Ltd. v Federation of Russia,* SCC V 079/2005, Award on Jurisdiction, November 2008, <http://ita.law.uvic.ca/documents/RosInvestjurisdiction_decision_2007_10.pdf> (last accessed 28 February 2009), paras 105–123. In this case (and disregarding the MFN aspect), if one follows Douglas' argument, the UK would arguably have been entitled to espouse the claim regarding the existence of expropriation but precluded to do so regarding the claim of compensation. While it could be said that the jurisdiction over responsibility is implicit in the jurisdiction over dispute (R Higgins, 'Issues of State Responsibility before the ICJ' in M Fitzmaurice and D Sarooshi (eds) *Issues of State Responsibility before International Judicial Institutions* (Hart Publishing, Oxford, 2004) 1, 3) and the tribunal would have had jurisdiction to rule on the wrongfulness of expropriation, the 'slicing' of the jurisdiction raises controversial issues in this context that could be evaded if the State's rights of invocation are deemed not to be affected at all.

[129] S Joseph, J Schutlz and M Castan, *The International Covenant on Civil and Political Rights* (2nd edn, Oxford University Press, Oxford, 2004) 21.

[130] Eg L Zwaak, 'General Survey of the European Convention' in P van Dijk et al, *Theory and Practice of the European Convention on Human Rights* (4th edn, Intersentia, Antwerpen, 2006) 47–51; in particular *Greece v UK* (App no 175/56 and 299/57) App no 175/56 and 299/57 Yearbook II 182 and 186; *Austria v Italy* (App no 788/60) (1961) Yearbook IV 161; *Ireland v UK* (App no 5310/71 and 5451/72) (1978) A 25, para 159; *Cyprus v Turkey* (App no 25781/94) (2001) Reports of Judgments and Decisions 2001-IV.

[131] Eg the cases on the responsibility of Turkey for the acts of the Turkish Republic of Northern Cyprus respectively from the individual and the home State's perspective, *Loizidou v Turkey* [GC] (App no 15318/89) (1996) Reports of Judgments and Decisions 1996-VI; *Cyprus v Turkey,* ibid; cf *Yearbook of the ILC 1998,* above n 107, 27, para 10 (Brownlie). While the respondent States objected to the jurisdiction of the Court, they did not argue that the existence of individual-State procedural avenues made the State-State claims impermissible (*Cyprus v Turkey*, ibid, paras 59–104, *Ireland v UK*, ibid), and this may be read as State practice to support the permissible parallelism of the individual

Finally, such a conceptualization seems more favourable to Douglas' broader thesis that concepts from diplomatic protection should not be lightly read into investment arbitration law. If investment arbitration has replaced diplomatic protection, one may reasonably wonder whether at least certain concepts of *lex generalis* do not remain relevant in informing, structuring and explaining the *lex specialis*.[132] However, if diplomatic protection maintains its parallel and conceptually distinct autonomous existence, there is no necessity for integration and synthesis. Therefore, it would seem that the legal entitlement to engage in diplomatic protection has not disappeared, even if for pragmatic reasons of efficiency the exercise of diplomatic protection has faded into the background.[133]

D. Diplomatic protection excluded by investment protection *law as* lex specialis

If the premise of Douglas' argument is that investment arbitration occupies a very different legal space from diplomatic protection, the ILC work on diplomatic protection arrived at the opposite conclusion that investment arbitration is a special rule *vis-à-vis* the general rule of diplomatic protection. This section will discuss the ILC debates on the issue and the validity of the *lex specialis* argument.

The ILC approach changed a number of times, fluctuating from Dugard's argument for diplomatic protection as parallel to investment arbitration to the argument for diplomatic protection as conflicting with investment arbitration. The ambiguity may be caused by a lack of clear distinction between an argument of interpretation and an argument of *lex specialis*. From the perspective of interpretation, the question is whether the law of diplomatic protection is relevant to the interpretation of the law of investment arbitration, effectively dealing with the scope of Article 31(3)(c) of the Vienna Convention on the Law of Treaties (VCLT)[134] (eg should the continuous nationality rule from diplomatic protection law be implied in investment arbitration).[135] From the perspective of *lex specialis*,

---

and State claims. This view is in line with Judge Fitzmaurice's discussion of 'non-exhaustion of the domestic remedies that might have been available to the affected persons acting individually' that he found to be potentially (although not ultimately) problematic for the domestic remedies, without even mentioning any relevance for the State's rights of the right for 'the affected persons acting individually', *Ireland v UK*, ibid, Separate Opinion of Judge Fitzmaurice, para 9.

[132]   Report of the Study Group of the ILC, 'Fragmentation of International Law: Difficulties Arising from Diversification and Expansion of International Law', above n 51, para 100.

[133]   *Diallo*, above n 10, para 88.

[134]   C McLachlan, 'The Principle of Systemic Integration and Article 31(3)(c) of the Vienna Convention' (2005) 54 *International and Comparative Law Quarterly* 279; R Gardiner, *Treaty Interpretation* (Oxford University Press, Oxford, 2008) 250–290. Report of the Study Group of the ILC, 'Fragmentation of International Law: Difficulties Arising from Diversification and Expansion of International Law', above n 51, para 2.

[135]   M Mendelson, 'Runaway Train: The "Continuous Nationality" Rule from the *Panavezys-Saldutiskis Railway* case to *Loewen*' in T Weiler (ed) *International Investment Law and Arbitration: Leading*

the question is whether the existence or invocation of investment arbitration within a treaty excludes the existence or invocation of a parallel and autonomous right of diplomatic protection. There is some superficial similarity between these two questions about the relationship of treaty and customary law, but there is a conceptual difference between applying diplomatic protection law as part of the applicable law for the interpretation of the treaty and excluding diplomatic protection law as the inapplicable *lex generalis*. The first argument goes to the content of the law of investment arbitration, while the second argument goes to the availability of the law of diplomatic protection.

Dugard's First Report addressed the latter aspect and endorsed the parallel existence, clearly distinguishing the pragmatic reasons for not exercising diplomatic protection and the existing legal right to do so:

Nor is [the State] obliged to abstain from exercising that right when the individual enjoys a remedy under a human rights or foreign investment treaty. In practice a State will no doubt refrain from asserting its right of diplomatic protection while the injured national pursues his international remedy. Or it may, where possible, join the individual in the assertion of his right under the treaty in question [the footnote refers to European Court of Human Rights (ECtHR) cases]. But in principle a State is not obliged to exercise such restraint as its *own* right is violated when its national is unlawfully injured.[136]

The Fourth Report concentrated on the former aspect, concluding that the investment arbitration law is *lex specialis* and as such will not be influenced by diplomatic protection law, but also appeared to draw somewhat questionable conclusions regarding the parallel existence of diplomatic protection.[137] The Fifth Report returned to the analytical clarity of the First Report, providing a persuasive policy rationale that:

Diplomatic protection, bilateral investment treaties and human rights treaties are all mechanisms designed to protect persons who have suffered injury as a result of an internationally wrongful act. They are meant to complement and support each other in the pursuit of this goal. The present articles should make it clear that these regimes are not in competition or exclusive of each other.[138]

The subsequent documents show a degree of confusion between the questions of interpretation and conflict of law. The Draft Articles adopted in first reading in 2004 contained a without prejudice clause for other remedies and procedures in Article 17, but also included Article 18 which

---

Cases from the ICSID, NAFTA, Bilateral Treaties and Customary International Law (Cameron May, London, 2005) 97.

[136] J Dugard, *First Report on Diplomatic Protection*, A/CN.4/506, para 74 (emphasis in the original).
[137] See Part III.B.
[138] J Dugard, *Fifth Report on Diplomatic Protection*, A/CN.4/538 20–21, para 44. Guinea (Pellet) presented a similar argument in the *Diallo* case: 'les deux institutions (de la protection diplomatique, d'une part, et de l'action directe des actionnaires, d'autre part) sont sous-tendues par la même considération fondamentale: l'impossibilité de laisser sans aucun espoir de protection les actionnaires étrangers de la société nationale d'un Etat auteur d'un fait internationalement illicite', *Diallo*, above n 10, <http://www.icj-cij.org/docket/files/103/13503.pdf> (last accessed 28 February 2009), 37 (para 11).

stated that '[t]he present draft articles do not apply where, and to the extent that, they are inconsistent with special treaty provisions, including those concerning the settlement of disputes between corporations or share-holders of a corporation and States.'[139] According to the Chairman of the Drafting Committee, the new Article 18 reflected the prevailing view that the relationship of diplomatic protection with investment protection was unlike the parallelism that existed in the human rights context. Rather, the relationship between the two was of a *lex specialis* nature, so that there was a need to focus on the obligation to resort to treaty procedures which would prevail to the extent that recourse to diplomatic protection was not excluded altogether.[140]

At the same time, Dugard's Seventh Report came closer to his earlier approach of parallel existence than to the 2004 ILC Articles, emphasizing that rules on diplomatic protection 'do not interfere with bilateral and multilateral treaties that may include different rules relating to the treat-ment of both individual and corporate investors'.[141] Article 17 of the 2006 ILC Articles provides, in rather similar terms to the old Article 18, that '[t]he present draft articles do not apply to the extent that they are incon-sistent with special rules of international law, such as treaty provisions for the protection of investments'. The commentary is unclear whether dip-lomatic protection is excluded, noting the practical advantages to the indi-viduals of investment arbitration and suggesting (in terms rather similar to those employed by Dugard) that the articles do not apply 'to the alternative special regime for the protection of foreign investors'.[142]

The 2006 ILC Articles reflect a compromise between Dugard's initial position and the 2004 ILC Articles. While the sentence on the general exclusion of diplomatic protection has been dropped and it is stated that the law of diplomatic protection 'does not influence' special regimes (rather than the latter excluding the former), the early emphasis on parallelism of differ-ent mechanisms does not reappear, and the special regimes are described as 'alternative'. The ILC articles do not necessarily have to be accepted at face value as accurate statements of international law,[143] and the International Court's increasingly cautious attitude towards the drafts is reflective of this careful approach.[144] The apparent problem with the ILC's argument is

---

[139] ILC, 'Title and Text of the Draft Articles Adopted by the Drafting Committee on the First Reading' A/CN.4/L.647, art 17.

[140] Diplomatic Protection: Statement of the Chairman of the Drafting Commitee, Mr. Rodriguez-Cedeño, <http://untreaty.un.org/ilc/sessions/56/Diplomatic_protection_statement_final.pdf> (last accessed 28 February 2009) 27–30.

[141] J Dugard, *Seventh Report on Diplomatic Protection,* A/CN.4/567, para 88.

[142] 2006 ILC Articles, above n 71, 89–90.

[143] DD Caron, 'The ILC Articles on State Responsibility: The Paradoxical Relationship between Form and Authority' (2002) 96 *American Journal of International Law* 857; F Berman, 'The ILC and its Relationship with the Sixth Committee' (2006) 49 *German Yearbook of International Law* 107, 127 fn 74; A Pellet, 'Article 38' in A Zimmermann, C Tomuschat and K Oellers-Frahm (eds) *The Statute of the International Court of Justice: A Commentary* (Oxford University Press, Oxford, 2006) 792.

[144] In the *Genocide* case, the Court did not decide on the customary law nature of Article 5 of the 2001 ILC Articles on State responsibility, *Case Concerning the Application of the Convention on the*

that it does not lead very far, since to say that diplomatic protection does not apply to the extent that it is excluded is only to point to the obvious solution in a conflict between custom and treaty.[145] In a sense, it begs the *a priori* question about the unarticulated assumption that there *is* a possibility of a conflict, without giving any indication whether, how and to what extent diplomatic protection can be inconsistent with investment protection.

For diplomatic protection and investment protection to be in the relationship of general and special rules, they would first of all have to address the same subject-matter[146] and there should be actual inconsistency or a discernible intention to exclude the other rules.[147] While it may be said that the subject matter is *grosso modo* the same in the sense of dealing with State responsibility for breaches of investment protection obligation, the particular rules are importantly different: diplomatic protection is a State's right to invoke State responsibility, while investment arbitration is an individual's right to invoke State responsibility.[148] As was argued above, the rules on the suspension of diplomatic protection in Article 27 of the ICSID Convention and the BIT practice suggest that the State's and investor's rights to invoke responsibility are in principle autonomous and distinct. Whether one takes the view that the investor's *rights* are direct or derivative,[149] the practice of express coordination strongly indicates the view of States that the *invocation* of responsibility is in principle autonomous and possible in parallel.[150]

Prevention and Punishment of the Crime of Genocide (Bosnia and Herzegovina v Serbia and Montenegro) [2007] ICJ Rep <http://www.icj-cij.org/docket/files/91/13685.pdf> (last accessed 28 February 2009), para 414, an approach evidencing extreme caution because the Court had earlier seemed to approve the customary nature of this Article in the *Congo v Uganda* case, see *Case Concerning Armed Activities on the Territory of the Congo (Democratic Republic of the Congo v Uganda)* [2005] ICJ Rep <http://www.icj-cij.org/docket/files/116/10455.pdf> (last accessed 28 February 2009), para 160. In the *Diallo* case, the Court did not decide on the customary law nature of Article 11 (b) of the 2006 ILC Articles, *Diallo,* above n 10, para 39, paras 91–93.

[145] Y Dinstein, 'The Interaction between Customary International Law and Treaties' (2006) 322 *Recueil des Cours* 243, 404–407.

[146] Pauwelyn *Conflict*, above n 51, 364–366, 389.

[147] ILC 2001 Articles, above n 13, art 55, Commentary 4.

[148] Simma and Pulkowski make precisely this point in their discussion of how the individual invocation of State responsibility impacts the State invocation of responsibility in human rights law: 'most of these [human rights] procedures do *not* constitute *leges speciales* to Articles 42 and 48. Individual claims procedures are not "concerned with the same substantive matter"—to pick up on Fitzmaurice's definition of special rules. The scope of the ILC Articles is limited to the rights of *states* to invoke responsibility of other states. They have no bearing on the question whether, and under which conditions, individuals are entitled to present claims or to request remedies. Vice versa, the mere existence of an individual claims procedure cannot warrant the conclusion that inter-state invocation is consequently precluded. Rather, the invocation of responsibility rests on two pillars', Simma and Pulkowski, above n 50, 525 (emphasis in the original). See discussion at Part V.A.5 on the possibility to rely on this argument in the investment law context.

[149] Cf the general discussion and argument in favour of treating investor's rights as direct rights, Douglas, above n 45, 167–184.

[150] Another type of argument in favour of excluding diplomatic protection (that the ILC did not utilize) would rely on the concept of agency to view investment arbitration as an 'in some sense institutionaliz[ed] and reinforce[ed] ... system of diplomatic protection', Crawford 'Retrospect', above n 119, 887–888. This argument would consist of three sub-arguments: first of all, that a BIT is an

The inconsistency that exists pertains only to the relevance that diplomatic protection law can play in the interpretation of investment arbitration law through Article 31(3)(c), but not to the continuing existence of the rights to diplomatic protection. Neither principle nor practice can influence the nuanced and persuasive position that Dugard initially adopted: there is no synthesis either way between the diplomatic protection and investment arbitration. The legal entitlement to the exercise of investment arbitration and diplomatic protection are each autonomously interpreted and maintain parallel existence (even if for pragmatic reasons the actual invocation of responsibility would overwhelmingly be carried out through investment arbitration).

agreement between the home State and the host State to authorize the investor to exercise diplomatic protection; secondly, that the authorization also modifies the procedure of exercise of the right; and thirdly, that the State loses its right to exercise diplomatic protection concurrently. While the suggested construction is certainly very artificial, there is no reason of principle why States would not be entitled to create such a regime if they wished to.

The 2006 ILC Articles do not address the concept of agency in express terms, but there exists practice of authorizing the exercise of diplomatic protection upon an agreement of all three States (the home State, the host State, and the agent State), E Borchard, *Diplomatic Protection of Citizens Abroad* (The Banks Law Publishing Co., New York, 1915) 471–475; AP Sereni, 'Agency in International Law' (1940) 34 *American Journal of International Law* 638, 642–644; AP Sereni, 'La représentation en droit international' (1948) 73 *Recueil des Cours* 69, 112–117. The consent of all the involved actors is essential, therefore the possible attempt to authorize diplomatic protection without the consent of third States in Article 20 of the Treaty Establishing the European Community is problematic from the *res inter alios acta* perspective, T Stein, 'Interim Report on "Diplomatic Protection under the European Union Treaty"' in *Report of the Seventieth ILA Conference* (ILA, London, 2002) 277–289; L Condorelli, 'La protection diplomatique et l'evolution de son domaine d'application' (2003) 86 *Rivista di diritto internazionale* 5, 12. The agency, including agency of diplomatic protection, may also in principle be compulsory, i.e. excluding the right of the principal to engage in the particular conduct, Sereni 'Agency', at 651. The problem with this argument is therefore not theoretical, but rather that it is very complicated to justify in terms of interpretation and State practice; as the *Corn Products* Tribunal put it, '[t]he notion that [NAFTA] Chapter XI conferred upon investors a right, in their own name and for their own benefit, to institute proceedings to enforce rights which were not theirs but were solely the property of the State of their nationality is counterintuitive,' *Corn Products*, above n 49, para 169.

Regarding the first argument, there is no express support in the treaty language for viewing investment arbitration as a case of delegated diplomatic protection. There is little interpretative authority to imply such a complex legal arrangement either. The consistent parallelism of State-State and investor-State dispute settlement clauses suggests a possibility of parallel exercise, since otherwise the ubiquitous State-State dispute settlement clauses would be rendered almost completely ineffective (an unacceptable result as a matter of treaty interpretation). The point is particularly persuasive in the historical context, with investor-State clauses supplementing the treaty models already containing the State-State clauses, the latter presumably remaining unchanged in the absence of express indication otherwise. Finally, there is the pragmatic point that neither the ILC nor the State comments even considered such a possibility.

Regarding the second argument, Douglas has shown that most aspects of investment arbitration suggest a qualitatively different approach from diplomatic protection, Douglas, above n 45, 167–184. In the absence of express suggestions to the contrary, it is more natural to read such aspects as pertaining to the nature of investment arbitration itself and not as modifications from the *ab initio* model of diplomatic protection. Regarding the third argument, even if the agency nature of investment arbitration is accepted, the presumption would still be that the principal State retains the right to exercise the conferred power, Sereni 'Agency', at 651–652. There is no express exclusion of the State's rights, and the existence of broadly worded State-State dispute clauses provides interpretative context for positively concluding that these rights are retained. Consequently, the argument is likely to fail on all three grounds: neither the agency, nor the modification, nor the waiver of concurrent exercise of conferred powers can be implied.

E. Diplomatic protection and the arbitral award

It was argued above that the right to diplomatic protection is not excluded in non-ICSID treaty arbitrations: the suspension of diplomatic protection is a treaty rule particular to the ICSID Convention and does not reflect customary law; while it is correct that the investor is entitled to directly invoke the host State's responsibility, it does not exclude its home State's right to do so; and investment arbitration does not replace diplomatic protection because, despite the factual resemblance, in legal terms they do not cover the same subject matter and States have not treated them in such a manner. To the extent that these arguments are followed, two further questions arise: the possibility of the home State engaging in diplomatic protection in response to breaches of the investment protection treaty and the influence of the arbitral award on this right. These questions will be considered in turn.

If the State is entitled to engage in diplomatic protection over breaches of primary rules that the other State owes to it, then *prima facie* it would appear irrelevant in legal terms that the investor is also entitled to invoke State responsibility, has already invoked it or has received an arbitral award. Since the right of invocation is different, there is no conflict but only support in the achievement of the goal of implementing State responsibility for the breach of the particular primary rule. Depending on the particular treaty that may provide for limitations or conditions, the home State would be entitled to pursue the claim through the State-State dispute settlement mechanisms or espouse the claim without referring to binding third-party procedures, claiming the responsibility for BIT breaches and non-compliance with the investor-State dispute settlement obligations.

The situation could (or should) arguably be different when the investor-State Tribunal has already rendered its award in the particular dispute. Strictly speaking, this award would not have any *res judicata* effect on the home State because the parties are clearly different.[151] At the same time, the State responsibility for the breach of the particular primary rule can be invoked both by the State and the investor.[152] As Simma and Pulkowski have noted, '[c]onceptually, the responsibility of States arises irrespective of who has the right to invoke it and in which fashion. The various procedures have no bearing on the question whether a state is responsible for a breach.'[153] It may be recalled that the *Reparation for Injuries* advisory opinion considered 'solutions inspired by goodwill and common sense' appropriate for concurrent claims of responsibility, therefore a pragmatic

---

[151] WS Dodge, '*Res Judicata*' in *Max Planck Encyclopaedia of Public International Law*, <www.mpepil.com> (last accessed 28 February 2009); *Genocide*, above n 144, paras 115–116; A Reinisch, 'The Use and Limits of *Res Judicata* and *Lis Pendens* as Procedural Tools to Avoid Conflicting Dispute Settlement Outcomes' (2004) 3 *Law and Practice of International Courts and Tribunals* 37, 44–48; B Cheng, *General Principles of Law as Applied by International Courts and Tribunals* (Stevens & Sons Limited, London, 1953) 339–347.

[152] Crawford 'Retrospect', above n 119, 887–888.

[153] Simma and Pulkowski, above n 50, 525.

and context-sensitive approach may be the preferable one, at least *de lege ferenda*.

Since States have agreed that State responsibility for breaches of specific primary rules owed to them can also be invoked by other entities, 'common sense' would suggest that the third-party binding determination of the breach of the relevant primary rule should also be accepted by the home State, even though invoked by another entity. To the extent that the cause and the object are identical, it may be said that the Tribunal's determination envelops the original breach of the primary rule. Support for such a rule appears to follow from Italy's comment to the ILC where it noted, in considering the procedures provided by instruments on human rights and investment protection, that:

> when an alternative procedure—whether resorted to by the State or by the individual to be protected—entails a binding decision adopted by a fully independent and impartial judge, the right to exert diplomatic protection should no longer exist. There should be no ground to exert the diplomatic action in such a case, since the action undertaken warrants a more secure elimination of the consequences of any wrongful act that might have been committed.[154]

It is possible to distinguish five situations. *First of all*, the investor's claim could be upheld. In this case, the argument about the award enveloping the claim applies with the greatest force, and it would make sense to permit the State to claim responsibility only for the failure to comply with the award.

Secondly, the investor's claim could be rejected on the merits. In this case as well, it could be argued that the State's right to claim diplomatic protection should be enveloped by the award, having been terminated regarding the claims that have been addressed and rejected on the merits. An indirect support for these propositions may be found in Model BITs that confirm the existence of diplomatic protection for cases where jurisdiction has been denied, thus implicitly excluding it from cases where jurisdiction has been confirmed.[155]

Thirdly, the investor's claim could fail for jurisdictional reasons related to the coverage of the particular treaty, eg because the *ratione personae*,[156] *ratione materiae*,[157] or *ratione temporis* criteria have not been

---

[154] ILC, 'Diplomatic Protection: Comments and Observations Received from Governments' A/CN.4/561/ Add. 2, 7–8.

[155] 1998 Malaysia Model BIT art 7(4), 1995 Switzerland Model BIT art 8(4) and 1991 UK Model BIT art 8(4) provide that '[n]either Contracting Party shall pursue through the diplomatic channel any dispute referred to the Centre unless (a) the Secretary-General of the Centre, or a conciliation commission or an arbitral tribunal [constituted by it—*not in the Swiss BIT*], decides that the dispute is not within the jurisdiction of the Centre'. This rule can be read either in support of a general principle or as reflecting the particular rule of Article 27(1) of the ICSID Convention.

[156] Eg because the investor was not an investor within the meaning of the treaty, *Soufraki v UAE*, ICSID Case No. ARB/02/7, Decision on Jurisdiction, July 7, 2004, <http://ita.law.uvic.ca/documents/ Soufraki_000.pdf> (last accessed 28 February 2009), paras 47–84.

[157] Eg because no investment had been made within the meaning of the treaty, *Bayview Irrigation District et al. v Mexico*, ICSID Additional Facility Case No. ARB(AF)/05/01, Award, June 19, 2007, <http://ita.law.uvic.ca/documents/bayview.pdf> (last accessed 28 February 2009), paras 81–124.

satisfied.[158] In these cases, the jurisdictional decisions are akin to a rejection on the merits, and the claim would be dismissed because no primary rule was binding on the host State in the first place. Arguably, the same solution as that under the rejection on the merits could be adopted.

Fourthly, the investor's claim could be rejected before it reaches the merits but for reasons that are not related to the applicability of the investment protection treaty. Particular dispute settlement rules may impose stricter criteria than those contained in the treaty containing the primary rules.[159] Such rejection of jurisdiction would be limited to the particular forum. Also, the jurisdiction of the Tribunals may be narrower than the substantive scope of the obligations.[160] The decision would again be without prejudice to the existence and compliance with the obligations outside the jurisdiction.[161] Investors may have failed to comply with the time limitations for the investment claim provided in the treaty[162] or taken the wrong turn at the fork-in-the-road.[163] More broadly, the inadmissibility of the claim could relate not to the lack of the State's consent but the inappropriateness of the particular forum at the particular time.[164] If the rationale of the termination of the right to exercise diplomatic protection is that it could have been identically invoked both by the investor and the State, in these cases the negative award of the Tribunal should not in

---

[158] Eg because the treaty was not in force at the time of the alleged breaches, *Empressas Lucchetti, S.A. and Lucchetti Peru S.A. v Peru,* ICSID Case No. ARB/03/4, Award, February 7, 2005, (2004) 19 *ICSID Review—Foreign Investment Law Journal* 359, 382 (paras 48–67).

[159] Eg 'ICSID investment' and 'ICSID nationality' that allegedly impose requirements over and above those contained in the BIT definition for those disputes that are brought to an ICSID Tribunal, respectively *Malaysian Historical Salvors, SDN, BHD v Malaysia,* ICSID Case No. ARB/05/10, Decision on Jurisdiction, May 17, 2007, <http://ita.law.uvic.ca/documents/MHS-jurisdiction.pdf> (last accessed 28 February 2009), paras 42–106; D Krishan, 'A Notion of ICSID Investment' in T Weiler (ed) *Investment Treaty Arbitration and Treaty Law* (JurisNet, LLC, New York, 2008) 61; and *Tokios Tokelés v Ukraine,* ICSID Case No. ARB/02/18, Decision on Jurisdiction, Dissenting Opinion of President Weil, April 29, 2004, (2005) 20 *ICSID Review—Foreign Investment Law Journal* 245; *TSA Spectrum de Argentina S.A. v Argentina,* ICSID Case No. ARB/05/5, Award, December 19, 2008, <http://ita.law.uvic.ca/documents/TSAAwardEng.pdf> (last accessed 28 February 2009), paras 134–154; Concurring Opinion of Arbitrator Abi-Saab, <http://ita.law.uvic.ca/documents/TSAAbi-SaabConcurring. pdf> (last accessed 28 February 2009), paras 11–20; A Sinclair, 'ICSID's Nationality Requirements' in T Weiler (ed) *Investment Treaty Arbitration and Treaty Law* (JurisNet, LLC, New York, 2008) 85.

[160] Eg NAFTA rules on investment protection with the exception of the rule on expropriation do not apply to financial services, *Fireman's Fund Insurance Company v Mexico,* ICSID Additional Facility Case No. Arb(02)/01, Decision on a Preliminary Question, July 17, 2003, <http://ita.law.uvic.ca/documents/ FiremansAward.pdf> (last accessed 28 February 2009), paras 61–75; *Fireman's Fund Insurance Company v Mexico,* ICSID Additional Facility Case No. Arb(02)/01, Final Award, July 17, 2006, <http://ita.law. uvic.ca/documents/FiremansFinalAwardRedacted.pdf> (last accessed 28 February 2009), fn 206.

[161] *Case Concerning Armed Activities on the Territory of the Congo, (New Application: 2002) (Democratic Republic of the Congo v Rwanda)* [2006] ICJ Rep <http://www.icj-cij.org/docket/ files/126/10435.pdf> (last accessed 28 February 2009), para 127.

[162] Eg the discussion in *Feldman v Mexico,* ICSID Additional Facility Case No. Arb(AF)99/01, Interim Decision on Preliminary Jurisdictional Issues, December 6, 2000, (2003) 18 *ICSID Review— Foreign Investment Law Journal* 469, 480 (paras 39–49).

[163] C Schreuer, 'Travelling the BIT Route: of Waiting Periods, Umbrella Clauses and Forks in the Road' (2004) 5 *Journal of World Investment and Trade* 231, 231–249.

[164] J Collier and V Lowe, *The Settlement of Disputes in International Law* (Oxford University Press, Oxford, 1999) 155–156.

principle prejudge the State's rights to diplomatic protection over breaches of primary rules that have not been adjudicated upon because of the inappropriateness of the particular forum.[165]

Fifthly, a less clear situation could arise when the remedies diverge, eg the investor asks for compensation and the State asks for restitution and satisfaction in the form of an apology. With all due caution, the 2001 ILC Articles on State responsibility and the Draft Articles on Responsibility of International Organizations address the situation of multiple entities injured by a single act which claim multiple remedies as having no clear answer, and provide merely for a plea for co-ordination and the preclusion of double recovery.[166] While the lack of clear rules prioritizing and coordinating remedies may be considered as an indication of the impermissibility of the parallelism of invocation, it is fairly reflective of the general situation in the decentralized international legal order. In the particular case, it would be necessary to consider the extent to which the remedies that the State is entitled to demand are qualitatively different: for certain remedies (eg apology) parallel invocation by the home State would be acceptable. The possibility of double recovery could be evaded by the common sense approach suggested by the Court in *Reparation for Injuries* that has been accepted by Tribunals.[167] In any case, in practice the home State will find it more convenient to concentrate on the non-compliance with the award so as to escape the requirement for the investor to exhaust local remedies.

F. Diplomatic protection and local remedies

If diplomatic protection can be exercised in the particular situation, it would be necessary to consider admissibility issues. The nationality of claims would be resolved relatively easily, because the treaty would function as an agreement by States regarding the nationality of investors *inter se*. The exhaustion of local remedies may be somewhat less straightforward, and would turn on the interpretation of the particular treaty. The *ELSI* case suggests that the waiver of the requirement to exhaust local remedies

---

[165] The latter situation could perhaps be distinguished from the former one as pertaining to the admissibility of the claim and not the State's consent to the Tribunal's jurisdiction, and thus not being capable of being invoked by the home State as well (because the forum would be similarly inappropriate for its claim). The distinction between jurisdiction and admissibility in investment arbitration is rather controversial, see I Laird, 'A Distinction Without a Difference? An Examination of the Concepts of Admissibility and Jurisdiction in *Salini v Jordan* and *Methanex v USA*' in T Weiler (ed) *International Law and Investment Arbitration: Leading Cases from the ICSID, NAFTA, Bilateral Treaties and Customary International Law* (Cameron May, London, 2005) 201–222; J Paulsson, 'Jurisdiction and Admissibility' in *Global Reflections on International Law, Commerce and Dispute Resolution: Liber Amicorum Robert Briner* (ICC, Paris, 2005) 601; DA Williams, 'Jurisdiction and Admissibility' in P Muchlinski, F Ortino and C Schreuer (eds) *The Oxford Handbook of International Investment Law* (Oxford University Press, Oxford, 2008) 919–928.

[166] 2001 ILC Articles on State responsibility, above n 13, 124; ILC Draft Articles, above n 124, art 50, Commentary 2.

[167] *CME v Czech Republic,* UNCITRAL Case, Partial Award, September 13, 2001, <http://ita.law.uvic.ca/documents/CME-2001PartialAward.pdf> (last accessed 28 February 2009), para 410.

should be express. It does not seem that the direct right to arbitration for the investor or eg a negotiation requirement for the home State would qualify as such an express waiver.[168]

The distinction should be drawn between the wrongful conduct of the host State regarding the substantive treatment of the investor and the non-compliance with the investor-State dispute settlement obligations. To take the latter case first, as Fawcett observed, '[w]here the act complained of is a breach of an international agreement or of customary international law, but not of the local law, the rule of the exhaustion of local remedies is not applicable and cannot support a preliminary object or defence to a claim'.[169] Since the obligation to comply with the award follows from the international treaty itself, it would seem that the requirement of exhaustion is not applicable. In the former case, *de lege lata*, if the requirement for the exhaustion of local remedies has not been waived, the exhaustion by the investor would have to be carried out in accordance with the general rules of international law, exhausting all available and effective remedies provided by the host State's legal order.[170]

De lege ferenda, it could be argued that the recognition of the right of individuals to invoke the responsibility of the host State before international courts and tribunals should extend the requirement of 'exhausting local remedies' to 'exhausting remedies', before the home State can engage in diplomatic protection. The classic position is stated in Article 14(2) of the 2006 ILC Articles in the following terms: '"Local remedies" means legal remedies which are open to the injured person before the judicial or administrative courts or bodies, whether ordinary or special, of the State alleged to be responsible for causing the injury.' It made perfect sense for a legal order where 'States only and exclusively are subjects of the Law of Nations'[171] to require individuals to exhaust the remedies provided by the sole subjects of international law before their injury became internationally admissible. It arguably makes less sense to maintain the emphasis on 'domestic' rather than 'remedies' when each investment protection treaty is 'marking another step in their [investors'] transition from objects to subjects of international law'.[172]

As Amerasinghe has noted, '[t]he general rule that local remedies must be exhausted does not exist in a vacuum but it is to be seen as an instrument of the international legal system and of international society'.[173] The rule of exhaustion of local remedies reflects the competing interests of a number

---

[168] Amerasinghe *Diplomatic Protection,* above n 73, 341.

[169] JES Fawcett, 'The Exhaustion of Local Remedies: Substance or Procedure?' (1954) 31 *British Yearbook of International Law* 452, 457–458.

[170] 2006 ILC Articles, above n 71, arts 14–15; Amerasinghe *Local Remedies,* above n 75, 385–421.

[171] L Oppenheim, *International Law* (Volume I, Longmans, Green, and Co., London, 1905) 341.

[172] *Plama Consortium Limited v Republic of Bulgaria,* ICSID Case No. ARB/03/24, Decision on Jurisdiction, February 8, 2005, (2005) 20 *ICSID Review—Foreign Investment Law Journal* 262, 304 (para 141); R Higgins, 'Conceptual Thinking about the Individual in International Law' (1978) 4 *British Journal of International Studies* 1.

[173] Cf Amerasinghe, *State Responsibility for the Injuries to Aliens* (Clarendon Press, Oxford, 1967) 170.

of participants: the host State's interest to resolve the dispute in its own courts to give justice and avoid publicity of the dispute; the alien's interest to obtain quick, cheap and efficient justice; the home State's interest to avoid litigation to the extent that the justice is indeed such; and the international community's interest in seeing the dispute being resolved fairly.[174] The contemporary rule should arguably focus on 'remedies' rather than 'local' and consider the speed and efficiency of the remedies available to the individual against the host State rather than the legal order within which the host State has chosen to situate them.

The reference to the 'domestic' nature of remedies simply makes the descriptive point that in the classic international legal order no others were available. One of the reasons for the local remedies rule was the home State's concern to avoid the burden of protection to the extent that effective remedies were provided at the individual-host State level, and this policy is equally valid for the remedies provided within international law. For the purpose of future law-making, it could make sense to extend the requirement to exhaust remedies also to international remedies provided to the individual against the host State that satisfy the qualitative criteria of efficiency and availability, acting as a bar to admissibility of the home State's espousal. In practice, it could mean that when the host State is a member of the Council of Europe, the ECtHR should be exhausted first, and that in the particular situation the investor would need to exhaust investment arbitration before its home State's claim would be admissible. In any event, *de lege lata* such a further requirement does not exist.

G. Countermeasures and procedural conditions of application

Taking into account the presence of the State-State dispute settlement clauses both in ICSID Convention and in most investment protection treaties,[175] it is appealing to imagine a kind of procedural framework that would permit resource to countermeasures only after the failure of all formalized methods of dispute settlement. If there is a compromissory clause in the particular treaty, it seems natural to require the State to take the dispute to an international adjudicative or arbitral body. It would increase the likelihood of resolving the dispute without resorting to the undesirable breaches of international law (even with precluded wrongfulness). It would also ensure, should all else fail, that the international wrongfulness is objectively established, not requiring the home State to take the risk of subjective appreciations. Leben has suggested the following kind of procedural sequencing:

si l'État refuse d'appliquer une sentence rendue par un tribunal arbitral dans le litige qui l'oppose à l'investisseur (premier niveau), l'État national de celui-ci

---

[174] Amerasinghe *Local Remedies,* above n 75, 59–62.
[175] Eg McLachlan, Shore and Weiniger, above n 69, 33; Ben Hamida, above n 104, 575–577; Schreuer, above n 104, 402–405.

pourra mettre en ouvre la clause de règlement des différends et saisir le tribunal arbitral prévu par le traité de protection (deuxième niveau). Si cette deuxième sentence est elle-même refusée, le refus pourra donner lieu à la mise en jeu de sa responsabilité au niveau inter étatique (troisième niveau), que ceci soit expressément prévu dans la traité ou non. ... un État peut être éventuellement habilité à recourir à des contre-mesures vis-à-vis de l'État responsable du fait illicite.[176]

While States would certainly be entitled to use State-State dispute settlement mechanisms before adopting countermeasures (and in policy terms third-party determination is certainly preferable to auto-determination), it is less obvious whether they would be required to do so under *lex lata*.

The relationship of countermeasures and dispute settlement mechanisms was one of the most controversial elements of the ILC work on State responsibility. A whole spectrum of views existed: from conditioning the exercise of countermeasures on the prior use of all peaceful dispute settlement mechanisms[177] or at least those where the particular treaty allegedly breached contained a compromissory clause,[178] to considering dispute settlement as a co-requisite of countermeasures rather than prerequisite,[179] to rejecting the obligation to resort to dispute settlement measures before taking countermeasures.[180]

The divergence of views was reflected in the documents produced and debated by the ILC, where the balance between unilateralism and third-party determination seemed to slowly shift in the direction of the former. While the early drafts and documents required, at different level of specificity, the State to exhaust available measures of peaceful settlement of disputes before adopting countermeasures,[181] Article 48 of the 1996 Draft Articles adopted in the first reading already recognized that 'the injured State may take countermeasures without any prior resort to third party dispute settlement procedures'.[182] In the ILC discussion of the second reading, there was broad support for a provision that did not require prior recourse to third-party dispute settlement,[183] and Article 52 as adopted in the 2001 Articles does not contain any such requirement.[184]

---

[176] Leben, above n 46, 695, 696.

[177] G Arangio-Ruiz, 'Counter-measures and Amicable Dispute Settlement' (1994) 5 *European Journal of International Law* 20, 20–53; O Schachter, 'Dispute Settlement and Countermeasures in the International Law Commission' (1994) 88 *American Journal of International Law* 471, 471–474.

[178] B Simma, 'Counter-measures and Dispute Settlement: A Plea for a Different Balance' (1994) 5 *European Journal of International Law* 102, 102–105; L Condorelli, 'Le règlement des différends en matière de responsabilité internationale des Etats: quelques remarques candides sur le débat a la C.D.I.' (1994) 5 *European Journal of International Law* 106, 106–115.

[179] Crawford, above n 19, 65–76.

[180] Tomuschat, above n 68, 77–88.

[181] Crawford, above n 19, 69–76.

[182] 1996 Draft Articles on State Responsibility with Commentaries Thereto Adopted by the International Law Commission on First Reading <http://untreaty.un.org/ilc/texts/instruments/english/commentaries/9_6_1996.pdf> (last accessed on 28 February 2009) 314.

[183] ILC, *Report of the Fifty-Second Session* (2000), A/55/10 52, 55–57.

[184] 2001 ILC Articles on State responsibility, above n 13, art 52.

Since an adoption of the 2001 ILC Articles on State responsibility in a treaty form appears neither likely in the nearest future nor desirable,[185] their legal relevance should be assessed against the benchmark of how accurately they codify customary law (or perhaps how much they have contributed to its development post-2001).[186] In probably the most authoritative post-War case on the issue, the *Air Service Agreement,* the Tribunal concluded that the US was entitled to take countermeasures (even though there was an obligation of negotiation and the possibility to submit the dispute to arbitration), but that the right would cease when the dispute was brought before a Tribunal.[187]

Article 52 of the ILC articles broadly follows this approach, requiring notification and the offer of negotiation in 52(1) and providing for suspension of the right to take countermeasures when the dispute is brought before a Tribunal in 52(3).[188] The ILC's project 'to superimpose procedural values of rectitude and transparency on state's assessments of countermeasures options' would operate in investment protection law similarly as in other areas of law, reflecting the individualistic interplay between customary and particular treaty law requirements.[189]

The most common approach in treaty practice appears to require six months[190] (or two months,[191] or twelve months[192]) of negotiations or consultations before the dispute can be submitted to arbitration. This rule would probably overlap with the customary law obligation to offer negotiations but would not preclude the subsequent application of countermeasures before the time limitation provided by treaty law expires.[193] Some treaty rules provide for negotiations and arbitration without specifying

---

[185] J Crawford and S Olleson, 'The Continuing Debate on a UN Convention on State Responsibility' (2005) 54 *International and Comparative Quarterly* 559, 559–571.

[186] S Olleson, The Impact of the International Law Commission's Articles on Responsibility of States for Internationally Wrongful Acts (BIICL, London, forthcoming 2009).

[187] *Air Service Agreement*, above n 21, 444 (paras 84–96).

[188] Simma and Pulkowski have argued that in the human rights context (that is arguably instructive for the present discussion as well) the availability of State-State procedures of a judicial character excludes the right to invoke responsibility though other channels, including countermeasures, above n 50, 526. This argument seems closer to Simma's 1994 argument in favour of requiring the use of specific dispute settlement measures rather than the *Air Services Agreement* and 2001 ILC Articles on State responsibility approach.

[189] DJ Bederman, 'Counterintuiting Countermeasures' (2002) 96 *American Journal of International Law* 817, 819.

[190] 2003 India Model BIT art 10; 2003 Ghana Model BIT art 11; Italy Model BIT art IX; Kenya Model BIT art 11; Uganda Model BIT art 11; Burkina Faso Model BIT art 11; Benin Model BIT Article 8; Burundi Model BIT art 9; Maurice Model BIT art 8; 1998 Mongolia Model BIT art 9; 2002 Sweden Model BIT art 9; 2001 Greece Model BIT art 9; 2001 Finland Model BIT art 9; 2000 Denmark Model BIT art 9; 2000 Peru Model BIT art 9; 2000 Turkey Model BIT art 9; 1999 France Model BIT art 11; 1998 Croatia Model BIT art8; 1998 South Africa Model BIT art 8; 1995 Switzerland Model BIT art 8; 1994 China Model BIT art 8; 1994 Chile Model BIT art 9.

[191] 2007 Norway Model BIT art 20.

[192] Romania Model BIT art 10.

[193] The distinction between the obligation to negotiate and the obligation to offer to negotiate seems to lie in the fact that in the former case the State is under a stronger obligation 'not only to enter into negotiations but also pursue them as far as possible with a view of concluding an agreement', *Railway Traffic between Lithuania and Poland (Poland v Lithuania)* [1931] PCIJ Rep Series A/B no. 42

the minimum time for negotiations.[194] The treaty rules may also require[195] or entitle the submission of the dispute to arbitration after the negotiations.[196] This difference would in the former case mean an effective cessation of countermeasures since willingness to apply them *sine qua non* suggests the existence of a dispute. Finally, some treaty rules may require a mandatory establishment of a Tribunal, and the right to apply countermeasures would then cease almost immediately.[197] At the end of the day, the limits and conditions of the right to apply countermeasures have to be assessed against the background of treaty rules relevant in each particular situation.

IV. Countermeasures as a Sword: ICSID Arbitration

A. Diplomatic protection and countermeasures

Most of the analysis regarding countermeasures in non-ICSID arbitrations applies *verbatim* to the ICSID arbitrations, with the important qualification regarding the legal effect of Article 27(1) of the ICSID Convention. Article 27(1) raises three general questions, regarding the points in time when the provision starts and ceases to apply, and its *ratione materiae* scope. These questions will be addressed in turn.

First of all, the provision starts to apply not when a treaty with an offer to ICSID arbitration comes into force but only when the investor actually perfects the consent by submitting the claim. Article 27(1) puts the *dies a quo* at the point in time when the investor and the host State 'consent[] to submit' or 'submit to arbitration'. The ordinary meaning suggests a requirement for a mutual consent (a submission of the investor's claim in treaty cases) and this reading is not disapproved by the context[198] and is confirmed

---

108, 116, Collier and Lowe, above n 164, 23. An obligation to *offer* negotiation is weaker and would probably require only a good faith effort to create an *opportunity* of negotiations.

[194] 2004 US Model BIT art 37; 2004 Canada Model BIT art 48; 1998 Malaysia Model BIT art 8; 1998 Germany Model BIT art 8; 1998 (1994 revised) US Model BIT art 10; 1998 Netherlands Model BIT arts 11–12; 1994 US Model BIT art 10; 1991 UK Model BIT art 9. Uganda Model BIT art 11 provides for the establishment of a joint commission between negotiations and arbitration.

[195] Eg 2003 India Model BIT art 10.

[196] Eg 2007 Norway Model BIT art 20(1)–(4).

[197] 2004 US Model BIT art 34 (8) (regarding failure to comply with the investor-State awards).

[198] It has been suggested regarding the consequences of the Bolivian denunciation of the ICSID Convention (S Manciaux, 'La Bolivie se retire du CIRDI' (2007) 4 (5) *Transnational Dispute Management*) that the requirement of 'consent' in Article 72 could also be satisfied by a particularly worded BIT arbitration offer even without a subsequent claim by the investor (E Gaillard, 'The Denunciation of the ICSID Convention' (2007) June 26 *New York Law Journal* 8; C Tietje, K Nowrot and C Wackernagel, 'Once and Forever? The Legal Effects of the Denunciation of ICSID' (2009) 6 (1) *Transnational Dispute Management* 28–30; OM Garibaldi, 'On the Denunciation of the ICSID Convention, Consent to ICSID Jurisdiction, and the Limits of the Contract Analogy' (2009) 6(1) *Transnational Dispute Management*). Without expressing a view regarding the correct reading of Article 72, it does not contain the explicit requirement of mutual consent, thus no *mutatis mutandis* argument is possible.

by the preparatory materials.[199] Consequently, Article 27 starts to apply only at the moment when the consent becomes mutual.[200]

Secondly, Article 27 would cease to apply if 'such other Contracting State shall have failed to abide by and comply with the award rendered in such dispute'. The ordinary meaning of the text within its context suggests that it is non-compliance with the award that stops the application of Article 27(1). Compliance with the award is a matter to be determined in accordance with the relevant rules of ICSID Convention.[201]

Thirdly, express reference to diplomatic protection would also appear to exclude countermeasures. Article 27 does not define diplomatic protection (except in negative terms by saying in Article 27(2) that diplomatic consultations are not diplomatic protection), so one would assume that the interpreter would have to fall back on other rules of international law binding between the parties to the ICSID Convention, ie general international law. The technique of interpreting the treaty term against the background of applicable customary law has been utilized by the International Court of Justice itself.[202] In the investment arbitration context, the meaning of eg 'deprivation',[203] 'unreasonable measures'[204] and (much more controversially) 'measures necessary'[205] has also been sought in customary law.[206]

As considered in greater detail above, in contemporary law diplomatic protection is addressed separately from countermeasures.[207] Classic international law did not maintain the analytical distinction between primary rules addressing the scope and content of the obligations and secondary

---

[199] In answering the Japanese delegate's question about a domestic law containing an offer to go to ICSID arbitration, Broches stated that 'it could, at least, be argued that until the investor had actually availed himself of the offer contained in the law there would be no agreement to accept the Centre's jurisdiction', *Convention: Documents,* above n 52, 527. The point seems to be *mutatis mutandis* applicable to a treaty containing an offer to go to ICSID arbitration.

[200] Schreuer, above n 104, 409.

[201] Ibid, 1076–1140; *Enron Corporation Ponderosa Assets, L.P. v Argentina,* ICSID Case No. ARB/01/3, Decision on Argentina's Request for a Continued Stay of Enforcement of the Award, October 7, 2008, <http://ita.law.uvic.ca/documents/Enron-Stay.pdf> (last accessed 28 February 2009), paras 61–78; *Sempra Energy International v Republic of Argentina,* ICSID Case No. ARB/02/16, Decision on Argentina's Request for a Continued Stay of Enforcement of the Award, March 5, 2009, <http://ita.law.uvic.ca/documents/Sempra-Stay.pdf> (last accessed 5 March 2009), paras 30–76; SA Alexandrov, 'Enforcement of ICSID Awards: Articles 53 and 54 of the ICSID Convention' (2009) 6(1) *Transnational Dispute Management.*

[202] *Oil Platforms (Islamic Republic of Iran v US)* (Merits) [2003] ICJ Rep 161, 182 (para 41).

[203] *Saluka Investment BV v Czech Republic,* UNCITRAL Arbitration Partial Award, March 17, 2006, <http://ita.law.uvic.ca/documents/Saluka-PartialawardFinal.pdf> (last accessed 28 February 2009), para 254.

[204] *BG,* above n 47, para 340.

[205] See above n 47 and n 48.

[206] The application of Article 31(3)(c) of VCLT to investment protection law falls beyond the scope of this contribution. It only needs to be noted that the analysis is far from a one-way-customary-law-incorporating-street. As Sir Michael Wood noted in the somewhat different context of UNCLOS, 'care is needed with the suggestion that a court or tribunal may find it necessary to resort to general international law to fill what might be termed gaps in the Convention. Some "gaps" may have been deliberate', M Wood, 'The International Tribunal for Law of the Sea and General International Law' (2007) 22 *Journal of Coastal and Marine Law* 351, 361.

[207] See above III.A.

rules addressing the legal consequences of the breach of the primary obligations, and there the linkage was much clearer. To consider a few examples, Borchard's 1915 treatise *Diplomatic Protection* discussed reprisals as one of the 'various agencies which serve states to fulfil their function of protecting citizens abroad'.[208] The Bases of Discussion regarding State responsibility of the 1930 Hague Codification Conference discussed primary rules on the treatment of aliens and secondary rules in an integrated manner. The Bases *inter alia* discussed reprisals as one of the circumstances in which 'a State is not responsible for the damage caused to a foreigner' together with such aspects of diplomatic protection as nationality and exhaustion of local remedies.[209] The ILC First Special Rapporteur on State Responsibility García-Amador also understood State responsibility to mean State responsibility for treatment of aliens, proposing an integrated project of these primary rules and rules on human rights, as well as secondary rules.[210] As he noted in his 1958 Hague lectures,

the "doctrine of diplomatic protection of citizens abroad" refers to a subject-matter also covered by the expression "responsibility of the State for injuries caused in its territory to the person or property of aliens"—that is, the expression which have been used in connexion with the codification of "State responsibility", both in the time of the League of Nations and more recently by the United Nations International Law Commission.[211]

Looking from the perspective of the contemporary understanding of the law of State responsibility, it is hard to disagree with Ago's 1939 characterization that 'du point de vue systématique, l'on ne saurait approuver une méthode susceptible de causer des confusions avec graves'.[212] In the ILC discussions, García-Amador's draft was subject to different criticisms, *inter alia* suggesting a shift of focus from the primary to secondary rules.[213] Ago became the Second Special Rapporteur on State Responsibility in 1962. From 1969 to 1980 he produced eight reports that set the structure of what was to become Part One of the 2001 Articles, embodying the distinction between primary and secondary rules and excluding diplomatic protection from this analysis.[214]

---

[208] Borchard, above n 150, 435, 453–455.

[209] S Rosenne (ed) *League of Nations Conference for the Codification of International Law [1930]* (Volume II, Oceana Publications, Inc., New York, 1975) 550–552, 558–567.

[210] FV García-Amador, 'State Responsibility in the Light of the New Trends of International Law' (1955) 49 *American Journal of International Law* 339, 339–346; FV García-Amador, 'The Role of State Responsibility in the Private Financing of Economic and Social Development' (1964–1965) 16 *Syracuse Law Review* 738, 739; FV García-Amador, *The Changing Law of International Claims* (Oceana Publications, Inc., New York, 1984).

[211] FV García-Amador, 'State Responsibility: Some New Problems' (1958) 94 *Recueil des Cours* 365, 426.

[212] Ago, above n 13, 468.

[213] *Yearbook of the ILC* 1957, above n 38, 156–157 (Ago), 164 (Fitzmaurice), 167 (Ago), 168 (Spiropoulus), 170 (Verdross); *Yearbook of the ILC* 1959, *Vol. I* A/CN.4/SER.A/1959 150 (Verdross, Ago).

[214] Crawford *Articles*, above n 123, 2–3.

With the benefit of hindsight, the beginning of the 1960s was the time when Ago's theoretical argument started gaining credence in international law. However, the change of perception was not instantaneous, and the distinction between primary and secondary rules was even long afterwards criticized as overly theoretical and unworkable, particularly by Anglo-American scholars.[215] The draft of the ICSID Convention was discussed and negotiated from 1961 to 1965, was opened for signature and ratification in 1965, and entered into force in 1966.[216] The contemporaneous approach to treaty interpretation directs the attention of the interpreter in the first instance to the elucidation of the meaning attributed to treaties at the time of their conclusion.[217] In this light, the concept of diplomatic protection (recognized by Broches himself as not altogether clear)[218] could be read against the pre-Ago state of debate and in light of the repeatedly expressed purpose of the drafters to exclude the political interference of the State in dispute settlement, thus also excluding countermeasures as an element of protection of aliens ultimately susceptible of politicizing the dispute.[219]

Alternatively, in the particular instance 'the meaning and scope of a term or expression used in the treaty should follow the development of the law' through an inter-temporal *renvoi*[220] because the generic term[221] carries with it an evolving meaning.'[222] It is not obvious that this is the case: what has evolved is not so much a new content of the rules of diplomatic protection and State responsibility, but rather a clearer conceptualization of their relationship in light of the doctrinal debate and successful efforts of codification. Indeed, State practice and the case law that the ILC relied

---

[215]   RR Baxter, 'Reflections on Codification in Light of the International Law of State Responsibility for Injuries to Aliens' (1964–1965) 16 *Syracuse Law Review* 745, 745–761; Lillich, above n 38, 373–379; MS McDougal, HD Lasswell and L-C Chen, 'The Protection of Aliens from Discrimination and World Public Order: Responsibility of States Conjoined with Human Rights' (1976) 70 *American Journal of International Law* 432, 454–456; C Warbrick, 'The Theory of International Law: Is There an English Contribution?' in W Butler (ed) *Perestroika and International Law* (Martinus Nijhoff Publishers, Dordrecht, 1990) 41, 50. The American scholarly perception appears to have changed, J Alvarez, 'International Organizations: Accountability or Responsibility?' Luncheon Address at the Canadian Council of International Law, October 27, 2006 <http://www.asil.org/aboutasil/documents/CCILspeecho61102.pdf> (last accessed 28 February 2009), 2.

[216]   *Convention: Documents,* above n 52.

[217]   G Fitzmaurice, 'The Law and Procedure of the International Court of Justice, 1951–4: Treaty Interpretation and Other Treaty Points' (1957) 33 *British Yearbook of International Law* 203, 212; HWA Thirlway, 'The Law and Procedure of the International Court of Justice 1960–1989 (Part Three)' (1991) 62 *British Yearbook of International Law* 1, 57; HWA Thirlway, 'The Law and Procedure of the International Court of Justice 1960–1989. Supplement, 2006: Part Three' (2006) 77 *British Yearbook of International Law* 1, 65.

[218]   *Convention: Documents,* above n 52, 434.

[219]   Ibid, 242, 273, 303, 372, 464.

[220]   HWA Thirlway, 'The Law and Procedure of the International Court of Justice—Part One' (1989) 60 *British Yearbook of International Law* 1, 134–143; Thirlway (1991), above n 217, 57, 60; HWA Thirlway, 'The Law and Procedure of the International Court of Justice 1960–1989. Supplement, 2005: Parts One and Two' (2005) 76 *British Yearbook of International Law* 1, 71–77.

[221]   R Higgins, 'Time and Law: International Perspectives on a New Problem' (1997) 46 *International and Comparative Law Quarterly* 501, 517–519.

[222]   McLachlan, above n 134, 316–318.

on in formulating rules on diplomatic protection and injured-State countermeasures reflect a rather conservative view of the international law-making process, illustrating gradual clarification and elucidation through classic case law[223] and nothing that could be characterized as a rupture with the earlier regimes.[224]

Even if the contemporary understanding of countermeasures and diplomatic protection is applied, it does not seem to change the conclusion that countermeasures could not be applied, even if the reasoning becomes slightly different. As was suggested above, the inapplicability of the diplomatic protection means that the invocation of responsibility remains inadmissible. Consequently, to the extent that Article 27(1) applies, States are not entitled to take countermeasures.[225]

B. After the host State's non-compliance

Article 27(1) expressly indicates the host State's failure to comply with the award as the moment when the right to take diplomatic protection reappears. It was suggested in the previous sections that the home State should be entitled to engage in diplomatic protection of the breaches both of the substantive rules on the treatment of investors and the host State's procedural obligations regarding dispute settlement, but that the investor-State Tribunal's award would envelop the former breach to the extent that the causes are identical. To the extent that the breaches of primary rules have not been adjudicated by the Tribunal, they may be protected separately and the investor would have to exhaust the local remedies. This section will consider whether the legal situation is similar in cases when the host State has failed to comply with an ICSID award.

The first unclear issue arises from identifying the possible causes of the diplomatic protection and countermeasures[226] or, more accurately, the breaches of the primary rules that could be protected through diplomatic

---

[223] The structure of diplomatic protection analysis follows such classic judgments as the 1924 *Mavrommatis* case and the 1970 *Barcelona Traction* case (see 2006 ILC Articles, above n 71, 25, 27, 29, 52 et seq., 73, 97), and the analysis of countermeasures is still to a large extent based on the seminal 1978 *Air Service Agreement* award (see 2001 ILC Articles on State responsibility, above n 13, 128–131, 134–136; Crawford 'Retrospect', above n 119, 883–884).

[224] To borrow the distinction from Judge Bennouna's discussion of inter-temporal law in a different context where he emphasized that in that particular case one could talk not only of 'de simple évolution des principes et des règles, mais d'une véritable rupture caractérisée par l'avènement du droit des peuples à disposer d'eux-mêmes', *Sovereignty over Pedra Branca/Pulau Batu Puteh, Middle Rocks and South Ledge (Malaysia/Singapore)* [2008] ICJ Rep, Déclaration du juge Bennouna <http://www.icj-cij.org/docket/files/130/14499.pdf> (last accessed on 28 February 2009), para 2.

[225] Despite reaching the right conclusion, the ILC Commentary seems to be inaccurate in asserting that Article 27(1) 'excludes all forms of invocation by the State of nationality, including the taking of countermeasures', 2001 ILC Articles on State responsibility, above n 13, 136. Countermeasures (Chapter II of Part III) are not a form of *invocation* of responsibility (Chapter I of Part III) but another form of *implementation* of responsibility (Part III). It would be more accurate to say that it is not the countermeasures that are excluded by Article 27 but the precondition for their application.

[226] I Brownlie, 'Causes of Action in the Law of Nations' (1979) 50 *British Yearbook of International Law* 13.

protection and countermeasures.[227] Article 27(1) provides in the relevant part that '[n]o Contracting State shall give diplomatic protection ... unless such other Contracting State shall have failed to abide by and comply with the award rendered in such dispute.' The effect of the rule can been read in two ways. On the one hand, Article 27(1) could be a *waiver* of the right to exercise diplomatic protection regarding breaches of primary rules that the investor and the State have consented to submit to arbitration, preserving only the right of the home State to claim responsibility for the breach of the primary rule regarding compliance with the ICSID awards.[228] From this perspective, failure to comply with the award is crucial because that is the only breach that the home State can claim responsibility for. On the other hand, Article 27(1) could be merely a *suspension* of the right to exercise diplomatic protection over the original breach that is lifted at a certain point in time. From this perspective, failure to comply is still a breach on its own but is not in any way relevant to the original breach, being merely a trigger for the revival of the right to exercise protection over the earlier breach. The distinction between these two issues has not always been clearly maintained.[229]

Looking at the ICSID Convention, an interpretation according to which the right to diplomatic protection would be only suspended and not waived seems more plausible. The ordinary meaning of the obligation not to 'give' diplomatic protection suggests that what is affected is the exercise of the right to claim the responsibility and not the right's existence.[230] The structure of the provision also supports this view: what the Convention seems to have in mind is the situation where a dispute arises between the investor and the host State, and the home State—albeit entitled to exercise diplomatic protection over the matters in dispute—holds back its hand and lets the investor-State arbitration take place uninterrupted. The *quid pro quo* logic of not giving diplomatic protection over a particular dispute for compliance with the arbitral award regarding the particular dispute becomes invalid when the latter part of the equation fails, and the legal situation returns to the initial entitlement.[231]

---

[227] Crawford 'Retrospect', above n 119, 876–879.

[228] A perfectly possible legal construction, since the right to diplomatic protection is the home State's *jus dispositivum* right and can accordingly be waived by it, including through treaty law, ILC 2001 Articles, above n 13, art 45(a).

[229] For example, Schreuer combines the view that 'the right of diplomatic protection will revive in case of non-compliance with the award' with seeing diplomatic protection purely in the context of enforcement of the award, Schreuer, above n 104, 411, 413. Amerasinghe states that 'Article 27 waives the right of the national State to exercise diplomatic protection until a certain point in the settlement of investment disputes', leaving it unclear whether what is waived is the exercise of the right until failure to comply (so it would not actually be a waiver *stricto sensu*) or the right to protect breaches that take place until the failure to comply, Amerasinghe *Diplomatic Protection*, above n 73, 334.

[230] In a different context, *Plama,* above n 172, 310 (para 155).

[231] Cf O Spiermann, 'Individual Rights, State Interests and the Power to Waive ICSID Jurisdiction under Bilateral Investment Treaties' (2004) 20 *Arbitration International* 179, 201–202; Condorelli 'La protection diplomatique', above n 150, 17–18.

The preparatory materials confirm this view. While possibly not without some ambiguity in this[232] and other contexts,[233] Broches maintained the language of suspension and revival of the right, stating in the Legal Committee that:

The closing phrase of [what was to become Article 27(1)] did not introduce a right of intervention by the investor's State but merely permitted such a right (if it existed) to revive if the State party to the dispute failed to comply with the award.[234]

This view is supported by the following exchange between the UK representative Philip Allott and Broches:

Allott: ... the wording of [what was to become Article 27(1)] appeared to suggest that if arbitration failed the only ground for action by the injured State would be in respect of failure to observe the Convention as though the right in respect of the original injury had somehow lapsed. Such an injury might have been per se a breach of international law, as, for example, in the case of expropriation. It seemed to him that in such a case there would be two causes of action for the injured State, and he wondered whether his understanding was correct.

The CHAIRMAN agreed that in the hypothetical case mentioned by the United Kingdom expert there would be two causes of action for the injured State.[235]

The result of the non-compliance is thus not (or more precisely not only) a new breach of a primary rule by the host State, but also a complete revival of the right to diplomatic protection to the extent that it existed before the investor consented to arbitration.[236]

If one accepts that the right to diplomatic protection of the original breach is not waived, the next question is whether the State is bound to follow the determination of the investment-State arbitral Tribunal regarding the dispute. Schreuer has suggested that '[u]nder the Convention, diplomatic protection after an award has been rendered is available exclusively

---

[232] The initial drafts of the Convention contained broader formulations, talking generally about alleged violations by the other State of any its obligations under the Convention with respect to the dispute, *Convention: Documents,* above n 52, 23–24 (Working Paper in the Form of a Draft Convention, art II (5)), 163–164 (First Preliminary Draft of the Convention, art IV(17)), 221 (Preliminary Draft of the Convention, art IV(17)). The provision was subsequently limited to the incompliance with the award, and some of the debates in this regard focused entirely on the entitlement to give diplomatic protection for breaches of the ICSID Convention, without apparent consideration of its role in reviving earlier right to protection, 349 (Broches), see also 527 (Broches), 764–765 (Broches).

[233] Article IV(17)(2) of the Preliminary Draft Convention is not relevant in the context. It provided a without prejudice clause regarding State-State disputes taking place at the same time as the investor-State arbitration (*Convention: Documents,* above n 39, 576 (Chairman's Report) regarding abstract treaty-law issues (ibid, 350 (Broches), 435 (Broches), 576–577 (Chairman's report)) and therefore not affecting the exercise of protection over breaches of the investor's rights. The clause was dropped as both superfluous and confusing (ibid, 577 (Chairman's report)).

[234] Ibid, see also 527 ('The investor State's right of espousal, which disappeared on the assumption that the investor had a remedy under the Convention, revived when that remedy was frustrated').

[235] Ibid, 433.

[236] As Alexandroff and Laird observe, '[c]learly, a claimant's state could espouse an independent international claim', Alexandroff and Laird, above n 57, 1186.

for the purpose of its implementation'.[237] This view is correct 'under the Convention' where 'Article 64 merely provides an additional procedure',[238] but it would appear to have no broader application. BITs could provide jurisdictional bases for State-State dispute settlement and the espousal of the claim can also be pursued through non-formalized means of peaceful dispute settlement.[239] It would seem that the position is similar to that suggested regarding non-ICSID arbitrations: to the extent that the breach of the primary rule complained of is identical, the State should follow the Tribunal's determination. The State practice in Model BITs supports this view, recognizing the rights of diplomatic protection regarding claims rejected on a jurisdictional basis, although it would be preferable to distinguish between those jurisdictional decisions regarding the general inapplicability of the treaty from those relying only on the inappropriateness of the particular forum.[240]

Regarding the exhaustion of local remedies, the host State's obligation to comply with the ICSID award flows from the ICSID Convention and the relevant investment protection treaty, so there should be no need to exhaust domestic remedies.[241] In respect of diplomatic protection over breaches that fall outside the consent to arbitration, the interplay of Articles 26 and 27 suggests that the waiver of the exhaustion of local remedies applies regarding disputes that the investor and the State have consented to submit to arbitration. To the extent that the claims were not adjudicated upon for reasons not pertaining to the merits, it could be suggested that parties did not consent to their arbitration within the meaning of this rule, and thus the exhaustion of local remedies is not waived. Consequently, in such cases remedies should be exhausted, in accordance with the applicable rules of general international law.[242]

C. *Before the investor's consent*

The *dies a quo* of Article 27 of the ICSID Convention is the mutual consent of parties to investment arbitration; for the purposes of investment treaty arbitration it would be the submission of the claim. Until the claim is submitted, Article 27 does not apply and the ICSID Convention is in

---

[237] Schreuer, above n 104, 413.

[238] Ibid, 412.

[239] ILC 2006 Articles, above n 71, art 1, Commentary 8.

[240] 1998 Malaysia Model BIT art 7(4), 1995 Switzerland Model BIT art 8(4) and 1991 UK Model BIT art 8(4) provide that '[n]either Contracting Party shall pursue through the diplomatic channel any dispute referred to the Centre unless (a) the Secretary-General of the Centre, or a conciliation commission or an arbitral tribunal [constituted by it—*not in the Swiss BIT*], decides that the dispute is not within the jurisdiction of the Centre'. This rule can be read either in support of a general principle or as reflecting the particular rule of Article 27(1) of the ICSID Convention.

[241] Even though Article 26 of the ICSID Convention expressly excludes domestic remedies, strictly speaking the remedies are excluded regarding the investor's access to arbitration, and the right to diplomatic protection by the host State is a conceptually different issue, Schreuer, above n 104, 411–413.

[242] ILC 2006 Articles, above n 71, arts 14–15; Amerasinghe *Local Remedies,* above n 75.

that sense not relevant. As Schreuer has noted, 'the investor retains the option to request diplomatic protection from its home State despite the fact that the ICSID arbitration is open to it. But in that case, the investor would first have to exhaust local remedies. If there is no valid consent to jurisdiction the waiver of the exhaustion of local remedies ... also does not apply.'[243]

D. Regarding abstract interpretation

The host State could also take countermeasures in a dispute regarding abstract interpretation of the treaty that would not (or at least would only marginally) involve the diplomatic protection of the injury to a particular alien. Since Article 27 only suspends the right of diplomatic protection of investors, the ordinary meaning *a contrario* suggests that other rights of the States are not affected, including those provided for in the bilateral treaties. The preparatory materials of the ICSID Convention confirm this view. In response to concern about the effect on investment protection treaties (containing only State-State clauses at that time),[244] Broches confirmed that there was no intention to abrogate bilateral treaties in similar fields and promised express language to that effect.[245] Subsequent drafts incorporated language stating that the suspension was without prejudice to the right of the State to arbitrate even the same facts under a bilateral treaty.[246]

The debate about the provision showed some confusion about the nature of the rights at issue in both cases, the relationship between the two dispute settlement procedures and the remedy that the State could ask for.[247] Broches' own position was somewhat ambiguous, since he seemed to accept that the home State could arbitrate the same facts giving rise to the investor-State dispute, though the relief would be only declaratory and would not influence the investor-State award.[248] After the regional discussions, Broches decided to exclude the provision as superfluous and confusing, clearly distinguishing between the two cases:

Section 17 (1) deals with the right of espousal, i.e., the right of a State to bring an international claim based on an alleged injury done to that State in the person of its national, whereas Section 17 (2) contemplates a situation in which a dispute arises with respect to one of the rights or obligations of the State itself under the inter-governmental agreement. Although from the wording of Section 17 (2) it could be implied that it was intended as an exception to the general rule in Section 17 (1), Section 17 (1) in fact deals with an entirely different case.[249]

---

[243] Schreuer, above n 104, 409.
[244] *Convention: Documents,* above n 52, 63 (Donner).
[245] Ibid.
[246] *Convention: Documents,* above n 52, 163–164 (First Preliminary Draft of the Convention, art IV(17)(2)), 221–222 (Preliminary Draft of the Convention, art IV(17)(2)).
[247] Ibid, 274 (Mpanjo, Brown), 434–435 (Rodoconachi).
[248] Ibid, 273–274, 350, 435.   [249] Ibid, 576–577.

To the extent that it is possible to draw a distinction between diplomatic protection for injury of aliens and the more abstract State's rights under the treaty, Article 27 would not exclude claims regarding the latter ones. As Broches noted in his subsequent Hague Academy lecture regarding the application of Article 27 to investment treaty arbitration:

> each State consents in advance and irrevocably to submit disputes with respect to measures allegedly contrary to the treaty to ICSID conciliation and arbitration at the request of a national of the other State who claims to be injured by those measures. The question may arise whether the same facts could give rise to two arbitrations, or put differently, whether the two procedures are or are not mutually exclusive? Without trying to answer that question, I want to give as my view that the answer will not be found in Article 27 of the Convention—since no question of diplomatic protection is involved—but by interpretation of the Belgium-Indonesia treaty.[250]

One reason for the confusion seems to have been the broader ambiguity about the nature of the primary rule the State was claiming had been breached in each particular circumstance. There does not appear to be any hard and fast rule on the issue. Article 14(3) of the 2006 ILC Articles points to the criterion of preponderance of the claim in order to distinguish between claims of interpretation of treaties and claims of diplomatic protection relating to the injury of aliens. This is a test that the ILC itself concedes will be 'in practice difficult to decide'[251] and would require examination of the nature of the claim and the nature of the remedy required.[252]

Treaty claims regarding the treatment of aliens involve particularly difficult questions of classification, as shown by the *ELSI* case where the US skilfully attempted to dress a diplomatic protection claim in a treaty interpretation request for a declaratory judgment.[253] During the negotiations of the Convention a more liberal view appears to have been taken about the right of the home State to ask for interpretation of treaties regarding treatment of aliens that would not amount to diplomatic protection, different from the stricter *ELSI* standard that 'the matter which colours and pervades the United States claim as a whole, is the alleged damage' to its nationals. The more robust distinction between abstract and non-abstract claims would enable drawing the line in a clearer manner, treating as non-precluded only those claims which do not address individual investors at all.

A matter not caught by Article 27 could be a claim for a declaratory award that a piece of domestic legislation is contrary to substantive investment protection rules, even though not yet applied to any particular investor.[254] A law providing authority to a governmental agency 'to expropriate foreign

[250]   Broches, above n 42, 377–378.
[251]   2006 ILC Articles, above n 71, 74.
[252]   J Dugard, *Second Report on Diplomatic Protection*, A/CN.4/514 12–14.
[253]   *ELSI*, above n 113, 41 (paras 51–52); see also the controversy in *Avena*, above n 106.
[254]   Douglas, above n 45, 190; see the discussion of the right to protest imminent or threatened loss at BA Wortley, *Expropriation in Public International Law* (Cambridge University Press, Cambridge, 1959) 72–75.

property without compensation if the purpose is sufficiently important, with the reasoning of the decision being confidential and not subject to appeal' would arguably be contrary to the rules on expropriation and fair and equitable treatment. Assuming for the sake of an argument that such a rule would be in breach of the investment protection treaty, and following the conditions relating to the adoption of countermeasures, it should be considered whether countermeasures could be adopted when reparation in the form of compensation is not being asked for by the home State. According to Kelsen,

the obligation to repair the wrong inflicted upon another State, whether directly stipulated by general international law or established by agreement between the two States concerned, is not a sanction—as it is sometimes characterised—but a substitute obligation which replaces the original obligation violated by the international delict. The non-fulfilment of the obligation to repair moral and material damage caused by a delict is the condition to which international law annexes its specific sanctions, reprisals and war.[255]

To put Kelsen's argument in modern terminology, after the breach of the primary rule secondary obligations of State responsibility come into force, and it is for the inducement of compliance with these rules that countermeasures can be used. Within a third-party dispute settlement process, the home State could ask for a declaratory award if no material damage has been caused.[256] A decision upholding such a claim would confirm the respondent State's obligations pursuant to Article 30 of the 2001 ILC Articles on State responsibility to cease the wrongful act and, if the circumstances so require, to offer appropriate assurances and guarantees of non-repetition. Since the obligations to cease and appropriately confirm non-repetition automatically follow from the breach of the primary rule even without their invocation, a declaratory award on the existence of the breach would confirm the scope of the secondary rules binding on the host State. The home State could also plausibly ask for reparation as satisfaction in the form of acknowledgment of breach, expression of regret or apology, since such forms of reparation would not prejudice its position as not engaging in diplomatic protection.[257] To the extent that the respondent State does not cease its breach (in the example above probably repealing legislation), the claimant State would be entitled to use countermeasures to induce compliance.

E. Taken by a different home State

As (now Sir) Elihu Lauterpacht stated on behalf of Belgium in the *Barcelona Traction* case, 'the pattern of corporate structure today is one

---

[255] H Kelsen, *General Theory of Law and State* (Russel & Russel, New York, 1961) 357–358.

[256] C Gray, *Judicial Remedies in International Law* (Clarendon Press, Oxford, 1987) 96–107.

[257] 2001 ILC Articles on State responsibility, above n 13, art 47; A Watts, 'The Art of Apology' in M Ragazzi (ed) *International Responsibility Today* (Martinus Nijhoff Publishers, Leiden, 2005) 107–116; R Bilder, 'The Art of Apology in International Law and Politics' (2006) 46 *Virginia Journal of International Law* 433.

in which it is neither abnormal nor improper for business to be done in one country by a subsidiary set up in another and owned by a parent in a third.'[258] The observation made in 1964 sounds even truer in 2009. The customary law of investment protection of the 1960s did not reflect the corporate and economic reality in the 1960s[259] and it does not appear to have changed nowadays,[260] only in exceptional cases providing right of protection to the shareholders of the company beyond the narrow and rather contested concept of direct rights of shareholders.[261] The situation is different in treaty law where 'shares' are a standard example of what investment protection treaties explain the 'investment' to be,[262] whatever their approach to the definition of 'investment' is more generally.[263] As the *GAMI* Tribunal observed, '[t]he fact that a host State does not expressly interfere with share ownership is not decisive. The issue is rather whether a breach of NAFTA leads with sufficient directness to loss or damage in respect of a given investment.'[264] Investment protection treaties may also extend (as they often do) such protection to indirect shareholders, holding shares through an intermediary in the home State,[265] in the host State,[266] in a third State[267] and even in a third State by a shareholder itself controlled by an investor in another third State.[268] As suggested earlier, the State responsibility that the investor may invoke is paralleled by that arising from the obligations owed to its home State. Consequently, to the extent that investors can invoke the State responsibility for breaches affecting their investment, their home State (or States) can invoke diplomatic protections for injury to aliens and exercise countermeasures. In other words, to take the most (in)-famous

---

[258] *Barcelona Traction, Light and Power Co, Limited, (New Application) (Belgium v Spain)*, I.C.J. *Pleadings,* Volume II 542.

[259] L Caflisch, *La Protection des Sociétés Commerciales et des Intérêts Indirects en Droit International Public* (Martinus Nijhoff, the Hague, 1969).

[260] 2006 ILC Articles, above n 71, arts 9–12.

[261] V Lowe, 'Shareholders' Right to Control and Manage: From Barcelona Traction to ELSI' in N Ando et al (eds), *Liber Amicorum Judge Shigeru Oda* (Volume I, Kluwer Law International, the Hague, 2002) 269.

[262] R Dolzer and M Stevens, *Bilateral Investment Treaties* (Martinus Nijhoff Publishers, the Hague, 1995) 28.

[263] N Rubins, 'The Notion of 'Investment' in International Investment Arbitration' in N Horn (ed) *Arbitrating Foreign Investment Disputes: Procedural and Substantive Legal Aspects* (Kluwer Law International, the Hague, 2004) 283–324.

[264] *Gami Investments, Inc. v Mexico*, 15 November 2004, UNCITRAL arbitration, Final Award, November 15, 2004, <http://ita.law.uvic.ca/documents/Gami.pdf> (last accessed 28 February 2009), para 33.

[265] *Siemens A.G. v Argentine Republic*, ICSID Tribunal, Case No. ARB/02/8, Decision on Jurisdiction, August 3, 2004, <http://ita.law.uvic.ca/documents/SiemensJurisdiction-English-3August2004.pdf> (last accessed 28 February 2009), paras 137–144.

[266] *Enron and Ponderossa Assets v Argentine Republic*, ICSID Tribunal, Case No. ARB/01/3, Decision on Jurisdiction, January 14, 2004, <http://ita.law.uvic.ca/documents/Enron-Jurisdiction_000. pdf> (last accessed 28 February 2009), paras 52–56.

[267] *Lauder v Czech Republic*, UNCITRAL Tribunal, Final Award, September 3, 2001, <http://ita.law.uvic.ca/documents/LauderAward.pdf> (last accessed 28 February 2009), para 154.

[268] *Aguas del Tunari, S.A. v Republic of Bolivia*, ICSID Tribunal, Decision on Respondent's Objections to Jurisdiction, October 21, 2005, (2005) 20 *ICSID Review—Foreign Investment Law Journal* 450, 515 (paras 214–333).

double-bite arbitration of *CME* and *Lauder,* it could just as well have been *CME* and *the US* or *the Netherlands* and *Lauder*, with the relevant home State engaging in diplomatic protection and countermeasures in accordance with the interplay of customary and relevant treaty rules.[269]

V. Countermeasures as a Shield

Along with the use of countermeasures as means to induce compliance with the obligations under investment protection treaties, countermeasures may also be applied against the investment protection treaties themselves. The role of countermeasures 'as a sword' was directly addressed in the investment law-making processes by suspending the exercise of diplomatic protection during ICSID arbitration. The role of countermeasures 'as a shield' does not appear to have received much explicit attention, so the issue has to be considered against the background of customary law. The argument will be made in two steps, considering whether investment protection rules are obligations not affected by countermeasures (A), or obligations excluding countermeasures (B).

A. Obligations not affected by countermeasures

Article 50 of the ILC 2001 Articles addresses obligations not affected by countermeasures. Investment protection treaties are not expressly mentioned as one of such rules. It will be further considered whether investment protection treaties are nevertheless covered by these rules or whether the rationale underpinning these rules could not be applied, *mutatis mutandis*, to investment protection treaties. The arguments for investment protection treaties being not affected will be taken in turn, starting from the least plausible and dealing with peremptory norms (1), humanitarian law (2), human rights argument in terms of substantive coverage (3), the nature of the legal obligations (4), and the nature of the legal rights (5).

Before considering these arguments in greater detail, it is necessary to note some general issues regarding the identification of obligations not affected by countermeasures. The problems with situating investment protection treaties within this Article are fourfold. First of all, there is a broader problem regarding the interpretative rules applicable to the 2001 ILC Articles on State responsibility, their Commentaries and other earlier draft documents and debates: despite the intuitive VCLT-reminiscent approach

---

[269] *CME,* above n 167 and below n 424; *Lauder,* above n 267. The *CME-Lauder* arbitrations are perhaps not the best example since they were conducted under UNCITRAL rules, thus not raising the question about the role of Article 27 of the ICSID Convention. The example has been used because of the general awareness of the corporate structure of the case. As was suggested above at Part III. B-D, in non-ICSID arbitrations there is no express exclusion of diplomatic protection, thus (depending on the interpretation of each particular treaty) there could have been *CME-the Netherlands-Lauder-US v Czech Republic* disputes.

of reading the ordinary meaning of the Articles and trying to confirm it in the Commentaries and drafts, the proper benchmark is the degree to which any of these propositions reflect customary international law, thus requiring equal attention to the earlier debates and drafts.[270] Secondly, there is a particularly perplexing inter-temporal twist in the apparent confirmation by the Court in its 1998 judgment in *Gabčíkovo-Nagymaros Project* case of the customary nature of the 1996 ILC Articles on counter-measures and not having given a similar approval to the 2001 ILC Articles on State responsibility subsequently.[271] It could be argued that on this particular issue the thoughts expressed in the first reading enjoy more authority than those expressed in the second reading. Thirdly, as Crawford recognized in his Fourth Report, '[t]he essential problem is that the list in Article 51 [now 50] appears to embody no clear principle.'[272] If the distinction between primary and secondary rules had been faithfully pursued, Article 50 should arguably have been reduced to *jus cogens* and *lex specialis* rules. By giving guidance on the most obvious exceptions, the ILC may have eliminated uncertainty in the particular context but also contributed to ambiguity more broadly regarding the criteria relevant for identifying such rules.[273] Fourthly, in addition to these broader problems, investment protection treaties have not been expressly considered in this context.

1. Investment protection law and peremptory norms

Article 50(1)(d) provides that 'countermeasures shall not affect … other obligations under peremptory norms of international law'. To the extent that the rules provided in investment protection treaties are *jus cogens,* countermeasures would not affect these obligations.[274] The treatment guaranteed in investment protection treaties does not generally have the character of *jus cogens.* The Court of First Instance of the European Communities in the *Yusuf* and *Kadi* cases has suggested that protection of property and the right to fair trial are *jus cogens,* but it is doubtful whether that is an accurate statement of contemporary international law.[275] The Third Restatement

---

[270] Caron, above n 143, 869–870; see preceding discussion at n 143 and n 144 above and surrounding text.

[271] *Gabčíkovo-Nagymaros Project*, above n 21, 55 (para 83).

[272] J Crawford, *Fourth Report on State Responsibility,* A/CN.4/51, para 64.

[273] Crawford *Articles,* above n 123, 51. The *Corn Products* Tribunal considered Article 50 to have no direct relevance for investment protection rules, *Corn Products,* above n 49, para 149.

[274] *Methanex Corporation v United States of America,* UNCITRAL Arbitration, Final Award, August 3, 2005 Part IV—Chapter C, <http://ita.law.uvic.ca/documents/MethanexFinalAward.pdf> (last accessed 28 February 2009), para 24.

[275] C Tomuschat, 'Case Note (*Yusuf* and *Kadi*)' (2006) 43 *Common Market Law Review* 537, 545–551; P Eeckhout, 'Community Terrorism Listings, Fundamental Rights, and UN Security Council Resolutions. In Search of the Right Fit' (2007) 3 *European Constitutional Law Review* 183, 194–197. The judgment of the European Court of Justice set aside the Court of First Instance judgment on other grounds and did not address the issue of *jus cogens,* but it is instructive that the UK, France, the Netherlands, and the Commission asked the Court to find that the particular fundamental rights did not have the character of *jus cogens,* Case 402/05 P and C 415/05 P *Yassin Abdullah Kadi and Al Barakaat International Foundation v Council* [2008] Judgment of 3 September 2008, paras 329 and 265.

of the Foreign Relations Law of the United States suggests that discrimination and discriminatory takings against nationals of the offending State are impermissible, but the argument is not linked to *jus cogens*.[276]

At the same time, it is possible that the treatment required by investment protection law may in particular instances have the character of *jus cogens*. As the 2001 ILC Articles on State responsibility themselves point out, genocide, racial discrimination and crimes against humanity are among the clearly accepted peremptory rules.[277] If racially discriminatory rules are applied to investors, they would simultaneously breach the national treatment rules in the investment protection treaty and the customary law obligation having *jus cogens* character. If investors and their property are mistreated as part of a State-controlled and inspired campaign of persecution as crimes against humanity, this would breach both obligations having *jus cogens* character and those contained in investment protection treaties regarding expropriation, fair and equitable treatment, full protection and security and national treatment. To consider a few historical examples, the persecution of Jews by Nazi Germany is an example of the latter situation, resulting *inter alia* in indirect expropriations through forced sales,[278] a legal situation also possible in investment law.[279] Another example can be found in the series of long-running disputes in the late XIX and early XX centuries about the compatibility of Russian anti-Jewish legislation with its treaty obligations with the US, the UK, France, Germany, and Switzerland. Russia argued that the national treatment clauses in the treaties did not require it to treat Jewish aliens differently from its Jewish nationals.[280] In contemporary international law conduct pursuant to such a treaty construction would probably be contrary to *jus cogens*. It may be concluded that while in particular circumstances the obligations provided in investment protection treaties would have the character of *jus cogens* because of the overlap with the *jus cogens* rule, this overlap is certainly not general.

2. *Investment protection law and humanitarian law*

Article 50(1)(c) provides that 'countermeasures shall not affect ... obligations of a humanitarian character prohibiting reprisals'. One could argue

---

[276] *Restatement (Third) of the Foreign Relations Law of the United States* (American Law Institute Publishers, St. Paul, Minn., 1987) § 905 Commentary b, § 711 f, g, § 712 f.

[277] 2001 ILC Articles on State responsibility, above n 13, 85.

[278] GC Christie, 'What Constitutes a Taking of Property under International Law?' (1962) 38 *British Yearbook of International Law* 307, 324; BH Weston, '"Constructive Takings" Under International Law: A Modest Foray into the Problem of "Creeping Expropriation"' (1975) 16 *Virginia Journal of International Law* 103, 141; R Higgins, 'The Taking of Property by the State: Recent Developments in International Law' (1982) 176 *Recueil des Cours* 259, 326.

[279] See the analysis of forced sales issues in investment protection context, *Desert Line Projects LLC v Republic of Yemen*, ICSID Case No. ARB/05/17, Award, February 6, 2008, <http://ita.law.uvic.ca/documents/DesertLine.pdf> (last accessed 28 February 2009), paras 148–194.

[280] N Feinberg, 'The National Treatment Clause in a Historical Perspective (A Controversy with Czarist Russia)' in *Recueil d'études de droit international en hommage à Paul Guggenheim* (Imprimerie de la Tribune de Genève, Geneva, 1986); Мартенс, above n 12, 348 fn 2.

that the long-established prohibition of property confiscation in wartime would *a fortiori* mean that reprisals should be forbidden in peace-time. Arangio-Ruiz proposed the *a fortiori* argument from the war-time treatment of property to the peace-time treatment of property as one of the ways to conceptualize countermeasures against private property.[281]

First of all, the premise of the argument is correct. As the ICRC *Customary International Humanitarian Law* states in Rule 51(c), '[i]n occupied territory ... private property must be respected and may not be confiscated ... except where the destruction or seizure of such property is required by imperative military necessity.' The commentary explains that '[t]he protection of private property against confiscation is a long-standing rule of customary international law.'[282] While not free from doubt (especially in the aftermath of conflicts in which practice contradicted the rule),[283] this seems to be an accurate statement of international law for the last century and before, codified in treaties and reflected in case law and legal writings.[284] At the same time, the rigour of the rules on the protection of property was limited by the rules on confiscation of contraband and the controversial right to capture belligerent property from neutral ships.[285]

Secondly, it seems that the *a fortiori* argument in favour of protection of property in peace-time does not accurately reflect the law-making processes of the 1920s and 1930s that moulded international practice into the rule on protection of property. In light of broader criticism of the protection of private property,[286] the *a fortiori* or *mutatis mutandis* arguments from war-time protection were employed.[287] They were not successful. While

---

[281] G Arangio-Ruiz, 'Third Report on State Responsibility' in *Yearbook of the ILC* 1991, *Vol. II(1)* A/CN.4/SER.A/1991/Add.1, para 111; see also Seidl-Hohenveldern, above n 64, 474–475; H Rolin, 'Avis' (1959) 6 *Netherlands International Law Review* 260, 274.

[282] J-M Henckaerts and L Doswald-Beck, *Customary International Humanitarian Law: Volume I: Rules* (Cambridge University Press, Cambridge, 2005) 178–181.

[283] Eg C Mullins, 'Private Enemy Property' (1918) 8 *Transactions of the Grotius Society* 89, 89–106.

[284] See Henckaerts and Doswald-Beck, above n 282, 178–181 (Article 46 of the Hague Regulations and relevant case law); also Wheaton, above n 28, 417; Oppenheim, above n 4, 146–150; JB Moore, 'International Law and Some Current Illusions' in JB Moore, *International Law and Some Current Illusions and Other Essays* (The MacMillan Company, New York, 1924) 21 et seq.; EC Stowell, *International Law: A Restatement of Principles in Accordance with Actual Practice* (Sir Isaac Pitman & Sons, Ltd., London, 1931) 520. The full compensation also applied to angary, C Bullock, 'Angary' (1922–1923) 3 *British Yearbook of International Law* 98, 98–129; H Lauterpacht, 'Angary and Requisition of Neutral Property' (1950) 27 *British Yearbook of International Law* 455, 455–459; H Lauterpacht (ed) *Oppenheim's International Law* (Vol II, 7th edn, Longmans, Green and Co., 1952) 759–766.

[285] On contraband Lauterpacht, ibid, 823–830; von Liszt, above n 12, 360–361; G Fitzmaurice, 'Modern Contraband Control and the Law of Prize' (1945) 22 *British Yearbook of International Law* 73, 73–95; JHW Verzijl, WP Heere and JPS Offerhaus, *International Law in the Historical Perspective: Part IX-C* (Martinus Nijhoff Publishers, Dordrecht, 1992) 331–370; on the treatment of enemy goods on neutral ships, Verzijl et al, at 299–330.

[286] Eg JF Williams, 'International Law and the Property of Aliens' (1928) 9 *British Yearbook of International Law* 1 et seq.; A Cavaglieri, 'La notion des droits acquis et son application en droit international public' (1931) 38 *Revue générale de droit international public* 257, 294–296 (against protection of property in international law); J Brierly, 'Règles générales du droit de la paix' (1936) 58 *Recueil des Cours* 5, 171 (uncertain about any rule for non-discriminatory expropriations).

[287] Bullington, who made probably the most sophisticated and erudite argument between the two World Wars for the existence of a rule on the protection of private property in the time of peace,

puzzling to the modern eye, express consideration of the protection of private property in the XIX and early XX century only existed for war-time,[288] most probably because of the tacit consensus on what it was in peace-time,[289] modelled on Anglo-Saxon rule of law ideas.[290] The Institute of International Law did not address the treatment of persons and property in peace-time before 1927[291] and, as late as 1926, the mind of an ASIL speaker on property protection naturally averted to confiscation in times of war.[292] The argument in favour of protection of property in war-time could thus be made simultaneously with one rejecting it in peace-time. At the League of Nations Committee of Experts for the Progressive Codification of International Law Special Rapporteur Guerrero famously argued for a very narrow concept of treatment of aliens outside national treatment rules, limiting it to the denial of justice.[293] While supporting compensation for expropriations during civil wars[294] and wars,[295] he rejected compensation in cases of non-discriminatory expropriations.[296]

The war-time analogy was certainly one of the possible law-making strategies[297] employed for justifying the existence of private property (together with the rules on State succession,[298] arguments deriving from general principles *in foro domestico*[299] or simply US law).[300] However, the more successful strategy turned out to be the argument of acquired rights.[301]

relied on the 'well-established rule of positive international law protecting the private property of alien individuals on land outside the zone of military operations' to argue that there was a general peace-time rule on protection of property, JP Bullington, 'Problems of International Law in the Mexican Constitution of 1917' (1927) 21 *American Journal of International Law* 685, 694–695.

[288] Eg Wheaton, above n 28, 378–388.

[289] G Schwarzenberger, 'The Protection of British Property Abroad ' (1952) 5 *Current Legal Problems* 295, 298–299.

[290] G Schwarzenberger, 'The Standard of Civilization in International Law' (1955) 8 *Current Legal Problems* 212, 227.

[291] G Fitzmaurice, 'The Contribution of the Institute of International Law to the Development of International Law' (1973) 138 *Recueil des Cours* 203, 227–228, 255.

[292] C Bouve, 'The Confiscation of Alien Property' (1926) 20 *ASIL Proceedings* 14, 14.

[293] S Rosenne (ed) *League of Nations Committee of Experts for the Progressive Codification of International Law [1925–1928]* (Volume II, Oceana Publications, Inc., New York, 1972) 120, 125–126.

[294] Ibid, 128.

[295] S Rosenne (ed) *League of Nations Committee of Experts for the Progressive Codification of International Law [1925–1928]* (Volume I, Oceana Publications, Inc., New York 1972) 96–97.

[296] Ibid, 98.

[297] On law-making strategies see M Byers, 'Pre-Emptive Self-Defence: Hegemony, Equality and Strategies of Legal Change' (2003) 11 *Journal of Political Philosophy* 171, 171–190; M Byers, 'Policing the Seas: The Proliferation Security Initiative' (2004) 98 *American Journal of International Law* 526, 526–545.

[298] Bullington, above n 287, 694–695.

[299] Ibid, 688–694.

[300] E Borchard, 'The "Minimum Standard" of the Treatment of Aliens' (1939) 33 *ASIL Proceedings* 51, 65 (Nielsen).

[301] *Case Concerning Certain German Interests in Polish Upper Silesia,* Ser A 7 4, 22; see also J-C Witenberg, 'La protection de la propriété immobilière des étrangers' (1928) 55 *Journal du droit international* 566, 570–572; 'Report of Dr. J. C. Witenberg to the Protection of Private Property Committee' in *International Law Association's Report of the Thirty-Sixth Conference* 1929 (Sweet & Maxwell, London, 1930) 305 *et seq.*; C Dupuis, 'Règles générales du droit de la paix' (1930) 32 *Recueil des Cours* 5, 160; G Kaeckenbeeck, 'The Protection of Vested Rights in International Law' (1936) 17 *British*

It was generally agreed at the time that countermeasures could be applied to the property of nationals of the wrongdoing State.[302] Even the broader argument in favour of protection of private property therefore recognized the applicability of reprisals. As Anzilotti put it in his expert opinion on the Italian Insurance Companies dispute,[303] 'je ne crois pas qu'il y ait dans tout le droit international de principe plus certain que celui-ci: L'État ne peut pas violer la propriété privée des étrangers, hors des cas spécifiquement déterminés (droit de guerre, représailles, etc.).'[304]

The distinction between the two strands of law-making is clearly confirmed by the State practice at the 1930 Hague Conference. In response to the question about reprisals as a circumstance in which a State is entitled to disclaim responsibility for injuries to aliens,[305] three States did not answer this question,[306] three States considered that reprisals should *de lege ferenda* be forbidden[307] or at least limited to acts similar to the anterior breach,[308] seven States confirmed the exercise of such a right with procedural qualifications,[309] and seven States fully confirmed the existence of such a right.[310] Against the background of the sufficiently clear legal situation in the 1920s and 1930s of impermissibility of war-time confiscations and apparently broad consensus on the permissibility of peace-time countermeasures, one would need to show some fundamental change of perception in the subsequent State practice that would bring these regimes into harmony.

Thirdly, it could be argued that the changing law of belligerent reprisals, providing extensive prohibitions of reprisals against the protected

Yearbook of International Law 1; G Kaeckenbeeck, 'La protection internationale des droits acquis' (1936) 59 *Recueil des Cours* 321; CC Hyde, 'Confiscatory Expropriation' (1938) 22 *American Journal of International Law* 759, 760; A McNair, 'The General Principles of Law Recognised by Civilized Nations' (1957) 33 *British Yearbook of International Law* 1, 16–18.

[302] Eg Phillimore, above n 3, 31; Мартенс, above n 12, 508; Oppenheim, above n4, 38; J Westlake, *International Law: War* (Cambridge University Press, Cambridge, 1907) 7; Halleck, above n 12, 505; Hall, above n 12, 433; von Lyszt, above n 12, 297. Fauchille considered such reprisals to be immoral and ineffective, but did not question their lawfulness, P Fauchille, *Traité de droit international public* (Librairie Arthur Rouseau, Paris, 1926) 692. The suggestion of the 1934 International Law Institute Paris Resolution that the effect of countermeasures on individual rights should be limited, 'Régime des représailles en temps de paix', above n 21, art 6(3), was not taken up either by States or legal writers (or alternatively it was simply assumed that no question of 'rights' arose regarding the treatment of individuals in such situations, merely one of interests).

[303] Fachiri, above n 32, 166–167; E Audinet, 'Le monopole des assurances en Italie et le droit des etrangers' (1913) 20 *Revue générale de droit international public* 5; O Hoijer, 'La Responsabilite internationale des etats en matiere d'actes legislatifes' (1929) 3 *Revue de droit international* 577.

[304] Cited from *Oscar Chinn* Case, above n 32, 53. Other writers also combined the arguments for protection of private property and applicability of countermeasures to private property, eg CC Hyde, *International Law, Chiefly as Interpreted and Applied by the United States* (2nd edn, Little, Brown and Company, Boston, 1947) 710–722, 1662.

[305] Rosenne *Conference* Vol II, above n 32, 550.

[306] Ibid, 550 (Germany), 552 (Poland, Siam).

[307] Ibid, 550–551 (Denmark), 551, (Netherlands).

[308] Ibid, 551 (Finland).

[309] Ibid, 550 (Belgium), 551 (Great Britain, India, New Zealand), 552 (Switzerland, Czechoslovakia), 680 (Canada).

[310] Ibid, 550 (South Africa, Australia, Austria), 551 (Hungary, Italy, Japan), 698 (US).

persons and their property, could stimulate the analogous development in the law of peace-time countermeasures. Classical international law recognized belligerent reprisals as a regrettable but indispensable means to limit illegitimate acts of warfare,[311] and even though humanitarian restrictions were considered necessary *de lege ferenda*,[312] it was only the 1929 Geneva Convention concerning the Treatment of Prisoners of War that prohibited the use of reprisals in the narrower area of treatment of prisoners of war.[313] The 1949 Geneva Conventions prohibited reprisals in international armed conflicts, including those against the property of civilians, and Additional Protocol I introduced a sweeping treaty law prohibition of reprisals also in the zone of military conflict.[314] Considered against this background, it could be argued that the position in the 1930s should not be determinative since the development of the prohibition of belligerent reprisals had only just started in 1929; the emergence of the sweeping prohibition on reprisals in contemporary international law (*inter alia* against property) should be reflected in a similar restriction of countermeasures. Such logic seems implicit in the argument from the opposite perspective adopted by the International Criminal Tribunal for Former Yugoslavia (ICTY) in *Prosecutor v Kupreškić* where it relied on the 1996 ILC Articles regarding restriction of countermeasures against basic human rights to support its conclusions on the general prohibition of belligerent reprisals.[315]

The argument is problematic on a number of levels. *First of all*, both classic international law and the discussion in *Kupreškić* show a distinction between the policies involved in countermeasures, taken to compel the responsible State to settle the particular difference, and more future-oriented and contextual belligerent reprisals, taken to compel the State to abandon unlawful acts of warfare and not repeat them, and the balance between military necessity and humanitarian considerations peculiar to the latter.[316] The policy differences may preclude the application of the developments in the law of belligerent reprisals to peace-time counter-measures. *Secondly*, the correctness of the ICTY's sweeping position and its legal rationale is subject to some doubt.[317] *Thirdly*, as will be further

---

[311] Oppenheim, above n 4, 259; L Oppenheim, *International Law* (Vol II, 2nd edn, Longmans, Green and Co., London, 1912) 305; RF Roxburgh (ed) *Oppenheim's International Law* (Vol II, 3rd edn, Longmans, Green and Co., London, 1921) 335–337.

[312] A McNair (ed) *Oppenheim's International Law* (Vol II, 4th edn, Longmans, Green and Co., London, 1926) 408.

[313] Kalshoven, above n 29, 78–82.

[314] T Meron, 'Humanization of Humanitarian Law' (2000) 94 *American Journal of International Law* 239, 250.

[315] *Prosecutor v Kupreškić* (Judgment) IT-95-16 (14 January 2000), paras 529, 534.

[316] H Lauterpacht (ed) *Oppenheim's International Law* (Vol II, 6th edn, Longmans, Green and Co., London, 1940) 446–447.

[317] CJ Greenwood, 'Belligerent Reprisals in the Jurisprudence of the International Criminal Tribunal for Former Yugoslavia' in H Fischer et al (eds) *International and National Prosecutions of Crimes under International Law* (Arno Spitz, Berlin, 2001) 331; F Kalshoven, 'Reprisals and the Protection of Civilians: Two Recent Decisions of the Yugoslavia Tribunal' in LC Vohrah et al (eds) *Man's Inhumanity to Man: Essays on International Law in Honour of Antonio Cassese* (Kluwer Law

explained, the debate preceding the 2001 ILC Articles on State responsibility showed that the limitations of countermeasures arising from humanitarian law stemmed from different considerations. The argument is thus initially suspect, and its transposition into the law of countermeasures is problematic and it is not apparent that it has been attempted. One probably has to follow Bowett's sobering view taken in 1972 that adoption of non-forcible self-help measures against individuals for their nationality State's breaches is an unattractive principle but one that would be unrealistic to attempt to change.[318]

Fourthly, the distinction between humanitarian law and other exceptions to countermeasures is confirmed by the ILC. The early documents supported a closer link between humanitarian law and human rights restrictions of countermeasures, reflected in Riphagen's[319] and Arangio-Ruiz's reports,[320] supported to some extent in the ILC[321] and included in the 1996 ILC Articles.[322] Crawford in his Third Report was critical about generalizations drawn from humanitarian law,[323] and with a few exceptions[324] the members of the ILC broadly supported maintaining the distinction.[325] The Commentary to the 2001 ILC Articles on State responsibility considers human rights and humanitarian law distinctly, while not free from ambiguity: it weaves together several strands of argument *inter alia* regarding humanitarian considerations present in restrictions existing in humanitarian law.[326] The most prescient reason for distinguishing between the two was provided by Crawford in the 2000 ILC debate:

There might, however, be situations when the human being was not the subject of the right, but, in some sense, the object. That had been true of the old prohibition of reprisals in humanitarian law, a prohibition which, unlike the situation in modern human rights, had been a pure inter-State obligation of which individuals were beneficiaries.[327]

International, the Hague, 2003) 481; UK Ministry of Defence, *The Manual of the Law of Armed Conflict* (Oxford University Press, Oxford, 2004) 420–421, fn 62. Cf the more cautious approach of the *Martić* Trial Chamber recognizing the principle of belligerent reprisals, *Prosecutor v Martić* (Judgment) IT-95-11-T (12 June 2007), paras 465–467, implicitly accepted by the Appeals Chamber, *Prosecutor v Martić* (Judgment) IT-95-11-A (8 October 2008), paras 263–267.

[318] D Bowett, 'Economic Coercion and Reprisals by States' (1972) 13 *Virginia Journal of International Law* 1, 10. Under contemporary law, the statement should be read subject to *lex specialis* and *jus cogens* rules.

[319] W Riphagen, *Fourth Report on State Responsibility* A/CN.4/366 17, paras 18–19.

[320] Arangio-Ruiz 'Third Report', above n 281, para 111; Arangio-Ruiz, 'Fourth Report', above n 64, para 78.

[321] *Yearbook of the ILC* 1992, *Vol. I* A/CN.4/SER.A/1992 166, para 8 (Tomuschat).

[322] 1996 ILC Articles, above n 182, 334, para 17.

[323] J Crawford, *Third Report on State Responsibility*, A/CN.4/507 Add.3, para 312.

[324] *Yearbook of the ILC* 2000, above n 68, 272, para 47 (Galicki), 274, paras 64, 66 (Pellet) (Pellet's argument should be read having regard to his minority position that *jus cogens* would cover all the exceptions, para 67, cf 275, para 76 (Crawford)), 286, para 32 (Momtaz).

[325] Ibid, 275, para 75 (Lukashuk), 275, para 79 (Dugard), 300, para 86 (Hafner).

[326] 2001 ILC Articles on State responsibility, above n 13, 132.

[327] *Yearbook of the ILC* 2000, above n 68, 271, para 39.

In humanitarian law, the rationale of prohibition seemed to flow from the unacceptability of arbitrariness of the mutually injurious conduct in breach of elementary precepts of humanity. Reflecting the maturity of the legal order of the time, the rules, while factually benefiting the individuals, did not grant them legally enforceable rights. In human rights law (and *mutatis mutandis* investment protection law), the policy of reducing mutually injurious conduct plays a lesser role, shifting the search for the possible rationale to the particular aspects of the rules, especially the legal nature of the obligations and the role the rights and remedies provided to individuals play.

3. *Investment protection law and human rights: the substantive argument*

Article 50(1)(b) provides that 'countermeasures shall not affect ... obligations for the protection of fundamental human rights'. If the rights protected by investment protection treaties could be considered to be both human rights and fundamental, countermeasures would be excluded on this basis. The issue will be considered in three steps, addressing the conceptual distinction between these branches of law, the possibility of using comparative arguments drawn from human rights law in investment protection law in general as well as in the particular instance.

First of all, there is a clear and conceptual distinction between the law of human rights and the law on treatment of aliens, reflected in post-Second World War law-making processes. The classic position of international law was to recognize only the rights of aliens and not fundamental human rights.[328] The post-War emergence of legal documents addressing human rights, therefore, created qualitatively new challenges regarding the conceptualization of the relationship between these branches of international law. At one end of the spectrum, it was argued with slightly differing emphases that a general standard of human rights should replace the international standard of rights of aliens, whether by transformation,[329] assimilation,[330] synthesis[331] or abandonment of the latter in favour of the former.[332] An intermediate position recognized the conceptually different nature of both standards, but called for some more nuanced relationship between the two, in particular by using human rights arguments to concretize and elucidate the content of the international standard.[333] At the

---

[328] H Lauterpacht, 'Law of Nations, Law of Nature, and Rights of Man' (1944) 29 *Transactions of the Grotius Society* 1, 27.

[329] PC Jessup, *A Modern Law of Nations* (Archon Books, Hamden, Connecticut, 1968) 97.

[330] H Waldock, 'Human Rights in Contemporary International Law and the Significance of the European Convention' in *The European Convention on Human Rights* (BIICL, London, 1965) 3.

[331] McDougal, Lasswell and Chen, above n 215, 454 et seq.

[332] García-Amador 'State Responsibility', above n 211, 433–437.

[333] Eg AV Freeman, 'Human Rights and the Rights of Aliens' (1951) 45 *ASIL Proceedings* 120, 125; P Guggenheim, 'Les principles de droit international public' (1952) 80 *Recueil des Cours* 1, 130; CT Eustathiadès, 'Les sujets de Droit international et le responsabilité internationale. Nouvelles tendances' (1953) 81 *Recueil des Cours* 397, 597, 599; RY Jennings, 'General Course on Principles of Public International Law' (1967) 121 *Recueil des Cours* 323, 488; A-C Kiss, 'La condition des étrangers

other end of the spectrum, in the immediate post-War period a sceptical view argued that acceptance of human rights standards would amount to the abandonment of any realistic protection.[334] García-Amador's proposals at the ILC embodied the first approach, calling for the creation of a new international standard of human rights.[335]

The ILC rejected this approach. While Lillich explained the rejection in light of the defence by developing and Communist States of the national treatment rule,[336] the actual debates demonstrate a widespread scepticism about the normative underpinnings of the project that cannot be explained away simply by ideological considerations. The UK member of the ILC Fitzmaurice pointed to the conceptually distinct nature of the regimes,[337] the US member Edmonds was sceptical about the place of human rights in international law,[338] and the Netherlands member François felt that human rights law was too vague to be of any assistance to the elucidation of the international standard.[339] Some of these criticisms have retained their relevance; to the extent that the international legal order has evolved further and rendered them partly redundant, they point to the appropriate authorities and methods to be taken into account in approaching the relationship of human rights and international standards on the treatment of aliens.

The sweeping rejection of García-Amador's ambitious proposal meant that the argument for unification of the law on the treatment of aliens and law of human rights had failed, and indeed it has not featured prominently in subsequent law-making processes. More recently, the Court appears to have accepted the distinction. In the *LaGrand Case*, Germany argued that the right to consular protection constituted a human right of aliens.[340] The Court accepted the anterior German argument that these rights were individual rights and thus left open the question of human rights, but the language the Court used ('additional argument') suggested that it viewed human rights as conceptually distinct.[341] When Mexico pressed the same argument in the *Case Concerning Avena and Other Mexican*

---

en droit international et les droits de l'homme' in *Miscellanea WJ Ganshof van der Meersch* (LGDJ, Paris, 1972) 505.

[334] AV Freeman, 'Recent Aspects of the Calvo Doctrine and the Challenge to International Law' (1946) 40 *American Journal of International Law* 121 et seq. See the sceptical view about the substantive and procedural aspects of human rights protection: Amerasinghe *State Responsibility*, above n 73, 4–6.

[335] Garciá-Amador, 'State Responsibility', above n 211, 438; *Yearbook of the ILC 1956, Vol. II A/CN.4/SER.A/1956/Add.1* 202; *Yearbook of the ILC 1957, Vol. II A/CN.4/SER.A/1957/Add.1* 113–114.

[336] Lillich 'Duties', above n 38, 377.

[337] *Yearbook of the ILC 1956, A/CN.4/SER.A/1956*, 243–234; see also *Yearbook of the ILC 1957*, above n 38, 164, 169 (Spiropoulus).

[338] *Yearbook of the ILC 1957*, above n 38, 160.

[339] *Yearbook of the ILC 1956*, above n 337, 243; see also *Yearbook of the ILC 1957*, above n 38, 163.

[340] *LaGrand Case (Germany v US)* [2000] ICJ Pleadings CR 2000/26 <http://www.icj-cij.org/docket/files/104/4649.pdf> (last accessed 28 February 2009) 59–62 (Simma); CR 2000/27 <http://www.icj-cij.org/docket/files/104/4649.pdf> (last accessed 28 February 2009) 8–13 (Simma).

[341] *LaGrand Case*, above n 106, 494 (para 78).

Nationals, the Court went further and stated that nothing supported Mexico's conclusions regarding the human rights nature of consular rights.[342] The distinction between human rights and the standard of treatment of aliens was confirmed in the *Case Concerning Ahmadou Sadio Diallo,* where the Court described human rights and the international standard as distinct primary rules that could give rise to diplomatic protection.[343]

Secondly, the conceptually distinct nature of the two regimes does not preclude valuable comparative analysis to explain the international standard through the prism of human rights. To recall the doctrinal debates of the 1950s and 1960s and the ILC discussion, García-Amador's project was rejected because of its overly ambitious reach as well as the uncertain and undeveloped nature of the law of human rights at the time. When placed in this context, the early debate on State responsibility shows not the irrelevance of human rights law for the law of treatment of aliens, but rather establishes the limits within which the human rights arguments may be used and the required specificity and clarity of the sources from which these arguments are sought.

The arguments suggest that a shift of methodological focus should be sought, abandoning the extremes of total rejection and total synthesis and adopting a careful comparative approach, always keeping in mind the systemic differences[344] and the key question of comparative analysis in international law: *to what extent* is it appropriate to employ these principles for the analysis of investment protection law?[345] Consequently, using comparative arguments 'as a useful if rough barometer'[346] may in principle assist in elucidating the meaning of investment protection rules,[347] to the extent that meaningful comparison between functionally similar matters can be made.[348] There is therefore no *a priori* reason for dismissing reliance on comparative human rights arguments.

---

[342] *Avena,* above n 106, 60 (para 124).

[343] *Diallo,* above n 10, para 39.

[344] Eg V Lowe, 'Regulation or Expropriation?' (2002) 55 *Current Legal Problems* 447, 463.

[345] D Sarooshi, *International Organizations and Their Exercise of Sovereign Powers* (Oxford University Press, Oxford, 2005) 16.

[346] *Mondev v United States of America,* UNCITRAL Arbitration, US Pleadings (Legum), May 23, 2002 <http://www.state.gov/documents/organization/15440.pdf> (last accessed 28 February 2009) 760.

[347] *Mondev v United States of America,* ICSID Case No. ARB(AF)/99/2, Award, October 11, 2002, (2003) 42 *International Legal Materials* 85, 112 (paras 138, 141, 143–144); *Técnicas Medioambientales Tecmed, S.A. v United Mexican States,* ICSID Case No. ARB(AF)/00/02, Award, May 29, 2003, <http://ita.law.uvic.ca/documents/Tecnicas_001.pdf> (last accessed 28 February 2009), paras 116, 122; *Azurix Corp. v Argentine Republic,* ICSID Case No. ARB/01/12, Award, July 14, 2006, <http://ita.law.uvic.ca/documents/AzurixAwardJuly2006.pdf> (last accessed 28 February 2009), para 311; *Saipem,* above n 63, paras 130, 132.

[348] As it could not be made in *Siemens* regarding the rules on compensation in human rights law, *Siemens A.G. v Republic of Argentina,* ICSID Case No. ARB/02/8, Award, February 6, 2007, <http://ita.law.uvic.ca/documents/Siemens-Argentina-Award.pdf> (last accessed 28 February 2009), para 354, cf more generally on the contextual differences S Ratner, 'Regulatory Takings in Institutional Context: Beyond the Fear of Fragmented International Law' (2008) 102 *American Journal of International Law* 475.

Thirdly, it does not appear that the comparative argument can be used in the particular situation. First of all, the use of the term 'fundamental' to qualify human rights does not lead very far. '[T]he phrase "fundamental human rights" has no settled meaning',[349] and to describe them as 'essential'[350] or 'core' rights does not assist much in identifying their identity and content.[351] The drafts of the ILC are also not very clear in this respect, changing without much conceptual debate Arangio-Ruiz's 1992 proposal of 'fundamental' human rights (evoking the preamble of the UN Charter) to 'basic' human rights in the 1996 ILC Articles (evoking *Barcelona Traction* list of *erga omnes* human rights),[352] and back to 'fundamental' human rights again in the 2001 ILC Articles on State responsibility. If what is meant by that is *jus cogens* then the rule itself is superfluous because peremptory norms are addressed in Article 50(1)(d); if what is meant is the importance of the right, one would be thrown into the controversial debate about the place of human rights in non-treaty law.[353] Revealingly, all States that commented on this issue considered the scope of these rights to be ambiguous.[354]

Secondly, to the extent that the fundamental human rights are identified by reference to their non-derogable treaty nature,[355] it is not entirely clear why this distinction is relevant in the particular context. The right to derogate is exercised by the State that is bound by a treaty in accordance with that treaty, while countermeasures are adopted by a State in breach of a treaty (or other rules of international law).[356] Moreover, the rules on derogations usually expressly preclude breach of other rules of international law.[357] Consequently, despite the superficial attraction of using derogability as the benchmark for identifying the most important rights worthy of not being subject to countermeasures, the legal nature of the procedures in question appears too distinct to permit any meaningful borrowing.

---

[349] Crawford *Fourth Report,* above n 272, 26, para 64.

[350] *Yearbook of the ILC* 1992 *Volume I* A/CN.4/SER.A/1992 166, para 8 (Tomuschat).

[351] Ibid, 188, para 60 (Arangio-Ruiz).

[352] 1996 Draft Articles, above n 182, 341, para 24.

[353] B Simma and P Alston, 'The Sources of Human Rights Law: Custom, *Jus Cogens* and General Principles' (1998–1999) 12 *Australian Yearbook of International Law* 82. Property protection as a human right would be particularly controversial, C Krause and G Alfredsson, 'Article 17' in G Alfreddson and A Eide (eds) *The Universal Declaration of Human Rights: A Common Standard of Achievement* (Martinus Nijhoff Publishers, the Hague, 1999).

[354] Crawford, *Third Report,* above n 323, para 317 (the US, the UK, Ireland). The comments of the States were made about 'basic' human rights.

[355] *Yearbook of the ILC* 1992 *Volume I* A/CN.4/SER.A/1992 179, para 60 (Careno); 1996 Draft Articles, above n 182, 341, para 23; Crawford *Third Report,* above n 323, para 317 (Ireland); 2001 Draft Articles, above n 13, art 50, Commentary 6.

[356] The distinct nature between countermeasures and the human rights regimes on restrictions and derogations taking into account emergencies is emphasized in Crawford, *Third Report,* above n 323, para 349.

[357] Eg A-L Svensson-McCarthy, *The International Law of Human Rights and States of Exceptions* (Martinus Nijhoff Publishers, the Hague, 1998) 624–639; Joseph et al, above n 129, 827–828; C Flinterman, 'Derogation from the Rights and Freedoms in Case of a Public Emergency (Article 15)' in P van Dijk et al *Theory and Practice of the European Convention on Human Rights* (4th edn, Intersentia, Antwerpen, 2006) 1067–1068.

Thirdly, the ILC itself appeared to be divided over the precise place that human rights were supposed to occupy in the scheme of counter-measures. In his Third Report, Crawford proposed drawing a distinction between obligations not subject to countermeasures and prohibited coun-termeasures, the latter including basic human rights and addressing situ-ations where the indirect effect of the countermeasures (eg sanctions) was consequential on individuals.[358] In the ILC debate, the distinction was generally rejected[359] and the 2001 ILC Articles on State responsibility pro-vide a unified regime for all obligations not subject to countermeasures.[360] At the same time, Crawford and Simma expressed the unchallenged view that apart from the reference to basic or fundamental human rights there was a general prohibition on applying countermeasures to human rights, a point that does not clearly emerge from the Articles and Commentaries.[361]

Fourthly, even if one accepts derogation as the proper criterion in this context, the rules on property protection and the right to fair trial, which occupy positions functionally analogous to rules on expropriation and fair and equitable treatment, are not generally included among the non-derogable rights.[362] Fifthly, the ILC itself appeared to reject catego-rizing of property rights as 'fundamental'. As Arangio-Ruiz noted in his Fourth Report:

> the human rights which should be considered inviolable by countermeasures—the "more essential" human rights—are not understood to include property rights. Recent State practice presents not only cases of expropriation of foreign property by way of countermeasure, but also rather frequent cases where the assets of foreign nationals have been "frozen" by way of reaction to a prior alleg-edly wrongful act by their State. It is not considered, therefore, that the provi-sion concerning humanitarian limitations should either explicitly include or be read as referring to property rights.[363]

Finally, in the pre-ILC writings it was suggested that a distinction could be drawn between impermissible confiscations of property and permis-sible lesser interferences with property.[364] Apart from the lack of support for this argument in the ILC and comments by States, it is not entirely

---

[358] Crawford, *Third Report*, above n 323, paras 349–351.

[359] Simma initially approved the distinction, *Yearbook of the ILC* 2000, above n 68, 271, para 30.

[360] Ibid, 274, para 64 (Pellet), 278, para 19 (Gaja), 283, para 52 (Rao), 284, para 5 (Dugard), 288, para 45 (Pambou-Tchivounda), 295, para 38 (Economides), cf Crawford's recognition that the prop-osition has failed 299, paras 71, 78.

[361] Ibid, 271, para 30 (Simma), para 39 (Crawford).

[362] Flinterman, above n 357, 1068. The International Covenants do not expressly provide for property protection at all, even though such issues have indirectly arisen in other contexts, Joseph et al, above n 129, 700–705, 746; see generally, Svensson-McCarthy, above n 357, 371–562. Ireland suggested the inclusion of the list of non-derogable human rights from the ICCPR, ILC, 'State Responsibility: Comments and Observations Received from Governments' A/CN.4/488 131.

[363] Arangio-Ruiz 'Fourth Report', above n 64, para 83; *Yearbook of the ILC* 1992, *Volume I* A/CN.4/SER.A/1992 169, para 19 (Al-Baharna), 179, para 60 (Carreno), although see 159, para 22 (Al-Khasawehn).

[364] Sicilianos, above n 13, 358–360; Zoller, above n 13, 73–74; Seidl-Hohenveldern, above n 64, 473; Elagab, above n 13, 111; Arangio-Ruiz 'Third Report', above n 281, para 112.

clear what the legal rationale for such a rule would be. To the extent that prohibition of confiscation is not a *jus cogens* rule, it is more plausible to read the criticism of particular actions in State practice as addressing the proportionality of the particular response (or lack of an earlier wrongful act, or incompliance with procedural requirements) rather than a substantive limitation for all countermeasures.[365] Whatever conceptual path one takes, it is hard to arrive at a conclusion that investment protection treaties can be excluded from countermeasures because of their substantive similarities to human rights.

4. *Investment protection law and human rights: the nature of obligations*

The nature of human rights treaty obligations can also provide a different rationale for excluding countermeasures from human rights treaties in general, surpassing the distinction between those rights that are fundamental, basic or non-derogable and those that are not. These arguments were also expressed during the ILC debates. Writing in 1983, Third Special Rapporteur Riphagen explained that 'there are other objective regimes which impose on States the respect of human rights, whatever the nationality of the person affected, and whatever the circumstances. Reprisals in breach of such rules are obviously inadmissible ... the requirement of reciprocity is definitely not part of those rules.'[366] In the 2000 ILC debate, Simma used somewhat different terminology to describe broadly the same phenomenon: 'while it was true that human rights must not be an object of countermeasures, human rights obligations, whether derived from a treaty or grounded in customary international law, were by definition "integral obligations" within the meaning of new article 40 bis. Performance of those obligations could accordingly not be bilateralized because that would impair the right of other States parties to the obligation to see the human right respected.'[367]

Such arguments in favour of excluding countermeasures from the law of human rights draw upon the distinction between obligations of a purely reciprocal and bilateralizable character (that even within a multilateral setting are essentially bundles of bilateral obligations) and interdependent and integral obligations that go beyond this classic *quid pro quo* logic.[368]

---

[365] O Schachter, 'General Course on Public International Law' (1982) 178 *Recueil des Cours* 9, 181–182.

[366] W Riphagen, 'Fourth Report on the Content, Forms and Degrees of International Responsibility (Part 2 of the Draft Articles)' in *Yearbook of the ILC* 1983, *Vol. II(1)* A/CN.4/SER.A/1983/Add.1 17, para 89.

[367] *Yearbook of the ILC* 2000, above n 68, 270, para 31; cf B Simma, 'From Bilateralism to Community Interest in International Law' (1994) 250 *Recueil des Cours* 217, 337–338, 364–376.

[368] B Simma, 'Bilateralism and Community Interest in the Law of state Responsibility' in Y Dinstein (ed) *International Law at a Time of Perplexity: Essays in Honor of Shabtai Rosenne* (Martinus Nijhoff Publishers, Dordrecht, 1989) 821–822; L-A Sicilianos, 'The Classification of Obligations and the Multilateral Dimension of the Relations of International Responsibility' (2002) 13 *European Journal of International Law* 1127, 1127–1145; J Pauwelyn, 'A Typology of Multilateral Treaty Obligations: Are WTO Obligations Bilateral or Collective in Nature?' (2003) 14 *European Journal of International Law* 907, 907–951; J Crawford, 'Multilateral Rights and Obligations in International Law' (2006) 319 *Recueil des Cours* 325, 344.

The work of the ILC relied on the multilateral dimension of responsibility in gradually moving beyond bilateralism[369] and distinguishing the rules of invocation of responsibility by different kinds of injured States and other States.[370] Since the post-War multilateral human rights treaties[371] are not bilateralizable but owed to all contracting States as obligations *erga omnes partes*, the breach of the obligations by one State would not permit other States to engage in responses that law of treaties and law of State responsibility provide for breaches of bilateral obligations.[372]

If the exclusion of countermeasures from human rights law can be explained solely in such terms,[373] then this argument has no apparent relevance for investment protection law. The obligations embodied in BITs are by definition bilateral. While the characterization of multilateral investment protection treaties as multilateral BITs may not necessarily be accurate in every case,[374] they do not seem to have moved beyond bundles of bilateral obligations.[375] At some level of seriousness of the breach, it could be argued that other contracting States could be treated as injured because the breach could raise questions about general multilateral investment protection.[376] However, this does not seem to have been the main concern in creating these rules, and States have not expressed such interest in practice. This view would also not move beyond the idea of injured States, nor would it change the situation regarding rules expressed in bilateral treaties that constitute the absolute majority.

5. *Investment protection law and human rights: the nature of rights*

The third way of looking at human rights and countermeasures that arguably is the most relevant for investment protection law would consider the

---

[369] G Nolte, 'From Dionision Anziloti to Roberto Ago: The Classical International Law of State Responsibility and the Traditional Primacy of a Bilateral Conception of Inter-State Relations' (2002) 13 *European Journal of International Law* 1083.

[370] J Crawford, 'Responsibility to the International Community as a Whole' (2000–2001) 8 *Indiana Journal of Global Legal Studies* 303, 319–321; Crawford *Articles,* above n 123, 38–43.

[371] The pre-War ILO conventions were sometimes conceptualized in contractual terms regarding the impact of competition on labour standards, J Klabbers, 'On Human Rights, Contractual Conceptions and Reservations' in I Ziemele (ed) *Reservations to Human Rights Treaties and the Vienna Convention Regime* (Martinus Nijhoff, Leiden, 2004) 149, 179.

[372] PM Dupuy, 'A General Stocktaking of the Connections Between the Multilateral Obligations and the Codification of the Law of Responsibility' (2003) 13 *European Journal of International Law* 1053, fn 64.

[373] Sicilianos, above n 13, 352–356.

[374] *The Canadian Cattlemen for Free Trade v Canada*, UNCITRAL Arbitration, Award on Jurisdiction, January 28, 2008, <http://ita.law.uvic.ca/documents/CCFT-USAAward_000.pdf> (last accessed 28 February 2009), paras 164–169.

[375] C Carmody, 'WTO Obligations as Collective' (2006) 17 *European Journal of International Law* 419, text at fns 76–77. The Energy Charter Treaty conceptualized as a bundle of 1,000 BITs in T Waelde, 'International Investment Law: An Overview of Key Concepts and Methodologies' (2007) 4(4) *Transnational Dispute Management* 48–49 fn 104.

[376] See on breaches of bilateralizable Vienna Convention on Consular Relations ILC 2001 Articles, above n 4, 118; cf the law of treaties perspective *Avena*, above n 106, 30 (para 47); H Thirlway, 'The Law and Procedure of the International Court of Justice 1960–1989. Supplement, 2007: Parts Four, Five and Six' (2007) 78 *British Yearbook of International Law* 17, 27.

role that the rights owed to individuals play in the adoption of counter-measures against their home State. The framework of international trea-ties addressing the substantive treatment of individuals, together with *ex ante* consent by States to the jurisdiction of international adjudicators, is reminiscent of the developments in regional human rights law during the second half of the last century. There are both similarities and crucial differences, therefore the argument needs to be both identified and trans-posed with care. The proposition will be taken in two steps, considering the argument and its criticisms in the human rights context and the possible relevance to investment law.

Crawford situated the relationship of human rights and countermea-sures within the broader rubric of law dealing with the effect of counter-measures on third party rights:

> countermeasures against a State by definition cannot permit the violation of non-derogable human rights, the beneficiaries of which are by definition third parties in relation to the target State, even if they are its nationals. ... The position with respect to human rights is at one level the same as the position with respect to the rights of third States. Evidently, human rights obligations are not owed to States as the primary beneficiaries, even though States are entitled to invoke those obli-gations and to ensure respect for them. ... Thus it is obvious that human rights obligations (whether or not qualified as "basic" or "fundamental") may not them-selves be the subject of countermeasures, in other words, that human rights obli-gations may not be suspended by way of countermeasures, and that conduct inconsistent with human rights obligations may not be justified or excused except to the extent provided for by the applicable regime of human rights itself.[377]

There appear to be three elements to this argument. First of all, in line with what was to become Article 33(2), Crawford recognized that rights under international law may accrue to non-State entities including indi-viduals. The second part of the argument emphasizes the *ratione personae* limits of countermeasures. Article 49(1) of the 2001 ILC Articles on State responsibility provides that '[a]n injured State may *only* take counter-measures against a State which is responsible for an internationally wrong-ful act' (emphasis added), and Commentary 4 explains that the word 'only' means that countermeasures may not be taken against a State which is not responsible. The preclusion of wrongfulness of countermeasures is thus not absolute but relative to the pre-existing wrongful act by the particular State. The lack of such an earlier act (because it has not been committed or because it has been committed by another State) would mean that coun-termeasures may not be applied. Thirdly, the obligations owed to indi-viduals could conceptually be assimilated to obligations owed to States under this rule, and since individuals are structurally incapable of breaching international obligations owed to States, the conditions for lawful appli-cation of countermeasures against them will never be fulfilled.

---

[377] Crawford *Third Report,* above n 323, paras 312d, 349.

There is support for Crawford's argument in the State practice. The UK comment to the ILC appears to be making the same point:

The fact remains, however, that most countermeasures are not directed at individuals, but are measures taken by one State against another State. It is therefore far from clear how any recognizable countermeasure in the understood sense of the term could amount to "conduct which derogates from" fundamental rights of this kind. Whether the same would be true of other generally recognized human rights, such as freedom of association, is not immediately apparent; nor is it apparent whether they would or would not be within the proposition in the draft article.[378]

Crawford's argument was criticized from a number of perspectives. Pellet 'utterly rejected the idea that individuals could be "third parties" in the context of inter-State responsibility'.[379] While the thrust of the argument is not completely clear, it appears to merely draw the attention to the limits of the particular ILC task of codifying the law of State responsibility in inter-State terms, leaving individual rights at a 'without prejudice' level to be dealt with by special rules.

Simma argued that 'it was dangerous to relieve States of the responsibility to secure performance of human rights obligations on the part of other States, thereby de-emphasizing the inter-State aspect of human rights obligations'.[380] The caution against turning human rights treaties into sanction-less caricatures by overemphasizing the aspect of individual remedies is correct,[381] but this concern would support a clear distinction between the two aspects of the obligations and not a rejection of the individual perspective.[382] The invocation of responsibility *erga omnes partes* would exist in parallel to the individual perspective of invocation.

Simma's further criticism concentrated on the inappropriateness of using the term 'third parties' to describe individuals that were usually not described by this term, who were parties to human rights obligations and not third parties, and who could be incorrectly implied as not involved.[383] The criticism can be partly explained by the different roles that similarly sounding terms occupy in the law of international obligations (and particularly in the law of treaties) and in the law of responsibility. In the law of treaties, third parties are not parties to the particular treaty (and one would assume that the same logic should also apply to customary law of non-general character), so in principle their legal position is unaffected and no legal obligations are owed to them.[384] In the law of responsibility,

---

[378] ILC, 'State Responsibility: Comments and Observations Received from Governments' A/CN.4/488 132.

[379] *Yearbook of the ILC* 2000, above n 68, 273, para 57.

[380] Ibid, 270, para 31.

[381] Simma, above n 367, 372.

[382] *Yearbook of the ILC* 2000, above n 68, 271, para 42.

[383] Ibid, 270, para 31.

[384] C Rousseau, *Principes généraux du droit international public* (A. Pedone, Paris, 1944) 453; A McNair, *The Law of Treaties* (Clarendon Press, Oxford, 1961) 309–310; I Sinclair, *The Vienna Convention on the Law of Treaties* (2nd edn, Manchester University Press, Manchester, 1984) 98–99;

third parties are owed obligations, but they have not committed the prior wrongful act that would entitle the adoption of countermeasures against them.

The individual will be a third party (in the negative sense of not being a party) *vis-à-vis* the creation of international law due to lack of law-making capacity but will lack the safeguard of consent for the purpose of alteration of its legal position.[385] At the same time, obligations may be directly owed to individuals under these rules thus making them third parties in the law of responsibility *vis-à-vis* the breaches committed by States and international organizations. As Crawford pointed out, 'human rights ... in reality were rights of third parties, when compared with State-State obligations, which were the subject of countermeasures'.[386] Even if the terminological criticism is accepted and rights accruing to individuals are not called 'third party rights', the conceptual argument remains unaffected. While the 2001 ILC Articles on State responsibility do not expressly confirm Crawford's proposal,[387] their silence can be explained by terminological controversies and the limited scope of the project, and not a fundamental disagreement with the proposition itself. Consequently, the rationale of non-applicability of countermeasures to human rights seems to lie in the 'quasi-third party' role of the individual who is structurally incapable of triggering the entitlement for the State to adopt countermeasures.

If the broader validity of the argument in the context of human rights is accepted, its introduction in the investment law context calls for a number of additional caveats. *First of all*, investors' rights under investment protection treaties can be conceptualized either as being the rights owed to their home States or rights accruing directly from international treaties.[388] The ILC did not take any view on the issue,[389] and 'the starting point must be that international legal theory allows for both possibilities'.[390] It is certainly more natural to explain the factual autonomy of the investors in the conduct of investment arbitration as reflecting the legal autonomy of their rights.[391]

P Reuter, *Introduction au droit des traites* (3e edn, PUF, Paris, 1995) 94–97; M Fitzmaurice, 'Third Parties and the Law of Treaties' (2002) 6 *Max Planck Yearbook of UN Law* 37 et seq.; A Aust, *Modern Treaty Law and Practice* (2nd edn, Cambridge University Press, Cambridge, 2007) 256–261.

[385] C Chinkin, *Third Parties in International Law* (Clarendon Press, Oxford, 1993) 13–14, 120–122. The *Corn Products* Tribunal used the ILC terminology of 'third parties' when discussing the rights of investors, *Corn Products*, above n 49, para 176.

[386] *Yearbook of the ILC 2000*, above n 68, 271, para 41.

[387] Merely making a *renvoi* to the rule on human rights in a footnote to the discussion of third States, 2001 ILC Articles on State responsibility, above n 13, fn 750.

[388] Ibid, art 33(2), Commentary 4; Douglas, above n 45, 160–193; Spiermann, above n 231; *SGS*, above n 63, para 154, fn 83; *ADM Award*, above n 49, 161–180; Concurring Opinion of Arbitrator Rovine, above n 49.

[389] Crawford 'Retrospect', above n 119, 888.

[390] Douglas, above n 45, 168.

[391] Z Douglas, 'Nothing if not Critical for Investment Treaty Arbitration: *Occidental, Eureko* and *Methanex*' (2006) 22 *Arbitration International* 27, 37–38; *Occidental Exploration & Production Company and the Republic of Ecuador* [2005] EWCA Civ 1116, para 18.

At the same time, there are also elements of treaty practice that support the derivative approach,[392] and at least theoretically it is not impossible to conceptualize investment arbitration as a case of agency of diplomatic protection with considerably modified content of rights.[393] Probably the strongest argument in support for the direct rights approach would draw upon the earlier analysis of the possibility of parallel exercise of the State's and investor's rights. The State practice of rules permitting parallel invocation of responsibility supports the direct nature of both rights, because it would be somewhat odd to create such a parallel framework for managing a single model of invocation.

In any event, the nature of the rights is not an abstract and irrebutable *a priori* proposition, and as a rule of *jus dispositivum* is open to amendment or reinterpretation, in particular through subsequent agreement and practice. The approach of the majority of the *ADM* Tribunal interpreting NAFTA rights as derivative rights, by relying on the subsequent pleading practice of the NAFTA States, is therefore at least in principle unobjectionable.[394] While in the absence of contrary practice it is more natural to interpret the rights as direct, the position taken in this contribution is that the nature of investors' rights may at least in principle differ in different investment treaty rules, having important consequences for the applicability of countermeasures.

Two NAFTA Tribunals have expressly considered the applicability of countermeasures to investment protection law. Both cases dealt with similar issues, sitting on the fault lines between investment law and the long running trade dispute between the US and Mexico regarding Mexican tax

---

[392] Eg the NAFTA regime regarding expropriatory taxation, where the home and host State fiscal authorities can by agreement block the investor's claim, WW Park, 'Arbitration and the Fisc: NAFTA's "Tax Veto"' (2001) 2 *Chicago Journal of International Law* 231. This regime would not make sense if the obligation in issue was owed to some other entity apart from the State, because then the State would be entitled to block the exercise of another entity's rights. The derivative approach also appears to have been accepted in these cases: *Loewen Group, Inc. and Raymond L. Loewen v US,* ICSID Case No. ARB(AF)/98/3, Award, June 26, 2003, (2003) 42 *International Legal Materials* 811, 846 (para 233); *ADM* Award, above n 49, para 176.

[393] See above n 150 for the argument why this proposition is likely to be unsustainable in practice.

[394] *ADM* Award, above n 49, para 176. It is less clear whether the pleadings were clear, concordant and consistent enough to constitute 'subsequent practice' that would need to be taken into account in the process of interpretation according to Article 31(3)(b) of VCLT, Gardiner, above n 116, 225–249. An additional question is the degree to which pleadings may be used for the purpose of subsequent practice, see the critical view in *Gas Natural SDG, S.A. v Argentina,* ICSID Case No. ARB/03/10, Decision on Preliminary Questions of Jurisdiction, June 17, 2005, <http://ita.law.uvic.ca/documents/ GasNaturalSDG-DecisiononPreliminaryQuestionsonJurisdiction.pdf> (last accessed 28 February 2009), fn 12; *Sempra,* above n 47, paras 385–386; and a more approving (and at least in principle more persuasive) view in *CCFT,* above n 374, paras 188–189. Arbitrator Rovine in his Concurring Opinion took the opposite view, relying on different international instruments dealing with individual rights, apparently suggesting that derivative rights are even theoretically impossible. The *Corn Products* Tribunal also examined subsequent practice of parties but did not find it relevant, *Corn Products,* above n 49, para 179. It should be noted that the *ADM* and *Corn Products* Tribunals examined different elements of practice in order to answer different questions: the *ADM* Tribunal was looking at pleadings and Article 1128 submissions to identify the nature of investors' rights (that it found to be derivative), while the *Corn Products* Tribunal was looking at the practice regarding trade countermeasures to identify the applicability of countermeasures to investors' rights (that it had already found to be direct).

on sweeteners[395] (that the US had won in the WTO).[396] The *ADM* and *Corn Products* Tribunals both found Mexican taxes to be in breach of NAFTA Article 1102 rule on national treatment, and proceeded to consider the Mexican argument that wrongfulness of the breach was precluded because of countermeasures. Both Tribunals rejected the argument, but took very different paths to arrive at the same conclusion, with one separate opinion to each decision further extending the spectrum of views.

At one end of the spectrum, the *ADM* Tribunal took the view that investor's rights were derivative and therefore countermeasures could apply in principle. However, even *arguendo* assuming a breach by the US, the particular measures did not comply with the substantive and procedural conditions for countermeasures set out in customary law.[397] An intermediate position was adopted by the *Corn Products* Tribunal, rejecting the countermeasures defence because countermeasures could not apply to the direct rights of the investor and because in any event Mexico had not proven that the US had committed an earlier wrongful act.[398] At the other end of the spectrum, the separate opinions in both cases were similarly unequivocal in rejecting the countermeasures because of the direct nature of the investors' rights, even if Arbitrator Rovine in *ADM* sought support for this in different instruments dealing with individual rights[399] while Arbitrator Lowenfeld in *Corn Products* considered 'traditional international law' analysis to be superfluous.[400]

Secondly, to the extent that investor's rights are its direct rights, it appears that Crawford's and the UK's argument about the impact of countermeasures on human rights can be transposed *verbatim*: obligations arising from investment protection are owed both to States and directly to the investors; countermeasures may not be adopted otherwise than in response to a prior breach of international law by the entity to which the obligation is owed; investors are structurally incapable of committing such a breach of international law; *ergo,* countermeasures may never be lawfully adopted regarding obligations owed to investors. Conversely, if obligations are owed only to the States and investor-State arbitration is diplomatic protection in disguise that is adopted merely for the sake of convenience, the third party problem does not arise since the only obligation is owed to the home State and countermeasures may be adopted in response to a breach by the home State. The mere fact that investors' interests would be affected is irrelevant; the WTO system shows how legally uncontroversial the effect

---

[395] Pauwelyn 'Spaghetti Bowl', above n 53, 2–7; N DiMascio and J Pauwelyn, 'Nondiscrimination in Trade and Investment Treaties: Worlds Apart of Two Sides of the Same Coin?' (2008) 102 *American Journal of International Law* 48, 49–50.

[396] WTO, *Mexico-Tax Measures on Soft Drinks and Other Beverages,* WT/DS308/R; WTO, *Mexico-Tax Measures on Soft Drinks and Other Beverages,* WT/DS308/AB/R.

[397] *ADM* Award, above n 49, paras 110–180.

[398] *Corn Products,* above n 49, paras 153–191.

[399] *ADM* Award, Concurring Opinion of Arbitrator Rovine, above n 49.

[400] *Corn Products*, Separate Opinion of Arbitrator Lowenfeld, above n 49, in particular para 3.

of countermeasures on involved industries and even 'innocent bystanders' can be.[401]

Thirdly, the existing State practice is not very helpful, apart from some indirect hints during the abortive negotiations of the Multilateral Agreement on Investments (MAI). While it does not appear that the States were attempting to codify customary law (and the reliance on the collective confirmation process of the WTO dispute settlement mechanism is pronounced),[402] the approach and concerns are instructive at least in terms of policies that States consider relevant when they engage in international law-making. The negotiators considered that the MAI obligation could in principle be suspended, but not regarding rules on expropriation and general treatment and 'should not include denial of other protections to *established* investment'.[403] The latter point could be read to suggest awareness by the States that the rights accruing to investors could not be suspended for breaches by their home State, thus supporting the direct right approach regarding countermeasures.

Fourthly, the direct rights approach appears preferable in order to exclude a controversial procedural debate about the *Monetary Gold* doctrine. The International Court of Justice has recognized in a number of cases that it is unable to exercise jurisdiction where the very subject-matter of the Court's decision would be the rights, obligations or international responsibility of a third State that has not consented to the Court's jurisdiction.[404] While decided within a particular procedural context of State-State adjudication in the International Court of Justice, *Monetary Gold* could arguably be said to reflect the broader principle of international dispute settlement that jurisdiction of the international adjudicator is derived from the consent of States, and therefore it cannot exercise jurisdiction over a dispute that A and B have submitted to regarding rights of the non-consenting State C. That seemed to be the way the *Larsen* Tribunal looked at the matter, stating that the *Monetary Gold* rule 'applies with at least as much force to the exercise of jurisdiction in arbitral proceedings'. It proceeded to find that it was precluded from considering an individual's

---

[401] M Bronckers and N van den Broek, 'Financial Compensation in the WTO: Improving the Remedies of WTO Dispute Settlement' (2005) 8 *Journal of International Economic Law* 101, 103–104; cf *Corn Products*, above n 49, paras 164–178.

[402] Y Kodama, 'Dispute Settlement under the Draft Multilateral Agreement on Investment' (1999) 16 *Journal of International Arbitration* 45, 69. See generally M Matsushita, TJ Schoenbaum and PC Mavroidis, *The World Trade Organisation: Law, Practice and Policy* (2nd edn, Oxford University Press, Oxford, 2006) 165–200.

[403] Draft Consolidated Text of the MAI, DAFFE/MAI(98)7/REV1, 22 April 1998, <http://www.oecd.org/daf/mai/pdf/ng/ng987r1e.pdf> (last accessed 28 February 2009), 68 (emphasis added); Selected Issues on Dispute Settlement, Note by the Chairman), DAFFE/MAI(98)12, 13 March 1998 <http://www.oecd.org/daf/mai/pdf/ng/ng9812e.pdf> (last accessed 28 February 2009), 4.

[404] *Case of the Monetary Gold Removed from Rome in* 1943 *(Preliminary Questions)* [1954] ICJ Rep 19, 31–33; Chinkin, above n 385, 198–212; HWA Thirlway, 'The Law and Procedure of the International Court of Justice 1960–1989 (Part Nine)' (1998) 69 *British Yearbook of International Law* 1, 37–39, 47–52; Collier and Lowe, above n 164, 158–161; C Tomuschat, 'Article 36' in A Zimmermann, C Tomuschat and K Oellers-Frahm (eds) *The Statute of the International Court of Justice: A Commentary* (Oxford University Press, Oxford, 2006) 603–604.

claim because it would have affected the rights and obligations of a State (the US) which was not a party to arbitration.[405]

If the host State is in principle entitled to apply countermeasures in breaching an investment protection treaty, the first question regarding the lawfulness of these countermeasures is the existence of a prior wrongful act by the home State. If the dispute comes before an investor-State Tribunal, it would be put squarely before the *Monetary Gold* problem: the very subject matter of its decision about lawfulness of the host State's countermeasure is the prior responsibility of the home State. To paraphrase *Monetary Gold,*

to determine whether [the host State] is entitled to [adopt countermeasures], it is necessary to determine whether [the home State] has committed any international wrong against [the host State] ... In order to decide such questions, it is necessary to determine whether [the home State's conduct] was contrary to international law. In the determination of these questions—questions which relate to the lawful or unlawful character of certain actions of character of certain actions of [the home State] vis-à-vis [the host State]—only two States, [the home State] and [the host State], are directly interested. To go into the merits of such questions would be to decide a dispute between [the home State] and [the host State]. The Court cannot decide such a dispute without the consent of [the home State].[406]

While different treaties provide different procedural models of the way how the home State could be involved in proceedings (NAFTA Article 1128 submissions being one of them), none of them appear to rise to the level of a party to arbitration.

One exception that the *Larsen* Tribunal pointed out was when a legal finding against the absent third party could be taken as a given, like when the Security Council has decided on the issue.[407] Arguably, the same logic should apply to an international judgment given against the State and, exceptionally, an express acknowledgment of the breach by the State itself. The *Request for Interpretation of the Judgment of 31 March 2004 in the Case concerning Avena and Other Mexican Nationals (Mexico v. United States of America)* can serve as an illustration of both of these scenarios. From the adjudicatory perspective, since the International Court's interpretation of its earlier judgment confirmed a breach of the obligations owed to Mexico by the US, the breach by the US could now be taken as a given.[408] From the unilateral perspective, the US has expressly conceded

---

[405]   *Larsen v Hawaiian Kingdom,* UNCITRAL Arbitration, Award, February 5, 2001, (2002) 119 International Law Reports 566, 588 (paras 11.8–11.24).

[406]   *Monetary Gold,* above n 404, 32. As was noted in the aftermath of the *Larsen* award, 'an international arbitral tribunal cannot exercise jurisdiction over a case where the lawfulness of a state's conduct implicates on the merits an evaluation of the lawfulness of the conduct of another state that is a nonparty to arbitration', D Bederman and K Hilbert, 'Lance Paul Larsen v The Hawaiian Kingdom' (2004) 1 *Hawaiian Journal of Law and Politics* 82, 90.

[407]   *Larsen,* above n 405, 592 (para 11.24).

[408]   *Request for Interpretation of the Judgment of 31 March 2004 in the Case concerning Avena and Other Mexican Nationals (Mexico v US) (Mexico v US)* (Judgment) [2008] <http://www.icj-cij.org/docket/files/139/14939.pdf> (last accessed 28 February 2009), paras 52–53.

that an execution without the required review would not be in compliance with the *Avena* judgment.[409] If Mexico chooses to apply countermeasures against the US by suspending NAFTA obligations in order to preclude further executions before review pursuant to *Avena*, the wrongfulness of the conduct of the US could arguably be taken as a given.

The other exception is where the finding is merely one of fact. The *Corn Products* Tribunal *obiter dictum* pointed out that Mexican argument would be rejected due to Mexican failure to prove the anterior wrongfulness of the US conduct, the option of staying proceedings while the issue is resolved being an impracticable one.[410] However, the factual exception argument would not necessarily apply to the particular circumstances where the question is not about the host State being able to prove the existence of certain conduct by the home State but the legal evaluation of the home State's acts as wrongful. The impracticability of staying the proceedings does not seem relevant in considering issues of admissibility, since a *Monetary Gold* objection in practice tends to fully end the adjudication rather than transfer it into a different forum. Impracticability is a *sine qua non* element of a successful objection and not a reason to limit its application. If this level of analysis is reached, one may reasonably wonder whether the Tribunal should not seriously reconsider the admissibility of the investor's claim, finding itself in the situation where it simultaneously has to decide on the host State's argument to rule on the case and cannot decide on the host State's argument because of the missing third home State. While one could argue that the *Monetary Gold* doctrine does not extend to investor-State arbitration[411] or attempt to split

---

[409] *Request for Interpretation of the Judgment of* 31 *March* 2004 *in the Case concerning Avena and Other Mexican Nationals (Mexico v US) (Mexico v US)* (Request for the Indication of Provisional Measures) [2008] <http://www.icj-cij.org/docket/files/139/14639.pdf> (last accessed 28 February 2009), para 76, Joint Dissenting Opinion of Judges Owada, Tomka and Keith <http://www.icj-cij.org/docket/files/139/14643.pdf> (last accessed 28 February 2009), paras 5, 16, Dissenting Opinion of Judge Skotnikov, <http://www.icj-cij.org/docket/files/139/14645.pdf> (last accessed 28 February 2009), para 2; ICJ Pleadings CR 2008/17 <http://www.icj-cij.org/docket/files/139/14596.pdf> (last accessed 28 February 2009), para 31 (Bellinger). Agents in international judicial proceedings have the authority to commit the State, as the Court and dissenting judges all agreed ibid; see also *CMS Gas Transmission Company v Republic of Argentina*, ICSID Case No. ARB 01/08, Decision of the *ad hoc* Committee on the Argentine Republic's Request for a Continued Stay of Enforcement of the Award, September 1, 2006, <http://ita.law.uvic.ca/documents/CMS-StayDecision.pdf> (last accessed 28 February 2009), para 49 and cases referred therein.

[410] *Corn Products*, above n 49, para 189–191. The main rationale for rejecting the countermeasures argument was the direct nature of investors' rights, therefore the issue of prior wrongfulness was considered in strictly *arguendo* terms.

[411] The *Larsen* arbitration dealt with a claim by a US national of Hawaiian origin against the Kingdom of Hawaii (that both parties considered still existing in international law because of the internationally wrongful way it was annexed by the US) regarding breaches of international law by the US that the Kingdom had not prevented. The Tribunal found that apart from the allegations regarding the non-party US, there was no actual dispute between the parties, so one could argue that the very peculiar procedural context should make one cautious against generalizations. Interestingly, (now Judge) Greenwood was both the President of the *Corn Products* Tribunal and one of the members of the *Larsen* Tribunal. While the implications of *Larsen* were not expressly considered by the *Corn Products* Tribunal, it is reasonable to assume that it was aware of the case and did not see it as relevant.

the legal issues so to exclude the express consideration of lawfulness of the home State's acts from the *ratio*,[412] it is preferable to evade the whole dispute altogether by accepting the direct rights approach.[413]

In the *ADM* case, the majority accepted the derivative rights approach, but rejected the Mexican claim of countermeasures because Mexico had not adopted the measures in response to a US breach and in order to induce the US to stop the breach, and because the countermeasures would not have been proportionate.[414] This argument is problematic on a number of levels. Deciding a case or at least part of the case on the basis of a breach of international law by the home State is precisely what *Monetary Gold* doctrine should preclude, and the discussion of the US breach in *arguendo* terms does not change that proposition. To consider the effect of the *ADM* approach, while glossing over *Monetary Gold* may be adequate for cases where the countermeasures argument appears only in the arbitral setting, it would not solve the situations where the procedural aspects of countermeasures are complied with. Had Mexico complied with the formal requirements, notifying the US about countermeasures, expressly enacting them in order to induce compliance and keeping within the broad parameters of proportionality,[415] it is difficult to see how the Tribunal could have evaded a finding of inadmissibility.[416]

---

[412] As the *ADM* Tribunal proceeded to do, assuming *arguendo* that the home State had indeed committed a wrongful act, but rejecting the host State's response because it did not comply with the procedural requirements and was disproportionate, thus not justifying the breach and not requiring the Tribunal to examine the point. Assuming for the sake of an argument that a third State has committed an internationally wrongful act is not very far from deciding upon it, and at least in *East Timor*, even quite imaginative issue-splitting was not successful, Thirlway (1998), above n 404, 52.

[413] The issue indirectly arose in the Iran-US Claims Tribunal case regarding *Queens Office Towers Associates*. While dealing with a contractual dispute and not with State responsibility, the Tribunal had to determine whether the Iranian respondent could invoke frustration of contract when the supervening event was the economic countermeasure adopted by the US against Iran for the taking of hostages in the Tehran embassy. The Tribunal decided that in adopting countermeasures the US had taken only one possible course of action, thus the supervening event was not attributable to Iran even though it was due to its actions. Arbitrator Holtzmann dissented and considered that the clear illegality of Iran's conduct recognized by the Court in *Tehran Hostages* meant that a lawful response could not interrupt the chain of causality, *Queens Office Tower Associates v Iran National Airlines Corp.* [1983] 2 IUSCTR 247, respectively 253–254, 256–258. The case highlights possible lines of arguments more generally: the allegedly non-State nature of the Iranian entity suffering from countermeasures, the place of measures extraneous to the Tribunal's jurisdiction in the adjudication of a particular dispute (and even specifically excluded in the particular case), the legal point taken as a given because of an adjudicator's (International Court's) judgment.

[414] *ADM*, above n 49, paras 134–160.

[415] The *ADM* Tribunal characterized the Mexican countermeasures as disproportionate because they were applied because of a breach of State-State obligations to suspend investment obligations, above n 49, paras 157–160. This argument appears to rely on the notion of reciprocal countermeasures that the ILC has expressly rejected: 'There is no requirement that States taking countermeasures should be limited to suspension of performance of the same or a closely related obligation', ILC 2001 Articles, above n 13, 129; C Annacker, 'Part Two of the International Law Commission's Draft Articles on State Responsibility' (1994) 37 *German Yearbook of International Law* 206, 239–240. Consequently, if the *ADM* Tribunal meant to limit the effect of its approach by suggesting that only breaches of rules regarding the treatment of investors can justify countermeasures regarding such rules, this argument is without clear basis in international law.

[416] Among other controversial pronouncements that make the coherence of the argument suspect, the *ADM* Tribunal relied on the *Tehran Hostages* case as an authority on proportionality, *ADM*,

The approach adopted by the *ADM* Tribunal also suggests that host States undertaking acts of doubtful compliance (or clear incompliance) with investment obligations can place strategic obstacles to admissibility of investment claims simply by framing them as countermeasures against the investors' home States. Since the rationale of investment arbitration is to legalize and depoliticize investment protection by isolating it from the political controversies between States, it suggests an error in the argument if its necessary implication directly subjects the investor to political risks by simultaneously taking away the most important procedural protection.

The consequences could be even graver if the focus is moved from classic injured-State countermeasures to third State countermeasures. The ILC Articles suggest at least *de lege ferenda* that third States would be entitled to adopt countermeasures in cases when *erga omnes* obligations are breached.[417] Aggression is one of the *Barcelona Traction* examples of *erga omnes* obligations,[418] and it would not be complicated to find instances of developed States that are parties to large numbers of BITs engaging in use of force of at the very least doubtful lawfulness (eg 1999 Kosovo and 2003 Iraq).[419] Since the treatment of foreign investment could often provide the only realistic leverage against the strategic policies of developed home States, it is possible to imagine consistent patterns of expropriations or mistreatments of foreign investors to prevent or stop eg an allegedly unlawful use of force by developed States. The third-State countermeasures would also make it easier for the host State to escape the *CME-Lauder* effect of corporate structuring of the investment at different levels of shelf companies, since many of the popular shelf-company home States have participated in such uses of force.[420]

These far-reaching consequences may provide a serious reason for certain developed States (US and Canada in particular) to reconsider their short-term arbitration and treaty-making strategies. Emphasizing the derivative nature of the rights may be perfectly understandable from the position of a host State in a particular case. In the NAFTA context, States have tended to emphasize the similarity of diplomatic protection and investment arbitration, in order to benefit from the limitations of customary law of diplomatic protection being implied into the treaties.[421]

---

above n 49, para 156, even though it is traditionally read as a case of *lex specialis* regime of diplomatic law, ILC 2001 Articles, above n 13, art 50(2)(b), Commentaries 14–15.

[417] 2001 ILC Articles on State responsibility, above n 13, art 54, see above n 15.

[418] *Barcelona Traction,* above n 94, 32 (para 34).

[419] Eg the different views about lawfulness in S Chesterman, *Just War or Just Peace?* (Oxford University Press, Oxford, 2001); T Franck, *Resource to Force* (Cambridge University Press, Cambridge, 2002) 135–191; Y Dinstein, *War, Aggression and Self-Defence* (4th edn, Cambridge University Press, Cambridge, 2005) 70–73, 297–300; C Gray, *International Law and the Use of Force* (3rd edn, Oxford University Press, Oxford, 2008) 30–55, 354–366; O Corten, *Le droit contre la guerre* (Editions Pedone, Paris, 2008).

[420] See *Legality of the Use of Force (Serbia and Montenegro v Netherlands)* (Preliminary Objections) [2004] ICJ Rep 1011.

[421] *ADM,* above n 49, para 176; also *GAMI,* above n 264, para 29.

However, the cost-benefit calculus may appear different if the possible consequence of general acceptance of the derivative rights doctrine would lead to an unravelling of the whole investment protection system, leaving investors substantively and procedurally helpless before host State countermeasures.

Arbitrator Rovine in the *ADM* case tried to distinguish these statements as not being made in cases where countermeasures were an issue.[422] The point that all the implications of the argument may have not been fully appreciated seems correct. However, there is no reason of principle why a logical implication of a particular legal position should not follow even if the logic was not expressly (or at all) considered when the position was originally taken. Now that the link between the theoretical nature of investors' rights and the applicability of countermeasures has been made in express terms, the States should be able to rethink their position and either to modify their practice or confirm it.

Fifthly, if one accepts the first approach alluded to above, it is important to identify its limitations. It does not mean that investors have safeguards to the alteration of their legal rights under the investment protection law analogous to those of third parties in the more accepted sense. Contracting States may agree on the interpretation of a treaty according to Article 31(3)(a) of the VCLT through pre-established institutions[423] or in an *ad hoc* manner;[424] they may engage in subsequent practice according to Article 31(3)(b)[425] or explain the understanding of the applicable rules of international law according to Article 31(3)(c);[426] they may also amend the treaty[427] or denounce it completely. The investor does not control these law-making processes. While it is not theoretically impossible to imagine a stabilization clause that requires the State to desist from changing treaty law (rather than domestic law), such an approach would be exceptional and would not follow from general principle.

The approach also does not mean that circumstances precluding wrongfulness are generally inapplicable to obligations owed to investors (leaving aside the possible *lex specialis*). Countermeasures would not apply because their precondition requires a breach of an international obligation owed to the particular State, and one would assume that the same logic would exclude the rules on self-defence. Conversely, those circumstances precluding wrongfulness that do not require an anterior breach (like necessity, distress, and *force majeure*) can in principle also apply to obligations owed

[422] *ADM,* Rovin, above n 49, para 70.

[423] *Methanex,* above n 274, Part IV Chapter C, paras 21–23.

[424] *CME v Czech Republic,* UNCITRAL Arbitration, Final Award, March 14, 2003, <http://ita.law.uvic.ca/documents/CME-2003-Final_002.pdf> (last accessed 28 February 2009), paras 87–93.

[425] *CCFT,* above n 374, paras 181–189.

[426] Eg the reference to customary law of expropriation in 2004 US Model BIT Annexes A and B, <http://www.ustr.gov/assets/Trade_Sectors/Investment/Model_BIT/asset_upload_file847_6897.pdf> (last accessed 28 February 2009).

[427] *Methanex,* above n 274, Part IV Chapter C, paras 20–21.

to investors.[428] Consequently, the application of law of necessity to obligations owed under the US-Argentina BIT is in principle uncontroversial: the protection of essential interests of the State is a circumstance that could preclude wrongfulness of an obligation owed also to individuals.

The approach also does not preclude host States from adopting unilateral measures against investors in accordance with the relevant primary rules with effects similar to those of countermeasures. To paraphrase Crawford, 'conduct inconsistent with [investment] obligations may ... be justified or excused ... to the extent provided for by the applicable regime of [investment law] itself'. One possible example of such a provision provided in the primary rules is the so-called 'denial of benefits' clause that provides the right of the host State to deny protection to shelf companies. There is some controversy whether the exercise of these rights in particular treaties can have retrospective[429] or only prospective effect.[430] In any case, there is no reason of principle why a properly worded clause could not completely alter the legal rights accruing to the investor with any temporal effect.

It is less clear what the situation would be in a case where States have agreed to a *lex specialis* regime of countermeasures as eg in the WTO context. Assuming that the WTO DSB authorizes countermeasures regarding WTO rules[431] that are also addressed in the BITs (IP rights being one example),[432] the relevance for investment protection rules may appear on a number of levels.[433] From the WTO perspective, since the WTO authorization of suspension applies to WTO-covered agreements,[434] the entitlement to suspend WTO obligations would not entitle the State to suspend non-WTO BIT obligations even if they have similar or identical substantive content. While the State would be entitled to suspend WTO rules, it would still remain bound by investment protection rules, thus its authorized breach of WTO rules would still be wrongful regarding the BIT obligation. From the investment protection perspective, even if the WTO panel has determined the breach, the WTO DSU is based on the

---

[428] ILC 2001 Articles, above n 13, arts 23–25.

[429] KJ Vandevelde, *United States Investment Treaties: Policy and Practice* (Kluwer, Boston, 1992) 53, 55–57; AC Sinclair, 'The Substance of Nationality Requirements in Investment Treaty Arbitration' (2005) 20 *ICSID Review—Foreign Investment Law Journal* 357, 385–388.

[430] *Plama*, above n 172, 309 (paras 152–165).

[431] Matsushita, Schoenbaum and Mavroidis, above n 402, 695–738; CM Correa, *Trade Related Aspects of Intellectual Property Rights: A Commentary on the TRIPS Agreement* (Oxford University Press, Oxford, 2007); RC Dreyfuss, 'Intellectual Property Law and the World Trading System' in A Lowenfeld, *International Economic Law* (2nd edn, Oxford University Press, Oxford, 2008).

[432] Eg CM Correa, 'Bilateral Investment Agreements: Agents of New International Standards for the Protection of Intellectual Property Rights?' (2004) 1(4) *Transnational Dispute Management*; F Weiss, 'Trade and Investment' in P Muchlinski, F Ortino and C Schreuer (eds) *The Oxford Handbook of International Investment Law* (Oxford University Press, Oxford, 2008) 196–199.

[433] WTO, *EC-Regime for the Importation, Sale and Distribution of Bananas (Article 22.6)*, WT/DS27/ARB/ECU, paras 65–165; WTO, *US-Measures Affecting the Cross-Border Supply of Gambling and Betting Services (Article 22.6)*, WT/DS285/ARB, paras 4.1–4.119, 5.1–5.13.

[434] Y Guohua, B Mercurio and L Yongjie, *WTO Dispute Settlement Understanding: a Detailed Interpretation* (Kluwer Law International, the Hague, 2005) 256–272.

presumption against unilateral enforcement, therefore States would not be entitled to breach BITs to enforce WTO rules.[435] There also do not seem to be conflicting obligations, because States can simultaneously comply with their WTO and investment protection obligations, simply by failing to exercise the authorized right to act in breach of WTO obligations.[436]

At the same time, if one adopts a broader concept of conflict of norms, it could be said that there is a conflict between an obligation (to grant IP treatment under BIT) and an exceptional right (to deny IP treatment under WTO).[437] Much would depend on the manner in which the case arose and was argued: different appreciations of the interplay between jurisdiction and applicable law; obligations conflicting in time and varying in generality and specificity; rules constituting or not constituting 'other rules of international law' because of their conclusion at different times and between different parties—these are only some of the arguments that make any hypothetical predictions about how the particular spaghetti bowl could be untangled increasingly difficult. If conflict rules are applied in favour of the WTO, the question should turn on whether these rules are conceptualized within primary rules analogously to denial of benefit clauses or within secondary rules analogously to the general rules on counter-measures, permitting their application in the former and permitting or precluding their application in the latter (and more persuasive) case, depending on the nature of investors' rights.

Finally, the approach does not mean that breaches of law by an investor cannot have important negative consequences for its successes in investment arbitration. While not without controversy, some tribunals have refused jurisdiction because of breaches of domestic law committed by the investor.[438] The conduct of the investor can play an important role in the analysis of the host State's compliance with the rules on indirect expropriation and fair and equitable treatment.[439] Conduct of the investor has also been taken into account in identifying the remedial consequences of

---

[435] A Lowenfeld, *International Economic Law* (2nd edn, Oxford University Press, Oxford, 2008) 195–211; G Marceau, 'WTO Dispute Settlement and Human Rights' (2002) 13 *European Journal of International Law* 753, 759–760; WTO, *US-Sections 301–310 of the Trade Act of 1974*, WT/DS152/R, para 7.59.

[436] Eg the classic argument in W Jenks, 'The Conflict of Law-Making Treaties' (1953) 30 *British Yearbook of International Law* 401, 451; and the modern exposition particularly regarding WTO in G Marceau 'Conflict of Norms and Conflict of Jurisdictions: the Relationship between WTO Law and Agreements and Other Treaties' (2001) 35 *Journal of World Trade* 1081, 1082–1086; Marceau, 'WTO Dispute Settlement and Human Rights', above n 435, 791–794.

[437] Pauwelyn, above n 51, 184–187; E Vranes, 'The Definition of 'Norm Conflict' in International Law and Legal Theory' (2006) 17 *European Journal of International Law* 395.

[438] *Inceysa Vallisoletana v Republic of El Salvador*, ICSID Case No. ARB/03/26, Award, August 2, 2006, <http://ita.law.uvic.ca/documents/Inceysa_Vallisoletana_en_000.pdf> (last accessed 28 February 2009), paras 190–264; *Fraport A.G. Frankfurt Airport Services Worldwide v Republic of Philippines*, ICSID Case No. ARB/03/25, Award, August 16, 2007, <http://ita.law.uvic.ca/documents/FraportAward.pdf> (last accessed 28 February 2009), paras 300–404; see also Dissenting Opinion of Arbitrator Cremades.

[439] P Muchlinski, 'Caveat Investor'? The Relevance of the Conduct of the Investor Under the Fair and Equitable Treatment Standard' (2007) 55 *International and Comparative Law Quarterly* 527.

the breach by the home State.[440] To conclude, exempting the investor from the effect of countermeasures does not mean that its dubious or wrongful acts would remain without appropriate eventual negative legal consequences in the domestic and the international legal orders; it merely removes it from a dispute that is a matter between the States concerned so as to avoid collective punishment.[441]

B. Obligations excluding countermeasures

The application of countermeasures may also be excluded by *lex specialis,* as it has occurred in the WTO and EC legal regimes. If investment protection treaties were such *lex specialis,* the argument for the adoption of countermeasures could be rejected *ab initio* without even entering into the discussion conducted above. The silence of most investment protection treaties on the applicability of rules of State responsibility is reminiscent of the broader analytical problem, since 'the wording of the special treaties (WTO, EC, human rights ...) can simply be read in both ways: as permitting or precluding application of the rules on state responsibility'.[442] Not surprisingly, the first publicly available award to discuss the applicability of circumstances precluding wrongfulness when the treaty was silent on the issue was careful to explain that its conclusions were valid whether the BIT excluded the particular circumstance or not, without indicating the solution it found more persuasive.[443]

There is a spectrum of views that one may take regarding the relationship of general and special in investment protection law. On the one hand, to the extent that the *lex specialis* nature of the regimes may be extrapolated from their integrated nature and the efficiency of their methods of enforcement, there are elements in investment protection law that would arguably point in a similar direction. To consider the latter point first, the absolute majority of investment treaty awards both in ICSID and non-ICSID arbitrations have been complied with voluntarily, and even in the small minority of cases where compliance has not been voluntary the awards have ultimately been fulfilled.[444] The system therefore seems to have worked in a remarkably efficient and successful manner. From the normative perspective, the recurring trends and patterns in investment treaty-making[445] as well as the synergy through arbitral case law[446] and

---

[440] *MTD Equity Sdn. Bhv. and MTD Chile S.A. v Republic of Chile,* ICSID Case No. ARB/01/07, Award, May 25, 2004, <http://ita.law.uvic.ca/documents/MTD-Award.pdf> (last accessed 28 February 2009), paras 242–246.

[441] Crawford *Third Report,* above n 323, para 312d.

[442] Simma and Pulkowski, above n 50, 505.

[443] *BG,* above n 47, paras 407–412.

[444] Alexandroff and Laird, above n 57. The one case where the systemic aspects of enforcement will possibly be tested is the case law regarding Argentinian crisis, Lowe 'Procedural Weaknesses', above n 56, 39.

[445] McLachlan, Shore and Weiniger, above n 69, 223–224.

[446] Above n 63.

most-favoured-nation (MFN) clauses[447] could be treated as reflecting a process leading to a common and integrated law of investment protection.[448] The same and different States follow similar patterns in treaty making. Investors, States, and Tribunals place great reliance on the analysis of previous arbitral Tribunals. The MFN clauses may serve to harmonize the divergences of the more technical character, where such exist between treaties. If investment protection treaties are sufficiently effective in ensuring compliance and creating a homogenous legal regime, they may also be sufficiently special to implicitly exclude countermeasures.

On the other hand, despite the trends in treaty practice and case law, in legal terms the investment protection rules do not seem to have moved beyond their bilateral origins to form a unified system. Historically, States have experimented with multilateral investment treaty-making, both in the aftermath of the Second World War and more recently regarding MAI,[449] but have always preferred customary law-making and (particularly post-*Barcelona*) bilateral treaty-making. This has been a conscious law-making choice and as such should be respected, rejecting the intuitive impulse of reliance on the interpretation of similar-sounding rules in treaties that have no direct interpretative relevance (but that would have had such relevance had the States instead concluded a single multilateral treaty).

Regarding the impact of case law, it appears that a mere jurisdictional decision admitting a Tribunal's right to consider sensitive regulatory issues played an importantly negative role for the multilateral treaty-making during the MAI negotiations.[450] If this reaction is considered in context with treaty awards issued on the merits within the last 10 years routinely dealing with matters such as health,[451] environment,[452] taxation,[453]

---

[447] *Rumeli Telekom A.S. and Telsim Mobil Telekomunikasyon Hizmetleri A.S. v Kazakhstan,* ICSID Case No. ARB/05/16, Award, July 29, 2008, <http://ita.law.uvic.ca/documents/Telsimaward.pdf> (last accessed 28 February 2009), para 575.

[448] S Schill, 'The Multilateralization of International Investment Law: The Emergence of a Multilateral System of Investment Protection on the Basis of Bilateral Investment Treaties' SIEL Online Proceedings Working Paper No 18/08 <http://papers.ssrn.com/sol3/papers.cfm?abstract_id=1151817> (last accessed 28 February 2009); S Schill, *The Multilateralization of International Investment Law* (Cambridge University Press, Cambridge, forthcoming 2009).

[449] SD Amarasinha and J Kokott, 'Multilateral Investment Rules Revisited' in P Muchlinski, F Ortino and C Schreuer (eds) *The Oxford Handbook of International Investment Law* (Oxford University Press, Oxford 2008) 125–129; van Harten, above n 36, 18–22.

[450] R Geiger, 'Regulatory Expropriation in International Law: Lessons from the Multilateral Agreement on Investment' (2003) 11 *New York University Environmental Law Journal* 94, 96–99.

[451] *Methanex,* above n 274.

[452] Ibid; *Metalclad v Mexico,* ICSID Case No. ARB(AF)/97/1, Award, August 30, 2000, (2001) 16 *ICSID Review—Foreign Investment Law Journal* 168.

[453] *Link-Trading Joint Stock Company v Moldova,* UNCITRAL Case, Award, April 18, 2002, <http://ita.law.uvic.ca/documents/Link-Trading-Moldova.pdf> (last accessed 28 February 2009); *Feldman v Mexico,* ICISD Case No. ARB(AF)/99/1, Award, December 16, 2002, (2003) 18 *ICSID Review—Foreign Investment Law Journal* 488; *Occidental Exploration and Production Company v the Republic of Ecuador,* LCIA Case No. UN3467, Final Award, July 1, 2004, <http://ita.law.uvic.ca/documents/Oxy-EcuadorFinalAward_001.pdf> (last accessed 28 February 2009); *EnCana Corporation v Republic of Ecuador,* LCIA Case No. UN3481, Award, February 3, 2006, <http://ita.law.uvic.ca/documents/EncanaAwardEnglish.pdf> (last accessed 28 February 2009); generally TW Wälde and

judicial administration,[454] economic emergencies,[455] and provision of important services to the general public,[456] willingness to create an integrated investment protection system with strong enforcement mechanisms is the least likely abstract attitude that could be attributed to States.[457]

When States have expressed their views regarding particular cases, they have been largely critical and have engaged in interpretative[458] and law-making efforts[459] to reach results different from those suggested in case law. Against this background, the interpretative analysis of Tribunals has focused on earlier arbitral awards interpreting *pacta tertii* treaties containing similar rules,[460] the interpretative role of which lies at best somewhere between the outer fringes of marginally relevant supplementary materials in Article 32 VCLT[461] and complete interpretative

A Kolo, 'Taxation and Modern Investment Treaties' in P Muchlinski, F Ortino and C Schreuer (eds) *The Oxford Handbook of International Investment Law* (Oxford University Press, Oxford, 2008) 324–352.

[454]   *Loewen*, above n 392; *Petrobart Limited v Kyrgiz Republic*, SCC Case No. 126/2003, March 29, 2005, <http://ita.law.uvic.ca/documents/petrobart_kyrgyz.pdf> (last accessed 28 February 2009); *LLC Amto v Ukraine*, SCC Case No. 080/2005, Award, March 26, 2008, <http://ita.law.uvic.ca/documents/AmtoAward.pdf> (last accessed 28 February 2009); *Victor Pay Casado* above n 63.

[455]   See above n 47.

[456]   *Azurix*, above n 347; *Siemens*, above n 348; *PSEG Inc. v Turkey*, ICSID Case No. ARB/02/5, Award, January 19, 2007, <http://ita.law.uvic.ca/documents/PSEGGlobal-Turkey-Award.pdf> (last accessed 28 February 2009); *Compañía de Aguas del Aconquija S.A. and Vivendi Universal v Argentina*, ICSID Case No. ARB/97/3, Award, August 20, 2007, <http://ita.law.uvic.ca/documents/VivendiAwardEnglish.pdf> (last accessed 28 February 2009); *Biwater Gauff (Tanzania) Ltd. v Tanzania*, ICSID Case No. ARB/05/22, Award, July 24, 2008, <http://ita.law.uvic.ca/documents/Biwateraward.pdf> (last accessed 28 February 2009); *Jan de Nul B.V. v Egypt*, ICSID Case No. ARB/04/13, Award, November 6, 2006, <http://ita.law.uvic.ca/documents/JandeNulNVaward.pdf> (last accessed 28 February 2009).

[457]   A finding on jurisdiction is clearly without prejudice to the responsibility on merits, J Paulsson, 'Avoiding Unintended Consequences' in KP Sauvant *Appeals Mechanism in International Investment Disputes* (Oxford University Press, Oxford, 2008) 248–250. However, the practice of the States at MAI negotiations showed that even the potential consideration of such issues was an argument against law-making, therefore (in the absence of a better alternative) the substantive aspects of the decided cases provide one benchmark for determining the presumable general attitude of the States.

[458]   Eg regarding fair and equitable treatment in the NAFTA Free Trade Commission's decision, *Methanex*, above n 274, Chapter C, paras 21–23; regarding the MFN clauses in the Panama-Argentina interpretative declaration, *National Grid Plc v Argentina*, UNCITRAL Case, Decision on Jurisdiction, June 20, 2006, <http://ita.law.uvic.ca/documents/NationalGrid-Jurisdiction-En.pdf> (last accessed 28 February 2009), para 85.

[459]   Eg regarding expropriation and fair and equitable treatment in the 2004 US Model BIT and 2004 Canada Model BIT, respectively S Schwebel, 'The United States 2004 Model Bilateral Investment Treaty: an Exercise in the Regressive Development of International Law' (2006) 3 (2) *Transnational Dispute Management*; A Newcombe, 'Canada's New Model Foreign Investment Agreement' (2005) 2 (1) *Transnational Dispute Management*.

[460]   See above n 63.

[461]   In any event, the legitimate reliance on such authorities is usually restricted to rather narrow circumstances, where different awards directly or indirectly explain or shed light on the same treaty rules, *Oil Platforms*, above n 202, Dissenting Opinion of Vice-President Schwebel 874, 882; *Aguas*, above n 268, 533 (paras 266, 288); *The Czech Republic v European Media Ventures* SA 2007 EWHC 2851 (Comm), paras 24–30; *Enron*, Decision on Argentina's Request for a Continued Stay of the Enforcement, above n 201, para 32; F Berman, 'Treaty Interpretation in a Judicial Context' (2004) 29 *Yale Journal of International Law* 315, 317, 318; Thirlway (2006), above n 217, 74–77; Aust, above n 385, 248. The argument for a general treatment of (any) awards as supplementary materials for interpretation of (any) investment treaties appears to confuse the subsidiary role of judicial decisions in terms of sources of law and supplementary means of interpretation of each particular treaty: the

irrelevance.[462] Such arguments are hard to conceptualize as directly relevant solely in treaty law terms. Therefore, only if the applicable law leads to the background customary law, can the development of investment law in a harmonious manner be legitimately justified.[463]

The MFN clauses also do not merge different rules into an integrated regime but simply 'determine[] ... obligations by means of a parameter which varies according to such undertaking as may be assumed by [States] in other respects'.[464] Moreover, the reach of MFN clauses is importantly limited by its application only to more or less favourable matters, thus excluding those concepts that cannot be situated on the spectrum of comparability. If considered in this light, the normatively expressed unwillingness of States to develop investment protection law beyond a substantively and procedurally decentralized framework (that is sometimes almost by accident pulled together by pre-existing customary law) makes the applicability of 'well-developed and integrated systems of enforcement' argument to exclude countermeasures by *lex specialis* very doubtful.[465]

Secondly, one could argue that countermeasures should be excluded because of the nature of the rules embodied in the particular regimes. To consider the substantive perspective, if there was ever a rule that would exclude arbitrary State interference (arbitrary *vis-à-vis* the investor) indirectly, it should surely be the one that excludes it expressly through the rules on indirect expropriation, indirect discrimination and fair and equitable treatment.[466] This argument is problematic on a number of levels. The modern rules on expropriation and fair and equitable treatment to a certain (if unclear) extent are inspired by and perhaps reflect the structure

fact the judgment and awards are subsidiary sources does not mean they can be introduced, even as a matter of Article 32 of VCLT, in interpretation of any unrelated treaty, *CCFT*, above n 374, paras 50–51; *Chevron Corporation and Texaco Petroleum Corporation v Ecuador*, UNCITRAL Case, Interim Award, December 1, 2008, <http://ita.law.uvic.ca/documents/Chevron-TexacovEcuadorInterimAward. pdf> (last accessed 28 February 2009), paras 119–124.

[462] *Oil Platforms*, above n 202, Separate Opinion of Judge Shahabuddeen 822, 836; *Sempra*, above n 47, para 381.

[463] C McLachlan, 'Investment Treaties and General International Law' (2008) 57 *International and Comparative Law Quarterly* 361, 364; M Paparinskis, 'Investment Protection Law and Sources of Law: A Critical Look' (2009) 103 *ASIL Proceedings* [forthcoming].

[464] P Reuter, *Introduction to the Law of Treaties* (2nd edn, Kegan Paul International, London, 1995) 106.

[465] Even though diverging on other issues, both *ADM* and *Corn Products* Tribunals were in agreement that countermeasures were not excluded by *lex specialis*, *ADM*, above n 49, paras 116–123; *Corn Products*, above n 49, paras 76, 161–179 (the latter Tribunal's view is implicit in its examination of the investors' rights: if the countermeasures were excluded *in limine* by *lex specialis*, such analysis would be unnecessary). Cf the *National Grid* Tribunal's view that the argument of necessity could in principle be applied to investment protection treaties, since 'by concluding the Treaty with the United Kingdom, the Respondent did not limit its powers that as a sovereign it would have under international law except to the extent provided in the Treaty', *National Grid*, above n 47, para 255; *CMS* annulment committee, above n 47, para 134. The *BG* Tribunal left the issue open, *BG*, above n 47, paras 407–412.

[466] The *Nicaragua* Court found that the abrupt termination of commercial intercourse breached the obligations implied in the FCN Treaty, a point arguably applicable also regarding arbitrary conduct of States under BITs, *Military and Paramilitary Activities in and against Nicaragua (Nicaragua v US)* (Merits) [1986] ICJ Rep 14, 138 (para 276).

(if not the embryonic content) of classic customary law obligations regarding the treatment of aliens.[467] At the same time, the classic law was unequivocal in permitting such countermeasures.[468]

Moreover, the particular substantive nature of the treatment provided in the particular obligation does not necessarily exclude countermeasures. The *Air Service Agreement* Tribunal recognized that 'the network of air services is in fact an extremely sensitive system, disturbances of which can have wide and unforeseeable consequences' but that did not alter its conclusion that the countermeasures were not prohibited.[469] In a different sense, it could be said that what distinguishes the present situation from the classic law and the *Air Service Agreement* are the direct rights granted to the investors. However, assuming that the direct rights approach is correct, this argument would not support exclusion of countermeasures *in toto* because that would be already taken care of by the third party status of the investor. Indeed, provided that the investor's rights are not affected, it is not clear why the host State should not be able to suspend other treaty obligations owed solely to the home State, including regarding future investors (provided there is no market access clause)[470] or *ratione materiae, temporis* or *loci* in a way that would not affect the existing investors.

Thirdly, whatever the situation is more generally, some treaty rules arguably incorporate or exclude countermeasures, in particular the NPM clauses where the reference to 'essential security interests' could apply to countermeasures to the same extent as necessity. There are three approaches to the interpretation of these clauses, treating them respectively in terms of primary rules (which seems most persuasive), in terms of *lex specialis* secondary rules and in terms of *lex specialis* secondary rules interpreted against the *lex generalis* background.

According to the first approach, '[t]he question arising ... is not ... whether such measures are ... justified counter-measures in general international law; the question is whether the measures in question are, or are not, in breach of the Treaty.'[471] The NPM clauses are then part of the particular primary rules, and the secondary rules of State responsibility regarding circumstances precluding wrongfulness have no direct relevance. If this approach is followed, the NPM clause would not affect the

---

[467] E Root, 'The Basis of Protection to Citizens Residing Abroad' (1910) 4 *American Journal of International Law* 517, 521; *The United States of America, on behalf of Margeruite de Joly de Sabla v The Republic of Panama* (1934) 28 *American Journal of International Law* 602, 611–612.

[468] See preceding discussion at n 3, n 6, n 302–n 304 and surrounding text.

[469] *Air Services Agreement,* above n 21, 445 (para 92).

[470] A Joubin-Bret, 'Admission and Establishment in the Context of Investment Protection' in A Reinisch (ed) *Standards of Investment Protection* (Oxford University Press, Oxford, 2008) 9; I Gómez-Palacio and P Muchlinski, 'Admission and Establishment' in P Muchlinski, F Ortino and C Schreuer (eds) *The Oxford Handbook of International Investment Law* (Oxford University Press, Oxford, 2008) 227.

[471] *Nicaragua* Jennings, above n 62, 541; *CMS* annulment committee, above n 47, paras 129–233; *Continental Casualty,* above n 47, paras 162–168.

application of countermeasures, the arguments being made respectively at the different levels of primary and secondary rules.

The second approach would treat the NPM clause as a secondary rule, implicitly situating the treaty in a relationship of a *lex specialis* secondary rule towards customary law.[472] It would seem to follow from this argument that the *lex specialis* excludes the *lex generalis,* thus the law of necessity would be replaced between the Contracting Parties by the NPM clause. To apply this approach to countermeasures, the customary law of counter-measures would be excluded by the *lex specialis* treaty rule. The impact of the measures on the investor would therefore depend upon the interpreta-tion of each particular treaty, and the law of countermeasures would not play any role at all.

The third approach would treat the NPM clauses as 'inseparable from the customary law standard insofar as the definition of necessity and the conditions for its operation are concerned'.[473] While the Tribunals do not fully explain their argumentative process, it seems that in a somewhat circular manner they first of all accept the NPM clause to be a *lex specialis* secondary rule replacing the customary law rule and then use VCLT Article 31(3)(c) to incorporate the customary law criteria from *lex generalis.* This approach, applying *mutatis mutandis* the necessity analysis to counter-measures, would bring in the customary law of countermeasures within the treaty. However, it would not change the conclusions reached above regarding the impact of countermeasures on the rights of the investors: even though countermeasures will be applicable in principle, the direct or derivative nature of the investors' rights will still influence the impact that they will have. To conclude, whether countermeasures remain unaffected, are replaced by treaty rules or are brought into the treaty interpretation, the conceptual arguments retain their validity.

It may be worthwhile to recall Simma's and Pulkowski's words about the different views of the international legal order that also influence the place on the spectrum between general and special on which each legal argument is situated.[474] While the different shades of speciality may lead to equally plausible alternative views, and particular relationships between treaty and customary law may lead to various conclusions, it does not appear that investment protection treaties fully exclude the law of State responsibility regarding countermeasures.[475] In policy terms, while the exclusion of measures of self-help from this particular field of contempo-rary international law serves an attractive purpose, the law does not yet appear to have developed in this direction.

---

[472] *LG&E,* above n 47, paras 245–261; *Patrick Mitchell v DRC,* ICSID Case No. ARB 99/7, Decision of the *ad hoc* Committee on the Application for Annulment, November 1, 2006, <http://ita.law.uvic.ca/documents/mitchellannulment.pdf> (last accessed 28 February 2009), para 55.

[473] *Sempra,* above n 47, para 376, also para 378; *CMS,* above n 47, paras 315–382; *Enron,* above n 47, para 334.

[474] Simma, above n 50, 506.

[475] *ADM,* above n 49, paras 113–123.

To put the analysis in perspective, even the much more nuanced and direct treatment of countermeasures 'as a sword' has left open many opportunities for their application. One should perhaps not expect an excessive degree of clarity of this other aspect of countermeasures, rather disregarded in the law-making process. Consequently, the debate about the exclusion of countermeasures hinges—as do many other issues in investment arbitration—on the nature of the investor's rights, and the law-making and elucidation efforts in both fields should be considered in parallel. To the extent that investors' rights are considered direct and untouched by countermeasures, the question about the exclusion of countermeasures becomes superfluous; to the extent that they are derivative and subject to countermeasures, one could expect reactions in State practice and case law to identify the substantive and procedural scope of protection (if any) still available in particular treaties. A clearer appreciation of these systemic consequences of the derivative rights arguments could also lead certain developed States to reconsider their long-term priorities in investment law-making.

VI. Conclusion

The purpose of this contribution has been to locate the seemingly archaic gunboat diplomacy-reminiscent instrument of countermeasures within the refined treaty structures of modern investment protection law. Even though diplomatic protection and the accompanying countermeasures have 'somewhat faded' from contemporary State practice, being factually replaced by investment arbitration, in legal terms the entitlement still very much maintains its parallel existence. Considered as a measure to induce compliance with investment protection law, despite express suspension in ICSID arbitrations, diplomatic protection and countermeasures do not appear to be precluded more generally, whether by customary law coordinating dispute settlement, imposing the investor's invocation over the State's, or by replacing the latter with the former. As a result, the project for completely removing the discretionary intervention by States in investment disputes is far from being fully successful. While States have been content to leave the precise scope of their legal powers unexplored while the investment arbitration has been operating relatively smoothly, the existence of these rights provides the important background for investor-State negotiations and arbitrations, and may become more relevant in the not improbable event if host States become unable or unwilling to fully fulfil the obligations according to the awards.

In its defensive capacity, the relationship between countermeasures as a circumstance precluding wrongfulness and investment protection obligations is not entirely clear, but the most plausible conceptualization would treat countermeasures as not excluded in principle but as not applicable to the investor's direct rights under the treaty. The analysis of different possible arguments for excluding countermeasures also assists in appreciating the place of investment protection rules and investors' rights in the international legal order. It also shows the impact that developments in other areas of law have had and may further have on investment protection law. The direct correlation between the nature of the rights and the applicability of countermeasures also provides a very pragmatic reason for States to adopt the direct rights approach, whatever the possible short-term tactical benefits of the derivative rights arguments in particular cases may be.

This may be an appropriate place to recall the perspective of the first author to have examined in detail the relationship of breaches of rights of aliens and countermeasures. De Legnano would probably find the framework of the present discussion quite familiar, with the individual being once again the subject most directly engaged in dispute settlement. While the right to take countermeasures has been divorced from the individual and rendered more humane, the questions of 2009 concerning the relationship of *jus cogens, lex specialis* and countermeasures are surely no less perplexing than those of 1393 about the possibility of applying reprisals to married clerks, people going to a festivals, or students on their way to studies.[476] It may be tentatively suggested that the law on the treatment of aliens and investors is likely to continue its co-existence with the law of countermeasures (as it has for at least the last six centuries). The particular mode of the relationship, however, will reflect the level of maturity of the international legal order and the wisdom of the law-makers at a given point in time.

The likelihood of conclusion of multilateral treaties dealing with the issues of countermeasures is and remains rather low. It is more probable that the development of law will take place through State practice (in particular in the form of pleadings), arbitral awards and doctrinal reappraisals. The clarification of the role of countermeasures in the implementation of international responsibility would be likely to depend on actual instances where the investor-State dispute settlement and State-State dispute settlement are unsuccessful, requiring the resort to the ultimate method of inducement. The clarification of the role of countermeasures as a circumstance precluding wrongfulness is more likely, considering the express link that the *ADM* and *Corn Products* Tribunals drew between the nature of rights and the applicability of countermeasures. The future practice both on countermeasures in particular and the nature of rights in general would be conducted against the background of this proposition, confirming one or the other approach to rights or even attempting to de-link the framework. The ambiguity about the precise mode of relationship in both guises of countermeasures suggests that there is much room for clarification and further development of law.

---

[476] *De Bello,* above n 25, 318–320.

THE FUNCTION OF LAW IN THE INTERNATIONAL COMMUNITY: 75 YEARS AFTER

By MARTTI KOSKENNIEMI[*]

I

What was the world like into which Hersch Lauterpacht's most important book *The Function of Law in the International Community*[1] appeared?

Fifteen million Americans were out of work as President Roosevelt took office in 1933. A World Monetary and Economic Conference met in the summer to debate a programme of currency stabilization and adjustment of inter-governmental debts. Even contemporaries understood that this was a 'Period of Crisis'.[2] They were right. 1933 was the year of Hitler's accession as *Reichskanzler* and Europe's definite turn to the path of darkness. By now Hitler had been joined by Mussolini who insisted Italy be treated as a Great Power, especially in terms of its colonial designs in Eastern Africa. Japan's attack on China had led to the establishment of the puppet regime of Manchukuo. Diplomats kept on talking about non-recognition and economic sanctions but with little effect. The Soviet Union turned unexpectedly away from the policy of world revolution. In the following year it would join the League where it would become a staunch opponent of "revision".

The League of Nations was in a bad way. The Manchurian situation had demonstrated the fragility of the Covenant's collective security provisions. The Disarmament Conference had been undermined by Hitler's accession and Japan's withdrawal. No country had worked more to support the conference than Britain. Against a general atmosphere of hopelessness Prime Minister Ramsay MacDonald suggested in the spring a new draft convention with definite levels of material and provision for conference in case of threatened violations of the peace.[3]

* Professor of International Law, University of Helsinki Arthur Goodhark Visiting Professor of Legal Science (2008–2009), University of Cambridge. This was a keynote address given at a conference in Cambridge on 11–12 July 2008 to celebrate the 80ᵗʰ birthday of Professor Sir Elihu Lauterpacht and the 25ᵗʰ anniversary of the Lauterpacht Centre for International Law which he founded in 1983. For the conference proceedings, see James Crawford and Margarat Young (eds) *The Function of Law in the International Community: An Anniversary Symposium* (2008), Proceedings of the 25ᵗʰ Anniversary Conference of the Lauterpacht Centre for International Law. Available at <http://www.lcil.cam.ac.uk/25th_anniversary/book.php>.
    [1] Hersch Lauterpacht, *The Function of Law in the International Community* (Clarendon Press, Oxford, 1933).
    [2] G M Gathorne-Hardy, *A Short History of International Affairs 1920–1939* (4ᵗʰ edn. Oxford University Press, Oxford, 1950), 258.
    [3] See eg F S Northedge, *The League of Nations. Its Life and Times 1919–1946* (Leicester University Press, 1986), 130–131.

The League's Codification conference had ended three years earlier in general disappointment. No significant progress had been made in the conclusion of multilateral treaties in order to solidify the basis of international law. In 1933 the Permanent Court of International Justice was faced with the trickiest problem it had so far encountered, namely the legality of the planned Austro-German customs union. Was the union or was it not contrary to the pledge of neutrality Austria had made in the Peace of Saint-Germain of 1919? The case immediately raised the problem that formed the main subject of *The Function of Law in the International Community*— namely the relationship between political developments and legal rules: was the growth of German hegemony in Europe a justiciable matter?

II

In 1933 Hersch Lauterpacht was 36 years old. He had received his doctorate in Vienna in 1922 and had arrived in Britain with his wife Rachel in the following year. He enrolled in the LSE where he began to collaborate with Arnold McNair for his London dissertation, *Private Law Sources and Analogies of International Law*. The work was published in 1927 and in the same year Hersch received an assistant lectureship that was upgraded to full lectureship in 1930. In the following year, he received British citizenship.[4] At this time, he was busily giving lectures and publishing articles on international law matters, including, for example, the treatment of the Manchurian situation by the League organs. In Lauterpacht's view, the organs had not strictly speaking violated the Covenant in failing to take effective action. The Covenant did leave them discretion. But they had failed in their *political* obligation to use that discretion so as to give effect to the purposes of the League.[5]

No doubt owing to his readiness to speak on politically interesting topics Lauterpacht's lectures were widely attended by students not working for a law degree. He also collaborated actively with the professor of international relations at the LSE, C.A.W. Manning. Even if the British legal community did not hold international law in very high value, a persistent strand of inter-war political idealism did. In the course of the 1930s, Lauterpacht worked to support the Disarmament Conference and participated in the drafting of the abortive Peace Act, proposed by Labour's Arthur Henderson and Lauterpacht's LSE colleague, Philip Noel-Baker. In a predominantly positivist legal environment, Lauterpacht was a natural lawyer—albeit one whose views were still more evident in his critique of sovereignty than any well-formulated normative theory. Unlike the

    [4] On these biographical facts, see my 'Hersch Lauterpacht 1897–1960', in Jack Beatson & Reinhard Zimmermann, *Jurists Uprooted. German-Speaking Emigré Lawyers in Twentieth–Century Britain* (Oxford University Press, Oxford, 2004), 604–616.
    [5] Hersch Lauterpacht, 'Japan and the Covenant' (1932) 3 *Political Quarterly,* 174–194.

Professor of International Law at the LSE, H.A. Smith, Lauterpacht was not a predominantly technical international lawyer law but returned constantly to the foundational questions. In 1932, for example, he lectured to the LSE's famous Sociological Club on 'Is International Law Different in Nature from Other Law'—a text that became the basis of Chapter 20 of *The Function of Law in the International Community*.

III

The Function of Law in the International Community[6] joins a wide European debate about the relationship between the 'political' and the 'legal' in the international world, a debate that had by that time received particular acuity in problems relating to the application of the League Covenant. After all, the Covenant's system of dispute settlement was based on the distinction between two kinds of disputes—those that were 'suitable for arbitration or judicial settlement' (Covenant 13.1 Article) and those that were not and were therefore to be directed to political organs such as the Council. The question of the 'nature' of particular disputes, and therefore of their justiciability, had been raised in practically every case in the Permanent Court that had not been submitted to it as a result of special agreement. It had been conventionally accepted that arbitration or judicial settlement were unsuitable for dealing with disputes over 'vital interests and honour', and many arbitration treaties contained a specific reservation to that effect. But although Lauterpacht dealt with the topic as it arose in the international realm, he was well aware that it was a general problem of jurisprudence, in particular the kind of jurisprudence that had been developed in German public law and that had peaked in the legal debates in Weimar Germany about the nature of sovereignty and the role of the republican constitution in times of economic and political crisis.

In a significant sense, much of the way we speak about international law has been received from German public law as it developed from constitutional commentaries about the nature of the Holy Roman Empire in the 17th century to the natural law of the 18th and the formalism of the 19th centuries. No legal tradition in this period compares with the German in the depth, complexity or sense of urgency of its questions. Lauterpacht had been brought up in that tradition. One of his teachers in Vienna had been Hans Kelsen who at the time of the publication of *The Function of Law* was intensively engaged in a debate about the relationship between law and political sovereignty under the Weimar Constitution—the application of the infamous Article 48 on emergency powers so as to strengthen the position of the Reich, and in particular the *Reichskanzler*, against deviating factions in the realm. The debate concerned the foundations of

---

[6] Lauterpacht, above n 1 (hereinafter *The Function of Law*).

the legal-constitutional order. For the legalists, Kelsen as their spokesman, law itself regulated the limits of its validity. When and how emergency powers, for example, could be used was a question of legal interpretation, properly within the jurisdiction of the constitutional court. For Kelsen's opponents, led by Carl Schmitt of the *Kronjurist* regime, the foundation of the constitutional order must necessarily lie outside that order itself. In particular, it must lie in a political sovereignty that can guarantee the efficiency of the constitution, if necessary by sending in the police.[7] For Kelsen, in other words, the political decisions needed to uphold the law must be received from the law (constitution). For Schmitt, the constitution is powerless in itself—its force and effect must lie in a prior political *decision* about whether to follow the constitution or to make an exception to it.

The question of the respective relations of law and politics in the international world had also been frequently dealt with in German doctrine. For instance, Karl Strupp in Frankfurt had devoted a good quarter of his 1922 *Habilitation* on State responsibility to the question of *Notrecht* and gave his trial lecture precisely on Article 48 of the Weimar Constitution.[8] More significantly, the question of the respective roles of law and politics in international dispute settlement was taken as the object of his 1929 doctoral dissertation by Strupp's most famous student, Hans Morgenthau, the future father of the discipline of international relations in the United States.[9] Morgenthau had argued that there were two kinds of international conflict—'disputes' that focused on well–defined single issues that could be made the object of legal settlement and what he chose to call 'tensions' that implicated a wider—political—antagonism and that could not usefully be submitted to legal mechanisms. There was no general rule by which the two could be identified. The 'political' nature of a problem depended simply on how intensely a State felt about it. When the intensity was high enough, a legal procedure would not only be useless but quite harmful.[10]

The Function of Law could only have been written from the inside of the German tradition, from a vivid sense of the urgency of the question of the legal system's ultimate foundation. Things seemed completely different in Britain. The validity of the British constitution, or of the legal system, was an unreflective second nature of British politics and in no need of elaborate doctrinal defense. In the troubled waters of the German and the international world of the 1930s, no such self-evidence was present. *The Function of Law* was German; not only in its sentence structure, but

---

[7] For one brief but useful description of this debate, see David Dyzenhaus, *Legality and Legitimacy. Carl Schmitt, Hans Kelsen and Hermann Heller in Weimar* (Clarendon Press, Oxford, 1997).

[8] For Strupp's treatment of the legal disputes/political disputes distinction in his various later works, see Sandra Link, *Ein Realist mit Idealen—Der Völkerrechtler Karl Strupp* (1886–1940) (Nomos, Baden-Baden, 2003), 241–247.

[9] Hans Morgenthau, *Die internationale Rechtspflege. Ihr Wesen und ihre Grenzen* (Noske, Leipzig, 1929).

[10] For Lauterpacht's positive review, *cf* (1931) *BYIL*, 229.

in the sensibility it transmitted to its readers. In an early essay on Spinoza, Lauterpacht had written that '[i]t is the ultimate results of the theory of the state which are resorted to by international lawyers as the foundation of their systems'.[11] Few assumptions can be more un-English, more German than that the law emerges as deductive inferences from the political philosophy of statehood.

This, however, is the perspective adopted in *The Function of Law*. It asks the question about the proper role of law in the international world, especially vis-à-vis that which is 'politics', often appearing under the vocabulary of 'sovereignty'. For, as Lauterpacht says at the outset of the book, the 'limitation of the place of law [is] an expression of the theory of sovereignty'.[12] The question is not approached in an openly philosophical or political theory vocabulary, however, but through a technique of legal argument that almost presupposes the answer that Lauterpacht will produce by it. The perspective taken here is legal-institutional. What, *The Function of Law* asks is, is the (legal) force of the claim, often raised in the practice of judicial and arbitral tribunals, that some disputes cannot be dealt with by law—that they are 'non-justiciable'—owing to their nature as 'political' disputes?

IV

The Function of Law in the International Community was an attack on the commonly held view that there were two types of international conflicts—legal and political disputes—and that, consequently, only some of them were justiciable whereas others were not. Lauterpacht had no sympathy with these distinctions. For him they were unfounded in logical, jurisprudential as well as practical terms. In fact, as he put it, the distinctions were ideological. They were '... first and foremost, the work of international lawyers anxious to give legal expression to the State's claim to be independent of law'.[13] Lauterpacht agreed with Morgenthau and Schmitt that it was impossible to draw a clear distinction between the political and the legal by a determinate rule. Anything can, from some perspective, be labeled 'political'. In particular, as he put it with special reference to Morgenthau's dissertation, '[t]he State is a political institution, and all questions which affect it as a whole, in particular in its relations with other States, are therefore political'.[14] But surely the mere fact that all disputes are 'political' in this way cannot provide a reason for regarding them as non-justiciable. In fact, says Lauterpacht, 'it is the refusal of the State to submit the dispute to judicial settlement, and not the intrinsic nature of the controversy, which makes it political'.[15] This is what it means

---

[11] Hersch Lauterpacht, 'Spinoza and International Law' (1927) VIII *BYIL*, 368.
[12] Lauterpacht, *The Function of Law*, above n 1, 3.
[13] Ibid, 6.   [14] Ibid, 153.   [15] Ibid, 164.

to say that the theory of non-justiciability is a consequence of the doctrine of sovereignty—it defers to the sovereign will of the State itself. But
if the will of the State were a *conditio sine qua non* for a dispute being justiciable, then it would always remain open for a State to opt out from the
law's constraint. Like Morgenthau and Schmitt, Lauterpacht thought
that the distinction between legal and political disputes, combined with
the principle that its application was dependent on the State's own view,
led international law beyond the vanishing point of jurisprudence.[16] But
where Morgenthau concluded that the absence of a delimiting rule meant
that everything was *politics*, Lauterpacht drew the contrary conclusion.
For him:

> ... all international disputes are, irrespective of their gravity, disputes of a legal
> character in the sense that, so long as the rule of law is recognized, they are capable
> of an answer by the application of legal rules.[17]

In other words, the fact that a State may feel strongly about some matter—
for example, that it relates to its 'vital interests'—does not exempt the matter from the law but on the contrary, calls for the application of legal rules
concerning precisely those kinds of (important) matters. *The Function of
Law* then goes methodologically through each of the four non-justiciability
doctrines that Lauterpacht was able to identify in the international debates,
showing how each attempt to delimit a realm of the 'political' outside the
'legal' in international affairs will eventually become an apology for unlimited freedom of action of States.

The first item dealt with is the claim that when there is 'no law' at all
a matter must be dealt with in a political way. To treat this issue Lauterpacht
chooses the jurisprudential vocabulary of 'lacunae'. What force is there
to the argument that in cases of 'gaps', judicial and arbitral bodies must
decline jurisdiction and declare '*non liquet*'? As he had already done in his
London doctoral dissertation of 1927, Lauterpacht shows that as far as
legal practice is concerned, courts and tribunals appear to constantly decide
cases by analogy, by general principles of law, balancing conflicting claims
or having recourse to abstract points about the needs of the international
community.[18] The alleged novelty of a dispute has never prevented a tribunal from giving a legal answer to it.[19] Of course situations must arise every
now and then for which the legislator has provided no prima facie applicable solution. No legislator will have prepared for every contingency. But
the fact of there not existing positive (in the sense of 'posited') law on every
conceivable aspect of human behaviour has not, at least not in practice,
led to a wide acknowledgement of the correctness of the theory of 'gaps'.

But Lauterpacht does not merely wish to demonstrate the absence of
cases of *non liquet* in international practice. He derives this state of affairs

---

[16] Morgenthau, above n 9.
[17] Lauterpacht, *The Function of Law,* above n 1158.
[18] Ibid, 110–35.   [19] Ibid, 105–135.

from a wider principle—namely the jurisdictional axiom 'that the judge is bound to give a decision on the dispute before him'.[20] There are no gaps for Lauterpacht. This does not follow from the (naive) assumption that the legislator would have foreseen everything. The completeness of the law is, instead, 'an *a priori* assumption of every system of law, not a prescription of positive law'. Though particular laws or particular parts of the law may be insufficiently covered, '[t]here are no gaps in the legal system as a whole'.[21] This is not a result of arguing from formal completeness of the Kelsenian type—that is to say, from the perspective of the assumption that in the absence of law, the plaintiff has no valid right and that *ergo*, his claim must be rejected.[22] For Lauterpacht, the very notion of 'law's absence' is untenable. For it presumes that law consists of isolated acts of State will that may or may not have extended to the matter under consideration. But this is not at all how Lauterpacht understands the law. He is, after all, a natural lawyer; although for good prudential reasons he refrained from trumpeting this in his British legal environment. But it led him to suggest that 'gaps' were in fact only *primae impressionis* difficulties to decide cases. If law is thought in terms of general principles, judicial balancing and social purposes—as Lauterpacht held it to be—then there is no principled difficulty to respond to novel situations in the end.[23] Even 'spurious gaps' may be filled: an unsatisfactory single rule may be by-passed to give effect to a major principle of law, the intention of the parties or the purposes of the legal system as a whole. In this way, even legal change is regulated by the law.[24]

A second, widely held view presupposed that only technical or otherwise minor disputes were amenable to legal settlement while 'important' issues needed to be dealt with in a political vein. *De maximis non curat praetor*. This was the view on which Morgenthau had written his doctoral dissertation, and had proposed the distinction between political 'tensions' and legal 'disputes'.[25] Sometimes, Morgenthau wrote, even a minor issue must be understood as a 'tension' rather than a dispute because it has become a *symbol* of the antagonism between the relevant states: the real issue is the political conflict, not the legal form it takes. Again, Lauterpacht begins by noting that since the *Alabama* case, tribunals have dealt with a wide number of important questions.[26] Having surveyed the practice of the Permanent Court of International Justice, he concludes that adhering to this principle 'would mean the speedy and radical liquidation of the

---

[20] Ibid, 135.   [21] Ibid, 64.   [22] Ibid, 77–8, 85–104.
[23] Hence McNair's apt characterization of Lauterpacht's writing as 'constructive idealism', A McNair, 'Hersch Lauterpacht 1897–1960', (1961) *Proceedings of the British Academy*, 378.
[24] Lauterpacht, *The Function of Law*, above n 1, 79–87, 254–7 and *passim. Cf* also 'The Absence of an International Legislature and the Compulsory Jurisdiction of International Tribunals', (1930) XI *BYIL*, 134, 144–54.
[25] Morgenthau, above n 9.
[26] Lauterpacht, *The Function of Law*, above n 1, 145–153.

activities of the Court'.[27] Again, however, the main argument is not about what tribunals may have done in practice. An issue of principle is involved. Lauterpacht agrees—perhaps surprisingly—with Morgenthau and even with Carl Schmitt that whether a matter touches on the State's 'vital interests' or 'honour' cannot be decided in abstraction from the State's own view of it.[28] These are purely subjective notions. If important issues were excluded from judicial settlement, and if the determination of the 'importance' of an issue were left to the party itself, then there would in fact exist an unlimited right to opt out from third party settlement. And this would be absurd.

On the other hand, Lauterpacht did not want to completely offset arguments about 'vital interests' or 'honour'. It was true that they had been widely used in arbitration treaties and they did reflect important concerns of States. To discard or ignore such references would be unrealistic and counterproductive. To avoid the absurdity of self-judgment, however, the decision on whether a matter in fact touches the 'honour' or 'vital interests' of a State must be allocated to the tribunal itself in which the claim has been made. That is to say, it should be dealt with no differently from any other treaty provision or customary law principle. As such, it is tantamount to calling for a decision on the merits of the claim. But this means, of course, that the matter is fully justiciable.[29] For instance, it is often held that issues of immigration are non-justiciable. 'In fact', responds Lauterpacht, 'they are typically appropriate subject for judicial settlement. An international court will in most cases invariably presume that the claim will be dismissed'.[30]

The third group of arguments that presumed a distinction between legal and political disputes had to do with the need of accommodating the needs of change in law. Sometimes—and Lauterpacht must have had the debate about the revision of the Versailles peace settlement in mind—law might represent an obsolete political situation, a status quo that no longer existed. An arrangement made long ago may have come to seem too burdensome or otherwise unjust for a party. Owing to the absence of an international legislature, it was impossible to correct the matter by formal means. In such cases—so that argument went—it would be unjust, counterproductive or even dangerous to insist on the application of the law.[31] For Lauterpacht, however, arguments about the clash between law, on the one hand, and justice or peace, on the other, are completely vacuous. The political realists mistake complexity for conflict. Problems of the obsolete or unjust rule may always be tempered by reference to the larger purposes of the law, *rebus sic stantibus*, abuse of rights or principles of equity.[32] The view that law lags behind and must therefore sometimes be offset by new 'political' objectives that provide a better response to the requirements of

---

[27] Ibid, 155.   [28] Ibid, 159.   [29] Ibid, 353–61.
[30] Ibid, 174.   [31] Ibid, 245–347.
[32] Ibid, 270 *et seq*.

the moment is again based on the old (positivist) idea that law is a matter of legislated rules—typically rules laid out by the sovereign legislator—that are carved in stone and become inevitably outdated as the reasons for their enactment have disappeared.

Yet it is a primitive legal theory that views the law in such a way. For as legal practice shows, judges and arbitrators have not lacked means to apply the law in innovative ways, and to set aside rules that appear to be obsolete or unjust: 'much of this amending process is actually and necessarily preformed by international judges in the ordinary course of their judicial function'.[33] It is a matter of the normal interpretation of the rules, and often by reference to their object and purpose. Rules operate in normative environments in which there are many kinds of interpretative techniques, principles of proportionality, and reasonableness and other argumentative resources that enable the adjustment of the law according to important needs. The concerns of realism are incorporated in the law for example by the State's undoubted right to determine the conditions of self-defence for itself and in the exception to the vitiating effect of duress in the law of treaties. The realists' main concern is that law might sometimes fail to give due regard to the liberty and the fundamental rights of the state. As Lauterpacht responds, however:

It is not sufficiently realized that fundamental rights of States are safe under international judicial settlement, for the reason that they are fundamental legal rights.[34]

The fourth and last group of arguments seeking to uphold the law/politics distinction made reference to the difference between 'disputes as to rights' and 'conflicts of interest'. This, too, is an empty distinction. Every right worth having makes reference to some interest, and merely having an interest in something is surely not a legitimate ground for imposing the burden of a legal duty on somebody. Legitimate and illegitimate interests, and the connected duty on somebody to contribute to the fulfillment of legitimate interest, can only be identified by making the distinction between 'raw' interests and interests upgraded into (legal) rights. If a state demands a piece of territory from another because this is vital for its development, it is easy to understand why it may want to deal with this as a conflict of interests rather than as a conflict of rights (because, it has no right). But if it were entitled to do this unilaterally—that is to say, if it had the opportunity to change the terms of the debate from 'rights' to 'interests' by an *ipse dixit*—then of course this would violate the interests of its opponent in a way that would be absurd. In fact, Lauterpacht says, to presume such a distinction 'very nearly amounts to a rejection of the institution of obligatory judicial settlement'.[35] For the same reason proposals to set up specialized institutions to deal with 'conflicts of interest' cannot be accepted. As 'interest' is not amenable to objective determination, this would only create

[33] Ibid, 344.   [34] Ibid, 173, and generally 177–82, 271.   [35] Ibid, 355.

a unilateral veto from juridical settlement and an authorization to discard the rights of others.[36]

V

The refutations of the distinction between legal and political disputes in *The Function of Law* turn on Lauterpacht's hermeneutic view on law— the assumption that no event is 'essentially' or in itself a legal or a political event. Its character as such is the result of projection, interpretation from some particular standpoint. If the distinction were upheld, it would always allow a State to present its unwillingness to submit to the legal process as a result of its 'application'. And:

[a]n obligation whose scope is left to the free appreciation of the obligee, so that his will constitutes a legally recognized condition of the existence of the duty, does not constitute a legal bond.[37]

That the problem of self-judgement (or autointerpretation) becomes the central problem of Lauterpacht's doctrinal work follows from his view that the law is always relative to interpretation. This was a basic tenet of German legal theory—both Kelsen and Schmitt shared it, as did such new streams of continental jurisprudence as Hermann Kantorowicz's 'free law'.[38] If rules do not have essential meanings but those meanings result from interpretation, then the project to chain States into the rule of law by legislation is insufficient. Instead, 'who judges?' (*Quis judicabit?*) becomes the key question. In *The Function of Law* , the lawyer—as judge and arbitrator— becomes the foundation of the rule of law. This is why Lauterpacht was lead to focus on their impartiality and to examine their ability to interpret the law so that everybody's vital interests are secured.[39] To us, an enquiry into judicial honesty and competence seems a somewhat facile solution for world peace. But Lauterpacht's rule-scepticism is ours, too. Our own pragmatism stands on the revelation that it is the legal profession (and not the rules) that is important. As Lauterpacht put it:

[36] Ibid, 372–377.
[37] Ibid, 189. This is, paradoxically, the very point E H Carr makes against Lauterpacht. Precisely because there can be no distinction between law and politics, the latter will always prevail, E H Carr, *The Twenty-Years' Crisis* 1919–1939 (2nd edn. Macmillan, London, 1981 [1946]) 195.
[38] In *The Function of Law*, there is only one reference to the free law school or to Kantorowicz himself. Nevertheless, Lauterpacht's discussion of 'spurious gaps'—that is, gaps that result from the unsatisfactory character of clear rules is practically indistinguishable from 'free law' arguments. For Lauterpacht, too, the distinction between 'real' and 'spurious' gaps is 'relative' (just like, he says, the difference between the legislator and the judge) and cases 'may occur in which a decision which at first sight is *contra legem* can be brought within the pale of law conceived as a whole'. Like Kantorowicz, Lauterpacht refrains from associating judicial freedom with arbitrariness. 'It is freedom within the law conceived as something more comprehensive than the sum total of its positive rules', *The Function of Law,* above n 1, 79, 80.
[39] Ibid, 202–41.

There is substance in the view that the existence of a sufficient body of clear rules is not at all essential to the existence of law, and that the decisive test is whether there exists a judge competent to decide upon disputed rights and to command peace.[40]

The Function of Law puts forward the image of judges of 'Herculean' gap-fillers by recourse to general principles and the law's moral purposes that is very similar to today's Anglo-American jurisprudential orthodoxy.[41] Moreover, it heralds the end of jurisprudence and grand theory in the same way legal hermeneutics does, by focusing on the interpretative practices of the legal profession.[42] Simultaneously, however, it remains hostage to and is limited by the conventions and ambitions of that profession. In this sense, *The Function of Law* is the last book on international theory— the theory of non-theory, the sophisticated face of legal pragmatism.

VI

And what has *The Function of Law in the International Community* to say to us today? Is the distinction between 'legal' and 'political' disputes still an important consideration invoked to decide the jurisdiction of particular international bodies of agencies? Of course it is. Many, though by no means all, constitutional systems subscribe to the distinction and exempt issues of foreign policy from the jurisdiction of domestic supreme courts.[43] The 'political questions doctrine' followed by the US Supreme Court is one well-known, though controversial example of the view of foreign policy being essentially non-justiciable.[44] An example of the contrary case is provided by Germany in which important foreign and even defence policy issues are regularly submitted to the scrutiny of the Constitutional Court (*Verfassungsgericht*).[45] In Britain, as is well-known, the matter came up in the *Pinochet* case where it was pointed out by Lord Nicholls that any suggestion that the matter might be non-justiciable was mooted by the Parliament's having specifically enacted upon it.[46] This presumes (*contra* Lauterpacht) that when there is no such (positive) legislation, there is also no jurisdiction. But in fact, non-justiciability reaches further. In a 2006

---

[40] Ibid, 424.

[41] I have argued about the essential similarity of Lauterpacht's constructivism and Ronald Dworkin's jurisprudence in my *From Apology to Utopia. The Structure of International Legal Argument. Reissue with a New Epilogue* (Cambridge University Press, Cambridge, 2005), 52–56.

[42] This point is emphasized in Anthony Carty, 'Why Theory? The Implications for International Law Teaching' in Allott et al. (eds) *Theory and International Law: An Introduction* (1991), 77, 78–99.

[43] See eg Thomas M Franck, *Political Questions/Judicial Answers. Does the Rule of Law Apply to Foreign Affairs?* (Princeton University Press, Princeton, 1992).

[44] For a recent case, See *Schneider v Kissinger*, 412 F.3d 190 (D.C. Cir. 2005).

[45] For a recent case concerning the violation of parliamentary procedure in a contribution by Germany of troops for a NATO–operation in Turkey in 1983, see *BVerfG*, 2 BvE 1/03 (7 May 2008).

[46] *Ex parte* Pinochet (No. 1), Lord Nicholls, 119 ILR (2002), 96.

case the Court of Appeals highlighted 'a general principle of the separation of powers between the executive and the courts, including the principle that there remain some areas which are essentially matters for the executive and not the courts'.[47]

International lawyers may have thought that the settled practice by the International Court of Justice of dismissing claims by parties according to which the Court would not enjoy jurisdiction owing to the 'political' nature of the case, should have finished with the matter internationally. The Court, it appears, has endorsed Lauterpacht's position and routinely asserts that the fact that a case has political implications does not mean that the Court could not pronounce on its legal aspects.[48] Nevertheless, that practice has now been nuanced by the partial *non liquet* given by the Court in the 1996 Advisory Opinion on the *Legality of the Threat and Use of Nuclear Weapons*.[49] Moreover, the debate in the 1990s over judicial review of Security Council decisions highlighted many of the aspects of the old debate and though it remained inconclusive, there has been marked hesitation (to put it no higher) among international lawyers to affirm the Court's jurisdiction over Council activities.[50] In the European Union, the exclusion of the jurisdiction of the European Court of Justice from matters of common foreign and security policy and, a *fortiori*, common security and defence policy, reflects precisely the kinds of arguments against which Lauterpacht wrote *The Function of Law*. Nevertheless, when the jurisdiction of the ECJ has been triggered in matters that are related to foreign policy—such as in the application of economic sanctions—a remarkable development has taken place from an outright refusal to deal with such matters to a close scrutiny of sanctions from the perspective of their conformity with human rights and due process standards.[51] The

---

[47] *R (on the Application of Gentle and Clarke) v Prime Minister, Secretary of State for Defence and Attorney General* (12 December 2006), 133 ILR (2008), paragraph 75 (p. 752).

[48] The "Lauterpachtian" language is particularly clear in the *Tehran Hostages* case where the Court pointed out that 'disputes between sovereign States by their very nature are likely to occur in political contexts' and that if the Court 'contrary to its settled jurisprudence' were to see this as a reason for refusing to deal with the case, 'it would impose a far-reaching and unwarranted restriction upon the role of the Court in the peaceful solution of international disputes'. *Tehran Hostages*, ICJ Reports 1980, 20 (para 37). The most exhaustive discussion of the matter is now in *Construction of a Wall* (Advisory Opinion), ICJ Reports 2004, 155–156 (para 41).

[49] Here the Court concluded that 'in view of the current state of international law, and of the elements of fact at its disposal, the Court cannot conclude definitively whether the threat or use of nuclear weapons would be lawful or unlawful in an extreme circumstance of self-defence, in which the very survival of a State would be at stake', *Threat or Use of Nuclear Weapons* (Advisory Opinion), ICJ Reports 1996, *Dispositif*, 266 (E).

[50] Out of the huge literature, see eg Kamrul Hossain, *Limits to Power? Legal and Institutional Control over the Competence of the United Nations Security Council under Chapter VII of the Charter* (Acta Universitatis Lapponiensis, 2007).

[51] For an overview of the attitude of the ECJ until 2002, see my 'Judicial Review of Foreign Policy Discretion in Europe', in Petri Helander, Juha Lavapuro, Tuomas Mylly (eds) *Yritys euroop-palaisessa oikeusyhteisössä* (Turun Yliopisto, Oikeustieteellinen tiedekunta 2002), 155–173. For more recent practice, see *Ahmed Ali Yusuf and Al Barakaat International Foundation and Yassin Abdullah Kadi v Council of the European Union and Commission of the European Communities*, Case T-306/01 and Case T-315/01 (21 September 2005).

European Court on Human Rights, too, has frequently dealt with cases in which respondent governments have claimed that the matter pertained to the exclusive jurisdiction of the domestic authorities. The Court has never adopted a formal non-justiciability doctrine—indeed, it would be hard to see how such would work in a human rights context. But it has often been sensitive to the concerns of member governments, endowing them with a wide margin of appreciation when they were conducting policies intended to safeguard national security.[52]

If the terms of the inter-war debate are applied to the question about the jurisdiction of the ECJ or the ECHR, it is possible to see that behind the apparently conceptual problem about the limits of the 'political' vis-à-vis the 'legal' is a more pragmatic concern about who should have the final say about foreign policy—and thus occupy the place political theory has been accustomed to calling 'sovereignty'. Kelsen, Schmitt, and Lauterpacht all had much to say about this, and very little that would have been both new and intelligent has been added to it thereafter. But to phrase this debate as being about 'sovereignty'—the 'Weimar' perspective—does not really lead far towards resolving it. In a fragmented world there simply is no such 'ultimate' place from which authoritative direction could be received for any and all disputes. Perhaps the whole question should be rather brought down from conceptual abstraction and the inconsequential debates about the 'nature' of particular grievances. Perhaps it could be examined in terms of a the subtle institutional politics that we witness in national administrations as well as international institutions—the jurisdictional tug of war between technical experts, lawyers, and policy–makers. A question of economic sanctions, for example, can be described and dealt with from the perspective of politics, economics, security, human rights, development, and international legality. Accordingly, it may trigger the expertise and jurisdiction of political and economic experts, security institutions, human rights bodies, and development organizations—as well as of course, international judicial or arbitral tribunals. Who should be entitled to decide? Framed in these terms, drawing a line between 'legal' and 'political' (or indeed such other fields as 'economics', 'security', 'human rights' etc.) by an abstract rule begins to seem increasingly less important than to accept that however it is done, the matter will remain controversial and will require attention to such institutional safeguards as representation, transparency, and accountability. Each of these various institutions and forms of expertise appears to itself as the 'ultimate' point from which matters ought to be decided. For those outside the institution—the expert

---

[52] In an early case, the Court held that 'having regard to the high responsibility that a government bears to its people to protect them against any threat to the life of the nation, it is evident that a certain discretion —a certain margin of appreciation—must be left to the government'. ECHR, *Lawless* case, Ser.B, 1960–61, para 90, p 82. In a 1993 case concerning terrorism and the derogation from rights under Article 15 of the Convention under public emergency, the Court affirmed that 'a wide margin of appreciation should be left to the national authorities'. Nevertheless, this margin was not unlimited and its use was examined by the Court. ECHR, *Brannigan and McBride*, Ser. A 258.B., 49 (para 43).

committee, the council of diplomats, the court or tribunal—however, it may be anything but self-evident which of them should have jurisdiction, and the privilege to decide.

Hersch Lauterpacht was committed to believe that international lawyers, in particular international judges, should rule the world. This was a part of what I have called the project of gentle civilizing. It was a legal but also a political project. Putting trust in the good sense and responsibility of lawyers for resolving international disputes has its advantages, of course. But judicalization also has its well-known disadvantages. It prefers some interests against others; some voices become heard in courts and tribunals whereas other voices only with difficulty if at all. There is still much work to be done on how interests and preferences get filtered in different institutions and thus contribute to form the structural bias of such institutions. I have said this before and I will say it again: *The Function of Law in the International Community* is the most important English-language book on international law in the 20th century. It is not so because of the invulnerability of its arguments, however, but because of the acute sensitivity it shows to institutional choices for the distribution of spiritual and material values in the world. We know now that neither lawyers nor diplomats should be bosses—should have the final say—in the absolute terms of the old debate. Instead, we should choose the available vocabularies, and institutional alternatives, with a keen eye on the foreseeable effects that this will have in the global games of power in the 21st century.

REVIEWS OF BOOKS

An International Relations Debacle: The UN Secretary-General's Mission of Good Offices in Cyprus, 1999–2004. By CLAIRE PALLEY, Oxford, Hart Publishing, 2005. 224 pp. £26.00.

Legal Aspects of the Cyprus Problem: Annan Plan and EU Accession. By FRANK HOFFMEISTER, Leiden, Martinus Nijhoff Publishers, 2006. xvi + 294 pp. $154.00.

A Functional Cyprus Settlement: The Constitutional Dimension. By TIM POTIER, Ruhpolding, Verlag Franz Philipp Rutzen, 2007. 764 pp. £37.00.

'Cyprus: Diplomat's Graveyard, Lawyer's Gold-mine'. This characterization of the so far unresolved international dispute over Cyprus by one of the three authors whose books are being reviewed is surely an apt one. Few issues have figured so long on the United Nations' agenda; few have been given such unremitting attention by the Security Council and the Secretariat in efforts at mediation and good offices; and yet the latest episode in this long and dispiriting saga (from 1997–2004) ended with rejection of the Annan Plan by three-quarters of the Greek Cypriots who voted, even if two-thirds of the Turkish Cypriots approved it. No less than five UN Secretary-Generals have grappled with the problem, Special Representatives and Advisors running into double figures have broken their teeth on its inherent intractability; now a sixth Secretary-General, Ban Ki-Moon, and another Special Adviser, Alexander Downer, the former Australian Foreign Minister, have been handed the baton. And, over that some forty-five year period, galaxies of international lawyers have participated in the series of negotiations which have taken place and even more have been prayed in aid by the different governments principally concerned to offer formal advice and opinions on the main legal questions in dispute, two amongst them being authors of the books being reviewed. This latest negotiating initiative, just getting under way, is a good reason for welcoming the appearance of these three books which focus on the last such initiative and its outcome, even if it is perhaps legitimate to note that they have arrived, like London buses, in a bit of a gaggle. But no one should imagine that they take similar points of view—far from it, their authors are, after all, distinguished lawyers!

The intractability of the Cyprus Problem, certainly relates in good part to the difficulty the two communities in Cyprus have in overcoming the traumas of their recent historical experiences; to the complex inter-relationships between those communities and their motherlands, Greece and Turkey; to the jockeying of great power politics during the Cold War and since; and to the personal characteristics of the leaders on both sides who, by mischance, never seemed to result in the bringing together at the same time of two men with an equal determination to see the negotiations through to an agreed outcome and with an equal willingness to reach compromises on the main issues at stake. But a further factor which has greatly complicated the negotiations, to which these three authors do ample justice, is the extraordinary complexity of the legal issues under consideration. This results from the overlap between a number of different legal considerations and systems; there are those derived from Cyprus' independence settlement in 1960, incorporated in the Treaties of Guarantee, of Alliance and of Establishment, which bind together Cyprus, Greece, Turkey, and the UK; there are those based on the UN Charter, the Universal

Declaration of Human Rights and innumerable Security Council Resolutions adopted since the dispute first flared up in 1963; there are those based on the Council of Europe's Convention on Human Rights and the jurisprudence of its Court; and then, in the most recent negotiations but not in earlier rounds, the whole panoply of European Union law that has come into play as a result of Cyprus' own membership of that organization and of Turkey's application to join. This cats-cradle of interlocking legal factors has to be addressed by anyone wishing to bring the dispute to a settlement; but the widely differing, indeed sharply contradictory, views of at least two of these three authors, Claire Palley and Frank Hoffmeister, show just how intractable that aspect of the problem is too.

No-one who, like the present reviewer, has had anything to do with the Cyprus Problem, can doubt, however, that efforts to resolve it have more to do with politics and diplomacy than with law. Each of the three authors finds a different way of handling this evident fact. Claire Palley simply throws caution to the winds and embarks on a full-blooded defence of the Greek Cypriot rejection of the Annan Plan, based as much on political considerations as on legal ones. She indulges in some polemical, at times rather vicious, criticism of the principal UN negotiators, whose legal advisers' chief defect was, it seems, their youth. And she glosses over the fact that two out of the three most recent Presidents of Cyprus whom she herself advised (Vassiliotl and Clerides) actually campaigned for and voted 'yes' in the referendum on the Annan Plan. For her, Papadopoulos could do no wrong, a view fortunately not shared by the Cyprus electorate in February 2008 when two-thirds of them voted for candidates who championed the re-opening of negotiations to settle the Cyprus Problem.

Frank Hoffmeister is more cautious about plunging into the political imbroglio and sticks firmly to the legal issues which have arisen in the period since Cyprus' post-independence settlement broke down in 1963 and most particularly those that arise from the drafting of the five different iterations of the Annan Plan and from the interlinked issues of European Union law. His book is a stout defence of the flexibility and ingenuity of the UN and EU Commission officials (of whom he was one) in finding ways of resolving the many problems; and a firm rejection of the Palley thesis that many of these ingenious devices were of dubious legal validity. His unremitting concentration on the legal aspects, to the exclusion of the politics does on occasion lead to an odd feeling that one is watching 'Hamlet without the Prince of Denmark'. For instance the significance of the looming invasion of Iraq at the end of 2002 and in the early months of 2003, the tensions to which it gave rise in relations between Turkey and the US/UK and within Turkey, and its impact on Turkish policy-making at the moment which was probably, looking back on it, the most propitious one to reach a settlement, is simply ignored.

Tim Potier for his part writes more or less as if the political considerations did not exist, or at least as if clear legal thinking could make them vanish; that, together with the fact that he limits his detailed examination to the governance of a re-united Cyprus, leaving aside issues such as property, security and the territorial adjustment of the boundaries of the Greek Cypriot and Turkish Cypriot constituent states, all matters of greater interest and combustibility for the protagonists than those of governance, does rather reduce its relevance either to past negotiations or to those which lie ahead. It is nonetheless a remarkably detailed analysis of those governance matters.

These three books illustrate, therefore, three quite conflicting views of the use and usefulness of legal considerations in the resolution of international disputes. For Claire Palley they are a tool, a weapon even, for use against the opposing party, a means of gaining redress, in court or at the negotiating table, for the wrongs and errors of the past. Hence the bitter sense of deprivation expressed when it became clear that the European Commission, after all the guardian of EU orthodoxy, set out to ensure that European Union law was not used, as many Greek Cypriots wished it to be, as a means of imposing on Turkish Cypriots, solutions which they had long resisted at the UN negotiating table, but rather as a flexible instrument for enabling negotiated solutions to work. Hence, too, her rather engaging admission that, faced with Turkish military superiority, the Greek Cypriots had few effective weapons other than international law. And hence also her astonishingly reductive view of the scope for the UN Secretary-General and his officials to try to broker solutions to deadlocked problems, a reductive view shared on the other side of the table by Rauf Denktash. For Frank Hoffmeister lawyers are there to advise and to help politicians and negotiators to shape up solutions on whose desirability they are mutually agreed. Naturally such solutions must be consistent with whatever form or forms of international law are applicable to the case in point, but he sees those forms, particularly European Union law, as capable of accommodating a good deal of flexibility, not as a strait-jacket. Tim Potier clearly hopes that the sheer logic and intellectual validity of well-designed legal solutions will overcome political prejudices and historical memories. Alas, he is the least likely of the three to see his precepts applied.

How relevant then is all this, admittedly quite recent, political and legal history to the negotiations for a re-united Cyprus which are now getting under way in Nicosia? More than you might expect from the aggressively confrontational rhetoric which poured forth from both sides and their backers in the immediate aftermath of the referendums on the Annan Plan in April 2004 and from the sterile deadlock of the last four years. The hard fact is that there is no real dispute about the overall objective of a bi-communal, bi-zonal federation which was settled as long ago as the High Level Agreements of 1977 and 1979. There is none, apart from those on the extremist fringes of politics on both sides, who do not really want a solution at all or at least not one on terms which could be conceivably negotiable with the other party, who believes seriously that an alternative constitutional structure for a re-born Cyprus is out there waiting to be discovered, that a reversion to the unitary state of 1960 or to Denktash's pipe-dream of a confederation is even remotely realistic. Moreover, during the final stages of those last negotiations and since serious contacts were resumed following the Greek Cypriot Presidential elections of February 2008 a large amount of the legal underpinning of such a federal state has been agreed. There are many hundreds, if not thousands, of pages of the federal laws of a United Cyprus Republic (as the federal state is likely to be called) which have been settled; there is a list of the international obligations which the UCR would inherit from its predecessors, including automatic membership of the UN, the European Union, the Council of Europe and a whole range of other multilateral international organizations; there is much of the structure for applying the acquis communautaire to the north of the island, including, since after the 2004 negotiations, the inclusion of the whole of Cyprus in the euro zone; there are even a whole panoply of flags and a whole cacophony of national anthems waiting to be chosen (currently, oddly enough, neither side has an anthem, each simply using that of the motherland, surely a historical relic which needs to be ended).

So does that mean that, at last, a settlement this time is a sure thing? Far from it. No one has yet lost money betting against a settlement in Cyprus. There are a number of really difficult problems which remain to be resolved in each of the main sections of the negotiations – governance, security, property, and territorial adjustment. The electorates on both sides, who will be the ultimate arbiters of any outcome, have long been nurtured on a diet of unachievable expectations and will not easily be reconciled to the no doubt messy compromises which will be needed on some issues. The curse of every Cyprus negotiation so far, the failure to have at the same time two leaders genuinely committed to reaching a negotiated settlement and an external context propitious to that, has not yet been banished beyond doubt, most obviously in Turkey. What can be said with a reasonable degree of likelihood is that, if this negotiation fails, it is not easy to see another succeeding or even being attempted in the foreseeable future. So there is much to be said for proceeding with care and caution, avoiding impatience and the early setting of deadlines; for suppressing too the temptations of playing the blame game, at which both sides are now adept; and for permitting a sufficient degree of transparency on what is being negotiated so as to avoid the upset that occurred in 2004 when, on the Greek Cypriot side at least, there was a lack of preparedness for what was on the table at the end.

There will have to be some changes in the arrangements negotiated on the last occasion; and they will have to meet problems raised on both sides, not just on the Greek Cypriot side. The most obvious change is the need to avoid the trap into which the UN and others, including Turkey, fell in 2003 when, in order to find a way round the immovable road-block imposed by Denktash, it was decided to put the Annan Plan to referendums without obtaining the signature and support of the leaders and governments on both sides. This, inadvertently, opened the door for Papadopoulos and the parties backing his government to campaign successfully for a 'no' vote. Next time it will surely be essential for the leaders to sign up formally to any agreement reached and to commit themselves, in advance, to campaigning for its endorsement in the subsequent referendums.

Beyond that there does need to be a cultural change away from the zero-sum mentality which has dominated every round of negotiations so far, away from the belief that Cyprus is just a pawn on the chess-board of power and towards a realization that a settlement would bring medium- and long-term benefits to both sides in Cyprus which would far exceed any sacrifices they would be asked to make. It is the unquestioned belief that any change made at the request of one side must, by definition, be of equal detriment to the other which has dogged the footsteps of successive UN negotiators. It is the failure to see the benefits which a reunited Cyprus, firmly embedded in the European Union, would bring not only to its own citizens but also to Greece and Turkey which could then hope to heal finally the wounds left by their own twentieth century history, which has overshadowed all the ingenuity of those negotiators. And it is the belief that whatever Cypriots on either side may do, they are simply at the mercy of others, which has bred an atmosphere of detachment and denial of the fact that Cypriots like Denktash and Papadopoulos have been every bit as responsible for the failure of previous attempts to reach a settlement as outsiders have been. Giving Cypriots and their leaders a greater say in the negotiations and a greater involvement in their development is one way of helping to bring about this cultural shift, so long as it is not supposed that Cypriots will, unaided and unsupported, be able to identify and broker the necessary compromises. To believe that would be a triumph of hope over experience; both the UN and the European Union will still have an important role to play, albeit more that of midwife than that of arbiter they played in 2004.

The main joker in the pack remains Turkey, and above all Turkey's fraught but crucial relationship with the European Union. Unpalatable though it is to most Cypriots to admit this, it really is hard to see the Cyprus Problem being solved if Turkey has been rebuffed by Europe, and its accession negotiations have failed or stalled completely. And, unpalatable though it is to most Turks, it is inconceivable that Turkey should actually join the European Union while Cyprus remains divided as it is today. Somewhere between these two extremes a way forward needs to be found, and not just a Micawberish approach of waiting for something to turn up. It can hardly be in Turkey's interest to push off the difficult decisions on Cyprus to the final stages of their own accession negotiations when other hard choices will have to be made; and it can hardly be in the interest of either side in Cyprus to leave the negotiations on the future of the island hanging in limbo until an indeterminate and uncertain date in the future. So the best policy mix would be to revive the momentum in the EU-Turkey accession negotiations, which has flagged so evidently during the recent constitutional crisis in Turkey, and at the same time to push forward purposefully but not too hastily with the resumed negotiations over Cyprus.

So politics and diplomacy have rather taken over this review from legal considerations as they tend to do when the issue of Cyprus comes up. Which is not to say that the legal issues are not of serious importance. They are; and, if disregarded or flouted, they will bite the negotiators' ankles just when they least want that. Claire Palley, in one of those copious footnotes, of which she is so fond, flattered me by attributing to me the phrase 'lawyers should be on tap, not on top'. The phrase is in fact Winston Churchill's, with a minor adjustment to substitute lawyers for experts. I doubt whether the great man would have objected to that.

DAVID HANNAY
FORMER BRITISH AMBASSADOR TO THE EU AND THE UN;
AND FROM 1996–2003 BRITISH SPECIAL REPRESENTATIVE FOR CYPRUS

Perspectives on the ICRC Study on Customary International Humanitarian Law. By ELIZABETH WILMSHURST and SUSAN BREAU (Editors), Cambridge, Cambridge University Press, 2007. 472 pp. £65.00.

The Handbook of International Humanitarian Law, Second Edition, by DIETER FLECK (Editor), Oxford, Oxford University Press, 2008. 812 pp. £95.00.

The feature both of these books share in substantive terms, apart from being edited collections of contributions by individual authors, is that both constitute, in their own ways, a general analysis of the state of international humanitarian law. While the volume edited by Dieter Fleck is essentially a handbook that can be used both by academics and practitioners, as well as a textbook to be used in classrooms, the other volume, edited by Wilmshurst and Breau, is essentially a reaction to a previous comparable effort conducted by the International Red Cross Committee (ICRC) with a view to identifying customary law standards in international humanitarian law.

In this sense, both volumes are more than timely. They have appeared at the right moment, when international humanitarian law finds increased reflection in State practice and the jurisprudence of national and international courts, as well as in the work of other international organs; in addition, the link between humanitarian law and human rights is increasingly acknowledged. There are a number of aspects of humanitarian law that have attracted a great deal of attention, for example, in the context of situations in and around Afghanistan, Iraq, Palestine, Sudan, and the Balkans. Analysis of the application of humanitarian law in these situations is essential to the development and continued effectiveness of humanitarian law.

In methodological terms, the law applicable to armed conflicts, that is *jus in bello*, is broader than humanitarian law. Part of *jus in bello* relates to what action belligerent States can undertake during a war. International humanitarian law is another part of *jus in bello*, and focuses on the protection of individuals affected during the armed conflict. These two parts of *jus in bello* are substantially different from each other: the law of belligerent actions is often dependent on the origin of armed conflict, which may determine the legality of a particular belligerent action. International humanitarian law, on the other hand, due to its focus on the protection of individuals, applies regardless of who initiated the armed conflict, and protects individuals even if they are the nationals of, or are fighting for, the State which has launched the aggressive war. Although the volume edited by Fleck is denoted as a handbook of humanitarian law, some of its parts, for instance the high-quality chapters on neutrality and law of armed conflicts at sea, are as much about the law governing belligerent action as they are about humanitarian law.

Sources of law and the problem of customary law are among the most intensively debated questions of humanitarian law, especially as the volume edited by Wilmshurst and Breau is about the customary law status of the relevant humanitarian law rules, having the ICRC's study on customary international law as its focus of analysis. Ever since the Hague Conventions were adopted in 1907, one of the main difficulties with ensuring implementation of humanitarian law standards is that the relevant treaties are not always ratified by those States whose conduct is at stake. Therefore, the customary law status of the relevant humanitarian law standards acquires essential importance for the general efficiency of and respect for the relevant law. Well into the twenty-first century, it is still the case that treaties so essential for maintaining the standard of humanity, especially preventing unnecessary loss of life and maintaining the particular aspects of the paramount distinction between civilian and military targets, such as I 1977 Additional Protocol, are not ratified by a number of States.

Iain Scobbie's essay criticizes the ICRC Study for not according sufficient relevance to State practice, and especially not confining itself to examining the practice of thirty or so States that are not parties to the relevant treaties, such as the 1977 Additional Protocols This way, Scobbie considers, the ICRC Study has privileged the practice of States who are conventionally bound by the Protocols anyway. Then the ICJ decision on *North Sea* is pointed to, in which the Court denied that the State which has not joined the relevant convention can still be regarded as bound by its principles unless the high burden of proof to the contrary effect is discharged. Focusing on the practice of non-parties to the Protocols would demonstrate that States are divided on what the law requires and neither uniform practice nor *opinio juris* exists (Wilmshurst and Breau, 33–34). Now, if States are really not agreed on what the legal position on the pertinent matter is, then there is simply no law on that matter. In that case, even if State practice is not, as Scobbie points out, crystallized around the Protocols' provisions, nor would the diverging State practice be enough to crystallize the relevant legal position for the very reason that States would be seen as divided on the issue. Thus the only outcome of pointing to the division of views in State practice is that there is no customary law on the matter on which State views are divided; not that the state of State practice can point to the pertinent legal position. In any case, what could be the impact of the practice of those thirty States against the background of the regulation of humanitarian law under international conventions and the Martens Clause? In order to have any impact on the legal position, this practice should be reasonably uniform and be accompanied by the legal conviction as to the content of particular rules. The alternative way is not to focus on State practice as such in the field extensively covered by treaties, but to adopt the interpretative presumption of the Martens clause and related factors, as the ICJ and ICTY have done in a number of cases.

In respect of the above, the essay of David Turns on Implementation and Compliance in relation to humanitarian law is relevant, especially in terms of examining the customary law status of the law of belligerent reprisals. Turns examines, for instance, the treatment in the ICRC Study of the issue of reprisals against persons protected by the Geneva Conventions, and examines the ICRC's view that in the context of the 1970 Friendly Relations Declaration (General Assembly resolution 2625) and the ICTY decision in *Kupreskic*, there is a trend towards outlawing belligerent reprisal against civilians, but no customary law to that effect yet exists. Turns approves this position by referring to the British position in the UK Ministry of Defence Manual on the law of armed conflicts. According to the manual, reprisals can be taken only in response to serious deliberate attacks in breach of Article 51 of the I Additional Protocol by the adverse part, and with clearance by the Ministry of Defence at the Cabinet level (Turns in Wilmshurst & Breau, 369–370; referring to the Ministry of Defence Manual, OUP 2003, section 16.19.1). This viewpoint invites two observations.

In the first place, the drawing of the connection, in the Ministry of Defence Manual, between Article 51 of the I Additional Protocol and the permissibility of reprisals is not free of problems. This goes against the structure and *raison d'être* of the I Protocol which outlaws attacks listed in Article 51 yet also outlaws belligerent reprisals against civilians. It is clear that the Protocol does not conceive the attacks listed in Article 51 as a right cause for reprisals against civilians, and it is rather curious that the MoD Manual considers that this may be the case. In addition, whatever kind of situations and attacks the authors of the Manual might have had in mind, it is also clear that the possible justification of belligerent reprisals against civilians by Article 51, and *a fortiori* excluding any other justification, will make it impossible to invoke the right to reprisal in wars conducted abroad, such as Iraq and Afghanistan.

In the second place, the entitlement to conduct a belligerent reprisal against civilians, even in response to serious breaches of Article 51, has little practical significance. As Cabinet clearance is required, which is a political decision of which the public knowledge would be expected, it is very unlikely that the British Cabinet would authorize attacks against civilians under whatever purpose or pretext. Thus, even if the MoD Manual, in principle, attempts to preserve the Government's right to resort to reprisals against civilians, it restricts this right procedurally so that the military commanders will not be able to take such a decision. It remains to conclude that the reference in the MoD Manual to right to resort to reprisals against civilians has little practical significance, its main implication being to encourage academic lawyers to assert that the element of reciprocity in humanitarian law still plays a significant role and the non-reciprocal character of humanitarian law does not by itself outlaw reprisals.

Criticism of *Kupreskic* is understandable because this decision of ICTY has formulated principles of custom-generation in international humanitarian law that were not commonly received in the legal discourse before. Still, due to its recourse to the structural and fundamental aspects of humanitarian law, as well as its general compatibility with the judicial treatment of custom-generation in the field of human rights and humanitarian law in the ICJ Judgment on *Nicaragua*, previous ICTY decisions such as *Furindzija* and *Delalic*, and US decisions from *Filartiga* onwards, *Kupreskic* is a right decision.

It has to be said that in the discourse on humanitarian law, the role of State practice in construing rights and obligations of States is very often considered important. State practice as an element of international law-making is not just anything States do. In order to be valid State practice, it has to be qualified in the sense of expressing the concordance of will of States, and also not consist in violation of rules deriving from sources other than custom. In humanitarian law the conduct of States does not necessarily constitute the valid State practice in terms of international law-making. Even consistent patterns of State behaviour in armed conflicts can constitute breaches of international law.

As another instance of a similar discourse, Michael Schmitt considers that the customary law status of the rule that requires warning civilians to leave the area that is going to be attacked is not part of customary law, because there is widespread practice of not warning such civilians (Wilmshurst & Breau, 166). Relying on State conduct as State practice in such contexts raises an important conceptual problem in terms of where do we stop regarding belligerent actions as valid State practice. If the failure to warn civilians is valid State practice undermining the customary law status of the rule obliging the issuance of warnings, then potentially so is the State practice consisting of the failure to prosecute war criminals, of undertaking reprisals against civilians, of denying prisoner of war status to captured combatants, of denying quarter to the population in captured towns, or of detaining prisoners of war for longer than the III Geneva Convention would allow, or even of torturing captured combatants and non-combatants. Hardly can it be denied that all that is frequently practised in armed conflicts, whether international or non-international. But this is not the same as regarding these patterns of behaviour as State practice that can generate legal regulation or impact on the content of existing legal regulation. Patterns of behaviour that go against treaty-based humanitarian law cannot validly count as aspects of custom-generation because even if they were to build customary rules, these would still be displaced by conflicting treaty rules.

Both volumes raise the questions as to when international humanitarian law becomes applicable. Christopher Greenwood specifies that a State may use only such force as is necessary to achieve the goals permitted by the right of self-defence. In this sense, *jus ad bellum* has an effect upon the conduct of hostilities as well as upon the initial use of force (Fleck, 37). While this is right, it has to be asked what the legal position is if the relevant belligerent is the aggressor which cannot claim the right to self-defence? If the matter were to be left to *jus in bello* only, then military necessity under humanitarian law would determine the legality of the aggressor's belligerent actions and rule, according to the humanitarian law criteria, some of them as lawful and others as unlawful. Yet, even in relation to the 'lawful' belligerent actions of the aggressor, the victim could suffer significant material damage for which it could not demand compensation if the governing law is only *jus in bello*. If this were the case, then *jus in bello* would conflict with, and legalize the situation unacceptable under, *jus ad bellum* under which the aggressor has to be denied of any rights deriving from the commission of the act of aggression. This situation requires adopting the line of reasoning according to which military necessity as part of *jus in bello* does not confer legality to any action of belligerents if they fight an aggressive war.

International humanitarian law is normally brought into operation when the conditions specified in the relevant treaties, such as the 1949 Geneva Conventions and their Additional Protocols, materialize. Both Christopher Greenwood (Fleck, 59), and Jelena Pejic (Wilmshurst and Breau, 96), emphasize the problems of the notion of the 'war on terror', Pejic particularly emphasizes the uncertainty of who is the other party in the 'global war' on terror. The involvement of terrorism cannot, according to Pejic, affect the characterization of the relevant conflict under international humanitarian law.

The relevance of terrorism in this field depends thus on how the law of armed conflicts classifies the relevant conflicts. Greenwood emphasizes that terrorist acts can bring international humanitarian law into operation, when these acts are attributable to the State and give rise to armed conflict between that State and the target of terrorist attacks. This can also happen when the author of the attack is not a State but it leads the victim State to take military action on the territory of another State, and brings about the fighting between the two States. Thus, the fighting between the US and Afghan forces in Afghanistan in 2001–2002 was an international armed conflict whether or not the Al-Qaeda attacks in New York and Washington were attributable to Afghanistan (Greenwood in Fleck, 59). In this case humanitarian law indeed applies to the relevant armed conflict, though the ultimate legal merit of the belligerent action would depend on whether the State which takes the fighting to the territory of another State has done so lawfully, especially in terms of the requirements regarding 'armed attack' under Article 51 of the UN Charter and the need to supply genuine proof that the State to whose territory fighting is taken is indeed behind the attack.

The applicability of international humanitarian law depends, *inter alia* on the status of entities involved in the relevant conflict. In terms of whom the US military has actually been fighting in Afghanistan, this conflict has been characterized as international, non-international, or even as being below the threshold of armed conflicts and not even subjected to the effect of the Common Article 3 of the 1949 Conventions. The US Supreme Court in the 2006 *Hamdan* decision rejected the view that Common Article 3 did not apply to the conflict in Afghanistan. The Supreme Court (see paragraphs 65–68 of the Judgment), used Common Article 3 as a sort of default provision which applies across the board in humanitarian law and covers all types of conflicts. The Supreme Court stated that the US had been fighting Al-Qaeda—a non-State actor and not a 'High Contracting Party' to the Convention—and the Convention did not extend to this type of conflict. This way the Supreme Court avoided determining whether the conflict in Afghanistan was international or internal.

In the *Hamdan* case it was allegedly sufficient for the Supreme Court to find Common Article 3 applicable because its due process guarantees could be used to affirm Hamdan's right to *habeas corpus*. But on a more general plane it has still to be clarified what type of conflict has been taking place in Afghanistan since 2001. The existing international jurisprudence of ICJ and ICTY on *Nicaragua, Tadic,* and *Bosnia/Serbia* dealt with the intervention of one State on the side of the rebels or similar entities in and against the government of another State. Afghanistan is allegedly different. The original intervention, that is the US fighting against the Taliban as the effective government was presumably an international conflict. But after the ousting of the Taliban and the installation of the Karzai Government, the US and NATO troops continue fighting the Taliban which is no longer an effective government. On this basis Dieter Fleck in his chapter on non-international armed conflicts (Fleck, 607), concludes that, as foreign troops operate in Afghanistan with the consent of the government, the conflict in Afghanistan is non-international. Jelena Pejic speaks of the 'two strands of the Afghan conflict' that involved the Taliban, the Northern Alliance and foreign troops (in Wilmshurst and Breau, 91).

Some questions necessarily arise. In relation to *jus ad bellum* it is known that the International Court characterized the foreign intervention in civil wars to support rebels against the government as the breach of the prohibition of the use of force. The intervention to support the government is thus permissible. But how does this position translate into *jus in bello*? If the fighting, albeit with the consent of the territorial government, is conducted between the rebels or a similar movement and foreign armed forces, the conflict is presumably not similar to the international armed conflict subsumable within Article 2 of the 1949 Geneva Conventions. But nor is it similar to a typically internal conflict where two domestic factions fight each other. But the characteristics of *jus in bello* require viewing such conflict as international, because the actual fighting is done by the foreign power. This foreign power takes decisions in terms of calculating military necessity, proportionality, collateral damage, distinction between civilian and military targets, treatment of prisoners, treatment of civilian population, and so on. If these decisions rest with the foreign power, then it is difficult to see the conflict like that in Afghanistan as an internal conflict, even as the US and NATO are not fighting against the government.

Now it is obvious that Article 2 of the 1949 Conventions refers to international armed conflicts between two High Contracting Parties, although it does not specify whether the identity of High Contracting Parties for the purposes of the applicability of the Conventions is the same as that of their established or recognized governments. Thus it could be arguable, tentatively at least, that Article 2 does not categorically exclude wars between the rebels in the relevant State and the foreign intervening forces. This may be seen as manipulating uncertainty, and presumably is not the absolutely certain solution either. But questions would necessarily arise from the other side too, if the internal character of the conflict in Afghanistan was asserted. The II Additional Protocol of 1977, which applies to internal conflicts, does not cover those like Afghanistan. As Article 1(1) of the II Protocol specifies, this instrument applies to conflicts which 'take place in the territory of a High Contracting Party between its armed forces and dissident armed forces or other organized armed groups which, under responsible command, exercise such control over a part of its territory as to enable them to carry out sustained and concerted military operations and to implement this Protocol.' Thus, the internal armed conflict cannot be the one in which the Taliban is fighting against the US and NATO forces, at least to the extent that these latter forces are engaged in the conflict on their own.

The solution can be dictated by comparing the texts of the 1949 Conventions, and *a fortiori* of the I Protocol, with that of the II Protocol. The II Protocol is less flexible in its terms, referring not only to particular actors but also to their armed forces, and thereby excludes Afghanistan from its ambit. Article 2 of the 1949 Conventions is, however, flexibly worded and refers to 'all cases of declared war or of any other armed conflict which may arise between two or more of the High Contracting Parties, even if the state of war is not recognized by one of them.' Thus, the Geneva Conventions apply to *all cases of any sort of armed conflict* between two States-parties. It does not positively specify whose forces shall be fighting in the conflict for that conflict to fall within the scope of the Convention, and does not expressly equate the conflict between the two States with that between the two governments. Furthermore, the purpose of the phrase 'even if the state of war is not recognized by one of them' is to secure the protection of the relevant persons and objects in the armed conflict even if one of the belligerents denies that there is war. Would this cover the situation where the Government of Afghanistan consents to the presence of NATO troops in that country? This certainly proves that there is no war between the governments. But there still is war in Afghanistan which does not qualify as an internal conflict under the II Protocol. The relative flexibility of the wording of the 1949 Conventions—though the lack of absolute precision in relation to the Afghanistan-like conflicts should be acknowledged—and the plain fact that there is international military involvement in Afghanistan, should be enough to conclude that if the choice is to characterize this conflict as international or internal, both in terms of law and fact the conflict in Afghanistan fits relatively better within the former than within the latter. This may be an argument that is vaguely right rather than plainly wrong, but this impression would be due to the fact that this specific question has not been judicially tested yet.

Both volumes deal with the concept of military necessity and limits on it. The distinction between civilian and military objects is cardinal and paramount. It cannot be compromised by way of balancing it against the competing considerations of military advantage. The multiplicity of circumstances involved in targeting, as evidenced by wars in Yugoslavia, Afghanistan, Lebanon, and Iraq, raises the issues as to which factors could be considered in terms of target selection and the way of attacking.

The criteria of necessity and proportionality under *jus ad bellum* set limits in terms of military action as to both civilian and military targets; it is about how far military response to armed attack can go. Once *jus in bello* comes in, necessity and proportionality apply to areas in which the hostilities can be validly conducted in the first place. Here the issues of mixed targets and collateral damage can become relevant. The concept of military necessity has long been fundamental in the law of armed conflicts, but there have also been several ways to understand this concept and exactly what it regards as necessary in terms of fighting a war. As Greenwood stresses, military necessity under *jus in bello* enables the victim of aggression to put an end to an attack on it and recover the territory occupied by the invader. In an extreme case the achievement of defensive goals can be secured only by the complete submission of the enemy but this will not normally be required. For instance, the British armed forces could not have lawfully attacked the Argentinian mainland to recover the Falkland Islands that had been invaded by Argentina (Greenwood in Fleck, 36). But still, military installations and supply lines on the mainland could in principle be attacked as legitimate targets. Another, more extreme, perspective on this issue is illustrated by Michael Schmitt by referring to the view expressed by a NATO general involved in the bombardment of the Federal Republic of Yugoslavia in 1999: to destroy power supply, all major bridges over the Danube, and water supply so that the citizens of Belgrade would stand up to the Government and oppose its policies in Kosovo (Schmitt in Wilmshurst and Breau, 139). Schmitt also takes the view that despite Article 51 of the I Protocol, and given that humanitarian law is a balance of humanitarian considerations and military necessity, even extensive collateral damage could be justified if required by military advantage (Schmitt, 158). However, one cannot use the necessity/humanity dichotomy to justify the outcome disapproved under the special provisions of a humanitarian law treaty. Schmitt's analysis effectively puts subjectively malleable policy reasons above the letter of the law.

During the campaigns in Kosovo, Afghanistan, and Iraq, military necessity was expressly or implicitly invoked to attack targets such as bridges far away from the hostility zones, or a national television station. Could anything that makes the adversary potentially stronger and capable to conduct war effort be attacked? Would military necessity justify destroying a farm that provides foodstuff for the war effort; or a religious site that strengthens the moral and psychological aspect of the war effort? That is why the I Protocol limitations, enshrined under Articles 51, 52, and 57, are so crucially important, emphasizing the actual use, location and function of the relevant object, instead of its potential and past uses. Humanitarian law is not about means of *finishing* war, but of *conducting* war; it is about *how*, not *for how long*. This underlines the need to adopt a consistent approach in determining the scope of military necessity in the sense that the distinction between legitimate and civilian targets is consistent and transparent at the moment of the attack.

Military objectives are those involved in pursuing war. However, as Stefan Oeter's chapter on Methods of Combat in Fleck explains, in its military manual the United States has substituted this concept with that of 'war-sustaining capability'. Such an interpretation would allow belligerents to declare nearly every civilian activity as indirectly sustaining the war effort, and thus goes too far. If the intention to directly influence the enemy population's determination to fight were to be recognized as a legitimate use of military force, then no limit on warfare would remain (Fleck, 179–180).

The imperatives of international humanitarian law, if this body of law is to retain its independent applicability in armed conflicts, require seeing the concept of military necessity as limited in two ways: in the first place to attacking only the objects that have military profile and are used for hostilities; in the second place to the objects that are used for hostilities at the time when the attack on them is launched. The temporal limitation included in Article 51(3) of the I Protocol is absolutely crucial to maintain the entire system of civilian/military targets distinction intact. In order to be workable, this distinction must identify straightforward criteria in terms of which targets can be attacked and which cannot. This, in its turn, is possible only if it is possible to make the distinction at the moment of attack. If anything or anybody that potentially or prospectively is viewed as a military target or unlawful combatant can be attacked, then any civilian target can be attacked because it always can potentially become, or has in the past been, part of combat action. Indeed as Oeter observes, the principle of distinction and of non-combatant immunity today constitutes one of the few peremptory norms of humanitarian law (*jus cogens*) (Fleck, 189).

In assessing the requirements to balance the expected military advantage against collateral damage, Oeter points to the complex nature of the circumstances and factors involved, and favours resorting to common sense in such circumstances (Fleck, 198). However, States can differ on what constitutes common sense, especially in such a sensitive field as armed conflict. To maintain legitimacy, the process of application of humanitarian law has to be in strict compliance with the requirements set out in detail in Article 51 of the I Additional Protocol, in terms of the nature, use and location of the relevant objects and the timing of attack. In this regard, more attention should be paid to the ICTY's application of the principles regarding military necessity and excessive collateral damage, for example, in the cases of *Kordic*, *Galic*, and *Hadjihasanovic*.

Yet another very topical and contemporary issue is that of belligerent occupation. Hans Peter Gasser's chapter in Fleck on the protection of the civilian population extensively and interestingly covers the issues of belligerent occupation. After examining the applicability of the law of occupation, the analysis proceeds to briefly focus on the applicability of the law of occupation to Iraq after the 2003 US-led invasion, and then concludes that a number of unclarified issues remain in relation to the cases of the US invasions of Grenada and Panama, the Soviet invasion of Afghanistan, and wars in Lebanon and the Congo (Fleck, 270ff.). But Gasser's analysis does not focus on the issues of the law of occupation in terms of the conflict in the Congo as examined by the International Court of Justice in the *Armed Activities* case in 2006. In this case the Court set out various parameters of the duties of the belligerent occupant which are highly relevant both as a matter of principle and practice.

It has to be concluded that whether and how far these two volumes clarify the above issues, they importantly raise them and attempt tackling them. Thus both volumes are indispensable parts of the discourse on humanitarian law. They should be consulted by anyone teaching or researching in this field.

ALEXANDER ORAKHELASHVILI
BRITISH INSTITUTE OF INTERNATIONAL AND COMPARATIVE LAW

International Investment Arbitration: Substantive Principles. By CAMPBELL MCLACHLAN, LAURENCE SHORE, and MATTHEW WEINIGER, Oxford, Oxford University Press, 2007. 600 pp. £155.00.

Principles of International Investment Law. By RUDOLPH DOLZER and CHRISTOPH SCHREUER, Oxford, Oxford University Press, 2008. 400 pp. £26.99.

The Fair and Equitable Treatment Standard in International Foreign Investment Law. By IOANA TUDOR, Oxford, Oxford University Press, 2008. 300 pp. £60.00.

Until recent years, publications on investment arbitration law focused primarily on procedural issues, lacking any detailed discussion on the substantive principles, which in essence are the core of investment arbitral awards. This is quite unusual given the number of investment arbitration cases, which now exceed 290.[1] The books by Dolzer and Schreuer, and McLachlan, Shore and Weiniger offer an in-depth analysis of international investment law, attempting to fill this gap in investment arbitration literature by placing an emphasis on substantive principles. Tudor's work concentrates on one substantive standard for protection of investors: the fair and equitable treatment (FET), but places FET in a broader context by assessing its interactions with other standards of protection. As the authors of this selection of books are renowned academics and practitioners in the field of international investment law, they barely need introduction. Professors Dolzer and Schreuer laid down the foundations of investment law with two essential studies: Bilateral Investment Treaties[2] and The ICSID Convention: A Commentary.[3] McLachlan, Shore and Weiniger are experienced practitioners in investment and commercial arbitration and authors of numerous studies in the field.[4] Tudor is a new presence, with an intriguing and difficult topic, but succeeds in delivering an outstanding piece of research. All three studies are clearly written and take a comprehensive approach of the major issues and principles of international investment law, by combining an analysis of the underlying principles of international investment law with an examination of investment arbitration cases. Consequently, the selection of books under review is a useful guide not only for novices in the field of investment law, but also for experienced practitioners since they represent a powerful reference tool. It must be noted that in such a sensitive area of international law, these books successfully manage to take a balanced approach to the

---

[1] According to UNCTAD: *Latest Developments in Investor-State Dispute Settlement*, IIA Monitor (1) 2008 International Investment Agreements.

[2] R Dolzer and M Stevens, *Bilateral Investment Treaties*, (Martinus Nijhoff Publishers, Leiden, 1995).

[3] C Schreuer, *The ICSID Convention: A Commentary*, (Cambridge University Press, Cambridge, 2001).

[4] C McLachlan, L. Collins, C Morse, D McClean, A Briggs, J Harris (eds.) *Dicey, Morris & Collins on the Conflict of Laws* (14th edn, Sweet & Maxwell, London, 2008); L Shore, 'What lawyers need to know about international arbitration' (2003) 20 *Journal of International* Arbitration 67; M Weiniger, 'Jurisdiction Challenges in BIT Arbitrations: Do You Read a BIT by Reading a BIT or by Reading into a BIT?' in J Lew and L. Mistelis, (eds.) *Pervasive Problems in International Arbitration,* (Kluwer Law International, 2006) 235.

theory and practice of investment law. Although the book by Tudor might prove more useful for counsel representing investors, it is nonetheless an excellent tool for arbitrators dealing with FET claims.

Given the amount of information offered and analysed by these distinguished authors, one might be tempted to include these books in the category of 'shelf books' that one uses only when necessary. It would be wrong to label these books as such. They are easy to read and give a clear and comprehensive presentation of the issues under review. It would also be wrong not to read them as a novel—from beginning to the end, because ultimately they are telling us the story of international investment law. These books will no doubt be a standard reference point on the substantive principles of international investment law for years to come.

This book review will commence with a brief presentation of the content of each book and will continue with a comparative review on the main issues analysed by the authors. As this review takes a comparative approach, it will not undertake to exhaust the matters addressed in these three books, but rather to concentrate on three topics: investment, fair and equitable treatment standard, and expropriation.

McLachlan, Shore and Weiniger set out the basics of investment protection. This book has benefited from the authors' personal experience as counsel and arbitrators in commercial and investment arbitration cases. Being the first book published on substantive principles of investment law, the authors assume a difficult mission in this untouched field. They first begin with an overview of investment law, concentrating mainly on treaty law, and continuing with highlights of investment treaties: the features of bilateral and multilateral investment treaties (BITs) and the dispute resolution provisions under them, placing a special focus on the ICSID Convention. The authors dedicate the second part of the book to the ambit of protection and address three controversial jurisdictional issues: parallel proceedings, nationality, and investment. In the final part of the book the authors explore the substantive rights of investors: fair and equitable treatment, full protection and security, national and most-favoured-nation treatments, and dedicate a special section to expropriation and compensation.

As Dolzer and Schreuer reveal, the 'aim of [their] book is mainly to elucidate the meaning of the central principles that govern current foreign investment law' (Dolzer and Schreuer, Foreword). This book is an exceptional guide for practitioners and students alike and an essential reference tool for investment arbitration cases.[5] The authors first present the nature of international investment law by putting investment law into an historical context. An extensive analysis is dedicated to the interpretation and application of investment treaties, with particular emphasis on the authority of 'precedents' and the relevant date for determining jurisdiction, especially under the ICSID Convention.

The authors continue with a standard-by-standard analysis: fair and equitable treatment; full protection and security; umbrella clauses; access to justice, fair procedure and denial of justice; emergency, necessity, armed conflicts and force majeure; arbitrary or discriminatory measures; national treatment; most-favoured-nation treatment.[6] They conclude with the rules of attribution and the settlement of investment disputes. The chapter on the settlement of disputes between investors and states is a useful guide for every practitioner embarking on this challenging but rewarding investment arbitration journey.

---

[5] The authors provide a comprehensive list of cases for each issue discussed (for example cases where tribunals invoked Article 31 of the Vienna Convention on the Law of Treaties 1969, 1155 UNTS 331, or cases where tribunals equated the standards of full protection and security with the fair and equitable treatment).

[6] The authors dedicate special chapters to access to justice, fair procedure and denial of justice; and arbitrary or discriminatory measures, while McLachlan, Shore and Weiniger and Tudor discuss them as part of the fair and equitable treatment standard.

The fair and equitable treatment standard is the focus of the monograph written by Ioana Tudor. Although a significant number of investment arbitration cases extensively rely on FET, this is the first book dedicated to an in-depth study of this standard. The reader will find a comprehensive analysis of the FET starting from the nature of this standard and continuing with the way in which FET is applied in concrete cases. Tudor also offers a short description of the historical background of FET and an identification of sources of international law that are later used to uncover the sources of the FET standard. This book proves to be a very useful instrument for both academics and practitioners, ingeniously combining theoretical and practical approaches. Of significant importance for practitioners dealing with the FET standard is the chapter dedicated to the interaction between FET and other standards of treatment of investors. This book offers a useful starting point for considering FET clauses in specific situations, as it deals with a review of the framework within which the FET standard operates. As the author suggests, '[the book] offers, instead, layers of novel methods and structures, through which its [the FET] contours become discernible' (Tudor, 6). In the final chapters of the book Tudor discusses the issues of compensation and enforcement of arbitral awards where tribunals have held that the FET standard has been violated. Although it is often argued that the FET standard favours investors, the author suggests here that '[t]he FET obligation [...] may create a more balanced situation by taking into account the behaviour of the Investor as well as the extreme financial or social situation of the State.' (Tudor, 228.)

I. INVESTMENT

The notion of investment 'has become increasingly important as a threshold jurisdictional question in treaty arbitration'. (McLachlan, Shore and Weiniger, 6.01) There is much debate on what constitutes an investment under Article 25 of the ICSID Convention since no definition of this notion is incorporated in the ICSID Convention.[7] The books by McLachlan, Shore and Weiniger and Dolzer and Schreuer provide a practical analysis of the notion of investment under investment treaties and the ICSID Convention, looking particularly at ICSID case law.

Examining what constitutes an investment, McLachlan, Shore and Weiniger focus on the ICSID Convention and bilateral and multilateral investment treaties. Special attention is paid to the timing and territorial issues related to investments, pre-contractual investments, admission of investments and direct/indirect investments. Dolzer and Schreuer discuss this concept under the ICSID Convention and its case law, and under investment treaties. They dedicate a special chapter to the admission and establishment of investments.

Despite the absence of a definition under the ICSID Convention, it is considered that the content of the notion of investment cannot be entirely decided by the parties in dispute. It is argued by scholars and ICSID tribunals that the notion of investment has objective limitations which cannot be ignored and the consent of the parties alone may not be decisive or sufficient for qualifying an investment. This is the so-called *objective approach*. McLachlan, Shore and Weiniger, as well as Dolzer and Schreuer seem to adhere to this understanding of the notion of investment. On the other hand, the *subjective approach* considers that the notion of investment is controlled by the consent of the parties, in the absence of a definition

---

[7] Despite many attempts to include a definition of investment in the ICSID Convention of 18 March 1965, 575 UNTS 159, the final draft provides no such definition. Article 25 of the ICSID Convention simply states that '[t]he jurisdiction of the Centre shall extend to any legal dispute arising directly out of an investment, between a Contracting State [...] and a national of another Contracting State, which the parties to the dispute consent in writing to submit to the Centre.'

of investment in the ICSID Convention. This means that if the parties to the dispute considered (in a direct or indirect manner) their transaction an investment, such determination of the parties should be sufficient for the purpose of Article 25 of the ICSID Convention. Few scholars and tribunals concurred with this approach.[8]

As McLachlan, Shore and Weiniger point out, Schreuer drew up the list of objective factors defining an investment back in 1996 in an article on the ICSID Convention which was later inserted in his commentary on the ICSID Convention.[9] These factors are: certain duration, regularity of profit and returns, specific risk undertaken by the parties, substantial commitment and significant contribution to the development of the host State. Dolzer and Schreuer remind us that '[t]hese criteria were restated clearly in *Salini v Morocco* in 2001 and have also been applied in subsequent decisions' (Dolzer and Schreuer, 68). In fact, the *Salini* decision[10] considered only four factors: contribution, a certain duration, risk, and contribution to the economic development of the host State. Within the objective approach, several ICSID tribunals took a broad view of the notion of investment, since 'a dispute that is brought before the Centre must be deemed to arise directly out of an investment even when it is based on a transaction which, standing alone, would not qualify as an investment under the Convention, provided that the particular transaction forms an integral part of an overall operation that qualifies as an investment'.[11] The books by McLachlan, Shore and Weiniger, and Dolzer and Schreuer offer an excellent review of the prominent ICSID cases discussing these objective criteria of investment. A book review of this type is not the appropriate place to consider these cases in detail, but probably a short comment on the economic development requirement should be put forward.

The authors argue that for an investment to be within the meaning of the ICSID Convention, certain criteria must be met, and one of these is the contribution to the economic development of the host State.[12] As briefly explained above, this requirement was upheld by several ICSID tribunals and most recently in *Noble Energy v Ecuador*,[13] but the existence of this criterion was put in the spotlight by the decision of the annulment committee in *Patrick Mitchell v Congo*.[14] The annulment committee in *Patrick Mitchell v Congo* held that 'the existence of a contribution to the economic development of the host State [is] an essential—although not sufficient—characteristic or unquestionable criterion of the investment'.[15] It would have been expected that the authors might bring more light on this controversial issue. Dolzer and Schreuer state that '[i]n case of an investment lawfully admitted and implemented, the very consistency of the project with the legal order

---

[8] Support for this approach can be found in the Preamble of the ICSID Convention and the Report of the Executive Directors on the ICSID Convention. Several ICSID cases, including *Philippe Gruslin v Malaysia* (ICSID Case No. ARB/99/3) and *Lanco International v Argentina* (ICSID Case No. ARB/97/6), adopted this approach.

[9] C Schreuer, *Commentary on the ICSID Convention*, 11 ICSID Rev.-FILJ 1996, 316 and later; C Schreuer, above note 3.

[10] *Salini Costruttori S.p.A. and Italstrade S.p.A. v Kingdom of Morocco* (ICSID Case No. ARB/00/4), Decision on Jurisdiction of 29 November 2004.

[11] *Ceskoslovenska obchodni banka, a.s. (CSOB) v Slovak Republic* (ICSID Case No. ARB/97/4), Decision on Objections to Jurisdiction of 24 May 1999, para 71.

[12] Without denying this approach, it must be pointed out that these *objective criteria* are the creation of scholarly writings and case law. Several studies engaged in discussing whether, in the absence of a *stare decisis* doctrine, this approach has sufficient legal support.

[13] *Noble Energy Inc. and MachalaPower Cía. Ltd. v Republic of Ecuador and Consejo Nacional de Electricidad* (ICSID Case No. ARB/05/12), Decision on Jurisdiction of 5 March 2008.

[14] *Patrick Mitchell v Democratic Republic of the Congo* (ICSID Case No. ARB/99/7), Decision of 1 November 2006 on the Application for Annulment of the Award. The committee considered that the activities of a US law firm in Congo did not contribute to the economic development of Congo.

[15] *Patrick Mitchell v Democratic Republic of the Congo* (ICSID Case No. ARB/99/7), above n 21, para 33.

of the host state should indicate the contribution to the development of the host state' (Dolzer & Schreuer, 69). No explanation is given for this consideration. The authors point out, however, that as soon as the contribution, duration and risk requirements are met, the economic development requirement 'should not be difficult to establish' Dolzer & Schreuer, 69).[16] McLachlan, Shore and Weiniger consider this criterion in light of the ICSID case law, without any comment as to the existence and legitimacy of this requirement.[17]

A hot topic for investment arbitration is whether pre-contractual investments (or rather pre-contractual expenditures) are included in the notion of investment under the ICSID Convention. This was, for instance, the case in *Mihaly v Sri Lanka*[18] where the tribunal had to decide whether, in the absence of a contract signed by the parties, the expenditures incurred by the investor in the preparation for the investment could constitute an investment for the purpose of Article 25 of the ICSID Convention. McLachlan, Shore and Weiniger consider that in the absence of a specific consent of the State, such pre-contractual expenditures are not covered by investment treaties and thus, the ICSID tribunals have no adjudicatory jurisdiction (McLachlan, Shore and Weiniger, 6.50). Dolzer and Schreuer are of a similar opinion that 'in the absence of a specific applicable treaty clause, the current understanding is that when the negotiations do not lead to a contract and no other type of investment is made, the potential investor is not in a position to raise a claim under a BIT' (Dolzer & Schreuer, 71). Arguably, excluding these pre-contractual expenditures from ICSID's jurisdiction discriminates against foreign investors and forces them to structure their investments accordingly in order to receive the protection of BITs. It is true that allowing discontented potential investors to submit their disputes to ICSID would be unreasonable and would add an unjustified burden on the States, but it is also a fact that the majority of ICSID cases do not rely on investment agreements. This is the reason why careful consideration must be given to the principles of equity and fairness among investors and their investments, as ICSID's jurisdiction should be made equally available to foreign investors.

As to the admission and establishment of investments, Dolzer and Schreuer indicate that '[f]rom the perspective of general international law, states are in no way compelled to admit foreign investments' (Dolzer & Schreuer, 79). It is also an expression of States' sovereignty to impose additional requirements to investments and investors or to consent to only certain types of disputes to fall under the jurisdiction of ICSID. Modern BITs usually provide protection only to investments made in accordance with the legislation of host States. Such provisions allow States to adapt their national laws on the admission of foreign investments in accordance with their economic or political interests or policies; nevertheless, these adjustments must be made in good faith, with the observance of obligations undertaken under international treaties. Investment treaties may also contain additional requirements regarding the approval or authorization of foreign investments by competent authorities of the host State. Investments made in breach of host State legislation or failing to obtain the approval or authorization of the local authorities, shall not be covered by the provisions laid down in the respective investment treaties. Such requirements are deemed as limitations to the consent of States. Consequently, the dispute resolution mechanism provided for by these treaties covers only investment disputes regarding investment legally made or authorized/approved in accordance with the legislation of the host State. McLachlan, Shore and Weiniger make clear that illegal investments are

---

[16] With reference to *LESI/Dipenta v Algeria* (ICSID Case No. ARB/03/8) and *Bayindir v Pakistan* (ICSID Case No. ARB/03/29).

[17] The authors refer to *Fedax v Venezuela* (ICSID Case No. ARB/96/3) and *Bayindir v Pakistan* (ICSID Case No. ARB/03/29).

[18] *Mihaly International Corporation v Democratic Socialist Republic of Sri Lanka* (ICSID Case No. ARB/00/2), Award of 15 March 2002.

disqualified from the protection of investment treaties and such disputes are not within the jurisdiction of arbitral tribunals (McLachlan, Shore and Weiniger, 6.63). As explained by Dolzer and Schreuer, 'investments made in violation of domestic rules may be outside the substantive guarantees contained in the relevant agreement, depending upon the nature and gravity of the violation' (Dolzer & Schreuer, 69). On the approval and authorization of investments, McLachlan, Shore and Weiniger are of the opinion that 'the question as to whether registration [of an investment] has been properly obtained will be considered under the domestic law of the State whose approval is required' (McLachlan, Shore and Weiniger, 6.106). As mentioned earlier, such requirements 'must be exercised subject to the overriding concerns of good faith contained in international law' (McLachlan, Shore and Weiniger, 6.106).

II. Fair and Equitable Treatment

Tudor traces the first reference to FET back to 1948 in the Havana Charter of the defunct International Trade Organization (ITO) which mandated the ITO 'to assure just and equitable treatment' to the investors of the Member States. After the failed Havana Charter, the standard was later incorporated in the Treaties of Friendship, Commerce and Navigation, and BITs. Tudor identifies thirty-four cases between 1997 and August 2007 where arbitral tribunals dealt with the FET standard. This number must be weighted against the total number of known investment arbitration cases of 290 counted between 1987 and 2007, bearing in mind that not all investment arbitration awards are public or published in full.[19] It is undisputed that FET became an indispensable tool for a successful claim in international investment arbitration. Tudor considers that the popularity of FET derives from the easy application of the standard to a broad range of situations and actions since it is 'contingent upon other standards or situations, [...] broad and vague, [...] it is a unilateral obligation of the home State, requiring no specific duties from the Investors' (Tudor, 10).

FET is a standard and therefore a precise definition is difficult to find. However, as Tudor points out, 'its shape and meaning is given by State practice, decisions of international tribunals and, more importantly, the circumstances of the case' (Tudor, 15). The State practice is reviewed with reference to the relevant BITs,[20] regional treaties[21] and multilateral instruments.[22] This overview reveals different drafting variants of the FET clause[23] which make the author conclude that the diversity among the FET clauses is not accidental. Dolzer and Schreuer agree that 'no single frozen version [of the FET] exists' (Dolzer & Schreuer, 121) and these variations of the FET clause must be interpreted in accordance

---

[19] See UNCTAD: *Latest Developments in Investor-State Dispute Settlement*, above n 1.

[20] The author reviewed 365 BITs concluded by Argentina, Australia, Bangladesh, Canada, France, Japan, Romania, Saudi Arabia, Switzerland, and the US.

[21] The regional instruments considered for the book are: Lomé IV Convention, the Energy Charter Treaty, the Economic Agreement of Bogotá, MERCOSUR, COMESA, NAFTA, ASEAN, the Agreement for Investment in Arab Capital, and the CARICOM and Cuba agreement.

[22] The multilateral instruments (including guidelines) reviewed for the book include: the Convention establishing the MIGA, the UN Code of Conduct on Transnational Corporations, the OECD Multilateral Agreement on Investment etc.

[23] Tudor identifies at least seven variations of the FET clause: FET not mentioned, FET mentioned alone, FET mentioned with the reference to 'international law', FET mentioned with reference to 'arbitrary and discriminatory' measures, FET mentioned with an example of impairment, FET mentioned together with 'full protection and security', FET mentioned with 'national treatment' or MFN clauses. The author gathers the empirical findings of this research under Appendixes I to VI.

with the principles of interpretation laid down in the Vienna Convention on the Law of Treaties. From the perspective of customary law, Tudor argues that the FET standard is part of the international minimum standard only when linked to it; otherwise, FET is an autonomous standard. The same opinion is shared by Dolzer and Schreuer. They consider that FET may overlap or be identical with the minimum standard based on the actual wording of the particular treaty.

Dolzer and Schreuer see the FET as a gap-filling clause: essentially, the FET clause will fill in the gaps 'left by the more specific standards, in order to obtain the level of investment protection intended by the treaties' (Dolzer and Schreuer, 122). Dolzer and Schreuer consider that although the FET standard may be viewed as incorporating two distinct standards—'fair' and 'equitable', they suggest that the general understanding is that the FET standard represents a 'single, unified standard' (Dolzer & Schreuer, 122). According to Tudor, a standard is a legal concept containing an objective and a subjective element. The objective element is the concept itself which must be assessed based on the circumstances of each case; while the subjective one is in fact the application of the standard. Reviewing the cases dealing with the FET standard, Tudor concludes that it is impossible to provide a clear-cut definition of the FET standard especially because 'generality and vagueness are an integral part of its content' (Tudor, 6).

McLachlan, Shore and Weiniger analyse the cases on the FET standard as falling into two categories: cases concerned with the treatment of investors by the courts of the host State and cases dealing with administrative decision-making (McLachlan, Shore and Weiniger, 7.76). They also provide an excellent overview of the factors which may give rise to a breach of the FET standard and the factors which may indicate that the standard was not breached. Among the factors indicating a FET breach, McLachlan, Shore and Weiniger consider the following: legitimate expectations and the state of law at the time of the investment, specific representations made to the investor, due process in administrative decision-making, discrimination, transparency, use of power for improper purposes, inconsistency, coercion and harassment by State authorities, and bad faith. On the opposite side, factors that may indicate the absence of a FET breach include: an objective basis for the decision, lack of disproportionate impact on foreign investor, absence of the alleged right and the investor's conduct and his duty to investigate. Dolzer and Schreuer discuss the specific application of the FET standard and similarly refer to transparency, stability and legitimate expectations, compliance with contractual obligations, procedural propriety and due process, good faith and freedom from coercion and harassment. It is often said that transparency overlaps with the FET standard.[24] Dolzer and Schreuer explain that '[t]ransparency means that the legal framework for the investor's operations is readily apparent and that any decisions affecting the investor can be traced to that legal framework'. Transparency will be implicitly (even if not expressly) included in investment treaties that provide for the FET standard.[25] The relation between transparency and the FET standard usually relates to the idea that a non-transparent decision and investment regime in general is not fair and equitable (Tudor, 177).

One important issue is how tribunals should assess the existence of a FET breach. Dolzer and Schreuer identify three approaches in the practice of ICSID tribunals. The first one implies that tribunals find a definition of the essential elements of the standard on the basis of abstract reasoning. The second one rejects such an abstract definition of the FET standard and tribunals rather attempt to 'decide ad hoc whether a certain conduct satisfies the requirement of the standard' (Dolzer and Schreuer, 133). Under the third

---

[24] UNCTAD Series on Issues in International Investment Agreements, *Fair and Equitable Treatment*, UNCTAD/ITE/IIT11 (Vol. III) at <http://www.unctad.org/en/docs/psiteiitd11v3.en.pdf> (last accessed 8 December 2008), 51.

[25] Ibid, 51.

approach, tribunals 'will attempt to base its decision primarily on previous decisions or will build upon relevant precedents by way of analogy or by drawing on the same principle' (Dolzer and Schreuer, 133).[26]

Tudor also takes a look at the interaction between the FET standard and other standards of treatment of investors: full protection and security, non-discrimination, most-favoured-nation clauses, pacta sunt servanda (umbrella clause), and the standard of non-impairment. The author concludes that special attention needs to be paid to the actual wording of the FET clause and the other standards under the specific investment treaty, as there might be cases where 'other standards may be indicative of minimum level of FET' (Tudor, 201) or, one could add, they could often overlap. For example, Tudor refers to the full protection and security standard and the FET and points out that '[t]he bridge between the two standards is built by the obligation of due diligence which is part of the FET' (Tudor, 185). However, the author adds, '[t]he difference between the two types of due diligence is that under the full protection and security obligation, it essentially refers to the protection of the Investor and his investments, hence, it relates mainly to the physical aspect, while the due diligence requirement as contained in FET is connected more to the environment in which the foreign investment is taking place and to its treatment as a more elaborated notion' (Tudor, 185).

III. Expropriation

Although being one of the most popular concepts in investment arbitration, expropriation has no precise definition under bilateral and multilateral investment treaties. Investment treaties usually refer to expropriation (and nationalization) in a general manner and, rather, focus on the conditions that should be met on behalf of States for such an action to be lawful. For instance, the Sweden-Mexico BIT in Article IV(1) provides that '[n]either Contracting Party shall expropriate or nationalise an investment of an investor of the other Contracting Party, either directly or indirectly through measures tantamount to expropriation or nationalisation (hereinafter referred to as 'expropriation'), except: (a) for a public purpose; (b) on a non-discriminatory basis; (c) in accordance with due process of law; and (d) on payment of compensation in accordance with paragraphs 2 and 3'.[27] No explanation is given for what expropriation or nationalization may comprise of. The situation is the same when considering multilateral treaties, for example NAFTA or the Energy Charter Treaty.

Back in 2002, Dolzer was writing that 'it is not unreasonable to assume that the legal issues in the foreign investment may, for the time being, be dominated by the definition of expropriation'.[28] However, since 2002, no investment treaties have incorporated a definition of expropriation. For McLachlan, Shore and Weiniger, 'the concept of expropriation is reasonably clear: it is a governmental taking of property for which compensation is required' (McLachlan, Shore and Weiniger, 8.03).

---

[26] It is interesting that here Dolzer and Schreuer refer to 'precedents'. As mentioned at note 19, there is no *stare decisis* doctrine in investment arbitration. In fact, Dolzer and Schreuer remind us at page 36 that 'it is also well-established that tribunals in investment arbitration are not bound by previous decisions of other tribunals'. Therefore 'precedents' are to be understood here as 'case law'.

[27] *Agreement between the Government of the Kingdom of Sweden and the Government of the United Mexican States Concerning the Promotion and Reciprocal Protection of Investments*, signed on 3 October 2000.

[28] R. Dolzer, 'Indirect Expropriation: New Developments?' (2002) 11 *New York University Environmental Law Journal* 64, 66.

It is accepted that States are entitled to expropriate foreign investments as long as they comply with certain requirements. Dolzer and Schreuer prompt us to the fact that 'state practice has considered this right [expropriation] to be so fundamental that even modern investment treaties [...] respect this position' (Dolzer and Schreuer, 89). As to the requirements that must be fulfilled for an expropriation act to be lawful, Dolzer and Schreuer refer to three (or four in some cases) cumulative conditions: the expropriation must serve a public purpose; the measure must not be arbitrary and discriminatory; some treaties explicitly refer to expropriation complying with principles of due process; and the measure must be accompanied by prompt, adequate and effective compensation. Looking at the ICSID case law, Dolzer and Schreuer conclude that the most controversial requirement is the measure of compensation. The assessment of expropriatory measures must be made in accordance with the principles and obligations under international law. Or as McLachlan, Shore and Weiniger refer to this, 'the fact that a 'taking' of that property by the host State may be legal under municipal law does not affect the question of whether the State's conduct is expropriatory under international law' (McLachlan, Shore and Weiniger, 8.65).

If direct expropriation is rare, indirect expropriations are becoming more and more frequent. Dolzer and Schreuer see the difference between direct and indirect expropriation in 'whether the legal title of the owner is affected by the measure in question' (Dolzer and Schreuer, 92). McLachlan, Shore and Weiniger remind us that '[s]everal terms, in addition to 'indirect', are used to describe indirect expropriation, for example 'de facto' or 'creeping' expropriation, or measures 'tantamount to' or 'equivalent to' expropriation' (McLachlan, Shore and Weiniger, 8.75). Dolzer and Schreuer view indirect expropriation as a form of expropriation that 'leaves investor's title untouched but deprives him of the possibility to utilize the investment in a meaningful way' (Dolzer and Schreuer, 92). The authors analyse in detail the issues related to indirect expropriation: the degree of interference in the use, enjoyment and disposal of the property, the intention to expropriate, the investor's expectations, date and duration of expropriation. On whether it is necessary for the State to have the intent to expropriate, several tribunals considered that the intention to expropriate is not decisive when assessing whether indirect expropriation occurred. Dolzer and Schreuer stress that '[t]he effect of the measure upon the economic benefit and value as well as upon the control over the investment will be the key question when it comes to deciding whether an indirect expropriation has taken place' (Dolzer & Schreuer, 101). It is probably useful to recall here the award in *Siemens v Argentina* where the tribunal held that '[t]he Treaty refers to measures that have the effect of an expropriation; it does not refer to the intent of the State to expropriate'.[29]

A sensitive issue is the so-called regulatory expropriation. If we take a look at Article 1 of the Protocol no. 1 of 1952 to the European Convention for the Protection of Human Rights and Fundamental Freedoms, it is expressly acknowledged that 'a State [may] enforce such laws as it deems necessary to control the use of property in accordance with the general interest or to secure the payment of taxes or other contributions or penalties'. This provision is not strange to most modern investment treaties. It is within State's sovereignty to adopt laws regulating the use of property as long as this interference is made, *inter alia*, in accordance with the principles of international law, the obligations assumed under international treaties and in a manner which is not arbitrary. In the *Sporrong and Lönnroth* case, the European Court of Human Rights interpreted Article 1 of the Protocol no. 1 mentioned above and retained that 'States are entitled, amongst other things, to control the use of property in accordance with the general interest, by enforcing such laws as they

---

[29] *Siemens A.G. v The Argentine Republic* (ICSID Case No. ARB/02/8), Award of 6 February 2007, para 270.

deem necessary for the purpose'.[30] Although it adds nothing new to the interpretation of Article 1, the Court made it clear that such regulations are a fundamental attribute of States. The Court also held that '[i]n the absence of a formal expropriation, that is to say a transfer of ownership, the Court considers that it must look behind the appearances and investigate the realities of the situation complained of' and 'it has to be ascertained whether that situation amounted to a de facto expropriation'.[31] In the *Lucas v South Carolina Coastal Council* case, the US Supreme Court recognized that regulatory activities may fall within the broad concept of expropriation.[32] The US Supreme Court also established that when a State deprives an owner of the full economic value of his property for some public purpose, it must be a compensable taking unless the use that is being taken away was never part of the ownership title in the first place. McLachlan, Shore and Weiniger talk about regulatory activities and expropriation and point out that 'several arbitral decisions have firmly held that regulatory activity is not, per se, outside the scope of expropriation' (McLachlan, Shore and Weiniger, 8.112).

McLachlan, Shore and Weiniger refer to the Separate Concurring Opinion in *SD Myers v Canada* of Dr. Bryan Schwartz to distinguish between expropriation and regulatory activities of the host State. According to Dr. Schwartz, there are three main differences between expropriation and regulation: (a) '[e]xpropriations tend to be severe deprivations of ownership rights; regulations tend to amount to much less interference';[33] (b) '[e]xpropriations tend to deprive the owner and to enrich—by a corresponding amount—the public authority that the property passes to, or the third party to whom the property is given. There is both unfair deprivation and unjust enrichment when an expropriation is carried out with compensation. By contrast, regulatory action tends to prevent an owner from using property in a way that unjustly enriches the owner';[34] (c) '[e]xpropriations without compensation tend to upset an owner's reasonable expectations concerning what belongs to him, in law and in fairness. Regulation is something that owners ought reasonably to expect. It generally does not amount to an unfair surprise'.[35]

Dolzer and Schreuer emphasize that a 'host state's sovereignty supports the argument that the investor should not expect compensation for a measure of general application' (Dolzer and Schreuer, 109). The view adopted by Dolzer and Schreuer suggest that as long as the regulatory activities are non-discriminatory and refer to general application, there is a strong indication that they do not amount to expropriation. However, these factors must be weighted in light of the facts of each case. For example, in *ADC v Hungary* the tribunal pointed out that 'while a sovereign State possesses the inherent right to regulate its domestic affairs, the exercise of such right is not unlimited and must have its boundaries'.[36] Moreover, the tribunal added that '[i]t is one thing to say that an investor shall conduct its business in compliance with the host State's domestic laws and regulations. It is quite another to imply that the investor must also be ready to accept whatever the host State decides to do to it.'[37]

---

[30] *Sporrong and Lönnroth v Sweden*, 23 September 1982, European Court of Human Rights, Series A no 52, para 61.

[31] *Sporrong and Lönnroth v Sweden, Supra* at note 64, para 63.

[32] *Lucas v South Carolina Coastal Council*, US Supreme Court 505 U.S. 1003 (1992).

[33] *S.D. Myers Inc. v Canada*, arbitration under the UNCITRAL Rules, Separate Concurring Opinion of Dr. Bryan Schwartz to the Partial Award of 13 November 2000, para 211.

[34] Ibid, para 212.

[35] Ibid, para 213.

[36] *ADC Affiliate Limited and ADC & ADMC Management Limited v Hungary* (ICSID Case No. ARB/03/16), Award of 2 October 2006, para 423.

[37] *ADC Affiliate Limited and ADC & ADMC Management Limited v Hungary*, above n 72, para 424.

Anyone interested in international investment law and investment arbitration will find these three books of exceptional value. The books are equally useful for counsel representing investors and states, arbitrators and negotiators of investment treaties, as they contain excellent information and references, as well as pertinent commentaries and stimulating ideas.

CRINA BALTAG
QUEEN MARY, UNIVERSITY OF LONDON

The Immunities of States and their Officials in International Criminal Law and International Human Rights Law. By ROSANNE VAN ALEBEEK, Oxford, Oxford University Press, 2008. 500 pp. £72.95.

One of the key controversies of international law at its present stage of development concerns the relationship between norms conferring jurisdictional immunities on States and their officials and norms providing for the protection of human rights. The controversy results from the fact that these two sets of rules impose potentially conflicting obligations on States. On the one hand, the principle of State immunity compels States to exempt other States and their officials from the jurisdiction of their courts and tribunals in relation to acts of a governmental or public nature. In addition, States are barred from exercising their adjudicative jurisdiction over certain classes of foreign officials, such as diplomatic agents and heads of State, in relation to acts they perform in their private capacity. On the other hand, States are bound by international human rights law to protect the rights and interests of individual human beings. This duty is reinforced by the rules of international criminal law, which require States to bring those responsible for serious human rights abuses to justice. A conflict between the two sets of obligations may arise when foreign officials benefiting from jurisdictional immunities violate human rights norms. In such cases, the authorities of the forum State may find that they cannot uphold the jurisdictional immunities of the foreign officials and their home State *and* remedy the alleged breach of international human rights law at the same time.

This dilemma is not an entirely novel one. Claims that war crimes are covered by the principle of State immunity were raised, and defeated, before the International Military Tribunal at Nuremberg and the Supreme Court of Israel in the *Eichmann* case. However, it is only in recent years that a relatively steady stream of cases concerning the compatibility of jurisdictional immunities with human rights norms has come before national and international courts, including the *Pinochet* case before the House of Lords, the *Al-Adsani* case in the European Court of Human Rights and the *Arrest Warrant* case before the International Court of Justice. It is indicative of the growing significance of this subject that as of early 2009 two cases are pending before the International Court of Justice at once which are directly concerned with the relationship between jurisdictional immunities and international humanitarian and human rights law (*Republic of the Congo v France* and *Germany v Italy*), together with a third case that touches on this issue incidentally (*Belgium v Senegal*).

Rosanne van Alebeek's work makes an important contribution to the debate concerning the compatibility of jurisdictional immunities with human rights. The principal question of her study is uncomplicated: are the rules exempting States and their officials from foreign adjudicative jurisdiction affected by the development of international human rights law and international criminal law? The answer she offers is more complex. Van Alebeek suggests that the arguments employed by those who proclaim the existence of a human rights exception to jurisdictional immunities and those who deny the existence of such an exception suffer from certain deficiencies. In particular, both camps proceed from problematic assumptions concerning the epistemology of customary international law and an insufficient theorization of the relevant immunity rules. Van Alebeek therefore develops her own thesis in two stages. She first sets herself the task of reconsidering the nature and substance of the rules of State immunity, functional immunity and personal immunity in order to develop a coherent analytical framework in which the scope of these different rules of immunity can be defined. She then proceeds to assess the impact of international human rights law and international criminal law on these immunity rules relying on the analytical framework developed earlier. Given the complexity and merit of van Alebeek's work, it is worth setting out her arguments in some detail.

Chapter 2 begins by reconsidering the conceptual foundations of the law of State immunity. Based on an overview of State practice, van Alebeek argues that the absolute theory of State immunity has never attained the status of a rule of customary international law. While this revisionist thesis should not raise many eyebrows today, the author draws several wide-ranging conclusions from it. The fact that the law of State immunity did not progress in a linear fashion from an absolute to a restrictive model means that it is misleading to conceive of the restrictive theory simply as the continuation of the absolute theory with certain exceptions attached to it. Such a view conceals the existence of significant qualitative differences between the two theories. Inspired by the writings of Robert Ago, the author suggests that the restrictive theory provides for immunities that are 'necessary' in the sense that they are required by the principle of the independence and equality (in short: the sovereign equality) of States. By contrast, the absolute theory provides for immunities that are 'voluntary' in as much as they are not required by any structural principle of the international legal system, but are created through the usual processes leading to the formation of customary international law.

Two important methodological points follow from this. First, 'necessary' immunity rules prevent the forum State from asserting its adjudicative authority over the exclusive competences of other States protected by the principle of sovereign equality. Consequently, these 'necessary' immunity rules reflect substantive, rather than procedural, limits imposed on the legal competence of the forum State by the very structure of the international legal system. The restrictive theory of State immunity is therefore in fact concerned with the lack of the forum State's jurisdictional competences, rather than the non-exercise of its existing competences as is commonly believed. Second, whereas the existence and scope of 'voluntary' rules of immunity can be determined only by way of inductive reasoning taking the form of an analysis of State practice and *opinio juris*, the scope of the 'necessary' rules of immunity may be derived from the principle of sovereign equality by means of deductive reasoning. In other words, logical reasoning concerning the independence and equality of States may be relied on as legitimate arguments for the purposes of determining the scope of immunity rules.

Chapter 3 turns to the functional immunities of State officials. Traditionally, the principle of State immunity is said to extend to individuals who act on behalf of the State as its agents. The immunity of State officials is therefore seen as a consequence of the immunity enjoyed by their home State. The principal difficulty with this view is that it fails to reflect the rationale of functional immunity. As van Alebeek explains, State officials benefit from functional immunity whenever they act on behalf of the State as it is generally accepted that in these circumstances liability should be borne by the State itself. The applicability of functional immunity therefore depends on a distinction between 'acts of State', that is, acts performed on behalf of the State, and private acts, serving the individual's own ends. However, this distinction does not mirror the distinction drawn by the restrictive theory of State immunity between *acta jure imperii* and *acta jure gestionis*. Foreign officials may enter into transactions on behalf of their home State which are of a private law character and therefore do not qualify as *acta jure imperii*, but which nevertheless are covered by functional immunity. This suggests that the functional immunity enjoyed by State officials and the principle of State immunity are in fact two separate concepts. Acts performed on behalf of the State may constitute *acta jure imperii*, in which case they attract both functional immunity and State immunity. However, such an overlap between functional immunity and State immunity is not inevitable. This leads van Alebeek to conclude that the applicability of functional immunity is a *prerequisite* for the applicability of State immunity, rather than functional immunity being a *consequence* of State immunity as the traditional doctrine would have it.

As regards the scope of functional immunity, van Alebeek argues that not every act performed by an individual under the direction of a State will attract functional immunity. Just as the principle of State immunity is restricted to those rules that are 'necessary' to safeguard the independence and equality of States, so the principle of functional immunity protects only those transactions of an individual which constitute an exercise of State authority as defined by public international law. This implies that a State cannot extend the functional immunity of its officials unilaterally: no functional immunity attaches to acts that are performed under the direction of a State, but which actually exceed the exercise of its legal authority under international law. The fact that the competence of States in international law is not unlimited thus imposes normative limits on the functional immunity of State officials. A second implication emphasized by the author is that functional immunity should be distinguished from State responsibility. Not every act that can be attributed to the State under the law of State responsibility will attract functional immunity. A State can direct its officials to perform acts that exceed its legal authority in international law. Whereas in such cases the officials do not benefit from functional immunity, the acts concerned nevertheless may engage that State's international responsibility.

Chapter 4 examines the personal immunities enjoyed by diplomatic agents and heads of State. In the light of the preceding two chapters, it is perhaps unsurprising that van Alebeek describes personal immunities as 'voluntary' immunity rules. Immunity *ratione personae* applies not only to official acts, but also extends to acts performed in a private capacity, subject to certain exceptions. Even though such personal immunities may serve functional purposes in that they enable their beneficiaries to perform their public functions free from foreign interference, the author suggests that this is not their exclusive purpose, nor are personal immunities limited to what is strictly necessary from a functional point of view. Personal immunities thus exceed the bounds of functional immunity as defined in Chapter 3. Their broad scope does not reflect the requirements of the structural principles of the international legal system, but is the result of the separate development of customary international law.

Having thus established a framework of analysis, van Alebeek turns her attention to the impact of international criminal law and human rights law on immunity rules. Chapter 5 is concerned with the effects of international criminal law. In essence, the author contends that by establishing the principle of individual criminal responsibility in conventional and customary international law, States have in effect limited the range of circumstances in which State officials are considered to act in the exercise of State authority. The principle of individual responsibility for crimes committed against international law serves to rebut the assumption that an official has acted within the scope of his or her official mandate. It is important to stress that van Alebeek does not suggest that the development of international criminal law has resulted in the recognition of an 'international crime exception' to the functional immunity of State officials. Rather, she argues more radically that international crimes are not acts that can be attributed to the State for the purposes of functional immunity in the first place. The fact that an official ostensibly acting under State authority has incurred individual criminal responsibility defeats the presumption that the official concerned was engaged in the performance of an 'act of State'. International crimes are not official acts of State for immunity purposes. As van Alebeek formulates, '[f]unctional immunity ends where individual responsibility begins' (at 241).

By treating the functional immunities of State officials as a consequence of State immunity, one of the difficulties that traditional doctrine encounters is that State immunity may extend to State officials in civil proceedings even though the officials concerned do not benefit from immunity in criminal proceedings for the same acts. Imbalances of this kind, as seen in the *Jones* case before the House of Lords, seem unreasonable and are difficult to justify. Van Alebeek avoids this difficulty by arguing, on the one hand, that functional immunity is conceptually distinct from State immunity and by suggesting, on the other hand, that international crimes fall outside the scope of functional immunity altogether. This position enables her to assert that a State official accused of international crimes does not benefit from immunity in either criminal or civil proceedings, but that the official's home State may continue to enjoy immunity from foreign adjudicative and enforcement jurisdiction in relation to those crimes. Nevertheless, proceedings instigated against State officials for international crimes may implicate their State indirectly, in particular in the case of crimes that entail some form of official involvement or sanction, such as crimes against humanity and genocide. Van Alebeek therefore suggests, without elaborating this point, that the absence of functional immunity may not suffice on its own to enable foreign courts to entertain cases against State officials implicated in international crimes. Different considerations apply to personal immunities. The principle that an individual's official capacity does not exempt that person from criminal liability merely extends the principle of individual criminal responsibility to State officials, but it does not thereby remove any personal immunities that they may enjoy. The author accordingly concludes that no human rights exception to personal immunities exists.

Finally, Chapter 6 considers whether the development of human rights law affects the validity and scope of immunity rules. Van Alebeek dismisses the normative hierarchy argument which declares that no immunity can be available for violations of norms of *jus cogens*. As the author rightly points out, this argument implies that the prohibition of certain conduct permits the enforcement of that prohibition through national courts. However, these are two distinct issues: the normative hierarchy argument remains unconvincing as *jus cogens* norms and immunity rules operate in different spheres. For good measure, van Alebeek suggests that the delimitation of the competences of States as a consequence of the principle of sovereign equality may itself be considered as a rule of jus cogens *avant la lettre*. The author also rejects the argument that the gross violation of human rights does not constitute a sovereign function of the State and for that reason is not covered by immunity. Van Alebeek seeks to refute this view by reiterating that the horizontal division of authority between national courts protects the exercise of the exclusive competences of the State from interference by other States. Entitling foreign courts to adjudicate on the exercise of the exclusive competence of another State would violate the independence of that State. However, this argument seems to suffer from circularity. While it is certainly one of the fundamental purposes of the principle of State immunity to protect the exclusive competence of States from outside interference, the scope of this exclusive competence cannot be derived from the principle of non-intervention that the law of State immunity is meant to serve. The principle of non-intervention merely protects the exclusive competences of the State, but it does not define them. More convincingly, van Alebeek goes on to suggests that no human rights exception to the principle of State immunity emerges from the secondary rules of international law, in particular the rules of State responsibility relating to breaches of *erga omnes* obligations and violations of *jus cogens* rules.

The final part of Chapter 6 considers the impact of human rights on the level of policy arguments. Based on a close reading of several relevant cases, the details of which cannot be recounted here, van Alebeek suggests that certain tensions exist between immunity rules and the protection of the fundamental rights of individuals. For instance, she criticizes the position adopted by the European Court of Human Rights in *Al-Adsani* that State immunity rules do not violate the right of access to court because such rules serve a legitimate aim and are proportionate to that aim in so far as they reflect international law on the grounds that this position fails to distinguish between 'necessary' and 'voluntary' immunity rules and for that reason also fails to engage in a proper balancing of the competing interest involved. However, while these competing interests could be balanced more effectively and in certain circumstances alternative remedies could be employed, the author eventually comes to the conclusion that the room for reconsidering immunity rules to better reflect the development of international human rights law is rather narrow.

It should be clear by now that van Alebeek makes a valuable contribution to the debate on jurisdictional immunities. The analytical framework developed in the first part of her study stands out as a particularly useful aspect of her work. The central element of her approach is the re-conceptualization of State immunity as a set of rules imposing substantive, rather than merely procedural, limits on the competence of the forum State. Although this approach is not original *per se*, the principal merit of her work lies in the fact that it draws out the full implications of this approach. However, in some respects this reconsideration of the rules of State immunity arguably goes too far. In particular, van Alebeek seems to exaggerate the link between sovereign equality and State immunity.

The principle of sovereign equality allocates to each State the exclusive competence to exercise its jurisdiction over matters falling within its reserved domain of domestic jurisdiction. Taken to its logical conclusion, the concept of sovereign equality implies that States lack the competence to prescribe and enforce legal norms in relation to matters which fall within the exclusive competence of another State. The principle of sovereign equality thus imposes substantive limits on the legal competences of States. Whereas the rules of State immunity serve to protect these limits, conceiving these rules purely as a reflection of sovereign equality risks aligning them too closely with that concept. The principle of State immunity is concerned with adjudicative and enforcement processes rather than the exercise of prescriptive jurisdiction. State immunity covers only one aspect of the division of competences between States that flows from the principle of sovereign equality. State immunity and sovereign equality thus do not overlap in all respects. Moreover, State immunity is not the only legal method or 'avoidance technique' employed by States to protect their respective jurisdictional competences. Diplomatic negotiations, non-justiciability, act of State doctrine and the requirement of reasonableness or moderation also play an important role in avoiding or mitigating jurisdictional conflicts. Like these other methods, State immunity serves not only to protect the exclusive competences of the State from foreign intervention, but also to balance their competing jurisdictional interests in other areas. For example, it is difficult to see how the various rules concerning immunity in employment proceedings can be derived from the principle of sovereign equality. Indeed, as one moves away from the level of the *acta jure imperii/acta jure gestionis* distinction to the more detailed immunity rules, it becomes increasingly more difficult to sustain that all of these are necessitated by the structural peculiarities of the international legal system as opposed to being the products of voluntary State practice.

Accordingly, it appears that the restrictive theory of State immunity cannot be fully explained solely by reference to the principle of sovereign equality. Such an explanation also appears to be ahistorical. The fact remains that just like the absolute doctrine of State immunity for a considerable time represented legal reality in many parts of the world, even though it may not have attained the status of customary international law, many judicial authorities have explicitly or implicitly characterized the rules of State immunity as procedural bars on existing jurisdictional competences and not as substantive non-competences. This important part of State practice cannot be simply reconceptualized. A theory of State immunity should attempt to accommodate this procedural understanding of State immunity, even if that means that no coherent account of State immunity as a whole can be given.

However, these points of criticism should not detract from the fundamental value of this book. Van Alebeek offers a bold re-interpretation of the immunities enjoyed by States and their officials under public international law that nevertheless remains grounded in legal reality. While her work is not going to be the last word on this subject or resolve all of its difficulties, it contributes a number of fresh insights and analytical tools to a long-standing debate and for that reason deserves to be widely read.

AUREL SARI
UNIVERSITY OF EXETER

Making People Illegal: What Globalisation Means for Migration Law. By CATHERINE DAUVERGNE, Cambridge: Cambridge University Press, 2008. 232 pp. £45.00.

Making people 'illegal' and the moral panic that accompanies 'illegal' migration is a global phenomenon of the twenty-first century. In this book Dauvergne examines what globalization means for migration and the law, as indicated by the title, but also makes the innovative argument that the current state of migration law is vital for understanding globalization. Dauvergne's main contention is that the 'worldwide crackdown' on illegal migration is a reaction by states to perceived loss of sovereignty under globalizing forces. The absence of international law and persistent predominance of national level law in migration matters is resulting in migration law as a key point of response, which is being transformed into the last bastion of sovereignty. The rights of illegal migrants are shadowed, despite the expansion of human rights norms. Dauvergne argues that the sovereign state (acting within a modernist framework) is actually incapable of preventing illegal migration and, in a post-modern world, presents a barrier to creatively extend rights protections to illegal migrants by prioritizing states' interests and endlessly creating categories of illegality. Thus, the core inquiry of the book is whether migration law can be unhinged from the state and whether it can have emancipatory potential by drawing its authority from authority beyond the state, that is, the rule of law (37). Dauvergne argues that migration law in the twenty-first century, re-imagined, is a harbinger of a paradigm shift in the rule of law.

The book contains eight chapters in addition to an introduction. Chapter Two presents the phenomenon of illegal migration as a legal construct in domestic law while Chapter Three sets the scene for globalization. The book attempts to link together several 'analytically distinct' themes relevant to illegal migration and globalizing trends. The methodology of core sampling is employed in an attempt to prevent superficiality. These core sample case studies (which are much more than case studies) take up a particular instance of illegal migration and are presented in Chapters Four to Eight. However, Dauvergne concedes that the case studies are not comprehensive (3). Indeed, they appear one-dimensional and their complexities glossed over in an attempt to portray sovereignty as the enemy, a waning concept in a post-modern world, and that migration laws are being transformed into the last bastion of sovereignty. Chapter Nine gathers the core samples in an attempt to decentre sovereignty and unhinge law from state in particular. The book does not provide a chapter with overall conclusions.

Chapter Two: 'On Being Illegal' introduces the reader to the global phenomenon of 'illegal' migration. Dauvergne proceeds to examine how and why the label 'illegal' migration works. Dauvergne's central argument is that under globalizing pressures 'nationness' is threatened across a range of policy areas and the label 'illegal' reinforces migration law's exclusionary capability to combat these threats (17). Thus, the law makes populations 'illegal' rather than legal; constructs an 'us-them' divide; and allows governments to exclude populations when the nation is unable to assert sovereignty by closing its borders. Globalization gives the appearance that illegal migration is a global problem which is resulting in the worldwide crackdown. The chapter then turns to the International Convention on the Protection of the Rights of All Migrant Workers and Members of Their Families, which entered into force in 2003, in an attempt to demonstrate the intertwining relationship of sovereignty and illegal migration. Dauvergne argues that the failure of the Convention and lack of international law in migration matters attests to the inability of human rights to protect migrants and migrants themselves are reduced to ingredients of globalized economic processes (27). Thus, sovereign interests are always prioritized over rights of migrants and the law constructs, but cannot erase, illegality.

Chapter Three: 'Migration in the Globalisation Script' demonstrates why migration law is an ideal setting for understanding and testing the nature of globalization and 'lays the foundation for the 'core sampling' chapters that follow' (29). The chapter proceeds not by examining critically the theories of globalization but instead by describing what are, according to Dauvergne, concerns that form the core of what can be called globalization theory. Dauvergne's main contention is that global pressures, particularly migration, threaten the concept of sovereignty and the rights of migrants become shadowed in state interests, despite the expansion of human rights norms (32). Dauvergne provides little critical analysis that sovereignty is under threat and simply suggests that 'the persistence of illegal migration affects the state at precisely this point—the ultimate definition of sovereign power—the border itself is breached' (48). Dauvergne argues that to have emancipatory potential, there is a need to look beyond the state. Dauvergne proceeds to conceptualize law within globalization. Reliance is placed on Boaventura de Sousa Santos, who argues that under legal globalization the law is facing a paradigm shift from modern to post-modern assumptions in which the law becomes emancipatory. In particular, three features of Santos' analysis are utilized: first, 'unthinking' of the law outside the boundaries of modern law which, according to Dauvergne, is key to 'unhinging' law from the state; second, within the paradigm of modernity the State is unable to address illegal; third, globalization of law brings with it the rule of law (36, 37). Dauvergne argues that the law can draw authority beyond the state, that is, the rule of law, which has emancipatory potential. For this, Dauvergne relies on the work of Peter Fitzpatrick who argues that international law grounds its authority from an existent ethical community which provides a source of rule of law norms unhinged from the nation itself. These theories are heavily relied upon throughout subsequent chapters, particularly Chapter Nine, but are presented one-dimensionally. Thus, their pluralist methodologies and epistemological frameworks and limitations are not examined, nor is the question of how they sit with one and other and in the wider literature. Nor does Dauvergne explain how unhinging occurs, where this ethical community derives and the effect emancipation will have on the broader theme of illegal migration.

Chapter Four: 'Making Asylum Illegal' provides the first core sampling case study which comes from the topic of refugee law. The core inquiry of this chapter is the *Tampa* incident in 2001 and the ensuing globalized 'rush to the bottom' in refugee law, led by Australia. Dauvergne's concern is the decreasing availability of asylum as Western countries limit their responsibilities towards refugees. This is a highly topical issue and situates aptly with contemporary literature. The Refugee Convention, asserts Dauvergne, is the most important constraint on sovereignty (56). The fact that states are not simply walking away from the Convention and are, instead, attempting to limit their obligations, demonstrates its binding authority. This, according to Dauvergne, is part of the transformation from statement of law to rule of law. The emancipatory potential of the Refugee Convention and its ability to effectively remedy illegality 'comes not from human rights norms alone, but from the willingness of states and courts to treat refugee law as rule of law' (67). The space to argue for the right to remain, asserts Dauvergne, is provided by rule of law arguments (67). Thus, Dauvergne argues that there is evidence that 'Courts are reaching out for a rule of law beyond their own borders ... [which] may signal the beginning of unhinging law and nation' (67, 68). Dauvergne's analysis is based on the assumption that the

Refugee Convention is a constraint on sovereignty and is presented as a form of international law beyond the state which creates space for rule of law arguments. This analysis is heavily relied upon in subsequent chapters but, unfortunately, is substantiated with little evidence. Indeed, it would appear that the terrorism cases Dauvergne is referring to here and in subsequent chapters primarily concern the positive obligations imposed by Article 3 ECHR, which is human rights, and not refugee, law, and procedural and not substantive legal issues. Analysis neglects the nature of international law and many would argues that, first, the Convention does not constrain sovereignty, second, that states may appear to adhere politically but not practically and, third, that the Convention is inherently derogable, despite real risk of refoulement.

Chapter Five: 'Trafficking in Hegemony' examines the phenomenon of human trafficking, the moral panic that accompanies it, legal responses and United States' leadership. In particular, Dauvergne argues that the Protocol to Prevent, Suppress and Punish Trafficking in Persons, Especially Women and Children (2003) is deficient. People who have been trafficked are victims, predominantly women. However, 'states are reacting to trafficking as a migration issue rather than a human rights issue' (79). This demonstrates that the law is unable to construct remedies for victims, who are themselves victims of human rights abuse, and are treated as migration law transgressors and returned home (83). Trafficking is the most sophisticated threat to sovereignty and not granting trafficked victims residency is a way of politically reasserting sovereign control (86). The worldwide crackdown on illegal migration simply exacerbates trafficking by making border crossing harder and sovereignty leads to failure to protect victims, even though it is transparent that the sovereign objective of sealing the border will not address the crux of the problem (88). The Protocol also neglects the root cause of trafficking and the role played by the massive American domestic market and its economic hegemony. Dauvergne argues that it is vital to un-think the law imaginatively to provide an alternative remedy for protecting victims. Once again, reliance is placed upon the Refugee Convention as a legal framework and the community of ethics to create a space for the rule of law to transform (92).

Chapter Six: 'The Less Brave New World' considers the security turn in migration discourse and its consequences for migration law. This chapter is well situated in the current debate of security and immigration and is one that (for the present author) is most interesting. The core inquiry is how courts are responding to indefinite detention of terrorism suspects in instances where the executive is unable to deport due to real risk of treatment contrary to Article 3 ECHR. In particular, Dauvergne draws attention to the British case of *A v Secretary of State for the Home Department* [2005] HL, whereby the House of Lords ruled in favour of the appellants that indefinite detention breached Article 8 ECHR. Dauvergne uses this as an example of the courts reaffirming the rule of law and reigning in Government policy. Thus, Dauvergne asserts that in this context there is potential emancipation as unhinging of law from nation occurs (117). Unfortunately, this chapter adds little to existing debates and Dauvergne struggles to avoid superficiality. Thus, analysis is based upon a minority of cases from the UK, US, Canada, and New Zealand and is scant evidence that globalization brings with it rule of law. Furthermore, Dauvergne does not explain what impact emancipation, if any, will have on the broader issue of illegal migration. But indefinite detention itself is a one-dimensional view of the way in which terrorism suspects are being dealt with and neglects subsequent developments, including control orders, automatic deportation, and designation. Conspicuously absent is the broader issue of Article 3 and key ECtHR cases, including *Chahal*, *Saadi* and *Ramzy*, which are influencing developments in immigration law, security and international cooperation within Europe. Dauvergne also appears to neglect that immigration law itself is being used to construct state security in response to terrorism.

Chapter Seven: 'Citizenship Unhinged' addresses the discourse between illegal migration and citizenship in creating the border of the nation and drawing lines of inclusion and exclusion. Indeed, the dirty work of policing the boundary of citizenship is left to migration law (123). 'Its central assertion is that citizenship as a formal legal status is enjoying a resurgence of authority at present and this is directly linked to the worldwide crackdown on illegal migration' (119). Thus, changes are being made to citizenship laws, including curtailing of birthright citizenship, extending membership beyond territory and the European innovation of making nations the arbiters of supranational citizenship (137). These changes make citizenship a more valuable prize and increase the role of migration law in discriminating access to citizenship and reinforce the migration law-citizenship law dichotomy. The global crackdown means that access to citizenship is increasingly closed to migrants who are increasingly defined illegal (138). Finally, Dauvergne examines the role that amnesties play in state responses to illegal migration and the way in which they bridge the citizenship law-migration dichotomy. Thus, rather than erase or challenge laws that make people illegal, illegal status is simply pardoned, thus having 'the effect of instant policy success for a government concerned about an inability to control its illegal population through border control measures' (139). However, amnesties are also tied to global economic discourse (140). Dauvergne concludes that law reforms providing citizenship beyond territory 'literally tear citizenship away from the territorial nation: unhinging law and nation at their most basic joint' (141). It is apparent, however, that Dauvergne is referring to legal reforms in Italy, Ireland, and India which have introduced overseas citizenship 'with those who have, in the ideologically charged language of migration, chosen to establish their lives elsewhere' (135). Implicit here is that the state is attempting to reassert sovereignty over denationalized populations. Dauvergne does not examine, however, how this equates with unhinging law from nation; on the contrary, it could reaffirm state sovereignty.

Chapter Eight: 'Myths and Giants' places discussion of the illegal migration themes in Chapters Four to Seven against the narrative of globalization in the context of the United States and the European Union. It proceeds by considering two core samples: first the way in which the EU is tackling illegal migration through harmonization of immigration law and procedure and, second, the American phenomenon of tolerance for an immense illegal population alongside initiatives at fortifying the US-Mexican border. In the case of Europe, Dauvergne argues that we are witnessing a 'rush to the bottom' of minimum standards in refugee matters, evidenced by the Qualification Directive (2004) and the Procedures Directive (2005). Dauvergne poses the question: 'there is no reason why these documents read as minimum standards, rather than simply as standards' (153). The simple answer is that they reflect state practice and attest to the dominance of sovereignty and not, contrary to Dauvergne, its scarcity. However, Dauvergne also makes the observation that 'Member states are only moving crackdown measures to the outer border of the union, while at the same time retaining control over desirable migration and over admission to the full membership of citizenship' (154). Both issues situate aptly within current debate. In the case of the US, the Bush administration was considering a fully fenced border to prevent illegal border crossing (158); 'More than any other core sample, the Mexican border demonstrates the failure of modern responses to illegal migration' (162). However, Dauvergne observes that American economic hegemony is an enormous part of globalization and a huge draw for migrants. Indeed, this superpower tolerates, and even fosters, an enormous illegal population for its immense economic contribution (167). In examining parallels between the US and EU, Dauvergne observes that moral panic about illegal migration is entrenched and fuels intertwining of migration and security; migration is dominating policy agendas and resulting in draconian measures; complete control over migration is not politically possible; and lack of control cannot be attributed to human rights of migrants (162). Dauvergne concludes that in global times, the US and EU illustrate that both sites contribute to globalization and illegal migration, and that 'the central conception of national sovereignty determines the realm of the possible—even when this is no longer coterminous with nation itself' (167).

Chapter Nine: 'Sovereignty and the Rule of Law in Global Times' gathers the core sample case studies and examines their relationship in an attempt to make the case that 'migration law is being transformed into the last bastion of sovereignty' (169). Thus, Dauvergne asserts that sovereign power, as the centrepiece of migration regulation, condemns policy to old ways of thinking, repetition and failure in matters of illegal migration in global times (170). Thus, there is a need to imaginatively re-think sovereignty in the collective imagination and to globalize the rule of law, only then can law be unhinged from the state and have emancipatory potential for illegal migrants. Dauvergne's central argument is that the potential for a paradigm shift in the rule of law and glimpses of unhinging are apparent in security cases (175). Commitment by courts to the rule of law, grounded in an existent community of ethics, evidences that the malleability of migration law is not infinite and shares Fitzpatrick's equality, freedom and impartiality (183). Thus, Dauvergne argues that we must have faith that rule of law has its own substance and logic which allows it to play against interests of power and create a space where people are not made illegal.

In summary, this book is highly topical and situates aptly with current literature. It highlights many of the problems associated with illegal migration and demands us to rethink refugee law. However, its underlying assumption is that eroding state borders and diminishing sovereignty are of mutual benefit to all. Theoretically, it offers unique insight into globalization, migration, and law. However, overwhelming and uncritical reliance is placed on the work of Fitzpatrick and Santos and the assumption of an existent ethical community with emancipatory potential. Indeed, the assumption that globalization and, in particular, illegal migration, is withering sovereignty and that migration laws are the last bastion of sovereignty is perhaps overestimated; in the same token, unhinging law from the state is oversimplified. Thus, the main contention that migration law is a harbinger of a paradigm shift in the rule of law largely hinges on a minority of security cases. There is also over reliance upon the Refugee Convention and its practical effect and constraint on sovereignty. Much of the analysis of migration, sovereignty, and law appear to be reduced to power and politics, to the neglect of more complex processes of state identities, adaptation and socialization. This is not a book tailored for specialists of international law, who are likely to feel certain unease about the lightness of Dauvergne's style and reliance on imagination, faith and profound optimism of international law. It is certainly the case that the book reflects neither state practice nor the complex realities of international law and relations. Precisely for this reason Dauvergne is forced to quote Fitzpatrick for the view that 'the need for 'gods' to shift the shape of international law' would be required (89).

Matthew Garrod
University of Sussex

UN Peacekeeping in Lebanon, Somalia and Kosovo: Operational and Legal Issues in Practice. By Ray Murphy, Cambridge, Cambridge University Press, 2007. 332 pp. £55.00.

Ray Murphy's excellent monograph on UN peacekeeping, *UN Peacekeeping in Lebanon, Somalia and Kosovo: Operational and Legal Issues in Practice*, comes at an important time in the UN's peacekeeping history. Now, more than ever before, the UN has lost its way as regards what it expects of its peacekeeping operations. Time-tested limitations on peacekeeping practice—using force only in self-defence, obtaining host state consent and acting impartially—are questioned, narrowly interpreted or simply cast aside when the Security Council deems it politically expedient to do so. In addition to more traditional functions, peacekeeping operations are, at times, being asked to act as *de facto* governments in ungoverned territories, charged with issuing travel documents or overseeing border controls, and as *de facto* enforcement operations, charged with the restoration of the peace in the face of considerable resistance.

Murphy's careful analysis of the selected operations—all very different in nature—gives the reader valuable insights into the legal and non-legal issues relating to their establishment, their command and their use of force. The book is divided into six chapters. In the first, Murphy introduces the work and addresses some of the complicated issues relating to definitions. In Chapter 2, he considers the establishment of the operations and, in Chapter 3, the legal issues (as well as the quasi-legal and non-legal issues) relating to their command structures. The use of force by the operations is addressed in the fourth chapter; however, the difficult issues relating to the use of force are very much at the heart of Murphy's analysis throughout. When, if ever, is it acceptable for peacekeepers to use offensive force and when is its use likely to be successful? Chapter 5 considers human rights and humanitarian law in the context of peacekeeping operations. Finally, in Chapter 6, Murphy offers his conclusions.

In view of the breadth of functions assigned to UN operations, it is little wonder that commentators—including Murphy—find it increasingly difficult to rely on the single word 'peacekeeping' to describe them. Murphy distinguishes between 'traditional' or 'first-generation' peacekeeping, on the one hand, and 'second-generation' or 'multi-dimensional' peacekeeping, on the other. The basis for the distinction is largely that the former is authorized to use force in self-defence whereas the latter has greater leeway as regards the use of force. In part on the basis that it was only authorized to use force in self-defence, Murphy characterizes the United Nations Interim Force in the Lebanon (UNIFIL) as traditional peacekeeping. Murphy also uses the term 'robust peacekeeping'—though it is not entirely clear whether it is used as a synonym to 'second generation' or 'multi-dimensional' peacekeeping or to connote an operation with an even more forceful mandate.

What is clear is that he uses the term 'peace enforcement' for an operation which comes closer to enforcement than peacekeeping (whether 'second generation', 'multi-dimensional' or 'robust' in nature); a peace enforcement operation is authorized by the Security Council under Chapter VII to use offensive force and the consent of the host state is not essential. Peace enforcement operations may be UN-led or led by states, regional organization or coalitions of the willing (COTWs). Murphy uses the term 'peace enforcement' for the robust UN-led, Chapter VII-authorized operation in Somalia (UNOSOM II), as well as for the robust US-led, Chapter VII-authorized force (UNITAF) that preceded it. As to the two operations in Kosovo, UN-led UNMIK and NATO-led KFOR, he describes them (jointly) as a 'quintessential multi-dimensional peacekeeping operation with a peace enforcement mandate.' It would seem that, broken down, he views UNMIK to be a multi-dimensional peacekeeping operation and KFOR to be peace enforcement.

Murphy notes that the operations were selected by him as 'representative of the types of operations undertaken by and on behalf of the UN, and as reflecting the problems that are associated with their establishment, deployment, command, use of force, and applicability of [international humanitarian law] and international human rights law. They also reflect operations conducted in three different geographic regions—Africa, the Middle East and Europe.' However, it was not self-evident why Murphy selected the operations he did; they were not necessarily the strongest examples of the types of peacekeeping they represented. For example, his decision to use UNIFIL as an example of 'traditional peacekeeping' was unusual, given that operation's relationship with the use of force. Similarly, his choice of UNOSOM II and UNITAF in Somalia as a means to explore the functioning of 'peace enforcement' operations was somewhat dated. After all, while UNOSOM II was among the first UN-led operation specifically authorized under Chapter VII (ONUC in the early 1960's was impliedly authorized thereunder), there has been much water under the bridge since the UNOSOM II experiment. Since then, there have been several UN-led or state/COTW-led operations (operating together or sequentially), authorized under Chapter VII which, like UNOSOM II and UNITAF, were authorized to use 'all necessary means'.

Moreover, Murphy's decision to analyse peacekeeping operations which are so pronouncedly different in nature—as well as his decision to include related operations which, while UN-authorized, are not UN-led—makes it difficult, at times, to draw clear conclusions about the nature of the current peacekeeping practice. To a large extent, this is unavoidable given the hydra-headed monster that UN 'peacekeeping' has become. Still, there was, arguably, scope for greater clarity at times. For example, the fact that Murphy sometimes considers the NATO-led KFOR and the UN-led UNMIK together (sometimes referring to 'KFOR/UNMIK'), without always drawing attention to the fundamentally different natures of the two operations, made for confusion at times. To a lesser extent, this problem was present in his treatment of the US-led UNITAF alongside the UN-led UNOSOM II.

Nevertheless, the diffuse nature of the operations considered by Murphy is one of the book's major strengths. Their variety makes clear to the reader that there is no such thing as a 'typical' UN peacekeeping operation. Peacekeeping operations are notoriously *ad hoc* in nature, making it nearly impossible to draw common conclusions about what limits should be imposed upon them or how their chances of success may be increased. Yet common themes do sometimes emerge. For example, Murphy observes that 'Each operation [he considered] shows that, whatever the nature of a peacekeeping operation, its role and effectiveness is dependent upon support from the Security Council. Without political support and adequate resources, especially at the time of its establishment, a UN force remains at the mercy of the parties to the conflict.'

The importance of political support, considered throughout the book, is perhaps most evident in the second chapter which provides a detailed analysis of the political and diplomatic background to the establishment of the operations, as well as an overview of their functioning. Here Murphy's careful analysis evinces not just on an expertise in international law and politics, but also the knowledge of someone who has participated hands-on in peacekeeping operations. (Murphy served as an infantry officer with the Irish contingent of UNIFIL.) Also of significant value to his analysis are the numerous interviews he has conducted with other participants in peacekeeping operations. In Chapter 2, Murphy begins the process—a process which continues throughout the book—of analysing where the operations succeeded and where they did not and why. Murphy illustrates that, perhaps more than any other factor, the—frequently capricious—wishes of the Security Council impact on whether an operation is established and, if so, whether it is given the support necessary to succeed.

As to the three situations considered, Murphy's assessment is mixed. He outlines the many obstacles to UNIFIL, including 'ambiguous and unrealistic objectives and terms of reference [which were] agreed to hastily in order to solve the immediate crisis'. Nevertheless, his conclusion on its work is favourable: 'Taking into account the essential nature of UNIFIL and the many constraints under which it operates, its success as an integrated and efficient military unit is remarkable. In any event, a peacekeeping mission must be judged primarily by how it fulfils its political purpose and not solely on its military efficiency.'[38] As to the intervention in Somalia, Murphy concludes that it must 'in all of its manifestations ... be judged a failure', whether in terms of military efficiency or political purpose. He attributes this to a wide variety of factors, many of them touched on by previous analyses, including the unwillingness of UNITAF to disarm the factions; a lack of resources, planning and political support for UNOSOM II; and the loss of UNOSOM II's impartiality. As regards the last point, he characterizes UNOSOM II as having become 'a party to the conflict'. Later, he observes that 'UNOSOM II embarked

---

[38] He does not consider in detail the events in the summer of 2006 that resulted in a new and very unclear mandate for that operation, as they occurred after the preparation of his final draft.

upon enforcement measures, but the indiscriminate use of force even in Chapter VII operations can result in crossing the line from that which is acceptable to achieve the mandate, and that which is indistinguishable from all-out war.' He is not much more optimistic about the operations in Kosovo. Here, however, he takes the view that the operations were too reticent in using force, at least at the outset. He outlines the Kosovo Liberation Army's attacks against minorities at the early stages of the operations' presence and faults UNMIK and KFOR for having been unprepared and unable to deal with the scale of violence at the outset, describing a 'kid gloves approach that contributed to the breakdown of law and order.' As to public perception, he observes that 'UNMIK is viewed as an inept and even corrupt international neo-colonial presence that has done little to stem the widespread crime, unemployment and poverty'.

In Chapter 3, Murphy considers the legal framework of UN peacekeeping. Unlike many legal analyses of UN peacekeeping, the work does not focus on the Charter basis for the Security Council's peacekeeping powers or the limits thereupon; rather, it appears to presume that the Security Council's actions in relation to UN peacekeeping are *intra vires*. In relation to the legality of the use of force, he notes 'Despite the dangers involved, the international community and the UN have a responsibility not to shy away from complex and dangerous situations. Esoteric debates on legal principles have a value, but they should not be allowed to detract from the establishment and deployment of peacekeeping operations as facilitators of conflict resolution.' Esoteric perhaps, but surely essential to a determination of the legality of the establishment and functioning of a peacekeeping operation. After all, everything the Security Council does must have its constitutional basis in the Charter, and—the importance of practice notwithstanding—that document contains some significant limitations on its powers.

Instead, Murphy devotes considerable attention to issues of command and control—issues which are more likely to be influenced by legal rules at the national level (his focus is on Canada and Ireland), semi-legal considerations or non-legal practices or traditions than by Charter interpretation. His careful analysis of such considerations, largely unexplored in the literature, makes the work extremely valuable to lawyers and politicians alike. While it may be difficult for international lawyers to accept, the fact is that much of the decision-making in relation to peacekeeping operations takes place based on non-legal (or semi-legal) factors, such as the doctrinal precedents set by previous Secretaries-General and (sometimes) endorsed by the Security Council, the precedents for use of force set in other operations, the Rules of Engagement, as well as certain directives, rules or regulations established by the Secretary-General or his staff. Even more difficult to predict (or take account of) are factors as changeable as the mood of the Security Council, the personalities of Force Commanders or the applicable military culture and military codes (written and unwritten) adhered to by participating national forces, as well as the skill and obedience levels possessed by them. Murphy concludes, depressingly, that where a unit commander decides that he is unwilling to go along with the orders of the Force Commander, he will suffer no recourse so long as he has the support of his government in making the decision. As Murphy observes, command and control is an area which, while ostensibly straightforward, is in fact 'fraught with difficulties arising from subjective human factors and objective legal constraints'.

If, as Murphy concludes, an effective system of command is a *sine qua non* for a military operation generally, it is *a fortiori* the case where the operation engages in the use of offensive force. And it is the use of force which is the subject of Murphy's fourth chapter. The issue also represents an important factor in his analysis in Chapter 5—eg where a peacekeeper uses enforcement-type force can she retain her protected status or does she become a combatant?—as well as in his concluding chapter. Of course, the issue of whether peacekeeping operations should be mandated to use force beyond self-defence and, if so, whether they are likely to be successful, is one which has been grappled with for many years.

It is also one which—with the Security Council's current practice of routinely bestowing peacekeeping operations with the power to use force beyond self-defence—has returned to the forefront of peacekeeping analysis today. For many years after ONUC was militarized in the early 1960s, the matter appeared relatively settled: force could be used only in self-defence. However, the fact that the UN adopted a policy of defining self-defence to include 'defence of the mission' meant that, depending on the nature of the mission's mandate, self-defence could be tantamount to offensive force. Nonetheless, offensive force was rarely used. In the case of UNIFIL Murphy argues that this was because the commanders on the ground were politically and militarily astute enough to realize that to do so would be disastrous. The negative consequences of bestowing peacekeeping operations with enforcement-type powers are outlined by Murphy in the context of the intervention in Somalia. Chiefly, the use of offensive force compromises an operation's impartiality and may result in the peacekeeping force being classed as 'the enemy'. He attributes UNOSOM II's use of 'coercive enforcement measures' as inevitably leading 'to its role as a third-party UN force being converted to that of factional participant.' Other factors associated with granting peacekeeping operations enforcement-type powers include the risk that a host state which had granted consent to the force's presence will revoke it, the risk that contributing states will recall their troops in the face of the deaths of their nationals, the risk the lives of the members of the forces and the possibility of alienating the Security Council member states.

Yet the question remains: Should peacekeepers ever use force beyond self-defence or enforcement powers? Murphy's conclusions here are complex. They appear to depend on the type of force in question. He premises his analysis on the view that 'strict adherence to the principle of self-defence is the only option available in traditional peacekeeping operations'. He posits that 'enforcement action of any kind is inconsistent with the principles of peacekeeping and Chapter VI operations should not have elements of enforcement in the mandate that could lead to the incremental adoption of a Chapter VII strategy. The quasi-enforcement approach in peacekeeping does not work; apart form its poor track record due to weak judgment and inadequate resources, it is inherently flawed.' At the same time, however, he endorses the fact that UNIFIL—which he characterizes as 'traditional'—was empowered to use considerable offensive force: 'If a peacekeeping force is denied limited *de facto* enforcement powers, this could have the effect of rendering it ineffective for the purpose of fulfilling the mandate. This was especially evident in the case of UNIFIL'.

What of non-traditional operations? Many of the factors Murphy outlines which led to the failure of UNOSOM II in Somalia were directly attributable to the UN assuming an enforcement role. These include not just that operation's loss of impartiality—the first casualty of a robust operation—but also the fact that the more enforcement-centred its tasks became, the less able the UN was to effectively command and control it and the more under-staffed and under-resourced it became. In Murphy's words: 'UN-controlled forces are generally not given adequate capabilities to intimidate or enforce'. Nevertheless, he is unwilling to rule out the use of offensive force: 'when there is no other option, the security component of a peace operation mandated to protect the local population will have no choice but to use minimum force to prevent ethnic cleansing and similar human rights abuses from occurring.' Even if one accepts Murphy's view that peacekeepers have no choice but to use force in circumstances of ethnic cleansing or similar conduct, there is little reason to be confident that the necessary elements for a successful enforcement operation—adequate financing, political will, good leadership and the provision of highly trained troops and the necessary military equipment—will be present. As Murphy observed about the missions in Rwanda, Somalia, and the former Yugoslavia, '[e]ach was ill-conceived and short-sighted, and essentially placed the peacekeepers in an impossible situation. The Council hesitated and prevaricated when faced with starvation in Somalia and genocide in Rwanda, and it refused to give UNPROFOR the resources required to protect itself, let alone the people whose very existence depended upon its protection'.

Has the international community's commitment to preventing atrocities improved since the bad old days of Rwanda, Somalia, and the former Yugoslavia? Murphy appears to think so: 'Events in Somalia should not be used to discredit second-generation peacekeeping, or to deny the imperative to respond that [sic] global human crises such as those of Rwanda, East Timor or Darfur. The offensive operations launched by UN peacekeeping against militia forces in the Democratic Republic of the Congo during 2005 and 2006 indicate that the UN has learned from the mistakes of the past.' However, if the current vain struggles to obtain troops and equipment by the AU-UN peacekeeping operation in the Darfur region of Sudan (UNAMID) is any indicator, there is little cause for optimism.

JAMES SLOAN
UNIVERSITY OF GLASGOW

The Irish Yearbook of International Law, Volume 1, 2006. By JEAN ALLAIN and SIOBHÁN MULLALLY (Editors), Oxford, Hart Publishing, 2008. xiv + 500 pp. £50 per volume.

The Irish Yearbook of International Law is intended to stimulate further research into Ireland's practice in international affairs and foreign policy. The first annual volume includes peer-reviewed academic articles and book reviews as well as correspondent reports on specific aspects of Irish international law and practice. There is also a documents section containing materials reflecting Irish practice on contemporary issues of international law. The editors-in-chief of the *Irish Yearbook of International Law* —Dr Jean Allain and Dr Siobhán Mullally—are, respectively, senior lecturers in law at Queen's University Belfast and University College, Cork. The eight member Editorial Board includes Professors Christine Bell, Christine Chinkin, and William Schabas.

David Ong's 57 page article entitled 'International Law's 'Customary' Dilemma: Betwixt General Principles and Treaty Rules' is given pride of place. Ong's article addresses 'the continuing *substantive* and *systemic* difficulties that undermine the development of international environmental law as a viable sub-discipline or branch of public international law' (page 4). Ong's article is an excellent example of doctrinal rigour in the best traditions of yearbook scholarship.

Only one article has a specifically Irish connection. J Paul McCutcheon and Gerard Coffey's 'Life Sentences in Ireland and the European Convention on Human Rights' (pages 101–119). The article, based on research conducted for the Irish Human Rights Commission, concludes that rulings by the European Court of Human Rights (ECtHR) on the temporary release or release under licence of life sentence prisoners 'strongly indicate that current Irish law is not compatible with the ECHR' (page 118). The authors acknowledge that the possibility that the Irish courts will declare the current legal position incompatible with the ECHR 'is a matter of speculation' (page 119) and, in October 2007, the Irish High Court rejected a challenge to the constitutionality of the mandatory life sentence for murder holding that rights under Articles 3, 5(1) and (4) and 6(1) of the ECHR were not infringed by the imposition of mandatory life sentences under section 2 of the 1990 Irish Criminal Justice Act (*Whelan v Minister for Justice, Equality and Law Reform* [2007] IEHC 374). The leading ECtHR authority on mandatory life sentences is now the Grand Chamber decision in *Kafkaris v Cyprus* (Application No.21906/04) 12 February 2008. See also *R. (on the application of Wellington) v Secretary of State for the Home Department* [2008] UKHL 72, [2009] 2 WLR 48.

The book reviews include three titles with a specifically Irish connection, the five volume *Documents on Irish Foreign Policy* (1998–2006) (edited by Ronan Fanning et al), Gernot

Biehler's *International Law in Practice: An Irish Perspective* (2005) and *Irish Perspectives on EC Law* (2003) (edited by Mary Catherine Lucey and Catherine Keville).

The 2006 correspondent reports cover *International Law Developments in Ireland* (where Ireland's role in the 'Global War on Terror' dominated the domestic and international agenda in 2006), *Irish Practice Abroad* (mainly Ireland's contribution within the United Nations and particularly peacekeeping missions undertaken by the Irish Defence Forces under UN auspices), *North-South Developments* (covering the activities of the bodies established as a result of the 1998 Good Friday/Belfast Agreements) and *Law of the Sea Developments in Ireland* (primarily the 2006 Irish Sea-Fisheries and Maritime Jurisdiction Act but also covering the Irish submissions to the Commission on the Limits of the Continental Shelf (CLCS) in 2005 and 2006). The Executive Summaries of both the 2005 partial submission and the 2006 joint submission (with France, Spain, and the United Kingdom) to the CLCS (including maps) are included in the documents section.

The documents section also contains the Department of Foreign Affairs Strategy Statement 2005–2007, the 2006 Department of Foreign Affairs Annual Report, an address by the Irish Minister of Foreign Affairs on the occasion of the 50th anniversary of Irish membership of the United Nations, the Irish response to the International Law Commission's Draft Articles on the Responsibility of International Organisations, the St. Andrews Agreement of 13 October 2006 and the Irish Republican Army Statement of 28 July 2005.

As the editors note (page xi) the launching of the *Irish Yearbook of International Law* is, in many ways, long overdue and it is very encouraging to see the creation of a new (reasonably priced) publication that is devoted to the exposition of all aspects of international law (as opposed to a particular sub-discipline) as well as the detailed documentation of state practice. Two issues are however a source of concern. First, yearbooks need to be published as soon as realistically possible after the end of the year under review. Ideally this would not be more than six to eight months later but, in any event, within twelve months. The 2006 volume was only published in February 2008 and the 2007 volume was only scheduled for publication in May 2009. Hopefully future volumes will be published more promptly to ensure that the coverage of Irish practice on contemporary issues of international law is as current as possible. Another concern is that the referencing lacks consistency. References to the ICJ Reports, for example, vary both within and between articles. Ong's article reflects this inconsistency in successive footnotes (page 16, footnotes 51 and 52). See also Alexander Orakhelashvili's article 'The Power of the UN Security Council to Determine the Existence of a 'Threat to the Peace'' (pp. 61–99) and the discrepancy in the referencing of the decision of the Appeals Chamber of the International Criminal Tribunal for the Former Yugoslavia in the *Tadic* case in footnotes 7 and 80. A more consistent practice regarding the use of full titles and abbreviations of journal titles also needs to be adopted. Compare the approach to the *AJIL* (page 10, footnote 25) and the *JCSL* (page 61, footnote 2). These concerns may only be teething problems but they still need to be addressed.

PAUL EDEN
UNIVERSITY OF SUSSEX

The Nature of Customary International Law. By AMANDA PERREAU-SAUSSINE and JAMES BERNARD MURPHY (Editors), Cambridge, Cambridge University Press, 2007. 335 pp. £50.00.

Customary law is an elusive subject, whether in national law, international law, or general jurisprudence. In international law particularly, it is well-nigh ubiquitous; but at the same time, there is a woeful lack of consensus as to its real nature. Is custom best seen as a source of law properly speaking—meaning that it operates as a sort of pool of practices from which rules of law are somehow drawn or derived? Or should it, instead, be seen as actually *constituting* law in its own right? Or is it best seen as following in the wake of law-making and providing evidence of what the law is? There is the question, too, as to whether custom is best seen in contractual terms (as tacit treaty-making), or in legislative terms (as the laying down of universal norms). Nor is the boundary between customary law and general principles of law at all clearly demarcated. The existence of so much uncertainty on such basic questions, on a subject so central to our discipline, has made the subject into an embarrassing conceptual muddle.

Fortunately, some substantial assistance—if not actual relief or resolution—is at hand, in the form of this stellar collection of essays on the general subject of customary law, in all of its guises. Of the thirteen substantive contributions, six relate either wholly or in sub-stantial part to international law. But international lawyers will benefit from consulting the other contributions as well. Ross Harrison, for example, treats customary law in the context of a sparkling clear discussion of the relationship between morality and convention. James Bernard Murphy very cogently presents custom as standing between natural law, on the one hand, and legislation, on the other. In the course of his chapter, he provides a first-rate exposition of Aristotle's conception of custom. Christoph Kletzer provides an extremely helpful exposition of the contribution made by the historical school of jurispru-dence. He points out that Savigny, in particular, averred that customary practices are not law in themselves but merely evidence of law—with the actual law-making power residing in the *Volksgeist*, the spirit or general will of the community.

In the area of public international law specifically, Brian Tierney lucidly discusses the treatment of custom by Vitoria and Suárez in the Sixteenth and Seventeenth Centuries. Suárez in particular provided the first real analysis of custom as a source of international law. This was largely in the context of the distinction between *ius gentium* and natural law—with *ius gentium* essentially equated with what we now think of as customary inter-national law. Suárez presented this *ius gentium* as being poised between natural law and civil law—resembling the former in being unwritten, and the latter in being man-made. This version of customary law was basically legislative in nature, binding the whole of the international community, although Suárez conceded that a local custom could be contrary to the general *ius gentium*—the germ of our present-day notion of the persistent-objector principle.

Randall Lesaffer makes a convincing case that, at least in the Seventeenth and Eighteenth Centuries, the view of customary law as tacit treaty-making became predominant. Gerald J. Postema, in contrast, emerges as a champion of the legislative position. In what is perhaps the densest piece in the book, he undertakes to refute what he calls the 'additive' view of customary law—the contention that customary law arises from a 'hooking together' or com-bining of two essentially independent elements, state practice and *opinio juris*. In place of this thesis, he offers, in the spirit of Savigny, a communitarian view of custom as the expres-sion of the collective consciousness, or general will, of a true community of nations.

Amanda Perreau-Saussine presents what she calls three different methods of presenting international law: the 'mid-wife' view, in which customary practices are simply endorsed and accepted as they stand; a natural-law view, in which customs are accepted or rejected as law, depending on their compatibility with external standards of justice; and finally, what she calls the 'noble liar' position, in which law and morals are claimed to have a distinct basis but in which they actually do not. Some readers will wonder whether the 'noble liar' stance is not simply a variant of the natural-law one.

A critical treatment of commonly held views of customary law is offered by John Tasioulas. With reference to the work of Ronald Dworkin, he presses for what he calls (somewhat oddly) an interpretative view of customary law. This involves rejecting the picture of state practice and *opinio juris* as independent components of custom—with, so to speak, a fixed minimum 'quantity' of each being required for the cooking-up of the cake of custom. He insists, instead, on a sort of sliding scale, such that the greater the volume of state practice, the less is required in the way of *opinio juris*, and *vice versa*. On this view, state practice and *opinio juris* can substitute for one another.

These brief summations give only the palest indication of the riches contained in this excellent book. Remarkably, every single one of the contributions is of high quality. They do not, of course, amount to the last word on this vast and amorphous subject (as all of the authors would undoubtedly concede). It only remains to note that the book, precisely because of the sophistication of the contributions, is not designed for beginners. The fact that the index includes only proper names and not subjects also makes the book rather difficult to dip into on a casual basis. It is, in short, a book for jurisprudes. But when it comes to thinking about customary international law, that is what all of us are—or should be—whether we wish it or not. That is why we should all be immensely grateful for this splendid book.

STEVEN NEFF
UNIVERSITY OF EDINBURGH

International Territorial Administration: How Trusteeship and the Civilizing Mission Never Went Away. By RALPH WILDE, Oxford University Press, Oxford, 2008. xxvii + 607 pp. £60.

There exists now an extensive body of literature on the international administration of territories, much of it spawned in recent years by scholarly and other interest in the prominent international administration projects of Bosnia and Herzegovina, Kosovo, and East Timor. Ralph Wilde has made very substantial contributions to scholarship in this area over the past decade. Parts of this book represent expanded and updated versions of his prior scholarship but the book is much more than a synthesis of his earlier work. It is also an attempt to establish that international territorial administration (ITA) is what he terms a 'policy institution' (36) and to locate this institution within the *longue durée* of international trusteeship, broadly conceived. The result is an admirably thorough analysis of ITA, which takes account of all of the major scholarship on the subject, together with a highly original though not entirely uncontentious interpretation of this intriguing historical phenomenon.

The strengths of Wilde's book are several. Chief among them is the corrective function that it performs. Wilde takes issue with the 'exceptionalist' tendency in the academic literature that treats ITAs—with recent experiences foremost in mind—as *sui generis* and unprecedented undertakings. As he demonstrates, there is a rich tradition of territorial administration by international actors that spans the twentieth century. While other scholars (eg Steven Ratner) have drawn attention to earlier cognate initiatives, Wilde deserves credit for rescuing some lesser-known experiences, such as the League of Nations administration of the Colombian town and district of Leticia, from relative obscurity (although he omits mention of what is arguably the earliest twentieth century ITA: the International Control Commission of Albania from 1913 to 1914).

Wilde also challenges the applicability of Méir Ydit's concept of 'internationalised territory'—where sovereignty over a territorial unit is vested in an international actor—demonstrating in precise detail that in no instance of ITA have the international actors exercising administrative control over territory enjoyed title or even claimed it. Clarifying the legal status of ITAs is important for, among other things, understanding the purposes associated with these projects. These, too, Wilde maintains, are often misconstrued. The tendency of contemporary scholars and other analysts is to associate ITA largely, if not exclusively, with post-reconstruction efforts. Yet as Wilde makes clear, ITA has not always been employed for purposes of post-conflict reconstruction; indeed it has not always been employed after conflict: the United Nations administration of West New Guinea (West Irian)

from 1962 to 1963 is a case in point. Wilde very usefully distinguishes between two broad
sets of purposes for which ITAs have been established: in response to a 'sovereignty'
problem, where, for example, ITA has been used to administer a territory pending resolution of a question regarding the territory's status (eg the Saar Basin and Kosovo), and
in response to a 'governance' problem, where ITA has been used to fill a governmental
'vacuum' or to ensure that particular policy objectives or a particular quality of governance
in a territory are achieved (eg Bosnia and Herzegovina).

Correcting these misperceptions is important not only for its own sake but also because
it allows Wilde to make a number of larger claims concerning the nature of ITAs: first,
that ITA is what Wilde terms a 'policy institution', which he defines as 'an established
practice that manifests certain elements of commonality as a matter of purpose or policy'
(436); and second, bearing the common purposes and policies of this institution in mind,
that the boundaries of analysis merit expansion. Within the ambit of ITA, Wilde thus
includes the international appointment of foreign nationals to courts, electoral commissions, and other local bodies; and, more unusually, the administration of refugee camps and
the operation of material assistance programmes, although the latter two activities receive
scant attention in the book. Wilde also sees conceptual links between these ITA projects
and other activities outside the boundaries of the institution, and argues for association of
ITA with this larger set of activities that includes colonialism (in its later stages), protection,
the Mandate and Trusteeship systems, administration by representative bodies, and occupation—all of which, when pursued on behalf of a territory and its people, can be viewed
collectively as 'international trusteeship', Wilde contends (363). Continuity of purpose
and activity thus allows Wilde to argue that trusteeship—and the 'civilizing mission' that
informs it—never went away, as the book's subtitle suggests, but that it has simply assumed
a new form, in spite of the delegitimizing effect of the norm of self-determination on
trusteeship.

Taking a broad view of ITA in this manner also brings into sharper focus a number of
normative issues with which the institution is implicated. Although Wilde maintains that
through his clarification of the policy role and the place in history of international territorial administrations he is only facilitating normative appraisal that others might undertake, the book contains several very interesting and insightful observations of its own in
this regard. For instance, the strengths and limitations of the legitimating arguments
commonly invoked in relation to ITA are more evident when they are examined alongside
the objectionable features of colonialism. Comparisons with colonial trusteeship invite
investigation into the identity of the administering actors—a key legitimizing feature of
ITAs—and their interests whereas the selflessness and good faith of these actors is more
likely to be taken for granted when such comparisons are ignored. Sceptics may argue,
however, that Wilde's emphasis on commonalities obscures important differences between
these institutions notwithstanding the pains he takes to acknowledge them.

Wilde's book is not a comprehensive analysis of international territorial administration.
It is selective in its examination of the many legal questions that arise in the context of
this activity and it is says little about the actual practice of ITAs, although it is extremely
rich in empirical detail. Rather, it endeavours—and succeeds—in shifting our perspective
on a familiar topic. It is an important book that deserves wide readership.

RICHARD CAPLAN
UNIVERSITY OF OXFORD

Human Rights and Non-discrimination in the 'War on Terror'. By DANIEL
MOECKLI, Oxford, Oxford University Press, 2008. xxvi + 271 pp. £60.00.

The response of liberal democracies to the so-called 'war on terror' has caused significant
political and legal debate about the relationship between liberty and security. This debate

and, in particular, the disproportionate impact of recent counter-terrorism measures on marginal groups, forms the focus of Daniel Moeckli's challenging critique. Through a detailed analysis of counter-terrorism measures in the United States, the United Kingdom, and Germany, Moeckli concludes that 'discrimination permeates the anti-terrorism efforts of all three states' (226). This conclusion is not particularly novel nor is it unexpected. However, Moeckli's analysis and his route to this conclusion is informative and, where necessary, insightful.

The book is based on the author's doctoral thesis, which was awarded in 2006. As with many such books, it does read, at times, like a doctoral thesis, although this should not be seen as an overtly critical remark. The book benefits from the rigour and detail expected of a doctoral thesis. However, it is only towards the end of the book that the author fully engages with the more complex, theoretical questions raised by the topic in a way that clearly bodes well for his future work. Thus, Moeckli's brief discussions of 'the normalisation of the extraordinary' (232–234) and 'the non-discriminatory alternative' (234–237) certainly draw on the preceding analysis but also set the reader up for future offerings by the author.

However, this is not to take away from the considerable merit of the book itself. The first chapter examines some of the concepts inherent in the analysis. Moeckli questions the language of 'balance' that is so routinely associated with the liberty/security debate. In relation to the concept of liberty Moeckli draws on the work of E.P. Thomson to assert that the guarantee of equality 'can be seen, and used as a safeguard to protect those who are most likely to be subjected to the worst excesses of state power' (6). Similarly, his conceptualization of security is at the 'weaker' end of the scale and is focused on 'human security' allowing him to assert that 'respect for individual liberty and human rights is not in opposition to security but at its very heart' (7). Having established the potential for a non-discriminatory relationship between liberty and security, Moeckli goes on to explain how 'the call for readjustment of the balance between liberty and security has affected respect for human rights and, more specifically, the right to non-discrimination' (11).

In Chapter 2 Moeckli addresses the concept of anti-terrorism regimes. He considers international, regional, and national regimes before questioning the need for special regimes. Moeckli covers a good deal of ground in this first section which briefly considers the problem of defining terrorism as well as including an analysis of the legality of Security Council Resolution 1373. As the Chapter progresses, Moeckli challenges the newness of the threat of terrorism, and questions its international character. He criticizes the speed of introduction of recent counter-terrorism legislation as well as the de-individualization of both the threat of terrorism and the anti-terrorism measures. He concludes that 'the danger of discrimination is intrinsic in the establishment of special anti-terrorism regimes' (56).

Moeckli then addresses 'the obligation not to discriminate' in Chapter 3. After consideration of the philosophical foundations of the principle, the Chapter proceeds to a careful and detailed analysis of a range of international human rights and humanitarian instruments as well as examples of 'soft law' and customary international law, regional law, and the domestic law of the three focus states. Moeckli concludes that in relation to the states considered in the book they each 'have an obligation under international, regional and national law to respect the right to non-discrimination when they adopt measures to combat terrorism' (93).

Chapters 4–7 then focus on specific examples of discriminatory behaviour by states. Moeckli thankfully eschews a country by country exposition and critique of the relevant regimes, favouring instead a more thematic approach. In Chapters 4 and 5, Moeckli considers discriminatory behaviour based on citizenship status, specifically executive detention of foreign terrorist suspects and trial of foreign terrorist suspects. In Chapters 6 and 7, the focus is on distinctions based on country of origin, or nationality, race, ethnicity and religion. In particular Moeckli considers directly the selective enforcement of immigration laws and selective use of police powers. In each of these chapters, Moeckli explains the

relevant concepts, considers the state of the law before September 11 2001 and then analyses the impact of the law introduced since September 11 in relation to the three states.
By focusing on these issues, Moeckli is able to explore and critically assess a wide range of
specific anti-terrorism responses, including, *inter alia*, executive detention, Guantanamo
Bay and military commissions; changing immigration policies and the increased use of
deportation; and the use of terrorist profiling. In addition to this broad subject-matter
coverage, the book engages well with the burgeoning academic literature relating to the
'war on terror' and, in particular, the relationship between liberty and security. To that
extent the book provides a very useful source of comment and debate on that literature
and will be of use to students and practitioners as well as academics.

Moeckli concludes by arguing that discriminatory anti-terrorism measures are harmful
to the state in the long term and, indirectly, calling for a reversal of discriminatory policies.
However, the willingness of states to reverse their current impulse to adopt increasingly
illiberal solutions to the threat of terrorism is unlikely quickly to be reversed. Indeed, it
seems that states are learning how to be illiberal from one another. Witness the introduction of the United Kingdom's Special Immigration Appeal Commission which is based on
a Canadian model, or the recent introduction of special immigration status in the United
Kingdom which at least is 'better than Guantanamo'. Nevertheless, Moeckli rightly draws,
in his final section, on the work of Jürgen Habermas which 'highlights the central role of
both democratic deliberation and the legal form in securing the legitimacy of law' (237).

J. Craig Barker
University of Sussex

Decisions of British Courts during 2008 Involving Questions of Public or Private International Law

A. Public International Law[1]

Extradition—double criminality rule—extradition crimes—Extradition Act 2003—whether conduct of which defendant accused or conduct constitutive of offence of which defendant accused must amount to offence in UK—whether conspiracy to operate cartel and conspiracy to obstruct justice extradition offences under Extradition Act 2003, section 137(2)

Case No 1 Norris v Government of the United States of America, 12 March 2008, [2008] UKHL 16, [2008] 1 AC 920, [2008] 2 WLR 673 (HL)

It is typical for certain conditions precedent to attach to the obligation to extradite under an extradition treaty. One classic condition is the rule of 'double criminality'—that is, the stipulation that the conduct in respect of which extradition is requested constitute a crime not only in the requesting but also in the requested State, and usually a crime of a specified minimum gravity. The requirement is not typically found in the text of extradition treaties *sub nomine* 'double criminality' but under the rubric 'extradition crimes' or 'extradition offences'. The precise application of the rule of double criminality is a matter for the law of each State.

The US government sought the defendant's extradition on four counts, the first (under the Sherman Act 1890) alleging his participation in a conspiracy to operate a price-fixing agreement or cartel, the other three alleging a conspiracy to obstruct justice by interfering with witnesses and destroying documentary evidence.

On appeal to the Lords, who delivered a composite opinion, it was held that—absent aggravating factors such as fraud, misrepresentation, violence, intimidation or inducement of a breach of contract, none of which was alleged here—the conduct specified in the first count would not, if proved, have constituted a criminal offence in England under either common law or statute at the time of its alleged commission, namely 1989–2000.[2] Moreover, it would be wrong in principle for any court now to hold that there is or was at the time of the events complained of such a common-law

[1] © Dr Roger O'Keefe, 2009.
[2] See [2008] 1 AC 920, 931–44, 945 and 947, paras 7–52, 55 and 62.

offence:[3] the rule of law demanded that a person not be punished for conduct that was not, in the words of Lord Bingham in *R v Rimmington*, 'clearly and ascertainably punishable when the act was done',[4] and, as emphasized in *R v Jones (Margaret)*, the recognition of new crimes was the preserve of Parliament, not the courts.[5] As regards counts 2 to 4, their Lordships first held that the current English law, represented in the context of extradition to the USA by section 137(2) of the Extradition Act 2003, requires merely that the conduct of which the defendant is accused, as opposed to the conduct constitutive of the offence of which he or she is accused, amount to an offence in the UK: there was no need to investigate the legal ingredients of the foreign offence.[6] Next, the Committee emphasized that the double criminality rule went to the essence of the alleged acts, rather than to 'adventitious circumstances connected with the conduct alleged'.[7] In the instant case, the substance of the criminality charged was not that the defendant obstructed a criminal investigation into price-fixing being carried out by a Pennsylvania grand jury, but that he obstructed a criminal investigation into the matter being carried out by the duly appointed body. The question for an English court, therefore, was whether obstructing in England a criminal investigation into price-fixing being conducted by the appropriate UK investigatory body constituted an offence under English law at the time of the defendant's alleged conduct.[8] Their Lordships reasoned that although price-fixing *per se* was not an offence under English law, it could, when combined with other elements such as deliberate misrepresentation, amount to offences such as fraud or conspiracy to defraud.[9] In this light, had the defendant, with the intention of obstructing an investigation by a duly appointed UK body into possible criminal conduct in relation to price-fixing, tampered with witnesses and evidence as he was alleged to have done, he would have been guilty of either obstructing or conspiring to obstruct justice, both of them offences punishable by 12 months' imprisonment and therefore extradition offences within the meaning of section 137(2)(b) of the Extradition Act 2003.[10]

The Lords' decision on both points is unimpeachable. But certain dicta raise, and not for the first time, questions as to the rationale for the requirement of double criminality. Prior to *R v Bow Street Metropolitan Stipendiary Magistrate, Ex parte Pinochet Ugarte (No 3)*,[11] the stipulation had been characterized as one of the public policy of the forum, which obviated the

---

    [3] Ibid, 944, para 52.
    [4] Ibid, para 53, quoting [2005] UKHL 53; [2006] 1 AC 459, 482, para 33. See also ibid, 945, para 56.
    [5] Ibid, 945, para 54, quoting [2006] UKHL 16; [2007] 1 AC 136, 162, para 29, (2006) 77 *BYIL* 472–81 (HL). See also ibid, para 57.
    [6] See ibid, 948–55, paras 65–91.
    [7] Ibid, 959, para 99.
    [8] Ibid.
    [9] Ibid, para 100.
    [10] Ibid, para 101.   [11] [2000] 1 AC 147, (1999) 70 *BYIL* 277–95 (HL).

invidious necessity for English criminal justice to lend its assistance to the punishment by a foreign State of the freedom to offend officialdom, the practice of Christianity, the legitimate pursuit of commercial advantage or, indeed, any conduct considered unworthy of criminal sanction by the law of England. In *Pinochet (No 3)*, however, the Lords, in holding that the time by reference to which double criminality was to be assessed was the time of the alleged offence rather than, as had been thought, the time of surrender, characterized the double criminality rule as a safeguard of the principle *nullum crimen nulla poena sine lege*, a guarantee of the defendant's entitlement to fair warning under the criminal law. The invocation of *Rimmington* in the present judgment and their Lordships' statement that 'the underlying rationale of the double criminality rule [is] that a person's liberty is not to be restricted as a consequence of offences not recognised as criminal by the requested state'[12] endorse this second view. But this view is open to doubt, for the reason that the criminal law under which a defendant to extradition proceedings will eventually be tried, and thus the law in relation to which any issues of fair warning would relate, is that of the requesting, not requested State—here, US, not English law. And there was never any suggestion in this case that the US offence of conspiracy to operate a price-fixing agreement or cartel was retroactive.

Relationship between international law and English law—European Convention on Human Rights 1950—Human Rights Act 1998—whether divergence possible between rights under ECHR and rights under HRA

Case No 2 R (Animal Defenders International) v Secretary of State for Culture, Media and Sport, 12 March 2008, [2008] UKHL 15, [2008] 1 AC 1312 (HL)

The appellants sought a declaration under section 4 of the Human Rights Act 1998 ('HRA') that the ban on political advertising on radio and television in section 321(2) of the Communications Act 2003 was incompatible with the freedom of expression guaranteed by article 10 of the European Convention on Human Rights 1950 ('ECHR'), as given effect in English law by the HRA. The disposal of the appeal by the House of Lords required a careful analysis of the judgment of the European Court of Human Rights ('ECtHR') in the closely analogous case of *Verein gegen Tierfabriken v Switzerland*[13] (*'VgT'*), in which the Strasbourg court struck down as unnecessary in a democratic society, within the meaning of article 10(2) of the ECHR, a Swiss ban on paid political advertising on television. In the event, all of the Lords were content to distinguish *VgT* and hold that the UK's ban was permissible. The case is significant for dicta which reveal at least a superficial divergence of approach between Lord Scott and the other Lords as to the relationship between judgments of the

---

[12] [2008] 1 AC 920, 954, para 88.   [13] (2001) 34 EHRR 159.

ECtHR under the ECHR and judgments of the House of Lords and future Supreme Court under the HRA.

Although concluding that it was not to be assumed from *VgT* that the ECtHR would have disagreed with the House of Lords' decision in the instant case,[14] Lord Scott nonetheless floated the possibility of a divergence between the respective views of Strasbourg and the Lords:

The possibility of such a divergence is contemplated, implicitly at least, by the 1998 Act. The 1998 Act incorporated into domestic law the articles of the Convention and of the Protocols set out in Schedule 1 to the Act. So the articles became part of domestic law. But the incorporated articles are not merely part of domestic law. They remain, as they were before the 1998 Act, articles of a Convention binding on the United Kingdom under international law. In so far as the articles are part of domestic law, this House is, and, when this House is eventually replaced by a Supreme Court, that court will be, the court of final appeal whose interpretation of the incorporated articles will, subject only to legislative intervention, be binding in domestic law. In so far as the articles are part of international law they are binding on the United Kingdom as a signatory [to] the Convention and the European court is, for the purposes of international law, the final arbiter of their meaning and effect. Section 2 of the 1998 Act requires any domestic court determining a question which has arisen in connection with a Convention right to take into account, *inter alia*, 'any ... judgment, decision, declaration or advisory opinion of the European Court of Human Rights': subsection (1)(a). The judgments of the European court are, therefore, not binding on domestic courts. They constitute material, very important material, that must be taken into account, but domestic courts are none the less not bound by the European court's interpretation of an incorporated article.[15]

It was, in his Lordship's opinion, 'important that that should be so and that its importance is not lost sight of'.[16] He quoted from the speech of Lord Hoffman in *Alconbury*, in which his Lordship stated that '[t]he House [was] not bound by the decisions of the European court' and that, if such decisions 'compelled a conclusion fundamentally at odds with the distribution of powers under the British constitution', he 'would have [had] considerable doubt as to whether they should be followed'.[17] Lord Scott continued:

Section 4 of the 1998 Act empowers the court to make a declaration of incompatibility if satisfied that the legislative provision in question 'is incompatible with a Convention right'. Does that mean incompatible with a Convention right as interpreted by the European court and binding on the United Kingdom under international law? Or does it mean incompatible with a Convention right as interpreted by the domestic courts of this country? An important purpose of a declaration of incompatibility is, as I see it, to draw the attention of the Government,

---

[14]   [2008] 1 AC 1312, 1351, para 43.
[15]   Ibid, 1351–2, para 44.
[16]   Ibid, 1352, para 45.
[17]   Ibid, quoting *R (Alconbury Developments Ltd) v Secretary of State for the Environment, Transport and the Regions* [2001] UKHL 23; [2003] 2 AC 295, 327, para 76.

Parliament and the United Kingdom public to an inconsistency between the provision of domestic legislation in question and the rights under domestic law conferred on the applicant for the declaration by the article of the Convention in question. However another purpose of a declaration of incompatibility would be to draw the attention of the Government and Parliament to an inconsistency between the legislative provision in question and the international law obligations of the United Kingdom as a signatory [to] the Convention. If it were to be the unfortunate case that a divergence emerged between the opinion of the European court and the opinion of this House (or, later, the Supreme Court) as to the application or scope of one or other of the articles of the Convention that have become part of our domestic law, it might become necessary for a decision to be taken as to which purpose should be regarded as the prime purpose. They could not both be achieved.[18]

But he did not think that the problem arose in the appeal before the House.[19]

Lord Bingham could not, 'with regret', concur in all that Lord Scott said on the point:[20]

It is true, of course, that the 1998 Act gave domestic effect to the Convention rights defined in section 1 and that, under section 2, the obligation of the courts is to take into account any Strasbourg decision, not to follow it as a strictly binding precedent. But section 6(1) makes it unlawful for a public authority, including a court, to act in a way which is incompatible with a Convention right. The House has held that in the absence of special circumstances our courts should follow any clear and constant jurisprudence of the Strasbourg court, recognising that the Convention is an international instrument, the correct interpretation of which can be authoritatively expounded only by the Strasbourg court: *R (Ullah) v Special Ajudicator* [2004] 2 AC 323, para. 20. As the law now stands, I see little scope for the competition between conflicting interpretations which my noble and learned friend appears to envisage.[21]

Baroness Hale expressly shared Lord Bingham's view on this point:[22]

The Human Rights Act 1998 gives effect to the Convention rights in our domestic law. To that extent they are domestic rights for which domestic remedies are prescribed: *In re McKerr* [2004] 1 WLR 807. But the rights are those defined in the Convention, the correct interpretation of which lies ultimately with Strasbourg: *R (Ullah) v Special Adjudicator* [2004] 2 AC 323, para. 20. Our task is to keep pace with the Strasbourg jurisprudence as it develops over time, no more and no less: *R (Al-Skeini) v Secretary of State for Defence (The Redress Trust intervening)* [2008] 1 AC 153, para. 106. This cautious approach to the interpretation of the Convention rights has been criticised, mainly on the ground that 'the Convention is a floor and not a ceiling'. It represents the minimum and not the maximum protection that member states should provide. There is, of course, nothing to stop our Parliament from legislating to protect human rights to a greater extent than the Convention and its jurisprudence currently require; nor is there anything to prevent the courts from developing the common law in

---

[18] Ibid, 1352–3, para 46. [19] Ibid, 1353, para 46.
[20] Ibid, 1349, para 37. [21] Ibid. [22] Ibid, 1354, para 53.

that direction. But we are here concerned with whether an Act of the United Kingdom Parliament is compatible with the Convention rights: if prima facie it is not, Parliament has given us the duty, if possible, to interpret it compatibly with those rights (Human Rights Act 1998, section 3(1)); and if that is not possible, the power to declare it incompatible: section 4. I do not believe that, when Parliament gave us those novel and important powers, it was giving us the power to leap ahead of Strasbourg in our interpretation of the Convention rights. Nor do I believe that it was expecting us to lag behind. The purpose, in my view, of a declaration of incompatibility is to warn Government and Parliament that, in our view, the United Kingdom is in breach of its international obligations. It is then for them to decide what, if anything, to do about it.[23]

Lords Carswell and Neuberger agreed with Lord Bingham's reasons, although did not refer explicitly to the point at issue between him and Baroness Hale, on the one side, and Lord Scott, on the other.

The debate between Lord Scott and their other Lordships reflects something of a tension underlying the Lords' respective visions of the HRA since it came into force, although the divergence of views is not as great as it may at first appear. On a technical level, there is general agreement, as seen in the instant case, that the HRA creates what as a formal juridical matter are domestic rights. In accordance with article 1(1) and (3) of the HRA, the 'Convention rights' in compatibility with which primary and subordinate legislation must, as far as possible, be read and given effect,[24] in respect of which an English court may make a declaration of incompatibility[25] and incompatibly with which a public authority may not act[26] are those specified rights set out in Schedule 1 to the Act, the text of which is taken verbatim from the ECHR. Their textual provenance is the ECHR, but they are domestic rights. The point has been made on several occasions. In *McKerr*, dealing with the temporal scope of rights under the HRA, Lord Nicholls pointed out how certain lower court decisions 'fell into error by failing to keep clearly in mind the distinction between (1) rights arising under the Convention and (2) rights created by the Human Rights Act by reference to the Convention':

These two sets of rights now exist side by side. But there are significant differences between them. The former existed before the enactment of the Human Rights Act 1998 and they continue to exist. They are not as such part of this country's law because the Convention does not form part of this country's law. That is still the position. These rights, arising under the Convention, are to be contrasted with rights created by the Human Rights Act. The latter came into existence for the first time on 2 October 2000. They are part of this country's law. The extent of these rights, created as they were by the Human Rights Act, depends upon the proper interpretation of that Act. It by no means follows that the continuing existence of a right arising under the Convention in respect of an act occurring before the Human Rights Act came into force will be mirrored by

---

[23] Ibid, 1355, para 53.   [24] See HRA, s 3.
[25] See ibid, s 4.   [26] See ibid, s 6.

a corresponding right created by the Human Rights Act. Whether it finds reflection in this way in the Human Rights Act depends upon the proper interpretation of the Human Rights Act.[27]

Similarly, Lord Hoffman stated:

62. In my opinion the reasoning which the Court of Appeal accepted does not sufficiently distinguish between the obligations under international law which the United Kingdom (as a State) accepted by accession to the Convention and the duties under domestic law which were imposed upon public authorities in the United Kingdom by section 6 of the 1998 Act. These obligations belong to different legal systems; they have different sources, are owed by different parties, have different contents and different mechanisms for enforcement.

63. ... Although people sometimes speak of the Convention having been incorporated into domestic law, that is a misleading metaphor. What the Act has done is to create domestic rights expressed in the same terms as those contained in the Convention. But they are domestic rights, not international rights. Their source is the statute, not the Convention. They are available against specific public authorities, not the United Kingdom as a state. And their meaning and application is a matter for domestic courts, not the court in Strasbourg.[28]

Analogous statements have been made in other cases,[29] including by Lord Bingham,[30] who in the present case disagreed with Lord Scott. These pronouncements have all been made, however, in cases relating to the scope of application, be it temporal or territorial, of the HRA *vis-à-vis* that of the ECHR, rather than in cases relating to the interpretation of 'Convention rights' versus rights under the Convention (although Lord Hoffmann in *McKerr* did refer in passing to the meaning of 'Convention rights' being a matter for the domestic courts). As regards interpretation, it is clear once more that the English courts are not, strictly speaking, bound by the Strasbourg case-law. As Lord Bingham highlighted in the present case, section 2(1) of the HRA obliges an English court or tribunal determining a question which has arisen in connection with a Convention right to 'take into account' any judgment or decision of the ECtHR: the Strasbourg jurisprudence does not constitute 'strictly binding precedent'.[31] The bone of contention between Lord Scott and the rest is quite what 'take into account' is to be taken to mean. For Lord Scott, as for Lord Hoffmann in *Alconbury* and *McKerr*, it means what it says, and no more.

---

[27] *In re McKerr* [2004] UKHL 12; [2004] 1 WLR 807, 815, para 25, (2004) 75 *BYIL* 411–19 (HL).

[28] [2004] 1 WLR 807, 826.

[29] See *R (Quark Fishing Ltd) v Secretary of State for Foreign and Commonwealth Affairs* [2005] UKHL 57; [2006] 1 AC 529, 546, para 36 (Lord Nicholls) and 552, para 62 (Lord Hoffmann), (2005) 76 *BYIL* 589–93 (HL); *R (Al-Skeini) v Secretary of State for Defence* [2007] UKHL 26; [2008] 1 AC 153, 179–80, paras 133–4 (Lord Brown), (2007) 78 *BYIL* 529–46 (HL); *R (Al-Jedda) v Secretary of State for Defence* [2007] UKHL 58; [2008] 2 WLR 31, 53–54, paras 51–54 (Lord Rodger), (2007) 78 *BYIL* 564–82 (HL).

[30] [2008] 1 AC 153, 178–9, para 10.

[31] [2008] 1 AC 1312, 1349, para 37.

Having treated the European Court's case-law as 'very important material'[32] to be taken into consideration, an English court is not constrained from reaching a different conclusion on the law, especially where domestic constitutional particularities are implicated. 'Convention rights' are, after all, domestic rights, the meaning and application of which is a matter for the English courts. Parliament can remedy any deficit, and a disappointed claimant can always go to Strasbourg. For the other Lords, section 2(1) of the HRA, while phrased as it is in formal acknowledgement of the European Court's judicial 'otherness', is really a legislative direction to follow Strasbourg's lead on points of law more or less[33] unswervingly. On this view, the domestic 'Convention rights' are merely ciphers for rights under the Convention. Should they be ill-suited to local conditions, it is up to Parliament to make adjustments.

Neither of these two schools of thought is obviously wrong, and the story looks set to run.

It should be stressed, however, that the narrowness of the point of difference means that the controversy is unlikely to have much practical consequence.[34] This is all the more so when one considers the many and varied ways in which a common-law court can distinguish a precedent (or 'precedent', as the case may be) when faced with a slightly different set of facts and a potentially unpalatable outcome. The present case is an example of precisely this sort of creative casuistry: the case of *TgV* was pretty much on all fours with the facts before their Lordships, but the UK's political tradition of seeking to minimize the influence of money on electoral choice made declaring incompatible with a Convention right the ban embodied in section 321(2) of the Communications Act a step too far in the direction of Strasbourg, and led the House to distinguish the European 'authority'. The margin of appreciation accorded Contracting States by the European Court adds a further degree of domestic judicial leeway.

Finally, there seems to have been a subtext to the instant spat, a clue to which can be found in a seemingly incongruous quotation in the speech

---

[32] Ibid, 1351–2, para 44.

[33] To some extent Lord Scott and the others are talking at cross-purposes. Lord Bingham's dicta are, after all, hedged about with qualifications—that the domestic courts should follow any 'clear and constant' jurisprudence of the European Court 'in the absence of special circumstances', and that there is 'little', rather than no scope for competition between conflicting interpretations. Similarly, Baroness Hale acknowledges that there is nothing to stop the courts from developing the common law in a manner more generous than Strasbourg would compel. But neither Lord Bingham nor Baroness Hale holds to the logic of these seemingly platitudinous dicta.

[34] See, for example, *R (RJM) v Secretary of State for Work and Pensions* [2008] UKHL 63; [2008] 3 WLR 1023, 1035, para 34, below 477–9(HL), where Lord Neuberger—having reached a certain conclusion 'bearing in mind this House's obligation under section 2(1)(a) of the Human Rights Act 1998 to "take into account ... any judgment ... of the European Court of Human Rights", as explained by Lord Bingham of Cornhill in *R (Animal Defenders International) v Secretary of State for Culture, Media and Sport* [2008] 2 WLR 781, para 37'—makes it clear that he would have reached the same conclusion 'even on the somewhat more flexible approach proposed by Lord Scott of Foscote in paras 44 and 45 of that case'.

of Lord Scott. Before reproducing Lord Hoffmann's words in *Alconbury*, his Lordship states:

Lord Bingham of Cornhill observed in *Brown v Stott* [2003] 1 AC 681, 703:

'the case law of the European court shows that the court has been willing to imply terms into the Convention when it was judged necessary or plainly right to do so. But the process of implication is one to be carried out with caution, if the risk is to be averted that the contracting parties may, by judicial interpretation, become bound by obligations which they did not expressly accept and might not have been willing to accept.'

(Lord Scott associates himself with this passage from *Brown v Stott* again in *Gentle*.[35]) If one reads the rest of what Lord Scott says through the prism of this quotation, what his Lordship appears to be suggesting is that the English courts might well choose to depart from Strasbourg's more inventive interpretations of the ECHR. This would certainly fit with the preference for original intent, be it that of the Convention's drafters in 1950 or of Parliament in 1998, subsequently exhibited by his Lordship in *R (Wellington) v Secretary of State for the Home Department*.[36] It may explain too Lord Bingham and Baroness Hale's insistence, by way of reply, that the 'correct' interpretation of the Convention can be expounded only by the European Court. This last, it has to be said, is an unfortunate dogma. Following Strasbourg's lead ensures that the UK is not in breach of its Convention obligations. But the correctness of this lead cannot be presumed.

Immunity of international organizations—United Nations specialized agencies—Convention on the Privileges and Immunities of the Specialized Agencies 1947—United Nations Educational, Scientific and Cultural Organization (UNESCO)—European Convention on Human Rights 1950, article 6 (right of access to courts)—whether immunity from legal process of UNESCO compatible with ECHR, article 6

Case No 3 Entico Corporation Limited v United Nations Educational, Scientific and Cultural Organization, 18 March 2008, [2008] EWHC 531 (Comm), unreported (QBD (Comm Ct), Tomlinson J)

Pursuant to article III, section 4 of the Convention on the Privileges and Immunities of the Specialized Agencies 1947,[37] the specialized agencies of the United Nations, along with their property and assets, enjoy immunity from every form of legal process except in so far as in any particular

---

[35] See *R (Gentle) v Prime Minister and others* [2008] UKHL 20; [2008] 1 AC 1356, 1374, para 29, below 422–8 (HL).

[36] [2008] UKHL 72; [2008] 2 WLR 48, 62, para 47, below, 493–9(HL).

[37] New York, 21 November 1947 (entered into force 2 December 1948), 33 UNTS 261. The Convention adopts a curious scheme of 'articles' and 'sections'.

case they have expressly waived it.[38] By virtue of Annex IV, the Convention applies to the United Nations Educational, Scientific and Cultural Organization (UNESCO). The UK has, in accordance with article XI, section 43 of the Convention, indicated its acceptance of the applicability of the Convention to the Organization. Article IX, section 31(a) of the Convention provides that each specialized agency shall make provision for appropriate modes of settlement of disputes arising out of contracts or other disputes of a private character to which the specialized agency is a party. UNESCO's immunity from legal process is implemented in English law by the combined effect of the International Organisations Act 1968, the Specialised Agencies of the United Nations (Immunities and Privileges) Order 1974 and the Specialised Agencies of the United Nations (Immunities and Privileges of UNESCO) Order 1974.

The claimant in the present case was a publishing company which claimed to have entered into a contract with UNESCO to print a calendar. The alleged contract was said to contain a clause specifying that any dispute between the parties was to be settled by negotiation and, failing this, by submission of the dispute to a single arbitrator in accordance with the UNCITRAL rules. On the basis of what it believed to be the contractual arrangement between the parties, the claimant expended considerable sums of money on the calendar, only for UNESCO to inform it in due course that the project would not go ahead. UNESCO denied any legal liability and, on the claimant's invocation of the arbitration clause, denied any obligation to submit the dispute to arbitration, arguing that no contract arose between the parties on the facts.[39] In the event, the claimant sought to sue UNESCO in the English courts,[40] arguing as a preliminary matter that the latter had repudiated the arbitration clause or, in the alternative, that arbitration would be a meaningless process.[41] In order to overcome the immunity from English legal process enjoyed by the Organization, the claimant argued that such immunity was incompatible with article 6(1) of the ECHR, guaranteeing access to the courts, as given effect in English law by the HRA. It contended that the immunity from suit granted to UNESCO and other UN specialized agencies by the International Organisations Act 1968 and the Specialised Agencies of the United Nations

---

[38] Article III, section 4 goes on to specify that waiver of immunity shall not extend to measures of execution.

[39] UNESCO did, however, state that it would have no objection if the claimant wished to have recourse to arbitration under the UNCITRAL rules, reserving its right, in the event that arbitral proceedings were to be initiated, to contest the existence of the contract. It also emphasized that, should an arbitrator render an award in the case, it would comply with it.

[40] Service on UNESCO's Paris headquarters having been refused by the French authorities on account of the Organization's immunity, the claimant was permitted to effect service by first-class post.

[41] The claimant contended that UNESCO would not, in all likelihood, participate and that the arbitrator would not have competence to determine that the contact arising between the parties did not contain the arbitration clause in the first place, as argued—in the alternative to the argument based on repudiation—by the claimant.

(Immunities and Privileges) Order 1974 did not pursue a legitimate aim, in that it was not necessary for its or their proper functioning and, in the alternative, imposed a disproportionate restriction on the right of access to a court secured by article 6(1).[42]

Tomlinson J, in the Commercial Court of the Queen's Bench Division, who was not called upon to determine if a contract in fact existed, found in favour of UNESCO. It was not, in the final analysis, necessary for him to consider the immunity point, but he did so on the urging of the claimant and the Secretary of State for the Foreign and Commonwealth Office as intervener.

His Lordship stressed at the outset that the grant to UNESCO of immunity from English legal process was 'solely to comply with the UK's obligations under public international law',[43] in the form of article III, section 4 of the Convention on the Privileges and Immunities of the Specialized Agencies. Nor was there anything in the Convention which made the enjoyment of the privileges and immunities conferred by article III, section 4 dependent on compliance with article IX, section 31.[44] Moreover, article IX, section 31 offered 'no criteria pursuant to which the appropriateness of a mode of settlement [was] to be judged', and did not require that the mode of settlement for which provision was to be made had to be effective.[45] In this light, it would have been 'wholly inimical to the international scheme envisaged if individual States Parties arrogated to themselves the power to determine whether the provision made by each specialized agency for the settlement of disputes [was] adequate, whether considered generally or by reference to the facts of a particular case'.[46]

As for the relationship between article III, section 4 of the Convention and article 6(1) of the ECHR, the Convention on the Privileges and Immunities of the Specialized Agencies had to be interpreted in accordance with the rules laid down in articles 31 to 33 of the Vienna Convention on the Law of Treaties, which require that a treaty be interpreted in good faith in accordance with the ordinary meaning to be given to the terms in their context and in the light of the treaty's object and purpose. Applying the Vienna Convention, article III, section 4 of the Convention was 'clear, unequivocal and unconditional', and plainly required the States parties 'to recognise and give effect to a broad jurisdictional immunity possessed by each specialized agency'.[47] There was 'no room for "reading down" the provisions of the 1947 Convention to take into the provisions of the subsequent ECHR', a treaty 'which was binding upon only a minority of the parties to the 1947 Convention'.[48] In addition, the ECHR was itself to be interpreted in the light of article 31(3)(c) of the Vienna Convention, which specifies that there shall be taken into account in the interpretation

---

[42] See ECHR, art 6(2).   [43] [2008] EWHC 531 (Comm), para 17.
[44] Ibid.   [45] Ibid.   [46] Ibid.
[47] Ibid, para 18.   [48] Ibid.

of a treaty 'any relevant rules of international law applicable in the relations between the parties';[49] and article 30(4)(b) of the Vienna Convention, regarding the application of successive treaties on the same subject-matter, 'ha[d] the effect that the need to comply with the requirements of the ECHR [did] not excuse compliance with an earlier convention to which more states are party than are party to the ECHR'.[50] It was, his Lordship concluded, 'in the highest degree implausible that when the states part[ies] drafted and acceded to the ECHR they intended thereby to place themselves in violation of their existing international obligations'.[51] These existing obligations, 'owed to many more states than were or are party to the ECHR, required them to recognise and to give effect to a broad and unqualified jurisdictional immunity enjoyed by each specialised agency', with the upshot that it 'would be surprising if Article 6 of the ECHR was intended to render this regime non-compliant, thereby plunging all states part[ies] to both the ECHR and the 1947 Convention into a position in which their obligations conflicted'.[52]

Finding as he eventually did that article 6 of the ECHR was not violated, his Lordship considered it unnecessary to determine whether article 6 of the ECHR was engaged at all.[53] He did recall, however, that, in the context of State immunity, Lord Millet in *Holland v Lampen-Wolfe*[54] and Lords Bingham and Hoffmann in *Jones v Saudi Arabia*[55] had held that there was not even a prima facie breach of article 6 if a State 'fails to make available a jurisdiction which it does not possess';[56] and he added that '[w]hen the UK became party to the ECHR it possessed no jurisdiction over UNESCO unless UNESCO chose to waive its immunity'.[57] Since acknowledgement of the immunity of an international organization was as much required by international law as was acknowledgement of State immunity, there was no reason to regard the approach taken by the Lords in respect of the latter as not equally applicable in respect of the former.[58] 'Certainly', his Lordship observed, citing *Waite and Kennedy*, 'when considering whether the grant of immunity to an international organization pursues a legitimate aim, the ECtHR has drawn no distinction'.[59]

Turning to consider what the situation would be if article 6 were engaged, Tomlinson J explained that the question whether the immunity of UNESCO and similar organizations pursued a legitimate aim was not to be answered by reference to whether that immunity was necessary for the proper functioning of these organizations. Rather, his Lordship

---

[49]   Ibid, para 19, citing *Bankovic v Belgium* (2001) 123 ILR 94, para 57.
[50]   Ibid.   [51]   Ibid.
[52]   Ibid.   [53]   Ibid, paras 23 and 25.
[54]   [2000] 1 WLR 1573, 1583, (2000) 74 *BYIL* 405–8 (HL).
[55]   [2006] UKHL 26; [2007] 1 AC 270, (2006) 77 *BYIL* 499–520 (HL).
[56]   [2008] EWHC 531 (comm), para 23, quoting [2007] 1 AC 270, para 64 (Lord Hoffmann).
[57]   Ibid.
[58]   Ibid, para 24.
[59]   Ibid, citing *Waite and Kennedy v Germany* (1999) 30 EHRR 261, para 63.

concluded, relying for support on the approach taken by the Grand Chamber of the ECtHR in *Al-Adsani, Fogarty,* and *McElhinney* respectively, that 'compliance with obligations owed in international law is of itself pursuit of a legitimate aim'.[60] It was true that in the earlier case of *Waite and Kennedy*, which concerned the immunity of an international organization, rather than State immunity, 'the ECtHR did not express itself in quite such stark terms'; but, as his Lordship had already pointed out, there could be no principled basis on which the approach in the two situations could be different.[61] It was also true that, in considering the proportionality of the restriction on article 6(1) of the ECHR represented by the immunity from legal process accorded to the relevant international organization by the respondent State in *Waite and Kennedy*, the European Court regarded as a material factor the availability of means of redress which represented a reasonable alternative to access to the courts of the respondent State, and took into account the alternative means of legal process available to the applicants in the case before it, namely an internal tribunal.[62] His Lordship noted, however, that 'the Court did not approach the matter upon the basis that it is a pre-requisite to the compatibility with Article 6 of organizational immunity that the organization provide an alternative forum for dispute resolution'.[63] Furthermore, in *Waite and Kennedy*, the Court 'was concerned only with the obligations of an ECHR State owed to other ECHR States and to an organisation created by such States long after they had acceded to the ECHR'; and '[i]n the light of the approach of the ECtHR in the subsequent trilogy of State immunity cases', namely *Al-Adsani, Fogarty,* and *McElhinney*, 'it [was] not ... safe to assume that the ECtHR would, in a case involving the immunity of a global organiza-tion created prior to the ECHR, adopt reasoning similar to that to be found in *Waite and Kennedy*'.[64] If, however, contrary to his Lordship's view, it was relevant to take into account the availability of an alternative forum, there was in fact an alternative mode of dispute resolution in the present case, namely arbitration under the UNCITRAL rules; and, for reasons already stated, it was inappropriate for an English court to assess the 'adequacy and likely efficacy' of recourse to this, although his Lordship wished to record that it had 'certainly not been established that it [was] an inadequate remedy'.[65] In this regard, UNESCO's immunity from execu-tion was not incompatible with article 6, as made clear by the ECtHR in *Kalogeropolou*, and was in any event irrelevant, since UNESCO had already stated that it would comply with any award.[66]

---

[60] Ibid, para 26, citing and quoting from a common passage in *Al-Adsani v United Kingdom* (2001) 34 EHRR 273, *Fogarty v United Kingdom* (2001) 34 EHRR 302 and *McElhinney v Ireland* (2001) 34 EHRR 323.

[61] Ibid, para 27.

[62] Ibid.

[63] Ibid.

[64] Ibid.

[65] Ibid, para 28.   [66] Ibid.

*European Convention on Human Rights 1950, article 2 (right to life)—
obligation to conduct inquiry into death through State's alleged failure to
take reasonable steps to safeguard life—legality of invasion of Iraq—armed
forces—whether government obliged to conduct inquiry into whether reasonable steps were taken to be satisfied that invasion was internationally lawful—'jurisdiction' within meaning of ECHR, article 1—extraterritorial
application of ECHR—whether ECHR applicable to UK armed forces in
Iraq—Soering jurisprudence—whether decision-making in UK relevant to
sending armed forces abroad bringing case within purview of ECHR*

Case No 4 *R (Gentle) v Prime Minster and others*, 9 April 2008, [2008]
UKHL 20, [2008] 1 AC 1356 (HL)

The facts of and arguments in the case have been recounted previously.[67]
The claimants appealed to the House of Lords, arguing that article 2 of
the ECHR obliged the government to establish an independent public
inquiry into whether it had taken reasonable steps to satisfy itself that the
invasion of Iraq in 2003 was internationally lawful. (They did not seek an
inquiry into whether the invasion was in fact internationally lawful.)

A nine-member House of Lords unanimously dismissed the appeal.

Lord Bingham, who gave the leading judgment, with which the other
Lords agreed, emphasized that the established 'procedural obligation'
under article 2 to set up an independent public inquiry into any death
occurring in circumstances where it appeared that one of the substantive
obligations imposed by article 2 may have been violated[68] was 'parasitic
upon the existence of the substantive right':[69] it could not exist independently. To make good their procedural right, the claimants had to show at
least an arguable case that the relevant substantive right, and correlative
obligation, arose on the facts. His Lordship concluded that they could
not.[70] The substantive obligation argued for in this case was the obligation
to establish a framework of laws, precautions, procedures and means of
enforcement which would, to the greatest extent reasonably practicable,
protect life.[71] In this regard, Lord Bingham stated:

It may be significant that article 2 has never been held to apply to the process of
deciding on the lawfulness of a resort to arms, despite the number of occasions
on which member states have made that decision over the past half century and

---

[67] See *R (Gentle) v The Prime Minister, Secretary of State for Defence and the Attorney-General*
[2005] EWHC 3119 (Admin), (2005) 76 *BYIL* 632–4 (QBD (Admin Ct), Collins J); *R (Gentle) v
The Prime Minister, Secretary of State for Defence and the Attorney-General* [2006] EWCA Civ 1689;
[2007] QB 689, (2006) 77 *BYIL* 548–53 (CA (Civ Div)). Note that the argument changed slightly in
the Court of Appeal. The arguments before the Lords mirrored those in the Court of Appeal.
[68] See *McCann v United Kingdom* (1995) 21 EHRR 97.
[69] [2008] 1 AC 1356, 1366, para 6.
[70] Ibid.
[71] See *Osman v United Kingdom* (2000) 29 EHRR 245, as explained in *R (Middleton) v West
Somerset Coroner* [2004] UKHL 10; [2004] 2 AC 182, para 2.

despite the fact that such a decision almost inevitably exposes military personnel to the risk of fatalities.[72]

There were, his Lordship thought, three main reasons for this. First:

(1) The lawfulness of military action has no immediate bearing on the risk of fatalities. ... In this case, ... Fusilier Gentle died after Security Council resolution 1546 had legitimated British military action in Iraq, so that such action was not by then unlawful even if it had earlier been so.[73]

Secondly:

(2) The draftsmen of the European Convention cannot, in my opinion, have envisaged that it could provide a suitable framework or machinery for resolving questions about the resort to war. They will have been vividly aware of the United Nations Charter, adopted not many years earlier, and will have recognised it as the instrument, operating as between states, which provided the relevant code and means of enforcement in that regard, as compared with an instrument devoted to the protection of individual human rights.[74] It must (further) have been obvious that an inquiry such as the claimants' claim would be drawn into consideration of issues which judicial tribunals have traditionally been very reluctant to enter-tain because they recognise their limitations as suitable bodies to resolve them.[75] ... [I]n deciding whether a right exists it is relevant to consider what exercise of the right would entail. Thus the restraint traditionally shown by the courts in ruling on what has been called high policy—peace and war, the making of trea-ties, the conduct of foreign relations—does tend to militate against the existence of the right: *R v Jones (Margaret)* [2007] 1 AC 136, paras 30, 65–67.[76] This consideration is fortified by the reflection that war is very often made by several states acting as allies; but a litigant would be required to exhaust his domestic remedies before national courts in which judgments would be made about the conduct of states not before the court, and even if the matter were to reach the European Court of Human Rights there could be no review of the conduct of non-member states who might nonetheless be covered by any decision.[77]

Thirdly and finally:

(3) The obligation of member states under article 1 of the Convention is to secure 'to everyone within their jurisdiction' the rights and freedoms in the Convention. Subject to limited exceptions and specific extensions, the application of the Convention is territorial: the rights and freedoms are ordinarily to be secured to those within the borders of the state and not outside. Here, the deaths of Fusilier Gentle and Trooper Clarke occurred in Iraq and although they were subject to the authority of the defendants they were clearly not within the jurisdiction of

---

[72] [2008] 1 AC 1356, 1366–7, para 8.

[73] Ibid, 1367, para 8. See also ibid, 1369, para 13 (Lord Hoffmann), 1371 and 1372, paras 22 and 24 (Lord Hope), 1376–7, para 43 (Lord Rodger), 1381, para 57 (Baroness Hale), 1383, para 65 (Lord Carswell) and 1385, para 73 (Lord Mance).

[74] See also ibid, 1369, para 13 (Lord Hoffmann), 1372, para 24 (Lord Hope), 1375–6, paras 37–8 (Lord Rodger), 1381, para 57 (Baroness Hale) and 1384, para 70 (Lord Brown).

[75] See also ibid, 1372, para 24 (Lord Hope).

[76] See also ibid, 1382, para 60 (Baroness Hale).

[77] Ibid, 1367, para 8.

the UK as that expression in the Convention has been interpreted: *R (Al-Skeini) v Secretary of State for Defence* [2008] 1 AC 153, paras 79, 129.[78] The claimants seek to overcome that problem, in reliance on authorities such as *Soering v United Kingdom* (1989) 11 EHRR 439, by stressing that their complaint relates to the decision-making process (or lack of it) which occurred here, even though the ill-effects were felt abroad. There is, I think, an obvious distinction between the present case and the *Soering* case, and such later cases as *Chahal v United Kingdom* (1996) 23 EHRR 413 and *D v United Kingdom* (1997) 24 EHRR 423, in each of which action relating to an individual in the UK was likely to have an immediate and direct impact on that individual elsewhere.[79] But I think there is a more fundamental objection: that the claimants' argument, necessary to meet the objection of extra-territoriality, highlights the remoteness of their complaints from the true purview of article 2.[80]

Even if, contrary to his Lordship's conclusion, the claimants had been able to establish an arguable substantive right under article 2, they would still have failed to establish a right to a wide-ranging inquiry such as the one they sought, since nothing in the Strasbourg case-law on article 2 appeared to contemplate such an inquiry.[81] Nor was it for their Lordships to read in such a right:

> The procedural right under discussion is … a product of implication, and while the implication of terms may be both necessary and desirable it is a task to be carried out by any court, particularly a national court, with extreme caution. This is because states ordinarily seek to express the terms on which they agree in a Convention such as this; terms which are not expressed may have been deliberately omitted; terms, once implied, are binding on all member states, and may be terms they would not have been willing to accept: *Brown v Stott* [2003] 1 AC 681, 703. I find it impossible to conceive that the proud sovereign states of Europe could ever have contemplated binding themselves legally to establish an independent public inquiry into the process by which a decision might have been made to commit the state's armed forces to war.[82]

For his part, Lord Scott 'particularly' associated himself with these last comments.[83]

Of the other Lords, Lord Hoffmann stressed at the outset that any attempt by the claimants to argue that article 2 of the ECHR gave rise to an obligation on the part of a Contracting State not to participate in a war not permitted by the United Nations Charter would have been 'a hopeless submission'.[84] He explained that the claimants therefore fell back on the claim that article 2 generated in the circumstances an obligation to

---

[78] See also Lord Carswell, who, although expressly not deciding the issue, thought *Al-Skeini* rendered it 'questionable' whether the claimants were within the jurisdiction of the UK: ibid, 1383–4, para 66.

[79] See also ibid, 1370, para 19 (Lord Hope) and 1384, para 66 (Lord Carswell).

[80] Ibid, 1367–8, para 8. See also ibid, 1384, para 66 (Lord Carswell).

[81] Ibid, 1368, para 9. See also ibid, 1373, para 27 (Lord Hope), 1377, para 44 (Lord Rodger) and 1384–5, para 70 (Lord Brown).

[82] Ibid, 1368, para 9.

[83] Ibid, 1373, para 29.   [84] Ibid, 1369, para 13.

take reasonable steps to investigate whether the invasion of Iraq would, as a matter of international law, be lawful or not since, if proper investigation had taken place, there was a good chance that the UK would not have taken part in the invasion or occupation and the soldiers would not have been killed.[85] The claim did not impress him:

15 My Lords, this is a 'for want of a nail …' argument which I cannot accept. There are all kinds of things which, if the Government had acted differently, might have resulted in the UK not taking part in the war. A different assessment of our diplomatic interests or financial resources might have led to a different conclusion. Did the Government have a duty under article 2 to use, in [counsel's] phrase, 'due diligence' in the investigation of all these matters? Of course not. The question is not whether a better inquiry might have led to a different decision but whether article 2 created a legal duty to the soldiers to undertake such an inquiry.

16 Unless article 2 creates a duty not to go to war contrary to the United Nations Charter (a proposition for which, as I have said, [counsel] does not contend) I cannot see how there can be an independent duty to use reasonable care to ascertain whether the war would be contrary to the Charter or not. What would be the purpose of such a duty if the Government owed no duty under article 2 to comply with the Charter?[86] Of course it is desirable for all kinds of reasons that the Government should not act contrary to international law and that it should take reasonable steps to discover whether it is about to do so. But not, as it seems to me, to comply with article 2. …[87]

Lord Hope explained at the start of his speech that the guarantee in article 2 of the ECHR that everyone's right to life shall be protected by law was not 'an absolute guarantee that nobody will be exposed by the state to situations where their life is in danger, whatever the circumstances':[88]

Those who serve in the armed forces do this in the knowledge that they may be called upon to risk their lives in the defence of their country or its legitimate interests at home or overseas. In *Engel v The Netherlands (No 1)* (1976) 1 EHRR 647, para. 54, the European court said that, when interpreting and applying the rules of the Convention, the court must bear in mind the particular characteristics of military life and its effects on the situation of individual members of the armed forces. … [T]he extent of [the] protection [afforded by the Convention] must take account of the characteristics of military life, the nature of the activities that they are required to perform and of the risks that they give rise to.[89]

He underlined that '[t]he proper functioning of an army in a modern democracy includes requiring those who serve in it to undertake the operations for which they have been recruited, trained and equipped, some of

---

[85] Ibid, para 14.
[86] See also ibid, 1376, para 41 (Lord Rodger), 1381, para 59 (Baroness Hale) and 1383, para 64 (Lord Carswell).
[87] Ibid, 1369. See also ibid, 1376–7, para 43 (Lord Rodger).
[88] Ibid, 1370, para 18.
[89] Ibid. See also ibid, 1382, para 60 (Baroness Hale) and 1383, para 65 (Lord Carswell).

which are inherently dangerous', and concluded on the point that '[t]he guarantee in the first sentence of article 2(1) is not violated simply by deploying servicemen and women on active service overseas as part of an organised military force which is properly equipped and capable of defending itself, even though the risk of their being killed is inherent in what they are being asked to do'.[90] Nor was Lord Hope persuaded by the claimant's recourse to what his Lordship had said in *Launder* to the effect that, where decision-makers had purported to reach their decisions by taking into account international law, the court was entitled to examine the international law in question to see whether those decision-makers had misdirected themselves:

[T]he context in which I made that observation was a case where the Secretary of State was dealing with the applicant's rights under domestic extradition law. He chose to do this by reference, among other things, to the Convention. If he misunderstood its provisions he was, according to the ordinary principles of domestic law, reviewable. Here the Attorney General was not dealing with rights or obligations in domestic law when he was considering what international law had to say about the legality of the invasion. The only question he was concerned with was whether the invasion was lawful in international law. That question as such is not, as [counsel] accepts, reviewable in the domestic courts. Nor can it be linked to the state's obligations under article 2(1). The Attorney General did not say, when he was considering the issue of legality, that he was addressing his mind to the Convention rights of the troops ...[91]

Lord Rodger was not taken either with what he called the claimants' 'artificial *pis aller* of a duty to hold an inquiry into the steps taken by the Government to satisfy itself of the legality of the invasion under international law'.[92] Among his several reasons for rejecting its supposed existence was the following:

The supposed obligation would elevate procedure over substance. If the invasion were lawful, a government which got the answer to the legal question right, but had not exercised due diligence in doing so, would be in technical breach of the obligation. On the other hand, if the war were unlawful, a government which got the answer wrong, but had exercised due diligence in doing so, would not be in breach of the obligation. Being, thus, merely procedural, the obligation would not go to the heart of the matter. An inquiry into the performance of that obligation would likewise not go to the heart of the matter and would satisfy nobody.[93]

He also drew attention to the fact that 'the advice on the legal position was only one of many factors—most of them, presumably, in the sphere of international politics—which were in play when the Government decided to take part in the invasion of Iraq'.[94] In this situation, his Lordship remarked, 'it would be simplistic to suppose that any lack of diligence in

90 Ibid, 1370–1, para 19. See also ibid, 1384, para 70 (Lord Brown).
91 Ibid, 1373, para 26.
92 Ibid, 1376, para 39.
93 Ibid, para 42.   94 Ibid, 1377, para 44.

investigating the legal position could be regarded as a relevant cause of the deaths of two specific soldiers ... for the purposes of article 2 of the Convention'.[95] For her part, Baroness Hale confessed that if the ECtHR wished to read into article 2 of the ECHR an obligation of the sort argued for by the claimants, she would have been 'surprised but not at all unhappy'.[96] But she did not think that the House of Lords could go this far:[97]

56 ... It goes way beyond what member states might have thought that they were committing themselves to in 1950. Although the Convention is a living instrument, not to be interpreted only according to its original intention, we must tread very carefully before implying obligations which are not already there: *Brown v Stott* [2003] 1 AC 681. This is not because any decision of ours would be binding upon the other member states of the Council of Europe: it would not. It is because we are interpreting the Convention rights in the light of the jurisprudence of the Strasbourg court as it evolves over time: see *R (Ullah) v Special Adjudicator* [2004] 2 AC 323, para. 20. Parliament is free to go further than Strasbourg if it wishes, but we are not free to foist upon Parliament or upon public authorities an interpretation of a Convention right which goes way beyond anything which we can reasonably foresee that Strasbourg might do.

57 I cannot reasonably foresee that Strasbourg would construct out of article 2 a duty not to send soldiers to fight in an unlawful war. ...[98]

Her Ladyship added:

A further reason not to spell such a duty out of article 2 is that it would require both the domestic courts of this country, and the European Court of Human Rights in Strasbourg, to rule upon the legality of the use of force against Iraq in international law. This is beyond our competence. The state that goes to war cannot and should not be the judge of whether or not the war was lawful in international law. That question can only be authoritatively decided, not by us or by Strasbourg, but by the international institutions which police the international treaties governing the law of war. But if there were such a right, the domestic courts would have to do their best to decide if it had been broken, because the Human Rights Act 1998 requires us to decide whether or not a public authority has acted compatibly with the Convention rights.[99]

But Baroness Hale noted that she had little difficulty with the proposition that the claimants' sons were within the jurisdiction of the UK for the purposes of article 1 of the ECHR when they died.[100] She reasoned, by reference to *R (Al-Skeini) v Secretary of State for Defence*,[101] that '[i]f Mr Baha Mousa, detained in a military detention facility in Basra, was within the jurisdiction, then a soldier serving under the command and control of his superiors must also be within the jurisdiction', since the UK '[was] in a better position to secure to him all his Convention rights ... than it [was] to secure those rights to its detainees'.[102]

---

[95] Ibid.   [96] Ibid, 1380, para 55.   [97] Ibid, para 56.
[98] Ibid, 1380–1.   [99] Ibid, 1381, para 58.   [100] Ibid, 1382, para 60.
[101] [2007] UKHL 26; [2008] 1 AC 153, (2007) 78 *BYIL* 529–46 (HL).
[102] [2008] 1 AC 1356, 1382, para 60.

The House of Lords' decision is sound. The claimant's argument was specious from the start, and it is testimony to the cleverness of counsel and the sympathy capable of being exhibited by their Lordships that leave to appeal (and to a nine-member House) was granted after its refusal by the Court of Appeal. There are only two points of note. First, unless he simply expressed himself poorly, Lord Bingham appears to labour under the misapprehension that a decision of a national court on a point of treaty interpretation can bind other States Parties,[103] a solecism thankfully corrected by Baroness Hale.[104] Secondly, the question whether the deceased soldiers were under the jurisdiction of the UK for the purposes of article 1 of the ECHR while they were deployed in Iraq is a difficult one, given the absence of Strasbourg case-law dealing with the extraterritorial application of the Convention to the nationals of the respondent State. It cannot be taken as read that Lord Bingham's straightforward transposition of the ECtHR and House of Lord's jurisprudence on the extraterritorial application of the Convention to non-nationals is the way to approach the matter. At the same time, Baroness Hale's glib answer does this problematic issue a disservice. It is an issue picked up, and sought to be answered in more detail, by Collins J in the Administrative Court of the Queen's Bench Division in his judgment delivered two days later in *R (Smith) v Oxfordshire Deputy Coroner*.[105]

Convention relating to the Status of Refugees 1951—definition of refugee— persecution—statelessness—Occupied Palestinian Territory—whether to deny a stateless person re-entry to country of his or her former habitual residence amounting to persecution for the purposes of Refugee Convention

Case No 5 MA (Palestinian Territories) v Secretary of State for the Home Department, 9 April 2008, [2008] EWCA Civ 304, unreported (CA (Civ Div))

The appellant was a stateless Palestinian from Tulkarm in the West Bank who had been denied the status of refugee, within the meaning of the Refugee Convention,[106] in the UK. The proposal, in accordance with established procedure, was to deport him to Jordan, from where he would need to cross the King Hussein Bridge to re-enter the Occupied Palestinian Territory. The crossing is controlled on the Palestinian side by Israel, which has a policy of refusing re-entry to the West Bank to Palestinians forcibly returned from abroad. The appellant submitted that, for the purposes of the definition of a refugee in article 1A(2) of the Refugee Convention, it amounted to persecution to deny a stateless person re-entry to the country of his former habitual residence.

---

[103] See ibid, 1368, para 9.   [104] Ibid, 1381, para 56.
[105] [2008] EWHC 694 (Admin); [2008] 3 WLR 1284, below 430–5 (QBD (Admin Ct), Collins J).
[106] Convention relating to the Status of Refugees, Geneva, 28 July 1951 (entered into force 22 April 1954), 189 UNTS 2545.

On appeal from the Asylum and Immigration Tribunal (AIT), the Court of Appeal rejected the appellant's argument and dismissed the appeal. Kay LJ gave the leading judgment, with which Lawrence Collins and Aldous LJJ agreed.

Kay LJ observed at the outset that, in accordance with the express wording of article 1A(2) of the Refugee Convention, a stateless person 'outside the country of his former habitual residence' was capable of enjoying the protection of the Convention.[107] But such a person still had to prove that he or she had, in the words of the provision, a well-founded fear of persecution. After a brief survey of the relevant Commonwealth authorities (which, apart from not being binding on the Court, 'at their highest [went] no further than acceptance that, in some circumstances, to deny a stateless person re-entry *may* amount to persecution', rather than 'the proposition that a denial of re-entry is in itself persecutory'[108]) and of the secondary literature (which was conflicting[109]), his Lordship came to the view that it was not persecutory to deny a stateless person re-entry to the country of his or her former habitual residence:

The denial does not interfere with a stateless person's rights in the way that it does with the rights of a national. There is a fundamental distinction between nationals and stateless persons in that respect. It is one thing to protect a stateless person from persecutory return to the country of his former habitual residence (as the Refugee Convention does), but it would be quite another thing to charac-terise a denial of re-entry as persecutory. The lot of a stateless person is an unhappy one, but to deny him a right that he has never enjoyed is not, in itself, persecution. Stateless persons are themselves the subject of an international treaty, namely the Convention relating to the Status of Stateless Persons (1954). The United Kingdom is a party to that Convention but it has not been incorporated into domestic law and [counsel] does not suggest that it protects the appellant in this case.[110]

In this light, Kay LJ held that the AIT 'did not fall into legal error when it held that the denial of re-entry to a stateless person is not in itself persecutory under the Refugee Convention'.[111]

---

[107] [2008] EWCA Civ 304, para 20. Article 1A(2) of the Convention provides: 'For the purposes of the Convention the term "refugee" shall apply to any person who ... owing to well-founded fear of being persecuted for reasons of race, religion, nationality, membership of a particular social group or political opinion, is outside the country of his nationality and is unable or, owing to such fear, is unwilling to avail himself of the protection of that country, or being outside the country of his former habitual residence as a result of such events, is unable or, owing to such fear, is unwilling to return to it.'

[108] [2008] EWCA Civ 304, para 23, original emphasis, citing *Altawil v Canada (Minister of Citizenship and Immigration)* (1996) 114 FTR 211, *Thabet v Minister of Citizenship and Immigration* [1998] 4 FC 21 and the decision of the New Zealand Refugee Status Appeals Authority in *Refugee Appeal No* 73861, 30 June 2005.

[109] Ibid, citing G S Goodwin-Gill & J McAdam, *The Refugee in International Law* (3rd edn, Oxford University Press, Oxford, 2007), 69–70 and J C Hathaway, *The Law of Refugee Status* (Butterworths, Toronto, 1991), 62–3.

[110] Ibid, para 26.   [111] Ibid, para 29.

The decision has since been followed in *MT (Palestinian Territories) v Secretary of State for the Home Department*[112] and *SH (Palestinian Territories) v Secretary of State for the Home Department*.[113]

European Convention on Human Rights 1950—'jurisdiction' within the meaning of ECHR, article 1—extraterritorial application of ECHR—ECHR, article 2 (right to life)—positive obligation to safeguard life—obligation to provide effective official investigation into death of next-of-kin through State's failure to safeguard life—armed forces—whether ECHR, article 2 applicable to UK armed forces off base in Iraq

Case No 6 R (Smith) v Oxfordshire Deputy Coroner, 11 April 2008, [2008] EWHC 694 (Admin), [2008] 3 WLR 1284 (QBD (Admin Ct), Collins J)

The claimant, the mother of a British soldier who had died of hyperthermia (overheating) in Iraq while carrying out duties off base, appealed the ruling of the coroner that the procedural obligation implicit in article 2 of the ECHR,[114] as secured at the domestic level by the HRA, did not apply to her son's death. The Secretary of State for Defence sought judicial review of the coroner's summing up on other grounds. The coroner subsequently consented to the quashing of his verdict, but the claimant requested that the court deal with the remaining issues. The Ministry of Defence conceded that the ECHR and HRA applied to the death, but on a basis considered too narrow by the claimant, namely, relying on *Bankovic*[115] and *Al-Skeini*,[116] that the relevant circumstances leading to the death took place within the geographical area of a British army camp[117] and British army hospital; that the deceased was at all times acting within the scope of his duties; and that no third-party national was involved in his death. The claimant submitted that the ECHR and HRA applied to British soldiers operating in Iraq wherever they may be within that country, provided they were not on a frolic of their own.

Collins J, in the Administrative Court of the Queen's Bench Division, agreed with the claimant that the ECHR and HRA applied to a member of the UK armed forces wherever he or she may be.

His Lordship prefaced his judgment by noting that, as emphasized by the Secretary of State, there was an absence of claims, whether domestic or before the ECtHR, in which a UK national had alleged a breach of the ECHR outside the territory of the UK (or of those of its dependent territories to which the Convention had been extended).[118] He also recalled

---

[112] [2008] EWCA Civ 1149.   [113] [2008] EWCA Civ 1150.
[114] See *McCann v United Kingdom* (1995) 21 EHRR 97.
[115] *Bankovic v Belgium* (2001) 11 BHRC 435.
[116] *R (Al-Skeini) v Secretary of State for Defence* [2007] UKHL 26; [2008] 1 AC 153, (2007) 78 *BYIL* 529–46 (HL).
[117] The deceased had reported sick on base.
[118] [2008] 3 WLR 1284, 1291, para 10.

the Strasbourg court's decision in *Bankovic* and the House of Lords' decision in *Al-Skeini*, in which it was laid down that the notion of 'jurisdiction' in article 1 of the ECHR was primarily territorial, any other basis being exceptional and requiring special justification.[119] He noted, however, that at the time of his death the deceased was operating under an order promulgated by the Coalition Provisional Authority whereby all personnel of the multinational force in Iraq were 'immune from Iraqi legal process' and 'subject to the exclusive jurisdiction of their sending states'.[120] His Lordship continued:

Thus the United Kingdom's jurisdiction over its own nationals was clearly maintained. In any event, members of the armed forces remain at all times subject to the jurisdiction of the United Kingdom. It would obviously be wholly artificial to regard a soldier sent to fight in the territory of another state as subject to the jurisdiction of that state.[121]

Next, '[t]hat a member of the UK armed forces should remain within the jurisdiction of the United Kingdom for the purposes of the Human Rights Act 1998', as distinct from the ECHR, was, his Lordship believed, supported by the reasoning of the majority in *Al-Skeini*.[122] He quoted several passages from the speech of Lord Rodger in that case[123] before concluding that they confirmed the application of the HRA to the deceased.[124] This was, he noted, 'entirely consistent' with the approach of the House of Lords in *Lawson v Serco Ltd*,[125] in which the Employment Rights Act 1996 was held to extend to an employee summarily dismissed from his employment at a Ministry of Defence military establishment in Germany.[126] Moreover, he observed, in *Al-Skeini* Lord Brown had made the point that if the British soldier who had ill-treated Mr Mousa had been court-martialled in Iraq, 'there would have been no good reason for requiring that soldier's article 6 rights to have had to have been taken to Strasbourg rather than to the courts of the United Kingdom'—which 'presuppose[d] that the Convention applied to the soldier'.[127] Furthermore, there was one Strasbourg case which 'point[ed] in the direction of jurisdiction', namely *Martin v United Kingdom*,[128] in which a soldier serving in Germany had been tried by court-martial there under military law. It 'was not suggested in that case (albeit no question of jurisdiction within article 1 of the Convention was raised) that the Convention did not

---

[119] Ibid, 1291–2, paras 10–1.
[120] Ibid, 1292, para 12, quoting CAP/ORD/26 June 2003/17, s 2(1)(4).
[121] Ibid.
[122] Ibid, para 13.
[123] See ibid, 1292–3, paras 13 and 15, quoting [2008] 1 AC 153, 193 and 195–6, paras 46, 47 and 53–5.
[124] Ibid, 1293, para 16.
[125] [2006] UKHL 3; [2006] 1 All ER 823.
[126] [2008] 3 WLR 1284, 1293, para 16.
[127] Ibid, 1293–4, para 16.
[128] Application No 40426/98, ECtHR, 24 October 2006 (unreported).

apply'.[129] In addition, in *W v Ireland*, the European Commission on Human Rights had held that 'the authorised agents of the state, including diplomatic or consular agents and armed forces, remain under its jurisdiction when abroad'.[130] In any event, his Lordship reasoned, the absence of cases dealing with circumstances such as the present could not be determinative of the correct answer, and such observations as there were were 'consistent with the exercise of jurisdiction' in such cases.[131]

In response to the Secretary of State's argument that the impossibility of affording soldiers on active service outside their bases the benefits of the HRA made its application to them wherever they were unfeasible and therefore implausible, Collins J—recalling that article 2 of the ECHR imposes a positive obligation to protect life, so that, 'where there is a known risk to life which the state can take steps to avoid or to minimise, such steps should be taken'—stated that '[w]hat can reasonably be done will depend on the circumstances of a particular case'.[132] The lives of members of the armed forces sent to fight or keep order abroad could not receive absolute protection.[133] But, his Lordship added, 'the soldier does not lose all protection simply because he is in hostile territory carrying out dangerous operations', so that, for example, 'to send a soldier out on patrol or, indeed, into battle with defective equipment could constitute a breach of article 2 of the Convention'.[134] He concluded:

So the protection of article 2 is capable of extending to a member of the armed forces wherever he or she may be; whether it does will depend on the circumstances of the particular case.[135]

This is the statement with which his Lordship's initial discussion of the scope of application of the ECHR and HRA finished.

Before confirming his judgment, however, Collins J heard argument as to the effect of the House of Lords' decision in *Gentle*[136] two days earlier. In the light of this, he added a postscript in which he addressed in particular the statement of Lord Bingham, with whom the other Lords agreed (but with whom Baroness Hale differed on the particular point at issue), in which his Lordship stated, citing *Al-Skeini*, that while the deceased soldiers, killed in Iraq off base, 'were subject to the authority of the defendants they were clearly not within jurisdiction of the United Kingdom as

---

[129] [2008] 3 WLR 1284, 1294, para 17.
[130] Ibid, quoting (1983) 32 DR 211, para 14.
[131] Ibid.
[132] Ibid, para 19.
[133] Ibid, 1294–5, para 19. His Lordship remarked that the approach under the HRA accorded with that taken by the Court of Appeal under the law of negligence in *Mulcahy v Ministry of Defence* [1996] QB 732.
[134] [2008] 3 WLR 1284, 1295, para 20.
[135] Ibid.
[136] *R (Gentle) v Prime Minster and others* [2008] UKHL 20; [2008] 1 AC 1356, above, 422–8 (HL).

that expression in the Convention has been interpreted'.[137] After recalling that he had already sought to explain why the speeches in *Al-Skeini* did not suggest that the jurisdiction of the UK did not extend to cover soldiers who were there under the authority of the Crown, Collins J argued as follows:

4 The fact is that those soldiers have to accept that they are subject to the jurisdiction of this country in relation to their activities so that, for example, if they commit offences they are subject to military discipline in the form of court-martial; indeed, generally they are subject to military discipline. In addition, it seems clear that they would have a right of action in tort following the abolition of the protection given to the Crown under section 10 of the Crown Proceedings Act 1947, although of course the circumstances might well mean that any claim would not succeed because there would not be in the circumstances a duty of care: see the *Mulcahy* case [1996] QB 732.

5 The fact is that the starting point must be whether the 1998 Act covers the activities of a soldier when sent abroad. Of course it is necessary—and indeed our jurisprudence indicates—that the scope of the 1998 Act should march with the scope of the Convention. But it is to be noted that article 1 is not incorporated into the 1998 Act. Furthermore although the European Court of Human Rights has made it clear that the principle is one of territoriality and that of course accords with the approach in the *travaux préparatoires*, none the less the word used is 'jurisdiction'.[138]

In support of his view, his Lordship emphasized a point he had made earlier:

The scope will be a relatively narrow one. It is only if the decision is one such as I have indicated, namely sending out with defective equipment or some such other failure that the protection could arise, and it would not if any action were taken based upon the exigencies of a situation which arose in having to deal with particular events. So much, as it seems to me, is recognised by paragraph (2) of article 2. It is only if the decision is one which could be said to be laid at the door of the Ministry of Defence that the possibility of the application of the Convention would arise.[139]

He added:

There is a degree of artificiality in saying that a soldier is protected so long as he remains in the base or in the military hospital but he is not protected should he step outside. It is difficult to see what is the rationale behind that so far as his protection is concerned. One could well understand the rationale so far as the effect on those who are dealt with by the soldiers, that is to say the nationals of the country in which they are sent to carry out whatever operations they have to carry out. But so far as their own protection is concerned the distinction is difficult to understand. It will depend on the circumstances. I am not suggesting that

---

[137] [2008] 3 WLR 1284, 1304, para 2 of postscript, quoting [2008] 1 AC 1356, 1367, para 8.
[138] Ibid, 1304, postscript.
[139] Ibid, 1305, para 8 of postscript.

the door is opened very widely in deciding whether article 2 or indeed the Convention generally can apply.[140]

As for Lord Bingham's words in *Gentle*, Collins J reasoned to the following effect:

7 In the *Gentle* case [2008] 1 AC 1356 the question whether a soldier would be able to take advantage of the Convention, subject obviously to the circumstances of any individual case, was not at the centre of the argument. Indeed the point was very much a peripheral one although it was undoubtedly raised by their Lordships in the course of argument. It was not a point that, as far as I can see, was necessary for the decision which was reached. It certainly was a point which could support the conclusion reached by their Lordships but it was certainly not essential. It is to be noted that neither Lord Brown of Eaton-under-Heywood nor Lord Carswell appears to accept that a soldier cannot be covered by article 2 of the Convention when in Iraq or indeed anywhere else as a result of being sent to war or to join in police action on behalf of the United Nations. ...

10 I am satisfied that what Lord Bingham said in the *Gentle* case, at para 8(3), is not part of the ratio of the decision. I appreciate that it comes from the highest possible source, and it appears that at least four of their Lordships agreed with him in the sense that they state they agreed with his reasoning. But to agree with the reasoning is not necessarily to constitute a firm agreement with every single part of that reasoning, particularly if a part is not necessary for the final decision that was reached.

11 In those circumstances I am satisfied that what I have said, having heard full argument on the point which their Lordships did not hear, should stand. Despite the observations of Lord Bingham to which of course I pay the greatest respect, I am not persuaded that I should change the judgment I have handed down.[141]

Accordingly, Collins J's decision stood.

If his Lordship's decision were to turn out to be right, it would not be for the reasons he adduces. For a start, his consistent conflation of the concept of jurisdiction for the purposes of the application of the military, criminal and tort law of the UK with the distinct and highly particular concept of 'jurisdiction' for the purposes of article 1 of the ECHR is remarkable, to say the least. A hostile combatant who attacked UK forces on foreign territory would fall within both the prescriptive and enforcement jurisdiction of the UK under both international law and UK military law, but would not, unless and until he or she was in the custody of those forces, be within the UK's 'jurisdiction' for the purposes of the scope of application of the ECHR. Secondly, to argue on the basis of Lord Rodger's general dicta on the potential scope of application of English law, and therefore on the potential scope of application of the HRA, that the ECHR applies to a given situation is to put the cart before the horse. As for the case of *Martin*, concerning the soldier tried by court-martial in Germany, this was clearly a case where the Convention applied by dint of the fact that the UK military base on which the proceedings were conducted

---

[140] Ibid, para 9 of postscript.   [141] Ibid, 1304–5, postscript.

fell within the territorial control of the UK, and thus within its article 1 'jurisdiction' in accordance within the *Bankovic* jurisprudence.

Seemingly central to Collins J's analysis is his argument that 'the protection of article 2 is capable of extending to a member of the armed forces wherever he or she may be [but] whether it does will depend on the circumstances of the particular case'.[142] This is, with respect, unsatisfactory. Either the Convention applies to a soldier wherever he or she may be or it does not. If it does, the content of the right to life in the military context is a logically subsequent consideration: the fact that article 2 of the ECHR does not guarantee the lives of soldiers sent to fight abroad, as acknowledged by his Lordship and as elaborated on by Lords Hope, Carswell and Brown and Baroness Hale in *Gentle*,[143] has no bearing on whether the article applies in the first place.

As for the various statements in *Gentle*, it is true that what Lord Bingham says is not essential to his decision. But it is not true that neither Lord Brown nor Lord Carswell 'appears to accept that a soldier cannot be covered by article 2 of the Convention when in Iraq or indeed anywhere else'.[144] Lord Brown says nothing about issue. Lord Carswell, although expressly not deciding the point, thought *Al-Skeini* rendered it 'questionable' whether the claimants were within the jurisdiction of the UK.[145]

Finally, it may well be artificial to say that soldiers are protected by the ECHR as long as they remain in their base or in a military hospital but are not protected should they step outside, but that would seem to be the upshot of the Strasbourg jurisprudence on the extraterritorial application of the Convention—or at least of the jurisprudence on the extraterritorial application of the Convention to non-nationals, which is all there is to go on for now.

Convention relating to the Status of Refugees 1951—*definition of refugee— conscientious objection—anti-personnel landmines—international humanitarian law—Convention on the Prohibition of the Use, Stockpiling, Production and Transfer of Anti-Personnel Mines and on their Destruction 1997—Geneva Conventions 1949, common article 3—international human rights law— International Covenant on Civil and Political Rights 1966, article 6 (right to life)—whether refusal to lay anti-personnel landmines in populated area during peacetime grounding refugee status*

Case No 7 BE (Iran) v Secretary of State for the Home Department, 20 May 2008, [2008] EWCA Civ 540, unreported (CA (Civ Div))

The appellant was a deserter from the Iranian army whose application in the UK for the status of refugee, within the meaning of the Refugee

---

[142] [2008] 3 WLR 1284, 1295, para 20.
[143] See [2008] 1 AC 1356, 1370–1, paras 18–9 (Lord Carswell), 1382, para 60 (Baroness Hale), 1383, para 65 (Lord Carswell) and 1384, para 70 (Lord Brown).
[144] [2008] 3 WLR 1284, 1305, para 7 of postscript.
[145] [2008] 1 AC 1356, 1383–4, para 66.

Convention,[146] had been rejected. He faced persecution back in Iran for his refusal, in an act of conscientious objection, to obey orders to continue, in his position as a specialist sapper, to lay anti-personnel landmines in a populated area of Iranian Kurdistan where no armed conflict existed. This refusal stemmed from a desire not to harm innocent civilians. He based his claim on the speech of Lord Bingham in *Sepet v Secretary of State for the Home Department*, where his Lordship stated that '[t]here is compelling support for the view that refugee status should be accorded to one who has refused to undertake compulsory military service on the grounds that such service would or might require him to commit atrocities or gross human rights abuses, or participate in a conflict condemned by the international community, or where refusal to serve would earn grossly excessive or disproportionate punishment'.[147] After several intermediate procedural stages, an appeal to the Immigration Appeals Tribunal was rejected on the ground that—since Iran was not a party to the Convention on the Prohibition of the Use, Stockpiling, Production and Transfer of Anti-Personnel Mines and on their Destruction (the 'Ottawa Convention'),[148] and since the rules of international humanitarian law depended on the existence of a state of armed conflict—the orders to which the appellant objected were contrary to neither national or international law, with the result that he faced no more than condign punishment for disobeying orders. A few more intermediate procedural stages later, the case came before the new Asylum and Immigration Tribunal (AIT), which held that none of the three limbs of Lord Bingham's statement in *Sepet* were engaged by the appellant's claim and that, even if the first had been, what the appellant had been ordered to do was not contrary to international law.

On appeal for the third time to the Court of Appeal, the appellant did not seek to circumvent the obstacle of Iran's non-participation in the Ottawa Convention by arguing that its provisions represented customary international law.[149] Rather, he referred to the Convention and to statements by the International Committee of the Red Cross 'to make good [his] submission that by 1999 the almost universal condemnation of anti-personnel landmines had placed their use in the category of atrocities or of gross abuse of the human right to life and bodily integrity', within the meaning of Lord Bingham's dictum in *Sepet*.[150] '[A]ccepting that international

---

[146] Convention relating to the Status of Refugees, Geneva, 28 July 1951 (entered into force 22 April 1954), 189 UNTS 2545.

[147] [2003] UKHL 15; [2003] 1 WLR 856, 863, para 8, citing *Zolfagharkhani v Canada (Minister of Employment and Immigration)* [1993] 3 FC 540; *Ciric v Canada (Minister of Employment and Immigration)* [1994] 2 FC 65; *Canas-Segovia v Immigration and Naturalization Service* (1990) 902 F 2d 717; and UNHCR, *Handbook on Procedures and Criteria for Determining Refugee Status under the 1951 Convention and the 1967 Protocol relating to the Status of Refugees* (1979, re-edited 1992), HCR/IP/4/Eng/REV.1, paras 169 and 171.

[148] Oslo, 18 September 1997 (opened for signature Ottawa, 3 December 1997; entered into force 1 March 1999), UN Treaty Reg No 35597.

[149] [2008] EWCA Civ 540, para 27.

[150] Ibid, para 41.

humanitarian law is formally confined to situations of armed conflict', he contended 'that by the end of the 20th century international human rights law had recognised that a state which in peacetime was prepared randomly to kill or maim its own citizens might be guilty of systematic abuse of human rights, and international refugee law had accepted that individuals who refused to obey their state's orders to commit abuses of such gravity were entitled to international protection'.[151]

The Court of Appeal (Civil Division), with Sedley LJ delivering the judgment of the Court, granted the appeal. It was common ground between the parties that, 'once it is established that the individual concerned has deserted rather than commit a sufficiently grave abuse of human rights, whatever punishment or reprisal consequently faces him will establish a well-founded fear of persecution for reasons of political opinion'.[152] In the Court's view, 'what th[e] appellant was seeking to avoid by deserting was the commission of what ... civilised opinion worldwide recognise[d] as an atrocity and a gross violation of human rights—the unmarked planting of anti-personnel mines in roads used by innocent civilians'.[153]

The Court agreed with the AIT that customary international humanitarian law did not forbid the use by Iran of anti-personnel landmines. Nor, as also held by the AIT, could there be 'any simple reading across into peacetime' of the restrictions placed on the use of anti-personnel landmines in warfare by international humanitarian law. But this did not necessarily render the Convention 'irrelevant to the argument from human rights to which *Sepet* points'.[154] As for common article 3 of the 1949 Geneva Conventions, which 'unconditionally prohibits violence to the life and person of non-combatants', while the Court was in 'no doubt ... that any belligerent state or group which sows and leaves unmarked anti-personnel landmines in a populated area violates this fundamental rule of human conduct', the absence of armed conflict in Iranian Kurdistan at the relevant time prevented the appellant's 'direct' reliance on the provision.[155] Again, however, it did not follow, as the AIT had held it did, that *any* reliance by the appellant on the provision was doomed to fail. He was 'still entitled to ask', as he did, 'why civilians should be entitled to expect less legal protection in time of peace than they would have if there were a war on'.[156] It was a question to which the respondent 'ha[d] been able to offer no answer of principle':[157]

His answer, like that of the AIT, is that for better or for worse the law of war and the law of peace have not marched in step. But the question for us is whether, in determining what the law of peace is in this context, the law of war has at least an analogical bearing. We see no reason why it should not, and very good reasons why it should. So did the International Court of Justice in the *Corfu Channel*

---

[151] Ibid.   [152] Ibid.   [153] Ibid.
[154] Ibid, para 28.   [155] Ibid, para 30.   [156] Ibid.
[157] Ibid, para 31.

case (ICJ Reports, 1949, 4) when it held that it was incumbent on a government which laid mines in its territorial waters to warn foreign shipping of their presence.

'Such obligations are based, not on the Hague Convention of 1907, No VIII, which is applicable in time of war, but on certain general and well-recognised principles, namely elementary considerations of humanity, even more exacting in peace than in war. ...'[158]

In the final analysis, however, it was to 'the normative corpus of human rights law, set in the foregoing context', that the appellant pinned his colours.[159] He pointed to article 6 of the International Covenant on Civil and Political Rights,[160] to which Iran was a party, which guarantees the right to life and, as such, prohibits arbitrary deprivation of life.[161] In this regard, it was relevant that the Court had held towards the beginning of its judgment that 'anyone who, and any state which, sows unmarked anti-personnel mines in terrain from which civilians are not excluded is responsible for the deaths and injuries which will result'.[162] As for the 'arbitrary' deprivation of life within the meaning of article 6 of the Covenant, the Court observed that 'few things could be more arbitrary than the death or maiming of a civilian, very probably a child, by the accidental detonation of an anti-personnel mine'.[163] In this light, the Court concluded:

It follows, in our judgment, that the order given to the appellant to plant anti-personnel mines in roadways was an order to commit a grave violation of human rights. If it is necessary to characterise such a violation as gross before it can rank as a sufficient breach to attract refugee protection, we would so characterise it. We would also characterise it, even in the absence of resultant deaths or maimings, as an atrocity. ... [A]s the courts have repeatedly recognised, no right is more fundamental than the right to life, and a state which embarks on a course which is bound sooner or later, save by pure chance, to rob innocent people of that right without any justification beyond the state's perceived self-interest is in our judgment—and, we say with some confidence, in the judgment of the community of nations—committing a grave breach of human rights.[164]

As for the respondent's argument, drawing on the words of Potter LJ in *Krotov v Secretary of State for the Home Department*,[165] that the breach of human rights law must be 'widespread or systemic, not isolated or localised', before a refusal to take part in it can ground a successful claim for refugee status, this was said 'in the context of a carefully drawn distinction between the law of war (which was what *Krotov* concerned) and the law of peace, which is at issue here':[166]

Where [the respondent] is entitled, as we have held, to rely on the distinction in order to block a simple transposition of principles from wartime to peacetime,

---

[158] Ibid.   [159] Ibid, para 33.
[160] New York, 16 December 1966 (entered into force 23 March 1976), 999 UNTS 171.
[161] He also pointed to article 7 of the Covenant, prohibiting cruel or inhuman treatment.
[162] [2008] EWCA Civ 540, para 18.
[163] Ibid, para 35.   [164] Ibid.
[165] Ibid, para 37.   [166] Ibid.

[the appellant], it seems to us, is equally entitled to rely on it to prevent the importation into the law of peace of restrictions apposite to the law of war. The restriction relied on by [the respondent] reflects the fact that the occurrence of atrocities in war is often the result of individual or local indiscipline, so that more—for example policy or system—is required if an objector is to be able to rely on his potential involvement in such abuses to secure international protection. But that has little if any bearing where, as here, the objector is a military specialist who has twice been ordered to carry out such atrocities.[167]

Moreover, the evidence was 'clearly indicative of policy and system': nothing suggested that the order to lay anti-personnel landmines was 'a one-off enterprise by a local commander', and a statement made a few years later by Iran to the explicit effect that it would continue to use such mines to protect its borders and to combat drug smugglers 'strongly suggest[ed] that it was not'.[168]

The Court of Appeal's judgment is essentially sound. Even leaving aside, as the Court might have done, the '[i]nternational morality'[169] reflected in the Ottawa Convention and common article 3 of the Geneva Conventions, it ought to be a relatively uncontroversial proposition that the laying of unmarked anti-personnel landmines in populated areas in time of peace amounts to a violation of the right to life. As for the application of Lord Bingham's dictum in *Sepet*, it might be noted that, while his Lordship was explicitly referring to the refusal to undertake compulsory military service, the appellant in the present case was a volunteer. But the distinction was not pressed by the Secretary of State. One might pause to wonder, however, whether Lord Bingham's statement in *Sepet* accurately reflects the current state of positive international law, given that a single Canadian case, a single US case and two paragraphs from UNHCR's *Handbook on Procedures and Criteria for Determining Refugee Status*—the authorities on his Lordship relies—do not, with respect, constitute 'compelling support' for the view that refugee status should be accorded to a person who has refused to undertake compulsory military service on the ground that such service would or might require him or her to commit atrocities or gross human rights abuses.[170] But the view itself—which amounts, for the purposes of the definition of a refugee embodied in article 1A(2) of the Refugee Convention,[171] to characterizing the prospective punishment of such a refusal as persecution by reason of one's political opinion—is a thoroughly

---

[167] Ibid.   [168] Ibid.
[169] See the heading to the passage beginning at ibid, para 21.
[170] See [2003] UKHL 15; [2003] 1 WLR 856, 863, para 8.
[171] Article 1A(2) of the Convention provides: 'For the purposes of the Convention the term 'refugee' shall apply to any person who ... owing to well-founded fear of being persecuted for reasons of race, religion, nationality, membership of a particular social group or political opinion, is outside the country of his nationality and is unable or, owing to such fear, is unwilling to avail himself of the protection of that country, or being outside the country of his former habitual residence as a result of such events, is unable or, owing to such fear, is unwilling to return to it.'

reasonable and enlightened one, and it is hard to imagine, given today's 'international morality', that too many States would contest it.

Convention relating to the Status of Refugees 1951, article 31(1)—protection from penalties on account of illegal entry or presence—penalty on account of illegal attempted departure—interpretation of treaties—Immigration and Asylum Act 1999, section 31— Criminal Attempts Act 1981, section 1(1)— statutory construction—abuse of process—whether Refugee Convention, article 31(1) providing protection from penalties on account of illegal attempted departure from transit State—whether Immigration and Asylum Act 1999, section 31 providing defence to charge under Criminal Attempts Act 1981, section 1(1) of dishonestly attempting to obtain air transportation services by deception

Case No 8 R v Asfaw, 21 May 2008, [2008] UKHL 31, [2008] 1 AC 1061 (HL)

Section 31 ('Defences based on Article 31(1) of the Refugee Convention'), paragraph 1 of the Immigration and Asylum Act 1999 provides that it is a defence for refugees charged with an offence to which the section applies, namely a range of offences to do with the falsification of documents, to show that, having come to the UK directly from a country where their life or freedom was threatened (within the meaning of the Refugee Convention[172]), they presented themselves to the authorities in the UK without delay, showed good cause for their illegal entry or presence, and made a claim for asylum as soon as was reasonably practicable after their arrival in the UK. Article 31(1) of the Refugee Convention, to which section 3(1) of the Act gives domestic effect, reads:

The Contracting States shall not impose penalties, on account of their illegal entry or presence, on refugees who, coming directly from a territory where their life or freedom was threatened in the sense of article 1, enter or are present in their territory without authorization, provided they present themselves without delay to the authorities and show good cause for their illegal entry or presence.

The appellant, an Ethiopian national, had left Ethiopia on a false Ethiopian passport, travelling with an agent, with the intention of claiming refugee status in the USA. After passing through immigration control with her in the UK, the agent provided her with a false Italian passport and a ticket for Washington, DC. When the appellant attempted to check in for her onward flight, the Italian passport was spotted as a fake, the police were informed, and she was arrested at the departure gate as she attempted to board the plane. During the ensuing police interview, she announced her wish to claim refugee status in the UK. She was prosecuted on two counts while her refugee claim was pending, the first of using a false instrument with intent contrary to section 3 of the Forgery and Counterfeiting Act

---

[172] Convention relating to the Status of Refugees, Geneva, 28 July 1951 (entered into force 22 April 1954), 189 UNTS 2545.

1981, the second, based on the same facts, of dishonestly attempting to obtain air transportation services by deception contrary to section 1(1) of the Criminal Attempts Act 1981. In response to the first, the appellant raised the defence provided for in section 31(1) of the Immigration and Asylum Act 1999, the offence with which she was charged being listed in section 31(3)(a) of the Act as one to which the defence was available. The jury acquitted her on this count. In response to the second count, she raised a preliminary objection that, although the offence with which she was charged was not listed in section 31 of the Act, she could nonetheless invoke article 31(1) of the Refugee Convention. The judge rejected the objection. The appellant pleaded guilty to the count, and was convicted and sentenced to imprisonment. The Court of Appeal upheld the conviction on the second count, but, having criticized the CPS for prosecuting it to conviction after the appellant's acquittal on the first count, substituted an absolute discharge for her sentence. In April 2007, almost thirteen months after the Court of Appeal's decision, the Home Office recognized the appellant as a refugee.

The appellant took her conviction on the second count to the House of Lords, where, in a change of tack, the Crown Prosecution Service (CPS) argued that neither of the charges fell within the scope of either section 31 of the Act or article 31(1) of the Convention, since they were committed in the course of trying to leave the UK and not in the course of entering it or as a result of the appellant's illegal presence in the country. There were accordingly two issues before the House, namely whether the appellant was entitled as a matter of international law to the protection of article 31(1) of the Refugee Convention and whether she was entitled as a matter of English law to the defence provided for in section 31(1) of the Immigration and Asylum Act 1999.

The House of Lords (Lords Rodger and Mance dissenting), answering both questions in the affirmative, allowed the appeal and quashed the appellant's conviction on the second count. Lords Bingham and Hope, with whom Lord Carswell agreed, made the substantive speeches for the majority.

Lord Bingham, directing his attention first to the interpretation of article 31(1) of the Refugee Convention, stated by way of preface that 'in construing any document the literal meaning of the words used must be the starting point' but also that 'the words must be construed in context' and that 'an instrument such as the Refugee Convention must be given a purposive construction consistent with its humanitarian aims'.[173] After recalling *inter alia* the judgment of Simon Brown LJ in the Divisional Court in *Adimi*[174] (which predated the 1999 Act), as well as the opinion of

---

[173] [2008] 1 AC 1061, 1079–80, para 11.
[174] The relevant passage of the judgment is to be found at ibid, 1083, para 18, quoting *R v Uxbridge Magistrates' Court, ex parte Adimi* [2001] QB 667, 687 (Simon Brown LJ).

Hathaway[175] and a memorandum of December 2005 submitted by the United Nations High Commissioner for Refugees (UNHCR) to a House of Commons select committee,[176] and having adverted to the fact that the appellant's claim for refugee status was ultimately accepted with the consequence that she was a refugee within the meaning of the Convention at the moment she preferred the forged Italian passport,[177] his Lordship concluded that '[o]n the facts of this case, as now established, the appellant should not in my opinion, consistently with article 31, have been subjected to any criminal penalty on either count of the indictment preferred against her'.[178] Lord Hope arrived at the same destination initially by more or less the same route,[179] although he added a few points of his own. 'As a general rule', he stated, citing *Shah*, 'it [was] desirable that international treaties should be interpreted by the courts of all states parties uniformly', so that 'if it could be said that a uniform interpretation was to be found in the authorities, it would be appropriate for the courts of this country to follow it'.[180] The problem, however, was that it was plain from the material before their Lordships that 'the situation in this case [fell] far short of that ideal', in that the Refugee Convention's *travaux préparatoires* were uninformative and there was no relevant judicial authority other than dicta in *Adimi*.[181] 'As for the rest', his Lordship continued, 'while weight [was to] be attached to the views of UNHCR in the light of its functions under article 35 of the Convention and to those of academics who specialise in this field, their assertions appear[ed] never to have been tested judicially elsewhere in the courts of the states parties'.[182] Lord Hope then came to the heart of the matter:

54 In this situation, as in *Shah*, I suggest that the best guide is to be found in the evolutionary approach that ought to be taken to international humanitarian agreements. It has long been recognised that human rights treaties have a special character. This distinguishes them from multilateral treaties that are designed to set up reciprocal arrangements between states. Humanitarian agreements of the kind to which the Convention belongs are entered into for a different purpose. Their object is to protect the rights and freedoms of individual human beings generally or falling within a particular description. As Judge Weeramantry said in *Case concerning Application of the Convention on the Prevention and Punishment of the Crime of Genocide (Bosnia and Herzegovina v Yugoslavia)* (1996) 115 ILR 1, 57 they represent a commitment of the states parties to certain norms and values recognised by the international community.

---

[175] Ibid, 1084, para 20, quoting JC Hathaway, *The Rights of Refugees under International Law* (Cambridge University Press, Cambridge, 2005), 372 n 412, 406 and 406 n 556.

[176] Ibid, para 21.

[177] Ibid, para 22.

[178] Ibid.

[179] See ibid, 1091–5, paras 43–52.

[180] Ibid, 1095, para 53, citing *R v Immigration Appeal Tribunal, Ex parte Shah* [1999] 2 AC 629, 657, (1999) 70 *BYIL* 295–301 (HL).

[181] Ibid.

[182] Ibid.

55 In *Shah*'s case the problem was whether Pakistani women accused of adultery were a 'particular social group' within the meaning of article 1A(2) of the Refugee Convention. Lord Hoffmann said, at p. 651 C-D, that the concept was a general one and that its meaning could not be confined to those social groups which the framers of the Convention may have had in mind. In this case a meaning has to be given to the words 'on account of their illegal entry or presence' in article 31(1) which identify the type of penalties that the contracting states are not to impose on refugees who satisfy the requirements of the article. I would not confine the meaning of that expression to the particular situations that the framers had in mind in this case either. The overall context is provided by the preamble to the Convention. It refers to the principle that human beings shall enjoy fundamental rights and freedoms without discrimination. It states that 'the United Nations has, on various occasions, manifested its profound concern for refugees and endeavoured to assure refugees the widest possible exercise of these fundamental rights and freedoms'. This is an indication that a generous interpretation should be given to the wording of the articles, in keeping with the humanitarian purpose that it seeks to achieve and the general principle that the Convention is to be regarded as a living instrument.[183]

In Lord Hope's view, 'the single most important point' that emerged from a consideration of the *travaux préparatoires* was 'that there was universal acceptance that the mere fact that refugees stopped while in transit ought not deprive them of the benefit of the article'.[184] In this light, 'it would be artificial in the extreme to deny [the appellant] the protection to which she would have been entitled had she reached the United States just because she was detected at Heathrow before she boarded her flight to Washington'.[185] The UK, having asserted jurisdiction over her on account of her presence within its territory, was obliged 'to assume responsibility for affording her the benefit' of article 31 of the Convention.[186]

Turning to section 31 of the Immigration and Asylum Act 1999, which postdated *Adimi*, Lord Bingham recounted statements made by the Attorney General during its drafting which indicated that the intention behind the provision was to give effect to the UK's obligations under article 31(1) of the Refugee Convention,[187] before concluding:

I am of the opinion that section 31 of the 1999 Act should not be read (as the respondent contends) as limited to offences attributable to a refugee's illegal entry into or presence in this country, but should provide immunity, if the other conditions are fulfilled, from the imposition of criminal penalties for offences attributable to the attempt of a refugee to leave the country in the continuing course of a flight from persecution even after a short stopover in transit. This interpretation is consistent with the Convention jurisprudence to which I have referred, consistent with the judgment in *Adimi*, consistent with the absence of any indication that it was intended to depart in the 1999 Act from the Convention or ... *Adimi*, and consistent with the humanitarian purpose of the Convention.[188]

---

[183] Ibid, 1095–6.   [184] Ibid, 1096, para 56.   [185] Ibid, para 58.
[186] Ibid.   [187] Ibid, 1086, para 24.
[188] Ibid, 1087, para 26. By 'jurisprudence', his Lordship means the views of scholars.

It followed that the jury in the present case was entitled to acquit the appellant on the first count 'even though the offence was committed when the appellant was trying to leave the country after a short stopover in transit',[189] the offence charged being stated in section 31(3) of the Act to be one to which the defence in section 31(1) applied.[190] But the offence charged in the second count, that provided for in section 1(1) of the Criminal Attempts Act 1981, did not feature in section 31 of the Act. Lord Hope—basing his view on a comparison between section 31(3) of the Act, applicable to England and Wales and to Northern Ireland, and section 31(4), applicable to Scotland,[191] and on the statements made by the Attorney General during the drafting of the Act[192]—thought that 'the absence of section 1(1) of the Criminal Attempts Act 1981 [had to] be regarded as an oversight', and not 'a deliberate omission from the list, designed to restrict ... the scope of the protection that was contemplated by Simon Brown LJ in *Adimi*'.[193] Whatever the origin of the omission, however, the upshot was a disparity between the scope of article 31(1) of the Convention and that of section 31 of the Act, 'and by no legitimate process of interpretation', declared Lord Bingham, '[could] those subsections be read as including the offence charged in count 2'.[194] This disparity could not be overcome by the contention, put forward by reference to *inter alia* the observations of Lord Keith in *Sivakumaran*[195] and Lord Steyn in *Roma Rights*,[196] that the Refugee Convention had been incorporated into domestic law:

It is plain from these authorities that the British regime for handling applications for asylum has been closely assimilated to the Convention model. But it is also plain (as I think) that the Convention as a whole has never been formally incorporated or given effect in domestic law. While, therefore, one would expect any government intending to legislate inconsistently with an obligation binding on the UK to make its intention very clear, there can on well known authority be no ground in domestic law for failing to give effect to an enactment in terms unambiguously inconsistent with such an obligation.[197]

It could not be successfully argued either that the appellant had a legitimate expectation that the UK would honour its international obligation under article 31 of the Convention: 'she [could] not, at the relevant time, have had any legitimate expectation of being treated otherwise than in

[189] Ibid.   [190] Ibid, para 27.   [191] Ibid, 1097–8, paras 61–3.
[192] Ibid, 1098–9, para 66.
[193] Ibid, 1099, para 67.
[194] Ibid, 1087, para 28.
[195] See *R v Secretary of State for the Home Department, Ex parte Sivakumaran* [1988] AC 958, 990 (the Refugee Convention having 'for all practical purposes been incorporated into United Kingdom law').
[196] See *R (European Roma Rights Centre) v Immigration Officer at Prague Airport* [2004] UKHL 55; [2005] 2 AC 1, 45, para 42, (2004) 75 *BYIL* 504–12 (HL) ('the Refugee Convention has been incorporated into our domestic law').
[197] [2008] 1 AC 1061, 1087, para 29.

accordance with the 1999 Act'.[198] Nor did the criminal defence of necessity stretch this far.[199] Lord Hope agreed on all three points,[200] adding:

The giving effect in domestic law to international obligations is primarily a matter for the legislature. It is for Parliament to determine the extent to which those obligations are to be incorporated domestically. That determination having been made, it is the duty of the courts to give effect to it. There can be no free-standing defence, nor can there be any legitimate expectation that one will be provided, where Parliament has chosen in its own words to set out the scope of the defence that is to be available. For the courts to add further offences of their own choosing to the list of those to which Parliament has said section 31 applies in England and Wales and Northern Ireland would not be to interpret the subsection but to legislate. Our constitutional arrangements do not permit this.[201]

Lord Bingham, however, continued:

31 The appellant also submitted that it was an abuse of the criminal process to prosecute her to conviction under count 2. That submission calls for closer consideration. It was not an abuse to prefer charges under both counts, since the respondent was entitled to question whether the appellant was a refugee, and if she was not neither the article nor the section could avail her. It is true that the two counts related to identical conduct and the second count served no obvious purpose, but the court could ensure, on conviction, that no disproportionate penalty was inflicted. If, however, the second count was included in the indictment in order to prevent the appellant from relying on the defence which section 31 [of the Act] would otherwise provide, ... there would be strong grounds for contending that this was an abuse of process. It is not at all clear what legitimate purpose was sought to be served by including the second count, and it must be questioned whether there was any legitimate purpose.

32 ... [T]here is an obvious inconsistency between [the trial judge's] grounds for rejecting [the appellant's preliminary] objection and his direction to the jury ... His grounds for dismissing the appellant's objection were also, in my opinion, wrong, since if the jury were to acquit the appellant on count 1 in reliance on section 31, it would be both unfair and contrary to the intention of the statute to convict her on count 2. The Attorney General expressly recognised that additional offences might have to be added to section 31(3), and when such offences, requiring addition to the list, arose in individual cases it would plainly be necessary to avoid injustice in those cases. There was in my opinion a clear risk of injustice in this case if the jury were to acquit on count 1 but convict on count 2.

33 ... It is ... apparent that counsel's preliminary objection to count 2 could only, consistently with article 31 [of the Convention] and the intention of section 31 [of the Act], have been fairly met by staying further prosecution of count 2 at that stage. If the jury acquitted the appellant on count 1, the stay on prosecuting count 2 should have been maintained. If the jury convicted the appellant on count 1, rejecting her section 31 defence, there would have been no objection in principle to further prosecution of count 2. But the appellant would be likely in

---

that situation to have pleaded guilty (as she did in response to the judge's ruling), and the question would arise whether further prosecution of count 2 could be justified: given that the judge had power to sentence the appellant to imprisonment for ten years on count 1, it could scarcely be suggested that his powers of punishment were inadequate to reflect the appellant's culpability.

34 … [I]n my opinion it was an abuse of process in the circumstances to prosecute her to conviction. On 14 February 2005 the appellant was, in the Attorney General's expressive phrase, 'still running away' from persecution. Once that was established, count 2 being factually indistinguishable from count 1, she should not have been convicted at all.[202]

Lord Hope took the same view. He conceded that '[t]he margin between declining to add to the list in section 31(3) and declaring that it was an abuse for the appellant to be required to plead guilty to an offence that [was] not on the list when she was still being prosecuted for an offence for which the defence under that section [was] available' was 'a narrow one'— but it was 'not illusory'.[203] He also acknowledged that the offences mentioned and the complainants named in each count were different—'[b]ut they were two sides of the same coin'.[204] 'As one attracted the section 31 defence and the other did not, the effect was to expose the appellant to the imposition of a penalty for doing something against which she was entitled to claim protection under that section.'[205] His Lordship concluded:

It seems to me to be plain that it was an abuse for the prosecutor to undermine the protection in this way. Section 31 must be read in the light of article 31(1) of the Convention, to which it was intended to give effect. There is no room in this context for the formalistic argument that the omission from section 31(3) of section 1(1) of the Criminal Attempts Act 1981 enabled the prosecutor to take this course. He was alleging that the appellant had committed one of the offences on the list. The fact that it was a listed offence was a sufficient indication that it was the intention of Parliament that she should have the article 31(1) protection against the imposition of a penalty for her illegal act, provided the requirements of section 31(1) and (2) were satisfied. She ought not to have been required to plead to the second count until the jury had delivered its verdict on the first count. As the jury found her not guilty on the first count, holding that the requirements of section 31(1) and (2) had been satisfied, her prosecution on the second count should not have been proceeded with. As it is, the way in which the prosecution was conducted in this case deprived her of the protection and it was an abuse.[206]

With this their Lordships allowed the appeal.

Lord Rodger, in the minority with Lord Mance,[207] had no truck with the claim that article 31(1) of the Convention extended to the appellant's case on either count:

82 My Lords, I should like to think that anyone who simply read the words of article 31, in either of the official languages, would be as surprised as I was to be

[202] Ibid, 1088–9.   [203] Ibid, 1099, para 70.   [204] Ibid, 1100, para 71.
[205] Ibid.   [206] Ibid.
[207] Lords Rodger and Mance expressly agreed with each other's reasoning.

told that it covered offences committed by a refugee in order to leave the country. On its face, the article is all about entry and presence and says nothing about leaving. And the starting point of any interpretation of the article must indeed be the language itself: *Adan v Secretary of State for the Home Department* [1999] 1 AC 293, 305, per Lord Lloyd of Berwick. ...

84 The fact that commentators and the High Commissioner support the interpretation of article 31 advocated by the appellant does not excuse your Lordships from the duty of forming a considered view of the proper scope of the article. Indeed, nothing in the relevant passages in the commentaries or other extra-judicial material cited by counsel actually grapples with the text of article 31 or shows how, on the preferred interpretation, article 31 fits into the overall scheme of the Convention. For my part, I have come to the clear conclusion that the interpretation favoured by the appellant is not only impossible on the language, but is actually at odds with the scheme of the Convention and with its true humanitarian philosophy.

The language of article 31 showed that what could not be penalized was a refugee's unlawful entry to, or presence in, a State.[208] As for the Refugee Convention's scheme and humanitarian philosophy, his Lordship first emphasized that, in order to enjoy the protection of article 31, refugees were required to present themselves to the authorities without delay and to explain to them why they had entered or were present illegally.[209] This did not, under the scheme of the Convention, expose them to return to the country of persecution, since article 33 prohibited *refoulement*. In this light, all refugees who presented themselves to the authorities could be thought of as claiming asylum, 'if not expressly, then at least impliedly', and this was reflected for the purposes of section 31(1) of the Immigration and Asylum Act 1999 in the definition of a 'claim for asylum' found in section 167(1) of the Act.[210] Lord Rodger continued:

92 It follows that a refugee makes a claim for asylum if he asks the authorities in a country not to throw him out or return him to the country of persecution, even though he simultaneously tells them that he does not wish to settle in their country, but wants to go on to another country. He is asking for temporary asylum until he can continue on his way. Indeed, any other interpretation of article 31 would be absurd, since it would force refugees to make a claim to settle in the country as a precondition to obtaining impunity for their illegal entry or presence. Yet, a major concern of those negotiating the 1951 Convention was that their governments would find themselves having to take more refugees than they could handle.

93 Commentators are agreed that the delegates who inserted the requirement for refugees to present themselves without delay to the authorities regarded it as important. Its purpose was to encourage refugees to come forward and regularise their position, rather than eking out an existence in an unlawful twilight world on the fringes of society.

---

[208] Ibid, 1105, para 89.
[209] Ibid, para 91.   [210] Ibid.

94 Indeed, the spirit behind the Convention is one of treating refugees humanely, as people having a recognised place in the legitimate world, not as beings who can exist only on the margins and by committing crimes which contracting states must then ignore. ...

95 It is wholly consistent with this scheme that contracting states need only overlook the initial offence of entering and being present illegally. After they arrive in a safe country, the refugees are to present themselves to the authorities who must then treat them in accordance with the Convention. In that situation the refugees have no justification for committing further offences to escape persecution and are bound by the criminal law, just like anyone else in the country concerned. ...[211]

The last point was made clear in article 2 of the Convention, which provides that '[e]very refugee has duties to the country in which he finds himself, which require in particular that he conform to its laws and regulations as well as to measures taken for the maintenance of public order'. Section 31(5) of the Act, which states that '[a] refugee who has made a claim for asylum is not entitled to the defence provided by subsection (1) in relation to any offence committed by him after making that claim', was consistent with article 2, and had the result that refugees 'cannot avoid punishment if they steal food on the pretext that they need it to feed themselves or their children, or if they break into a house to provide themselves or their children with accommodation, or if they use a forged ticket to travel by bus or train to the docks in order to get a ship to another country, or if, to catch a flight, they take a taxi to the airport and run off without paying the fare'.[212] 'In each and all of these situations', Lord Rodger stated, 'article 31 is quite deliberately silent and article 2 applies'.[213] He continued:

Equally deliberately, article 31 is silent and article 2 applies if refugees reach the departure gate in the contracting state and present false documents with the intention of travelling to another country in order to claim asylum and settle there. If they present false passports or visas in order to persuade the airline to carry them, they are practising a deception on the airline which could result in it being subject to severe penalties in the destination country, under the equivalent of section 40 of the 1999 Act. Not only would it require clear language to oblige contracting states to grant refugees immunity from an offence that could have such potential consequences for a third party, but it would be contrary to the philosophy of the Convention. Refugees who are in a safe country and who want to travel on to another country have no more right than anyone else to use criminal means to do so. To suggest otherwise is to treat them as a breed apart, not as legitimate members of society.[214]

His Lordship then considered the text, rationale and circumstances of drafting of article 28 of the Refugee Convention, in accordance with which Contracting States to are obliged to issue refugees lawfully staying

---

[211] Ibid, 1105–6.   [212] Ibid, 1106, para 95.
[213] Ibid.
[214] Ibid, para 96.

in their territory travel documents for the purpose of travel outside their territory,[215] before concluding:

> It is, accordingly, as plain as it is unsurprising that those who drafted the Convention did not overlook the plight of refugees who found themselves in a safe state but wanted to settle in another safe state. On the contrary, they designed a system that would allow refugees to continue their journey lawfully, even though they had no passport. The very last thing that the representatives would have contemplated was undermining this noble and humanitarian initiative by extending the provisions of article 31 to refugees who ignored the system and resorted to criminal means to achieve the same objective. As would be expected, therefore, none of the legislation of countries implementing article 31 ... covers anything other than offences relating to entering and being present in the country in question. [216]

Nor could Lord Rodger agree with the reasoning of Simon Brown LJ in *Adimi*,[217] which he would have overruled.[218] (There the Divisional Court had held that persons who transited a third State en route from the State of persecution to the intended State of refuge were still to be considered as 'coming directly' to the latter and so were not to be denied refugee status there; and that since, on this logic, the defendants would have been entitled to refugee status in their State of intended destination, they were not to be prosecuted for using false passports while in transit in the UK in order to board their onward flight.) First, as emphasized by UNCHR and illustrated by the Dublin Convention,[219] nothing in the Convention gave refugees the right to choose where to claim asylum, so that the appellant 'had no right to choose to claim asylum in America or to try to exercise such a right by committing offences in the United Kingdom in breach of her duty under article 2 of the Refugee Convention'.[220] Secondly, while there was 'no doubt that a refugee [could] spend time en route in an unsafe third country and still be regarded as "coming directly" to the receiving country for the purposes of article 31',[221] it did not follow 'that the same applies where a refugee stops in a country where he is safe':[222]

> In such a situation the refugee is no longer in danger of persecution. Rather, he is in a position to take the necessary steps to regularise his position by presenting himself without delay to the authorities. If he intends to do so, but is caught before he can, then he will not be deprived of the benefit of article 31. But where, as in the case of Mr Sorani, Mr Kaziu [the appellants in *Adimi*] and Ms Asfaw, the refugee does not present himself to the authorities and has no intention of

---

[215] Ibid, 1107–8, paras 97–100.

[216] Ibid, 1108, para 101, citing E Feller, V Türk & F Nicholson (eds) *Refugee Protection in International Law: UNHCR's Global Consultations on International Protection* (Cambridge University Press, Cambridge, 2003), 234–52.

[217] Ibid, 1110, para 108.

[218] Ibid, 1111, para 114.

[219] Convention determining the State responsible for examining applications for asylum lodged in one of the Member States of the European Communities, Dublin, 15 June 1990, OJ C 254, 19.8.1997, p. 1.

[220] [2008] 1 AC 1061, 1110, para 109.

[221] Ibid, para 110.   [222] Ibid, 1111, para 111.

doing so, the very terms of article 31 show that it does not apply so as to entitle him to immunity from punishment, even for entering and being present in the country illegally.[223]

Nor could it be assumed that the appellants in *Adimi* would have been entitled to immunity from prosecution for illegal entry in Canada, the State of intended refuge, since—given that they could have asked the UK authorities for a travel document on which to proceed to Canada lawfully, but did not—they may not have been able to show, to the satisfaction of the Canadian authorities, good cause for their illegal entry, as required by article 31 of the Refugee Convention:

Entitlement to refugee status and entitlement to impunity under article 31 are different matters and the relevant criteria are different. In these circumstances it cannot be assumed that Mr Sorani and Mr Kaziu would necessarily have been entitled to rely on article 31 in Canada. So the initial premise of Simon Brown LJ's argument—that they could have invoked article 31 in Canada—is not well founded. The conclusion—that they must therefore have been able to invoke article 31 to cover their offences en route in this country—is accordingly not well founded, either.[224]

'Furthermore', his Lordship added, 'the requirement for a refugee to present himself to the relevant authorities without delay is quite specifically designed to ensure that refugees regularise their position and obtain official assistance rather than proceeding by illegal stratagems and using the illegal services of shady agents'.[225] In this light, a failure to comply with the requirement '[could] not be brushed aside on the basis that the refugees would have been eligible for asylum in any event'.[226] Lord Rodger then came to his conclusion on article 31(1) of the Convention:

I would … hold that article 31 of the Convention has no application to a refugee, such as Ms Asfaw, who has entered the United Kingdom unlawfully and who then, very shortly afterwards, uses a forged passport to try to leave, in order to travel to another country where she would like to claim asylum and settle. According to the scheme of the Convention, having entered a safe country which is a party to the Convention, she had to obey the laws of that country. If she wanted to travel on to the United States, she had to ask the British authorities for a travel document and had to try to persuade the United States immigration authorities to admit her. If that approach is regarded as unrealistic or as otherwise inappropriate for the world of today, then the necessary change can only be made by the contracting States agreeing to amend the Convention and, in particular, article 2—in a way that would profoundly affect its basic philosophy and have a significant impact on the integrity of the criminal law of the States.[227]

This being so, sections 31(1), (3), and (4) of the Immigration and Asylum Act 1999 '[were] to be interpreted according to the ordinary meaning of the words in their context'; and there was no reason why the offence

[223] Ibid.   [224] Ibid, para 112.   [225] Ibid, para 113.
[226] Ibid.   [227] Ibid, 1111–2, para 114.

charged in the second count, that provided for in section 1(1) of the Criminal Attempts Act 1981, should have been listed in section 31(3) of the 1999 Act.[228] When the effect of article 31 of the Convention was properly understood, the abuse of process argument fell away, since it was for the prosecuting authorities, in consultation with the immigration authorities, to decide, in the usual way, whether it was in the public interest to prosecute a person in the appellant's position and, if so, on what the counts should be, and in the event that the refugee pleaded guilty or was convicted after trial, it was for the judge to decide what sentence was appropriate.[229]

Lord Mance similarly underlined that there was nothing on the face of article 31(1) of the Refugee Convention to suggest that the provision afforded protection to a refugee who committed an offence not of illegal entry or presence but, when leaving a transit State, of deceiving or attempting to deceive an airline or the like. The question was whether it was nonetheless 'implicit in [article 31(1)'s] aims, scope and language that such conduct be covered by immunity'.[230] To answer this, his Lordship turned to '[t]he starting point for the interpretation of an international treaty', namely articles 31 and 32 of the Vienna Convention on the Law of Treaties 1969,[231] emphasizing at the outset that '[t]he primary canon is ... interpretation in accordance with the ordinary meaning in context and in the light of the Convention's object and purpose' and that there was not, in the present case, 'any explicit suggestion of subsequent State practice establishing the meaning of the parties regarding the Convention's interpretation, although reference was made to views expressed by the United Nations High Commissioner for Refugees and by certain commentators which mention *inter alia* the practice of "some states"'.[232] After a painstaking analysis of the *travaux*, of statements by UNHCR and of academic opinion,[233] Lord Mance arrived at the judgment of Simon Brown LJ in *Adimi*, which he took to task. He started:

That a refugee may have some element of choice is undoubtedly true. There may be a range of countries of refuge to which he or she can travel directly from the country of persecution. But that does not mean that a refugee has any entitlement to travel indirectly via an intermediate safe country to a final country of refuge, and still less, to my mind, does it mean that a refugee has any immunity in the event that she or he seeks to achieve this by breaking the law of the intermediate country in order to leave it. The broad aim of article 31(1), with its requirement of 'coming directly from a territory where their life or freedom was threatened in the sense of article 1', was, as pointed out above, to counter any suggestion that refugees have a right to move voluntarily from one safe intermediate country to another and then claim asylum in the latter.[234]

---

[228] Ibid, 1112, para 115. [229] Ibid, para 116. [230] Ibid, 1114, para 124.
[231] Ibid, para 125, referring to Vienna Convention on the Law of Treaties, Vienna, 23 May 1969 (entered into 27 January 1980), 1155 UNTS 331.
[232] Ibid, 1115, para 126.
[233] See ibid, 1116–20, paras 27–35 and 1124–7, paras 147–54 (appendix).
[234] Ibid, 1120, para 137.

'What [was] absent from the discussion in *Adimi*', his Lordship continued, '[was] reference to any responsibility on the part of the refugee to
regularise his or her position in the intermediate state and to seek travel
papers there, if he or she wishes to move on to another destination'.[235] As
for the argument that the appellants in *Adimi* were entitled in the UK to
the protection of article 31 because they would have been entitled to it in
Canada, he stated that 'the suggested logic [did] not exist and [was] not
supported by either the drafting history or the final text of the Convention'.[236]
'Standing back from the detail', Lord Mance concluded his discussion of
article 31(1) of the Refugee Convention:

140 ... I agree with Lord Rodger ... that article 31(1) of the [Refugee] Convention
is not on its face concerned with offences committed in order to leave a safe
intermediate country for a preferred final destination. ...

143 [W]hatever view is taken of the width of the phrase 'coming directly' when
considering the position of a refugee who has reached his or her final destination
..., and even if one goes as far in this respect as the Divisional Court did in
Adimi, it does not follow that article 31(1) provides immunity if such a refugee is
apprehended seeking to leave the intermediate country by using false documents
to deceive the relevant authorities or airline. Article 2 of the [Refugee] Convention
provides:

'Every refugee has duties to the country in which he finds himself, which require
in particular that he conform to its laws and regulations as well as to the measures
taken for the maintenance of public order.'

Article 28 (in the case of refugees lawfully within a country) or article 31(2) (in
the case of refugees unlawfully entering or present in a country) entitles such
refugees to travel documents or facilities. Article 31(1) gives freedom from penalties
on account of illegal entry or presence. That connotes freedom from penalties
for use of false documents to enter or stay in a country where asylum could be
and was claimed. But nothing in its history or language suggests that its drafters
contemplated, or that article 31(1) covers or affords immunity in respect of, the use
by refugees of illegal means in an unsuccessful attempt to leave an intermediate
country, let alone one where such refugees were free both to claim and obtain
asylum.[237]

As for section 31(1) of the Immigration and Asylum Act 1999, 'construed
as a whole and in the light of its clear intention to give effect to article
31(1)' it was to be read as restricted to offences committed 'on account ...
of illegality entry or presence', in the words of the latter provision.[238] In
this light, moreover, there was no reason why section 31(3) of the Act
should have included reference to section 1(1) of the Criminal Attempts
Act 1981.[239] Finally, given that article 31(1) did not apply to the appellant's
case, any argument as to abuse of process was irrelevant.[240]

---

[235] Ibid, 1121, para 139.   [236] Ibid.   [237] Ibid, 1121–3.
[238] Ibid, 1123, para 145.   [239] Ibid.
[240] Ibid, para 146.

The majority's decision and reasoning on both main issues is, with respect, suspect. Lords Bingham and Hope's interpretation of article 31(1) of the Refugee Convention, like Simon Brown LJ's in *Adimi*, shows scant regard for the ordinary meaning of the terms[241] or, insofar as their Lordships depart from this, for the near-total absence of any subsequent judicial or other practice of the States Parties in the application of the provision which might support their reading.[242] (Lord Rodger's account of the context provided by article 28, on the issuing of travel documents, is also persuasive.) Lords Bingham and Hope's approach, with its vesting of generative powers in the 'humanitarian' character of the Convention, also stands in stark contrast to their firm refusal to read words into section 31(1) of the Immigration and Asylum Act 1999.[243] As for Lord Hope's characterization of the Convention as a 'living instrument', this vapid Strasbourgese is no more than a recognition of the fact that, in accordance with the ordinary rules of interpretation reflected in articles 31 and 32 of the Vienna Convention on the Law of Treaties,[244] the meaning of any treaty provision is not restricted to that envisaged by its drafters, and even less are the examples of its possible application so limited. Rather, the generally applicable rules on treaty interpretation permit a degree of evolutive construction[245] by privileging over the preparatory works[246] factors such as the ordinary meaning of the terms—insofar as this may have diverged over time from the original meaning and as distinct from any specific instances of the provision's application in the minds of the drafters—and any subsequent agreement between the parties as to the meaning of the provision[247] or subsequent practice of the parties in its application. Alternatively, even where the meaning of a provision does not change, its application may.[248] Calling the Refugee Convention a 'living

---

[241] See Vienna Convention on the Law of Treaties, art 31(1).

[242] See ibid, art 31(3)(b).

[243] It further contrasts with Lord Bingham's conservative dicta on the interpretation of treaties in *R (Corner House Research) v Director of the Serious Fraud Office* [2008] UKHL 60; [2008] 3 WLR 568, 584–5, para 44, below 459–67 (HL), although these were made in the context of a treaty with attached monitoring body (and, as it is, are overblown).

[244] The rules of treaty interpretation contained in articles 31 and 32 of the Vienna Convention have been recognised as consonant with customary international law: see *Territorial Dispute (Libya/Chad)* [1994] ICJ Rep 6, 21, para 41 and numerous cases since.

[245] The 'carefully and subtly graduated elements' of the rules on treaty interpretation (P Reuter, *Introduction to the Law of Treaties* (2nd Eng edn, J Mico & P Haggenmacher trans, Kegan Paul International, London, 1995), para 142) seek to reconcile the competing claims of stability and dynamism in treaty relations. See the final commentary to what became, almost unchanged, articles 31 and 32 of the Vienna Convention on the Law of Treaties, ie articles 27 and 28 of the International Law Commission's Articles on the Law of Treaties, in *Year book of the International Law Commission* 1966–II, 217–23.

[246] In accordance with article 32 of the Vienna Convention, the *travaux préparatoires* are merely a supplementary means of treaty interpretation, to be used only in order to confirm the meaning resulting from the application of article 31 or to determine the meaning when the application of article 31 leaves it ambiguous or obscure or leads to a result which is manifestly absurd or unreasonable.

[247] See Vienna Convention on the Law of Treaties, art 31(3)(a).

[248] See eg *Sepet v Secretary of State for the Home Department* [2001] 1 WLR 856, 862, para 6 (Lord Bingham).

instrument' (which every treaty is) is no licence for its judicial amendment, as Lord Rodger underlines. Equally, the non-synallagmatic character of the Convention's undertakings is irrelevant to their interpretation. As for the majority's reliance on the abuse of process jurisdiction to quash the second charge brought against the appellant, this is strained. For a start, Lords Bingham and Hope effectively hold that the CPS was obliged to consider legally dispositive of whether the appellant was a refugee the jury's implicit (and, for all anyone knew at the time, quite possibly ill-founded) belief that she was, rather than the Secretary of State's formal, then-pending determination of her claim. Secondly, the effective suppression of the second count via a finding of abuse of process sits awkwardly with *Rimmington*, in which the House of Lords ruled that it is not open to the courts to abolish existing offences.[249]

State immunity—immunity from execution—exception to immunity from execution in respect of property in use or intended for use for commercial purposes—State Immunity Act 1978, sections 3(3), 13(2), 13(4) and 17— whether monies held on behalf of State pursuant to World Bank Revenue Management Programme immune from execution

Case No 9 Orascom Telecom Holding SAE v Republic of Chad and another, 28 July 2008, [2008] EWHC 1841 (Comm), unreported (QBD (Comm Ct), Burton J)

In order to enforce an arbitral award rendered in its favour by an International Chamber of Commerce tribunal, the claimant sought a final Third Party Debt Order in respect of monies held by Citibank on behalf of the first respondent, the Republic of Chad. The relevant background is that in the 1990s the World Bank lent Chad approximately US $300 million to enable it to construct a pipeline across its own and Cameroonian territory to facilitate the distribution of Chadian oil, exploited commercially by several multinational oil companies, to international markets. A condition of the loan, designed to secure and facilitate its repayment, was the imposition of a 'Revenue Management Programme' (RMP) whereby all direct and indirect revenues generated by the oil and the pipeline were paid into an escrow account established at Citibank in London known as the 'Transit Account', from which amounts were set aside each month to service the repayment of Chad's debts to, *inter alia*, the World Bank. In addition, ten percent of direct revenues were transferred into a 'Fund for Future Generations'. The remaining funds in the Transit Account then passed into Chad's 'Borrower's Account', from which it was moved into a special oil revenue account held in Chad with a commercial bank, from where it would be transferred directly to Chad's central bank for use by

---

[249] See *R v Rimmington (Anthony)* [2005] UKHL 53; [2006] 1 AC 459, 480, para 31 (Lord Bingham) and 492–3, para 53 (Baroness Hale). The author is grateful to Professor John Spencer for this insight.

the government. The Third Party Debt Order was sought only in respect of the Borrower's Account. Section 13(2)(b) of the State Immunity Act 1978 ('SIA'), however, provides that the property of a State shall not be subject to any process for the enforcement of an arbitral award. But an exception to this is found in section 13(4), which states that execution is permitted 'in respect of property which is for the time being in use or intended for use for commercial purposes'. The term 'commercial purposes' is defined in section 17(1) of the SIA, in accordance with which 'commercial purposes' means 'purposes of such transactions or activities as are mentioned in section 3(3)' of the Act. Section 3(3), which in turn defines the term 'commercial transaction' for the purposes of section 3(1) (a),[250] reads:

(3) In this section 'commercial transaction' means—

    (a) any contract for the supply of goods or services;

    (b) any loan or other transaction for the provision of finance and any guarantee or indemnity in respect of any such transaction or of any other financial obligation;

    (c) any other transaction or activity (whether of a commercial, industrial, financial, professional or other similar character) into which a State enters or in which it engages otherwise than in the exercise of sovereign authority...

The question to be decided by the court was whether the monies in the Borrower's Account fell within the exception to immunity from execution provided for in section 13(4) of the SIA—in other words, whether they were property which was for the time being in use or intended for use for the purposes of such transactions or activities as are mentioned in section 3(3) of the Act. The first respondent submitted that it did not, arguing that the Borrower's Account was effectively a second transit account in respect of monies derived from the Transit Account proper, the ultimate destination of the funds from which was Chad's central bank, 'where it would then be used for sovereign purposes'.[251]

Burton J, in the Commercial Court of the Queen's Bench Division, held that Chad's Borrower's Account was not immune from execution.

His Lordship began by noting that the only subparagraphs of section 3(3) relevant to the instant case were subparagraphs (a) and (b),[252] so that the question was whether the Borrower's Account and its contents 'were for the time being in use or intended for use for the purposes of a contract for the supply of goods or services, or [for the purposes] of a loan or other transaction for the provision of finance'.[253] He also noted, recalling the judgments of Sir John Donaldson MR in the Court of Appeal and Lord

[250] Section 3(1)(a) of the SIA provides that a State is not immune from the jurisdiction of the English courts in respect of proceedings relating to a commercial transaction entered into by the State.
[251] [2008] EWHC 1841 (Comm), para 17.
[252] Ibid, para 14.   [253] Ibid, para 15.

Diplock in the House of Lords in *Alcom Ltd v Republic of Colombia*, that, since the words 'otherwise than in the exercise of sovereign authority' applied only to subparagraph (c) of section 3(3), the contracts or transactions referred to in subparagraphs (a) and (b) fell within the commercial transaction exception to immunity 'even if they [were] entered into or engaged upon by the State in the exercise of sovereign authority'.[254] He returned to the last point later,[255] where he further observed, relying for support on scholarly writing, that the language of section 3(3)(a) was 'very broad' and that the provision of finance referred to in section 3(3)(b) could be either by or to the State in question.[256] Without further ado, his Lordship then concluded:

I am entirely satisfied that this account, the Borrower's Account, was established by the RMP, and has been operated, specifically for the purposes of a commercial transaction, namely:

(i) so as to receive the proceeds of a contract for the supply of goods or services; and/or

(ii) so as to be part of a system specifically established for the purposes of (repayment of) the loans by the World Bank *etc* to Chad.[257]

With this, he made the Third Party Debt Order against Citibank.

His Lordship's strikingly brusque determination is far from obviously correct. While the monies in the Borrower's Account—the property in question for the purposes of sections 13(2) and 13(4) of the SIA—were certainly the proceeds of a contract for the supply of goods or services, it is hard to see how this makes them property which is for the time being 'in use or intended for use for' a contract for the supply of goods or services, in the words of sections 13(4). They were the product of, not the resources for, such a contract. Similarly, the monies in the Borrower's Account may well have been 'part of a system specifically established for the purposes of (repayment) of the loans by the World Ban *etc* to Chad',[258] but this does not mean that they were 'in use or intended for use' for those loans. They were what was left after sums destined for the repayment of the loans had been set aside. In all of this, the dicta of Sir John Donaldson MR and Lord Diplock in *Alcom* are nothing to the point. In the final analysis, the sums in the Borrower's Account were not themselves in use for anything, and were intended for use, after their transfer into the account in Chad and their further transfer directly to Chad's central bank, for sovereign purposes.

---

[254] Ibid, para 14, citing [1984] 1 AC 580, 586–7 (CA, Sir John Donaldson MR) and 603 (HL, Lord Diplock), (1984) 55 *BYIL* 340–3 (HL).

[255] Ibid, para 21.

[256] Ibid, para 22, citing A Dickinson, R Lindsay and J P Loonam, *State Immunity: Selected Materials and Commentary* (Oxford University Press, Oxford, 2004), 359, para 4.030.

[257] Ibid, para 23.

[258] Ibid.

*Extradition—abuse of process—Extradition Act 2003—whether plea bargain
by requesting State rendering extradition proceedings an abuse of process*

Case No 10 McKinnon v Government of the United States of America, 30
July 2008, [2008] UKHL 59, [2008] 1 WLR 1739 (HL)

The US government requested the appellant-defendant's extradition for
his having allegedly hacked, from his home computer in London, into 97
high-level US government computers operated by various branches of
the military and by the Department of Defense, intentionally causing considerable damage and network disruption and copying data and files to his
own computer. In accordance with US practice, the US prosecutor offered
the defendant a plea bargain whereby, in return for not contesting extradition and agreeing to plead guilty to two of the counts against him, the latter
would likely be sentenced to three to four years' imprisonment in the US
and, after six to twelve months, repatriated to serve the remainder of his
sentence in the UK. Given that he would be eligible for release after serving half his time, and released as of right after two-thirds, he might, according to the deal envisaged, spend as little as eighteen months to two years in
prison. If, on the other hand, he were to resist extradition and defend the
charges, the likelihood was that he would be sentenced to eight to ten years,
maybe longer, would not be repatriated and would be eligible for at most a
15% remission. It was also possible that he would serve his time in a maximum security prison. Subsequently, however, a US government attorney
swore an affidavit that the defendant's repatriation would not be opposed
were he to contest his extradition. The defendant declined the proposal. He
then challenged his extradition on the ground that, in view of the proposed
plea bargain, the proceedings amounted to an abuse of the English court's
process and that, as held by the Divisional Court in *R (Bermingham) v
Director of the Serious Fraud Office*[259] and *R (Government of the United
States of America) v Bow Street Magistrates' Court*,[260] the District Judge
(Magistrates' Court) enjoyed a jurisdiction under the Extradition Act 2003
to stay extradition proceedings permanently and discharge the defendant
in order to protect the integrity of the statutory regime.

On appeal to the House of Lords, where Lord Brown (with whom the
other Lords agreed) gave the leading judgment, the appellant's argument
was rejected. The 'essential questions' to be asked were—borrowing from
United States of America v Cobb,[261] in which the Supreme Court of Canada
reinstated an extradition judge's stay of proceedings in the context of a
plea bargain—as follows:

Did the US prosecuting authority here 'attempt to interfere with the due process
of the court'? Did it place 'undue pressure [on the appellant] to forego due legal

---

[259] [2006] EWHC 200 (Admin); [2007] QB 727, 764, para 97, (2006) 77 *BYIL* 464–9 (QBD (Div Ct)).
[260] [2006] EWHC 2256 (Admin); [2007] 1 WLR 1157, 1181, paras 82–3, (2006) 77 *BYIL* 520–3
(QBD (Div Ct)).
[261] [2001] 1 SCR 587.

process' in the UK and so disentitle itself from pursuing extradition proceedings? Would extradition in this case 'violate those fundamental principles of justice which underlie the community's sense of fair play and decency'? Would the appellant following extradition be paying 'an unconscionable price ... having insisted on exercising [his] rights under [English] law'?[262]

To be taken into consideration in answering these questions was the fact that English law was 'replete with statements of the highest authority counselling ... the need in the conduct of extradition proceedings to accommodate legal and cultural differences between the legal systems of the many foreign friendly states with whom the UK has entered into reciprocal extradition arrangements'.[263] With this in mind, Lord Brown unhesitatingly answered the questions posed in *Cobb* in the negative:

[T]he gravity of the offences alleged against the appellant should not be under-stated: the equivalent domestic offences include an offence under section 12 of the Aviation and Maritime Security Act 1990 for which the maximum sentence is life imprisonment. True, the disparity between the consequences predicted by the US authorities dependent upon whether the appellant co-operated or not was very marked. It seems to me, however, no more appropriate to describe the pre-dicted consequences of non-co-operation as a 'threat' than to characterise the predicted consequences of co-operation as a 'promise' (or, indeed, a 'bribe'). In one sense all discounts for pleas of guilty could be said to subject the defendant to pressure, and the greater the discount the greater the pressure. But the discount would have to be very substantially more generous than anything promised here (as to the way the case would be put and the likely outcome) before it constituted unlawful pressure such as to vitiate the process. So too would the predicted con-sequences of non-co-operation need to go significantly beyond what could prop-erly be regarded as the defendant's just deserts on conviction for that to constitute unlawful pressure.[264]

The differences between the instant case and that of *Cobb* were striking: there the trial judge himself had threatened, in the event of non-cooperation, 'the absolute maximum jail sentence' that the law permitted him to give, and the prosecutor had effectively threatened that the defendant would be subjected in prison to homosexual rape.[265] In conclusion, his Lordship stated:

In my judgment it would only be in a wholly extreme case like *Cobb* itself that the court should properly regard any encouragement to accused persons to surrender for trial and plead guilty, in particular if made by a prosecutor during a regulated process of plea bargaining, as so unconscionable as to constitute an abuse of proc-ess justifying the requested state's refusal to extradite the accused. It is difficult, indeed, to think of anything other than the threat of unlawful action which could fairly be said so to imperil the integrity of the extradition process as to require the

---

[262]   [2008] 1 WLR 1739, 1748–9, para 33.
[263]   Ibid, 1750, para 37.
[264]   Ibid, para 38.
[265]   [2001] 1 SCR 587.

accused, notwithstanding his having resisted the undue pressure, to be discharged irrespective of the strength of the case against him.[266]

The present was 'far from being such a case'.[267]

The Lords' decision cannot be faulted, and is supported, by way of analogy, by the case-law relating to the inherent jurisdiction on the part of the High Court to remedy executive abuse of process, as recognized in *Bennett*.[268] Cases like *Latif*[269] and *Mullen*[270] make it clear that the exercise of the *Bennett* abuse-of-process jurisdiction involves a weighing of the seriousness of the crime against the seriousness of the abuse of process. And in the present case, the appellant's deliberate deletion of critical operating systems files 'shut down the entire US Army's Military District of Washington network of over 2,000 computers for 24 hours, significantly disrupting Governmental functions', while his deletion of 'logs from computers at US Naval Weapons Station Earle, one of which was used for monitoring the identity, location, physical condition, staffing and battle readiness of Navy ships, ... render[ed] the base's entire network of over 300 computers inoperable at a critical time immediately following 11 September 2001 and thereafter leaving the network vulnerable to other intruders'.[271]

An application by Mr McKinnon to the ECtHR[272] was struck out on 28 August 2008.

Relationship between international law and English law—unincorporated treaty provision—administrative decision—judicial review—OECD Convention on Bribery, article 5—whether judicial review by reference to unincorporated treaty provision lying where decision-maker claiming to have taken provision into account

Case No 11 *R (Corner House Research) v Director of the Serious Fraud Office*, 30 July 2008, [2008] UKHL 60, [2008] 3 WLR 568 (HL)

Under article 1 of the Convention on Combating Bribery of Foreign Public Officials in International Business Transactions 1997,[273] known as the OECD Convention on Bribery,[274] each State Party is obliged to take such

---

[266] [2008] 1 WLR 1739, 1750–1, para 41.

[267] Ibid, 1751, para 42.

[268] *R v Horseferry Road Magistrates' Court, ex parte Bennett* [1994] 1 AC 42, (1993) 64 *BYIL* 447–52 (HL).

[269] *R v Latif* [1996] 1 WLR 104, 112–3, (1996) 67 *BYIL* 569–72 (HL).

[270] *R v Mullen* [2000] QB 520, 534–7.

[271] [2008] 1 WLR 1739, 1743–4, para 13.

[272] Application No 36004/08.

[273] Paris, 21 November 1997 (entered into force 15 February 1999), UKTS No 107 (2000), Cm 4852.

[274] The Convention 'is not strictly speaking an OECD Convention but a Convention negotiated within the OECD framework', and is open to states that are not OECD Members: N Bonucci, 'Article 12. Monitoring and Follow-up', in M Peith, L A Low & P J Cullen (eds) *The OECD Convention on Bribery. A Commentary* (Cambridge University Press, Cambridge, 2007), 445, 449. At the same time, in an 'unusual institutional [arrangement]', monitoring of States Parties' compliance with the Convention 'is entrusted to a full-fledged OECD body', namely the Working Group on Bribery in

measures as may be necessary to establish as a criminal offence the intentional offer, promise or gift of any undue pecuniary or other advantage to a foreign public official in order to obtain or retain business or other improper advantage in the conduct of international business. In accordance with article 5 of the Convention, investigation and prosecution of the bribery of a foreign public official shall be subject to the applicable rules of each State Party and shall not be influenced 'by considerations of national economic interest [or] the potential effect upon relations with another State'. The UK gives effect to its obligation under article 1 of the OECD Convention on Bribery by means of sections 108 to 110 of the Anti-terrorism, Crime and Security Act 2001, which render the common law of bribery and parts of the Public Bodies Corrupt Practices Act 1889 and the Prevention of Corruption Act 1906 applicable to the situations covered by article 1 of the OECD Convention. Article 5 is not incorporated into domestic law. For its part, article 12 of the OECD Convention obliges the States Parties to co-operate in carrying out a programme of systematic follow-up monitoring and to promote the full implementation of the Convention within the framework of the OECD Working Group on Bribery in International Business Transactions, unless otherwise decided by consensus among the Parties.

Exercising his powers under the Criminal Justice Act 1987,[275] which are subject to the superintendence of the Attorney General,[276] the Director of the Serious Fraud Office (SFO) initiated an investigation in 2004 into allegations that the UK arms manufacturer BAE Systems plc had procured by means of corrupt payments to Saudi public officials an extremely lucrative arms deal known as the 'Al Yamamah' contract—for which it was the main contractor—between the UK government and the government of the Kingdom of Saudi Arabia. The launch of the SFO investigation coincided with negotiations between the UK and Saudi Arabia for an extension to the contract by which the UK would supply Typhoon fighter aircraft. In 2006, the SFO attempted to investigate certain bank accounts in Switzerland in order to determine whether BAE had made payments in connexion with the Al Yamamah contract to an agent or public official of Saudi Arabia. In response, the Saudi authorities issued an explicit threat that they would withdraw from ongoing bilateral counter-terrorism co-operation arrangements with the UK, withdraw co-operation in relation to the UK's strategic interests in the Middle East and call off negotiations for the Typhoon aircraft. Her Majesty's ambassador to Saudi Arabia subsequently informed the Director of the SFO that the threats posed to national and international security by any such action by the Saudi government,

---

International Business Transactions, which serves a 'hybrid' function as both a 'body fully integrated into the OECD hierarchy', operating under the supervision of the OECD Council 'acting as the supreme governing body', and a 'Conference of the Parties' to the Convention: ibid.

[275] See Criminal Justice Act 1987, s 1(3)(5).
[276] Ibid, s 1(2).

the risk of which was acute, were very grave, stating that 'British lives on British streets were at risk'.[277] Similarly, the Prime Minister—basing his judgment on the highest-level intelligence and the assessment of the Permanent Under-Secretary at the Foreign and Commonwealth Office of the importance of Saudi Arabia to UK efforts to secure peace and stability in the Middle East—wrote a personal minute to the Attorney General in which he drew the latter's attention to the considerations at stake. In the event, after involved discussions within Whitehall, the Director of the SFO, referring to 'the need to safeguard national and international security' and the necessity of balancing 'the rule of law against the wider public interest',[278] announced his decision to discontinue the Al Yamamah investigation. Stating that he had taken account of and was acting in accordance with article 5 of the OECD Convention, he noted that '[n]o weight ha[d] been given to commercial interests or to the national economic interest'.[279] On the same day, the Attorney General made a statement to Parliament, in which he cited the 'clear view' of the Prime Minister, the Secretary of State for Defence, the Secretary of State for the Foreign and Commonwealth Office, the heads of the security and intelligence agencies and the ambassador to Saudi Arabia that 'continuation of the investigation would cause serious damage to UK/Saudi security, intelligence and diplomatic co-operation, which [was] likely to have seriously negative consequences for the United Kingdom public interest in terms of both national security and [its] highest priority foreign policy objectives in the Middle East'.[280] He indicated that article 5 of the OECD Convention on Bribery precluded him and the Director of the SFO from taking into account considerations of the national economic interest or the potential effect on relations with another State, and stated that they had not done so.

The second of the two issues before the House of Lords[281] centred on the Director of the SFO's public claim to have acted in accordance with article 5 of the OECD Convention.[282] The applicant-respondents argued, on the basis of *Launder*[283] and *Kebilene*,[284] that it was, as a result of this claim, open to the English courts to review the correctness in law of the Director's decision by reference to article 5 of the OECD Convention; that the Director's interpretation of article 5, *viz* that the expression 'the potential effect upon relations with another State' did not encompass threats to national and international security, should be held to be incorrect; and

---

[277] [2008] 3 WLR 568, 574, para 14 and 576, para 21.
[278] Ibid, 577, para 22.
[279] Ibid.
[280] Ibid, quoting Hansard (HL Debates), 14 December 2006, cols 1711–3.
[281] The first was a question of pure domestic law.
[282] The parties agreed that, had the Director of the FCO not taken the provision into account, his decision could not have been challenged for inconsistency with it, since article 5, an unincorporated treaty provision, did not sound in domestic law.
[283] *R v Secretary of State for the Home Department, Ex parte Launder* [1997] 1 WLR 839, 867 (Lord Hope, with whom the other Lords agreed), (1996) 67 *BYIL* 548–51 (HL).
[284] *R v Director of Public Prosecutions, Ex parte Kebilene* [2000] 2 AC 326, 367 (Lord Steyn).

that the Director's decision should therefore be quashed. The Director, who obviously believed that his construction of article 5 was correct, gave unequivocal evidence that he would have arrived at the same decision even if he had believed that discontinuing the investigation was incompatible with article 5.

The Lords rejected the respondents' argument.

Lord Bingham[285] was not convinced by the respondent's reliance on *Launder* and *Kebilene*, in both of which the court was prepared to review the consistency with the then-unincorporated ECHR of a decision claimed to be consistent with it. He pointed out that there was no issue between the parties in *Launder* as to the interpretation of the relevant articles of the ECHR, while in *Kebilene* 'there was a body of Convention jurisprudence on which the court could draw in seeking to resolve the issue before it'.[286] It was, in his Lordship's view, 'at least questionable' whether, had there been 'a live dispute on the meaning of an unincorporated provision on which there was no judicial authority, the courts would or should have undertaken the task of interpretation from scratch'.[287] 'It would, moreover', he added, 'be unfortunate if decision-makers were to be deterred from seeking to give effect to what they understand to be the international obligations of the United Kingdom by fear that their decisions might be held to be vitiated by an incorrect understanding'.[288] Moreover, in the instant case, account had to be taken of article 12 of the OECD Convention, on follow-up and implementation under the aegis of the OECD Working Group on Bribery in International Business Transactions. While this did not provide for binding judicial interpretation of the Convention, it did provide 'a forum in which and a means by which differences of approach to the interpretation and application of the Convention [could] be discussed and either reconciled or resolved'.[289] His Lordship thought it in the interests of a 'highly desirable' uniformity of interpretation and application among the States Parties that 'a national court should hesitate before undertaking a task of unilateral interpretation where the contracting parties have embraced an alternative means of resolving differences'.[290] As for the correct interpretation of the phrase 'the potential effect upon relations with another State' found in article 5 of the OECD Convention, Lord Bingham reflected as follows:

Clearly the investigator or prosecutor is not to be deterred by the prospect or occurrence of a cooling of relations between his state and that of the allegedly corrupt official, even if this escalates into a diplomatic stand-off involving (for instance) the denial of visas, the cutting off of cultural and sporting exchanges,

---

[285] Lord Hoffman agreed with Lord Bingham, and Lord Rodger agreed with Lords Bingham and Brown. Lord Brown himself agreed with Lord Bingham but added a few words of his own.
[286] [2008] 3 WLR 568, 584, para 44.
[287] Ibid, 584–5, para 44.
[288] Ibid, 585, para 44.
[289] Ibid, para 45.   [290] Ibid.

the obstruction of trading activities, the expulsion of diplomats and the blocking of bank accounts. But can the negotiators have intended to include multiple loss of life within the description 'potential effect upon relations with another state'? And can they, if so, have intended to deny to member states the right to rely on a severe threat to national security? ... The extreme difficulty of resolving this problem on a principled basis underlines the desirability of resolving an issue such as this in the manner provided for in the Convention.[291]

As it was, his Lordship found it 'unnecessary and undesirable to resolve these problematical questions', since it was clear that the Director had based his adherence to article 5 on the belief that it allowed him to take into account, as a public interest consideration, threats to human life, and he had, furthermore, given incontrovertible evidence that he would have taken the same decision even had he believed it was contrary to the OECD Convention.[292]

The Director's forthright evidence as to what he would have done had he believed that article 5 did not permit him to take account of threats to British lives also persuaded Lord Rodger, who likewise held it 'unnecessary, even supposing that it would be competent, for the House to interpret article 5'.[293] Baroness Hale took the same view, and noted that, as matter of domestic law, the Director was entitled to reach such a decision.[294]

Lord Brown accepted at the outset that, as *Launder* and *Kebilene* illustrated, 'there are indeed occasions when the court will decide questions as to the state's obligations under unincorporated international law'.[295] 'Why, then', he asked rhetorically, 'should the court here not accede to the respondents' invitation to construe article 5 and, if it accepts the respondents' contended for construction, quash the Director's decision and require it to be redetermined?'[296] His Lordship provided his own reply:

64 There is not to my mind any one simple answer to this question although I am perfectly clear that the invitation must be declined ...

65 Although, as I have acknowledged, there are occasions when the court will decide questions as to the state's obligations under unincorporated international law, this, for obvious reasons, is generally undesirable. Particularly this is so where, as here, the contracting parties to the Convention have chosen not to provide for the resolution of disputed questions of construction by an international court but rather (by article 12) to create a Working Group through whose continuing processes it is hoped a consensus view will emerge. Really this is no more than to echo ... Lord Bingham's opinion. For a national court itself to assume the role of determining such a question (with whatever damaging consequences that may have for the state in its own attempts to influence the emerging consensus) would be a remarkable thing, not to be countenanced save for compelling reasons.[297]

[291] Ibid, 585–6, para 46.   [292] Ibid, 586, para 47.
[293] Ibid, para 51.   [294] Ibid, 588, para 56.
[295] Ibid, 589, para 62.   [296] Ibid, 590, para 63.
[297] Ibid, 590–1.

No such compelling reasons existed here.[298] There were, for a start, 'very real differences' between the present case and *Launder* and *Kebilene*:

66 ... As Lord Bingham points out, ... there is a marked distinction between seeking to apply established Convention jurisprudence to the particular case before the court (as there) and determining, in the absence of any jurisprudence whatever on the point, a deep and difficult question of construction of profound importance to the whole working of the Convention (as here). Secondly, it seems to me tolerably plain that the decision-makers in both *Launder* and *Kebilene*, deciding respectively on extradition and prosecution, would have taken different decisions had their understanding of the law been different. In each case the decision-maker clearly intended to act consistently with the United Kingdom's international obligations whatever decision that would have involved him in taking. That, however, was not the position here. Although both the Director (and the Attorney General) clearly believed—and may very well be right in believing—that the decision was consistent with article 5, it is surely plain that the primary intention behind the decision was to save this country from the dire threat to its national and international security and that the same decision would have been taken even had the Director had doubts about the true meaning of article 5 or even had he thought it bore the contrary meaning. All that he and the Attorney General were really saying was that they believed the decision to be consistent with article 5. This clearly they were entitled to say: it was true and at the very least obviously a reasonable and tenable belief.

67 The critical question is not, as the respondents' arguments suggest, whether the Director's successor would make the same decision again once the courts had publicly stated that this would involve a breach of the Convention; rather it is whether the court should feel itself impelled to decide the true construction of article 5 in the first place. It simply cannot be the law that, provided only a public officer asserts that his decision accords with the state's international obligations, the courts will entertain a challenge to the decision based upon his arguable misunderstanding of that obligation and then itself decide the point of international law at issue. For the reasons I have sought to give it would certainly not be appropriate to do so in the present case.[299]

His Lordship continued by quoting from Sales & Clement, 'International Law in Domestic Courts: The Developing Framework' (2008) 124 *LQR* 388, 405–6, his subsequent reading of which had 'strongly confirmed' the view he had already formed:

'Part of the problem here is that the executive may not have any practical option but to direct itself by reference to international law, and if the rule of law in *Launder* is treated as unlimited it will lead to very extensive direct application of treaties and international law in the domestic courts, thereby for practical purposes undermining the basic constitutional principle about non-enforceability of unincorporated treaties. One solution might be for the domestic courts, in recognition of the limits of their competence to provide a fully authoritative ruling on the point, the limits of their competence under domestic constitutional arrangements to rule on the subject-matter in question and the dangers posed to the national interest

---

[298] Ibid, 590, para 66.   [299] Ibid, 590–1.

by them ruling definitively on the point at all, either to decline to rule or to allow the executive a form of 'margin of appreciation' on the legal question, and to examine only whether a tenable view has been adopted on the point of international law (rather than ruling on it themselves, as if it were a hard-edged point of domestic law). This is the approach which has been adopted by the ECtHR, when it has to examine questions of international law which it does not have jurisdiction to determine authoritatively itself. Adoption of a 'tenable view' approach would be a way—under circumstances where the proper interpretation of international law is uncertain, the domestic courts have no authority under international law to resolve the issue and the executive has responsibility within the domestic legal order for management of the United Kingdom's international affairs (including the adoption of positions to promote particular outcomes on doubtful points of international law)—to allow space to the executive to seek to press for legal interpretations on the international plane to favour the United Kingdom's national interest, while also providing a degree of judicial control to ensure that the positions adopted are not beyond what is reasonable.'

The article goes on to suggest that the *Launder* approach must indeed be subject to limitations, dependent perhaps upon 'the intensity of judicial scrutiny judged appropriate in domestic law terms in the particular context'. I have no doubt this is so and that the question will require further consideration on a future occasion.[300]

Lord Brown equally had no doubt 'that in this particular context the "tenable view" approach [was] the furthest the court should go in examining the point of international law in question', and it was clear that the Director held 'at the very least a tenable view' of the meaning of article 5 of the OECD Convention.[301]

Particularly if one reads Lord Brown's estimable speech first, the House's decision is defensible, subtle and probably even sensible. It represents their Lordship's first attempt to peg out the parameters of the rule laid down in *Launder* and *Kebilene*, a rule which manages where *Brind*[302] did not to hold executive decision-making to the standards of the UK's unincorporated treaty obligations—and thus a rule with implications for the constitutional separation of powers. Perhaps the most persuasive argument against judicial review along *Launder* and *Kebilene* lines in the present case is that put by Lord Brown where—in an appeal to policy on a point on which the Lords remain unencumbered—he asserts that '[i]t simply cannot be the law that, provided only a public officer asserts that his decision accords with the state's international obligations, the courts will entertain a challenge to the decision based upon his arguable misunderstanding of that obligation'.[303] There is, as his Lordship in effect points out in the previous paragraph, a world of difference between a case where the decision-maker's understanding of the relevant treaty provision is the basis of the impugned decision and one where, as in the case of the Director

---

[300] Ibid, 591–2, para 68.   [301] Ibid, 592, para 68.
[302] *R v Secretary of State for the Home Department, Ex parte Brind* [1991] 1 AC 696, (1991) 62 *BYIL* 437–40 (HL).
[303] [2008] 3 WLR 568, 591, para 67.

of the SFO's decision, it is extraneous to, albeit cited in connection with, it. The question must be whether, in the words of Lord Hope in *Launder*, 'a decision ... is flawed because the decision-maker has misdirected himself on the [treaty] which he himself says he took into account'.[304] If, despite the decision-maker's having misconstrued the treaty, the decision can be considered rational, for the reason that the construction of the treaty was immaterial to that decision and the material motivation was rational, the decision must surely stand.

More broadly, however, while there is an element of wisdom in the Lords' general comments as to the chariness with which domestic courts should approach the interpretation of treaties, especially when the States Parties have established an international forum for the resolution of differences, it is best not to overstate the point. To imply, as Lord Bingham does, that the English courts should shy away from deciding a point of treaty interpretation in the absence of a *jurisprudence constante* from the relevant international body is almost to forget that international law is treated as law in the English courts, which are presumed to know its content. To say that '[f]or a national court itself to assume the role of determining such a question ... would be a remarkable thing' is to imply that the national court would be usurping the role of any international counterpart (or, in this case, crypto-quasi-counterpart), when the reality is that, while decisions of international courts constitute subsidiary sources of international law in accordance with article 38(1)(d) of the Statute of the International Court of Justice, a decision of a national court on a point of treaty interpretation is merely one voice in the Babel of States Parties' subsequent practice for the purposes of article 31(3)(b) of the Vienna Convention on the Law of Treaties.[305] And to hint that a national court should restrain itself, when acting within its rightful constitutional province, for fear of the 'damaging consequences [its decision] may have for the state'—for which read 'the executive'—'in its own attempts to influence [an] emerging consensus' on the interpretation of a given treaty provision[306] goes close to a counsel of judicial abdication. All this said, in cases such as the present where it is unnecessary for the determination of the case before it for an English court to engage in the 'unilateral interpretation'[307] of a treaty, discretion may be the better part of valour.

By way of postscript, it is worth noting that the OECD Working Group on Bribery in International Business Transactions has taken a keen interest in the halting of the investigation into the Al Yamamah contract. In a press release of 14 March 2007, 'it maintain[ed] its serious concerns as to whether the decision was consistent with the OECD Anti-Bribery Convention', in

---

[304] [1997] 1 WLR 839, 867 (Lord Hope).
[305] Vienna, 23 May 1969 (entered into force 27 January 1980), 1155 UNTS 331.
[306] [2008] 3 WLR 568, 590–1.
[307] Ibid, 585, para 45.

particular article 5.[308] As a result of the discontinuation of the investigation, which served to highlight concerns previously expressed as to the UK's compliance with the Convention,[309] the Working Group undertook a so-called 'Phase 2*bis*' supplementary review of the relevant UK law and practice, which considered, *inter alia*, the House of Lords' decision in the present case, reporting on it as follows:

One ground for distinguishing *Launder* is … of particular concern. In the Al Yamamah case, the then SFO Director did consider Article 5 and thought that he acted in accordance with it. The House of Lords distinguished *Launder*, however, based at least in part on the Director's further assertion that he would have taken the same decision to discontinue the case even if he had thought that it was contrary to Article 5. The same argument could be made if the Director considered Article 5, but decided that in his/her view the national economic interest nonetheless prevailed. The UK government has not explained how such action would be consistent with the Attorney General's commitment to the Working Group that Article 5 will apply …[310]

As regards the status of article 5 of the Convention in UK domestic law, the report states:

The lead examiners consider that Article 5 must be equally applicable in all member states of the Working Group. Because the Article addresses investigation and prosecution decisions taken in the domestic legal order, it must apply with full force and effect in that sphere, both as a practical and legal matter, in order for its purposes to be achieved.

The lead examiners consider that the uncertain application of Article 5 in the domestic sphere as a substantive matter is inconsistent with the Convention. Rather than being generally applicable, Article 5 may only apply at most in highly specific factual contexts of uncertain boundaries. … The lead examiners accordingly recommend that the UK take all necessary measures to ensure that Article 5 applies to all investigation and prosecution decisions in foreign bribery cases.[311]

On 19 November 2008, the Law Commission published a report entitled *Reforming Bribery*,[312] in which the Commission recommended the repeal of the common law of bribery and its replacement with statutory offences, including a discrete offence of bribery of a foreign public official.

---

[308] 'OECD to conduct a further examination of UK efforts against bribery', OECD press release, 14 March 2007.

[309] See OECD Working Group on Bribery in International Business Transactions, *United Kingdom: Phase 2 Report on the Application of the Convention on Combating Bribery of Foreign Public Officials in International Business Transactions and the 1997 Recommendation on Combating Bribery in International Business Transactions*, 17 March 2005.

[310] OECD Working Group on Bribery in International Business Transactions, *United Kingdom: Phase 2bis Report on the Application of the Convention on Combating Bribery of Foreign Public Officials in International Business Transactions and the 1997 Recommendation on Combating Bribery in International Business Transactions*, 16 October 2008, 26, para 98.

[311] Ibid, 28.

[312] Law Commission, *Reforming Bribery*, Law Commission Report No 313, HC 928, 16 November 2008.

Prohibition on torture—prohibition on cruel, inhuman or degrading treatment or punishment—evidence obtained by means of torture—Convention against Torture and Other Cruel, Inhuman or Degrading Treatment or Punishment 1984, article 15—customary international law—jus cogens—obligations erga omnes—relationship between customary international law and English law—whether Secretary of State obliged to disclose documents allegedly evidencing torture on part of foreign governmental authorities

Case No 12 R (Mohamed) v Secretary of State for Foreign and Commonwealth Affairs, 21 August 2008, [2008] EWHC 2048 (Admin), unreported (QBD (Div Ct))

The claimant—an Ethiopian national resident in the UK but held by the US authorities at Guantánamo Bay, where he faced trial before a military commission—sought disclosure in confidence to his lawyers of certain exculpatory or otherwise relevant documents in the possession of the Secretary of State. It was common ground that the claimant had been held incommunicado between April 2002 and May 2004 by US authorities. He alleged that, during this time, he had been subjected to torture and cruel, inhuman and degrading treatment by US operatives in Pakistan, then irregularly rendered by the CIA to Morocco, where he was subjected to more of the same before being irregularly rendered by the CIA again, this time to Afghanistan, for another dose of such cruelty. He contended that he was transferred in May 2004 to Bagram in Iraq, where the mistreatment continued, as a result of which he had confessed to anything his tormentors wanted him to say and signed statements put before him by the US authorities. He submitted that he had done the same, for the same reasons, after his transfer to Guantánamo Bay in September 2004. It was on the basis of the statements made by him at Bagram and Guantánamo that he was charged with offences potentially carrying the death penalty and faced trial at Guantánamo before a US military commission. The documents he sought from the Secretary of State were alleged to corroborate his account of the circumstances under which he signed the incriminating statements.

The claimant's case was two-pronged. First, and principally, he sought a *Norwich Pharmacal* order, so named after Lord Reid's holding in *Norwich Pharmacal v Customs and Excise Commissioners* that 'if through no fault of his own a person gets mixed up in the tortious acts of others so as to facilitate their wrong-doing he may incur no personal liability but he comes under a duty to assist the person who has been wronged by giving him full information and disclosing the identity of the wrongdoers'.[313] The allegation was that the UK government was involved, however innocently, in the alleged wrongdoing by the US. Secondly, the claimant contended that customary international law gave rise to an independent common-law

---

[313] [1974] AC 133, 175 (Lord Reid).

obligation on the part of the Secretary of State to disclose the relevant documents. This contention was itself two-pronged. The first submission was that article 15 of the Torture Convention[314] imposed an obligation to disclose documents in order to ensure that evidence obtained as a result of torture was not invoked in legal proceedings in another State; that article 15 had become a rule of customary international law; and that, since customary international law was part of the common law, the Secretary of State owed a common-law obligation of disclosure in this case. Article 15 of the Torture Convention provides:

Each State Party shall ensure that any statement which is established to have been made as a result of torture shall not be invoked as evidence in any proceedings, except against a person accused of torture as evidence that the statement was made.

The second submission relevant to the alleged common-law duty of disclosure was that the status of the prohibition on torture as *jus cogens* binding on States *erga omnes* gave rise to an obligation of disclosure on the part of the UK, which passed into the common law as an obligation of disclosure on the part of the Secretary of State.

The Divisional Court made the requested *Norwich Pharmacal* order in respect of some of the information held by the Secretary of State, but found against the claimant on the alleged common-law obligation of disclosure. Thomas LJ delivered the judgment of the Court.

In considering whether to make the *Norwich Pharmacal* order, the Divisional Court 'attach[ed] particular significance to the nature of the prohibition on State torture' which was alleged to have been violated.[315] The prohibition on State torture had achieved the status of a norm of *jus cogens*, and generated an obligation owed by States *erga omnes*.[316] It was also clear that, although acts constituting torture had been 'regarded with particular abhorrence', 'a State's acts comprising cruel, inhuman or degrading treatment or punishment [were] also the subject of international prohibition and stigmatism'.[317] Accordingly the Court was 'bound to give great weight to these considerations' in the exercise of its discretion to make the order.[318]

As for the alleged common-law right based on article 15 of the Torture Convention, the Court acknowledged that the contents of a provision of a multilateral treaty could in time attain the status of a rule of customary international law, as had been explained by the International Court of Justice in the *North Sea Continental Shelf Cases*.[319] In terms of the contents

---

[314] Convention against Torture and Other Cruel, Inhuman or Degrading Treatment or Punishment, New York, 10 December 1984 (entered into force 26 June 1987), 1465 UNTS 112.
[315] [2008] EWHC 2048 (Admin), para 142.
[316] Ibid.
[317] Ibid, para 143.
[318] Ibid, para 144.
[319] Ibid, para 164, quoting *North Sea Continental Shelf Cases (Federal Republic of Germany/Denmark; Federal Republic of Germany/Netherlands)* [1969] ICJ Rep 3, 41–3.

of the provision in question, the Court remarked that it may well have been the case that the exclusionary obligation contained in article 15 of the Torture Convention had attained the status of a rule of customary international law, although it also noted that the House of Lords in *A (No 2)* did not endorse a submission to this effect.[320] In the final analysis, however, the Court was not required to rule on the issue, since it came to the 'clear conclusion' that, in any event, article 15 did not create, expressly or impliedly, the obligation of disclosure for which the claimant (referred to by his initials 'BM') contended:[321]

BM seeks to derive from Article 15 an obligation in customary international law on a State to disclose to a victim of torture information in its possession which demonstrates that evidence which another State intends to use against that victim was in fact obtained by torture. Applying the principles of interpretation of treaties set out in the Vienna Convention on the Law of Treaties, 1969, Article 15 does not, in our view, contain either expressly or by implication the obligation for which BM contends. ... [W]e have come to the clear conclusion that the obligation under Article 15 is directed to a State's control of proceedings within its jurisdiction and applies only to prevent the invocation of evidence procured by torture in proceedings for which that State is responsible. The obligation imposed is a high one. It is a duty to ensure that a specific result shall be achieved, to ensure that any statement obtained by torture shall not be admissible. A State clearly has the power to bring about and to ensure such a state of affairs within its own legal system but it would normally be powerless to ensure such a result within the legal system of another State. Indeed, the reading of Article 15 for which BM contends would require a very high degree of intervention by one State in the legal system of another State, a matter traditionally regarded as essentially within the exclusive jurisdiction and responsibility of the forum State. In the absence of clear evidence that it was intended to impose such a startling obligation to intervene in the domestic legal system of another State—and we are told by counsel that the *travaux préparatoires* of the Torture Convention provide no support for such a conclusion—we are unable to accept the exceptionally wide reading of Article 15 for which BM contends.[322]

The Court recalled that it had not been referred 'to any evidence of State practice, judicial decisions or writings of publicists which support[ed] the wide reading of Article 15' for which the claimant contended.[323] On the contrary, it was 'fortified' in its conclusion as to the scope of article 15 by the observations of the Committee against Torture in *PE v France*.[324]

---

[320]   Ibid, para 166, citing *A and others v Secretary of State for the Home Department (No 2)* [2005] UKHL 71; [2006] 2 AC 221, (2005) 76 *BYIL* 615–26 (HL).

[321]   Ibid.

[322]   Ibid, para 167.

[323]   Ibid, para 168.

[324]   Ibid, quoting (2002) 10 IHRR 42, para 6.3, emphasis added by the Divisional Court ('The Committee considers in this regard that the generality of provisions of Article 15 derive from the absolute nature of the prohibition of torture and imply, consequently, an obligation for each State party to ascertain whether or not statements constituting part of the evidence *of a procedure for which it is competent* have been made as a result of torture. The Committee finds that the statements at issue

It observed that, in the present case, the obligation under article 15 to exclude evidence obtained by torture was 'clearly directed at the United States of America, in respect of legal proceedings for which it [was] responsible'.[325] It was not possible 'to fashion from Article 15 an implied duty of disclosure on the United Kingdom of the kind contended for'.[326]

Turning to the claimant's second line of argument going to a common-law duty of disclosure, namely 'that the duties which necessarily flow from the status of the prohibition on torture as a rule of *jus cogens* imposing obligations *erga omnes* include a duty on a State to disclose to a victim material in its possession which would demonstrate that evidence which another State intends to use in proceedings against the victim was obtained by torture',[327] the Court considered it to be 'beyond dispute that the fact that a rule, such as the prohibition on torture, has achieved the status of a rule of *jus cogens erga omnes* in customary law gives rise to certain special consequences in international law'.[328] But '[t]he precise extent of those consequences ha[d], however, been more controversial'.[329] The Court undertook an extensive survey of the relevant domestic and international case-law,[330] as well as of the International Law Commission's Articles on Responsibility of States for Internationally Wrongful Acts[331] and commentaries thereto,[332] before summing up as follows:

179 The legal obligations ancillary to the prohibition of torture identified in the authorities referred to above are extensive. None of these authorities purports to provide a comprehensive statement of the legal consequences flowing from the *jus cogens* status of the primary rule. Nevertheless, it is significant that there is no suggestion in any of these passages of the existence of an obligation resembling that for which BM contends. There is, so far as we are aware, no judicial authority which supports the existence of such a wide obligation of disclosure. BM has certainly not identified any. This, of itself, is not necessarily fatal to BM's contention, in particular when one has regard to the rapidly developing nature of international law in this field. Nevertheless, BM's submission at present lacks any judicial support.

constitute part of the evidence of the procedure for the extradition of the complainant, and *for which the State party is competent. ...*').

[325] Ibid, para 169.
[326] Ibid.
[327] Ibid, para 170.
[328] Ibid, para 171.
[329] Ibid.
[330] See ibid, paras 171–8, citing *Al-Adsani v United Kingdom* (2002) 34 EHRR 11; *Jones v Saudi Arabia* [2006] UKHL 26; [2007] 1 AC 270, (2006) 77 *BYIL* 499–520 (HL); *Armed Activities on the Territory of the Congo (New Application 2002) (Democratic Republic of the Congo v Rwanda)*, *Jurisdiction and Admissibility*, 3 February 2006; *Prosecutor v Furundzija* (2000) 121 ILR 213; *A and others v Secretary of State for the Home Department (No 2)* [2005] UKHL 71; [2006] 2 AC 221; *Legal Consequences of the Construction of a Wall in the Occupied Palestinian Territory, Advisory Opinion* [2004] ICJ Rep 136; *R (Al-Rawi) v Secretary of State for Foreign and Commonwealth Affairs* [2006] EWCA Civ 1279; [2008] QB 289, (2006) 77 *BYIL* 523–33 (CA).
[331] UN Doc A/RES/56/83, 12 December 2001, Annex.
[332] International Law Commission, *Report on the work of its fifty-third session (23 April-1 June and 2 July-10 August 2001)*, UN Doc A/56/10, 30–143.

180 Furthermore, it does not appear to us that such an obligation is, as a matter of principle, a necessary corollary to the primary rule or to any of the ancillary obligations identified in the authorities. Lord Bingham's conclusion in *A (No 2)* that there is reason to regard it as a duty of States, save possibly in exceptional and limited circumstances, to reject the use of evidence obtained by torture is readily explicable as one aspect of the duty, identified, for example, in *Prosecutor v Furundzija* and in the Advisory Opinion on *Legal Consequences of the Construction of a Wall in the Occupied Palestinian Territory*, to deny recognition and effect to a state of affairs brought about in violation of the primary rule. By contrast, it seems to us that the ancillary obligation contended for by BM in the present case—an obligation on all States to disclose to any person claiming to be a victim of torture material which might support his objection to the admission of evidence said to have been obtained by torture in proceedings against him in another State—goes considerably beyond denying recognition or effect to a state of affairs brought about in violation of the primary rule. To employ the terminology of Lord Hoffmann in *Jones v Saudi Arabia* (at paragraph 45) the obligation contended for by the BM is not entailed by the prohibition on torture.

The Court continued:

181 There is, so far as we are aware, no support in any treaty for the existence of a duty of disclosure similar to that for which BM contends. In particular, we draw attention to our conclusion that no such obligation has been undertaken by the States parties to the Torture Convention. It would be surprising if customary international law imposed wider duties of disclosure than those undertaken by the parties to that Convention. The other treaties on which BM relies are identified ... above. They are, with one exception, all concerned with procedures before international tribunals. They are expressed in terms which provide no support for BM's case on this point. The exception is Article 10 [of the] Inter-American Convention to Prevent and Punish Torture 1985[333] ... The very general terms of this provision take the matter under consideration no further.

182 BM has not produced any evidence of State practice to support his contention. There is before us no evidence of the necessary widespread and general State practice or of the necessary *opinio juris* in relation to the obligation for which BM contends required for the creation of a new rule of customary international law. Similarly, we have not been shown any writings of publicists supportive of the obligation of disclosure in international law for which BM contends.

In this light, the Court was unable to conclude that there existed a rule of customary international law which required the UK to disclose the relevant documents to the claimant.[334]

The Court's judgment is beyond reproach, and its level-headed attitude to the '*jus cogens erga omnes*' argument, like that of the Lords in *Jones v*

---

333   Cartagena, 9 December 1985 (entered into force 28 February 1987), OASTS No 67. Article 10 reads: 'No statement that is verified as having been obtained through torture shall be admissible as evidence in a legal proceeding, except in a legal action taken against a person or persons accused of having elicited it through acts of torture, and only as evidence that the accused obtained such statement by such means.'

334   [2008] EWHC 2048 (Admin), para 183.

Saudi Arabia, is particularly welcome. A great pity from an academic point of view, however, is that, as a consequence of its finding that no rule of customary international law imposed on the UK an obligation of disclosure, the Court was not required to decide on the Secretary of State's submission on the relationship between customary international law and the common law, which ran as follows:

It was submitted, on [the Secretary of State's] behalf, that even if the obligations claimed by BM could be derived from customary international law, they do not enter into the common law in such a way as to create absolute rights in the manner for which BM contends. While customary international law is a source of the common law, the precise manner in which it is received into English law is a question determined by English law. It is said that duties owed by one State to another under customary international law do not automatically entail the existence of individual rights in English law to compel the United Kingdom Government to act in accordance with its duties under customary international law. In this regard reliance was placed upon *R v Jones (Margaret)* [2006] UKHL 16, [2007] 1 AC 136, in particular on the speeches of Lord Bingham at paragraphs 11 and 23 and Lord Hoffmann at paragraphs 65–66.[335]

It would have been interesting to see what good judges, such as those in the present case, would have done with this.[336]

European Convention on Human Rights 1950, article 8 (right to respect for family life) and article 14 (non-discrimination in application of Convention rights)—deportation to State not party to ECHR—family law aspects of Shari'a law—whether, on particular facts of case, deportation to non-Convention State where Shari'a law dictated surrender of custody of child a violation of ECHR, article 8

Case No 13 EM (Lebanon) v Secretary of State for the Home Department, 22 October 2008, [2008] UKHL 64, [2008] 3 WLR 931 (HL)

The claimant, a Lebanese woman, had married and subsequently divorced in Lebanon under *Shari'a* law, which dictated that she was entitled to remain living with her young son only until he reached the age of seven, after which physical custody would pass to the father (her former spouse) or one of his male relatives,[337] leaving her with mere rights of supervised access. Before the child's seventh birthday, the claimant fled with him to the UK, where her claim for recognition of refugee status was rejected. She sought to resist deportation on the ground that her return to Lebanon would amount to a violation by the UK of the right to respect for family life guaranteed to her by article 8 of the ECHR, as given effect under English law by the HRA. The Court of Appeal had

---

[335] Ibid, para 184.
[336] For more on the relationship between customary international law and the common law, see R O'Keefe, 'The Doctrine of Incorporation Revisited', above 7–85.
[337] Legal custody had vested in the father immediately upon divorce.

ruled that the claimant's involuntary return to Lebanon would not violate her right under article 8, whether read alone or in conjunction with the non-discrimination clause in article 14 of the ECHR, in that—given that she would have some right to contact with her son after his surrender to the father—her right to respect for family life would not be completely denied. When the case came before the House of Lords, the son, who had reached the age of twelve, who continued to live with his mother and who had not had contact with his physically abusive father since the latter came to the hospital on the day the former was born with a view to taking him to Saudi Arabia, was granted the right to participate as intervener.[338]

The Lords unanimously granted the appeal, holding that the claimant's deportation to Lebanon would constitute an infringement by the UK of article 8 of the ECHR, as secured to the claimant as against the Secretary of State by section 6 of the HRA. Lords Bingham and Hope gave the leading judgments, Baroness Hale and Lord Carswell agreeing with the reasoning of the former and Lord Brown with that of both.

Their Lordships recalled the case of *Ullah*[339] (the principles laid down in which were reiterated in *Razgar*, delivered the same day[340]), in which the House had ruled unanimously that articles of the ECHR other than article 3, among them article 8, could in principle be engaged by the removal of an individual from the UK. *Ullah* had also made clear, however, 'that the threshold of success in such a case was a very high one'.[341] While the precise test to be applied had been put different ways, the various formulations 'ha[d] been used to describe the same test, not to lay down a different test'.[342] Expressions such as 'flagrant denial or gross violation' of a right,[343] 'flagrant violation of the very essence of [a] right',[344] 'flagrant breach or violation' of a right,[345] 'flagrant, gross or fundamental breach of [an] article such as to amount to a denial or nullification of the rights conferred by it',[346] 'complete denial or nullification' of a right[347] and 'flagrant or

---

[338]   The Secretary of State acknowledged that the son might have had a separate claim of his own under article 8.

[339]   *R (Ullah) v Special Adjudicator* [2004] UKHL 26; [2004] 2 AC 323, (2004) 75 *BYIL* 439–44 (HL).

[340]   *R (Razgar) v Secretary of State for the Home Department (No 2)* [2004] UKHL 27; [2004] 2 AC 368, (2004) 75 *BYIL* 444–50 (HL).

[341]   [2008] 3 WLR 931, 946, para 33 (Lord Bingham). See also ibid, 954, para 57 (Lord Carswell), speaking of 'a stringent test, which will only be satisfied in very exceptional cases'.

[342]   Ibid, 947, para 34 (Lord Bingham).

[343]   Ibid, 946, para 33 (Lord Bingham) and 953, para 55 (Lord Carswell), quoting [2004] 2 AC 323, 352, para 24 (Lord Bingham), quoting in turn *Devaseelan v Secretary of State for the Home Department* [2002] UKIAT 702; [2003] Imm AR 1, para 111.

[344]   Ibid, 947, para 33 (Lord Bingham) and 953, para 55 (Lord Carswell), quoting [2004] 2 AC 323, 362, para 50 (Lord Steyn).

[345]   Ibid, 947, para 33 (Lord Bingham), quoting [2004] 2 AC 323, 367, para 69 (Lord Carswell).

[346]   Ibid, quoting [2004] 2 AC 323, 367, para 70 (Lord Carswell).

[347]   Ibid, 948, para 35 (Lord Bingham), echoing ibid, 946, para 33 (Lord Bingham), quoting [2004] 2 AC 323, 352, para 24 (Lord Bingham) and [2004] 2 AC 323, 367, para 69 (Lord Carswell), both quoting in turn *Devaseelan v Secretary of State for the Home Department* [2002] UKIAT 702; [2003]

fundamental breach of [an] article, which in effect constitutes a complete denial of [the claimant's] rights'[348] were to be assimilated to each other.[349] They also encapsulated the same test as that applied by Judges Bratza, Bonello, and Hedigan of the ECtHR in their joint partly dissenting opinion in *Mamatkulov and Askarov v Turkey*, where—recalling the requirement, in deportation cases engaging article 6 (the right to fair trial) of the ECHR, of a 'flagrant' breach of the right in the receiving State—they held that 'what the word "flagrant" is intended to convey is a breach ... so fundamental as to amount to a nullification, or destruction of the very essence, of the right guaranteed by [the relevant] article'.[350] The question to be determined in the present case was accordingly whether, on the particular facts, there was a real risk[351] that the removal of the claimant and her son to Lebanon would 'so flagrantly violate her, his and their article 8 rights as to completely deny or nullify those rights there'.[352] Lord Carswell cautioned that this did not mean, as the Court of Appeal had thought, that if the claimant 'retained any vestige of those rights her claim must fail': this formula was 'excessively restrictive and set[] the bar too high'.[353] The various statements in *Ullah* and *Razgar* and in *Mamatkulov* indicated that the correct criterion was 'the destruction of the very essence of the right guaranteed by article 8'.[354] Applying the test, then, to the appeal before them, all of their Lordships agreed without difficulty that, on 'the highly exceptional facts of the case',[355] the claimant's right to respect for family life under article 8 of the ECHR would be violated by her deportation to Lebanon.[356]

Four of their Lordships went on to express scepticism, purely *obiter*, towards potential claims in deportation cases founded on the combination of the right to respect for family life secured by article 8 and article 14's guarantee against the discriminatory application of Convention rights

---

Imm AR 1, para 111. See also [2008] 3 WLR 931, 953, para 56 (Lord Carswell), quoting *Government of the United States of America v Montgomery (No 2)* [2004] UKHL 37; [2004] 1 WLR 2241, 2252, para 26 (Lord Carswell), (2004) 75 *BYIL* 464–7 (HL).

[348] [2008] 3 WLR 931, 953, para 56 (Lord Carswell), emphasis omitted, quoting [2004] 2 AC 368, 403, para 72 (Lord Carswell).

[349] Ibid, 948, para 35 (Lord Bingham). See also ibid, 935, para 4 (Lord Hope) and 952–4, paras 53–7 (Lord Carswell).

[350] Ibid, 948, para 34 (Lord Bingham), quoting (2005) 41 EHRR 494, 537, para O-III14. See also ibid, 934–5, para 3 (Lord Hope), 951, para 45 (Baroness Hale), and 952–3 and 953–4, paras 54 and 57 (Lord Carswell).

[351] Ibid, 934, paras 2–4 (Lord Hope).

[352] Ibid, 949, para 38 (Lord Bingham). See also ibid, 934–5, paras 2–3 (Lord Hope).

[353] Ibid, 952, para 53.

[354] Ibid, 952–3 and 953–4, paras 54 and 57. See also ibid, 951, paras 45 and 46 (Baroness Hale).

[355] Ibid, 954, para 60 (Lord Brown). See also ibid, 940, para 18 (Lord Hope) ('a very exceptional case'), 941, para 19 (Lord Bingham) ('exceptional facts'), 951, para 47 (Baroness Hale) (a 'case so different from the general run of child abduction cases') and 954, para 58 (Lord Carswell) ('very exceptional' facts).

[356] Ibid, 940, para 18 (Lord Hope), 949, para 41 (Lord Bingham), 951, paras 46–7 (Baroness Hale), and 952 and 954, paras 52 and 58 (Lord Carswell).

where the argument was that the claimant would be subject to the family-law aspects of *Shari'a*. Lord Hope stated:

14 As this case shows, the principle that men and women have equal rights is not universally recognised. ... As the court said in *Soering* 11 EHRR 439, para 91, [however,] there is no question of adjudicating on or establishing the responsibility of the receiving state, whether under general international law, under the Convention or otherwise. Everything depends on the extent to which responsibility can be placed on the contracting states. But they did not undertake to guarantee to men and women throughout the world the enjoyment without discrimination of the rights set out in the Convention or in any other international human rights instrument. Nor did they undertake to alleviate religious and cultural differences between their own laws and the family law of an alien's country of origin, however extreme their effects might seem to be on a family relationship.

15 The guidance that is to be found in [its] decisions indicates that the Strasbourg court would be likely to hold that, except in wholly exceptional circumstances, aliens who are subject to expulsion cannot claim an entitlement to remain in the territory of a contracting state in order to benefit from the equality of treatment as to respect for their family life that they would receive there which would be denied to them in the receiving state. The return of a woman who arrives here with her child simply to escape from the system of family law of her own country, however objectionable that system may seem in comparison with our own, will not violate article 8 read with article 14. ... On a purely pragmatic basis the contracting states cannot be expected to return aliens only to a country whose family law is compatible with the principle of non-discrimination assumed by the Convention.[357]

Lord Bingham took a similar view:

Considerable emphasis was laid in argument ... on the arbitrary and discriminatory character of the family law applied in Lebanon, and it is plain that this would fall foul of both article 8 and article 14. But Lebanon is not a party to the European Convention, and this court has no standing to enforce observance of other international instruments to which Lebanon is party. Its family law reflects a religious and cultural tradition which, in one form or another, is respected and observed throughout much of the world. This country has no general mandate to impose its own values on other countries who do not share them. I would therefore question whether it would avail the appellant to rely on the arbitrary and discriminatory character of the Lebanese custody regime had she not shown, as in my opinion she has, that return to Lebanon would flagrantly violate, or completely deny and nullify, her and [her son]'s right to respect for their family life together.[358]

---

[357] Ibid, 939, the last sentence echoing *F v United Kingdom*, Application No 17341/03, ECtHR, Decision on Admissibility, 22 June 2004 (unreported), quoted by Lord Hope at ibid, 938, para 11. His Lordship also discussed *N v United Kingdom*, Application No 26565/05, ECtHR (Grand Chamber), Decision on Admissibility, 27 May 2008 (unreported) and *Z and T v United Kingdom*, Application No 27034/05, ECtHR, Decision on Admissibility, 28 February 2006 (unreported).

[358] Ibid, 949, para 42.

Lord Carswell agreed with both:

In deciding this appeal by the application of article 8 of the European Convention on Human Rights the House is applying the domestic law of this country, as it is bound to do. We have to do so by reference to the values enshrined in the Convention, the common values of the states who are members of the Council of Europe. We are not passing judgment on the law or institutions of any other state. Nor are we setting out to make comparisons, favourable or unfavourable, with Shari'a law, which prevails in many countries, reflecting, as Lord Bingham has said ..., the religious and cultural tradition of those countries. For this reason I share the doubts expressed by Lord Bingham and by my noble and learned friend, Lord Hope of Craighead, about the appellant's right to rely on a claim of discrimination under article 14 of the Convention.[359]

Lord Brown's views were of a piece with these others.[360]

The House of Lords' decision is a pioneering one. As acknowledged more than once in the various speeches, Strasbourg is yet to hold that any of the Convention rights capable of restriction has been violated on the facts of what has come to be known in the UK as a 'foreign' case—that is, on the facts of a case where a Contracting State's obligations under the ECHR are engaged by the extradition or deportation of the applicant to a State outside the Convention's *espace juridique*. Their Lordships' respective judgments are sound, even if Lord Carswell was alone in really grasping where the Court of Appeal had got it wrong.

European Convention on Human Rights 1950—*European Court of Human Rights*—*Human Rights Act* 1998—*doctrine of precedent*—*whether doctrine of precedent to be modified in cases of inconsistency between domestic authority and subsequent decision of European Court of Human Rights*

Case No 14 *R (RJM) v Secretary of State for Work and Pensions*, 22 October 2008, [2008] UKHL 63, [2008] 3 WLR 1023 (HL)

The claimant was on income support, in which was included a disability premium. As a result of his becoming homeless, the disability premium was cut off, in accordance with paragraph 6 of Schedule 7 to the Income Support (General) Regulations 1987. The claimant challenged the decision, arguing that the non-contributory premium was a possession within the meaning of article 1 of Protocol 1 to the ECHR. His claim was dismissed on the basis of the Court of Appeal's 2004 decision in *Campbell v South Northamptonshire District Council*,[361] which had not been overruled by the House of Lords. The Secretary of State conceded the point, however, before the Court of Appeal, in light of the 2005 decision in *Stec v United Kingdom*,[362] in which a Grand Chamber of the ECtHR had ruled

---

[359] Ibid, 952, para 52.
[360] Ibid, 954, para 60.
[361] [2004] EWCA Civ 409; [2004] 3 All ER 387.
[362] (2005) 41 EHRR SE 295.

that a legally enforceable right to receive a social security or welfare benefit was a possession for the purposes of article 1 of Protocol 1. The Court
of Appeal made clear, however, that but for the Secretary of State's concession, it would have felt bound to follow its own previous decision in
Campbell, leaving it to the Lords to overrule it. The relevant principle
was that laid down by Lord Greene MR in *Young v Bristol Aeroplane Co
Ltd*[363] (as approved by the Lords[364] and reaffirmed in *Davis v Johnson*[365])
in which his Lordship held that the Court of Appeal was bound to follow
one of its own decisions unless there were two conflicting decisions, unless
the decision '[could] not stand' with a decision of the House of Lords or
unless the decision was given *per incuriam*. The Court of Appeal also
distinguished the decision in *Kay*,[366] in which the House of Lords ruled
that when faced with a prior decision of the House and a subsequent
inconsistent decision of the ECtHR, the Court of Appeal was to abide by
the doctrine of precedent and leave it to the Lords to overrule themselves
(except in a single 'very exceptional' circumstance, which constituted the
'one partial exception'[367]). In the event, the claimant's appeal was upheld,
and the Secretary of State appealed to the House of Lords, where the
concession in relation to article 1 of Protocol 1 was withdrawn.

   The House's decision is not itself important for present purposes. Of
interest is the dicta of Lord Neuberger (with whom the other Lords agreed)
as to what the Court of Appeal should do when faced with one of its previous
decisions and a subsequent contrary decision of the ECtHR.

   In Lord Neuberger's opinion, there was a difference between the situation in *Kay*, where the Court of Appeal was confronted by a decision of
the House of Lords, and the present case, where the earlier English decision was its own.[368] In the former case, the Court of Appeal was (except
in the 'wholly exceptional circumstances' specified in *Kay*) to follow the
House of Lords' decision: '[a]s a matter of principle, it should be for th[e]
House, not for the Court of Appeal, to determine whether one of its earlier
decisions has been overtaken by a decision of the ECtHR'.[369] But both *Young*
and more recent jurisprudence on the notion of '*per incuriam*' showed that
the Court of Appeal was 'freer to depart from its earlier decisions than
from those of th[e] House'.[370] His Lordship continued:

The principle promulgated in *Young* [1944] KB 718 was, of course, laid down at
a time when there were no international courts whose decisions had the domestic
force which decisions of the ECtHR now have, following the passing of the 1998
Act, and in particular section 2(1)(a). In my judgment, the law in areas such as
that of precedent should be free to develop, albeit in a principled and cautious

---

[363]   [1944] KB 718, 729–30.
[364]   [1946] AC 163, 168.
[365]   [1979] AC 264, 323–4, 336 and 349.
[366]   [2006] UKHL 10; [2006] 2 AC 465, (2006) 77 *BYIL* 469–72 (HL).
[367]   See [2006] 2 AC 465, 497–8, para 45.
[368]   [2008] 3 WLR 1023 1042, para 63.
[369]   Ibid, para 64.   [370]   Ibid, para 65.

fashion, to take into account such changes. Accordingly, I would hold that, where it concludes that one of its previous decisions is inconsistent with a subsequent decision of the ECtHR, the Court of Appeal should be free (but not obliged) to depart from that decision.[371]

His Lordship noted that his reasoning and conclusion on the point was not dissimilar to those of Jacob LJ (giving the judgment of the Court) in *Actavis UK Ltd v Merck & Co Inc*,[372] where the latter held that the Court of Appeal should be free to depart from one of its previous decisions if satisfied that it is inconsistent with a subsequent decision of the European Patent Office (EPO) Board of Appeal. Lord Neuberger agreed with Jacobs LJ to this extent.[373] But he disagreed on two other points. First, he did not, for the reasons outlined in *Kay* and underlined by his Lordship in the present case, believe that the Court of Appeal was free to depart from a decision of the House of Lords which the former considered inconsistent with a subsequent decision of the EPO Board of Appeal. This was for the House of Lords alone to do.[374] Secondly, he did not think that there was any reason for having a different rule for decisions of the EPO Board of Appeal, on the one hand, and of the ECtHR, on the other. He did accept, however, 'that (particularly in relation to decisions which are not of the Grand Chamber) the Court of Appeal may be less ready to depart from one of its earlier decisions which is inconsistent with a decision of the ECtHR than one which is inconsistent with a decision of the [EPO] Board [of Appeal]'.[375]

United Nations Security Council resolutions 1267 (1999), 1333 (2000) and 1390 (2002)—Al-Qaida and Taliban Sanctions Committee—United Nations Security Council resolution 1373 (2001)—United Nations Act 1946—Al-Qaida and Taliban (United Nations Measures) Order 2006—Terrorism (United Nations Measures) Order 2006—asset freezing—whether Al-Qaida and Taliban (United Nations Measures) Order and Terrorism (United Nations Measures) Order ultra vires the United Nations Act

Case No 15 A, K, M, Q and G v HM Treasury, 30 October 2008, [2008] EWCA Civ 1187, unreported (CA (Civ Div))

United Nations Security Council resolutions 1333 (2000) of 19 December 2000 and 1390 (2002) of 16 January 2002, adopted under article 41 of the UN Charter, oblige UN Member States to freeze the funds and other financial assets and economic resources of Usama bin Laden, members of the Al-Qaida organization and the Taliban, and of other individuals, groups, undertakings and entities associated with bin Laden. The specific persons against whom such measures are to be taken are designated by the Committee established under paragraph 6 of resolution 1267 (1999) of

---

[371] Ibid, para 66.   [372] [2008] EWCA Civ 444; [2008] 1 All ER 196.
[373] [2008] 3 WLR 1023 1042–3, para 67.
[374] Ibid 1043, para 67.   [375] Ibid.

15 October 1999, known as the 'Al-Qaida and Taliban Sanctions Committee', which adds their names to a Consolidated List kept by it. The Committee designates persons on the basis of lists transmitted to it by Member States.[376] Removal of names from the Consolidated List is also possible. Serious questions of due process have been raised in relation to persons and organizations listed in accordance with resolutions 1333 (2000) and 1390 (2002).[377] The Committee, which meets in closed session, exercises effectively unrestrained discretionary powers and, despite the severity of the measures at stake, there are no genuine procedural safeguards built into the programme. Persons to be listed have no right to be heard by the Committee and no formal power to challenge a decision. Their only hope of international recourse until recently was to convince their State of nationality to seek the removal of their names. Where it is that very State which has sought their listing in the first place, this is generally unrealistic. Things have been ameliorated in theory by the creation of the so-called 'focal point' mechanism via Security Council resolution 1730 (2006) of 19 December 2006, but the improvement is more cosmetic than real.[378]

Security Council resolution 1373 (2001) of 28 September 2001, also adopted under article 41 of the UN Charter, obliges UN Member States to '[f]reeze without delay funds and other financial assets or economic resources of persons who commit, or attempt to commit, terrorist acts or participate in or facilitate the commission of terrorist acts; of entities owned or controlled directly or indirectly by such persons; and of persons and entities acting on behalf of, or at the direction of such persons and entities, including funds derived or generated from property owned or

---

[376] The mandate and *modus operandi* of the Committee have evolved over time, via SC res 1452 (2002), 20 December 2002; SC res 1455 (2003), 17 January 2003; SC res 1526 (2004), 30 January 2004; SC res 1617 (2005), 29 July 2005; SC res 1730 (2006), 19 December 2006; SC res 1735 (2006), 22 December 2006; and SC res 1822 (2008), 30 June 2008. For the current state of play, see SC res 1822 (2008), 30 June 2008 and Security Council Committee established pursuant to Resolution 1267 (1999) concerning Al-Qaida and the Taliban and Associated Individuals and Entities, *Guidelines of the Committee for the Conduct of Its Work* (as amended 9 December 2008), <http://www.un.org/sc/committees/1267/pdf/1267_guidelines.pdf>.

[377] See eg Parliamentary Assembly of the Council of Europe Resolution 1597 (2008), 23 January 2008 ('United Nations Security Council and European Union blacklists') and Parliamentary Assembly of the Council of Europe Recommendation 1824 (2008), 23 January 2008 ('United Nations Security Council and European Union blacklists'); *Kadi and Al Barakaat International Foundation v Council of the European Union and Commission of the European Communities*, Joined cases C-402/05 P and C-415/05 P, Judgment of the Court (Grand Chamber), 3 September 2008.

[378] It should be borne in mind that the measures specified in Security Council resolutions 1333 (2000) and 1390 (2002) are not formally punitive, but rather preventive, as highlighted in the preamble to SC resolution 1822 (2008) of 30 June 2008, where the Security Council reiterated that the measures imposed by the 1273/1333/1390 regime 'are preventative in nature and are not reliant upon criminal standards set out under national law'. The distinction, however, may be lost on the individual targeted, as noted by the Grand Chamber of the European Court of Justice in *Kadi and Al Barakaat*, para 358, where the Court stated: 'Th[e relevant] freezing measure constitutes a temporary precautionary measure which is not supposed to deprive those persons of their property. It does, however, undeniably entail a restriction of the exercise of Mr Kadi's right to property that must, moreover, be classified as considerable, having regard to the general application of the freezing measure and the fact that it has been applied to him since 20 October 2001.'

controlled directly or indirectly by such persons and associated persons and entities'.[379] The terms 'terrorism', 'terrorists' and 'terrorist acts' are not defined in resolution 1373 (2001). Whether or not a given individual or organization is characterized as terrorist for the purposes of the resolution is determined by each Member State—and not by the so-called Counter-Terrorism Committee established pursuant to paragraph 6 of resolution 1373 (2001). The last represents a point of distinction between the 1267/1333/1390 regime and the 1373 regime.

The UK government gives domestic effect to its UN sanctions obligations by means of Orders in Council made under powers conferred by section 1(1) of the United Nations Act 1946, which provides as follows:

If, under Article forty-one of the Charter of the United Nations signed at San Francisco on the twenty-sixth day of June, nineteen hundred and forty five (being the Article which relates to measures not involving the use of armed force) the Security Council of the United Nations call upon His Majesty's Government in the United Kingdom to apply any measures to give effect to any decision of that Council, His Majesty may by Order in Council make such provision as appears to Him necessary or expedient for enabling those measures to be effectively applied ...

The 1267/1333/1390 regime of asset-freezing was given domestic effect by means of the Al-Qaida and Taliban (United Nations Measures) Order 2006 ('the Al-Qaida Order'), the 1373 regime by means of the Terrorism (United Nations Measures) Order 2006 ('the Terrorism Order'). The Al-Qaida Order provides in relevant Part:

3. Designated persons

    (1) For the purposes of this Order—

        (a) Usama bin Laden,
        (b) any person designated by the Sanctions Committee, and
        (c) any person identified in a direction, is a designated person.

    (2) In this Part 'direction' ... means a direction given by the Treasury under article 4(1).

4. Treasury's power to designate persons

    (1) Where any condition in paragraph (2) is satisfied, the Treasury may give a direction that a person identified in the direction is designated for the purposes of this Order.

    (2) The conditions are that the Treasury have reasonable grounds for suspecting that the person is or may be—

        (a) Usama bin Laden;
        (b) a person designated by the Sanctions Committee;

---

[379] SC res 1373 (2001), 28 September 2001, para 1(c). See also, subsequently, SC res 1377 (2001), 12 November 2001; SC res 1456 (2003), 20 January 2003; SC res 1566 (2004), 8 October 2004; and SC res 1624 (2005), 11 September 2005.

(c) a person owned or controlled, directly or indirectly, by a designated person; or

(d) a person acting on behalf of or at the direction of a designated person.[380]

In accordance with what was then article 5(4) of the Al-Qaida Order,[381] an application to the High Court to set aside a direction by HM Treasury under article 4(2) could be made by the person identified in the direction or by any other person affected by the direction. Since a person's automatic designation for the purposes of English law, pursuant to article 3(1)(b) of the Order, on account of his or her international designation by the Al-Qaida and Taliban Sanctions Committee did not involve a direction by the Treasury, no express right of High Court challenge lay in this respect. For its part, the Terrorism Order provides, as relevant:

3. Designated persons

(1) For the purposes of this Order a person is a designated person if—

(a) he is identified in the Council Decision [*i.e.* Council Decision 2006/379/EC], or

(b) he is identified in a direction.

(2) In this Part 'direction' … means a direction given by the Treasury under article 4(1).

4. Treasury's power to designate persons

(1) Where any condition in paragraph (2) is satisfied, the Treasury may give a direction that a person identified in the direction is designated for the purposes of this Order.

(2) The conditions are that the Treasury have reasonable grounds for suspecting that the person is or may be—

(a) a person who commits, attempts to commit, participates in or facilitates the commission of acts of terrorism;

(b) a person identified in the Council Decision;

(c) a person owned or controlled, directly or indirectly, by a designated person; or

(d) a person acting on behalf of or at the direction of a designated person.

---

[380] The difference between article 3(1)(a) and (b) and article 4(2)(a) and (b) is apparently that the latter provides a basis for domestic designation if there is some question as to whether the individual in question actually is Usama bin Laden or is internationally designated by the Sanctions Committee: see [2008] EWCA Civ 1187, para 15.

[381] Article 5(4) has since been revoked by Counter-Terrorism Act 2008, Schedule 9(4), para 1 (in force 16 February 2009 for repeals specified in SI 2009/58, art 2(j); not yet in force otherwise) and replaced by the fuller provisions of section 63 of that Act. Like article 5(4) of the Al-Qaida Order, section 63 of the 2008 Act applies only to decisions of the Treasury, as made clear in section 63(1).

Article 5(4), as it then was,[382] empowered the High Court to set aside a direction made by the Treasury on the application of the person identified in the direction or any other person affected by the direction.

In the present case, applicant G, whose assets had been frozen pursuant to both article 3(1)(b) of the Al-Qaida Order (on international designation by the Al-Qaida and Taliban Sanctions Committee) and article 4(2)(a) of the Terrorism Order (on a direction by HM Treasury) sought to have both Orders quashed as *ultra vires* the United Nations Act 1946, while the four other applicants, whose assets had been frozen pursuant to article 4(2)(a) of the Terrorism Order, sought the quashing of this Order alone on the same ground. Both applications were successful at first instance before Collins J of the Administrative Court of the Queen's Bench Division.[383] HM Treasury appealed his decision.

The Court of Appeal (Civil Division) granted the appeal for the most part. It severed three words from the Terrorism Order but (Sedley LJ dissenting) otherwise upheld it, and upheld the entirety of the Al-Qaida Order, adding, however, that applicant G was entitled to a merits-based judicial review of the latter.

Sir Anthony Clarke MR focused first on the Terrorism Order. The applicants had submitted that article 4(2) of the Order—in accordance with which the Treasury is empowered to direct that a person be designated for the purposes of UK law where it has 'reasonable grounds for suspecting that the person is or may be' a person who commits, *etc* terrorist acts—was *ultra vires* the United Nations Act, which operated in this context by reference to Security Council resolution 1373 (2002), in that neither the criterion of 'reasonable grounds for suspecting' nor the words 'may be' was found in resolution 1373 (2002). In response, the Master of the Rolls, accepting that the words 'necessary or expedient' in section 1(1) of the United Nations Act were disjunctive and gave the Crown 'a wide discretion', and that 'the court should not lightly declare a provision made pursuant to such a wide power to be *ultra vires*',[384] stated:

SCR 1373 is silent on the standard of proof to be satisfied on the question whether a particular person 'commits, or attempts to commit, terrorist acts ...' before a State must freeze his assets within paragraph 1(c) ... In my opinion a State could properly conclude that it was expedient to provide that reasonable grounds for suspicion was an appropriate test. ... [S]uch a test has been accepted by the ECtHR in relation to a similar problem arising out of the risk of terrorism. In these circumstances I would accept such a test as lawful provided that the person concerned has a proper opportunity to challenge the decision made against him.[385]

---

[382] Like article 5(4) of the Al-Qaida Order, article 5(4) of the Terrorism Order has since been replaced by section 63 of the Counter-Terrorism Act 2008.

[383] See *A, K, M, Q and G v HM Treasury* [2008] EWHC 869 (Admin).

[384] [2008] EWCA Civ 1187, para 39.

[385] Ibid, para 42, quoting SC res 1373 (2001), para 1(c) and referring to *Fox, Campbell and Hartley v United Kingdom* (1990) 13 EHRR 157, para 32, quoted previously by his Lordship at [2008] EWCA

Nor, provided again that the relevant person's right to challenge the decision was preserved, did the 'conclusion that the "reasonable grounds for suspecting" test [was] within the ambit of the general power expressed in the United Nations Act' fall foul of the principles enunciated in a range of English cases cited by Collins J,[386] most notably *Pierson*[387] and *Simms*,[388] which laid down that fundamental rights could be overridden only by express language or necessary implication and not by general words. Sedley LJ agreed,[389] as did Wilson LJ,[390] and what went in this regard for the Terrorism Order went equally for the Al-Qaida Order.[391] When it came, however, to the inclusion of 'or may be' in article 4(2) of the Terrorism Order, all of their Lordships agreed that the legal complexion was different. Sir Anthony Clarke MR stated:

48 [T]he principles which I have just stated are of fundamental importance. The judge said at [39] that, in his view, if Parliament was not to be involved, it was necessary for the Order in Council to go no further than to apply what the SCR required. I agree. In the case of 'reasonable grounds for suspicion' it did not, in my opinion, go further than SCR 1373 required, whereas, by adding 'may be', it did.

49 There is no warrant in the language of the SCR for the addition of 'may be' in the Taliban Order. There is scope for argument as to how much difference this will make but I would accept the argument advanced on behalf of the applicants that it makes the test very wide indeed. In response to the submission that it was 'expedient' within the meaning of section 1 of the United Nations Act to express the test in such wide terms, the judge expressed his conclusion thus at [40]:

'[Counsel for HM Treasury] submits that it is expedient, which has a wider meaning. In *R (Gillan) v Commissioner of Metropolitan Police* [2006] 2 AC 307, the distinction between necessary and expedient was considered in the context of powers of random search conferred by s. 44 of the Terrorism Act 2000. Lord Bingham at paragraph 14 said that Parliament had used the word deliberately recognising that the powers were desirable in the interest of combating terrorism. But Lord Bingham drew attention to the close regulation of the exercise of the statutory power. There is no such regulation here and I do not accept that the extension to those who are suspected of possible involvement is properly within the scope of what is authorised by s.1 of the 1946 Act.'

I agree.

Civ 1187, para 40 via the Court of Appeal's judgment in *Secretary of State for the Home Department v MB* [2006] EWCA Civ 1140; [2007] QB 415, para 59.

[386]   Ibid, para 46, referring to [2008] EWHC 869 (Admin), paras 21 to 25.

[387]   *R v Secretary of State for the Home Department, Ex parte Pierson* [1998] AC 539, 575 (Lord Browne-Wilkinson), quoted at [2008] EWCA Civ 1187, para 43 (Sir Anthony Clarke MR).

[388]   *R v Secretary of State for the Home Department, Ex parte Simms* [2000] 2 AC 115, 131 (Lord Hoffmann), quoted at [2008] EWCA Civ 1187, para 44 (Sir Anthony Clarke MR).

[389]   [2008] EWCA Civ 1187, para 135.

[390]   Ibid, paras 151 and 155.

[391]   Ibid, para 107 (Sir Anthony Clarke MR).

Sedley LJ described the words 'or may be' as 'a bridge too far',[392] and Wilson LJ agreed that they were 'neither necessary nor expedient', within the meaning of section 1(1) of the United Nations Act, 'in relation to the objective of achieving effective implementation of the requisite measures' specified by the Security Council in resolution 1373 (2002).[393] All three of their Lordships also agreed that the offending words were severable from the Terrorism Order.[394]

In the event, however, only the Master of the Rolls and Wilson LJ actually severed the impugned words from the Terrorism Order. Sedley LJ held that, since prior primary legislation—namely the Terrorism Act 2000 and the Anti-Terrorism, Crime and Security Act 2001—already gave the government the power to freeze suspected terrorists' assets, and since the Order made 'no proper provision ... for according due process to those against whom it [was] deployed', the Terrorism Order could not be said to be expedient, within the meaning of article 1(1) of the United Nations Act, so that it had to be quashed in its entirety.[395] In contrast, Sir Anthony Clarke MR was unconvinced that a designated person's interests could not be 'suitably protected by procedures to be worked out on a case by case basis', for example by the use of special advocates, so that it was 'wrong to hold that it was not open to HM Treasury to conclude that it was expedient to make the Order' and 'wrong to quash the Terrorism Order itself', as distinct from the offending words 'or may be'.[396] Wilson LJ went further. Unpersuaded by the applicants' reliance on the Terrorism Act 2000 and the Anti-Terrorism, Crime and Security Act 2001, he held that the remainder of the Terrorism Order and the whole of the Al-Qaida Order ought to be considered 'not just expedient but necessary in relation to [the relevant Security Council resolution's] objective'.[397]

For its part, the Al-Qaida Order raised a further problem, namely the nature and scope of the challenge that could be mounted against it when, as was the case with applicant G, a person was subject to the Order, by way of article 3(1)(b), by sole virtue of the fact that he or she had been internationally designated by the Al-Qaida and Taliban Sanctions Committee.[398] In this regard, Sir Andrew Clarke MR recounted that G had had no contact with the Committee, had no idea on what evidence its decision to designate him had been based[399] and, absent the Al-Qaida

---

[392] Ibid, para 136.   [393] Ibid, para 155.

[394] Ibid, paras 151–3 (Sir Anthony Clarke MR), para 138 (Sedley LJ) and paras 151 and 157 (Wilson LJ).

[395] Ibid, para 144.

[396] Ibid, para 78 (Sir Anthony Clarke MR).

[397] Ibid, para 155.

[398] Ibid, para 107 (Sir Anthony Clarke MR).

[399] Ibid, para 108. Since it was the UK government which had requested that applicant G be internationally designated, the evidence was presumed to be the same as that relied on by the Treasury when making a direction for his (other) domestic designation under the Terrorism Order—evidence 'said to be so sensitive that G could not be given details': ibid.

Order, would not have been able to challenge his inclusion on the Committee's Consolidated List.[400] As for the position under English law, he would not have been affected by his inclusion on the Committee's List were it not for the Al-Qaida Order, and, because his domestic designation was not the result of a direction by HM Treasury under article 4(2) of the Order, he enjoyed no express right to challenge this designation in the High Court.[401] His Lordship continued:

113 The question is whether the court is powerless to achieve a solution whereby a person in the position of G can challenge the underlying basis of the case against him. The question is thus whether he can do so through judicial review. If he can do so under the Terrorism Order, it would to my mind be very strange if he could not do so in the case of the Al-Qaida Order in a case where the evidence against him appears to be the same in both cases. If he cannot, I would be inclined to hold that the Al-Qaida Order was unlawful, by reason of the application of the principles [laid down in *Pierson* and *Simms*].

114 The argument addressed to the [first instance] judge by [counsel] on behalf of G was that there must be implied into the Al-Qaida Order a right of access to the court by way of judicial review. That is not in dispute. It is the extent or content of the right that is in dispute.

His Lordship recalled (as Collins J had done) what Lord Bingham had said in *Al-Jedda*, namely that the only way to reconcile the maintenance of international peace and security, 'a fundamental purpose of the UN' in accordance with which the Security Council was empowered to mandate measures by UN Member States, with respect for human rights, another of the Organization's fundamental purposes, was to rule that the UK government could lawfully act in accordance with its Charter obligations but was obliged to ensure that the rights of the person against whom the relevant measures were taken were not infringed to any greater extent than was inherent in the measures mandated by the Council.[402] Sir Anthony Clarke MR recalled too Lord Carswell's analogous statement in *Al-Jedda* that measures undertaken pursuant to Security Council mandate had to be exercised in such a way 'as to minimise the infringements of the [target person's] rights'.[403] The Master of the Rolls agreed with Collins J that the reasoning of Lords Bingham and Carswell 'was clearly applicable to the inevitable breaches of property rights and infringement of Article 8 [of the ECHR] rights resulting from the application of the Al-Qaida Order to G'.[404] In this light, his Lordship concluded:

119 I would accept the submission that the court has power to consider an application for judicial review by a person to whom the Al-Qaida Order applies as a result of designation by the Committee and, on such an application, ... so far as

---

[400] Ibid, para 110.   [401] Ibid.
[402] Ibid, para 116, citing *R (Al-Jedda) v Secretary of State for Defence* [2007] UKHL 58; [2008] 1 AC 332, para 39, (2007) 78 *BYIL* 564–82 (HL).
[403] Ibid, quoting [2008] 1 AC 332, para 136.
[404] Ibid, para 118.

it can, to consider what the basis of the listing was. This will not be a challenge to the Al-Qaida Order itself but, if—to take the example of G—it were held that G should not have been listed, I see no reason why HM Treasury (or the relevant government body) should not, as the judge put it, be bound to support delisting. ...

120 So far as possible in the circumstances, G should be put in the same position as he is as a subject of a direction under the Terrorism Order, with the right to challenge it under article 5(4) of it. There must be procedures to enable him, again so far as possible, to discover the case against him, so that he may have an opportunity to meet it. This may involve, as in the case of the Terrorism Order, appropriate use of a special advocate. How the system will work in a particular case will depend upon the circumstances, as the House of Lords held is appropriate in the control order cases in *MB* and *AF*. There may be greater difficulties in a case where HM Treasury knows nothing of the facts upon which the designation was made by the Committee. I would leave the possible problems in such a case to be solved when they arise. Here there is no such problem because HM Treasury knows all the facts relevant to the Terrorism Order and must know either all or most of the facts which led to G's designation by the Committee.

121 In these circumstances, I would not set aside the Al-Qaida Order as the judge did. Although I would answer the question whether the Al-Qaida Order was unlawful in the negative, I would hold that G is entitled to a merits based review of the kind I have indicated.

Sedley LJ did not dissent from this,[405] and Wilson LJ agreed with Sir Anthony Clarke MR's 'creative solution', namely 'merits-based judicial review of the executive's response to a person's application to it that it should request, or support his own request, for de-listing by the Sanctions Committee'.[406]

Finally, Collins J had understood one of the applicants to have argued that section 1(1) of the United Nations Act did not enable the government to take measures enforceable against individuals. His Lordship had rejected the contention, as he understood it, as follows:

[Counsel for the applicants] submitted that s. 1 of the 1946 Act should apply only to inter-state relations and not to sanctions to be imposed on individuals within a state. He relied on statements in Parliament when the Bill was being considered. It may well be that no one at the time thought that Article 41 would be used against individuals, but that is nothing to the point. The Charter clearly requires Member States to take the action needed to carry out decisions of the Security Council ... The wording of s. 1 of the 1946 Act is clear: it applies to any measure which the Security Council calls upon the UK to apply under Article 41. The resolutions in question focus on individuals and it is not nor could be suggested that they are *ultra vires* Article 41. It follows that, whatever may have been the belief in 1946, s. 1 of the Act can apply to the Resolutions which require the freezing of the assets of those who fall within the scope of the Resolutions.[407]

---

[405] Ibid, para 147.   [406] Ibid, para 157.
[407] Ibid, para 122 (Sir Anthony Clarke), quoting an unreferenced passage from [2008] EWHC 869 (Admin).

Sir Anthony Clarke MR found it 'not difficult to agree with the judge's reasoning in this respect'.[408]

The Court of Appeal's judgment, which is clearly correct on the 'reasonable grounds to suspect' and state-versus-individual points, is certainly plausible on the 'or may be' issue. More challenging is the majority's ruling that merits-based judicial review—by which is presumably meant a consideration not just of the formal *vires* of the relevant decision but also of whether it is rational in the *Wednesbury* sense—is available to a person internationally designated by the Al-Qaida and Taliban Sanctions Committee. For a start, the argument that what goes for the Terrorism Order should, where the evidence against the designated person is the same, go for the Al-Qaida Order[409] is a furphy, and even more so is the argument that '[s]o far as possible in the circumstances, G should be put in the same position as he is as a subject of a direction under the Terrorism Order, with the right to challenge it under article 5(4) of it'.[410] The court is mixing apples and pears. There is a cardinal difference between the two Orders, which is that there is no facility under the Terrorism Order such as that provided for in article 3(1)(b) of the Al-Qaida Order for a person's automatic domestic designation on his or her international designation by the relevant Security Council sanctions committee. (The reason for this is plain: the relevant Security Council sanctions committee in the context of the Terrorism Order, namely the Counter-Terrorism Committee established pursuant to resolution 1373 (2001), does not designate persons; rather, the identification of persons to whom the measures mandated by resolution 1373 (2001) are to apply is a matter for each UN Member State.[411]) Leaving aside the effect of EU Council Decision 2006/379/EC, the only way a person can be made subject under the Terrorism Order to the measures required by Security Council resolution 1373 (2001) is by way of a direction by HM Treasury on the basis of evidence available to it, in respect of which a right of application to the High Court lies under article 5(4) of the Terrorism Order. But while an identical right of challenge is available, under article 5(4) of the Al-Qaida Order, to a person made subject under the Order to the measures required by resolutions 1333 (2000) and 1390 (2002) by means of a direction by HM Treasury, no such right exists for those to whom the Order applies by virtue of their international designation by the Al-Qaida and Taliban Sanctions Committee. In short, the posited identity between a person caught by the Terrorism Order thanks to HM Treasury and a person caught by the Al-Qaida Order thanks to the Al-Qaida and Taliban Sanctions Committee is doubly false. But perhaps even more problematic is the question of exactly what decision

---

[408] Note that Wilson LJ entered a general concurrence in the Master of the Rolls' reasoning: ibid, para 151.

[409] See ibid, para 113 (Sir Anthony Clarke MR).

[410] Ibid, para 120 (Sir Anthony Clarke MR).

[411] In the case of EU Member States, it is also a matter for the Council of the European Union.

persons domestically designated, via article 3(1)(b) of the Al-Qaida Order, by sole virtue of their international designation by the Al-Qaida and Taliban Sanctions Committee would seek review. The Master of the Rolls holds that 'the court has power to consider an application for judicial review by a person to whom the Al-Qaida Order applies as a result of designation by the Committee and, on such an application, ... so far as it can, to consider what the basis of the listing was', clarifying that this would 'not be a challenge to the Al-Qaida Order itself'.[412] To what, however, would it be a challenge? Presumably not to the Committee's decision. This is patently beyond the jurisdiction of an English court; moreover, it would be odd to order HM Treasury to make amends for the Committee's irrational decision, as his Lordship's suggestion that the Treasury could 'be bound to support delisting'[413] could be taken to suggest. One relevant decision that an English court could impugn would be the decision by the UK government to recommend the designated person's international designation by the Al-Qaida and Taliban Sanctions Committee, but this is a decision very probably not taken by HM Treasury, for which it could not be made to answer, let alone atone; and even where it was the Treasury which recommended the person's international designation, questions of causation would remain, given that the actual decision to include a person on the Committee's Consolidated List— the decision giving immediate rise to domestic legal effects under the Al-Qaida Order—would have been taken by the Committee. The answer to the riddle would seem to be found not in Sir Anthony Clarke MR's judgment but in that of Wilson LJ, where his Lordship refers to what he calls the Master of the Rolls' 'creative'[414] solution, namely 'judicial review of the executive's response to a person's application to it that it should request, or support his own request, for de-listing by the Sanctions Committee'.[415] This would be a decision capable of challenge in an English court on *Wednesbury* grounds, but it is again unlikely to be a decision taken by, or indeed within the remit of, the Treasury. In short, 'creative' the majority's solution surely is. Welcome it will be too, at least to anyone concerned by the Kafkaesque situation in which the objects of the 1267/1333/1390 sanctions regime often find themselves. But compelling it is not.

Non-justiciability—foreign act of State doctrine—'Buttes' non-justiciability—whether subject-matter non-justiciable on account of potential to embarrass foreign State

Case No 16 Korea National Insurance Co v Allianz Global Corporate & Speciality AG, 2 December 2008, [2008] EWCA Civ 1355, unreported (CA (Civ Div))

The claimant, a North Korean State-owned insurance company, sued the defendant, the company's reinsurer, in the Commercial Court in London

---

412 Ibid, para 119.   413 Ibid (Sir Anthony Clarke MR).
414 Ibid, para 157 (Wilson LJ).   415 Ibid.

to enforce a judgment to the value of over 43 million euro rendered by the Court of Pyongyang in North Korea. In the course of the proceedings, the judge struck out two defences sought to be raised by the respondent, both of which alleged criminality on the part of the North Korean government. In the first, it was alleged that the judgment of the Court of Pyongyang was unenforceable as it was procured by a fraud instigated or approved by the government of North Korea and implemented with the knowledge or participation of the claimant. The argument, supported by evidence, was that the underlying insurance claim in respect of which the claimant sought payment from the defendant by way of reinsurance was a fraud perpetrated by the claimant at the behest of the North Korean government as a means of accruing hard currency for the State; and that the Court of Pyongyang, in full knowledge of this, lent itself to the fraud, again at the behest of the North Korean government. In the second, related defence, it was argued that the judgment was unenforceable on grounds of public policy, in that the North Korean judiciary was not independent of the North Korean government, which instigated or approved of the fraudulent procuration of the judgment. The judge did not seek the view of the Foreign and Commonwealth Office as to whether adjudication of the issues would embarrass diplomatic relations between the UK and North Korea (and it subsequently declined to offer its view). He held, by reference to Lord Wilberforce's speech in *Buttes Gas and Oil Co v Hammer (No 3)*[416] and to the judgment of the Court of Appeal delivered by Brooke LJ in *Kuwait Airways*,[417] that the allegations raised in the defences were non-justiciable. Judicial restraint was called for 'where the court is asked to decide matters the investigation into which and adjudication thereon would embarrass the country's foreign relations', and 'the investigation into and adjudication on the reinsurers' allegations that the North Korean State ... fraudulently procured the North Korean judgment and that this was of a piece with and [was] to be inferred from many other criminal acts committed by the North Korean State ha[d] an obvious potential for embarrassing the foreign relations between Her Majesty's Government and the Government of North Korea'.[418] While the case continued in the Commercial Court, the defendant applied to the Court of Appeal for permission to appeal the strike-out of its defences. The case was listed urgently, with appeals to follow if permission were granted. Neither party sought to uphold the judge's decision: in what was held to be a considered decision, the claimant was content for the defences to be contested on the merits.

The Court of Appeal, in a judgment delivered on the same day as argument, granted the appeal, holding that 'the judge should not have ruled

[416] [1982] AC 888, 931, (1982) 53 *BYIL* 259–68 (HL).
[417] *Kuwait Airways Corpn v Iraqi Airways Company* [2001] 3 WLR 1117, (2000) 71 *BYIL* 408–12 (CA).
[418] [2008] EWCA Civ 1355, para 27, quoting para 30 of the judgment of Field J in the Commercial Court.

that any of the allegations were non-justiciable and certainly should not have done so without some indication from the Foreign and Commonwealth Office that some embarrassment might be caused to the diplomatic relations between the United Kingdom and North Korea if the court did adjudicate the issue'.[419] Waller LJ gave the leading judgment, with which Rix and Thomas LJJ agreed.

Waller LJ took the view that the judge had misunderstood what Lord Wilberforce was saying in *Buttes* and what Brooke LJ was saying in *Kuwait Airways*.[420] There was 'no general rule that if an allegation might embarrass a foreign sovereign it follow[ed] that that will also embarrass diplomatic relations with the United Kingdom and that thus such embarrassing issues are non-justiciable'.[421] While Lord Wilberforce had come to the conclusion that English law recognized a general principle that 'the courts will not adjudicate upon the transactions of foreign sovereign states', it was noteworthy that his examples had related to 'sovereign acts done within the sovereign territory or situations in which the issue would impinge upon international relations at state level'.[422] Moreover, his ultimate conclusion had been that there were 'no judicial or manageable standards by which to judge [the] issues' before the House.[423] Neither Lord Wilberforce's words nor those of Brooke LJ in *Kuwait Airways* gave support to the view 'that, where in a commercial context allegations are made against the state, not in relation to some sovereign act carried out within its own jurisdiction but in relation to acts which affect the rights of a party under a commercial contract, the court should exercise restraint to the extent of not being prepared to decide the same, at least without some indication from the executive that a decision will embarrass the diplomatic relations between the United Kingdom and that State'.[424] If, his Lordship observed, a foreign State were an insured under an insurance contract, the insurers would not be precluded from alleging a fraudulent claim simply because that might embarrass the foreign State, and it could not, he asserted, be any different if a State entity made the claim and it was argued that both the entity and the State, its owner, were involved in the fraud.[425]

There is nothing wrong with the Court of Appeal's statement that no rule of English law renders a subject-matter non-justiciable solely on the ground that its adjudication may embarrass a foreign State. It is obvious, however, that their Lordships' judgment was rendered 'at speed', without 'full (or any adversarial) argument on the precise limits of the law on non-justiciability'.[426]

For a start, as is frustratingly common[427] but in contrast to the judgment of Brooke LJ in *Kuwait Airways*, the judgment conflates two distinct

---

[419] Ibid, para 28 (Waller LJ).   [420] Ibid, para 29.   [421] Ibid, para 30.
[422] Ibid.   [423] Ibid.   [424] Ibid, para 32.
[425] Ibid.
[426] Ibid, para 5.
[427] See, for example, *Kuwait Airways Corpn v Iraqi Airways Company (Nos 4 and 5)* [2002] UKHL 19; [2002] AC 883, (2002) 73 *BYIL* 400–4 (HL).

doctrines and their distinct rationales, namely the foreign act of State doctrine proper and the doctrine of judicial abstention coined by Lord Wilberforce in *Buttes*. The first is a rule, originally enunciated in *Duke of Brunswick v King of Hanover*[428] and founded on the sovereign equality of States, whereby an English court will not enquire into the legality, whether under national or international law, of the sovereign acts of a foreign State within its own territory. The second is a broader and territorially unlimited rule according to which an English court will not question the legality, again whether under national or international law, of the 'transactions of foreign sovereign states'[429] or 'acts done abroad by virtue of sovereign authority',[430] the reason being a lack of 'judicial or manageable standards' by which to judge such issues.[431]

Secondly, and perhaps more significantly for practical purposes, the ruling that potential embarrassment to a foreign State does not render a subject-matter non-justiciable in the English courts ought not to have been dispositive of the case. It might also have been asked whether the foreign act of State doctrine nonetheless applied, and the answer to this is not obvious. One could argue that it should have.[432] The doctrine serves to prevent an English court sitting in judgment of the sovereign acts of a foreign State performed within its territory; the impugned act here was the judgment of the Court of Pyongyang; and the passing of judgment by a court is surely a sovereign act. In short, respect for the sovereign equality of States would appear to dictate that an English court be precluded from deciding whether a foreign judgment was fraudulent. That said, there is an established exception to the foreign act of State doctrine which provides that an English court will not give effect to a foreign law or other sovereign act where to do so would be contrary to English public policy. It might, at first, be doubted whether the exception would have come into play on the facts of the instant case, given that the gist of the public policy argument would have been that the courts of North Korea knowingly and willingly perpetrated fraud on behalf of the State—the very contention that the foreign act of State doctrine says is non-justiciable. But there is conceivably a distinction to be drawn between foreign sovereign acts consummated in the foreign sovereign's territory and foreign sovereign acts, such as the unexecuted judgment in the present case, which require the assistance of the English courts for their consummation. As regards the latter, it is not unreasonable to suggest that, for self-evident public policy reasons, the English courts

---

[428] (1848) 2 HL Cas 1.
[429] [1982] AC 888, 931 (Lord Wilberforce).
[430] Ibid, 932 (Lord Wilberforce).
[431] Ibid, 938 (Lord Wilberforce).
[432] As for *Buttes*, it is not clear that there were no judicial or manageable standards by reference to which the court could have adjudicated the case, although any such adjudication would probably have called for expert evidence as to the North Korean law of fraud and as to the alleged fraudulent practices of the North Korean regime, including its courts.

are not compelled by the foreign act of State doctrine to perfect a foreign sovereign act without first ascertaining whether it is lawful.

European Convention on Human Rights 1950, *article 3 (prohibition on torture and inhuman or degrading treatment or punishment)—extradition*—Soering *jurisprudence—whether desirability of extradition to be taken into account in deciding whether extradition exposes individual to inhuman or degrading treatment or punishment*

Case No 17 *R (Wellington) v Secretary of State for the Home Department,* 10 December 2008, [2008] UKHL 72, [2008] 2 WLR 48 (HL)

The US government requested, and the Secretary of State granted, the appellant's extradition to stand trial in the State of Missouri on, *inter alia*, two counts of first-degree murder, for which the mandatory pre-scribed punishment was life imprisonment without eligibility for parole,[433] although the State governor retained a power to order release. The appellant challenged the Secretary of State's decision, arguing that in agreeing to his extradition, the Secretary of State had acted contrary to the HRA,[434] in that mandatory life imprisonment without eligibility for parole amounted to inhuman or degrading treatment or punishment within the meaning of article 3 of the ECHR, and the *Soering*[435] jurisprudence provided that a Contracting State to the Convention breached article 3 if it returned a person within its jurisdiction to a non-Contracting State where he or she would be subject to treatment which, if meted out by a Contracting State, would violate that provision.

On appeal to the House of Lords, it was held unanimously, dismissing the appeal, that the appellant's imprisonment in Missouri would not have constituted inhuman or degrading treatment or punishment within the meaning of article 3, since it was, in principle, liable to reduction by the governor of Missouri.[436] It is, however, the Lords' dicta on an additional, hypothetical point—namely what the situation would have been had the sentence been irreducible—that is mainly of interest for present purposes. On this their Lordships divided three to two. Worth noting too is some striking reasoning by Lord Scott on another point.

Lord Hoffmann, with whose reasoning Baroness Hale and Lord Carswell agreed, opened his consideration of the hypothetical point by quoting from, and emphasizing certain words of, a passage from the judgment in *Soering* where the Strasbourg court stated that 'the beneficial purpose of extradition in preventing fugitive offenders from evading justice cannot

---

[433] The death sentence was also prescribed, but the Missouri prosecuting authority undertook not to seek it.

[434] See HRA, s 6.

[435] *Soering v United Kingdom* (1989) 11 EHRR 439.

[436] See [2008] 2 WLR 48, 58, para 34 (Lord Hoffmann), 61–2, paras 43–7 (Lord Scott) and 62, para 49 (Baroness Hale).

be ignored in determining the scope of application of the Convention *and of article 3 in particular*.[437] His Lordship elaborated:

I have emphasised the last few words of this passage because they make it clear that in cases of extradition, article 3 does not apply as if the extraditing state were simply responsible for any punishment likely to be inflicted in the receiving state. It applies only in a modified form which takes into account the desirability of arrangements for extradition. The form in which article 3 does apply must be gathered from the rest of the judgment and subsequent jurisprudence.[438]

He explained how the ECtHR distinguished in *Soering* between torture, on the one hand, and inhuman or degrading treatment or punishment, on the other. It would always be a violation of article 3 of the Convention for a Contracting State to extradite a fugitive to a requesting State where there were substantial grounds for believing that he or she was in danger of being tortured, 'however heinous the crime allegedly committed'.[439] But the position as regards inhuman or degrading treatment or punishment was 'more complicated', with what amounted to such treatment or punishment depending on 'all the circumstances of the case'.[440] After quoting again from the judgment in *Soering*,[441] Lord Hoffmann interpolated:

The passage makes it clear that the desirability of extradition is a factor to be taken into account in deciding whether the punishment likely to be imposed in the receiving state attains the 'minimum level of severity' which would make it inhuman and [*sic*] degrading. Punishment which counts as inhuman and degrading in the domestic context will not necessarily be so regarded when the extradition factor has been taken into account.[442]

He further quoted the ECtHR's reference to 'the search for the requisite fair balance of interests and to the proportionality of the contested extradition decision in the particular case'.[443] His Lordship then continued:

A relativist approach to the scope of article 3 seems to me essential if extradition is to continue to function. For example, the Court of Session has decided in *Napier v Scottish Ministers* 2005 SC 229 that in Scotland the practice of 'slopping out' (requiring a prisoner to use a chamber pot in his cell and empty it in the morning) may cause an infringement of article 3. Whether, even in a domestic context, this attains the necessary level of severity is a point on which I would wish to reserve my opinion. If, however, it were applied in the context of extradition, it would prevent anyone being extradited to many countries poorer than Scotland, where people who are not in prison often have to make do without flush lavatories.[444]

---

[437] Ibid, 55, para 21, giving no citation. The emphasis is Lord Hoffmann's.
[438] Ibid, para 22.
[439] Ibid, para 23, quoting (1989) 11 EHRR 439, para 88. See also ibid, 63, para 50 (Baroness Hale) and 66, para 58 (Lord Carswell).
[440] Ibid, 55, para 23, quoting (1989) 11 EHRR 439, para 89.
[441] Ibid, quoting (1989) 11 EHRR 439, para 89. See also, identically, ibid, 63, para 50 (Baroness Hale) and 65, para 57 (Lord Carswell).
[442] Ibid, 55, para 24. See also ibid, 65–6, paras 57–8 (Lord Carswell).
[443] Ibid, 56, para 25, quoting (1989) 11 EHRR 439, para 110.
[444] Ibid, para 27.

He added that treating article 3 'as applicable only in an attenuated form' if the question arose in the context of extradition or other forms of removal to a foreign State was consistent with the European Court's jurisprudence on the applicability of other articles of the Convention 'in a foreign context'.[445] It was not sufficient, for example, that the fairness of any trial in the requesting State would not meet the requirements of article 6 of the ECHR; rather, there had to be a risk of a 'flagrant denial of justice'.[446] His Lordship was satisfied, therefore, that there was nothing in the Strasbourg jurisprudence 'to qualify the principle laid down in *Soering* that torture is a contravention of article 3 whether the context is domestic or foreign but that such context may affect whether other punishment or treatment is regarded as sufficiently severe to contravene'.[447] He noted that a 'similar relativist approach' was taken by the Supreme Court of Canada.[448] Turning, then, to the case before the House, Lord Hoffmann held that, even if the sentence imposed in the State of Missouri were thought irreducible, it would violate article 3 of the ECHR in the context of extradition only 'if one would be able to say that such a sentence was likely, on the facts of the case, to be clearly disproportionate' or, synonymously, 'grossly disproportionate'.[449] And on the facts of the case before their Lordships, 'it could not be said that a sentence of life without parole would be so grossly disproportionate to the offence as to meet the heightened standard for contravention of article 3 in its application to extradition cases':[450]

Unlike *Soering* 11 EHRR 439, there is no other jurisdiction in which the appellant can be tried. If he is not extradited to Missouri, he will be entitled to remain in this country as a fugitive from justice. The standard of what amounts to inhuman and degrading treatment for the purposes of article 3 must therefore be a high one. The offence which he is alleged to have committed is one for which an English judge might well impose a whole life sentence ... It is true that the English judge would do so as a matter of judicial discretion, whereas in Missouri the sentence is mandatory. ... But in my opinion it is irrelevant. The mandatory nature of the sentence would be very important if we were concerned with the validity of a domestic rule imposing such a sentence ... But we are not concerned with the validity of the Missouri law. The fact that a life sentence without parole is mandatory in Missouri is relevant only in enabling the English court to predict the punishment which the appellant will receive if he is convicted of first degree murder.[451]

The question was whether such a sentence would be 'obviously disproportionate' to the crime of which the appellant in this particular case was accused.[452] Lord Hoffmann's answer was that it was not. But 'if the facts were that a prisoner was charged with the kind of mercy killing postulated by ... Lord Brown', it might well have been.[453]

---

[445] Ibid, para 28.
[446] Ibid, para 29, quoting *Drozd and Janousek v France and Spain* (1992) 14 EHRR 745, para 110.
[447] Ibid, 57, para 30.   [448] Ibid, para 32.
[449] Ibid, para 35.   [450] Ibid, 58, para 36.
[451] Ibid, 58–9, para 36.   [452] Ibid, 59, para 36.
[453] Ibid.

In contrast to Lord Hoffmann's relativist approach to article 3 in the context of return to a foreign country, Lord Brown adopted what Lord Scott, who agreed with his reasoning, called an 'absolutist'[454] stance. His Lordship opened his discussion of the point as follows:

In and in so far as Lord Hoffmann would hold that where, as here, it is obviously desirable that the appellant be extradited and tried for his alleged crimes rather than be able to invoke article 3 to secure safe haven here, the threshold of what amounts to inhuman and degrading treatment or punishment is heightened, I would respectfully disagree.[455]

He took the view that *Chahal v United Kingdom*, 'a decision strongly reaffirmed by the Grand Chamber's recent unanimous judgment in *Saadi v Italy*', had rejected just such relativism:[456]

86 There is, I conclude, no room in the Strasbourg jurisprudence for a concept such as the risk of a flagrant violation of article 3's absolute prohibition against inhuman or degrading treatment or punishment (akin to that of the risk of a 'flagrant denial of justice'). By the same token that no one can be expelled if he would then face the risk of torture, so too no one can be expelled if he would then face the risk of treatment or punishment which is properly to be characterised as inhuman or degrading. That, of course, is not to say that, assuming for example 'slopping out' is degrading treatment in Scotland, so too it must necessarily be regarded in all countries ...; or that leaving asylum-seekers totally destitute would necessarily constitute article 3 ill-treatment in, say, a poor (warm) country as the House [has] held it to be here ...; or, indeed, that a particular punishment (or the particular conditions in which any term of imprisonment would be served) that might be regarded as inhuman or degrading in a Convention state is necessarily to be so regarded in a state not party to the Convention—the Strasbourg court has repeatedly said that the Convention does not 'purport to be a means of requiring the contracting states to impose Convention standards on other states' (*Soering*, para 86) and article 3 does not bar removal to non-Convention states (whether by way of extradition or simply for the purposes of immigration control) merely because they choose to impose higher levels or harsher measures of criminal punishment.

87 Nor is it to say that a risk of article 3 ill-treatment, the necessary pre-condition of an article 3 bar upon extradition, will readily be established. On the contrary ... Whilst, however, I readily accept that there is a good deal of flexibility in the concept of inhuman and degrading treatment and punishment with many factors in play in determining whether it attains the minimum standard required and whether the risk of such ill-treatment is satisfied, I cannot accept that the expelling state's desire to extradite the person concerned (legitimate though clearly it is) can itself properly be one such factor.[457]

Applying these principles to the case before the House, Lord Brown concluded that '[i]f a mandatory life sentence would properly be regarded as

---

[454] Ibid, 60, para 39.   [455] Ibid, 75, para 85.
[456] Ibid, citing (1996) 23 EHRR 413 and Application No 37201/06, ECtHR (Grand Chamber), 28 February 2008 (unreported) respectively.
[457] Ibid, 75–6.

violating article 3 in a domestic case, so too … would the risk of it preclude expulsion of the defendant from this country in a foreign case'.[458] Indeed, this seemed to follow from the Strasbourg court's judgment in *Einhorn v France*.[459] Lord Scott, agreeing with Lord Brown, added some words of his own:

It is accepted that the absolute nature of the article 3 bar on torture would bar extradition to a country where the extradited person would face torture and that that which would constitute torture for article 3 purposes in Europe would constitute torture for those purposes everywhere. But it is suggested that treatment or punishment that might for article 3 purposes be inhuman or degrading in Europe would not necessarily need to be so categorised if it were treatment or punishment likely to be faced in the requesting country by a person faced with extradition to that country for crimes committed there. But, if that is so, how can it be said that article 3 rights not to be subjected to inhuman or degrading treatment are absolute rights? If, in an extradition context they can be 'relativist' rights, why should they not also be 'relativist' rights in other contexts where the public interest were equally engaged and would be advanced by the removal to his home country of the individual in question? This might often be so in immigration or deportation cases.[460]

It struck his Lordship that '[t]he paradox created by categorising article 3 rights not to be subjected to inhuman or degrading treatment or punishment as absolute and at the same time authorising or applying a "relativist" approach to the interpretation of those rights in an extradition context could … be resolved in two alternative ways':[461]

41 … One way would be to distinguish between treatment that constituted 'torture' for article 3 purposes and treatment or punishment that was merely 'inhuman or degrading', the former being absolutely prohibited by article 3, the latter, too, being prohibited absolutely in a domestic context but not necessarily preventing removal to his home country of a person likely in that country to face such treatment or punishment. The problem with this approach to article 3 is that the language of the article provides no basis at all for distinguishing between that which would qualify as sufficiently inhuman or degrading, and therefore prohibited by article 3, in an extradition context and that which would be prohibited by article 3 in a domestic context but could be overlooked in an extradition context, or for distinguishing between treatment that would be sufficiently inhuman or degrading to bar removal to a foreign country in an immigration context but insufficiently in order to bar removal to that country in an extradition context. It seems to me that the standard of treatment or punishment apt to attract the adjectives 'inhuman or degrading' for article 3 purposes ought to be a constant. I do not see how otherwise the article 3 prohibition regarding such treatment or punishment can be regarded as an absolute one. This, I think, and respectfully agree with, is Lord Brown's point.

42 The other way of resolving the paradox would be to adopt a uniformly strict approach to what constitutes 'inhuman or degrading treatment or punishment'

---

[458] Ibid, 76, para 88.
[459] Reports of Judgments and Decisions 2001-XI, 275.
[460] [2008] 2 WLR 48, 60, para 40.
[461] Ibid, para 41.

for article 3 purposes. It must, in my respectful opinion, be borne in mind that article 3 was prescribing a minimum standard of acceptable treatment or punishment below which the signatory nations could be expected not to sink but not as high a standard as that which many of those nations might think it right to require for every individual within their jurisdiction, and therefore entitled, even if only temporarily, to their protection. Article 3 was prescribing a minimum standard, not a norm. It must be open to individual states to decide for themselves what, if any, higher standard they would set for themselves. Lord Hoffmann referred ... to a decision of the Court of Session which ruled that in prisons in Scotland the practice of 'slopping out' was, or might be, an infringement of article 3. This decision illustrates very well the point I am trying to make. It would, of course, be unexceptionable for the courts of Scotland, or the courts of any other jurisdiction, or their prison authorities to rule that the practice of slopping-out was unacceptable and should cease. But to give that ruling as an interpretation of an article 3 obligation would, in my opinion, undermine the absolute nature of the obligation in question. It would be unthinkable to rule that in no circumstances could slopping-out in a prison, or comparable institution, be tolerated. Whatever view one might have about the objectionable quality of slopping-out, that view could not, in my opinion, be carried forward into an acceptable interpretation of an absolute obligation in article 3.[462]

With that, his Lordship turned to other questions.

Neither of the positions staked out is wholly satisfactory, but this is as much a function of the conceptual incoherence of the Strasbourg jurisprudence on extradition and expulsion as it is of their Lordships' own reasoning. Not even Lords Hoffmann and Brown can make a silk purse out of a *Soering*.

Also of note in the case is how Lord Scott came to the conclusion that the mandatory life sentence without parole faced by the appellant in Missouri would not have amounted to inhuman or degrading treatment or punishment if done by the UK. His Lordship stated:

A full life term of imprisonment without parole would not, I believe, have been regarded as a *per se* inhuman and degrading sentence in the 1950s when the Convention was signed, nor in 1998 when the United Kingdom enacted the Act that incorporated article 3 into the domestic law of this country. If such a sentence would not have been so regarded in 1998, there is no justification, in my opinion, for so regarding it now.[463]

He dismissed the appeal on this ground without mentioning *Kafkaris v Cyprus*,[464] the Grand Chamber case from 2005 on which the other Lords focused in relation to the first and determinative issue before the House.

Lord Scott's approach to the application of the ECHR is, with respect, flawed or at least poorly articulated. Even leaving aside the trumpeted notion of the Convention as a 'living instrument', the application of a treaty

[462]   Ibid, 60–1.
[463]   Ibid, 62, para 47.
[464]   Application No 21906/04, ECtHR (Grand Chamber), 12 February 2008 (unreported).

provision is not restricted to that which its drafters would have given it. This is not even the case as regards its interpretation.[465] His Lordship's dicta in *Animal Defenders*[466] and *Gentle*[467] suggest that his (wholly legitimate) concern is the judicial reading of obligations into the Convention. But resisting this does not require an insistence on original intent. Articles 31 and 32 of the Vienna Convention on the Law of Treaties are all that is needed. As for Lord Scott's approach to the HRA, this overlooks section 2(1)(a) of the Act, which compels an English court determining a question of Convention rights to take into account any judgment—and not just pre-1998 judgments—of the ECtHR. Section 2(1)(a) manifests Parliament's intent that the date of passage of the HRA is not that by which its intent in passing the Act is to be assessed.

State responsibility—organs of a State—territorial units of a State—irrelevance of internal law—United Kingdom—England and Scotland—European Convention on Human Rights 1950, article 6 (right to hearing within reasonable time)—whether English and Scottish police forces distinguishable for purposes of ECHR, article 6

Case No 18 *Burns v Her Majesty's Advocate*, 15 December 2008, [2008] UKPC 63, 2009 SLT 2 (PC (S))

Article 6(1) of the ECHR guarantees a hearing within a reasonable time. Pursuant to cross-border co-operation between the Scottish and English police, the appellant, a resident of Glasgow, was arrested on 18 February 2003 in Luton, England, where he was staying with his sister. He was detained for 24 hours and interviewed under caution by the Metropolitan police on suspicion of involvement in a paedophile ring. His sister's house in Luton and his own house in Glasgow were simultaneously searched, the latter yielding his computer, with internet connection, which was seized and examined. The officers from the Met told him that they would be recommending that proceedings be brought against him, in either England or Scotland, depending on which of the two had jurisdiction. He was released on bail. The Crown Prosecution Service subsequently advised that the Scottish courts had jurisdiction. The accused's case papers were passed to the Strathclyde police, who made an initial report to the procurator fiscal in October 2003, but a full report was not made until October 2004. A warrant for the appellant's arrest was granted in November 2004, and he appeared in answer to it on 17 December 2004. With the agreement of the defence, extensions of the twelve-month period for bringing the case to trial were granted. Eventually, at a trial diet at Glasgow sheriff

---

[465] See the discussion above 453.

[466] See *R (Animal Defenders International) v Secretary of State for Culture, Media and Sport* [2008] UKHL 15; [2008] 1 AC 1312 1352, para 45, above 411–7 (HL), quoting from *Brown v Stott* [2003] 1 AC 681, 703 (Lord Bingham).

[467] See *R (Gentle) v Prime Minister and others* [2008] UKHL 20; [2008] 1 AC 1356, 1374, para 29, above 422–8 (HL).

court in June 2007, the appellant submitted that, by bringing him to trial, the Crown was, on account of delays on its part, acting incompatibly with article 6(1) of the ECHR, as given domestic effect by the HRA (Scotland). He argued that time began to run from the date of his being informed of the Met's recommendation that charges be brought against him. The sheriff and, on appeal, the High Court of Justiciary rejected the appellant's argument, holding that time began to run on 17 December 2004, when he appeared in answer to the charges brought by the competent authority in Scotland. The English and Scottish criminal justice systems were distinct from each other.

On appeal, under devolution arrangements, to the Privy Council in right of Scotland, the Board unanimously allowed the appeal, holding that it would be artificial to treat the actions of the prosecuting authorities in Scotland as divorced from those of the Metropolitan police in February 2003. For the purposes of article 6(1) of the ECHR, the appellant was 'charged' on 19 February 2003. Of relevance for present purposes is a dictum from Lord Rodger.

Lord Rodger—having held that the distinction between the Scottish and English criminal justice systems 'was a legal technicality which could not possibly have reduced [the appellant's] anxiety or uncertainty', so that he 'required the protection of the article 6(1) guarantee from that time onwards'[468]—continued:

This is consistent with wider considerations. The United Kingdom, rather than Scotland or England, is the party to the European Convention. In terms of article 1, the United Kingdom has undertaken to secure to everyone within its jurisdiction, *inter alia*, the rights defined in article 6. Of course, the United Kingdom is free to make what internal constitutional arrangements it pleases, but, whatever arrangements it adopts, it remains bound to fulfil that obligation. Suppose a case where someone is 'charged' in Scotland for article 6(1) purposes and his trial in Scotland is then delayed for a period which is unreasonable. The United Kingdom will be in breach of article 6(1). Suppose, instead, that he is 'charged' in Scotland and his trial in England on substantially the same matter is then delayed for the same period. The same result must follow. In other words, the way that the United Kingdom has chosen to distribute its criminal jurisdiction cannot impair or defeat an accused's right to be tried on a criminal charge within a reasonable time. In a case like the present, therefore, when applying article 6(1), it is appropriate to look at the sum total of the actions of the competent English and Scottish authorities.

The other Lords agreed with the reasons given by Lord Rodger.[469]

Lord Rodger's dictum is a textbook application of articles 4(1) and 32 of the Articles on Responsibility of States for Internationally Wrongful Acts.[470]

---

[468] 2009 SLT 2, 7, para 27.
[469] Lady Cosgrove, who agreed with Lord Rodger's reasons, also gave a substantive speech, with the reasoning of which the other Lords, including Lord Rodger, also agreed.
[470] UN Doc A/RES/56/83, Annex, 12 December 2001.

DECISIONS OF BRITISH COURTS 2008

B. PRIVATE INTERNATIONAL LAW

By Adrian Briggs*

1. Mutual judicial assistance in cross-border insolvency: *Re HIH Casualty and General Insurance Ltd, McGrath v Riddell*[1]

Some cases suggest that when the legislature has intervened to alter by statute what was perceived to be the common law, it is for the common law, by which is meant the judiciary, to stand still and let Parliament have its way. All the more, it may be supposed, where the legislatures in question are the Parliament at Westminster *and* the competent organs of the European Union. Even less should the common law develop—which means that the judges should not assume the mantle of legislators—to abrogate rights conferred by Parliament on individuals. Thus it was that the English statutory reform of choice of law for claims in tort was held, only last year, to paralyse judicial development of those parts of the common law which were left outside the reforming provisions of the legislation.[2] The fact that Parliament may have moved too cautiously for the liking of some grants no judicial licence to do anything at all. So when Parliament has enacted a scheme for the distribution of the assets of an insolvent,[3] and has enacted a regime to identify when and how an English court may cooperate with the proper bodies acting under a foreign liquidation,[4] and has gone no further; and when legislation from Europe[5] and from UNCITRAL[6] allows for a measure of coordination in certain cases of cross-border insolvency, one could be forgiven for thinking that that was that. A bare majority of the House of Lords in *Re HIH Casualty and General Insurance Ltd, McGrath v Riddell* probably agreed, though a vigorous contradictory view challenges that assumption and supports the rival contention that though Parliament may enact new laws, its doing so does not prevent the judicial development of the common law, even where this has the appearance of repealing part of the legislation. The case was one in which the desirable answer was pretty obvious, but the path to it was not so easily seen.

* Professor of Private International Law, Oxford University; Fellow & Tutor in Law, St Edmund Hall, Oxford; Barrister.

[1] [2008] UKHL 21, [2008] 1 WLR 852, [2008] Bus LR 905 (Lord Hoffmann, Lord Phillips of Worth Matravers, Lord Scott of Foscote, Lord Walker of Gestingthorpe and Lord Neuberger of Abbotsbury), reversing [2006] EWCA Civ 732, [2007] Bus LR 250.

[2] *Harding v Wealands* [2006] UKHL 32, [2007] 2 AC 1 (noted this Year Book 77 (2006), p 565).

[3] Insolvency Act 1986, and rules made thereunder.

[4] Section 425 of the 1986 Act.

[5] Council Regulation (EC) 1346/2001, [2000] OJ L160/1.

[6] UNCITRAL Model Law on Cross-Border Insolvency, implemented in Great Britain by Insolvency Act 2000 and the Cross-Border Insolvency Regulations 2006, SI 2006/1030.

HIH was an Australian insurance company[7] which got itself into such a financial pickle that proceedings for its judicial liquidation and winding up were instituted before the Supreme Court of New South Wales. Among the assets of HIH were the proceeds of certain policies of reinsurance placed on the London market, and which funds were understood to be within the territorial jurisdiction of the English courts. Provisional liquidators were therefore appointed in England. As a matter of Australian law, in such circumstances, proceeds of reinsurance form an asset for the benefit of the relevant insurance creditors, and do not fall into the general pool for distribution according to the rules as these apply to non-reinsurance assets. But English law contained no such rule; and if the assets found in England were to be distributed according to the statutory scheme of the Insolvency Act 1986, they would follow a different path to a different destination. The Australian liquidators therefore sought to have the English provisional liquidators directed to get in and hand over the English assets, for eventual distribution according to the scheme of Australian law. They made several attempts to bring this about; but in the end the Supreme Court of NSW made a request under section 426(4) of the Insolvency Act 1986, which allows the court 'having jurisdiction in relation to insolvency law in [England to] assist the courts having the corresponding jurisdiction in [Australia]'.[8] The immediate objection to making the orders applied for was that some of those who stood to benefit as creditors in the English liquidation of HIH stood to be prejudiced if the assets passed out of the control of the English provisional liquidators and the English statutory distribution scheme. They might point to their rights under the English statutory scheme, and oppose any order which would have the effect of setting them aside. David Richards J saw the point as one which led him to the conclusion that he had no power to accede to the request of the NSW Court. The Court of Appeal took the view that it did have the power, but that it would be wrong in the circumstances to exercise it. The House of Lords held that the provisional liquidator should be directed to do as the NSW Court had requested, but divided on the question whether the source of the power so to direct the provisional liquidators was to be found in the common law or in the Insolvency Act 1986. This suggests that there was no right answer waiting to be found, only a range of imperfect solutions to a problem—that of seeking to reduce the overall cost and to increase the overall coherence of cross-border insolvency— which struck the various judges in different ways.

The problem is that there are impossibly contradictory demands which need to be organized as best one can. For it is widely held that although legislative schemes for insolvent liquidations work according to their

---

[7] The facts have been simplified for the purpose of this Note, for 'HIH' was in fact a group of companies incorporated under Australian law. But nothing turns on this, and HIH may be referred to as though it were the single and sole Australian entity.

[8] Australia being a country designated by the Secretary of State under s 426(11) of the 1986 Act.

terms for insolvencies which are territorially confined, they are not well designed to meet the distinct needs of those more complex insolvencies which cross national lines. Those who make international insolvency the centre of their daily attention tend to reduce the available philosophies to two: universalism and territorialism. The former has as its ambition that where there is an insolvency with international elements, the law should strive to produce a result which is equally fair to everyone;[9] the latter promotes the view that each state should deal with and apply its own law to the component of the insolvency over which it has territorial jurisdiction, and should not seek to do otherwise in search of a broader result.[10] Each approach is coherent in its pure form; equally, each is unattractive in its pure form, and as a result, tends to be advocated in a modified, watered-down form. As with all compromises, the modified doctrines have fewer sharp edges and inflict fewer wounds; but they look messy, irresolute and not completely predictable. The Insolvency Act 1986 is itself a good example of an irresolute statutory provision. Apart from making provision in section 426(4) for cooperation with the competent authorities in designated countries, the statute also allows the application of the law of another country, but in terms which are perplexing. Section 426(5) provides that:

For the purposes of subsection (4) a request made to a court...by a court...in [Australia] is authority for the court to which the request is made to apply, in relation to matters specified in the request, the insolvency law which is applicable by either court in relation to comparable matters falling within its jurisdiction. In exercising its discretion under this sub-section, a court shall have regard in particular to the rules of private international law.

The meaning of this is far from obviously clear: the English court may apply English law, and may apply Australian law, in dealing with the object of the request for assistance, but in doing either of these, shall have regard to the rules of private international law.[11]

One analysis of the issue in *re HIH* was, therefore, that s 426(5) authorized the English court to apply Australian insolvency law, and that this therefore allowed it to direct the provisional liquidators to collect and remit the English assets for Australian distribution. In doing so, would the English court be applying Australian law? Lord Hoffmann, in characteristically forthright terms, said not: the application of Australian law would be done by the Australian court, not the English court.[12] This, however, is to play with words. Of course the Australian liquidators would apply Australian insolvency law, but that does not preclude the contention that the English court

---

[9] For those helped by illustration drawn from popular culture, the universalist position calls to mind the famous seventies advertisement for Coca-Cola in which a smiling multi-ethnic crowd warbles about how each person present would: 'like to teach the world to sing; In perfect harmony...'.

[10] In the same vein, the territorialist approach calls to mind the BBC television series 'The League of Gentlemen' and the unnerving siblings, Edward and Tubbs, who were memorable for telling outsiders that 'This is a local shop for local people; there's nothing for you here...'.

[11] For the question of which country's private international law this might be, see further below.

[12] At [27].

is also applying Australian law in ordering the provisional liquidators to remit the assets to Australia for distribution according to the Australian scheme. The only rule of law which directs that distribution is a rule of Australian law, and it therefore follows that the English court, in making such an order, is applying Australian law. If this does not persuade, one may read 'apply' in the sub-section in its common legal sense of 'apply or cause to be applied'. This view of section 426(5) was favoured by a bare majority of the House; and it appears to be correct. Section 426(5) empowered to the English court to direct the provisional liquidator to collect and remit the assets for distribution according to Australian insolvency law; and the majority were right to say that it did.

But to give the court power is not to answer the further and separate question of how it should exercise that power. Two issues immediately arise. The first is how can this be done when its effect will be to deprive some who have an interest[13] in the assets of the expectation of receipt? For there is no doubt that when assets leave England, general creditors (or in the end, contributories) will lose out; and the outcome will be that the scheme for distribution in the 1986 Act will not be applied to the English assets. Scott V-C (as he then was) had wrestled with this in *Re BCCI (No 10)*,[14] and had come to the uneasy conclusion that he did not have power to make any order which had the effect of dis-applying a statutory part[15] of the English scheme. The trouble with this is, as it was then, that it had the potential[16] to emasculate the duty and power given by section 426. This is because the English scheme for distribution of assets in an insolvent winding up is exhaustive: every penny of the assets collected in will go somewhere: there will be no remainder left over and unclaimed. The logic of Scott V-C's conclusion is,[17] as it was then, that it will never be a proper exercise of the power for a court to order remission to a foreign liquidator unless the outcome will be identical with the distribution which would result from non-remission, which makes the whole thing useless. It is hard to accept that this would be a rational interpretation of

[13] Of course, much turns on the real nature of that interest. If the creditors have rights properly so called, it is hard to see that these can be overridden by a judicial discretion. If, on the other hand, they do not have rights in this sense, but have merely or instead an interest in the proper administration of the insolvency, then they have much less of a basis for objecting to the exercise of discretion by the court. One interpretation of *Cambridge Gas Transport Corp v Official Committee of Unsecured Creditors of Navigator Holdings plc* [2006] UKPC 26, [2007] 1 AC 508 (noted this Year Book, 77 (2006), p 575) is that insolvency is not concerned with the determination or vindication of rights, but with the organization of collective execution against assets of the insolvent: see esp at [14]. If that is accepted, the complaint of the English creditors that their rights were being abrogated misses the target: their rights are not in question, but the issue is how to organize the enforcement of all the rights of all those who have them; and on that, individual creditors do not have a veto.

[14] [1997] Ch 213.

[15] In that case, the insolvency set-off in Insolvency Rules, SI 1986/1925, rule 4.90.

[16] But only the potential. In *re BCCI*, the main insolvency was in Luxembourg, which had not been designated by the Secretary of State under section 426(5). As a result, any power to make an order cooperating with the Luxembourg insolvency proceedings had to be justified by the common law.

[17] Though Scott V-C did not appear to accept that it would necessarily be so.

the intention of the legislature as expressed in section 426 of the Act. The question is then how to make sense of section 426(5), while not losing sight of the objection that English creditors will have ground for objection if assets leave the control of the English provisional liquidator before they get their hands on them.

The second issue points to the answer. The sub-section requires the court to have regard to the rules of private international law. This cannot be taken as a reference to those rules which bind the court and tie the hands of the judges in any event, for there is no point in telling a judge that he should have regard to laws by which he is directly bound. Those rules of private international law which determine whether a contractual claim is valid, whether A has a valid claim against B for damages for a tort, whether property belongs to C or D, and so forth, retain their effect, and nothing in section 426(5) will bear on the point. But there was a principle of the common law of private international law, to the effect that an English court might consider its liquidation to be ancillary to one taking place in another jurisdiction and might, as a consequence of that characterization, act in a particular way.[18] In fact, the idea that an English liquidation was ancillary to another, and that this was legally as distinct from factually significant, seems to lack a proper pedigree. But despite this shadowy parentage, the idea has taken hold, and nowadays no-one would have trouble with the notion that the English liquidations in *re BCCI (No 10)*, and the English provisional liquidation in *re HIH*, were to be seen as ancillary to something much bigger, taking place before the courts of the place of incorporation. This seems to be a principle of private international law, at least according to the common law. And not only that: the idea of dominant and servient liquidations finds its echo in the Insolvency Regulation,[19] where the terminology is that of 'main' and 'secondary' insolvency proceedings, and in the UNCITRAL Model Law, where it is expressed, even more prosaically, as 'main' and 'non-main' proceedings. Seen in this light, the idea that there are principal and ancillary insolvencies is part of the private international law of the law of nations, and not just a piece of common law. If one interprets the words at the end of section 426(5) in this way, it becomes easier to see why the majority was right to understand the sub-section as providing authority for the making of the order sought by the Australian court: private international law acknowledges that a court may act differently according to whether its proceedings are principal or ancillary, main or secondary, main or non-main. One might venture the view that Lords Scott and Neuberger made rather heavy weather of a rather short point,[20] but when Lord Hoffmann[21] is taking an

---

[18] See Lord Hoffmann at [8]; *re Matheson Bros Ltd* (1884) 27 Ch D 225.

[19] Regulation (EC) 1346/2000.

[20] Lord Phillips confined himself to the conclusion that Lords Scott and Neuberger had identified a legislative basis for their decision, with which he agreed; and said no more.

[21] With whom Lord Walker expressed unconditional agreement.

opposing view, some judges will feel the need to labour the point in which they see the right answer.

And there is this. Those who dealt with HIH, or with Australian companies in the HIH group, knew or should have known that they were making an agreement with an Australian company. When they chose to place themselves in the position of potential creditor of an Australian company, they did so with eyes which must be deemed to have been wide open. They knew or ought to have known that they would, in some respects, have the rights which Australian law gave them. They would have other rights as well, such as those which were created under the laws which governed any contractual relationship with HIH. But just as with shareholders in HIH, they entered into a voluntary relationship with HIH which therefore had a natural connection to Australian law. Indeed, if one were to have asked these putative creditors which law they would have expected to determine whether HIH might be wound up, the answer is likely to be Australian law. If the Australian courts had wound up HIH, or if the Australian statutory procedure for corporate reconstruction had been implemented,[22] with the consequence that HIH disappeared and was reincarnate in a new corporate form, most people would have little difficulty in accepting that if you contract with an entity incorporated under Australian law, Australian law can also put it to sleep. And if the entity is destroyed by Australian law, the financial consequences which result from this will naturally be those which Australian law provides.[23] To put it a little crudely: if you contract with an Australian corporation, and it goes bust and is wound up, what law do you expect to regulate the share-out of what remains after the preferred creditors have taken that which counts as theirs? The answer is Australian law; and this piece of common sense ought to have reassured the majority in the conclusion to which it came.

Lord Hoffmann saw the problem from a different angle. He has, for some considerable time, promoted the idea that judges can, by international judicial cooperation, bring about a coordination of cross-border insolvency which legislatures either had not, or cannot, achieve for themselves. His conclusion that the common law allows for this creative judicial management can be traced back to the problems generated by Robert Maxwell's inter-continental frauds,[24] but it also motivated his conclusion in *Cambridge Gas Transport Corp v Official Committee of Unsecured Creditors of Navigator Holdings plc*[25] that a Manx court could and should direct the cancellation of shareholdings in a Manx company, just because an American court requested it as part of its process of corporate reconstruction. No statutory

---

[22] Financial Sector (Business Transfer and Group Restructure) Act 1999 (Cth).

[23] There is more than an echo of the view that where the *lex contractus* of a supposed contract determines that the contract was originally or became void as a source of legal obligation, that same law should regulate the remedial consequences of that conclusion, and all the more so if the *lex contractus* was expressly chosen by the parties to the supposed contract.

[24] *Barclays Bank plc v Homan* [1992] BCC 757 (CA).

[25] [2006] UKPC 26, [2007] 1 AC 508 (noted this Year Book, 77 (2006), p 575).

rule of Manx law provided for such a thing; but the Privy Council, speaking through Lord Hoffmann, thought it to be, or to contribute to, the best way to sort the mess into which a company had got itself. In *re HIH*, the thinking of Lord Hoffmann appeared to be that the legislation did not authorize the order which the court was asked to make, but the common law could come to the conclusion that this was really an Australian insolvency, and act accordingly. Some may see echoes of a principle analogous to that of *forum non conveniens*, which so transformed the rigidity of the jurisdictional rules of the English common law: the development of a cousin-principle of *concursus non conveniens*, perhaps? In *re HIH* the solution was to order the assets to be remitted to Australia;[26] in the *Cambridge* case, by making an order which could only be made effective by a Manx court. But the unease which attended the decision in the *Cambridge* case, as shareholders found themselves deprived of their property when a Manx court acceded to a request made as a result of American judicial proceedings in which they had not been involved, does not altogether go away until one understands and accepts that those who enter into a relationship with an artificial person need to realize that the law which created the counterparty may also un-create it; and in the process of un-creation, that foreign law may also determine the financial consequences of that un-creation. If this works badly for them, that's just too bad. No-one forced them into this relationship.[27] If you become a temporary member of an Australian club or society, you take the risk that Australian law will apply to you so long as you remain bound to it, and that you may not like it: *qui sentit commodum, sentire debet et onus*; in for a penny, in for a pound.[28]

The result was that the decision of the House of Lords was what it should have been: this was an Australian liquidation, and the assets should have been dealt with[29] as though they were Australian assets, even if they happened to be in England. Lord Hoffmann's justification is, perhaps, not sufficiently persuasive or predictable to be preferred; though next time a similar issue arises in relation to an insolvency in a country which has not been designated for the purposes of Section 426, it will have to be faced up to, for there will be nothing else to hand. As it was, the majority rested their conclusion on the correct legal rule, though in their interpretation of it they may have missed the best way forward. The view preferred here is that this is another context in which the general principle, that those who enter into relationships with artificial persons should not be taken by surprise when the law under which that person was created un-creates it

[26] In fact, there was no need to order a remission, for two schemes had been settled: one on the footing that cooperation with the Australian court was to be ordered, the other on the basis that it was not.

[27] This may not be entirely correct: if the creditor has a claim in tort against the insolvent company, the proposition that the relationship was voluntarily created may not be completely correct. But the general principle holds.

[28] Or, given what the general creditors stood to recover, in for a pound, out for a penny.

[29] Subject to the claims of any preferred creditors under English insolvency law.

and defines the consequences of the un-creation, would have responded best to the question why these English assets should be remitted to Australia for distribution according to the scheme of Australian insolvency law.

2. Special jurisdiction at the place of delivery of goods sold: *Scottish & Newcastle International Ltd v Othon Ghalanos Ltd*[30]

Article 5(1)(b) of the Brussels I Regulation gives special jurisdiction, in matters relating to a contract for the sale of goods, to the courts of the place in a Member State where, under the contract, the goods were delivered or should have been delivered. When a Cypriot buyer ordered barrels of cider from the English manufacturer of alcoholic drinks, it was agreed that the cargo be shipped from England and delivered 'CFR Limassol'. The clear impression from the pro-forma invoices was that the sale was on f.o.b.[31] terms. Bills of lading were to be issued in the buyer's name and mailed to them immediately upon shipment. The cider arrived in Cyprus, but the buyer did not pay the price. The seller brought proceedings in England, claiming that this was the place of delivery of the goods, which were then shipped from Liverpool for transport to Limassol. The buyer objected to the jurisdiction, contending that the place of delivery was Limassol. At first instance, and on appeal, and in the House of Lords, the conclusion was that the seller was entitled to sue in England. The references in the documentation to Limassol made it clear that Limassol was the end-point of the transportation, where the goods would be discharged from the ship, but did not disturb the conclusion that the contract of sale was expressed to be governed by English law, and was on f.o.b. terms. Under this, as a matter of English law, which was the *lex contractus*, the seller transferred property and risk at Liverpool, which was where the goods were delivered to the sea-carrier as agent for the buyer. Upon that delivery, the seller held the bill of lading as agent for the buyer. Delivery under the contract of sale therefore took place at Liverpool, and the challenge to the jurisdiction failed.[32]

Given the clarity and certainty with which each of the courts came to the conclusion which it did, it is perhaps surprising that the case made its way to the House of Lords. The case makes it clear that for the purposes of Article 5(1)(b), the task of the court is to identify the terms of the contract of sale, and to ask where this contract required the goods to be delivered. In the context of the present case, this required two points to be

---

[30] [2008] UKHL 11, [2008] 2 All ER 768, [2008] Bus LR 583: Lord Bingham of Cornhill, Lord Rodger of Earlsferry, Lord Brown of Eaton-under-Heywood, Lord Mance and Lord Neuberger of Abbotsbury, dismissing the appeal from [2007] 2 Lloyd's Rep 341.

[31] 'Free on board'. These acronyms, of which more are encountered below, are a mere shorthand to describe the division of duties in the sale, transport, and delivery of goods in international trade. Their precise meanings are of no importance to this Note.

[32] It is not possible to discern from the report whether the proceedings were begun in the High Court at Liverpool, or in London. Article 5(1) would appear to specify Liverpool as the place, rather than the United Kingdom as the state, in which proceedings may be brought; but it is not known whether there was a point to be taken on this distinction.

particularly noticed. First, the contractual relationship into which the parties had entered may be more complex than that of sale: a seller may undertake to sell, to arrange transport, to insure, and to do all manner of other things. But Article 5(1)(b) asks where the contract of *sale* required delivery of the goods to be made, not where the contract for the transportation of the goods required the plane, boat, or plane to carry them to. If the contract said, in terms, that the goods would be delivered to the buyer's agent at Liverpool, but transported to Limassol for discharge, that made the place of delivery under the contract of sale Liverpool. Second, the specification of the place of delivery is a matter over which the buyer and seller are sovereign. More fool them if they act in such a way that they do not understand what they have done, or if they subscribe to a kind of contract which they do not fully understand. But it is up to them; and it is no-one else's business to settle it. In particular, it is not for some 'autonomous interpretation' of where this particular contract required the delivery of the goods: the same would be true if the parties had not identified a particular place, but had opted for the default rule of the *lex contractus*. Every now and then there is an attempt to undermine this simple truth, which is vouched for by *Industrie Tessili Italiana Como v Dunlop AG*;[33] and every time[34] the European Court repels the challenge, even when this involves departing from the advice of its Advocates-General.[35] So the question in the instant case was whether the claimant could show the court, or could be said to have much the better of the argument, that the parties' contract of sale called for the delivery of the goods to be at Liverpool. He could, and that was that.

As it was common ground that the contract was governed by English law, English law would specify the provisions of the contract which the parties left blank. Section 32(1) of the Sale of Goods Act 1979 provides that:

'where, in pursuance of a contract of sale, the seller is authorised or required to send the goods to the buyer, delivery of the goods to the carrier (whether named by the buyer or not) for the purpose of transmission to the buyer is prima facie deemed to be a delivery of the goods to the buyer'.

Nothing in the contract provided otherwise, with the consequence that the delivery to the carrier in Liverpool was the delivery of the goods sold under the contract of sale. Mercifully, Lord Rodger declined to spend too long on the distinctions to be drawn between different kinds of contracts for the sale of goods, known in the trade by their initials but serving to mystify everyone else.[36] He advised that one should simply concentrate

---

[33] Case 12/76 [1976] ECR 1473.
[34] For example, Case C-288/92 *Custom Made Commercial Ltd v Stawa Metallbau GmbH* [1994] ECR I-2913.
[35] Case C-440/97 *Groupe Concorde v Master of the vessel 'Suhadiwarno Panjan'* [1999] ECR I-6307 and Case C-420/97 *Leathertex Divisione Sintetici SpA v Bodetex BVBA* [1999] ECR I-6747.
[36] See at [13] on whether the contract was cfr, cif or fob.

on the terms, and if one did that, both section 32 and the fact that on a true construction of the contract under English law, the seller disposed of its entire interest in the goods when handing them over at Liverpool, meant that the English court had special jurisdiction under Article 5(1)(b).

Lord Mance was more ambitious, prepared to go further than Lord Rodger and lay down some broader rules.[37] His analysis of why it was correct to see the contract as providing for delivery of the goods at Liverpool was more elaborate than that of Lord Rodger, but it came down to the same, single point: as a matter of the construction of the individual contract and as a matter of English law as set out in section 32 of the Act, when the buyer parted with possession at Liverpool, it no longer retained any interest in the goods, and had therefore delivered them; it having acted in accordance with the contract, it could be seen that the contract called for delivery of the goods at Liverpool. He went on to consider the case, of which this was not one, where the seller might retain 'symbolic possession' through the bills of lading, after parting with the physical goods to the carrier. This might be thought to open the door to an argument that there was no delivery of the goods until the documents of title were surrendered (and at that time, delivery might indicate the location of the cargo or of the documents), or no delivery in a single place, or something different again. Mercifully, he came back to the conclusion that the place at which the physical goods were handed over to the carrier would still be a good guide to the place of delivery, this being identified (if it be in doubt) as a matter for the *lex contractus* to decide. He then, in the present submission, spoiled everything by suggestion that, as an alternative, the court could locate the place with special jurisdiction by 'engaging in autonomous conceptions of delivery'.[38]

One hopes that this throwaway line, at the tail end of the judgment, will be quietly forgotten. The place where the contract requires the goods to be delivered is a matter for the parties, if they wish, to specify for themselves, and if they do not wish to specify, to be supplied by the law which they chose to govern the contract which they made, and if they did not wish to choose, by the law of the country with which the contract has its closest connection.[39] Autonomous definition has no part to play in this. It is just possible, it is admitted, that one may ask for an independent definition of what it means to deliver goods under a contract for the sale of goods, but it difficult to imagine that the answer to the question would be substantially at variance with the 'voluntary transfer of possession from one person to another', which is the definition given by Sale of Goods Act 1979 s 61(1). Under this contract, that was required to be done in England,

---

[37] Lord Brown and Neuberger expressed their agreement with Lord Mance, but noticeably not with Lord Rodger. Lord Bingham shared the reservations of Lord Rodger about the obiter dicta in the judgment of Lord Mance.

[38] At [55].

[39] Rome Convention (Contracts (Applicable Law) Act 1990, Sch 1), Art 4(1).

at Liverpool. Were the contract to provide for the delivery to be at several places within England, this would still suffice to give special jurisdiction to the courts for any of the places where delivery was due.[40]

Needless complication will also arise, as Lord Mance may unintentionally have demonstrated, if we adopt sub-rules to identify the place of delivery as a matter of law under the various contracts encountered in international trade. The mistake would be to suppose that each of these is utterly monolithic, so that the place of delivery can be identified by category. Not so: Lord Rodger, as previously mentioned, observed that the contract in the case before him did not fit easily and only into the one alphabetic type. Lord Mance was clearer still:

'there is considerable flexibility both within and between the categorisations such as fob, cfr (or c&f), cif and ex ship.'[41]

The individual contract in the present case was considered to be 'in all essential respects an f.o.b. contract. All the indicia of an f.o.b. contract are present'.[42] But what this goes to demonstrate is that there is no advantage whatsoever in trying to shoehorn contracts, which may be infinitely variable, into too small a number of pigeonholes, for the purpose of deriving an answer from the individual pigeonhole rather than from the content of the individual contract. We may have just learned that in relation to jurisdiction clauses, which are variable in all sorts of ways, and which risk being denatured if we are told that they must be either exclusive or non-exclusive and that there is no *tertium quid*. We need to remember that the way one identifies the place where, under the contract the goods were to be delivered is, and is only ever, by reading and if necessary construing the terms of the individual contract. There are no shortcuts; there are only false trails.

It remains to say a further word about the methodology, correct and adopted by all of their Lordships, of identifying the place of delivery as a term of contractual art by reference to the *lex contractus*. It has been noted above that this approach to the interpretation and location of contractual terms was established by the European Court in 1976, and has not been displaced in its subsequent jurisprudence. This is striking, for the *Tessili* decision has been the target of endless sniping from many sides.[43] The basis for the objection appears to be that *Tessili* leaves special jurisdiction as remaining dependent on a question being answered by reference to the

---

[40] Case C-386/05 *Color Drack GmbH v Lexx International Vertriebs GmbH* [2007] ECR I-3699 (claimant may sue at the principal place of delivery, failing which at any place of delivery which it chooses within the Member State in question).

[41] At [34].

[42] At [36].

[43] See for example Magnus & Mankowski, *Brussels I Regulation*, p 134–5. The most recent example may be found in Hare & Hinks [2008] LMCLQ 353.

lex contractus and, as the various Member States may[44] not be of a single mind on the question of what the *lex contractus* is, *Tessili* opens the door to divergence in judicial view about the place of performance for the purpose of Article 5(1). There appears to be neither limit nor end to the production of such nonsense. Whatever those who complain about *Tessili* may pretend, the jurisdictional rule in Article 5(1)(b) directs attention to where, *under the contract*, the goods were (to be) delivered. The material question is not: 'where were the goods delivered?', which is a question which just might have been understood and answered in purely factual terms,[45] but which was not posed by the legislation. It asks, instead, where *under the contract* this happened (if it did) or was to happen (if it did not but should have). That is not a question about a matter of fact; it is a question about a legal stipulation, a legal obligation. The interpretation of any, of every, contractual obligation is a matter for the law which governs that contract.[46] That is as illuminating a truth today as it was in 1976, and it remains so even if those in the darkness comprehend it not. As to the contention that the modified language, now set out as Article 5(1)(b) of the Brussels I Regulation, was intended to break the link between special jurisdiction and the *lex contractus*, two things need to be said. First, it may well have been the intention of some, but if it was, they failed to consecrate their intention in the legislative wording used. It is well known and understood that the wording agreed as Article 5(1)(b) did not emerge as the logical destination to which lengthy prior discussion had been leading,[47] but was a back-of-the-envelope jotting which was accepted to sidestep the irreconcilability in national positions and allow everyone to

[44] Though this is an increasingly unlikely possibility as choice of law for contractual obligations is harmonized.

[45] Although it would require an autonomous interpretation of 'delivered', which will be more easily done with some contracts than others.

[46] Cf Fawcett Harris & Bridge, *International Sale of Goods in the Conflict of Laws*, para 3.194, assert that this requires the court to look at the *contract* but to be blind to the law which governs that contract and provides the meaning of the terms used in it. There appears to be no merit in such a suggestion.

[47] The article by Hare & Hinks, at 357, appears to assume that the final text of Article 5(1)(b) was adopted to give effect to the original intention of the European Commission as expressed in its proposal for legislation. This is not correct. Neither is their suggestion that the continued applicability of *Tessili* within Art 5(1)(b) was overcome by Case C-386/05 *Color Drack GmbH v Lexx International Vertriebs GmbH* [2007] ECR I-3699. Paragraph [30] of the judgment simply observes that Article 5(1)(b) determines the international and the national jurisdiction of the court under this rule. This is the sense in which the Article excludes reference to national law. At [39] the judgment makes clear that special jurisdiction is no longer determined by reference to 'each of the obligations' in the contract, and varying be reference to the particular one upon which the claimant bases his claim: instead, the place of contractual delivery is competent no matter the particular obligation on which the claim is based. In short, nothing in this decision casts proper doubt on the *Tessili* methodology.
It is also to be observed in the judgment in *Color Drack* that, according to the Court, Article 5 of the Regulation specifies and determines the international *and* national jurisdiction. If that is so, it will mean that where it specifies the courts of a part of the United Kingdom, there will be no residual power in the court so identified to stay proceedings in favour of the courts of another part of the United Kingdom. The view to the contrary, to the broad affect that nothing in the Regulation served to prevent a court in one part of the United Kingdom staying proceedings in favour of a court in another part is, therefore, disapproved: see on this Briggs & Rees, *Civil Jurisdiction and Judgments*

get to bed.[48] Second, the dominant intention of those who considered it to be necessary to re-write the rule which had existed as Article 5(1) of the Brussels Convention was an entirely different one: to prevent an unpaid seller being able to seise the courts of his home jurisdiction by arguing that the obligation upon which he founded his claim was that of the buyer to pay; that according to the contract or the *lex contractus* payment was due at the seller's place of business, and therefore the courts at that place had special jurisdiction. It is historically accurate, and clear, that this was the target of the legislative reform, and the reform succeeded in its aim: the unpaid seller can no longer seise the courts for the place where payment was to be made unless this is also the place where, under the contract, the goods were delivered, *et cetera*. Further than that the reform did not go; further than that it would have been daft for it to have tried to get. It would be nice to think that we have heard the last of this anti-*Tessili* nonsense, but the naysayers have allowed neither the constant jurisprudence of the European Court and the House of Lords, nor the text of the legislation, to dissuade them, and it is probably too much to hope for now. More's the pity of it.

3. Precedence of proceedings in the seisin race: *Phillips v Symes (No 3);*[49] *Olafsson v Gissurarson;*[50] *Kolden Holdings Ltd v Rodette Commerce Ltd;*[51] *Bush v Bush*[52]

As is well known, the general scheme of the Brussels Convention and Regulations adopts a rule to control the outbreak of parallel litigation of claims. So long as the proceedings are in respect of the same cause of action and between the same parties, and subject to immaterial exceptions, the court which is first seized has jurisdiction, and the court seized second does not. If the prize for winning the race to institute proceedings first is clear, and may be substantial, the penalty for a foot fault in the process of service, or of giving the game away—careless talk costs *lis*, as one may say—before service is attempted, is potentially immense. It is no surprise that some expensive attention has been given to the question of the precise date upon which a court was seized. The fact that this may be accompanied by judicial disapproval is a curious incident of modern adjudication.

(4th ed, 2005), para 2.231; Dicey, Morris & Collins, *The Conflict of Laws* (14th edn, 2006), para 12–024 and Second Cumulative Supplement, para S12–024.

  [48] See Beaumont in Fawcett (ed) *Reform and Development of Private International Law*, pp 15–21.
  [49] [2008] UKHL 1, [2008] 1 WLR 180: Lord Bingham of Cornhill, Lord Rodger of Earlsferry, Baroness Hale of Richmond, Lord Brown of Eaton-under-Heywood and Lord Mance: the case is also reported as *Phillips v Nussberger*: reversing [2006] EWCA Civ 645, [2006] 1 WLR 2598 (noted this Year Book, 77 (2006), 595).
  [50] [2008] EWCA Civ 152, [2008] 1 WLR 2016: Sir Anthony Clarke MR, Dyson and Jacobs LJJ.
  [51] [2008] EWCA Civ 10, [2008] 1 Lloyd's Rep 434: Tuckey, Lawrence Collins and Rimer LJJ, affirming [2008] 1 Lloyd's Rep 197.
  [52] [2008] EWCA Civ 865, [2008] 2 FLR 1437: Thorpe, Lawrence Collins and Rimer LJJ.

The facts of *Phillips v Symes* will, by now, be well known. The issue was whether the English courts were seized prior to those of the Swiss canton of Zürich. The problem had arisen because the package of English papers ultimately served on Mrs Nussberger by a Swiss judicial officer did not include the original writ which, by English administrative error, had been stamped with the legend 'not for service out of the jurisdiction'. She saw her chance to institute proceedings in Zürich. In due course, Peter Smith J made an order declaring that the English court had been seized as from the date of incomplete service, and dispensing the claimant from the need to (re-)serve the writ. This meant that the date on which the English proceedings were definitively pending was held to be sooner than the date on which the Zürich proceedings had been commenced. The Court of Appeal reversed him, on the ground that the English proceedings were not definitively pending until the date on which Peter Smith J had made his order and that, whatever else the order did, it did not rewrite history. This would have left the Zürich proceedings with temporal priority. The House of Lords restored the judgment at first instance, holding that the original service, even if not perfect in every material particular, was more than sufficient to establish that service had been made and that, if this were taken to be the date on which an English court was seized, the English court had been seized first. It is not known what effect this has had on the proceedings in Zürich, though the answer ought to be clear.

Parallel litigation as between the courts of the United Kingdom and Switzerland is controlled by the Lugano Convention which, until amended,[53] means that a court is seized when proceedings are 'definitively pending' before it. Two issues therefore arose. One was as to the application of the rule on the footing that definitively pending, in the context of English proceedings, meant on service of process. The second was whether an English court was seized for this purpose on service or on some other, earlier, occasion, such as the issue of proceedings or the making of orders for interlocutory relief prior to service. As to the first of these, there was little to constrain the court which, it may be surmized, took a dim view of the behaviour of Mrs Nussberger and found no sufficient reason to allow her to get away with it. Lord Brown took the view that when Peter Smith J declared the original imperfect service to have been effective, he was not rewriting history to deem service to have been made on a day on which it was not made, but was determining that the service made on that day should stand as good service. It is difficult to find fault with this. It responds to a sense that when she received the package of documents from the duly-appointed Swiss process server, Mrs Nussberger was left in no doubt that

---

[53] The process of amending the Lugano Convention to bring its content into line with the Brussels I Regulation is well underway: the text is at 2007 OJ L339/1. It will enter into effect six months after being ratified by the EU and one of the three (Iceland, Norway, and Switzerland) Contracting States.

proceedings had been instituted against her in the English courts. An approximate trend in the modern case-law has shown the European Court to be unreceptive to arguments raised by persons complaining that there were deficiencies in the paperwork or the service which lead to the supposed consequence that the initial error invalidated everything which followed. The most striking recent example was in *ASML Netherlands BV v SEMIS*,[54] where it was specifically held that a defendant, upon whom a judgment had not been served, had still been given enough information for him to be able to learn that the judgment had been given and to be expected to challenge it if so advised. The defendant's contention, which amounted to saying that as the service had been less than perfect he was to be treated as though there had been no service at all, was unattractive and was rejected. Nothing in the *ASML* decision supported the contention, effectively advanced by Mrs Nussberger, that unless and until there had been an act of service, or acts of service, perfect in every detail, the English court was not seized. Nor did it appeal to Lord Brown, who came very close[55] to saying that it was up to English law to decide what was needed to satisfy a requirement that a case be 'definitively pending', and that offshore contribution was not helpful. Nor was it necessary for Lord Brown to consider that his decision, or that of Peter Smith J, involved the English proceedings in 'jumping the seisin queue', as Pill LJ had put it below.[56] All that had happened was that the original service of process, over which a question mark may been thought to hang, was confirmed as having been good and effective.

All that being said, there is something unsettling about the proposition that the original service was deemed to have been good: one does not have to be Lord Mildew to consider that there can be 'too much of this damned deeming'.[57] Perhaps the proper response is that nothing was deemed, or deemed to have happened at any time other than that which it did happen. The effect of *Phillips v Symes* is that an English court is seized, for the purpose of the Lugano Convention, on the date of effective service, which is to say service which is held to have been sufficient for the purposes of the civil procedure rules. Not on the date of perfect service, or on the date of perfected service, but on the date of service whether perfect or tolerably imperfect. It was, as Lord Brown, a matter for English law to determine the date on which it considered the proceedings to be definitively pending. Unless the law is to descend to a hunt for minute discrepancies and loopholes, this decision was surely inevitable. So long as the approach of the

---

[54] Case C-283/05, [2006] ECR I-12041. Oddly, perhaps, the decision does not appear to have been cited to the House of Lords.

[55] At [35].

[56] Though Lord Brown, at [35], did express the view that if this was what was happening, he was untroubled by it. This is not, perhaps, a helpful contribution to the analysis.

[57] Megarry, *Miscellany-at-Law* (London, 1955), p 361, attributes this to A P Herbert's report of *Travers v Travers*, which was not one of the fictional cases collected and published in Herbert, *Uncommon Law* (London, 1935).

court is consistent with the principle that a defendant needs to be able to understand that a case has been commenced, or that judgment has been given, against him, before his position may be taken as having been affected, which it was, there is no need to ask for any more when answering the question whether the proceedings are definitively pending for the purposes of the Lugano Convention.

It was therefore unnecessary for the House of Lords to consider whether the Court of Appeal had been correct in *Dresser UK Ltd v Falcongate Freight Management Ltd*[58] to hold that an English court was seized for the purposes of the Convention on service rather than on issue, and correct in *The Sargasso*[59] to hold that there were no exceptions to this rule which might otherwise have supported the argument that an English court was seized on the making of orders against a defendant prior to service of the claim form. If clarity were the principal concern—as well it might be, given that the rule has to be one which a foreign court may understand as part of its decision whether it was seized before or after the English court—the inevitable answer was the one the Court of Appeal gave: that service was required, and no exceptions could be permitted. But if the dominant principle was to ask whether something had happened to put the defendant on notice that proceedings were in the offing, there was no need to require service of the claim form. Service of an *ex parte* order, such as a freezing injunction, would suffice to get that message across, even before the claim form arrived, borne by a competent process server. Lord Mance[60] was not prepared to stop where Lord Brown had. His view was that an English court should consider itself to be seized on issue of the claim form, or on the making of an order such as an interlocutory injunction prior to any service of the claim form. Service, as he saw it, came much later than the point at which proceedings could first be said to be definitively pending. The attraction of issue is that it has become the date of seisin of an English court under the Brussels I Regulation; the attraction of the date on which a judicial order is made is that it is, at that stage, jolly difficult to contend that the English court is not seized of something. But each point can be answered. Provisional and protective measures are not founded on the same cause of action as the substantive claim; their availability is governed by rules which lie outside those otherwise listed in Title II of the Convention; jurisdiction to grant them is not dependent on the court having jurisdiction over the merits of the substantive claim. A court which has been asked to grant such relief may never be seized with a substantive claim, and it is just too difficult if the law is to hold that a court may be seized of a substantive claim which is never in fact commenced. Given all this, it is difficult to the point of being impossible to see how a court could be said to be seized merely by virtue of its having made an order for provisional measures. As the issue is of virtually no

---

[58] [1992] QB 502, CA.   [59] [1994] 3 All ER 180, CA.
[60] With whom Baroness Hale agreed.

practical significance, given the immediate realignment of the Lugano Convention with the Brussels I Regulation in general and with its Article 30 in particular, no more needs to be said. But the disparaging of *The Sargasso* was, in the present submission, unjustified. Whether an English court should have been seen as seized on issue, rather than service, will be a detail of legal history.

Irregularity in service, and the effect on the fact or date of seisin for the purposes of the Lugano Convention, arose also, if peripherally, in *Olafsson v Gissurarson*. An Icelandic businessman complained of libel on the English website of the Icelandic defendant, a university professor and right-wing controversialist. Process was served in Iceland on the defendant in person by HM Consul in Reykjavik. But the defendant was not asked to sign a receipt for the summons and, as a result, the service failed to conform to the technical requirements of Icelandic law. It followed that service had not been 'duly made' and the defendant, acting on legal advice which may not have been wholly sound, ignored the summons. Judgment was entered in default of appearance; an application to set it aside was dismissed by the Master who purported to 'cure' any irregularity in service. This was, in due course, set aside by the judge, whose decision that the judgment be set aside was not appealed. The claimant then sought to start again, but to avoid the need to re-serve the writ by applying for an order dispensing him from the need to re-serve it. It was necessary for him also to apply for and obtain an extension of time for such service, for the claim was now out of time for issue of a fresh claim form. There were at no point any proceedings instituted before the Icelandic court, and therefore no question of the claimant's being accused of attempting to disrupt the order of seisin, but the decision of the Court of Appeal on the application to extend the validity of the claim form and the time for its service, would determine whether the Icelandic defendant could be sued in England. The case therefore had less of an international dimension than *Phillips v Symes*, or the next case which we will note; but the court still applied the jurisprudence on the Lugano Convention to it.[61] By the time it came to give its judgment, it had the benefit of the decision in *Phillips v Symes*. The broad theme of the latter, that if the defendant had been sufficiently served (in the sense that it was not unfair to him for the English court to overlook any imperfection), then the service would be regarded as having been effectively made, pointed inescapably to the conclusion that service on the defendant should be regarded as sufficient. It therefore held that the judge had been entitled

---

[61] There was a second argument advanced on behalf of the defendant, that Article IV of the First Protocol to the Lugano Convention restricted the means of service which could be utilized for the delivery of English process in Iceland, and that this precluded the operation of a procedural rule of English law to overcome any deficiencies in service. The court rejected the analysis of Article IV which led to this supposed conclusion, not least because there is no bilateral Convention between the United Kingdom and Iceland, of any multi-partite Convention to which both are party, to which Article IV could make reference. However, the importance is not such as to merit further attention here.

to rule that the defendant had been duly served. The question was really no more than whether an irregularity in service could be forgiven on application to the court. The court saw no reason in principle not to forgive it in accordance with clear and established principles of English domestic law, and found nothing in the Lugano Convention to cause it to have second thoughts.

One may wonder whether we are moving, more or less deliberately, to a position in which 'served' in the context of the Convention and Regulations means 'sufficiently served'. This makes sense in a case like the present, where an English-speaking defendant could point only to the lack of a signature to support his contention that he had not been duly served, that this was fatal to the claimant, and that it was now too late for anything to be done about it. There was no sense in *Olafsson* that the claimant was indulging in sharp practice in the way exemplified by Mrs Nussberger in *Phillips v Symes*. But other cases will not be so clear-cut, and a judgment which seemed inevitable on its facts seems just as likely to unlock the door to further controversy in future.

Another case in which it was necessary to thwart the antics of a litigant prepared to play disreputable games, but this under the rules of the Brussels I Regulation, arose in *Kolden Holdings Ltd v Rodette Commercial Ltd*. A had a claim against R, which was commenced in the English courts. At some point, A assigned its interests to K, notified R, and made an application to have K substituted for A as claimant against R in the English proceedings. But in the gap between the notification of the assignment, and the application for permission to amend coming on for hearing, R launched proceedings against K in Cyprus, for a declaration of non-liability. The Cypriot court, sensibly enough, seemed disposed to wait and see whether the English courts considered themselves to be the courts first seized, notwithstanding that according to R, the first action which has involved K as a party was the one brought by it in Cyprus. The Court of Appeal, affirming Aikens J, held that as the English action as commenced by A was first in time, and as the substitution of K for A had the effect of making K party to the proceedings from the date of their inception, the English action was at all material times and in all material respects prior to the Cypriot proceedings. It followed that Article 27 of the Regulation did not require the English court to consider itself, in relation to the proceedings before the Cypriot court, to be seized second. Of course, it would be for the Cypriot court to decide for itself whether to conclude that it was seized second in relation to the English proceedings, but as the decision of the Court of Appeal was a judgment in a civil or commercial matter, the obligation on the Cypriot court to recognize it, imposed by Chapter III of the Regulation, was likely to be conclusive.

The answer reached by the Court of Appeal was so obviously right that there is little to be said about it. The contention of the defendant was that K, which did not become added as a party to the proceedings until an order to that effect had been made, was a defendant to the claim in Cyprus before it was claimant in the English proceedings. Had it been a simple matter of looking in K's diary, to see which of the two events in which it was involved had been recorded first, this would have been correct. But the question is not so simple, for Article 27 asks when each court was seized of the proceedings before it, always assuming that these are between the same parties and founded on the same cause of action.[62] As to that, the English court was seized of the claim in the original claim form on the issue of the original claim form, and K was legal proprietor of that claim.[63] Its interest in the proceedings was the same interest as that of A: to put it in the idiom of the European Court, the interests of A and K were 'identical to and indissociable from' one another in relation to the subject matter of the two disputes, not least because judgment against K would be *res judicata* so far as A might be concerned.[64] On the date the Cypriot proceedings were instituted before that court, the English court was already seized of a claim founded on the same cause of action, and which was as a matter of English law between the same parties. It may be justified by looking to the substance rather than the form,[65] or by the need to take a pragmatic view of whether proceedings involve the same parties, with a view to preventing as far as possible the difficulty of parallel proceedings leading to the non-recognition of judgments.[66] It does not matter: the outcome is all the same. The European Court has already held that two separate legal entities may be 'the same party' for the purpose of Article 27.[67] As the original contract gave rise to a single obligation, the position of A on the one hand, and of K on the other, in relation to it, was one of complete identity. It followed that on the date on which the Cypriot proceedings were instituted, the English proceedings were already pending between the same parties; and subsequent confirmation by the English court that K was the proper claimant under them was simply that: confirmation of what had already taken place, a year before. That this served to frustrate the disreputable behaviour of R, as claimant in the spurious Cypriot proceedings,

---

[62] For a decision that this condition is not satisfied when (i) the foreign proceedings are brought despite an agreement on jurisdiction, and the jurisdiction of that foreign court is challenged by reference to that jurisdiction agreement, and (ii) the English proceedings claim damages for breach of the jurisdiction agreement, see *Lloyd's Syndicate 980 v Sinco SA* [2008] EWHC 1842 (Comm), [2008] 2 CLC 187. Beatson J saw the plain differences between the relief sought in the two jurisdictions as decisive, and regarded the fact that 'the validity of the jurisdiction agreement' was common to the two sets of proceedings as insufficient to attract the rule in Article 27.

[63] More complicated questions arise when a claim in English proceedings is added by amendment into an earlier-issued claim form. In the *Sinco* case, above, the judge held that it would subvert the certainty provided by Article 30 for it to be held that the English court had been seized of the added-in claim from the date of the original writ, even where the amendment was one which was open to be made without the need to obtain permission to make it.

[64] This test derives from Case C-351/96 *Drouot Assurances SA v Consolidated Metallurgical Industries* [1998] ECR I-3075; this summary is taken from the judgment of the Court of Appeal at [33].

[65] At [85].

[66] At [81], [85].

[67] Case C-351/96 *Drouot Assurances SA v Consolidated Metallurgical Industries* [1998] ECR I-3075.

was simply a benefit. There was no apparent reason save vexation for R's preferring to hijack the venue and have the case heard in Cyprus,[68] and the only consequences of accepting the submission of R, that it had managed to displace the prior seisin of the English proceedings, were 'anomalous and arbitrary' ones.[69]

The court did not refer to its earlier judgment in *Moore v Moore*,[70] which is perhaps a surprise. In that case the court had dealt with the contention that where an English court has ruled at first instance that it had no jurisdiction, and has dismissed a claim on that ground, it was immediately disseized, with the result that if proceedings were thereupon begun before the courts of another Member State, then by the time that the English dismissal was reversed on appeal, the English court would be bound to find that it was now the court seized second, and required to decline jurisdiction on that new ground. Such a conclusion would have done no credit to the law; and the nonsense advanced on behalf of K in the present case was in substance just the same. When proceedings are begun, they are to be regarded as begun as of that date, notwithstanding hiccups or *faux pas* in the starting process, or interim decisions made during the whole process of establishing the jurisdiction of the English court. In the context of English law and the Brussels I Regulation,[71] this means that the court is seized when the claim form is issued, assuming that an act sufficient to count as service takes place afterwards; and that there is no hiatus (i) created by imperfections in the process of issue or service, or (ii) until the final determination of the decision whether the court has jurisdiction. If this is not the view taken, chicanery will be the inevitable response. Whether these recent English decisions may also be seen as part of a broader development, collecting around a principle which allows a court to override abusive procedures, or exercises of procedure, taken before a court in another Member State,[72] is perhaps too early to say. But it has been a good twelve months for those who wish to see jurisdictional sharp practice stamped out by robust and rational judicial adjudication. The intellectual spirit which animated the anti-suit injunction is not dead yet.

By way of postscript to this examination of the mechanics of the first seized rule, and the twists and turns which it invites the parties to inflict upon each other, and the courts, one may look at the jurisdictional scheme for certain matter of child responsibility contained in the Brussels II*bis* Regulation. Though this Regulation imposes a strict rule of priority for the court first seized in relation to divorce, it adopts a more sensitive jurisdictional approach to jurisdiction to determine certain issues of responsibility

---

[68] At [6].

[69] At [95].

[70] [2007] EWCA Civ 361, [2007] 2 FCR 353 (noted this Year Book, 78 (2007), 606).

[71] As explained above, the Lugano Convention will be aligned with this aspect of the Brussels I Regulation during 2008, or so it is supposed.

[72] Or in the English courts, if this is the correct interpretation of *Knauf UK GmbH v British Gypsum Ltd* [2001] EWCA Civ 1570, [2002] 1 WLR 907.

for children. According to Article 8, the general rule is that the courts of
the Member State within which the child is habitually resident shall have
jurisdiction, but Article 12 permits the parents to agree[73] that these matters be dealt with by the court which has matrimonial jurisdiction. In
addition, Article 15 permits a court which finds that it has jurisdiction
over a matter of child responsibility to stay the proceedings and direct
the parties to invoke the jurisdiction of the other court, or may itself
request the other court to exercise jurisdiction. The legislative thinking
obviously is that the best interests of the child, and the sense that they
may be served by proceeding in the court most appropriate to determine
these specific issues, will not necessarily coincide with the outcome of the
jurisdictional battle which the parents set about fighting. In *Bush v Bush*,
the children of the separating parents had their habitual residence in
Spain. The mother had, however, commenced divorce proceedings in
England where, it is fair to suppose, she hoped to obtain better financial
provision than might have been available to her in Spain. The father
brought proceedings in Spain to seek to ensure that the children remained
in Spain; but for reasons not completely clear,[74] the Spanish judge stayed
the proceedings before her to allow them to be joined with the matrimonial proceedings in England. The Court of Appeal plainly saw this as an
insufficient justification for the issues of parental responsibility to be dealt
with in England rather than Spain. It therefore held that the Spanish
court should deal with these, because that was in the best interests of the
child, was the more appropriate forum, and because in any event the parents had not expressly or unequivocally agreed to the child jurisdiction of
the English courts. In part, at least, it called for an application of the
principles of forum non conveniens in the special context of parental
responsibility.[75]

The decision was undoubtedly right in its interpretation of the Brussels
II*bis* Regulation, and it serves to make one wonder whether it really was
wise to yoke the sensitive issues of child welfare to the plotting and schem-
ing which too frequently characterizes the scramble to establish spousal
jurisdiction.[76] Whether or not it makes sense, though, the legislation
allows a court which considers itself, in the instant case, to be *forum non
conveniens* to do something direct about it. It is, to be sure, a long way
from the question of which court should deal with the welfare of infants,
to the harder-edged issues of jurisdiction which arise in commercial litigation, but Brussels II*bis* may yet point the way to a modest loosening of
Brussels I.

---

[73] The agreement must be unequivocal or express.
[74] It appeared to the Court of Appeal that the Spanish judge had based her decision on Article 28
of the Brussels I Regulation, and made no reference to the Brussels II*bis* Regulation. It was not
known how this seeming error had come to pass: see at [36].
[75] At [44].
[76] But in cases where the spouses have not declared war on each other, there is undoubted sense in
allowing a court to deal with the issues of child, as well as adult, law.

4. Enforcing and re-enforcing an English judgment: *Masri v Consolidated Contractors International Co SAL*[77]

For a number of years there has been a rumbling tension between some of the civil procedural techniques of the Brussels Regulation and the common law. At bottom, the conflict arises because the technique of the common law is to make its orders against an individual over which it has established personal jurisdiction, and to focus any measures of constraint on the individual who refuses to do as he has been ordered. Thus it is that Mareva injunctions do not freeze assets but order the owner of the assets to behave in relation to them in a particular way; an Anton Piller order does not licence entry onto land, but requires the person in occupation to open his doors and drawers to the claimant's agent; an anti-suit injunction does not stop judicial proceedings before a foreign court but orders the party bringing the proceedings to discontinue them; a receivership order does not seize debts but order the owner of the debt to cooperate in having it paid to the receiver, and so forth. Most of these are equitable in nature, and when it is said that equity operates *in personam*, this is what it means. The common law did not. Writs of execution apply directly to property, but can therefore be issued only in relation to property within the territorial jurisdiction of the court. A garnishee order, seizing a debt and requiring the debtor to pay it to the judgment creditor, with the promise of discharge from the claims of his creditor if he does so, can only be made in relation to property within the jurisdiction. This brilliant, stereoscopic, combination of remedies and enforcement measures of different type is one of the things which makes English judicial orders so much more effective than those available from a system which sees the issues with only one eye. It also means that those from outside the common law can be unable to understand what they are looking at. And this in turn can mean that remedies which are perfectly justifiable when taken on their own terms become equally unjustifiable when (mis-)translated into civilian legal language.

Almost every one of these misunderstandings came up for inspection after a judgment of the Commercial Court which awarded Mr Masri damages in the eventual sum of $55m against a number of entities in the

---

[77] Three separate decisions of the Court of Appeal are noted here: The first is [2008] EWCA Civ 303, [2009] 2 WLR 621: Ward LJ, Lord Neuberger of Abbotsbury and Lawrence Collins LJ, affirming [2007] EWHC 3010 (Comm), Gloster J. The second is[2008] EWCA Civ 625, [2009] 2 WLR 669: Sir Anthony Clarke MR, Longmore and Lawrence Collins LJJ, affirming [2007] EWHC 1510 (Comm), HH Judge Mackie QC. The third is [2008] EWCA Civ 876, [2009] 2 WLR 669 Sir Anthony Clarke MR, Longmore and Lawrence Collins LJJ, varying the order of Master Miller (appealed direct to the Court of Appeal under CPR r 52.14). This was appealed to the House of Lords; the outcome of the appeal will be reported next year. In addition, the appeal from the decision of the Court of Appeal at [2005] EWCA Civ 1436, [2006] 1 WLR 830, was listed to be heard by the House of Lords in July 2008. The appellants, Consolidated Contractors, failed to comply with various orders made by the House of Lords, with the result that the appeal was struck out in July 2008. An order for the reinstatement of the appeal, conditional upon the appellants paying into court the full sum ordered by Gloster J to be paid as damages, was made on July 30th 2008, failing which the appeal would be dismissed without further order. It remained struck out.

Consolidated Contractors Group. The group was Lebanese, but certain of its members may have had a domicile in Greece; and it had assets in several places outside Lebanon. The source of its wealth was an interest in an oil concession in South Yemen, and the profits to be derived from contracts of sale of the oil to third party buyers. No sooner had the judgment been given—though it will have been apparent from long before—the defendants made it plain that they had not the slightest intention of honouring their judgment debt. Prime among these demonstrations was the bringing of proceedings before the Yemeni courts for a declaration that they owed no liability to Masri. Masri therefore went back to court and applied for a number of orders designed to assist him in the execution of his judgment. These included (1) an anti-suit injunction to restrain the proceedings in Yemen; (2) a freezing injunction coupled with an order for the disclosure of assets;[78] (3) the appointment of a receiver by way of equitable execution; and (4) an order that certain of the judgment-debtor's office-holders attend court in England to give evidence relating to the judgment debtor's assets. The defendants objected at every point. As to (1), it was contended that the Yemeni court should decide for itself whether, among other things, the English judgment had any bearing on the issue of liability which was (according to the defendants) still contested. And insofar as one of the defendants had a domicile in Greece, such a claim had to be reconciled with the jurisdictional rules of the Brussels Regulation, which it could not be. As to (2), it was said that the freezing order was made in relation to assets outside the territorial jurisdiction of the English court, and that there was therefore no right to make such an order in respect of an issue— the enforcement of a judgment—which fell within the jurisdiction of the place where enforcement was sought. As none of the assets of the defendants were in England, the order should not have been made. As to (3), the order was one which struck and demanded payment of debts which were outside the jurisdiction of the English court. In that respect, the recent authority of the House of Lords on third party debt orders meant that only the courts at the situs of the debt had jurisdiction to make the order. As to (4), it was contended that as these office-holders were domiciled in

[78] In further proceedings, [2008] EWHC 2492 (Comm), the Commercial Court was called upon to deal with the defendants' refusal to comply with the obligation to make disclosure (so as to frustrate the freezing injunction), and their attempt to postpone the date on which trade customers were obliged to pay for oil supplied (so as to frustrate the receivership). It was therefore asked to extend the scope of both orders. Tomlinson J observed that the defendants had, if anything, become even more determined to avoid complying with the court's judgment, and made the orders applied for. The decision raised some novel legal questions, but they do not need to be separately noted here, the decision being more or less wholly justified by the principles established by the Court of Appeal. It also recited some of the manoeuvering executed by the defendants before the courts of the Lebanon and having the apparent aim of preventing compliance with disclosure orders by reason of an act force majeure which they had themselves sought: see at [28]-[29]. This succeeded for a while (see the interlocutory judgment of David Steel J at [2008] EWHC 1159 (Comm), [2008] 1 CLC 878), but when the facts were more completely exposed, Tomlinson J was reassuringly undistracted by such nonsense. If it is part of the common law of contract that self-induced acts do not frustrate a contract, there is good reason to consider that self-inflicted foreign judicial orders should not be allowed to frustrate an English judgment.

other Member States, Article 2 of the Brussels Regulation insulated them from the jurisdiction of the English courts, and that any such application was required to be made in the form of a request to the Greek court to take the evidence, under Regulation 1206/2001.

As was to be hoped, these arguments were all rejected. What is truly heartening is the manner in which the Court of Appeal repudiated the underlying contention of the judgment debtor, that the Brussels apparatus stymied the enforcement of the judgment of the Commercial Court. As to point (1), there was undoubtedly a conflict of laws, but as the English court was entitled to make ancillary orders which protected its jurisdiction, an ancillary order which supported the enforcement of its judgment was well within its power. The injunction was not made in relation to proceedings before the courts of another Member State, and it was therefore and otherwise unobjectionable. As to point (2), the order was not made in relation to specific assets, but operated *in personam* against a judgment debtor who had submitted to the jurisdiction of the court and who had no ground to oppose the making of orders which were ancillary to the exercise of jurisdiction over the substance of the claim. As to point (3), the appointment of a receiver by way of equitable execution of the judgment made no claim to affect title to debts or other assets, and was entirely different from a third party debt, or garnishee, order. All it did was to appoint a receiver and to require the judgment debtor to cooperate in the recovery of assets by the receiver. As the order made no claim on, or of entitlement to, property outside the jurisdiction of the English court, because it made no claim to any particular property anywhere, it could not be said to infringe a rule[79] which gave exclusive jurisdiction to the courts for the place where the property was. And as to point (4), the office-holder who was summoned to give evidence could not be said to be 'sued' for the purpose of the rule in Article 2 of the Regulation, which was therefore quite beside the point. Moreover and in any event, as the order was one which was ancillary to proceedings over which the court had and had exercised substantive jurisdiction, there was no external limitation on the power of the court to act.

The result was that the English court was able to grant orders which had the aim of preventing judicial proceedings taken overseas and designed to undermine the English judgment before the courts of a foreign country, and was able to ensure, to the extent that any court is able to ensure by the expedient of making judicial orders, that assets located outside its territorial jurisdiction were disclosed, preserved, and made available for the satisfaction of an English judgment. The foundations of this were simple and robust. The defendant had submitted to the jurisdiction of the English court in relation to the substantive claim, and the English court therefore had jurisdiction to make orders against him which were ancillary to its trying

---

[79] Whether found in Article 22(5) of the Brussels Regulation, or in a principle of common law private international law.

the case on its merits. The three judgments perfectly illustrated the wisdom and consequence of the fact that as equity operates *in personam*, all it requires is that the party against whom the order is to be made be subject to its jurisdiction. Once the order is made, what happens next is primarily matter for the respondent, and only secondly a matter for the judge.

It will be seen from this introduction that the Brussels Regulation was, in fact, peripheral to the issues which the court needed to decide. The defendants' principal asset was an oil concession in Yemen; the assets which the receiver was expected to seek to recover were contractual debts owed or to be owed by entities purchasing the oil derived from that concession. These purchasers were not located in Member States (a substantial part of the oil was sold to Singapore), so the possibility that the enforcement would have much or any effect in the territory of a Member State was probably small. But, subject to one point, it would not have mattered much if it had. The principle confirmed in *Van Uden Maritime BV v Deco Line*,[80] that a court with jurisdiction over the merits of a claim has jurisdiction to make ancillary orders is untrammelled by the Regulation. It means that such orders may be made even though they are made against a person not otherwise subject to the jurisdiction. The one exception is that an anti-suit injunction may not be made in respect of civil or commercial proceedings before the courts of another Member State. This is so, even though the English court does have jurisdiction under the Regulation,[81] or even though the proceedings before the English court are completely outside the material scope of the Regulation.[82] Whether one approves or not of this limitation, the limitation is itself narrow and confined to a single remedial order. That apart, an English court with jurisdiction over the merits may bring to bear the full range of its procedural powers in order to make its adjudication more effective.

The most difficult problem was, therefore, one of perception: the court was making orders which had an effect, and were expected to have an effect, overseas. But in all cases, they sought to bring this about by indirect means: the orders were made to appoint individuals, or to require individuals to attend, in London. In that respect, not only did they not infringe the Regulation, but they did not overstep the limitations which the principle of international comity places on national courts in international litigation. And in this sense, the court was building upon foundations which it had laid the year before. In dealing with recognition and enforcement of foreign laws laying claim to cultural artefacts, the court identified the line between foreign laws to which it would and would not give the legal effect they were designed to have by having regard to the principle of comity, the principle which represents the outer limit of what a legislator or court

---

[80] Case C-391/95, [1998] ECR I-7091.
[81] Case C-159/02 *Turner v Grovit* [2004] ECR I-3565.
[82] Such as where they are brought solely to enforce the terms of an agreement to arbitrate: Case C-185/07 *Allianz SpA v West Tankers Inc* [2009] 1 Lloyd's Rep 413.

may properly expect to regulate by its act. Although it has been doubted whether 'comity' is useful, in the sense of having edges which are hard and clear enough to be used in definition, recent judgments have shown its utility in providing an underpinning for decisions which may be rested on technical grounds. So where a foreign company has chosen to submit to the jurisdiction of a court, there is no overreaching when it is required to act in accordance with the same rules which would have applied to an English company in the same position: 'in for a penny, in for a pound', as one might say. To put it another way, when a foreign defendant has submitted to the jurisdiction, though its submission may be taken, in effect, to be restricted to the broad subject matter of the particular dispute, and is not to be taken as putting it in the same position as a local defendant whose liability to the jurisdiction is unrestricted, in relation to that subject matter and those proceedings, the submission is unreserved.

And that brings us to another point. It is easy enough to understand the nature and consequences of submission where the submission is by an individual, a natural person. By contrast, where the submission is by a company or other corporation, a fictitious person, there are two categories of natural person whose legal position may be affected even though they, as individuals, were not summoned and did not submit: directors (and other office-holders), and shareholders.

The principle of separate corporate personality is fundamental to English law. Ever since *Salomon v Salomon & Co Ltd*,[83] it has been an article of legal faith that companies have a personality which is separate and distinct from that of the corporators. From time to time, the courts find it necessary to repeat the message. So it was that the International Tin Council was identified as having a legal personality separate and quite distinct from the states which belonged to or created it. So also was separateness of Cape plc from its subsidiaries the reason why a judgment from the Texas courts against a subsidiary was of no effect as against the parent company.

But this is sometimes an awkward conclusion. Of course, if the incorporation is a fraud, it is permitted to lift the corporate veil and see the naked truth behind it. But it is not just a matter of fraud. When a Manx company submitted to the jurisdiction of an American court, and the American court made an order purporting to divest the shareholders of their interest in the company, a letter of request from the American court to the Manx authorities, asking that the shares be cancelled and new shares issued in their place, was acceded to. The Privy Council denied that it was enforcing a judgment against the shareholders: it accepted that the shareholders had not submitted to the jurisdiction of the American court, but also considered that there was no good reason not to comply with the request. It might as well have said that, if people subscribe for shares in a corporation, they accept the risk that the corporation will act, and will

---

[83] [1897] AC 22.

assume obligations, which are contrary to their individual interests. So if the Manx company submits to the jurisdiction of the American court, and orders are made by that court which damage the interests of the shareholders, that it just too bad. So far as the shareholders are concerned, *qui sentit commodum sentire debet et onus*: you take the rough with the smooth, the bitter with the sweet. It is not unreasonable to suppose that where your company has submitted to the jurisdiction of a foreign court you cannot, as shareholder, claim to be wholly immune from the consequences of the judgment: *Cambridge Gas Transport Corp v Official Committee of Unsecured Creditors of Navigator Holdings plc* makes this clear, and the only interesting task which remains is that of mapping the limits of the principle.

So also the directors of the judgment debtor: it was entirely right and proper that they be summoned to give evidence about the business and assets of the judgment debtor. It could hardly be maintained that although the company had submitted to the jurisdiction, this was *res inter alios acta* as far as the directors and office-holders were concerned. Natural persons they may have been, but they were the eyes and ears, and hands, of the company; and they were placed fairly within the grasp of the English court when the company chose to submit to its jurisdiction. The decision in the third *Masri* case was plainly correct; and the fact that the directors may have been domiciled in other Member States should have been neither here nor there, as their company had already submitted. For the court to rest its conclusion on the proposition that they were not being sued was unobjectionable, not least because it was true; but it may be advantageous to recognize that this was only one of a number of good and sufficient justifications for the orders which were made.[84]

Even so, it shows that we probably need to develop a clearer view of this ancillary or consequential submission. It is hardly a new idea, though the recent case-law shows that it remains to be properly understood and explained. For one, the original *Mareva* injunction was thought to lie only against those who were party to the proceedings as defendants; but before very long it was recognized that, to achieve its intended effect, the order would need to be capable of extension to others closely associated with the defendant, and who may also have control of the assets at which the order is indirectly aimed. For another, the *Norwich Pharmacal* version of the interlocutory injunction is directed at those who have got themselves mixed up in another's wrongdoing. What all these procedures share is a sense that it is not always a good and sufficient pleading for A to state, truthfully, that the claim is against B, and B is a different person. For a third, costs orders may be made against non-parties (it is endless, frustratingly,

---

[84] Also to be noted is the decision in *Vitol SA v Capri Marine Ltd* [2008] EWHC 378 (Comm), [2009] Bus LR 271, which held that an order made against the officer of a corporate judgment debtor is not an order made against the judgment debtor itself, a conclusion which was material to the question whether such an order could be served out of the jurisdiction under what was then CPR r.6.30(2). It is unclear whether this decision would have been the same under the new rule in CPR r.6.38.

misleading to describe them as 'third parties') at the conclusion of a case
in which they have supported the losing side. What these have in common
is a sense that the non-party was sufficiently involved for this to overcome
the legal fact, also correct, that they were not party to the proceedings,
whether by submission or otherwise. Any sense that a non-party was 'sufficiently involved' needs to be capable of definition and measurement if it
is to be allowed to overcome the conclusion which B, the non-party, invites
the court to draw. The third *Masri* decision does not furnish us with the
answer, but it does draw attention to the practical necessity of focussing
on the question.

5. Ancillary measures in support of secondary proceedings: *Kensington
International Ltd v Republic of Congo*;[85] *Mobil Cerro Negro Ltd
v Petroleos de Venezuela SA*;[86] *ETI Euro Telecom International
NV v Republic of Bolivia*.[87]

If the *Masri* litigation illustrates the private international law of measures
which may be used to enforce and reinforce an English judgment, it is useful to contrast this with the law which governs whether and how an English
court may grant relief in support of proceedings being brought in other
courts. In two cases in particular, the Court of Appeal had to consider what
an English court could properly be asked to do in aid of proceedings before
foreign courts. In each case the point of departure was Civil Jurisdiction
and Judgments Act 1982, s 25, which gives an English court power to grant
interim relief in support of substantive proceedings in other jurisdictions.

      In *Kensington International Ltd v Republic of Congo*, K had obtained
several English judgments against the Congo[88] which the latter had not
paid and showed every sign of intending never to pay. K sought to enforce
its judgments by seizing debts owed and to be owed by entities who pur-
chased oil from the state. In England this would have been by third party
debt order, so far as the debts were situated in England; outside England
it was by attachment of the debts wherever they could be found. To this
end, K brought proceedings in Geneva, taking its first step by petitioning
the court for an interim attachment of debts said to be owed to the state
by V SA, the Swiss parent of a complex of companies trading in oil. The
Swiss court made the interim attachment against V SA, but not against
English entities in the group. Two English companies were therefore joined
to the English proceedings,[89] to obtain interim injunctions against them
which would prevent their acting to discharge V SA's debts to the state

---

[85] [2007] EWCA Civ 1128, [2008] 1 Lloyd's Rep 161: May, Carnwath and Moore-Bick LJJ.
[86] [2008] EWHC 532 (Comm), [2008] 1 Lloyd's Rep 684: Walker J.
[87] [2008] EWCA Civ 880, [2009] 1 WLR 665: Tuckey, Lawrence Collins and Stanley Burnton
LJJ.
[88] Congo-Brazzaville, the former French colonial territory. Not to be confused with the entity
which had carried on business as Belgian Congo, Zaïre, and, most recently and tragically, as the
Democratic Republic of Congo.
[89] This must have meant the substantive English proceedings.

and so forestall any frustration of K's attempt to enforce the judgment in its favour. The Court of Appeal found no real difficulty in upholding the injunction made by Gloster J below.

It could not be argued that the English companies were not subject to the jurisdiction of the English court; but it was argued that s 25 of the 1982 Act did not justify making the order applied for. Part of the argument was that English law did not allow a court to seize future debts, that is, those which had not arisen at the date of the order. The response of the court was, however, that the relief was to be granted in support of the substantive Swiss proceedings; that the Swiss proceedings[90] provided for an attachment of future debts, and that the English court should therefore make an order which mirrored this width of scope. The fact that interim relief of this width would not normally be granted in support of an English application for a third party debt order was of no relevance.[91] It must have been accepted that an order that future debts not be paid was an order which English procedural law allowed an English court to make; given that it was, the only question was whether this was the right order to be making in support of the proceedings in Geneva. Given, in particular, the evidence which showed the willingness of V SA to engineer a scheme to allow the state to avoid paying the sums due on the judgment, it was held that it was.

Each step in the argument seems correct. The relief was sought in support of Swiss proceedings; these were substantive;[92] the order was one within the judicial power of an English court; and the order reflected the proceedings in the Swiss courts. Yet the result was that interim relief was ordered which was wider than would have been appropriate if it had been sought in aid of an application for a third party debt order. The underlying judgment was English, and the Swiss proceedings were, but were only, to secure the enforcement of that English judgment. Yet the effect of instituting the enforcement application in Geneva appears to have widened the material reach of the court's order for interim relief. Perhaps it shows the lengths to which a court is prepared to allow itself to be led when it considers that the attempts to avoid the payment of judgment debts are simply beyond the pale.

The proposition that an English court has jurisdiction to grant interim relief in support of an ICC arbitration was tested in *Mobil Cerro Negro Ltd v Petroleos de Venezuela*. When the government of Venezuela decided to move its oil resources closer to state ownership, by legislating for such

---

[90] At least arguably: the true scope of the Swiss attachment was yet to be determined by the Swiss court.

[91] At [21].

[92] But see below. In *ETI Euro Telecom International NV v Republic of Bolivia*, at [75], it was observed that the question whether the proceedings before the Swiss courts were substantive had not actually been before the Court. It is a little hard to see how this can have been correct; it may be that the point was simply conceded without argument. In *ETI v Bolivia*, however, the court agreed that the proceedings before the Swiss court in *Kensington v Congo* were substantive for the purposes of section 25.

assets to be held by companies which had a majority Venezuelan sharehold-
ing, one of the companies which considered itself to have been unjustly
done to was Mobil. It commenced an ICSID arbitration against Venezuela,
but also sought to enforce the terms of a guarantee from Petroleos de
Venezuela by commencing an ICC arbitration in New York. It applied
in London for a worldwide *Mareva* injunction in support of the ICC
arbitration,[93] relying on Arbitration Act 1996, s 44, as the basis for the
order which it sought from the court. While accepting that he had power
to grant relief, as the parties' agreement did not contain terms which showed
an intention to make it inapplicable, Walker J declined to do so, on the
ground that there was so little connection to England that it was inconsistent with the principles of comity for him to make the order applied for.
In determining whether to make the order, the judge's reasoning paid close
attention to the parallel analysis which has to be undertaken when an application is made under Civil Jurisdiction and Judgments Act 1982, s 25, in
support of litigation before the courts of another country, and in particular the analysis in *Credit Suisse Fides Trust v Cuoghi*[94] and *Motorola Credit
Corp v Uzan (No 2)*.[95] According to this authority, if the defendant is not
resident or otherwise present in England, and the assets are mostly outside England, it will generally not be expedient to grant the relief. Where
there is no basis for an allegation that the defendant has engaged in fraudulent conduct, the likelihood of being able to obtain a worldwide injunction
is even lower. So it proved in this case; the decision is an entirely orthodox
application of general principle—and none the worse for that. It also had
the beneficial side effect that the English courts avoided being dragged
into a dispute between the Venezuelan state and an American oil company.

ETI Euro Telecom International NV v Republic of Bolivia was, however, rather different. It also arose from a South American legislative act
of nationalization, into which the court found no legal justification for its
intervention. Quite apart from that, though, it suggests that, by contrast
with *Kensington v Congo*, the willingness of a court to find the limits of the
law is less pronounced when there has not yet been a final judgment to
establish the liability of a defendant. In 2006, the government of Bolivia
embarked upon the re-nationalization of a telephony company, Entel, of
which ETI, a Dutch entity, was majority shareholder. In due course, ETI
instituted an ICSID arbitration against Bolivia, which ignored the fact
and pressed on with its nationalization. ETI then obtained from the US
District Court in New York a provisional attachment of assets of Entel
held in New York, this 'in aid of arbitration'.[96] It was not clear how quickly
this order would be confirmed or set aside, but almost immediately, ETI
applied for interim relief from the English courts. Entel had $50m or so
on deposit with a bank in London, and an injunction was sought against

---

[93] The significance of its not seeking relief in relation to the ICSID arbitration emerges below.
[94] [1998] QB 818 (CA).
[95] [2003] EWCA Civ 752, [2004] 1 WLR 113.   [96] At [30].

Entel (whose credit it was) and Bolivia (which was about to become owner of Entel) to restrain the removal of the fund. It was contended that the judicial basis of the claim was that the English court had power to make the order under Arbitration Act 1996 s 44, and under Civil Jurisdiction and Judgments Act 1982, s 25. The substantial basis for the claim was that there was an ICSID arbitration against Bolivia; Bolivia would soon be able to transfer the funds standing to the credit of Entel out of reach of ETI, and that this justified making the order against Bolivia[97] and Entel. Though the relief was granted *ex parte*, the orders were set aside by Andrew Smith J, and the appeal against his decision was dismissed by the Court of Appeal. Though the hearings before the judge and the Court of Appeal were completed within a month, the judgments are excellent in every respect. It is sometimes necessary to acknowledge, with simple admiration, the way the system can work. No wonder litigants are still drawn to London for the resolution of commercial disputes.

The principal aspect of the decision, for our purposes, was that the proceedings before the US District Court were not of the kind in relation to which section 25 gave the court power to act, for the US proceedings were not 'on the substance of the matter' in dispute between the parties.[98] Relief could not be granted in support of proceedings which were themselves in support of proceedings before another court or tribunal, and though in *Kensington v Congo* the proceedings before the Swiss court were substantive (with the consequence that the court was entitled to grant relief under section 25), those before the New York court in *ETI v Bolivia* were not. It is not clear whether this was because the proceedings in New York were targeted only at assets in New York, and not at assets in England, or because the proceedings in New York did not seek the resolution of any dispute, or both. In principle, though, the correct answer must be that the New York proceedings were not brought for the resolution of any issue between the parties. If it were not so, and the reason the English court had no power to act had been because the New York attachment was not aimed at assets outside the territorial jurisdiction of the New York court, the law would be counter-intuitive. In those cases where the foreign court had purported to reach outside its territorial jurisdiction, the English court would be able to grant relief, but where the foreign court had no such power, confining itself to local assets, the English court would have no power to assist. That would make English law a pallid reflection of foreign law on interim relief, which seems unnecessary and undesirable.

ETI's fallback position was that section 25 empowered the court to grant the relief applied for, not in aid of the New York judicial proceedings, but in support of the ICSID arbitration, a proposition which would render the New York proceedings irrelevant to the application. This too

---

[97] The issues arising from Bolivia's immunity from legal process as a state is not examined in this Note as it raises issues of public, not private, international law.
[98] At [70].

failed, for the simple enough reason that Parliament had not acted upon the power given by section 25(3)(c) to extend the provision of the section to arbitration proceedings[99] before that sub-section was itself repealed[100] and superseded by Arbitration Act s 44. The power to extend section 44 to ICSID arbitrations had not been activated by the Lord Chancellor, so section 44 offered no hope, either.[101] Quite separately from this, the court could not easily identify the basis on which relief had been sought against Entel, with which ETI had no dispute. There being no basis to treat Entel and Bolivia as the same body, there was no obvious reason for the ordering of relief against Entel.

The obstacles which the legislation put in the way of ETI's application for support in relation to the arbitration were insuperable, but predominant was the point that there was no statutory basis on which the relief could be rested. Given the peculiar nature of ICSID arbitration, it is no surprise that the ordinary support mechanisms of the Arbitration Act 1996 have not been extended to them. And section 25 of the 1982 Act provided no support for the view that 'proceedings' could, in this context, include 'arbitration proceedings'. But the unavailability of section 25 in support of the proceedings before the New York court was, at first sight, less expected. It is, however, quite right. It was unexpected in the light of *Kensington v Congo*. If *Kensington v Congo* is correct, it is because the Swiss proceedings were substantive, as the Court of Appeal accepted. Section 25 allows a court to act in support of substantive proceedings; it does not allow it to act in support of a court which is itself acting in support of substantive proceedings elsewhere. If it is correct that *exequatur sur exequatur ne vaut*,[102] that is, an order for enforcement sought on the basis of an order for enforcement is not possible, the same spirit leads to the conclusion that order in support of an order in support is not permissible either. The English court was right to conclude that it could not make orders in support of the New York attachment which, unlike the attachment in Geneva, was not the precursor to substantive proceedings. But there is more difficulty when one examines what it was that made *Kensington v Congo* correct. The Swiss proceedings in that case were for the enforcement of an English judgment; there was a clear sense in which they were not substantive: they were in support of the original proceedings in England. They might have been substantive if it had been held that the Swiss court was being asked to try the substance of the claim, but it was not being asked to do that. It was being asked to grant exequatur in respect of the English judgment. It may be even more correct to say that the Swiss proceedings fell under Title III of the Lugano Convention, for the recognition and enforcement

---

[99] Section 25(3) gave it that power; no such order had been made.
[100] Arbitration Act 1996 Sch 3. The reason for the repeal was that the powers of courts to grant relief in relation to disputes which were being resolved by arbitration was to be set out in the 1996 Act itself: see at [91].
[101] See at [94].
[102] Kegel, in Dieckmann (ed) *Festschrift für Wolfram Müller-Freienfels* (1986), 337.

of an English judgment. Yet if that were so, the Swiss court was strictly forbidden to enter upon the substance of the dispute.[103] Seen in that light, there is some awkwardness in considering the Swiss proceedings to be substantive; and if this adjective is indeed a strict limitation upon the power of an English court to make orders in support of a foreign procedure, this aspect of *Kensington v Congo* may require reconsideration. Even so, the case, and the vigour of the judgments, does suggest that where there has been a final judgment, a court will be inclined to pull out all the stops. In *ETI v Bolivia*, by contrast, there was no judgment, no award. There may also have been a perception that steps taken by the government of a sovereign state to take into public ownership an essential piece of physical infrastructure, which was wholly within the territorial jurisdiction of the state, was not the context in which the court could properly be asked to extend the reach of an English court. However it is looked at, the decision in *ETI v Bolivia* is unassailable. That in *Kensington v Congo* ought to be right, but is far from being easy to support.

6. The law which governs a trust: *Gomez v Gomez-Monche Vives*[104]

Article 5(6) of the Brussels I Regulation gives an English court special jurisdiction over a Spanish domiciliary if she is sued 'as settlor, trustee or beneficiary of a trust created by the operation of a statute or by a written instrument, or created orally and evidenced in writing' if the United Kingdom is the Member State in which the trust is domiciled. Accordingly, when allegations of breach of trust were raised by the children against their mother, the defendant and widow of the settlor (who had at all material times been domiciled in Spain), who was herself domiciled in Spain, it was necessary for the claimants to satisfy the court on two matters. The first was that the trust in question, which was established in writing in 1984, was domiciled in the United Kingdom; the second was that the defendant was sued in the particular capacity stated in the Article. We may take the points in that order.

Article 60(3) directs an English court, called upon to determine whether a trust is domiciled in the United Kingdom, to apply its own rules of private international law. These are set out in para 12(3) of Schedule 1 to the Civil Jurisdiction and Judgments Order 2001,[105] and require a court to identify the system of law with which the trust has its closest and most real connection. The court, quite correctly, observed the distinction between this formulation and the separate and irrelevant question of the country with which the trust had its closest connection; and just as correctly, concluded that where the trust had been established with English law chosen as its governing law, English law was the Law with which the trust was most closely connected. Its conclusion is unassailable, notwithstanding

---

[103] Article 30.
[104] [2008] EWCA Civ 1065, [2009] 2 WLR 950: Jacob and Lawrence Collins LJJ, Lewison J, allowing in part and dismissing in part appeals from [2008] EWHC 259 (Ch), [2008] 3 WLR 309 (Morgan J).
[105] SI 2001 No 3929.

that the trust was administered in Liechtenstein, its accounting books were located there and the preponderance of its trustees were in or of Liechtenstein. It was an English law trust, and that was that.

The judgment set out in detail the reasoning which led to its conclusion. Prominent was the provision in the Hague Convention on the Recognition of Trusts, that a trust is governed by the law chosen by the settlor. As the settlor had made his choice, the only argument open to the defendant was that the trust, though governed by English law, was more closely connected to the law of another country. The proposition only has to be written down to reveal its hopelessness; but the court went further. It drew[106] a telling distinction between the law which is chosen to govern a commercial contract, and that chosen to govern a trust. Whereas the former may be readily understood as a choice of the law which the parties wish to have applied to the resolution of any dispute between them, part of the dispute-resolution matrix and not generally important during the existence and performance of the contract,[107] the law which governs a trust is an altogether different animal. The trust will vest powers and duties in the trustees, in particular; and there needs to be some law by reference to which they may decide how to invest or divest, distribute or accumulate, vary or otherwise manage the terms of the trust, and so forth. There is an active[108] management obligation imposed on the trustees of a kind wholly absent from the ordinary commercial contract; the trustees will need to check, every time they take or do not take a particular decision, that this is in accordance with the law which governs the trust and their duties in relation to it. There is certainly room for debate about whether it makes sense to speak of 'a contract' or of 'an English contract'; but there is no similar debating space where one is dealing with a trust. The institution established by the settlor in 1984 was an English-law trust; and though the trustees had been replaced as time had gone by, no attempt had ever been made to alter the original specification of English law as the expressly chosen law. Saving the possibility of 'evasive' choices of law, which this could not possibly have been seen to be, this was an English law trust, because that was what the settlor established; and the presence of factual connections with Liechtenstein could not possibly overcome the express choice of law by the settlor as determining the law with which it was most closely connected.

The reference to evasive choices of law is significant, for there is more than a suspicion that the whole international trusts industry is evasive by nature: whether it is tax or transparency, trusts are all too commonly the vehicle by which laws are evaded. It is therefore appropriate for the courts to have a general reserve power to find that a trust chosen to be governed

---

[106] At [64].
[107] See generally Briggs, *Agreements on Jurisdiction and Choice of Law* (2008).
[108] Indeed, where the trust is governed by English law, a better adjective might be 'demanding' or even 'ferocious'.

by a law other than English law may not be sufficient to overcome the view that the trust is most closely connected to English law. But in practice, it is very hard to conceive of a set of facts in which the trust would be expressed to be governed by a dubious law yet not have this bolstered by the establishment of additional connections, such as the presence of local trustees: Liechtenstein may be tiny, opaque, and addicted to secrecy, but it does not seem to have a shortage of willing, able, and faceless would-be trustees. It is hard to imagine a case in which the choice of governing law of such a haven will stand alone, and therefore hard to imagine that it may be generally[109] overridden on the ground that there is a closer connection with another law.

The second question was, therefore, whether the defendant was sued as beneficiary. The complaint was that she had received income and capital from the trustees who had made the distribution in breach of trust; and that as she had been aware of the breach of trust, she was obliged to reconstitute the trust fund. Significantly, perhaps, the pleading was that she had received the distributions as a volunteer, and was on that account liable as a constructive trustee.[110] In a second complaint, it was alleged that the defendant had misused a power in the trust deed by making herself the Appointor of the trust, though the relief sought in relation to that complaint was that she be removed as Appointor and replaced by someone else. It is instantly clear how these facts pose problems for the jurisdictional rule in Article 5(6) of the Regulation. The claimants asserted that the payments were unlawful, that the defendant had no right to receive or to retain them, that she was therefore a volunteer with guilty knowledge, and was on that account liable to restore them: she was not a beneficiary but a stranger who had no right to receive. That would have placed the claim outside the formulation in Article 5(6), as she was being sued, not as beneficiary, but as improper recipient. The defendant, by contrast, seemed likely[111] to defend the claim on the basis that the payments were properly made to her, that she was entitled to benefit from the distribution, and that she was therefore a beneficiary, but a beneficiary who could not be sued as she had no case to answer. To put it another way: the claimant sued the defendant but not as beneficiary; the defendant defended as beneficiary who owed no liability.

Though the point of departure for the court was that Article 5(6) should receive a restrictive construction, it is hard to see that this pointed the way forward. As Article 5(6) does not apply to the resulting or constructive trust which ensues which fills the gap when something goes wrong, the only question for the court was whether the defendant was sued as beneficiary of the 1984 trust. Perhaps mindful of the topsy-turvy reasoning which would result from taking each side at its word, the court was able

---

[109] As distinct from being inapplicable in the face of mandatory laws of the forum, for example.
[110] See at [29], setting out the pleading.
[111] As she was challenging the jurisdiction, no defence had been filed.

to reason that the defendant was being sued as overpaid beneficiary, and not as stranger to the trust; for this reason the claim was made against her as beneficiary. The pleading referred to above was, fortunately for those who drafted it, not as jurisdictionally damaging to the claim as it might well have been. Another view, however, is that the case was analogous to that which arises when the claimant asserts the non-existence of a contract as the ground for its entitlement to relief, and the defendant pleads the existence of a contract. In such cases, generically thought of as negative declaratory in character, the dominant view is that they still relate to a contract, even though the claimant denies it: the validity of the contract represents and defines the issue which is live between the parties, and the pleading of the claimant, that there is no valid contract, does not pull the rug from beneath its own feet. All that being so, it was not difficult to see the issue in *Gomez* as being whether the defendant could justify her receipt and retention by establishing that she was entitled to receive and retain as beneficiary. That ought to be determined in the court which would certainly have had jurisdiction if there had been no dispute that the parties were trustee and beneficiary of a written trust; and this intelligent appreciation of what was at stake must have encouraged the court to find that a dispute about an English-law trust should be resolved before an English court. The contrary conclusion would have represented a triumph of formalism over common sense; and the court was having none of it. After all, the claim arose out of and involved 'what Professor Schlosser called the problems arising in connection with the internal relationships of the trust'.[112]

All of which makes the conclusion of the court on the issue of whether the defendant had acted properly or improperly in appointing herself, the donee of the power, as the Appointor of the trust, perplexing. The issue for eventual determination was whether as a matter of the law of trusts it had been open to the defendant to make the appointment of herself. The judge had held that at this point she was not being sued as trustee or beneficiary, and that Article 5(6) did not extend to this aspect of the claim. Coming as it did after the judge's conclusion that in the receipt claim the defendant was not being sued as beneficiary, there was a strategic advantage in the conclusion which he reached. But once the Court of Appeal had reversed the judge on the receipt claim, there was every practical reason to reverse him on the appointment claim. Its decision not to do so was therefore most unwelcome. As matters were left to stand, the receipt claim could proceed in England, but the appointment claim would need to be brought before a Spanish court. At this point, one quietly recites the prayer for mutual trust,[113] and hopes for the best if and when the finer points of the law on fiduciary powers are raised, translated, and debated before the judge in Madrid. It is not, one respectfully ventures to suggest, a happy outcome. This aspect of the dispute concerned whether the defendant was

---

[112] Judgment at [90], referring to Schlosser 1979 OJ C59/71 at [109]-[111].
[113] Case C-159/02 *Turner v Grovit* [2004] ECR I-3565.

entitled to appoint herself the Appointor, and if that was not also 'a problem arising from the internal relationships of the trust', it is hard to see
what it was. The justification given for the particular conclusion was that
the need to adopt a conservative interpretation of the special jurisdictional rules in Article 5 meant that persons sued as appointors, protectors,
and other new-fangled creations of the international trust industry, was
not within Article 5(6). As to this, several short and dissenting observations
may be made. First, when the rule in Article 5(6) was devised, it is practically certain that the words used—'as settlor, trustee or beneficiary'—
were intended to include the players within the organization of the written
trust. It if far from clear that there was a conscious, still less rational, decision to exclude the donee of a fiduciary power from this list: the words of
Article 5(6) should not be understood *ejusdem generis*. Second, the institution of the 'protector' was invented in the money laundries and tax havens
of the Caribbean as part of the legislative apparatus by which it was sought
to reassure the settlor that after the settlement he would still have control
of the levers of power, at the same time as telling the outside world that
this was an institution which ought to be regarded as a trust. It is even
further from clear that claims against the 'protector' were intended to be
excluded from Article 5(6), or that such disputes[114] do not involve the
internal relationships of the trust. Third, these embarrassing and rather
malodorous species of alleged trust raise real and novel issues of fiduciary
law[115] which belong in the Chancery Division. The idea that they may
better be brought before the courts of a jurisdiction which does not have
English as its mother tongue or the common law as its mother law is, frankly,
not rational. Fourth, the risk of irreconcilable decisions if the courts of
England and Spain each have a look at the merits of the dispute is, surely,
far from fanciful; and fifth, the cost and expense of the parallel litigation
of the claims is not desirable. While the general instruction to construe
the special jurisdictions in Articles 5 and 6 narrowly is vouched for by the
European Court, and while the Court of Appeal could be seen to be doing
only what it was told, the tail end of the judgment, which is otherwise
wholly persuasive, is certainly the least convincing.

7. Jurisdiction to establish the validity of foreign intellectual property
rights: *Satyam Computer Services Ltd v Upaid Systems Ltd;*[116]
Lucasfilm Ltd v Ainsworth.[117]

There is something undeniably old-fashioned about the legal rule that the
English courts have no jurisdiction to determine the validity of foreign
intellectual property rights; and a string of decisions which have managed

---

[114] On the other hand, it will be unusual for a trust governed by English law to have a protector, so
the problem is, at the moment, perhaps more apparent than real.
[115] Such as whether they really count as trusts at all.
[116] [2008] EWHC 31 (Comm): Flaux J. The point principally examined here was not the subject of
appeal to the Court of Appeal, whose decision at [2008] EWCA Civ 487 is only briefly noted below.
[117] [2008] EWHC 1878 (Ch), [2009] FSR 103: Mann J.

to sidestep it are now piling up in the law reports. The pressures against the rule come from several places. If it is understood as a common law rule of jurisdiction,[118] it may have been overcome by the Brussels Convention and Brussels I Regulation where the claim is made against a defendant over whom these instruments would otherwise confirm the jurisdiction of the court. If it is understood as an early and primitive form of the developed principle of *forum non conveniens*, that is equally inapplicable where the Brussels rules provide that there is personal jurisdiction over the defendant. Alternatively, it may be understood as having its roots in choice of law. The common law provided no remedy for violation of foreign intellectual property rights. The reason was that infringement of a Ruritanian patent would not have been actionable as a tort if the acts had taken place in England, so the claim would be defeated by the rule requiring a claimant to demonstrate double actionability.[119] Moreover, as the jurisdictional rule was established for matters requiring a court to determine title to foreign land, not everyone will see that the same rule should apply to foreign intellectual property rights.[120] If the rule does apply to patents, which are in some sense the most formal and exclusive, it might not be so obviously applicable to others, such as copyright. And anyway: there may be cases in which the court cannot give judgment unless it takes a view about the validity or otherwise of a foreign intellectual property right, but in which it is not straightforward to say that the court is determining the validity of the right, against the world, as it were.[121] There is an intuitive distinction, but may also be a principled distinction, between an incidental (though essential) determination of validity, and a ruling which is to be binding *in rem*.[122] And on top of all that, judges who relish the duties of the office do not always accede uncomplainingly to a submission that they have no jurisdiction to answer a question which is plainly in dispute and which, if they do not decide it, will continue as a source of trouble. Given all that, it is no surprise that the rule that an English court has no jurisdiction to determine the validity of a foreign intellectual property right is insecure.

In *Satyam v Upaid*, a more-than-averagely complicated complaint of breach of contract was advanced. Part of the subject matter of the agreement had been American patents; among the allegations was the complaint that the grantor had purported to grant rights which were not valid and

---

[118] *British South Africa Co v Companhia de Moçambique* [1893] AC 602; *Hesperides Hotels v Aegean Turkish Holidays Ltd* [1978] AC 508.

[119] All the above is discussed in *Pearce v Ove Arup Partnership Ltd* [2000] Ch 403 (CA), though it is not the only case to have looked at the question.

[120] *Pearce v Ove Arup Partnership Ltd* [2000] Ch 403, in this respect not following *Potter v Broken Hill Pty Ltd* (1906) 3 CLR 479. The issue is perhaps whether the rule, expressed as referring to immovable property, is in fact confined to land.

[121] *Griggs (R) Group Ltd v Evans (No 2)* [2004] EWHC 1088 (Ch), [2005] Ch 153.

[122] Ibid.

that their invalidity had caused loss to the claimant.[123] Among other issues, the question arose whether the English court had or would exercise jurisdiction in circumstances in which a claim for damages would require it to determine the validity of the US patents. The question precisely arose because the claim was for damages, but the assessment of any right to damages could not be undertaken without the court making a ruling on the validity of the patent. Flaux J took the view that there was no impediment to the action proceeding in the English courts. Even assuming there to be a jurisdictional rule which applied to foreign patents as it applied to foreign land, it did not prevent his making a finding which would be material only for the purpose of resolving a personal claim, or of having effect *in personam* on the parties to the litigation alone. It was, he thought, *a fortiori* where the validity of the patent was relevant only to the computation of damages.

Though the judge was willing to make a determination of the validity of an American patent, which might have been thought to lie outside his jurisdiction, the arguments in support of his conclusion are probably stronger. There always has been a jurisdiction to enforce a contract between the parties even though that contract has foreign land or intellectual property as its subject matter, because the personal obligations of the contract will bind only the parties to it.[124] The same principle applies to those bound by personal equities, though no analogous principle was developed by the common law to apply to claims in which the claimant accused the defendant of commission of a tort concerning foreign land.[125] This, after all, was why a court was taken to have no jurisdiction at common law to try a patent infringement claim where the defence raised by the alleged infringer was invalidity of the right.[126] But as the claim in *Satyam v Upaid* was that the obligations of a contractual transferor had been breached, the rule in *Penn v Baltimore* justified the court in exercising jurisdiction to determine the consequences.[127] Any assessment of validity or invalidity was really incidental to that. This is not to say that it was minor or peripheral, for much of the claim for relief was predicated on a finding that the transferor had breached its obligation to transfer rights in a valid patent. It was, however and as a matter of legal analysis, an incidental issue. It is possible that the persuasiveness of the judge's analysis was why the appeal

---

[123] Specifically, it had had to settle (for a large sum) an infringement claim brought against it by another.

[124] *Penn v Baltimore* (1750) 1 Ves Sen 444.

[125] This distinction, between personal equities and common law wrong, can give rise to real difficulty where the personal equity responds to wrongful conduct: see *Griggs (R) Group Ltd v Evans (No 2)* [2004] EWHC 1088 (Ch), [2005] Ch 153. Civil Jurisdiction and Judgments Act 1982 s 30 enacts a statutory rule to give the court jurisdiction to try claims based on torts relating to foreign land, but this has not been extended by Parliament to foreign intellectual property.

[126] *Coin Controls Ltd v Suzo International (UK) Ltd* [1999] Ch 33.

[127] For the unsurprising but useful view that a court with jurisdiction under the *Penn v Baltimore* principle may find that, as the law to be applied to determine the issue in dispute is not the lex fori then it may accede to an application for a stay on *forum non conveniens* grounds, see *Murakami v Wiryadi* [2008] SGCA 44.

to the Court of Appeal restricted itself to the interpretation of the various agreements on jurisdiction and dispute resolution, which was dealt with by the unremarkable application of orthodox principle, adding nothing to the private international law of intellectual property.

Lucasfilm Ltd v Ainsworth was another thing altogether. A long time ago in a factory far, far away, Mr Ainsworth designed for the claimant film company the distinctive headgear to be worn by the 'Imperial Stormtroopers' in the film 'Star Wars'. He kept his original moulds. When, decades later, Ainsworth made tentative steps to exploit that which he had created, making sales[128] in the United States of almost $14,600,[129] the empire struck back. And how. In a splendid example of life imitating cartoon,[130] it attacked with overwhelming force, and on several fronts at once.[131] It sued in the United States for infringements of copyright, infringement of trademark and competition, demanding and obtaining $5m for the copyright claim; a further $5m for the trademark and competition claim which was then trebled by virtue of the Lanham Act: all of which came to a nice round $20m. It followed this up with English proceedings in which it complained of infringement of its United Kingdom and US copyright. It sought in the first instance to enforce its US judgment, though limiting its claim to $10m; but in the event that the law on foreign judgments did not permit this,[132] it sought relief by original action on its English and US copyright. The detail of the claim based on English copyright is of no professional interest to private international lawyers,[133] though devotees of the films may wish to add it to their collection of assorted memorabilia.

The judge's approach to issues of private international law was not exactly what one might have expected. He considered that insofar as the claim arose out of the US copyright, the English court was not being required to rule on the validity of the copyright, and there was therefore no sustainable objection to its jurisdiction to deal with the US copyright claim. Any exclusionary rule was to be confined to cases in which the validity of the right was required to be determined. Such rule would not necessarily apply to all such rights, and least of all to copyright.[134] The judge was of the opinion that any exclusionary rule should be no wider than that applicable to foreign land. The absolute *Moçambique* rule in relation to jurisdiction

---

[128]   *Sic*: not profits.

[129]   Double *sic*.

[130]   The writer understands that these children's films were not cartoons in the traditional sense. But it is just asking too much to refer to them in writing as art.

[131]   It was probably even more expensive to run than were the helmets to make.

[132]   This raised questions concerning the enforcement of foreign judgments, which are examined below.

[133]   Yet one may still learn something from the guidance, proposed by the judge at [134], which asks whether the helmet and armour of an Imperial Stormtrooper was something which William Morris would have recognized as contributing to what the Arts and Crafts Movement were seeking to achieve. Evidently the answer is negative.

[134]   Which does not require registration or deposit and is, therefore, the least formally tied to the state of protection.

to determine title to foreign land had been trimmed when Civil Jurisdiction and Judgments Act 1982 s 30 removed the jurisdictional bar for torts claim in relation to foreign immovable property unless the claim was one which principally concerned the question of title to that property. The judge could 'see no reason why the same should not apply to copyright';[135] he was free to take that view because the exclusionary rule was really an articulation of English public policy,[136] and the question of whether adjudication would conflict with English public policy was for him to say.

Quite apart from the merits of the result, it is appropriate to express surprise at the notion that because Parliament has done A, and the judge sees no reason why it should not have done B, the judge may interpret the law as though B had been done and proceed from there. But the judge saw no reason not to improve the law which Parliament has made: with the bit so firmly between his teeth, a submission that he should acknowledge the restraint by which he was bound had little chance. And so it proved. He took the view that whether there had been infringement of the US copyright was a matter which he was entitled to determine; and had it been necessary to determine the validity of that copyright, this would not have affected his answer.

If the judge is right, the net effect is that in an action *in personam*, the High Court has jurisdiction to determine whether a foreign intellectual property has been infringed or, with the possible exception of patents, is valid. This new principle will not be limited to cases founded on a contract or other equity between the parties. Though the judgment does not yet allow it to be said that an English court now has jurisdiction to make a determination of the validity or otherwise of a patent, in the sense that it will direct the Registrar or other office to annul the deposit or record, it remains unclear whether it will invariably exercise jurisdiction over an infringement claim to which a defence of invalidity is raised in apparent good faith.[137] The European Court has made it clear, however, that where the patent or other right is granted under the law of another Member State, such a defence may not be adjudicated by the court hearing an infringement claim, but must be left to be decided by the court of the Member State under which the right was granted.[138] That the jurisdictional consequences should be radically different where the right is granted under the law of a non-Member State would be surprising, though whether Article 22(4) of the Brussels I Regulation, or the 2006 decisions of the European Court,[139] apply by analogy[140] remains to be determined. The judge took

---

[135] At [266].
[136] At [265].
[137] A court must have power to find such a defence to be spurious and disregard it accordingly.
[138] Case C-4/03 *GAT v LuK* [2006] ECR I-6509; Case C-539/03 *Roche Nederland BV v Primus* [2006] ECR I-6535.
[139] Case C-4/03 *GAT v LuK* [2006] ECR I-6509; Case C-539/03 *Roche Nederland BV v Primus* [2006] ECR I-6535. The judge does not appear to have been taken to these decisions.
[140] Or apply 'with reflexive effect', as translation from the French of M. Droz would have it.

the view[141] that the principle of *forum non conveniens* might be pressed into service to save the English court from having to adjudicate on the validity of certain foreign intellectual property rights, though he does not appear to have been invited to explain how this could be squared with the decision in *Owusu v Jackson*[142] which is completely hostile to any such solution, no matter how urgent the need to find one. The law is, it seems, in a transitional phase, or a muddle.

Having improved upon section 30 of the Civil Jurisdiction and Judgments Act 1982 the judge turned his attention to the enforcement of the US judgment. He came to the conclusion, entirely orthodox, that Ainsworth had not been subject to the international jurisdiction of the American court, as none of the law laid down in *Adams v Cape Industries plc*[143] could be prayed in aid of the contention that he was present within or had submitted to the jurisdiction of the American court. An invitation to sweep away the restrictions of that case, at least for those judgment debtors who attract and do business over the internet, was mercifully repelled: heaven only knows where that could have been expected to lead. The judge appeared to believe that it was for Parliament to make any changes to settled law as laid down in *Adams v Cape*. That meant that the issue about the enforcing judgments for multiple damages was moot. But the judge gave his opinion, which does rather go against his view that changes to settled law are for Parliament to make.

The judgment that Ainsworth pay $20m comprised $5m for copyright, plus a second $5m for trademark and competition rights which had then been trebled, to make a grand total of $20m. If otherwise entitled to recognition and enforcement,[144] this American judgment was enforceable as to the first $5m; and was certainly unenforceable as to the $10m which represented the process of multiplication: the former was established in *Lewis v Eliades*,[145] and the latter the inescapable conclusion following from section 5 of the 1980 Act. That left the sum of $5m in respect of trademark and competition rights, to which the prohibited multiplication had been applied. Section 5(1) of the Act left no obvious room for doubt. It provided that:

[a judgment for multiple damages][146] shall not be registered under Part II of the Administration of Justice Act 1920 or the Foreign Judgments (Reciprocal Enforcement) Act 1933, and no court in the United Kingdom shall entertain proceedings at common law for the recovery of any sum payable under such a judgment.

---

[141] At [269].

[142] Case C-281/02, [2005] ECR I-1383.

[143] [1990] Ch 433 (CA).

[144] There was an analysis of whether Ainsworth was, for the purposes of English private international law, subject to the international jurisdiction of the American court.

[145] [2003] EWCA Civ 1758, [2004] 1 WLR 692.

[146] This wording being taken from sub-section (2)(a).

The claim to recover the second (and then multiplied) sum of $5m was therefore plainly within the prohibition put in place by Parliament in relation to the recovery of 'any sum payable' under the judgment. That the Act produced this result was the very point upon which objection had been raised, clearly and precisely, in correspondence between the United States Ambassador in London and HM Government. The same objection had been noted and dismissed, just as clearly, by the United Kingdom in correspondence between HM Ambassador in Washington and the United States Government.[147] It was as plain as plain could be that the government had procured legislation which did exactly what it wanted and which did exactly what the United States objected to. In a parliamentary democracy, one might think that that settled the debate about what the law actually was, but by now the judge was prepared to let the force be with him. He took the view, in effect, that Parliament had been irrational in legislating as it had.[148] What it should have done, according to the judge, was to prohibit the recovery of the $10m which was the excess above the sum assessed as compensation, but not to touch the underlying $5m. The legislation being found to be defective, the judge was free[149] to 'read in the concept'[150] that compensatory judgments ought to be enforceable, and thereby recast the statute as though it had said what Parliament should have said. Perhaps one ought not rise to the bait when all it amounts to are a few dicta from a puisne judge on the very last day of the summer term, but this really does take the biscuit.

8. Russian oligarchs and the conflict of laws: *OJSC Oil Co Yugraneft v Abramovich;*[151] *Cherney v Deripaska;*[152] *Re OJSC ANK Yugraneft; Millhouse Capital UK Ltd v Sibir Energy plc.*[153]

The year was one in which the business of the rich and powerful men of Russia gave the English courts[154] plenty to think about. From a luridly rich seam of private international legal material, a number of items stand out as worthy of attention on the ground that though the decisions were

---

[147] The diplomatic correspondence is published in Lowe, *Extraterritorial Jurisdiction* (1983), 177.
[148] The reference is to *Associated Provincial Picture Houses Ltd v Wednesbury Corporation* [1948] 1 KB 223, which sets the standard for judicial review of reviewable bodies.
[149] His justification, that this question had not been decided in *Lewis v Eliades*, does not deserve to be taken seriously. The point was not raised in that case because it was irrelevant to the claim advanced; and the wording of the statute was so clear that argument about it before the Court of Appeal would in any event have been futile.
[150] At [230].
[151] [2008] EWHC 2613 (Comm), Christopher Clarke J.
[152] [2008] EWHC 1530 (Comm), [2009] 1 All ER (Comm) 333: Christopher Clarke J.
[153] [2008] EWHC 2614 (Ch), [2009] 1 BCLC 298: Christopher Clarke J.
[154] To say nothing of the English news media, about which nothing will be said. In addition to the cases noted here, though *Berezovsky v Abramovich* [2008] EWHC 1138 (Comm) raised no real issue of private international law, *Berezovsky v Russian Television and Radio Broadcasting Co* [2008] EWHC 1918 (QB) did. Eady J refused to find that he had no jurisdiction over a claim alleging defamation, on the ground the pleading alleged a publication in England and that the claimant could not be regarded as a libel tourist. Being a libel refugee (see at [1]) is, quite another matter.

reached at first instance only, their importance is high. The complexity of the facts which gave rise to the legal issues under discussion is not important, and is not recited here. It is sufficient to note that tales of corporate activity involving the turbulent de-nationalization of the natural resources of Russia,[155] and corporate entities in Russia, Cyprus, Jersey, the British Virgin Islands, and litigation in most of them, are unlikely to be fit for broadcast before the watershed.

One of several such claims led to the Commercial Court, in which Yugraneft, a Russian joint stock company, brought proceedings against three defendants, including one Abramovich, a Russian national with business interests around the world and proprietor of the Chelsea Association Football Club. One says Russian, but while Yugraneft was a Russian corporation now in liquidation, the web of business transactions which underpinned its claim to have been defrauded by Abramovich implicated entities created under the laws of the jurisdictions mentioned above. Abramovich himself, though retaining his Russian citizenship and holding the Governorship of a vast area of the Russian Far East,[156] had links to a large number of countries. Service of process was made out of the jurisdiction without the permission of the court. The claimant justified having done so by contending that Abramovich was domiciled in the United Kingdom for the purpose of Article 2 of the Brussels I Regulation,[157] and that permission was therefore not required.[158] The substance of the claim against him was formulated in equitable terms, alleging dishonest assistance of another's breach of trust, and knowing receipt of trust property. There was a further allegation of unjust enrichment; and pleadings which alleged that various laws of the Russian Federation, civil and criminal, had been violated. In a judgment of impressive rigour the judge, among other things,[159] explained why Abramovich was not domiciled in the United Kingdom; that the substance of the claims against him was governed by Russian law, according to which they were all fatally[160] barred by lapse of time; and that if an application were to be made for permission to serve Abramovich out of the jurisdiction, it would be refused.

It is convenient to start with the domicile point, for though it is in one respect the mainspring of the Brussels I Regulation, decisions on its meaning

---

[155] The most notorious is routinely referred to as the 'aluminium wars'; the struggle for control of the oil and gas production industry was scarcely more dignified.

[156] The Chukotka Autonomous Okrug.

[157] According to the rules in Article 59 of the Brussels I Regulation and SI 2001 No 3929, Sch 1, para 9.

[158] CPR r 6.19(1), which from 1st October 2008 was substantially remade as CPR r 6.33.

[159] The constraints of size mean that this note cannot deal with the question of whether estoppel resulted from judicial proceedings in the British Virgin Islands and various Russian courts, nor with the equitable proprietary claim.

[160] In the sense that Russian law produced this result, Foreign Limitation Periods Act 1984, s 1 applied Russian law on this point, and section 2 of the same Act was unavailable to contradict the application of Russian law which was neither contrary to English public policy or otherwise liable to do injustice to the claimant.

are few. It was necessary for the claimant to show, in the sense of its having the better of the argument about it, that when the proceedings were instituted the defendant was resident in the United Kingdom, and that the nature and circumstances of his residence indicated a substantial connection with the United Kingdom. The rhetorical strength of the claimant's case was that if the defendant's ownership of substantial houses in Belgravia and in Surrey, where his former wife and their children lived, and of the Chelsea Football Club, did not demonstrate a substantial connection to the United Kingdom—more marketable substance than most of the rest of us are ever likely to acquire—then it was hard to see what else might be required. But as a matter of immigration control, Abramovich did not have leave to remain, instead entering the United Kingdom on a business visa; as a matter of tax law, Abramovich was not regarded by HMRC as resident[161] for the purpose of United Kingdom taxation; and as a matter of balance sheet accounting, Abramovich could show that his English houses represented less than 1% of his 'net worth'.[162] He could also show that he spent no more that one night a week in an English bedroom, and the dates of his presence in the United Kingdom were strikingly similar to the home fixture list of the Chelsea Football Club. According to the judge, the sum of this evidence did not show that Abramovich was resident in the United Kingdom; it followed that he could not be found to be domiciled in the United Kingdom. The judge was fortified in his view by taking a commendably rational view of what 'residence' meant for the purpose of the domiciliary rule in Article 2 of the Regulation. Proceeding from the fact that jurisdiction established on the basis of the defendant's domicile could not be stayed on the ground that the natural forum for a claim lay elsewhere,[163] it ought to follow that the residence which underpinned a finding of domicile had to be sufficiently substantial to justify the jurisdiction of the English courts even in circumstances where, as in the instant case, there may be no real or substantial connection to England.[164] Setting the height of the bar by reference to the consequences which flowed from a finding of domicile, the judge was easily able to dismiss the contention that Abramovich was resident in the United Kingdom. It was an admirable piece of analysis of the position of the peripatetic businessman, and

---

[161] From which a conclusion that his residence disclosed a substantial connection was impossible to be drawn.

[162] When the economy of the United Kingdom collapsed late in 2008, this valuation may have become inaccurate. The 'net' worth of people in the position of Abramovich was, it appeared, rather harder to calculate. The sound proposition that Chelsea Football Club was only English in a technical sense, with its manager and almost all its playing staff being foreigners, was not apparently advanced.

[163] Case C-281/02 *Owusu v Jackson* [2005] ECR I-1383.

[164] At [444]. Much the same point had, however, been made by Langley J in *Ministry of Defence of Islamic Republic of Iran v Faz Aviation Ltd* [2007] EWHC 1042 (Comm), [2008] 1 All ER (Comm) 372, a case where domicile was determined for the purpose of Article 60 of the Regulation.

one which should now stand as the primary source of English law on the law of domicile under the Regulation.[165]

Service in purported accordance with the Regulation having been set aside, the judge quickly dismissed any thought that an application for permission to serve out would have had a better chance of success. The natural forum for the claims made was Russia, and even if Abramovich was said to be a proper party to the claim, which was also advanced against an English defendant, the English defendant was little more than a husk, appearing on the Claim Form only in order to provide a hook on which to seek to hang a claim against the non-English defendant. The judge saw it for the ruse it was,[166] and that was the end of that. Even so, he was pressed with the argument that Yugraneft should be allowed to serve out, even though Russia may be the natural forum, on the authority of his own decision in *Cherney v Deripaska*.[167] In that case, the judge had upheld an application for permission to serve out of the jurisdiction in another claim against a Russian businessman which arose from the turbulent world of Russian raw materials. He upheld permission on the ground that though Russia was the natural forum for the claim, the claimant's fears that he could not get a fair trial in Russia were sufficient to overcome the fact that *Spiliada Maritime Corp v Cansulex Ltd*[168] required a claimant to show that England was the natural forum before service out could be authorized. The decision in *Cherney* was the first occasion on which the court had found that it was justified in authorizing service out even though the foreign court was the natural forum. The fact that the judge gave leave to appeal was justified by the obvious novelty in the judgment. But the encouragement that it gave to claimants to argue that the foreign courts were not to be trusted to do justice according to their law is much more controversial. Evidence that a foreign court may[169] not do justice, or will deliver corrupted justice, has almost always been excluded from jurisdictional applications. It flies in the face of the judicial injunction against fighting jurisdictional applications by disparaging the quality of adjudication in other states;[170] it invites the court into an area in which it is required

[165] In this respect, superseding *High Tech International AG v Deripaska* [2006] EWHC 3276 (Comm) and *Cherney v Deripaska* [2007] EWHC 965 (Comm), with which the present judgment is entirely consistent.

[166] At [490].

[167] [2008] EWHC 1530 (Comm), [2009] 1 All ER (Comm) 333.

[168] [1987] AC 460.

[169] After all, the cases in which evidence will demonstrate that the foreign court *will not* do justice will be rarer. It is usually a matter of prediction or speculation, which a court may be reluctant to make. By contrast, the contention that a state did not do justice, or was chronically incapable of doing justice, may properly be advanced in answer to a claim to enforce a foreign judgment, and is not obstructed by the dubious principle that certain matters are non-justiciable where they involve allegations of criminal behaviour against a foreign government: *Korea National Insurance Co v Allianz Global Corporate and Specialty AG* [2008] EWCA Civ 1355, [2008] 2 CLC 837, (allegations of criminal conspiracy made against judgment creditor and foreign government to defraud judgment debtor).

[170] The cases are summarized in Dicey, Morris & Collins, *The Conflict of Laws* (14th edn), para 12–031.

to make judgments by reference to standards which are not judicially manageable;[171] it restores the principle, hitherto repudiated, that an English court may find that it is a superior form of tribunal; and it will run the risk of causing embarrassment to the executive in its conduct of foreign affairs.[172] An exception may be made for instances—mercifully rare—which speak for themselves, but the judge was not being asked to stay proceedings in favour of Nazi Germany or the Democratic Republic of Congo.[173] Life and times in Russia are, no doubt, sometimes a bit rough around the edges, but for the judge to find that a particular claimant was justified in impugning the Russian legal system was altogether unexpected. However, the judge was unwilling to make any similar finding in relation to Yugraneft, even though the company had appeared to wish to sue anywhere except Russia. No doubt its protestation of lack of confidence in the Russian system was based on something, but it was not anything which found favour with the judge. There is room for the view that the judge took a false step in *Cherney v Deripaska*, but *Yugraneft* added nothing to the argument.

The issues of choice of law for the claims formulated as equitable and restitutionary were dealt with in exemplary fashion.[174] The judge was not

---

[171] Cf (on judicially manageable standards) *A-G (UK) v Heinemann Publishers Australia Pty Ltd* (1988) 165 CLR 30.

[172] This consideration, if ever it underpinned an exclusionary legal rule, is an issue which is now of sharply reduced significance. An English court, called upon to implement the European Convention on Human Rights, may be required to deal with evidence about the behaviour of a foreign country, government or legal system which is (or ought to be) deeply embarrassing.

[173] In *889457 Alberta Inc v Katanga Mining Ltd* [2008] EWHC 2679 (Comm), [2009] 1 Lloyd's Rap 213 the court refused a stay in respect of the first defendant which was domiciled in the United Kingdom (Articles 60 and 2 of the Brussels I Regulation), and authorized service out on the second and third defendants as necessary or proper parties to the claim: this fact served also to satisfy the further requirement that England was the natural forum for the claim. The further finding of the judge in relation to the alternative court, that the Democratic Republic of Congo was not an available forum, as law and order had effectively broken down and had been left unrepaired, was not one which he needed to act on. Tomlinson J noted the decision in *Cherney v Deripaska* without comment, but had no need to rely on it. As a matter of interest, on the date on which the judgment was handed down, the Foreign and Commonwealth Office was advising against any travel to certain parts of the Congo, and against all but essential travel to the rest of the country. The conclusion that the Congo was not an available forum should, therefore, have been an easy one to reach: if this is the nature of the advice of the FCO, it is very hard to see that a stay in favour of the foreign court could ever be granted. The question whether a claim against a defendant served out of the jurisdiction, which claim has its natural forum in the Congo, should nevertheless be allowed to be brought, was not touched by the judgment.

The decision in *Cherney v Deripaska* was applied by the Staff of Government Division of the Manx High Court, and service out authorized on appeal, reversing the decision of the Deemster below, even the natural forum was in Kyrgyzstan, in *Kyrgyz Mobil Tel Ltd v Fellowes International Holdings Ltd* (28 November 2008). The conclusion of the court was that as there was a risk that the particular claim might not be dealt with properly according to the law—the evidence for this lying in the fact that previous decisions of the Kyrgyz judicial system had been perverse and irrational—it had not been shown that justice could be done in Kyrgyzstan. How this overcame the fact that the Isle of Man was no more a natural forum than had been the English court in *Cherney v Deripaska* was unexplained.

[174] It was surprising that the judgment's intellectual indebtedness to Yeo, *Choice of Law for Equitable Doctrines* (2004), from which this aspect of the analysis must have been derived, was not expressly acknowledged.

particularly hemmed in by authority—that which existed was notable neither for clarity nor for internal coherence—and not much constrained by analysis in the textbooks.[175] He therefore observed that there was no separate and distinct choice of law category for 'equitable claims',[176] and that the causes of action set out in the pleadings had to be accommodated within the orthodox categories for choice of law. That eliminated the possibility that an equitable claim could be governed entirely by the *lex fori*, or by the *lex fori* 'with allowance made' for the points of factual contact with foreign law. It was much more persuasive to see equitable claims resulting from a prior relationship between the parties as governed by the law of that relationship, and those founded on allegations of wrongdoing as governed by the choice of law rule for torts.[177] That this analysis prefigured the law to be stated in the Rome II Regulation[178] was an uncovenanted-for bonus. His immense labour may be contrasted with the view of superficial impression, which will be as far as many will go: this was a Russian claim, between Russian parties, arising from Russian business practices, and where the claims of Russian law to be the law which should sort out the mess were, beyond any question or pleading, self-evident. Only the huge sums of money at stake could have explained the complexity of the story and manner of its telling. It was about Russia, and really only about Russia.

The judge's analysis will soon be overtaken by the Rome II Regulation but, while it remains authoritative it stands as a textbook example of how to deal with a disputed question of choice of law. It also encourages those who believe that the common law is not well served by an approach which allows a claimant to assert a number of causes of action, arising from a common factual source, but alleged to give him the opportunity of pointing to a number of different choice of law opportunities. For the judge to find that the allegations were all based on wrongdoing, and comprehended

[175] For dishonest assistance as a matter of common law authority, *Arab Monetary Fund v Hashim* (29th July 1994), *Dubai Aluminium Co Ltd v Salaam* [1999] 1 Lloyd's Rep 415, *Grupo Torras SA v Al Sabah* [1999] CLC 1469, rev'd [2001] CLC 221, and *Kuwait Oil Tanker Co SAK v Al Bader* [2001] 2 All ER (Comm) 271. The sum total was that the defendant could not be liable as a matter of English private international law unless it was also liable, to the same degree, under the law of Russia where the alleged wrong was done: the applicable rule for choice of law was, in effect, one of double actionability, as it was for tort claims. The claims founded on dishonest assistance were therefore within the material scope of the Private International Law (Miscellaneous Provisions) Act 1995, which would use slightly different reasoning to reach the same conclusion that liability under Russian law was required. For claims based on wrongful receipt and unjust enrichment, which the judge correctly considered to be functionally identical, the judge followed the advice in Dicey, Morris & Collins, *The Conflict of Laws* (14th edn, 2006) in the Commentary to Rule 230, to discount the applicability of the law of the place of enrichment (with a reservation for cases in which there was no prior relationship between the parties to indicate some other choice of law: see at [247]) and to apply instead the law which governed the relationship which the parties had established between themselves. That was Russian law. As the claims were barred in Russian law by lapse of time, they were not actionable in England.
[176] The point of departure for which may be Dicey Morris & Collins, para 2–035.
[177] Especially at [246]–[247].
[178] Regulation (EC) 864/2007, [2007] OJ L199/40, in force from 11th January 2009.

by the choice of law rule for tort claims, was therefore very welcome. Other judges have seen the attraction of a similar approach,[179] though individual decisions at first instance cannot be taken to have settled the matter so far as the common law is concerned. Even so, when English private international law is restated in the twin Regulations of Rome I[180] and Rome II, it is most improbable that cumulative and alternative characterization of claims will be permitted. It will be the imposition of a *Pax Romana*, but that is preferable to common law anarchy.

It followed from all of this that there was no claim capable of being asserted in the English courts. This meant that the court in *Re Yugraneft, Millhouse Capital UK Ltd v Sibir Energy plc* did not have to decide whether it would have acceded to a petition to wind up Yugraneft, an unregistered company as far as English law is concerned and which was being wound up in Russia. Insolvency Act 1986, section 221, allows the English court to wind up an unregistered company, but the case-law establishes that this will not be done unless there is a point to it, such point most usually being demonstrated by the presence of assets in England upon which the order for winding up could usefully bite and from which local creditors could gain.[181] The judge came to the wholly predictable conclusion that if he had not set aside service of the claim form in the proceedings just noted, he would have allowed the petition for the winding up of the unregistered company to proceed, the gigantic claim for compensation (on that hypothesis) before the English courts constituting a local asset which gave purpose to the winding up.[182] It seems to be an entirely orthodox application of established law.

9. The common law of domicile: *Barlow Clowes Ltd v Henwood;*[183] *HMRC v Gaines-Cooper.*[184]

It can come as a slight surprise to discover that there are still areas of the law, matrimony aside, in which the common law of domicile still plays a decisive part. But when Barlow Clowes Ltd sought to enforce a judgment debt against H, who had been adjudged to be implicated in the dishonest

---

[179] *Trafigura Beheer BV v Kookmin Bank Co* [2006] EWHC 1450 (Comm), [2006] 2 Lloyd's Rep 455, where a separate choice of law for a tort committed within the framework of a contractual relationship was denied.

[180] Regulation (EC) 593/2008, [2008] OJ L177/6.

[181] See *Re Compania Merabello San Nicholas SA* [1973] Ch 75, *Re Latreefers Inc, Stocznia Gdanska SA v Latreefers Inc* [1999] 1 BCLC 271, *Re Latreefers Inc, Stocznia Gdanska SA v Latreefers Inc (No 2)* [2001] 2 BCLC 116, *Re Drax Holdings Ltd* [2004] 1 WLR 1049.

[182] The judge's further conclusion, however, was that the material misleading of the court by non-disclosure on the original application for the appointment of a provisional liquidator, would have justified the setting aside in any event of the order appointing the provisional liquidator. This reinforcement of the law on full and frank disclosure, which seems on occasion to be treated with unsettling laxity, is valuable, even though it establishes no new point of principle.

[183] [2008] EWCA Civ 577: Waller V-P, Arden and Moore-Bick LJJ.

[184] [2007] EWHC 2617 (Ch), Lewison J. Permission to appeal was refused by the Court of Appeal, in notably strong language: [2008] EWCA Civ 1502.

processing of monies stolen from the company, and sought to bankrupt him, H objected to the petition on the ground that he was, as he said, no longer domiciled in England.[185] H had been sued to judgment in the Isle of Man on account of his misdeeds; the judgment had been confirmed by the Privy Council. Its enforcement in England was unchallengeable; and the method chosen by the judgment creditor was to make the statutory demand and then petition for the bankrupting of the judgment debtor. On the footing that the judgment was to be taken at face value, H had little legitimate claim to the benefit of any doubt.

The point of departure was that H had an English domicile of origin. He claimed to have had a miserable childhood, and it was not disputed that had certainly established a domicile of choice on the Isle of Man. He had abandoned this when the fraud which was the Barlow Clowes affair, and his part in it, became a matter of public Manx scandal. He spent more time in France, where he had a substantial house, but where H did not seek to persuade anyone that he had established a domicile of choice. He also spent some time in Mauritius, where he took a lease from year to year of a rather more modest dwelling; he did not seek to purchase a more substantial interest in land, and did not have indefinite leave to remain.[186] Quite by chance, it appears, Mauritian law on bankruptcy was unexpectedly favourable to H, at least so long as he did not set up business in Mauritius. Evans-Lombe J, however, had held that H had acquired a domicile of choice in Mauritius, and had not relinquished it by or before the date of presentation of the petition. He appears to have reached this conclusion on the basis that once a domicile of choice has been acquired, the next step, if there is one, will be the acquisition of another domicile of choice. The Court of Appeal disagreed, holding that H had an English domicile, by revival, on the relevant date. Its judgments, however, had to grapple with the slippery story told by H in his attempt to avoid the petition, and the strangeness of the law itself. But the conclusion, reached at some considerable length by Arden LJ, more concisely by Moore-Bick LJ and most concisely by Waller V-P, was that H had failed to establish a further domicile of choice after he had left the Isle of Man for good. When he waved a final goodbye to that fogbound tax-raid-shelter, he had not reached the decision to make his home, indefinitely or permanently, in France, or in Mauritius, or in any other single place. As a matter of ancient common law doctrine,[187] in such circumstances the domicile of origin will revive, no matter how uncongenial that may have been for the respondent, no matter how deep-seated his reasons for claiming to have suppressed it with a Manx domicile of choice.

---

[185] Insolvency Act 1986 s 265 gave the court jurisdiction to make the order if the respondent were domiciled in England but not otherwise.
[186] At [119]. It is not clear whether he had even applied for such leave.
[187] *Udny v Udny* (1969) LR 1 Sc & D 441.

The minutiae of the evidence which supported, or contradicted, the proposition that H had decided to reside, chiefly[188] and indefinitely, in Mauritius was recited at length. It was almost entirely self-serving: if ever there was an issue on which the quality of the advocacy was likely to sway the outcome of the case, a dispute as to domicile is likely to be it: there will usually be more than enough in the life of the propositus to suggest that he is a fugitive from civil or criminal justice (or injustice); that the fiscal advantages of a particular domicile never entered his mind and, until the litigation was commenced, were something of which he knew nothing; that he has decided to make his home in the haven of choice although, being rather rich, he cannot be expected to have given up travelling around, because that is what the rich naturally do. It was all there, set out in and occluding Arden LJ's judgment: H professed an intention to live, die, and to be interred in Mauritius, but spent less than one-fifth of the average year there, and could not remember the denomination, never mind the name, of the church in whose burial ground he said he wished to be laid. It was pretty unedifying stuff, as the naked evasion by debtors of their liabilities usually is. In the end, the question might have been put to H in the following essential form: 'do you really expect the court to believe that you had decided to settle in Mauritius for good, until the end of your days?'

In the light of this, it is necessary to say only a little about the strangely similar case of *HMRC*[189] *v Gaines-Cooper*. The taxpayer,[190] who had an English domicile of origin, who had retained his status as a British citizen, and was only a British citizen, sought to persuade HM Revenue & Customs that for the years of assessment he had acquired a domicile of choice in the Seychelles: sunny islands with which he claimed to have fallen in love and in which he also wished to be taxed: alive, dead and buried. The Special Commissioners considered the evidence—the usual junky collection of car-boot-sale material—which was assembled by and on behalf of the taxpayer and HMRC.[191] They concluded that the taxpayer had not established a Seychellois domicile of choice which might displace his domicile of origin. On the taxpayer's appeal on point of law, the judge upheld the decision below. In effect, he found that the protestations and demonstrations of love for the Seychelles went only so far. As the taxpayer had at all times maintained a residence in England, in order for him to establish a domicile

---

[188] A person cannot have two domiciles of choice, and so if there are two contenders for the title of domicile of choice, each one satisfying the minimum criteria of residence coupled with an intention to remain indefinitely, the tie must be broken by finding one to be the chief and the other not.

[189] Her Majesty's Revenue & Customs has assumed the responsibilities previously discharged by the Inland Revenue Commissioners among others.

[190] The correct term would really be tax avoider, but as far as the law is concerned, his duty is to pay.

[191] This included the startling information that he had planted a coco-de-mer (*Lodoicea Maldivica*) tree in his Seychellois garden, and that this could be seen to vouch for his intention to reside there indefinitely, for the species was notoriously slow growing. The notion that one acquires a domicile of choice by putting down roots is all very well as far as it goes, but unless there was unrecorded irony in the submission, the idea of doing it through the agency of a tree was a bit much.

of choice in the Seychelles, it was incumbent upon him to establish that what he had established in the Seychelles was his principal or chief residence.[192] On the evidence, which was as voluminous as it was tendentious, the Special Commissioners had not erred in law in reaching the conclusion that he had not done so. If it can be summed up in a single line, it would be that it is not a matter of where you love, but where you live. In the case of Mr Gaines-Cooper, he may have loved the Seychelles, with its benevolent sunshine, slow-growing flora, and laws, but it was not there that he lived, at least in the sense that he had not made the Seychelles the principal of his two residences. And that was that.

10. Mental incapacity and forced marriage: *KC v City of Westminster Social & Community Services Dept*[193]

Marriage is one of those areas of private international law in which some people's cultural sensitivities can make life difficult. The present case was one. Marriage, as a characterization category in private international law, certainly needs to be wider in scope, more accommodating, than the domestic English version. For example, a marriage to which one party was fifteen,[194] or in which the participants came within one of the remoter degrees of kindred and affinity, cannot be any the less a marriage, at least until we know more about it. Marriages can be in varying degrees forced,[195] sham, or arranged: it would be daft to exclude from the characterization as marriage those unions which are not exactly the same as we are now supposed to do it at home. Parliament, of course, can establish particular rules for individual institutions, as it did for civil partnerships:[196] a characterization category which, as a matter of English private international law, encompasses and characterizes as civil partnership unions which other systems, less in thrall to ancient superstition or more modern bigotry, have simply defined as marriage.[197] But if the courts were to consider that, say, polygamous unions were not marriages,[198] or the thrice-repeated dismissal: 'I repudiate you (as I can, because God made me the man and you the woman)' was not a divorce,[199] all manner of consequential questions would arise when

---

[192] If it is necessary to ask whether the propositus has established a residence in a new country at the same time as he maintains a residence in the old, the test must be understood to ask whether he has established in the new country a principal residence: *IRC v Plummer* [1988] 1 WLR 292.

[193] [2008] EWCA Civ 198, [2009] Fam 11: Thorpe, Wall, and Hallett LJJ.

[194] After all, the age of consent in many European countries is lower than 16. In *Mohamed v Knott* [1969] 1 QB 1, the wife was 13 but the marriage, which was in every respect Nigerian, was not invalid.

[195] Statute now provides some person protection from being pressed into such things, but does not appear to make the marriage independently invalid: Forced Marriage (Civil Protection) Act 2007.

[196] Civil Partnership Act 2004.

[197] Section 213 and schedule 20 to the Act. For example, same sex marriage under the law of Belgium or the Netherlands is for English purposes a civil partnership; the same is true for same sex marriage under the laws of Spain and Canada: *Wilkinson v Kitzinger (No 2)* [2006] EWHC 2022 (Fam), [2007] 1 FCR 183.

[198] See *Hyde v Hyde* (1866) LR 1 P&D 130.

[199] 'Talaq, talaq, talaq': see *Chaudhary v Chaudhary* [1985] Fam 19 (CA) regarded it as a divorce but not as one entitled to be recognized in the particular case.

it came to be decided whether there was capacity to do it, and so on. For this reason, the common law really had no choice but to include polygamous unions, and unions between uncle and niece[200] as marriages; it had also to regard religiously-based repudiations of spouses[201] as divorces. That, at least, pointed the way to the individual rules for choice of law, in these tricky areas, which need to be developed to regulate the effect of these things in English law. Whether this is culturally inclusive or insensitive is an interesting or political question,[202] but it is not one with which the common law could have seriously engaged without losing its way.

Marriage, therefore, must have an irreducible core meaning for the purposes of private international law: just as a contract without consideration is still a contract, the marriage of one's kin, or a divorce without the respondent having any right to object, may still qualify as a marriage or a divorce. After all, it is not as though we are bestowing approval: we are just trying to fit the world into the categories envisaged by our private international law. But it is harder to state precisely what that irreducible core is. The union of male and female is, as a matter of statutory clarification, part of it. Once we have decided it is a marriage, the law then attaches conditions: there may be restrictions of form, of how, of where, the ceremony takes place. There are rules which determine whether an individual is personally competent to enter into marriage, and others which determine whether the opposite spouse is legally available to him or her. There are rules which determine whether it is necessary to be willing and able to have sexual relations, whether the marriage can be rescinded or treated as void when some problem or unpleasant surprise comes to light. And, for the most part, these are determined by the domiciliary law of the party with the problem.

In the unsettling and unhappy case of *KC v Westminster*, C was the child of a couple of Bangladeshi extraction but who were domiciled and resident in England. C was in his twenties, though autism and other disability had retarded his mental development to being that of someone no older than three. He had been born in England, and had an English domicile of origin and dependency. His local authority had played an active part in his

---

[200] *Cheni v Cheni* [1965] P 85.
[201] We await the wise judge who will say that such barbarity offends the Human Rights Act 1998, and that the pretended justification of recognition of religious freedom is as unavailing as it is repellent. Every year brings us one year closer. In *EM (Lebanon) v Secretary of State for the Home Department (AF (A Child) intervening* [2008] UKHL 64, [2008] 3 WLR 931, the Court expressed the view that the position of married women under muslim (sharia) law was such that to deport the applicant to Lebanon would in the circumstances amount to a flagrant breach of her rights under Article 8 of the Convention. The court denied that such an argument was available to any woman who arrived at Heathrow without permission to enter the country, but did accept that the arbitrary and discriminatory rules of this aspect of Lebanese law made it unlawful to deport the applicant, who was in the United Kingdom as an asylum seeker, to Lebanon (it is obvious that the distinction between the two categories of case is a very uneasy one). The wider implications of the judgment remain to be seen. The court accepted that Lebanon was not to be regarded as though it were bound by the obligations of the ECHR, but did accept that the question was whether the *English* court could properly make a deportation order where the known consequences were so disgraceful.
[202] See in particular Wall LJ at [44].

care; and in 2007 instituted proceedings for a declaration of his (in)capacity to marry. But before this came on for hearing, C's parents arranged for him to be married, 'in Bangladesh' and in muslim form. In fact, C's participation was by telephone from London; what he understood of the whole business was unknown and unknowable. Though he lacked capacity to enter into any marriage as a matter of English law, it was contended by the parents that he had capacity under the law of Bangladesh, and that the result of the arrangement was, as a matter of Bangladeshi law, a legally effective marriage. The Court of Appeal rejected the contention of the parents, holding the so-called marriage to be without effect as a matter of English private international law.

In coming to its conclusion, though, the court was troubled by whether C's condition was to be characterized as raising the objection of absence of consent, which would make the marriage voidable,[203] or as lack of capacity, which makes a marriage void.[204] Whichever it was to be, the court rejected the proposition that there was, in this case at least, any exception to be made in favour of the recognition of this as a Bangladeshi or muslim marriage, dismissing any suggestion that public policy might call for the recognition of the legal validity of this extraordinary arrangement. It expressed no view about the proposition, accepted below for the sake of argument, that this was a marriage celebrated in Bangladesh. Though the question of whether the marriage was voidable, rather than void, was not handled clearly, the conclusion that this lamentable series of events did not result in a marriage is plainly correct. Even if it were to be contended that the law of Bangladesh saw this as a form of marriage which was actually for the welfare of the impaired party, it is hard to see that an English court could have reached any other conclusion than the one it did.

Perhaps the largest question was whether the marriage was voidable or void. Thorpe LJ was of opinion that it followed from Matrimonial Causes Act 1973, s 12, that lack of consent due to unsoundness of mind rendered a marriage voidable. This interpretation of the section had been confirmed in *Re Roberts (dec'd)*.[205] He was fortified in this interpretation by the fact that Family Law Act 1986 s 55 prevents the court making a declaration that a marriage was void from its inception: such a ruling has to be obtained on a petition for nullity. By contrast, the Act allows the making of a declaration of the voidability of a marriage. Thorpe LJ therefore preferred the view that this marriage was voidable. Wall LJ, on the other hand, interpreted this as a case where C's lack of personal capacity to marry under the law of his domicile made the marriage void. He seems to have considered that to allow section 55 to intrude into the substantive analysis, as distinct from its impact being confined to the order which a court may

---

[203]   Matrimonial Causes Act 1973, s 12.
[204]   Ibid, s 11.
[205]   [1978] 1 WLR 654 (CA).

make, would be to allow the remedial tail to wag the substantive dog. Hallett LJ, less than altogether helpfully, agreed with both judgments.

On the analysis of consent and capacity, the approach of Wall LJ is much to be preferred. On the facts as found by the court, there was certainly an issue whether C had capacity to marry, and a question whether he had consented to the marriage: the process of characterization identified these two questions as potential impediments to the marriage. But the answer to the former was, plainly and on any view of the matter, that C had no capacity for marriage. The union was therefore a nullity from its inception. For all that it may have been a religious something, it was a legal nothing. As a result, the question of whether C had consented to enter into it was incoherent: there was no 'it' for him to have consented to. The provision in section 12 of the 1973 Act, which makes lack of consent a reason for a marriage to be voidable, is applicable only if and after it has been found that the person concerned did have capacity to enter into a marriage in the first place. The impediments listed in section 12 are those which give the parties the option of deciding to affirm the validity of the marriage by choosing not to seek an annulment of it. This was not the way to view the impediment which afflicted C. According to his personal law, C had no capacity to marry anyone; and the proposition that he could have been party to a voidable[206] marriage is as unsound as it is unsettling. The declaration made by the court, in the end, sidestepped this difference of analysis, and section 55, by stating that the marriage was not recognized as valid as a matter of English law. That conclusion was beyond reproach.

The judgments, but more especially that of Wall LJ, examined the extent to which a court should exercise a degree of cultural tolerance, or manipulate its public policy, with a view to finding that a questionable marriage was valid. They should not have done so. English public policy may invalidate a marriage which is by reference to the ordinary rules for choice of law a valid one. But it will only do so *in extremis*. So it was that the marriage of uncle to niece in *Cheni v Cheni*,[207] found to be valid according to the Egyptian law of each party's domicile, was not invalidated. Likewise, the marriage of an adult to a child in *Mohammed v Knott*[208] was not invalidated. But it is generally understood that a marriage of brother and sister, of the marriage of a child too young for school, could not be recognized as valid, whatever the domiciliary laws might say. Cases in which English public policy might validate a marriage liable to be found invalid by the ordinary rules have tended to focus on foreign rules of invalidity of a kind abhorrent to English standards of common

---

[206] With its silent suggestion that he might avoid the marriage when he recovered from and became aware of his disability.
[207] [1965] P 85.
[208] [1969] 1 QB 1.

decency. Invalidities based on racial prejudice[209] or on religious bigotry[210] are unfit for recognition through the ordinary rules for choice of law. But the fact that Bangladeshi law conferred capacity on the wife to marry a person incapable of understanding what was going on was not the point. It was his incapacity, not her capacity, which was the problem.

The party who was domiciled in England was denied capacity according to the law of his English domicile. It is obvious that English public policy cannot be utilized to contradict the answer given by a rule of English domestic law. The only escape would have been to discover that the applicable choice of law looked not to the law of C's domicile, but this was hopeless on the facts. Even if there had been judicial support for the application of the law of the intended matrimonial home, which there was not,[211] the matrimonial home intended by C's parents was England in any event. And the truth was rather the opposite: if C had been domiciled in Bangladesh as well, with the consequence that each party had domiciliary capacity to marry the other, it must have been very likely indeed that the marriage would have been regarded as ineffective as a matter of English private international law: public policy would surely have been repelled by the idea of a marriage even more culturally challenging than that in *Cheni v Cheni*. The conclusion is that in giving so much attention to the question, the court was, one may suggest, trying a little too hard to appear to be sensitive.

Was the marriage celebrated in Bangladesh? The question went unanswered, as the decision on capacity and consent was sufficient. But the proposition that the place of celebration was Bangladesh was factually, and surely legally, wrong. It took place partly in Bangladesh, where the wife, her family, and a khazi[212] were, and partly in London, where C, his family, and an imam[213] were in attendance. There was a telephone at each end. How anyone could contend that this was a marriage celebrated in Bangladesh and not in England is not at all clear. The private international law of divorce got itself into a terrible tangle a little while ago, as the choice of law rules for the recognition of divorces are evidently drafted on the assumption that all divorces are obtained in *a* country, even though it is perfectly clear that some are trans-national in nature. The law on the recognition of divorces has it that if a divorce is trans-national, it may not

---

[209] Discussed, in relation to the racial laws of the American South, in *Sottomayor v De Barros* (1877) LR 3 PD 1; (1879) LR 5 PD 94; *Chetty v Chetty* [1909] P 67 (a case on caste). The racial laws of Nazi Germany are an obviously stronger case. But the case-law is not completely coherent: see *Corbett v Corbett* [1957] 1 WLR 486 (recognition of an annulment which had been declared on the ground that a Jew could not lawfully marry a Christian).

[210] Dicey states at 17–115 that under the laws of some countries in which the doctrines of the Roman Catholic church still hold sway, the marriages of priests or nuns are prohibited: no such country is identified, however. The recognition of such impediments to marriage would be contrary to English public policy: *Sottomayor v De Barros (No 2)* (1879) 5 PD 94, 104.

[211] *Radwan v Radwan (No 2)* [1973] Fam 35 was prepared to use the law of the intended matrimonial home to save the validity of a marriage otherwise in danger of falling foul of English law which denied capacity to contract a polygamous marriage. As authority it stands alone.

[212] A religious functionary.   [213] A religious functionary.

be recognized, at least if one of its component parts is in England.[214] If there is an analogy to be drawn, and there probably is, it would be that a marriage which is in part celebrated in England is either invalid unless it complies with English law, or is invalid unless it complies with English domestic law *and*, one would suppose, the law of the other place of part-celebration. Thorpe LJ[215] was inclined to think that if it were possible to marry by telephone at all, the marriage would need to comply with the laws of each country, at the very least in point of form, and with the whole of English law if one of the places of celebration is England. As to whether it is possible for someone to marry *in absentia*, the rules which seem to have recognized marriage by proxies would suggest so.[216] Indeed, one case suggests that a marriage can be validly celebrated in the absence of both spouses, which is even more challenging,[217] and may cross the line which delimits the characterization category of marriage. But in *KC v Westminster*, the requirement that the marriage conform to the requirements of Bangladeshi form,[218] and of English form and substance, would seem rational.[219] If the choice of law rules of the common law require an answer to the question where was the marriage celebrated, and the answer is in two places at once, what else can the law do but require compliance with the laws of each on any issue for which the rules of private international law call for compliance with the law of the place of celebration?

11. Resolution of disputes about dispute-resolution agreements: *Elektrim SA v Vivendi Holdings 1 Corp;*[220] *The 'Kallang', Kallang Shipping SA Panama v Axa Assurances Senegal;*[221] *The 'Duden', Sotrade Denizcilik Sanayi ve Ticaret AS v Amadou Lo;*[222] *ACP Capital Ltd v IFR Capital plc;*[223] *UBS AG v HSH Nordbank AG;*[224] *Deutsche Bank AG v Asia Pacific Broadband Wireless Communications Inc;*[225] *CMA CGM SA v Hyundai Mipo Dockyard Co Ltd.*[226]

---

[214] See the law as analysed in *R v Secretary of State for the Home Department ex parte Fatima* [1986] AC 527.

[215] At [36]-[42]. At [50], Wall LJ shared the doubt.

[216] *Apt v Apt* [1948] P 83.

[217] *McCabe v McCabe* [1994] 1 FLR 410 (CA): neither party was physically present in Ghana; they just sent a bottle of gin and some money to Ghana, where some kind of ceremony took place. This was apparently enough to constitute a marriage according to the custom of the wife's tribe, but the proposition that the place of the marriage was Ghana, which was what the Court of Appeal said, is just too surreal to be taken for law.

[218] The need to meet the requirements of a foreign *lex loci* is confined to issues characterized as formal.

[219] There is a general view, though lacking decisive authority, that a marriage celebrated in England must probably comply with English law as to capacity as well as form: Dicey, Rule 67, Exception 3.

[220] [2008] EWCA Civ 1178, [2009] 1 Lloyd's Rep 59: Sir Anthony May P (QBD); Hallett and Lawrence Collins LJJ.

[221] [2008] EWHC 2761 (Comm), [2009] 1 Lloyd's Rep 124: Jonathan Hirst QC.

[222] [2008] EWHC 2762 (Comm), [2009] 1 Lloyd's Rep 145: Jonathan Hirst QC.

[223] [2008] EWHC 1627 (Comm), [2008] 2 Lloyd's Rep 655: Beatson J.

[224] [2008] EWHC 1529 (Comm), [2008] 2 Lloyd's Rep: Walker J.

[225] [2008] EWCA Civ 1091, [2008] 2 Lloyd's Rep 619: Laws, Keene, and Longmore LJJ.

[226] [2008] EWHC 2791 (Comm), [2009] 1 Lloyd's Rep 213: Burton J.

A final note, which cannot avoid being fragmentary, is required to deal with the aftermath of *Premium Nafta Products Ltd v Fili Shipping Co Ltd*,[227] which we noted last year.[228] That decision, it will be recalled, demanded a fresh start be taken to the construction of arbitration and jurisdiction agreements, and established that a dispute should still be referred to arbitration even though one party had sought to rescind the contract in which the agreement was, in some sense, contained. The use of 'in some sense' is deliberate, and reflects the legal interpretation which holds that the provisions which deal with dispute resolution are severable from the substantive contract, and are not invalidated by a plausible challenge to the validity of the substantive contract. So although the shipowners sought to disavow a contract procured, as they said, by the bribery of their agent, they were still required to make their case before the arbitrator and not before the court. It was only a few years before that the House of Lords[229] had made it clear that, as far as it was concerned, agreements on choice of court should, like agreements to arbitrate, be enforced by specific order and with a minimum of fuss. All this represented a restatement of the common law in favour of the effectiveness of dispute resolution agreements; but it would have been unrealistic to suppose that there would not be ripples or aftershocks. Five[230] of these should be noted.

The facts of *Elektrim SA v Vivendi Holdings 1 Corp* are too complicated to justify telling. The touchpaper was lit by the collapse of a rickety Polish entity with interests in telephony which set off an explosion of litigation right around the globe. The particular issue on this application was whether an anti-suit injunction should be ordered to restrain proceedings which were pending before the courts in Florida. The legal basis for the claim was that the parties were bound by a contractual term according to which a bondholder would not bring proceedings against the issuer. The bondholder brought proceedings before the Florida courts, alleging fraud. The Court of Appeal had little difficulty in construing the no-proceedings clause in broad terms, on the understanding that this was the way to give commercial meaning to them. It reasoned that, though framed in tort, the claim sought compensation for the non-delivery of expected contractual benefits, and therefore fell within the material scope of the contractual no-proceedings clause. It had no more difficulty in enforcing the broken agreement by injunction. Once it has been decided that the party bringing proceedings has promised not to bring them, and is now in breach, there is little left to argue about.

---

[227] [2007] UKHL 40, [2007] Bus LR 1719. The case is also reported as *Fiona Trust & Holding Corp v Privalov*, which was its designation in the courts below. It appears that this is the name by which it is to be known in the profession, so this is the usage adopted here.

[228] This Year Book, 78 (2007), 588.

[229] *Donohue v Armco Inc* [2001] UKHL 64, [2002] 1 Lloyd's Rep 425.

[230] The decision in *Cavell USA Inc v Seaton Insurance Co* [2008] EWHC 3043 (Comm) is lengthy, but may be fairly described as an orthodox application of the decision in *Fiona Trust*. It calls for no further examination.

The same robust reasoning was deployed in two cases generated by a nasty outbreak of something best described as insurance claim piracy.[231] In *The Kallang* and *The Duden* the facts were substantially the same, and equally depressing. A charterparty contained a London arbitration clause, and the bills of lading issued by the master expressly[232] incorporated it. When the cargo was discharged in Senegal the cargo insurer alleged that it had found fault, and threatened to arrest the vessel. When the relevant P&I club proffered security and undertook to answer to English law and jurisdiction, the insurer spurned the offer, procured a Senegalese order for the arrest of the vessel, and arrested the vessel. In due course the P&I club issued another letter which, because it could be construed as submitting to Senegalese jurisdiction, was sufficient to procure the release of the vessel.[233] That accomplished, the shipowner sued the cargo owner for breach of the arbitration clause, and sued the insurer for tortiously procuring the breach of contract. The judge found that the Senegalese arrest had not been for the sole purpose of obtaining security for the claim to be made in the English arbitration, but had sought to try to force the litigation into the Senegalese court. Such a breach of contract, and its wrongful procuring or inducement, was actionable in damages, and did not require the implication of a term to warrant it. That the behaviour of the insurer might have been lawful under the law of Senegal was presumably so irrelevant that no mention was made of it. Although the judge recited in his judgment the long list of instances which suggested that a tawdry little 'claims industry' was developing in Senegal,[234] he simply and correctly drew the conclusions which followed from the fact that the express agreement on dispute resolution had been breached, and that damages was the appropriate remedy for it.

In *ACP Capital Ltd v IFR Capital plc*, an application was made for the stay of a counterclaim in proceedings pending before the English courts, on the ground that it fell within a choice of court agreement for the courts of Jersey. An agreement (advisory contract) had been made by the parties which had provided for the Jersey courts to have jurisdiction; thereafter further agreements (loan agreements) had been made which provided for English jurisdiction. Although it was argued that the proceedings before the English courts should be allowed to determine all the issues between the parties, on the basis that the English court could offer one-stop shopping and the English jurisdiction clause could be construed as being wide enough to justify it, the judge disagreed. He declined to find in *Fiona Trust* a principle that, so long as there was a jurisdiction agreement for the English courts, that swept all before it and concentrated jurisdiction

---

[231] The judge preferred not to call it blackmail (*The Kallang*, at [53]; *The Duden*, at [42]), so an alternative expression, which was not put to the judge, has been adopted here.

[232] *The Kallang*, at [66]. There was therefore no need to debate the issue of whether incorporation could be achieved by general words.

[233] In addition, injunctions were at that stage obtained from the English courts.

[234] *The Kallang*, at [52]-[54]; *The Duden* at [41].

in the English courts. Rather, where sophisticated and legally-advised parties have bargained at arms' length for a series of agreements, each having its own provision for dispute resolution and these not being all for the one jurisdiction, the result of their negotiation should not be overridden by ascribing an undue width to the English jurisdiction agreement. This would be so, even if it meant that claims which could otherwise have been concentrated in the English proceedings would be determined separately. True, the court does have a discretion to override an agreement on jurisdiction, as *Donohue v Armco Inc* made clear, but the invitation to exercise that discretion is not properly founded on anything available for extraction from *Fiona Trust*. A similar analysis of a case concerning disputes arising from financial transactions which had involved a number of contracts was taken in *UBS v Nordbank*. The judge, in a very short analysis, considered that the advantages of 'one-stop shopping' in England were insufficient to outweigh the rival contention, that certain claims fell within the parties' express agreement to litigate in a foreign court. In complex transactions, there is always a risk that the parties' drafting will leave them with a patchwork of agreements on jurisdiction. If they have, they are likely to be left to deal with it. Especially where the jurisdiction agreement for the English courts is validated by Article 23 of the Regulation, but also generally, the preference for upholding agreements for the resolution of disputes, even untidy ones, is stronger than ever.[235]

The cases just mentioned are authoritative on the approach of the common law to dispute-resolution agreements, and in particular where there is a dispute about the dispute-resolution agreement. Whether they shine any light on the corresponding problem which arises where the disputed jurisdiction agreement is one to which Article 23 of the Brussels I Regulation would apply is not clear. For there is no particular reason to suppose that the common law preference for one-stop shopping and severability is part of the complex scheme put in place by the Regulation, and in which Article 23 may be seen to enjoy a lower priority than equivalent agreements are given at common law. In the fourth case, *Deutsche Bank AG v Asia Pacific Broadband Wireless Communications Inc*,[236] a loan agreement contained a jurisdiction agreement for the English courts, and as one party to the agreement was domiciled in a Member State, the exclusively Taiwanese connections of the other did not prevent the application of Article 23. What might have done was the assertion of the defendant that the agreement had been made by a corporate officer who lacked authority to make it and

---

[235] That said, the revival of interest in the discredited case-law on the meaning of 'arising out of', and so forth, revealed by the judgment in *UBS v Nordbank*, suggests that the fresh start dictated by *Fiona Trust* was more easily said than done.

[236] The writer appeared for the defendant before the Court of Appeal. The case is therefore noted in deliberately neutral terms in order to draw attention to what is, on any view, an important decision; it is not intended to offer any personal view or individual assessment of what the Court of Appeal should have done, or of what any other court might do. A petition for leave to appeal to the House of Lords was dismissed.

to bind the defendant. Though the defendant had initially submitted to the jurisdiction of the English courts when proceedings were issued claiming to enforce the agreement, it opposed an application to amend to add a claim for restitution which was posited on, and only on, the proposition that the defendant was not bound by the agreement which its officer had purported to make on its behalf. The contention succeeded before the judge, who saw an impossible contortion in a claimant seeking to assert (i) that the contract was a nullity, (ii) that this was the legal basis for its claim for relief, but (iii) that the claim could be brought in the court designated by a term of the contract which, on the claimant's own showing, was devoid of legal effect. His conclusion was reversed by the Court of Appeal which interpreted the defendant's contention as one which sought to argue (i) that the substantive contract was not binding on the defendant, as it had been concluded by a person who lacked authority from the defendant to bind him to it, then (ii) as far as the defendant was concerned, it had not made any agreement that the claim in question should be brought in the nominated court, and as (iii) the validity of the jurisdiction agreement was impugned on the same ground which was said to render the substantive contract invalid as against the defendant, (iv) the defendant's contention infringed the common law principle of severability of dispute-resolution agreements as well as the jurisprudence of the European Court.[237]

It is obvious, as *Fiona Trust* amply showed, that legal policies are in conflict. The common law has committed itself to the view that where there is genuine dispute about the legal validity of a dispute-resolution agreement, it should be presumed to be effective, and the decision whether it really is binding be one taken by the designated court or tribunal. As a rule it has an arbitrary aspect, for it seems to take one party's side sooner in the debate than this has been shown to be correct. On the other hand, there are excellent reasons of policy in support of this approach, at least in a case where there is a proper basis for the contention that the agreement was made, and the dispute is (merely) whether it is valid and binding upon the party charged with it. It is, however, far from clear that the European learning has reached such a point of development. All the European Court has said so far is that a court called upon to exercise jurisdiction under what is now Article 23 is not prevented from doing so by the defendant's simple assertion that the substantive contract is not binding upon him.[238] All the European Court has done so far is to declare one line of argument inadmissible. Its reasoning does not cover the case in which a claimant advances a claim in which the invalidity of the substantive contract is common ground, yet its provision for the resolution of disputes is still held to be valid and binding. This is not to say that that

---

[237] Case C-269/95 *Benincasa v Dentalkit srl* [1997] ECR I-3767.
[238] See also, for the principles of the operation of Article 23 in relation to non-parties, *Knorr-Bremse Systems for Commercial Vehicles Ltd v Haldex Brake Products GmbH* [2008] EWHC 156 (Pat), [2008] 2 All ER (Comm) 448.

the European Court could not, one day, reach such a conclusion; it is simply to observe that the authority of *Benincasa* falls way short of establishing it. Nor is it to deny that there is a case to be made for the more general acceptance within the Brussels scheme of auxiliary jurisdiction: that is, of the argument that if the court has jurisdiction over one claim, this should be sufficient to give it jurisdiction over another which is closely connected to it, even though the latter claim, if advanced in proceedings all by itself, would not have been within the jurisdiction of the court. But that would require a cultural change on the part of the European Court, and there is little sign of that on the horizon. One may read in the decision of the Court of Appeal the sub-text that, if it was directing the course of European law, that law would be aligned or realigned[239] to conform to the commercial common sense of the commercial common law. But that leads nowhere at all.

Last, but assuredly not least, is the decision in *CMA v Hyundai*. A Korean shipyard had agreed to build four vessels for a German buyer. The German buyer wished to transfer its contracts to C, a French entity. It proposed to do this by a novation of the shipbuilding contract, which provided that the consent of the shipyard was required, this not to be unreasonably withheld. When the shipyard nevertheless withheld its consent, C brought proceedings against it before the French courts, alleging that the withholding amounted to a tort against C;[240] and although the shipyard did later consent to the novation, C still pressed the French proceedings to judgment. The French court ordered the shipyard to pay several million euros in damages.[241] But the shipbuilding contract contained a provision for London arbitration. The shipyard, smartly as one may think, thereupon instituted an arbitration against C, seeking an award which would reverse the monetary effect of the French judgment. The arbitrators made the award. The judge, dismissing a challenge to the award, ruled in favour of the shipyard on the ground that (i) once the novation had taken place C stood in the shoes of the original contracting party as though from the original date of the contract, (ii) according to the arbitration agreement in the contract to which C had become a party, a dispute about whether consent to novation had been wrongly withheld fell within the very wide material scope of that agreement, (iii) the continuation of the French proceedings by C had therefore become an actionable breach of the contract to resolve the matter by arbitration, (iv) damages were recoverable to reverse the payments made under the French judgment on the simple ground that a contract-breaker was not to be permitted to profit from its breach, and (v) this did not infringe the Brussels I Regulation, as arbitral

---

[239] Which is correct is the issue which lay at the heart of the appeal.

[240] The proposition that a *non*-party to a contract may bring a claim against a contracting party accusing the latter of unreasonably refusing to enter into direct contractual relations with it is, to English eyes, quite extraordinary. That the claim and the judgment included an additional €10,000 for the 'slur' cast on C only went to highlight the egregious nature of C's behaviour.

[241] It was common ground that there had been no submission to the jurisdiction of the French court: at [7].

tribunals had no obligation under that Regulation[242] to recognize the judgments of a court in a Member State which had not in any event contradicted the allegation that there was a breach of the agreement to arbitrate.
It was a pretty bracing judgment which rests a single, simple enough, point:
if you bind yourself to an agreement for the resolution of disputes, and you
breach it, you may be made liable in damages for all the loss which flows
from it, not excluding loss which takes the form of payment of damages
under the order of a foreign court.

The construction of the agreement to arbitrate, and its application to
parties who 'repeople'[243] the original contract by novation, raises no issue
of private international law. As *Fiona Trust* means that an agreement to
arbitrate is to be interpreted as broadly as its wording will bear, the judge
was certainly entitled to find that the arbitrators had interpreted it correctly. On its true construction, C had put itself in the position of becoming obliged to discontinue any claim which now fell within the agreement
to arbitrate, even though C had committed no wrong when it instituted
those proceedings:[244] it may be a severe construction, but it was simply
the legal effect of the novation which C had itself sought. Did it then follow that the damages which the shipyard had been ordered by the French
court to pay, and which it had paid, were recoverable as losses caused by
what was now to be seen as a breach of the arbitration agreement? The
arbitrators had seen some difficulty with giving a simple affirmative answer,
but the judge did not: the French proceedings should not have been brought
or prosecuted to judgment and the damages which were ordered to be paid
constituted the losses which flowed from the breach. The only legal justification which was proposed was that a party in breach of contract was
not entitled to gain from its breach, a principle ascribed to *New Zealand
Shipping Co Ltd v Société des Ateliers et Chantiers de France*.[245] Though
the authority given in support of the conclusion was far from what one
might have expected, for the principle attributed to *New Zealand Shipping*
is in the broadest of terms, the judgment itself is clear that where quanti-
fiable financial loss has resulted from a breach of contract, it is recoverable
as damages, and that is that, and the fact that the financial loss consists of
the paying of damages under foreign judicial order does not prevent its
being seen as loss.

---

[242] Whether they were obliged to do so according to the law which governed the arbitration and
the tribunal was a separate question on which the Regulation was not the controlling instrument.

[243] At [23].

[244] For the future, the claim of C would now be seen as founded on a non-contractual obligation,
and so as governed by the Rome II Regulation (above, n 178). It would therefore be governed by the
law which governed the contract, or which would have governed the intended contract, between C
and the shipyard. That contract providing for English arbitration, it would be probable that the non-
contractual claim would also have been governed by English law, which would not have seen any form
of liability on these facts.

[245] [1919] AC 1, a case on whether a contract which provided that it was to be void in the event of
conduct which would otherwise have amounted to a breach was to be interpreted in that sense: held
not, as it would allow a party in breach to profit from his wrong.

The judge dealt equally clearly with the submission that this conclusion was beyond the reach of the arbitrators as the judgment of the French court was required by the Brussels I Regulation to be recognized, and contradicted the conclusions which the arbitrators were being asked to reach. Not so said the judge: the issue in the arbitration was simply whether the arbitration agreement had been broken, and it had been. The French court had not made a finding on that point, so its judgment provided no basis for an estoppel in the claim in arbitration. And even if it had, arbitrators are not bound to apply the Brussels I Regulation, because arbitration falls outside the material scope of the Regulation. Even if an English court would not be obliged to ignore such a judgment as a French court might have given, the arbitrators were not required by the Regulation to be inhibited by a Regulation which had no application in the procedure with which they were concerned.

Had the claim for damages been brought before an English court rather than a tribunal, and had that court treated the French judgment as evidence and proof of breach and of the damage resulting from it, as distinct from being a bar to the claim in the first place, its judgment would also have been correct[246] if controversial. However, the fact that the arbitrators were free in a way the courts are not is vouched for by the wording of the Regulation, and supported by the Opinion of the Advocate-General in *Allianz SpA v West Tankers Inc*,[247] and consistent with the approach of the Cour de Cassation[248] which implements the view that the exclusion of arbitration from the material scope of the Regulation means exactly what it says in the absolutest of terms. And it just goes to show that when one approaches agreements for the resolution of disputes as self-contained, fully-enforceable, common-or-garden commercial agreements governing the parties' behaviour *inter se*, the award of damages for their breach raises no real issue of rational contention.

---

[246] See Briggs, *Agreements on Jurisdiction and Choice of Law*, at para 8.63 *et seq.*

[247] Case C-185/07. The judgment of the court given on 10 February is reported at [2009] 1 Lloyd's Rep 413; it does not deal directly with this point.

[248] *Republic of Congo v Groupe Antoine Tabet* (Cass Civ I, 4 July 2007) *Rev Crit* 2007, 882, [2008] ILPr 622.

United Kingdom Materials on International Law 2008

Compiled by Kaiyan Kaikobad,[1] Jacques Hartmann,[2] Sangeeta Shah[3] and Colin Warbrick[4]

1. This selection of UK materials on international law is made from published sources. It does not purport to include everything that could be of interest to an international lawyer but it is not wholly restricted to materials that could be called 'state practice' in the strictest sense: some context is provided.

We have to make very considerable exclusions of material that we know would be of interest to some international lawyers. We bear in mind first, the need to avoid the purely ephemeral, and second, to exclude materials that are concerned mainly with the UK's implementation of the international law of co-operation, particularly at the general level. We are very sparing with matters of EU law, though we report some EU positions on questions of international law with which the UK is associated.

There is only limited material on UK treaties because the texts and explanatory memoranda are readily available on the web: **<www.fco. gov.uk/treaties>.**

Extracts are generally reproduced in their original form, which leads to inconsistencies, eg in spelling ('judgement'/'judgment') or capitalization 'UN charter' or designation ('Chapter Seven'/'Chapter VII'/ 'Chapter 7').

Introductory material is printed thus:

'The Foreign Secretary wrote to the FAC ...'

---

[1] Brunel Law School
[2] Lauterpacht Centre for International Law, Cambridge
[3] School of Law, Nottingham University
[4] The Birmingham Law School

Material from documentary sources is printed thus:

'We have signed a Memorandum of Understanding ...'

We have inserted a small amount of editorial material in the form '[... Ed.]' where it appears to be helpful to do so.

Cross-references to the present edition of UKMIL are written 'See **16/14**' and to previous editions of UKMIL are written, 'See **UKMIL [2008] 16/1**'.

2. Hansard references are to the Web version. There may be minor discrepancies between the column references in the Web edition and the bound volumes.

References to Hansard are given in the following forms:

Commons—HC Deb 13 November 2001 Vol 374 c345 or c134W or c101WH or c1WS, where W, WH and WS stand for Written Answers, Westminster Hall and Written Statements;

Lords—HL Deb 8 October 2002 Vol 639 or 16 October 2003 Vol 653 cWA125, where WA stands for Written Answer or HL Deb 29 January 2003 Vol 643 cGC170 where GC stands for Grand Committee.

3. Some sources are given as <www.fco.gov.uk>. These are references to Press Releases or Speeches on the FCO website. The appropriate link should be followed to the date given for the item in the text.

4. From its start in 1978 and up to and including 1996 the materials in UKMIL were classified on the basis of the Model Plan for the Classification of Documents concerning State Practice in the Field of Public International Law adopted by the Committee of Ministers of the Council of Europe in its Resolution (68) 17 of 28 June 1968. The Committee of Ministers considered that developments in public international law since 1968 made it necessary to amend the Model Plan. Accordingly, by Recommendation (97) 11 of 12 June 1997, it adopted an Amended Model Plan as a contribution by the Council of Europe towards implementing General Assembly Resolution 2099 (XX) on technical assistance to promote the teaching, study, dissemination and wider understanding of international law. The present issue of UKMIL is based on the 1997 Amended Model Plan.

5. We are glad to acknowledge the assistance of Joanna Foakes and Diana Brookes and their colleagues in the Legal Adviser's Department of the Foreign & Commonwealth Office.

6. We are grateful for financial assistance in the preparation of UKMIL to the Whittuck Trust.

INDEX

C. Types of States
    1. Unitary States, federal States and confederations
    2. Personal and real unions
    3. Protected States
D. Formation, continuity, extinction and succession of States
    1. Conditions for statehood
    2. Formation
    3. Identity and continuity
    4. Extinction
    5. Succession
        (a) Cases of State succession
            (i) Union with or without the demise of the predecessor State
            (ii) Dismemberment
            (iii) Separation
            (iv) Newly independent States
        (b) Effects of State succession
            (i) Territory and other areas under national jurisdiction
            (ii) Nationality
            (iii) Succession in respect of treaties
            (iv) Archives
            (v) Debts
            (vi) Property
            (vii) Responsibility
            (viii) Other rights and obligations
E. Self-determination

II. International organizations
  A. In general
    1. Status and powers
        (a) Personality
        (b) Privileges and immunities of the organization
        (c) Power, including treaty-making power
    2. Participation of states in international organizations and in their activities
        (a) Admission
        (b) Suspension, withdrawal, expulsion
        (c) Obligations of membership
        (d) Representation of States, including privileges and immunities
    3. Legal effect of the acts of international organizations
    4. Personnel of international organizations

Part One: International Law in General

Part Two: Sources and Codification of International Law

Part Two: I.B. *Sources and Codification of International Law—Sources of international law—Custom*

2/1 [See also **[2005]** UKMIL **1/2**]
In a debate in the Sixth Committee of the General Assembly on the Status of the Additional Protocols to the Geneva Conventions on the Law of Armed Conflict 1949, the UK representative said:

General Assembly resolution 61/30 offered one of the few opportunities for States to report on compliance with their obligations in the field of international humanitarian law. Unfortunately, the number of replies to the Secretary-General's request for information under the resolution had thus far been disappointing; her own delegation, after some delay, had just submitted its own reply and she urged other States to follow suit. ICRC was said to be considering whether a standard template would be helpful, and she encouraged it to pursue that initiative.

At the thirtieth International Conference of the Red Cross and Red Crescent, held in 2007, which had set that movement on a good course for the next four years, one of the commissions had been asked to consider the role of national societies as auxiliaries to the public authorities in the humanitarian field. Partnerships between governments and national societies would, of course, vary widely, but they could be fruitful for both sides; her delegation therefore welcomed the inclusion in resolution 61/30, for the first time, of a reference to the role of those societies.

The preamble to the draft resolution under the agenda item referred to the ICRC study entitled "Customary International Law". While her Government recognized that there might be cases in which such law could supplement the extensive range of treaties in that field, it had reservations about volume I of the study. In particular, some of the examples provided were not, in its view, properly to be regarded as State practice for the purpose of the rules relating to the formation of customary international law. Furthermore, the study sometimes jumped too quickly to the conclusion that a rule had entered into the corpus of that law without sufficient evidence of State practice. On the other hand, volume 2 of the study was a valuable research tool which brought together a large amount of material that would otherwise be difficult to locate. She welcomed the update of that volume being conducted at the Lauterpacht Centre for International Law, in the University of Cambridge, with funding from the British Red Cross.

The draft resolution also referred to the Montreux Document on Pertinent International Legal Obligations and Good Practices for States related to Operations of Private Military and Security Companies during Armed Conflict, in the drafting of which the United Kingdom had participated. In general, private companies provided a very good and, in some cases, indispensable service; however, the document's recapitulation of the legal obligations of States and list of potential good practices that they might wish to consider when deciding upon regulation in that field would prove useful.

The four Geneva Conventions had as much relevance to the modern world as at the time of their adoption in 1949; they were among the very few, if not the only, treaties to which all States were parties. However, it was also necessary to implement them as fully as possible in the interests of those who suffered during armed conflicts. The United Kingdom was, or had committed itself to becoming, a party to all the treaties in the field of international humanitarian law. In particular, it strongly supported and hoped soon to ratify Additional Protocol III to the Geneva Conventions, which had introduced the red crystal as a further humanitarian symbol, and was pleased that it had entered into force.

Her Government attached great importance to the role of journalists in reporting armed conflict and to their position under the Geneva Conventions. As civilians, journalists must be protected and deliberate attacks on them must be forcefully condemned. At the same time, journalists should respect the human dignity of those captured or interned during armed conflicts and ensure that they were not made the object of "public curiosity", a concept which, although mentioned in the Conventions, might be difficult to interpret in the current age of instantaneous media reporting. Guidance for the media on the relevant provisions of the Conventions, produced jointly by her Government and the British Red Cross, was posted on the website of the Permanent Mission of the United Kingdom to the United Nations.

(UN Doc. A/C.6/63/SR.13, General Assembly Sixty-third session, 7 November 2008)

Part Two: I.C. *Sources and Codification of International Law—Sources of international law—General principles of law*

2/2

Speaking in the Sixth Committee of the General Assembly on the Report of the ILC [A/63/10, Ed.], the FCO Legal Adviser, said:

I turn now to the statement of the United Kingdom on chapter IV of the International Law Commission's Report, dealing with the topic of shared natural resources.

The United Kingdom notes that the Drafting Committee of the Commission adopted at this year's session a preamble and an entire set of 19 draft articles on transboundary aquifers, as well as commentaries to the aforementioned draft articles. The United Kingdom also notes the Commission's recommendation that the General Assembly take note of the draft articles in a resolution, to recommend that relevant States make appropriate bilateral or regional arrangements for the proper management of their transboundary aquifers on the basis of the principles enunciated in the draft articles, and to consider at a later stage the possibility of concluding a convention on the basis of the draft articles.

The United Kingdom has in the past refrained from making substantive comments on this topic, primarily as we are not directly affected by this aspect of the Commission's work. We have, however, followed the Commission's work closely, and recognise the importance of this issue. With this in mind, the United Kingdom supports the Commission's recommendation that the General Assembly takes note of the draft articles in a resolution, and would likewise encourage States to continue to arrive at mutually beneficial bilateral arrangements on these issues. A convention could be considered at a later stage, if thought useful and necessary at that time.

The United Kingdom observes that the Special Rapporteur and the Commission have had a lengthy debate on whether or not, and how, the Commission might cover the issue of shared oil and gas resources. We have previously expressed the view in this Committee, as have other delegations, that any study on oil and gas would entail great complexity, and we are also uncertain about the existence of, or need for, any universal rules on this question. Like many other States, we have a lot of experience in dealing with cross-boundary oil and gas fields. In general, bilateral discussions with neighbouring States are guided by pragmatic considerations, based on technical information. Our general approach to these issues is that States should co-operate in order to reach agreement on the division or sharing of such cross-boundary fields.

With this in mind, the United Kingdom is not convinced, at this stage, that there is a pressing need for the Commission to elaborate a set of draft articles or guidelines on shared oil and gas resources.

(Text supplied by FCO)

Part Three: The Law of Treaties

Part Three: I.B. *The law of treaties—definition, conclusion, and entry into force—conclusion, including signature, ratification, and accession*

3/1

A Minister wrote:

All 27 member states must ratify the Lisbon Treaty before it can enter into force. In the UK, the EU (Amendment) Bill received Royal Assent on 19 June.

Article 6 of the Lisbon Treaty provides that:

"This Treaty shall be ratified by the High Contracting Parties in accordance with their respective constitutional requirements. The instruments of ratification shall be deposited with the Government of the Italian Republic."

Ratification is the process by which the UK indicates its consent to be bound by a treaty under international law. The procedure for ratification of the Treaty of Lisbon on behalf of the UK is the same as that for previous EU amending treaties. An instrument of ratification is drafted and submitted for the signature of Her Majesty the Queen. This is then sealed and bound and forwarded to our embassy in Rome for delivery to the Italian Government as depositary.

The administrative arrangements for ratification of the Lisbon Treaty were initiated following the granting of the Royal Assent to the EU (Amendment) Bill on 19 June 2008. The completion of these arrangements normally takes a number of weeks.

(HC Deb 1 July 2008 Vol 478 cW780–781)

Part Three: I.C. *The law of treaties—definition, conclusion, and entry into force—reservations, declarations, and objections*

[See also **6/45, 6/46, 6/54, 6/99**]

3/2
Under cover of a Diplomatic Note No 08/07 dated 12 February 2007, the Department of Foreign Affairs and Trade of the Commonwealth of Australia, in its capacity as depositary, circulated the following communication from the government of the UK; Government of the Commonwealth of Australia Department of Foreign Affairs and Trade No. 01/2007

The Foreign and Commonwealth Office of the United Kingdom of Great Britain and Northern Ireland Present its compliments to the Department of Foreign Affairs and Trade of the Commonwealth of Australia and has the honour to acknowledge the Depositary Notification date 10 October 2006 from that Office, enclosed with Note No.22/06 of 11 October from the Australian High Commission, Notifying the ratification of the Agreement on the Convention of Albatrosses and Petrels by the Government of the Argentine Republic and the accompanying Argentine Statement. The United Kingdom firmly rejects the Argentine statement concerning the United Kingdom's extension of the Agreement on the Conservation of Albatrosses and Petrels to the Falkland Islands, South Georgia and South Sandwich Islands and British Antarctica. The United Kingdom has no doubts about its sovereignty over the Falkland Islands, South Georgia and South Sandwich Islands and the surrounding maritime areas. The United Kingdom reiterates that there can be no negotiations on sovereignty of the Falkland Islands unless and until such time as the Falkland Islanders so wish. The United Kingdom has no doubts about British sovereignty over the British Antarctic Territory, and notes the Argentine reference to article IV of Antarctic Treaty, to which both the Government of Argentine Republic and the Government of the United Kingdom of Great Britain and Northern Ireland are parties.

(Treaty Series No.14 (2008) Ratifications etc, Second Supplementary List ... Cm 7496)

3/3
On 7 February 2008, the Secretary-General of the United Nations, as depositary, received a communication relating to Gibraltar, from the government of Spain, as follows; [*Translation: Original Spanish*]

The Permanent Mission of Spain to the United Nations presents its compliments to the Secretary-General of the United Nations and has the honour to refer to note verbale no. 54/IPE/ac sent by this Permanent Mission on 17 January 2008 with regard to the United Nations Convention against Transnational Organised Crime, which was opened for signature in December 2000, and transmitting a unilateral declaration of Spain pertaining to that Convention, following its extension to Gibraltar by the United Kingdom on 27 November 2007.

The Permanent Mission of Spain wishes to inform the Secretary-General that on 19 December 2007, following an exchange of letters between their Permanent

Representatives to the European Union, the English and Spanish versions of which are annexed to the present document, the Kingdom of Spain and the United Kingdom reached agreement on the "Agreed Arrangements relating to Gibraltar Authorities in the Context of Mixed Agreements (2007)" (annex I). The text of the "Agreed Arrangements relating to Gibraltar Authorities in the Context of European Union and European Community Instruments and Related Treaties" of 19 April 2000 is also annexed in both languages (annex II).

The procedure envisaged in the arrangements relating to Gibraltar authorities in the context of Mixed Agreements (2007), which was agreed by Spain and the United Kingdom on 19 December 2007, applies to the United Nations Convention against Transnational Organised Crime, since it is a mixed agreement.

The Permanent Mission of Spain to the United Nations should be grateful if the Secretary-General would inform the States parties to the United Nations Convention against Transnational Organised Crime of the content of this note verbale and of the texts annexed.

ANNEX I

AGREED ARRANGEMENTS BETWEEN THE KINGDOM OF SPAIN AND THE UNITED KINGDOM RELATING TO GIBRALTAR AUTHORITIES IN THE CONTEXT OF MIXED AGREEMENTS 19 DECEMBER 2007

[Translation: Original Spanish]
Brussels, 19 December 2007

Sir,

I am writing to thank you for your letter of 19 December setting out your Government's view on arrangements relating to mixed agreements that have been extended to Gibraltar and which, for the purposes of their implementation, could give rise to the intervention of Gibraltar authorities.

I am pleased to confirm that the arrangements set out in your annexed letter are acceptable to the Government of Spain and that your letter and the present reply constitute the official expression of both our Governments' understanding on this matter, which shall be known as "Agreed Arrangements relating to Gibraltar Authorities in the Context of Mixed Agreements (2007)" and shall be applicable as of today.

I also agree that, once you receive my reply, we should both transmit a copy of our exchange of letters/notes verbales to the Secretary-General of the Council of the European Union, with the request that he distribute the aforementioned correspondence to the Permanent Representatives of the other member States and to the other European Union institutions for information.

The present arrangements and any activity or measure undertaken in implementation or as a consequence thereof do not imply any change whatsoever in the Kingdom of Spain's and the United Kingdom's respective positions on the question of Gibraltar or on the boundaries of that territory.

Yours sincerely,

(Signed) Carlos Bastearreche

Permanent Representative of Spain to the European Union

19 December 2007

HE Carlos Basterreche

Spanish Permanent Representative to the European Union

Dear Carlos

I refer to the discussions we have had regarding the applicability of the Agreed arrangements relating to Gibraltar authorities in the context of EU and EC instruments and related Treaties of 19th April 2000 to Mixed Agreements which have been extended to Gibraltar, and which, for the purpose of implementation, may result in the intervention of Gibraltar authorities. ('Mixed Agreement' means an international instrument that contains provisions some elements of which fall within Community competence and some of which fall within the competence of the Member States, and to which the Community—if that is permissible under the instrument in question—and the Member States are Parties, following a Council Decision).

It is the understanding of my Government following these discussions that for these mixed Agreements the system of 'post boxing' in the 2000 arrangements will apply for communications between Spanish authorities and a Gibraltar body, authority or service but not for communications between the authorities of other States and Gibraltar.

Notwithstanding the above, for instruments covered by paragraphs 5a–5d of the 2000 arrangements, "postboxing" as set out in those arrangements will, for the time being, remain in place. If the arrangement set out above regarding mixed agreements is acceptable to the Government of Spain. I suggest that this letter and your reply will place on record the understanding of our two Governments which will be known as the 'Agreed arrangements relating to Gibraltar authorities in the context of mixed Agreements (2007)" and will be implemented as of the date of your reply. I propose that, on receipt of your reply, we should each send a copy of our exchange of letters / notes to the Secretary General of the Council of the European Union with the request that he circulates the aforementioned communication to the Permanent Representatives of the remaining Member States and to the other institutions of the European Union for their information.

These arrangements or any activity or measure taken for their implementation or as a result of them do not imply either on the side of the United Kingdom or on the side of the Kingdom of Spain any change in their respective positions on the question of Gibraltar or on the limits of that territory.

Yours

H. E. Mr. Kim Darroch

Permanent Representative of the United Kingdom to the European Union

ANNEX II

AGREED ARRANGEMENTS BETWEEN THE KINGDOM OF SPAIN AND THE UNITED KINGDOM RELATING TO GIBRALTAR AUTHORITIES IN THE CONTEXT OF EUROPEAN UNION AND EUROPEAN COMMUNITY INSTRUMENTS AND RELATED TREATIES 19 APRIL 2000

The Permanent Representative United Kingdom

Permanent Representation to the European Union

19 April 2000

HE Mr Javier Elorza
Permanent Representative of Spain to the European Union

Dear Ambassador

I refer to the discussions which have taken place between our two Governments to resolve certain difficulties which have arisen relating to Gibraltar authorities in the context of EU and EC instruments and related treaties. I now attach to this letter arrangements, as agreed in those discussions, relating to Gibraltar authorities in the context of EU and EC instruments and related treaties ("the" arrangements) in the English and the Spanish languages, both texts having equal validity, which will take effect on 01 June 2000.

If the Government of Spain confirms its agreement to the arrangements, they will form an understanding to which our two Governments are committed. I propose that, on receipt of your reply, we should each copy the arrangements, together with our exchange of correspondence, to the Secretary General of the Council with the request that he circulates the arrangements, together with this exchange of correspondence to the Permanent Representatives of other Member States and to the other institutions of the European Union in accordance with paragraph 8 of the arrangements for their information and for the purposes indicated in them.

Yours sincerely

Stephen Wall

ARRANGEMENTS RELATING TO GIBRALTAR AUTHORITIES IN THE CONTEXT OF EU AND EC INSTRUMENTS AND RELATED TREATIES

19 April 2000

Taking account of the responsibility of the United Kingdom of Great Britain and Northern Ireland as the Member State responsible for Gibraltar, including its external relations, under the terms of Article 299.4 of the Treaty establishing the European Community, when in an instrument or treaty of the type specified in paragraph 5 a provision is included whereby a body, authority or service of one Member State of the European Union may communicate directly with those of another EU Member State or may take decisions with some effect in another EU Member State, such a provision will be implemented, in respect of a body, authority or service of Gibraltar (hereinafter referred to as "Gibraltar authorities"), in accordance with the procedure in paragraph 2 and in the cases specified therein, through the authority of the United Kingdom specified in paragraph 3. The obligations of an EU Member State under the relevant instrument or treaty remain those of the United Kingdom.

In order to implement such a provision, formal communications and decisions to be notified which are taken by or addressed to the Gibraltar authorities will be conveyed by the authority specified in paragraph 3—under cover of a note in the form attached for illustrative purposes in Annex 1. The authority specified in paragraph 3 will also ensure an appropriate response to any related enquiries. Where decisions are to be directly enforced by a court or other enforcement authority in another EU Member State without such notification, the documents containing those decisions by the Gibraltar authority will be certified as authentic by the authority specified in paragraph 3. To this effect the Gibraltar authority will make the necessary request to the authority specified in paragraph 3. The certification will take the form of a note based on Annex 1.

1 The authority of the United Kingdom mentioned in paragraphs 1 and 2 will be The United Kingdom Government/Gibraltar Liaison Unit for EU Affairs of the Foreign and Commonwealth Office based in London or any United Kingdom body based in London which the Government of the United Kingdom may decide to designate.

2 The designation by the United Kingdom of a Gibraltar authority in application of any instrument or treaty specified in paragraph 5 that includes a provision such as that mentioned in paragraph 1 will also contain a reference to the authority specified in paragraph 3 in the terms of Annex 2.

3 These arrangements will apply as between EU Member States to:

(a) any present or future European Union or Community instrument or any present or future treaty concluded within the framework of the European Union or European Community;

(b) any present or future treaty related to the European Union or European Community instrument to which all or a number of EU Member States or all or a number of EU and EFTA/EEA states are the only signatories or contracting parties;

(c) the Council of Europe Conventions mentioned in the Convention of 19 June 1990 implementing the Schengen Agreement;

(d) the following treaties related to instruments of the European Union:

The Convention on the Service Abroad of Judicial and Extrajudicial Documents in Civil or Commercial Matters done at the Hague on 15 November 1965.

The Convention on the Taking of Evidence Abroad in Civil or Commercial Matters done at the Hague on 18 March 1970.

The Convention on the Civil Aspects of International Child Abduction done at the Hague on 25 October 1980 (when extended to Gibraltar)

(e) other treaties to which both sides agree that these arrangements should apply. Where there is no such agreement, the two sides will nevertheless seek to avoid and to resolve any problems which may arise.

In respect of the treaties specified in sub-paragraphs (a) and (b) these arrangements will also apply as between all the contracting parties to those treaties. Paragraphs 1 and 2 of these arrangements will be construed accordingly.

6 The spirit of these arrangements will be respected to resolve questions that may arise in the application of any provision of the kind described in paragraph 1, bearing in mind the desire of both sides to avoid problems concerning the designation of Gibraltar authorities.

7 These arrangements or any activity or measure, taken for their implementation or as a result of them do not imply on the side of the Kingdom of Spain or on the side of the United Kingdom any change in their respective positions on the question of Gibraltar or on the limits of that territory.

8 These arrangements will be notified to the EU institutions and Member States for their information and for the purposes indicated in them.

ANNEX I

SPECIMEN NOTE FROM THE AUTHORITY SPECIFIED IN PARAGRAPH 3

On behalf of the United Kingdom of Great Britain and Northern Ireland as the Member State responsible for Gibraltar, including its external relations, in accordance with Article 299.4 of the Treaty establishing the European Community, I attach a certificate in respect of (the company), signed by the Commissioner of Insurance, the supervisory authority for Gibraltar.

In accordance with the Article 14 of the Directive 88/357/EEC, as amended by Article 34 of Directive 92/49/EEC, the (name of company) has notified to the Commissioner of Insurance in Gibraltar its intention to provide services into (name of EU Member State). The process envisaged by Article 35 of Directive 92/49/EEC is that within one month of the notification the competent authorities of the home Member State shall communicate to the host Member State or Member State within the territory of which an undertaking intends to carry on business under the freedom to provide services:

(a) A certificate attesting that the undertaking has the minimum solvency margin calculated in accordance with Article 16 and 17 of Directive 73/239/EEC.

(b) The classes of insurance which the undertaking has been authorised to offer.

(c) The nature of the risks which the undertaking proposes to cover in the Member State of the provision of services.

ANNEX II

FORMULA TO BE USED BY THE UNITED KINGDOM WHEN DESIGNATING A GIBRALTAR AUTHORITY

In respect to the application of the (name of instrument) to Gibraltar, the United Kingdom, as the Member State responsible for Gibraltar, including its external relations, in accordance with Article 299.4 of the Treaty establishing the European Community, designates (name of Gibraltar authority) as the competent authority for the purposes of (relevant, provision of the instrument). In accordance with arrangements notified in Council documents [xxx of … **2000**]

One or more of the following alternatives will be used as appropriate any formal communications required under the relevant provisions of (name of instrument) which come from or are addressed to (name of Gibraltar authority) any decision taken by or addressed to (name of Gibraltar authority) which is to be notified under the relevant provisions of (name of instrument) will be conveyed by (name of UK authority) under cover of a note. The (name of UK authority) will also ensure an appropriate response to any related enquiries.

Where decisions are to be directly enforced by a court or other enforcement authority in another Member State without the need of a formal previous notification.

The documents containing such decisions of (name of Gibraltar authority) will be certified as authentic by the (name of UK authority). To this effect the (name of Gibraltar authority) will make the necessary request to the (name of UK authority). The certification will take the form of a note.

[Courtesy translation Original: Spanish]

Brussels, 19 April, 2000

His Excellency Sir J. Stephen WALL

Ambassador, Permanent Representative of the United Kingdom to the European Union.

Thank you for your letter dated 19 April to which are attached arrangements, as agreed in the discussions to which you refer, relating to Gibraltar authorities in the context of EU and EC instruments and related treaties ("the arrangements").

I confirm the agreement of the Government of Spain to the arrangements, which will form an understanding to which our two Governments are committed. I agree that, on your receipt of my reply, we should each copy the arrangements, together with our exchange of correspondence. to the Secretary General of the Council with the request that he circulates the arrangements, together with this exchange of correspondence, to the Permanent Representatives of other Member States and to the other institutions of the European Union in accordance with paragraph 8 of the arrangements for their information and for the purposes indicated in them.

(signed) Javier ELORZA

Ambassador, Permanent Representative of Spain to the European Union

(Treaty Series No.14 (2008) Ratifications etc, Second Supplementary List ... Cm7496)

3/4

In answering a number of questions about human rights, a Minister wrote in answer to one asking whether or not the UK planned to dispense with its power to make reservations to or derogations from the ECHR:

It would be impossible for the Government to do so. The United Kingdom already has no power to make reservations in relation to its existing obligations under the Convention. Reservations may only be entered by a state at the time at which it signs or ratifies (or equivalent processes for other states through which treaty obligations are accepted) the Convention. Therefore, the United Kingdom could only enter a reservation at such time as it signs or ratifies an additional Protocol to the Convention; it is not possible for the United Kingdom to dispense with this power.

(HL Deb 29 September 2008 Vol 703 cWS181)

3/5

In the debate on the Report of the ILC [UN Doc. A/63/10, Ed.] in the Sixth Committee of the General Assembly, and referring to 'specific issue questions' posed by the ILC on the matter of reservations to treaties, the representative of the UK said:

On reservations to treaties, the United Kingdom has followed with interest the work of the Commission and the Special Rapporteur, Mr Pellet, and believes that a Guide to Practice in this area will be very useful, given that the Vienna Convention on the Law of Treaties does not cover interpretative declarations and that there is a dearth of examples to illustrate national practice. However, given this dearth of State practice, we think that great care should be given even when formulating non binding guidelines.

The United Kingdom considers that it is appropriate to deal with interpretative declarations alongside reservations to treaties, believing that there is link between the two. For example, in some cases interpretative declarations are disguised reservations, where a treaty instrument may expressly forbid the making of reservations. However given the differences between reservations and interpretative declarations, the United Kingdom suggests that the title of Chapter VI be expanded to make specific reference to interpretative declarations. The United Kingdom agrees that separate terminology be used where possible, since reservations are juridicially different to interpretative declarations.

The United Kingdom welcomes Guidelines that support the following principles:

1 non-parties can make interpretative declarations, even though their declaration may not be determinative of interpretation under Article 31(3) of the Vienna Convention on the Law of Treaties;

2 interpretative declarations can be made at any time, and should not be subject to a definitive time-frame: an interpretation issue may not arise for some considerable time after a treaty has entered into force, or after Consent to be Bound has been given;

3   interpretative declarations should be made in writing; we note however, that the reasons for an interpretative declaration may be complex and not capable of simple definition.

The United Kingdom does not agree that silence as a response to an interpretative declaration necessarily constitutes acquiescence. The second paragraph of draft guideline 2.9.9 either needs deletion (thus leaving the issue of acquiescence to be ascertained by reference to international law) or further elaboration. If a Contracting State makes an interpretative declaration, and no time limit for reactions to declarations exists, at what point is the silence of other Contracting States deemed acquiescence? It is possible to envisage acquiescence by silence more readily in the case of a multilateral treaty with a small number of parties, who might be expected to be aware of the position of the State making the interpretative declaration, and react accordingly or if an interpretative declaration is obviously a disguised reservation, to which other States might be expected to object. However there could be other motivations for remaining silent to the effect that acquiescence cannot be presumed. In answer to specific issues question 26(a) we therefore do not see how silence can constitute acquiescence when there is no duty to react. It is very hard to ascertain when a State is expected to react and by when. On question 26(b) we cannot think of any circumstances in which silence in response to an interpretative declaration can be taken definitively to constitute acquiescence. On question 26(c) we do not think silence should play a part in the legal effects of interpretative declarations.

On the consequences of interpretative declarations and specific issues question 27 (a) for the author of the interpretative declaration, the declaration acts as an aid to interpretation; if it is not withdrawn, revised or supplemented it is possible that some issues of estoppel may arise. Likewise on question 27(b) for other States or organisations that have approved the interpretative declaration, the declaration acts as an aid to interpretation and it is also possible that some issues of estoppel may arise. On question 27(c) for States or organisations that have been silent, no acquiescence can be presumed; the declaration does not act as an aid to interpretation for that State or organisation. Likewise for States or organisations that have opposed, the declaration is not to be of any guidance; ordinary principles of treaty interpretation apply.

On reservations to treaties, with regard to draft Guideline 2.1.9, the United Kingdom strongly supports any move towards the provision of greater clarity in the making of reservations, whilst recognising that there is no obligation on States to do so. The making of reservations of a general and unspecific character frequently results in other States tabling objections to the same on those grounds. The number of such objections could potentially be reduced if the Parties to a treaty have greater insight to the reasons behind a State's reservation: they may then come to a clearer judgement on an appropriate response.

With regard to "reservations" to bilateral treaties, the United Kingdom agrees that the unilateral statements described in draft Guideline 1.5.1[1.1.9][See A/CN.4/ L.575, YbILC (1999-I) 214, saying that unilateral statements of whatever form made before a bilateral treaty came into force were not "reservations", Ed.] do not constitute a reservation within the context of the present Guide to Practice. In practice, the United Kingdom would normally seek to avoid making such statements, whatever their effect, or non-effect.

The United Kingdom trusts that the points we have raised will make some positive contribution to the valuable work being undertaken by the Commission and
Special Rapporteur in this area.

(Text supplied by FCO)

Part Three: II.B. *The law of treaties—observance, application, and interpretation application*

3/6
An FCO legal adviser told the FAC:

Generally, treaties that are concluded within the UN tend to not to have territorial application provision because there is a reluctance in that forum to talk about
colonies or to recognise that states have "colonies"—that is what they are often
called. Such forums tend to be silent on that, which means that we take the position that we decide ourselves whether we want to extend the treaty to the territory or not. Other conventions, usually in Europe, tend to have territorial
application provisions that set out the mechanism for extending treaties to the
territories.

Generally speaking, there is not an automatic application of a treaty to a territory.
That is something we usually look at and take a decision on. I do not know what
happened 50 years or more ago, but nowadays we never extend a treaty to the territories without consulting them. We have the power to do so—we could extend
a treaty if we wanted to—but we always have consultation. We tend to be accused
of not consulting properly but to my knowledge, we never extend anything without consultation.

To answer the question, there is a de minimis consideration because not all treaties are extended to all territories. Sometimes the territory says no because it does
not have the infrastructure or facilities in place to have it applied. Therefore, we
do not extend it. I could give examples of treaties that have not been extended.

There is consultation at the time of extension. Sometimes, the problem is that
the territories lose sight of what applies to them. But we have lists in our treaties
section. They can ask, and we can give them the information. (Qs. 324–325)

(FAC Report, Overseas Territories, HC 147-II (2008))

Part Three: II.C. *The law of treaties—observance, application, and
interpretation – interpretation*

3/7
Speaking in the Sixth Committee of the General Assembly on the Report
of the ILC [UN Doc. A/63/10, Ed.], the FCO Legal Adviser said:

I turn finally to the very interesting paper at Annex A of the Commission's Report
on treaties over time and thank Georg Nolte for his work on this topic. The
United Kingdom agrees that this is a topic of interest and appropriate to the work

of the Commission. Legal issues concerning the interpretation and application of treaties have historically been amongst the most successful and enduring work of the Commission and we anticipate that further work by the Commission on this subject could be equally useful.

The topic of treaties over time is potentially very broad and the United Kingdom notes that the report proposes that focus should be directed in the first instance to the issues of subsequent agreement and subsequent practice. The United Kingdom agrees that it would be appropriate to limit the focus at this point to these two areas. The United Kingdom also agrees with the two goals identified in the report, namely, of producing a repertory of practice and thereafter of identifying some guidelines and conclusions that might be drawn from that repertory. The issues of subsequent agreement and subsequent practice in the interpretation and application of treaties must quintessentially be rooted in what States actually do, rather than in theories of living instruments and the evolutionary character of particular kinds of treaties. The United Kingdom thus supports an endeavour, and an approach, that would be rooted in the practice of States and identifying whether there are indeed any general guidelines that may be drawn from this practice.

(Text supplied by FCO)

Part Three: IV.C. *The law of treaties—invalidity, termination and suspension of operation—termination and suspension of operation, denunciation, and withdrawal*

3/8

Speaking in the Sixth Committee of the General Assembly on the Report of the ILC [UN Doc. A/63/10, Ed.], the FCO Legal Adviser said:

I turn next to Chapter V of the Report on the effects of armed conflicts on treaties.

With the benefit of reviewing the draft articles in their present form, the United Kingdom would like to raise a question regarding how the draft articles might work in practice. Article 8 creates an obligation on a State Party to notify the other State Party or other States parties to the treaty of its intention to terminate or withdraw from a treaty or suspend its operation. The UK questions whether it will always be practical for the State Party withdrawing from or terminating the treaty to carry out this obligation by making the necessary notification, particularly if the other State Party or other States Parties and the depositary are belligerents.

Regarding draft article 4, it would be helpful to expand on the indicia in paragraph (b) by referring not just to the subject matter of the treaty but to its provisions, including the subject matter. As we have said before, it would also be very helpful to include a reference to the intention of the parties among the "indicia".

Article 12 provides that the resumption of the operation of a treaty suspended as a consequence of an armed conflict shall be determined in accordance with the indicia referred to in draft article 4. This leaves unclear however whether the decision to resume the operation of the treaty is the unilateral decision of the party which suspended its operation or whether the other parties to the treaty are also involved in the decision to resume.

We also suggest the following three textual amendments to the draft:

First, in Article 1, we wonder whether, instead of describing the draft articles as "applying to" the effects of an armed conflict in respect of treaties, it would be preferable to describe them as "dealing with" the effects of an armed conflict in respect of treaties, since this is what the draft articles in fact do. It would also be helpful to make it clear in this article that the draft articles are without prejudice to the role of international humanitarian law as the "lex specialis" applying to armed conflict. This would in turn help to reinforce the point that the definition of "armed conflict" in draft Article 2(b) is specific to the draft articles and the effects of armed conflicts on treaties.

Second, in draft article 6, paragraph 2, the inclusion of the word "lawful" to qualify agreements which may be concluded is somewhat surprising. The United Kingdom questions why it is thought necessary to include it, and suggests its deletion.

Thirdly, Article 18 provides that the draft articles are without prejudice to the right of States Parties to an armed conflict to regulate, subsequent to the conflict, on the basis of agreement, the revival of treaties terminated or suspended as a result of armed conflict. It is unclear why withdrawal is not included in this article, given that the provision deals with treaties which have been terminated or suspended and in the light of Articles 4, 8, 9, 10 and 11 which do include withdrawal.

(Text supplied by FCO)

Part Four: Relationship between International Law and Internal Law

Part Four: II. *Relationship between international law and internal law—Application and implementation of international law in internal law*

4/1
A Minister said:

... it is very important that the public at large, and children in particular, are made very much aware of their rights under the UN Convention [on the Rights of the Child]—one of the most popular conventions that there has ever been. We have a number of programmes on raising awareness ... We are committed to operating a number of web-based portals, enabling children and adults to access information about the convention. For parents and young people, Directgov has a popular section on it. For children under 10, DirectgovKids has a section on it. We also have specific training on the convention for all those who work with children.

(HL Deb 31 January 2008 Vol 698 c738)

4/2
The Northern Ireland Secretary wrote to the FAC:

INTERGOVERNMENTAL AGREEMENT WITH IRELAND

Following the successful restoration of devolution in Northern Ireland yesterday, I am pleased to enter into an Intergovernmental Agreement with Ireland. This treaty reaffirms both Governments' commitment to protect, support and where appropriate implement the provisions of the Belfast Agreement, subject to the alterations to the operation of the institutions agreed at St Andrews.

As you may be aware, this Agreement was signed on 22 March and laid before Parliament as a Command Paper (Cm 7078) on 18 April in the wake of the 26 March breakthrough and Easter recess. Copies of the Agreement and its accompanying Explanatory Memorandum have already been distributed to members of your Committee.

As you know, the tenets of this Agreement have been considered by Parliament during the passage of the Northern Ireland (St Andrews Agreement) Act 2006. Following the successful restoration of devolution to Northern Ireland on 8 May, I consider it appropriate in these circumstances to truncate the standard 21-day laying period under the Ponsonby Rule to ensure the Agreement can be brought into force as soon as possible. This will provide swift formal clarity to the agreed alterations to the arrangements and institutions established by the Belfast Agreement of 1998, and ensure a shared understanding of the St Andrews Agreement commitments across these islands. To that effect, notes of completion will therefore be exchanged today with the Irish Government.

I will make a Written Ministerial Statement to Parliament today explaining my reasons for truncating the Ponsonby laying period on this occasion, and I am writing in similar terms to the Northern Ireland Affairs and Public Accounts Committees.

The Ministerial statement read:

Following the successful restoration of devolution in Northern Ireland, I am pleased to enter into an intergovernmental agreement with Ireland.

This treaty reaffirms both Governments' commitment to protect, support and where appropriate implement the provisions of the Belfast agreement, subject to the alterations to the operation of the institutions agreed at St. Andrews. The conditions laid out in legislation for the restoration of the devolved institutions in Northern Ireland have now been met. In this historic context, it is fitting that these commitments are formalised promptly with the Irish Government and the Government welcome this opportunity to provide a shared understanding of these arrangements across these islands.

This agreement was laid before Parliament as a Command Paper (Cm 7078) on Wednesday 18 April. The tenets of this agreement have been considered by Parliament during the passage of the Northern Ireland (St. Andrews Agreement) Act 2006 and, following the successful restoration of devolution to Northern Ireland on 8 May, the Government consider it appropriate to truncate the standard 21-day laying period under the Ponsonby rule to ensure the agreement can be brought into force as soon as possible. This will provide swift formal clarity to the agreed alterations to the arrangements and institutions established by the Belfast agreement of 1998.

(HC Deb 9 May 2007, Vol 460 c14WS)

4/3

In answering a number of questions about human rights, a Minister wrote about unincorporated international human rights treaties:

Our dualist legal system means that international treaties are not enforceable in our domestic courts unless they have been expressly incorporated into our domestic law, as happened in respect of ECHR through the Human Rights Act 1998. The Government believe that this system remains appropriate to the United Kingdom's constitutional traditions, and have no plans to change it. There are nevertheless limited circumstances in which our domestic courts can have regard to our international treaty obligations, including international human rights treaties, most notably where a court interprets an ambiguous statutory provision by reference to the assumption that Parliament, in the absence of an express indication to the contrary, does not intend to legislate so as to place the United Kingdom in breach of its international obligations.

(HL Deb 29 September 2008 vol 479 cWS181)

Part Five: Subjects of International law

Part Five: I.A.2. *Subjects of international law—states—status and powers—sovereignty and independence*

5/1

The Government were asked if they would participate in debates on Scottish sovereignty. The Advocate-General for Scotland said:

Under the Treaty of Union of 1707 both England and Scotland ceded sovereignty to form the basis for the United Kingdom. The Government have no intention of discussing the break-up of the union.

(HL Deb 24 January 2008 Vol 698 c329)

5/2
Cyprus

The Government were asked what the status was of the pound sterling, European euro and Turkish lira in each of the two United Kingdom sovereign territories on the island of Cyprus. A Minister wrote:

In appendix O to the treaty establishing the Republic of Cyprus, the UK Government agreed that "the currency of the Republic will be legal tender in the sovereign base areas". From 1960 the sovereign base areas, including a large number of Cypriot citizens as well as the British military personnel who reside there, have used the Cyprus pound. The Republic of Cyprus replaced the Cyprus pound with the euro on 1 January 2008. At the same time the sovereign base areas adopted the euro as legal tender. The use of a currency in the sovereign base areas other than that circulating in the Republic of Cyprus would be impractical, and would run counter to our 1960 commitments.

(HL Deb 17 January 2008 Vol 697 cWA277)

5/3
Georgia [See also 16/5–16/7]

The Foreign Secretary made the following Ministerial Statement:

The Prime Minister made a statement on 10 September on the conflict in Georgia. [See 16/5]

Since then, the Government have been actively engaged in multilateral efforts to resolve the conflict, both in supporting the Georgian Government and people as they try to recover, and in making it clear to Russia that we expect it to abide by its agreement with President Sarkozy. We have supported efforts by the Organisation for Security and Co-operation in Europe (OSCE), the UN and EU to establish mechanisms that will provide independent monitoring of the situation on the ground in Georgia. I have made clear in discussions with Russian Foreign Minister Lavrov that we reject unilateral Russian recognition of the breakaway territories and continued Russian military presence in Georgia. I have also visited both Georgia and Ukraine and assured them that the UK stands by their rights as sovereign countries to determine their own futures. My right hon. Friends the Prime Minister and the Chancellor of the Exchequer and I met the Georgian Prime Minister during his visit on 19 September and discussed specific measures to help the Georgian economy. On 27 September, I met with President Saakashvili in New York and discussed the international peace talks to be held in Geneva on 15 October, reconstruction efforts and the importance of Georgia continuing its domestic reform programme.

We have engaged in intensive discussions with international partners, including through the UN, EU, NATO, G7 and OSCE, in order to help bring peace and stability to the region, to achieve a settlement based on recognition of and respect for Georgian sovereignty and territorial integrity, as well as to address critical humanitarian needs, which includes the voluntary return of over 100,000 people displaced by the conflict. Whatever the wisdom of Georgian actions on 7 August, Russia's response was entirely disproportionate. It has been widely condemned by EU, NATO and G7 Foreign Ministers. The encroachment of Russian military forces deep into Georgian territory beyond South Ossetia and Abkhazia during the fighting violated Georgian sovereignty and territorial integrity. Russian actions, including recognition of South Ossetia and Abkhazia, breach a number of UN resolutions that Russia has itself signed. The most recent was UN Security Council Resolution 1808, adopted with Russian support in April 2008, which explicitly "Reaffirms the commitment by all member states to the sovereignty, independence and territorial integrity of Georgia within its internationally recognised borders".

In the EU, the comprehensive review of EU-Russia relations has begun and will continue up to the next EU-Russia summit in Nice on 14 November. Negotiations on a new EU Partnership and Co-operation Agreement (PCA) with Russia also remain suspended.

The agreement reached on 8 September between Presidents Sarkozy and Medvedev secured Russia's commitment to withdraw its troops from Georgian territory outside the regions of Abkhazia and South Ossetia, in line with the six-point ceasefire plan brokered with the parties to the conflict on 12 August. Russia committed also to international discussions on future security modalities. On 15 September EU Foreign Ministers agreed to deploy an EU monitoring mission to the region adjacent to South Ossetia and Abkhazia. That mission is now on the ground. The UK has contributed 19 monitors, two headquarters personnel and four armoured vehicles. The mission has a one year mandate to operate throughout Georgia. Its purpose is to monitor compliance with the ceasefire plan, with the aim of supporting efforts to ensure lasting peace and security in the region. More specifically, the mission will help to ensure the free movement of people and goods, as well as monitoring the human rights situation in Georgia and progress on the return of those displaced by the conflict. As such, it is vital that international monitors are afforded the access they need in order to enable them to carry out their mandate.

This mission meets the EU's commitment to provide at least 200 unarmed civilian EU monitors to deploy to zones adjacent to South Ossetia and Abkhazia by 1 October. We expect Russia to meet its commitment to withdraw its forces to their pre-conflict positions by 11 October. The UK is committed to the EU-led conference process due to start in Geneva on 15 October and which will examine ways to ensure security and stability in the region, to ensure protection of civilians, and to settle the issue of refugees and internally displaced persons on the basis of internationally recognised principles and established post-conflict resolution practice.

The UK will continue to work with international partners to ensure that effective support is given to Georgia and towards a lasting, peaceful solution.

(HC Deb 6 October 2008 Vol 480 c2WS-3WS)

5/4 (See also 5/11–5/28)
Kosovo

The Government were asked what the terms of reference of EULEX were. An FCO Minister wrote:

The Joint Action, adopted on 4 February, sets out the European Union Rule of Law Mission in Kosovo's (EULEX Kosovo) mission statement. This is that EULEX Kosovo shall assist Kosovo authorities, judicial authorities and law enforcement agencies in their progress towards sustainability and accountability and in further developing and strengthening an independent multi-ethnic justice system and multi-ethnic police and customs service, ensuring that these institutions are free from political interference and adhering to internationally recognised standards and European best practices. EULEX Kosovo, in full co-operation with the European Commission assistance programmes, shall implement its mandate through monitoring, mentoring and advising, while retaining certain executive responsibilities.

(HL Deb 10 March 2008 Vol 699 cWA201)

5/5

The Government were asked whether the terms of reference of the NATO Kosovo Force would be changed; and, if so, to what extent. An FCO Minister wrote:

The Kosovo Force (KFOR) is mandated under UN Security Council Resolution (UNSCR) 1244. On 18 February 2008, the North Atlantic Council agreed that KFOR should continue to remain in Kosovo on the basis of UNSCR 1244, unless the UN Security Council decides otherwise. The North Atlantic Treaty Organisation's responsibility and capability to ensure a safe and secure environment in Kosovo remain unchanged.

(HL Deb 10 March 2008 Vol 699 cWA207)

5/6

The Government were asked whether EULEX would seek to arrange secure access between Serbia and Serbian Orthodox monastic houses in Kosovo, particularly for principal religious festivals. An FCO Minister wrote:

The EU's European Security and Defence Policy (ESDP) mission in Kosovo, EULEX, will assist with policing and rule of law. It will also work closely to ensure that all communities and their religious and cultural heritage are protected and promoted in line with the UN special envoy's comprehensive proposal for a Kosovo status settlement.

The proposal provides extensive safeguards for non-Albanian communities, especially the Kosovo Serbs and guarantees a special status for the Serbian Orthodox Church and protection of its religious sites.

The main responsibility to ensure the security of Kosovo's religious and cultural heritage, including secure access for pilgrims, will lie with the Kosovo Police Service (KPS). The ESDP rule of law mission, in consultation with the Kosovo Force (KFOR), will monitor, mentor and advise the KPS in this task.

(HL Deb 10 March 2008 Vol 699 cWA208)

5/7
Somaliland

The Foreign Secretary was asked what the Government's policy was on claims of independence by Somaliland. An FCO Minister wrote:

The UK does not recognise Somaliland as an independent state. The Government's policy on Somaliland's claims of independence is that the Somaliland authorities should negotiate with the Transitional Federal government to determine their future relationship.

He wrote further:

No assessment has been made of the effect of Somaliland being recognised as independent on the safety of shipping using the Gulf of Aden and port of Berbera.

The incidents of piracy and risks to shipping in the region are a result of insecurity in parts of Somalia and limited maritime security capacity provided by the governing authorities. Addressing these issues will have the greatest impact on improving the safety of shipping. [See **19/43**]

(HC Deb 8 May 2008 Vol 475 c1105W-1106W)

5/8
West Papua

The Foreign Secretary was asked whether he had discussed West Papua with the Indonesian Minister for Finance, H. E. Dr. Sri Mulyani Indrawati, during his visit to the UK on 14 and 15 January 2008. An FCO Minister wrote:

I met Indonesian Finance Minister, Dr. Sri Mulyani Indrawati, in London on 15 January. I discussed with her a range of bilateral and multilateral issues, including ... the situation in Papua.

The Government's position on Papua is longstanding. We support the territorial integrity of Indonesia and do not therefore support calls for independence for Papua. We believe that full implementation of existing Special Autonomy legislation is the best way to address outstanding areas of concern and ensure the long-term stability of Papua.

The overall human rights situation in Indonesia has improved dramatically in recent years. Indonesia is opening itself up to scrutiny by the international human rights framework, including through the UN Human Rights Council's process of Universal Periodic Review. Indonesia has a flourishing free media and a parliament that is increasingly holding the government to account. However, we recognise that challenges remain, particularly in Papua. I discussed the situation in Papua and raised human rights with Papua Governor Barnabus Suebo whom I met in London on 25 October 2007. Our embassy in Jakarta monitors the situation in Papua closely and continues to support those working to improve human rights across Indonesia.

(HC Deb 17 March 2008 Vol 473 c865W)

Part Five: I.A.3. *Subjects of international law—states—status and powers— domestic jurisdiction.*

5/9

The Government were asked whether they would make representations to the Government of Indonesia to allow freedom of expression and the right to peaceful assembly under the International Covenant on Civil and Political Rights, with particular reference to the right of West Papuans to raise their independence flag. An FCO Minister wrote:

The Foreign and Commonwealth Office does not intend to make representations to the Government of Indonesia in support of raising the Papuan independence flag. Flying the Papuan national "Morning Star" flag is currently illegal under Indonesian law. Special autonomy legislation allows for the use of Papuan symbols and anthems, but the local legislation that is required to confirm the chosen symbols and anthems has yet to be passed. The UK supports the territorial integrity of Indonesia and therefore does not support independence for Papua …

We believe that the best way to resolve the issues in Papua is through promoting peaceful dialogue between Papuan groups and the Indonesian Government. We are in regular contact with Papuan activist groups in the UK, and encourage dialogue between them and the Government of Indonesia. Our embassy in Jakarta regularly discusses human rights issues, including in Papua, with the Indonesian Government. My honourable friend the Parliamentary Under-Secretary of State for Foreign and Commonwealth Affairs, Meg Munn, met the Governor of Papua, Barnabas Suebo, when he visited London on 25 October. They discussed the situation in Papua, including human rights and the implementation of the special autonomy law.

(HC Deb 9 January 2008 Vol 697 cWA204)

Part Five: I. A.6. *Subjects of international law—states—status and powers— state immunity (see Part Seven: IV.A, below)*

5/10

The Chancellor of the Exchequer was asked whether sovereign wealth funds were exempt from taxation in the United Kingdom. A Minister wrote:

Where a sovereign wealth fund is an integral part of the government of a foreign sovereign state it will benefit from immunity from UK tax. As a result of this immunity, no taxation will have been received from sovereign wealth funds.

The United Kingdom recognises the principle of international law known as sovereign immunity whereby one sovereign state does not seek to apply its domestic laws to another sovereign state. In accordance with this principle, current UK practice is to regard as immune from direct taxes all income and gains which are beneficially owned by the head of state and the Government of a foreign sovereign state recognised by the UK.

(HC Deb 28 April 2008 Vol 475 c144W)

Part Five: I.B.1. *Subjects of international law—states—recognition of states*

5/11
Kosovo [See also **5/4**]

The FAC, in its Report, *Global Security: Russia*, concluded on the subject of Kosovo that:

[W]hilst in principle we support the concept of 'supervised independence' for Kosovo, we are concerned that the Government may have underestimated the damage to the authority of the Security Council, to bilateral relations with Russia, and to the very fragile democracy in Serbia. (Paragraph 263)

The Government said in response

66. [It] welcomes the Committee's support for the concept of "supervised independence" for Kosovo. The Government believes that the UN Special Envoy's Comprehensive proposal for the Kosovo Status Settlement (recommending *inter alia* that Kosovo should be independent subject to international supervision) offers the best way forward for Kosovo and the region as a whole. The Comprehensive proposal sensibly recognises the political realities arising from Kosovo's recent history and it represents a judicious balance between acknowledging the aspirations of the overwhelming majority of Kosovo's population on the one hand, whilst providing extensive and far-reaching protections for Kosovo's non-Albanian communities on the other.

67. The Government is highly conscious of the importance of acting in a way which protects and reinforces the authority of the UN Security Council. The UN Status Process for Kosovo is itself mandated by UN Security Council Resolution 1244. The process was initiated following a UN Comprehensive Review of the Situation in Kosovo, which concluded that the status quo was unsustainable and that the risks of a "wait and see" approach outweighed those of addressing Kosovo's future status. The process was taken forward by a UN Special Envoy appointed by the UN Secretary General. As the Committee has noted, both the decision to move to a status process and the appointment of a UN Special Envoy were endorsed by the UN Security Council.

68. The Comprehensive proposal of the UN Special Envoy received the support of the UN Secretary General and indeed a clear majority of the UN Security Council. It was however rejected by Russia. Despite strenuous efforts in New York, involving several iterations of a draft resolution aimed at addressing Russian concerns, agreement on a Security Council Resolution was not possible and indeed Russia clearly indicated it would obstruct the passage of any resolution allowing for implementation of the UN Special Envoy's proposal.

69. In a further effort to address Russian concerns and to leave no stone unturned in the search for an agreed approach, additional negotiations (under Contact Group auspices, in EU/Russia/US Troika format) took place between August and December 2007. These led to a report from the Troika, forwarded by the Contact Group to the UN Secretary General on 6 December 2007, making clear that, despite the period of further negotiations, the parties were not able to reach agreement on the final status of Kosovo. Discussions in the UN Security Council on 19 December 2007, on the basis of the Troika's report, demonstrated that the Security Council remained unable to agree on the way forward.

70. The Government's preference has always been that the Kosovo Status Process should be completed on the basis of a negotiated settlement endorsed by the UN Security Council. But it is clear both that a negotiated settlement is out of reach and that the Security Council is deadlocked over the way forward because of Russia's opposition to the UN Special Envoy's proposal. Given the clear view of the UN Secretary General, the Contact Group and the EU that the status quo is unsustainable, the Government's view is that the only realistic way forward is to move in a careful and co-ordinated manner towards a settlement for Kosovo. The Government is confident this can be done in a way consistent with UN Security Council Resolution 1244, thereby upholding the authority of the UN Security Council.

71. In the Government's opinion the divergence of view between Russia and the UK on Kosovo has had limited impact on the current state of the bilateral relationship, where other problems, highlighted elsewhere in the Committee's Report, have been more powerful factors. A key point is that over Kosovo, Russia's differences are not primarily with the UK but rather with an approach endorsed by most European countries and the US. Despite differences over Kosovo, the Government has worked closely with Russia on this issue both within the Contact Group and bilaterally, in a spirit of openness about our different perspectives.

72. The Government agrees with the Committee on the strategic importance of strengthening Serbia's democratic orientation. The Government wants Serbia's democracy to thrive and Serbia and its neighbours to fulfil their European destiny as quickly as possible. The Government strongly supports Serbia's European perspective and welcomes the agreement reached at the European Council on 14 December 2007 that, if the necessary conditions are met by Serbia, progress on Serbia's road towards the EU can be accelerated. The Government believes this process will help embed European democratic standards in Serbia.

73. The Government recognises that resolution of Kosovo's status is likely to be painful both for Serbia's political establishment and for the wider public. On occasions, the pace of the UN Status Process for Kosovo has been sensitively adjusted in the light of political developments in Serbia (for example the UN Special Envoy's decision in November 2006 to delay presentation of his proposal until after parliamentary elections in Serbia). However, leaving outstanding legacy issues from the conflicts of the 1990s unresolved and festering is itself an impediment to completion of Serbia's democratic transition. It would mean that domestic politics in Serbia would continue to revolve around nationalist issues from the past, rather than around the reform and European integration challenges that are critical for Serbia's successful future. In the Government's view, resolution of Kosovo's status is essential if Serbia is to move forward from its past to a future in which it is successfully integrated into European and Euro-Atlantic structures. The Government agrees with the UN Comprehensive Review of the Situation in Kosovo of October 2005 which concluded that, "For Belgrade, determining the future status of Kosovo will remove an important source of internal political instability and facilitate the realisation of Serbia's European perspective".

(Second Report from the Foreign Affairs Committee Session 2007–08, Global Security: Russia. Response of the Secretary of State for Foreign and Commonwealth Affairs, Cm 7305)

5/12

The FAC had also written in its Report, *Global Security: Russia*:

We regret that, eight years after the Kosovo conflict, disagreement over the province may once again cause the UN to be sidelined. We conclude that Russia may be adopting an intransigent position now on the Ahtisaari plan for Kosovo in order to demonstrate its strength. It may also be using the issues as a way to encourage division within the European Union. However, Moscow would find it much harder to do so had the plan been accepted by Serbia. We conclude that the Government underestimated Russia's likely opposition to the Ahtisaari plan.

We recommend that in its response to this Report, the Government inform us of the steps it is taking to try to win Kosovar Albanian and Serbian acceptance of a modified version of the Ahtisaari plan and to prevent a further outbreak of violence taking place. (Paragraph 264)

The Government replied:

74. The Government always assessed that firm Russian opposition within the Security Council to implementation of the Comprehensive proposal was possible. Although the Government worked intensively to secure Russia's support for (or acquiescence to) the outcome of the UN Status Process, this was never taken for granted.

75. The Russian position itself did not crystallise until negotiations in New York were underway. It is worth noting that at various points in the UN Status Process for Kosovo, Russia committed itself to principles subsequently reflected in the UN Special Envoy's Comprehensive proposal. Russia, together with the rest of the Contact Group, has stated that it sees the status quo as unsustainable and an early resolution of the status issue as crucial. In successive Contact Group statements, Russia acknowledged that any settlement should be acceptable to the people of Kosovo (the overwhelming majority of whom clearly want independence). In a joint statement of 20 September 2006, Contact Group Ministers, including the Russian Foreign Minister, agreed that "striving for a negotiated settlement should not obscure the fact that neither party can unilaterally block the status process from advancing". In that same statement, Contact Group Ministers urged the UN Special Envoy to prepare a proposal for Kosovo's status, a request which was duly discharged by the UN Special Envoy's Comprehensive proposal for the Kosovo Status Settlement.

76. The Government has worked hard to address Russia's concerns about the UN Special Envoy's Comprehensive proposal. Nonetheless, the Government believes that, in a situation where the status quo is unsustainable, it would be irresponsible to risk regional stability by allowing the UN Status Process to be blocked from completion. Therefore, the Government believes the right policy approach would remain the same: to consider the UN Special Envoy's Comprehensive proposal thoroughly in the UN Security Council; to test fully the degree of flexibility in the Russian position; to find a way forward on the basis of a new UN Security Council Resolution if possible; but, if not, to move forward on the basis of UN Security Council Resolution 1244 having gone the last mile to demonstrate that options for a negotiated settlement have been exhausted.

77. The Government has been intensively engaged both with Belgrade and Pristina, encouraging both sides to participate fully and constructively in the further negotiations conducted by the EU/Russia/US Troika. The Government has equally emphasised in the strongest terms the importance of both sides demonstrating their commitment to a peaceful and non-violent approach to this issue. The Government welcomes the commitments secured by the Troika from both sides to refrain from provocative words and actions and has made clear to both sides that it expects these commitments to be honoured. The Foreign Secretary emphasised these points strongly during his meetings with the Kosovo Unity Team on 9 October 2007 and with the Serb Foreign Minister on 4 December 2007. The Contact

Group Ministerial meeting in New York on 27 September, chaired by the UK, underlined these points in its joint statement.

78. The Government strongly and actively supported the Troika process, and regrets that further negotiations did not lead to agreement either on the basis of the UN Special Envoy's Comprehensive proposal or on any other model. The Government agrees with the assessment of the EU and US representatives on the Troika that the potential to reach a negotiated settlement is now exhausted and that the parties would not be capable of reaching agreement on this issue if negotiations were to be continued, whether in the Troika format, or in some other form.

79. The Government will continue to make a strong practical contribution to the security and stability of Kosovo through its contributions to the NATO force in Kosovo (KFOR) and to the UNMIK policing contingent. These international presences play a key role in preventing and deterring further outbreaks of violence in Kosovo.

(Second Report from the Foreign Affairs Committee Session 2007–08, *Global Security: Russia*. Response of the Secretary of State for Foreign and Commonwealth Affairs, Cm 7305)

5/13
The FAC asked the Foreign Secretary about Kosovo:

On 17 February, Kosovo declared independence and with it declared a situation that had effectively been in place for years. Are you in any way disappointed that some big countries—India, Brazil, New Zealand, Israel—have not yet recognised Kosovo? As of 8 June, only 42 countries have recognised Kosovo.

He said:

I think it is 43, but that is a difference without substance. Would I like there to be more? Yes. Is 43 in the space of three months quite substantial? I would also say yes. If you think back to the history of the recognition of Bangladesh in the early 1970s, it took nine months for Britain to recognise it. It was quite a slow process, and it took three or four years for Bangladesh to gain a UN seat. I have talked about this with a lot of different countries, and there are a lot of countries looking to move as a bloc. They take significant sustenance from the fact that 21 European countries, with the addition of the Czech Republic, have now recognised Kosovo-so two thirds-plus of the European Union has recognised it-and they recognise that it is our back yard.

I tried to make a very strong case, including to some of the Muslim countries, that this is a very significant opportunity to help to bring stability to the Western Balkans, in the unique situation where a country—the Former Yugoslavia—has disappeared. I would like to see the number going up, and we are working to achieve that, but I do not think it is at all nugatory to have 43 recognitions. [Q.31]

5/14
The Foreign Secretary was asked:

… can that reconfiguration you mentioned—UNMIK into EULEX—happen without a Security Council resolution being needed?

He said:

In our view it can—very much so. We have the UN Security Council foundation in resolution 1244. We now have the Secretary-General making decisions rather than referring to the Security Council for resolutions. I think that the Secretary-General has been doing a very good job of talking to everyone, including his own people, but it is now approaching the time when he is going to want to take decisions. The more one looks at resolution 1244, the stronger it is as a foundation for this, because it envisages the political process, but does not prescribe the outcome. I think that is important. [Q.33]

5/15
The Foreign Secretary was asked about partition in Kosovo. He said:

I do not want to say that there is de facto partition for a number of reasons. First, there is not a partition of population, in that 60% of Kosovo Serbs are south of the Ibar in enclaves, so it is not partition in that sense. Secondly, there are border presences on the Serb border of the international mission. Those are just two examples. Equally ... it would not be true to say that there is equal consistency in international presence right across the country. It is important that we insist that there should be international presence across the country, but it is not consistent across the country. I think it is right to think about a transition that involves a shift from UNMIK's exclusive role, to working with EULEX, to EULEX taking over. But it is a transition-one that needs to be managed. That is what we are trying to achieve and what the Secretary-General and the EU representative are trying to achieve. [Q.34]

It was put to the Foreign Secretary that Serbs north of the River Ibar were not prepared to recognize international presences not directly authorized by the Security Council, which was a significant obstacle to the integration of these Serbs with the rest of Kosovo. He said:

The difficulties here are shown in part by the use of the word integration. Integration to some can sound like an enforced dilution of their identity, whereas the Ahtisaari plan was strong on continuing to recognise the distinctive identities of minorities right across Kosovo. That is just one example of why this is difficult terrain, but there is a clear direction, which is from UNMIK to EULEX. There is a clear international basis for the new country of Kosovo to operate. That is provided on the foundation of resolution 1244, and on the follow-through with the Ahtisaari plan. There are very detailed discussions to be had-in fact they are ongoing-about the exact nature of the relationship between UNMIK and EULEX. That is one reason why I am relatively cautious about what exactly I want to say in public on this. However, it is very important that I say that the direction of travel is clear, the onus on the Secretary-General is clear, and the determination of the European Union to provide an anchor for all the countries of the Western Balkans is very clear. [Q.35]

(Foreign Affairs Committee Report on Lisbon Treaty, Uncorrected Evidence, 11 June 2008, <www.publications.parliament.uk/pa/cm200708/cmselect/cmfaff/uc713-i/uc71302.htm>)

5/16

A press release introducing the Prime Minister's statement on the recognition of Kosovo on 18 February said:

Speaking to journalists in Downing Street, the Prime Minister said that the move would "close the chapter" following the break-up of Yugoslavia and help carry Kosovo to "a prosperous future". The UK understood Serbian sensitivities around the change and remained committed to Serbia's "European future", he added.

"I have written to President Sejdiu to tell him that Britain will now formally recognise Kosovo as an independent sovereign state … I believe this is a step forward for the international community and this follows the meeting that has already just finished with the European Union Foreign Ministers."

Mr Brown said that the decision to recognise independence had depended on assurances that minorities within Serbia would be protected under any new administration. The UK will continue to provide support through the presence of soldiers with the NATO mission, police officers with the EU representation and financial aid for the next three years, the PM added.

Kosovo issued its declaration of independence on Sunday after nine years under NATO control following the expulsion of Serbian troops in 1999. Following a meeting of EU foreign ministers in Brussels today several countries, including the UK, pledged their support. Key United Nations members such as China and Russia are opposed to the move.

(<www.number10.gov.uk/Page14594>)

5/17

In a debate on the declaration of independence by Kosovo in the Security Council, the UK representative said:

The Council meets today in unusual circumstances. A new state has been established in Europe, against the wishes of its former parent state and of a permanent member of this Council. This new state is being recognized today by many governments in Europe and beyond, including my own. Formal letters of recognition have today been delivered to the President of Kosovo by British Government representatives.

It is important to understand how this has come about, and to understand why the events of recent months, of yesterday and today, and of the weeks and months to come are inevitable as well as exceptional.

At the heart of today's controversy is a resolution adopted at this table in June 1999. In that resolution, our Council took an unprecedented step. It effectively deprived Belgrade of the exercise of authority in Kosovo.

It did so because the then regime in Belgrade had not just unilaterally deprived Kosovo of its powers of self-government, thereby triggering a rebellion. It had tried in 1999 to expel the majority population from Kosovo. Hundreds of thousands of men, women and children were driven from Kosovo by the state security forces of Slobodan Milosevic. People being herded onto trains provoked images from the 1940s. The events of 1999 shaped the events we see now.

In Resolution 1244, the Council recognized that the human rights of the people of Kosovo and the stability of the region could be secured only if Serbia did not govern Kosovo.

It established a UN mission to serve as Kosovo's interim government. This mission had two crucial tasks. First to help Kosovo establish its own institutions of self-government and to pass authority progressively to those institutions. Second, to facilitate a process to determine Kosovo's future status, taking into account the Rambouillet accords, which had specified that such a settlement had to be based on the will of the people of Kosovo.

1244 placed no limits on the scope of that status outcome. Paragraph 11(a) is clear that the substantial autonomy which Kosovo was to enjoy within the FRY was an interim outcome "pending a final settlement".

Within two years of the Resolution's passage a new democratic government came to power in Belgrade. That government and its successors have wrestled with the legacy of Milosevic's war crimes. They are right to argue that they should not be punished for those crimes. But equally, they have a duty to help resolve the problems caused by Milosevic, and they must accept that the legacy of Milosevic's oppression and violence has made it impossible for Kosovo to return to control by Belgrade. When, in the middle of the final status process, the government of Serbia changed its constitution to exclude any future for Kosovo outside Serbia it effectively ended any chance of a negotiated settlement. The international community cannot be party to a settlement that is opposed by over 90% of a territory's population: apart from anything else, it would be contrary to our overriding priority of upholding peace and security.

My government is convinced that the proposal of the UN's Special Envoy for supervised independence, which the Kosovo Assembly has embraced and committed itself to implement, is the only viable way forward. It commits Kosovo to protect its minority populations. Other than the Kosovo Serbs, all of them— Roma, Jews, Turks and others—have endorsed the Ahtisaari plan. That speaks for itself.

The UK urges Kosovo's Serb population to play a full part in the political, economic and social life of Kosovo. The UN mission, the EU and NATO will work to ensure that the commitments made by Prime Minister Thaci on 17 February, and the far-reaching provisions to protect minorities in the Ahtisaari plan, are implemented in full. Kosovo's progress towards the EU will depend, inter alia, on how well she treats her minorities. We also expect the Serbian authorities and Kosovo Serb leaders to take no action to promote the separation of the North of Kosovo from the rest of the country. Excluding Kosovo's government from majority Serb areas of Kosovo will not be accepted. Kosovo Serb leaders should work with the Government in Pristina and with the international presences.

The Ahtisaari plan also commits Kosovo to accept extensive and continuing international supervision. NATO has agreed to continue to provide security in Kosovo. And the European Union has agreed to deploy a rule of law mission to oversee the build-up of Kosovo's capacity in this crucial area.

One delegation has sought to argue that the EU mission can only deploy with the express agreement of the Security Council. The United Kingdom disagrees.

The EU has been part of the international civilian presence in Kosovo from the outset. The UN mission has evolved and developed, adapting to changing circumstances within its original broad mandate, without requiring any new decisions from this Council. I do not want to repeat once again our views on the legal position, but for the sake of clarity, these are attached to the circulated copy of my statement. [See **5/18**.]

The European Union is committed to a better future for the region as whole. My government applauds the European vision for Serbia that President Tadic has consistently displayed. As the European Council said in December 2007, a stable and prosperous Serbia integrated into the family of European nations is important for the stability of the region. That is the future open to Serbia and my government calls on its leaders to look ahead and to focus on that prize.

More immediately, we call on Serbia's leadership, religious as well as political, to encourage restraint, refrain from provocative words or actions, and to desist from punitive measures or threats against Kosovo. We are concerned about the violent demonstrations against some Embassies in Belgrade, and about the attack on international offices in North Mitrovica.

I began by saying that this Council was facing an extraordinary set of circumstances. It is not ideal for Kosovo to become independent without the consent of Serbia and without consensus in this Council. My government believes that the unique circumstances of the violent break-up of the former Yugoslavia and the unprecedented UN administration of Kosovo make this a sui generis case, which creates no wider precedent, as all EU member states today agreed.

My delegation hopes the Council in the weeks and months to come can recover its unity of purpose on this issue, and that the UN on the ground will continue to make its contribution to stability, security and prosperity in the Balkans, alongside the EU, NATO and others, with the active backing of the Security Council.

(UN Doc. S/PV.5839, 18 February 2008)

5/18
Annex to statement in the Security Council

Kosovo: Legal Questions

Compatibility of Kosovo's declaration of independence with Resolution 1244

Resolution 1244 provided for Kosovo to enjoy substantial autonomy within the FRY as an interim solution, pending Resolution of its final status (paragraph 11(a) and Annex 2). The Resolution does not preclude Kosovo's independence because it does not predetermine or delimit final status.

Paragraph 11(e) of 1244 asks the UN to facilitate a final status process, "taking into account the Rambouillet Accords". These did not make a final settlement conditional on Serbian agreement and refer to final settlement "based on the will of the people of Kosovo".

The reference (in PP10 of 1244) to the commitment of Member States to the sovereignty and territorial integrity of the FRY is a preambular reaffirmation of a general principle applicable to all States. This provision does not create additional rights for Serbia. Nor does it impose a binding obligation on other States. This reference is also qualified in a way which makes clear that the reaffirmation of territorial integrity applies only to Kosovo's interim phase not to final status.

Kosovo is a special case as a consequence of the violent and non-consensual break-up of Yugoslavia, and in particular the humanitarian crisis which led to the conflict in 1999, the long period of international administration, and the final status process called for by UNSCR 1244. Recognition of its independence, which is a matter for individual States to decide, is not therefore a precedent for any other situation.

Legality of deployment of EU rule of law mission

The EU decided in its Joint Action of 4 February to launch a Mission to enhance the EU's contribution to justice, the rule of law and policing capacity in Kosovo. The Joint Action makes clear that the EU envisages acting under the mandate conferred by Resolution 1244, specifically paragraphs 11(f) and 11(i), and will work with the UN, not replace the UN.

No new decision of the Security Council is required to authorise deployment of the EU Mission. Paragraph 10 of Resolution 1244 authorised the Secretary-General to establish an international civil presence without specifying what the composition of the international presence should be. That was left to the Secretary-General to decide. The authorisation to the Secretary-General also included the remit to establish the civil presence with the assistance of relevant international organisations. The role of the EU in Kosovo, which was already established in 1999, was specifically welcomed in paragraph 17 of Resolution 1244, and the EU has been part of UNMIK from the beginning.

The Secretary-General set out in an initial report to the Security Council in June 1999 the "preliminary operational concept" for the overall organisation of UNMIK. At the request of the Secretary-General, the Security Council signified its general approval to this. However, the subsequent detailed concept of operations for UNMIK (S/1999/779) was not submitted for approval by the Council. Moreover, the structure and functions of the various components of UNMIK as outlined in the Secretary-General's initial report have been modified on several subsequent occasions without Council approval (see for example, S/2000/878 and S/2001/565). The current format of UNMIK is not therefore the format described in the Secretary-General's initial report.

It follows that there is no basis for the contention that deployment of the EU Mission in Kosovo requires a new Council decision. The organisation of the international civil presence is a matter for the Secretary-General to determine pursuant to the authority conferred on him by Resolution 1244 and there is no basis for arguing that he is required to seek authorisation from the Security Council before making changes to its structure, in accordance with the UN's usual practice.

(<http://ukun.fco.gov.uk/en/newsroom/?view=News&id=3297487>)

5/19

The EU Council issued the following statement after a special meeting of the Council with the Foreign Minister Jeremić of Serbia on 19 February 2008.

We have listened very carefully to what Mr Jeremić has said here today about the future of Kosovo. This is an issue which is of crucial importance to Serbia, to future stability in the Balkans and to the security of Europe as whole. EU Foreign Ministers met yesterday in the General Affairs and External Relations Council to discuss this matter in Brussels.

The Council adopted the following conclusions: "On 17 February 2008 the Kosovo Assembly adopted a resolution which declares Kosovo to be independent. The Council takes note that the resolution commits Kosovo to the principles of democracy and equality of all its citizens, the protection of the Serb and other minorities, the protection of the cultural and religious heritage and international supervision. The Council welcomes the continued presence of the international community based on UN Security Council resolution 1244.

The Council notes that Member States will decide, in accordance with national practice and international law, on their relations with Kosovo.

The Council recalls the European Union's longstanding commitment to the stability of the Western Balkans region. The Council reiterates the European Union's readiness to play a leading role in strengthening stability in the region, and recalls the European Union's commitments contained in the conclusions of the European Council of 14 December 2007, as well as the agreement to Joint Actions establishing an ESDP Police and Rule of Law mission and appointing an EU Special Representative in Kosovo. The European Union will continue to cooperate with the UN, KFOR, OSCE and other international actors in order to preserve stability in the region.

The Council reaffirms its commitment to fully and effectively support the European perspective for the Western Balkans. It asks the Commission to use community instruments to promote economic and political development and to propose to the broader region concrete measures in order to advance in that direction.

The Council reiterates the EU's adherence to the principles of the UN Charter and the Helsinki Final Act, inter alia the principles of sovereignty and territorial integrity and all UN Security Council resolutions. It underlines its conviction that in view of the conflict of the 1990s and the extended period of international administration under SCR 1244, Kosovo constitutes a sui generis case which does not call into question these principles and resolutions.

The Council also condemned recent acts of violence in Belgrade, Mitrovica and other places, in particular against foreign diplomatic missions and urged respective authorities to ensure security and safety of EU citizens and their property. The Council called on Belgrade and Pristina to respect previous commitments to refrain from any activities or statements which might endanger the security situation.

The EU strongly believes that the OSCE should continue to play an important role in supporting a peaceful, democratic and multi-ethnic Kosovo, with full respect for the rule of law, the protection of minorities and of Kosovo's cultural and religious heritage, as well as the highest level of internationally recognised human rights and fundamental freedoms. The protection of minorities is critical for Kosovo's communities in order to feel more secure about their future and role in Kosovo society. The test of this will be at the local level, where property rights, access to services and inter-ethnic communication are key challenges.

The European Union reiterates its appreciation for the essential work done by the OSCE Mission in Kosovo through its headquarters in Pristina as well as its broad field presence. The EU continues to believe that the OSCE should maintain its current presence, which is in the interest of all the people of Kosovo, and the Serb community in particular. We made our commitment clear in our interpretative statement of 21 December 2007 on the extension of the mandate of the OSCE Mission in Kosovo.

(Text supplied by FCO)

5/20

In response to a question, the Foreign Secretary wrote:

On 17 February the Parliamentary Assembly of Kosovo was convened for an extraordinary session at which Prime Minister Thaçi read out Kosovo's declaration of independence. The declaration made clear that Kosovo was a democratic, secular and multi-ethnic republic and that its leaders would promote the rights and participation of all communities in Kosovo. The declaration in particular committed Kosovo to implementing fully the obligations contained in UN Special Envoy Ahtisaari's Comprehensive Proposal for a Kosovo Status Settlement, including its extensive minority safeguards. And the declaration invited and welcomed an international civilian presence to supervise implementation of the Comprehensive Proposal, an EU rule of law and police mission (EULEX) and a continuation of NATO's Kosovo Force (KFOR). The declaration was endorsed by all Parliamentary members present.

The declaration took place following exhaustive negotiations between Belgrade and Pristina aimed at finding a mutually agreed resolution to Kosovo's status. UN Special Envoy Ahtisaari had presided over 14 months of intensive negotiations before concluding an agreement was out of reach. An EU-Russia-US Troika facilitated an additional four months of talks, with EU member Ambassador Ischinger concluding that the parties would not be capable of reaching agreement if negotiations were to be continued, in whatever format.

My statement of 11 December noted that, against this backdrop of inconclusive negotiations, almost all in the international community were agreed that the status quo in Kosovo was unsustainable. This is a point that had been underlined by the European Union, the UN Secretary General and the Contact Group. My statement made clear that we could not therefore allow the status process to grind to a halt, having learned in the 1990s the cost of an indecisive international response to developments in the Balkans. In the view of the Government, it would be important for the EU to play a leading role in bringing the status process through to conclusion. The UN Special Envoy's Comprehensive Proposal, balancing independence with strong minority safeguards and international supervision, remained in our view the only viable way forward.

Since my statement, the Government have worked hard to ensure the necessary international community resolve and engagement to solve the Kosovo issue. The Government strongly supported the decision at the December European Council that the EU should play a leading role in implementing a settlement defining Kosovo's status.

Against this background, the General Affairs and External Relations Council met on 18 February, the day following Kosovo's declaration of independence. EU Ministers agreed that the EU should play a leading role in strengthening stability in the region. The EU has given effect to this commitment through a series of steps:

In terms of ensuring security and justice sector reform, the EU has agreed on the deployment of an ESDP Policing and Rule of Law Mission (EULEX) consisting of 2,200 international personnel. This will be the largest civilian ESDP mission to date.

In terms of ensuring Kosovo's political development and good governance, the EU has now agreed on the appointment of an EU Special Representative to Kosovo.

The EU has agreed to make a major contribution to the international civilian office which will oversee settlement implementation.

The EU has committed itself to the promotion of Kosovo's economic and political development. The Commission will use community instruments to take this forward and is planning to organise a donors conference.

EU Ministers were clear in their view that Kosovo constituted a sui generis case which did not set any precedent.

Taken together, these decisions amount to a clear and united EU approach towards contributing to Kosovo's future and to delivering stability in the Western Balkans region. I welcome the leadership that the European Union has shown in tackling this European foreign policy challenge.

EU Ministers also discussed the issue of recognition. There was agreement that this is a matter for national governments and the Council acknowledged that it was for member states to decide, in accordance with national practice and international law, on their relations with Kosovo.

Bringing all these elements together—the unsustainable status quo; Kosovo's commitment to the stringent safeguards in the UN Special Envoy's Comprehensive Proposal; and the international support for settlement implementation and, increasingly, recognition—the Government considers that UK recognition of Kosovo is fully justified. Our firm view is that it is the best way of resolving Kosovo's status, ensuring regional stability and solving this last remaining issue from the breakup of the Former Yugoslavia. The Prime Minister wrote to President Sejdiu on 18 February indicating to the Kosovo government that the United Kingdom recognises Kosovo's independence. I have also written to Prime Minister Thaçi proposing the establishment of diplomatic relations. At least 16 other countries, including France, Germany, Italy, the US and Turkey, have also either recognised Kosovo or indicated their intention to do so.

Kosovo's independence will bring a long-awaited certainty and permanence to Kosovo's identity, marking an end to nearly nine years of political and economic limbo But it will also be just the beginning of a challenging journey ahead, building a stable, sustainable, multi-ethnic and democratic country. It will be important for Kosovo's Assembly and Government to adhere faithfully to the undertakings made in their declaration of independence. It will also be important for all sides to refrain from action that risks provoking or increasing ethnic tensions.

The UK will make a full contribution in support of Kosovo's efforts. The UK will second approximately 70 personnel to the ESDP mission and about 10 to the International Civilian Office. We will maintain our current contribution of around 140 troops to KFOR as well as maintaining a battalion on stand-by as part of the NATO operational reserve force. And in terms of development, the UK has committed £23 million in bilateral assistance to Kosovo over the next three years.

As Kosovo moves forward, there will remain a need to address the regional dimension. We recognise how difficult an issue Kosovo's independence is for Serbia. Despite the difference of view with Belgrade on Kosovo, the Government will remain keen to maintain a cooperative and warm bilateral relationship. We will also want to assist Serbia and the other countries of the region to move towards European standards and EU accession. The interim political agreement offered to Serbia following the January General Affairs and External Relations Council was a sign of the EU's commitment to Serbia's progress. There remains a compelling strategic case for enlargement to the Western Balkans as a whole so that this region can share in the security, stability, and prosperity that the EU offers.

(HC Deb 19 February 2008 Vol 472 c19WS-22WS)

5/21

After criticism of the EU statement on Kosovo dated 19 February 2009 (see **5/20**), the Foreign Secretary said:

It would only have been a failure if it were for the European Union to recognise the new country of Kosovo. There are divisions within EU countries about whether or not to recognise Kosovo, but it is a matter for individual countries to decide. The matter at hand for the EU is not about recognition and I am sure that he would agree with me that it would be quite wrong to move into a world where the EU starts recognising countries when it is in fact a responsibility of member states. In matters that are the responsibility of the EU—first, the deployment of a European mission; secondly, the partnership arrangements between all the countries of the western Balkans; and thirdly, the ultimate objective of EU membership—there should be and is European cohesion.

(HC Deb 20 February 2008 Vol 472 c372)

5/22

The Foreign Secretary was asked about the situation in the western Balkans. A Minister wrote:

On 17 February the Kosovo Assembly passed a resolution declaring Kosovo to be independent. On 18 February the Prime Minister and Foreign Secretary announced that the UK recognised Kosovo as a sovereign and independent state and would establish diplomatic relations in accordance with the Vienna Convention.

On 18 February the European General Affairs and External Relations Council called on Belgrade and Pristina to respect previous commitments to refrain from any activities or statements which might endanger the security situation. At a meeting of the North Atlantic Council, the North Atlantic Treaty Organisation (NATO) also reaffirmed that Kosovo Force (KFOR) will continue to ensure a safe and secure environment.

Since the Kosovo declaration of independence, there have been demonstrations in Belgrade and amongst the Serb communities in Kosovo. There was some damage to property caused by demonstrators outside the US and Slovenian embassies in Belgrade. There have been small explosions near the EU offices in North Mitrovica. There are no reported casualties.

The UK remains fully committed to safeguarding the region's security and contributes to KFOR, and the EU forces in Bosnia. We remain ready to fulfil our obligations to NATO's pan-Balkans Operational Reserve Force (ORF), and we stand ready to send the UK ORF battalion, currently at highest readiness, if requested by the NATO Commander. The UK will also contribute approximately 80 personnel to the European Security and Defence Policy Police and Rule of Law mission currently deploying to Kosovo and the International Civilian Office overseeing settlement implementation.

(HC Deb 21 February 2008 Vol 472 c828W)

5/23
An FCO Minister told the House of Commons in a debate on the recognition of Kosovo:

I turn to United Nations Security Council resolution 1244. It left Kosovo within Serbia on an interim basis, pending the outcome of a process to determine Kosovo's final status. The nature of that outcome is not constrained in any way by that resolution. The status process was duly taken forward by the UN special envoy Ahtisaari. It resulted in his proposals for supervised independence. References to the territorial integrity of the Federal Republic of Yugoslavia in resolution 1244 are related to that interim stage, but not to Kosovo's final status.

On the question of EU unity and EU action, on 18 February the General Affairs and External Relations Council set out a clear EU response to developments in Kosovo. It agreed to a range of political and practical assistance to Kosovo, including the deployment of an EU special representative to Kosovo, and the deployment of a European security and defence policy mission to assist with reform of policing and the justice sector. It will also provide support for Kosovo's political and economic development, in line with the EU perspective for the region. That, the largest EU deployment of its kind, was agreed unanimously. It is not for the European Union or the United Nations to recognise nation states bilaterally. It is for other sovereign nations to do so, which is why the United Kingdom, with 20 other nations thus far, recognises Kosovo's independence.

The question was posed whether that sets a precedent ... In the case of Kosovo, given its tragic recent history, there is a range of circumstances that are not replicated anywhere else in the world.

Security Council resolution 1244 has provided for a political process to determine Kosovo's final status. That process has taken place and it resulted in the proposal for supervised independence. That, of course, was not agreed to unanimously because

Russia indicated throughout the process that it would not allow a UN process to be concluded. It has now been agreed that the Ahtisaari proposals should be the bed-rock for the principles and specifics of what needs to be delivered on the ground. They propose extensive powers for local government, and they guarantee thresholds of representation in Parliament, a police force, a judiciary and a civil service that reflect Kosovo's ethnic diversity. The House will be aware that the majority of Serbs in Kosovo do not live in that northern region, but 60 per cent. live in the south. [The debate was brought to an end for procedural reasons, Ed.]

(HC Deb 26 February 2008 Vol 472 c224WH)

5/24

The Foreign Secretary was asked what representations he had received from the government of Serbia in relation to the Government's recognition of the inde-pendence of Kosovo. An FCO Minister wrote:

The Serbian government has made clear, both orally and in writing, their disa-greement with the UK on recognition of Kosovo's independence.

Their representations have included an official démarche delivered by the Serbian chargé d'Affaires on 19 February and several letters of protest.

(HC Deb 22 May 2008 Vol 476 c518W)

5/25

In a debate on Kosovo in the Security Council, the UK representative said:

Of course, that dialogue [between the Secretary-General's Special Representative and the Government of Serbia, Ed.] does not represent the beginning of a new negotiation process; the time for talking about Kosovo's status is past. The United Kingdom and many other countries with interests in and commitment to the Balkan region have recognized Kosovo as an independent State, and that is not going to change.

We congratulate the Kosovo Government on the progress made since its declara-tion of independence in adopting and enacting priority legislation on minority rights and decentralization and on the entry into force of the new Constitution on 15 June.

(UN Doc. S/PV.5944, 25 July 2008)

5/26
A Minister wrote:

So far, 51 countries have recognised the Republic of Kosovo including 22 EU member states and all of the G7. We have been engaging actively in both bilat-eral discussions and multilateral forums, working closely with and alongside the Government of Kosovo, and with like-minded international partners to encour-age further recognitions. We have also engaged with the Government of Kosovo to help them take forward their efforts on recognition.

(HC Deb 20 October 2008 Vol 481 c98W)

5/27

Her Majesty's Government were asked whether diplomatic relations have been established between the UK and Kosovo since its declaration of independence. In reply, a Minister wrote:

The UK recognised Kosovo on 18 February and the British office in Pristina became the British embassy. Our current ambassador, Mr. Andy Sparkes, presented his credentials on 28 April. The Government of Kosovo have nominated Mr. Muhammet Hamiti as chargé d'affaires in London. He is expected to take up his appointment shortly.

(HC Deb 30 October 2008 Vol 481 c1212W)

5/28

In a debate in the Security Council on the Secretary-General's Report on Kosovo, the UK representative said:

I would like to say at the outset that our view is that Kosovo independence is irreversible. It is also indivisible. I think one of the important things about the proposals set out in the Secretary-General's report today is that they show that the risk of partition is receding.

I am very pleased to hear such clear support from Council members for the Special Representative's intentions, for the reconfiguration that the Secretary-General has set out, and also the clear support for full deployment of the European Union Rule of Law Mission (EULEX) throughout Kosovo. That is very welcome news to those of us in the European Union who have Kosovo and Serbia as our neighbours.

In June the Secretary-General decided that, given the changed situation on the ground in Kosovo, it was right to reconfigure the international civilian presences. I think events have borne out that that decision was the right one. We are very pleased that the reconfiguration is now properly under way. We note that the Special Representative says that when EULEX fully deploys, UNMIK will be able to review its tasks. That is very welcome. The Rule of Law Mission is set to reach initial operating capacity in early December. With the Secretary-General's report envisaging an acceleration of reconfiguration in the coming period, it is very important, as a number of colleagues have made clear today, that the European Union and the United Nations continue to work closely together. EULEX will implement its mandate as set out in the relevant European Union Joint Action, while operating under the overall authority of the Untied Nations.

I wanted to say two particular things about the report. The first is factual and for the record. I just wanted to note that there is a factual error in paragraph 21 of the report. It refers to the executive authority of the Special Representative of the Secretary-General. That does not, in fact, derive from resolution 1244 (1999). It derives from the later, constitutional framework, which was not endorsed by the Security Council, and there is no provision in the new Kosovo constitution for the constitutional framework.

The other thing I wanted to say is that in paragraph 27 of the report the Secretary-General makes clear that the dialogue and consultations set out in the report have been conducted with Belgrade and Pristina without prejudice to their positions on the status issue and in the spirit of the United Nations Charter. I think we should all bear that in mind as we move forward.

The United Nations is engaged with both Pristina and Belgrade on the so-called six points, the transitional arrangements in areas important for Kosovo's Serbian community. We also know that there have been differing views on those transitional arrangements and concerns, particularly in Pristina, as to their implications. We are very pleased to see that the Secretary-General's report acknowledges those real concerns and provides reassurance that the implementation of transitional arrangements will be on the basis of continuous consultation and coordination and that commitment to consultation and coordination constitutes a strong assurance to Pristina. At the same time, the commitment to the transitional arrangement also provides a strong assurance to Kosovo/Serb and other minority communities ...

I want to be clear in the light of some views expressed in the Council: it is from the European Union (EU) that EULEX derives its mandate. It will implement its mandate as set out in the relevant European Union joint actions while operating under the overall authority of the United Nations. EULEX also constitutes the EU's largest ever civilian mission. Its work will be to the benefit to all of Kosovo's people and those United Nations Members who sit on the Peacebuilding Commission will note the value of integrating missions between justice and police sectors. And that is something that EULEX will do. So its work will be important in terms of lessons learned for the wider United Nations community.

EULEX will support multi-ethnicity, and we welcome Kosovo's cooperation with EULEX deployment throughout the whole of Kosovo. We also welcome the Government's assurances that it will continue to take into account the concerns of all of Kosovo's communities. Obviously, that is extremely important.

The Security Council did not take a view on Kosovo's status. It had no vote and it issued no statement. The best one could conclude is that it was neutral on the issue, though it is worth noting that a majority of its members have recognized Kosovo. So I do not think there can be any question of defiance of the Council.

I would also like to talk briefly about minority communities in Kosovo. All the minority communities except the Kosovo Serb community have supported where we are on status. I think that it is incumbent on all of us who worry about minority communities in Kosovo to uphold the rule of law in the north of Kosovo. We must do everything we can to ensure that the deplorable attacks that we witnessed on international officials of the UNMIK police and on the Kosovo Force in March of this year are never repeated and that the perpetrators are brought to justice.

(UN Doc. S/PV.6025, 26 November 2008)

5/29
Abkhazia and South Ossetia (See also 16/5)

In a debate in the Security Council on the Russian recognition of Abkhazia and South Ossetia as States, the UK representative said:

Since the outbreak of fighting in Georgia on 7 August, the United Kingdom's approach has been based on two basic principles: first, full support for Georgia's sovereignty and territorial integrity; and secondly, full support for efforts to end the violence and lay the foundations for a peaceful and enduring settlement to the conflict that is acceptable to all the parties. We supported French-led efforts to secure an immediate end to the fighting, efforts that culminated in the six-point agreement signed by Russia and Georgia, together with the agreed clarifications issued by President Sarkozy. We support it, and we continue to support efforts to ensure the full implementation of that agreement, including the full withdrawal of Russian forces back to the positions occupied prior to 7 August ...

Let me be clear. Russian military action and Russia's recognition of Abkhazia and South Ossetia constitute a unilateral attempt to redraw the borders of a neighbouring country through the use of force. It is our view that that is entirely unacceptable and unjustified. It is in direct contravention of the founding principles of the United Nations and is in defiance of numerous resolutions adopted by the Council. It is also a flagrant breach of point 6 of the agreement signed by President Medvedev. Condemnation of Russia's actions has come not only from the foreign ministers of the Group of Seven (G7), Russia's partners in the G8, but from many parts of the international community, as the enormous implications of Russia's actions sink in.

Russia's decision has grave humanitarian and political implications. We have heard justifications for Russia's actions based on the need to prevent humanitarian catastrophe. But what we have seen in recent weeks is ethnic Georgians being pressured to flee from their homes in South Ossetia and Abkhazia.

Tuesday's decision by Russia will encourage those in South Ossetia and Abkhazia who are bent on violence and intimidation, and there is already credible evidence that they have accelerated their work.

We call on Russia to do three things: first, to abide by international law as the basis for resolving this crisis; secondly, to act now to ensure full and free humanitarian access to Abkhazia and South Ossetia and to prevent violence and intimidation against ethnic Georgians—and that does not mean requiring ethnic Georgians to accept Russian citizenship as the price of remaining in South Ossetia; and thirdly, to implement urgently and in full its undertakings under the six-point agreement, including withdrawal of its forces to the positions occupied prior to 7 August. It is unacceptable that, over two weeks since the agreement was signed, Russian forces continue to occupy parts of Georgia well beyond the conflict zones.

We look to Russia to facilitate the deployment of international observers, as prefigured in point 5 of the six-point plan, to speed up the Russian pullback. The use of force, violence and intimidation against civilians and de facto annexation cannot be the basis for a peaceful and durable settlement to this or any other conflict. Future arrangements in South Ossetia and Abkhazia can be agreed only through international negotiations involving all the parties, as envisaged in point 6 of the six-point plan. The United Nations has already expressed its willingness to help take forward this initiative, in cooperation with other international actors. We encourage the Secretary-General to begin consultations to that end as a matter of urgency.

(UN Doc. S/PV.5969, 28 August 2008)

5/30

As part of a written statement to Parliament on 10 September 2008, the Prime Minister wrote:

... on 26 August, Russia unilaterally recognised the independence of South Ossetia and of Georgia's other separatist region, Abkhazia. Russia also refused to withdraw its forces from Georgia and in some cases moved to reinforce them.

It was in this context that I and the Foreign Secretary attended the Extraordinary European Council on 1 September, convened by French President Nicolas Sarkozy, in his capacity as current Presidency of the EU, to discuss the current crisis in Georgia.

At this meeting the European Council unanimously condemned Russia's decision to recognise the independence of Abkhazia and South Ossetia; and expressed its grave concern about the consequences of the conflict and Russia's disproportionate military action. Russia's actions were in clear breach of international law and of successive UN Security Council Resolutions.

In response to Russian actions, the Council decided to conduct a comprehensive review of EU-Russia relations. This evaluation has begun and will continue in the run up to the next EU-Russia Summit scheduled to take place in Nice on 14 November 2008. The EU has decided to suspend negotiations with Russia on the new EU Partnership and Co-operation Agreement (PCA) until Russian troops withdraw from Georgia to their pre-conflict line. We strongly support this decision. As I made clear during Council discussions, although the EU should continue discussions with Russia on areas of interest and concern to the EU, it cannot be "business as usual". This review will allow us to take a considered decision about the future of EU-Russia relations.

(HC Deb 10 September 2008, Vol 479 c127WS)

Part Five: I.B.2. *Subjects of international law—states—recognition of governments*

5/31

Her Majesty's Government were asked why they continue to recognise certain Governments after they have secured power in a manner deemed not to be free and fair; yet do not recognise certain other elections that were deemed to have been free and fair. In reply, a Minister wrote:

Lord Carrington, then Foreign Secretary, stated in the House of Lords in April 1980 (*Official Report*, col. 1121 WA), (see **[1980]** UKMIL pp367–368)

"We have decided that we shall no longer accord recognition to governments. The Government recognises States in accordance with common international doctrine ... the policy of successive Governments has been that we should make and announce a decision formally 'recognising' the new government. This practice has sometimes been misunderstood, and, despite explanations to the contrary, our 'recognition' interpreted as implying approval ... we shall continue to decide the nature of our dealings with regimes which come to power unconstitutionally in the light of our assessment of whether they are able of themselves to exercise effective control of the territory of the State concerned, and seem likely to continue to do so".

Our policy has not changed.

(HL Deb 7 July 2008 Vol 703 cWA61WA-62)

5/32
Kenya

The Government were asked whether they recognised Mwai Kibaki as the legitimately elected President of Kenya. An FCO Minister wrote:

We share the concerns of the international community over the conduct of the presidential election. Concerns were highlighted in independent election observer mission reports, including those from the Commonwealth, the East African Community, domestic observers, as well as in the initial findings of the European Union's mission.

The Government recognise states, not Governments. Given that none of the independent international observers to the elections believes the tallying met international standards it is difficult to have any confidence in the announced result. Against that background, we are supporting the mediation efforts of Kofi Annan and his African colleagues to ensure an agreement between the two sides in Kenya on a Government that will enjoy Kenyan and international confidence.

(HL Deb 30 January 2008 Vol 698 cWA127)

5/33
Transitional Federal Institutions of Somalia

An FCO Minister wrote:

Neither the UK nor the EU provide any political, diplomatic or military support for Ethiopia for its role in Somalia.

Both the UK and the EU maintain full diplomatic relations with Ethiopia. Neither the UK nor the EU provide any military support, but where suitable opportunities arise and we are satisfied that human rights concerns are being met, the UK remains interested in assisting Ethiopia to develop its internal security infrastructure.

Both the UK and the EU support the Transitional Federal Institutions of Somalia as established by the Transitional Federal Charter, including the Transitional Federal Government. The UK does not currently have formal diplomatic accreditation to Somalia, but we maintain a high level of contact with members of the Somali Government. Neither the UK nor the EU provide (sic) any military support to Somalia.

(HC Deb 15 May 2008 Vol 475 c1780W)

5/34

The Foreign Secretary was asked what representations he had made to the government of Ethiop ia and the Transitional Federal Government in Somalia on their obligations to ensure that their armed forces comply with international humanitarian law. An FCO Minister wrote:

We regularly raise the issue of compliance with international humanitarian law with both the Ethiopian Government and the Transitional Federal Government of Somalia, including at the highest level.

While Ethiopia's troops remain in Somalia, we urge them to use only appropriate force, adhere to international humanitarian law, respect human rights and to ensure that their forces should leave the country as soon as is practical without creating a security vacuum.

(HC Deb 15 May 2008 Vol 475 c1780W)

5/35
Zimbabwe

The Foreign Secretary made a statement to the House of Commons on the situation in Zimbabwe, following disputed elections there. He said:

The failure is not of the opposition but of the Government. Robert Mugabe and his thugs made an election impossible, and certainly made the notion of a free and fair election farcical. It is clear that the only people with democratic legitimacy are those who won the parliamentary majority on 29 March, and who took most votes in the first round of the presidential election, and that was of course the opposition.

We do not—repeat not—recognise the Mugabe Government as the legitimate representative of the Zimbabwean people. We will not "de-recognise" the state of Zimbabwe, because that would mean the withdrawal of diplomatic representation and all that goes with it, but the Prime Minister could not have been clearer that we do not believe that a Government who have clubbed their way to victory and defied the constitution, which requires a second round within 30 days of the first round of the election, can claim to be the legitimate representative of the Zimbabwean people.

(HC Deb 23 June 2008 Vol 478 c43)

5/36

The Government were asked why, given that the Zimbabwean run-off election had been held outside the time-limit fixed by the Constitution and that (President) Mugabe and his party had been beaten in earlier elections, it did not simply withdraw recognition of Mugabe's regime. A Minister said:

It is extremely tempting to do so, but we have to think very carefully whether that is sensible at this time. All options are possible. We recognise states, not governments, and Mugabe is not a legitimate president. However, 14,000 or so

British citizens live in Zimbabwe. At present, we believe that it would be wrong not to have some representation for those people, especially given the very difficult circumstances that I have tried to outline.

(HL Deb 30 June 2008 Vol 703 c3)

5/37 (See also **15/26**)
During a debate, the Foreign Secretary stated:

I think that we agree that the elections of 27 June were a sham. The United Nations Secretary-General has said that the outcome did not reflect the true and genuine will of the Zimbabwean people. The G8 expressed its disgust at the Foreign Ministers' meeting that I attended in Japan last week. Many African voices are now speaking out against Mugabe, too—not just President Mandela but representatives of Botswana and Kenya. Many of us will believe that the recent AU summit did not meet the aspirations and hopes of the Zimbabwean people for a strong statement, but it is relevant to point out that the AU stated that the elections were not free and fair, and were scarred by violence. Sad as it is to say, that is an unprecedented judgment by the AU.

....

Our goal is simple: to ensure that the Government of Zimbabwe reflect the will of the people of Zimbabwe. This is not about Britain versus Zimbabwe, still less about establishing a new British Government in Zimbabwe, but about having a Zimbabwean Government who deliver for their own people. The opposition have recognised the need for a broad-based Government and called for the formation of a transitional Government, recognising the unique political circumstances that now exist. For that Government to be credible, it must be based on the outcome of the 29 March election ... whatever the final composition of that transitional Government, Robert Mugabe cannot be in control of it.

(HC Deb 3 July 2008 Vol 478 c1037)

5/38
He continued:

Thirdly, through the UN and the EU and bilaterally, we must step up the pressure on Mugabe and his cohorts, including through targeted sanctions. In our view, those sanctions must be focused on punishing those within, or associated with, the regime, and if at all possible not on hurting ordinary Zimbabweans. Building on the statement by the UN Security Council on 23 June, we will continue to push for a UN Security Council resolution calling for further sanctions, including an arms embargo, a travel ban and an assets freeze on key regime figures, as well as a strong role for the UN in a substantive political dialogue ...

Within the EU, at our meeting later this month, Foreign Ministers will decide how to widen and deepen existing EU-targeted measures. We will push for an extension of the EU assets freeze to cover further individuals whose actions are contrary to a political settlement. We will also push for an extension of targeted measures to include farms and businesses owned by those individuals already the subject of targeted sanctions. We will support measures that prevent regime members from attending international events within the EU.

It is important to be honest about the fact that we need to strike a delicate balance. We have no evidence of breaches of the current sanctions regime by British or other businesses. I reckon that it is a relatively easy choice to try to prevent direct succour and support from being given to members of the regime. It is an easy choice to try to keep employment and sustenance being provided to the people of Zimbabwe. But where both the regime and the people are benefiting from economic engagement, difficult choices must be made on a case-by-case basis.

(HC Deb 3 July 2008 Vol 478 c1038–1039)

5/39
A Minister said:

I hope that our position on Zimbabwe is absolutely clear. We condemn the violence and do not recognise the outcome of the second round of the sham presidential election. We call for a new transitional Government who reflect the will of the Zimbabwean people as shown on 29 March, and we call on all members of the international community to work towards the restoration of democracy in that country.

(HL Deb 17 July 2008 Vol 703 cGC173)

Part Five: I.B.6 *Subjects of international law—states—recognition—acts of recognition—Non-recognition and its effects*

5/40
Northern Cyprus (See also 5/50)

The Government were asked whether, given that the United Kingdom was a guarantor power under the 1960 Treaty of Guarantee, they had authorized the police in the United Kingdom to pursue normal international co-operation with the police in Northern Cyprus; how such co-operation operates in light of the United Kingdom's lack of recognition of, and normal relations with, Northern Cyprus; and whether the Northern Cyprus authorities reciprocate that co-operation at all times. An FCO Minister wrote:

The UK maintains a dialogue with the Turkish Cypriot community on a range of issues, including international organised crime. We have urged the Turkish Cypriot leadership to tighten anti-money-laundering controls and welcome recent steps in this direction. While we do not recognise the "Turkish Republic of Northern Cyprus", we have co-operated informally on a number of specific cases that have a direct impact on the UK. Co-operation has generally been good and has made a real contribution to our fight against organised crime.

(HL Deb 19 February 2008 Vol 699 cWA36)

5/41

The Government agreed a Memorandum of Understanding with the Government of Cyprus about the Treaty of Guarantee, 1960:

MEMORANDUM OF UNDERSTANDING BETWEEN THE REPUBLIC OF CYPRUS AND THE UNITED KINGDOM—5 JUNE 2008

The President of the Republic of Cyprus and the Prime Minister of the United Kingdom hereby establish a framework for developing a stronger relationship between the UK and the Republic of Cyprus.

A reunited Cyprus will bring an end to conflict in the island and lead to greater prosperity for the people of Cyprus. A united Cyprus will be able to contribute further to the stability of the region and strengthen the EU's ability to respond to global challenges.

Therefore the UK commends the leaders of the two communities on the process agreed on 21st March and 23rd May.

The Republic of Cyprus and the United Kingdom will cooperate in the following areas:

Both countries commit themselves to working together to reunify the island. The aim is a comprehensive and durable settlement based on a bi-zonal, bi-communal federation and political equality, as defined by the relevant UN resolutions and the principles upon which the EU is founded. This settlement must be based on a single sovereignty, international personality and a single citizenship.

Both countries support the on-going process under the Good Offices of the Secretary-General, including the move to full negotiations on a date agreed by the two leaders.

The UK and the Republic of Cyprus will work with the UN, with relevant support from the EU, to ensure a successful conclusion to the on-going process and the achievement of an agreed, negotiated solution, between the two communities, as soon as possible.

The two countries reiterate their commitment to their respective obligations under the Treaties signed in 1960.

The UK reiterates its commitment to its obligations as a Guarantor Power. The UK will continue fully to respect existing UN resolutions on Cyprus, including UNSCRs 541 and 550. Therefore the UK will not support any moves towards the partition of the island or the recognition or up-grading of any separate political entity on the island.

In addition, the two countries will continue to work together in a constructive manner on all issues emanating from the Treaty of Establishment.

The UK and the Republic of Cyprus reaffirm their support for measures aimed at the economic integration of the island in accordance with the 26 of April 2004 EU Council Conclusions and helping to prepare the Turkish Cypriot community for reunification and the full application of the acquis communautaire on the basis of Protocol 10 of the Treaty of Accession.

The UK commends the measures taken and proposed by the Republic of Cyprus for the benefit of the Turkish Cypriot community. The UK will work with the Republic of Cyprus to help promote further contact between the Greek Cypriot and Turkish Cypriot communities in order to support the reunification of the island.

The UK recognises the positive proposal made by the Republic of Cyprus towards the establishment of an accreditation process for enabling the Turkish Cypriot higher education institutions to participate in international co-operation programmes.

The UK undertakes to continue to inform its citizens on the legal situation prevailing in Cyprus regarding the properties issue and relevant ECHR judgments.

The Republic of Cyprus and the UK will establish a programme of bilateral co-operation on a range of priority issues. It will identify common interests between the two countries, based on the common legal framework, administrative structures, economic complementarity, people-to-people ties and shared strategic interests.

This co-operation will be developed through exchange of best practice and direct co-operation in specific areas. The sectors to be covered will be identified, developed and adjusted by the diplomatic representatives in London and Nicosia. Initial priorities include:

Education and Health: schools, higher education, technical, vocational education and training;

Police and security issues: organised crime, counter-terrorism, illegal immigration, road safety and football hooliganism;

Economic and commercial issues: competitiveness, research and development, financial services, energy and environment;

The Millennium Development Goals: The Republic of Cyprus has today joined the Call to Action. The UK and the Republic of Cyprus strongly support the need for an EU action plan to be agreed at the June Council;

The Olympics: we will work together to identify areas for co-operation as the UK prepares for the 2012 London Olympics.

The Republic of Cyprus and the UK will establish closer dialogue in Brussels, London and Nicosia on EU issues where they have shared interests (e.g. to promote a more effective social dimension and co-operation on issues such as Justice and Home Affairs (JHA), taxation, budget reform, climate change).

As the Republic of Cyprus prepares for its EU Presidency in 2012, the UK will offer to share its experience, including through inward secondments.

The two countries will also hold a regular dialogue on EU/Turkey, where they share the objective of full membership once full conditions have been met. Both countries agree on the need for Turkey to fulfil its outstanding obligations towards all member states in accordance with the Negotiating Framework and the 21st September 2005 EU Declaration. The two countries will pursue dialogue by discussing issues relating to the negotiations at an early stage to clarify and resolve outstanding difficulties.

This programme of action will be delivered through six-monthly reviews at Ministerial level in Nicosia or London and regular discussions between High

Commissions and Governments in capitals. It will also be delivered through contact between Representations in Brussels and New York. The UK and Cyprus will also aim to hold an annual Cyprus/UK Forum to address specific issues of mutual interest.

Gordon Brown, Prime Minister of the United Kingdom

Demetris Christofias, President of the Republic of Cyprus

(<http://ukincyprus.fco.gov.uk/content/en/article/2008/3672787/Memorandum-understanding>)

5/42

The Government were asked what investigations they were undertaking into the purchase by British nationals of property, the title of which was disputed, in the Turkish-occupied sector of Cyprus; and what representations they had made to the Turkish Cypriot authorities on these matters. An FCO Minister wrote:

The Government are not undertaking any investigations into potentially disputed property bought by British citizens in northern Cyprus. However, in response to inquires from members of the public, and through our travel advice on the Foreign and Commonwealth Office website ..., we strongly advise anyone thinking of purchasing property in the northern part of Cyprus to seek independent legal advice before buying any land or property. We also highlight the risks associated with buying property in the northern part of Cyprus.

In our contacts with the leaders of the Turkish Cypriot community, we recognise the Turkish Cypriots' need for economic development in support of reunification. But we urge them to ensure that any property development that takes place does so in a manner that is both environmentally sustainable and does not complicate an eventual solution. Ultimately we believe that the difficult issue of property is likely to be fully resolved only in the context of a comprehensive settlement. We continue to urge both sides to engage constructively with the United Nations and to show the political will necessary to make decisive progress towards a comprehensive settlement in 2008.

(HL Deb 4 March 2008 Vol 699 cWA166)

[See now, *Apostolides v Orams* (2009) ECJ C-420/07 GC, Ed.]

5/43
Abkhazia and South Ossetia (see also 5/29)

During a debate in the House of Commons, the Foreign Secretary said:

The international community has made its view most clear in its failure to follow the Russian lead on recognition of Abkhazia and South Ossetia. Two countries followed the Russian lead, and Hamas also recognised them, but otherwise the world has been united in refusing to recognise a country created on the basis of force. A clear signal has been given that it must be the rule of law that decides the future map of Europe and its neighbourhood, not force.

(HC Deb 7 October 2008 Vol 480 c137)

Part Five: I.E. *Subjects of international law—states—self-determination*

5/44
Overseas Territories-General

The Government was asked whether an overseas territory would be granted independence without a referendum taking place in the territory. An FCO Minister said:

The Government's position is that that is the way by which we would expect a territory to indicate that it wanted to have independence, but that does not rule out other mechanisms that might be acceptable—for example, if a political party went into an election on the basis that it would pursue independence and there was a clear majority for that party. We would have to look at each circumstance, but our position is that a referendum is the preferred route. (Q.270)

(Foreign Affairs Committee Report, Overseas Territories, HC 147-II (2008))

5/45
British Indian Ocean Territory

The Foreign Secretary was asked what recent representations he had received from the Government of Mauritius on *(a)* the use of Diego Garcia and *(b)* the future military use of the Chagos Islands. An FCO Minister wrote:

The Prime Minister of Mauritius, Dr. Navinchandra Ramgoolam, last raised the issue of sovereignty of the British Indian Ocean Territory with the Prime Minister in the margins of the Commonwealth Heads of Government meeting in Kampala in November 2007. The Government have no doubt about their sovereignty over the British Indian Ocean Territory, but the Prime Minister agreed to establish a dialogue between the Mauritian high commission in London and officials at the Foreign and Commonwealth Office on issues relating to the British Indian Ocean Territory.

(HC Deb 27 February 2008 Vol 472 c1701W)

5/46
East Timor

An FCO Minister said, referring to the deaths of five journalists in East Timor in 1975:

The FCO files from the period indicate that the Government's policy was not to intervene directly in the controversy surrounding the future of East Timor but to engage the Indonesian Government on the need for democratic outcomes. The United Kingdom never recognised the Indonesian annexation of the country. We constantly worked through the United Nations to seek a resolution that would fully protect the interests of the people of East Timor.

(HC Deb 27 February 2008 Vol 472 c318WH)

5/47
Falklands

The Foreign Secretary was asked what recent assessment he had made of
(a) UK relations with Argentina and *(b)* the situation in the Falkland
Islands. An FCO Minister wrote:

The UK values its relationship with Argentina as an important international
partner. We have a close and productive relationship on a range of bilateral and
multilateral issues, including human rights, sustainable development and counter-
proliferation. We are keen to establish a constructive relationship with the new
Argentine Government on South Atlantic issues and believe we have much to
gain from working together.

However, the Argentine sovereignty claim to the Falkland Islands casts a shadow
over the bilateral relationship. The UK has no doubts about its sovereignty over the
Falkland Islands. We support the Falkland Islanders' right of self-determination
and will not discuss sovereignty unless and until they so wish. The UK has good
relations with the Falkland Islands' Government, which has continued to develop
and diversify its economy over recent years, particularly in the areas of fisheries,
renewable energy and tourism. My hon. Friend the Parliamentary Under-Secretary
of State for Foreign and Commonwealth Affairs, visited the Islands from 3 to 5
January and took the opportunity to assure the Falkland Islands Government
of the Government's commitment to their self-determination and economic
development.

(HC Deb 5 February 2008 Vol 471 c969W)

5/48

A Minister wrote:

The United Kingdom is responsible for the Falkland Islands' foreign relations. The
UK values its relationship with Argentina as an important international partner.
We have a close and productive relationship on a range of bilateral and multilateral
issues, including human rights, sustainable development and counter-proliferation,
and continue to look for practical ways to co-operate with Argentina on a range of
South Atlantic issues. However, the Argentine sovereignty claim to the Falkland
Islands and the Argentine refusal to recognise the democratically elected Falkland
Islands Government, casts a shadow over our relationship. The principle of self-
determination, enshrined in the Charter of the United Nations, underlies our
position on the Falkland Islands.

(HC Deb 28 October 2008 Vol 481 c799W)

5/49 (See also 3/3)
Gibraltar

During a debate in the House of Commons, a Minister stated:

The UK Government's position on sovereignty is clear, and forms the important
overall context in which to view the points raised by the hon. Gentleman. In an
otherwise excellent speech, the comments that he made about the actions of this
Government and the reference he made to raising the Spanish flag above the Rock

are without foundation. The British Government have never sought to impose a constitutional arrangement on Gibraltar. I state clearly for the record that the UK will never enter into arrangements under which the people of Gibraltar would pass under the sovereignty of another state against their freely and democratically expressed wishes. Furthermore, the UK will not enter into a process of sovereignty negotiations with which Gibraltar is not content. That could not be clearer. The Government stand by that public commitment to Gibraltar, which is reflected and enshrined in the 2006 constitution and its accompanying dispatch.

...

The 2006 constitution provides for a modern and mature relationship between Gibraltar and the UK. Although it gives Gibraltar much greater control over its internal affairs, it does not in any way diminish British sovereignty over Gibraltar and the UK retains full international responsibility for Gibraltar, including for Gibraltar's external relations and defence. The UK is the member state responsible for Gibraltar in the European Union.

The people of Gibraltar exercised their right to self-determination in line with the treaty of Utrecht when they approved the constitution by referendum in November 2006. That is an important point to make to some of the international critics of the constitutional settlement as regards Gibraltar. The fundamental issue is the right to self-determination, which is absolutely in accord with the principles of the United Nations.

(HC Deb 7 October 2008 Vol 480 c520–521)

5/50

The Government were asked by the FAC whether there were risks in increasing and maximizing the level of self-government to an overseas territory, such as for Gibraltar under its new Constitution. An FCO Minister said:

In Gibraltar's case specifically, the new constitution that it agreed to by referendum is about the right balance. It does not jeopardise UK sovereignty, and that is very clear. There is general acceptance of that, and that was the basis of the understanding around the agreement and the referendum. It changes the relationship, while not jeopardising sovereignty, and shows that the UK is involved only when it is appropriate to be involved. It gives the Gibraltar Government a greater formal role in the governance of Gibraltar in an important and sensible way. It is a modernisation, and it has been described by others as an end to the colonial relationship, although I have never described it in those terms. It is a modernisation and improvement, and a sensible move forward, while establishing and protecting the principle of British sovereignty.

On Gibraltar, the fact is that the "UN Special Committee of 24" process is still there. We do not think it reflects the modern sentiment between the United Kingdom and Gibraltar. We continue to argue the case, but we continue to co-operate on the fantastically titled "form 73E" ... on the basis, first, that it is part of the UN Charter and, secondly, that it shows a determination to continue to co-operate in a process and sea change. It is important, not just in Gibraltar, but in terms of the UN's posture on that committee. Generally, the committee's colonial description does not reflect the modern reality of Gibraltar ... Generally,

I do not think it does, and we should move away from that UN process. We continue to argue that. (Q.245)

5/51 (See also **5/11, 5/40**)
Northern Cyprus

The Government were asked whether, in the light of the declaration of independence of Kosovo, they would review the right to self-determination of the Turkish Republic of Northern Cyprus; and whether their position on any such right was affected by the practicalities of retaining military bases in the south of Cyprus. An FCO Minister wrote:

The independence of Kosovo does not set a precedent. There is no universal blueprint that can be applied to every post-conflict scenario; each is unique and different criteria apply. We should give no comfort to those looking to exploit Kosovo in relation to unrelated agendas, either in the Balkans or further afield.

Our long-standing policy on the non-recognition of the so-called "Turkish Republic of Northern Cyprus" will not change. Our objective in Cyprus is to achieve a comprehensive and viable settlement, based on a bizonal, bicommunal federation with political equality. We welcome the continued commitment of the leaders of both sides to these basic principles. Our continued support for a settlement is not affected by the presence of the sovereign base areas.

(HL Deb 12 March 2008 Vol 699 cWA229)

5/52

Tibet

In reply to a question on Tibet's right to national self-determination, a Minister wrote:

Successive Governments have regarded Tibet as autonomous while recognising the special position of the Chinese authorities there. We have consistently informed the Chinese Government of our view that greater autonomy should be granted to the Tibetans. But like all other EU members, we do not support Tibetan independence.

We have emphasised that the current political difficulties in Tibet can best be resolved through dialogue between the Chinese Government and the Dalai Lama. The Dalai Lama has stated publicly that he opposes violence and does not seek independence, but greater autonomy for Tibet. We consider that this provides a basis for a negotiated settlement to the issue of Tibet.

[T]he Prime Minister had talks with both Premier Wen and President Hu while in China for the Olympic games. He reiterated our desire that the next round of the dialogue between the Chinese Government and representatives of the Dalai Lama should take place in a constructive manner and produce positive outcomes.

(HC Deb 22 October 2008 Vol 481 c390W-391W)

[See also HC Deb 29 October 2008 Vol 481 c30WS-32WS]

5/53
Western Sahara

The Foreign Secretary was asked what discussions he had had with his Moroccan counterpart on the human rights situation in Western Sahara. An FCO Minister wrote:

The UK is concerned about the welfare of the people of Western Sahara. While the Foreign Secretary has not discussed human rights in Western Sahara with his Moroccan counterpart, I have discussed a range of issues regarding conditions on the ground in Western Sahara with the Moroccan Foreign Minister, Fassi Fihri, most recently in July 2007. Officials in Rabat, London and New York are in regular dialogue with the Moroccan authorities, civil society and other interested parties regarding Western Sahara, including on human rights.

The UK also remains concerned that the issue of the status of Western Sahara remains unresolved, with consequent problems for the people of the region. The UN Security Council unanimously adopted resolution 1783 on 31 October 2007, which renewed the mandate of the UN Mission for the Referendum in Western Sahara until 30 April 2008. The resolution also calls upon the parties to continue negotiations under the auspices of the UN Secretary-General, without preconditions and in good faith. The UK fully supports these negotiations, with a view to achieving a just, lasting and mutually acceptable political solution, which will provide for the self-determination of the people of Western Sahara.

(HC Deb 4 March 2008 Vol 472 c2361W)

5/54

The Foreign Secretary was asked whether he had received representations from the UN on Morocco's claim of sovereignty over the territory of Western Sahara. An FCO Minister wrote:

The UK has not received representations from the UN on Morocco's claim of sovereignty over the territory of Western Sahara. The UK regards the sovereignty of Western Sahara as undetermined pending UN efforts to find a solution. The UK fully supports the efforts of the UN Secretary-General and his Personal Envoy to the Western Sahara, Peter van Walsum, to achieve a just, lasting and mutually acceptable political solution, which will provide for the self-determination of the people of Western Sahara.

UN Security Council Resolution 1813 of November 2007 [Res. 1813 was passed in April 2008, Ed.] extended the mandate of the UN Mission for the Referendum in Western Sahara and called on the parties to continue negotiations under the auspices of the UN Secretary-General. The UK fully supports these negotiations and has called on the parties to continue to engage in the process in a spirit of realism and compromise.

The UK maintains regular contact with Mr. van Walsum, both at the UN in New York and when he has visited the UK.

(HC Deb 26 June 2008 Vol 478 c539W)

5/55

The Government were asked what recent representations they had made to the Moroccan Government, with particular reference to mineral rights. In reply, a Minister wrote:

No representation has been made to Morocco regarding the use of mineral resources in Western Sahara. The UK's long standing position remains that Morocco, the de facto administering power of Western Sahara, is obliged under international law to ensure that economic activities under their administration do not adversely affect the interests of the people of Western Sahara, and this includes their de facto control over most of the territory and maritime resources of Western Sahara.

(HC Deb 21 July 2008 Vol 479 c879W)

5/56

A Minister wrote:

The UK welcomes closer co-operation between the EU and Morocco, including the proposal for an Advanced Status Agreement currently under discussion between EU member states, the Commission and Morocco. The issue of Western Sahara, while not discussed within the context of the advanced status, remains part of the political dialogue between the EU and Morocco. We expect that both Western Sahara and human rights will be discussed as part of the political dialogue at the next EU-Morocco Association Council on 13 October.

The UK continues to believe that progress towards a negotiated solution to the dispute in Western Sahara providing for the self-determination of the people of Western Sahara, is best achieved under the auspices of the UN. To this end and in accordance with UN Security Council Resolution 1813 of 30 April, the UK fully supports the efforts of the UN Secretary-General and his staff, and the negotiation process currently under way. We hope a further round of talks will take place later this year.

(HC Deb 21 October 2008 Vol 481 c216W-217W)

5/57 (See also **11/10**)

The Government were asked what steps were being taken to ensure that the indigenous people of Western Sahara receive licensing revenues or aid derived from the EU-Morocco Fisheries Agreement as a result of UK trawlers' fishing activity in the waters of the occupied Western Sahara. In reply, a Minister wrote:

Morocco, as the de facto administering power in the Western Sahara, has an obligation under international law to ensure that economic activities carried out under its administration in the territory do not adversely affect the interests of the people of the Western Sahara. This includes revenues from the EU-Morocco Fisheries Agreement 2006. Trawlers from the UK and those from other EU member states fishing in the waters off Morocco or the Western Sahara must act in accordance with the provisions of this agreement.

(HC Deb 6 October 2008 Vol 480 c227W)

5/58

Her Majesty's Government was asked whether they regard the waters off the coast of Western Sahara as international waters; and what the status is of UK fishing vessels fishing in those waters under the terms of the EU fisheries agreement with Morocco. In reply, a Minister wrote:

The EU-Morocco Fisheries Agreement was agreed in 2006 and sets out the terms for which UK and other European fishing vessels may fish in the waters off the coast of Western Sahara. The agreement does not prejudice the issue of the status of Western Sahara, which the UK regards as undetermined pending UN efforts to find a resolution. Nor does the agreement represent recognition of Morocco's sovereignty over the maritime waters of Western Sahara.

(HC Deb 6 October 2008 Vol 480 c227W)

Part Five: II.A.1.(a). *Subjects of international law—international organisations—general—status and powers—personality*

5/59

The Foreign Secretary was asked whether the legal personality accorded to the EU under the Treaty of Lisbon would enable the EU to agree defence treaties with third countries. An FCO Minister wrote:

The EU already has the legal personality to conclude international agreements under Article 24 of the Treaty on the EU. For example, on 10 December 2002, the EU signed an agreement with the Republic of Iceland to enable its participation in the EU Police Mission in Bosnia and Herzegovina. The Lisbon Treaty does not give the EU any new powers to conclude international agreements. Any decision to sign a treaty with defence or security implications would require a decision by the Council acting in unanimity.

(HC Deb 19 March 2008 Vol 473 c1187W)

Part Five: II.A.2.(b) *Subjects of international law—international organisations—general—participation of states and international organisations in international organisations and in their activities—suspension, withdrawal, expulsion and deportation*

5/60
Commonwealth

In a debate on the UK and the Commonwealth, an FCO Minister said:

The Commonwealth is unique among international organisations in having the Commonwealth ministerial action group, of which we are a member. The group has the power to suspend members who have breached the Harare principles of democracy and good governance that guide all member states. We are hopeful that in future the group will do more as an early warning mechanism, providing peer pressure and mediation support in conflict situations ...

Last November, the Commonwealth ministerial action group responded to the state of emergency in Pakistan by setting five conditions to be met within a given time-table. When the conditions were not met, it suspended Pakistan from the councils of the Commonwealth. I think that was helpful in Pakistan. The attempt by violent extremists to derail the democratic process was faced down by the Pakistani people. They showed courage, and in doing so have given Pakistan the chance to build a stable, secure and prosperous future. The Prime Minister has said that Pakistan should return to the fold of the Commonwealth and I hope we can see that process through in the coming weeks.

(HC Deb 20 March 2008 Vol 473 cs1100–1101)

Part Five: II.B. 1. *Subjects of international law—international organisations—particular types of organisation—universal organisations*

5/61
The Foreign Secretary was asked what steps he was taking at the United Nations to support the initiative announced by the Prime Minister on 21 January to include India as a permanent member of the United Nations Security Council. An FCO Minister wrote:

The UK is a long-standing supporter of India's candidacy for permanent membership of the UN Security Council. We also support Brazilian, German, Japanese and African permanent representation.

The eventual size and form of an enlarged Security Council requires agreement from the UN membership, as set out in the charter of the UN. The UK has consistently championed the need for a reformed Council to represent emerging powers in the modern world. The UK continues to engage actively in debate over Security Council reform both in New York and with UN partners world-wide, and we have voiced our support for initiatives by the President of the General Assembly to drive forward the reform process.

(HC Deb 29 January 2008 Vol 471 c221W)

5/62
The Government were asked about their assessment of proposals to establish a league of democracies composed of all democratically ruled countries. A Minister wrote:

We would not want any multilateral organisations to undermine the United Nations because it clearly remains the most important international organisation. It is at the heart of the multilateral architecture. Its universal membership gives it an unparalleled political legitimacy.

(HL Deb 24 June 2008 Vol 702 c1330)

Part Five: IV.B. *Subjects of international law—international organisations— entities and groups other than states and international organisations— dependencies*

5/63
British Overseas Territories—General

The Government was asked by the FAC about human rights in the Overseas Territories. An FCO Minister said:

In terms of UN [sc. Human rights] conventions, the British Government are responsible for those, including in the territories, so we want the territories to be able to sign up to them and to have them as part of their legislation and the like. That has been one of the things that I have been particularly concerned about. At the Overseas Territories Consultative Council we discussed the fact that some territories had not signed up, particularly to some key conventions, and we want that to happen. In terms of the constitutions that are now being discussed for territories that have not put new constitutions in place, our view is that they should include issues relating to human rights, so that is part of the negotiation. Where there is a difference, we do not intend to say that territories must enact, for example, civil partnerships. That is not something we have gone that far with currently. It is an issue that I was questioned about at great length when I visited Cayman, which expressed concern that signing up to human rights within its constitution would automatically mean that it would have to have civil partnerships. That was not our view. (Q.264)

(Foreign Affairs Committee Report, Overseas Territories, HC 147-II (2008))

5/64 (See also **5/45 and 11/3**)
British Indian Ocean Territory

The Government were asked what measures were in place to protect fish stocks in waters around the British Overseas Territories. A Minister wrote:

UK Overseas Territories with a commercial fishery within their waters engage in the management and conservation of fish stocks by participating in applicable regional fisheries management organisations. Where appropriate, UK Overseas Territories also participate in bilateral discussions on the management and conservation of straddling stocks. Certain UK Overseas Territories with commercial fisheries protect their resources utilising a range of measures including fisheries protection vessels, aircraft surveillance, satellite-based vessel monitoring systems and the deployment of observers.

(HL Deb 20 February 2008 Vol 699 cWA59)

5/65
On the question of the use of Diego Garcia, the Government wrote to the FAC:

Thank you for letter of 25 January in which you requested information on British Government appointments to the Overseas Territories and on the UK's agreement with the US on Diego Garcia.

DIEGO GARCIA

The Committee have asked for confirmation that: (i) the use of Diego Garcia by the US will *automatically* continue beyond 2016 unless either the UK or US gives notice that they no longer want this arrangement to continue and (ii) that it would be sufficient for the agreement to expire if only the UK were to give notice that it wished to terminate it. The Committee has also asked for information on the form in which this notice would have to be given.

The 1966 Exchange of Notes by which the British Indian Ocean Territory was set aside for the defence purposes of the UK and the US will continue in force for a further period of 20 years beyond 2016, unless it is duly terminated. However, the UK and US would of course continue to consult closely on their mutual defence needs and expectations well in advance of that time. The 1966 Exchange of Notes may be terminated by either Government giving notice of termination, in accordance with its terms. The form of such notice would most appropriately be a formal diplomatic note or letter from one Government to the other.

(FAC Report, Overseas Territories, HC 147-II (2008))

5/66
Falklands

The Government was asked about the application of international obligations to Overseas Territories, in particular concerning the application of the Ottawa Convention on the Prohibition of the Use etc of Anti-Personnel Mines and their Destruction to the Falklands and whether it was possible to treat Overseas Territories in a way different from the UK itself because of the limited resources of some Overseas Territories. An FCO Minister said:

We are aware of our obligation under the Ottawa Convention. We are also aware of the difficulties that there are and, having been to the Falkland Islands, I am aware of the views of the Falkland Islanders that you have expressed. We have had a feasibility study done to assess how practicable de-mining would be in relation to the Falkland Islands and whether it could actually be done. Anyone who has been there knows that the terrain is quite difficult. Having had that report done, we have to reflect on that matter and consider whether we should go ahead, what the time scales would be and other such issues. That is actively under consideration at the moment.

(Foreign Affairs Committee Report, Overseas Territories, HC 147-V (2008))

5/67

The Foreign Secretary was asked a number of questions about the Falkland Islands. An FCO Minister wrote:

The Governor of the Falkland Islands is also the Commissioner for South Georgia and South Sandwich Islands, but the two positions are separate and distinct. He has no responsibility for any of the other Overseas Territories in the south Atlantic, nor South Orkney, which is administered as part of the British Antarctic Territory. The Falkland Islands government has no responsibilities in relation to South Georgia, the South Sandwich Islands, South Orkney or any other territories in the south Atlantic.

The Governor/Commissioner maintains a regular dialogue with Foreign and Commonwealth Office officials to ensure that the priorities set out in the 1999 White Paper on the Overseas Territories are being met.

… the Government will play a role in supporting the secure development of oil and gas exploration facilities in the Falkland Islands territorial sea and continental shelf. The Government are responsible for the external security and defence of the Falkland Islands. The provision of routine security and policing of oil rigs is a matter for the Falkland Islands government and the oil exploration companies.

The Government hold regular discussions with the Falkland Islands Government on issues including the exploration for oil and gas in Falkland Islands waters. Most recently, these have included meetings between the Foreign and Commonwealth Office's (FCO) Director General for Defence and Intelligence and other FCO officials with representatives of the Falkland Islands Government in January and February 2008.

There have been no discussions, with the Argentine Government, on the exploration for oil and gas in Falkland Islands waters since the South West Atlantic Hydro Carbons Commission ceased to meet in July 2000. On 27 March 2007, the Argentine Government announced its repudiation of the 1995 Joint Declaration on hydrocarbon exploration in the special co-operation area. We regret the Argentine decision, which makes future co-operation in this area more difficult. But we remain committed to promoting practical cooperation with Argentina in the South Atlantic and on broader international issues.

(HC Deb 29 February 2008 Vol 472 c2022W-2023W)

5/68 (See also 11/10)

The Foreign Secretary was asked what measures the Government were taking to protect the fisheries around the Falkland Islands from unauthorized fishing by foreign vessels. An FCO Minister wrote:

The Falkland Islands Government exercise responsibility for protecting fisheries around the Falkland Islands from unauthorised fishing. In order to achieve this task the Falkland Islands Government have two maritime surveillance aircraft, a chartered fisheries protection vessel and a satellite based vessel monitoring system. Additionally, a small number of fisheries observers are deployed on the commercial fleet. Their primary role is the collection of scientific data but they also monitor compliance with regulations.

Since the introduction of the first fisheries conservation zone around the Falkland Islands in 1986 and the beginning of the regulated fishery, fin fish stocks in the Falkland Islands have been relatively stable. Squid stocks are less stable due to their short life cycle (one-year) and dependence on favourable environmental conditions. After a period of decline, stocks of the main squid species now appear to have returned to normal levels. Apart from the noted volatility of squid stocks, we expect conservation action to generally maintain stock levels and catches at current levels.

We have had no recent discussions with the Argentine Government on the issue of licences to fish in Falkland Islands waters. The Falkland Islands Government has responsibility for the licensing of fishing in its waters, in line with international best practice. We do participate in fisheries discussions with Argentina through the South Atlantic Fisheries Commission. We last met the Argentine Government to discuss the mandate of the South Atlantic Fisheries Commission in March 2007.

The Falkland Islands Government license commercial fishing in Falkland Islands waters in line with their legislation on conservation and management of fish stocks. The legal and regulatory framework in which the Falkland Islands' fishery operates has been modernised and re-stated recently with the enactment of the Fisheries (Conservation and Management) Ordinance 2005. These regulations are similar to those used in other fisheries around the world where international best practice is adhered to.

The issuing of fishing licences by the Falkland Islands Government has generated the following amounts for each of the calendar years since 1989 (the earliest year for which figures are available):

Income generated from fishing licences (£)

1989	29,001,223
1990	27,942,586
1991	26,360,901
1992	26,513,702
1993	21,073,205
1994	26,690,547
1995	20,348,929
1996	21,977,242
1997	21,296,309
1998	19,577,548
1999	20,182,480
2000	24,780,401
2001	27,685,053
2002	26,552,083
2003	20,466,419
2004	11,912,319
2005	10,552,357
2006	14,401,541

Figures for income generated by the sale of licences specifically to foreign vessels is only available for the last three years. These amounts are:

Income generated from fishing licences to foreign vessels (£)

2005	5,268,712
2006	7,655,134
2007	8,788,340

The Falkland Islands Government Fisheries Department supplied these figures. The responsibility for the sale of fishing licences lies with the Falkland Islands Government.

(HC Deb 6 February 2008 Vol 471 c1162W)

Part Five: IV.C. *Subjects of international law—international organisations— entities and groups other than states and international organisations—special regimes*

5/69 (See also **3/3**)
The Foreign Secretary wrote:

I wish to make a statement to the House on the issue of mixed competence conventions. As the then Minister for Europe, reported to this House in April 2007, the outstanding issue blocking the ratification of a number of mixed competence conventions by the EU was the arrangements for communicating with competent authorities in Gibraltar which Spain had questioned.

I am delighted that, with the agreement of the Government of Gibraltar and in the spirit of ongoing co-operation, we have now concluded a set of arrangements with Spain which will allow the EU to move ahead and ratify all such instruments. Among the conventions covered are the 1996 Hague Convention on the Protection of Children and the 2001 Cape Town Convention on International Interests in Mobile Equipment and its protocol on aircraft.

In future under the 'Agreed arrangements relating to Gibraltar authorities in the context of mixed agreements' a system of 'post-boxing' will apply for communications between Spanish and Gibraltar authorities but not for communications between the authorities of other states and Gibraltar. The same arrangements will also apply for communications between Gibraltar and Spain in the context of the 'Agreed arrangements relating to Gibraltar authorities in the context of certain international treaties'.

(HC Deb 8 January 2008 Vol 470 c7WS)

Part Five: IV.F. *Subjects of international law—international organisations— entities and groups other than states and international organisations—others (eg indigenous peoples, minorities, national liberation movements)*

5/70
The Foreign Secretary was asked what recent representations his Department had made to the Botswana government on the Botswana

High Court ruling in December 2006 that the Botswana government had illegally removed Kalahari bushmen from their tribal lands; and whether his Department had received recent reports on the Botswana government's response to this ruling. An FCO Minister wrote:

A Minister raised the court ruling with President Mogae of Botswana when he visited in June 2007. Our high commissioner in Gaborone followed this up by raising it with both the Botswana Vice President and the Foreign Minister. Since then our high commission in Gaborone, working closely with EU partners, has maintained regular contact with the Government of Botswana on the issue of the San community. We continue to encourage the Government of Botswana to take an inclusive approach to finding a sustainable solution to the future use of the Central Kalahari Game Reserve, underlining the importance of dialogue and negotiation with the San (Bushmen).

Our high commission is in regular contact with representatives of the San Community and non-governmental organisations, through whom they receive assessments on the implementation of the court ruling.

(HC Deb 22 February 2008 Vol 472 c1056W)

Part Six: The Position of the Individual (including the Corporation) in International Law

Part Six: I. *The individual (including the corporation) in international law—nationality*

6/1

The Government were asked in the context of determining British citizenship what was their definition of 'Irish citizen'. A Minister wrote:

Those who were citizens of Eire on 1 January 1949 could opt to remain a British subject under Section 4(2) of the British Nationality Act 1948. Such people continue to have that right under the British Nationality Act 1981.

For this purpose, "citizens of Eire" were defined by the Irish Nationality and Citizenship Act 1935 and the Irish Nationality and Citizenship (Amendment) Act 1937.

Those who have no claim to British subject status would need to naturalise, in the same way as other foreign nationals, in order to become British citizens. For this purpose, the term "Irish citizen" would refer to those recognised by the Irish Government under their current legislation as being their nationals. When applying for citizenship, this would normally be demonstrated by possession of an Irish passport.

(HL Deb 11 March 2008 Vol 699 cWA220)

6/2

The Defence Secretary was asked when he planned to update the guidance letter issued to South Africans in the British Army dated 20 February 2008 on South African legislation on mercenaries and membership of other nations' armed forces; when guidance on this subject was issued to South African personnel in *(a)* the Royal Navy and *(b)* the RAF; whether South African personnel would be able to continue to serve in the British armed forces on a conditional or qualified basis on terms set out by the South African government when the legislation came into force; what meetings had been held between (i) officials and (ii) Ministers and the South African government to discuss the issue; and whether South African personnel in the armed forces would be granted UK citizenship if barred from membership of the UK armed forces by the legislation. A Defence Minister wrote:

Letters are sent out to serving South African personnel at regular intervals updating them on the latest situation with regards to the South African legislation on mercenaries and membership of other nations' armed forces. The last letters to Royal Naval personnel were sent out on 31 January 2008 and letters to RAF personnel were sent on 15 February 2008. Further updates will be sent in due course if and when there are further developments.

We are urgently investigating the potential consequences for South African personnel currently serving in the UK armed forces, so that we can support those who may be affected. Our overriding aim is to secure the continual service of South African personnel in the UK armed forces and for them to be able to deploy on operations. We hope to send a team of officials to South Africa to hold face to face discussions with the officials who will be drafting the new regulations as it is the details of these underlying regulations that will allow us to understand what real effect the new Act, when it comes into force, will have on personnel.

Representations have been made by the Secretary of State for Defence to the South African Defence Minister, Mr Lekota, on the potential implications the legislation would have on recruitment and retention of personnel into the UK armed forces. The Secretary of State for Defence wrote to Mr Lekota in August 2006 and followed this up with a telephone conversation in December 2006 and he wrote again in April 2007. Our high commissioner to South Africa, Paul Boateng, has also made representations to the Government of South Africa on several occasions. His last letter was sent to Mr Lekota on 22 January 2008.

The Mercenary Act was discussed at the UK-South Africa bilateral Defence Staff talks held in the MOD on 3–4 March 2008 with the aim of securing a date for an officials visit at the earliest opportunity.

Under current rules eligible SA citizens serving in the British armed forces can apply for British citizenship if they have been resident in the UK for a five year period, or three years if married or in a civil partnership to a British citizen. Service in the armed forces, at home and abroad, counts towards the residential qualifying period. We are discussing other options with the Home Office should South African personnel be barred from membership of the UK armed forces.

We cannot say precisely what the implications of the legislation are for our people until the details of the regulations are divulged to us.

(HC Deb 2 June 2008 Vol 476 c695W)

6/3

In answering a number of questions about nationality law, a Minister wrote:

Although there is no absolute right within British law to British nationality, there are provisions about the acquisition of citizenship by a stateless person which enable us to meet our obligations under the 1961 United Nations Convention on the Reduction of Statelessness. Under Section 1 of the British Nationality Act 1981, a child born in the United Kingdom to a parent who is a British citizen or "settled" in the United Kingdom will become a British citizen. Section 1 also provides that any child born here who was not British at birth but whose parent becomes British or settled after their birth to [sc "may"] be registered as a British citizen while a minor. Similarly, any child born in the United Kingdom and who lives here for the first 10 years of his or her life may register as a British citizen. Schedule 2 of the Act also provides that a person under the age of 22 who has lived in the United Kingdom for a continuous period of five years may register as a British citizen; this provision is more generous than that prescribed in Article 1 of the United Nations Convention, which permits states to impose a 10-year residence requirement. The Government believe that it is reasonable to ensure that those who benefit from British citizenship demonstrate a real link with this country through a substantial period of residence here, in addition to the location of their birth.

Further to this, there are also provisions in the 1981 Act allowing for the registration of stateless children of British nationals, and for the registration of people born stateless before 1983 who can demonstrate one of a set of defined connections to the United Kingdom or its current or former overseas possessions or territories. There are provisions in the 1981 Act which allow the Home Secretary to deprive a person of their British citizenship. If this is done on the basis that it is "conducive to the public good", there is a requirement that the person should not be left stateless as a result.

The British Nationality Act 1981, in providing for the acquisition of citizenship since 1983, does not discriminate on grounds other than nationality. Previous legislation was discriminatory in that British women were not able to pass on citizenship to their children born in the United Kingdom. The 1981 Act provided that, from 1 January 1983, women could pass on citizenship in the same way as men. This was not made retrospective at the time because of complications which could have arisen in suddenly giving people, many of whom were adults, British nationality. Section 4C of the 1981 Act provides for people born to British mothers between 1961 and 1983, who would have become British automatically if women had been able to pass on citizenship in the same way as men at that time, to be registered as British citizens. We now recognise that those born before 1961 are at a disadvantage compared to the children of British men and are planning to amend this section to remove the 1961 cut-off date, so that people born before that date will be able to apply for registration.

(HL Deb 29 September 2008 Vol 703 cWS190)

6/4

A Minister wrote:

The China Center of Adoption Affairs (CCAA) has taken the position that adoptions under Chinese domestic law by British citizens resident in China cannot proceed without a guarantee of automatic conferral of British citizenship on the child.

Although UK adoption law has provisions that recognise adoptions effected in China, British nationality legislation provides that a child will not be a British citizen if the adoption is not made under the 1993 "Convention on Protection of Children and Co-operation in Respect of Intercountry Adoption", or the adoptive parents were not habitually resident in the United Kingdom at the time the adoption was certified under the convention. Children in such cases can apply for registration as a British citizen at the Home Secretary's discretion under section 3(1) of the British Nationality Act 1981.

In light of the position taken by the CCAA, the Home Office has considered whether it would be possible to give an indication to the Chinese authorities of the likely outcome of an application for citizenship by a child adopted in China. The Home Office concluded that this is not possible because the Home Secretary is unable to fetter her discretion by undertaking to grant citizenship in advance of receiving an application.

Citizenship is a matter for the Home Office. However, officials from the Department for Children, Schools and Families are working with Home Office colleagues and Foreign and Commonwealth Office representatives in Beijing, to try and establish with the CCAA a mutually acceptable way forward, through the provision of text for a certificate which may be used in such adoption applications.

(HC Deb 17 October 2008 Vol 480 c1580W)

Part Six: II. *The individual (including the corporation) in international law—diplomatic and consular protection (see also Part Thirteen II.A.1.(c), below)*

6/5

The Government responded to the FAC Report on Foreign Policy Aspects of the Lisbon Treaty. The Committee had recommended that:

25 ... in its response to the present Report, the Government sets out its reaction to the proposals that there should be "common offices" of EU Member States in third countries and that the new EU delegations may take on consular tasks. We also recommend that the Government clarifies the role and responsibilities of EU delegations in countries where the UK has no Embassy or High Commission. (Paragraph 203)

The Government said that it:

... shares with other EU Member States the view that the provision of consular assistance to their citizens is primarily a matter for national authorities. We welcome efforts to improve co-operation and co-ordination between Member States in this area, including those under Article 20 TEC, which requires Member States to treat requests for consular assistance by unrepresented nationals of Member States on the same basis as requests by their own nationals.

This is not a new provision. EU citizens have been able to seek consular assistance from other Member States, where their own country has no representation, since 1993. This supplements the high standard of consular assistance already available from British embassies and consulates. The UK enjoys a similar arrangement with Commonwealth partners. We are aware that, in some parts of the world, delivering consular assistance to British nationals is only possible through the consular and diplomatic networks of our EU Partners.

The concept of "common offices" for EU consular work in third countries, which is included in the Commission's Green Paper of November 2006 and the Commission's Action Plan of December 2007, has not been clearly defined. Co-location of Member States' consular offices already takes place in a number of countries, as do local arrangements for allocation between Member States' missions of unrepresented EU nationals. However, these and any other such arrangements for co-operation are for the Member States concerned to decide on.

While the UK welcomes the role of the Union in facilitating co-operation and ensuring non-discrimination in the provision of consular assistance, the provision of consular assistance remains a matter for Member States.

(Government Response to the Foreign Affairs Committee Report on 'Foreign Policy Aspects of the Lisbon Treaty' (Third Report of Session 2007–08) Cm 7332)

6/6

The Government were asked what representations they had made about the journalist and cameraman who have been arrested and imprisoned in the north of Niger, and who may face the death penalty. An FCO Minister said:

I understand the question refers to the case of Mr Dandois, a French-British dual national, and his colleague, a French national. Mr Dandois was travelling in Niger on his French passport. As such his interests are primarily being looked after by the French Government, as are those of his colleague.

The Government have been working closely with the French embassy in Niger, through its representative in Niamey, to clarify the status of and charges against Mr Dandois. If Mr Dandois is indeed charged with a potentially capital offence, the Government would join France in making formal representations to the Government of Niger. The death penalty remains on the statute book in Niger, even though no execution has taken place since 1976.

(HL Deb 16 January 2008 Vol 697 cWA261)

6/7

An FCO Minister wrote:

The joint Foreign and Commonwealth Office-Home Office Forced Marriage Unit helps British nationals in the UK and overseas facing the threat of and living with the consequences of forced marriage. The unit works closely with other agencies in the UK, such as the Ministry of Justice, the police, social services and specialist non-governmental organisations. Our embassies overseas provide direct support to victims and potential victims of forced marriage. This can include rescue and repatriation to the UK. The unit has published guidelines for agencies working with forced marriage victims. These will be placed on a statutory footing with the implementation of the Forced Marriage (Civil Protection) Act later this year. The unit carries out an extensive outreach programme to raise awareness of the issue and of the support services that they offer.

(HL Deb 4 February 2008 Vol 698 cWA155)

6/8
Simon Mann

The Foreign Secretary was asked what steps he proposed to take to ensure that Simon Mann does not face the death penalty in Equatorial Guinea. An FCO Minister wrote:

We understand that the Government of Equatorial Guinea provided assurances to the Government of Zimbabwe that the death penalty would not be implemented should Simon Mann be extradited to Equatorial Guinea. The Attorney-General of Equatorial Guinea, Jose Ole Obono, publicly stated on 10 May 2007 that, 'the death penalty will not apply in this case'.

We are currently seeking urgent consular access to visit Mr Mann in prison and have underlined to the Government of Equatorial Guinea their obligations to respect Mr Mann's human rights during his detention.

The UK is opposed to the death penalty in all circumstances and works closely with the EU to promote abolition of the death penalty around the world.

(HC Deb 7 February 2008 Vol 471 c1407W)

6/9 (See also 15/25)

The Foreign Secretary was asked what sanctions the Government had considered taking against *(a)* Equatorial Guinea and *(b)* Zimbabwe to ensure the safe return of Simon Mann. An FCO Minister wrote:

The Government have no plans to apply sanctions on the Governments of Equatorial Guinea or Zimbabwe in response to Simon Mann's removal. Our main concern must be for Mr Mann's immediate welfare.

(HC Deb 18 February 2008 Vol 472 c180W)

6/10

The Foreign Secretary was asked if he would make representations to the United States Administration requesting it to exert its influence on Equatorial Guinea to secure the safe return of Simon Mann. An FCO Minister wrote:

The Government have no plans to make representations to the United States in relation to Simon Mann.

United States officials visited Simon Mann in Black Beach Prison on 6 February 2008, at the invitation of the Equatorial Guinean authorities. While the visit by the United States afforded an opportunity to check on Mr Mann's welfare and safety, we nevertheless made clear to the government of Equatorial Guinea that such a visit was not a substitute for UK consular access.

UK consular access to Mr Mann was granted on 12 February.

(HC Deb 18 February 2008 Vol 472 c181W-182W)

6/11

The Government were asked whether they would summon the ambassadors of Equatorial Guinea and Zimbabwe to explain the apparent abduction of Simon Mann from Zimbabwe to Equatorial Guinea; and what action they planned to take to secure his safe return. An FCO Minister wrote:

I met the Equatorial Guinean ambassador to the UK, Mr. Agustin Nze Nfumu, on 7 February to discuss Simon Mann's case and request immediate consular access. I then telephoned the ambassador on 11 February to reiterate this request and stress the need for UK officials to be granted access to Mr Mann. Consular access was granted on 12 February. UK officials will be in touch with the ambassador of Equatorial Guinea as the need arises.

Our concerns were conveyed to the Zimbabwean ambassador, prior to Mr Mann's removal. Our primary concern at this point must be for Mr Mann's immediate welfare.

Our deputy high commission in Lagos provides consular assistance to British nationals in Equatorial Guinea. Our consul in Lagos travelled to Equatorial Guinea on 5 February, as soon as it was confirmed that Mr Mann had been extradited. We were granted consular access to Mr Mann and visited him on 12 February. We expect the authorities in Equatorial Guinea to treat him in line with international standards. The authorities have offered assurances that he will be treated well while in detention.

We will continue to visit Mr Mann in prison in line with our consular policy. We will also discuss with EU partners what assistance they may be able to provide.

(HL Deb 20 February 2008 Vol 699 cWA65)

6/12

The next day, the Minister added:

Our consul in Harare visited Simon Mann regularly. We reminded the Zimbabwe authorities of their obligations under the International Covenant on Civil and Political Rights when considering an extradition request. We received assurances that due process would be followed regarding Mr Mann's extradition. We understand from Mr Mann's lawyer that he had indicated an intention to further appeal his extradition. In the event, Mr Mann was removed from Zimbabwe without a further appeal being considered and is now in Equatorial Guinea. Our consul in Lagos visited him in prison in Equatorial Guinea on 12 February.

(HL Deb 21 February 2008 Vol 699 cWA81)

6/13

The Foreign Secretary was asked a number of questions about the treatment of Simon Mann who was detained in Equatorial Guinea after being extradited from Zimbabwe. A Minister wrote:

… the Government's main concern is for Mr Mann's immediate welfare.

Our objective in dealing with the Equatorial Guinean authorities is to maintain open lines of communication, with a view to regular access to Simon Mann and ensuring that he is treated in line with international standards.

We do not believe that sanctions would be conducive to facilitating dialogue with the Equatorial Guinean government …

The issue of the legality of Mr Mann's removal from Zimbabwe and its implications for any subsequent trial are a matter for Mr. Mann's legal representatives to take forward in Zimbabwe and Equatorial Guinea.

We have expressed our concern to the Zimbabwean authorities following Mr Mann's transfer to Equatorial Guinea.

The Equatorial Guinean authorities have assured us that Mr. Mann will receive a fair trial, in accordance with international law, and that he will be free to appoint a lawyer.

(HC Deb 25 February 2008 Vol 472 c1139W)

6/14

The Foreign Secretary was asked about the consular assistance provided to Simon Mann who was detained in Equatorial Guinea. An FCO Minister wrote:

We are providing consular assistance to Mr Mann, including with regard to his treatment and welfare. In considering whether he is being treated well, the Government will refer to international instruments, such as the International Covenant on Civil and Political Rights, to which Equatorial Guinea is a party. We will also refer to non-binding instruments, such as the UN Standard Minimum Rules on the Treatment of Prisoners, that provide guidance for appropriate conditions of detention.

(HC Deb 26 February 2008 Vol 472 c1375W)

6/15

A Minister said in a debate concerning the position of two UK nationals who were wanted for alleged offences in Cyprus:

I welcome the opportunity briefly to emphasise the role that our consular staff in Cyprus and London have played in following the cases of Mr Binnington and Mr Atkinson and in providing them and their families with consular assistance.

The British high commission in Nicosia was officially informed by the Cypriot authorities on 21 August 2006 that Mr. Binnington and Mr. Atkinson had appeared in Larnaca district court on 19 August, when an eight-day remand order was issued. Both men were being investigated for, but not yet charged with, conspiracy to kill, premeditated murder and attempt to kill.

The duty officer at the British high commission visited both men on 19 August, following notification of their court appearance, and they both had proper legal representation. They did not need anyone in the UK to be contacted.

Let me move on to deal with extradition. I am liaising closely with the Minister for Europe, as this matter falls between our responsibilities—he representing the Foreign and Commonwealth Office and me the Home Office. The fact is that if the supreme court has decided as it has on a prison sentence, a warrant will be issued for the extradition of the two men back to Cyprus if they do not return willingly. That is a matter for the courts in both the UK and Cyprus; it is not something that Ministers can get directly involved in.

Consular staff from the British high commission in Nicosia attended the hearing yesterday at the supreme court, where the three presiding judges agreed on an adjournment because certain documents were unavailable. Consular staff in Cyprus also spoke to the defendants' lawyer, who confirmed that because of the behaviour of the victim's family at previous court hearings, he did not intend to address the next court hearing orally, but to provide the judges with written statements and evidence.

[I was] asked whether the Government could intervene on [sc "with"] the Cypriot Government to fend off a possible extradition request. As I have already said, however, that is a matter for the courts. It is not the role of Her Majesty's Government to interfere in the internal affairs of another state, including in their judicial proceedings. Our own proceedings are, quite rightly, protected in a similar way ... challenging the issues of legality within Cyprus is taking the right route, as Her Majesty's Government cannot be expected, and are unable, to intervene.

Encouraging the Cypriot Government to institute a full review of the case is another [request]. The defence lawyer for both Mr Atkinson and Mr Binnington has not raised with the Government any questions about the conduct or fairness of the supreme court hearings. Where appropriate, however, the Foreign and Commonwealth Office will consider approaching the local authorities if a British national is not treated in line with internationally accepted standards. The FCO will also consider approaching the local authorities where a trial does not follow internationally recognised standards for a fair trial or where it is unreasonably delayed. I hope that that explains the Government's remit in this area.

As I have already explained a couple of times, Ministers have no role in the extradition process. Whether or not to order extradition is a matter for the courts, and the courts must decide whether extradition would be compatible with the convention rights within the meaning of the Human Rights Act 1998.

The men's lawyers will be able to put all their arguments to the court, should an extradition request be made and referred to it. In extradition requests, the legal niceties are all dealt with properly and formally. Extradition warrants have been well conducted and well rehearsed for some time now—we have good conventions within the EU on the matter.

[The question was] raised about article 6 of the European Convention on Human Rights, which protects the right to a fair hearing but does not require that an accused be tried by jury. Mr. Harrington's sentence being disproportionate to the offence is a difficult matter for us to comment on. It is difficult for the Government to know the full facts of the case and all the factors that the judge took into account in sentencing. That is a matter for the judicial authorities in Cyprus.

The honorary legal adviser in Nicosia advised that the ruling of the supreme court is not contrary to Cypriot law, but noted the possibility of an appeal to the European Court of Human Rights.

The primary role of the Foreign and Commonwealth Office in assisting British nationals arrested or detained overseas is to support them and take an interest in their welfare. The Home Office has a responsibility to ensure that the European arrest warrant is conducted in a proper manner, but without interference from Ministers. We ensure that the process happens as it should, and in my experience as a Minister looking at other European arrest warrants, it works well and fairly. We have respect for each other's legal systems, which is the bedrock of the process.

We can take up any justified complaint about ill treatment, personal safety or discrimination, with a British national's permission, but consular staff in Cyprus and London will, of course, continue to support Mr. Binnington and Mr. Atkinson and their families, within those limitations.

(HC Deb 14 March 2008 Vol 473 cs593–596)

6/16
The Foreign Secretary was asked about allegations of ill-treatment of UK citizens in Pakistan. A Minister wrote:

Of these six cases, two were mono British nationals and four were dual British/Pakistani nationals. We sought consular access to the two mono British nationals and were given full consular access in one case. We have also requested, but are yet to be given, consular access to one dual national on exceptional grounds in accordance with our published policy on the death penalty.

Of the six cases mentioned, four have alleged mistreatment whilst in Pakistani custody.

(HC Deb 16 May 2008 Vol 475 c1816W)

6/17 (See also 6/93)
He was asked again about allegations of ill-treatment of UK citizens. A Minister wrote:

The Government take allegations of mistreatment very seriously. Where allegations of mistreatment are made by British nationals in Pakistani custody or following release from Pakistani custody and when we are asked to do so by the individual affected, we can raise those allegations with the appropriate authorities.

Of the six detainees referred to in the earlier answer, [6/16] one remains in Pakistani custody.

British officials sought and were granted access to the two mono British nationals. Priority was given to the welfare of the detainees.

The answer provided to the earlier question [6/16] does not take into account allegations of mistreatment other than those made to UK officials.

Consular access was not sought in all of the six cases, as four of the individuals were dual Pakistani/British nationals in the country of their other nationality. The Pakistani authorities are under no obligation to inform us of the detention of a dual Pakistani/British national or to provide consular access. We are exceptionally seeking access to one dual national in accordance with our published policy on the death penalty, but this is yet to be given.

(HC Deb 4 June 2008 Vol 476 c1006W)

6/18

The Foreign Secretary was asked what representations the Government had made on behalf of British citizens imprisoned in the United Arab Emirates. An FCO Minister wrote:

There are currently 43 British citizens imprisoned in the United Arab Emirates (UAE). Consular officers can consider approaching the local authorities only if a British citizen is not treated according to internationally accepted standards. This may include where a trial does not follow internationally recognised standards for a fair trial or is unreasonably delayed compared to local cases. We have no record of any such approaches having been made in the UAE in recent years.

Additionally, with the prisoner's permission, consular officers can take up any justified complaint about ill treatment, personal safety, or discrimination with the police or prison authorities. We have no record of any such issues having been raised in recent times with UAE authorities. However, we have on occasion brought welfare concerns to the attention of prison authorities. These usually involve dietary and medical issues raised by prisoners. Our consulate in Dubai has taken up four cases of ill treatment with the Dubai authorities in the last three years. Posts also continue to liaise with the authorities in Sharjah and Abu Dhabi to ensure that the appeals are progressing.

(HC Deb 26 June 2008 Vol 478 c538W)

6/19

The Government were asked whether they were making representations to the Government of Goa regarding the reinterpretation of existing property legislation and amendment to the Indian Registration Act 1908 that is resulting in seizure of United Kingdom citizens' properties. A Minister wrote:

Our High Commission in New Delhi has raised the issue with both the authorities in Goa and at a national level. In particular, we have made it clear that there should be no confiscation of property acquired legally by British citizens.

The Government will continue to reiterate this message to the Indian authorities. Our travel advice has been updated to warn British citizens of the potential problems they could face in buying property in India. This can be accessed at the Foreign and Commonwealth Office's website at: <www.fco.gov.uk/en/travelling-and-living-overseas/travel-advice-by-country/>.

(HL Deb 29 September 2008 Vol 703 cWA399)

Part Six: VII. A. *The individual (including the corporation) in international law—immigration and emigration, extradition, expulsion, asylum—immigration and emigration*

6/20

The Home Secretary was asked to which countries there was currently no safe route of return for failed asylum seekers. A Minister wrote:

There are no countries to which the United Kingdom does not remove failed asylum seekers on the basis of the safety of the route. Officials consider not only the merits of the individual case but also the most effective means of achieving a safe and successful return. While there is no policy not to return to any country or territory, our ability to return may of course from time to time temporarily be affected by legal challenge. This is currently the case with Zimbabwe, where we have undertaken to the High Court that we will not enforce the return of failed asylum seekers to Zimbabwe until the current country guidance litigation is resolved, and that remains the case.

(HC Deb 28 April 2008 Vol 475 c73W)

Part Six: VII. B. *The individual (including the corporation) in international law—immigration and emigration, extradition, expulsion, asylum—extradition*

6/21
Iran

A Minister said:

The Foreign and Commonwealth Office regularly raises concerns with Iran in the context of individual cases, most often around methods of punishment used by that regime. Representations are also made through the EU, as this has been found to be the most effective way of making such representations. The Border and Immigration Agency enforces the return of Iranian gay men only when we are satisfied that they are not in need of protection. We do not seek to enforce returns to Iran unless our decision-making processes and the independent courts are satisfied that it is entirely safe to do so.

(HL Deb 11 March 2008 Vol 699 c1399)

6/22
Rendition

The Foreign Secretary made a statement on US rendition operations.

On 12 December 2005, in response to a parliamentary question ... the then Foreign Secretary, updated the House on the subject of terrorist suspects and rendition, stating:

"Careful research by officials has been unable to identify any occasion since 11 September 2001, or earlier in the Bush administration, when we received a request for permission by the United States ... for a rendition through UK territory or airspace, nor are we otherwise aware of such a case." [*Official Report*, 12 December 2005; Vol. 440, c. 1652W.]

That was supplemented by two further statements in January 2006 and a letter of 6 February 2006 to [an MP].

In March 2007, the then Prime Minister gave an assurance to the Intelligence and Security Committee that he was satisfied that the US had at no time since 9/11 rendered an individual through the UK or through our overseas territories. In its report on rendition of 28 June 2007, the ISC said:

"We are satisfied that there is no evidence that US rendition flights have used UK airspace (except the two cases in 1998 referred to earlier in this Report) and that there is no evidence of them having landed at UK military airfields."

The Government welcomed those conclusions in their response to the report in July 2007. Parliamentary answers, interviews and letters followed that evidence. I am very sorry indeed to have to report to the House the need to correct those and other statements on the subject, on the basis of new information passed to officials on 15 February 2008 by the US Government.

Contrary to earlier explicit assurances that Diego Garcia had not been used for rendition flights, recent US investigations have now revealed two occasions, both in 2002, when that had in fact occurred. An error in the earlier US records search meant that those cases did not come to light. In both cases, a US plane with a single detainee on board refuelled at the US facility in Diego Garcia. The detainees did not leave the plane, and the US Government have assured us that no US detainees have ever been held on Diego Garcia. US investigations show no record of any other rendition through Diego Garcia or any other overseas territory, or through the UK itself, since then.

Yesterday, US and UK legal teams discussed the issue, and I spoke with Secretary Rice. We both agree that the mistakes made in those two cases are not acceptable, and she shares my deep regret that the information has only just come to light. She emphasised to me that the US Government came to us with the information quickly after they discovered it.

The House and the Government will share deep disappointment at the news, and about its late emergence. That disappointment is shared by our US allies. They recognise the absolute imperative for the British Government to provide accurate information to Parliament. I reaffirm the Government's commitment to that imperative today. We fully accept that the United States gave its earlier assurances in good faith. We accepted those assurances, and indeed referred to them publicly, also in good faith.

For the avoidance of doubt, I have asked my officials to compile a list of all the flights where we have been alerted to concerns regarding rendition through the UK or our overseas territories. Once it is ready we will be sending the list to the US and seeking their specific assurance that none of those flights was used for rendition purposes.

Our counter-terrorism relationship with the United States is vital to UK security. I am absolutely clear that there must and will continue to be the strongest possible intelligence and counter-terrorism relationship with the US, consistent with UK law and our international obligations. As part of our close co-operation, there has long been a regular exchange with the US authorities, in which we have set out, first, that we expect them to seek permission to render detainees via UK territory and airspace, including overseas territories; secondly, that we will grant that permission only if we are satisfied that rendition would accord with UK law and our international obligations; and thirdly, how we understand our obligations under the UN convention against torture. Secretary Rice has underlined to me the firm US understanding that there will be no rendition through the UK, UK airspace or overseas territories without express British Government permission.

The House will want to know what has become of the two individuals in question. There is a limit to what I can say, but I can tell the House the following. The US Government have told us that neither of the men was a British national or a British resident. One is currently in Guantanamo Bay. The other has been released. The House will know that the British Government's long-standing position is that the detention facility at Guantanamo should be closed.

My officials and their US counterparts continue to work through all the details and implications of this information. We will keep procedures under review to ensure that they meet the standards that we have set, and I will, of course, keep the House updated.

... He said further that the practice was established in the 1990s for permission to be sought, and in 1998 it was sought in four cases, in two of which rendition occurred and in two of which it did not. There was also a preliminary inquiry, which was referred to in the letter that was sent to him on 6 February 2006 about the 2004 case. I associate myself entirely with his view that rendition to torture would be quite wrong and is something that the UK Government should never participate in and certainly not instigate.

I can tell the House that in this case we have been told that the two individuals involved were not taken to a secret detention facility or subject to water-boarding or other similar forms of interrogation. [A speaker] talked about the importance of advocating an international standard of definition, and that is what we do through our signature of international conventions on torture and through our adherence to our definition of it. We will certainly continue to do that.

... the ISC addressed that issue in a way that the Government recognised and agreed with, which is that so-called extraordinary rendition to torture is always wrong—it is illegal and immoral—but it is not the case that all rendition is, by definition, illegal. I referred earlier to the 1998 cases, two of which were accepted and two of which were refused. They were renditions to the US system, and there were full legal rights for the accused in those cases, although two were refused.

(HC Deb 21 February 2008 Vol 472 cs547–558)

6/23

The Foreign Secretary was asked whether the recent discovery that facilities on Diego Garcia had been used for the rendition of two individuals had been preceded by a specific request by the UK to the US authorities to review their records in this respect. He wrote:

 As set out in my statement to the House on 21 February 2008 (**6/22**), new information was passed to UK officials by the US regarding rendition flights through Diego Garcia on 15 February. This was not preceded by a specific UK request to the US authorities to review their records in this respect. However, it follows regular dialogue on these issues, including assurances provided by the US in September 2007 at annual political-military talks in relation to the US Naval Support Facility at Diego Garcia.

(HC Deb 6 March 2008 Vol 472 c2785W)

6/24

The Foreign Secretary was asked what recent assessment his Department had made of the adequacy of the permissions system that operates on rendition flights through the UK. An FCO Minister wrote:

We would consider all the circumstances of a request for rendition through the UK or our Overseas Territories and we would only grant permission if we were satisfied that it would accord with our domestic law and international obligations.

We continue to keep procedures under review to ensure that they meet the standards that we have set. Our officials are currently looking at the proposals of the all party parliamentary group on extraordinary rendition in light of the two cases of rendition through Diego Garcia in 2002. Once we have established more of the details and implications of these renditions we will take a decision on whether these proposals are necessary.

[See letter from the Chairman of the Parliamentary Group of 22 April 2008 and reply of the Foreign Secretary of 5 June 2008 at <www.extraordinaryrendition.org>, Ed.]

(HC Deb 7 May 2008 Vol 475 c934W)

6/25

The Foreign Secretary made the following Ministerial Statement:

On 21 February I made a statement to the House regarding new information we had been passed by the United States Government regarding rendition. Contrary to earlier assurances that Diego Garcia had not been used for rendition flights, United States investigations had revealed two occasions, both in 2002, when this had in fact occurred. Since February, I have corresponded with Secretary Rice on this issue and our officials have continued to work through the details and implications of the new information.

I promised the House that, as part of this process, my officials would compile a list of flights where we had been alerted to concern about rendition through the UK or our overseas territories. The list which they have compiled, containing 391 flights, reflects concerns put to us by hon. Members, members of the public, multilateral organisations and non-governmental organisations. Inclusion on this list does not represent an official endorsement of any allegations about a particular flight. On the contrary, US Government flights—as with other Government flights—occur regularly for a variety of purposes. Our intention was to collate in one place those concerns that had been put to us directly. The list was passed to the US on 15 May. I undertook in February to publish the list and have today placed a copy in the Library of the House and published it on the FCO website at <www.fco.gov.uk>.

The US Government received the list of flights from the UK Government. The US Government confirmed that, with the exception of two cases related to Diego Garcia in 2002, there have been no other instances in which US intelligence flights landed in the United Kingdom, our overseas territories, or the Crown dependencies, with a detainee on board since 11 September 2001.

Our US allies are agreed on the need to seek our permission for any future renditions through UK territory. Secretary Rice has underlined to me the firm US understanding that there will be no rendition through the UK, our overseas territories and Crown dependencies or airspace without first receiving our express permission. We have made clear that we would only grant such permission if we were satisfied that the rendition would accord with UK law and our international obligations. The circumstances of any such request would be carefully examined on a case-by-case basis.

Our intelligence and counter-terrorism relationship with the US is vital to the national security of the United Kingdom. There must and will continue to be the strongest possible intelligence and counter-terrorism relationship between our two countries, consistent with UK law and our international obligations.

(HC Deb 3 July 2008 Vol 478 c58WS-59WS)

6/26

The Government were asked by the FAC whether the UK had sought reassurance from the United States concerning allegations, made in the context of the discussion of rendition, that ships outside the territorial waters were being serviced from Diego Garcia. An FCO Minister said:

Just to be clear about ships generally, because that came up in the statement, we have had no evidence to suggest that any ships outside the territorial waters of Diego Garcia have been involved in rendition, nor that they have been serviced from the island ... We have no evidence to suggest that that is the case. The issue in relation to the territorial waters is more complex. There is an issue about how far outside the territorial waters they are if they are outside them. We are still in the process of putting together the information that will go to the US in relation to a whole range of issues. I do not know whether this would be one of the specific issues that we would ask. If they are outside our territorial waters our responsibilities are different from if they are inside.

He continued:

No [we have not sought reassurance from the US] and as you will be aware, we want to do an extremely thorough job in relation to the whole issue of Diego Garcia. So where there are any suggestions or there have been any allegations or any concerns about any possible flights and the like, all that information has been put together and will be passed on to the US. That information has not yet gone. [Qs.304–306]

The Minister was asked whether [the Government had given any consideration or had any discussion with the US about the possibility of terminating the agreement concerning US use of Diego Garcia in 2016 when it would be automatically extended for a further 20 years unless terminated.

The Minister said:

No [Q.307] nor had there been any discussions about increasing UK oversight if the agreement were extended. [Q.308].

(Foreign Affairs Committee Report, Overseas Territories, HC 147-II (2008))

6/27
The Foreign Secretary wrote to the FAC about rendition through Overseas Territories.

Thank you for your letter of 28 February concerning the new information that we have received from the US on rendition through Diego Garcia. I agree that this new information and the Government's response to it are relevant to your broader inquiry into the Overseas Territories.

Your questions cover a range of issues that officials in my Department are currently working on. The US Government recognises the absolute imperative for the British Government to provide accurate information to Parliament and we are working closely with our US allies on the details and implications of this new information. This process will take some further time and therefore, at this stage, I will not be able to provide all the details you seek.

However, I am pleased to be able to provide you with a response to the specific points on which we do have clarity. I will write to you again when officials have concluded their work on this issue.

DIEGO GARCIA

— The Government has no record of any request having been made by the US regarding the rendition of the two individuals through Diego Garcia.

— The Government previously received assurances from the US in 2005, 2006 and 2007 that no detainees had been transferred through the territorial waters of Diego Garcia. These assurances were given at the annual Diego Garcia political-military talks.

— I enclose copies of the initial agreement of 1966 and the subsequent agreement of 1976, a note explaining UK supervision of activities on Diego Garcia and details of UK military personnel stationed on the island.

TURKS AND CAICOS ISLANDS

— The Government had received assurances from the US in respect of rendition through all UK territories or airspace (ie including the Turks and Caicos Islands) in November 2005.

— We will be referring all flights where concerns have been raised to the US. This includes flights through the UK and its Overseas Territories (ie including the Turks and Caicos Islands).

LIST OF ALL FLIGHTS BEING SENT TO THE US

— The list of flights where the Government has been alerted to concerns about rendition is nearing completion. I will forward a copy to you as soon as possible. The list is based on information provided by my Department, the Department for Transport, the Ministry of Defence, the Home Office, Members of Parliament, members of the public and non-governmental organisations. Once complete, it will be sent to the US as a matter of urgency.

— The list contains all specific flights where concern has been raised about rendition, but not more general allegations that lack sufficient data to be verified. The flights on the list include instances where concerns have been raised that planes may have been on their way to or from a rendition operation. However, our purpose here is to identify whether rendition (ie of an individual) through UK territory or airspace in fact occurred. We do not consider that an empty flight transiting through our territory falls into this category.

— Although the list contains the names of individuals who are alleged to have been rendited [sic] on specific flights, we are seeking clarification on the flights and not the individuals at this stage.

I hope that I have addressed most of your concerns. I would be glad to receive any follow-up questions you may have. However, I must state again that officials are still analysing the implications of the new information received from the US and I may have to defer any further questions until we have established more of the detail surrounding this issue.

EXTENT OF UK SUPERVISION

UK personnel on Diego Garcia provide Customs and Immigration cover, policing and a range of other civil functions including Magistrate, Coroner, Development Control and Registration of Births, Deaths and Marriages, in order to ensure that UK Law, supplemented by specific BIOT ordinances, is upheld.

A wide range of activities are conducted by US personnel on Diego Garcia which are routine in nature and are covered by entries in the Exchange of Notes. These activities are not normally supervised by UK personnel, nor at 42 personnel is there capacity to do so. Any extraordinary use of the US base or facilities, such as combat operations or any other politically sensitive activity, requires prior approval from Her Majesty's Government and would attract a greater level of involvement by UK personnel both on Diego Garcia and in the UK.

(FAC Report, Overseas Territories, HC 147-II (2008))

6/28

An FCO Minister was asked by the FAC about rendition.

When it was revealed in February that two detainees had been transported on US flights that had refuelled at Diego Garcia, the Committee wrote to the Foreign Secretary asking a number of questions. He said, "We do not consider that an empty flight transiting through our territory falls into this category". By "this category", he meant rendition. What legal advice have the Government taken on whether they have a duty in relation to flights on the way to or from rendition when there is not a detainee on board?

The Minister said:

Obviously the case of Diego Garcia shows that we do indeed conclude that we have a duty. I think that our policy is clear—it is not just that we ourselves do not render people in breach of legal obligations, but we consider all circumstances in requests for rendition through the UK or the Overseas Territories. We would grant permission only if it was in accordance with our domestic law and our international obligations. That is why we are so anxious to ascertain whether our territory has been used for other cases of rendition. [Q.58]

When it was put to him that the Foreign Secretary had said that empty flights were 'more or less okay', the Minister said:

I do not think that it is more or less okay, but there is a limit to what we can do effectively to monitor empty planes, whose purposes it is not really reasonable for us to investigate. If an American military flight requests refuelling or access and is empty of any passengers, I am not sure that it is possible for us to demand what it might be doing on its return flight. [Q.59]

(Foreign Affairs Committee Report, Human Rights Report 2007, HC533 (2008))

6/29

The Government replied to the FAC Report on the Annual Human Rights Report 2007 on the matter of rendition. The FAC had concluded:

47.. ... that the Government has a moral and legal obligation to ensure that flights that enter UK airspace or land at UK airports are not part of the "rendition circuit", even if they do not have a detainee on board during the time they are in UK territory. We recommend that the Government should immediately raise questions about such flights with the US [authorities in order to ascertain the full scale of the rendition problem, and inform the Committee of the replies it receives in its response to this Report.

The Government wrote:

The Foreign Secretary explained in his letter to the Chairman of 18 March that our purpose in submitting a list of flights to the US was to identify whether rendition of an individual had in fact occurred. The Government does not consider that a flight transiting UK territory or airspace on its way to or from a rendition operation constitutes rendition. Nor do we consider that permitting transit or refuelling of an aircraft without detainees on board without knowledge of what activities that aircraft had been or would be involved in, or indeed whether or not those activities were unlawful, to be unlawful in itself. There are more than two million flights through UK airspace annually. It would be unreasonable and impractical to check every aircraft transiting UK airspace on the basis that it may have been, at some point in the past, and without UK knowledge, involved in a possible unlawful operation. Instead an intelligence-led approach is and must be employed. If individuals are reasonably suspected of committing criminal offences, or if there are reasonable grounds to suspect that aircraft are being used for unlawful purposes, then action can be taken. The nature of that action would depend on the facts and circumstances of any case.

(Foreign Affairs Committee Session 2007–08 Annual Report on Human Rights 2007, Response of the Secretary of State for Foreign and Commonwealth Affairs Cm 7463)

6/30
The FCO wrote to the FAC:

US AIRCRAFT USED IN RENDITION OPERATIONS

Your letter asks whether US aircraft used in rendition operations have called at airfields in the UK or its Overseas Territories en route to or from a rendition operation. You further refer to the Intelligence and Security Committee (ISC) Report on Rendition and its reference to the allegations made by Stephen Grey in his book "Ghost Flights", including that "on up to four occasions since 9/11, aircraft that had previously conducted a rendition operation overseas transited UK airspace during their return journeys (without detainees on board)". The ISC concluded that "The Committee has not seen any evidence that might contradict the police assessment that there is no evidential basis on which a criminal inquiry into these flights could be launched".(Conclusion GG p.62)

You ask whether the Government were informed by the US authorities of the four flights referred to. The answer is no. There are more than two million flights through UK airspace annually. The ISC report concluded that "We consider that it would be impractical to check whether every aircraft transiting UK airspace might have been, at some point in the past, and without UK knowledge, involved in a possibly unlawful operation...." (Conclusion HH p.62). The Government agrees that it would not be possible to check every flight—instead an intelligence-led approach is employed. If individuals on board are reasonably suspected of committing criminal offences, or if there are reasonable grounds to suspect that an aircraft is being used for unlawful purposes, then action can be taken.

As has previously been explained, our policy on rendition is clear. We have not approved and will not approve a policy of facilitating the transfer of individuals through the UK to places where there are substantial grounds to believe they would face a real risk of torture. If we were requested to assist another State in a rendition operation, and our assistance would be lawful, we would decide whether or not to assist taking into account all the circumstances. We would not assist in any case if to do so would put us in breach of UK law or our international obligations. (See also **[2006]** UKMIL **6/17–6/19**.)

(Second Report from the Foreign Affairs Committee Session 2007–08, *Global Security: Russia,* Response of the Secretary of State for Foreign and Commonwealth Affairs, Cm 7305)

Torture

6/31

In a debate on the Torture (Damages) Bill, a Justice Minister said:

Clearly, this is a matter of great significance, but it also requires us to consider various principles of international law, as well as the United Kingdom's diplomatic and legal relations with other states. I shall draw attention to certain challenges and difficulties that would need to be faced.

The Government unreservedly condemn torture in all its forms, wherever it occurs in the world. We work hard with our international partners to eradicate this abhorrent practice, although … we can never afford to be complacent. International action has been a priority for the Government since the launch of the 1998 UK anti-torture initiative. My colleagues in the Foreign and Commonwealth Office have intensified their efforts to combat torture, wherever it occurs, through diplomatic activity, practical projects and funding for research.

Between 2005 and 2007, we funded Penal Reform International to implement a project to strengthen national mechanisms to prevent torture and ill-treatment in Kazakhstan. It has established a network of public monitoring boards across the country, which were responsible for providing public control of prisons as well as helping victims of torture in pre-trial detention centres and police cells. As a result, in December 2006, three police officers were sentenced for torturing suspects in pre-trial detention centres. There are further examples of the UK's action and international action in supporting such initiatives and actions.

We abide by our commitments under international law and expect all countries to comply with their international legal obligations. We encourage other countries to adopt and to adhere to international standards in this area, particularly the United Nations Convention against Torture and the European Convention for the Prevention of Torture, which has been much spoken about in this debate. We also support the work of the Association for the Prevention of Torture, an NGO working for the ratification and implementation of the UN Convention.

We have taken the lead internationally. In 2003, we ratified the optional protocol to the UN Convention. We were the third country in the world and the first European Union country to do so. We are now close to completing the establishment of the national preventive mechanism that it requires, which will possess powers to visit unannounced any place of detention in the United Kingdom …

[I was asked] about superior orders being a defence to torture, to Section 134 of the Criminal Justice Act 1988 where the only defence to a prosecution for torture is that the pain or suffering was inflicted with lawful authority, which gives effect to Article 1 of the UN Torture Convention. I also refer … to Article 2.3 of the convention, which clearly states:

"An order from a superior officer or a public authority may not be invoked as a justification of torture".

We take seriously our obligation to give refuge to people fleeing persecution or torture, but it is important to ensure that our asylum system is fair and capable of distinguishing between legitimate and illegitimate claims.

Under the UN Convention Against Torture, states party to it are required to establish jurisdiction in their criminal law over the offence of torture wherever in the world that torture is alleged to have occurred ... Section 134 of the Criminal Justice Act 1988 fulfils this obligation in respect of the United Kingdom.. It means that if a person who is alleged to have committed torture is present in our territory, they should either be extradited to face trial overseas or tried in our domestic courts. A number of noble Lords recalled the successful prosecution in 2005 of Faryadi Zardad for torture offences committed in Afghanistan. He is now serving 20 years' imprisonment. [It has also been] pointed out that while universal criminal jurisdiction over torture is mandated by our international obligations, universal civil jurisdiction is not so required.

(There were references to the case of *Jones against Saudi Arabia* [2006] UKHL 26. The issues in the case were, first, whether state immunity applies where civil compensation is being sought for torture and, secondly, whether officials should be able to rely on the immunity of the state. The Government of Saudi Arabia argued that they were entitled to immunity under the State Immunity Act 1978 and well established rules of international law. The two leading judgments were given by Lord Bingham and Lord Hoffmann, with the rest of their Lordships concurring, and they found that an English court does not have jurisdiction to entertain proceedings brought here by claimants against a foreign state and its officials in relation to alleged torture carried out in the territory of the foreign state [where the foreign State insists on its immunity or that of its officials, Ed.]).

The general principle of international law remains that one state is not subject to the jurisdiction of another except in certain recognised circumstances. I understand the argument that the exceptional nature of torture is one where such a recognised circumstance would come to the fore. However, the exercise of extraterritorial jurisdiction, even where states and state officials are not involved, remains at the least a difficult area. States have to respect the limits imposed by international law on the authority of an individual state to apply its laws beyond its territory.

On the question of civil jurisdiction, there is as yet no evidence that states have generally recognised or given effect to any obligation to exercise universal civil jurisdiction over claims arising from alleged torture. When the United Nations Convention against Torture was negotiated, the option of creating an international civil course of action was accordingly not pursued. Furthermore, the United Nations adopted in 2004 the Convention on Jurisdictional Immunities of State and Their Property after a period of prolonged negotiation, which, as I have said, the United Kingdom[signed in 2005. That Convention also makes no exception in respect of civil actions for personal injury or death alleged to have occurred outside the territory of a state. Although the Convention is not yet in force, I recall that the noble and learned Lord, Lord Bingham, described it as,

> "the most authoritative statement available on the current international understanding of the limits of state immunity in civil cases".

[It was suggested that the passage of the Bill] would mark the beginning of a journey rather than the end. While the Bill could make it possible for those who claim to have suffered torture to seek an award of damages, it would remain essentially impossible to enforce a judgment against a foreign state. I should also point out that any attempt to seize the property or assets of a state would be particularly controversial and liable to lead to potential retaliatory action against United Kingdom interests.

[It had been argued that the potential issues regarding international relations should yield to human rights considerations, Ed.] The Minister said:

I understand the point; [it was] suggested that the importance of this Bill is that it sends a signal to the international community. I well understand that, but unilateral action in the manner proposed in the Bill might also be significantly damaging to the international relations of the United Kingdom. However, the Government are alert to the possibility that in the future a new international consensus may develop and prompt changes to the law in appropriate places. That is what happened in relation to universal criminal jurisdiction as reflected in the UN Convention against Torture.

[There was not time to proceed with the Bill in session 2007–2008. It was reintroduced in session 2008–2009, Ed.]

(HL Deb 16 May 2008 Vol 701 cs1225–1228)

Part Six: VII.C. *The individual (including the corporation) in international law—immigration and emigration, extradition, expulsion, asylum—expulsion*

6/32

In the debate on the Report of the ILC in the Sixth Committee of the General Assembly [A/63/10, Ed.], the representative of the UK said:

Turning to the topic of expulsion of aliens, we thank the Special Rapporteur, Mr Maurice Kamto, for his fourth report. As we explained in our statement last year, this is a difficult and complex issue and we remain of the view that it is a problematic topic for the Commission to address. We continue to have real doubts about this topic being one that is suitable for codification or consolidation at the present time. We therefore support the cautious approach of the Special Rapporteur in this regard.

In particular we support the Special Rapporteur's conclusion that he remains unconvinced of the advisability of preparing draft articles on issues relating to nationality. We also continue to have doubts about the appropriateness or need for a draft article on non-expulsion of nationals.

(Text supplied by FCO)

6/33 (See **6/41**)

The Home Secretary was asked what representations her Department had made in the Council of Europe on revision by international instrument of Article 3 of the European Convention of Human Rights as it applied in deportation cases. She wrote:

None. As I made clear when I wrote to the chair of the Joint Committee on Human Rights in August, the Government are not seeking to amend the text of Article 3 of the European Convention on Human Rights.

(HC Deb 7 January 2008 Vol 470 c269W)

6/34

In a debate on the Prevention of Terrorism Act 2005 (Continuance in Force of sections 1 to 9) Order, a Home Office Minister said:

If we cannot prosecute suspected terrorists and they are foreign nationals, we aim to deport them. The European Convention on Human Rights currently does not allow us to deport suspected terrorists back to their country of origin if there are grounds for believing that there is a real risk that they might be tortured or subjected to inhuman or degrading treatment on return. Therefore, to provide the necessary assurance as to treatment, we have agreed, and are continuing to negotiate, appropriate arrangements with other countries to protect deported individuals' human rights.

Separately, we are also working to persuade the European Court of Human Rights to reconsider current jurisprudence on the deportation of terrorist suspects in order to ensure that the rights of the individual are appropriately balanced by the interests of national security.

Despite these advances, there remain a very small number of suspected terrorists whom we can neither prosecute nor deport. Control orders remain the best available means of dealing with these individuals. Since their introduction in 2005, control orders have been an important part of our fight against terrorism. A tailored set of obligations, such as restrictions on their finances or communications equipment, can be applied which help to prevent, restrict and disrupt individuals engaging in terrorism-related activity.

Control orders are not imposed arbitrarily. A judge must agree that they are necessary and proportionate, and they are subject to regular and rigorous review. As of today, only 11 control orders are in force and only 31 individuals have ever been subject to a control order. They are an important tool in protecting the public from the very real threat from terrorism.

Over the past year, there has been continued support for control orders from outside government. First, there was the landmark judgment by the Law Lords in October last year. Crucially, they upheld the control order system, although we were disappointed that they did not agree with the Government on every issue.

On Article 5 of the European Convention on Human Rights, the Law Lords judged that no control order then in effect needed to be weakened. Indeed, the judgment puts the Government in a stronger position than before, as the Law Lords effectively indicated that a 16-hour curfew does not breach Article 5.

On Article 6, the judgment was more complex and has been widely misreported. The Law Lords did not say that any case before them had breached the right to a fair trial. They said that in some, possibly exceptional, cases, the current provisions in the Act might breach Article 6. The Act was therefore "read down" to ensure that the procedure adopted under it would be compatible with Article 6 in every case. They concluded that the High Court should consider the point on a case-by-case basis. This forms part of the mandatory review of each individual control order by the High Court—one of the many safeguards in place to secure the rights of the individual. We therefore remain firmly of the view that the legislation, and the order before us today, are fully compliant with the ECHR.

Secondly, the independent reviewer of the operation of the Prevention of Terrorism Act, the noble Lord, Lord Carlile of Berriew, continues to view control orders as necessary. He states that:

> "as a last resort (only), the control order system as operated currently in its non-derogating form is a justifiable and proportional safety valve for the proper protection of civil society".

Both the other statutory consultees—the Intelligence Services Commissioner and the Director-General of the Security Service—share this view. I place on record my, and the Government's, thanks to the noble Lord, Lord Carlile, for another thorough report, which I am sure will add a great deal to today's debate. A formal reply will of course be produced in due course.

Let me be clear that control orders are not ideal. They are a last resort for those involved in facilitating or executing acts of terrorism who cannot be prosecuted or deported. However, over the past year, much hard work has gone into improving them. For example, exit strategies continue to be sought for those currently on control orders. Although I am not convinced by the suggestion of the noble Lord, Lord Carlile, that there should be an arbitrary end date for individual control orders—in part because each order addresses individual risk—I am firmly of the view that control orders should be imposed for as short a time as possible, in line with the risk posed. Exit strategies are considered as an integral part of the formal quarterly review for every control order, and an order can be renewed only if it is necessary to do so. Indeed, over the past year, we have seen two control orders revoked and another two orders not renewed. Deportation is another exit strategy. Previously, nine individuals who were at one time subject to control orders have been served with notices of intention to deport, and six of them have been deported.

... there are currently five individuals who have been subject to control orders for longer than two years. Two further cases would have reached the two-year point on Saturday. However, those control orders have now lapsed, as the orders were those imposed on two of the individuals who absconded in May 2007.

[The Order was approved as SI 559/2008. See, The Government Reply to the Report by Lord Carlile of Berriew Q.C., Report on the Operation in 2007 of the Terrorism Act 2000 and of Part 1 of the Terrorism Act 2006, Cm 7429, Ed.]

(HL Deb 27 February 2008 Vol 699 cs720–721)

6/35

In a debate on the Criminal Justice and Immigration Bill, a Minister explained the purpose of certain provisions in the Bill. He said:

... these provisions are being introduced in response to a ruling by the High Court in 2006—subsequently confirmed by the Court of Appeal—in relation to the men who seized control of an aircraft on an internal flight in Afghanistan in early 2000 and forced the pilot to fly to Stansted. [The men's convictions were set aside by the Court of Appeal in 2003, Ed.]

The High Court and the Court of Appeal ruled that, as these men had won their appeals against the decision to refuse them leave to enter the United Kingdom, it was not open to the Government to leave them on a "temporary admission" because under Schedule 2 to the Immigration Act 1971 temporary admission is not intended to be used in those circumstances. [*S & Others v Secretary of State for the Home Department* [2006] EWCA Civ 1157, Ed.] In giving judgment, the Court of Appeal commented that, if the Secretary of State wanted to be able to withhold immigration leave, it was open to him—as was then the case—to legislate to that effect. The then Home Secretary announced his intention to do so, and here we now are. That intention translates into eight clauses covering some four and a half pages …

At issue is what immigration status should be accorded to an individual whose actions are such as to warrant his deportation from the UK but who cannot be removed because to do so would be contrary to our obligations under the ECHR. At present, following the ruling by the Court of Appeal, the practice is to grant short periods of leave—usually for six months at a time. At the end of the period granted, the person has to apply for further leave, his position is reviewed and, if it is still not possible to remove him, there is no option but to grant an extension of that leave.

I remind the Committee that we are talking here about people with no entitlement to remain beyond the fact that they cannot lawfully be removed. They are here not because they qualify to remain here under the Immigration Rules; they are here by default. As I say, at present there is no alternative but to grant them leave of some sort, and the practice is to grant short, time-limited periods of leave. It would be possible to grant longer periods, or even indefinite leave, but to do so would effectively be to reward bad behaviour. However, at present even the short periods of limited leave granted carry with them certain benefits, such as access to employment and to the mainstream benefits system. The result is that the group in question enjoy the advantages of an immigration leave to which they have no entitlement beyond the fact that, at present, there is no alternative. The right to work, in particular, represents a financial advantage to them. It also allows them to establish roots in the UK which may make it much harder to deport them if and when the original barrier to removal has been overcome …

The Government do not accept that we should be forced to grant immigration leave to someone whom—for good, objective reasons—we do not want in the country at all. That is the argument in a nutshell. Should the Government be compelled to grant immigration leave to those people who are liable to be deported because of their actions but who cannot be deported because their removal would breach their human rights?

This is not in any way to suggest that those rights are not important. They are; they are fundamental. Even so, there are limits to what is required, and it is perfectly legitimate to ask whether we should be forced to grant immigration leave to a person who is liable to deportation because of his conduct simply because he would face torture or ill-treatment in his country of origin and there is no other country to which he can be sent. We consider that in those circumstances it is sufficient not to remove the person concerned, but there is no need to go beyond that and to take the additional step of conferring immigration leave.

We could discuss where to draw the line. I believe that the Bill draws it in the right place; others may disagree. However, the fundamental point is, in my view, sound: there are some people who do not qualify for leave to enter or remain under the Immigration Rules and who, because of their actions, simply do not deserve to be given it. We are therefore creating a new statutory category to accommodate them.

Even if the designated person cannot be removed at the moment, removal remains the ultimate objective, and I see no justification for allowing the sort of people for whom special immigration status is intended to enjoy the benefits of immigration leave in the mean time. The future removal of the individuals concerned is a key factor. The purpose of the conditions that can be imposed is to help to maintain contact and to prevent them establishing roots in the UK which will make their eventual removal much more difficult.

It may be helpful if I remind the Committee to whom the new status is intended to apply. Clause 181 creates the power to designate foreign criminals who are liable to deportation but who cannot be removed due to a human rights barrier. This power also applies to members of a foreign criminal's immediate family—that is, their spouse or civil partner and any minor dependent children—and I should like to take a moment to explain the reason for this.

The reason—and the only reason—that the Bill provides for family members to be designated is to deal with the situation where an individual applies for leave under the Immigration Acts and his or her family members apply for leave "in line". In effect, they are saying, "My application for leave to enter or remain stands or falls with his or hers. Treat me in the same way". In those circumstances, it would be illogical for someone whose application for leave to remain rides on the coat-tails of another to end up in a better position than the person wearing the coat.

As a matter of policy, at present the Border and Immigration Agency does not grant someone who applies in line leave that is more favourable than the leave given to the principal applicant. However, unless the Bill provides for family members to be designated, that policy will be breached once the provisions in this part come into force and someone who is a principal applicant is designated. That is the only reason we have extended the provision beyond the "foreign criminal" himself or herself. I repeat the assurance given by the Minister in Committee in another place, that we will not designate family members unless we designate the main applicant. I repeat also that there is nothing to prevent family members applying for and being granted leave in their own right either before they are designated or after they have been designated.

Clause 182 defines the term "foreign criminal" for the purposes of Part 12. It includes any foreign national who has received a custodial sentence of two years or longer for any offence, or a custodial sentence of any length for one of the offences listed in the 2004 order made under Section 72 of the Nationality, Immigration and Asylum Act 2002, or who is excluded from refugee status by Article 1F of the 1951 refugee convention.

As I have just explained, for technical reasons, special immigration status will also apply to the family members of such persons where they have applied for leave "in line", but in all cases it will apply only where the foreign criminal cannot be deported for human rights reasons. Designation will not apply to British citizens, who of course cannot be deported; to recognised refugees; or to persons exercising rights under the European Community treaties.

I am aware that concern has been expressed by some commentators about the fact that exclusion under Article 1F of the refugee convention is a condition which can result in designation. They take the view that if we are going to take the serious step of refusing to grant immigration leave, we should do so only in cases where the person's wrong-doing has been established beyond reasonable doubt. The Government do not agree. To take such an approach is to apply the wrong test and to treat special immigration status as essentially a criminal justice measure. As the name suggests, special immigration status is an immigration provision that is intended to be used in cases where the person is liable to deportation but cannot be removed from the United Kingdom for human rights reasons.

I remind your Lordships of the exact wording of Article 1F, which states that the provisions of the convention,

> "shall not apply to any person with respect to whom there are serious reasons for considering that:
>
> (a) he has committed a crime against peace, a war crime or a crime against humanity, as defined in the international instruments drawn up to make provision in respect of such crimes;
>
> (b) he has committed a serious non-political crime outside the country of refuge prior to his admission to that country as a refugee;
>
> (c) he has been guilty of acts contrary to the purposes and principles of the United Nations".

Where there are serious reasons for considering that a person has acted in a way that would result in his exclusion from the refugee convention, there are, in my view, proper grounds for considering that their deportation would be "conducive to the public good", which is—as I am sure I do not need to remind the Committee—the test which applies when taking deportation decisions under Section 3(5)(a) of the Immigration Act 1971. So the sort of person we are dealing with is someone whose actions are, on the face of it, sufficiently serious to warrant deportation, but who cannot actually be removed for human rights reasons. The position at present is that if we are unable to remove such a person, we find ourselves constrained to grant them immigration leave and, with that, access to the benefits that flow from having such leave.

In my view, if there are serious reasons for considering that a person has acted in a way that leads to their exclusion from the refugee convention, which means they are denied the protection of the international community, that is just as strong a ground for deportation as a criminal conviction of the kind described in the other two conditions in this clause. It follows that we consider the case for their designation is equally strong. The Government's position is that where such people can be deported, they should be deported, and where they cannot be removed for human rights reasons, it should be possible to designate them under this part of the Bill. As Clause 183 makes clear, a designated person does not have leave to enter or remain in the United Kingdom, although he will not be regarded as being here in breach of the immigration laws …

As I said, designation is discretionary, not mandatory, and so does not have to be used in the case of someone who has been trafficked even if they have been prosecuted and received a custodial sentence for one of the offences listed in the 2004 order, and if the person wishes to challenge their designation as unreasonable, they can do so by way of judicial review.

I am also aware of the concerns of the UNHCR about Section 54 of the Immigration, Asylum and Nationality Act 2006. It expressed its concerns at the time of the 2006 Act. Our position then—and our position now—was that Section 54 was essentially declaratory and that the construction set out in that section and accepted by Parliament in passing the provision had always applied. If UNHCR is concerned that people are being excluded from the protection of the refugee convention when they should not be, the appropriate response is to challenge the decision to exclude, not to say that people who have been correctly excluded should nevertheless be granted immigration leave.

[The provisions were enacted as ss.130–137 Criminal Justice and Immigration Act 2008, Ed.]

(HL Deb 10 March 2008 Vol 699 cs1348–1352)

6/36

The Government were asked what procedures existed to ensure that victims of human trafficking who were repatriated had access to relevant civil society organizations in their countries of origin. A Minister wrote:

Victims of trafficking who have no basis of stay in the United Kingdom may be repatriated either via the government-funded voluntary assisted returns programme run by the International Organisation for Migration (IOM) or as an enforced return. However, voluntary returns are always the preferred option; removal action is only ever considered as a last resort. Victims of trafficking are routinely encouraged to make use of the assisted voluntary return (AVR) programme available to them.

The IOM's network of offices work in co-operation with local non-government organisations and generally provide specialist reintegration assistance for victims of trafficking where necessary. The assistance may include shelter, medical assistance/psychological counselling and vocational training. IOM monitor the provision of such services themselves. However, the availability of such services in a given country depends on what sort of provision the Government of that country have agreed can be made available.

There is no post-return monitoring or sustainability programme for those persons who choose not to return as part of an AVR package and whose subsequent removal from the UK is enforced.

(HL Deb 25 June 2008 Vol 702 cWA256)

6/37

A Minister made the following written statement:

Pursuant to my answer of 2 June to [a] question … (*Official Report*, 2 June, col WA15), we have continued our search for the records relating to an answer given by [a Foreign Office Minister] on 6 January 2004. [The question had been: Whether any prisoners captured in Iraq have been held within 100 miles of Diego Garcia;

if so, when were they held there; and by whom. To which the Minister replied: No prisoners captured in Iraq are, or ever have been, under detention either on Diego Garcia or on any of the islands of the British Indian Ocean Territory (BIOT), or anywhere in the territorial waters belonging to BIOT. Nor have any such prisoners been detained on board any vessel, wherever it may be, after it has in some way transited through any place in BIOT. (HL Deb 6 January 2004 Vol 656: cWA31)]

We have now located the records concerned. The answer was drafted by the Overseas Territories Department and approved by the FCO Minister concerned in the normal way. The background to this answer states that assurances on this issue were given at the annual British Indian Ocean Territory US-UK political-military talks in June 2003, and that officials had tested this assurance with the US embassy in London, the State Department in Washington and the US Commanding Officer on Diego Garcia.

(HC Deb 1 July 2008 Vol 478 cWS49)

6/38
Diplomatic Assurances

A Minister wrote:

Memoranda of understanding on deportation with assurances were signed with Jordan, Libya and Lebanon in 2005. Separate arrangements, set out in an exchange of letters in July 2006, apply in respect of Algeria.

The Government are pursuing agreements regarding deportation with assurances with a number of countries. Identification of the parties would prejudice these negotiations. Copies of any agreements concluded will be placed in the Library in due course, as has been done previously.

Since July 2006, no one has been deported to Jordan, Libya or Lebanon on grounds of either national security or unacceptable behaviour. Six men have been deported to Algeria since that date, all on national security grounds.

(HL Deb 22 July 2008 Vol 703 cWA243)

6/39

An FCO Minister was asked by the FAC about the value of diplomatic assurances since the Government had lost cases in the Court of Appeal. The Minister said:

Those Court of Appeal cases were obviously setbacks, but they were very case-specific. The assurances were thought not to be adequate in those countries at this time. We still have other cases that are moving ahead, so I do not think that the policy is dead. We do think that the courts have set the bar high, and frankly that is probably a good thing ...

Asked if he thought that it might be better simply to accept that there was an absolute bar on the possible return of deportees to a country where torture is practiced, the Minister said:

With some of the deportee cases, accepting that individuals who have done—or incited people to do—terrible things here in the UK are on our hands indefinitely is not a reasonable Government policy. There will be cases where we will prevail, but we are a country of laws and courts. The fact that we lose a couple of cases shows the strength of the procedures, rather than invalidating them all. [Q.76]

He went on:

Again, the courts have accepted the process as legitimate. They were careful to say that it was the particular conditions, in Libya in one case, and Jordan in the other, relevant to the individuals, which determined their decision. [Q.77]

[The Minister sent a note to the FAC: I said that the Jordan and Libya cases were the first to reach the Court of Appeal. Some Algerian cases have also reached the Court of Appeal so this is incorrect.]

The Minister was asked for his response to the suggestion from Human Rights Watch that the UK was trying to undermine the laws on non-refoulement, returning a person to a country that employs torture, relying on the Government's intervention in *Saadi v Italy* ECtHRs [(2008) No.37201/06].

The Minister said:

In a globalised world where we are trying to deal with cases of this kind, we must go on pressing to find a way of returning people that functions legally and works. For it to work legally, there must be the assurance that any individual being returned will have proper protection of their rights. The alternative is to accept that we are stuck with people who have this kind of history, and that is not a politically accept-able solution. [Q.80]

[See now *RB (Algeria) v Secretary of State for the Home Department* [2009] UKHL 10, upholding removals from the UK on the basis of diplomatic assurances, Ed.]

(Foreign Affairs Committee Report, Human Rights Report 2007, HC533 (2008))

6/40
The FCO wrote to the FAC following an FCO Minister's oral evidence to the Committee.

Does the Government accept that the Convention Against Torture obligation of non-refoulement is absolute and that there should never be a balancing exercise with national security when there is a risk of torture?

Article 3.1 of the Convention Against Torture is quite clear that no State Party shall expel, return ("refouler") or extradite a person to another State where there are substantial grounds for believing that he/she would be in danger of being sub-jected to torture, and the Committee established by Article 17 has made it equally clear that, where this is the case, no other considerations can be taken into account.

Whether or not there are substantial grounds for believing that a person would be in danger of being subjected to torture is a judgement that has to be made on the basis of the circumstances of the individual case, including any specific infor-mation and any assurances provided by the receiving State.

The Government has made it clear that, if there is a real danger that an individual will be subject to torture on return, we will not deport them, even if we have a framework agreement on assurances in place.

(Foreign Affairs Committee Report, Human Rights Report 2007, HC533 (2008))

6/41

The FAC had concluded in its Report on the Annual Human Rights Report 2007 that:

... in the case of *Saadi v. Italy* (ECtHRs (2008) No.37201/06), the Government clearly attempted to water down its anti-torture commitments. We also conclude that it is disturbing and surprising that such arguments were made in the name of the UK [and we believe this gives cause for serious concern. (Paragraph 72)

The Government wrote:

The Government, in its intervention in the European Court of Human Rights case of *Saadi vs. Italy*, did not attempt to water down its anti-torture commitments. The UK consistently and unreservedly condemns the use of torture. We work hard with our international partners to eradicate this abhorrent practice. The Government has made it clear that we would not deport an individual if we believed that there was a real risk of their being tortured on return.

The Government is committed to respecting and promoting human rights, not just because it is the right thing to do but also because it is one of the most effective ways to undermine terrorism. In the UK's interventions to the European Court in *Saadi v. Italy* and two other cases (*Ramzy v the Netherlands* and *A v the Netherlands*), we were not arguing that any individual should be deported no matter what risk he or she might face on return. The UK argued that it should be possible to take account of the risk posed by an individual to the community as a whole as well as the possible risk to the individual on return when considering a deportation on the grounds of national security. The UK also argued that where an applicant presents a threat to national security, stronger evidence must be adduced to prove that the applicant would be at risk of ill-treatment in the receiving country. The Court rejected these arguments and we respect their judgment. We fully expect the Court to deal with the matter in the other existing cases, to the extent it needs to, consistently with its decision in *Saadi*. We are not currently planning to make any further interventions on this issue.

(Foreign Affairs Committee Session 2007–08 Annual Report on Human Rights 2007, Response of the Secretary of State for Foreign and Commonwealth Affairs Cm 7463)

6/42

The Government were asked, further to the Prime Minister's Statement of 14 November 2007 on national security, how many of the 24 foreign nationals then subject to deportation proceedings on national security grounds *(a)* have been deported, *(b)* have not been deported following a decision by a court, *(c)* have been given the right to remain in the UK and *(d)* have cases which are outstanding. In reply, a Minister wrote:

Since the Prime Minister's statement of 14 November 2007, of the 24 foreign nationals then subject to deportation proceedings on national security grounds:

Twelve are no longer the subject of deportation proceedings following the Court of Appeal's ruling on the test cases of two Libyan nationals. Of these 12, eight previously had the right to remain in the UK and continue to do so. All 12 of the cases are under review as to their future immigration status. Twelve others remain subject to ongoing deportation proceedings and are at various stages of the appeals process.

(HC Deb 1 September 2008 Vol 479 c1553W)

Part Six: VII. D. *The individual (including the corporation) in international law—immigration and emigration, extradition, expulsion, asylum—asylum*

6/43

In reply to a question concerning Christian and other minorities in Iraq seeking asylum in the UK, a Minister wrote:

The United Kingdom considers all asylum claims, including those from Iraqi nationals, on their individual merits in accordance with our obligations under the 1951 UN Refugee Convention. All claims are considered against the background of the latest country information and country guidance case law as decided by the Independent Asylum and Immigration Tribunal.

(HC Deb 14 July 2008 Vol 479 c100W)

Part Six: VIII. *The individual (including the corporation) in international law—human rights and fundamental freedoms*

6/44
Afghanistan

The Foreign Secretary was asked about the transfer of detainees in the custody of UK forces in Afghanistan to the Afghan authorities. He wrote:

Information available to 29 January shows that a total of 74 detainees have been transferred from UK forces to the Afghan authorities under the terms of the bilateral memorandum of understanding on the transfer of detainees [See **(2007) UKMIL 6/49**, Ed.] Of those, 13 remain in Afghan custody.

The UK's bilateral memorandum of understanding on the transfer of detainees to the Afghan authorities does contain provisions about respecting the human rights of detainees.

The Afghan government has shown that it is fully aware of its obligations and takes its human rights responsibilities seriously. The arrangements for access to detainees by our officials and by human rights organisations to monitor their treatment were restated in an exchange of letters between the Afghan government and the governments of Canada, Denmark, the Netherlands, Norway, the UK and the United States in 2007.

We have a constructive relationship with the Afghan government on detention issues and are working closely with them on a number of projects to improve facilities and governance.

(HC Deb 4 February 2008 Vo 471 c758W)

6/45
Child

The Government were asked who is conducting the review of the UK's reservation against Article 37(c) of the UN Convention on the Rights of the Child; and when the review will be published. In reply, a Secretary of State wrote:

The review has been conducted by officials from the Joint Youth Justice Unit and the Ministry of Justice, to enable Ministers with responsibility for youth justice in England and Wales to decide whether or not the reservation remains relevant to the secure estate for children and young people in England and Wales. The officials' advice includes legal advice: in accordance with normal practice, we are not planning to publish it. [We shall] announce our conclusion in due course.

The reservation against Article 37(c) applies to the United Kingdom as a whole. Any decision to withdraw it would also require agreement from Scotland and Northern Ireland.

(HC Deb 7 July 2008 Vol 478 c1418–1419W)

6/46

The Government were asked what reservations the UK has entered to the United Nations Convention on the Rights of the Child and its optional protocols; and which of those reservations are under review by the Government. In reply, a Secretary of State wrote:

The Government currently hold two reservations to the United Nations Convention on the Rights of the Child. The reservations are against Article 22 and Article 37(C). The Government are currently reviewing both reservations. The Government have no reservations against the Convention's optional protocols.

(HC Deb 7 July 2008 Vol 478 c1419W)

6/47

The International Development Secretary was asked what support his Department provided to civil society in developing countries to hold their governments to account on their observance of United Nations Convention on the Rights of the Child obligations. A Minister wrote:

In several developing countries, the Department for International Development funds civil society specifically to hold governments to account for meeting commitments made under the United Nations Convention on the Rights of the Child (UNCRC). This commonly takes the form of strengthening local groups representing children to demand that governments take all available measures to make sure children's rights are respected, protected and fulfilled.

The UK Government also support child-focused international non-government organisations (NGOs) such as Save the Children and Plan International who work to strengthen international mechanisms and develop indicators to measure governments' compliance with the UNCRC and other international law.

(HC Deb 3 March 2008 Vol 472 c2079W)

6/48

The Minister for Children made the following Ministerial Statement:

On 3 October 2008 the United Nations Committee on the Rights of the Child published their Concluding Observations on the United Kingdom's report on the implementation of the United Nations Convention on the Rights of the Child (UNCRC). Publication of the Concluding Observations follows the submission of the UK Government's written report to the Committee in July 2007 and an Oral Hearing with the Committee on 23 and 24 September 2008.

The United Kingdom's delegation entered into a frank and open discussion with the Committee. This was recognised both in the Committee's closing remarks at the Oral Hearing and the Concluding Observations. I am pleased that the Committee has also recognised the significant progress we have made in the implementation of the convention and the emphasis we have placed on improving the well-being of children and young people.

I broadly welcome the Concluding Observations and, while areas of difference with the Committee remain, we will give the Committee's recommendations the careful consideration they deserve. This process will include a dialogue with non-governmental organisations and the four United Kingdom Children's Commissioners. Our "Children's Plan", published in December 2007, sets out our ambitions and strategies to tackle many of the issues the UN Committee has highlighted. Later this year we will report on progress against the commitments made in the children's plan.

(HC Deb 7 October 2008 Vol 480 c7WS)

6/49
Death Penalty

The Foreign Secretary was asked what recent discussions he had had on the use of the death penalty with the governments of *(a)* China, *(b)* Iran, *(c)* Saudi Arabia, *(d)* Pakistan, and *(e)* the USA. An FCO Minister wrote:

The UK opposes the death penalty in all circumstances as a matter of principle and we are committed to working with all EU partners towards universal abolition.

In China, we welcome the Supreme People's Court's central review of death penalty cases since 1 January 2007 which has reportedly led to a reduction in executions, but continue to urge the Chinese government to make public statistics and to reduce the scope of the death penalty. We did this most recently at the UK-China Human Rights Dialogue at the end of January. The Prime Minister also raised the death penalty with Chinese Premier Wen during his visit to China in January.

We are deeply concerned by the increasing use of the death penalty in Iran and its continued use for juvenile offenders and we regularly raise this with the Iranian authorities in bilateral meetings and through the EU. Most recently, in a meeting with the Iranian ambassador on 1 April, the Minister for the Middle East, called on Iran to limit its use of the death penalty and raised concerns about articles of Iran's draft penal code which would make apostasy punishable by death. We have supported several EU statements and demarches this year about the general use of the death penalty in Iran and individual death penalty cases.

The Minister for the Middle East raised the issue of the death penalty during his visit to Saudi Arabia in February 2008.

The UK delegation to the UN Human Rights Council raised the issue of the death penalty with Pakistan as part of the Universal Periodic Review that Pakistan underwent on 8 May. The UK delegation urged the Government of Pakistan to review the use of the death penalty, with a view to a moratorium and abolition, in order to implement the UN General Assembly resolution adopted in December 2007 calling for a moratorium on the use of the death penalty. The UK, with our EU partners, will continue to lobby the Government of Pakistan against the use of capital punishment.

Our officials in the US continue to monitor the use of the death penalty in the US and make representations bilaterally or with EU partners on specific cases where the circumstances warrant them. The EU last took action in the case of Lynd v Georgia on 2 May 2008, sending a letter to the Georgia Board of Pardons and Paroles appealing for clemency. [Lynd was executed on 6 May 2008, Ed.]

(HC Deb 22 May 2008 Vol 476 c513W)

6/50

The Foreign Secretary was asked what recent representations his Department had made to the Chinese government on the publication of statistics on its use of the death penalty. An FCO Minister wrote:

In March a Chinese court official reported that, since recovering the right of review over all death sentences, the Supreme People's Court had rejected 15 per cent of original verdicts from lower-level courts. However, unless China is more transparent about the application of the death penalty, we cannot verify its claims that the number of executions has fallen. We continue to urge China to reduce the scope of death penalty crimes and to allow transparency of statistics. We did so most recently at the UK-China Human Rights Dialogue at the end of January.

(HC Deb 22 May 2008 Vol 476 c514W)

6/51

The Government were asked whether the Slovenian presidency of the European Union had received a response from the Government of Iran following its statement of 4 June on the death sentences imposed on Behnood Shojaee, Mohammad Fadaei, and Saeed Jazee, who were aged under 18 at the time of their alleged offences; and whether they would make representations to the Government of Iran about their obligations under international covenants on death sentences. An FCO Minister wrote:

Following the 4 June statement about planned juvenile executions in Iran, the EU presidency issued a further statement on 10 June calling for the Iranian authorities to halt the execution of juvenile offenders Mohammad Fadaei, Behnood Shojaee and Saeed Jazee. The embassy of the Republic of Slovenia in Tehran also spoke to an official from the Iranian Judiciary to make further representations and draw attention to the EU's statement. The executions of Fadaei and Shojaee, which had been scheduled for 11 June, were subsequently stayed for one month to allow time for further negotiations with the respective families. However, a 17 year-old juvenile offender, Mohammad Hassanzadeh, was executed on 10 June and Saeed Jazee's execution remains scheduled for 25 June.

The position of the EU and the Government on the death penalty is clear, and the execution of juveniles is against all international human rights standards. The EU issued a further statement on 13 June which strongly condemned the execution of Mohammad Hassanzadeh in direct contravention of international law and Iran's obligations as set out in the International Covenant on Civil and Political Rights and the Convention on the Rights of the Child. The statement reiterated that there is "absolutely no justification for the use of the death penalty by the Iranian authorities in the case of juvenile offenders" and called for an end to all executions of juvenile offenders, a moratorium on the use of the death penalty in all instances and for Iran to bring her own legislation in line with the international human rights conventions into which she entered freely and indeed ratified.

We will continue to make representations to the Government of Iran regarding their obligations on these matters.

(HL Deb 30 June 2008 Vol 703 cWA15)

6/52 (See also 6/22–6/27)
Detention—British Indian Ocean Territory

The Government were asked what reports his Department had received of allegations relating to the USS Peleliu; and what discussions he had had with his US counterpart on the matter. In reply, a Minister wrote:

We have received allegations relating to detainees being held on US naval vessels, including the USS Peleliu, from human rights non-governmental organisations. We have asked the US to clarify their position on detainees being held on ships and to verify previous assurances that detainees had never been held on ships in the territorial waters of Diego Garcia.

The US confirmed to us that no detainees have been held on ships within Diego Garcia's territorial waters since 11 September 2001. They also informed us that they do not operate detention facilities for terrorist suspects onboard ships, although US naval vessels were used in the early days of Operation Enduring Freedom in Afghanistan to screen and temporarily hold a very small number of individuals pending their transfer to land-based detention facilities. These ships were not located within the territorial waters of Diego Garcia. We have no information to suggest that these ships were supplied from the island.

(HC Deb 6 October 2008 Vol 480 c220W)

6/53

The Foreign Secretary was asked if he would place in the Library the response received to the request made to the US Secretary of State for clarification on a number of specific issues about detention on and transit through Diego Garcia. In reply, a Minister wrote:

[T]he Foreign Secretary's letter to US Secretary of State Rice relating to the two renditions through Diego Garcia in 2002, the US have informed us that:

there have been no other instances in which US intelligence flights landed in the UK, our overseas territories or the Crown dependencies, with a detainee on board since 11 September 2001;

no detainees have been held on ships within Diego Garcia's territorial waters since 11 September 2001; and

no non-US service personnel have been held on Diego Garcia or within its territorial waters since 11 September 2001.

The US have also underlined their firm understanding that there will be no rendition through the UK, our overseas territories and Crown dependencies or airspace without first receiving our express permission.

(HC Deb 6 October 2008 Vol 480 c220W-221W)

6/54
Disabilities Convention

During a debate on the Disabilities Convention, it was put to the Government that:

It is easy enough to ratify the Convention, but if it is amended with all sorts of qualifications and reservations it could become meaningless.

In reply, a Minister stated:

[That] would be absolutely right if we had a whole raft of reservations that fundamentally undermined the Convention; but only reservations that are compatible with the Convention can be made. I stress again that it is important that, when we ratify the Convention, we are in a position fully to implement it. That is why we must have this review of our laws and procedures.

(HL Deb 8 July 2008 Vol 703 c631)

6/55

Her Majesty's Government was asked how the Department for International Development plans to ensure that his Department meets its obligation under the Convention on the Rights of Persons with Disabilities to *(a)* make development assistance inclusive and *(b)* include disabled people in all programme evaluations and reviews on ratification of the Convention. In reply, a Minister wrote:

The information is as follows:

(a) Inclusive development assistance

The Department for International Development (DFID) is aware of the importance of international cooperation [co-operation] as stated in Article 32 of the UN Convention. We understand the need to find ways to promote the inclusion of disabled people into mainstream development as well as looking for ways to build the capacity of representative organisations of disabled people. Our Civil Society Challenge Fund identifies disability as a cross-cutting issue so all applications need to demonstrate how they are engaging with disabled people. The latest round of applications saw a record number of projects with disability as the main focus (22 out of 145) which indicates that more international organisations are becoming aware of the need to promote the rights of disabled people.

We are supporting several initiatives aimed at increasing the capacity of disabled people's organisations. We have a Programme Partnership Agreement (PPA) with UK-based Action on Disability and Development which is working directly with disabled people's organisations (DPOs) in eight countries across Africa and Asia. Recently we also committed to providing substantial support to a new Disability Rights Fund (DRF) set up to empower DPOs to participate effectively in the implementation and monitoring mechanisms set out in the UN Convention. This is one of the first foundations to support organisations run by disabled people in the developing world.

As suggested by Article 32 DFID is also looking at ways to increase the amount of disability related research. We are currently funding the Southern Africa Federation of Disabled People Research Project (SRP) which is an innovative project designed and run by disabled people in the region. This project is helping local DPOs to research issues linked to disability and poverty and is already starting to produce evidence of the kinds of barriers disabled people face when trying to access basic services.

(b) Inclusion of disabled people in programme reviews and evaluations

All major country and thematic reviews are now quality assured to ensure they will address the exclusion of different groups. This includes disability as well as for example, gender and people affected by HIV and AIDS. Currently we are developing a new strategy for evaluation which will include reference to disability. The strategy will be available for public consultation.

(HC Deb 6 October 2008 Vol 480 c123W-124W)

6/56
Discrimination

The Foreign Secretary was asked what steps the Government had taken with its international counterparts to end the criminalization of homosexuality in other countries. An FCO Minister wrote:

The Government have adopted an international policy of prioritising work on lesbian, gay, bisexual and transgender rights where there is complete illegality, or there are moves to introduce criminalisation, and seek ways to lobby for [run-on] decriminalisation.

The then Minister for Trade, Investment and Foreign Affairs and I, as the then Deputy Minister for Women and Equality, issued a joint statement pledging our support for worldwide protests against homophobia planned to mark the International Day against Homophobia on 17 May 2007.

The UK has long been at the forefront of encouraging the EU to speak out in favour of promoting and protecting the rights of lesbian, gay, bisexual and transgendered people. At the Organization for Security and Co-operation in Europe Human Dimension Implementation Meeting in September 2007, the EU delivered a speech that condemned the fact that relationships between adults of the same sex are criminal in two participating states, namely Uzbekistan and Tajikistan.

In the past year we have also lobbied in support of the UN-Economic and Social Council continuing to grant consultative status to lesbian, gay, bisexual and trans-gender non-governmental organisations. We also lobbied to persuade Rwanda not to criminalise same sex acts in the revised penal code, and Nigeria not to outlaw advocacy in favour of lesbian, gay, bisexual and transgender rights.

An FCO Minister intends to raise this issue when he visits the Human Rights Council in Geneva.

We also raise this issue bilaterally. For example, our high commissioner in Singapore went to see Singapore's Attorney General on 26 October 2007 about various human rights issues, including the decriminalisation of homosexuality.

(HC Deb 5 March 2008 Vol 472 c2569W)

6/57

A Minister wrote:

We strongly support the right to freedom of religion or belief, including full imple-mentation of those norms laid out in the 1981 UN Declaration on the Elimination of all Forms of Intolerance and of Discrimination Based on Religion or Belief. We condemn all instances of violence and discrimination against individuals and groups because of their faith or belief, wherever they happen or whatever the religion of the individual or group concerned. We have made representations in several countries bilaterally and in conjunction with EU partners. More detailed information is contained in the Foreign and Commonwealth Office's Annual Report on Human Rights that can be found at:

<www.fco.gov.uk/resources/en/pdf/human-rights-report-2007>.

(HC Deb 2 July 2008 Vol 478 c1007W)

6/58
Female genital mutilation

During a debate in the House of Commons, a Minister said:

The UK Government condemn female genital mutilation as an extreme violation of women's and girls' human rights—a violation to which the World Health Organisation estimates up to 140 million women and girls have been subjected.

We work through international organisations to eradicate the practice, which is now a criminal offence in the UK.

(HC Deb 7 October 2008 Vol 480 c132W)

6/59
Guantanamo

An FCO Minister was asked by the FAC what could be done about non-EU national detainees in Guantanamo who could not be returned to their countries of nationality because they were not accepted by their Governments or because there was a risk that if they were returned, they would be seriously ill-treated. The Minister said:

We think that this is in a sense a self-made problem. Once you take people out of normal legal process and put them in something like Guantanamo, it becomes very hard to undo and get them back into a proper legal process that allows conventional solutions between the US and other countries about whether people should be returned. We have probably more than carried our weight on this. We requested the return of the so-called five British residents, although as you know, not all of them had a right to live here. We were trying to do our bit to deplete the case load. Certainly we have kept a careful eye on others. You will recall that there are at least two who might have come back but did not. We are trying to work with the US wherever we can be helpful to bring down that case load. We remain concerned about their habeas corpus rights in the meantime. [Q.84]

It was put to the Minister that he had said that the Government had requested the return of the five non-British citizens but only three of them had come because of the reluctance of the US to release the other two.

The Minister said:

That is correct, due to security concerns ... I do not think that you could possibly argue that the reason Guantanamo remains open is solely that there is nowhere to put people. That is one factor but there are also, in American eyes, hard-core security cases for which they have not found another solution. [Qs.87, 88]

(Foreign Affairs Committee Report, Human Rights Report 2007, HC533 (2008))

6/60

In its Report on the Annual Human Rights Report 2007, the FAC had concluded that:

13 overdue closure of the detention facilities at Guantánamo Bay. We welcome the Government's representations on behalf of the five British residents in Guantanamo Bay. Given its decision to intervene in their cases, we recommend that the Government should express particular concern over the prospective trial of Binyam Mohamed under the Military Commissions Act and lobby strongly against any use of the death penalty if he is found guilty. We recommend that the Government should continue to press for the return of Binyam Mohamed and Shaker Aamer to the UK. (Paragraph 77)

The Government wrote:

The Government notes the Committee's conclusion on the role that the European Union could play in assisting the United States to close the detention facility at Guantanamo Bay. We will continue and where possible, ramp up, our engagement with EU Member States on this issue.

Our position on the death penalty is well known. However, our present understanding is that the Military Commissions Prosecutors at Guantanamo Bay have indicated that they will ask for a sentence of life imprisonment if Mr Mohamed is found guilty by a Military Commission. That said, it is far from clear that the jury would agree to such a sentence, as the recent *Hamdan* case illustrates.

The Government continues to press for the release of Mr Mohamed from Guantanamo Bay and return to the UK. In parallel to the current Judicial Review proceedings brought by Mr Mohamed's lawyers relating to information held by the Government which may assist him in a future Military Commission trial, we have also gone to considerable lengths to ensure he is able to access this information through the US legal system. The Government's position on the Military Commissions Act remains that we have outstanding concerns about a number of its aspects.

We are no longer in active negotiations for the return of Shaker Aamer to the UK although we continue to discuss his case with the US authorities. Our request for his release and return to the UK remains open should the US position change.

[See, *Mohamed, R (on the application of) v Secretary of State for Foreign & Commonwealth Affairs* [2008] EWHC 2048 (Admin); *Mohamed, R (on the application of) v Secretary of State for Foreign & Commonwealth Affairs (3)* [2008] EWHC 2519 (Admin); *Mohamed, R (on the application of) v Secretary of State for Foreign & Commonwealth Affairs* [2009] EWHC 152 (Admin); *BM, R (on the application of) v Secretary of State for Foreign & Commonwealth Affairs* [2009]EWHC 571 (Admin), Ed.]

(Foreign Affairs Committee Session 2007–08 Annual Report on Human Rights 2007, Response of the Secretary of State for Foreign and Commonwealth Affairs Cm 7463)

6/61
The Defence Secretary was asked what the Government's policy was on recording *(a)* requests for the transfer of individuals to the detention facility at Guantanamo Bay and *(b)* the transfer of individuals to the detention facility at Guantanamo Bay for which the UK Government's consent was not requested. He wrote:

Any request made by the US authorities for approval to transfer to Guantanamo Bay an individual previously detained by UK forces but passed into their jurisdiction would be recorded …. we have no record of any such requests having been made and no record of any such individual being transferred without our consent.

(HC Deb 31 January 2008 Vol 471 c524W)

6/62

During a debate in the House of Commons, a Minister said:

In the US, we have had serious discussions with the Administration on all aspects of counter-terrorism and human rights issues, including rendition, Guantanamo Bay and the handling of detainees. The US is well aware of our views on water-boarding, for example, and has actively engaged in a dialogue with us on the issues. That frank approach helped secure the release in 2004 and 2005 of all nine of the British nationals detained at Guantanamo Bay as well as four individuals who had formerly resided lawfully in the UK. Continued close co-operation with the US is critical to our ability to counter the threat posed to the UK by global terrorism. Dialogue on the importance of human rights to our counter-terrorism efforts is a critical part of that.

(HC Deb 13 October 2008 Vol 480 c571)

6/63
Humanitarian intervention

In the debate on the Report of the ILC [A/63/10, Ed.] in the Sixth Committee of the General Assembly, the representative of the UK said:

In relation to Chapter IX of the Report on the protection of persons in the event of disasters, the United Kingdom welcomes the careful consideration given by the Commission to the scope and parameters of this relatively new but important topic. We also thank the Special Rapporteur, Mr. Valencia-Ospina, for the thorough and thoughtful treatment he has given in his report to the preliminary issues raised.

At this early stage, the United Kingdom will address some general comments to the issues identified by the Commission and the Special Rapporteur. No doubt, as the Commission's work progresses, there will be suitable opportunities in the future to provide more detailed views.

The regularity with which the international community faces disasters that adversely affect large populations is, [run-on] unfortunately, too frequent. The United Kingdom recognises that the needs of affected persons are best addressed when those involved in the provision of relief and assistance—States, international organisations, non-governmental organizations, commercial entities—operate and coordinate [co-ordinate] in accordance with appropriate and agreed principles and practices. We anticipate that the Commission's work will provide useful guidance to States and other actors engaged in disaster relief. In particular, the United Kingdom would welcome the identification of areas of common ground on important aspects of disaster relief, such as: preventative measures, readiness and capacity building; the co-ordination of actors providing assistance and relief; the provision of technical assistance and expertise in addition to assistance to meet the immediate humanitarian needs of affected persons; and, reasonable and appropriate cost-sharing arrangements between States providing and receiving disaster assistance.

The United Kingdom that, as recently as November 2007, the 30th International Conference of the Red Cross and Red Crescent adopted *Guidelines for the*

Domestic Facilitation and Regulation of International Disaster Relief and Initial Recovery Assistance. The United Kingdom supports the Guidelines and greatly values the preparatory work undertaken by The International Federation of Red Cross and Red Crescent Societies. We hope the Commission, without duplicating this work, will take account of the Guidelines and their reception and use by States and others engaged in international disaster relief.

The United Kingdom does not see any reason in principle for the Commission to restrict the scope of this topic to *natural* disasters. Recognising the difficulty in distinguishing disasters caused by natural phenomenon from those caused by human activity, and acknowledging that disasters may have multiple and complex causes, its seems appropriate for the scope of the topic to be shaped by factors such as the nature, magnitude, imminence and duration of the threat posed by disasters, the needs of those affected, the capacity of the affected State to deal with the disaster effectively, and the role and co-ordination of actors, rather than the cause or causes of disasters. No doubt the Commission can take account of relevant, existing work, for example in the nuclear and maritime fields.

Notwithstanding this broad scope, we agree with the views expressed by the Special Rapporteur and some members that the protection of persons in armed conflict should remain outside the scope of the Commission's work, given its primary regulation by international humanitarian law. Similarly, we would urge that in developing principles of broad application care is taken not to undermine or hinder existing regimes for responding to specific kinds of disasters of aspects thereof. The United Kingdom also considers assistance provided by States to their nationals abroad pursuant to established mechanisms and practices, such as consular assistance, to be distinct from the humanitarian relief and assistance provided generally to all persons who are victims of a disaster, which is the subject of this topic.

We note from the Report that the origin of the term "protection" in the title of this topic remains unclear. The United Kingdom is reluctant to draw any particular interpretation of the topic based on the use of the term. We would encourage the Commission to consider the term as generally synonymous with "relief" or "assistance".

With regard to the substantive principles highlighted in the Report, the United Kingdom would urge the Commission to approach the notion of a right to humanitarian assistance with caution, particularly given the need to respect the principles of humanity, sovereignty and non-intervention.

Finally, regarding the form of the Commission's work, the United Kingdom believes that the codification or progressive development of comprehensive and detailed rules is likely to be unsuitable for this topic, particularly given the relative scarcity of applicable treaties in force and the general absence of rules of customary international law arising in this context. In our view, the development of non-binding guidelines or a framework of principles for States and others engaged in disaster relief is more likely to be of practical value and enjoy widespread support and acceptance.

(Text supplied by FCO)

6/64
ICCPR

The Government were asked whether they would accept the right of individual petition under the Optional Protocol to the United Nations International Covenant on Civil and Political Rights. In reply, a Minister wrote:

The Government remain to be convinced of the practical value to the United Kingdom citizen of rights of individual petition to the United Nations. The UN committees that consider petitions are not courts, and they cannot award damages, or produce a legal ruling on the meaning of the law. In 2004, we acceded to the Optional Protocol to the Convention on the Elimination of All Forms of Discrimination Against Women. One of our reasons for doing so was to enable us to consider, on a more empirical basis, the merits of the right of individual petition. We are currently reviewing the United Kingdom's experience under the optional protocol.

(HL Deb 16 July 2008 Vol 703 cWA176)

6/65

The Government were asked how they considered the United Nations Human Rights Committee and the international community should deal with violations of human rights by the lower tiers of government in federal systems of government. A Minister wrote:

When a federal state becomes party to a human rights treaty, all parts of that state are bound by its provisions. Article 50 of the International Covenant on Civil and Political Rights (ICCPR) states that "the provisions of the present Covenant shall extend to all parts of federal States without any limitations or exceptions".

The UN Human Rights Committee, set up to monitor adherence to the ICCPR, should deal with violations by all tiers of government in the same way. In advance of a state's examination, the committee selects five members of the committee to look into that state's record. Drawing on the periodic report prepared by the state under review, they are able to consult widely, including using the UN network of experts and special rapporteurs, to help determine a list of issues that will be put to the state as well as the questions that the committee will ask on the day of the examination. Non-Governmental Organisations are also able to feed their concerns in to the UN Human Rights Committee in advance of the oral examination.

In addition, when a state fails to comply with its obligations, other states can raise concerns in the UN Human Rights Council or in the UN General Assembly, either by making statements, formulating resolutions or calling for special sessions or action by special procedures.

A new innovation in the UN Human Rights Council is the creation of a universal periodic review which is a state-to-state peer review mechanism with every UN country's human rights record being examined over a four-year period, on a rolling basis. This process has just started. The UK is aiming to ensure that all states participate actively in the process and use it as an opportunity to be self-critical about their own human rights record and commit to make improvements. It will take time and effort to build this system into a mechanism that can deliver real improvements in the human rights situation on the ground. However, the UK was one of the first to undergo the process and was therefore in a privileged position to be able to lead by example. We are now working with other states coming up for review to encourage them to engage positively in the process.

(HL Deb 29 September 2008 Vol 703 csWA398-WA399)

6/66
Iran

[These items about Iran are examples of similar answers about human rights concerns in individual foreign States. They are not comprehensively reproduced in UKMIL because the details are readily available in the FCO's Human Rights Report—<www.fco.gov.uk/resources/en/pdf/human-rights-report-2008>, Ed.]

In its reply to the FAC Report, *Global Security: Iran*, the Government said that:

It is deeply concerned by the progressive deterioration in the human rights situation in Iran, particularly the increase in the use of the death penalty and its continued use against juvenile offenders, the reappearance of flogging, stoning and amputation sentences, growing pressure on human rights defenders and increased censorship of print and electronic media. We are disappointed by Iran's refusal to engage constructively with the international community to address these concerns. In the absence of any genuine commitment on the part of the Iranian Government to improve the situation we, along with our EU partners, continue to raise our concerns about these issues with them on a regular basis. In 2007, the EU raised human rights concerns with the Iranian authorities twenty-eight times in meetings and statements, and we did so bilaterally on at least eight occasions. We also encourage debate and action in UN fora, and for the last five years have supported a resolution on the human rights situation in Iran at the UN General Assembly. This resolution was adopted in December 2007 for the fifth consecutive year, highlighting the strength of international concern at the situation.

The Government welcomes and takes note of the Committee's recommendation that it should ensure that human rights are not treated as a secondary concern to the nuclear issue, and recognises the concerns about this. The Government agrees that treating human rights as a secondary concern to other issues would be counterproductive. The Government remains committed to a broad policy approach towards Iran, which is designed to address a range of concerns including human rights, proliferation, support for terrorism and role in the wider region. Our policy, in respect of each of these concerns, is aimed at encouraging Iran to take its place as a responsible member of the international community that can be relied upon to respect its international obligations (including the human rights conventions that it has signed). We will continue to attach importance to human rights alongside the nuclear issue and other concerns.

The Iranian Government often claims that international concern about human rights in the country is an attempt to discredit and undermine the Islamic Republic, rather than a reflection of its failure to meet its freely undertaken human rights commitments. In that context the Government is grateful for the Committee's analysis of the situation, as an independent Parliamentary body, and we greatly welcome the fact that the Committee raised its own concerns with Iranian inter-locutors during the course of the members' visit to Iran.

We fully agree with the Committee that sanctions are acting as a disincentive for Iran to continue with its nuclear programme, and that a united front from the UN Security Council and the EU is extremely important in holding Iran to its obligations, as demonstrated recently with the adoption of UNSCR 1803 with a vote of 14-0, with one abstention. We judge that the sanctions introduced so far have sent a clear political signal to the Iranian regime. We will continue to work closely with our UN and EU colleagues on this issue.

We have always made clear that sanctions are not an end in themselves, but they are an important means for the international community to make clear that Iran's current policies are unacceptable and will entail an increasing cost for Iran if they do not change course. Ultimately, our aim is to present Iran's leaders with a clear choice between co-operation, and a renewed relationship with the interna-tional community, or further isolation.

While there is a clear risk that the sanctions regime could allow some in the regime to deflect attention from Iran's economic problems, it is worth noting that the economic policies of the Government are the subject of regular public criticism. Even the Supreme Leader himself recently criticised the Government's initial position on the distribution of domestic gas supplies. But the limited preelection debate did not focus on the nuclear question.

(Fifth Report of the Foreign Affairs Committee Session 2007–08, *Global Security: Iran*: Response of the Secretary of State for Foreign and Common-wealth Affairs Cm 7361, paras. 35–40)

6/67

The Foreign Secretary was asked what representations he had made to the Iranian authorities in respect of the Iranian Government's proposed Bill for Islamic penal law, with particular reference to section 5 and those of non-Muslim faiths. An FCO Minister wrote:

We are aware that a new draft Islamic penal code is currently being considered by the Iranian Parliament. We have concerns about this draft law; in particular the provisions set out in section 5 in relation to apostasy, heresy and witchcraft, which stipulate that these offences should be punishable by death. If the draft is adopted, it would be the first time that the death penalty is set down in Iran's criminal law for apostasy. We are concerned that these articles would constitute a violation of Iran's international human rights obligations, such as the right to freedom of reli-gion and belief, and the provision that in countries that retain death penalty, the sentence of death may be imposed only for the most serious crimes. We are par-ticularly concerned about the impact the new law, if adopted, would have on non-Muslim faiths in Iran. We are following developments closely and are currently discussing with our EU partners what representations to make on this matter.

He wrote further about the protection of the Baha'i community in Iran:

The Government remain very concerned by the situation of the Baha'i commu-nity in Iran. The Baha'i faith is not recognised as an official minority religion under the Iranian Constitution and Iranian Baha'is face systematic discrimination and persecution. We regularly raise our concerns about the treatment of Baha' is with the Iranian authorities, bilaterally and through the EU. On 22 January, the EU presidency, with strong UK support, raised specific concerns about the treatment of the Baha'i community in Iran during a meeting with the Iranian Ministry of Foreign Affairs. In this meeting the EU expressed opposition to all forms of discrimination, in particular regarding freedom of religion. Most recently, on 7 February, the EU presidency issued a public statement expressing concern about the deteriorating situation of the Baha'i minority. We have also taken action at the UN; in December 2007 the UN General Assembly adopted a resolution about the human rights situation in Iran. The resolution, which was co-sponsored by the UK and all other EU member states, expressed very serious concern about increasing discrimination against religious minorities in Iran and the situation of the Baha'is in particular. We will continue to urge the Iranian authorities to uphold the right to freedom of religion and belief as described in Article 18 of the International Covenant on Civil and Political Rights, to which Iran is a state party.

(HC Deb 22 February 2008 Vol 472 c1057W-1058W)

6/68

The Government were asked if the serious concerns about the treatment of Baha'is in Iran warranted an emergency resolution by the Human Rights Council. An FCO Minister said:

I agree that it warrants one; we will have to consider whether we can achieve it. It is possible to ask for a special session of an emergency resolution at the Human Rights Council, but to date the way that we have had most success on Iran, including on the Baha'is issue, has been through the third committee of the UN General Assembly. We have used the Human Rights Council to raise issues of the treatment of the Baha'is, using the thematic special rapporteurs …

(HL Deb 22 May 2008 Vol 701 c1556)

6/69

The Government were asked about its policy of returning Christians to Iran. A Minister said:

We recognise that persons who actively display their faith in public may attract adverse attention from the Iranian [run-on] authorities and we believe that they have an absolute right legally to show their faith publicly. However, we have not found—the Country of Origin Information Service looked into this—that there is systematic persecution of them all. Current case law from the Asylum and Immigration Tribunal concludes that an ordinary convert will not face persecution. The issue of Christian converts was closely considered again as a result of a hearing in May 2008 [See *SZ and JM (Christians, FS confirmed) Iran CG* [2008] UKAIT 00082 (12 November 2008), Ed.]. We will alter our guidance if necessary based on the awaited determination from that study and review.

The COI Service—gathers together all the data, which are compiled from a wide range of sources, including the UN High Commissioner for Refugees, human rights organisations, NGOs, news, media and the Foreign and Commonwealth Office. The data are updated frequently and significant changes in country conditions are communicated quickly to decision-makers. It would be a little over the top if I said that we are absolutely sure all the time that every single bit of evidence is there, but we try to get all the evidence that there is.

(HL Deb 9 June 2008 Vol 702 cs363–364)

6/70

The Foreign Secretary was asked what representations he had made to the Iranian Government on its practice of holding peaceful dissenters in detention without trial under national security legislation. An FCO Minister wrote:

We are very concerned by the growing clampdown on dissent in Iran, including through the use of national security legislation.

In the last year, a large number of human rights defenders have been accused of

"acting against national security".

This has included trade unionists, such as Mansour Ossanlou and Mahmud Salehi, peaceful protesters including teachers protesting for a living wage, a large number of women arrested in spring/summer 2007 for protesting in favour of equal rights, and other human rights activists such as Emaddedin Baghi, an anti-death penalty campaigner.

Others have been sentenced for related offences such as

"propaganda against the system"

Most recently, a group of 54 Baha'is, but also a number of students arrested in July 2007 in connection with an article in a student magazine.

We have raised all of these cases through the EU, highlighting the fact that individuals have essentially been sentenced for non-violent protest, and calling on the Iranian Government to support the right to freedom of expression, as it is committed to under the International Covenant on Civil and Political Rights.

The UN General Assembly passed a resolution about the human rights situation in Iran in December last year [A/62/168 (73-53-55), Ed.], expressing very serious concern about

"ongoing, systemic and serious restrictions of freedom of peaceful assembly and association, and freedom of opinion and expression ... and increasing harassment, intimidation and persecution of political opponents and human rights defenders from all sectors of Iranian society".

(HC Deb 4 February 2008 Vol 471 c763W)

6/71

The Foreign Secretary was asked about representations made by the Government to the Government of Iran about the death penalty. An FCO Minister wrote:

The Government remain deeply concerned by the increasing use of capital punishment in Iran. We regularly make representations to the Government of Iran, in our bilateral contacts and through the EU, to express general concern about the use of the death penalty in Iran and to raise individual execution cases. In 2007, the EU presidency did this on more than 20 occasions in both meetings and public statements. The EU has issued two further declarations on the death penalty in Iran already this year. We also discuss human rights issues bilaterally with Iranian officials in London and Tehran. In the last 12 months we have raised serious concerns about the use of death penalty on seven separate occasions. This has included specific instances when capital punishment has been carried out in Iran, for example the executions of Mohammad Moussavi, Jafar Kiani, Makwan Moloudzadeh and Mohammad Reza Tork.

We are extremely worried by the growing numbers of executions taking place in Iran. We understand that approximately 300 executions were carried out in 2007, compared with 177 in 2006 and 94 in 2005. This has included growing numbers of public and collective executions (eg the execution of two men in central Tehran in August 2007), and the first confirmed execution by stoning for five years in July 2007. Iran continues to execute juvenile offenders—at least four were put to death in 2007. We have concerns that not all death sentences are the result of a fair trial and that capital punishment continues to be applied for charges such as adultery, rape and drug related offences. The Government will continue to raise concerns with the Iranian authorities about executions and the use of the death penalty in Iran. We will continue to press Iran to uphold its international human rights obligations including the International Covenant on Civil and Political Rights which states that

"in countries which have not abolished the death penalty, the sentence of death may be imposed only for the most serious crimes"

and that

"no-one shall be subjected to torture or to cruel, inhuman or degrading treatment or punishment".

The EU presidency, with strong UK support, has issued two statements about the use of the death penalty in Iran this year.

(HC Deb 26 February 2008 Vol 472 c1372W-1373W)

6/72

The Foreign Secretary was asked what representations he had made to the Government of Iran on its decision to prevent reformist candidates from standing in the recent elections. An FCO Minister wrote:

The UK strongly supports the EU presidency statement of 15 March 2008 which said that the recent parliamentary elections in Iran were 'neither free nor fair' and that 'the Iranian people deserve a genuine democratic choice about their country's future'. We were deeply disappointed that Iran's Interior Ministry and Guardian Council disqualified over a third of all prospective candidates who registered to stand, including a large proportion of reformist candidates. This denied the Iranian electorate their right to choose from candidates representing the full range of political views in their country and make a genuine democratic choice about how they are governed. We do not wish to take sides in Iran's internal debates, but together with the EU we will continue to stand up for the internationally recognised principles to which many Iranians aspire including freedom of speech and transparent, genuinely democratic and accountable government.

(HC Deb 27 March 2008 Vol 474 c407W)

6/73

The Foreign Secretary was asked what steps he *(a)* had taken and *(b)* planned to take at the United Nations on the statements made by the President of Iran on denial of the Holocaust. An FCO Minister wrote:

The Government have consistently condemned President Ahmadinejad's statements questioning the Holocaust, and has made clear that these statements are wholly unacceptable, abhorrent, and have no place in civilised political debate. In December 2006, under the guise of an academic exercise, the Iranian Government hosted a conference to which they invited a number of well-known Holocaust deniers. The aim of the conference was to cast doubt on whether the Holocaust took place in an attempt to undermine Israel's existence. Former Prime Minister ... Tony Blair, publicly condemned the conference in the strongest terms and I summoned the Iranian Ambassador to express the Government's anger at the event. In January 2007 the UN General Assembly adopted a resolution condemning without reservation any denial of the Holocaust. The UK strongly supported this resolution. Iran was the only country that chose to disassociate itself from the consensus shared by all other UN members on this issue.

(HC Deb 5 March 2008 Vol 472 c2571W)

6/74

The Government were asked whether they would make representations to the European Union to deproscribe the People's Mujaheddin Organisation of Iran. An FCO Minister said:

The House will be aware that the People's Mujaheddin Organisation of Iran is currently on the domestic list of proscribed organisations. The House might also be aware that the Proscribed Organisations Appeal Commission recently determined that it should be removed from this list. Proscription at the EU level is based in part on the UK's domestic proscription. Her Majesty's Government are appealing the decision of the Proscribed Organisations Appeal Commission and the domestic proscription will remain in force until that appeals process is complete. [The Court of Appeal rejected the Home Secretary's appeal—*Secretary of State for the Home Department v Lord Alton of Liverpool & Ors* [2008] EWCA Civ 443, Ed.]...

We continue to believe that the PMOI was responsible for a number of serious military attacks over a very long period of time and that its disarming was entirely pragmatic—in the event of the coalition forces forcing it to disarm after the intervention in Iraq. We have seen no evidence that the organisation has publicly renounced violence and terrorism. We have to be consistent in our views of terrorists. When we like the people whom terrorists attack, we call them "terrorists"; when it is the civilians of Iran who are attacked, we have a bad habit of thinking of them as liberation fighters. Terrorism and its tactics are objectionable irrespective of the target.

The Government were asked whether the Minister could assure the House that the Government were consistent in their definition of terrorists? We have had a great variety of exiled groups in London—Tamils, Kurds, people from the north and south Caucasus and so on. We host those groups, although a number of them support opposition groups in their own countries that are not always non-violent.

The Minister said:

In the case of the Tamils, the LTTE is a proscribed organisation. It is quite difficult determining which groups in this country fall on which side of the line—and which support peaceful change in their countries and which support violent change and finance it. We look very carefully at that issue on a continuing basis.

… we have always objected, most recently in the case of Ireland, to unwarranted attacks on civilian targets. There is a big difference between military campaigns that fall within the Geneva conventions and the rest of international law and abusive campaigns that target asymmetrically civilians. I hope we have a consistent policy towards such groups.

(HL Deb 5 February 2008 Vol 698 cs948–950)

[The Government introduced an order deproscribing POMI after the appeal, The Terrorism Act 2000 (Proscribed Organisations) (Amendment) Order 2008 No. 1645, Ed.]

6/75

Later, the Government were asked how they had voted on the proposal to keep the People's Mujaheddin Organisation of Iran on the European Union's list of banned terrorist organisations at the Council of Ministers meeting on 16 July. An FCO Minister said:

The continued listing of PMOI on the new EU list of persons and entities subject to the EUCT assets freeze was supported in the Council of Ministers by the overwhelming majority of member states. The renewed listing was based on new information brought to the Council's attention by another EU member state. However, respecting the UK court judgment, we abstained in the vote.

The Minister continued:

I felt it enormously important that the UK Government respected the undertakings we had given your Lordships in this House, and that we ourselves were therefore not party to a vote at the European level on continuing this listing. I urge the supporters of the PMOI, who were successful here in overturning the view of the Government through court action, to similarly take advantage of the Court of First Instance action in Europe to pursue a similar legal strategy there to secure redress.

We were determined to respect that court decision, which is why we were not able to support the Government who brought to the table new information that had not been available earlier, on the basis of which they were able to persuade many Governments of Europe to support them. As to why we abstained rather than opposing the listing, the difficulty is that it is a total list with all terrorist

organisations on it, and you have to vote up or down on that list. We were therefore faced with the unpalatable situation that either the old list would be retained,
which would have done no good because the PMOI would have remained on it,
or we would have been left with no listed terrorist organisations in Europe. We
felt that was an unacceptable threat to the people of Britain as well as the rest of
the Continent.

The Council is required to defend its decision and make clear its actions. It may
be of some small comfort to noble Lords to know that although the Council decision has led to an asset freeze, because of the situation we faced before the court
decision, it is no longer illegal in this country to be a member of the PMOI; it is
only an issue of the assets of the PMOI, which are under threat from the European
ruling.

[The Court of First Instance found that the Council's decision was
unlawful—*People's Mojahedin Organization of Iran v Council (Common
foreign & security policy)* [2008] EUECJ T-284/08, Ed.]

(HL Deb 22 July 2008 Vol 703 cs1650–1652)

6/76
A Minister wrote:

We remain very concerned about the overall treatment of Iran's Baha'i community and, in particular, the continued detention without charge of seven members
of their informal leadership since May. We have consistently voiced our concern
about this and urged the Iranian government to release them unconditionally.
Following a UK recommendation, the EU issued a public statement on 21 May
expressing serious concern at the discrimination and harassment of Baha'is in Iran
and calling for the release of the Baha'i leaders. In statements to the UN Human
Rights Council in Geneva on 6 June and 16 September, the UK once again called
on Iran to release the detained Baha'is. Most recently, and again with strong UK
support, the EU issued a further public declaration on 26 September about the
increasing pressure on people belonging to religious minorities in Iran in recent
months. This declaration set out that the EU was

'deeply disturbed'

by the arrests of members of the Baha'i community and called for their

'immediate and unconditional release'.

We will continue to press Iran to fully uphold the right to freedom of religion and
to end the persecution of Baha'is in Iran.

(HC Deb 6 October 2008 Vol 480 c225W)

6/77
Iraq

The Defence Secretary was asked what monitoring and administration of
individuals in detention was necessary; and what the UK's reporting

obligations were to the International Committee of the Red Cross. He wrote:

In order to ensure that we can effectively administer individuals while they are detained by the UK armed forces, it is necessary to obtain and record some personal details. This is important, for example, to enable the relevant persons, such as their next of kin, to be informed of their detention and the location in which they are being detained. We collect information on an individual throughout their time in our detention, including their date of capture, medical records, and the date of release or transfer.

We are obliged, as laid out in the Coalition Provisional Authority Memorandum Number 3 (Revised), to report to the International Committee of the Red Cross (ICRC) information on individuals we have in our detention in Iraq and to grant the ICRC access to them.

(HC Deb 8 May 2008 Vol 475 c1133W)

6/78

The Defence Secretary wrote in a Ministerial statement:

In February 2005, the then Defence Secretary undertook to publish the findings of the review instigated by General Sir Mike Jackson into the cases of deliberate abuse of Iraqi citizens in 2003 and 2004. I am pleased to announce that the report, entitled "The Aitken Report: An Investigation into Cases of Deliberate Abuse and Unlawful Killing in Iraq in 2003 and 2004" is today being released in full.

The report by Brigadier Aitken is critical in places, and rightly so; only the highest standards are acceptable to the Army and to the Ministry of Defence as a whole.

Since the events that Brigadier Aitken has examined in his report, the Army has already done a great deal to improve its procedures. I am satisfied that the Army is doing everything possible to ensure that its personnel do not repeat the appalling acts that were perpetrated in these cases. I believe that Brigadier Aitken has demonstrated this in his report, but we must not be complacent.

The report makes three broad recommendations:

The Army needs to ensure that it learns and implements lessons from the disciplinary process in the same way that it does for wider operational issues;

The Army needs to find better ways to inculcate its core values of selfless commitment, courage, discipline, loyalty, integrity, and respect for others and its standards of behaviour and discipline, into the everyday lives of its personnel;

The Army must educate itself to ensure that they are using administrative action correctly.

The report is part of a continuing process of review, investigation and continuous professional development for the Army. It details the work that has already been completed, or is in progress, to ensure such acts as are examined by the report are not repeated. This work includes enhancements to training packages for both routine and specific training, and the implementation of a standard operating procedure for use in Operation Telic, which includes the treatment of detainees and prisoners.

I am proud to acknowledge that the vast majority of our personnel who have served in Iraq have conducted themselves to the highest standards of behaviour—some displaying extraordinary qualities of courage, self-discipline, integrity and selfless commitment far and above what might reasonably have been expected under the circumstances they faced.

One of the cases of abuse examined by Brigadier Aitken and referred to in his report is that of Mr. Baha Mousa. In September 2003, an Iraqi civilian, Mr. Baha Mousa, lost his life while in British military custody. He and eight other Iraqis had been subjected to varying degrees of abuse. I should like to take this opportunity to also update the House on recent developments in this case.

Last year, the court-martial of seven British Army officers and soldiers concluded. That trial resulted in the conviction of one individual, who had pleaded guilty to the inhuman treatment of prisoners; the other defendants were acquitted.

Following the trial, and in line with normal procedures, the Royal Military Police (Special Investigation Branch) reviewed the case to establish if there was any new evidence (including evidence from the trial) and any further lines of criminal inquiry into the death of Mr. Mousa and ill-treatment of other Iraqi nationals. They reported their findings to the Army Prosecuting Authority, who, in turn, having considered the report, consulted the Attorney-General.

The criminal review concluded that no further criminal lines of inquiry could be pursued on the basis of the existing evidence. This does not mean that a further investigation will not be instigated should new evidence be made available. Those individuals who were under investigation, and Mr. Mousa's family, have been informed that no further disciplinary action will be taken based on the current evidence. The Army's chain of command is now considering whether individuals should face administrative action.

The next step is to consider what form any future inquiry into these appalling incidents should take. I have agreed to receive representations from the legal representatives for Mr. Mousa's family, and I will make a further statement when a decision has been made. The conclusions of Brigadier Aitken's work and the subsequent actions already carried out by the Army will then be taken into account in this process.

[The Aitken Report is at <www.mod.uk/DefenceInternet/AboutDefence/CorporatePublications/DoctrineOperationsandDiplomacyPublications/Op erationsInIraq/TheAitkenReport.htm>, Ed.]

(HC Deb 25 January 2008 Vol 470 c65WS-66WS)

6/79
Israel

The Foreign Secretary was asked whether action by Israel in the occupied territories were breaches of the human rights provisions of any EU trade agreements. An FCO Minister wrote:

The European Commission does not consider that Israel's actions are in breach of the human rights provisions of any EU trade agreements.

Dialogue between the parties continues to be the best hope of a peaceful and secure future for both Israel and the Palestinians. We will continue to raise our concerns about human rights issues with Israel and the Palestinian Authority both bilaterally and with EU partners. The EU's relationship with Israel provides the framework for free and frank discussion of issues of concern, including human rights.

(HC Deb 29 February 2008 Vol 472 c2024W)

6/80

The Government were asked when they would next make representations to the Government of Israel on the continued long-term detention of Palestinian prisoners without due process. An FCO Minister wrote:

We continue to monitor the situation with regard to all Palestinian prisoners. Most Palestinian prisoners have been tried by Israeli courts and have the right of appeal. However, we do have concerns about Palestinian prisoners that are being held in administrative detention. All Palestinian prisoners should have access to a fair trial and we call on Israel to ensure that any actions are in accordance with international law. We will continue to raise our concerns with the Israeli authorities.

We are in close contact with the International Committee of the Red Cross, which monitors conditions in Israeli prisons. Where appropriate we raise our concerns with the Israeli authorities. The Israeli Prison Service has stressed its commitment to honouring its international obligations with regard to the humane and dignified treatment of prisoners.

(HL Deb 4 February 2008 Vol 698 cWA156)

6/81

The Government were asked what steps they planned to take to ensure that information shared between the EU and Israel under the Co-operation in Justice and Home Affairs Initiative of the EU-Israel Association Council has not been obtained in circumstances which would be defined as torture in UK law. In reply, a Minister wrote:

The UK abides by its commitments under international law, including the UN Convention Against Torture, and expects all other countries to comply with their international obligations.

We have made it clear that all intelligence received from foreign sources, in whatever forum, is carefully evaluated, particularly where it is clear it has been obtained from individuals in detention.

(HC Deb 7 October 2008 Vol 480 c634W-635W)

6/82
United Nations

In its reply to the FAC Report on the Annual Report on Human Rights 2007, the Government said, concerning its policies within the UN:

8. Our overall priority during the next three years is to see the Human Rights Council take action aimed at creating genuine improvements in human rights.

We will argue in favour of the Council taking a pro-active, progressive approach to human rights. We will continue to support country specific action, despite a number of countries seeking to downgrade the Council's ability to do such work. Among the many thematic human rights issues on which we engage, we will pay close attention to the work the Council does on freedom of expression and freedom of religion.

9. We will continue to defend the independence of the Office of the High Commissioner for Human Rights against those who wish to see the Council have more control and use this control to silence criticism of human rights violations.

10. We will look to use the Council to advance the Government's international human rights priorities, including abolition of the death penalty and the fight against torture. We will continue to consult widely with Non-Governmental Organisations to ensure that their views enrich policy-making and that we seize the opportunities to work together to achieve shared goals. We will also continue to look for opportunities to work with countries outside the Western European group, either as part of the EU or nationally, on issues of mutual importance.

11. The new Universal Periodic Review mechanism, which began early in 2008, will be a particularly important priority for the Government. We believe that the United Kingdom set a good example for others in the way we approached our review in April. We are engaged with a range of other countries that will be reviewed to share our experience. Many UN members are concerned that the Universal Periodic Review will be used to "name and shame" them, and are likely to be defensive in response. Our aim is to encourage all countries to engage constructively with the review. We will encourage them to consult widely at the national level before compiling their reports; to receive positively recommendations for improvement; and to be willing to implement such changes domestically.

12. If the majority of states approach the Universal Periodic Review in this way, we believe this will make a significant contribution to the success of the Human Rights Council as a whole. The Government will continue to contribute to each country review and ensure that both human rights achievements and challenges are reflected, along with constructive recommendations for improvement.

13. The Human Rights Council faces a significant number of challenges. Nonetheless, it is uniquely placed to promote global improvements in human rights. The Government is committed to helping it to do so.

(Foreign Affairs Committee Session 2007–08 Annual Report on Human Rights 2007, Response of the Secretary of State for Foreign and Commonwealth Affairs Cm 7463)

6/83
An FCO Minister wrote:

The UN Human Rights Council (HRC) is now fully up and running after an institution building phase begun in 2006. Achieving UK human rights priorities remains difficult with the majority of members wishing to prevent the body effectively tackling country specific problems. However, the HRC has, largely through UK/ EU action, taken some encouraging steps, including special sessions on Burma and Darfur and discussions of a wide range of country specific situations during open session. These sessions are webcast and open to Non-Governmental Organisations and interest groups.

The introduction of the HRC's Universal Periodic Review marks the first time that every UN member's human rights record will be systematically examined. The UK was one of the first countries to be examined in April. We used this opportunity to provide a model for engagement that we encourage others to follow, including by addressing the challenges we face.

The UK remains committed to seeing complementary action on human rights in other parts of the UN, in particular through the General Assembly's Third Committee. We will continue to resist those who argue that human rights are only a matter for the HRC in Geneva. They must be promoted in all parts of the UN.

We continue to see the HRC as a body that can deliver valuable results in human rights on the ground. It will take time and effort to realise this aim. The UK is ready to engage fully to see the Council increasingly fulfil its potential.

(HC Deb 19 May 2008 Vol 476 c77W)

6/84
A Minister said:

The 60th anniversary of the United Nations Declaration of Human Rights will take place in December. It is a reminder that some values and aspirations are universal and that states can come together and agree a set of common standards. Those standards, in turn, have been codified into a series of legally binding obligations. "Obligation" is a serious word, meaning something more than an aim or aspiration. The older UN texts, such as the convention on torture and the international human rights covenants, and the newer texts are binding on the states that have ratified them. That means that all of us, the UK included, must respect them.

Of course, it is tempting to set out in this debate the large raft of legislation flowing from our international commitments that is before us in the UK at any one time, but this is a debate on foreign policy so I shall stick to the rest of the world. Another hugely significant aspect of the legal framework set out in the UN and other places is that it opens each of us to the scrutiny of other states party to the treaties. Without that scrutiny, the many pages of promises would be worthless. We in the UK support more action to monitor countries' performance on human rights, for example in the UN Human Rights Council and the General Assembly. Unfortunately, that work can be undermined if it is seen simply as a process of recrimination and of putting country X in the dock. Sometimes that may be necessary, but rarely. The vast bulk of countries, the UK included, benefit from discussion about the merits of their domestic legislation and, importantly, their actions.

... The frameworks, conventions and declarations on human rights therefore form the backbone of the international system. It is the responsibility of our generation to ensure that they are more than pieces of paper, and that they are genuine commitments backed up with action—a point reflected in the interventions today.

We also need to ensure that the UN General Assembly is more than a talking shop. When the UN works it is a powerful instrument for good, as the recent success on the arms trade shows—how many lives will be saved because of this piece of paper?—but these successes must become more frequent and more assured. We want to reform the international system to ensure that the words are matched with actions.

(HC Deb 13 October 2008 Vol 480 c567–569)

6/85

A Minister wrote:

The UK expects every member of the UN Human Rights Council to act in accordance with the spirit of UN General Assembly Resolution 60/251 in upholding the highest standards of human rights promotion and protection and co-operating fully with the Council.

(HC Deb 28 October 2008 Vol 481 c801W)

6/86

The FCO wrote to the FAC following an FCO Minister's oral evidence to the Committee.

Does the Government support the introduction of mandatory mechanisms to ensure international businesses protect human rights?

The UK does not support the introduction of specific mandatory mechanisms to ensure businesses protect human rights. We believe that, at present, voluntary mechanisms and other non-legal approaches have more to offer in this field. States have an obligation to protect their populations from human rights abuses, which is why HMG is keen to mobilise international opinion to support practical political initiatives and encourage private sector good practice. We have supported initiatives bringing together governments, NGOs and businesses to facilitate the promotion of human rights, since we believe this to be the most effective way to address this important issue. For example, we led the development of the Kimberley Process, an international initiative with 48 participants designed to stop the world wide trade in illicit/conflict diamonds.

(Foreign Affairs Committee Report, Human Rights Report 2007, HC533 (2008))

6/87
Torture

The Government were asked whether they would ask the Council of Europe's Committee for the Prevention of Torture to publish its findings on the Imrali Island Prison in Turkey. An FCO Minister wrote:

The Government publish the Council of Europe's Committee for the Prevention of Torture (CPT) reports on the UK, and we would encourage the Turkish Government to publish the CPT reports for Turkey, including any findings on the Imrali Island prison. They have done so with an earlier report in 2005. (<www.cpt.coe.int/documents/tur/2006-30-inf-eng.pdf>).

The situation in Imrali Island prison is a matter for the Turkish Government, but we urge the Turkish Government to ensure that conditions of detention and the treatment of all prisoners are in line with European Court of Human Rights standards.

(HL Deb 28 January 2008 Vol 698 cWA98)

6/88

A Minister wrote:

Although a large number of states have ratified various international conventions prohibiting torture, torture continues to be committed with impunity in many parts of the world. The UK remains fundamentally opposed to torture and continues to be one of the most active countries in the world in the fight to eradicate it.

For example, we continue to support wider ratification of the UN Convention Against Torture (CAT) and its Optional Protocol (OPCAT) through bilateral lobbying campaigns, EU demarches and our work in UN forums such as the Human Rights Council. We also use a combination of project work and diplomatic activity to encourage implementation of OPCAT, including by the establishment of national preventative mechanisms. Since OPCAT was opened for signature on 4 February 2003, 61 states have become a signatory. As of July 2008, 35 states have ratified OPCAT, most recently Guatemala in June 2008. This marks significant progress, although there is of course more to be done.

Further information on the Foreign and Commonwealth Office's (FCO) work in this field can be found in the FCO's 2007 Annual Human Rights Report, which is available on the FCO's website at: <www.fco.gov.uk>

(HC Deb 7 July 2008 Vol 478 c1543W)

6/89

A Minister wrote:

The UK is opposed to torture and is one of the most active countries in the world in the fight to eradicate it. We provide consular assistance to British nationals detained abroad, which includes taking an interest in their welfare. We take allegations of mistreatment—including torture—very seriously and, with the permission of the individual concerned, can take up such allegations with the relevant authorities in the host state.

From 1 April 2005 we have collated statistics on the number of cases where we have, with the permission of the British national concerned, raised concerns with the detaining authorities over allegations of mistreatment, ranging from a lack of water to physical abuse. Records were not collated prior to April 2005.

Cases have been raised as follows:

April to December 2005: 39 allegations raised;

January to December 2006: 69 allegations raised; and

January to December 2007: 75 allegations raised.

Collated data are not broken down into specific details of the alleged mistreatment.

(HC Deb 17 July 2008 Vol 479 c681W)

6/90
The following was put to an FCO Minister by the FAC:

You will have read, as we have read, that water-boarding involves the pinioning of a detainee to a board, so that they are incapable of movement, then filling up the detainee's lungs with water, so that they are terrorised into revealing information under imminent fear of death by drowning. You will also know that it is the American Government's view that this is not a form of torture. Indeed, President Bush has made specific provision to be able to authorise water-boarding, should it become necessary. The British Government rightly regard this is as a form of torture.

He was then asked:

Could you tell us what steps the British Government are taking to persuade the American Government that water-boarding is indeed a form of torture, that it should not be engaged in by any civilised country and that the information so obtained, under such extreme duress, may well not be very reliable in any event?

The Minister said:

First, we have made it clear in the House of Commons and in all appropriate contacts with allies that in our view water-boarding is torture—period. There is no ambiguity about that. We are very clear, just as we have also been very clear that Guantanamo Bay should be closed. Our position on this is right, and we have conveyed that to the US. Certainly in any UK court proceedings, any information found out by torture would be utterly dismissed, out of hand, and found not admissible. Our position is clear. Obviously, it is for the US to arrive at its own decisions having heard the view of ourselves and other allies. [Q.62]

(Foreign Affairs Committee Report, Human Rights Report 2007, HC533 (2008))

6/91
The Government replied to the FAC Report on the Annual Human Rights Report 2007. The FAC had concluded that:

53 ... the Foreign Secretary's view that water-boarding is an instrument of torture is to be welcomed. However, given the recent practice of water-boarding by the US, there are serious implications arising from the Foreign Secretary's stated position. We conclude that, given the clear differences in definition, the UK can no longer rely on US assurances that it does not use torture, and we recommend that the Government does not rely on such assurances in the future. We also recommend that the Government should immediately carry out an exhaustive analysis of current US interrogation techniques on the basis of such information

as is publicly available or which can be supplied by the US. We further recommend that, once its analysis is completed, the Government should inform this
Committee and Parliament as to its view on whether there are any other interrogation techniques that may be approved for use by the US Administration
which it considers to constitute torture.

The Government wrote:

24. The Committee will be aware that the UK unreservedly condemns the use of
torture as a matter of fundamental principle. The Government ensures that relevant UK co-operation with the US, as with any other partner, would be lawful by
reference to our domestic law and applicable international law. We do not simply
rely on general assurances a State might give on the use of torture. For example,
the UK carefully evaluates any intelligence received from foreign sources, including the US, where it is clear it has been obtained from individuals in detention.

25. The US are fully aware of our views on water-boarding and have actively
engaged in a dialogue on all aspects of counter-terrorism and human rights issues,
including the handling of detainees. It should be noted that it was the US Government itself that made public its use of water-boarding and the fact that the technique was used in a small number of specific cases in the past. Continued close
co-operation with the US is absolutely critical to our ability to counter the threat to
the UK posed by global terrorism. We consider that our ongoing dialogue with the
US on counterterrorism and human rights issues to be the appropriate course.

26. The UK legislation criminalising torture (implementing the UN Convention
Against Torture) defines it as any act which causes severe pain or suffering, whether
physical or mental, which is intentionally inflicted on a person. But whilst in some
cases it will be clear that a certain technique constitutes torture, in other cases it
will not be possible to determine whether the use of a particular technique is torture without taking into consideration all the circumstances of the case. For this
reason the Government judges that an analysis along the lines that the Committee
suggests would not be meaningful.

(Foreign Affairs Committee Session 2007–08 Annual Report on Human
Rights 2007, Response of the Secretary of State for Foreign and
Commonwealth Affairs Cm 7463)

6/92 (See 6/17)

An FCO Minister was asked by the FAC for an assurance that the Pakistan
Inter-Service Intelligence agency did not use torture in interrogations.
He said:

In the case of Pakistan, we made it absolutely clear at every level of government,
both the previous Government and this one, that we view torture as an absolutely
abhorrent and inappropriate technique for extracting information. Obviously, we
pressed extremely hard for return to civilian, democratic government to the extent
that that strengthens [our opposition] but, as for individuals, we have looked into
allegations made in the [HRW] report and, behind the issue of hundreds, those
of six nationals—if I am right—were specifically raised.

We have looked into those cases and, of them, two were joint British-Pakistan citizens who we gained consular access to because we were concerned about their situation. They made no complaints of ill treatment when we met them, until after their release. A third individual was a UK national who complained similarly only after his release of his treatment in detention. We are vigilant when cases are brought to our attention, and we are concerned to use our consular access to ensure that there is no torture. Our position is that we do not know of any cases of torture. [Q.65]

The Minister was asked why consular access had not been obtained to all British prisoners. He said:

Because of the other five cases, all were joint Pakistan-UK citizens. In such cases the bar for demanding access is higher, in that we need to be convinced—as they are after all under their own domestic jurisdiction—that indeed there is a reasonable concern. So we got access to two ... one British national and two Pakistan-UK joint nationals. [Qs.67–69]

The Minister went on:

I do not think that it is a particular problem in the sense that wherever evidence was obtained, if we felt that it had been obtained through torture we would not use it. We are as conscious as anyone of the allegations, and we absolutely deny the charge that we have in any way outsourced torture to Inter-Services Intelligence as a way of extracting information, either for court use or for use in counter-terrorism. [Q.70]

(Foreign Affairs Committee Report, Human Rights Report 2007, HC533 (2008))

6/93

The Government replied to the FAC Report on the Annual Human Rights Report 2007. The Committee had concluded that:

62 ... it is extremely important that the veracity of allegations that the Government has "outsourced" interrogation techniques involving the torture of British nationals by Pakistani authorities should be investigated. Irrespective of these allegations, we recommend that the FCO should immediately seek full consular access in all cases where it is aware of mono- or dual-national British citizens being detained by the Pakistani authorities, and in particular by the Inter-Services Intelligence agency. We conclude that it is not acceptable for the Government to use an individual's dual nationality as an excuse to leave him or her vulnerable to the prospect of possible torture.

The Government wrote:

The Government absolutely denies the serious allegation that it has "outsourced" torture as a way of extracting information. We unreservedly condemn the use of torture and our clear policy is not to participate in, solicit, encourage, or condone the use of torture or inhuman or degrading treatment for any purpose.

28. The Government takes allegations of mistreatment very seriously. As the Foreign Secretary told the House on 17 July, "the Security Service has checked for any

relevant information in light of the media allegations and informed [him] that there is nothing to suggest that it has supported torture in Pakistan or anywhere else".

29. If there was a question of any person acting in an official capacity being engaged in an act of torture then this would be a matter for the police. If any individual believes that their Human Rights have been infringed as a result of actions carried out by, or on behalf of, any of the intelligence services then they should take their case to the Investigatory Powers Tribunal.

30. The Government agrees with the Committee's recommendation that the FCO should seek consular access in all cases where it is aware of mono-national British citizens being detained by the Pakistani authorities. Indeed it is our policy to do so.

31. In line with consular policy, we would not normally offer consular assistance to dual nationals in their country of other nationality. However, we do make an exception to this rule if, having looked at the circumstances of the case, we consider that there is a special humanitarian reason to do so. Such circumstances might include cases involving minors, forced marriage, an offence which carries the death penalty or other concerns such as allegations of torture.

32. When we do seek access to a detained dual national in the country of their other nationality, that access, and any help we can provide, will depend on the agreement of the state of other nationality.

33. It should be noted that we may not be aware that a dual national is being held or that there may be allegations of torture, as the detaining authorities may not inform us of the detention, or to allow the person to contact our consular staff.

(Foreign Affairs Committee Session 2007–08 Annual Report on Human Rights 2007, Response of the Secretary of State for Foreign and Commonwealth Affairs Cm 7463)

6/94

In its Report on the Annual Human Rights Report 2007, the FAC had recommended that:

63 ... in its response to this Report, the Government should explicitly state whether UK officials met any of the four dual nationals to discuss non-consular matters and should also state why non-consular access was granted to one UK national, but not consular access. We also recommend that the Government should further tell us whether it was aware of all six individuals at the time of their detention, and whether intelligence or evidence gained by the Pakistani authorities in its interrogation of any of these men led in whole, or in part, to further investigations or charges in the UK. We further recommend that the Government should describe its collaboration with the Inter-Services Intelligence agency, and its human rights concerns about this organisation, in its response to this Report.

The Government replied:

34. The Government is currently aware of eight cases of British or dual British/ Pakistani nationals having been detained on suspicion of terrorist offences in Pakistan since 2000 (and took steps to amend an earlier Parliamentary answer on this question as soon as its inaccuracy came to light). It is difficult to give precise

numbers as we are not always given consular notification of the detention of dual British nationals in the country of their other nationality.

35. Consular officials were aware of six of the eight individuals at the time of their detention. Consular access was sought and given for both UK mono-nationals. In one case our request was initially denied, but subsequently access was given before deportation. Consular access was also sought, in two of the six dual national cases. In one of these cases access was not granted before the individual was released. The other individual remains in Pakistani custody and we continue to press for consular access.

36. The Government notes the Committee's recommendation but can neither confirm nor deny whether UK officials met any of these eight individuals to discuss nonconsular matters.

37. The Government notes the Committee's interest in our collaboration with the Inter-Services Intelligence Directorate. It is the Government's long standing policy not to comment on intelligence-related issues. This includes details of UK intelligence agency collaborations with foreign intelligence services. All intelligence received from foreign sources is carefully evaluated, particularly where it is clear it has been obtained from individuals in detention. Evidence obtained as a result of any acts of torture would not be admissible in criminal or civil proceedings in the UK.

38. The Government shares the Committee's concerns about allegations that the Inter-Services Intelligence Directorate (ISI) has mistreated detainees and we are aware of several NGO reports of human rights abuses perpetrated by Pakistan's intelligence and police authorities. We encourage the Government of Pakistan to meet its human rights obligations through bilateral contact and regular EU representations. We also ensure that our programme of support for building Pakistan's counter-terrorism capacity addresses the importance of compliance with internationally agreed human rights standards. We work closely with the Government of Pakistan to support its counter extremism efforts through development support, institutional capacity building work to improve governance and through increased investment in education. We are also engaged in projects to help build improved capacity for counter-terrorism, for example through legislative mechanisms and practical training on forensics, terrorist financing and crisis management.

39. We continue to press the Government of Pakistan to ratify the Convention against Torture (CAT) which Pakistan signed in April of this year. We hope the Government of Pakistan will make urgent progress by incorporating the obligations under CAT into domestic law.

(Foreign Affairs Committee Session 2007–08 Annual Report on Human Rights 2007, Response of the Secretary of State for Foreign and Commonwealth Affairs Cm 7463)

6/95

The Foreign Secretary was asked if he would make representations to the US Government requesting the disqualification of evidence extracted by torture in the trial of 9/11 suspects. An FCO Minister wrote:

The Military Commissions Act, the US legislation which applies to the Military Commissions designed to try "unlawful enemy combatants" held at Guantanamo

Bay, mandates that evidence obtained under torture is inadmissible. Admissibility of evidence in practice will be for the Military Commissions themselves to determine with respect to the individual cases brought. The Foreign and Commonwealth Office has raised concerns about the implementation of the Military Commissions process with the US.

(HC Deb 2 June 2008 Vol 475 c708W)

6/96
Trafficking

The Government were asked what progress had been made towards meeting the Government's deadline to ratify the Council of Europe Convention on Human Trafficking by the end of 2008. In reply, a Minister wrote:

Good progress has been made. We are on track to ratify the Council of Europe Convention on Action against Human Trafficking ("the Convention") by the end of the year. We have made the necessary legislative changes and a Command Paper and supporting documents were laid before Parliament on 7 October setting out the Government's plan.

[The UK ratified the Convention on 17 December 2008 and it came into force for the UK on 1 April 2009, Ed.]

(HC Deb 21 October 2008 Vol 481 c265W-266W)

6/97
Women's Rights—Convention for the Elimination of All Forms of Discrimination Against Women

The FCO wrote to the FAC following an FCO Minister's oral evidence to the Committee.

Why are issues relating to women's human rights not explicitly included in the FCO's policy goals?

The promotion of all human rights—including women's rights—and good governance are, and will remain, a vital part of this Government's international agenda. The new policy goals do not downgrade their importance. Human rights are essential to achieving all the new policy goals, for example, in countering the risk of violent extremism and in preventing and resolving conflict.

Our gender commitments include: tackling all forms of gender based violence; full implementation of UN Security Council Resolution 1325 on Women, Peace and Security; encouraging ratification of UN Human Rights instruments to which we are party, including Convention on the Elimination of all forms of Discrimination Against Women; achievement of all the Millennium Development Goals (MDGs) including MDG 3 (promoting gender equality and empowerment of women) and MDG 5 (improving maternal health).

(Foreign Affairs Committee Report, Human Rights Report 2007, HC533 (2008))

6/98

The Foreign Secretary was asked which countries were represented on the Committee for the Elimination of All Forms of Discrimination Against Women; and what the terms of reference for the Committee were. An FCO Minister wrote:

Countries are not represented on the Committee on the Elimination of Discrimination against Women (CEDAW). Committee Members are nationals of States Parties to the Convention on the Elimination of All Forms of Discrimination Against Women and serve on the basis of their personal expertise. They do not represent governments. However, consideration is given to equitable geographical distribution, the representation of different cultures and principal legal systems. A list of the current members of the Committee can be found at:

<www.ohchr.org/english/bodies/cedaw/membership.htm>

The Committee's functions are set out in the Convention on the Elimination of All Forms of Discrimination Against Women. Essentially they are to monitor States Parties' implementation of the Convention and make recommendations on how this can be improved. Monitoring is done primarily through a public reporting and examination process. States Parties to the Optional Protocol to the Convention have also given the Committee competence to receive complaints from individuals alleging that their rights under the Convention have been violated. The UK is party to the Protocol as well as the Convention.

CEDAW monitors implementation of the whole Convention. The Convention concerns the elimination of discrimination against women in a wide range of areas, including in respect of health care. While the Convention itself does not explicitly mention abortion or reproductive rights, Articles 12 and 14 refer to access to health care services, including those related to family planning. It is possible that a Committee might address issues relating to abortion and/or reproductive rights when examining a State Party's implementation of the Convention. But this is for the Committee to decide.

In addition to making recommendations to individual States Parties on implementing the Convention, the Committee is also able to issue general guidance to all States Parties focussing on specific aspects of the Convention. These are produced periodically in the form of non-binding "General Recommendations". A number of these General Recommendations relate to health matters. In particular, General Recommendation 24 from 1999, relates to "Women and Health". This does address, among other things, issues relating to sexual and reproductive rights ...

There is no UK representative on the Committee on the Elimination of Discrimination Against Women (CEDAW).

CEDAW's 23 members are elected by the States Parties to the Convention for the Elimination of All Forms of Discrimination Against Women. States Parties nominate candidates from among their own nationals, but members serve in a personal capacity and do not represent governments. The Convention states that CEDAW should consist of experts of "high moral standing and competence in the field covered by the Convention".

(HC Deb 5 March 2008 Vol 472 c2567W)

6/99

A Minister wrote:

The United Kingdom signed the United Nations Convention on the Elimination of all forms of Discrimination Against Women (CEDAW) in 1981, and ratified with reservations in 1986. The UK reservations in 1986 were general reservations (a–d), and specific reservations on Article 1, 2, 9, 10, 11, 15 and 16. Since that time the Government have not sought any new reservations on the Convention and have withdrawn a number of reservations, most notably in 1995 and 1996.

The UK's sixth periodic report to the CEDAW committee on progress towards the implementation of the Convention was submitted on 1 May 2007. The report notes that the UK has withdrawn the CEDAW reservation relating to immigration and has modified the reservation relating to the throne and the armed forces. The UK currently has reservations on: general reservations (a, c, and d), and specific reservations on article 9, 11, 15(3) and 16.

The current reservations will be reviewed in 2008–09 as part of the follow up plan from the UK's examination by the CEDAW Committee in July 2008.

(HC Deb 28 October 2008 Vol 481 c803W)

6/100

A Minister said:

The review of the experience of the United Kingdom under the Optional Protocol to the United Nations Convention for the Elimination of Discrimination Against Women, announced on 25 June 2007 has been concluded.

The CEDAW optional protocol allows women in the UK to submit complaints directly to the United Nations Committee for the Elimination of Discrimination Against Women if they feel that their rights have been violated. The Government accepted the optional protocol to reaffirm our commitment to women's rights and gender equality, and to gain greater empirical evidence on the value of individual petition to the UN generally.

The review of CEDAW was carried out by Professor Jim Murdoch of Glasgow University School of Law. Professor Murdoch finds that: the CEDAW OP has not yet provided women in the UK with real benefits; Non-Governmental Organisations in the UK have not used the optional protocol in advancing the cause of women; and the quality of the UN committee's adjudication on admissibility of complaints can appear inconsistent.

Government expenditure on cases involving the UK has been calculated at just over £4,000 per case.

Professor Murdoch's findings suggest that the first three years have not provided sufficient empirical evidence to decide either way on the value of other individual complaint mechanisms. We will need further evidence, over a longer period, to establish what the practical benefits are. In the meantime, the Government will consider the merits of other individual complaints mechanisms on a case-by-case basis.

[For Professor Murdoch's Report, see <www.justice.gov.uk/publications/docs/un-optional-protocol-women.pdf>, Ed.]

(HL Deb 4 December 2008 Vol 706 WS24)

6/101
Women's Rights—Security Council

A Minister wrote:

Eight years after the adoption of UN Security Council resolution (UNSCR) 1325, the resolution has had a positive impact on the inclusion of women in post-conflict negotiations and reconstruction. It has drawn international attention to the issue, it has resulted in greater inclusion of women in political dialogue in countries where the UN Peacebuilding Commission is operating, and mandates for UN peacekeeping missions now routinely request that the role of women is fully recognised. But we recognise that work must continue to ensure the systematic involvement of women at all stages of the conflict cycle. The adoption of UNSCR 1820 in June this year was a significant step forward in strengthening previous calls to address women's under-representation. In September, the UN Security Council held an Open Debate on 'mediation' in conflict resolution reiterating this call and in October, the UN Security Council Open Debate will focus on the need to enhance the role of women in peace processes.

The UK is at the forefront of international efforts to ensure the comprehensive and effective implementation of UNSCR 1325. We were among the first countries to draw up a national Action Plan setting out action for Government personnel and Departments to implement UNSCR 1325 and have encouraged other countries to do the same. Several European countries have since developed their own action plans. We regularly review the plan in partnership with civil society. We are raising awareness of gender in conflict by ensuring references in all relevant UN Security Council resolutions and in the mandates of peacekeeping operations, and are promoting the role of women in conflict prevention, conflict resolution and peacebuilding through forums in a range of conflict affected countries.

The UN Peacebuilding Commission was established in 2005, to offer technical assistance to countries emerging from conflict and provide catalytic financial support for reconstruction efforts. The UK is a member of the Commission and has been instrumental in ensuring that UNSCRs 1325 and 1820 are mainstreamed through the Commission's engagement with countries on its agenda.

(HC Deb 27 October 2008 Vol 481 c771W)

Part Six: IX. *The Position of the Individual (Including the Corporation) in International Law—Crimes under international law*

6/102

The Government were asked whether they recognized the existence of genocide in Armenia in 1915. An FCO Minister wrote:

The position of the Government on this issue is long-standing. The Government acknowledge the strength of feeling about this terrible episode of history and recognise the massacres of 1915–16 as a tragedy. However, neither this Government nor previous Governments have judged that the evidence is sufficiently unequivocal to persuade us that these events should be categorised as genocide as defined by the 1948 UN Convention on Genocide.

As the then Minister for Europe said in a debate in Westminster Hall on 7 June 2006 (*Official Report*, col. 137WH), the work of establishing the truth must be conducted as a joint exercise by the parties directly involved if it is to help towards reconciliation. There needs to be a truth and reconciliation process owned by the people of Armenia and Turkey. Outsiders can commend the idea to the parties, but they should not try to do the work for them—undertaking this is an important part of the confidence-building and reconciliation process for the parties themselves. The Government will continue to encourage the parties to embark on such a process. In the mean time, we should resist the temptation to pre-empt its conclusions.

(HL Deb 4 March 2008 Vol 699 cWA165)

6/103

The Foreign Secretary was asked what assessment his Department had made of the ability of the Uganda Special Court to provide trials for the leaders of the Lords Resistance Army in accordance with the principles of international humanitarian law. An FCO Minister wrote:

As the Final Peace Agreement between the Ugandan Government and the Lord's Resistance Army has yet to be signed, the method of justice for those that perpetrated war crimes and human rights abuses during the conflict has not been finally agreed. Should a special division of the Ugandan High Court be established, the Government will press for it to be fully compatible with the Rome Statute and international law.

(HC Deb 4 June 2008 Vol 476 c1008W)

6/104

During a debate in the House of Lords, a Minister said:

[U]nlike six months ago, there is now no doubt that Mr Mugabe and those around him have committed crimes which deserve referral to the International Criminal Court (ICC). In the past, the crimes were of such ancient origin that they preceded the establishment of the court and were not covered by it. Any referral of a non-signatory such as Zimbabwe would be via the UN Security Council. At this stage, the Security Council is seized with sanctions. If the object of those sanctions—a change of Government in Zimbabwe—is not achieved, I suspect that this is one of several steps we would want to bring to the Council as a possible next round of pressure.

(HL Deb 8 July 2008 Vol 703 c631)

6/105

The Government were asked what assessment they had made of the differences between rights abuses allegedly committed by the forces of Jean-Pierre Bemba, ex-Vice President of the Democratic Republic of Congo, for which he will face trial at the International Criminal Court in The Hague,

and the rights abuses allegedly committed by the armed militias and supporters of President Mugabe of Zimbabwe; and whether they would take
the necessary steps at the earliest opportunity to have President Mugabe
similarly arraigned. In reply, a Minister wrote:

The allegations of war crimes and crimes against humanity faced by Jean-Pierre
Bemba and the suffering witnessed in Zimbabwe are extremely serious. Jean-
Pierre Bemba is in custody following an investigation by the ICC into crimes
committed during armed conflict in the Central African Republic and the issue
of a warrant for his arrest. There has been no such investigation into events in
Zimbabwe, which is not a state party to the ICC. Neither do we wish to pre-empt a
decision that is properly the prerogative of a successor Government in Zimbabwe.

(HL Deb 15 July 2008 Vol 703 c631)

Part Seven: Organs of the State and their Status

Part Seven: II. *The State and its organs—ministers*

7/1

In the debate on the Report of the ILC in the Sixth Committee of the
General Assembly [A/63/10, Ed.], the representative of the UK said:

The UK welcomed the introduction of the topic of immunity of state officials
from foreign criminal jurisdiction on to the work programme of the International
Law Commission. This is an important subject which offers an opportunity for
the Commission to provide valuable clarification on a matter of real practical
concern for both States and individuals. The work is still at a very early stage but
the UK would like to take this opportunity to congratulate the Special Rapporteur
on the excellent start made in his preliminary report and to thank the Secretariat
for the very useful memorandum it has produced on this matter.

If progress is to be made on this topic, it will be important for the Commission
not to become embroiled in arid and contentious debates about what the law
should be. Accordingly, the UK fully endorses the approach taken by the Special
Rapporteur—in particular his expressed aim not to formulate abstract proposals
as to what international law might be but to work on the basis of the evidence of
existing international law in the field.

Whilst acknowledging that national laws and the decisions of national courts
may constitute evidence of the existence of customary international law, the
United Kingdom also welcomes the Special Rapporteur's primary focus on the
international law in this field. In this connection, the United Kingdom agrees
with the view that the decision of the International Court of Justice in the Arrest
Warrant Case constitutes a sound basis on which to proceed.

The United Kingdom notes that the Special Rapporteur has indicated his intention to consider existing practice in relation to immunity from foreign civil jurisdiction. Whilst recognising that such immunity may have some common features
with the present topic, the United Kingdom supports the view that there are

some very different considerations in play in such cases. For this reason, it would like to sound a note of caution in this regard.

As to the persons to be covered under this topic, there is clearly work to be done on the immunity *ratione personae* enjoyed by a limited category of officials. There is now broad acceptance that a serving Head of State, Head of Government and Foreign Minister enjoy such immunity but, as the Special Rapporteur has rightly observed, the question as to whether such immunity may extend to other high ranking officials is less clear. Two cases in the United Kingdom courts have shown the courts' willingness to recognise the personal immunity of a foreign Defence Minister and a foreign Trade Minister respectively but the precise rationale and criteria on which entitlement to such immunity may be based is unsettled. This is an area on which the Commission's work could usefully focus and, in this connection, the United Kingdom agrees that the identification of criteria rather than an enumerative approach is more likely to prove fruitful.

In carrying out this aspect of its work, the Commission should, in the view of the United Kingdom, adopt a cautious approach and, in identifying relevant criteria, should remain mindful of the existence of separate rules of customary international law under which State officials may be entitled to immunity, most notably those relating to special missions.

The United Kingdom supports the view of the Special Rapporteur and some members of the Commission that the topic should, in principle, cover all State officials who enjoy immunity *ratione materiae*. It should also cover former State officials who retain such immunity after leaving office. In the view of the United Kingdom, there could be considerable value in a close and balanced study of the precise limits of such immunity particularly within the context of criminal acts committed in the territory of the forum State and of the distinction between public and private acts. However, in handling such a broad and potentially contentious subject it will be important for the Commission to clearly identify and delimit the scope of the questions to be addressed and to keep in mind the Special Rapporteur's stated aim not to formulate abstract proposals as to what international law might be but to work on the basis of existing international law.

The United Kingdom supports the view that the subject of recognition is a separate and preliminary question of international law and should not be included in this topic. It is also inclined to agree with the Special Rapporteur that the position of family members is, generally speaking, outside this topic. However, the topic may have some relevance to the limited category of Heads of State (particularly sovereigns) and, for this reason, the United Kingdom would suggest that, if it is decided to proceed without further consideration of this matter, the Commission do so on the basis of an appropriate savings clause in this regard. As regards the suggestion that the Commission should also consider the question of immunity of military personnel, the United Kingdom would note that such personnel are often the subject of specific agreement between States, particularly when stationed abroad. However, insofar as such personnel are not covered by specific agreement, the United Kingdom sees no reason why they would not be covered by the topic just as any other State official may be.

Finally, the United Kingdom would like to take this opportunity to emphasise its support for the general approach and methodology proposed by the Special

Rapporteur. In undertaking work on this particular topic, the Commission must be only too aware of its importance and potential impact on international relations. In our view, it is only on the basis of a very careful and thorough analysis of the *lex lata* and its policy rationale that the Commission can hope to provide real clarification of the relevant immunities and reflect the delicate balance of interests they represent. We wish the Commission every success in this important task and look forward to its next Report.

(Text supplied by FCO)

Part Seven: IV. *The State and its organs—diplomatic missions and their members*

7/2

The Government were asked on how many occasions in the past 12 months civil action in respect of the commercial obligations of foreign diplomats accredited to the United Kingdom had been blocked because of the respondent's diplomatic immunity; and what were the countries concerned. An FCO Minister wrote:

We are not aware of any such occasions in the past 12 months. There is no obligation on the courts or parties to a civil dispute to notify us of such cases.

The 1961 Vienna Convention on Diplomatic Relations states that diplomats should not practise any professional or commercial activity for personal profit. We would therefore not expect diplomats posted to the UK to become involved in civil cases of a commercial nature.

The Government were asked further whether accredited foreign diplomats might use diplomatic immunity to avoid enforcement of commercial debts and obligations incurred in the course of business trading; and what steps they take if such an individual abuses diplomatic immunity to avoid commercial obligations.

The Minister wrote:

The Diplomatic Privileges Act 1964 provides that foreign diplomats do not enjoy immunity from civil or administrative jurisdiction for actions relating to any professional or commercial activity exercised by diplomats outside their official functions. It would therefore not be possible for an individual to abuse diplomatic immunity to avoid commercial obligations.

And further what steps had the Government taken to ensure that fully accredited diplomats are present in the United Kingdom solely or principally for undertaking diplomatic activity; and whether an individual with diplomatic status might be present in the United Kingdom principally for the purpose of carrying out business activity.

The Minister wrote:

We would take a serious view of any foreign diplomat breaching the provisions of Article 42 of the 1961 Vienna Convention on Diplomatic Relations that "a diplomatic agent shall not in the receiving state practice for personal profit any professional or commercial activity".

Appointments of foreign diplomats are notified to the Foreign and Commonwealth Office on forms signed by the head of mission or their designate. Where necessary, we seek further clarification on appointments from the head of mission.

(HL Deb 24 June 2008 Vol 702 cWA226)

7/3

The Government were asked why, following the finding of the House of Lords that Mr. Hany Salaam was dishonest in a $50 million fraud, he was subsequently accredited to the United Kingdom as a diplomat with full diplomatic status, whilst continuing to conduct business transactions from an office in London. An FCO Minister wrote:

Mr Salaam's appointment to the embassy of Gabon was notified to the Foreign and Commonwealth Office in September 2006. Article 7 of the Vienna Convention on Diplomatic Relations 1961 allows a sending state to

"freely appoint the members of staff of the mission".

The formal process of agreement applies only to heads of mission, and we do not conduct background checks on members of the mission.

We take a serious view of any foreign diplomat breaching the provisions of Article 42 of the Vienna Convention that

"a diplomatic agent shall not in the receiving state practise for personal profit any professional or commercial activity".

We are seeking further information about Mr. Salaam's role at the embassy of Gabon, and I shall write to the noble Lord when we have further information.

(HL Deb 29 September 2008 Vol 703 c309)

7/4

The Foreign Secretary was asked how many offences committed by diplomats resulted in the diplomatic representative subsequently leaving the United Kingdom in each year from 2003 to 2007. In reply, a Minister wrote:

As a result of Foreign and Commonwealth Office representations, the following number of diplomats left the UK during the period 2003–07.

	Number
2003	1
2004	2
2005	2
2006	1
2007	5

(HC Deb 6 October 2008 Vol 480 c221W)

7/5
A Minister wrote:

We expect all diplomatic missions to meet their national non-domestic rate obligations, and the vast majority do so. The Valuation Office Agency of HM Revenue and Customs sends monthly statements to all diplomatic missions which have outstanding debts. The Foreign and Commonwealth Office has an annual process of formally raising outstanding debts with missions, and urging prompt settlement. Failure to do so leads to the missions appearing on the written ministerial statement which ... the Foreign Secretary makes to Parliament each year.

The total amount of national non-domestic rates owed by foreign Missions in the UK fell by more than 50 per cent between 2006–07 and 2007–08.

(HC Deb 21 October 2008 Vol 481 c213W)

7/6
The Foreign Secretary wrote:

In 2007, there were 6,241 recorded outstanding parking and other minor traffic violation fines incurred by diplomatic missions and international organisations in the United Kingdom. These totalled £656,275. In March this year the Foreign and Commonwealth Office wrote to all diplomatic missions and international organisations concerned, giving them the opportunity to either pay their outstanding fines or appeal against them if they considered that the fines had been issued incorrectly. As a result of subsequent payments totalling £27,300 and formal appeals lodged, there remains a total of 5,093 (£538,745) unpaid fines for 2007. The table below details those diplomatic missions and international organisations that have outstanding fines totalling £1,000 or more:

[The table is not reproduced]

Congestion Charge

The number of outstanding fines incurred by diplomatic missions in the United Kingdom [UK]for non-payment of the London congestion charge since its introduction in February 2003 until 14 May 2008 was 175,482. The table below shows the 10 diplomatic missions with the highest value of outstanding fines:

Mission	Number of fines outstanding	Value (£)
USA	23,188	2,347,205
Japan	13,062	1,334,560
Russian Federation	12,765	1,308,720
Germany	11,213	1,149,050
Nigeria	11,096	1,120,650
Sudan	7,984	793,300
Kenya	5,084	502,630
Tanzania	4,654	461,080
India	3,949	409,360
South Africa	4,098	406,480

(HC Deb 26 June 2008 Vol 478 c32WS-33WS)

7/7
The Foreign Secretary wrote:

The majority of diplomatic missions in the United Kingdom pay the national non-domestic rates requested from them. They are obliged to pay only 6 per cent. of the total national non-domestic rates (NNDR) value, which represents payment for specific services such as street cleaning, lighting, maintenance and fire services. The total amount outstanding from all diplomatic missions is approximately £424,700.51. However, as at 31 March 2008 the missions listed below owed over £10,000 in NNDR. One additional diplomatic mission, which owes £10,000 or more in NNDR, has made arrangements with the Valuation Office Agency to clear their outstanding debt and has not been included in this list:

[The list is not reproduced]

(HC Deb 26 June 2008 Vol 478 c34WS)

7/8
The Foreign Secretary wrote:

In 2007, 20 serious offences allegedly committed by people entitled to diplomatic immunity were drawn to the attention of the Foreign and Commonwealth Office. 'Serious offences' are defined as offences that would, in certain circumstances, carry a penalty of 12 months or more imprisonment. Some 24,000 people are entitled to diplomatic immunity in the United Kingdom.

The table below lists those foreign missions whose diplomats allegedly committed serious offences and the type of offence from 2003–2007:

[The table is not reproduced but, in the five-year period, there were only two occasions when more than one member of a single mission was convicted of a serious offence in a single year, on both occasions, there were offences by members of the same mission, Kazakhstan and Malawi, driving under the influence of alcohol, Ed.]

(HC Deb 26 June 2008 Vol 478 c34WS-36WS)

Part Seven: V. *The State and its organs—consulates and their members*

7/9 [See also 6/5]
The Foreign Secretary was asked what arrangements were in place to provide alternative consular services in the case of each of the embassies, high commissions and consulates closed since May 1997. He wrote:

Where a non-sovereign post (British consulate or British consulate general) has closed, consular services will be provided by either the sovereign post (embassy or high commission), or the nearest non-sovereign post in the country concerned, possibly through an honorary consul.

Should a sovereign post close, an honorary consul supervised by a neighbouring post will normally be appointed. In some countries where we have no representation, under reciprocal arrangements, either an EU member state or a Commonwealth country that has representation in the country concerned may provide consular services in an emergency. Under Article 20 of the treaty establishing the European Community, EU nationals in a country where their own state is not represented are entitled to consular protection from an embassy or consulate of another member state, on the same conditions as the nationals of that state.

[A list of closures was appended, not reproduced here, Ed.]

(HC Deb 9 January 2008 Vol 470 c557W)

Part Seven: VII. *The State and its organs—trade and information offices, trade delegations etc*

7/10 [See also 19/24]
The Foreign Secretary said:

I should like to make a statement on the Russian Government's actions against the British Council in Russia. The House will recall that in October 2007 the Russian Government threatened to close the British Council's operations outside Moscow from 1 January 2008. That was confirmed on 12 December and again last week with the threat of a series of administrative measures against the British Council, including tax measures in St Petersburg and visa restrictions against British Council staff in St Petersburg and Yekaterinburg. The Russians also threatened to take measures against the British Council in Moscow, up to and including the removal of accreditation of British Council staff working in Russia.

On Tuesday this week, the Prime Minister's foreign policy adviser held what we believed were productive talks in Moscow about a range of international and bilateral issues, including the British Council. Yet on the same day, the Russian Government exerted further pressure on the British Council. The Russian security services summoned more than 20 locally engaged members of British Council staff in St Petersburg and Yekaterinburg one by one for interviews. Ten members of staff were interviewed late at night in their homes after calls by the Russian tax police. Questioning ranged from the institutional status of the British Council to personal questions about the health and welfare of family pets. These Russian citizens have chosen to offer their skills and hard work to promote cultural contact between the people of Russia and the UK. As a result, they have been the subject of blatant intimidation from their own Government.

I think that the whole House will agree that such actions are reprehensible, not worthy of a great country and contrary to the letter and spirit of the legal framework under which the British Council operates—notably international law, including the Vienna conventions and the UK-Russia 1994 bilateral agreement on cultural co-operation, which Russia has ratified.

Russia has failed to show any legal reasons under Russian or international law why the British Council should not continue to operate. It has also failed to substantiate its claims that the British Council is avoiding paying tax. The British Council is in fact registered for tax in Russia and has complied with all requests of the tax authorities in respect of its activities. Instead of taking legal action against the British Council, the Russian Government have resorted to intimidation of its staff. I am confident that the whole House will share the anger and dismay felt by this Government at the actions of the Russian Government. We saw similar actions during the cold war but thought, frankly, they had been put behind us.

The British Council's first priority is, rightly, the safety of its own staff, yet the actions of the Russian Government have made it impossible for staff to go about their work in a normal way. British Council offices in Yekaterinburg and St Petersburg have been prevented from operating, so the British Council has, with great regret, taken the decision to suspend its operations in those two cities. The Council is making an announcement to this effect as I speak. The staff concerned will continue to be supported while the Council considers its next steps.

There has already been strong international condemnation of Russia's actions. Following my conversation last night with the Slovenian Foreign Minister in his capacity as presidency of the EU, an EU presidency statement has just been issued on behalf of all European Governments. The statement makes it clear that the EU is

"very concerned at Russia's demand to close British Council regional offices"

and

"deeply regrets the harassment of British Council staff"

and other measures taken. It calls on Russia to

"allow the British Council to operate freely and effectively in Russia".

The Government of the United States have issued a statement of support, calling for the British Council to be able to continue its good work in Russia, and the Canadian Government are also expressing their concerns in Moscow about these developments. I am grateful for the many expressions of support that the British Council has received from Russians who have benefited from working with it.

The Russian Foreign Minister stated publicly on 14 December what the Russian Government had been saying to us in private—that their attacks on the British Council were linked to the Litvinenko affair. I announced to the House on 16 July a list of measures that the Government had decided to adopt in response to Russia's failure to co-operate with our efforts to secure justice for Alexander Litvinenko. These included introducing visa restrictions for Russian officials travelling to the UK and suspending our visa consultations. The House can rest assured that those measures will continue to be administered rigorously.

We regard as entirely separate the issues surrounding Mr. Litvinenko's murder and the activities of the British Council to build links between British and Russian schools and universities, to support English language teaching in Russia and Russian studies in the UK and to promote the best of British drama, writing, music and art. Nor do we believe that cultural activities should become a political football. In fact, educational and cultural activities are important ways of bringing people together. That is why I have decided not to take similar action against Russia's cultural activities in the UK—for example, by sending back Russian masterpieces scheduled for show at the Royal Academy or by taking measures against the two Russian diplomats at the Russian embassy who are dedicated to cultural work. We have nothing to fear from these contacts; we welcome and encourage them.

The immediate cost to the Russian people of the Russian Government's actions is their lack of access to the benefits of British Council activity. The longer-term cost is their country's standing in the world as a responsible international player. The British Council will continue its work in Moscow, meeting the demand from as many as possible of the 1.25 million Russian citizens who used the council's services last year.

The British Council's experience in Russia is not repeated in any of the more than 100 British Council operations elsewhere in the world. Russia's actions therefore raise serious questions about her observance of international law, as well as about the standards of behaviour she is prepared to adopt towards her own citizens. That can only make the international community more cautious in its dealings with Russia in international negotiations and more doubtful about its existing international commitments.

Russia remains an important international player in addressing key global issues and challenges, including climate change and energy security, as well as others such as Iran and Kosovo, but I hope the whole House will agree with me that Russia's actions against the British Council are a stain on Russia's reputation and standing that will have been noted by countries all around the world.

(HC Deb 17 January 2008 Vol 470 c1095–1097)

7/11

Answering questions about the operation of British Council offices in Russia, the Foreign Secretary said:

On 12 December the Russian authorities announced that they planned to shut down the British Council offices in St. Petersburg and Yekaterinburg on 1 January 2008. I made it clear in my written ministerial statement of 13 December that the Russian Government's threat against the British Council was illegal [UKMIL (2007) **7/11**]. It is therefore the intention of the British Council to remain open and operational in St. Petersburg and Yekaterinburg …

The independence of the British Council is asserted on both sides of the House. Certainly it is not a political football from our point of view, and our message to the Russian Government is that they should not use the British Council as a political football. I hope that that can be a united message, because 1.25 million Russians benefited from the activities of the British Council last year, and that must be in both our countries' interests …

The first thing to say is that, while a threat was issued on 12 December, it has not yet been carried out. Our first priority is to send a clear message to the Russians that this is illegal and there is nothing to be gained by them—in fact, there is everything to be lost, in terms of services for Russian people and of the reputation of Russia around the world—in carrying out this threat. Certainly, my conversations with European and other G8 colleagues suggest that there is unanimous incomprehension at the proposal of the Russian Government to crack down on the British Council. Our duty of care to our staff is obviously something that we take seriously and the offices are in the first instance a matter for British Council management. … both at official level in Russia and at ministerial level, we take the duty of care to both sets of staff extremely seriously …

We can at least say that there is absolutely no foundation to those allegations. The legality of the British Council activity seems to me to be clear. It may be worth reading into the record that the British Council's activities are fully compliant with not just international law, but Russian law. Its presence and its activities are specifically endorsed by a 1994 cultural centres agreement signed by Russia. I give my absolute assurance on the independence and legality of the British Council's work ...

First, let us not yet talk about Russian actions. There have been threats, but there have not yet been actions against the British Council outside Moscow, and we should continue to urge the Russian Government not to take any actions. Secondly, we need to continue to give the Russian Government the clear message that we will continue to take the Lugovoi issue seriously; the request for his extradition remains in force, and it remains a commitment of ours to see justice done in this country. At the same time, we are determined to work with Russia on a range of international and bilateral issues. We must continue to make that twin-track message clear.

(HC Deb 8 January 2008 Vol 470 cs141–143)

7/12
The Foreign Secretary wrote:

I made clear in my Written Statement on 12 December, and again in oral questions on 8 January, that the Russian Government's threatened action against the British Council in Russia was illegal, and that the British Council intended to remain open and operational in St. Petersburg and Yekaterinburg. The British Council has done so.

I regret to inform the House that, on 14 January, the Russian authorities informed the British Ambassador in Moscow that Russia intends to take a series of administrative measures against the British Council. These include tax measures against the British Council in St. Petersburg and visa restrictions against British Council staff in St. Petersburg and Yekaterinburg. Russia has further stated that it may take further action against the British Council in Moscow, including visa restrictions against UK diplomatic staff. Such threats can only make matters worse. It is not in the interests of either the UK or Russia for flourishing cultural, educational and scientific links to be held hostage to unrelated issues in this way.

As the Government have repeatedly made clear to the Russian authorities, the British Council's activities in St. Petersburg, Yekaterinburg and across Russia are fully compliant both with Russian and international law, under the Vienna conventions. Its presence and activities are also specifically sanctioned by a 1994 UK-Russia Agreement on Co-operation in Education, Science and Culture, signed by Russia.

The Government will consider these latest actions by Russia carefully and will continue to engage with our international partners on them. We will respond to the Russian Government shortly.

(HC Deb 15 January 2008 Vol 470 c27WS)

7/13
An FCO Minister said:

In respect of the British Council's legal position, the 1994 cultural agreement is legally binding. So far as I understand it, the British Council's Moscow offices have not yet been targeted but there have indeed been threats. I understand that Russia has not sought a new status in respect of a cultural agreement or a new agreement for the British Council. The council does not need a new agreement to operate in Russia. However, interestingly, for the past nine years, the UK has been keen to conclude a further cultural centres agreement with Russia. The Russians have not seen fit to co-operate on that yet, but I stress that the council does not need a new agreement, and the 1994 agreement does not stipulate that it does. I am glad to report that I do not believe that any other British organisations have been affected in any way to date ...

Of course the British Government agree with my noble friend that the real reason for the actions of the Russian state—it is the Russian state—against the British Council is not to do with the legality of the British Council but more to do with the Litvinenko case. The Russians have made that connection very clear. We have been trying to keep those matters apart; they made it very clear that they are linked.

(HL Deb 17 January 2008 Vol 697 c1468–1470)

Part Seven: VIII. *The State and its organs–armed forces, including visiting forces*

7/14 (See 16/15)
The Defence Secretary was asked if he would list those *(a)* establishments and *(b)* parcels of land where the US authorities had been granted exclusive occupation by his Department. A Minister wrote:

The United States Visiting Force has never been granted exclusive occupation of UK bases; rather they are made available under the terms of the NATO Status of Forces Agreement 1951, and other arrangements. The following establishments in the United Kingdom are currently occupied by the USVF under the terms of the NATO SOFA of 1951:

[There followed a list, not reproduced.] ...

UK nationals work in a variety of roles at all the principal USVF bases. At RAF Menwith Hill and the Joint Maritime Facility at RAF St. Mawgan there is a joint UK-US mission, where UK nationals are also employed in an operational role.

(HC Deb 15 January 2008 Vol 470 c1136W)

7/15
During a debate in the House of Commons, the Prime Minister said:

On 1 January 2009, with the expiry of United Nations resolution 1790, Iraq will regain its full sovereignty. Yesterday in Baghdad, I told Prime Minister Maliki, and he agreed, that British forces in Iraq should have time to finish the missions that I have just outlined. In the past three weeks, concluding with our talks yesterday, we have made substantial progress with the Government of Iraq. We have defined: first, the tasks that need to completed; secondly, the authorisations needed to complete them; and thirdly, a way to provide a firm legal basis for our forces. At all times, we have worked closely with President Bush and the Americans, and our other coalition partners.

On 16 December, the Iraqi Council of Ministers agreed to submit to the Council of Representatives a short draft law to give the presence of UK forces a legal basis after 1 January. The law is now going through the Iraqi Council of Representatives; it had its first reading yesterday and is scheduled to have its second reading on 20 December. We expect the process to be complete before UN resolution 1790 expires. In the event of the process not being complete, the Iraqis have told us that Coalition Provisional Authority order 17, which confers protection on coalition troops, will remain in place. Our troops will therefore have the legal basis that they need for the future.

Once we have completed our four tasks, including training for the headquarters and specialists of 14th Division—with the precise timing of its completion decided by commanders on the ground—the fundamental change of mission that I described in the House last summer will take place by 31 May 2009 at the latest. At that point, we will begin a rapid withdrawal of our troops, taking the total from just under 4,100 to under 400 by 31 July. The majority of the remaining troops will be dedicated to naval training.

Yesterday, Mr. Maliki and I agreed that Britain's future role will focus on continuing protection against attack of Iraqi oil platforms in the northern Gulf, together with long-term training of the Iraqi navy—work that I saw for myself at the port—and support for training the officers of the Iraqi armed forces. In other words, that is the realisation of a normal defence relationship, similar to those we have with our other key partners in the region, which I agreed with Mr. Maliki in July was our joint objective for 2009.

Of course, that relationship will be one strand of a broader, enduring relationship with democratic Iraq, which I also discussed yesterday with the Prime Minister. Our future relationship will be one of partnership. We agreed to continue the shift of focus to economic, commercial, cultural and educational relationships. We will maintain a large embassy headed by a senior ambassador in Baghdad and maintain small missions in Basra and Erbil. The embassy in Baghdad will expand its commercial office and the Department for International Development will expand its programme of economic advice in Baghdad. We have discussed a plan with Prime Minister Maliki for British companies to provide expertise to the Iraqi Ministry of Oil, and Britain can help Iraq's plans to give 10,000 Iraqi students scholarships overseas.

The Prime Minister continued:

… The Right Hon. Gentleman asked about the agreement between our forces and the Iraqi Government. The agreement provides the conditions under which, following the expiry of the UN resolutions, our forces can be protected while in the country. I will place in the Library the document that is going to the Iraqi provisional assembly, the Council of Representatives. It contains means by which, if there are disputes on these matters, they can be resolved, and it maintains that if a case came up, any person concerned would remain in British detention, not Iraqi detention, during the period of the investigation. It is similar but not entirely similar to the United States' agreement. We should remember that the United States' presence will be longer. It is engaged more than we are in combat operations, and the discussions with the Iraqi authorities were different from the very special discussions that we had with the Iraqi authorities.

(HC Deb 18 December 2008 Vol 485 c1234–1238)

Part Eight: Jurisdiction of the State

Part Eight: I.A. *Jurisdiction of the State—bases of jurisdiction—territoriality*

8/1

A Treasury Minister wrote:

Domicile and residence are separate concepts and domicile is not affected by visits to the UK whereas residence may be. If someone is neither resident nor domiciled in the UK, they are subject to tax only on UK-source income. It is only when someone establishes that they are resident in the UK that their domicile becomes relevant for UK tax purposes.

Under the changes announced at the Budget, from 6 April 2008, any day where an individual is present in the UK at midnight will be counted as a day of presence in the UK for residence test purposes.

An exemption will apply in the case of transit passengers. This will provide that days spent in transit, which could include being in the UK at midnight, will not be counted as days of presence so long as during the transit the individual does not engage in activities that are to a substantial extent unrelated to their passage through the UK.

(HL Deb 14 March 2008 Vol 699 cWA263)

8/2

A Minister wrote:

Foreign security officials who come to the United Kingdom in support of sporting events are subject to United Kingdom laws. Foreign security officials who commit a criminal offence while in the United Kingdom, including assault on a member of the public, are liable to investigation and prosecution in the same way as those who are resident in the United Kingdom.

The Independent Police Complaints Commission deals with complaints and conduct matters against police officers and staff in England and Wales. The Government have no plans to extend the jurisdiction of the Independent Police Complaints Commission.

(HL Deb 1 July 2008 Vol 703 cWA27)

Part Eight: I.B. *Jurisdiction of the State—bases of jurisdiction—personality (active and passive)*

8/3
It was put to the Minister of Defence:

As you know legislation has been introduced over the years which has made it completely illegal for any corrupt practices to take place and for some sort of extraterritoriality. The allegations that have been made to this Committee took place over 30 years and the Government has actually defended all those allegations going way back to the 1960s. The responses have not relied upon Part 12 of the Anti-Terrorism, Crime and Security Act 2001. That statute provided extraterritorial reach ... in respect of acts of bribery by UK citizens overseas but the MoD said that for many years prior to the introduction of the 2001 Act UK civil servants were already subject to extraterritorial jurisdiction for criminal offences if all the elements of the offence were committed overseas by virtue of the Criminal Justice Act of 1948. The implications that we drew were that if a civil servant was engaged in corruption overseas he or she would have been prosecuted under the 1948 Act. Is that a correct construction to put on the MoD's position?

He said:

My understanding, from the enquiries that I have made and the advice I have received, is that Section 31 of the Criminal Justice Act 1948 creates just that jurisdiction. So far as public officials were concerned in terms of activity abroad we did not need to wait until 2001 until there was a jurisdiction including activities beyond the shores of the United Kingdom [UK]. The answer to your question is that for a prosecution there needs to be a complaint, evidence and an investigation. I am not aware of any complaint and investigation that took place in relation to the 1948 Act so if you draw the inference that the absence of a prosecution meant that there was no breach of it, then you are entitled to do that. I am not suggesting that to you. I do not know if, at any time between the 1970s and now, somebody made a complaint. I don't know. Can I also say to you, just for completeness' sake, that my understanding—and I accept this advice—is in law that this extraterritoriality, this jurisdiction went beyond the public servants and in fact there was in the common law such a jurisdiction relating to people who were not public servants. [Q.16]

(Quadripartite Committee Report, Scrutiny of Arms Export Control, HC 254 (2008))

Part Eight: I.D. *Jurisdiction of the State—bases of jurisdiction—universality*

(See **6/31**)

8/4
The Home Secretary was asked what plans her Department had to enhance the powers of *(a)* border and *(b)* other officials to stop people on

the grounds that they suspect them to be victims or perpetrators of human trafficking. A Minister wrote:

To help meet the increased challenge from organised crime and terrorism the Prime Minister announced in November the creation of the United Kingdom Border Agency which will bring together into a single organisation the work of UK visas, the Border and Immigration Agency and the border work of HM Revenue and Customs. The UK Border Agency will give officers the power to detain people not just on suspicion of immigration offences or for customs crime but also for other criminal activity. Powers are also being given to airline liaison officers to cancel visas where justified.

To assist in punishing facilitators or traffickers Section 31 (1) of the UK Borders Act 2007 came into force on 31 January 2008. This will give border staff powers to ensure that we can prosecute traffickers and facilitators operating anywhere within the secure areas of ports, whether they commit an act here or overseas and regardless of their nationality.

Increased training and awareness raising, including that provided by other expert organisations, means that our front-line staff are better equipped than ever to identify potential victims at an early stage.

[The UK Borders Act 2007, s 31(1) amends the Asylum and Immigration (Treatment of Claimants etc) Act 2004, s.4 by making it an offence to traffick people for exploitation regardless where the conduct takes place or the nationality of the defendant, Ed.].

(HC Deb 18 February 2008 Vol 472 c443W)

Part Eight: III.A. *Jurisdiction of the state—extra-territorial exercises of jurisdiction—general*

8/5
A Business Minister wrote in reply to a question about US jurisdiction of UK companies:

We are aware of the concerns of industry with regard to US extra-territorial legislation, which are raised by representatives of industry and their legal advisors on a regular basis.

...

The UK opposes the excessive use of extra-territorial legislation, and we regularly express our concerns when Washington embassy officials meet relevant US officials.

In addition, the UK has made two recent formal representations in a demarche to the State Department and in a letter from Sir Nigel Sheinwald to Secretary of State Rice concerning an Alien Tort Statute case being considered by the Supreme Court against companies dealing with South Africa in the apartheid era.

[Sir Nigel Sheinwald is the British Ambassador to the US; the case, *American Isuzu Motros et al v Ntseobeza et al (07-919)*, was returned to the District Court by the US Supreme Court on 12 May 2008 because the Supreme Court did not have a quorum to decide whether or not the application was well founded under the ATCA, Ed.]

(HC Deb 15 May 2008 Vol 475 c1753W)

8/6

The Business Secretary was asked with respect to USA: bank services, what progress had been made on establishing guiding principles for intervention in extraterritoriality cases since July 2008. In reply, a Minister wrote:

While discussions on guiding principles are still ongoing, we continue to oppose the excessive use of extra-territorial legislation. There has been continued regular contact with UK companies about the applications of US extraterritoriality, and we continue to raise the issue with US interlocutors of the excessive extraterritorial reach of US jurisdiction as appropriate.

(HC Deb 21 October 2008 Vol 481 c216W)

8/7

A Minister wrote:

The Department periodically receives representations from businesses, business representatives and individuals usually, but not exclusively, in respect of US trade sanctions against Cuba.

The Government are opposed to excessive assertions of extraterritorial legislation and jurisdiction and frequently makes their views known in contacts with the US.

We have made our opposition to US policy clear through our vote every year against the US embargo on Cuba at the United Nations General Assembly, most recently on 30 October 2007, and UK officials raised the issue again with US officials in Washington in May. The UK and the US agree that though they share the same policy aim, peaceful transition to pluralist democracy, they differ on how to achieve that aim. The US favours isolation of Cuba, while the EU prefers constructive engagement and dialogue.

(HC Deb 21 October 2008 Vol 481 c206W-207W)

Part Nine: State Territory

Part Nine: II.A. *State territory—boundaries and frontiers—delimitation*

9/1

The Defence Secretary was asked whether all NATO member states with forces serving in Afghanistan recognized the same international border between Afghanistan and Pakistan for military operations. He wrote:

All contributing nations to the ISAF mission in Afghanistan agree to be bound by the definition of the joint area of operations contained within the operational plan. Consequently the international border between Afghanistan and Pakistan is viewed consistently by all these nations

(HC Deb 7 January 2008 Vol 470 c16W)

9/2

The Foreign Secretary was asked whether the United Kingdom recognized the 1893 Durand Line as the international border between Afghanistan and Pakistan. An FCO Minister wrote:

We regard the treaties establishing the Durand Line as an international border as valid. However, it has a complicated history and there are sensitivities in the region surrounding its status. It is therefore for the sovereign parties concerned to determine their territorial border and any related disputes.

(HC Deb 7 January 2008 Vol 470 c87W)

Part Ten: International Watercourses

Part Eleven: Seas and Vessels

Part Eleven: II. *Seas and vessels—territorial sea, including overflight*

11/1

The Environment Secretary was asked what responsibilities *(a)* his Department and *(b)* the Scottish Executive had within the (i) six and (ii) 12 nautical miles limit around Scotland. A Minister wrote:

Activities in the marine area out to both six and 12 nautical miles are controlled under a variety of regimes. Responsibilities under these regimes in different parts of our territorial sea are subject to the devolution settlements and other management arrangements agreed with the devolved administrations. As a consequence, DEFRA responsibilities across the marine area vary and some of those responsibilities are shared with other Government Departments and agencies.

Responsibilities within those parts of the territorial sea adjacent to Scotland are defined under the Scotland Act 1998. The Scottish Executive has responsibility in that area for all matters not reserved to the UK Government by virtue of that Act, and for any reserved matters which have been executively devolved to the Scottish Ministers.

(HC Deb 14 January 2008 Vol 470 c865W-866W)

11/2
Fishing

The Environment Secretary was asked how many non-UK vessels had historic rights to fish within the UK 12 nautical mile limit, broken down by country of origin; and what the quota of each is. A Minister wrote:

There is no stipulation of the number of non-UK vessels that are entitled to fish within the UK's six to 12 nautical mile zone. However, vessels are restricted entry to our inshore waters on the basis of country and gear type. Those countries who have historic rights to fish are laid down in Annex 1 of the Framework Regulation for the Common Fisheries Policy (Council Regulation (EC) No 2371/2002 of 20 December 2002 on the conservation and sustainable exploitation of fisheries resources under the Common Fisheries Policy), which can be found at:

<http://eurlex.europa.eu/LexUriServ/LexUriServ.do?uri=CELEX:32002R2371: EN:NOT>

Quota is allocated to member states on the basis of the International Council for the Exploration of the Sea (ICES) sea areas. There is no specific quota for the six to 12 mile zone. Details of the quotas for each species that individual countries have access to can be found in Council Regulation (EC) No 40/2008 of 16 January 2008 fixing for 2008 the fishing opportunities and associated conditions for certain fish stocks and groups of fish stocks, applicable in Community waters and, for Community vessels, in waters where catch limitations are required, which can be accessed at:

<http://eurlex.europa.eu/LexUriServ/LexUriServ.do?uri=OJ:L:2008:019:0001: 0203:EN:PDF>

(HC Deb 28 February 2008 Vol 472 c1861W)

11/3

The Secretary for the Environment was asked (1) whether *(a)* UK and *(b)* other EU member states' fishing vessels were permitted to engage in pair-trawling in the six to 12 mile band of UK waters; and (2) what assessment he had made of the effects of pair-trawling in UK waters on *(a)* bass and *(b)* dolphins; and what steps he planned to take to reduce adverse effects. An Environment Minister wrote:

In 2004 we banned pelagic pair trawling for bass by UK vessels within 12 miles of the south west coast of England (within ICES area VIIe) as this fishery was shown to have relatively high levels of cetacean by-catch. Other bass fisheries, such as gillnetting and hand lining, and pair trawl fisheries targeting other species have not been affected.

The UK asked that the ban on pelagic pair trawling for bass be extended to the vessels of other member states, who are currently permitted to fish between six and 12 miles off the south west English coast (under Article 9 of Council Regulation EC No. 2371/2002), but this was turned down by the European Commission. We could therefore only take unilateral action for our own vessels out to 12 miles.

There is ongoing research funded by the Department and carried out by the Sea Mammal Research Unit to monitor by-catch in all relevant UK fishery sectors, including the bass pair trawl fishery, and to research by-catch mitigation measures in order to identify measures that are effective at deterring cetaceans over the long-term and that are safe and cost-effective for the industry. Further analysis of the effectiveness of the 12 mile ban of sea bass pair trawling will be undertaken as further data becomes available.

The scientific advice from the International Council for the Exploration of the Sea (ICES) in 2004, based on analytical assessments of UK inshore bass stocks, suggest that the bass stock is fished sustainably. Updated assessments have been carried out by the Centre for Environment, Fisheries and Aquaculture Science (CEFAS), in 2006 and 2008. These confirm the earlier assessment indicating that current levels of both bass landings and biomass are high.

The 2007 UK report to the European Commission on observed cetacean by-catch levels in certain fisheries, as required by Council Regulation (EC) 812/2004, includes estimates of common dolphin and harbour porpoise by-catch in the south-west for 2005 and 2006 in gillnet, tangle net and bass mid-water pair trawls. The UK is not due to report to the European Commission on 2006–07 observed by-catch levels until June. It is for each member state to monitor by-catch on their own vessels and submit their findings to the European Commission.

(HC Deb 15 May 2008 Vol 475 c1747W)

11/4
Iran/Iraq territorial waters

The Government were asked what procedure was followed in (a) delineating, and (b) publishing the boundary line between Iraqi and Iranian territorial waters in the North Arabian Gulf. An FCO Minister wrote:

The present boundary between Iran and Iraq was originally agreed in the Constantinople Protocol of 17 November 1913. A further treaty was agreed in 1937 which reaffirmed the boundary in the Shatt al-Arab as established by the Constantinople Protocol. On 6 March 1975 a joint communiqué was issued in Algiers by Iran and Iraq relative to the resolution of the problems of their common boundary as follows: to undertake the final demarcation of their land boundaries on the basis of the Constantinople Protocol of 1913; and to delimit their river boundary according to the thalweg (deep water channel) line. Following World War II, problems continued along the boundary and Iran was keen to establish the actual position of the thalweg in the Shatt al-Arab. This process became a Treaty Relating to the State Boundary and Good-Neighbourliness between Iran and Iraq with three protocols and their annexes and was signed in Baghdad on 13 June 1975. The protocol relating to the river boundary included an annex of four admiralty charts of the Shatt al-Arab containing co-ordinates of the thalweg boundary. The boundary as agreed in these treaties was effectively ignored by Iraq during the Iran/Iraq war, but was reinstated in 1990. The boundary as defined in the 1975 treaty is therefore the present ratified boundary between Iran and Iraq and is depicted on our charts and maps.

(HL Deb 29 April 2008 Vol 703 cWA19)

11/5

The Government were asked whether any steps had been taken to define and announce any exclusion zone or line of blockade or similar maritime boundary in relation to Iraqi waters in the North Arabian Gulf. An FCO Minister wrote:

There is no naval blockade of Iraqi territorial waters. An exclusion zone has been established around two Iraqi oil platforms, situated in Iraq's territorial waters. Within these, the right of innocent passage is suspended. This has been formally promulgated by a notice to mariners. The Government of Iraq are negotiating with Kuwait and Iran to agree maritime boundaries.

(HL Deb 19 May 2008 Vol 701 cWA166)

Part Eleven: VI. *Seas and vessels—exclusive economic zone, exclusive or preferential fisheries zone*

11/6

The Foreign Secretary was asked what progress had been made in negotiations with the Maldives on maritime demarcations between Maldive territorial waters and those around the Chagos Archipelago. An FCO Minister said:

There is no overlap of territorial waters between the Maldives and the British Indian Ocean Territory.

A draft agreement on the boundary between the Maldives Exclusive Economic Zone (EEZ) and the British Indian Ocean Territory Fishery Zone was agreed at technical level in 1992, but it has never been signed and is not in force. Since 1992, the Maldives has replaced its 1976 legislation on the EEZ with Act No 6/96 dated June 1996. Notwithstanding the changes to this EEZ legislation, which introduces archipelagic baseline points, it seems to respect the boundary agreed in draft in 1992.

The draft agreement reached in 1992, which would set out the maritime boundary between the Maldives Exclusive Economic Zone and the British Indian Ocean Territory Fishery Zone, is based entirely on the equidistance principle with no adjustment.

Representatives of the Government of the Republic of Maldives and the Government met in November 1992 to discuss the delimitation of the maritime boundary between the Maldives and the British Indian Ocean Territory. Disclosure of the minutes to this meeting, together with a copy of the draft agreement attached thereto, could only be made after consultation with the Government of the Maldives.

(HC Deb 9 January 2008 Vol 470 c559W)

11/7

A Minister wrote:

According to Article 73(3) of the United Nations Convention on the Law of the Sea (UNCLOS):

"Coastal State penalties for violations of fisheries laws and regulations in the Exclusive Economic Zone may not include imprisonment, in the absence of agreements to the contrary by the States concerned, or any other form of corporal punishment".

The penalties in the shark-finning order derive from the Sea Fish (Conservation) Act 1967, and these do not include imprisonment in line with UNCLOS.

Obstruction of British sea-fishery officers at sea or on land is treated very seriously. Where this amounts to assault or compromises safety at sea, offences will be prosecuted under the appropriate legislation.

(HL Deb 20 May 2008 Vol 701 cWA176)

11/8

The Environment Secretary was asked which measures concerning pelagic pair trawling which he had *(a)* introduced and *(b)* proposed to the European Commission under (i) Article 8, (ii) Article 9 and (iii) Article 10 of Council Regulation 2371/2002 had been approved. A Minister wrote:

In January 2005, the UK invoked Article 9 of Council Regulation 2371/2002. In its proposals, the UK sought a ban on pelagic pair trawling by all member states within 12 nautical miles of the English coast within The International Council for the Exploration of the Sea (ICES) Area VIIE. The European Commission rejected the proposal and the ban on pelagic pair trawling remains applicable to UK vessels only under the South-West Territorial Waters (prohibition of Pair Trawling) Order 2004.

The Environment Secretary was asked further what measures which EU Member States had *(a)* introduced and *(b)* proposed to the European Commission under (i) Article 8, (ii) Article 9 and (iii) Article 10 of Council Regulation 2371/2002 had been approved. The Minister wrote:

To the best of my knowledge, none of our neighbouring member states have invoked, or had approved, measures that have a significant effect on the UK fishing industry under Articles 8 and 9 of Council Regulation 2371/2002. A more complete answer to this question can be obtained from the European Commission as the Article 8 and 9 measures are only notified to the Commission, concerned member states, and the relevant regional advisory council.

Article 10 measures are applicable solely to fishing vessels flying the flag of the member state invoking the article and are therefore not notifiable to other member states.

(HC Deb 24 January 2008 Vol 470 c2124W)

11/9

The Environment Secretary was asked what vessels from other EU member states undertook fisheries protection and enforcement within UK fishery limits. A Minister wrote:

Patrol vessels from other member states may operate in UK waters in the following circumstances:

1. when taking part in Joint Deployment Plans organised by the Community Fisheries Control Agency.

2. when taking part in joint exercises organised by the UK and one or more other member states.

3. when inspecting their own vessels under their own initiative after notifying the UK authorities in accordance with EC Reg. 1042/2006.

4. when inspecting OMS vessels under their own initiative, when permission from the UK must be sought in accordance with EC Reg. 1042/2006.

To date, vessels from France, Belgium, Netherlands, Germany and Denmark have taken part in joint operations under options 1. and 2. France have notified the UK and inspected their own vessels under option 3. No vessels have or sought our permission to carry out operations under option 4.

(HC Deb 7 March 2008 Vol 472 c2879W)

11/10 [See also **5/68**]

In reply to a question on fishing in the waters of Western Sahara, a Minister wrote:

All fishing in the waters of Morocco or Western Sahara must be conducted in accordance with the EU-Morocco Fisheries Agreement 2006. EU member states and the European Commission engaged in detailed discussion about the legality of the Agreement before it was finalised. The EU's Legal Service opinion was that the Agreement was in accordance with international law, including Chapter XI of the Charter of the UN which requires of administering powers that the development of their economic activities in a non-self governing territory does not adversely affect the interests of its peoples. All British vessels and those from other EU member states fishing in the waters of Morocco or Western Sahara are obliged to act in accordance with the terms of the Agreement.

(HC Deb 6 October 2008 Vol 480 c237W)

Part Eleven VII. *Seas and vessels—continental shelf*

11/11

A Minister wrote:

In accordance with article 76 of the UN Convention on the Law of the Sea, on 9 May 2008, the UK submitted to the Commission on the Limits of the Continental Shelf, information on the limits of the continental shelf beyond 200 nautical miles from the coastline of Ascension Island.

Under the Rules of Procedure of the Commission, the executive summary of the submission was made public and circulated to all UN member states (a copy can be found at:

<www.un.org/Depts/los/clcs_new/submissions_files/submission_gbr.htm>

A period of at least three months then had to follow before the submission could be formally heard by the Commission, during which time any and all member states of the United Nations had the right to transmit Notes Verbale making observations on, or objecting to, the submission.

No such observations or objections having been made, the UK formally presented its submission to the Commission in New York on 27 August 2008.

We expect that the Commission will now proceed to establish a sub-commission of seven members to examine the UK submission. The time scale for this will depend on the overall work load of the Commission. There is no deadline for a decision.

Once satisfied, the Commission will make its recommendations to the UK regarding the establishment of the outer limits of the continental shelf around Ascension Island. In line with the provisions of the convention, the limits subsequently established shall be final and binding in international law.

In 2006, the UK made another submission to the Commission—jointly with France, Ireland and Spain—in respect of the sea bed in the Bay of Biscay. We await the Commission's recommendations.

UK officials and scientists are also in the process of examining two further areas of continental shelf where the geological conditions may exist to justify further submissions—in the 'Hatton Rockall Area' of the North East Atlantic, and around the Falkland Island islands and South Georgia. In both instances, the UK will take appropriate action before May 2009, as required by the convention.

The UK has confirmed to the Commission that it is not submitting data for the continental shelf around the British Antarctic Territory, but that it reserves the right to do so in future.

The UK—and many other countries—is taking these actions in order to safeguard for the future its sovereign rights over its continental shelf, where the conditions laid down by the convention allow. It is an orderly process, entirely in line with international law, and recognised by the UN General Assembly.

(HC Deb 13 October 2008 Vol 480 c959W-960W)

11/12

The Environment Secretary was asked when he next planned to discuss the Marine Bill with the devolved administrations; if he would discuss the control of the seabed to the 200 nautical miles limit around Scotland; whether he intended to use the Marine Bill to give the Scottish Executive control over that seabed. A Minister wrote:

DEFRA officials and I meet regularly with our counterparts in the devolved administrations to discuss marine issues, including the Marine Bill. Proposals for the draft Marine Bill respect the current devolution settlement with Scotland. It is for the UK Government as a whole to consider any proposals for changes in responsibility for the control of the seabed to the 200 nautical mile limit around the whole of the UK.

(HC Deb 14 January 2008 Vol 470 c865W)

11/13

Part Eleven VIII.A. *Seas and vessels—high seas—freedom of high seas, including overflight*

The Business Secretary was asked what minimum safety and security requirements applied to vessels carrying nuclear material by sea for a distance of *(a)* less and *(b)* more than 500 miles. A Minister wrote:

The security of nuclear material on board a UK-flagged vessel is regulated by the Office for Civil Nuclear Security (OCNS) in accordance with the Nuclear Industries Security Regulations 2003 (NISR). These regulations, which ensure that the UK's obligations under the Convention on the Physical Protection on Nuclear Material (CPPNM) are met and which take full account of international recommendations in this area, are supplemented by a Technical Requirements Document which details minimum security standards. This document is protectively marked; it is not Government policy to release precise details of security measures since this information could be of use to those with malicious intent.

In terms of security arrangements for the transport of nuclear material, distance is not the factor which sets the level of security. The overall security posture will be dictated by the category of the material being carried and the threat pertaining. The mode(s) of transport, packages to be used and other physical, procedural and administrative measures based on the principles of defence-in-depth and graded approach will also be relevant in designing a security system combining deterrence, detection, delay and response measures, complemented by other measures for mitigating the consequences of malicious acts, including recovery and for minimizing the radiological consequences of any theft, sabotage or other malicious act.

Vessels transporting nuclear material by sea are required to operate in compliance with the requirements of prevailing international law on the safety of ships, most notably the International Convention for the Safety of Life at Sea (SOLAS, found at <www.imo.org/Conventions/contents.asp?topic_id=257&;doc_id=647>). Additionally they are required to comply with supplementary measures contained in the International Code for the Safe Carriage of Packaged Irradiated Fuel, Plutonium and High Level Radioactive Wastes on board ships (the INF code, found at <www.imo.org/Safety/mainframe.asp?topic_id=354>) which deal specifically with the carriage of nuclear material.

(HC Deb 26 March 2008 Vol 474 c290W)

11/14

The Transport Secretary was asked what obligations ship owners are under to inform the Maritime and Coastguard Agency of cargoes lost overboard in *(a)* British and *(b)* international waters. A Minister wrote:

Reporting requirements for the loss of polluting goods, containers or packages overboard are addressed under the Merchant Shipping Vessel Traffic Monitoring and Reporting Requirements) regulations 2004/2110.

All vessels operating in UK controlled waters must inform the Coastguard of any such losses from the vessel itself or of sightings of containers and packages drifting at sea.

For UK vessels operating in international waters a report must be made to the authority of the coastal state of any losses of polluting goods, containers or packages which pose a threat to the coastline or a related interest of that state.

(HC Deb 22 May 2008 Vol 476 c432W)

Part Eleven VIII.B. *Seas and vessels—high seas—visit and search*

11/15

The FCO sent the following memorandum to the Quadripartite Committee in response to questions raised by the Committee:

The UK plays a significant part in the Proliferation Security Initiative which aims to stop illegitimate trade in weapons of mass destruction and WMD technology. Does the UK Government have the necessary powers to interdict ships and their cargoes on the high seas?

ANSWER

At present the UK has no powers to seize goods subject to export controls on the high seas, or to interdict ships on the grounds that they are carrying such goods.

The 2005 Protocol to the 1988 Convention for the Suppression of Unlawful Acts Against the Safety of Maritime Navigation (the SUA Protocol) will strengthen the international legal basis to impede and prosecute the trafficking of WMD, their delivery systems and related materials on the high seas in commercial ships by requiring state parties to criminalize such transport. The Protocol also establishes a mechanism to facilitate the boarding in international waters of vessels suspected of engaging in these activities.

In broad terms, once the SUA Protocol comes into force and the UK has ratified, UK enforcement officers will be able to board a ship on the high seas and seize goods, where there is reasonable grounds to suspect the ship is transporting WMD, or equipment that could be used for WMD. Consistent with existing international law and practice, SUA boardings can only be conducted with the express consent of the flag state of the vessel to be boarded.

The SUA Protocol will only come into force after ratification by 12 countries. Currently only three countries (Spain, Cook Islands and St Kitts and Nevis) have ratified. The UK has signed the Protocol but has not yet ratified.

PSI is a practical, highly effective mechanism for addressing the very real threat of illicit trafficking in WMD and related materials. The UK continues to participate actively in PSI. We recently hosted a meeting of the PSI Operational Experts Group in London (February 2008), and sent a strong cross-departmental team to the PSI 5th Anniversary events in Washington (May 2008). The initiative that led to the creation of the SUA Protocol was driven by PSI nations, and at the recent Washington meetings PSI participants adopted a declaration which encouraged all signatories to the Protocol to work towards ratifying it.

Does the Government require legislation to give legal effect to the Protocol to the Convention for the Suppression of Unlawful Acts Against the Safety of Maritime Navigation? When will the legislation come forward?

ANSWER

Legislation is required to enable the UK to ratify the SUA Protocol. The necessary legislation is contained in the Transport Security Bill, which has a place in the Draft Legislative Programme for the fourth session of Parliament. The Department for Transport has led preparation of the Bill. [No Bill has yet been introduced, Ed.]

(Quadripartite Committee, Scrutiny of Arms Export Control, HC 254 (2008))

Part Eleven VIII.D. *Seas and vessels—high seas—piracy*

11/16

The Defence Secretary was asked whether pirates arrested at sea by the Royal Navy were *(a)* taken on board Her Majesty's ships and *(b)* rendered to UK jurisdiction; and what discussions his Department had had with officials in the Home Department on the potential for such pirates to claim asylum in the United Kingdom. A Minister wrote:

Our records suggest that no pirates have been arrested by the Royal Navy since the Second World War. If a pirate were to be arrested, they would remain in UK custody until such time as they were either lawfully transferred to another nation or returned to the UK criminal justice system.

(HC Deb 22 May 2008 Vol 476 c401W)

11/17

A Minister wrote:

Ministers from the Departments responsible for countering piracy have recently agreed that HMG should take a more proactive stance on dealing with this issue, recognising that this will be best achieved with international partners including NATO, the EU and coalition forces already in the Gulf of Aden.

We continue to work with our EU partners on measures to implement UNSCRs 1816 and 1838. In September we supported the establishment of an EU cell that aims to co-ordinate military escorts to World Food Programme shipping. We have also supported EU planning for a counter-piracy naval operation off the coast of Somalia, and on 14 October the EU Political and Security Committee decided to accept the offer made by the UK to provide the Operation Commander (Rear Admiral Phil Jones) and the Operation HQ (the Multinational Headquarters at Northwood).

A formal decision from the EU member states to allow planning for the opera-tion to proceed to the next stage is expected in the next ten days. We have made it clear that the UK offer is conditional on sufficient forces being generated for the mission to be effective. Current estimates are for the operation to be launched towards the end of 2008, probably in December, once force generation and detailed planning is complete.

The key task of the operation will be to ensure the safe delivery of World Food Programme and other vital humanitarian deliveries to Somalia, but also to deter attacks on European and other shipping. EU partners are agreed that the ESDP operation is closely co-ordinated with other actors in the region, including Combined Task Force 150 and NATO.

The ESDP operation will not solve the long-term problems of Somalia which are the root causes of piracy, and we will continue working with our international partners to restore governance.

(HC Deb 21 October 2008 Vol 481 c192W-193W)

11/18
During a debate in the House of Lords, a Minister said:

All Royal Navy vessels and those of other countries have a responsibility to tackle piracy under the United Nations Convention on the Law of the Sea. We are tak-ing a more proactive role along with other partner nations because of the severity of the problem and the concern that it is causing. The Transitional Federal Government in Somalia are very unstable, and the situation is very difficult. We and other allies are offering aid. There is a problem about what will happen to anybody who is apprehended because we do not want to see the Royal Navy hav-ing to bring back a lot of individuals to this country. Part of our purpose is deter-rence, but we are also seeking a memorandum of understanding with coastal states in the area to see what possibility there is of landing anybody who is appre-hended on those shores for local action.

(HC Deb 5 November 2008 Vol 705 c216)

11/19
The Government were asked what powers they had under international law for preventing piracy. In reply, a Minister wrote:

The Government have powers to act against piracy under Article 105 of the UN Convention on the Law of the Sea, which provides that any warship may seize a pirate ship or aircraft, and arrest persons and seize the property on board.

Under the international law of the sea, piracy only occurs on the high seas, or a place outside the jurisdiction of any state. The high seas would include parts of the Gulf of Aden and the Indian Ocean. Piracy on the high seas is a crime of universal jurisdiction; the alleged pirate may be charged, tried and punished by any nation into whose jurisdiction he enters.

Under international law, piratical acts in territorial seas come within the coastal state's jurisdiction. States, therefore, may only take action against pirates in territo-rial seas if authorised by the coastal state, and in accordance with its domestic law.

There are separate international instruments which call on states to outlaw other related acts, such as armed robbery at sea, most notably the Convention for the Suppression of Unlawful Acts Against the Safety of Maritime Navigation.

(HC Deb 5 November 2008 Vol 705 cWA72)

11/20

In a debate on piracy off the coast of Somalia, the Foreign Secretary said, in explanation of the vote of the UK in favour of SC resolution 1851:

The United Kingdom has voted in favour of the resolution adopted because we support robust action to address the serious threat to international navigation, including deliveries of humanitarian aid to the people of Somalia, posed by piracy and armed robbery off the coast of Somalia.

The authorization conferred by paragraph 6 of the resolution to permit States cooperating with the Transitional Federal Government to use "all necessary measures that are appropriate in Somalia, for the purpose of suppressing acts of piracy" enables States and regional organizations, with the consent of the Transitional Federal Government, to act, using force if necessary, against pirate activities on land in Somalia. This is an important additional tool to combat those who plan, facilitate or undertake acts of piracy from the territory of Somalia. The United Kingdom considers that any use of force must be both necessary and proportionate. These concepts include an assessment that the measures taken must be appropriate to the circumstances to which they are directed.

[Paragraph 6 of resolution 1851 says:

In response to the letter from the TFG of 9 December 2008, [the Council] *encourages* Member States to continue to cooperate with the TFG in the fight against piracy and armed robbery at sea, *notes* the primary role of the TFG in rooting out piracy and armed robbery at sea, and *decides* that for a period of twelve months from the date of adoption of resolution 1846, States and regional organizations cooperating in the fight against piracy and armed robbery at sea off the coast of Somalia for which advance notification has been provided by the TFG to the Secretary-General may undertake all necessary measures that are appropriate in Somalia, for the purpose of suppressing acts of piracy and armed robbery at sea, pursuant to the request of the TFG, provided, however, that any measures undertaken pursuant to the authority of this paragraph shall be undertaken consistent with applicable international humanitarian and human rights law., Ed.]

(S/PV.6046, 16 December 2008)

Part Eleven VIII.E. *Seas and vessels—high seas—conservation of living resources*

11/21

The Environment Secretary was asked about the Government's policy on the conservation of whales. A Minister wrote:

The UK forms part of a core anti-whaling grouping within the International Whaling Commission (IWC) and supports the IWC's moratorium on commercial whaling. The UK remains strongly opposed to any attempt to lift or weaken the moratorium and, in the longer term, wishes to see it strengthened. We will be meeting with the core anti-whaling group in the run up to IWC60. Posts abroad will also lobby a wide range of governments prior to the meeting to ensure support for the moratorium.

The UK has led efforts to recruit more conservation-minded countries to the IWC through our publication 'Protecting Whales—A Global Responsibility'. This publication has recently been updated and was re-released on 21 December 2007. In the coming weeks, posts will deliver the updated version to host governments, and will continue to engage in discussion with their counterparts on whaling at every appropriate opportunity.

This year, the Secretary of State will write to 18 countries encouraging them to join the IWC for the greater protection of whales.

The UK Government have consistently voiced their opposition to Japanese "scientific" whaling. Most recently, on 8 January, I called in the deputy ambassador from the Japanese embassy in London to express the UK's outrage and urge Japan to end its slaughter of whales.

On 21 December 2007, the UK along with 29 other countries took part in a demarché to the Japanese Government calling on Japan to

> "cease all its lethal scientific research on whales, and assure the immediate return of the vessels which are implementing JARPA II" (the Japanese 'scientific' Research Programme in the Antarctic).

(HC Deb 16 January 2008 Vol 470 c1243W)

11/22

An FCO Minister visited Tokyo from 17–19 January. During his discussion with the Japanese Foreign Minister, the Minister reiterated the UK's strong opposition to Japan's whaling programme.

The Government believe whaling is inherently cruel and continue strongly to urge Japan to cease its whaling activities. In December last year our ambassador in Tokyo took part in a 30 country (plus the European Commission) demarche to the Japanese Ministry of Foreign Affairs to protest against Japan's whaling programme. An Environment Minister met with the deputy head of mission at the Japanese embassy in January and robustly challenged Japan's policy on whaling, pointing out that the UK would continue to state our opposition on this issue publicly.

(HC Deb 4 March 2008 Vol 472 c2357W)

11/23

A Minister wrote:

The right of Governments to issue permits for the killing of whales for scientific purposes is enshrined in Article VIII of the 1946 International Convention for the Regulation of Whaling (ICRW), the parent treaty of the International Whaling Commission (IWC). We doubt that the authors of the ICRW envisaged that parties would seek to conduct research on the scale now practised by Japan, but whether

Japan's activities in this regard can be said to constitute an abuse of the rights granted by Article VIII of the ICRW is a matter which only the courts could determine—were anyone prepared to stand the cost of asking.

Whether or not 'scientific' whaling is legal, we certainly regard it as undesirable since it undermines the IWC's moratorium on commercial whaling and contributes little or nothing to our knowledge of the size and structure of whale populations.

The UK takes every appropriate opportunity to make its opposition to Japan's 'scientific' whaling operations clear to the Japanese Government. We have participated in a number of high level diplomatic protests in recent years and on 8 January this year I called in officials from the Japanese embassy in London to express the UK's outrage over Japan's whaling activities. At this year's IWC meeting in June the UK Commissioner to the IWC made it clear that we saw no justification for lethal scientific research on whales and called for Special Permit whaling to be brought within IWC control and phased out as quickly as possible.

(HC Deb 7 July 2008 Vol 478 c1205W)

11/24

The Government were asked what discussions they had had with the Government of Iceland on the resumption of commercial whaling by Iceland. In reply, a Minister wrote:

[T]he Prime Minister met the Icelandic Prime Minister on 24 April 2008 and during the meeting made clear the UK's disappointment and strength of feeling on this issue.

(HC Deb 7 July 2008 Vol 478 c1336W)

Part Eleven XIII. *Seas and vessels—protection of the marine environment*

11/25

The Environment Secretary was asked if he would make a statement on the recent co-operation between the Government and the Government of the Republic of Ireland on the monitoring of pollution in the Irish Sea. A Minister wrote:

The Irish Sea is bounded by England and Wales, Scotland, Northern Ireland and the Irish Republic and these regions will all have their specific mechanisms for monitoring and reporting on pollution in the Irish Sea.

Partnership-working on the state of the Irish Sea is carried out in the framework of the OSPAR Convention for the Protection of the North East Atlantic to which the UK and the Republic of Ireland are Contracting parties. Regular assessments are carried out, information gathered by the various organisations is brought together and assessments are made and published in the OSPAR Quality Status Report (QSR). The last QSR was published in the year 2000, and included a regional report on the Celtic seas. The next QSR will be published in 2010.

(HC Deb 16 January 2008 Vol 470 c1238W)

11/26

Speaking on a private member's bill to regulate transfer of materials, especially oil, between ships at sea, a Transport Minister said:

The United Kingdom has a highly successful record in maritime safety and the prevention of pollution, and we appreciate the importance of both issues. In particular, we have a highly developed strategic approach to protecting the UK's seas and coasts from ship-source pollution, which involves all of the following steps and measures. We have put in place a network of shore-based stations around the UK coastline to monitor vessel traffic, using automatic identification system technology. We achieve agreement in the forum of the International Maritime Organisation on ships' routing measures which will reduce the risk of groundings or collisions. We ensure that powerful tug boats—commonly referred to as "emergency towing vessels"—are available, so that they can go out and assist ships that lose motive power. We have established arrangements under which a ship that requires assistance, and whose condition needs to be stabilised, can be brought into a place of refuge. We have a highly effective structure for command and control of an incident, in which the Secretary of State's representative for maritime salvage and intervention—SOSREP—plays a major role. We have a fully developed national contingency plan, consistent with the 1990 international convention on oil pollution preparedness, response and co-operation—the OPRC convention. We participate actively in international assistance and co-operation arrangements of a bipartite, multipartite or regional nature—again consistent with the OPRC convention.

In addition, the United Kingdom takes specific actions to give effect to the international convention for the prevention of pollution from ships—the MARPOL convention—notably by the following: ensuring that, in UK ports, reception facilities are available for the types of waste that are generated on board ship, thereby leaving no excuse for ships to resort to discharging their waste illegally at sea; carrying out surveillance, either aerial or satellite, to identify ships carrying out acts of pollution; and having an effective enforcement regime in place, so that ships that have been identified carrying out acts of pollution are prosecuted.

However … I must say that we oppose the Bill on the basis that it goes about that in the wrong way, and the desired control over ship-to-ship oil transfers can be achieved without the need for a Bill.

We have been working for some time on producing regulations under section 130 of the Merchant Shipping Act 1995 to control ship-to-ship oil transfers within UK territorial waters and to ensure that any such transfers are subject to appropriate environmental scrutiny. It is our intention to lay such regulations before Parliament this year, so placing an obligation on the Secretary of State to do so would achieve nothing of value. On the contrary, working on this Bill could only delay the introduction of those regulations by diverting the attention of all concerned.

[The bill was withdrawn, Ed.]

(HC Deb 25 January 2008 Vol 470 c1795–1798)

11/27

The Environment Secretary was asked what plans he had to call upon the Standing Committee of the Convention on International Trade in Endangered

Species to examine the compliance of the Japanese whaling industry with the provisions of the Convention. A Minister wrote:

Following the recent announcement that Japan intended to take 50 Humpback whales in the southern ocean as part of its JARPA II whaling programme, the UK Convention on International Trade in Endangered Species (CITES) Management Authority wrote to the CITES Secretariat asking for clarification on the legal position. We have drawn the contents of the reply to the attention of the EU CITES Management Committee, which will consider it at its next meeting in April.

(HC Deb 1 February 2008 Vol 471 c709W)

11/28

A Minister later wrote:

Following the recent announcement that Japan intended to take 50 humpback whales in the Southern Ocean as part of its JARPA II whaling programme, the UK Convention on International Trade in Endangered Species (CITES) Management Authority wrote to the CITES Secretariat asking for clarification on the legal position. In their response, the CITES Secretariat stated that they were not in a position to issue a statement to the effect that the introduction from the sea of humpback specimens violates article III of the convention. We have drawn the contents of their reply to the attention of the EU CITES Management Committee that will consider it at its next meeting in April.

(HC Deb 18 February 2008 Vol 472 c279W)

11/29

A Minister wrote:

The Government are currently in the process of transposing the existing Annex VI (International Convention for the Prevention of Pollution from Ships) of MARPOL into UK law and will be following this legislation with the implementation of the EU Sulphur Content of Liquid Fuels Directive.

These measures have been agreed internationally and regionally and establish standards for the sulphur content of marine fuels. MARPOL Annex VI applies to all vessels equally while the EC measure targets emissions in port and from vessels engaged in regular service between EC ports.

In implementing Annex VI, the Government have undertaken a series of consultations and sought to ensure that the measures are applied in a fair, transparent and equal manner across the maritime sector to ensure a level playing field for the industry. A further consultation on the EC Directive will be carried out in the spring of 2009.

Additionally the revisions to Annex VI of MARPOL have been developed as a result of work by an International Maritime Organisation (IMO) group of experts and take account of the cost and availability of fuel. The implementation of this will in due course be subject to UK consultation.

(HC Deb 9 October 2008 Vol 480 c792W-793W)

Part Eleven XV. *Seas and vessels—cables and pipelines*

11/30
Speaking on the Energy Bill, the Business Secretary said:

Current offshore legislation was designed principally for oil and gas production or extraction. As a result, there is no single piece of legislation that covers the new kind of offshore gas infrastructure that we in the UK need. The current regulatory process is therefore complex and fragmented. It must be improved and streamlined if new investment is to take place in the time scale that we are discussing. Through clauses 1 to 15, the Bill creates a new regulatory and licensing framework specifically designed for offshore gas storage and offshore LNG—liquefied natural gas—unloading projects. That will simplify the regulatory process and will, I hope, create greater clarity and certainty for investors. The Planning Bill, which I have already mentioned, will streamline the consenting processes for onshore gas projects. The Energy Bill will create a fit-for-purpose regime for offshore gas projects.

This part of the Bill also creates a new regulatory framework for offshore carbon dioxide storage projects. Fossil fuels will continue to be part of the UK's diverse energy mix for decades to come. On present policies, global energy demand could be more than 50 per cent higher in 2030 than it is today. With a significant percentage of that being met by fossil fuels, energy-related greenhouse gas emissions could be around 55 per cent higher than today. Finding a way to reduce the emissions from fossil fuel generation is therefore absolutely essential if we are to meet the challenge of climate change. That is why the Government are supporting a competition for the demonstration of carbon capture and storage. Clauses 16 to 34 will establish a licensing framework that allows storage of carbon dioxide under the sea bed. Without the new legislation, I do not believe that that demonstration project could proceed.

In addition to making provision on licensing, the Bill will also assert the UK's rights to store carbon dioxide beneath the UK sea bed and extend relevant existing offshore legislation—on the decommissioning of offshore gas installations, for example—to future facilities that might be used for carbon dioxide storage. That is a key part of enabling the long-term development of carbon capture and storage. Once constructed, the demonstration project, which we hope will be operational by 2014, will be one of the world's first commercial scale power stations with carbon capture and storage. Our aim is to drive forward the development of a technology that has the potential to reduce carbon emissions from fossil fuel power stations by as much as 90 per cent.

[See Energy Act 2008, ss 1–16 (gas storage); ss.17–35 (carbon dioxide storage), Ed.]

(HC Deb 22 January 2008 Vol 470 cs1365–1366)

Part Eleven XVIII. A.1.(c) *Seas and vessels—vessels—legal regime—merchant vessels*

11/31
The Government were asked whether they claimed ownership of the wreck of HMS Ontario. In reply, a Minister wrote:

I undertook to write to you in answer to your Parliamentary Question on 3 July 2008 (Official Report, column 1040W), about the ownership of HMS ONTARIO, whose wreck has apparently been discovered by a Canadian dive group at the bottom of Lake Ontario on the US-Canada border.

HMS ONTARIO, a 22 gun sloop, foundered in a storm on Lake Ontario on October 31 1780 during the American Revolutionary War—it is uncertain how many lives were lost (estimates range from 88 to over a 120) as the ship may have been carrying some American prisoners of war in addition to British soldiers and her British and Canadian crew. There were no survivors. The dive group, who located the wreck using side-scanning sonar and an unmanned submersible, say that it is virtually intact, it is thought that the cold, fresh water of the lake has acted as a preservative with the lack of light and oxygen slowing decomposition of the ship's timbers. In addition to being effectively the last resting place of those who perished in the sinking, the remains of the ONTARIO undoubtedly represent an important item of underwater cultural heritage. The dive group apparently have no plans to attempt to raise the wreck or remove artefacts from it and have not publicised its position.

The ONTARIO was launched from Carleton Island shipyard on Lake Ontario in May 1780. A King's Ship, she was part of the Provincial Marine, a coastal protection service on the Great Lakes operated and staffed by the Royal Navy. This service with the Provincial Marine complicates the question of ownership as it is possible that rights to the wreck may have transferred to Canada when she became an independent nation and the assets of the Provincial Marine were made over to it. This issue is being investigated but as you can appreciate, it is likely to take some time to resolve.

That said, the issue of who actually owns the wreck may, in this case, be moot. The remains of HMS ONTARIO appear to lie in United States territorial waters and the United States have already indicated that they are willing to use US legislation to protect the wreck from unauthorised interference—a stance that the United Kingdom is entirely comfortable with. The United Kingdom is unlikely to object to appropriate archaeological investigation of the find—however, any such investigation would be a matter for the Canadian and United States authorities in the first instance given that these two countries control access to the site. We shall of course continue to monitor developments and liaise with our Canadian and United States counterparts, but it seems clear that all State parties involved are united in their wish to see the wreck of HMS ONTARIO properly protected.

(HC Deb 1 September 2008 Vol 479 c1403W-1465W)

Part Eleven XVIII. C.4. *Seas and vessels—vessels—jurisdiction over vessels—exercises of jurisdiction other than by flag, coastal, and port state*

11/32

In reply to a question on the Nairobi International Convention on the Removal of Wrecks of 2007, a Minister wrote:

Her Majesty's Government support ratification and early entry into force of the Nairobi International Convention on the Removal of Wrecks 2007, and the implementing provisions to allow the UK to ratify the convention were included in the draft marine navigation Bill, which recently underwent parliamentary scrutiny.

Subject to parliamentary time being available the Government intend to introduce legislation to implement the convention which will allow it to be ratified as soon as possible.

Should the UK ratify the convention, the Government intend to make use of the option to extend its scope to include our territory and territorial sea and to inform the secretary-general of the International Maritime Organisation (IMO) accordingly.

The convention will only enter into force 12 months after the 10th state has deposited an instrument of ratification, acceptance, approval or accession with the secretary-general of the IMO. To date only one state has deposited an instrument of ratification of this convention.

(HC Deb 4 November 2008 Vol 705 c36WA)

Part Twelve: Airspace, Outer Space and Antarctica

Part Twelve: I.A. *Airspace, Outer Space and Antarctica—Airspace— Status*

12/1

Answering a question about the tax status of the aviation industry, a Transport Minister said:

Taxing aviation involves international issues, which are dealt with in the Chicago Convention. The Government are trying to ensure that the convention is renegotiated; that is not an easy task. They are also pursuing—with some success, and hoping for a final decision soon—the inclusion of aviation in the European Union emissions trading system ...

She said later:

... we are trying to gather an international consensus to amend the Chicago Convention, which is now anachronistic.

(HC Deb 6 March 2008 Vol 472 cs1902–1903)

Part Twelve: I.B. *Airspace, Outer Space and Antarctica—Airspace—Uses*

12/2

The Defence Secretary was asked what records his Department held on (*a*) the testing of weapons in space by other Governments over the last 10 years, (b) the volume of debris in low earth orbit which relates to such testing and (c) the potential effects of such debris. A Minister wrote:

We have no evidence suggesting that any state has conducted tests of space-based weapons in the past 10 years. China conducted a successful anti-satellite (ASAT) missile test against its own space asset on 11 January 2007, but the missile itself was ground launched and hence, not stationed in space. The UK has expressed its concern to China about the potential impact of the additional debris this ASAT test created.

The British National Space Centre (BNSC) conducts regular assessments of the volume of space debris in orbit and the potential threat this poses to UK assets.

(HC Deb 10 January 2008 Vol 470 c707W)

12/3
In reply to a question on a no-fly zone for Darfur, a Minister wrote:

We are not currently proposing a no-fly zone for Darfur. We assess that a no-fly zone would restrict essential humanitarian operations and be a major logistical challenge due to the size of Darfur and the lack of available air assets. The United Nations-African Union Mission in Darfur (UNAMID) is mandated to monitor military activity, including flights prohibited by UN Security Council Resolution 1591. We continue to press all parties for the rapid and full deployment of UNAMID

(HC Deb 21 October 2008 Vol 481 c216W)

Part Twelve: III.A. *Airspace, Outer Space and Antarctica—Antarctica—Status*

12/4
The Foreign Secretary was asked whether he planned to make a territorial claim on Antarctica; and what advice he had received on potential conflicts with the Antarctic Treaty Act. An FCO Minister wrote:

The UK has no plans to make any new territorial claim on Antarctica; nor would it do so as that would be contrary to the Antarctic treaty.

The UK has not made any announcements, or final decisions, about any approach to the UN Commission regarding delineation of the outer limits of the continental shelf pertaining to the British Antarctic Territory. The UK will make its intentions known to the Commission prior to the deadline in 2009.

In making any decision to submit information to the UN Commission for the limits of continental shelf, we will of course respect our obligations under the Antarctic treaty and related agreements. We remain fully committed to the treaty, including its protocol on Environmental Protection 1991, which prohibits indefinitely all activity related to mineral resources, other than scientific research, within the treaty area.

(HC Deb 8 January 2009 Vol 470 c443W)

Part Twelve: III.B. *Airspace, Outer Space and Antarctica—Antarctica—Uses*

12/5
The Foreign Secretary was asked whether he had raised concerns with the Antarctic Treaty Secretariat on pollution from the sinking of a passenger cruise vessel in Antarctic waters. An FCO Minister wrote:

The UK has not raised any concerns with the Antarctic Treaty Secretariat on this issue as the Secretariat has no executive powers to take action. This is a matter for Treaty Parties. We have consulted experts from the British Antarctic Survey, whose initial view is that the environmental impacts from the vessel are likely to be minimal. The M/S Explorer used marine gas oil, which is a light non-persistent fuel. The ship sank in open water, some 50 nautical miles from the nearest point of land and any penguin or seabird colonies. There have been reports of fuel leakage, but this has been dissipating quickly and evaporating in the open water. HMS "Endurance" is due to arrive in Antarctica shortly and she will use swath bathymetry to accurately locate the position of the vessel on the seabed and report on any visible signs of pollution.

Tourism and cruise ship safety in Antarctica will be major discussion topics at the next Antarctic Treaty Consultative Meeting in Kiev in June 2008. The UK will continue to engage fully with other Treaty Parties in these discussions and will pursue its proposals for measures to strengthen the contingency plans of cruise ships in the Antarctic.

(HC Deb 8 January 2008 Vol 470 c442W)

Part Twelve: III.C. *Airspace, Outer Space and Antarctica—Antarctica—Protection of the Environment*

12/6
The Foreign Secretary was asked what reports he had received on oil exploration and research in the Antarctic by other countries. An FCO Minister wrote:

We have received no such reports on oil research and exploration in the Antarctic. The UK is fully committed to upholding the provisions of the Antarctic Treaty including the Protocol on Environmental Protection and its clear prohibition on any activity related to mineral resources, other than scientific research.

(HC Deb 6 February 2008 Vol 471 c1160W)

Part Thirteen: International Responsibility

Part Thirteen: II.D. *International responsibility—General issues of international responsibility—Consequences of Responsibility (restitution in integrum, damages, satisfaction, guarantees)*

13/1

The Defence Secretary was asked if the Government would take steps to sequester assets of the government of Iran in the UK to the value of the British military equipment which had been seized in *(a)* 2004 and *(b)* 2007. He wrote:

We will continue to pursue diplomatic means for the return of the boats and equipment seized by Iran in 2004 and 2007.

(HC Deb 7 January 2008 Vol 470 c47W)

13/2

A Minister wrote:

The conclusion of a Government-to-Government agreement between the US and Libya on 14 August will provide for compensation for many of the victims of Libya's past sponsorship of terrorism, while ruling out the possibility of legal action against Libya before the US courts as regards allegations of Libyan involvement in terrorism before 30 June 2006. The Government regard inclusion of the British families of the victims of the bombing of PanAm flight 103 over Lockerbie in 1988 in the recipients of compensation as welcome news for these families, but it is regrettable that the deal will not benefit all UK nationals with cases in US courts against Libya.

During the course of negotiations between the US and Libya, the Government made representations to the US Administration that the families of Lockerbie victims and existing UK claimants, with claims before US courts against Libya for its past sponsorship of Irish Republican Army (IRA) terrorist acts (the McDonald case), should be included as recipients of any compensation package. In the event, it proved not possible to include the McDonald case claimants in the recipients of compensation under the US/Libya Agreement. The Government did not make representations to the US Administration regarding the Berlin bombing as there are no UK nationals with cases in US courts against Libya regarding this attack.

A key reason for not including the McDonald claimants in the compensation package was that international and US law do not permit the US Administration to espouse the claims of foreign nationals. Also relevant to the US decision was their assessment of how likely it would be that claims would fall within the jurisdiction of US courts and how likely it would be that they would succeed. We understand from the US that US courts would not have jurisdiction to hear such actions by British nationals against Libya.

It was possible for the UK victims in the Lockerbie case to receive payments from the compensation fund due to the unique circumstances of that case. The Lockerbie bombing was subject to a UN Security Council resolution which required that Libya accept responsibility for the Lockerbie bomb and pay victims' families appropriate compensation. On this basis, the US assisted in bringing closure to that case on behalf of the entire international community and the Libyan Government agreed in 2003 to the payment of compensation to the victims' families. The sums to be paid to those families under the terms of the recent US/Libya agreement reflect the final (so far unpaid) tranche of the previously agreed settlement payments. There is no such mechanism, settlement or court judgment in place in relation to the legal actions regarding the supply of arms by Libya to the IRA.

The Government have already openly responded to queries on the US/Libya deal and will continue to do so. Therefore, we consider that a statement from my right hon. Friend the Foreign Secretary is not necessary.

(HC Deb 6 October 2008 Vol 480 c235W-236W)

13/3
During a debate in the House of Commons, a Minister stated:

Reference was made to the fact that the United States and Libya signed a comprehensive claims settlement agreement on 14 August. The important point is that that followed an explicit approach by Libya to the US to resolve outstanding compensation claims in order to improve their relations. Under the agreement, compensation will be paid from a humanitarian fund to several categories of victims. Libya's sovereign immunity before the US courts will be restored, and terrorism-related legal action, prior to June 2006, before the US courts will be barred.

It is true, however, that those who will receive compensation will be of either US or Libyan nationality, with the exception of those involved in the Lockerbie case. Although the provision of the outstanding compensation to the families of the 52 British victims of Lockerbie is welcome—I am sure that the hon. Gentleman would acknowledge that—I am of course disappointed that the agreement between the US and Libya could not provide compensation for all British claimants in the US proceedings regarding Libyan-sponsored terrorism.

I assure the hon. Gentleman, and all others with an interest in this issue, that the UK Government recognised the importance to the UK victims of their US legal claims, which is why we made real efforts to raise their interests with the US Government. When it became clear that the negotiations were taking place between the US and Libya, the UK Government made a number of diplomatic representations urging the US Government to include, on the list of recipients of any compensation package, UK claimants who had brought cases in the US against Libya. We attempted to do that, but regrettably it did not prove possible for the UK claimants to be included in the US-Libya agreement. A key reason for that, as the Prime Minister explained in writing to H2o—the law firm representing the claimants—was the US view that international and US law did not permit the US Administration to espouse as its own the claims of non-US nationals. The US Administration was precluded by law from espousing the claims of UK nationals as part of the compensation agreement. Also relevant to the US decision was its assessment—I must underline that it was its assessment—of how likely the cases were to succeed in the US courts.

Why Lockerbie and not the IRA victims? Although I am sure that the hon. Gentleman would welcome the inclusion of British Lockerbie victims among the recipients of compensation, it is worth emphasising that they have been able to benefit from this agreement because of the unique circumstances of the case. Unlike Libya's support to the IRA, the Lockerbie bombing was subject to a UN Security Council resolution that required Libya to accept responsibility and pay victims' families appropriate compensation. Libya agreed to do so in 2003 following negotiations between the victims' families and Libya. The sums paid to the Lockerbie families under the US-Libya agreement represent the last unpaid tranche of previously agreed settlement payments. Regrettably, no such mechanism, settlement or court judgment is in place in relation to the legal actions regarding the supply of arms by Libya to the IRA. I wish that things were different, but those are the facts of the case.

The hon. Gentleman has urged the Government to open bilateral negotiations with Libya to seek compensation for the British victims of Libyan-sponsored IRA terrorism. The Government considered that very carefully at length and on a number of occasions, and we understand that it is a difficult and sensitive matter for those involved. Although the Government made diplomatic representations to the US Government about their agreement with Libya, the Government's position remains—I respect his view, of course—that we will not seek to enter into a bilateral discussion with Libya on this matter.

...

He continued:

 I do not absolve Libya from its responsibilities for its past actions, but it is incontestable that there has been a transformation in our relations with the Libyan Government to the benefit of people throughout the UK. Libya has renounced its support for international terrorism.

In 1995, Libya explained to the UK Government the extent of its support to the IRA. It has also complied with UN Security Council resolutions and handed over the Lockerbie suspects for trial, in return for which all UN and EU sanctions against Libya have now been lifted. With the support of the British Government, Libya has now returned to the international community—that is in everyone's interest—and has built normal co-operative relations with those countries to which it was formerly hostile, and we believe that it is right to seek to build on this improvement in relations. Libya is now an essential partner for the UK on wide-ranging issues, in particular in the fight against today's terrorist threats. It is vital for the UK's present and future security that that co-operation continues.

For its part, Libya considers this matter closed. [Interruption.] Let me continue. In 1995, Libya explained to the UK Government the extent of its support to the IRA. We should not underestimate the significance of that explanation, because it helped the Government accurately to assess the true material capacities of the IRA. Without that agreement and information, it would have taken us longer to make progress in Northern Ireland. The Libyan Government have subsequently made it clear to us that they now consider this matter closed and that they would be strongly opposed to reopening it. It is therefore this Government's considered assessment that Libya would not support a bilateral settlement of these cases with the UK Government. That is an important point given that in the US, Libya actually initiated the agreement.

(HC Deb 22 October 2008 Vol 481 c98W-100W)

13/4

Her Majesty's Government were asked whether they would assist British nationals seeking compensation from Libya in the courts of the United

States in respect of crimes committed by terrorists trained or armed by Libya. In reply, a Minister wrote:

The conclusion of a government-to-government agreement between the US and Libya on 14 August will provide for compensation for many of the victims of Libya's past sponsorship of terrorism including the British families of the victims of the bombing of Pan Am flight 103 over Lockerbie in 1988. While this is welcome news for these families, it is regrettable that the deal will not benefit all UK nationals with cases in US courts against Libya.

During the course of negotiations between the US and Libya, the Government made representations to the US Administration that existing UK claimants with claims before US courts against Libya for its past sponsorship of IRA terrorist acts (the McDonald case) should be included in the recipients of any compensation package. But, in the event, this proved not to be possible.

A key reason for this was that international and US law do not permit the US Administration to espouse the claims of foreign nationals. Also relevant to the US decision was their assessment of how likely it would be that claims would fall within the jurisdiction of US courts, and how likely it would be that they would succeed. We understand from the US that US courts would not have jurisdiction to hear actions by British nationals against Libya.

(HC Deb 19 November 2008 Vol 705 cWA203–204)

Part Thirteen: III.A. *International responsibility—responsible entities—states*

13/5

The Government were asked what reports they had received of Iranian funding of the Revolutionary Guard Qods Force in Iraq. In reply, a Minister wrote:

The Qods Force (QF) is a branch of the Iranian Revolutionary Guards Corps (IRGC), and as such is an agency of the Iranian state. We assess that the IRGC and the IRGC-QF is involved in training, equipping and supplying Iraqi armed groups. Any Iranian support to armed groups operating outside the political process in Iraq is unacceptable. Both the Government and the sovereign Government of Iraq have made this clear to the Iranian authorities on many occasions.

(HC Deb 2 July 2008 Vol 478 c1005W)

Part Thirteen: III.B. *International responsibility—responsible entities—international organisations*

13/6

The Foreign Secretary was asked what recent discussions he had had with the UN troop contributor Governments on the conduct of troops on

UN missions, including their treatment of women. An FCO Minister wrote:

We believe strongly that UN personnel must uphold the highest standards of behaviour. The vast majority of UN peacekeepers uphold those standards while doing important work in difficult and dangerous circumstances.

The UN is responsible for tackling any individual allegations of misconduct with troop contributing countries. We have therefore not raised this with Governments, but we do pursue the issue with the UN. The UK played a key role in the 2006 negotiations that established a model Memorandum of Understanding (MoU) between the UN and troop contributing countries, which lays out the actions that will be taken if any troops fall short of prescribed standards of conduct. We were also involved in negotiations last year which made the MoU more robust. We support the UN Secretary-General's 'zero-tolerance' policy towards sexual exploitation and abuse by UN personnel and we press for language supporting that policy, and call for troop contributing countries to take appropriate preventative action, to be included in all UN Security Council resolutions on peacekeeping missions. The peace support operations training that the UK provides for troops of other countries also covers matters of conduct, including the importance of protecting civilians (including women) in accordance with international law.

(HC Deb 19 May 2008 Vol 476 c79W)

13/7

In the debate on the Report of the ILC in the Sixth Committee of the General Assembly [A/63/10, Ed.], the representative of the UK said:

The United Kingdom welcomes the Sixth Report on Responsibility of International Organizations, and acknowledges the efforts of the Commission and of its Special Rapporteur, Giorgio Gaja, on this topic. The United Kingdom notes that the Commission provisionally adopted eight draft articles and accompanying commentaries at its 60th session. These provisions deal with the invocation of the international responsibility of an international organization, and will constitute Chapter I of Part Three of the draft articles.

In the past, the United Kingdom has expressed some concern about how closely the Commission's work on this topic has been following the Commission's Articles on State Responsibility. The United Kingdom recognises, however, that there are some issues where it is sensible to have regard to the equivalent provision in the Articles on State Responsibility. This is the case as regards several of the draft articles which were adopted by the Commission during this year's session.

Nevertheless, the United Kingdom questions whether it is correct to state, as do draft articles 46 and 52, that an international organisation is entitled to invoke the responsibility of another international organisation, if the obligation breached is owed to 'the international community as a whole'. These provisions essentially follow the wording of articles 42 and 48 of the Articles on State Responsibility. The United Kingdom is of the view that it is difficult to consider international organisations as having the same right as States to present a claim in the event that an international organisation commits a breach of an obligation which is owed to the international community as a whole. This is because there is a wide

variety of international organisations, some with more limited functions, mandates, and membership than others, and it is not clear that all international organisations can properly be considered to be members of the "international community".
The United Kingdom recognises that the invocation of responsibility by an
international organisation under these draft articles is dependent on further criteria, but considers that further consideration should be given to this issue.

With regard to draft article 48, the United Kingdom agrees with the Commission
that it is important to include a provision dealing with nationality of claims and
exhaustion of local remedies. It notes that the phrase 'local remedies' refers to
'any available and effective remedy provided by that organisation', which might
include remedies available before arbitral tribunals, national courts or administrative bodies where the international organisation in question has accepted their
competence to examine claims.

Finally, Mr. Chairman, as regards the draft articles on countermeasures, the United
Kingdom notes that these have not yet been adopted by the Commission, and
that these will be considered next year. The United Kingdom recalls that it
expressed reservations on the provisions concerning countermeasures in the
Articles on State Responsibility in its comments in 2001 (see UN Doc A/CN.4/
515, at p. 76ff). In those comments, the United Kingdom observed that the provisions concerning countermeasures were a 'striking anomaly' in the Articles on
State Responsibility. Alone among the circumstances precluding wrongfulness
in Part One, Chapter V, they were singled out for lengthy elaboration. The United
Kingdom considered that there was no good reason why countermeasures should
be treated in this way, while self-defence, *force majeure* and necessity were not.
The same applies in respect of the Commission's work on the Responsibility of
International Organisations. Without prejudice to its views on the individual
provisions, the United Kingdom urges the Commission to reconsider whether a
separate Chapter is necessary for the topic of countermeasures.

(Text supplied by FCO)

Part Fourteen: Peaceful Settlement of Disputes

Part Fourteen: II.A. *Peaceful settlement of disputes—means of settlement—
negotiations*

14/1

A Minister wrote about the situation on the Eritrea-Ethiopia border:

The Military Co-ordination Commission (MCC) last met on 31 July 2006.

The meetings of the MCC ceased when the Government of Ethiopia said they
would only participate if Eritrea withdrew its military forces from the Temporary
Security Zone. The Government of Eritrea said they would continue with the
MCC meetings once Ethiopia agreed to participate.

As a bilateral mechanism, established under the Agreement on Cessation of
Hostilities, 18 June 2000, between Ethiopia and Eritrea, they both bear the responsibility to re-activate the work of the MCC. The Government are prepared to

support any initiative which will assist the parties in doing this and resolving the border dispute peacefully.

(HC Deb 7 July 2008 Vol 478 c1334W-1335W)

14/2
A Minister wrote:

The UK's policy towards the Ethiopia-Eritrea border dispute is based on three principles: to avoid any return to war, which would be unacceptable; for the border to be demarcated; and for the parties to normalise their relations. Ethiopia and Eritrea should agree a way forward to allow demarcation to proceed and for a normalisation process to begin, as set out in the Algiers Agreements of June and December 2000, to which both Ethiopia and Eritrea are signatories.

We have set out this policy to both Ethiopia and Eritrea, including in November 2007 when the Foreign Secretary met Ethiopian Foreign Minister Seyoum Mesfin. The former Minister for the Middle East most recently discussed the border situation when he met Ethiopian Prime Minister Meles Zenawi in June and the Eritrean ambassador in July. In addition, Foreign and Commonwealth Office officials continually reiterate these messages to both the Ethiopian and Eritrean ambassadors to London and to their interlocutors in the Governments of Ethiopia and Eritrea in Addis Ababa and Asmara respectively.

Even with the termination of the UN Mission in Ethiopia and Eritrea (UNMEE) on 31 July the UNSC made clear the Algiers Agreements remain in force. The UN Secretary-General will continue to monitor the situation and consult both parties in an effort to (1) achieve a comprehensive and lasting settlement of their border dispute, and (2) help the countries to normalise their relations.

We will continue to pursue the policy above with our international partners, including through the efforts of the United Nations with the parties, to which UK efforts are closely aligned and to which we give our support.

(HC Deb 20 October 2008 Vol 481 c96W-67W)

Part Fourteen: II. D. Peaceful settlement of disputes—means of settlement—mediation

14/3
A Minister wrote:

The UK's policy towards the Ethiopia-Eritrea border dispute is based on three principles: to avoid any return to war; for the border to be demarcated; and for the parties to normalise their relations. Ethiopia and Eritrea should agree a way forward to allow demarcation to proceed and for a normalisation process to begin, as set out in the Algiers Agreements of June and December 2000, to which both Ethiopia and Eritrea are signatories.

As part of the above policy, we continue to request Eritrea to remove its forces from the Temporary Security Zone—the demilitarised zone established along the border between Ethiopia and Eritrea.

An FCO Minister set out this policy to the Eritrean ambassador on 10 July. The UK's policy has equally been conveyed to the Government of Ethiopia, notably by my right hon. Friend the Foreign Secretary to the Ethiopian Foreign Minister Seyoum Mesfin in November and by my noble Friend the Minister for Africa, Lord Malloch-Brown, to Ethiopian Prime Minister Meles in January in Addis Ababa.

In addition, Foreign and Commonwealth Office officials continually reiterate these messages to both the Ethiopian and Eritrean ambassadors to London and to their interlocutors in the Governments of Ethiopia and Eritrea in Addis Ababa and Asmara respectively.

(HC Deb 21 July 2008 Vol 479 c868W)

Part Fourteen: II.G.1. *Peaceful settlement of disputes—means of settlement—judicial settlement—International Court of Justice*

14/4 [See also **5/11–5/28**]
In the General Assembly debate on 8 October 2008 on a proposal to ask the ICJ for an advisory opinion on the declaration of independence by Kosovo, the UK representative said:

Let me start by making clear that the United Kingdom is a strong supporter of the International Court of Justice. We have for many years accepted the Court's compulsory jurisdiction: we are one of only 65 States with a current optional clause declaration under Article 36(2) of the ICJ Statute giving the Court jurisdiction over a wide range of matters. We support the use of the Court by Member States to resolve their disputes and the right of United Nations institutions to seek advisory opinions on questions affecting the performance of their functions.

Why, you might ask, are we now raising questions about the Serbian request? The reason is that the Serbian request is primarily for political rather than legal reasons. It is designed to slow down Kosovo's emergence as a widely recognised independent nation, playing its part in the international institutions of the world. Many members of the United Nations emerged into independence at what, at the time, were controversial circumstances. These circumstances normalise over time, and the clock of history is rarely turned back. Kosovo's independence is, and will, remain a reality.

The Government of Serbia will have to decide how it comes to terms with that reality. Kosovo's independence has now been recognised by 22 out of the 27 member states of the European Union—an organisation that Serbia aspires to join. We too want to see Serbia as a member of the European Union. To that end, Serbia will need to work constructively with its future EU partners to maximise stability in the region, including in Kosovo, so that we can achieve our goal of bringing the whole region and its peoples to a stable and more prosperous future.

I have set out in Security Council debates on this issue that the United Kingdom is confident in our legal position as a State which has recognised the independence of Kosovo following the final status process which was conducted pursuant to Security Council Resolution 1244.

In terms of the draft Resolution before us, my delegation regrets that our Serbian colleagues have declined to seek a consensual way forward. They have, on the contrary, decided to press this Resolution through the General Assembly with minimal debate about the issues. This is not the custom in the General Assembly, and it is regrettable that Serbia has decided to pursue that course. In the light of our reservations on matters of both substance and procedure, the UK will abstain on this Resolution.

If the Resolution is adopted, the question will need to be addressed against the background of the full context of the dissolution of Yugoslavia in so far as it affects Kosovo, starting with Belgrade's unilateral decision in 1989 to remove Kosovo's autonomy, through to the present day. Serbia complains of the unilateral declaration of Kosovo in February 2008. But it was Serbia who, in a unilateral move of its own, rendered successful negotiations impossible. In November 2006, while the UN Status Envoy was conducting talks, Serbia brought forward a new Constitution that unilaterally re-asserted control over Kosovo. That Constitution was narrowly approved by a referendum; but well over a million Kosovo Albanians-people whom Serbia was by its new Constitution claiming as its own—were effectively excluded from voting. And the effect of the Constitution was to tie the hands of the Serbian negotiators to the point where they could not even accept a status-neutral proposal put forward by the European Union.

That status-neutral proposal, in December 2007, represented the last chance for a negotiated settlement, and it was rejected by Serbia. So, in co-ordination with many of the countries most closely involved in stabilising the Balkans, Kosovo's Assembly declared Kosovo independent on 17 February 2008. The declaration committed Kosovo to full implementation of the UN Envoy's Comprehensive Settlement Proposal, including the most extensive safeguards for minority communities anywhere in Europe, together with international supervision. In the last eight months, 48 countries have recognised Kosovo as a sovereign independent State, and that number is set to grow.

If this Resolution is adopted, my delegation invites the Court to proceed in accordance with the principle that, without prejudice to the advisory opinion being sought, all parties with an interest, including the Government of Kosovo, should be able to present arguments on an equal footing.

My Government's overwhelming concern in its policies towards the Balkans over this last eighteen years has been to provide for peace and stability and to build a basis for long-term prosperity in the region. Those principles continue to guide us today. The people of Serbia have made a strategic choice in their recent election, one that my Government welcomes. We will do what we can to facilitate Serbia's integration into Europe. But we will expect, in return, the Government of Serbia to co-operate fully with the European Union in achieving stability in the southern Balkans, for generations to come. Our disagreement with Serbia over the tactics that it is adopting on this particular issue will not distract us from our strategic objectives that we believe are widely shared and advance the interests of the people of the Balkans as a whole.

(<http://ukun.fco.gov.uk/en/newsroom/?view=News&id=7233681>)

14/5

After the vote that was in favour of asking the ICJ for an advisory opinion (GA resolution 63/3), the UK gave an explanation of its abstention on the resolution. Its representative said:

... in my statement in the debate I set out a number of reservations on the part of the United Kingdom with regard to the draft resolution which has just been adopted. Those reservations led us to abstain in the vote, notwithstanding our long-standing support for the International Court of Justice. It is striking that more Member States felt unable to support the Resolution than voted in favour of it. We might infer from this that we are far from alone in having deep reservations.

The United Kingdom welcomes the use of the advisory jurisdiction of the ICJ in appropriate cases, but we question the utility of the question which has been proposed by Serbia. An advisory opinion cannot in itself be determinative of Kosovo's status. The position of the United Kingdom reflects our conviction that implementation of the Comprehensive Settlement Proposal by an independent Kosovo under international supervision offers the best chance for Kosovo, Serbia and the region to achieve peace, stability and prosperity.

The United Kingdom also regrets the lack of substantive debate within the General Assembly on the draft Resolution, including on the context and formulation of the question, and on the desirability of signalling, in the interests of fairness, that Kosovo should be allowed to present its arguments to the Court.

For all these reasons, the United Kingdom abstained on adoption of the Resolution. Nevertheless, we recognise that the question which the General Assembly has decided to ask the Court raises significant issues of international law. We are confident of our legal position as a State which has recognised the independence of Kosovo following the final status process which was conducted pursuant to Security Council Resolution 1244. The United Kingdom looks forward to engaging constructively with the Court to assist in its consideration of these important issues. In parallel, we look to Serbia to engage constructively with the European Union on promoting stability in the region.

(<http://ukun.fco.gov.uk/en/newsroom/?view=News&id=7233398>)

14/6

The UK had written to the General Assembly before the vote. It said:

Annex to the letter dated 1 October 2008 from the Permanent Representative of the United Kingdom of Great Britain and Northern Ireland to the United Nations addressed to the President of the General Assembly "Request for an advisory opinion of the International Court of Justice on whether the unilateral declaration of independence of Kosovo is in accordance with international law"

Note of issues

1. By a letter dated 15 August 2008 (A/63/195), the Permanent Representative of Serbia to the United Nations transmitted a letter from Vuk Jeremić, Minister for Foreign Affairs of the Republic of Serbia, to the Secretary-General requesting "the inclusion in the agenda of the sixty-third session of the General Assembly, under heading F, 'Promotion of justice and international law', of a supplementary

item entitled 'Request for an advisory opinion of the International Court of Justice on whether the unilateral declaration of independence of Kosovo is in accordance with international law', with subsequent consideration of the item directly at a plenary meeting of the General Assembly". An explanatory memorandum was attached.

2. The General Assembly agreed by consensus on 19 September 2008 to include the item on the agenda for consideration at a plenary meeting. The United Kingdom joined the consensus, reflecting the United Kingdom's practice of supporting the inclusion of agenda items that merit debate. Serbia has now circulated a draft resolution under this agenda item (A/63/L.2).

3. The United Kingdom is a strong supporter of the International Court of Justice. It has a long-standing Optional Clause Declaration under article 36(2) of the Court's Statute giving the Court compulsory jurisdiction in a wide range of matters. It has taken an active part in all the recent advisory proceedings of the Court. It has also been a party in a number of contentious proceedings before the Court in recent years. The role of the Court as the principal judicial organ of the United Nations is important, both within the United Nations system and more widely. The advisory jurisdiction of the Court is an important mechanism for affording guidance to the General Assembly, Security Council and other bodies on questions of law relevant to the performance of their functions. Advisory opinions have contributed much to the work of the Organization and to the development of international law.

4. The view is sometimes expressed that there is intrinsic merit in requesting an advisory opinion from the Court on contentious issues of law. Notwithstanding its strong support for the Court, the United Kingdom does not subscribe to this view if the consequence of this approach would be to request an advisory opinion without a clear sense of purpose and the practical utility of an opinion for the requesting body.

5. The United Kingdom nevertheless recognizes that the proposed request for an advisory opinion engages important questions of international law. We also recognize the sensitivity of the issues for Serbia's internal political debate. Notwithstanding the United Kingdom's well-known position on the underlying issues of substance, including its recognition of Kosovo, it looks forward to engaging constructively in the General Assembly debate on this item in due course and, to this end, identifies below some of the questions that it believes would merit closer consideration.

6. If an advisory opinion is to be requested, it will be important to ensure that the resolution sets the context of the question posed in order to assist the Court in its consideration of the issues. Previous requests for advisory opinions from the General Assembly have set the question to be addressed in its wider legal and political context. The resolution requesting an advisory opinion on the Legal Consequences of the Construction of a Wall in the Occupied Palestinian Territory (General Assembly resolution 10/14 of 8 December 2003) illustrates this. In the matter under discussion, any consideration of the issues by the Court would necessarily have to take place in the context of the events associated with the wider dissolution of the former Socialist Federal Republic of Yugoslavia in the period from 1991. It would facilitate the task of the Court, therefore, for

further contextualization to be added by expanding the preambular paragraphs of the draft resolution.

7. The United Kingdom would also welcome consideration of the formulation of the question in the draft resolution. The agenda item proposed by Serbia requests an advisory opinion on the question of whether "the unilateral declaration of independence of Kosovo is in accordance with international law". In contrast, the question formulated in the draft resolution is cast in terms of whether "the unilateral declaration of independence by the Provisional Institutions of Self-Government of Kosovo [is] in accordance with international law". It would be useful to know whether Serbia is seeking to focus on a narrower question about the competence of the Provisional Institutions of Self-Government of Kosovo, and, if so, precisely how that question relates to Kosovo's status at the present time.

8. Beyond this, Serbia's explanatory memorandum states that the object of the request for an advisory opinion is to enable States to make a more thorough judgement of the issue. Separate from any question of whether this object is appropriate to the advisory role of the Court, it would be useful to consider whether the question as formulated is best suited to this objective. Many States emerged to independence in what at the time were controversial circumstances. An advisory opinion addressing the emergence to independence of Kosovo could not therefore by itself be determinative of Kosovo's present or future status or the effect or recognition of that independence by other States.

9. The ability of all those who have an interest in a matter at issue before a court to be represented and to present arguments is a cardinal principle of fairness in legal proceedings. The proposed advisory opinion would put in issue the legality of the declaration of independence of Kosovo. Without prejudice to the answer to this question, if an advisory opinion is requested, it would be appropriate for the resolution referring the matter to the Court to signal that the General Assembly considers that fairness dictates that Kosovo should be permitted to be represented in the proceedings and to present arguments in its own name.

10. In raising these issues for consideration, the United Kingdom emphasizes both its commitment to the International Court of Justice and to a constructive discussion of the issues. The United Kingdom has recognized Kosovo's independence and considers that the pragmatic reality of the circumstances warrant wider recognition of this status. If a question is referred to the Court for an advisory opinion, the United Kingdom would engage constructively in the proceedings, as it has done in previous advisory opinions. The United Kingdom is not, however, currently persuaded of the utility of the proposal or that some of the issues of detail that it considers to be important have been fully addressed. This note is circulated with the object of raising relevant issues in a transparent fashion for wider consideration.

(Text supplied by FCO)

14/7

In a debate in the Security Council on Kosovo, the UK representative said:

The other point I would like to make concerns [Serbia's] reference to General Assembly resolution 63/3, requesting an advisory opinion from the International

Court of Justice. It is not the case that the General Assembly approved Serbia's position on Kosovo's status in adopting the draft resolution submitted by Serbia requesting the advisory opinion. The General Assembly merely agreed that the International Court of Justice should be asked to opine on the question which Serbia had asked and this does not prejudge the answer to that question, on which the United Kingdom's views are well known and were set out in the document that the United Kingdom circulated at the time (A/63/461).

(UN Doc. S/PV.6025, 26 November 2008)

Part Fourteen: II. G.2. *Peaceful settlement of disputes—means of settlement—judicial settlement—courts and tribunals other than the International Court of Justice*

14/8
Democratic Republic of Congo

An FCO Minister wrote:

The arrests of Mathieu Ngudjolo, Germain Katanga and Thomas Lubanga send a strong message that the international community is determined to hold those guilty of atrocities in the Democratic Republic of Congo (DRC) to account for their actions. Efforts to prosecute militia leaders who commit the most serious abuses against the civilian population in DRC should continue, both as a matter of justice for their victims and to serve as a deterrent against future acts of violence. There is no evidence that the inquiries into Ngudjolo, Katanga and Lubanga by the International Criminal Court have had any impact on security in DRC.

(HC Deb 13 March 2008 Vol 473 c642W)

14/9
In reply to a written question, the Foreign Secretary wrote:

The UK is ready to provide whatever assistance may be required to ensure that those accused of the most serious crimes by the International Criminal Court (ICC) are brought into custody. Co-operation between the Government of the Democratic Republic of Congo (DRC) and the ICC has already led to the arrest of three DRC nationals, as part of the ICC's investigations into the situation in the DRC. We expect the Government of the DRC to provide the same level of co-operation over the arrest of Bosco Ntaganda.

(HC Deb 15 July 2008 Vol 479 c223WS)

14/10
European Court of Human Rights

The Government were asked whether they had considered the judgments of the European Court of Human Rights in cases of enforced disappearance in Turkey and Chechnya in Russia; and, if so, how those judgments will affect future policy towards and dialogue with these countries. An FCO Minister wrote:

The UK regularly considers progress in the Council of Europe's Committee of Ministers on the implementation of judgments by the European Court of Human Rights against a number of states. The committee last did so in December 2007. The Government fully support the work of the European Court of Human Rights and full implementation of its judgments by Council of Europe member states.

In EU and bilateral human rights consultations with the Russian Government, the UK regularly raises its concerns over ongoing human rights violations, including cases of enforced disappearances in the North Caucasus region. We have consistently urged the Government of Turkey to pursue a comprehensive policy of reforms to ensure comprehensive alignment with EU standards and we will continue to do so.

It is important to stabilise the North Caucasus region. To this end, we have assisted development through our £1 million bilateral Global North Caucasus Education Initiative, the European Commission's €20 million technical aid to the Commonwealth of Independent States programme for the North Caucasus as well as by supporting specific projects through dedicated funds such as the Global Conflict Prevention Pool.

(HL Deb 4 February 2008 Vol 698 cWA153)

14/11

The Government were asked whether they would seek ways to improve and allocate the processing of cases pending from Russia before the European Court of Human Rights. An FCO Minister wrote:

The European Court of Human Rights is an independent judicial body. Allocation and processing of cases is a matter for the court. The UK is a consistent supporter of the European Court of Human Rights and a strong advocate of reform measures to improve its effectiveness. An efficient court is essential for the promotion and protection of human rights.

Both the UK and Russia agree on the need for reform of the court to ensure that it functions more effectively. The UK believes that Protocol 14 to the European Convention on Human Rights must be implemented to achieve this goal. We are disappointed that Russia is the only Council of Europe member state not to have ratified the protocol. We, in concert with the majority of Council of Europe member states, the EU presidency and other EU member states have called on Russia to ratify Protocol 14 swiftly.

(HL Deb 4 February 2008 Vol 698 cWA160)

14/12
International Criminal Court [See **14/8, 14/9, 14/16, 14/17, 14/19–14/22**]

In its reply to the FAC Report on the Annual Human Rights Report 2007, the Government wrote:

21. The Government agrees with the Committee's conclusion that progress made by the International Criminal Court is to be welcomed. The Government shares

the Committee's view that international criminal law will be most effective if applied in a systematic and consistent way. The Government works with EU partners towards achieving universality of the Rome Statute of the International Criminal Court, and looks forward to discussing this issue with the next US Administration.

22. The Government does not share the Committee's view that we should seek to extend the ambit of the International Criminal Court. The Government notes that the crimes over which the International Criminal Court has jurisdiction are defined in the Rome Statute. Many "gross life-taking and life-threatening violations of human rights" already fall within the existing broad scope of the definition of crimes against humanity, which includes murder, extermination, torture, slavery and rape when committed as part of a widespread or systematic attack against a civilian population.

(Foreign Affairs Committee Session 2007–08 Annual Report on Human Rights 2007, Response of the Secretary of State for Foreign and Commonwealth Affairs Cm 7463)

14/13
International Criminal Tribunal for Yugoslavia

A Minister wrote:

The Government believe that the arrest and transfer of Radovan Karadzic was a significant step forward in Serbia's co-operation with the International Criminal Tribunal for the former Yugoslavia (ICTY). ICTY Prosecutor Serge Brammertz visited Belgrade from 10–11 September and briefed the EU General Affairs and External Relations Council on 15 September. His next report to the UN Security Council is due in December.

In itself, the arrest of Karadzic does not equate to 'full co-operation'. In our view, evidence of full co-operation would be a period of committed and sustained activity by the Serbian Government, demonstrating hundred per cent effort and political will. Co-operation with the Tribunal covers efforts in a range of areas including: tackling support networks; in meeting requests for documents; in allowing access to archives; in ensuring protection of witnesses; as well as in locating and transferring the two remaining indictees, Goran Hadzic and Ratko Mladic.

Our assessment is that the Serbian Government are working actively to ensure the transfer of the remaining indictees, including Ratko Mladic, to The Hague. We call upon them to make every effort to ensure that transfer takes place as soon as possible.

(HC Deb 6 October 2008 Vol 480 c224W)

14/14

The Government were asked about an alleged agreement by the US to afford Radovan Karadzic immunity from arrest. In reply, a Minister wrote:

No discussions have taken place with the US Government on allegations by Radovan Karadzic that the US offered him immunity from arrest. The US

Department of State issued a statement on 31 July in response to these allegations, available on its website:

<www.state.gov/r/pa/prs/ps/2008/07/107615.htm>.

The UK strongly supports the efforts of the International Criminal Tribunal for the former Yugoslavia to complete its mandate by prosecuting those alleged to be most responsible for serious violations of international humanitarian law in the former Yugoslavia, such as Radovan Karadzic.

We continue to urge all States, particularly those of the former Yugoslavia, to fully co-operate with the Tribunal so that the remaining fugitive indictees, Ratko Mladic and Goran Hadzic, can be apprehended and made to face international justice as soon as possible.

(HC Deb 22 October 2008 Vol 481 c390W)

14/15
Lebanon

An FCO Minister said:

The special tribunal for Lebanon has the United Kingdom's strong support. Achieving a swift and just outcome to the investigation into the death of former Prime Minister Rafik Hariri will be vital to demonstrate that acts of political violence in the middle east will not go unpunished. The United Kingdom co-sponsored Security Council resolution 1757, which brought into force the agreements necessary to establish the tribunal. We also committed $1 million to getting the special tribunal up and running. That underlines our commitment to promoting the rule of law in Lebanon.

The United Kingdom will continue to work strenuously with international partners for a resolution of the current political crisis, as well as on the wider challenges that Lebanon faces. Of course, the Lebanese must ultimately take responsibility for resolving their political crisis, but it is crucial that Lebanon's international friends play a supportive role. Lebanon should not once again become a battlefield in which countries with opposing interests play out their differences, and fight their wars by proxy. It is not in the interests of Lebanon, its neighbours, or the region for the dangerous political vacuum there to drag on.

(HC Deb 28 January 2008 Vol 471 c145)

14/16
Uganda

An FCO Minister wrote:

The Government strongly support the International Criminal Court and believe that its investigation in Uganda has helped to bring the Lord's Resistance Army (LRA) to the negotiating table. We welcome the progress made by the Government of Uganda and the LRA and are encouraged by reports that the two sides will sign a final peace agreement by the end of the month. Justice is an essential part of a sustainable peace and it is vital that those responsible for the terrible crimes committed during the conflict in northern Uganda are held to account.

(HC Deb 13 March 2008 Vol 473 c650W)

14/17

The Foreign Secretary was asked what reports he had received of an approach by the Ugandan government to the UN Security Council to suspend the International Criminal Court warrants for the arrest of leading members of the Lord's Resistance Army. An FCO Minister wrote:

We have received no reports that the Ugandan government has approached the UN Security Council to request suspension of the International Criminal Court (ICC) warrants against the leading members of the Lord's Resistance Army (LRA). We note that in the peace agreement, the LRA leadership has asked the Ugandan government to request a deferral of the ICC warrants and establish national mechanisms to try those alleged to have committed crimes against humanity and war crimes as an alternative to the ICC. We believe that justice is an essential part of a sustainable peace and it is vital that those responsible for the terrible crimes committed during the conflict in northern Uganda are held to account. It is up to the Ugandan government to convince the ICC that any new national mechanisms are in line with the Rome Statute and are sufficient to allow the ICC to lift the warrants issued for the arrest of LRA leaders.

(HC Deb 18 March 2008 Vol 473 c1036W)

14/18
Security Council Tribunals

In a debate in the Security Council on the Ad Hoc International Criminal Tribunals, the UK representative said:

A number of speakers this morning have referred to the question of transfer to national jurisdiction. I would just like to set out the United Kingdom's view on that subject, which is that it is suitable, whether in the case of the ICTR or the ICTY, for lower-level cases. It is absolutely not suitable for the highest-level fugitives, including Mladić.

The full and active cooperation of States is essential to enable the Tribunals to complete their work. We would like to take this opportunity once more to remind all States of their obligation to cooperate with the Tribunals under Security Council resolutions 1503 (2003) and 1534 (2004).

A number of speakers have also referred to the arrest of Radovan Karadzic. That arrest, together with the arrest of Zupljanin, was a milestone for the ICTY, and their capture was the result of the coordinated efforts of key authorities in Serbia. My Government applauds this success, and we salute those modernizers in Serbia who have brought this change about. We also welcome the Prosecutor's assessment in his report that Serbia has made substantial progress in cooperation since the last report. We urge Serbia to step up this cooperation in the areas that the Prosecutor has identified, and obviously and in particular, to increase efforts to locate and capture Ratko Mladić and Goran Hadžić. I just want to stress that this will mean needing to ensure that each and every part of the relevant Serbian bodies are doing their utmost and are tasked to do their utmost to this end …

Turning to the ICTR fugitives, it is an issue of concern to us that so many individuals remain at large. We are disappointed in particular that there has been no significant progress in tracking the whereabouts of Félicien Kabuga. We urge Kenya and other States in the region to cooperate fully with the ICTR's efforts to secure the arrest and surrender of the fugitive indictees. It is vital that all remaining fugitive indictees from both Tribunals be brought to trial.

As we approach the end of the completion strategies, it is important to focus on preserving the legacy of the Tribunals for future generations. We commend the work of the Tribunals and the international community to strengthen the capacity of domestic judicial institutions in the regions. A high priority is to reach agreement on the establishment of a residual mechanism, which will be necessary to carry out certain essential functions of the Tribunals in the post-completion phase. These functions include the prosecution of remaining indictees, the protection of witnesses, the enforcement of sentences and the management of the Tribunals' archives to ensure the widest possible accessibility.

(UN Doc. S/PV.6041, 12 December 2008)

14/19
Sudan

The Foreign Secretary wrote:

Under article 14 of the Rome Statute, a State Party can refer to the Prosecutor of the International Criminal Court (ICC) for investigation, a situation in a third State in which one or more crimes within the ICC's jurisdiction appear to have been committed. The effect of article 13 of the Rome Statute is that such a referral can only be made where the third State is a party to the Rome Statute. The UN Security Council (UNSC), acting under chapter VII of the UN charter, can also refer a situation to the ICC Prosecutor. The UK has made no unilateral referrals, but we played a leading role in the UNSC's adoption of UNSC resolution 1593 (March 2005) which referred the situation in Darfur to the ICC.

(HC Deb 7 July 2008 Vol 478 c1337W)

14/20
A Minister wrote:

On 14 July the International Criminal Court (ICC) Prosecutor announced his application to the ICC judges for an arrest warrant against President Bashir of Sudan for genocide, crimes against humanity and war crimes. The Prosecutor is completely independent and the court has its own procedures. It would therefore be inappropriate and premature to comment or speculate on the outcome of the ICC deliberations.

The UK has a long standing position of support for the work and purposes of the ICC. We also have a long standing position of calling on the Government of Sudan to co-operate with the ICC over the two existing indictments. [T]the Foreign Secretary reiterated this to the Sudanese President during his visit to Khartoum on 9 July.

We continue to urge all sides to show restraint, continue to implement the Comprehensive Peace Agreement and engage in the African Union-UN led political process for Darfur.

(HC Deb 17 July 2008 Vol 479 c688W)

14/21

A Minister wrote:

As a State Party to the International Criminal Court, the UK has regular contacts with the court at official level, including with the Prosecutor and his Office, over a range of matters, including the on-going investigation into the situation in Darfur referred to the Prosecutor by UN Security Council Resolution 1593 (2005). All contacts with the Prosecutor and his Office, and with others at the court, take place on the clear understanding of the court's, and the Prosecutor's, independent status and competence. It would be inappropriate and premature at this stage to comment or speculate on the outcome of the court's deliberations and the range of possible diplomatic and political implications.

We continue to urge all sides to show restraint, to implement the Comprehensive Peace Agreement, and to engage in the African Union/UN-led political process for Darfur.

(HC Deb 21 July 2008 Vol 479 c874W)

14/22

The Government were asked which Sudanese officials, identified for investigation by the International Criminal Court for crimes against humanity, had travelled to the United Kingdom in the past four years; what were the purposes of their visits; and what restrictions would be placed on their future visits to the United Kingdom. An FCO Minister wrote:

In 2007 the International Criminal Court (ICC) issued arrest warrants for two individuals, Ahmed Harun and Ali Kushayb, on charges of war crimes and crimes against humanity. On 14 July 2008 the ICC prosecutor applied to the court for a further warrant, for Sudanese President Bashir, on charges of war crimes, crimes against humanity and genocide. None of these individuals has travelled to the UK in the past four years. Before allowing any individual under investigation by the ICC into the UK we would consider our legal obligations under the Rome statute, including our obligation to arrest and surrender to the ICC any individual for whom there was an outstanding warrant.

(HL Deb 29 September 2008 Vol 703 cWA320)

Part Fifteen: Coercive Measures short of the Use of Force

Part Fifteen: I.A. *Coercive measures short of the use of force—unilateral measures—retorsion*

15/1 [See also **6/104, 6/105**]

The Foreign Secretary wrote:

The EU and US have an embargo on the sale of arms to Zimbabwe. We encourage all countries to adopt this approach and support the call for a temporary moratorium on all arms sales until Zimbabwe has a democratic Government in place.

We have lobbied the Chinese about the sale of arms to Zimbabwe and we, and other EU partners, have lobbied southern African Governments. We also raised this in the UN Security Council on 29 April 2008.

(HC Deb 4 June 2008 Vol 476 c1008W)

15/2

The Foreign Secretary was asked if he would request the European Commission to investigate whether the delivery of paper by MK Airline for the printing of Zimbabwe dollar bearer cheques was in breach of EU rules relating to Zimbabwe. An FCO Minister wrote:

The EU targeted measures consist of a travel ban and assets freeze against 131 named individuals and an arms embargo. There are no economic sanctions against Zimbabwe and therefore nothing to investigate in this instance.

(HC Deb 4 June 2008 Vol 476 c 1008W)

Part Fifteen: I.B. *Coercive measures short of the use of force—unilateral measures—counter-measures*

15/3

The FCO sent the following memorandum to the Quadripartite Committee in response to questions raised by the Committee:

Does the behaviour of the Chinese authorities in Tibet justify a strengthening of the arms embargo?

ANSWER

We continue to have serious concerns about human rights in China. We cover human rights issues in depth with the Chinese during our regular biannual UK-China Human Rights Dialogue, (the last round of which took place in Beijing in January 2008). The December 2004 European Council conclusions sent a strong political signal of the continued importance of human rights in assessing EU arms exports to China. The Code of Conduct, which is the primary means of controlling arms exports, has set criteria regarding human rights. In line with Criterion 2, HMG would not permit the export of goods if there was a clear risk the export might be used for internal repression.

On Tibet in particular, we continue to urge substantive dialogue between the Chinese authorities and the Dalai Lama to resolve the underlying human rights issues there. We believe that engagement with China, not isolation, is the best way to encourage this. Strengthening the arms embargo would do nothing to encourage dialogue, and would risk isolating the Chinese Government in a way which would make it significantly more difficult for us to raise human rights concerns.

The Government's approach has been to engage in dialogue with China. What has the UK to show for its efforts at dialogue with China?

ANSWER

By engaging with China on arms and export issues, we are able to share our best practice knowledge on export licensing controls. We have been involved in an EU pilot project with the Chinese, which has resulted in the production of guidance for Chinese industry on internal compliance procedures. Continued dialogue was also influential in allowing us to lend our voice to that of African civil society when lobbying the Chinese on the arms shipment to Zimbabwe throughout April this year. Overall, we judge that the human rights situation has improved significantly in China since 1989. The US has now dropped China from its list of "countries of concern" in its annual human rights report. By entering into dialogue with the Chinese we can encourage greater transparency and foster the modernising of arms export regulations and communicate our concerns openly; something we could not do if we were not willing to engage with the Chinese on arms issues. However, this willingness to enter into dialogue does not influence our policy on arms exports to China. In line with Code of Conduct criteria for arms exports, the UK does not approve export of goods to the region if they would adversely affect regional stability in any significant way. This includes the potential for equipment to enhance significantly the effectiveness of existing capabilities or to improve force projection.

(Quadripartite Committee Report, Scrutiny of Arms Export Control, HC 254 (2008))

Part Fifteen: I.E. *Coercive measures short of the use of force—unilateral measures—other unilateral measures*

15/4
Cuba

The Foreign Secretary was asked about the effect of US sanctions against Cuba. An FCO Minister wrote:

The UK does not support US economic sanctions on Cuba and makes its opposition to them clear through its Annual vote at the United Nations General Assembly. The last vote took place on 30 October 2007. The sanctions have had little positive impact on the regime. The UK and the US share the same goal over Cuba, transition to democracy, but differ on how to achieve it. The UK, through the framework of the EU Common Position, engages in dialogue with the Cuban Government and aims to encourage a peaceful transition to pluralist democracy, greater respect for human rights and unconditional release of all political prisoners.

(HC Deb 26 February 2008 Vol 472 c1365W)

15/5

The Government were asked what recent discussions they had had with their United States counterparts on the position of UK firms which trade with Cuba. In reply, a Minister said:

My Department has not received any formal complaint from UK-based firms affected by US trade sanctions against Cuba. The Foreign and Commonwealth

Office makes the Government's position clear every year by voting against the US trade embargo on Cuba—including aspects of its extraterritorial legislation—at the United Nations General Assembly. The last such vote was on 30 October 2007.

[A General Assembly resolution urging the end of the embargo against Cuba, A/63/7 was passed by 185-3-2 in October 2008, Ed.]

(HC Deb 3 July 2008 Vol 478 c1013)

15/6
Zimbabwe

A Minister wrote:

There is no legal authority for a blanket freeze of all Zimbabwean assets in the UK but we are looking at a range of targeted options which impact on those specifically responsible for the crisis in Zimbabwe. This could include extending the existing EU targeted measures which have already frozen the bank accounts and prevented the travel to the EU of 131 named regime members. In considering these options we shall take full account of the likely impact of any new measures on ordinary Zimbabweans.

(HC Dep 9 July 2008 vol 478 c1661W)

Part Fifteen: II.A. *Coercive measures short of the use of force—collective measures—United Nations*

15/7
Arms Export

The Business Secretary was asked about plans to strengthen controls over the export of arms. A Minister wrote:

On 6 February 2008 the Government published their initial response to a public consultation carried out as part of the 2007 review of export control legislation. The response can be viewed on BERR's website at:

<www.berr.gov.uk/europeandtrade/strategic-export-control/legislation/export-control-act-20Q2/review/index.html>

The initial response commits the Government to (1) extending export laws to control the brokering and trafficking, by UK persons anywhere in the world, of small arms, man portable air defence systems (MANPADs), and those cluster munitions that cause unacceptable harm to civilians; (2) extending controls on the export and trading of torture equipment to include sting sticks; (3) starting ED negotiations to introduce a new EU-wide torture end use control, which would enable all EU states to make licensable—and therefore refuse—the export of any equipment believed to be for use in acts of torture; and (4) rationalising the licensing treatment of long range missiles and unmanned air vehicles.

(HC Deb 22 February 2008 Vol 472 c1027W)

15/8
China

The Foreign Secretary was asked what recent assessment he had made of the effectiveness of the EU-China arms embargo; what his policy is on proposals to end the embargo and place the arms trade with China under a strengthened EU Code of Conduct. An FCO Minister wrote:

The EU-China Arms Embargo and EU Code of Conduct are separate. The European Council text on the embargo is politically binding and does not have the force of law. The embargo is narrowly defined by most major European exporters as covering lethal exports only. The UK's interpretation of the embargo was set out in a written answer the then Minister of State, Foreign and Commonwealth Office gave on 3 June 1998, *Official Report*, columns 246–47W. The EU Code of Conduct is the primary means of controlling arms sales and the UK regularly meets with its EU partners to discuss, enforce and strengthen it.

There is currently no consensus within the EU to end the arms embargo. The European Council in December 2003 agreed to launch a review of the embargo, which is still under way … As set out in the December 2004 European Council Conclusions, the result of any decision on the embargo should not be an increase in arms exports from EU member states to China, either in quantitative or qualitative terms. The Government continue to fully implement the embargo.

(HC Deb 25 March 2008 Vol 474 c134W)

15/9
Ethiopia and Eritrea

The Foreign Secretary was asked what reports he had received of Eritrean co-operation with the United Nations Mission in Ethiopia and Eritrea, with particular respect to fuel supplies. He wrote:

We are dismayed by Eritrea's refusal to resume fuel shipments to the UN Mission in Ethiopia and Eritrea (UNMEE), or to allow it to import its own fuel. This refusal threatens UNMEE's ability to carry out its mandate. We strongly condemn Eritrea's actions in this regard.

Eritrea's action is in direct contravention of the demands of the UN Security Council (UNSC), as set out in paragraph seven of UNSC Resolution 1798, adopted unanimously on 30 January 2008, and the UNSC press statement of 4 February 2008. The UK strongly supports the UNSC's demands.

Our ambassador in Asmara emphasised the UK's condemnation of Eritrea and support for the UNSC's demands to the Eritrean Government on 14 February 2008. An FCO Minister did the same with the Eritrean ambassador to the UK on 18 February 2008.

(HC Deb 20 February 2008 Vol 472 c707W)

15/10
Intelligent sanctions

The Foreign Secretary was asked what representations had been made to his Department on the appropriateness and equity of the targeting of

UN sanctions under chapter VII of the UN Charter on persons within the UK; and whether there were reasonable opportunities for the subjects of sanctions to appeal. An FCO Minister wrote:

The Foreign and Commonwealth Office has received representations from legal representatives of designated individuals seeking assistance in challenging their listing by the UN Security Council or requesting exemptions to meet basic or extraordinary expenses. Important reforms have been made in recent years to the Security Council's procedures for considering such requests, including the establishment of a focal point for receiving delisting petitions by UN Security Council resolution 1730 (2006). This has increased the opportunities for designated individuals to make their views known to the Security Council. The Government will continue to give representations on such matters due consideration.

There are currently 16 UK residents subject to sanctions by the UN Security Council and one UK resident subject to sanctions by the European Union. A further UK resident was removed from the UN Security Council list and another from the European Union list in 2005.

(HC Deb 6 February 2008 Vol 471 c1165W)

15/11
Iran

The Foreign Secretary was asked (1) what steps would be taken by UK authorities as a result of the inclusion of Iranian banks Melli and Mellat in UN Security Council Resolution 1803 (2008); and (2) what steps the Government planned to take to exercise vigilance over the activities of financial institutions in the UK with all banks domiciled in Iran, as required in UN Security Council Resolution 1803 (2008). A further question asked what assessment had been made of the possible links between Iranian banks Melli and Mellat, including their branches and subsidiaries abroad, and activities contributing to proliferation of sensitive activities in Iran. A Treasury Minister wrote:

In October 2007 HM Treasury, following agreement by the Financial Action Task Force (FATF), advised the financial sector to consider applying increased scrutiny and due diligence to transactions associated with Iran due to deficiencies in Iran's anti-money laundering and counter-terrorist financing regimes. We reiterated this on 29 February 2008 following a second FATF statement.

On 4 March 2008 HM Treasury published a notice on its website again advising caution and alerting the UK financial sector to the financial measures in UN Security Council Resolution 1803, which mentions banks Melli and Sanderat. The notice is available at <www.hm-treasury.gov.uk/media/9/C/fin_sanctions_iran_notification_040308.pdf>;

The UK also monitors the activities of UK financial institutions with all banks domiciled in Iran, in accordance with its international commitments.

Banks Melli and Saderat, rather than Melli and Mellat, are mentioned in the text of UN Security Council Resolution 1803.

The UK shares the concerns of the UN Security Council about bank Melli's and bank Saderat's links to the Iranian nuclear and missile programmes. The Security Council has called upon all states to exercise vigilance over the banks to prevent Iran from proliferating nuclear sensitive material. The UK continues to monitor banks Melli and Saderat in accordance with its international commitments.

(HC Deb 11 March 2008 Vol 473 c330W-331W)

15/12
The Foreign Secretary was asked whether detailed criteria had been agreed that would trigger the inspection of cargoes to and from Iran as stipulated in UN Security Council Resolution 1803 (2008) or whether this was a matter for the judgment of individual states. He wrote:

UN Security Council resolution 1803 (2008) requires states to inspect the cargoes to and from Iran, of aircraft and vessels, at their airports and seaports, owned or operated by Iran Air Cargo and Islamic Republic of Iran Shipping Line, where there are reasonable grounds to believe that the aircraft or vessel is transporting embargoed goods. It is up to states to decide when they believe the criteria is [sc, are] met.

(HC Deb 18 March 2008 Vol 473 c1032W)

15/13
The Defence Secretary was asked about Iranian support for dissident groups in southern Iraq. He said:

Evidence suggests that a significant proportion of the equipment and armaments being used by insurgents in Iraq is of Iranian origin or has been transited through Iran. Any Iranian links to armed groups in Iraq outside the political process— either through the supply of weapons or through training and funding—is unacceptable. With our allies, we are seeking to challenge that in a number of ways. Through our support for the Department of Border Enforcement, we seek to interdict the transfer of any such weaponry from Iran into southern Iraq; and through supporting the searches conducted by Iraqi security forces, we have discovered, seized and destroyed a large amount of weaponry that appears to have been sourced from Iran. By seeking to influence the Iranian Government diplomatically in a number of ways, including involving other influential countries in the region, we are trying to get it across to Iran that it is not in its long-term interests to have instability in southern Iraq or any part of Iraq at all. We are also endeavouring to deal with the insurgent and other groups that the Iranians seek to support in Iraq—and we have done so very successfully recently.

(HC Deb 28 April 2008 Vol 475 c6)

15/14
The Foreign Secretary was asked whether it was UK policy to secure the multilateral withdrawal of export credit provision to Iran by European Union countries and what UK policy was on *(a)* monitoring the activities

of Iranian financial institutions and *(b)* a European ban on the operations of Iranian banks Melli and Mellat. He wrote:

United Nations Security Council resolution (UNSCR) 1803, adopted on 3 March 2008, "calls upon all States to exercise vigilance in entering into new commitments for public provided financial support for trade with Iran, including the granting of export credits". The first step will be a new EU Common Position implementing the provisions of UNSCR 1803, including those on export credits. I will inform the House when this has been adopted. We are also discussing with EU partners the scope for further action in this area. The UK's Export Credit Guarantee Department has stopped processing applications for new export credit cover to Iran;

and

The UK has implemented the provisions in previous UN Security Council resolutions that relate to named Iranian banks. HM Treasury and the Financial Services Authority monitor the activities of these and other Iranian institutions closely. Building on UN Security Council resolution 1803, which was adopted in March, we are pressing for a new Common Position to implement it at EU level, including the provision on increased vigilance over the activities of Iranian financial institutions, including Banks Melli and Meillat. On 23 June the EU listed more Iranian entities, including Bank Melli, which imposed an EU-wide freeze of their funds and other financial assets.

[The new common position was not forthcoming. For the present position, see www.fco.gov.uk/en/business-trade/export-controls-sanctions/country-listing/iran, Ed.]

(HC Deb 30 June 2008 Vol 478 c674W)

15/15
A Minister wrote:

All funds belonging to, owned, held or controlled by Bank Sepah Iran and Bank Sepah International plc. in the UK are frozen in accordance with UN Security Council resolutions 1737 (2006), 1747 (2007) and 1803 (2008). No other entities designated by these measures hold funds in the UK. We do not provide details of individual entities' funds, whether they are natural or legal persons, as this would breach their confidentiality.

Since the introduction of these measures, HM Treasury has licensed payments out of the frozen funds in accordance with the exemptions provided in the UN Security Council resolutions.

(HC Deb 9 July 2008 Vol 478 c1564)

15/16
The Foreign Secretary wrote:

The UK is robustly implementing the provisions of UN Security Council Resolution (UNSCR) 1803. The Resolution already contains criteria for making inspections on the basis of having "reasonable grounds to believe" the aircraft or vessel is transporting prohibited goods. UK authorities routinely inspect cargoes from Iran. The EU is currently negotiating a new Common Position which the Government hope will build on the measures in UNSCR 1803.

(HC Deb 17 July 2008 Vol 479 c684W)

15/17
The Foreign Secretary wrote:

The UK is fully implementing all provisions of UN Security Council Resolution (UNSCR) 1803 (2008). The EU has already banned the supply of dual-use items covered in the resolution. Assets of individuals and entities named in the annex have been frozen by virtue of an Order in Council and the individuals have been added to the visa warnings index. The Export Credits Guarantee Department has stopped processing applications for new export credit cover for Iran. Bank Melli Iran was named as a bank of particular concern in UNSCR 1803. The UK has worked with EU partners to secure the designation of Bank Melli Iran and its subsidiaries and branches at EU level. Following designation on 24 June 2008, all assets belonging to, owned, held or controlled by Bank Melli Iran and Melli Bank Plc in the UK are frozen. HM Treasury issued guidance to financial institutions on 29 February 2008 advising them to take the risk arising from the deficiencies in Iran's anti-money laundering/counter-terrorist financing regime into account for enhanced due diligence. HM Revenue and Customs has enhanced its compliance and enforcement activity for consignments destined for Iran.

(HC Deb 21 July 2008 Vol 479 c869W)

15/18
In reply to a question on sanctions against Iran pursuant to Security Council Resolution 1803, a Minister wrote:

UK authorities undertake daily inspections of cargoes to and from Iran on the basis of risk and intelligence. UK authorities have undertaken no inspections in accordance with UN Security Council resolution 1803 since March 2008. Inspections in the UK are triggered at a lower level of confidence than the wording of the resolution which calls upon states to undertake inspections only where there are 'reasonable grounds to believe'.

(HC Deb 21 October 2008 Vol 481 c214W)

15/19
Kimberly Process

The Foreign Secretary was asked about the Government's support for the 'Kimberly Process' on conflict diamonds. An FCO Minister wrote:
The UK is fully committed to implementing the Kimberley Process Certification Scheme. The Government Diamond Office sits within the Foreign and Commonwealth Office and works closely with HM Revenue and Customs, the UK diamond industry and civil society groups to ensure effective implementation of the provisions of the Kimberley Process Certification Scheme.

In the past year, an official from the Government Diamond Office has taken part in Kimberley Process review visits to Romania and Bulgaria. A staff member of the Government Diamond Office also formed part of last year's extraordinary review mission to Ghana, as part of wider efforts to ensure full compliance of the Kimberley Process Certification Scheme among all participants in order to eradicate the trade in conflict diamonds.

In 2007, the UK supported the European Union's chairmanship of the Kimberley Process Certification Scheme by funding a non-governmental organisation secondee to provide logistical support to European Commission.

(HC Deb 28 January 2008 Vol 471 c56W)

15/20
Russia [See **[2007]** UKMIL **7/11–7/13** and **19/21** and **[2008]** UKMIL UKMIL **7/11** and **19/24**]

An FCO Minister wrote:

In his oral statement to the House on 16 July 2007 on measures the Government would impose in response to Russia's failure to answer satisfactorily our request for the extradition Andrey Lugovoy, the Foreign Secretary agreed that he would keep Parliament informed of any changes to our visa regime for Russian officials.

One of the measures imposed in July last year was to restrict visas for Russian officials to being single-entry and time-limited. This brought UK practice into line with Russian practice for issuing visas to UK officials. I wish to inform Parliament that, by agreement between the UK and Russia, official couriers will be issued with multiple-entry visas, which accords with recent Russian visa practice towards UK couriers. The change is aimed at maximising the efficiency and efficacy of our network of couriers, and will enable our couriers to support better our diplomatic posts in Russia.

(HC Deb 20 March 2008 Vol 473 69WS)

15/21
Sudan

The Prime Minister, speaking about action in Darfur, said:

I welcome UN Secretary-General Ban Ki-moon's 5 February agreement with President Bashir to accelerate the deployment of UNAMID. UNAMID is already behind schedule and the sooner the United Nations and the African Union secure prompt and effective deployment, the sooner the situation on the ground can stabilise. President Bashir must honour these commitments.

In considering additional measures, beyond UNAMID, we would need to assess the logistical challenges of implementation and their impact on humanitarian efforts. We have not ruled anything out including the imposition of no-fly zones. UNAMID is mandated to monitor military activity, including flights prohibited by UN Security Council resolution 1591.

The prospect of further United Nations sanctions, as advocated by the United Kingdom and the United States, combined with persistent persuasion by the

UN Secretary-General among others, helped bring the Government of Sudan to agree to UNAMID in 2007. So I will continue to be clear that we will pursue further targeted sanctions against any party that undermines resolution of the crisis in Darfur, including by impeding UNAMID deployment. This was a key element of my discussion with Premier Wen when I visited China in January, and I will continue to make the case with other members of the Security Council that sanctions must be one of a range of measures to bring resolution of the crisis in Darfur.

I continue to believe that the UN arms embargo on Darfur should be extended to the whole of Sudan. The United Kingdom delegation to the United Nations, most recently in the UN Sanctions Committee meeting of 6 November 2007, is pursuing this initiative. We have the support of our United States and European allies, but we do not have the consent of all members of the Security Council. That is why we continue to make the case, especially to permanent members of the Security Council, that extending the arms embargo should be part of a range of measures to bring resolution of the crisis in Darfur.

(HC Deb 18 February 2008 Vol 472 c128W)

15/22

The Foreign Secretary was asked what assessment had been made of regional compliance with the UN arms embargo on Darfur; and whether plans are being considered to extend the embargo to the whole of Sudan. An FCO Minister wrote:

The UN Panel of Experts, established by UN Security Council Resolution 1591, is responsible for monitoring the arms embargo on Darfur. In its latest report, published on 3 October 2007, the panel established that violations of the arms embargo continued, both by the Government of Sudan and non-state armed groups, during the period of the report, from 29 September 2006 to 29 August 2007. The panel reported that weapons, specifically heavy weapons (artillery pieces), small arms, ammunition and other military equipment were entering the Darfur states in breach of the embargo from several countries including regional neighbours.

The UK proposed in the UN Sanctions Committee of 6 November 2007 to extend its arms embargo on Darfur to all of Sudan, but not all Security Council members agree. We will continue to press for an extension of the arms embargo. The EU has implemented an arms embargo on the whole of Sudan via Common Position 2005/411/CFSP, adopted 30 May 2005.

(HC Deb 11 March 2008 Vol 473 c334W)

15/23

A Minister wrote:

The UK asked the UN Sanctions Committee of 6 November 2007 to extend its arms embargo on Darfur to all of Sudan, but not all UN Security Council (UNSC) members agreed. Since then, we have raised the issue whenever Sudan has been discussed in the UNSC and elsewhere, for example at the UN/African Union led talks on Darfur in Geneva on 5 June.

On 12 June 2008, the UK reiterated in the UNSC the need for all parties to adhere to the arms embargo on Darfur. We will continue to press for an extension of the arms embargo.

The EU continues to operate an arms embargo on the whole of Sudan.

(HC Deb 10 July 2008 Vol 478 c1828W)

15/24
Travel ban

The Government were asked how many foreign nationals were subject to a travel ban to the United Kingdom, broken down by country; and whether there were any names of foreign nationals subject to a travel ban to the United Kingdom which they were not prepared to disclose; and, if so, on what criteria. A Minister wrote:

The names and nationalities of those foreign nationals who are subject to a United Nations or European Union travel ban are available via the following websites:

<www.ec.europa.eu/external_relations/cfsp/sanctions/measures.htm>

<www.un.org/sc/committees/index.shtml>

All individuals who are subject to a UN or EU travel ban are normally barred from entering the United Kingdom.

Separately, since July 2005, Home Secretaries have excluded a total of 221 individuals from the United Kingdom. We have a legal responsibility to handle personal information fairly and would not normally disclose the names of those individuals excluded from the United Kingdom unless it was necessary to do so for a legitimate purpose.

(HL Deb 26 February 2008 Vol 699 cWA120)

15/25 (See also 5/37)
Zimbabwe

Asked about President Mugabe, the Prime Minister stated:

I talked to the Secretary-General of the United Nations only this morning about what I believe are the responsibilities of the United Nations in this area. Given that the only credible election that has taken place was the one in which the Movement for Democratic Change actually recorded a victory, and given that the second round was a travesty at the hands of what is a blood-stained regime, I am pleased that, yesterday, the African Union called for an end to violence, set up a system of mediation and talked about a transitional Government in Zimbabwe. Having talked to the UN Secretary-General this morning, I think that it is right that the UN send an envoy to Zimbabwe. In the absence of real change, we will step up our sanctions and ask other countries to do so. We will press for tough action on Zimbabwe at the Security Council later today, and we will do so at the G8 in coming days. There will not be support for reconstruction in Zimbabwe until democracy is restored.

(HC Deb 2 July 2008 Vol 478 c855)

15/26

The Foreign Secretary said:

Since the sham election on 27 June, conditions in Zimbabwe have deteriorated. International agencies estimate that 36,000 people have been displaced internally since the first round in March, at least 103 have been murdered and many thousands have received treatment for the injuries they have been dealt by the security forces. In spite of the promise of the authorities that the ban on their activities was temporary, aid agencies are still denied access to large swathes of the country, a restriction that means that 1.5 million people are still unable to access food aid and vital medicines that they need.

We have been clear that words are simply not enough, and that the international community as a whole must act. We have said openly that Zimbabwe's crisis is one that the world has a responsibility to respond to. That is why we supported the United States in their decision to table a resolution at the Security Council and to take that resolution to a vote on 11 July. The draft resolution had the nine votes that it needed to pass into law. It was co-sponsored by two African states—Liberia and Sierra Leone. Burkina Faso—an African member of the council—also voted in favour of it. All European and South American council members and the USA were behind it. That it was vetoed by Russia and China despite this clear and broad majority is something that the ordinary people of Zimbabwe—the victims of that violence and those who are denied that food and medicine—will not be able to understand.

I believe that it is right when one believes in a cause that should push others to be clear on their attitude to it. That Russia agreed to a G8 statement calling for further measures, including precisely the targeted sanctions that we were advocating but then—the same week—chose to vote against that resolution is now for them to explain. The terms of the draft UN resolution were widely discussed within the Council. Sufficient opportunity was given to explain reservations and to table amendments. Russia chose not to engage in that debate. China's decision to veto was deeply disappointing, too. We will continue to work with both states to persuade them to take a different course and to use their influence both in Zimbabwe and in the wider region to resolve the crisis.

The draft resolution did not cut across negotiations that the African Union had advocated in its own conclusions at its summit in Sharm el Sheik. We believe that dialogue between the parties can provide a way forward for Zimbabwe's crisis. But we need to be clear about the basis on which dialogue can be developed. At present we have one party that won a popular mandate in the parliamentary elections of 29 March, but whose members and supporters have been intimidated by the violence unleashed on them by the state and by ZANU-PF militia. We have another party that has refused to cede power, and that has used the full force of the state security apparatus to intimidate its citizens and turn the presidential run-off into a farce. To turn this context into one in which credible negotiations might begin, pressure is needed and the threat of an alternative approach that demonstrates what is at stake, personally, for the very people who believe they have least to gain from engaging in a process leading to democratic reform. That is why we will continue to advocate further targeted sanctions that focus on not just the 14 who would have been affected by the draft UN resolution but those around them and those who depend on them.

The UN itself estimates that 5 million people will need food aid in Zimbabwe by the end of 2008 if conditions do not improve. Given the humanitarian situation on the ground, the incalculable hyper-inflation and the increasing violence, the end of 2008 may bring a greater catastrophe still—for both Zimbabwe and the region—if the international community does not act to prevent it.

At the EU General Affairs and External Relations Council on 22 July, we will press for EU Foreign Ministers to agree to extend the number of persons on the EU visa ban and asset freeze list, for the first time to target companies and entities owned by such persons, and to tighten further the exemptions which allow Zimbabweans on that list to travel to the EU. This first wave of targeted measures will aim to act as a stimulus on the regime to engage in meaningful dialogue with the opposition. The regime and some of its sympathisers try to portray the 'talks about talks' that have occurred in South Africa last week as a breakthrough. We will not regard those talks as a breakthrough until they lead not just to agreements on paper but to implemented changes on the ground, and in particular a transitional Government who reflect the will of the people as they voted on 29 March. Meanwhile, we shall work with like-minded partners to root out the sources of the regime elite's foreign currency and target their personal wealth. With our partners, we shall work with banks and financial institutions to underline the unacceptability of harbouring the cash of those who are directing or profiting from Zimbabwe's meltdown.

The opposition MDC and their leader Morgan Tsvangirai have been clear that basic preconditions must be met before any real negotiation can begin. Their demands are reasonable: the cessation of violence; the release of political prisoners; and the unfettered access of NGOs to the people who need them most and for whom the regime has long since forgotten its responsibilities. The onus now is on the region—the Southern Africa Development Community—and the African Union to demonstrate that they are serious about making dialogue work. We will also continue to advocate the appointment of a UN envoy to support President Mbeki's efforts to negotiate, and to investigate and report on human rights abuses on the ground.

For the first time in the election on 27 June, we saw all three major African election observer groups underline their public dissatisfaction with the vote and the outcome. It is now for Africa and its leaders to show that it will not accept the 27 June result as the basis for any future settlement, and that its commitment to democracy and to reform is real. We will support them in that goal. But calls for space and for time for negotiation to work can be taken seriously only when the conditions on the ground are conducive to meaningful dialogue. The current violence makes that impossible. Newly elected MDC MPs today are in hiding in Harare and elsewhere and are afraid to take up their roles. They are right to be afraid, and Africa and its leaders have a responsibility to respond to their concerns and to their constituents' concerns and remove the causes of that fear.

Robert Mugabe described his election campaign as a war. Morgan Tsvangirai was clear that the people of Zimbabwe did not want to join Mugabe's war. Zimbabwe's independence has been won long ago. No one is challenging its sovereignty or its right to be a nation. Our concern is that its people should have the right to choose who leads it and how it is governed, and that their choice be respected. Our twin-track approach of applying pressure on the regime elite via targeted sanctions and keeping the ordinary people of Zimbabwe alive through our contribution as the second largest bilateral donor of aid will continue. We will continue to meet our responsibilities on both, and we will press others to join us in that approach. The price of not doing so—in terms of the dead and the dying in Zimbabwe—means that we have no option but to continue.

(HC Deb 15 July 2008 Vol 479 c11WS-13WS)

Part Fifteen: II.B. *Coercive measures short of the use of force—collective measures—Outside the United Nations*

15/27
Burma

The Foreign Secretary was asked what criteria were used in deciding to establish EU sanctions against Burmese companies. An FCO Minister wrote:

The EU Common Position on Burma dates back to 1996 and imposes restrictive measures on members of the military regime, the military and security forces, the military regime's economic interests and other individuals, groups, undertakings or entities associated with the military regime who formulate, implement or benefit from policies that impede Burma's transition to democracy, and their families and associates.

In November 2007, the EU strengthened the Common Position to add further state economic enterprises to the investment ban extant on Burmese state owned enterprises. Further restrictive measures include a ban on trade and investment in the timber, gemstones and other extractive industries, which provide a source of revenue for the military regime, including companies trading in these commodities.

In drawing up these measures, the aim of the EU is to target those closely associated with the regime and to minimise the impact on ordinary Burmese citizens.

(HC Deb 27 March 2008 Vol 474 c404W)

15/28
European Union

The Defence Secretary was asked whether under the treaty of Lisbon the European Court of Justice would have jurisdiction over any aspect of the UK's foreign and defence policies; and what the definition of common foreign and security is in the Treaty. An FCO Minister wrote:

The jurisdiction of the European Court of Justice (ECJ) over the Common Foreign and Security Policy (CFSP) is explicitly excluded with two limited exceptions. The ECJ will be able to monitor the boundary between the CFSP and other EU external action, as is currently the case; it will, in addition, be able to ensure that the CFSP cannot be affected by other EU policies as a distinct and equal area of action. In addition, individuals who are subject to CFSP sanctions will be able to challenge these in court. Individuals can already challenge economic sanctions to which they are subject and the Government welcome this closing of the gap in the judicial protection of the individual.

The Maastricht treaty established that the Union should define a CFSP covering all areas of foreign and security policy. The treaty of Lisbon reconfirms that the CFSP shall cover all areas of foreign policy and all questions related to the Union's security. It further specifies that the CFSP shall be defined and implemented by the European Council and the Council.

(HC Deb 17 March 2008 Vol 473 c815W)

15/29

The Defence Secretary was asked what obligations in international law on the UK would be created by *(a)* Article 11(3) and *(b)* Title V of the Treaty of Lisbon; and how would they be enforced. An FCO Minister wrote:

The duty of loyal co-operation as described in Article 11(3) (Article 24(3)) in the consolidated version of the treaties (as amended by Lisbon) is not new. It was introduced by the Maastricht treaty and it has not prevented the UK from pursuing its own foreign policy when required to. The language is identical to that currently used in Article 11(2) of the EU treaty with the addition of the phrase that member states "shall comply with the Union's action in this area". The latter is a statement of the obvious point that when—and only when—member states decide on Common Foreign and Security Policy (CFSP) action they must abide by what they agree—a point which is already reflected in current EU treaty provisions on the CFSP.

Title V of the treaty of Lisbon sets out the general provisions on the Union's external action and specific provisions on the CFSP. The CFSP will remain intergovernmental: when EU members all agree, we act together, but where we do not, the UK acts independently.

The European Court of Justice will not have jurisdiction over the CFSP, except for those limited areas set out in [**15/28**]. And the Commission will not be able to commence infraction proceedings against member states under Title V.

(HC Deb 17 March 2008 Vol 473 c817W)

15/30 [See also **6/74**]
Iran

The Government were asked how they voted on the proposal to keep the People's Mujaheddin Organisation of Iran on the European Union's list of banned terrorist organisations at the Council of Ministers meeting on 16 July. In reply, a Minister said:

[T]he continued listing of PMOI on the new EU list of persons and entities subject to the EUCT assets freeze was supported in the Council of Ministers by the overwhelming majority of member states. The renewed listing was based on new information brought to the Council's attention by another EU member state. However, respecting the UK court judgment, we abstained in the vote.

...

We were determined to respect that court [Court of Appeal] decision, which is why we were not able to support the [French] Government who brought to the table new information that had not been available earlier, on the basis of which they were able to persuade many Governments of Europe to support them. As to why we abstained rather than opposing the listing, the difficulty is that it is a total list with all terrorist organisations on it, and you have to vote up or down on that list. We were therefore faced with the unpalatable situation that either the old list would be retained, which would have done no good because the PMOI would have remained on it, or we would have been left with no listed terrorist organisations in Europe. We felt that was an unacceptable threat to the people of Britain as well as the rest of the Continent.

(HL Deb 22 July 2008 Vol 703 c1650–1651)

15/31

The Government were asked what assessment they had made of the effect on commercial relations with Iran of changes in staffing levels in the commercial section of the British Embassy in Tehran. In reply, a Minister wrote:

UK policy is to support UN and EU sanctions by making clear to those in the Iranian regime that it cannot be business as usual as long as they fail to comply with UN Security Council resolutions and co-operate fully with the International Atomic Energy Authority. We are prepared to risk any impact the reduction in trade promotion activities may have on British business with Iran in order to maintain pressure on the Iranian regime over its nuclear programme. It is too early to judge the effect that these changes may have on our wider commercial relationship with Iran. We look forward to the day when we can return to business as usual, to the benefit of the UK and Iran. But a decision to reach that state rests with the Iranian regime. It is of note that trade between the UK and Iran fell by 8 per cent. over the first four months of this year.

(HC Deb 20 October 2008 Vol 481 c97W)

15/32
Zimbabwe

A Minister wrote:

There has been a military arms embargo against Zimbabwe since 2000. The Government did not therefore grant any licences for export to Zimbabwe of military cryptography equipment or software in 2007.

The Government publish detailed information on export and trade control licences issued, refused and revoked, including the overall value and a summary of the items covered by these licences, in its annual and quarterly reports on strategic export controls. The quarterly reports covering 2007 are available on the FCO website at:

<www.fco.gov.uk/en/about-the-fco/publications/publications/annual-reports/export-controls1>

The 2007 annual report is expected to be published shortly.

Previous annual reports, since 1997, are available from the House of Commons Library, and all the annual reports from 2003 onwards, plus the quarterly reports covering 2007, are available on the Foreign and Commonwealth Office (FCO) website via the link above.

(HC Deb 1 July 2008 Vol 478 c799W)

15/33
The Foreign Secretary said:

The House will have seen news of the political agreement reached between the parties in Harare on 15 September to form an interim coalition Administration. Three weeks have passed since that moment and still no cabinet has been appointed. The positive momentum generated by the signature is fast evaporating, Zimbabwe's economic and political situation is deteriorating, inflation continues to mount and the people of Zimbabwe are still suffering.

That is why there must be no further delay in the appointment of a Zimbabwean Government. The people of Zimbabwe have made their choice. They had the courage to vote on 29 March in spite of the threats and political violence they faced then. They wanted a Government that represented change and reform. Robert Mugabe and ZANU(PF) spent five weeks suppressing the results of that vote. Time was used as a weapon to drag out the election and avoid the transfer of power. The same tactic is being employed now and it is unacceptable.

We and other donors are continuing to provide vital humanitarian relief to the people of Zimbabwe. The UK remains the second largest bilateral donor. We are providing seeds, fertiliser and other agricultural inputs. Via the Department for International Development, we have already given an additional £9 million to the World Food Programme over the summer. The cruel and inhuman ban on the operation of NGOs has been lifted and so our aid is now finally reaching the most vulnerable in Zimbabwe. But some local restrictions remain in place and the situation for ordinary Zimbabweans remains precarious.

Humanitarian relief is vital but it is not the long-term solution in Zimbabwe. We and others want to help the people of Zimbabwe and a new inclusive Administration deal with the root causes of those problems. For that to happen a new and genuinely representative Government must be put in place and they must commit themselves to reform and change. Evidence of that commitment will be simple to see, in the first instance: full and equal humanitarian access without any political or other restrictions; an end to all political violence and the threat of violence; independent media being allowed back in to Zimbabwe and permitted to report freely; freedom of association for all; and a new Government that shows itself committed to macroeconomic stability and reviving the economy.

Morgan Tsvangirai and the MDC have already said they are committed to taking these kinds of steps. They are no more than the Zimbabwean people deserve and need. In New York at the UN General Assembly, Robert Mugabe said that his party will abide by the spirit and letter of the agreement he had signed. We and others are prepared to help and to judge a new Government by their actions, not by their history. The process of development and reform must be Zimbabwean-led and owned and must come out of Harare. A Government who demonstrates by their actions that they are committed to the rights and welfare of its people will attract substantial assistance from the UK and the international community.

Former President Mbeki worked hard to bring the political parties together. Follow-through on the agreement reached in Harare depends on the parties themselves but South Africa, the region and the African Union can all play a positive role in resolving the current impasse and in overseeing the implementation of the agreement. We continue to encourage them to do so. Zimbabwe's problems are far from over. The agreement may mark a step forward but without fair and even-handed implementation it will not be the decisive step needed by the people of Zimbabwe.

Until a new Zimbabwean Government are appointed and that Government show by their action their commitment to reform, EU targeted measures will remain in place. I will discuss the situation in Zimbabwe again with EU Foreign Ministers when we meet on 13 October. We will continue to work within the EU and UN and with African partners to help resolve Zimbabwe's crisis and to support a positive transition to reform on the ground.

Our commitment to the people of Zimbabwe has never been in question and remains constant. What matters now is whether Robert Mugabe and ZANU(PF) can support an agreement that will bring those people relief.

(HC Deb 6 October 2008 Vol 480 c3WS-4WS)

Part Sixteen: Use of Force

Part Sixteen: I. *Use of force—prohibition of the use of force*

16/1
Colombia

Answering a question about terrorism in Colombia, a Minister said:

… the measures taken by states to combat terrorism must be legal, proportionate and justifiable. We in the UK abide by our commitments under international law and we expect all countries to comply with their international legal obligations. It is vital for all states to provide security against atrocities carried out by terrorists, while, of course, respecting the rule of law.

(HL Deb 12 March 2008 Vol 699 c1515)

16/2
Djibouti border

A Minister wrote:

There has been fighting on the Djibouti/Eritrea border after an incursion of Eritrean forces into the disputed Djibouti border region. This has led to casualties on both sides. We supported the UN Security Council (UNSC) presidential statement of 12 June condemning Eritrea's military action and urging both sides to show maximum restraint.

On 24 June, the UNSC renewed its call to Eritrea and requested it to withdraw its troops from the front-line with Djibouti. The Security Council asked for a UN factfinding mission to the disputed region.

We call on Djibouti and Eritrea to enter into a bilateral dialogue to resolve peacefully any outstanding issues and avoid escalating tension and further military action.

We remain concerned about security and stability in the Horn of Africa region. The clashes along the Djibouti-Eritrea border contribute to the instability in this region, but we have not seen any read [sic] across to the Ethiopia-Eritrea border situation.

(HC Deb 7 July 2008 Vol 478 c1334W)

16/3 [See also 5/3, 5/29]
Georgia

In a debate on the situation in Georgia in the Security Council, the UK representative said:

We support Georgia's sovereignty and territorial integrity, and I would like to take this opportunity to call on all members of the Security Council and other colleagues to reaffirm that. I would also like to take the opportunity to reiterate calls for a ceasefire and for withdrawal. We look to the Georgians, the Russians, the South Ossetians and other fighters to desist from violence and to use all means to ensure the safety and security of peacekeepers and of civilians

Humanitarian assistance cannot be used as a pretext for the presence of non-Georgian troops, and a return to the status quo ante, which is obviously desirable, must be such that it too is effective on non-Georgian as well as Georgian forces. We also call for international engagement in a South Ossetian peace process.

(UN Doc. S/PV.5952, 8 August 2008)

16/4

In a debate in the Security Council on the situation in Georgia, the UK representative said:

I think the facts make it clear that this is a conflict between Georgia and Russia. Russian spokesmen try to present the problem as a conflict between Georgia, South Ossetia and Abkhazia, with Russia's role one of peacekeeper. That claim was always doubtful. The last two weeks have demonstrated beyond any doubt that Russia is a party to the conflict. Indeed, Russia's letter last week, saying that they were acting under Article 51 of the United Nations Charter, confirmed that they are a party to the conflict, and Russian actions since 7 August have gone way beyond those of a peacekeeper or mediator. So let us not pretend that this is anything other than a conflict between Russia and Georgia, a conflict which Russia has clearly won militarily. Russian forces in Georgia are now, in effect, an army of occupation, and they will remain so until they withdraw to the positions held prior to 7 August and force levels return to those that prevailed then.

(UN Doc. S/PV.5961, 19 August 2008)

16/5
The Prime Minister said:

Between 8 and 12 August, Russian and Georgian troops clashed in Georgia's separatist region of South Ossetia. The resulting conflict led to a tragic loss of civilian life, and the displacement of over 100,000 people.

From the start of the conflict, the UK and its international partners have been involved in intensive discussions, including through the UN, EU, NATO, G7 and OSCE, to agree a ceasefire and to find a durable and peaceful way forward. I spoke to Russian President Medvedev and to other Heads of State, including Presidents Bush and Sarkozy, to try to find a way forward. My right hon. Friend the Foreign Secretary visited Georgia where he met President Saakashvili and Members of his Government.

On 12 August, the EU and OSCE were able to broker a ceasefire between the parties and agreement to a way forward. This agreement included six key principles:

the parties not to resort to the use of force;

the parties to stop all military actions for good;

the parties to allow free access for humanitarian aid;

Georgian armed forces to return to their places of usual permanent deployment;

Russian armed forces to withdraw to the line they occupied before the start of military actions. Until such time as an international mechanism is created, Russian peacekeeping forces to implement additional security measures;

the parties to engage in international discussions on the modalities of security and stability in Abkhazia and South Ossetia.

Despite this plan, on 26 August, Russia unilaterally recognised the independence of South Ossetia and of Georgia's other separatist region, Abkhazia. Russia also refused to withdraw its forces from Georgia and in some cases moved to reinforce them.

It was in this context that I and the Foreign Secretary attended the Extraordinary European Council on 1 September, convened by French President Nicolas Sarkozy, in his capacity as current presidency of the EU, to discuss the current crisis in Georgia.

At this meeting the European Council unanimously condemned Russia's decision to recognise the independence of Abkhazia and South Ossetia; and expressed its grave concern about the consequences of the conflict and Russia's disproportionate military action. Russia's actions were in clear breach of international law and of successive UN Security Council Resolutions.

In response to Russian actions, the Council decided to conduct a comprehensive review of EU-Russia relations. This evaluation has begun and will continue in the run up to the next EU-Russia summit scheduled to take place in Nice on 14 November 2008. The EU has decided to suspend negotiations with Russia on the new EU Partnership and Co-operation Agreement (PCA) until Russian troops withdraw from Georgia to their pre-conflict line. We strongly support this decision. As I made clear during Council discussions, although the EU should continue discussions with Russia on areas of interest and concern to the EU, it cannot be "business as usual". This review will allow us to take a considered decision about the future of EU-Russia relations.

Russia's actions in Georgia illustrate the need for Europe to intensify efforts to ensure its long-term energy security. The European Council tasked the EU with examining initiatives to be taken to this end. We should explore all options for the diversification of energy supply in the EU, including increased support for infrastructure that diversifies energy sources, an increased commitment to renewable energy, measures to improve energy efficiency and measures to improve the internal market.

The international community must support Georgia in rebuilding the damage caused by the conflict. The European Council made clear the EU's commitment to supply humanitarian aid and support for Georgia's long-term reconstruction efforts, including in Abkhazia and South Ossetia. The Council and the Commission have been tasked to start preparations for an international conference to bring focus to reconstruction efforts. The UK will play its part. We have already committed £2 million to Georgia in humanitarian aid. The EU has pledged to step up its relations with Georgia, including through visa facilitation measures, appointing an EU special envoy and the possible establishment of a full and comprehensive free trade area as soon as the conditions are met.

At the European Council, the EU unanimously called on the parties to implement the EU/OSCE peace plan in full. On 8 September, President Sarkozy, EU Commission President Barroso and EU High Representative Solana travelled to Moscow to press Russia to abide by its commitments. I welcome the agreement reached during this meeting that Russia will withdraw its troops from Georgian territory outside Abkhazia and South Ossetia and that Russia will commit to international discussions on future security modalities. This is a good first step towards peace and security. But it is only the start; Russia must now implement these commitments and must engage fully in finding a lasting solution to the crisis.

The international community will support efforts to ensure lasting peace and security in the region, including through the presence of observers on the ground. In line with the EU Council conclusions and the 8 September Moscow agreement, the European Union will contribute to these efforts. EU Foreign Ministers will discuss the deployment of EU monitors at the General Affairs and External Relations Council (GAERC) on Monday, 15 September. It is vital that international monitors are given free and unfettered access by all sides to carry out their mandate.

The EU's response to this crisis must also consider the implications for the EU's common neighbourhood. On 27 August the Foreign Secretary travelled to Kiev where he made a speech on the need for closer ties between the EU and the region. I am pleased that the Council agreed that the EU should strengthen its relations with the region, including Ukraine. I welcome the successful EU—Ukraine summit which took place yesterday (9 September). I look forward to the Commission's proposals for enhancing EU relations with the region, due in December this year.

The UK will continue to work with international partners to ensure that effective support is given to Georgia and that a lasting, peaceful solution is reached as soon as possible.

(HC Deb 10 September 2008 Vol 479 c127WS-130WS)

16/6

In reply to a question on South Ossetia, a Minister wrote:

In a statement published on 8 August 2008, the Government joined international calls for an immediate ceasefire in South Ossetia after Georgia launched a military offensive to regain control of the breakaway province. The Foreign and Commonwealth Office said that it was "monitoring" developments and called for an immediate ceasefire in the fighting in South Ossetia and for a resumption of direct dialogue between all the parties.

On 8 August, our ambassador in Tbilisi called on the Georgian Foreign Minister, Eka Tkeshelashvili to urge restraint and cooperation with the international peace efforts and convey our support for Georgia's territorial integrity within the internationally recognised borders.

In a statement on 9 August, the Foreign Secretary said: "The UK Government are deeply concerned by the violence in Georgia. The escalation in fighting is dangerously destabilising and there is also the threat of civilian losses on a large scale. I am today holding high level consultations with European Foreign Ministers and with the US Secretary of State. The UK will be discussing with all our partners how to stop the spread of violence, secure a ceasefire and get talks underway."

On 15 August, the Prime Minister spoke with the Georgian President Mikheil Saakashvili urging cooperation and implementation of the peace plan brokered by the EU and the Organisation for Security and Cooperation in Europe.

The Government's response to the crisis has remained the same—urging all parties to the conflict to work with the international community towards a sustainable resolution of the conflict based on territorial integrity, rule of law and respect for human rights.

I refer my hon. Friend to the Prime Ministerial written statement after the Extraordinary European Council on the crisis in Georgia on 1 September 2008 for further details of our response to the crisis, Official Report, 10 September 2008, columns 127–30WS [**16/5**].

(HC Deb 17 October 2008 Vol 480 c1598W-1560W)

16/7
Israel

The Foreign Secretary was asked what assessment he had made of the effects of the recent increase in rocket attacks by the Palestinian Islamic Jihad on the security situation in Israel. An FCO Minister wrote:

The UK is deeply concerned by rocket attacks from Gaza against Israeli citizens. The launching of rockets against Israeli civilian targets and all forms of violence must stop. Violence serves only to undermine the prospects for peace and security in the region.

The Government continue to call on all Palestinian factions to stop attacks, including rocket attacks, which target civilians and only escalate an already tense situation. At the same time, Israel must ensure its actions are in accordance with international law. It is important for both sides to exercise the utmost restraint and refrain from the use of force.

(HC Deb 28 April 2008 Vol 475 c19W)

16/8
Turkey

The Government were asked what their response was to the Declaration for a Democratic Solution to the Kurdish Question, published by the

Democratic Communities of Kurdistan in November 2007. An FCO Minister wrote:

We are aware of the Declaration for a Democratic Solution to the Kurdish Question, published by the Democratic Communities of Kurdistan in November 2007. It is in the interests of all parties to achieve security and stability in south-east Turkey. We continue to encourage the Government of Iraq and the Kurdish Regional Government to work with Turkey to tackle the Kurdistan Workers Party (PKK) presence in Northern Iraq.

(HL Deb 28 January 2008 Vol 698 cWA98)

Part Sixteen: II.A. *Use of force—legitimate use of force—self-defence*

16/9
Iraq

A Minister wrote:

UK forces are operating in Iraq as part of a multi-national coalition at the request of the Iraqi Government. The coalition and the Iraqi Government have routinely followed a policy of dialogue with insurgent groups, where it is judged they can be persuaded to renounce violence and participate in the legitimate political process. The offer of engagement is open to groups across the political spectrum and it has been an essential element of the counter-insurgency strategy to bring peace and security to Iraq.

In 2007, with the full knowledge and support both of our coalition partners and the Iraqi Government, UK forces conducted a dialogue with a range of militia leaders in Basra—including Jaish al-Mahdi—in accordance with the Iraq-wide reconciliation strategy. Neither these discussions, nor their outcome, prevented UK forces from providing military support to the Iraqi Security Forces.

(HC Deb 27 October 2008 Vol 481 c634W)

16/10
Israel

The Foreign Secretary was asked what representations he had made to the Palestinians on rocket and mortar attacks from Gaza into Israel. An FCO Minister wrote:

I issued statements on 27 and 28 February condemning unreservedly the barrage of rockets on southern Israel that left one man dead and several others injured that day. There can be no justification for the almost daily rocket and mortar attacks on Sderot and the surrounding area. The Government continue to call on all Palestinian factions to stop attacks, including rocket attacks, which target civilians and only escalate an already tense situation. At the same time, Israel must ensure its actions are in accordance with international law. It is important that all parties find a way to restore calm, stopping the reciprocal attacks, for the sake of the populations on both sides.

(HC Deb 6 March 2008 Vol 472 c2788W)

Part Sixteen: II.B.2. *Use of force—Legitimate Use of Force—Collective Measures—outside the United Nations*

Ballistic missile defence

16/11

Answering a question, an FCO Minister said:

The fact is that the United Kingdom welcomes the US expansion of the ballistic missile defence into Europe. We think that the sitings in the Czech Republic and Poland are an important protection against a potential attack by a rogue state. It is clear that the system offers no challenge whatever to Russia's strategic missiles, in terms of either its location or its capacity. That is generally accepted. The fact is that the US has offered to share the information, importantly, with Russia and with NATO allies. We welcome that very much indeed. We should not be criticising the US for seeking to deal with the threat; instead, we should be showing a united effort in trying to deal with those rogue states that the missile defence system is designed to protect us from.

(HC Deb 25 March 2008 Vol 474 c18)

16/12
European Union

The Defence Secretary was asked if he would make it his policy to ensure that British armed forces will not come under the command of *(a)* the European Union and *(b)* other European states' armed forces. An FCO Minister wrote:

The decision to launch any EU military operation can be taken only by unanimity among member states. Whether to contribute British forces to any operation is a voluntary decision for the UK Government to take case by case.

Any British forces contributing to an EU operation are likely, depending on the arrangements made for it, to come under the operational control of the Military Operation Commander, who may be a national of any EU member state and who would be chosen by the Council of Ministers of the European Union acting unanimously. The Lisbon Treaty will not change this position.

In the same way, British forces contributing to a NATO operation are placed under the operational control of the NATO Military Operation Commander.

(HC Deb 18 March 2008 Vol 473 c10140W)

16/13
Israel

The Foreign Secretary was asked what reports he had received on the recent conflict between Israel and Palestine in Gaza and consequent civilian deaths. A Minister wrote:

The Government remain deeply concerned about the recent escalation of violence in Gaza and southern Israel. My right hon. Friend the Foreign Secretary issued a statement on 2 March, regarding the rise in the number of rocket attacks into Israel. The statement stressed the need for all sides in the conflict, and the international community to keep the political process alive. We also support the UN Secretary-General's call for all parties to step back from the brink of even deeper and more deadly clashes.

The full text of the statement is available on the Foreign and Commonwealth Office website at:

<www.fco.gov.uk/servlet/Fron?pagename=OpenMarket/Xcelerate/ShowPage&;c=Page&cid=1007029391629&a=KArticle&aid= 1203947188494>.

He was asked also on which occasions his Department had issued criticisms of *(a)* Hamas and *(b)* Hezbollah for firing rockets into the State of Israel. The Minister wrote:

An FCO Minister issued statements on 27 and 28 February condemning unreservedly the barrage of rockets on southern Israel from Gaza, that left one man dead and several others injured. In addition, the Foreign Secretary issued a statement condemning the rocket attacks on 2 March. There can be no justification for the almost daily rocket and mortar attacks on Sderot and the surrounding area. The Government continue to call on all Palestinian factions to stop attacks, including rocket attacks, which target civilians and only escalate an already tense situation. At the same time, Israel must ensure its actions are in accordance with international law. It is important that all parties find a way to restore calm, for the sake of the populations on both sides.

During the 2006 conflict between Hezbollah and Israel the UK issued numerous statements condemning the firing of rockets by Hezbollah into Israel. During the 2006 conflict we also repeatedly called on Israel to ensure its response was proportionate and avoided civilian casualties. Since the 2006 conflict between Israel and Hezbollah, we are not aware of any instances when Hezbollah has fired rockets into Israel.

(HC Deb 13 March 2008 Vol 473 c646W-647W)

16/14
Republic of Congo

The Government were asked whether they would place in the Library of the House a copy of the agreement with the Government of the Republic of Congo to allow the deployment of British forces for the possible evacuation of British citizens from the Democratic Republic of Congo; and on what assessment of the peace process in the Democratic Republic of Congo this agreement was reached. An FCO Minister wrote:

The agreement signed with the Republic of Congo on 22 January 2008 is intended to facilitate the evacuation of British nationals in the Democratic Republic of the Congo in the event of a crisis. The UK entered into the agreement as a routine precaution. It forms part of the consular contingency plan of our embassy in Kinshasa and is not connected with efforts to end the conflict in the Democratic Republic of the Congo.

We will consult the Government of the Republic of Congo as to whether they are content for a copy of the agreement to be placed in the Library of the House.

[The agreement is reproduced below **16/15**, Ed.]

(HL Deb 4 February 2008 Vol 698 cWA151)

16/15

MEMORANDUM ON COOPERATION

Concerning the stationing of a British military contingent in Brazzaville

(Republic of Congo)

The Government of the Republic of Congo and the Government of the United Kingdom of Great Britain and Northern Ireland hereinafter "The Participants" have reached the following understandings:

Paragraph 1

The present Memorandum defines the provisions governing the stationing of the British military contingent in Brazzaville, which is to support the plan for the evacuation of British nationals in the Democratic Republic of Congo.

Paragraph 2

The Republic of Congo will provide facilities for the stationing of the British contingent operating as part of this evacuation plan.

Paragraph 3

The British military contingent will be stationed at the Brazzaville Air Base in accordance with the provisions of the present Memorandum.

Paragraph 4

The personnel forming the British military contingent will respect the laws and regulations of the Republic of Congo and will refrain from any action or activity incompatible with the aims of their mission.

I—General rules and regulations

Paragraph 5

Movement of personnel, equipment, land vehicles, aircraft and vessels forming part of the British military contingent will require authorisation issued by the appropriate Congolese military authorities.

Paragraph 6

The vehicles, aircraft and vessels operated by the British military contingent will carry soldiers in national uniform, evacuated entitled persons and the material and equipment necessary to carry out their mission.

Paragraph 7

Personnel of the British military contingent may carry individual weapons for the purpose of self-defence on condition that they are authorised to do so by their orders and after consulting the Congolese authorities.

Paragraph 8

In the case of aircraft, the information concerning each flight, as listed in the Annex, will be notified to the Congolese Participant at least 72 hours before the flight. However, for operational reasons, this flight information may in exceptional cases be notified only one (1) hour before take-off.

Paragraph 9

(1) The personnel forming the British military contingent will enjoy immunity from arrest and their equipment will not be seized.

(2) Personnel forming the British military contingent will enjoy immunity from legal proceedings in the Republic of the Congo.

Paragraph 10

If exceptional circumstances so demand, the Congolese Participant reserves the right to make unannounced checks. The British military contingent will be required to facilitate such checks.

Paragraph 11

Any dispute arising from damage caused by the contingent to persons or property of the Republic of Congo will be settled amicably.

Paragraph 12

The British military contingent will carry out operations to rescue its personnel or repair its equipment within the territory of the Republic of the Congo only after informing the Congolese authorities.

Paragraph 13

The aircraft and personnel of the British military contingent will be exempt from charges and/or fees levied by the Congolese Participant. However, they will be required to pay for any commercial services they may use.

II—Responsibilities of the Participants

Paragraph 14

The British Participant will:

• in its request for transit or landing by aircraft, provide the information required by the Congolese authorities, as listed in the Annex

• appoint a liaison officer responsible for liasing with the Congolese military authorities.

Paragraph 15

• The Congolese Participant will:

• ensure the security of the British military contingent, particularly in the area in which it is stationed.

• protect the confidentiality of information required.

- appoint a liaison officer responsible for liaising with the British military contingent.

Paragraph 16

This Memorandum will take place from the date of the signature and will cover a period of one (1) year.

It may be extended at the request of the British Participant.

Paragraph 17

Any provisions which may prove necessary and which have not been included in the present Memorandum may be added in an Addendum following the consent of both Participants.

Paragraph 18

Any disputes regarding the interpretation or application of this Memorandum will be resolved only by consultation between the Participants and will not be referred to a national or international tribunal or other third party for settlement.

Signed in duplicate at

On 22 January 2008

In the English and French languages, both texts having equal validity.

[ANNEX—Information to be provided in a request for overflight and/or landing in the Republic of Congo, not reproduced.]

<www.parliament.uk/deposits/depositedpapers/2008/DEP2008-0548.doc>

16/16
The Security Council

An FCO Minister was asked if he agreed that the responsibility to protect is now generally accepted in principle but frequently fails to deliver in practice; and the Government were asked whether or not they would urge on the UN Security Council the need to address the slaughter, disease, displacement, famine and slavery in the area, if necessary by direct international intervention. The Minister said:

[It] is right to say that the responsibility to protect unfortunately remains a doctrine recognised more in principle than in practice. All of us who were involved in its development had hoped that Sudan, particularly the Darfur region, would be one of the first places for its effective application. Instead we face continuing conflict throughout Sudan which ... humanitarian assistance alone cannot address. The UN Security Council, under the joint leadership of the British ambassador to the Council, has just been in Sudan trying to achieve political progress on Abyei and more generally on north/south and Darfur issues. We continue to press for a political solution here because Darfur and Sudan as a whole remains a blot on the collective international conscience.

(HL Deb 9 June 2008 Vol 702 c369)

16/17
Turkey

The Foreign Secretary was asked what representations he had made to the government of Turkey on its decision to engage Kurdish forces in the North of Iraq. An FCO Minister wrote:

The Foreign Secretary has urged his Turkish counterpart that Turkey should conclude this operation as quickly as possible, and then withdraw its troops from northern Iraq. We have also pressed Turkey to take all possible steps to avoid causing harm to civilians. We continue to encourage the Turkish government, the Iraqi government and Kurdish Regional authorities to work together to resolve this issue through dialogue.

(HC Deb 4 March 2008 Vol 472 c2361W)

16/18
Uganda

A Minister wrote:

We support a political solution to end the conflict between the Lord's Resistance Army (LRA) and the Government of Uganda. International backing for a peaceful solution will be vital.

UN Security Council (UNSC) resolution 1794 in December 2007 renewed the mandate for the UN Mission in the Democratic Republic of Congo (DRC) (MONUC). It included a call for militia groups present in eastern DRC, including the LRA, to lay down their arms. MONUC works alongside the Congolese armed forces to contain the threat of the LRA and ensure the protection of civilians.

We note the UN Secretary-General's analysis in his report of 3 July to the UNSC that a strengthening of MONUC's capacity would be required, should the mission be tasked beyond its current activities against the LRA. In its discussions with UNSC partners and the UN on the mandating of peacekeeping missions, the Government carefully weighs political needs and capacity and budgetary implications. We believe that MONUC has the necessary resources to fulfil its current mandated tasks.

(HC Deb 17 July 2008 Vol 479 c690W)

16/19
Zimbabwe

The Government were asked in what circumstances they would support a United Nations-sponsored military intervention in Zimbabwe. In reply, a Minister wrote:

We do not believe military intervention is the best way in the current circumstances to bring change and reform to Zimbabwe. African regional organisations and neighbouring countries continue to lead political and diplomatic efforts to resolve the crisis.

(HL Deb 3 July 2008 Vol 703 cWA56)

16/20

During a debate in the House of Lords, the Government were asked, in light of the fact that Zimbabwe was more a state in institutionalised chaos than it was a functioning sovereign state, whether it would be legitimate under international law for the UK to intervene for humanitarian reasons. In reply, a Minister stated:

[L]et me adamantly say that we have not received such advice. Let me remind the noble Lord that, as recently as July, a resolution, which certainly did not even call for force but called for a much milder set of sanctions against Zimbabwe, failed in the UN Security Council. The Security Council resolution, which is normally taken as the basis for such intervention, is, in our view, not achievable at this time.

(HL Deb 10 December 2008 Vol 706 c379)

Part Sixteen: III. *Use of force—disarmament and arms control*

16/21

In a debate on National Security Strategy, the Prime Minister said:

I can tell the House that Britain will be at the forefront of diplomatic action on nuclear weapons control and reduction, offering a new bargain to non-nuclear powers. On the one hand, we will help them, and we have proposed the creation of a new international system to help non-nuclear states to acquire the new sources of energy that they need, including through our proposed global enrichment bond, and we are today inviting interested countries to an international conference on these important themes later this year.

In return, we will seek agreement on tougher controls aimed at reducing weapons and preventing proliferation—first, by ending the stalemates on the fissile material cut-off treaty and the comprehensive nuclear test ban treaty and, secondly, by achieving, after 2010, a more robust implementation of the nuclear non-proliferation treaty with the aim of accelerating disarmament among possessor states, preventing proliferation and, ultimately, freeing the world from nuclear weapons. And, as a new priority to meet the dangers both of proliferation to new states and of material falling into the hands of terrorists, we propose not only tougher action against potential proliferators such as Iran but new action against suppliers. We are seeking to strengthen export control regimes and build a more effective forensic nuclear capability in order to determine and expose the true source of material employed in any nuclear device. Having already reduced the number of our operationally available warheads by 20 per cent. and made our expertise available for the verifiable elimination of warheads, I can confirm that we, Britain, are ready to play our part in further disarmament.

(HC Deb 19 March 2008 Vol 473 c927)

16/22

In a debate on the Atomic Weapons Establishment, Aldermaston, a Defence Minister said:

In compliance with the comprehensive nuclear test ban treaty, we are committed to maintaining the existing Trident warhead stockpile safely and effectively throughout its intended in-service life without recourse to nuclear testing. That commitment is supported by replacement facilities such as those necessary for handling high explosives, enriched uranium and non-nuclear warhead components. My hon. Friend complains about some of the expenditure at AWE, but in part it is used towards our commitments under the nuclear test ban treaty.

(HC Deb 26 March 2008 Vol 474 c118WH)

16/23

The Foreign Secretary was asked what recent steps had been taken by the Government towards nuclear disarmament under the terms of Article VI of the Nuclear Non-Proliferation Treaty. An FCO Minister wrote:

The UK is strongly committed to the Nuclear Non-Proliferation Treaty (NPT) and we are fulfilling all of our Treaty obligations, including those on disarmament under Article VI. We have reduced our nuclear platform to one delivery system, Trident, and have significantly reduced the operational status of that system. We have recently met our commitment to a further 20 per cent. reduction in the stockpile of operationally available warheads, contributing to a 75 per cent. reduction in the explosive power of the UK nuclear arsenal since the end of the Cold War.

In addition the UK is pursuing a programme to develop expertise in verifying the reduction and elimination of nuclear weapons internationally. The aim of the study has been to examine and trial potential methodologies which could be used in a future multilateral nuclear disarmament regime. This work is continuing at the Atomic Weapons Establishment and will be presented to the 2008 NPT Preparatory Committee in Geneva.

(HC Deb 7 May 2008 Vol 475 c933W)

16/24

The Foreign Secretary wrote:

The Director General of the International Atomic Energy Agency (IAEA), Dr. ElBaradei, issued a report on Iran's nuclear activities on 26 May. The report says that Iran has failed to suspend enrichment-related activities, has made no progress on the transparency measures the UN Security Council and the IAEA have called for and has failed to answer the IAEA's questions relating to studies with a possible military dimension. It notes that the alleged studies are a matter of "serious concern" and that "clarification of these is critical to an assessment of the nature of Iran's past and present nuclear programme". We have called on Iran to cooperate fully with the IAEA, fulfil its obligations under UN Security Council resolutions and to implement the additional protocol.

(HC Deb 4 June 2008 Vol 476 c1004W)

16/25

The Government were asked what factors are taken into account when deciding whether to sign the protocols of nuclear-free zones. In reply, a Minister wrote:

The UK supports the creation of nuclear weapon-free zones in accordance with the Principles and Guidelines in annex I of the report of the 54th session of the UN Disarmament Commission (<http://disarmament.un.org/undiscom.htm>). These principles and guidelines state, for example, that the nuclear-weapon states should be consulted during the negotiations of each treaty and its relevant protocol/protocols.

(HC Deb 3 July 2008 Vol 478 c1128W)

16/26

Her Majesty's Government were asked to which protocols of nuclear-free zones the UK was a signatory. In reply, a Minister wrote:

The UK has signed and ratified the protocols to the treaties of Tlatelolco (Latin America and the Caribbean) and Raratonga (South Pacific) as well as the relevant protocols of the treaty of Pelindaba (Africa), collectively giving treaty-based negative security assurances to over 100 countries.

(HC Deb 3 July 2008 Vol 478 c1128W)

16/27

The Government were asked what plans there are to sign the protocols of those nuclear-free zones for which the UK is not yet a signatory. In reply, a Minister wrote:

The UK supports the principle of both the South-East Asia and Central Asia nuclear weapon-free zones. The UK continues to seek ways to overcome the difficulties that pertain to the treaties of Bangkok and Semipalatinsk so that we can ratify protocols to these treaties. Foreign and Commonwealth Office officials continue to have discussions with representatives of members of the Association of South-East Asian Nations and the Central Asian States (the C5) to resolve these difficulties.

(HC Deb 3 July 2008 Vol 478 c1128W)

16/28

During a debate in the House of Lords, the Government were asked whether they would propose a new treaty, under which, pending full nuclear disarmament, states possessing nuclear weapons would undertake not to use them to attack states without nuclear weapons. In reply, a Minister said:

[T]he most appropriate way to provide treaty-based security assurances is through the relevant protocols to nuclear weapons-free zones. These provide credible, regional, internationally binding legal instruments. The UK remains fully committed to the negative security assurance we gave to the non-nuclear weapons states parties to the Nuclear Non-Proliferation Treaty in our 1995 letter to the UN Secretary-General, subsequently noted in Security Council Resolution 984.

(HL Deb 22 July 2008 Vol 703 c1648)

16/29

The Government were asked about their position on a nuclear-free Arctic. In reply, a Minister said:

[A] at the moment there are three existing treaties that create these nuclear-free zones, covering Latin America, the south Pacific and Africa. There are two more treaties, covering south-east Asia and central Asia, that need further work for us to be able to support them fully. The same principles apply to the Arctic. We are in favour of as many of these regional agreements as possible, so long as they are sensibly drafted to ensure that all countries are bound by them and that they apply in an equal way the principle of non-nuclear use.

(HL Deb 22 July 2008 Vol 703 c1650)

16/30

A Minister wrote:

The UK will work intensively with international partners before, at and after the 2009 Nuclear Non-Proliferation Treaty (NPT) Preparatory Committee to iden-tify areas of convergence that can form the basis of a successful outcome to the 2010 NPT Review Conference. In particular we will submit proposals to strengthen the NPT in all its aspects, promoting zero tolerance of proliferation, upholding the rights of all States party to the NPT to benefit from the peaceful uses of nuclear energy and reinvigorating the commitment of NPT Nuclear Weapons States to nuclear disarmament.

(HC Deb 6 October 2008 Vol 480 c229W-230W)

16/31

The Government were asked about the decision by the Nuclear Suppliers Group to support a nuclear agreement between the USA and India on the operation of article II of the Nuclear Non-Proliferation Treaty. A Minister wrote:

We assess that the decision by the Nuclear Suppliers Group (NSG) to allow an exemption for India to the NSG guidelines will not have any effect on the opera-tion of article II of the Nuclear Non-Proliferation Treaty. Article II prohibits the transfer of nuclear weapons or other nuclear explosive devices; the NSG exemp-tion for India does not allow for such transfers.

(HC Deb 6 October 2008 Vol 480 c230W)

16/32

The Government were asked about the compatibility with the United Kingdom's obligations under Article 1 of the Nuclear Non Proliferation Treaty (NPT) when deciding to invite Norway to participate as a non-nuclear state party to the NPT in the disarmament laboratory project on nuclear warhead dismantlement at AWE Aldermaston. In reply, a Minister wrote:

The joint research between the UK's Atomic Weapons Establishment, several Norwegian laboratories and the non-governmental organisation VERTIC on the verification of warhead dismantlement is being conducted in full accord with the mutual obligations under Articles I and II of the NPT. The underlying aim of the research is to investigate, under a hypothetical future verification regime, what technical evidence and assurances could be demonstrated to third parties without undermining national security or releasing proliferation sensitive information. The research is specifically designed to examine issues of verification while avoiding the use of sensitive design information or materials; constraints, necessarily levied by the NPT, that inspired the initiative.

(HC Deb 6 October 2008 Vol 480 c260W-260W)

16/33

During a debate in the House of Commons, a Member of Parliament said:

Would [the Foreign Secretary], on behalf of Her Majesty's Government, make it clear that an attack on Iran by Israel would trigger off uncontrollable, convulsive and irreversible consequences that would damage not only the region, but the entire global system, and that such an attack must not take place?

In reply, the Foreign Secretary said:

He will know that almost from my first day in this job I have emphasised that we are 100 per cent committed to a diplomatic course with Iran and to a process of making it a serious offer that presents it major economic—never mind political—benefits, but that we must be insistent that a uranium enrichment programme in defiance of not only the UN Security Council, but of Iran's obligations under the non-proliferation treaty is a serious danger to stability in not just the middle east, but in the world. The middle east has enough problems without a nuclear arms race, and it is very important that we address that matter diplomatically on all fronts.

(HC Deb 7 October 2008 Vol 480 c120W)

16/34

A Minister wrote:

While there is no internationally agreed definition of a "thermobaric" weapon, weapons of this nature would be controlled under UK Military List (entry ML4) and exports from the UK would require an export licence. All export licence applications are carefully considered on a case by case basis against the Consolidated EU and National Arms Export Licensing Criteria.

(HC Deb 14 October 2008 Vol 480 c1242W)

16/35

The Government were asked what discussions they had had with the United States and Russia on their obligations under Article VI of the nuclear non-proliferation treaty. In reply, a Minister stated:

We regularly discuss with the United States and Russia the importance of action to reinforce the nuclear non-proliferation treaty, including through demonstration of our commitment to Article VI. Under their bilateral strategic arms control arrangements, by 2012 both countries will have reduced their total stockpiles of strategic nuclear warheads by around 80 per cent. since the end of the cold war. We have welcomed that progress, and encouraged both countries to reduce their nuclear arsenals even further in due course.

(HC Deb 22 October 2008 Vol 481 c398W)

Part Seventeen: The Law of Armed Conflict and International Humanitarian Law

Part Seventeen: I.B.6. *The Law of Armed Conflict and International Humanitarian Law—International armed conflict—The Law of International Armed Conflict—Distinction between combatants and non-combatants*

17/1
A Minister wrote:

We do not routinely collate data on the number of insurgents killed by UK forces in Afghanistan. Collecting and verifying data is extremely difficult given the nature of the conflict. As we have said repeatedly, our long-term strategy towards defeating the insurgency in Afghanistan is through a wide range of military and non-military activity and not through an attritional, purely military campaign.

We regret incidents where civilians are accidentally killed as a result of actions by international forces. Procedures are in place, and being constantly updated in the light of experience, both to minimise the risk of these casualties occurring and to investigate any incidents that do happen. Wherever possible, local populations are warned of impending operations. We should remember the insurgents are the real threat to the safety and security of the Afghan people by their indiscriminate use of violence. ISAF forces are not present on a permanent basis in many parts of Helmand province, which makes it difficult to monitor atrocities against the civilian population by the Taliban. It is therefore impossible to estimate with any confidence the number of civilian casualties in Helmand province in 2007–08 that have been caused by the current conflict.

(HC Deb 27 October 2008 Vol 481 c623W)

Part Seventeen: I.B.7. *The Law of Armed Conflict and International Humanitarian Law—International armed conflict—The Law of International Armed Conflict—International humanitarian law*

17/2
Afghanistan

Her Majesty's Government were asked about civilian deaths due to air attacks by NATO forces in Afghanistan. In reply, a Minister wrote:

The Ministry of Defence does not collate data relating to reports or complaints of civilian casualties where these do not relate to incidents allegedly caused by

UK forces. Any such reports are passed to the NATO chain of command or the respective national authorities for investigation.

Over the last 12 months, my Department has received formal notification of two occasions on which UK aircraft were involved in incidents in which civilian casualties are believed to have occurred. One occurred in March 2008 and the second in September 2008. In both cases, the incidents were subjected to a thorough and detailed investigation. There is no reason to believe that UK forces behaved inappropriately in either incident. We do not collate or publish figures for civilian casualties in Afghanistan because of the immense difficulty and risks of collecting robust data.

(HC Deb 20 October 2008 Vol 481 c118W)

17/3
Israel [See also **16/10, 16/13**]

Asked to agree that the treatment by Israel of the population of Gaza was a collective punishment, an International Development Minister said:

We constantly call on all sides in the dispute and conflict to adhere to international law and to respect human rights. Israeli security and justice for the Palestinians will not be achieved by cutting off fuel, closing crossings, or firing rockets. That is a recipe for continued misery on all sides.

(HC Deb 30 January 2008 Vol 471 c303)

17/4
An FCO Minister said about the situation in Gaza:

The Government recognise the impact and scale of the problems and the need to address all of them. We understand the political and economic pressures that nurture and drive them, and that, for example, Israel has a right to defend itself against rocket attacks. I join my hon. Friend in deploring the fact that so-called rejectionist Palestinian groups—including Hamas, I am afraid—fire those rockets indiscriminately from Gaza, with the intention of killing and wounding Israeli civilians. However, in the course of self-defence, it is imperative that Israel remain committed to undertaking its obligations under international law. The United Kingdom continues to monitor the humanitarian situation in Gaza, and my right hon. Friend the Foreign Secretary has said clearly that restrictions on fuel supplies will not achieve Israeli security. He is dead right. Nor will the political aspirations of the Palestinian people be furthered by rocket attacks, so the United Kingdom urges restraint on all parties ...

We consider settlement building anywhere in the occupied Palestinian territories illegal under international law, including Israeli settlements in both East Jerusalem and the west bank. Settlement construction is an obstacle to peace. We support President Bush's view that there should be a complete freeze on settlement construction and that outposts should be removed ...

A reformed Palestinian security force will continue to be the key to the success of the peace process. Militias and gangs that fire rockets and mortars indiscriminately at Israeli civilian targets must be prevented from carrying out their murderous activities by the Palestinians themselves. Israeli security and Palestinian hardship can be tackled only through a political process that creates an economically and socially viable Palestinian state, at peace with Israel.

(HC Deb 30 January 2008 Vol 471 c94WH-96WH)

17/5

The Government were asked what their assessment was of the extent to which the post-Annapolis processes would help Israel to show an increased willingness to comply with United Nations resolutions past and present, and the United States to avoid future vetoes of such resolutions. An FCO Minister wrote:

We welcome the commitment shown by Israel, the Palestinians and the United States at Annapolis. On 30 November, the UN Security Council warmly welcomed Annapolis and encouraged the parties to pursue their obligations, and will be following developments carefully. This marks the start of a process. We have to work to ensure that the process leads to a comprehensive peace settlement. All our efforts are behind this. As both parties have made clear, it is for them to work out a solution.

We continue to call on the Government of Israel and the Palestinian Authority to adhere to international law and respect all UN Security Council resolutions. We press for the implementation of all Security Council resolutions by all the parties, and we remain committed to their aims. We continue to support a peaceful negotiated, two-state solution in keeping with the road map and Security Council resolutions 242, 338, 1397, 1435 and 1515.

(HL Deb 7 January 2008 Vol 697 cWA169)

17/6
A Minister wrote:

Israel has an obligation to adhere to the international humanitarian law. It may take reasonable measures for the protection of its own security and that of the population of the Occupied Territories, but such measures must be proportionate, taking account of an assessment of the threat and of the impact on the civilian population.

The only sustainable way to reduce suffering is for the relaxation on humanitarian imports into Gaza, and we will continue to call on the Government of Israel to take this action. The quartet has also reiterated its concerns, most recently during the UN General Assembly on 26 September.

(HC Deb 19 November 2008 Vol 705 cWA246)

17/7
Protection of Civilians

In a debate on the Protection of Civilians in Armed Conflict in the Security Council, the UK representative said:

As well as protecting civilians in situations of armed conflict, the international community has committed itself to assist States that are under stress before crises and conflicts break out. In that regard, we reaffirm our support for the concept of the responsibility to protect, as agreed by Member States at the World Summit in 2005. It is an important commitment, which should result in earlier and more decisive action to prevent genocide, war crimes, ethnic cleansing and crimes against humanity.

(UN Doc. S/PV.5898, 27 May 2008)

17/8
Sri Lanka

A Minister wrote:

The UK's view is that there must be inclusive political negotiations for a just settlement that could satisfy the legitimate aspirations of all communities in Sri Lanka and promote democracy, stability and the observance of internationally accepted human rights principles.

The Government have grave concerns about the human rights situation in Sri Lanka. Issues of concern include the targeting of civilians, the recruitment of child soldiers in violation of international law, reports of mistreatment and of the intimidation of the media and continuing abductions and disappearances. Tamils are disproportionately affected.

(HC Deb 16 July 2008 Vol 479 c426W)

17/9

During a debate in the House of Commons, an FCO Minister said:

It is important not to forget that the LTTE is a ruthless terrorist organisation, which is responsible for serious human rights abuses against civilians throughout Sri Lanka.

The LTTE has no democratic mandate to represent the Tamil population. It is reported to recruit civilians, including children, into its ranks forcibly, to extort food and money from an already impoverished people, to abduct and kill Tamil civilians who disagree with its views or methods and to break all norms of international humanitarian law by preventing civilians from leaving conflict areas, effectively holding them as a human shield. The LTTE has conducted a terrorist campaign across the whole of Sri Lanka for nearly three decades, deliberately targeting thousands of individual civilians, as well as assassinating Government figures.

(HC Deb 18 December 2008 Vol 485 c1348–1349)

17/10

A Minister stated:

The Government welcome the commitment of the Government of Sri Lanka to protect civilian populations and have continued to lobby for all parties in the conflict to respect their obligations under international humanitarian law. Those include the protection of the civilian population and humanitarian workers, the preservation of humanitarian space, and ensuring free and unfettered access to all affected areas by neutral, impartial humanitarian actors. Unless those basic requirements are met, funding will not ease the plight of IDPs and other vulnerable residents.

(HC Deb 14 October 2008 Vol 480 c246WH)

Part Seventeen: I.B.8. *The Law of Armed Conflict and International Humanitarian Law—International armed conflict—The Law of International Armed Conflict—Belligerent occupation*

17/11
Cultural Property

Government Response to the Culture, Media and Sport Committee Reports on the Draft Heritage Protection Bill and Draft Cultural Property (Armed Conflicts) Bill. A Minister wrote:

Today I am publishing and laying before Parliament a draft of the Cultural Property (Armed Conflicts) Bill for pre-legislative scrutiny. The Bill will help to ensure the security of the nation's most important cultural property in the event of armed conflict and will send a signal to the international community that the UK takes seriously its obligations under international humanitarian law to respect and safeguard the cultural property of other nations.

The Bill is required to enable the UK to ratify the 1954 Hague convention for the Protection of Cultural Property in the Event of Armed Conflict (The Hague Convention) and accede to its two protocols (1954 and 1999). The convention, adopted following the massive destruction that took place during the second world war, provides a system to protect cultural property from the effects of international and domestic armed conflict. Parties to the convention are required to respect cultural property situated within the territory of other parties by not attacking it, and to respect cultural property within their own territory by not using it for purposes which are likely to expose it to destruction or damage in the event of armed conflict.

[The Bill was not introduced, Ed.]

(HC Deb 7 January 2008 Vol 470 c1WS)

17/12 (See also 17/6]
Israel

An FCO Minister was asked by the FAC if he would confirm that it was the Government's position that Israel's policy towards the Palestinian population as a whole in Gaza of interrupting energy supplies, and blockading food supplies, medical supplies and other essentials of life was contrary to international law. He said:

I certainly will, in the sense that we have made repeatedly clear our extreme concern about the humanitarian situation. The Foreign Secretary has been in frequent touch with his Israeli counterparts about that. We are willing to be a very generous supporter to Gaza and are very clear that what concerns us, above all, is the current failure by Israel to allow movement and access, and the squeezing of energy and other vital supplies that are needed for Gaza. Of course, that is as well as our objections to the continued construction of settlements and the barrier in the West Bank. Let me also say, for the record, that we are obviously equally concerned about Hamas-sponsored rocket attacks against Israeli civilians. But yes, we think that the actions by Israel are deeply damaging and that they indeed contravene its obligations. [Q.106]

Given his answer, the Minister was asked whether he could tell the Committee in which court he considered the issue could be made the subject of legal proceedings. He said:

Our position is clear. We have, on a number of issues, declared Israeli action to be excessive, disproportionate and against international law. We have chosen not to take the next step of saying which court and under which terms, and we have no intention of sponsoring any effort to take Israel to any international court. We do not think that that would be the way forward, and we are extremely nervous about the political symbolism of such an act. We do not think that pursuing that kind of strategy would contribute to the necessary building of trust and peace-building steps between the two sides. [Q.107]

He went on:

First, one would have to decide which court and on which grounds. As far as I know, neither Israel nor Hamas is a signatory to the International Criminal Court, and I am not sure that the actions would even fall within the ICC's jurisdiction. Even if you could find a court that had jurisdiction, the issue really is that this is a problem that begs a political solution. We would press for success with the Annapolis process, backed by the Quartet, which put out a good statement when it met here in London last Friday expressing concern on exactly those points. An effective political process with a strong political will behind it strikes us as the best way forward. [Q.108]

(Foreign Affairs Committee Report, Human Rights Report 2007, HC533 (2008))

17/13

The Government were asked what action they and the quartet would take to prevent the closing down of the electricity plant in Gaza; what was their assessment of the humanitarian consequences of the absence of electricity there; and whether, following 72 deaths of patients unable to leave Gaza for medical treatment elsewhere, they would secure exit permits for all urgent cases. An FCO Minister wrote:

The Government continue to believe that Israeli security and Palestinian suffering and hardship need to be addressed together, and they can be addressed only through mutual recognition, which will be vital to long-term stability in the area.

As the Foreign Secretary and Secretary of State for International Development said on 21 January: "The recent escalation of violence between Gazans and Israelis is extremely grave. ... The rising number of rocket and sniper attacks from Gaza into Israel is unacceptable, as is the number of Palestinian civilian casualties. We do not support Israel's decision to close all crossings into Gaza, preventing the delivery of vital humanitarian supplies as well as fuel to the Gaza power station. Reports that electricity has been cut due to fuel shortage are particularly alarming and require urgent attention. Continued fuel shortages will have immediate humanitarian consequences, including on the supply of clean water". On 17 December 2007, the quartet called for the "continued provision of essential services, including fuel and power supplies".

Israel allowed limited fuel and humanitarian supplies to resume on 22 January. Some Palestinians have also been allowed to leave for medical treatment. We continue to call on Israel to fulfil its obligations to provide essential services, including medical treatment.

(HL Deb 28 January 2008 Vol 698 cWA83)

17/14
The International Development Secretary said:

… we unreservedly condemn the rocket attacks that continue to affect Sderot and the Negev in the southern part of Israel, but we are equally clear that we do not support the decision taken by the Israeli Government to close the crossings, restricting the flow of humanitarian supplies such as the ones the hon. Gentleman describes. It is also the long-standing position of the British Government that any response by Israel should be in accordance with international law, including the fourth Geneva Convention. We also, of course, deplore civilian casualties on both sides of the conflict.

The Minister was asked whether, given the British Government had consistently said that Israel's actions and response to violence from Hamas and others must comply with international law and meet United Nations humanitarian standards, the British Government had assessed whether the Israeli Government's recent actions meet those standards.

The Minister said:

There are appropriate bodies to adjudicate on international law. I assure the hon. Gentleman that in conversations with Defence Minister Barak of the Government of Israel we made it clear that we are keen to see Israel adhere to international law, whether in relation to the barrier or settlements or in terms of its response more generally. The issue is the subject of continuing discussion between the British Government and the Government of Israel.

(HC Deb 12 March 2008 Vol 473 cs267–268)

17/15
An FCO Minister said:

The Government consider Israeli settlement-building anywhere in the occupied Palestinian territories to be illegal under international law. That includes settlements in both East Jerusalem and the west bank. The road map makes it clear that Israel should freeze all settlement activity, including the natural growth of existing settlements, and dismantle all outposts erected since March 2001. That view has been expressed many times … We must make the position very clear.

I turn to the arguments that we have heard this morning, which I totally under-stand, about Israel having to defend itself against the horror of suicide bomb-ings. There is no way of rationalising that: it is the most foolish thing that any defender of the Palestinian cause can do …

Yes, Israel must defend itself, and if it wants to build a barrier, let it build a barrier, but it must be along the route of the 1967 ceasefire line. It must not arbitrarily incorporate tracts of Palestinian land. It might be that when the final negotiations are conducted, there will be land for peace trading. That was the fundamental theme of discussions, and there is no reason why it should not happen. Perhaps there will be agreement with the representatives of the Palestinian people along the lines of, "That can stay there, but we'll need a little bit of this." Similar arguments con-tinue on many borders across the world … Those arguments can continue; the issue is finding a way to avoid violence.

(HC Deb 25 March 2008 Vol 472 c270WH)

17/16

In his observations on a petition about the security barrier constructed by Israel, the Foreign Secretary wrote:

The Government are concerned at the impact the barrier has on the lives of Palestinians, and deplore the destruction of Palestinian homes and the confisca-tion of Palestinian land associated with its construction. We are concerned about the effects the building of the barrier has on the Palestinian community of Jayyous and their access to agricultural land and water. The Foreign Affairs Committee had a briefing on Jayyous during their trip to Israel and the Occupied Palestinian Territories from 28–30 March 2007. The EU has raised this issue with the Israeli Government. Our Embassy in Tel Aviv and Consulate-General in Jerusalem continue to monitor the situation in the West Bank and raise our concerns when appropriate.

The Government continue to make clear that Israel should halt the construction of the barrier on Palestinian land. This practice is contrary to international law and threatens the viability of an agreed two-state solution. The Israeli Government should not create facts on the ground, which might prejudice final status nego-tiations. We fully recognise Israel's right to self-defence and agree that a barrier is a reasonable way to achieve this. However, we call for the barrier to be built either on or behind the Green Line. The route, which the Israeli Cabinet approved on 20 February 2005, takes in a number of Israeli settlements, illegal under interna-tional law. It also contributes to the fragmentation of the West Bank, which in turn undermines prospects for a negotiated two-state solution.

(HC Deb 25 March 2008 Vol 474 c3)

17/17

The Foreign Secretary was asked what international status the Government ascribed to the Gaza Strip. An FCO Minister wrote:

The Government continue to regard the Gaza Strip as occupied Palestinian territory.

(HC Deb 7 May 2008 Vol 475 c933W)

17/18

The Government were asked what discussions they had had with the Government of Israel and the International Court of Justice about the status of Gaza. An FCO Minister wrote:

The Foreign Secretary has had many discussions with the Israeli Government regarding the status of Gaza. [He] discusses Gaza frequently with Israeli Foreign Minister Livni. At the Ad Hoc Liaison Committee meeting in London on 2 May, the humanitarian crisis in Gaza was discussed by members of the delegation. We have not spoken to the International Court of Justice recently regarding the status of Gaza. We unequivocally condemn the rocket and sniper attacks on Israel from Gaza. But any response by Israel should be in accordance with international law, including the Fourth Geneva Convention. We deplore civilian casualties on both sides. All parties must abide by their commitments under international law.

(HL Deb 12 May 2008 Vol 701 cWA111)

17/19

During a debate, a Minister said:

I would like to take this opportunity to set out the Government's legal view on the barrier; to say something about its impact on Palestinians; and to set out what the Government are doing to influence the Israeli Government's actions in relation to the barrier.

The Government agrees with the conclusion of the International Court of Justice that building a barrier along the current route is unlawful. Building the barrier on occupied land is contrary to international law. The Government therefore supported the United Nations General Assembly resolution that acknowledged the ICJ's advisory opinion on the legal consequences of the construction of the barrier in occupied Palestinian territory. While we recognise fully Israel's right to self-defence and agree that, if it decides that it wants to build a barrier it should be able to do that, we call for the barrier to be built either on or behind the green line. I take this opportunity to reiterate that call, which I have made many times in this place and in other places.

The Government are seriously concerned about the impact of the barrier on the lives of Palestinians, and deplore the destruction of Palestinian homes and the confiscation of Palestinian land associated with its construction. We are concerned about the effects of building the barrier on the Palestinian community and its access to agricultural land and water. ...

It is abundantly clear that the barrier has had a huge negative impact on the daily lives of many ordinary Palestinians. Nevertheless, as the right hon. Lady knows, the barrier is popular among a lot of Israelis. They have seen a huge decline in the numbers of suicide bombings and, as a consequence, a decline in the number of innocent people who have died at the hands of murderers and terrorists. That is, in a sense, the essence of the problem. The barrier is popular inside Israel and unpopular almost everywhere else.

In the continued debate, the Minister was asked:

If the wall was built on the 1967 boundary, it would have the same effect deterring terrorist attacks and would be legal.

The Minister replied:

Absolutely.

The Minister was then asked:

So to use that argument to justify it is to justify the breach of international law.

The Minister replied:

No. I do not know if the right hon. Lady heard me. I said precisely that the Government believe that that wall should not incorporate Palestinian land and should be on the 1967 line or behind it. I reiterate that point for her. Nevertheless, I stick to my argument, which is that, in the meantime, since parts of the wall or barrier have been built, that mentality has grown up inside Israel and is a new factor that we must take into consideration. I am not trying to justify the stealing of any land as a consequence of the wall's construction.

As the right hon. Lady knows, there are major impediments to access and movement on the west bank—she mentioned some of those difficulties—and Palestinians' ability to move on the west bank has deteriorated significantly in recent years. Checkpoints, curfews, road blocks and the permit system have all contributed to that. The permit system has resulted in delays for some of our consulate staff in Jerusalem—I experienced that when I was there—as well as for people going to and from work daily. The permit and checkpoint restrictions have isolated west bank residents from east Jerusalem, which is an important consideration.

The Government continue to make it clear to Israel that it should halt the construction of the barrier on Palestinian land. When explaining that to the Israeli Government, we have made it clear that they should not create facts on the ground— that is what they are—which will prejudice future final-status negotiations. The route that the Israeli Cabinet approved on 20 February 2005 takes in a number of Israeli settlements, which are illegal under international law. This morning, I asked Foreign Office officials how much land has been encompassed, and was told that it was 10 per cent of the Palestinian territory. That is a huge amount of land.

The barrier also contributes to the fragmentation of the west bank. I have a map which shows the mess. I am not sure whether it looks like a Swiss cheese, which is how President Bush described it, but one can see why the right hon. Lady made the point about cantonisation or bantustans. It has always disappointed me to hear all sorts of excuses when I have spoken to Israeli Ministers, about how someone from Bethlehem, for example, can get to Ramallah, which is not far away. The whole area is tiny, but the journey involves going the best part of the way to Jericho, and back up the road to Ramallah. They have sometimes said that they will build tunnels, but that is not good enough and does not address the aspirations of Palestinians who live in the area, and it means the cantonisation of the sovereign state that we want to be created.

The route does nothing to enhance the move towards the creation of a two-state solution, and we will continue to raise that—we do so regularly—with the Israeli Government. In our discussions with Israel, we have focused on those parts of the barrier's route that we believe are most problematic. They include the settlement of Ariel, which cuts 20 km deep into the west bank at a point where it is only 45 km wide. At Ma'ale Adumim, the barrier threatens territorial contiguity between the northern and southern parts of the west bank. That is a very deep cut, which contains a large number of new houses, many of which are still being built.

We have also raised with the Israeli Government our concerns about Israeli policies in Jerusalem, which threaten to cut off east Jerusalem from the west bank. Those policies include the routing of the barrier on occupied territory, settlement activity both within and around east Jerusalem, and increasingly restricted access to Jerusalem for Palestinian residents. We have also worked to raise those issues through the EU.

It is vital that we take this opportunity to focus on the wider picture—this debate has an important bearing on it—and notably the opportunity that the Annapolis process has provided to move the peace process forward. Since November's Annapolis conference, for the first time in seven years, we have been able to talk about a real process—perhaps not progress, but at least a process. At the conference, we saw substantial political movement from both sides. President Abbas and Prime Minister Olmert committed themselves to fortnightly meetings, and both restated their commitment to their road map obligations, meaning improved Palestinian security and a freeze on Israeli settlements. The US undertook to monitor the process, and all parties agreed to conclude negotiations by the end of 2008.

The conference was a signal of renewed international commitment to the peace process, and was remarkable for the strong Arab attendance, showing that the Arab world is prepared to be meaningfully involved in the process. The UK is deeply committed to supporting the peace negotiations. The Foreign Secretary and the Prime Minister have been engaged in supporting the process, and both have spoken regularly to the key actors involved and have been very clear in their message. We expect all parties to fulfil their road map obligations. That means that Israel must freeze all settlement activity and that the Palestinians must work to improve their security sector. I believe that the Palestinians are trying to do that.

As my ... Friend the Prime Minister said in the House on 18 June, it is essential that Israel

> "stop the settlement programme that is causing so much distress among the Palestinians."— [*Official Report*, 18 June 2008; Vol. 477, c. 945.]

The United Kingdom has been deeply engaged in supporting the political process. On 2 May, London hosted the ad hoc liaison committee and a meeting of the Quartet. Those were the first meetings on the middle east peace process in 2008. Since then, the Foreign Secretary visited Lebanon and the occupied Palestinian territories on 8–9 June, which was his second visit this year. More recently, I met Palestinian Prime Minister, Salam Fayyad, and the Foreign Minister on 23 June on the margins of an important peace conference in Berlin on Palestinian security.

Last Monday, I met the Israeli social welfare Minister and former housing Minister under the Ariel Sharon Government, Isaac Herzog. I tried to convey to Minister Herzog the Government's great concern at news of the planned construction of yet more illegal dwellings on Palestinian occupied territory.

I want to make it clear to the right hon. Lady that we do not believe that a series of bantustans or a fragmented parody of a state will do. Palestine must come out of the process as a sovereign state in every sense with control of its external borders. If that does not happen, the conflict will continue, as the right hon. Lady said, because the aspirations that have so often been voiced will not have been met.

(HC Deb 2 July 2008 Vol. 478 c258WH-262WH)

17/20

The Government was asked if they would instruct the British Embassy in Tel Aviv not to entertain leaders of settler communities in the West Bank at public expense. In Reply, a Minister wrote:

The Government's view on settlements is clear: all settlements are illegal under international law. Reports of recent settlement expansion are at odds with Israel's roadmap commitments—which call for a freeze on all settlement construction—and threaten negotiations on a two-state solution. As I made clear in an answer to the House on 24 June, the presence of settlers at the recent party at our embassy in Tel Aviv—celebrating Her Majesty the Queen's birthday—did not send out helpful signals in our efforts to hold Israel to its roadmap commitments on settlements.

(HC Deb 7 July 2008 Vol 478 c1338W)

17/21

A Minister wrote:

The 15 November 2005 Agreement on Movement and Access (AMA) does not specify levels of supplies to Gaza. The UK continues to call on both parties to implement the AMA and has repeatedly raised its concerns about the continued restrictions on access to Gaza with the Israeli Government, in public and in private. Most recently, we and other EU member states expressed concerns about access restrictions faced by the UN in providing assistance to Palestinian refugees in a letter from the European Union presidency and the European Commission to the Israeli authorities on 27 June. More tangibly, the UK will also support a UN access team to help get humanitarian supplies and personnel through crossings and checkpoints.

Moves towards a ceasefire in Gaza are very welcome. The ceasefire is an important first step to improve the daily lives of ordinary people on both sides. We hope that the militant groups will fulfill their commitment to cease attacks on Israel, and that Israel will ease restrictions on Gaza in line with its own commitments, ensuring that humanitarian aid and supplies can get through. We need to build on the opportunity that the ceasefire represents by working towards the reopening of the crossings between Israel and Gaza, under the control of the Palestinian Authority.

(HL Deb 22 July 2008 Vol 703 cWA270)

17/22

The Government were asked what was their response to a recent report by the United Nations Office for the Co-ordination of Humanitarian Affairs which claimed that Israel had put in place an additional 41 checkpoints and other physical limitations on the movement of Palestinians in the West Bank since September 2007. An FCO Minister wrote:

Movement and access restrictions have a significant impact on the daily life of ordinary Palestinians. While we understand Israel's security concerns, more should be done to ease movement and access restrictions to stimulate economic activity and improve daily life. We welcomed Israeli Defence Minister Barak's announcement in March to remove 50 obstacles. However, of these only five were assessed as "significant" obstacles by the UN. The Office for the Co-ordination of Humanitarian Affairs (OCHA) reports in its latest humanitarian monitor that, as of the end of June, the number of physical obstacles and checkpoints was 602.

We have repeatedly raised our concerns about the continued access restrictions with the Israeli Government in public and in private. We continue to call for the full implementation of the 2005 agreement on movement and access.

(HL Deb 29 September 2008 Vol 703 cWA370)

17/23

The Government were asked whether they regarded the blockade in Gaza as a collective punishment of Gazans; whether they viewed it as disproportionate; and whether they regarded it as a violation of international law. In reply, a Minister wrote:

We have serious concerns about the Israeli restrictions on Gaza and the impact they have on the lives of Gazans. Although there is no permanent physical Israeli presence in Gaza, given the significant control that Israel has over Gaza's borders, airspace and territorial waters, Israel retains obligations under the Fourth Geneva Convention as an occupying power. The Fourth Geneva Convention is clear that an occupying power must co-operate in allowing the passage and distribution of relief consignments. The restrictions currently imposed on the passage of relief supplies are, as we see it, a disproportionate response to the security threat.

The extent of Israeli restrictions, and the threat to Israel from militants in Gaza, varies constantly. Rather than focus on whether the restrictions at any given time amount to collective punishment, we have consistently pressed the Israeli Government to comply with their obligations under international law and allow passage of relief supplies. This was the message my right honourable friend the Foreign Secretary delivered in his meetings with Israeli leaders during his recent visit to the region.

(HC Deb 26 November 2008 Vol 705 cWA320)

17/24
Cluster munitions

The FCO wrote to the FAC:

In my letter of 28 May I undertook to write further after the Dublin Diplomatic Conference on cluster munitions ...

As the Prime Minister announced on 28 May, and Lord Malloch-Brown confirmed in the House of Lords on 3 June (*Hansard* Columns 78–80), the

United Kingdom has withdrawn from service all its cluster munitions. This includes the M85 sub-munition.

The conference ended on 30 May with the adoption of the text of a new Convention on Cluster Munitions, a copy of which I enclose, and which is available on the conference website: <www.clustermunitionsdublin.ie/pdf/ENGLISHfinaltext. pdf>. Under the new Convention the M85 sub-munition is prohibited.

(Foreign Affairs Committee Report, Human Rights Report 2007, HC533 (2008))

17/25

An FCO Minister was asked by the FAC what was the Government's position on cluster bombs—did it wish to see a complete ban on their production, stockpiling and use. The Minister said:

There are two negotiating tracks. The first is a more conventional track, which involves a wide range of Government parties. The second involves the hawks, who are pressing for a treaty—known as the Oslo process—that is as broad as possible, as soon as possible. We are part of that process. It began last year and it is hoped that a draft treaty will be ready for countries to ratify before the year is out. We are one meeting away from the completion of that process and there are some outstanding issues. One is the definition of what range of cluster munitions should be banned. At the moment we are holding to line that it is not the category of weapons per se that needs to be banned, but those weapons that cause unacceptable harm to civilians because of two particular features. Those features are first, the lack of a self-destruct mechanism and secondly, an aiming system that essentially means that they are fired blind, without those who fire them being able to see the target—something that is another cause of indiscriminate civilian casualties.

Why are we taking a narrower definition than just the whole category? There are a number of reasons. First, there are still cluster munitions in the British arsenal. They have not been used recently by the British in either Iraq or Afghanistan, due to the nature of the conflict in those two theatres. In asymmetrical warfare, where those attacking are in the midst of civilian populations and are not themselves employing heavy armament, cluster munitions are inappropriate weapons, as they are essentially supposed to be used against people in tanks and other armaments of that kind.

We were reluctant to give up the ability to use any such weapons in case we found ourselves again in a war against people using vehicles such as tanks and other equipment against us. Secondly, we were also extremely worried by the interoperability issue, and we would not want to rule out the use of weapons that other NATO members were using—I am told that that poses real military difficulties for us. Thirdly, there are issues about responsibility for dealing with the aftermath of the use of these weapons. Those are not consistent with how it was dealt with in the landmines treaty, and it opens up issues and exposes countries to unreasonable claims. These are all negotiating issues that we hope can be resolved in the final meeting of the Oslo process. Countries such as Norway, which does not have such weapons, understand our issues and, in the desire to get a universal treaty that we can all sign, will come sufficiently far towards us so that we can have a meeting of minds and get a treaty. [Q.53]

17/26
The Minister was asked about the cluster munitions system called CRV-7, which was helicopter launched and possessed by the British forces but it did not self-neutralize or self-destruct. The Minister said:

Of the two issues that I raised earlier, one was the self-destruct mechanism, which ... the CRV-7 does not have. The second was the issue of line of fire, so that someone can see who they are targeting. It is when neither of those conditions are in place that we believe the weapons count as so-called "dumb" cluster munitions. We feel that because this example does not have that second feature, it can be used responsibly. It is used as nine shells in a weapon that has more rounds in it and is fired ... from a helicopter. There is a debate about whether it is properly called a cluster munition or a sub-munition ... we are looking at the issue because we would not want this treaty to fail on a point such as that. At the moment, it is in the Army's armoury, so to speak. It is not being used currently, but at the moment it has a retirement date of 2020. [Q.54]

The Minister said further:

These CRV-7s apparently have a less than 2% failure rate, which means that only a very small proportion of them would be lying on a battlefield unexploded. The M85s that were used in southern Lebanon had something like a 25 or 30% failure rate and were used in crowded civilian areas. The battle context was different and the failure rate very high.

In the House of Lords, I used the term "unacceptable casualties", which falls into the same category as "responsible". That term was derived by the Oslo process because ultimately all weapons are dangerous; you never want to use them and there are nearly always tragic, collateral casualties among innocent civilians. It is always a matter of balancing what weapon you think it is reasonable to use and what weapon is likely to minimise, although unfortunately never eliminate, civilian casualties. [Q.55]

The Minister was asked about "interoperability", especially with the US. He said:

If you got to the point of having a reasonable treaty ready for global ratification that took a balanced view on some of these issues and was not just a complete blanket ban with a very broad definition of what counted as a cluster munition, to the point that the US and others felt that their ability to wage conventional warfare against a conventional opponent would [not] be compromised, our profound hope is that we could carry the US and others with us. [Q.57]

(Foreign Affairs Committee Report, Human Rights Report 2007, HC533 (2008))

17/27
In its reply to the FAC Report on the Annual Human Rights Report 2007, the Government said:

16. On 28 May, the Prime Minister announced the Government's support for a ban on cluster munitions, including UK cluster munitions currently in service. This confirmed the Government's commitment to address the humanitarian concerns

that cluster munitions raise, and helped to ensure the successful conclusion of the Oslo Process in Dublin earlier this year. The Government is delighted at the outcome of the Dublin Diplomatic conference and proud of the role the United Kingdom played in bringing about the new Convention on cluster munitions that was adopted by over 100 countries in Dublin on 30 May 2008. The Government believes the new Convention is strong and will help to make the world a safer place. The Government plans to sign the Convention when it opens for signature on 3 December in Oslo, and we are studying the text to establish what legislation is needed before we can proceed with ratification.

17. The Prime Minister wants to see the widest possible adherence to the norms of the Convention. The Government is leading by example by taking significant steps towards implementing its norms prior to ratification. The armed forces have withdrawn from service their remaining cluster munitions, the M85 and CRV-7 Multi Purpose Sub Munition, and have started the disposal process.

18. As the Prime Minister said to the house on 4 June it is the Government's ambition to have a global treaty on cluster munitions. With this aim in mind, the Government will work with our international partners to promote the widest possible support for the future convention. Universalisation is a long-term aim. The major users and producers, including the United States, have shown no interest in joining the Convention in the near future, but they are actively engaged in the ongoing process within the Certain Conventional Weapons Convention. Our immediate effort with these countries is therefore focused on securing a credible Protocol on cluster munitions within the Certain Conventional Weapons Convention that will deliver a strong humanitarian result. The Government welcomes the announcement in July of changes to United States' policy on cluster munitions as a positive step towards this shared goal.

19. It is the Government's view that Article 21 of the new Convention ensures that the UK will be able to fully participate in Chapter VII, NATO, EU and other coalition operations with partners not party to the Convention. The Government is pleased that participants in the Oslo Process recognised the necessity of such a provision and the Government believes that the article contains sufficient safeguards to ensure that states parties will abide by the Convention's spirit and norms.

(Foreign Affairs Committee Session 2007–08 Annual Report on Human Rights 2007, Response of the Secretary of State for Foreign and Commonwealth Affairs Cm 7463)

17/28

The Defence Secretary was asked by the Quadripartite Committee:

At the end of the war in the Lebanon in 2006 there was a 72-hour window between the passing of the United Nations Security Council resolution for a ceasefire and that ceasefire coming into effect. In that period the Israelis dropped a larger number of cluster munitions in that 72-hour period than has ever been recorded. You will also be well aware that that has resulted in a significant number of subsequent civilian deaths and maimings. The Committee … in its previous report very much welcomed the Government's decision to phase out dumb cluster munitions, but those of us who have been … to the Southern Lebanon—and have talked to the UN mine clearance personnel trying to remove these cluster munitions, have been very struck by the fact that not only do dumb cluster munitions have a significant failure rate (in other words do not detonate on impact) but we were surprised to discover that so-called smart cluster munitions also have a significant failure rate of up to approximately 10%. Given the fact that it is the Government's stated policy to stop the use of cluster munitions which in the Government's words "cause unacceptable harm to civilians", do you not agree that the Government should be seeking to phase out as soon as possible the use of smart cluster munitions as well?

He said:

I made the decision in March of last year to phase out two of the four cluster munitions that we had, to discontinue their use and to destroy them; they are now destroyed. We have taken the lead internationally in the context both of the CCW and the Oslo negotiations. In the process of delivering that commitment we have destroyed those two munitions. We still have two other munitions that are a cause of discussion. This whole process is bedevilled of course by a lack of clarity as to what is a cluster munition. There is no agreement internationally as to the definition of a cluster munition, never mind one that does unacceptable harm and parties are left to make their own view about that. In the absence of an international agreement on this which we strive for because we would like to see all cluster munitions phased out across the world, but I have responsibilities to balance military effectiveness and capability—including the very important imperative that I have to protect those forces whom I deploy into very difficult environments—with the humanitarian issues and concerns and I think it is important that people understand that I was able to make the decision that I made because the military advice, which I accepted, was that the purpose for which we had those munitions was able to be met in terms of military effectiveness and military protection—including force protection—by developments in other munitions. We strive to develop munitions which can replace those munitions that we have that some others define as dumb or smart cluster munitions; we make that differential ourselves because that has become a term of discussion. I think what I am saying is that I agree with you that we should have that ambition and I do have that ambition and our government does have that ambition, but subject to that very difficult balance between the military capability which we need for effectiveness, particularly for the protection of our forces, and these very obvious humanitarian considerations, some of which manifested themselves in Southern Lebanon in that 72-hour period. Can I also say that I am well aware of the work that the Norwegians did in that area and the conclusions they came to about the remnants of those weapons being used. We have ourselves ... done some other work and the advice that I received from that work is that the weapon that we hold has a failure rate of 1%. I know there is some dispute but that is part of the problem and that is part of why these processes—the CCW process and the Oslo process—are so important because I think we have to deal with these issues about definitions, about the evidential phase, about decisions that need to be made. The short answer to your question is yes because I think you asked me if I share that ambition and I do share that ambition. [Q.8]

The Minister was then asked:

Do you agree that using cluster bombs which have a significant failure rate is the equivalent of sowing anti-personnel landmines which the Government has, by treaty, now said that it would not use and, further, what were the technological prospects of achieving 100% detonation rates for cluster munitions?

The Minister said:

I share that ambition. Personally—although I believe I speak for the Government on this—I share the broader ambition of being able to do with anything that could be classed as a cluster munition what we were able to do with the two munitions that we have removed from our armoury and destroyed, and that is replace them with weaponry which provides the capability that cluster munitions presently do but without them being of that design. [Q.9]

The Minister was asked what he meant by using cluster munitions for force protection. He said:

Can I just say first of all that we do not deploy these munitions into any theatre of operations that we are presently engaged in. We neither deploy them in Iraq nor Afghanistan. They are not, in our view, appropriate or necessary for either of those two operational environments. However, they are appropriate in certain circumstances when you seek to take out either a number of armoured vehicles or alternatively a dispersed force in a particular area. So they are an area weapon and presently they are part of our capability should we be faced with that sort of challenge either to win the battle—which is what we would seek to do in war—or alternatively to protect our forces from that threat. The alternative, if we took them out, would be that we would have to bomb quite extensively the area and that risks a significant degree of collateral or civilian damage if we were to deploy a large amount of force over a large area in order to achieve the same objective. The bottom line is that I take very seriously—as do the military in the United Kingdom—and all previous governments have our obligation only to have and use weapons that conform with international humanitarian law. Weapons require not to be indiscriminate, careless or negligent; to the extent that they are then we have to be able to make the balance and all of this is a balance. I have tried to articulate that balance and by our actions and decisions shown how we can affect it. [Q.10]

It was put to the Minister that the Military authorities ought to be seeking alternatives to cluster weapons, rather than preserving the option to use them in some circumstances.

The Minister continued:

This Committee's evidence should not be left with the impression that the military are not seeking alternatives to these weapons. That is the state of mind of our military and that is the state of mind of our ministers. We are seeking alternatives to those weapons. There is an unhelpful vocabulary in relation to these weapons in terms of definition, in terms of phraseology, which is difficult to define unless you define it by reference—as I do—to international humanitarian law. I am very conscious of my responsibility in this regard. I can only reiterate that I have in government taken certain steps; I have an ambition to be able to take other steps. There will of course continue to be a debate in the military and this is a very healthy position; the use of vehicles, the use of all sorts of weaponry, about tactics, about concepts. The debate goes on. There is a settled view in the military in relation to the need for this capability presently. My view is that

I need to keep it in our armoury presently for the eventuality that I may have to deploy forces into certain circumstances; presently we are not doing that [Q.11].

(Quadripartite Committee Report, Scrutiny of Arms Export Control, HC 254 (2008))

17/29
The Quadripartite Committee requested a memorandum from the MOD prior to the evidence session with the Defence Secretary. The MOD wrote:

CLUSTER MUNITIONS

Cluster munitions deliver suppression and destruction capabilities against dispersed and mobile armoured targets, other combat forces and military facilities in a defined footprint of terrain. There may be situations where using a larger number of unitary munitions causes more collateral damage than would be the case with cluster munitions. The UK Armed Forces only use cluster munitions in strict accordance with International Humanitarian Law. Having carefully considered the military and humanitarian factors regarding cluster munitions, the Government took steps domestically to address them on 20 March 2007 when the Defence Secretary announced the immediate withdrawal from service of two of the UK's cluster weapon systems: the air-launched BL-755 and the ground-launched MLRS M26. These two "dumb" systems had neither target discrimination nor fail-safe capabilities. The UK continues to urge other countries to take similar action.

The Government is retaining certain types of cluster munitions that have a valid role in modern warfare. A ban on the use of all types of sub-munitions would adversely impact on the UK's operational effectiveness, impose serious capability gaps on our Armed Forces and take away one element of force protection.

UK policy addresses humanitarian concerns while at the same time retaining the capabilities essential for operational effectiveness. The UK shares the humanitarian concern about certain basic types of cluster munitions, which the Government also believes should be subject to a defined prohibition. The UK is engaged in the Conference on Certain Conventional Weapons (CCW). The UK supports the UN Secretary General's call to address cluster munitions in the CCW. The UK has also declared its support for the "Oslo Process" which aims to prohibit the use of those cluster munitions which cause unacceptable harm to civilians. The UK view is that this does not mean a total ban but a ban on certain types, such as the so-called "dumb" cluster munitions that the Government took out of service in March of this year.

(Quadripartite Committee Report, Scrutiny of Arms Export Control, Memorandum from Ministry of Defence, HC 254 (2008))

17/30
The FCO sent the following memorandum to the Quadripartite Committee in response to questions raised by the Committee:

20. *What is the UK Government's view of the proposal that the emerging international treaty, currently being discussed within the Oslo process, should only prohibit cluster munitions that do not have self-destruct mechanisms or that do not meet a*

fixed maximum percentage of failure, such as 1 %. Does the Government support such a proposal?

The aim of the Oslo Process, as expressed in the February 2007 Oslo Declaration, is to conclude a legally binding international instrument that will prohibit cluster munitions that cause unacceptable harm to civilians. One of the key tasks at the final Oslo Process meeting in Dublin (19–30 May) will be to define what types of cluster munitions might be prohibited by the Convention. It is the harm to civilians caused by unexploded ordnance from cluster munitions that we are all seeking to address.

Extensive discussions have taken place in previous Oslo Process meetings, including on the impact and reliability of self-destruct mechanisms, but no consensus has yet been reached. The UK has tabled its own proposal for what types of cluster munition might be prohibited or excluded by the Convention. We believe that self-destruct mechanisms can minimize the post-conflict risk posed by cluster munitions to civilians. We have therefore suggested that we need to consider the elements and characteristics that should exempt a sub-munition from a prohibition within specified reliability and accuracy benchmarks, including munitions which incorporate a failsafe mechanism.

(Quadripartite Committee Report, Scrutiny of Arms Export Control, HC 254 (2008))

17/31

The FCO sent the following memorandum to the Quadripartite Committee in response to questions raised by the Committee:

The Government supports a legally binding instrument to prohibit those cluster munitions that cause unacceptable harm to civilians. How does the Government define unacceptable harm to civilians?

ANSWER

"Unacceptable harm" was a phrase conceived for the purposes of the Oslo Declaration. The key task for those engaged in the Oslo Process, and the wider international community, was to find a balanced solution whereby those cluster munitions which caused unacceptable harm were clearly defined and prohibited. The humanitarian issue to address is minimising the potential exposure of civilians to the post-conflict hazard of unexploded sub-munitions. We are delighted that the text of the Convention on cluster munitions adopted at Dublin achieves that objective. In fact it does not seek to define unacceptable harm—instead it defines and prohibits all cluster munitions. Article 2 of the Convention makes clear that other munitions which have sub-munitions, but which meet a set of cumulative criteria designed to avoid indiscriminate area effects and the risks posed by unexploded sub-munitions, are not cluster munitions.

(Quadripartite Committee Report, Scrutiny of Arms Export Control, HC 254 (2008))

17/32

The Government were asked whether they would ask the Government of the United States to remove the maximum possible amount of American cluster munitions stored in the United Kingdom during the first two years of the agreed eight-year period [the Oslo Convention]. In reply, a Minister wrote:

Bilateral discussions with the United States on the implications of the Oslo Convention on US cluster munitions stockpiled on UK territory are continuing. We expect to reach a mutually satisfactory conclusion soon.

(HL Deb 17 July 2008 Vol 703 cWA182)

17/33
The Government were asked whether they will ensure that their cluster munitions, including those equipped with improved technology, are included in the terms of the Dublin Convention. In reply, a Minister wrote:

All UK cluster-munitions, as defined by the adopted text of the Oslo convention, are subject to the terms of the convention as agreed in Dublin.

(HL Deb 18 July 2008 Vol 703 cWA194)

17/34
The Government were asked what restrictions were in place to prevent the export of cluster munitions, as defined in the Trade in Goods (Categories of Controlled Goods) Order 2008 (SI 2008/1805), prior to that Order coming into force; and whether such restrictions are sufficient to prevent the export of those munitions. An FCO Minister wrote:

Cluster munitions are currently controlled under entries ML3 and ML4 of Part I of Schedule 1 to the Export of Goods, Transfer of Technology and Provision of Technical Assistance (Control) Order 2003 ("The Military List") and therefore cannot be exported from the UK without a licence granted by the Secretary of State for Business, Enterprise and Regulatory Reform (BERR).

I would like to clarify the Government's commitments in this area: at the recent Dublin conference, the UK was one of over 100 states which agreed to adopt the text of the new Convention on Cluster Munitions. That convention has yet to be ratified, but will include a ban. Until that ban is in place, any application to export cluster munitions from the UK would be rigorously assessed against the Consolidated EU and National Arms Export Licensing Criteria, which cover, among other things, exports which would be used in the perpetration of human rights abuses or would exacerbate regional or internal conflicts in the destination country; and would be refused if any of these criteria were breached. As the noble Lord will be aware, the convention does however permit the transfer of cluster munitions between states party to the convention for the purposes of destruction, and for the development of and training in cluster munition and explosive submunition detection, clearance or destruction techniques; or the development of cluster munition counter measures. My understanding is, however, that no cluster munitions are produced in the UK, therefore it is unlikely that an application to export will arise in practice …

No cluster munitions have been exported or licensed or approved for export from the UK since 30 May 2008.

(HL Deb 29 September 2008 Vol 703 cWA391)

17/35
Convention on Certain Conventional Weapons

The Government were asked what assessment they had made of the financial and legal liabilities that would arise from ratification of Protocol V to the United Nations Convention on Certain Conventional Weapons. An FCO Minister wrote:

There is no retrospective liability. Potential future liability is unquantifiable. Discussions among the government departments involved are ongoing in order to work out arrangements for managing this potential future liability. In the mean time, we follow the principles enshrined in Protocol V.

(HL Deb 23 January 2008 Vol 698 cWA54)

17/36
Depleted uranium

The Foreign Secretary was asked how the United Kingdom had voted on the United Nations General Assembly Resolution on the effects of the use of armaments and ammunitions containing depleted uranium, A/C.1.62/L.18/REV/i, on 5 December 2007; which other states voted in the same way; and what the reasons were for the UK vote. An FCO Minister wrote:

The UK opposed the resolution on the effects of the use of armaments and ammunitions containing depleted uranium at the UN General Assembly's First Committee. Israel, US, Netherlands and the Czech Republic also voted against the resolution.

The current consensus of scientific and medical experts, including reports published by the Royal Society, is that the use of depleted uranium for military purposes has not had any significant impact on the health of veterans or civilian populations. The UK is also aware that the US National Academy of Sciences is currently carrying out an independent review of the type mentioned in the resolution.

(HC Deb 15 January 2008 Vol 470 c1143W)

17/37
Landmines

The Government was asked what the position was on the removal of unexploded landmines and other ordnance still lying in the Falkland Islands following the 1982 conflict. An FCO Minister wrote:

A joint UK-Argentina feasibility study into de-mining in the Falkland Islands was completed in October 2007. It concluded that clearance will be challenging but technically possible.

The Government are now considering the options for clearance before deciding on next steps. Any clearance operation would remove all unexploded ordnance contained in mined areas.

The Minister was asked about international obligations bearing on the mine clearance. She said:

The UK is a state party to the Ottawa convention and its obligations, and we are very well aware of them. A feasibility study was concluded in October. The UK is now considering options before deciding on next steps. Since the end of hostilities in 1982, the landmines have been clearly marked, fenced off and monitored, and there have been no civilian casualties ...

It has taken time to get to this stage—a feasibility study that is now being looked at extremely seriously and will be put in front of Ministers very shortly—because we have been working alongside the Argentinean people on this ... that that has meant that negotiations on de-mining the Falklands have been detailed, complex and extensive. However, we now hope to be looking seriously at the next steps.

(HL Deb 29 January 2008 Vol 698 c544)

Part Seventeen: II. *The Law of Armed Conflict and International Humanitarian Law—Non-international armed conflict*

17/38
The Foreign Secretary was asked what steps the Government were taking to encourage the Colombian Government to investigate alleged murders of civilians by the Colombian army. An FCO Minister wrote:

Whilst the majority of murders in Colombia are committed by illegal armed groups, we regularly call on the Colombian Government, privately and in public, to ensure procedures are in place to fully investigate alleged abuses against civilians by the Colombian army. [An FCO Minister] did so with the Colombian Defence Minister and Vice President during their visits to the UK last year, and he repeated these concerns when visiting Colombia in November 2007. We have been impressed at the Colombian government's commitment to tackling this problem, but we recognise that more needs to be done. This is why the UK continues to provide the Colombian armed forces with human rights training and practical advice on military justice reform—which includes forging a closer working relationship between the Colombian Attorney General's Office and the Colombian armed forces—so to promote their adherence to international humanitarian law.

(HC Deb 10 January 2008 Vol 470 c790W)

Part Eighteen: Neutrality and Non-Belligerency

Part Nineteen: Legal Aspects of International Relations and Co-operation in Particular Matters

Part Nineteen: I.A. *Legal Aspects of International Relations and Co-operation in Particular Matters—General economic and financial matters—Trade*

19/1
Conventional arms

A Minister wrote:

The Government are strongly in favour of establishing common international standards for the export, import and transfer of conventional arms. That is why the UK has taken an international lead in establishing an Arms Trade treaty (ATT). Together with six other countries, we have been pressing for such a treaty to be agreed at the UN. At this year's First Committee of the UN General Assembly, the UK has co-authored a resolution proposing further work at the UN in 2009 aimed at establishing an ATT. Achieving an ATT is a complex process, which will take time, but we have made good progress, and we will continue to work actively towards achieving our goal.

... [T]he Foreign Secretary launched a new phase of the UK's campaign towards an ATT by hosting a meeting of key stakeholders from industry, civil society, academia and the media in London on 9 September. In addition, I hosted a briefing on 9 October for the London-based Diplomatic Corps setting out the Government's support for an ATT and encouraging active international engagement in the UN process.

(HC Deb 30 October 2008 Vol 481 c1227W)

19/2
Discriminatory legislation

The Business Secretary was asked what representations he had made to the United States administration on the enforcement of legal restrictions on the operation of UK businesses in the US. A Minister wrote:

We intervene with the US authorities where and when appropriate, when we consider the commercial interests of UK business to be adversely affected by discriminatory US legislation. Most recently we intervened with the Office of the US Trade Representative in relation to the withdrawal of commitments relating to gambling under GATS Article XXI.

(HC Deb 22 May 2008 Vol 476 c432W)

19/3
Economic Partnership Agreement

The Business Secretary was asked when he expected transitional agreements to be available to countries not ready to sign up for an economic partnership agreement by 1 January 2008. A Minister wrote:

35 countries from the African, Caribbean and Pacific (ACP) Group signed up to an Economic Partnership Agreement (EPA) before the end of 2007. These countries now receive duty free quota free access for their products into the EU. Of the countries which did not agree an EPA, 32 are classified as Least Developed Countries (LDCs) which makes them eligible for the Everything But Arms scheme (EBA) which provides for duty free access into the EU on all products

except for arms. 10 other countries can utilise the Generalised System of Preferences scheme (GSP) which is available to all developing countries and provides for a reduction in the standard rate of duty for products entering the EU. These schemes were already in existence and so these countries have been able to utilise them since the beginning of this year.

The UK continues to work with the European Commission and ACP Governments to ensure that these agreements benefit regional integration and deliver for development.

(HC Deb 4 February 2008 Vol 471 c895W)

19/4
Export Credit Agency

The Government were asked what standards were used to identify nations that qualify as poor countries under the expanded guidelines of the Export Credit Agency. In reply, a Minister wrote:

In January 2008, the Export Credit Group of the Organisation for Economic Cooperation and Development (OECD) adopted a set of "Principles and Guidelines to promote Sustainable Lending Practices in the Provision of Official Export Credits to Low Income Countries"—see:

<http://www.oecd.org>

Alongside all other OECD member Export Credit Agencies (ECAs), the Export Credits Guarantee Department (ECGD) is implementing these principles and guidelines (taking into account its own existing 'Productive Expenditure' guidelines), which seek to ensure that ECAs support export credits responsibly to those poor countries that are especially vulnerable to debt servicing problems.

The relevant countries are defined and listed in the OECD Principles and Guidelines. They are mainly those that have access to assistance from the International Development Association (IDA), part of the World Bank, and include most of the heavily indebted poor countries (HIPCs) as classified by the International Monetary Fund and World Bank.

(HC Deb 8 July 2008 Vol 478 c1566W-1567W)

19/5
Israel

The Chancellor of the Exchequer was asked on how many occasions since January 2007 HM Revenue and Customs had intercepted goods produced in Israeli settlements in the West Bank being imported to the UK claiming the preferences of the EU-Israeli Association Agreement; and what steps had been taken in consequence. A Treasury Minister wrote:

Since January 2007, there have been 202 occasions where claims to preference for goods produced in Israeli settlements in the West Bank and imported into the United Kingdom have been rejected. These goods were confirmed as incorrectly claiming a preferential rate of duty under the EU/Israel Association Agreement. A demand for the full rate of import duty was sent to every importer concerned.

(HC Deb 22 January 2008 Vol 470 c1958W)

19/6 (See also **6/79**)

The Foreign Secretary was asked what criteria were used in determining whether Israel's actions are compliant with human rights provisions in EU trade agreements. An FCO Minister wrote:

There are no formal criteria used by the EU Commission. The Commission draws on its own observers on the ground, non-governmental organisations, and member states' posts to determine the compliance of Israel's actions in accordance with Article 2 and in the context of Article 76 of the EU/Israel Association Agreement.

I share, and frequently raise, many of my hon. Friend's concerns over Israeli actions. However, on balance, I support the Commission's assessment that Israel is not in breach of the terms of the agreement ... I remain strongly of the opinion that active engagement with Israel through the EU provides a valuable forum through which to continue to raise human rights concerns. In 2007 the EU-Israel human rights working group, established under the framework of the Association Agreement, provided the opportunity to discuss: inter alia minorities; respect for human rights including respect for religious freedom and belief; Israeli settlement expansion; administrative detention including individual cases; international humanitarian law; as well as questions related to the UN Human Rights Council; and thereby established a closer bilateral dialogue on these issues.

(HC Deb 18 March 2008 Vol 473 c1033W)

19/7
Most-favoured-nation clause

Speaking in the Sixth Committee of the General Assembly on the Report of the ILC [A/63/10, Ed.], the FCO Legal Adviser, said:

I turn now to the report of the Commission's working group on the topic of the most-favoured-nation clause. The United Kingdom welcomes this report and the useful historical review it provides. As the Commission notes, the ILC previously considered this topic in the 1970s, and adopted draft articles in 1978, although the General Assembly took no action in relation to them. As the report of the working group indicates, there have been some significant developments with regard to practice in this field in recent years. These developments include the creation of the World Trade Organisation, which has seen the extension of the application of Most-Favoured-Nation treatment beyond trade in goods to cover trade in services and intellectual property; the sharp rise in the negotiation and conclusion of bilateral and regional free trade agreements, which include provisions on Most-Favoured-Nation treatment; and, particularly, the development of the field of investment treaty arbitration, which sees individuals bringing claims against States under Investment Promotion and Protection Agreements, which usually contain Most-Favoured-Nation clauses, and the interpretation by arbitral tribunals of such clauses.

The United Kingdom is supportive of further work in this area. As the working group report notes, issues going to the interpretation of MFN clauses engage public international law more generally. The United Kingdom would be cautious, however, about an exercise that proceeded on the basis of a 'one-size-fits-all' appreciation to the interpretation of MFN clauses. It is clear that not all MFN Nation clauses are drafted in the same terms. In particular, the problem identified in paragraphs 23–24 of Annex B of the Commission's report concerning the *Maffezini* case is one that might simply be regarded as a question of treaty interpretation. This can be seen in the wording of the MFN clause at issue in that case; the relevant provision in the Argentina-Spain Bilateral Investment Treaty applied to 'all matters subject to this Agreement', which permitted the Tribunal to adopt an expansive view of the provision's scope of application. In contrast, in the *Salini* case, which is cited by the Commission at paragraph 25 of Annex B, the Tribunal was faced with a differently worded MFN clause, which enabled it to reach a different conclusion from the Tribunal in *Maffezini*. In this regard, the United Kingdom agrees that some guidance on the interpretation of MFN clauses would be interesting and useful, but would encourage the Commission to be flexible concerning the final form of its work.

The United Kingdom welcomes the establishment of a Study Group for the consideration of this topic. As the work of the Study Group progresses, the United Kingdom hopes that States will be provided with suitable opportunities to comment on its reports. The United Kingdom looks forward to following the Commission's work on this topic with much interest.

(Text supplied by FCO)

19/8
TRIPS

A Minister wrote:

The Department for International Development (DFID) fully supports the right of developing countries to use all the flexibilities in the Trade Related Intellectual Property Rights (TRIPS) Agreement, notably to ensure affordable access to medicines to meet public health needs. In particular the DFID aims to ensure that EU agreements with developing countries avoid, as a matter of course, imposing intellectual property obligations that eliminate these flexibilities.

Over the last five years DFID has spent over £1.6 million on enhancing developing countries' knowledge of and capability to use the TRIPS agreement, as well as their flexibilities within it. In September 2007, an additional £1.35 million was committed over three years, to assist developing countries implement intellectual property policies in ways that support sustainable development. This includes support through the International Centre for Sustainable Development and the United Nations Conference on Trade and Development (UNCTAD).

(HC Deb 7 July 2008 Vol 478 c1214W)

Part Nineteen: I.F. *Legal Aspects of International Relations and Co-operation in Particular Matters—General economic and financial matters—Development*

19/9

An International Development Minister wrote:

The UK attaches great importance to the work of the OECD Development Assistance Committee in developing best practice guidance for donors whether in the form of principles, guidelines or policy statements. Where appropriate we will continue to work with others to ensure such guidance is associated with clear commitments and targets for its implementation.

For example, the Paris principles (partner country ownership, alignment, harmonisation, managing for results and mutual accountability) provide an organising framework for the commitments set out in the Paris Declaration on Aid Effectiveness. The international community agreed 12 targets to monitor the implementation of these commitments, and most recently reviewed progress in doing so at the Third High Level Forum on Aid Effectiveness held in Accra on 2–4 September. The Accra Agenda for Action, which resulted from that meeting, represents an important further means to accelerate progress towards the Paris Declaration targets set for 2010.

UK delivery of the Paris Declaration commitments and targets now forms part of the Department for International Development's (DFID) Departmental Strategic Objectives rather than of a separate action plan. There are therefore no costs associated with fulfilling a separate plan. Our progress in meeting our Paris Declaration commitments and targets is subject to DFID's normal management and reporting mechanisms.

(HC Deb 7 October 2008 Vol 480 c583W-584W)

19/10

A Minister wrote:

At the Third High Level Forum on Aid Effectiveness, held in Accra, Ghana from 2–4 September 2008, strong UK leadership helped to secure an ambitious 'Accra Agenda for Action' which will speed up implementation of the Paris Declaration.

Donors and developing countries commitments include:

A step change in donors' use of partner government systems to deliver aid, with a new target to channel 50 per cent of government-to-government aid through country systems, thus improving alignment;

Strengthening of national, and for the first time international, mutual accountability mechanisms, allowing donors and partner countries to better hold each other accountable for meeting their commitments, with a milestone agreed for 2009;

Donors agreed to respect and support partner country-led efforts to agree a better division of labour between donors at country level—and for the first time at international level too; we agreed to start dialogue on international division of labour by June 2009. This will reduce transaction costs for partner countries and help address the issue of under-aided countries;

For the first time and beginning now, donors will provide partner governments with forward expenditure or implementation plans for the following three to five years, allowing partner countries to integrate the information in their medium-term planning and macroeconomic frameworks. This will help developing countries plan to use aid to implement their own priorities, e.g. recruiting nurses and teachers; and

Partner countries will improve their information systems, with support from donors to develop national statistical capacity. The UK announced £50 million support for a new multi-donor Statistics for Results Facility. Donors will use these systems to manage development results.

These steps will help achieve the targets set for 2010.

(HC Deb 7 October 2008 Vol 480 c585W-586W)

19/11

A Minister wrote:

The Government are working closely with our European partners to press for the restoration of democracy in Mauritania following the coup d'etat on 6 August. The Cotonou agreement covers political relations, trade and development co-operation between the EU and 78 Africa, Caribbean and Pacific (ACP) countries, and is a central focus of our current work on Mauritania. Article 96 of the agreement provides for appropriate measures when the essential and fundamental elements of the agreement (such as democracy) have been infringed. The EU wrote to the Mauritanian regime in September to initiate the process and met with Mauritanian officials on 20 October to discuss the procedures. The Mauritanians failed to provide acceptable proposals for the restoration of democracy, and were given one month to do so.

Should the Mauritanians fail to provide acceptable proposals within this timeframe, consultations will be closed and the EU will consider appropriate measures including targeted sanctions. These measures may cover any aspect of the EU-ACP relationship (including development assistance, trade, financial and economic co-operation, political dialogue, humanitarian and emergency assistance).

The UK is also working with other international partners to try to secure a return to democracy in Mauritania. NATO allies suspended military activities to be carried out with Mauritania in September, and are reviewing activities on a case by case basis.

(HC Deb 5 November 2008 Vol 705 cWA67-WA68)

19/12
Aral Sea

In answer on the condition of the Aral Sea, an FCO Minister wrote:

According to the World Bank, the next step is to improve the irrigation efficiency of the land in the Kazakh part of the Aral sea basin. Additional waterworks are also planned to restore wetlands and fishing lakes in the delta region. A World Bank project to this end began in 2007.

Details of the World Bank project can be found at:

<www.worldbank.org.kz/external/projects/main?pagePK=64283627&;piPK=7 3230&theSitePK=361869&menuPK=361901&Projectid=P046045>

The Aral sea is an international problem which will require an international solution. In its "Strategy for Central Asia", which will be adopted at the European Council on 21–22 June, the EU commits itself, inter alia, to support the implementation of the EU Water Initiative for safe water supply and integrated water resources management; promotion of transboundary river basin management and regional co-operation and support the integrated management of surface and underground transboundary water resources, including the introduction of techniques for more efficient water use particularly in irrigation.

(HC Deb 6 February 2008 Vol 471 c1160W)

19/13
Convention on the prevention of marine pollution

A Minister wrote:

The issue of ocean fertilisation has been considered under the convention on the prevention of marine pollution by dumping of wastes and other matter (London convention 1972) and its protocol, global legal instruments to which the UK is a contracting party. In 2007 the convention's scientific group released a statement of concern that

> 'knowledge about the effectiveness and potential environmental impacts of ocean fertilisation currently was insufficient to justify large-scale operations'.

This statement was endorsed at the meeting of the convention and protocol in November 2007. A legal intercessional correspondence group has been set up, coordinated by DEFRA, which is working with our international colleagues to review how the framework of the convention and its protocol would apply to fertilisation. Its findings will be considered at the next meeting of the London convention and protocol in October.

(HC Deb 14 July 2008 Vol 479 c32W)

19/14
Convention on Watercourses

The International Development Secretary was asked for what reasons the Government had not signed the UN Convention on Watercourses. An International Development Minister wrote:

The Department for International Development (DFID) has undertaken an analysis of the development benefits of UK accession to the UN Convention on the Non-Navigational Uses of International Watercourses. DFID has also discussed this with other bilateral agencies and specialist water agencies, and sought views from other Government Departments to reach a joint conclusion. On the basis of the evidence available, the development benefits identified have not been shown to be significant. After 10 years only 16 countries have ratified or acceded to the convention. With 35 countries required there is little immediate prospect of it entering into force.

DFID recognises that the existence of the convention is helpful and its principles have been applied. DFID provides support to regional water initiatives in South Asia, the Nile Basin and the Middle East and is considering support in other shared waters. In none of the cases where we provide support is accession to the convention considered necessary.

(HC Deb 17 March 2008 Vol 473 c828W)

19/15
Endangered species

The Secretary for the Environment was asked what recent steps the Government had taken to increase the protection of endangered species. A Minister wrote:

Species protection has both national and international facets to it, and recent steps to improve protection have included the following ...

On the wider international stage, at the 2007 Conference of Parties to the convention on international trade in endangered species (CITES), the UK fully supported the increased protection of a range of species affected by international trade including the slow loris, the European eel and brazilwood. During 2007–08, DEFRA provided funding of around £1 million towards the operation of CITES and other major conventions, most notably the convention on biological diversity (CBD) including targeted funding for specific projects to protect and conserve albatrosses and petrels, migratory sharks, African elephants, Indian ocean marine turtles and tigers. In addition, DEFRA provided £75,000 for the Flagship Species Fund, which included projects on endangered sea turtles, primates and conifers.

(HC Deb 7 May 2008 Vol 475 c908W)

19/16
Ivory trade

A Minister wrote:

The global ban on international commercial trade in ivory remains firmly in place. The UK fully supports this and is absolutely clear that illegal and unsustainable trade in ivory should not be permitted.

However, we draw a distinction between one-off sales of ivory which is legally held by governments, for the benefit of their wildlife conservation programmes, and a general return to commercial trading in ivory, where we are not convinced that current conditions will ensure proper protection for elephants.

(HC Deb 13 October 2008 Vol 480 c926W)

19/17
National Wildlife Crime Unit

A Minister wrote:

In the UK, the Government are working with the National Wildlife Crime Unit (NWCU), HM Revenue and Customs and the police to establish the extent of trade taking place over the internet that is illegal, and to find effective ways to tackle this. The issue is one of five priority areas for consideration by the NWCU as part of its delivery of obligations to assist the Government to apply the requirements of the Convention on International Trade in Endangered Species (CITES). Additionally, DEFRA has been working with the trade, website owners, enforcement experts and other stakeholders to establish a Code of Practice for internet providers and users.

The issue, however, transcends borders and we believe a global approach is required. The UK was instrumental in proposing that CITES convenes a special workshop to consider the issue, and provided funds for this to occur. I am pleased to report that this meeting will take place next February in Canada. The workshop will review what is known about the scale and nature of illegal internet trade in wildlife globally and then consider ways to tackle illegal activity there. In addition to providing financial support to the workshop we have also contributed evidence of our current knowledge of illegal wildlife trade over the internet.

(HC Deb 29 October 2008 Vol 481 c1185W)

19/18 (See also 11/21–11/24]

Whaling

A Minister wrote:

The Foreign and Commonwealth Office has not discussed the specific issue of an illicit trade in whale meat from Japan's scientific whaling programme with the Japanese Government but has taken note of the allegations made by Greenpeace. The Government continue to oppose all forms of whaling apart from some limited subsistence whaling when there is a substantiated need. The UK has also protested against Japan's whaling operations, which we argue are unjustified, cruel and unnecessary, at every appropriate opportunity. Most recently the UK maintained its strong anti-whaling position at the annual International Whaling Commission meeting which was held in Santiago, Chile, in June 2008.

(HC Deb 17 July 2008 Vol 479 c684W)

Part Nineteen: VII. *Legal Aspects of International Relations and Co-operation in Particular Matters—Cultural matters*

19/19
Part 6 of the Tribunals, Courts and Enforcement Act 2007, SS 134, 135, provides protection for foreign cultural objects on loan to institutions in the UK.

The Explanatory Memorandum with the Bill said:

BACKGROUND

538. Under the previous law, the United Kingdom has only given immunity to objects which are covered by the provisions of the State Immunity Act 1978. The absence of a more general immunity for works of art and other cultural objects which are lent to temporary exhibitions in this country has made museums and private owners in other countries increasingly reluctant to lend to such exhibitions without a guarantee that their art treasures will be returned. Provisions in Part 6 will enable such a guarantee to be given.

COMMENTARY ON CLAUSES: PART 6

Clause 129: Protected objects [Now S.134, Ed.]

539. Clause 129 defines the conditions that need to be met for an object to be protected from seizure and specify where and for how long the protection will be given.

540. *Subsection (2)* provides that an object will only be protected if five conditions are satisfied: the object must usually be kept outside the United Kingdom; it must not be owned by anyone resident in the United Kingdom; the import of the object must comply with the law on the import of goods; it must be brought to the United Kingdom to be displayed to the public in a temporary exhibition at a museum or gallery and the museum has complied with regulations requiring publication of information about the object. The Secretary of State is given power to make such regulations.

541. *Subsection (4)* provides for the extent of the protection. An object must only be in the United Kingdom for the permitted purposes (defined further in subsection (7)) and, with one exception, the protection will only last for twelve months. It is only intended to protect from seizure objects which are being lent for the purposes of a temporary exhibition. Objects on long term loans to museums will not be protected.

542. *Subsection (5)* provides for the single exception to this rule. Where an object has been damaged since coming to the United Kingdom, and is being repaired, conserved or restored in this country, it will continue to be protected until it has left the United Kingdom following the completion of the repair, conservation or restoration.

543. *Subsection (7)* ensures that objects will only be protected if they are on display in a temporary exhibition at museums, undergoing related repair, conservation or restoration, or travelling to or from the place where they are being displayed or repaired/restored. *Subsection (8)* defines the repairs, conservation or restoration which will be considered to be related for these purposes.

...

Clause 130: Effect of protection [Now S.135, Ed.]

546. *Clause* 130 defines the effect of the protection and sets out the limited circumstances under which it will not be given.

547. *Subsection (1)* ensures that where seizure or forfeiture of an object is required to enable the *UK* to comply with its obligations under EU or international law, the object concerned will not be protected. This could apply where,

for example, the court is asked to enforce an order for the seizure of an object made by the courts of another country to confiscate proceeds of crime.

548. *Subsection (2)* ensures that the protection given to an object loaned to an exhibition does not give any protection from prosecution to those dealing with the object, where the dealing in question constitutes an offence.

549. *Subsection (3)* clarifies the extent of the protection which will be given to objects under this Bill. It includes immunity against all forms of execution which might be made against an object protected under the Bill, any order made in civil proceedings and any measure taken in criminal proceedings (or for the purposes of a criminal investigation) which might affect the control or custody of an object. The protection given is intended to exclude any form of seizure or detention of an object lent to an exhibition in this country whether by a claimant to the object, a creditor or by law enforcement authorities.

(Tribunals, Courts and Enforcement Act 2007)

19/20

The Government were asked what assessment they had made of the cultural effects of ratification of the UNESCO Convention on the Protection of the Underwater Cultural Heritage. In reply, a Minister wrote:

The UK Government have already adopted the Annex of the Convention on the Protection of the Underwater Cultural Heritage as best practice for archaeology. Although we keep the matter under review. We do not believe that the case for ratification by the UK has been made.

(HC Deb 21 July 2008 Vol 479 c805W)

Part Nineteen: VIII. *Legal Aspects of International Relations and Co-operation in Particular Matters—Legal matters (for example judicial assistance, crime control, etc.)*

19/21
Comprehensive convention on international terrorism

The Foreign Secretary was asked what steps the Government planned to take to reach international agreement on a comprehensive convention on international terrorism. The Foreign Secretary wrote:

Negotiations on a Comprehensive Convention on International Terrorism have been taking place since 2000 with the active support and involvement of the UK. We have made the case throughout for a clear text consistent with the 13 existing sectoral counter-terrorism conventions as well as with international humanitarian law. A comprehensive convention could contribute to a more unified global response to terrorism and we will work closely with our European allies and other international partners to try to reach agreement in the next round of negotiations this autumn.

(HC Deb 30 June 2008 Vol 478 c676W)

19/22
Convention on Combating Bribery

The FCO sent the following memorandum to the Quadripartite Committee in response to questions raised by the Committee:

The Committees understand that the OECD investigation in respect of corruption is a "Phase Two" examination—a procedure that, so far, only three countries, Ireland, Luxembourg and Japan, have been subjected to. Does the Government consider that the investigation is far from routine and brings into question the UK's laws and enforcement arrangements for combating corruption?

ANSWER

The OECD recognises that our law is in accordance with the minimum requirements of the OECD Convention on Combating Bribery of Foreign Officials in International Business Transactions, and that the UK has fully or partially implemented 17 of the 20 recommendations by the OECD Working Group set out in their Phase 2 report published March 2005.

In light of concerns raised by the OECD in their Phase 1 evaluation of the UK, the Government legislated in the Anti-terrorism, Crime and Security Act 2001 amending the existing law.

Following this, the OECD Working Group on Bribery concluded that "the UK law now addresses the requirements set forth in the Convention".

However, we recognise that the existing legal framework is fragmented and in need of modernisation. We have been striving to bring forward a new bribery law for some time. This has not proved an easy task, but it is vital we get it right. We look forward to receiving the Law Commission report [The Law Commission (Law Com No 313) Reforming Bribery HC 928, Ed.] and draft Bill this autumn and our intention is to introduce a draft Bill for pre-legislative scrutiny in the fourth session, as noted in the draft Legislative Programme. This is the best and most effective means to work up proposals for a new law.

With respect to enforcement, the UK has strengthened its systems to combat foreign bribery by establishing the Overseas Anti-Corruption Unit in the City of London Police in November 2006. Working closely with the Serious Fraud Office, they have successfully increased the number of enquiries and investigations. There are now 20 foreign bribery enquiries ongoing, and 46 allegations under preliminary investigation. BERR has recently provided further resources to increase the number of officers in the unit to 12

[See *Corner House Research & Ors, R (On The Application of) v The Serious Fraud Office* [2008] UKHL 60, Ed.]

(Quadripartite Committee Report, Scrutiny of Arms Export Control, HC 254 (2008))

19/23
Convention on Mutual Assistance in Criminal Matters

A Minister wrote:

We are aware of just one joint investigation team operation having been established under the provisions of the Convention on Mutual Assistance in Criminal

Matters 2000 involving United Kingdom law enforcement. This was a joint United Kingdom and Netherlands drugs investigation which took place in 2005, to which there was a successful outcome.

All members of a joint investigation team would be subject to the laws of the country in which the team is operating. Law enforcement officials from another member state act in a support and advisory capacity and would not have police powers when the team is operating in the United Kingdom. Teams operating in the United Kingdom would be under the strict control of a United Kingdom team leader.

(HC Deb 29 September 2008 Vol 479 c2350W)

19/24
Extradition

The FAC had concluded in its Report on Global Security: Russia that:

the Government was correct to send a strong signal regarding Russia's refusal to extradite Andrey Lugovoy. We recommend that in its response to this Report, the Government detail as far as possible the considerations which led it to take the specific measures announced on 16 July 2007, and the discussions which it has had—if any—with its Russian counterpart about possible ways of working around Russia's constitutional ban on the extradition of its nationals.

We further recommend that in its response the Government update us on any practical impact that the UK and Russian measures are having on government-to-government cooperation, on progress in the UK's review of cooperation with Russia, and on its discussions with EU partners on including issues arising from the Litvinenko case in the EU-Russia dialogue. (Paragraph 124)

The Government said:

33. We welcome the Committee's support for the need to send a strong signal to Russia following its failure to extradite suspected murderer Andrey Lugovoy. The Crown Prosecution Service stated that there is a case for Mr Lugovoy to answer. A full application for extradition and significant information was sent to the Russian authorities sufficient for the purposes of extradition. We are yet to receive a satisfactory response to the extradition request. We remain open to constructive proposals from the Russian government that will see this crime, which was committed in the UK, brought to justice in a UK court. At the June EU General Affairs and External Relations Council, Ministers agreed that there should be an annex to the EU negotiating mandate for a successor to the EU-Russia Partnership and Cooperation Agreement, highlighting EU concerns about the Litvinenko case. The EU has also expressed its concerns on this issue under the terms of the existing EU-Russia Agreement. The EU Troika raised the Litvinenko case in the Justice and Home Affairs Permanent Partnership Council in November 2007.

34. We have not taken our course of action without considering all the options, including trial in Russia or in a third country. Our international obligations, including under the European Convention on Human Rights, prevent us from accepting Russia's offer to consider a prosecution in Russia. Both the UN and the EU have raised concerns about the independence of the judiciary in Russia. Trials

in a third country would fall foul of Russia's constitutional bar on extradition and on the trial of Russian citizens by Ad Hoc Tribunals.

35. Before the decision to take the measures announced on 16 July 2007 careful consideration was given to the importance of the case and the need for an appropriate response to Russia's failure to co-operate in finding a solution. Account was taken of a wide range of relevant factors, including the impact of those measures on our bilateral relations. But our priority then, as it remains now, was to ensure the integrity of our legal process in order to secure justice for Mr Litvinenko.

36. Bilateral relations in some areas remain difficult in the wake of Russia's failure to extradite Lugovoy, the measures announced by the Foreign Secretary on 16 July 2007 and Russia's retaliation. Russia's unjustified and illegal action against the British Council has further exacerbated the strain on UK-Russia relations.

37. Nevertheless, government to government co-operation in other areas has continued. Despite bilateral differences the UK's economic relations with Russia remain strong and trade is growing. In the first half of 2007 Britain was the single largest investor in Russia.

(Second Report from the Foreign Affairs Committee Session 2007–08, Global Security: Russia. Response of the Secretary of State for Foreign and Commonwealth Affairs, Cm 7305)

19/25

The FAC had said in its Report, Global Security: Russia:

We are deeply concerned about the termination of British Council English language teaching in Russia, and the difficult environment that the British Council has faced in Russia in recent years. We recommend the FCO does all it can with its Russian interlocutors to secure conclusion of a new Cultural Centres Agreement as soon as possible. (Paragraph 137)

The Government said:

42. Russia demanded on 25 October 2007 that the British Council freeze its remaining operations outside Moscow with effect from 1 January 2008. It is clear from the later statement by Foreign Minister Lavrov on 14 December that this is politically motivated and linked directly to its Litvinenko retaliation. On 14 January 2008 the Russian Deputy Foreign Minister informed the British Ambassador to Moscow that Russia would take a series of administrative measures against the British Council if it persisted in operating from premises in St Petersburg and Yekaterinburg. We deeply regret that the Russian authorities have chosen to pursue a separate bilateral disagreement in a wholly inappropriate way.

43. The Foreign Secretary made clear in his Written Ministerial Statement of 13 December [[2007] UKMIL 7/11] that the Russian Government's threatened action against the British Council is illegal. The British Council's presence in Russia is entirely consistent with international law, including the Vienna Conventions. Its presence and activities are also specifically sanctioned by a 1994

UK/Russia Agreement on Cooperation in Education, Science and Culture, signed and ratified by Russia, and which binds both the UK and Russia. The British Council is the designated agent of the British Government for the implementation of the agreement.

44. For the past nine years, the UK has been keen to conclude a Cultural Centres Agreement with Russia. Such an agreement could potentially clarify, for example, Russian acceptance of English language teaching in Russia and facilitate the establishment of a Russian Cultural Centre in the UK. Pending such an agreement being reached, the 1994 Agreement remains in force. The British Council does not need a new agreement to operate in Russia. It should be emphasised that the British Council's announcement on re-structuring in Russia in September 2007 flows from the Council's 2010 Global strategy, based on key judgements on how the Council can best deliver its programmes in support of the Government's international priorities. In Russia, as elsewhere, for example in Western and Central Europe, this has meant a shift away from bricks and mortar in country, towards innovative ways of working, such as local partnerships and remote targeting of audiences. But Russian pressure forced the unplanned suspension of the Council's operations outside Moscow.

45. Despite the Prime Minister's Foreign Policy Adviser holding what we believed were productive talks in Moscow on 16 January on a range of international and bilateral issues, including the British Council, the Russian Government was simultaneously exerting further pressure on the Council by harassing locally engaged staff. Such action is totally unacceptable and made it impossible for the Council to continue its regional operations from 17 January.

46. As the Foreign Secretary told Parliament in his Oral Ministerial Statement of 17 January 2008 Russia's recent actions raise serious questions about Russia's observance of international law, as well as the standards of behaviour she is prepared to adopt towards her own citizens.

(Second Report from the Foreign Affairs Committee Session 2007–08, Global Security: Russia. Response of the Secretary of State for Foreign and Commonwealth Affairs, Cm 7305)

19/26

The Foreign Secretary was asked what recent discussions he had had at meetings of the Council of Ministers on (a) the European Union response to the murder of Alexander Litvinenko and (b) the refusal of the Russian authorities to extradite Andrei Lugovoi. An FCO Minister wrote:

We have been working at all levels with our partners in the EU to maintain EU pressure on Russia to ensure Andrei Lugovoi faces charges in connection with the assassination of Alexander Litvinenko in the UK. Our EU partners support our view that this is an issue which needs to be pursued within the framework of the EU's relations with Russia. We continue to demand that Lugovoi should stand trial in the UK. We have made clear to partners that Lugovoi remains charged with murder in the UK and is liable to prosecution here.

(HC Deb 1 February 2008 Vol 471 c711W)

19/27

In the debate on the Report of the ILC in the Sixth Committee of the General Assembly [A/63/10, Ed.], the representative of the UK said:

In relation to Chapter XI of the ILC's report on the issue of the obligation to extradite or prosecute, the United Kingdom thanks the Special Rapporteur, Mr. Galicki, for his third report and remains grateful to the Special Rapporteur and the Commission for their work in this area.

At the outset, the United Kingdom has the following general remarks about the direction of the Commission's work.

As we stated last year, we remain of the position that any obligation to extradite or prosecute arises as a result of treaty obligations and that we have not yet reached the stage at which the obligation can be regarded as a rule or principle of customary international law. In view of the UK position that any obligation to extradite or prosecute arises under the terms of international agreements, those terms must govern both the crimes in respect of which the obligation arises and the question of whether the custodial state has discretion as to whether extradition or prosecution should take priority.

The United Kingdom would furthermore note that, if contrary to its position, the ILC believes that such an obligation does now arise under customary international law it does so only in relation to a very narrow category of offences. We would furthermore agree with the view (reflected at paragraph 96 of the Special Rapporteur's report) that, if the ILC is nonetheless to continue its consideration of this area of law, it should conduct a systematic survey of the relevant international treaties, national legislation and judicial decisions prior to carrying out further work on draft articles.

As regards universal jurisdiction, the United Kingdom is of the view that, while there may be some correlation between the incidence of universal jurisdiction over an offence and the existence of a duty to extradite or prosecute in respect of that offence, the existence of universal jurisdiction is not a necessary pre-condition to the existence of the obligation to extradite or prosecute. It would for example be perfectly possible for states concluding a bilateral extradition treaty to specify that the obligation to extradite or prosecute should arise in relation to any offence in respect of which concurrent jurisdiction could be exercised. This would cover any offences over which universal jurisdiction could be exercised but also any offences in respect of which concurrent jurisdiction could be exercised on any other basis, for example where the crime had a territorial link to both states. The UK continues to take the view that the ILC should avoid examining the issue of universal criminal jurisdiction.

Finally, we would wish to re-iterate our position that the so-called "triple alternative", that is to say the issue of transfer to an international tribunal, should not be considered by the ILC as there are specific rules expressly covering such transfers. We welcomed the Special Rapporteur's confirmation last year that the Commission's further work on this issue would not examine the "triple alternative" and we note that in this year's report the Rapporteur considers that this decision might have been premature. We would continue to encourage the ILC to refrain from examining further this specific element.

(Text supplied by FCO)

19/28

An FCO Minister wrote in answer to a question about the extradition of UK nationals:

It is long-standing policy and practice to neither confirm nor deny the existence of an extradition request ahead of a person's arrest. Table 1, as follows, sets out how many UK citizens have been arrested pursuant to extradition requests made to England and Wales since 1 January 2003; and how many UK citizens have been extradited.

Since 1 January 2004, the UK has been operating the Framework Decision on the European arrest warrant (EAW) with other member states of the EU. The Home Office has no involvement in the operation of the EAW. The Serious Organised Crime agency is the designated UK authority for the receipt and transmission of EAWs in the UK. Table 2, as follows, gives the number of UK nationals (a) arrested and (b) surrendered under the EAW procedure.

Table 1: Extradition Statistics

	Arrests pursuant to the extradition requests received	*Extradited*[1]
2003	21	12
2004	31	18
2005	5	1
2006	14	6
2007	6	0
Total	77	37

Table 2: European Arrest Warrant Statistics

	EAWs received	*Extradited*[1]
2004	12	5
2005	42	11
2006	49	26
2007[2]	48	22
Total	151	64

[1] A person is not always extradited in the same year an extradition request/EAW is made. [2] These figures are from January to October 2007.

(HC Deb 4 February 2008 Vol 471 c808W)

19/29

The Government were asked a number of questions about extradition arrangements with the United States. A Home Office Minister said:

Her Majesty's Government are entirely satisfied with the current extradition arrangements between the United Kingdom and the United States. Recent court judgments have not persuaded us that a change is either necessary or desirable.

... it is worth saying that the US is a mature democracy; it has a system based on the Bill of Rights, which came from our Magna Carta; and it is one of many countries that this applies to. It would be bizarre—or should I say perverse?—if we did not demand a prima facie case for places such as Albania, Ukraine and other countries in Europe, but demanded it of the United States. On concurrency of jurisdiction, the Attorney-General has talked with her American counterpart about how that should be taken forward in British courts.

... my confidence in the US judicial system has been reinforced by the fact that the US Supreme Court has ruled that foreign nationals detained in Guantanamo Bay without charge were entitled to bring legal actions in the US federal civilian courts challenging their captivity. I have been reassured by the US legal system.

Before the arrangements were changed they were definitely unbalanced in that we were demanding a prima facie case whereas all that was needed from us was probable cause. Therefore I do not think that the arrangements are unbalanced. I think that on the whole they are balanced. Fifty-two people have been extradited from this country since 2004—in four years, 52 people—and 17 people have been moved the other way.

(HL Deb 20 February 2008 Vol 699 csWA174-WA175)

19/30
The Solicitor-General was asked what the reasons had been for the decision not to prosecute the NatWest Three in the UK. She wrote:

In serious fraud cases it is common for allegedly criminal conduct to occur in more than one country. In such cases inevitably proceedings are commenced in one country rather than the other. In this case, investigations had begun in the USA and there had been no complaint by anyone in this country.

When the Serious Fraud Office came to consider whether to investigate, it decided not to do so because the main evidence was in the USA (the co-conspirators); the conspiracy took place there; the alleged fraud could not have occurred without the complicity of the Enron executives; the American case was advanced and it was in the overall interests of justice for it to be dealt with by one court.

[See *Bermingham & Ors v Director of the Serious Fraud Office & Anor* [2006] EWHC 200 (Admin), Ed.]

(HC Deb 18 March 2008 Vol 473 c1037W)

19/31
The Government were asked what information they had received from the authorities in Spain about the extradition of Mr Farid Hilali in February; in particular, whether he had been or will be charged with an offence; and whether any proceedings in Spain would conform with the ruling of the House of Lords in his case. A Minister wrote:

Mr Hilali, a Moroccan national, was extradited to Spain on 8 February, under the European arrest warrant (EAW) procedure. He was extradited in relation to charges of conspiracy to commit murder of persons in the US and of destroying, damaging or endangering the safety of aircraft—contrary to Section 2 of the Aviation Security Act 1982.

Once a person has been surrendered to another member state, their case is deemed to have been concluded as far as the UK is concerned. There is no obligation on the requesting member state to keep the UK informed of progress of proceedings against the surrendered person, just as there is no obligation on the UK to inform other member states of developments in proceedings against people surrendered to this country.

I understand the Spanish authorities are fully aware of the House of Lords' judgment and have confirmed that they are proceeding against Mr Hilali in strict conformity with it.

[There were controversial aspects of Hilali's removal to Spain, some of which were ventilated after he had been returned, see *Hilali, Re* [2008] UKHL 3, Ed.]

(HL Deb 29 April 2008 Vol 703 cWA17)

19/32

In reply to a question on extradition proceedings, a Minister wrote:

It is not the normal policy or practice, to confirm or deny the existence of any extradition request ahead of a person's arrest. With that caveat in mind, the following table shows the number of persons arrested in the UK on such charges pursuant to extradition requests received since 2000. In all cases, the alleged conduct was carried out in the requesting state. There have been no European Arrest Warrants issued to the UK for persons accused of conduct falling within the scope of this question. The EAW has been in operation in the UK since 1 January 2004.

Extradition requests

Year received[1]	Number of requests	Conduct	Requesting state
2000	—	—	—
2001	—	—	—
2002	1	War Crimes	Croatia
2003	—	—	—
2004	—	—	—
2005	—	—	—
2006	1	War Crimes	Croatia
	4	Genocide	Rwanda

[1] One extradition request from Spain for offences allegedly committed in Chile was received before 2000, but was refused by the then Home Secretary in March 2000.

(HC Deb 14 October 2008 Vol 480 c1260W)

19/33
Prisoner transfer agreements

In a debate on the Criminal Justice and Immigration Bill, a Home Office Minister said:

[I was] asked about prisoner transfer agreements. It is true that it remains a voluntary process, which accounts for the small number of foreign national prisoners who were repatriated last year under such agreements; that stood at 111. The UK currently has prisoner transfer agreements with 98 countries and territories. We have negotiations for further bilateral agreements with Vietnam, Ghana, Libya, Nigeria, Botswana and Kenya. I understand that we hope to begin negotiations with China later this year; agreements with Jamaica and Pakistan were signed in 2007, and are subject to ratification. We expect the agreement with Pakistan to enter into force early this year, while the Jamaican agreement cannot enter into force until amendments have been made to Jamaican law.

On consent, in 2006 Parliament amended the Repatriation of Prisoners Act 1984 to remove the need for prisoners to consent to transfer. Prisoner consent is still required under all our existing agreements, but the Government intend to seek to put in place future agreements that do not require that. The success of it will depend largely on the willingness of other countries to enter into such agreements.

[See Criminal Justice and Immigration Act 2008, s.94, amending s.4 Repatriation of Prisoners Act 1984, adding new s.4A, (5)(b), Ed.]

(HL Deb 26 February 2008 Vol 699 c646)

Part Nineteen: IX. *Legal Aspects of International Relations and Co-operation in Particular Matters—Military and security matters*

19/34
Arms dealing

The Foreign Secretary was asked what information the Government collated on the activities of individual arms dealers, with particular reference to those who are reported to have *(a)* broken UN sanctions and *(b)* supplied countries where UK armed forces are operating. An FCO Minister wrote:

The Export Control Organisation at the Department for Business, Enterprise and Regulatory Reform is the licensing authority for strategic exports in the UK. It sets out the regulatory framework under which licence applications are considered, and the Secretary of State for Business, Enterprise, and Regulatory Reform takes the formal decision to issue or refuse export licences or refuse export licence applications in accordance with the appropriate legislation and announced policy. Information about arms brokers who have had their proposed export licence application either refused or revoked is shared with HM Revenue and Customs and the Revenue and Customs Prosecution Office to ensure that the decision is enforced. Where the Government receives information that an exporter has attempted to circumvent export control rules, the relevant Government departments and agencies will take action. For example, the arms broker John Knight was recently jailed for four years for breaching export controls relating to a brokered transaction between Kuwait and Iraq. This case illustrates that the legislation introduced under the Trade in Goods (Control) Order 2004 is making an impact.

The UK has one of the most rigorous and transparent export licensing regimes in the world. All licence applications are assessed on a case-by-case basis against "The Consolidated EU and National Arms Export Licensing Criteria". The criteria cover in detail how we assess each case. Specifically criterion 5b states:

"the risk of the goods concerned being used against UK forces". If there appears to any risk of this being the case, a licence will not be issued.

(HC Deb 1 February 2008 Vol 471 c711W)

19/35
Arms trade

The Government were asked various questions about the arms trade. A Minister wrote:

On 6 February 2008 the Government published their initial response to a public consultation carried out as part of the 2007 review of export control legislation. The response can be viewed on BERR's website at <www.berr.gov.uk/europeantrade/strategic-export-control/legislation/export-control-act-2002/review/index.html>.

The initial response makes a number of specific commitments to enhance the controls and covers the issues raised at points (a) and (b). However, as stressed in that response, there are a number of areas where further research and analysis is required.

The Government are extending the current extraterritorial controls to encompass the activities of UK persons anywhere in the world in relation to small arms. It is currently considering extending this beyond small arms to possibly encompass other weapons. In doing so, it will need to ensure that any new regulations are proportionate to the risk.

The Government's initial response states that they remain of the view that to attempt to control directly the activities of UK-owned foreign subsidiaries—in effect to treat them as though they are based in the UK—is not legally viable and would be virtually impossible to enforce.

Similarly on point (c), the Government are not convinced that requiring exporters to seek re-export approval from the UK authorities is necessary or feasible, since such a system would be onerous to operate and extremely difficult to enforce in practice outside the UK's legal jurisdiction.

It is however possible that the Government's continuing analysis will result in further changes that will impact on these issues. The Government aim to issue a further response later in 2008.

On point (d), the Government consider that Criterion 8 of the Consolidated EU and National Arms Export Licensing Criteria, which requires the Government to take into account "whether the proposed export would seriously undermine the economy or seriously hamper the sustainable development of the recipient country" already provides adequate protection against the risk that exports of controlled goods will prejudice the development of poor countries.

(HL Deb 22 February 2008 Vol 699 cWA87)

19/36
Export licenses

The FCO wrote to the Quadripartite Committee in reply to the following inquiry:

The Committees would be grateful for more information on the following licences issued during the third quarter (January to March) of 2007:

* * *

(n) Libya: SIELs for armoured personnel carriers and water cannons; more specifically how the Government was satisfied that these exports would not breach Criterion 2;

The Government was satisfied that these exports would not breach Criterion 2.

The Government placed a proviso on the licence that the goods were to remain in the control of the exporter until the end-user, the Libyan Police, had successfully completed, and been assessed against, appropriate training on the use of this equipment and best practice in public order situations. One aspect of the training was the 'underpinning theories and models related to Human Rights and the proportionality of response'. Independent assessors from the UK MoD Police and the Humberside Police evaluated this training.

HMG considered the level of risk that the goods would have been used contrary to Criterion 2 to have been mitigated to an acceptable level by the training and evaluation.

(<www.publications.parliament.uk/pa/cm200708/cmselect/cmquad/memo/254/ucqmo602.htm>)

19/37
India

The Foreign Secretary wrote to the Quadripartite Committee:

Thank you for your letter of 26 July about reports from NGOs of India selling advanced military helicopters to Burma, containing components from the UK.

As you rightly point out ... India has confirmed that it does not intend to sell this equipment to the Burmese.

Since then, on 27 July the EU Troika in New Delhi delivered a demarche on the Indian Government about the reported sale of such equipment to Burma. The Indians reiterated that no such deal was under consideration. The Troika reminded the Indian government of the long-standing Common Position on Burma and Europe's deep concern about the situation there. I hope that these representations will have reinforced with the Indian Government the seriousness with which the EU, including the UK, views the EU arms embargo on Burma.

You also asked about what measures the Government can take to prevent re-exports to Burma. ... we consider all applications for the export of military equipment on a case by case basis against the Consolidated EU and National Arms Export Licensing Criteria. This includes an assessment of whether there is a risk that the goods in question will be diverted within the buyer country or re-exported under undesirable conditions. If a licence application is deemed inconsistent with the Criteria, a licence will not be issued.

(<www.publications.parliament.uk/pa/cm200708/cmselect/cmquad/memo/254/ucqm0202.htm> (August 2007))

19/38
Iran

The FAC had concluded in its Report on Global Security: Iran that:

Iran has a legal obligation established by a number of Security Council resolutions to halt its enrichment activities. We also welcome the offers of enriched uranium to Iran by Russia, deliveries of which have already commenced, and the international community. These offers are significant. We further conclude that Iran must not be allowed to develop a nuclear weapon. (Paragraph 39)

The Government said that it:

9 ... agrees with the Committee's conclusion that Iran has a legal obligation to halt its uranium enrichment programme, as now demanded by four successive Security Council resolutions. We fully agree that Iran must comply with its obligations and not be allowed to develop a nuclear weapon. This is the primary goal of UK, and E3+3, policy on Iran.

(Fifth Report of the Foreign Affairs Committee Session 2007–08, Global Security: Iran Response of the Secretary of State for Foreign and Commonwealth Affairs Cm 7361)

19/39

The Chancellor of the Exchequer was asked what steps were planned to be taken through the Financial Action Task Force to ensure that certain Iranian banks cannot abuse the international banking system to support proliferation activities and terrorism. A Treasury Minister wrote:

The Financial Action Task Force (FATF) has expressed concern that the Islamic Republic of Iran's lack of a comprehensive regime for anti-money laundering and combating the financing of terrorism (AML/CFT) represents a significant vulnerability within the international financial system. In addition to its role in setting and monitoring standards for AML/CFT in general, the FATF has warned the financial sector of the risks posed by Iran and advised jurisdictions on implementation of the financial provisions of UN Security Council Resolutions relating to Iran's nuclear activities.

The FATF issued statements on Iran in October 2007 and February 2008. These statements warn businesses in the financial sector about the heightened risks of money laundering or terrorist financing arising from the deficiencies in Iran's AML/CFT regime, and recommend that they apply increased scrutiny and due diligence to transactions associated with Iran. The FATF has also met Iranian authorities to discuss measures to improve Iran's AML/CFT regime. The FATF is keeping the risk posed by Iran under review and discussed progress at its meetings in London this month. In response to these FATF statements, HM Treasury has issued advisory notices to UK businesses on the heightened risk of money laundering or terrorist financing from Iran.

At its June 2008 meeting in London, the FATF reaffirmed its public statement of 28 February 2008 regarding the anti-money laundering and countering the financing of terrorism risks posed by Uzbekistan, Iran, Pakistan, Turkmenistan and São Tomé and Principe, and the northern part of Cyprus. It welcomed the actions taken by its members to advise their financial institutions of these risks, and noted it was concerned about the lack of progress by, in particular, Uzbekistan and Iran. The FATF will continue to assess the situation and take further actions in October, as necessary, to protect the international financial system.

The FATF has also produced guidance on implementation of the financial provisions of UN Security Council Resolutions relating to Iran's nuclear activities. The FATF published Guidance in July 2007 on "Implementing Financial Provisions Of UN Security Council Resolutions To Counter Proliferation Of Weapons Of Mass Destruction", including guidance on implementing targeted asset freezes as required by UNSCR 1747. In October 2007 the FATF published "Guidance Regarding The Implementation Of Activity-Based Financial Prohibitions Of United Nations Security Council Resolution 1737"; advising jurisdictions on preventive measures to guard against the use of the financial system to support Iran's nuclear programmes.

A new mandate for the FATF has been agreed under the UK presidency which recognises its increased role in combating proliferation finance. The FATF will shortly publish a typology study on proliferation finance, detailing the extent of the threat and the methodologies used by proliferators.

(HC Deb 26 June 2006 Vol 478 c464W)

19/40
Iraq

The Government were asked what recent reports it had received on the *(a)* detention and *(b)* status of Abdul Razzaq Ali al-Jedda; and what representations he had received on the case.

In reply, a Minister wrote:

Mr. al-Jedda was released from UK custody in December 2007.

Prior to his release Mr. al-Jedda was held as a security internee by UK forces in Iraq because it was assessed that he posed a threat to the lives of Multi-National Forces personnel, Iraqi security personnel and Iraqi civilians. In December 2007, on the basis of the latest intelligence and security assessment, it was decided that it was no longer necessary to intern Mr. al-Jedda and he was released to a safe location in Iraq.

[Mr. al-Jedda's internment was pursuant to UNSCR 1546 and subsequent resolutions, and was found to be lawful by the House of Lords. [[2007] UKHL 58 Ed.]

(HC Deb 6 October 2008 Vol 480 c259W)

19/41

The Government were asked what their policy was on the legal immunity of private military contractors in the successor agreement to the UN mandate for Iraq. In reply, a Minister wrote:

The Government use private military and security companies to provide security for our diplomatic posts and for civilian officials in Iraq. As such, they play an important role in enabling us to achieve our objectives in Iraq. Although we have held initial discussions with the Government of Iraq on ways of securing a legal basis for activities by UK armed forces in Iraq following the anticipated expiry of UN Security Council Chapter VII authority, these have focussed on UK armed forces' operations and immunities. The issue of private military and security companies will be considered, if appropriate, in any future negotiations with the Government of Iraq.

(HC Deb 21 July 2008 Vol 479 c871W)

19/42
National Security Strategy

In a debate on National Security Strategy, the Prime Minister said:

As great a potential threat and as demanding of a co-ordinated international response is, of course, the risk from failing and unstable states. Again, the national security strategy published today proposes a new departure—and, again, it is a lesson learned from recent conflicts ranging from Rwanda and Bosnia to Iraq, Afghanistan and Somalia. It proposes to create a stand-by international civilian capability so that for fragile and failing states, we can act quickly and comprehensively by combining the humanitarian, peacekeeping, stabilisation and reconstruction support that those countries need. In the same way as we have military forces ready to respond to conflict, we must have civilian experts and professionals ready to deploy quickly to assist failing states and to help rebuild countries emerging from conflict, putting them on the road to economic and political recovery.

(HC Deb 19 March 2008 Vol 473 c927)

19/43 [See also 11/16–11/24]
Piracy

In reply to a question on counter-piracy measures, a Minister wrote:

We have been working with EU and North Atlantic Treaty Organisation (NATO) partners to consider options to counter-piracy in the region, both directly and through development activity to undermine it at its roots. In support of UN

Security Council resolution 1816, the EU has set up a cell in Brussels to co-ordinate EU activity in the region, and the EU and NATO are considering options to undertake further naval action. We have also supported the French drafting of a new UN Security Council resolution which aims to strengthen the international community's response to piracy.

(HC Deb 13 October 2008 Vol 480 c962W)

19/44
Small arms

A Trade Minister was asked by the Quadripartite Committee whether the Government was prepared to fill in the gaps in the criminal law in this area to extend extra-territoriality to all the items that are broadly within the definition of weapons to ensure that British residents overseas who seek to breach arms controls in a way that would be criminal offences if committed from within the UK are themselves made liable to the criminal law. The Minister said:

I think we have moved in the right direction on small arms which many people in the past have described accurately as the true weapons of mass destruction in places like Africa. We have moved forward on that and on MANPADS and on cluster weapons. It is a question of do we now need to move further. There is a working group … involving some of the NGOs and the industry who are looking at this to see whether some consensus can be reached and then no doubt advice can be put to both this Committee and to Government. As far as I am concerned, the door is wide open on this for us to take further steps should we deem that necessary. I guess in all of these things it is a question of degree. Perfectly properly under British law we reserve extra-territorial interventions for some of the most heinous crimes that exist—we track down paedophiles, for example—and, perfectly properly, those British people dealing in lethal weapons are also tracked down. [Q.145]

[See (2007) UKMIL **19/30**]

(Quadripartite Committee Report, Scrutiny of Arms Export Control, HC 254 (2008))

19/45
Sri Lanka

A Minister wrote:

The Liberation Tamil Tigers of Eelam (LTTE), also known as the Tamil Tigers, have been listed as proscribed as a terrorist organisation from 2001 under the Terrorism Act 2000. It is a criminal offence for a person to belong to or to invite support for the LTTE in the UK. The UK Government is in contact with the Sri Lankan authorities, law enforcement agencies and other Government Departments concerning preventing the transfer of funds from this country to the LTTE in Sri Lanka.

(HC Deb 7 July 2008 Vol 478 c1249W)

19/46
Trade Co-operation Treaty

The Quadripartite Committee requested a memorandum from the MOD prior to the evidence session with the Defence Secretary. The MOD wrote:

US/UK DEFENCE TRADE CO-OPERATION TREATY

The Defence Trade Cooperation Treaty will simplify and make more effective the controls on transmission of military goods, technology and information between the United Kingdom and United States, in support of our joint operations around the world and collaborative efforts aimed at developing future defence capabilities.

Currently, controlled information and material supplied by the US to the UK is passed under an individual export licence, which is issued by the US Government to the exporter. This process is time consuming and can add significant delays to procurement projects. It also makes it difficult for UK and US companies to work together to develop new defence capabilities.

Under the treaty, the need for individual licences from the US will be removed. Instead, US material will have a UK security classification attached to it, meaning that its handling will be subject to the Official Secrets Act. HMG will take enforcement action in the event of any unauthorised disclosure. This builds on the many years of the UK and US protecting shared information under the overarching security agreement between the two countries. The current system for exporting equivalent material from the UK to the US, including under Open General Export Licence, will not be changed.

Only material that is destined for UK and US sole end-use, in support of UK/US joint operations, cooperative defence and security programmes, and certain HMG-only projects that rely on US material, will be covered by the treaty. The treaty will only cover material listed for export control on the US Munitions List, and will include a small number of additional restrictions on certain sensitive technologies.

The treaty will allow for such material to pass without additional authorisation within an "Approved Community" of UK and US Government establishments and UK and US companies that have met certain criteria, including the ability to protect classified material. Only personnel who meet appropriate security standards and have a need to know will be able to access material.

(Quadripartite Committee Report, Scrutiny of Arms Export Control, Memorandum from Ministry of Defence, HC 254 (2008))

19/47

The Minister of Defence was asked about the UK/US Defence Trade Cooperation Treaty. He was told that:

The Committee has received evidence from Saferworld expressing some concerns about the impact on arms exports and particularly suggesting that the Treaty puts the UK/US relationship into some imbalance in the sense that it allows the US to determine which goods are included in the Treaty and allows the US to override the UK arms exports controls and impose their own in terms of end use of particular goods. Would you like to comment on that?

He said:

It's easier to answer the last part of the question first. The integrity of our own arms export control system is entirely intact and the United States has no role to play in that; it is still our responsibility. It no way weakens it and no way affects it. It is a misunderstanding of the Treaty if people think that it does. The other part of the question is designed to identify that there are some sensitive technologies (which is a phrase that is used in the Treaty) which will be excluded from the Treaty. The fact that the Americans will identify certain technologies that they will exclude from the Treaty and they will do that in consultation with us in the implementation arrangements does not in my view in any way undermine or imbalance the Treaty. In fact the whole purpose of the Treaty is to bring the processes into alignment so that we can speed up and simplify the delivery of equipment to the UK but also to US troops who operate together around the world which is a longstanding policy of both countries. Since we have deployed together and operated together and are valued allies of each other that seems to me to be an appropriate and reasonable objective and it is in our interests as well as in theirs. In relation to the sensitive technologies, there will be about three or four of them. I am not able to specify what they will be but they will be a comparatively small number. I think given the advantages there will be in the treaty which will be manifest ... then this comparatively small area of restriction which is perfectly understandable because of the sensitivities of the technologies does not in any way undermine it. [Q.32]

He was asked about the process of ratification of the treaty. He said:

The current position in relation to the Treaty ... is that the Treaty has gone through the parliamentary process here. The congressional process is an integrated process in the sense that both the Treaty and the implementing arrangements will be presented to Congress. The negotiation of the implementing arrangements is going on at the moment. I have in my mind a kind of timeline in relation to that but I do not think it would necessarily be helpful to the negotiations for me to publicly say that we expect them to be concluded on a particular day. However, they are advanced, they are going well; we have no reason to believe that they will not be concluded successfully in a reasonable timeline and then we will be in a position to present the Treaty to Congress. We hope to be able to do that at an early date and we are working with the American authorities to be able to do that. In case you ask me when I think we will get it through congress, I do not necessarily think it would be helpful to that process for me to say from here and feed into that process; I think we need to leave it to them.

(Quadripartite Committee Report, Scrutiny of Arms Export Control, HC 254 (2008))

TABLE OF CASES

INDEX